Amalia Bar-On and Dorit Ravid (Eds.)
Handbook of Communication Disorders

Handbooks of
Applied Linguistics

Communication Competence
Language and Communication Problems
Practical Solutions

Editors
Karlfried Knapp
Daniel Perrin
Marjolijn Verspoor

Volume 15

Handbook of Communication Disorders

—

Edited by
Amalia Bar-On and Dorit Ravid

Elitzur Dattner, Editorial Associate

DE GRUYTER
MOUTON

ISBN 978-1-5015-1935-2
e-ISBN (PDF) 978-1-61451-490-9
e-ISBN (EPUB) 978-1-5015-0094-7

Library of Congress Control Number: 2018934562

Bibliographic information published by the Deutsche Nationalbibliothek
The Deutsche Nationalbibliothek lists this publication in the Deutsche Nationalbibliografie;
detailed bibliographic data are available on the Internet at http://dnb.dnb.de.

© 2019 Walter de Gruyter Inc., Boston/Berlin
This volume is text- and page-identical with the hardback published in 2018.
Typesetting: RoyalStandard, Hong Kong
Printing and binding: CPI books GmbH, Leck

www.degruyter.com

Preface to the Handbooks of Applied Linguistics Series

The present handbook constitutes Volume 15 of the De Gruyter Mouton *Handbooks of Applied Linguistics*. This series is based on an understanding of Applied Linguistics as an inter- and transdisciplinary field of academic enquiry. The *Handbooks of Applied Linguistics* provide a state-of-the-art description of established and emerging areas of Applied Linguistics. Each volume gives an overview of the field, identifies most important traditions and their findings, identifies the gaps in current research, and gives perspectives for future directions.

In the late 1990s when the handbook series was planned by its Founding Editors Gerd Antos and Karlfried Knapp, intensive debates were going on as to whether Applied Linguistics should be restricted to applying methods and findings from linguistics only or whether it should be regarded as a field of interdisciplinary synthesis drawing on psychology, sociology, ethnology and similar disciplines that are also dealing with aspects of language and communication. Should it be limited to foreign language teaching or should it widen its scope to language-related issues in general? Thus, what *Applied Linguistics* means and what an Applied Linguist does was highly controversial at the time.

Against this backdrop, Gerd Antos and Karlfried Knapp felt that a series of handbooks of Applied Linguistics could not simply be an accidental selection of descriptions of research findings and practical activities that were or could be published in books and articles labeled as "applied linguistic". Rather, for them such a series had to be based on an epistemological concept that frames the status and scope of the concept of Applied Linguistics. Departing from contemporary Philosophy of Science, which sees academic disciplines under the pressure to successfully solve practical everyday problems encountered by the societies which aliment them, the founding editors emphasized the view that was only emerging at that time – the programmatic view that Applied Linguistics means the solving of real world problems with language and communication. This concept has become mainstream since.

In line with the conviction that Applied Linguistics is for problem solving, we developed a series of handbooks to give representative descriptions of the ability of this field of academic inquiry and to provide accounts, analyses, explanations and, where possible, solutions of everyday problems with language and communication. Each volume of the *Handbooks of Applied Linguistics* series is unique in its explicit focus on topics in language and communication as areas of everyday problems and in pointing out the relevance of Applied Linguistics in dealing with them.

This series has been well received in the academic community and among practitioners. In fact, its success has even triggered competitive handbook series by other publishers. Moreover, we recognized further challenges with language and communication and distinguished colleagues keep on approaching us with proposals to edit further volumes in this handbook series. This motivates both De Gruyter Mouton and the series editors to further develop the *Handbooks of Applied Linguistics*.

Karlfried Knapp (Erfurt), Founding Editor
Daniel Perrin (Zürich), Editor
Marjolijn Verspoor (Groningen), Editor

Table of contents

Preface to the Handbooks of Applied Linguistics Series —— v

Amalia Bar-On, Dorit Ravid, and Elitzur Dattner
Introduction —— 1

I Linguistic acquisition

Section 1: Phonology and speech

Liat Kishon-Rabin and Arthur Boothroyd
1 The role of hearing in speech and language acquisition and processing —— 19

Derek M. Houston and Andrea Warner-Czyz
2 Speech perception and auditory development in infants with and without hearing loss —— 43

Outi Bat-El and Avivit Ben-David
3 Developing phonology —— 63

Section 2: Lexical knowledge

Suvi Stolt
4 Early lexicon and the development that precedes it and the development that follows – A developmental view to early lexicon —— 91

Li Sheng
5 Typical and atypical lexical development —— 101

Herbert L. Colston
6 Figurative language acquisition and development —— 117

Fataneh Farnia
7 Figurative language development: Implications for assessment and clinical practice —— 137

Britta Biedermann, Nora Fieder and Lyndsey Nickels
8 Spoken word production: Processes and potential breakdown —— 155

Section 3: Grammatical constructions

Michael Ramscar, Melody Dye, James Blevins and Harald Baayen
9 **Morphological development** —— 181

F. Nihan Ketrez
10 **Acquisition of an agglutinative language under adverse neonatal condition** —— 203

Batia Seroussi
11 **Later morpho-lexical acquisition** —— 219

Ruth A. Berman
12 **Development of complex syntax: From early-clause combining to text-embedded syntactic packaging** —— 235

II Oral and written communication

Section 4: Communication and discourse

Vanessa Schell and Mark Sabbagh
13 **Theory of mind and communication: Developmental perspectives** —— 259

Beyza Ş. Ateş and Aylin C. Küntay
14 **Socio-pragmatic skills underlying language development: Boundaries between typical and atypical development** —— 279

Edy Veneziano
15 **Learning conversational skills and learning from conversation** —— 311

Ayhan Aksu-Koç and Aslı Aktan Erciyes
16 **Narrative discourse: Developmental perspectives** —— 329

Ageliki Nicolopoulou and Sarah Trapp
17 **Narrative interventions for children with language disorders: A review of practices and findings** —— 357

Julie Radford
18 **Helping language learning in inclusive classrooms** —— 387

Section 5: Linguistic literacy

David R. Olson
19 **What is literacy? And what is a literate disability?** —— 405

Dorit Aram
20 Promoting early literacy of children from low socioeconomic backgrounds in preschool and at home —— 415

David L. Share
21 Foundations for a universal model of learning to read —— 437

Séverine Casalis
22 Acquisition of spelling: Normal and impaired/disordered populations —— 461

Dominiek Sandra
23 The role of morphology in reading and writing —— 477

Julia Schindler and Tobias Richter
24 Reading comprehension: Individual differences, disorders, and underlying cognitive processes —— 503

Liliana Tolchinsky and Naymé Salas
25 Grammar for writing and grammar in writing —— 525

III Environmental effects

Section 6: Socio-economic status

Adriana Weisleder and Virginia A. Marchman
26 How socioeconomic differences in early language environments shape children's language development —— 545

Kylie Schibli, Nina Hedayati, Hannah Hobbs, Amina Sheik-Ahmed and Amedeo D'Angiulli
27 Cognition and language in different socioeconomic and environmental settings —— 565

Carolyn Letts
28 Language disorder versus language difference: The impact of socioeconomic status —— 585

Section 7: Multilingualism

Annick De Houwer
29 Input, context and early child bilingualism: Implications for clinical practice —— 601

Sharon Armon-Lotem
30 SLI in bilingual development: How do we approach assessment? — 617

C. Patrick Proctor and Rebecca Louick
31 Development of vocabulary knowledge and its relationship with reading comprehension among emergent bilingual children: An overview — 643

Susan Gass
32 Factors affecting second language acquisition: Successes and nonsuccesses — 667

IV Language and communication disorders

Section 8: Developmental and neurological disorders

Jan de Jong
33 The changing profile of Specific Language Impairment — 689

Lara R. Polse, Samantha M. Engel and Judy S. Reilly
34 Neuroplasticity and development: Discourse in children with early focal lesions and children with language impairment — 705

Naama Friedmann and Max Coltheart
35 Types of developmental dyslexia — 721

Rachel Schiff, Eli Vakil, Yafit Gabay and Shani Kahta
36 Implicit learning in developmental dyslexia as demonstrated by the Serial Reaction Time (SRT) and the Artificial Grammar Learning (AGL) tasks — 753

Steven Gillis
37 Speech and language in congenitally deaf children with cochlear implants — 765

Sara Ingber and Tova Most
38 Parental involvement in early intervention for children with hearing loss — 793

Esther Dromi, Yonat Rum and Jessica Goldberg Florian
39 Communication, language, and speech in young children with autism spectrum disorder (ASD) — 811

Yonata Levy
40 Language in people with Williams syndrome — 829

Sigal Uziel-Karl and Michal Tenne-Rinde
41 Making language accessible for people with cognitive disabilities: Intellectual disability as a test case —— 845

Section 9: Disorders in aging

Eve Higby, Dalia Cahana-Amitay and Loraine K. Obler
42 **Brain and language in healthy aging** —— 863

Rosemary Varley and Vitor Zimmerer
43 **Language impairments in acquired aphasia: Features and frameworks** —— 881

Frédéric Assal and Ariane Laurent
44 **Language in neurodegenerative diseases** —— 899

Index —— 919

Amalia Bar-On, Dorit Ravid and Elitzur Dattner
Introduction to the Handbook of Communication Disorders: Theoretical, Empirical, and Applied Linguistic Perspectives

1 Introduction

Communication Disorders (CD) is a clinical profession aimed at facilitating language, speech, hearing and oral motor functions by diagnosis, treatment and therapy. In the last few decades, the domain of CD has grown exponentially, having come to encompass much more than the important domains of audiology, speech impediments and early language impairment. The realization that most developmental and learning disorders are language-based or language-related has brought insights from theoretical and empirical linguistics and its clinical applications to the forefront of CD science. This shift is reflected in the numerous studies encompassing every facet of linguistic knowledge – side by side with atypical linguistic development and processing – in thematic disorders journals, cognition- and language-oriented journals, and journals specializing in language acquisition. The central role that spoken and written language, discourse and literacy now occupy in CD research highlights the value of the language sciences in providing accounts of and solutions for cognitive, developmental and learning problems within both educational and clinical contexts. As a direct result, CD practitioners (SLPs = Speech – Language Pathologists) now expect to gain the available language-based knowledge for the identification, diagnosis and therapy of a broad range of disabilities across the life span. These changes in the scope and orientation of the CD profession underscore the need for the current handbook, providing a robust psycholinguistic, neurolinguistic, and sociolinguistic foundation for the understanding and treatment of communication disabilities at different stages of human development and in various social and communicative contexts.

The *Handbook of Communication Disorders* targets speech-language pathologists as a state-of-the-art reference book during their academic studies. It is also designed to be a constant companion in their further specialized training and lifetime learning. In a broader perspective, this Handbook is offered to academics who work in the language, learning and communication fields, such as cognitive and developmental sciences, clinical, applied, socio- and psycholinguistics, language acquisition and development, communication sciences, psychology, education, special education, and

Amalia Bar-On, Dorit Ravid and Elitzur Dattner, Tel Aviv University

learning disabilities. Researchers in these fields now work in a multi-discipline arena which requires updated information about theoretical, empirical, and clinical aspects of CD.

1.1 How language interfaces with Communication Disorders

CD professionals and practitioners have always assumed that knowledge arises from experience and have sought ways to diagnose and treat the disorder but also recognize its cognitive and neurological sources. CD leaders nowadays consider it critical for SLPs to gain command of language sciences so as to understand the bases of language disorders (Bishop and Norbury, 2008; Jarmulowicz and Taran, 2013). Like psychologists, CD researchers rely on linguistic-generated insights as the evidence-based scientific framework against which language disabilities are conceptualized and clinical solutions are sought. Consequently, diagnosis and therapy innovation in CD is often driven by integrative research about the various facets of language abilities, as well as how they relate to general cognitive processes (McArthur, Ellis and Atkinson, 2009; van der Lely, 2005). However, the Handbook does not reflect the traditional structure of the science of linguistics – that is, phonology, morphology, lexicon, syntax, semantics and pragmatics. This is because imposing this taxonomy on CD might obscure the complex nature of disorders, which virtually always spans both linguistic and non-linguistic mechanisms, and very often involves more than one linguistic domain.

The most typical example of this claim is the case of *Developmental Language Disorders* and the debate reflected in the acronyms by which it is best known – *Specific Language Impairment (SLI), Language Impairment (LI)* (or *Language Learning Impairment, LLI*). According to proponents of hard-wired, modular brain and cognition, "The notion of *specific* in specific language impairment is at the heart of the matter" (Crago and Paradis, 2003; de Villiers, 2002): it is only the language module, or specific sub-modules within it, such as syntax, that are impaired, and therefore need to be treated. Diagnosis under this view should follow the exclusion of all other possible sources of language disorders. But this view is under constant revision, as a complex disorder, or a complex of disorders, which calls for description, assessment and explanation at more than a single level. Recently, a special issue of the *International Journal of Language and Communication Disorders* titled *The SLI debate: diagnostic criteria and terminology* offered a state of the art review of the case for LI, given the absence of empirical evidence for SLI (Bishop, 2014; Reilly et al., 2014). This has led to seeking inclusionary, rather than exclusionary, criteria for the diagnosis of developmental language disorders.

There are other, less controversial examples of the multi-dimensional properties of language-related disorders. For example, *Central Auditory Processing Disorder*, affecting about 5% of school-aged children, is a hearing/processing mismatch where the brain is able to detect speech sounds normally but does not process and interpret auditory information well enough in less than perfect hearing contexts. Although phonology is the closest linguistic domain, this disorder is not strictly phonological but rather has to do with what is termed in CD science "speech and auditory processing". *Autism Disorders*, a second example, mainly affect a person's communication and social interaction skills, which linguistically translates into pragmatic disability. However again, this complex spectrum of disorders encompasses both linguistic and non-linguistic socio-cognitive behaviors across development in ways that require us to treat it as a broad phenomenon that is not restricted to a single linguistic domain.

From a different perspective, vast research fields currently recognized as central to the diagnosis and therapy of numerous CDs are now viewed as language-related, yet best treated outside the strict confinement of formal linguistics: Written language, discourse construction and comprehension, second language learning, bilingualism, and language in different socio-economic environments. Researchers now recognize that many difficulties diagnosed early on as language-related take on more specific facets with growth in age and schooling, as in the case of *Language Impairment* re-emerging as *Dyslexia*. This is a disorder having to do with the processing of written language, which is typically diagnosed during the school years, but it is also manifested in spoken language performance (Ravid and Schiff, 2013; Schiff et al., 2016). In other cases, mild language-related disabilities may not even reach the threshold for diagnosis until the complex requirements of academic learning such as written discourse, to take one example, and second/foreign language learning, to take another, enhance them in school (Berman, Nayditz and Ravid, 2011; Nippold and Scott, 2009). Finally, a well-known cause of language communication failure is the less than optimal exposure to language in environmentally deprived contexts such as a person's low socio-economic background (Fernald, Marchman and Weisleder, 2012; Rowe, 2008). Evidence has been amassing regarding the deep effect of reduced language engagement in children raised in poverty (Hart and Risley, 1995), leading to a disturbing similarity to the effects of language impairment (Levie, Ben Zvi and Ravid, in press).

1.2 Linguistic theory and Communication Disorders

While each of these arenas is a discipline in its own right, their relevance to the field of CD is undisputed, as is the obvious connection to the science of linguistics, which has undergone upheavals in the last decades. The Chomskyan revolution in linguistics ushered in the cognitive era in psychology (Isac and Reiss, 2013; McGilvray, 2014), highlighting questions relating to the human adaptation in language, the nature of the language and cognition interface, and the role of innateness in language acquisition. However, in the wake of recent debates in the linguistic world and the rise of post-Chomskyan linguistic theory, perspectives have shifted on the role of universals in language and specific language typologies (Bybee, 2006, 2010; Evans and Levinson, 2009). Current usage-based models of language structure and use (Christiansen and Chater, 2008; Ibbotson, 2013), deriving from the Cognitive and Functional Linguistics traditions (Lakoff, 1991; Langacker, 1987), assume language knowledge to be a non-autonomous cognitive faculty (Bod, 2006; Croft and Cruse, 2004), extremely sensitive to other cognitive domains and to environmental factors. These changes in linguistic theory from the perception of language as a narrow grammatical faculty to its construal as a broadly based cognitive faculty have brought about a concurrent shift in CD science. Accordingly, even more connections can now be pointed out between language analysis and its clinical applications, encouraging SLPs to broaden treatment from language structure and meaning to its use in different communicative contexts. Usage-based theories regard linguistic acquisition as a data-driven, bottom-up task strongly leaning on mind-reading socio-cognitive abilities on the one hand, and the changing nature of linguistic input, on the other (Rowland et al, 2012; Tomasello, 2003). Thus, it is extremely important for CD researchers and SLPs to gain information about patterns of use in naturally occurring language, from morpho-phonology through syntax to discourse structures and their functions, so as to base study design and subsequent treatment on valid data.

1.3 Research methodologies

The field of CD has long relied on rigorous, data-driven, empirical studies of participants' behavior, both quantitative and qualitative, in the quest for clinical applications based on sound scientific investigation (Ball, Müller and Nelson, 2014; Nelson, 2016). The felicitous cooperation between CD and applied, socio- and psycholinguistics now relies on the same rigor in linguistic investigation. Two research methodologies are especially relevant, reflecting the shift to evidence-based linguistic data collection and analysis. One is the experimental, task-oriented elicitation of language behavior from participants, especially those applying multiple paradigms to ensure covering various facets of the investigated phenomena (Ambridge and Rowland, 2013; Phakiti, 2014; Saffran, Senghas and Trueswell, 2001). Another is the systematic investigation of features of produced discourse, which identifies both frequent, conventional patterns, and less frequent, novel uses of language – making it possible for SLPs to set goals for both oral and literate language gains (Berman and Ravid, 2008; Hoff, 2012; McNamara, Crossley, and McCarthy, 2010). Discourse analyses are most often statistically based, taking the corpus to be a representation of one's experience with language, including the role of memory and frequency (Bybee, 2010; Gries and Stefanowitsch, 2007). In other cases, exhaustive, word-by-word analyses of vocabulary and constructions within their contexts are undertaken (especially in studies of language development) to determine the effect of the ambient language in corpora on children's language production and comprehension. They also trace the changes internal language knowledge undergoes, as evidenced in the observed variation in the corpora (Behrens, 2009; Clark, 2016).

1.4 Language typology

A final, critical perspective on the interface of CD and language analysis is *ecological validity*, that is, taking into account different language typologies and the way they affect language learning and processing (Frost, 2012). Typology, in linguistics, is the search for patterns "that occur systematically across languages" (Croft, 2003:1) with the goal of reaching genuine typological generalizations (Comrie, 1989; Song, 2011). Linguistic thinking was dominated for a long time by the specific properties of English, which are not necessarily shared by the world's languages (Chung, 2009; Evans and Levinson, 2009; Haspelmath, 2012). From a CD perspective, the typology of a language has been found to be crucial for the understanding of language development and language disorders (Ravid, Levie and Avivi Ben-Zvi, 2003). Specifically, typological structure has been shown to account for the severity of morphological impairment in languages of differential morphological complexity (Dromi, Leonard, and Shteiman, 1993). In the same way, the study of the characteristics of orthographies other than English in conjunction with phonological and grammatical structures of languages in possession of these orthographies has contributed immensely to theories and application of reading, writing and spelling (Frost, 2012; Gillis and Ravid, 2006; Ravid, 2012; Perfetti, 2003; Share, 2008; Share and Bar-On, in press). Corpus-based linguistic analyses examine usage patterns of the same conceptual space in a variety of languages, thus accounting for the diversity of languages in a *typological* perspective, with immense benefits for psychological, clinical and educational applications. Taking an ecological validity stance and addressing the linguistic typological impact on language learning and CD, the handbook should thus be useful for readers from a variety of languages and language families.

2 Book structure

The book structure represents what we perceive as the current structure of the field of Communication Disorders. The over-arching objective of the handbook, which constitutes its major organizing principle, is to construct the interface between language and cognition as contextualizing Communication Disorders, disrupted abilities and behaviors. Given the realization that many disorders are developmental in nature, the handbook first covers language and literacy acquisition from infanthood through the school age – Parts I and II respectively, *Linguistic acquisition* and *Oral and written communication*. These set the stage for the two factors underlying communication disorders – Parts III and IV respectively, *Environmental effects* and *Major communication disorders*. Each part consists of a number of sections, each in turn comprising several chapters.

Part I *Linguistic acquisition:* Sections 1–3

The first part of the handbook focuses on the three core-language domains of phonology, lexicon and grammar. This structure also parallels the traditional sequencing of language acquisition from phonemes to words to structures. It is our conviction that the empirical and applied aspects of identification, diagnosis, treatment and therapy of disorders are based on understanding the nature of the disrupted domain. Therefore, each of the sections (1)-(3) contains chapters presenting the conceptual architecture of the domain and related areas, as well as chapters presenting theoretical and empirical information about typical and atypical development in the area.

Section 1: Phonology and speech

The first section of *Linguistic Acquisition* relates to phonology as the domain most relevant to speech perception and production, with three chapters. Starting with the very basic and primary key to early cognitive, social-cognitive, communication, language, and speech development, **Kishon-Rabin** and **Boothroyd** delineate the important role hearing plays in speech and language acquisition and processing. As knowledge of the mechanisms, functions, and roles of hearing is critical for any clinician working in CD, the chapter provides the readers with a review of the relation between hearing, and cognitive, language and speech functions. Following this, the complex way in which auditory development and speech perception development interact is explained by **Houston** and **Warner-Czyz**, who present data on the acquisition of infant hearing capacities, including implications for both infants with normal hearing and infants with hearing loss. Tracing the thread from hearing to phonology, the first section ends with **Bat-El** and **Ben-David** taking a generative approach to describe the role of universal principles in the acquisition of phonological structures within the word. The authors show that different effects of constraints in adults' and children's grammars yield different surface forms, and the relation between these surface forms is expressed in terms of phonological processes in language acquisition.

Section 2: Lexical knowledge

Knowledge, acquisition, learning, processing and deficits of lexical knowledge, a critical language domain, are presented in five chapters. The first two chapters deal with early lexical development. **Stolt** provides an overview on how early lexical acquisition is linked to the development that precedes and follows it. She then presents a discussion illustrating what kind of predictions one may make on the basis of early lexical development in children at-risk for weak language skills. In the next chapter, **Sheng** presents a description of the typical course of lexical development, addressing the rate of learning, the composition of the early lexicon, and child-level and environmental-level factors that lead to individual differences in lexical development. The influence of perceptual and cognitive variables on lexical development is demonstrated, as well as the role of environmental input on vocabulary learning.

The following two chapters address figurative language as a prominent feature of later lexical development. The chapter by **Colston** offers a review of recent research in figurative language acquisition – metaphors, proverbs, hyperbole, idioms, verbal irony and metonymy – in typical development, across the full range of relevant age groups and cross-linguistic comparisons. Issues such as early- versus late-development perspectives, stage versus continuity of development, differential acquisition and development rates of various figures are discussed, ending with the controversy regarding a unitary process versus separate accounts of figurative language comprehension and use. From a different point of view, **Farnia** discusses figurative language in the context of later language development. The chapter describes the developmental changes in language and communicative competence throughout childhood and adolescence. It highlights the roles of higher order/figurative language in adolescents' academic achievement, social relationships and ability to connect with peers and adults, the neurobiological and cognitive underpinnings of impairment in this domain and the overlap of figurative language impairment with socioemotional difficulties.

The section on *Lexical knowledge* ends with **Biedermann, Fieder** and **Nickels** chapter on spoken word production impairment. Comparisons are introduced and drawn between the most influential models of spoken word production, followed by an outline of impaired word production in adults with acquired language impairments and in language acquisition. Focus is on the characteristics of the errors that occur, with illustrations of how treatment of language impairments can inform theory development.

Section 3: Grammatical constructions

The third section covers morphology and syntax under the title of Grammatical Constructions. The section opens with **Ramscar, Dye, Blevines** and **Baayen** proposing *basic discriminative learning mechanisms* in language acquisition. By presenting a model of the learning of noun morphology, the authors show that the learning problem facing children is resolved as a result of the discriminative nature of human learning systems and the properties of the linguistic environment. The implications of these learning mechanisms can enrich the readers with a broader understanding of language and learning.

In the second chapter **Ketrez** addresses the effect of preterm birth on morphological development of preterm children in Turkish, a topic and a language offering a unique window on early grammatical acquisition. By using naturalistic recordings of parent-child conversations, Ketrez shows that children who experience adverse neonatal conditions lag behind their full-term and normal birth weight peers in the number of words in an utterance, but not in terms of agglutinative-morphological complexity, a central typological feature of Turkish.

Moving to later morphological development, **Seroussi** presents the role of derivational morphology in increasing both the breadth and depth of lexical knowledge. The chapter disambiguates relevant terms with a high degree of overlap – morphological knowledge, morphological awareness, and morphological processing, discussing pioneering and contemporary studies of the many facets of the acquisition of derivational morphology in English. The author highlights the interrelations of derivational morphology with a range of other domains, including the mental lexicon, syntax, and literacy, as mediated by factors such as form-meaning dependency, frequency, transparency, and salience.

In the last chapter of this section, **Berman** traces the developmental route of complex syntax, in the sense of combining clauses into more complex constructions from its emergence at around age two years to mastery of text-embedded so-called "syntactic packaging" at late school-age. Analysis of various communicative settings in English and Hebrew reveals a lengthy developmental path from early, highly scaffolded co-construction of complex sentences in adult-child interactions to autonomous topic elaboration as a means of intra-textual packaging of information in narratives and other contexts of extended discourse.

Part II Oral and written communication: Sections 4–5

Bottom-up language components alone cannot explain nor provide analytic and therapeutic means for all language- and communication-related disorders. This is because language learning and processing are anchored to the communicative context in which it is produced and comprehended. Moreover, some disorders have milder forms or may only be noticed in complex situations requiring the integration of several capacities. Part II thus focuses on oral and written communication, with Sections 4 and 5 providing information about pragmatic and textual development that scaffolds the following handbook parts concerning non-optimal and disordered acquisition of spoken and written skills. Part II also ushers in the shift from earlier to later language development in terms of the challenges and obstacles in acquiring the academic language skills necessary for functioning in the global, multi-cultural contexts of the 21st century.

Section 4 revolves around oral discourse in early development and during the school years, providing pragmatic contexts of typical and atypical language behavior, acquisition, and processing. Section 5 encompasses facets of written language knowledge, designated *linguistic literacy*, from basic literacy skills to reading, writing and spelling.

Section 4: Communication and discourse

Theory of Mind, which underlies human communication, develops over the preschool years, when children come to understand the representational nature of mental states. The first chapter of this section by **Schell** and **Sabbagh** discusses ToM and communication, showing that developments in domain-specific mental state understandings are related to domain-general advances in executive functioning. The authors present evidence suggesting that these advances entail advances in communicative development, concluding with speculations on how some aspects of communication might be affected by the biological and experiential factors that affect ToM development during the preschool years.

Ateş and **Küntay** assume that human infants develop a unique combination of socio-pragmatic skills enabling them to learn language and effective communication from interactions in social engagement with others in the first two years of life. Their chapter covers cross-linguistic and cross-cultural work on how infants use nonverbal devices to achieve successful communication, and how they translate pragmatic skills into more advanced forms such as joint engagement and referential interaction. The authors propose that children with atypical developmental profile have problems in interpreting relevant socio-pragmatic cues regarding their social partners' mental states.

These early socio-pragmatic devices lay the foundations for later conversational skills. **Veneziano** describes the relation between conversation and language development from two perspectives. One perspective concerns the acquisition of the conversational skills that are necessary to become a competent speaker of a language, and the second concerns the contribution of conversational functioning to children's acquisition of language knowledge. The author claims that the unfolding and effects of conversational exchanges result depend heavily on children's level of linguistic competence.

Narrative is another major mode of discourse in everyday social life and in academic achievement. **Aksu-Koç** and **Erciyes** trace developmental changes in narrative competence in typically developing children between early preschool and the school years. The chapter focuses on the course of structural developments in personal and fictional narratives, with quantitative and qualitative changes in expressive skills. Referential skills and evaluative language are considered as aspects of narrative competence that contribute to communicative adequacy, together with processing and socio-cognitive demands.

Given the complex coordination of lexical, morpho-syntactic, and pragmatic elements required for narration, it is not surprising that children with language impairment show difficulties in producing and comprehending narratives. Relevant information is provided by **Nicolopoulou** and **Trapp** who critically review published articles that assess the outcomes of narrative-based interventions for preschool and school-age children.

This well-rounded picture of communication and discourse is completed by the last chapter in this section by **Radford**, who emphasizes the importance of classroom discourse in academic development. She illustrates how to increase the participation of children with special educational needs through effective classroom discourse. The author discusses the advantages of dialogic teaching over recitation and refers to scaffolding as key in explaining high quality classroom discourse.

Section 5: Linguistic literacy

For more than four decades there has been a consensus regarding the central role of language in reading, with accumulating evidence indicating the high correlation between language and reading and writing abilities. As a result, SLPs, who traditionally perceived themselves mostly responsible for diagnostic and treatment of oral language, are now becoming more and more aware of their role in reading and writing skills. This section provides an overview on various aspects of linguistic literacy. It starts with the chapter by **Olson** on the nature of literacy and literacy disabilities, expressing the ideas that "literacy is much more than a skill" and that "learning to be literate involves conceptual changes in thinking about language and thinking about a world organized around writing." In accordance with these ideas, the author construes the notions of reading and literacy, presenting implications for literacy teaching with specific attention to the way in which literacy difficulties are diagnosed and treated.

The chapter by **Aram** provides evidence that literacy knowledge emerges before the formal instruction of reading and writing, showing that linguistic knowledge, phonological awareness, and alphabetic skills in kindergarten are chief predictors of literacy abilities in school. The chapter describes the nature of the major early literacy components and discusses recommended early literacy activities and the optimal ways for promoting them.

The chapter by **Share** focuses on the road to skillful, rapid and effortless reading. The questions of how this feat is accomplished has occupied many studies, however, most of them dominated the English of native English-speaking readers/writers. Against the Anglocentric and Alphabetic bias, the chapter by Share lays the foundations for a universal framework of learning to read.

Following reading acquisition, the chapter by **Casalis** turns to typical and atypical spelling acquisition. In addition to phoneme-to-grapheme correspondences and whole-word form retrieval, the chapter presents the contributions of orthographic properties and morphological information to accurate spelling. The author suggests that intervention studies should emphasize both phonological and morphological processing. Likewise, the important role of morphology in reading and writing is in the focus of the chapter by **Sandra**. By presenting an overview of cross-linguistic findings concerning morphological processing during spelling and reading in children and adults, the author explores their reliance on morphemes when dealing with morphologically complex words.

This section ends with two chapters on the integrative topics of text production and comprehension. **Schindler** and **Richter** elaborate the cognitive processes underlying reading comprehension, from word recognition to establishing local and global coherence. The authors conclude that dyslexic readers or poor comprehenders cannot be defined by one specific cognitive deficit. Instead, the sources and symptoms of poor reading comprehension are multifaceted and heterogeneous, and these individual patterns of deficits need to be considered when planning intervention programs. Text production is presented by **Tolchinsky** and **Salas** from a viewpoint of the connection between grammatical competence and text quality, which has not been robustly associated to date. The authors relate these findings to methodological problems, such as the chosen grammatical tasks or the way in which writing quality is defined, and call for future research that will formulate the exact relationship between the two.

Part III Environmental effects: Sections 6–7

The role of social, cultural and linguistic contexts in acquiring communicative and linguistic abilities has been amply demonstrated in the last decades. This part addresses the two major contexts detrimental to making optimal gains in language and literacy learning. One is the effect of SES (Socio-Economic Status), referring to the financial, educational and familial resources of the family a child grows in. Another is the situation in which an individual is in possession of more than one language (bi- and multi-lingualism), in many cases in the context of minority languages and migration. In both cases, the ambient language and literacy contexts are critical to optimal acquisition. The literature indicates numerous cases in which children from low SES background and children growing up in minority cultures and languages present with characteristics similar to those of language and learning disorders. While low SES requires enhancement of linguistic and literacy components in the input, multi-lingualism, if treated correctly, is a blessing for a child's developing cognitive and linguistic abilities and for an old person's maintenance of cognitive skills. The information in the sections on SES and multi-lingual backgrounds will enable professionals to recognize these two contexts, make the necessary diagnoses and select the appropriate remediation.

Section 6: Socio-economic status

Three chapters discuss the effects of SES on child development from different perspectives. In a chapter on the effects of SES differences on early language development, **Weisleder** and **Marchman** review research regarding the role of family environments, language experience and processing skills in this development. A second chapter by **Schibli, Hedayati, Hobbs, Sheik-Ahmed** and **D'Angiulli** reviews the contextual factors associated with poverty from a developmental neuroscience perspective, examining the relationship between SES, children's language and cognitive development. In the third chapter, **Letts** presents a problem that has occupied researchers since the 1970's, regarding the relationship between SES and child language acquisition and impairment. The chapter ends inconclusively on this topic, recommending that professionals consider carefully any assumptions regarding input and abilities of children from SES background.

Section 7: Multilingualism

Four chapters cover the many facets of multilingualism. The first two chapters provide readers with information and tools for language assessment of bilingual children. **De Houwer** highlights the main aspects of language development in children under six who are exposed to more than one spoken language. The chapter defines different pathways for early bilingual development and suggests a step-by-step language screening protocol. The chapter by **Armon-Lotem** addresses a problem bothering both parents and care providers, who struggle to disentangle the effects of SLI and bilingualism in the case of bilingual children who also have language impairment. The chapter offers information and diagnostic techniques regarding these children. **Proctor** and **Louick** present a thematic literature review on vocabulary and its relationship with reading comprehension among bilingual learners. The analysis reveals low initial levels of vocabulary development trajectories with a growth that rarely eliminates language gaps. The last chapter in this section by **Gass** deals with difficulties in adults' learning of a second language, which often falls short of complete mastery of the target language. The chapter presents an overview focusing on linguistic and non-linguistic factors that affect second language learning.

Part IV Language and communication disorders: Sections 8–9

This final part of the handbook addresses the major disordered domains and populations that are too extensive and diverse to be linked to specific linguistic areas or developmental stages. The common thread relating its two sections is the language-related character of most developmental and neurological disorders.

Section 8: Developmental and neurological disorders

The section opens with **De Jong**'s historical review of the changes in definitions of Specific Language Impairment, based on theoretical considerations. He describes how the search for clinical markers of SLI resulted in narrowing the picture of the disability mostly to verb inflection, claiming that while a specific clinical marker can serve to identify SLI, it is not enough for an in-depth diagnosis needed for intervention. A second chapter on language impairment concerns brain neuroplasticity. **Polse, Engel** and **Reilly** compare discourse and narrative performance of children with SLI and with early focal brain injury. Data from language trajectories across a wide age range contributes to a better understanding of the neural and behavioral plasticity for language and the complementary issue of neural specialization.

Two subsequent chapters deal with Developmental Dyslexia, demonstrating different approaches to the same problem. **Friedmann** and **Coltheart** express the idea that one source cannot account for all kinds of developmental dyslexia, given the different properties and error types shown by readers with dyslexia. Accordingly, the chapter outlines a classification of different types of Developmental Dyslexia and their underlying cognitive features. The chapter by **Schiff, Vakil, Gabay,** and **Kahta** brings evidence from studies of implicit learning, showing that readers with dyslexia have difficulties in picking up and assimilating the statistical properties and systematic patterns of a structured environment. The findings support the notion that reading impairment mainly reflects a deficiency in the general capacity of statistical learning.

The next five chapters portray populations with neurological disorders. Children with hearing loss are in the focus of the first two chapters. The chapter by **Gillis** provides readers with a broad overview on the language acquisition and development in deaf children with a cochlear implant, highlighting the large variation of this population resulting from auditory, child-related and environmental factors. From a different perspective, **Most** and **Ingber** discuss the value of parental involvement in early intervention for young children with hearing loss and define the domains of children's development that are affected by this involvement.

Three more chapters address other major communication disorders. Children who suffer from primary impairments in attachment and dyadic communication are associated with Autistic Spectrum Disorders, with many referred for diagnosis before the age of two. **Dromi, Rum** and **Goldberg – Florian** present a five-component developmental model constructed for a detailed evaluation of communication, language and speech behaviors in young children with ASD. Application of the model is also presented, using real examples of clinical cases.

Williams Syndrome, a relatively rare genetic disorder, is in the focus of the chapter by **Levy**. Individuals with WS typically show better verbal IQ than performance IQ, so that language is considered a relative strength. Following recent studies on different language aspects of WS, the chapter describes the disorder as a model case in the ongoing debate between modular and general cognition approaches, concluding in favor of the latter approach. Section 8 ends with the chapter by **Uziel-Karl** and **Tenne-Rinde**, highlighting the importance of making language accessible for people with cognitive disabilities. They outline the major guidelines for language accessibility and illustrate how these guidelines are implemented, pointing out dilemmas along the way.

Sections 9: Disorders in aging

Three chapters on age-related communication disorders constitute this last section, one on language in the healthy aging brain, another on acquired aphasia and a third regarding neurodegenerative diseases. **Higby, Cahana-Amitay** and **Obler** review evidence of brain-language changes and highlight the links among neural structure, brain function, and linguistic behavior in aging. They describe hemispheric contributions to decline in lexical retrieval and sentence comprehension, concluding with the assumption that linguistic and nonlinguistic neural networks work in concert to support language performance.

Varley and **Zimmerer** outline the critical neural systems for language processing, describing the features of aphasic language impairment that result from lesions in these substrates. They explore theoretical approaches to aphasia, concluding with a contemporary perspective on aphasia research. The last chapter by **Assal** and **Laurent** provides the readers with tools for diagnosing primary progressive aphasia, as well as selected therapeutic approaches. Overlaps of progressive aphasias with other clinical diseases are discussed, presenting language deficits in terms of clinical markers of the main neurodegenerative diseases.

References

Ambridge, Ben & Caroline F. Rowland. 2013. Experimental methods in studying child language acquisition. *WIREs Cognitive Science* 4. 149–168.

Ball, Martin J., Nicole Müller, and Ryan L. Nelson. (eds.). 2014. *Handbook of qualitative research in communication disorders.* New York: Psychology Press.

Behrens, Heike. 2009. Usage-based and emergentist approaches to language acquisition. *Linguistics* 47. 383–411.

Berman, Ruth A. & Dorit Ravid. 2008. Becoming a literate language user: Oral and written text construction across adolescence. In David R. Olson and Nancy Torrance (eds.), *Cambridge handbook of literacy*, 92–111. Cambridge: Cambridge University Press.

Berman, Ruth A., Ronit Nayditz & Dorit Ravid. 2011. Linguistic diagnostics of written texts in two school-age populations. *Written Language & Literacy* 14. 161–187.

Bishop, Dorothy V. M. & Courtenay Frazier Norbury. 2008. Speech and language impairments. In Michael J. Rutter, Dorothy Bishop, Daniel Pine, Stephen Scott, Jim S. Stevenson, Eric A. Taylor, and Anita Thapar. (eds.), *Rutter's Child and Adolescent Psychiatry*, 782–801. Oxford: Wiley-Blackwell.

Bishop, Dorothy V. M. 2014. Ten questions about terminology for children with unexplained language problems. *International Journal of Language and Communication Disorders* 49 (4). 381–415.
Bod, Rens. 2006. Exemplar-based syntax: How to get productivity from examples. *The Linguistic Review* 23. 291–320
Bybee, Joan L. 2006. *Frequency of use and the organization of language*. Oxford: Oxford University Press.
Bybee, Joan L. 2010. *Language, usage and cognition*. Cambridge: Cambridge University Press.
Christiansen, Morten H. & Nick Chater. 2008. Language as shaped by the brain. *Behavioral and Brain Sciences* 31. 489–558.
Chung, Sandra. 2009. Are lexical categories universal? The view from Chamorro. *Theoretical Linguistics* 38. 1–56.
Clark, Eve V. 2016. *First language acquisition* (3rd edn). Cambridge: Cambridge University Press.
Comrie, Bernard. 1989. *Language universals and linguistic typology* (2nd edition). Chicago: University of Chicago.
Crago, Martha & Johanne Paradis. 2003. Two of a kind? Commonalities and variation in languages and language learners. In Yonata Levy & Jeannette C. Schaeffer (eds.), *Language competence across populations: Towards a definition of specific language impairment*, 97–110. Mahwah, NJ: Erlbaum.
Croft, William & David A. Cruse. 2004. *Cognitive linguistics*. Cambridge: Cambridge University Press.
Croft, William. 2003. *Typology and Universals* (2nd edn). Cambridge: Cambridge University Press.
de Villiers, Jill G. 2002. Defining SLI: A linguistic perspective. In Yonata Levy & Jeannette C. Schaeffer (eds.), *Language competence across populations: Towards a definition of specific language impairment*, 425–447. Mahwah NJ: Lawrence Erlbaum.
Dromi, Esther, Laurence B. Leonard & Michal Shteiman. 1993. The grammatical morphology of Hebrew-speaking children with specific language impairment: Some competing hypotheses. *Journal of Speech and Hearing Research* 36. 760–771.
Evans, Nicholas & Stephen C. Levinson. 2009. The myth of language universals: Language diversity and its importance for cognitive science. *Behavioral and Brain Sciences* 32. 429–448.
Fernald, Anne, Virginia A. Marchman & Adriana Weisleder. 2013. SES differences in language processing skill and vocabulary are evident at 18 months. *Developmental Science* 16. 234–248.
Frost, Ram. 2012. Towards a universal model of reading. *Behavioral and Brain Sciences* 35. 263–279.
Gillis, Steven & Dorit Ravid. 2006. Typological effects on spelling development: a crosslinguistic study of Hebrew and Dutch. *Journal of Child Language* 33. 621–659.
Gries, Stefan Thomas & Anatol Stefanowitsch. (eds.). 2007. *Corpora in cognitive linguistics: Corpus-based approaches to syntax and lexis*. Berlin: Mouton de Gruyter.
Hart, Betty & Todd R. Risley. 1995. *Meaningful differences in the everyday experience of young American children*. Baltimore MD: Paul H. Brookes.
Haspelmath, Martin. 2012. Escaping ethnocentrism in the study of word-class universals. *Theoretical Linguistics* 38. 91–102.
Hoff, Erica. 2012. *Guide to research methods in child language*. London: Blackwell-Wiley.
Ibbotson, Paul. 2013. The scope of usage-based theory. *Frontiers in Psychology* 4. 255.
Isac, Daniela & Charles Reiss. 2013. *I-language: An introduction to linguistics as cognitive science* (2nd edition). New York: Oxford University Press.
Jarmulowicz, Linda & Valentina L. Taran. 2013. Lexical morphology: Structure, process, and development. *Topics in Language Disorders* 33. 57–72.
Lakoff, George. 1991. Cognitive linguistics versus generative linguistics: How commitments influence results. *Language and Communication* 11. 53–62.
Langacker, Ronald W. 1987. *Foundations of cognitive grammar: Theoretical prerequisites*, Vol. 1. Stanford CA: Stanford University Press.

Levie, R.onit, Galit. Ben Zvi & Dorit Ravid. 2016. Morpho-lexical development in language-impaired and typically developing Hebrew-speaking children from two SES backgrounds. *Reading and Writing*, 1–30.

McArthur, Genevieve, Carmen Atkinson & Danielle Ellis. 2009. Atypical brain responses to sounds in children with language and reading impairments. *Developmental Science* 12. 768–783.

McGilvray, James. 2014. *Chomsky: Language, mind, politics* (2nd edn.). Cambridge: Polity.

McNamara, Danielle S., Scott A. Crossley & Philip M. McCarthy. 2010. Linguistic features of writing quality. *Written Communication* 27. 57–86.

Nelson, Lauren K. 2016. *Research in communication sciences and disorders: Methods for systematic inquiry* (3rd edn.). San Diego: Plural Publishing.

Nippold, Marilyn A. & Cheryl M. Scott. 2009. *Expository discourse in children, adolescents, and adults: Development and disorders*. Hove, UK: Psychology Press.

Perfetti, Charles A. 2003. The universal grammar of reading. *Scientific Studies of Reading* 7. 3–24.

Phakiti, Aek. 2014. *Experimental research methods in language learning*. London: Bloomsbury Academic.

Ravid, Dorit & Rachel Schiff. 2013. Different perspectives on the interface of dyslexia and language: Introduction to the special LLD issue on Dyslexia and Language. *Journal of Learning Disabilities* 46. 195–199.

Ravid, Dorit. 2012. *Spelling morphology: The psycholinguistics of Hebrew spelling*. New York: Springer.

Ravid, Dorit, Ronit Levie & Galit Avivi-Ben Zvi. 2003. Morphological disorders. In Ludo Verhoeven & Hans van Balkom (eds.), *Classification of developmental language disorders: Theoretical issues and clinical implications*, 235–260. Mahwah, NJ: Erlbaum.

Reilly, Sheena, Bruce Tomblin, James Law, Cristina McKean, Fiona K. Mensah, Angela Morgan, Sharon Goldfeld, Jan M. Nicholson & Melissa Wake. 2014. Specific language impairment: A convenient label for whom? *International Journal of Language and Communication Disorders* 49 (4). 416–451.

Rowe, Meredith L. 2008. Child-directed speech: Relation to socioeconomic status, knowledge of child development and child vocabulary skill. *Journal of Child Language* 35. 185–205.

Rowland, Caroline F., Franklin Chang, Ben Ambridge, Julian M. Pine & Elena VM Lieven. 2012. The development of abstract syntax: Evidence from structural priming and the lexical boost. *Cognition* 125. 49–63.

Saffran, Jenny R., Ann Senghas & John C. Trueswell. 2001. The acquisition of language by children. *PNAS* 98 (23). 12874–12875.

Schiff, Rachel, Miki Cohen, Elisheva Ben-Artzi, Ayelet Sasson & Dorit Ravid. 2016. Auditory morphological knowledge among children with developmental dyslexia. *Scientific Studies of Reading* 20. 140–154.

Share David L. 2008. On the anglocentricities of current reading research and practice: The perils of overreliance on an "outlier" orthography. *Psychological Bulletin* 134. 584–615.

Share, David & Amalia Bar-On. 2017. Learning to read a Semitic Abjad: The triplex model of Hebrew reading development. *Journal of Learning Disabilities*. Doi: 10.1177/0022219417718198.

Song, Jae Jung. (ed.). 2011. *The Oxford handbook of linguistic typology*. Oxford: Oxford University Press.

Tomasello, Michael. 2003. *Constructing a language: A usage-based theory of language acquisition*. Cambridge MA: Harvard University Press.

Van der Lely, Heather K.J. 2005. Domain-specific cognitive systems: Insight from Grammatical-SLI. *Trends in Cognitive Sciences* 9. 53–59.

I Linguistic acquisition

Section 1: Phonology and speech

Liat Kishon-Rabin and Arthur Boothroyd
1 The role of hearing in speech and language acquisition and processing

1 Introduction: Terminology

As with many disciplines, terminology changes as knowledge increases. Unfortunately, researchers and clinicians do not always agree on the appropriate vocabulary. In addition, words with certain meanings in the general vocabulary may carry different, or more precise, meanings in a professional context. In this chapter:

i. Hearing refers to the process by which we detect, analyze, and interpret sound.
ii. Hearing impairment refers to any disorder of the process by which we detect, analyze, and interpret sound.
iii. Hearing loss refers to a deficit in the detection of sound, resulting in an elevated threshold whose severity can be expressed in decibels (dB).
iv. Sound stimulus refers to an acoustic signal reaching the ears.
v. Sound sensation refers to the resulting auditory impression experienced by the listener.
vi. Auditory processing refers to the organization of sound sensations and their conversion to sensory evidence in the auditory cortex – to be used in perception.
vii. Auditory perception refers to the process of making decisions about the most probable cause of, and implications of, the acoustic stimuli on the basis of sensory evidence, contextual evidence, and prior knowledge.
viii. The term resolution is used, here, to refer to the ability of the peripheral hearing mechanism to preserve, in the information it sends to the brain, the details of the sound patterns it receives.
ix. Speech perception requires the inclusion of speech and language in the listener's prior knowledge. It also includes knowledge of the world of people and the way they use spoken language to satisfy intent.
x. A primary disorder is the one most responsible for an observed communication deficit.
xi. A secondary disorder may contribute to the consequences of the primary disorder but, by itself, would not have the same effects. For example, an autistic child may have a primary disorder of social-cognitive function leading to a disorder of

---

Liat Kishon-Rabin, Tel Aviv University
Arthur Boothroyd, San Diego State University

language, cognition, and social cognition. At the same time, he could have a secondary impairment of hearing that, by itself, does not explain the absence of language but does present a challenge for diagnosis and intervention.[1]

2 The many roles of hearing

The importance of hearing in human development and function cannot be over emphasized. At a very basic level and at all stages of life, hearing serves as a "watchdog" sense – monitoring the environment and alerting us to potentially important events. In infancy, hearing is also key to early cognitive, social-cognitive, language, and speech development (Boothroyd, 1997). Once spoken language is developed, hearing remains a primary avenue for continuing cognitive, social-cognitive, and language development (Boothroyd and Boothroyd-Turner, 2002). In the school years, hearing contributes to the development of literacy and plays an important role in education. In adult life, cognitive, social-cognitive, and vocabulary, development continue at a slower pace, but with hearing still playing a major role. Congenital or early-acquired hearing loss can have serious and far-reaching effects on development (Boothroyd and Gatty, 2012). Loss of hearing in adult life can have devastating effects on leisure, employment, and socialization. In short, hearing permeates human development and human function, especially in those areas related to communication.

We do not mean to imply that development and function are impossible without hearing. The deaf child can use vision and sign in place of hearing and speech. In communication environments where signed language is the norm, developmental and life opportunities are unimpaired. But this text is about disorders in individuals whose communicative environment is one of spoken language – hence the focus of this chapter on hearing.

For persons working in communication disorders, knowledge of the mechanisms, functions, and roles of hearing is important for at least four reasons:
i. Hearing impairment can be a primary cause of communication disorders.
ii. Hearing impairment can be present in individuals who have a primary disorder of cognition, social-cognition, or language, and may explain some of the difficulties demonstrated by those individuals.

---

[1] The distinction between primary and secondary disorders is not always clear. Two disorders can contribute equally to a communication deficit, or they can interact in such a way that the combined effect is greater than the sum of the two separate effects. Pragmatically, the primary disorder often refers to the title of the professional who is leading the intervention team. The potential contribution of hearing to any communication disorder, however, should always be explored and, if necessary, treated.

iii. Identification, evaluation, and management of a secondary disorder of hearing is a critical part of intervention planning and implementation.
iv. Standard practice often relies on hearing as a primary medium for intervention and remediation when dealing with non-auditory disorders of communication.

It follows that an understanding of hearing, its role in development and function, and the ways in which it can be impaired must be in the armamentarium of clinicians who deal with the diagnosis, evaluation, remediation, and prevention of communication disorders.

3 Sound and hearing

3.1 Sound

Sound is the physical stimulus to which hearing responds. Sound usually consists of tiny fluctuations of air pressure.[2] The simplest sound pattern is that of a pure tone which has just two properties:
  i. Amplitude, which refers to the size of the pressure fluctuations. Amplitude is usually expressed in decibels (dB) rather than units of pressure.
  ii. Frequency, which refers to the rate at which the fluctuations repeat themselves. Frequency is expressed in cycles per second, or Hertz (Hz).

In young normally hearing people, pure tones with frequencies between 20 and 20,000 Hz are capable of stimulating the sense of hearing. The lowest audible amplitude for a typical young adult with normal hearing is referred to as the normal threshold of hearing and is given a value of 0 dB HL. The HL stands for Hearing Level and is used when the reader needs to know that the average normal hearing sensitivity is being used as the 0 dB reference.[3]

Most of the sounds we hear (including the sounds of speech) are complicated mixtures of pure tones. A complete description of the frequencies and amplitudes of the tones in such a mixture is known as its spectrum. The mixture can have an overall amplitude and, for musical sounds and spoken vowels, it can have a basic

---

[2] We say "usually" because physical vibration of the skull and soft-tissue conduction (Sohmer, 2014) can also stimulate hearing and spontaneous sound sensation is even possible without a sound stimulus, as in tinnitus (ringing in the ears).

[3] There are other references. We use dB SL (Sensation Level) when the 0 dB reference is the individual listener's own threshold and dB SPL (Sound Pressure Level) when the 0 dB reference is based on a standard pressure amplitude. When talking about hearing loss or hearing aid gain, we can simply use dB because the 0 dB reference is implicit.

(or fundamental) frequency. The spectrum of speech sounds is strongly related to their articulation while they are being produced. Changes in the vocal tract such as position of the tongue and extent of oral constriction influence the frequency regions in the spectrum that are being enhanced by resonance (the formants). Another important property of complex sounds is the way in which the amplitude and the spectrum vary with time (Raphael, Borden and Harris, 2007).

3.2 Hearing as a process

Hearing is the sense that responds to sound.[4] It does so by creating a sound sensation in the consciousness of the listener. The sound stimulus and the sound sensation are obviously related, but they are not the same. Changes of frequency in the sound stimulus are heard as changes of pitch in the sound sensation, changes of amplitude are heard as changes of loudness, and changes of spectrum and time pattern are heard as changes of sound quality.

Although there are situations in which listeners focus on sound sensation, the usual goal of auditory perception is to learn about the source of the sound stimulus. To achieve this goal certain pre-requisites in processing must be achieved: These include:

i. Detection. Detection occurs when a sound stimulus generates a sound sensation. As indicated earlier, threshold is the lowest stimulus amplitude at which this occurs. When an individual's threshold is more than 20 dB HL, we refer to a hearing loss.

ii. Resolution. Resolution occurs when different sound stimuli produce different sound sensations. It can be quantified in terms of the smallest change in an aspect of the stimulus that produces a detectable change in the corresponding aspect of the sound sensation. For example, we may refer to: the smallest change in amplitude that produces a detectable change of loudness (amplitude resolution), the shortest silent gap in an ongoing stimulus that is detectable (temporal resolution), or the smallest change in frequency that produces a detectable change of pitch (frequency resolution).[5]

iii. Recognition. Recognition occurs when the event that caused the sound stimulus is correctly identified. Indeed, the word recognition (re-cognition) literally means knowing again. Recognition deficits may follow directly from deficits of detection and/or discrimination. They can also occur independently in the form of

---

4 Note the circular definition. Sound is defined by hearing and hearing is defined by sound.
5 The term frequency-resolution has also been used to refer to the ability to respond to a single frequency in an acoustic stimulus when other frequencies are present. Readers may be more familiar with the term discrimination which depends on resolution but also involves processes beyond the periphery. It has been used to refer to the ability to differentiate and/or recognize words and speech sounds.

auditory-processing disorders (APD) or of general perceptual-processing disorders such as those related to the storage in memory of speech sounds and their accurate and efficient retrieval. A common task for assessing recognition is the repetition of words. When listening conditions are good then repetition of single words can be achieved with minimal knowledge of the language (phonological knowledge is sufficient). In challenging listening conditions, such as listening in noise, or with more complex speech stimuli, reliance on acoustic detail is not enough and knowledge of the language is essential for correct word repetition. In the clinic, the most common speech perception assessment task is the repetition of monosyllabic words in Phonetically-Balanced (PB) lists. Performance on this task at an optimal listening level is often referred to as PBMax and may be described as "speech discrimination ability". When this ability is significantly poorer than normal, we may refer to a discrimination loss.

iv. Comprehension. Comprehension implies deduction of the implications of a recognized sound in the general context of the individual's cognitive and linguistic status and in the immediate context. Clearly, comprehension involves prior knowledge of the world, of people, and of language – including its phonology, vocabulary, grammar, and pragmatics. We may, for example, recognize a knock on the door but we comprehend that a person is present and desires entry. In the context of language, we may recognize words and intonation patterns but we comprehend sentence meaning. Depending on our social-cognitive status, we may also comprehend the implications of the meaning, including the intent of the talker in expressing it.

Each aspect of perception is a pre-requisite for the next. Without detection, there can be no resolution. Without resolution, there can be no recognition. And without recognition, there can be no comprehension. The exceptions are instances where the speech stimulus is highly redundant and implementing previous knowledge of the language and world may result in comprehending the message despite minimal acoustic information (Nittrouer and Boothroyd, 1990). This issue needs to be considered when interpreting performance of speech recognition tests. It reminds us again of the connections among hearing, cognition, social cognition, and spoken language. It should also be noted that there can be confusion and inaccurate use of terminology among professionals. Using the terms 'speech intelligibility' and 'speech comprehension' can be misleading when based solely on the results of a test involving repetition of isolated words.

3.3 Hearing for monitoring the environment

The impact of hearing on communication may be our main focus, but we should not ignore the role of hearing in monitoring the auditory scene. The properties of the sound make it possible for us to perceive events at distance, almost as soon as they occur, and even when the objects involved cannot be seen. From slight differences in the sound amplitude and time of arrival at the two ears, we can also determine the direction the sound came from. And our ears never close. Hearing can still monitor and respond to sound when we sleep.

The watchdog role of hearing is apparent in neonates who may demonstrate attention to sound by reducing activity – including sucking. They may even turn their head in the direction of a sound. At an early age, infants respond to sound by turning to look at the source so as to gain the fine spatial information needed for learning about the objects and events involved. As the child matures, hearing consolidates its role, not just as a first indicator of a potentially important event but as a source of ongoing information about the activities of objects and people in the surroundings. The source of this information has been referred to as the "auditory scene" (Bregman, 1990). Thus, emerging environmental awareness represents an early stage of cognitive development on which language development is based.

Difficulties in monitoring the auditory scene may alert us to auditory processing problems despite normal hearing sensitivity. Such problems may co-occur with language deficits. Children with recurring ear infections may lose primacy of hearing for this role and become auditorily inattentive – with repercussions on communicative development and formal education. Indeed, it has been suggested that auditory attention deficits may be one of the causes of Auditory Processing Disorders (Moore et al., 2010).

3.4 Hearing as a mechanism

The hearing mechanism responsible for detecting and interpreting sound patterns has four major components:
1. The conductive component consists of the visible ear, the ear canal, the eardrum, and three tiny bones in the middle ear (the ossicles), with their associated tendons and muscles. Its role is to detect tiny fluctuations of air pressure, convert them into movements of the tympanic membrane (eardrum), and deliver (conduct) them as efficiently as possible to the sensory component.
2. The sensory component is the cochlea – a small snail-shaped cavity containing fluids, membranes, and around 16,000 tiny hair cells. Around 4000 of these cells are referred to as inner hair cells and are connected to around 95% of the fibers of the auditory nerve. The inner hair cells are responsible for converting patterns of movement into patterns of nerve activation, while preserving the details needed for resolution. The remaining 12,000 hair cells are involved in sharpening the frequency-resolution of the cochlea and they increase sensitivity to allow listening at low sound intensities (Purves et al., 2001).

3. The neural component begins with the auditory nerve, and is followed by several inter-connected relay stations or auditory pathways. Their role is to extract information from the patterns of stimulation and to pass it on, as new patterns of activation, to the central component.
4. The central component consists of the auditory cortex and associated regions of the brain. Its role is to generate sound sensations and to make decisions about their probable cause, their probable meaning, and appropriate responses.

Some further observations on the hearing mechanism:

   i. The boundaries between the four components described above are not clear. The conductive component involves part of the cochlea; the cochlea contains the first stage of the auditory nerve; many of the fibers in the auditory nerve and auditory pathways are carrying information in the reverse direction (efferent pathways), as if the four components are in conversation; and perceptual decisions cannot be made solely in the neural and central components of hearing.

   ii. Regions which are considered "non-auditory" cortical areas of the brain, such as the anterior lateral, frontal, and parietal lobes of the cerebral cortex, show widespread activation in response to sounds and have also been implicated in decision making and other aspects of responding to sounds (Moore, 2012). They have reciprocal connections with the recognized auditory cortex (Hackett, 2011), and thus form the origins of the 'top-down', descending, 'efferent' auditory system. Efferent pathways are active early in life and are involved in the maturation and maintenance of hearing (Moore, 2012).

   iii. Impairments can occur in any part of the hearing mechanism, leading to deficits in one or more aspects of the hearing process. These include:

   a) Conductive impairments occur when the external and middle ears fail to deliver sound energy efficiently to the fluids and membranes of cochlea. Such impairments can be temporary or permanent and are often amenable to surgical or pharmaceutical intervention. They can usually be corrected successfully with hearing aids. Conductive impairments reduce sound detection, producing a hearing loss. There is, however, usually no loss of resolution for those sounds that are strong enough to produce a sound sensation.

   b) Sensory impairments[6] occur when sound patterns reaching the cochlea are not adequately reproduced as patterns of stimulation of the auditory nerve. The most common cause is loss of, or damage to, the hair cells. These impairments are not usually amenable to surgical or pharmaceutical intervention. Sensory impairments produce a loss of sensitivity (which can

---

[6] It should be noted that loss of hair cells is often accompanied by (or may even result in) loss of auditory nerve fibers. For this reason, deficits of cochlear function are generally referred to as sensorineural impairments.

often be corrected with hearing aids) and a loss of discrimination (which cannot). In general, listeners with greater sensory hearing loss tend to have poorer resolution and, therefore, to gain less benefit from hearing aids. When the impairment is severe enough, cochlear implants are a viable solution for replacing the function of the cochlea. Although they cannot restore normal hearing, the results are often remarkably good.

c) Neural impairments occur when the auditory nerve and other auditory pathways carry incomplete patterns of activation from the cochlea to the auditory centers of the brain. Such impairments may or may not affect detection but they typically affect resolution, recognition, and comprehension. In pathological cases where there is no auditory nerve, auditory brainstem implants are considered an option – but with limited results.

d) Central impairments occur when the perceptual-processing centers of the brain fail, or are too slow, to properly interpret auditory sensory evidence.

iv. There are clinical tools that help to assess the integrity of the different components of the hearing mechanism. For example, the difference in thresholds between air and bone conduction (air-bone gap) and the results of tympanometry or acoustic reflex testing provide information about middle ear function; otoacoustic emissions (OAEs) provide information about cochlear function (specifically the function of outer hair cells); and auditory brainstem responses (ABR) provide information about the synchrony of the responses of the auditory nerve to auditory stimuli (Katz, 1994).

v. In children, in the absence of appropriate intervention, hearing loss (i.e., elevated thresholds) due to any of the components cited above, is known to impede language development, impact daily communication, restrict learning and literacy, and compromise educational achievement and later employment opportunities (e.g., Kral and O'Donoghue, 2010; Perez and Kishon-Rabin, 2013). Hearing aids or cochlear implants (depending on the severity of the hearing loss) provide access to acoustic information in the speech signal. This information stimulates the neural and cognitive substrates for speech and language processing and consequently facilitates distributional learning of speech patterns, word segmentation, and the acquisition of basic skills for language and cognitive development (e.g., Eisenberg 2007; Houston 2011). The children with congenital hearing loss with the best speech and language outcomes are those that received proper auditory rehabilitation prior to the age of 6 months. Any delay in the provision of hearing aids or cochlear implants after this age may result in an irreversible delay in spoken language skills and cognitive abilities (Yoshinaga-Itano, 2006).

vi. There are intriguing cases where, in the presence of normal hearing sensitivity, there are abnormal results on specific clinical diagnostic tests along with impaired language and/or literacy. Examples include: highly variable neural responses of ABR in children with dyslexia (Hornickel and Kraus, 2013);

delayed neural responses and prolonged brainstem conduction times of ABR in infants at high risk for autism (Ari-Even Roth et al, 2012); abnormal efferent feedback pathways to the auditory periphery as measured by acoustic reflex thresholds and transient OAEs in children with selective mutism (Muchnik et al, 2013); and severely abnormal or absent ABR in the presence of normal cochlear functioning in the case of auditory neuropathy spectrum disorder (ANSD) (Rance and Barker, 2008). As implied earlier, the abnormality of certain auditory functions in these examples (except for ANSD) do not fully account for the deficits in language abilities. They may, however, aggravate the communication deficit and compromise remediation. In some cases, addressing the auditory problems may assist in improving the deficit resulting from the primary disorder. In children with dyslexia, providing them with frequency-modulation (FM) assistive listening devices (to improve access to the speech signal in relation to the background noise) has been shown to result in more consistent ABR responses, enhanced attention, and improved reading performance (Hornickel et al, 2012). In children with selective mutism, it has been suggested that aberrant efferent auditory function creates difficulty in listening while vocalizing. Such children may face the dilemma (consciously or subconsciously) of choosing between speaking and listening (Muchnik et al, 2013). In the final example of ANSD, the pathology often involves a pre-neural deficit such as loss or malfunction of inner hair cells or disruption of the synaptic connection between these cells and the auditory nerve. In some such cases, cochlear implants have been found to be beneficial – possibly because they restore neural synchrony (Rance and Barker, 2008).

4 Hearing and motor-speech development

With his first cry, the neonate begins to learn the association between movements of his speech mechanism and the resulting sound sensations. This association becomes more refined in the next few months as he experiments with sound. Evidence of the coupling between auditory perception and motor-speech production can be found in the attempts of the infant to imitate speech sounds. Vocalizations (babbling) move from a language universal pattern to one that is specific to the ambient language of the infant (de Boysson-Bardies & Vihman, 1991). This pattern of vocalization follows the infant's changes in hearing sensitivity to speech sounds that are not part of his native language. In the first six months of his life, the infant is exposed to the phonemic patterns of his native language but shows similar sensitivity to sounds of his language compared to those that are not. Towards the end of the infant's first year of life, there is a decline in auditory discrimination for phonemes that are not part of his native language (Werker & Tees, 1984). At the same time, the infant's productions become more speech-like and resemble the phonemes of his language. These changes in auditory perception and early speech-like productions are attributed to the infant's development of higher level of processing in which perceptual decisions are based on learned categories. He is no longer treating sound as sound – something to be attended to and explored – but as evidence of something in his emerging knowledge base of the world, of people, and of speech. Moreover, he has started to understand that he can produce sequences of these sounds and by doing so he can control the environment to satisfy his needs. Once the infant acquires words and begins to combine and use them in communication, the roles of phonemic contrasts in determining word and sentence meaning will become increasingly apparent to him. His phoneme system matures. It may, however, take a few years for phonology to reach a fully mature state (longer for some languages than for others) (Kishon-Rabin et al, 2002).

Establishing basic auditory-motor associations in the first year of the infant's life has been found crucial not only for developing language and intelligible speech but also for setting the basis of speech perception skills. In a Motor Theory of speech perception, Liberman et al. (1967) suggested that listeners reconstruct the vocal tract movements themselves when the auditory pattern is decoded. The revised version of this theory suggests that the listeners learn to reconstruct the talker's intended gestures (Liberman & Mattingly, 1985). That is, the infants learn to perceive the articulatory plans that control the vocal tract movements that would produce a perfect exemplar of the talker's intended utterance. The relationship between speech movement and speech sound is not simple. Perception of speech is more than recognition of acoustic sound patterns. There is not a one-to-one relationship between the phonetic categories and their acoustic correlates. Thus, the intended motoric gestures of speech are assumed to be the only invariant property that unites the phonemic message through differences in rate of speech, talker, dialect or other speaker characteristics. It is, therefore, the only invariant property the infant can pick up from the speech signal and add to his newly acquired knowledge of how to make speech sounds in order to recognize them (Hawkins, 1999). A more recent developmental account emphasizes the role of experience with speech patterns in the ambient language for establishing the correspondence of motor-sound pairs that have been learned through babbling (Vihman, 1993). It is suggested that the experience of frequently self-producing consonant-vowel (CV) syllables alerts infants to similar patterns in their ambient language, making these forms more salient as potential building blocks for first words. Thus, the coupling between the development of the representations of articulatory parameters and auditory perception is not only experience-dependent but it is also assumed to be the basis for phonological development in the infant babbling phase (Westermann and Reck Miranda, 2004).

Neurobiological data provide strong support for the connections between auditory perception and speech production. Emergence of auditory mirror neurons[7] for acoustic stimuli is thought to strengthen neural connections between the motor and auditory map based on the co-variance between articulatory parameters and the auditory consequences when babbling sounds are made. Therefore auditory experience coupled with the production of the same sounds produce simultaneous activity of auditory and motor units which continue to strengthen these connections. The result is that sounds from the ambient language selectively reinforce the sounds from the infant's babbling inventory (Vihman, 2002). Further support for these strong connections arise from electrophysiological and imaging data which demonstrate activation of speech-related muscles during the perception of speech (Fadiga, Craiqhero, Buccino, & Rizzolatti, 2002) and overlap between the cortical areas that are active during speech production and those active during passive listening to speech (Pulvermuller et al., 2006). Indeed, auditory-to-motor stream, a parietal-frontal network predominantly in the left hemisphere which interfaces auditory and articulatory representations of speech (Démonet et al., 2005) is considered today one of two major parallel pathways that has been implicated in the processing of auditory stimuli, speech, and phonological and linguistic information (Hickok & Poeppel, 2000; Scott & Johnsrude, 2003).

Immediate implication of the auditory-motor associations is that motor practice should have an effect on auditory perception, and vice versa. For example, infants with normal hearing that could not babble due to tracheotomy showed abnormal patterns of vocal expressions that persisted even one year after the tracheostomy was removed (Bleile, Stark, & McGowan, 1993; Locke & Pearson, 1990). Similarly, individuals with cerebral palsy and speech deficits show difficulties in recognizing strings of nonsense words (Bishop, Brown, & Robinson, 1990). Conversely, auditory deprivation in infants with hearing loss has been shown to impede development of normal speech production. At six months of age, the vocalizations of hearing-impaired (HI) infants have been found to deviate from normal behavior, coinciding with the same age that hearing babies start babbling (Koopsman-van Beinum et al., 2001; Oller & Eilers, 1988). It has been shown that profound hearing loss resulted in delays of 5 to 19 months in the onset of babbling in HI infants (Oller & Eilers; 1988). Koopsman-van Beinum et al. (2001), for example, reported that none of their profoundly HI infants babbled before the age of 18 months. Finally, when the HI infants started babbling, their phonemic repertoire was usually limited and restricted to those language sounds that were visible (e.g., bilabials), acoustically salient (e.g., vowels) and/or provided tactile feedback (e.g., laryngeals) (Fletcher, 1992). It also

---

[7] Auditory mirror neurons are considered an extension to visual mirror neurons which were found to fire both when the animal acts and when it observed the same action performed by others (Galantucci, Fowler, & Turvey, 2006).

has been shown that certain stages in vocalization development, such as reduplicated babbling, were absent in infants with profound hearing loss (Moeller et al., 2007). It is important to note that early provision of auditory feedback, via cochlear implants for example, resulted in improved early pre-verbal vocalizations (e.g., Kishon-Rabin et al., 2005). These findings together with today's ability to indentify infants at risk for speech and language delay suggest that close monitoring of infants vocalizations in their first year can provide us with important information regarding their speech and language developmental processing as well as indications of the need for early intervention.

Some further observations on the role of hearing for speech development:

i. The intrinsic relation between auditory perception and production manifests itself in strong predictive values between auditory perception and vocalizations of infants already at the preverbal stage. Thus, the quality and quantity of the vocalizations of infants serve as an indirect measure of auditory perception (e.g., Kishon-Rabin et al., 2005; Moeller et al., 2007).

ii. Infants 2–7 months show preference to their language compared to other sounds or foreign languages (Kishon-Rabin et al, 2010; Vouloumanos and Werker, 2004, 2007). This ability, allowing infants to tune to the relevant environmental input, has been found to facilitate rapid language acquisition (Gervain and Werker, 2008; Sebastian-Galles, 2007).

iii. It is true that the smaller dimensions of the child's speech mechanism make it impossible for her to match, exactly, the speech she hears. But what is important is the speech patterns – the organized relationships among the details. Intonation patterns, for example, are characterized by the variation of pitch over time, not by the average pitch. Vowels are characterized by the relationships among the frequencies of the major spectral resonances (formants), not by their separate values.

iv. Another aspect of auditory input and feedback occurs in modeling. Parents will often respond to a child's communication by including a more correct pronunciation in cases of distortion, omission, or substitution.

v. The role of hearing in the mastery of phonology continues throughout childhood but its contribution diminishes as ongoing speech control is taken over by learned motor skills and proprioceptive feedback.

vi. After puberty, it becomes increasingly difficult to acquire the phonology of a new language and the influence of the native language seldom disappears.

vii. Adults who lose hearing do not suddenly lose speech production skills. The immediate effects are likely to be loss of loudness control – a task for which hearing remains important. It takes many years, however, for articulatory precision to deteriorate. Even then, there is usually no loss of intelligibility but only some loss of finesse in articulation (e.g., Kishon-Rabin et al., 1999). Thus, hearing is necessary for learning speech-motor skills in childhood but not for preserving those skills in adult life.

viii. Children and adults with normal hearing but with reading impairment have been found to have neurophysiologic dysfunctions along the auditory-to-motor stream (as opposed to the auditory-meaning stream). Although disorders of auditory-to-motor mapping are not considered to be the basis of reading impairments, they might possibly aggravate the phonological and literacy problem (Boets et al., 2007). This observation supports the notion that for many individuals, abnormal speech and language processing emerge prior to their manifestation in reading difficulties, possibly in the first year of life.

5 Hearing speech

In the context of spoken-language communication, the principal role of hearing is for speech perception. The model of this process, presented in Figure 1, drives our theoretical understanding of the process and suggest guidelines for assessment and intervention.

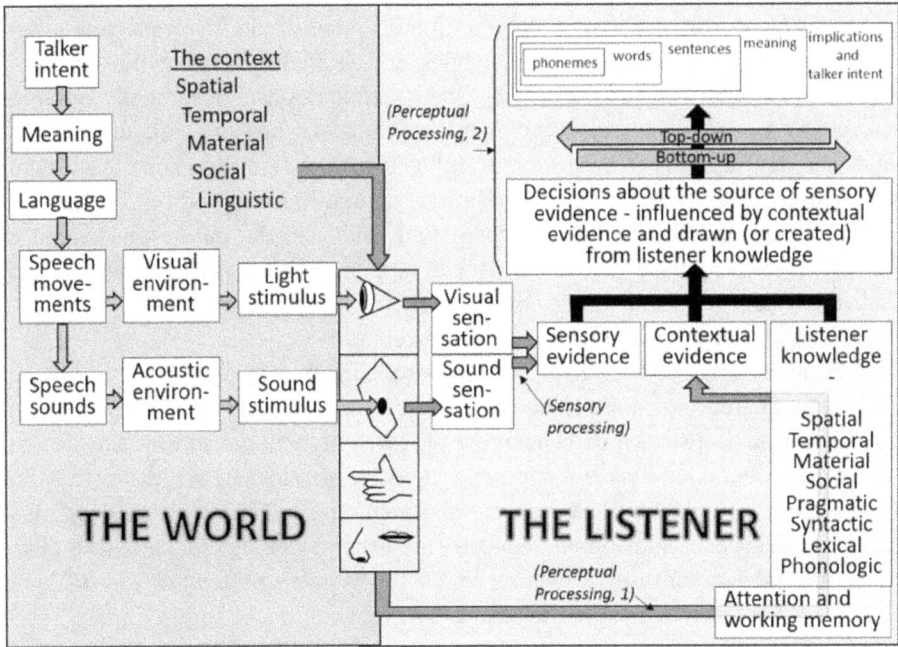

Figure 1: A conceptual model of speech perception

Speech communication begins with the talker's intent. The talker chooses a meaningful message to satisfy this intent and expresses it in language form, using patterns of speech movements to generate patterns of speech sound. After modification by the acoustic environment, the sound patterns arrive at the listener's ear as sound stimuli and are converted into patterns of sound sensation. The sensation patterns provide the listener's brain with sensory evidence about their source. In face-to-face communication, direct observation of speech movements can add to the sensory evidence, adding to motor evidence. Sensory evidence alone, however, is not enough. Its interpretation is strongly influenced by contextual evidence. This evidence comes from the actual context and is filtered by such things as the listener's sensory capacities, attention, working memory, and prior knowledge.

The listener's task is to make decisions about the most likely source of the sensory evidence. These decisions could involve things like the talker's gender, age, emotional state, health, or region of origin. In the context of communication, however, our main interest is in the language patterns (phonemes, words, sentences), their meaning, and their implications. When making perceptual decisions, maximum use of contextual evidence promotes both speed and accuracy. Note, also, that the possible decisions come from the listener's prior knowledge. In summary, successful perception relies on a combination of sensory evidence, contextual evidence, cognitive abilities, and prior knowledge.

In the context of speech perception, theorists have distinguished between "bottom-up" and "top-down" processing. Bottom-up processing would involve testing lower-level decisions first (e.g., about phonemes and words) and using the results to influence higher-level decisions (e.g., about sentences and meaning). Top-down processing would involve testing higher-level decisions first (e.g., about sentences and meaning) and using the results to influence lower-level decisions (e.g., about phonemes and words). The balance of bottom-up and top-down processing depends on the nature of the sensory and contextual evidence, the nature and extent of activity in other systems (e.g. vision, attention, memory, emotion), as well as on the individual's experience, and age (Moore, 2012).[8]

Some further observations on speech perception:

i. Some theories of speech perception describe it as "special", meaning that it uses different processes from those involved in general perception. We suggest, however, that speech perception uses the same functional substrate as general perception. What makes it special is the nature of the source. As illustrated in Figure 1, the source has many levels, including talker-intent, message, language, speech, and sound. Moreover, the listener can also function as a talker (recall the motor theory). In other words, the listener's prior knowledge includes all the levels that exist in the source.

---

[8] Consider the sentence "John *alks too fast" in which one sound is masked by a sudden noise. If three of you are out for a stroll and John is way ahead, you would have no difficulty deciding that the missing sound is /w/ (top- down processing). But if a friend is telling you about her new love interest, you would need to identify the missing sound before you could decide between /w/ and /t/ (bottom-up processing).

ii. In communication situations the intent of the talker is usually one of control. Declarative sentences seek to control the listener's knowledge. Imperatives seek to control the listener's behavior. Interrogatives seek to control the listener's speech output. And, in some cases, the talker's intent is to control the listener's emotional status.

iii. Theorists have made distinctions between auditory processing and perceptual processing. In the present model, auditory processing occurs when sound sensations are converted to sensory evidence. Perceptual processing occurs when contextual input is converted to contextual evidence and when the sensory evidence, contextual evidence, and prior knowledge are used to arrive at perceptual decisions.

iv. Among the things that make speech perception different from other kinds of perception (including reading) is that perceptual speed is controlled not by the listener, but by the talker. When the rate of speech input exceeds that of the perceptual processing, communication fails.

v. On the same point, successful speech perception involves a compromise between speed and accuracy. We can increase perceptual speed by making increased use of context (e.g., accepting what we expect to hear without checking it against the sensory evidence) but we then increase the risk of error. Alternatively, we can reduce the chance of error by paying close attention to the sensory evidence but this takes time. Successful speech perception requires a balance in the use of sensory and contextual evidence, which is also a balance between bottom-up and top-down processing and between speed and the risk of error. Competence may involve a shift in this balance to adapt to the demands of the communication situation. Top-down processing and maximum reliance on context may work well in a casual conversation with a friend but more bottom-up processing and increased reliance on sensory evidence will be needed when following a lecture.

vi. Recent studies emphasize the role of general cognitive abilities in speech perception (e.g., Conway et al., 2014; Pisoni, 2000; Moore, 2012). These, including attention, learning, and memory are thought to be mutually interdependent and cannot be divided up into separate subsystems. Understanding auditory perception (speech perception in particular) requires awareness and appreciation of the contributions of these cognitive factors. Listening experience and auditory feedback are assumed to be necessary for developing cognitive abilities. This assumption is based on the findings of poor general cognitive capabilities found in children with congenital and prelingually acquired hearing loss (Conway et al., 2011, 2014; Pisoni, 2000).[9]

---

[9] In this chapter, we addressed the influence of hearing only on spoken language and cognition. Findings of deaf children who use manual language for communication suggest that children without spoken language can think and reason well (e.g., Furth, 1966).

vii. The speech perception system modelled in Figure 1 has finite capabilities (Miller, 1956). This major limitation requires listeners to develop capabilities that will allow "information reduction". Attention or selective attention is an example of an ability that allows attending to a target signal while ignoring other competing sounds, also known as the "cocktail party effect". This ability allows the listener to switch and attend to a sound that a moment ago was irrelevant while ignoring (inhibiting) other incoming sounds that may have been relevant in a previous social interaction. Without this capability, the listener would have been "flooded" with an enormous amount of sensory information, only some of which is relevant at a particular moment in time, while overloading and "clogging" those channels that should be available for incoming relevant auditory information for further processing. Thus, selective auditory attention is an example of an auditory capability that allows for efficient listening in the presence of a system with limited capacity. It develops at an early age and allows typically-developing infants to selectively attend to the words of their language from an ongoing stream of background noises and irrelevant speech. It also allows children in school to attend to the voice of the teacher or to the voice of one of their classmates even when there is much background talk going on. For adults, selective auditory attention allows attention to a particular speaker in the presence of others in everyday activities such as work meetings, social gatherings, and team sports. Thus, an individual who has reduced capability of efficient listening will not only show difficulties in recognizing the targeted speech in noise but there is also great likelihood that he would be overwhelmed by the amount of incoming information to the point that he may shut himself from the environment. Such behavior is demonstrated, for example, by those on the autistic spectrum whose inefficient listening may also lead to poor language development and social interaction (Christ et al., 2007). From a physiological aspect, general deficits in frontal-lobe function known to be responsible for lack of inhibitory control are thought to be responsible for reduced selective attention in the elderly (Andres et al., 2006; Anderson et al., 2013).
viii. It is important to note that difficulties in perceiving speech in the presence of noise can also result from auditory peripheral factors, such as, reduced frequency resolution at the cochlear level or by inability to use linguistic knowledge when listening to a degraded acoustic signal (as in second language users or young typically developing children), and not only from impaired cognitive capabilities.
ix. As implied in the model (Figure 1), all aspects of auditory perception, in particular speech perception, "involve some kind of storage or memory system that preserves selected aspects of the initial sensory stimulation" (Pisoni, 2000). The role of working memory in the speech perception process is described as an episodic buffer which matches phonological information in the incoming speech signal with the existing representations stored in long-term memory.

Degraded acoustic input from environmental factors (e.g., noise) or auditory devices (e.g., cochlear implants, hearing aids) may result in a mismatch between the auditory signal and information in the mental lexicon in long-term memory. The ease of language understanding model (ELU) assumes that when this occurs, conscious processing resources, such as, shifting, updating, and inhibition need to be brought into play (Ronnberg et al., 2013). The role of these processes is to bring together ambiguous signal fragments with relevant contextual information that remains available during the time taken for testing and for accepting possible decisions (Rudner & Lunner 2014). Inhibition may be required to suppress irrelevant interpretations, while updating may bring new information into the buffer at the expense of discarding older information. Shifting may involve realignment of expectations. Thus, "there is a constant interplay between predictive kinds of priming of what is to come in a dialogue and postdictive reconstructions of what was missed through mismatches with the lexicon in semantic long-term memory" (Rudner & Lunner 2014). Not surprisingly, working memory was found to be strongly associated with speech perception in adverse listening conditions (Akeroyd, 2008; Besser et al., 2013), as well as, with speech perception in hearing impaired children with cochlear implants (Cleary et al., 2002; Dawson et al., 2002).

6 Speech perception assessment

It is our role as communication disorders clinician to identify the stage in the hearing process where the problem occurs in order to intervene appropriately.

Assessment of hearing has traditionally focused on sensory perception skills (bottom-up processing reflecting primarily the sensitivity and resolution of the cochlea and acoustic-sensory-neural-phonetic transformation) versus the use of material, social, and linguistic context (top-down processing). The former focused on the ability to perceive acoustic detail in the speech signal where minimal linguistic constraints are imposed whereas the latter has been subdivided to use of lexical, syntactic and semantic information, as well as world knowledge (Boothroyd and Nittrouer, 1988; Nittrouer and Boothroyd, 1990). This approach has led to the development of tests of speech perception capacity such as the Speech Pattern Contrast (SPAC) test, the Imitative SPAC (IMSPAC) test, its On- Line version (OLIMSPAC), the minimal pairs test, the Visual Response Audiometry SPAC (VRASPAC) test, and the Three-Interval Forced-Choice Test (THRIFT) (Boothroyd, 1984, 1991, 1995, 1997, 2009; Kosky and Boothroyd, 2003; Boothroyd, Eisenberg, and Martinez, 2010; Eisenberg, Martinez, and Boothroyd, 2007; Martinez et al., 2008). These and other tests, many of which have been adapted to different languages such as Hebrew (Kishon-Rabin and Henkin, 2000; Kishon-Rabin et al., 2002) and Arabic (Kishon-Rabin and Rosenhouse, 2000), are designed to evaluate the ability of the listener to detect differences in the acoustic patterns of speech signals that mediate differences in the meanings of the words. With older children and adults a simple test of word repetition is typically used to give an impression of discrimination at the phonetic level. It is the change of an articulatory feature such as the presence of vocal fold vibration (voicing), position of the tongue in the oral cavity (place of articulation), the extent and location of the oral constriction and/or the involvement of the nasal cavity (manner of articulation) in the production of the speech that lead to an acoustic change in the temporal, spectral and intensity domains that signal a change in meaning. The minimal word pairs /bat–bad/, /pick–peck/, /sea–tea/ are examples of word pairs that differ by one feature (final-consonant voicing, tongue-height, initial-consonant manner, respectively). The importance of these tests is that they provide information regarding the sensory analyzing capabilities of the auditory system that are the basis of the acoustic-to-phonetic transformation. Moreover, they are not dependent on previous acquired linguistic knowledge other than phonology of the language. Comparing performance on these tests with word recognition in isolation and in sentences provides information regarding the use of linguistic constraints. Such information is crucial for understanding the point of "breakdown" in the speech perception process in order to provide the appropriate intervention. If a child, for example, is able to perceive phonological contrasts of his/her language but fails to identify isolated words correctly, it is possible that the problem is in his/her ability to make use of the language for correct word identification. This may stem from limited vocabulary, inability to retrieve stored lexical information and/or delays in general cognitive abilities and basic learning mechanisms. Conway et al (2014), for example, showed that hearing-impaired children with cochlear implants repeated quite accurately words they heard but were unable to use sentence context in comparison to normal-hearing peers. It was suggested that these children treated words in sentences "as strings of unrelated words" (Eisenberg et al., 2002). Such information is important for designing intervention protocols for these children. It suggests that while these children may have access to the auditory speech signal and identifying it correctly when produced in isolation (thus confirming adequate auditory capacity), they have difficulty in recognizing the sentence structure and how words co-occur with each other thus in need for language intervention (Conway et al., 2014).

In contrast, the elderly have been shown to have good word identification in sentences but with poorer performance when words were presented in isolation. This is in keeping with the hypothesis that the elderly have age-related hearing deficits that influence their ability to identify the temporal and spectral information in the speech signal (deficits in bottom-up processing) but are able to compensate them by using life-long stored linguistic information (good top-down processing) (Schneider, Pichora-Fuller & Daneman, 2010; Sommers & Danielson, 1999). Additional studies showed, however, that deficits in the memory abilities of the elderly limited their ability to take advantage of this knowledge (Wingfield, 1996).

7 In summary

In this chapter, we have tried to emphasize the complex nature of hearing as both a mechanism for generating sensory evidence from a sound stimulus and as a process for using that evidence to make decisions about the most likely source of the stimulus. The generation and interpretation of sensory and contextual evidence depend on a combination of sensory capacity, cognitive skills, prior knowledge of the material and social worlds, and prior knowledge of the language used by people to refer to both. In short, hearing involves an intimate association among sensory function, cognition, social-cognition, language, and perceptual processing. This association exists at the level of development, at the level of function and, in the case of communication disorders, at the level of remediation. The simple phrase "I hear you" is not about detecting sound but about the perceptual, cognitive, and linguistic skills that make us human.

In the field of communication disorders, it is dangerous to seek a single cause for a developmental delay or disorder. Instead, a multifactorial approach is often more appropriate. In many communication disorders, hearing difficulties are involved – sometimes as a primary disorder, sometimes as a secondary disorder, and sometimes as a symptom. As in medicine, attention to underlying defects can often result in better clinical outcome than approaches that focus solely on remediation of symptoms. There is much research to be done, however, on the optimal way to describe, diagnose, and manage communication disorders. Whatever the results, it is clear that hearing will play a critical role.

References

Anderson, Samira, Travis White-Schwoch, Alexandra Parbery-Clark & Nina Kraus. 2013. A dynamic auditory-cognitive system supports speech-in-noise perception in older adults. *Hearing Research* 300. 18–32.

Pilar, Andrés, Fabrice B.R. Parmentier & Escera Carles. 2006. The effect of age on involuntary capture of attention by irrelevant sounds: A test of the frontal hypothesis of aging. *Neuropsychologia* 44. 2564–2568.

Akeroyd, Michael A. 2008. Are individual differences in speech reception related to individual differences in cognitive ability? A survey of twenty experimental studies with normal and hearing-impaired adults. *International Journal of Audiology* 47(2). S53–S71.

Ari-Even Roth, Daphne, Chava Muchnik, Esther Shabtai, Minka Hildesheimer & Yael Henkin. 2012. Evidence for atypical auditory brainstem responses in young children with suspected autism spectrum disorders. *Developmental Medicine and Child Neurology* 54(1). 23–29.

Besser, Jana, Thomas Koelewijn, Adriana A. Zekveld, Sophia E. Kramer & Joost M. Festen. 2013. How linguistic closure and verbal working memory relate to speech recognition in noise – Areview. *Trends in Amplification* 17. 75–93.

Bishop, V. M. Dorothy, B. Brown & J. Robson. 1990. The relationship between phoneme discrimination, speech production and language comprehension in cerebral-palsied individuals. *Journal of Speech and Hearing Research* 33. 210–219.

Bleile, Ken M. Rachel E. Stark & Joy McGowan Silverman. 1993. Speech development in a child after decannulation: Further evidence that babbling facilitates later speech development. *Clinical Linguistics and Phonetics* 7(4). 319–337.

Boets, Bart, Jan Wouters, Astrid Van Wieringen & Pol Ghesquière. 2007. Auditory processing, speech perception and phonological ability in pre-school children at high-risk for dyslexia: A longitudinal study of the auditory temporal processing theory. *Neuropsychologia* 45. 1608–1620.

Boothroyd, Arthur. 1984. Auditory perception of speech contrasts by subjects with sensorineural hearing loss. *Journal of Speech, Language, and Hearing Research* 27. 134–144.

Boothroyd, Arthur & Susan Nittrouer. 1988. Mathematical treatment of context effects in phoneme and word recognition. *Journal of Acoustical Society of America* 84. 101–114.

Boothroyd, Arthur. 1991. Speech perception measures and their role in the evaluation of hearing aid performance in a pediatric population. In Judith A. Feigin & Patricia G. Stelmachowicz (eds.), *Pediatric amplification*, 77–91. Nebraska: Boys Town National Research Hospital: Omaha.

Boothroyd, Arthur. 1995. Speech perception tests and hearing-impaired children. In Geoff Plant & Erik K. Spens (eds.), *Profound deafness and speech communication*, 345–371. London: Whurr Publishers.

Boothroyd, Arthur. 1997. Auditory development of the hearing child. *Scandinavian Audiology* 26, (Supplementrum 46). 9–16.

Boothroyd, Arthur, Laurie S. Eisenberg & Amy S. Martinez. 2010. An imitative test of speech-pattern contrast perception (OlimSpac): developmental effects in normally hearing children. *Journal of Speech, Language, and Hearing Research* 53. 531–542.

Boothroyd, Arthur & Dorothy Boothroyd-Turner. 2002. Post-implant audition and educational attainment in children with prelingually-acquired profound deafness. *Annals of Otology, Rhinology and Laryngology* 111(189). 79–84.

Boothroyd, Arthur. 2009. Assessment of auditory speech-perception capacity. In Laurie S. Eisenberg (ed.), *Clinical management of children with cochlear implants*, 189–216. San Diego: Plural Publishing.

Boothroyd, Arthur & Janice Gatty. 2012. *The deaf child in a hearing family: Nurturing development*. San Diego: Plural Publishing.

Broadbent Donald E. 1958. *Perception and communication*. Oxford: Pergamon Press.

De Boysson-Bardies, Bénédicte & Marline M. Vihman. 1991. Adaptation to language: Evidence from babbling of infants according to target language. *Language: Journal of the Linguistic Society of America* 67(2). 297–319.

Shawn, E. Christ, Daniel D. Holt, Desirée A. White & Leonard J. Green. 2007. Inhibitory control in children with autism spectrum disorder. *Autism Developmental Disorders* 37(6). 1155–65.

Cleary, Miranda, David B. Pisoni & Keren I. Kirk. 2002. Working memory spans as predictors of spoken word recognition and receptive vocabulary in children with cochlear implants. *The Volta Review* 102(4). 259–280.

Conway, M. Christopher, Joanne A. Deocampo, Anne A. Walk, Esperanza M. Anaya & David B. Pisoni. 2014. Deaf children with cochlear implants do not appear to use sentence context to help recognize spoken words. *Journal of Speech, Language, and Hearing Research* 57(6). 2174–2190.

Conway, M. Christopher, David B. Pisoni, Esperanza M. Anaya, Jennifer Karpicke & Shirley C. Henning. 2011. Implicit sequence learning in deaf children with cochlear implants. *Developmental Science* 14(1). 69–82.

Dawson, P.W., P.A. Busby, C.M. McKay & G.M. Clark. 2002. Short-term auditory memory in children using cochlear implants and its relation to receptive language. *Journal of Speech, Language, and Hearing Research* 45. 789–801.

Démonet, F. Jean, Guillaume Thierry & Dominique Cardebat. 2005. Renewal of the neurophysiology of language: Functional neuroimaging. *Physiology Review* 85(1). 49–95.

Eisenberg, S. Laurie, Amy S. Martinez, Suzanne R. Holowecky & Stephnine Pogorelsky. 2002. Recognition of lexically controlled words and sentences by children with normal hearing and children with cochlear implants. *Ear and Hearing* 23(5). 450–462.

Eisenberg, Laurie S. 2007. Current state of knowledge: Speech recognition and production in children with hearing impairment. *Ear and Hearing* 28. 766–772.

Eisenberg, S. Laurie, Amy S. Martinez & Arthur Boothroyd. 2007. Assessing auditory capabilities in young children. *International journal of pediatric otorhinolaryngology* 71. 1339–1350.

Fadiga, Luciano, Laila Craiqhero, Giovanni Buccino & Giacomo Rizzolatti. 2002. Speech listening specifically modulates the excitability of tongue muscles: A TMS study. *European Journal of Neuroscience* 15. 399–402.

Fletcher, Samuel G. 1992. *Articulation: A physiological approach*. San Diego: Singular Publishing Group.

Furth, Hans G. 1966. *Thinking without language: Psychological implications of deafness*. New York: Free Press.

Galantucci, Bruno, Carol A. Fowler & Michael T. Turvey. 2006. The motor theory of speech perception reviewed. *Psychonomic Bulletin and Review* 13(3). 361–377.

Gervain, Judut & Janet F. Werker. 2008. How infant speech perception contributes to language acquisition. *Language & Linguistic Compass* 2(6). 1149–1170.

Hackett, A. Troy. 2011. Information flow in the auditory cortical network. *Hearing Research* 271(1–2). 133–146.

Hawkins, Sarah. 1999. Looking for invariant correlates of linguistic units: Two classical theories of speech perception. In James M. Pickett (ed.), *The acoustics of speech communication: Fundamentals, speech perception theory and technology*, 198–231. Boston: Allyn & Bacon.

Hickok, Gregory & Poeppel David. 2000. Towards a functional neuroanatomy of speech perception. *Trends in Cognitive Sciences* 4(4). 131–138.

Hornickel, Jane & Nina Kraus. 2013. Unstable representation of sound: A biological marker of dyslexia. *Journal of Neuroscience* 33(8). 3500–3504.

Hornickel, Jane, Steven G. Zecker, Ann R. Bradlow & Nina Kraus. 2012. Assistive listening devices drive neuroplasticity in children with dyslexia. *Proceedings of the National Academy of Sciences of the USA* 109(41). 16731–16736.

Houston, Derek. 2011. Infant speech perception. In Richard Seewald & Anne M. Tharpe (eds.), *Comprehensive handbook of pediatric audiology*, 47–62. San Diego: Plural Publishing.

Katz, Jack (ed.). 1994. *Handbook of clinical audiology* (4th edn.). Baltimore: Williams & Wilkins.

Kishon-Rabin, Liat, Tammy Harel, Minka Hildesheimer & Osnat Segal. 2010. Listening preference for the native language compared to an unfamiliar language in hearing and hearing-impaired infants following cochlear implantation. *Otology and Neurotology* 31(8). 1275–1280.

Kishon-Rabin, Liat & Yael Henkin. 2000. Age-related changes in the visual perception of phonological contrasts. *The British Journal of Audiology* 34(6). 363–374.

Kishon-Rabin, Liat & Judith Rosenhouse. 2000. Speech perception test for Arabic-speaking children. *Audiology* 39(5). 269–277.

Kishon-Rabin, Liat, Riki Taitelbaum-Swead, Ruth Ezrati-Vinacour & Minka Hildesheimer. 2005. Prelexical vocalizations in normal hearing and hearing-impaired infants before and after cochlear implantation and its relation to early auditory skills. *Ear & Hearing* 26(4). 17S–29S.

Kishon-Rabin Liat, Riki Taitelbaum, Chava Muchnik, Inbal Gehtler, Jona Kronnenberg & Minka Hildesheimer. 2002. Development of speech perception and production in children with cochlear implants. *Annals of Otology, Rhinology, and Laryngology* 111(5, part 2). 85–90.

Kishon-Rabin Liat, Riki Taitelbaum & Osnat Segal. 2009. Prelexical infant scale evaluation (PRISE): From vocalization to audition in hearing and hearing-impaired infants. Chapter 12 in Laurie S. Eisenberg (ed.), *Clinical management of children with cochlear implants*, 325–368. San Diego: Plural Publishing.

Kishon-Rabin, Liat, Riki Taitelbaum, Yishai Tobin & Minka Hildeshaimer. 1999. The effect of partially restored hearing on speech production of postlingually deafened adults with cochlear implants. *Journal of the Acoustical Society of America* 106(5). 2843–2857.

Koopmans-van Beinum, Florien J. Chris J. Clement & Ineke van den Dikkenberg-Pot. 2001. Babbling and the lack of auditory speech perception: A matter of coordination? *Developmental Science* 4(1). 61–70.

Kral, Andrej & Gerard M. O'Donoghue. 2010. Profound deafness in childhood. *New England Journal of Medicine* 363(15). 1438–50.

Liberman, Alvin M. Franklin S. Cooper, Donald P. Shankweiler & Michael Studdert-Kennedy. 1967. Perception of the speech code. *Psychological Review* 74(6). 431–46.

Liberman, Alvin M. & Ignatius G. Mattingly. 1985. The motor theory of speech perception revised. *Cognition* 21(1). 1–36.

Locke, John L. & Dawn M. Pearson. 1990. Linguistic significance of babbling: Evidence from atracheostomized infant. *Journal of Child Language* 17(1). 1–16.

Martinez, Amy, Laurie Eisenberg, Arthur Boothroyd & Leslie Visser-Dumont. 2008. Assessing speech pattern contrast perception in infants: Early results on VRASPAC. *Otology and Neurotology* 29(2). 183–188.

Miller, George A. 1956. The magical number seven, plus or minus two: Some limits on our capacity for processing information. *Psychological Review* 63. 81–97.

Moeller, Mary P. Brenda Hoover, Coille Putman, Katie Arbataitis, Greta Bohnenkamp, Barbara Peterson, Sharon Wood, Dawna Lewis, Pat Stelmachowicz, Andrea Pittman & Mary P. Moeller. 2007. Vocalizations of infants with hearing loss compared with infants with normal hearing: Part I – Phonetic development. *Ear & Hearing* 28(5). 605–627.

Moore, David R. Melanie A. Ferguson, Mark A. Edmonson-Jones, Sonia Ratib & Alison Riley. 2010. The nature of auditory processing disorder in children. *Pediatrics* 126(2). 382–390.

Moore, David R. 2012. Listening difficulties in children: Bottom-up and top-down contributions. *Journal of Communication Disorders* 45(6). 411–418.

Muchnik, Chava, Daphne Ari-Even Roth, Minka Hildesheimer, Miri Arie, Yair Bar-Haim & Yael Henkin. 2013. Abnormalities in auditory efferent activities in children with selective mutism. *Audiology and Neurotology* 18(6). 353–361.

Nittrouer, Susan & Arthur Boothroyd. 1990. Context effects in phoneme and word recognition by young children and older adults. *Journal of the Acoustical Society of America* 87(6). 2705–2715.

Oller, Kimbrough D. & Rebecca E. Eilers. 1988. The role of audition in infant babbling. *Child Development* 59(2). 441–449.

Pennington, Bruce F. 2006. From single to multiple deficit models of developmental disorders. *Cognition* 101(2). 385–413.

Perez, Ronen & Liat Kishon-Rabin. 2013. Surgical devices (Cochlear Implantation-Pediatric). In Stilianos E. Kountakis (ed.), *Encyclopedia of otolaryngology, head and neck surgery*. Berlin/Heidelberg: Springer-Verlag. 2676–2687.

Pisoni, David B. 2000. Cognitive factors and cochlear implants: Some thoughts on perception, learning, and memory in speech perception. *Ear and Hearing* 21(1). 70–78.

Pulvermüller, Friedemann, Martina Huss, Ferath Kherif, Martin Del Prado, Moscoso Fermin, Olaf Hauk & Yury Shtyrov. 2006. Motor cortex maps articulatory features of speech sounds. *Proceedings of the National Academy of Sciences* 103(20). 7865–7870.

Purves, Dale, George J. Augustine, David Fitzpatrick, Lawrence C. Katz, Anthony S. LaMantia, James O. Mcnamara & Mark S. Williams (ed.). 2001. Two kinds of hair cells in the cochlea. Sunderland, MA: Sinauer Associates. http://www.ncbi.nlm.nih.gov/books/NBK11122/

Rance, Gary & Elizabeth J. Barker. 2008. Speech perception in children with auditory neuropathy/dyssynchrony managed with either hearing aids or cochlear implants. *Otology & Neurotology* 29(2). 179–182.

Raphael, Lawrence J. Gloria J. Borden & Katherine S. Harris. 2007 (5th). *Speech Science Primer*. Philadelphia: Lippincott Williams & Wilkins.

Rönnberg, Jerker, Thomas Lunner, Adriana Zekveld, Patrik Sörqvist, Henrik Danielsson, Björn Lyxell, Örjan Dahlström, Carine Signoret, Stefan Stenfelt, Kathleen M. Pichora-Fuller & Rudner Mary. 2013. The ease of language understanding (ELU) model: Theory, data, and clinical implications. *Frontiers in Systems Neuroscience* 7.

Schneider, Bruce A. Kathy Pichora-Fuller & Meredyth Daneman. 2010. Effects of senescent changes in audition and cognition on spoken language comprehension. In Sandra Gordon-Salant, Robert D. Frisina, Arthur M. Popper & Richard R. Fay (eds.), *The aging auditory system*, 167–210. New York: Springer.

Scott, Sophie K. & Ingrid S. Johnsrude. 2003. The neuroanatomical and functional organization of speech perception. *Trends in Neurosciences* 26(2). 100–107.

Sebastian-Galles, Núria. 2007. Biased to learn language. *Developmental Science* 10. 713–718.

Sohmer, Haim. 2014. Reflections on the role of a traveling wave along the basilar membrane in view of clinical and experimental findings. *Eur Arch Otorhinolaryngol*. 1–5.

Sommers, Mitchell S. & Stephanie M. Danielson. 1999. Inhibitory processes and spoken word recognition in younger and older adults: The interaction of lexical competition and semantic context. *Psychology and Aging* 14(3). 458–472.

Vihman, Marline M. 1993. Variable paths to early word production. *Journal of Phonetics* 21(1–2). 61–82.

Vihman, Marline M. 2002. The role of mirror neurons in the ontogeny of speech. In Maksim Stamenov & Vittorio Gallese (eds.), *Mirror neurons and the evolution of brain and language*, 305–314, Amsterdam: John Benjamin.

Vouloumanos, Athena & Janet F. Werker. 2004. Tuned to the signal: the privileged status of speech for young infants. *Developmental Science* 7(3). 270–276.

Vouloumanos, Athena & Janet F. Werker. 2007. Listening to language at birth: Evidence for a bias for speech in neonates. *Developmental Science* 10. 159–171.

Werker, F. Janet & Richard C. Tees. 1984. Cross-language speech perception: Evidence for perceptual reorganization during the first year of life. *Infant Behavior and Development* 7(1). 49–63.

Westermann, Gert & Eduardo R. Miranda. 2004. A new model of sensorimotor coupling in the development of speech. *Brain and Language* 89(2). 393–400.

Wingfield, Arthur. 1996. Cognitive factors in auditory performance: Context, speed of processing, and constraints of memory. *Journal of the American Academy of Audiology* 7(3). 175–182.

Yoshinaga-Itano, Cristine. 2006. Early identification, communication modality, and the development of speech and spoken language skills: Patterns and considerations. In Patricia E. Spencer & Marc Marschark (eds.), *Spoken language development of deaf and hard of hearing children*, 298–327, New York: Oxford University Press.

Derek M. Houston and Andrea Warner-Czyz
2 Speech perception and auditory development in infants with and without hearing loss

1 Introduction

Despite the intricate link between the development of auditory skills and refinement of speech perception abilities, there have been few attempts to review these two perspectives simultaneously (although see Saffran, Werker, and Werner, 2006). This chapter examines the acquisition of infant hearing capacities from both perspectives, including implications for both infants with normal hearing (NH) and infants with hearing loss (HL). To understand how HL affects speech perception, we first must understand the complex relationship between auditory development and early speech perception.

Little is known about how auditory development and speech perception development interact. In some ways, they seem to develop quite differently. For example, hearing newborns have reduced primary auditory abilities (e.g., frequency, intensity, and localization) relative to older children and adults (Werner, 1996). The enhancement of auditory skills occurs in several dimensions, as described in the subsequent sections. In contrast, several reports show younger infants demonstrate the ability to discriminate phoneme contrasts that older infants and adults seemly cannot discriminate (e.g., Best, McRoberts, and Sithole, 1988; Werker and Tees, 1984). The goal of this chapter is to address that apparent discrepancy.

The chapter begins by reviewing auditory development, speech perception, and word recognition in NH infants. Next, we review current work assessing speech perception in infants with HL using hearing aids (HA) and cochlear implants (CI). Finally, we discuss future directions for better understanding speech perception in infants with HL.

2 Auditory development

2.1 Intensity

Auditory response to sound occurs along a continuum from sound awareness to comprehension of sound. This chapter will focus on the earliest developing auditory skills: *Detection*, the awareness of sound versus silence, and *discrimination*, the recognition of differences in stimuli contrasts.

Derek M. Houston, The Ohio State University Wexner College of Medicine
Andrea Warner-Czyz, The University of Texas at Dallas

Infants exhibit elevated responses thresholds to auditory stimuli relative to adults (Northern and Downs, 2002; Werner and Gillenwater, 1990; Werner and VandenBos, 1993). These elevated responses thresholds may not represent the infant's true audiometric thresholds, but the lowest intensity at which the infant responds (i.e., *minimum response level*) (Matkin, 1977). Behaviorally, the minimal audible intensity for a hearing newborn to respond to sound is 40–50 dB poorer than adult thresholds, which converge at 0 dB Hearing Level (Eisele, Berry, and Shriner, 1975; Werner and Bargones, 1992; Werner and Gillenwater, 1990; Werner and VandenBos, 1993). Detection of sound improves to within 30–40 dB of adult thresholds at 1 month and within 15–30 dB of adult thresholds at 3 months (Olsho, Koch, Carter, Halpin, and Spetner, 1988; Tharpe and Ashmead, 2001; Trehub, Schneider, Thorpe, and Judge, 1991; Werner and Bargones, 1992; Werner and Gillenwater, 1990; Werner and Mancl, 1993). However, sound detection varies by frequency such that high frequencies have elevated response thresholds through the first three months of life (Olsho et al., 1988; Tharpe and Ashmead, 2001; Trehub et al., 1991; Werner and Bargones, 1992; Werner and Gillenwater, 1990). Minimum response levels for 6-month-old infants listening to pure-tone stimuli exceed adult thresholds by 10–15 dB, with similar response levels in the high frequencies (Spetner and Olsho, 1990; Tharpe and Ashmead, 2001; Werner and Bargones, 1992). Pure-tone thresholds more closely approximate adult thresholds between 8 and 12 months of age and, by 24 months, infant thresholds mirror those of adults across frequencies (Werner and Bargones, 1992; Parry, Hacking, Bamford, Day, and Parry, 2003). Electrophysiological measures confirm behavioral findings that auditory immaturities resolve as a function of age. Werner and colleagues (1993) report that 3- and 6-month-old infants exhibit adult-like auditory brainstem response thresholds at 1,000, 4,000, and 8,000 Hz. Other studies confirm mature electrophysiological responses by three years of age (Kaga and Tanaka, 1980; Klein, 1984; Schneider, Trehub, and Bull, 1979; Salamy and McKean, 1976; Teas, Klein, and Kramer, 1982).

Infants need not only to detect sound, but also to discriminate sound based on intensity. Detection, which forms the lower level of the dynamic range, affects sound awareness. Intensity discrimination underlies the number of discriminable steps from the threshold of detection to the threshold of pain, and influences loudness growth. The terms *difference limen, just perceptible difference*, and *just noticeable difference* describe the smallest detectable change in a parameter such as intensity. Difference limens depend on several factors including signal intensity, duration, and type (e.g., pure tone versus narrowband noise). For example, the difference limen improves (i.e., gets smaller) with increased stimulus intensity levels, longer stimuli durations, and broadband versus narrowband stimulus frequency (Jesteadt and Bilger, 1974; Jesteadt, Wier, and Green, 1977; Steinhardt, 1936).

Infants exhibit immature intensity resolution relative to adults, who have an intensity difference limen of 0.5–2 dB (Sinnott and Aslin, 1985). Five- and 6-month-old infants can discriminate a 10 dB change in a 500 Hz tone (Moffitt, 1973). Slightly older infants (7–9 months) need a comparable intensity difference of 3–12 dB to perceive intensity change of a 1,000 Hz tone (Sinnott and Aslin, 1985). Intensity resolution improves throughout childhood, approximating adult norms by around age 12 years (Maxon and Hochberg, 1982). More recent electrophysiological studies using mismatch negativity (MMN) and magnetic mismatch responses (MMR) confirm statistically significant responses to intensity changes in the acoustic signal, though the direction of the deflection does not always match that of adults (Partanen et al., 2013; Sambeth et al., 2009).

In summary, both behavioral and electrophysiological response thresholds for infants require higher intensities, particularly in the high frequencies, but age-related changes asymptote around 6 months of age and reach adult levels at all frequencies by 24 to 36 months of age. Infants improve their ability to discriminate differences in intensity as a function of age, but do not reach adult performance levels until adolescence.

2.2 Frequency

Like intensity, infants' ability to detect and discriminate stimulus frequency improves over time, particularly during the first year of life (Abdala and Folsom, 1995; Olsho, 1984; Olsho, Koch, and Halpin, 1987). This section details development of frequency detection, specificity, and resolution.

Infants show less sensitivity to high frequency stimuli than adults (Tharpe and Ashmead, 2001; Werner and Gillenwater, 1990). Werner and Gillenwater (1990) report that very young infants (2-5 weeks) show behavioral thresholds elevated by 42–47 dB between 500 and 4,000 Hz relative to adults, with larger group differences at higher frequencies. High frequency thresholds improve to within 35 dB of adult norms at age 1 month, within 19–30 dB at 3 months, and within 15 dB at 6 months (Tharpe and Ashmead, 2001; Werner and Gillenwater, 1990; Folsom and Wynne, 1987). Low frequency thresholds also improve over time: 3-month-olds' thresholds exceed adult thresholds by 23 dB at 500 Hz (Olsho et al., 1988).

Not only does frequency affect detection, but also specificity. Psychophysical tuning curves offer a way to measure how an individual resolves a low-intensity pure-tone test signal in the presence of competing noise, called a masker. The intensity of the masker is increased until the individual no longer can detect the test signal. Several factors, including the frequency composition of the masker relative to the test signal, affect the masker intensity required to eliminate signal detection. Maskers similar in frequency to the test signal likely engage similar neural activity as the test signal itself, thereby requiring less intensity to eradicate detection of the test signal; conversely, spectrally disparate maskers require more intensity to eliminate response to the test signal. A narrow psychophysical tuning curve reflects good resolution, or tuning, of frequency; and a broad psychophysical tuning curve indicates poor frequency resolution. Infants exhibit poorer frequency specificity relative to adults. Three-month-old infants have broader psychophysical tuning curves than adults at 500 and 1,000 Hz (Spetner Olsho, 1990). Six-month-old infants possess psychophysical tuning curve widths and critical bands similar to adults, suggesting comparable levels of frequency specificity at suprathreshold intensities (Schneider, Morrongiello, and Trehub, 1990; Olsho, 1985). Thus, frequency specificity may reach maturity by six months of age.

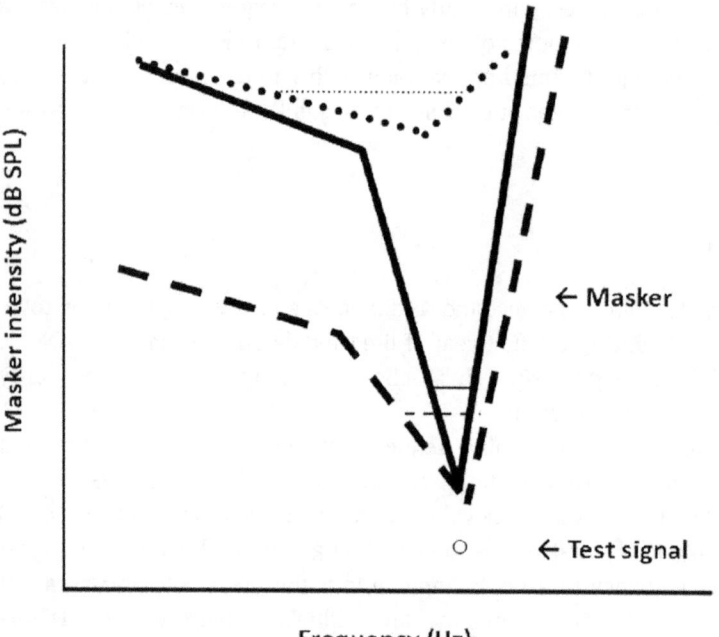

Figure 1: Schematic of psychophysical tuning curve
Figure 1 shows three psychophysical tuning curves plotted as a function of frequency on the x-axis and intensity on the y-axis. The small circle represents the frequency and intensity of a test signal. The three lines represent the intensity of the masker needed to eliminate detection of the test signal. The solid line depicts a normal psychophysical tuning curve that requires less intensity of the masker at frequencies similar to the frequency of the test signal and greater intensity of the masker at frequencies dissimilar to the frequency of the test signal. The width of the psychophysical tuning curve that leads to the tip specifies its resolution. A narrow tuning curve with a sharp point, as shown with the solid line, implies good frequency resolution. The broader tip of the tuning curve with the dashed line reflects poorer frequency resolution relative to the tuning curve with the solid line. The dotted line illustrates a psychophysical tuning curve with both an abnormal threshold, evident in the level of the masker required to eliminate perception of the test signal, and abnormal frequency resolution, evident in the width of the tuning curve

An individual's frequency resolution reflects attunement of their auditory system to specific frequencies, evidenced in the width of the psychophysical tuning curves.

One would expect frequency resolution to coincide with frequency discrimination such that individuals with better frequency specificity (i.e., narrower psychophysical tuning curves) can identify changes in frequency better than individuals with poorer frequency specificity. A mature human auditory system detects a difference limen equal to 1% change in frequency (Olsho, Schoon, Sakai, Turpin, and Sperduto, 1982). That is, adults can discriminate a 20 Hz change for a 200 Hz stimulus and a 200 Hz change for a 2,000 Hz stimulus. Better discrimination in the low versus high frequencies likely reflects attention to periodicity information in the signal rather than excitation information from the cochlea (Moore, 1973a; Moore, 1973b). Infants experience greater difficulty discriminating frequency compared to adults (Bargones, Werner, and Marean, 1995; Schneider, Trehub, Morrongiello, and Thorpe, 1989; Werner and Boike, 2001). Three-month-old infants require a frequency difference limen of 2–3% across the frequency range (Olsho et al., 1987). For example, 3-month-old infants require at least a 120 Hz change to discriminate a difference in a 4,000 Hz tone (Olsho et al., 1987). Five- to 12-month-old infants demonstrate frequency difference limens similar to 3-month-olds in the low and mid frequencies (250 Hz and 3,000 Hz), but comparable to adults in the high frequencies (4,000 and 8,000 Hz) (Olsho et al., 1982; Olsho et al., 1987; Sinnott and Aslin, 1985; Olsho, 1984).

Despite the fact that infants demonstrate better sensitivity to low versus high frequencies (Tharpe and Ashmead, 2001; Werner and Gillenwater, 1990; Olsho et al., 1988), young infants are able to discriminate both phonemes that differ primarily in low-frequency acoustic information (e.g., vowels; Kuhl, 1979; Trehub, 1973) and phonemes that differ primarily in high-frequency acoustic information (e.g., /s/ vs /ʃ/; (Eilers and Minifie, 1975) – at least under quiet laboratory conditions. Differences in fine-grained spectral resolution may not affect infant speech discrimination in quiet, but it may influence infant speech perception in adverse listening conditions such as background noise and perception of musical characteristics such as melody and timbre as shown in adults (Dorman, Loizou, Fitzke, and Tu, 1998; Fu, Shannon, and Wang, 1998; Won, Drennan, Kang, and Rubinstein, 2010).

Immaturities in frequency detection and discrimination likely relates to development of the middle ear system and higher order auditory pathways over the first few months of life. Differences in the efficiency and effectiveness of the middle ear system decrease its sensitivity to high frequencies, which match adult thresholds by 12 months of age (Keefe and Levi, 1996). Immaturity of the auditory brainstem and slower processing in higher order auditory pathways also may contribute to decreased sensitivity to high frequencies during infancy (Werner, Folsom, and Mancl, 1994).

2.3 Temporal

Temporal resolution underlies several aspects of auditory perception, including discrimination and recognition of speech, localization of sound, and listening in adverse conditions such as noise. Few studies have examined detection of temporal properties, instead focusing on the ability to discriminate differences in temporal aspects of sound.

Young infants respond reliably to gaps in stimuli, but need longer gap durations. For example, 3- and 6-month-olds require 40–60 ms longer gaps relative to adults at 500, 2,000, and 8,000 Hz (Werner, Marean, Halpin, Spetner, and Gillenwater, et al., 1992). Morrongiello and Trehub (1987) found similar results: 6-month-old infants detect gaps of 25 ms, 67% longer than gaps identified by five-year-old children (15 ms) and more than twice as long as gaps identified by adults (10 ms). Even though infants need longer gaps, they show a parallel pattern to adults with poorer gap detection in the low frequencies and better gap detection in the high frequencies (Werner et al., 1992). Three-month-old infants and adults perform similarly with a long temporal separation (200 ms), but differ with shorter temporal separations (5, 10, and 25 ms) (Marean and Werner, 1991). That is, shorter durations of temporal separation (5, 10, 25 ms) yielded a greater difference in masked versus unmasked thresholds for infants, but not adults.

Very young infants can discriminate voice onset time (VOT), the duration of time between the release of the stop consonant and the onset of vocal fold vibration (see Section 3.2.1. for details). Several researchers have shown that infants can discriminate voiced versus voiceless syllables (e.g., /ba/ vs. /pa/) within the first four months of life (Eimas, Siqueland, Jusczyk, and Vigorito, 1971; Eimas, 1974; Trehub and Rabinovitch, 1972). Infants' ability to perceive VOT cues emerges in spite of immature temporal resolution, as evidenced by measures such as gap detection and forward masking (Marean and Werner, 1991; Morrongiello and Trehub, 1987; Werner et al., 1992). Young infants can discriminate durational patterns, but their abilities do not quite match those of older children and adults. Progressive improvement throughout infancy suggests immaturity in temporal processing, but also may indicate immaturity in other realms such as attention and memory.

Infants with NH demonstrate immature auditory sensitivity across intensity, frequency, and temporal domains, but improve to more adult-like auditory capacities within the first 2 to 3 years of life. During the same period of life, infants develop sophisticated speech perception skills. It would be tempting to assume that improvements in auditory sensitivities will lead to increased perceptual sensitivity of speech. However, as we will see below (Section 3), the relationship between psychoacoustic abilities and speech perception abilities is much more complex than that.

3 Infant speech perception

At the same time that their auditory system is developing increased sensitivity to intensity, frequency, and temporal domains, infants develop perceptual skills to accomplish a seemingly simple but truly challenging task: To recognize acoustically different instances of the same word as phonologically equivalent, and, at the same time, differentiate words that may be acoustically very similar. The word *oil* produced by a man from Georgia in an angry mood is likely very different acoustically from the same word produced by a woman from New Hampshire in a happy mood, whereas two words like *peak* and *beak* produced by the same talker in the same mood are acoustically very similar. How humans recognize phonological differences and equivalences from the acoustic signal is far from straightforward.

This section reviews the current state of the field of infant speech perception as it relates to word recognition. Two speech perception processes form the foundation for recognizing words in natural speech: (1) identifying where words begin and end in continuous speech (i.e., *speech segmentation*) and (2) comparing candidate words segmented from continuous speech to stored representations of words in the mental lexicon (i.e., *discrimination/categorization*).

3.1 Speech segmentation

Most speech directed to infants occurs in the form of multiword utterances rather than isolated words (van de Weijer, 1998). Even when explicitly instructed to teach words to their infants, parents rarely provide words in isolation (Woodward and Aslin, 1990). Because no reliable acoustic cues to word boundaries exist in natural speech, infants segment words from fluent speech using a combination of several probabilistic cues informed by the ambient language (Cole and Jakimik, 1980).

3.1.1 Early-learned words

Young infants take advantage of existing knowledge to segment words from fluent speech. Six-month-olds use recognition of early-learned, highly familiar words (e.g., *Mommy*), which often occur in isolation, as boundary markers for candidate words (Bortfield, Morgan, Golinkoff, and Rathbun, 2005). This finding contrasts with earlier research showing that six-month-olds could not segment words from fluent speech without such markers (Jusczyk and Aslin, 1995).

3.1.2 Rhythmic properties

Although early-learned words may support segmentation by infants in some cases, infants consistently use cues related to the acoustic-phonetic organization of the ambient language to separate words from the speech stream. Infants show sensitivity to one suprasegmental aspect of speech, the rhythmic properties of words, at very young ages – even before birth. Fetuses at 33–41 weeks gestational age respond to a change from their ambient language to another language, likely reflecting sensitivity to rhythmic properties of speech transmitted *in utero* (Kisilevsky et al., 2009). Newborns can discriminate languages that differ in rhythmic structure even without *in utero* experience with either language (Nazzi, Bertoncini, and Mehler, 1998).

Sensitivity to rhythmic properties of speech influences speech segmentation between 6 and 12 months, at least for English-learning infants. Most bisyllabic words in English begin with a strong stressed syllable (e.g., *doctor*) versus a weak unstressed syllable (e.g., *guitar*). Jusczyk et al. (1999) found that 7.5-month-old English-learning infants could segment strong/weak but not weak/strong words from fluent speech, suggesting that English-learning infants treat strong syllables as beginnings of words and a strong-weak bisyllables as a cohesive unit. Infants learning other languages use other types of rhythmic information for word segmentation (Nazzi, Iakimova, Bertoncini, Fredonie, and Alcantara, 2006). Thus, experience drives awareness of rhythmic properties within words, which subsequently influences word segmentation.

3.1.3 Statistical learning

Noticing that one syllable consistently follows another syllable exemplifies "statistical learning" (Saffran, Aslin, and Newport, 1996). Learning the probability that syllables co-occur represents a powerful domain-general learning skill that plays a significant role in segmenting words from fluent speech.

3.1.4 Other acoustic properties

Infants refine their sensitivity to rhythmic cues and syllable co-occurrences to include segmental and subsegmental (e.g., coarticulatory) properties of their native language. Nine-month-old English-learning infants are sensitive to phonotactic properties such as the likelihood of consonant clusters occurring within or between word boundaries in their ambient language (Mattys, Jusczyk, Luce, and Morgan, 1999). Older infants (11 months) use allophonic and coarticulatory cues to identify word boundaries (Johnson, 2003; Jusczyk, Hohne, and Bauman, 1999). By the end of the first year of life, infants exhibit proficiency at segmenting words from fluent speech regardless of their rhythmic properties (Jusczyk, Houston, and Newsome, 1999).

3.2 Word recognition

To correctly recognize a word, an infant must discriminate it from other words and categorize it with other variants of the same word. As indicated above, this task goes beyond a simple determination of overall acoustic similarity to include identification of the acoustic-phonetic properties that afford discrimination of different words and categorization of the same word.

3.2.1 Word discrimination

The earliest infant speech perception work focused on which aspects of speech infants could discriminate (Eimas et al., 1971). Within the first weeks of life, infants can differentiate syllables based on single features such as consonant voicing, place of articulation, and manner of articulation (Eimas, 1974; Eimas, 1975; Eimas and Miller, 1980b; Eimas and Miller, 1980a; Eimas et al., 1971). Infant discrimination patterns often approximate those of adults. For example, both infants and adults demonstrate categorical perception of voicing contrasts when differences in voice onset time (VOT) cross a category boundary (e.g., 20 vs. 40 ms VOT) but not when VOT differences fall within the same category (e.g., 0 vs. 20 ms) (Eimas et al., 1971; Liberman, Harris, Kinney, and Lane, 1961).

Adult-like discrimination of speech contrasts by young infants challenge the notion that ambient language experience guides perception. Werker and Tees (1984) investigated English-learning infants' discrimination of a Hindi contrast, [da] vs. [ḍa] (retroflex "d", produced by pulling the tongue back from the teeth) which has no linguistic relevance in English. In contrast to Hindi-learning infants, who discriminate the native language contrast regardless of age, English-learning infants show age differences in discrimination. Younger infants (6–8 months) discriminate the non-native language contrast, but older infants (10–12 months) – like adults – do not.

Multiple studies confirmed this age-related pattern in discrimination of linguistically irrelevant language contrasts across multiple studies (Best et al., 1988; Kuhl, Williams, Lacerda, Stevens, and Lindblom, 1992; Trehub, 1976; Tsushima et al., 1994; Werker and Lalonde, 1988). This convergence of results led to widespread adoption of the *Universal Theory* of infant speech perception, which posits that infants emerge with the ability to discriminate all linguistically relevant contrasts of all the world's languages (Aslin and Pisoni, 1980). Exposure to the ambient language(s) causes infants to lose the ability to discriminate non-native, linguistically irrelevant contrasts but retain the ability to discriminate contrasts linguistically relevant to the ambient language(s) (e.g., Eimas, Miller, and Jusczyk, 1987; Werker and Pegg, 1992).

The fact that discrimination of non-native speech sounds becomes poorer seems to contrasts with the fact that psychoacoustic skills become more refined over the course of infancy. How can the auditory and speech perception systems develop in opposite directions? More recent work reviewed below suggests that while the auditory system becomes more acute over development, the complexity of the speech perception system exceeds that proposed by the Universal Theory.

Accumulating evidence suggests infants' categories realign rather pare down for phonemic contrasts. For example, listeners perceive stimuli with shorter VOT as voiced and longer VOT as unvoiced, but exact VOT boundaries differ across languages (Lisker and Abramson, 1964). Lasky and colleagues (1975) report that 4- to 6.5-month-old infants from monolingual Spanish-speaking homes exhibit discrimination patterns consistent with the English, not the Spanish, VOT boundary, suggesting the VOT boundary shifts to the ambient language sometime between infancy and adulthood. More recent work reports this boundary shift occurs around 8–10 months (Burns, Yoshida, Hill, and Werker, 2007; Hoonhorst et al., 2009; Liu and Kager, 2015). A similar realignment occurs with fricatives (Aslin and Pisoni, 1980; Eilers and Minifie, 1975; Eilers, Wilson, and Moore, 1977; Tsao, Liu, and Kuhl, 2006).

Other evidence supporting improved discrimination abilities during development directly contrasts the tenets of the Universal Theory. Sato et al. (2010) and Narayan et al. (2010) found only older infants (9–12 months), not younger infants (4–8 months), discriminate a linguistically relevant contrast of vowel duration and consonant place cue, respectively. Thus, for some acoustically similar yet linguistically relevant contrasts, infants are not born ready to discriminate them but need at least eight months of auditory experience with their ambient language.

3.3 Word categorization

To correctly recognize words, infants must not only discriminate different words, but also correctly categorize different variants of the same word. Some categorization emerges as a byproduct of discrimination processes. When an infant cannot discriminate between two variants of the same word, we can assume the infant on some level categorizes the variants as one unit. However, lexical categorization requires listeners to categorize variants of words that they *can* discriminate, a skill affected by qualities of the talker (e.g., gender, dialect, mood, and speaking rate) and its context within an utterance. These indexical properties are easily discriminable yet listeners categorize variants of words that differ in these properties. Moreover, the acoustic properties that convey indexical and phonological information are highly integrated (Hawkins, 2010), creating a challenge for developmental scientists to determine how infants learn to recognize variants of words across indexical properties.

The evidence to date suggests that word categorization develops throughout infancy. For example, 7.5-month-olds recognize words across two female or two male talkers, but not across male *and* female talkers (Houston and Jusczyk, 2000). Older 10.5-month-old infants, however, recognize words across gender boundaries. Similar patterns arise with different affective qualities of voice and dialect (Schmale and Seidl, 2009; Singh, Morgan, and White, 2004). In sum, by age 12 months, infants can cope with substantial indexical variability in recognizing the sound patterns of words.

Older infants' ability to recognize words across indexical properties suggests lexical representations develop to accommodate more acoustic variability, but these representations may sometimes become too flexible in accepting variability. Stager and Werker (1997) found 8-month-old infants notice switches in word-object pairings with phonologically similar words (e.g., *bih* and *dih*), but 14-month-old infants did not. A separate experiment confirmed that both sets of infants could discriminate *bih* and *dih* when not paired with objects, implying the older infants attend less to acoustic-phonetic information or have looser criteria in word recognition tasks. Other studies suggest 14-month-olds can differentiate phonologically similar words in other recognition tasks (Fennell and Werker, 2003; Fennell and Waxman, 2010; Fennell, 2011; Yoshidaet al., 2009). This overgeneralization of lexical representations extends beyond acoustic variability to phonological variability. 2.5-year-olds treat phonological neighbors of real words (e.g., *vish*) as variants of the real words (e.g., *fish*) rather than as novel words (Swingley, 2015).

In summary, infants refine discrimination skills over time. Categorization begins as an exclusive entity (e.g., cannot recognize words across different talkers) but expands with knowledge of word-object associations. That is, children accept not only indexical variability in representations of words, but also phonological variability, even though they maintain refined phonetic discrimination. Eventually, infants' category boundaries must become tighter as they acquire are increasing number of similar-sounding words.

4 Speech perception in infants with hearing loss

The advent of early identification of hearing loss and early intervention affords the opportunity to investigate speech perception of infants with HL. Assessing speech perception beyond hearing thresholds after receiving a hearing aid or cochlear implant (CI) provides essential knowledge of the adequacy of device fitting for optimal development of spoken language. However, very few studies have assessed speech perception skills in infants and toddlers with HL.

There are several reasons to hypothesize that speech perception abilities in infants with HL will differ from those of infants with NH, even after invention with an HA or CI. First, the devices do not provide the same information as natural hearing, especially the spectral degradation and broad excitation pattern of CIs. Second, because sensorineural hearing loss is due to atypical functioning of the cochlea and/or auditory nerve tract, responsiveness to speech input is also atypical. Third, speech perception involves a combination of bottom-up and top-down processes that may develop differently in infants with HL compared to NH infants.

Suprasegmental perception emerges early in infants with HL. Deaf infants with 1–2 months of CI experience can discriminate basic speech pattern differences (e.g., *hop hop hop* vs. *ahhh*) and prefer their native language to a foreign language (Kishon-Rabin, Harel, Hildesheimer, and Segal, 2010; Houston, Pisoni, Kirk, Ying, and Miyamoto, 2003). Preference for infant- versus adult-directed speech in infants and toddlers with hearing loss positively correlates with duration of device experience, particularly after six months of device use (Robertson, von Hapsburg, and Hay, 2013; Segal and Kishon-Rabin, 2011).

Investigations of phoneme discrimination in infants with hearing loss yield mixed results. Some studies report discrimination of several vowel and consonant contrasts, but difficulty with place of articulation (e.g., /z/–/v/) within the first year of CI use (Schauwers, Gillis, Daemers, De Beukelaer, and Govaerts, 2004; Uhler, Yoshinaga-Itano, Gabbard, Rothpletz, and Jenkins, 2011). Others indicate highly inconsistent segmental discrimination, especially for consonants (Eisenberg, Martinez, and Boothroyd, 2004; Eisenberg, Martinez, and Boothroyd, 2007; Martinez, Eisenberg, Boothroyd, and Visser-Dumont, 2008).

Finally, a few studies investigate auditory-visual speech perception. Infants with HL using hearing aids or CI can match auditory and visual components of speech with at least three months of device experience, but cross-modal integration depends on degree of hearing loss (Barker and Tomblin, 2004; Bergeson, Houston, and Miyamoto, 2010; Horn, Houston, and Miyamoto, 2007).

The studies conducted over the past fifteen years provide valuable information about speech perception in infants with HL. One particularly interesting aspect of these studies is that none report better speech perception in early- versus late-implanted infants, as long as cochlear implantation occurs before two years of age. The lack of an age-at-CI advantage is surprising when considering emerging evidence of better receptive and expressive language outcomes in children receiving CIs before one year versus between one and two years of age (Colletti, 2009; Colletti, Mandalà, Zoccante, Shannon, and Colletti, 2011; Dettman, Pinder, Briggs, Dowell, and Leigh, 2007; Holt and Svirsky, 2008; Holman et al., 2013; Houston and Miyamoto, 2010; Leigh, Dettman, Dowell, and Briggs, 2013; Nicholas and Geers, 2013). Studies of toddlers and older children with CIs report no age effect on speech perception skills if implanted by age two years (Grieco-Calub, Saffran, and Litovsky, 2009; Holt and Svirsky, 2008; Houston and Miyamoto, 2010; Leigh et al., 2013; Lesinski-Schiedat, Illg, Heermann, Bertram, and Lenarz, 2004). In other words, no evidence thus far definitively supports improved speech perception outcomes with CI before one year versus two years of age (for a different view, see Colletti, Mandalà, and Colletti, 2012).

What can explain the discrepancy between the effects of very early CI on language outcomes and the lack of effects on speech perception? One possibility centers on the mechanisms by which children who receive CIs early achieve better receptive and expressive language outcomes. Better linguistic outcomes may not stem from advanced speech perception skills, but rather from an improved ability to learn associations between what they perceive auditorily and what they experience through other modalities. Indeed, Houston et al. (2012) report that toddlers implanted before 14 months had better word-learning skills (i.e., learning associations between novel words and novel objects) than toddlers who receive CIs later. Moreover, performance on the word-learning task correlated with later measures of receptive and expressive language, suggesting that improvements in word-learning skills may play a more substantial role in language outcomes than speech perception alone.

Another possible explanation for the lack of an effect of very early implantation on better speech perception relates to the lack of sensitivity in current speech perception tests to detect the differences. Word-recognition tasks typically provide an overall accuracy rate and do not provide more subtle information about perception of specific acoustic-phonetic information. The few existing studies involving phoneme discrimination have very small sample sizes and vary in methodology (Eisenberg et al., 2004; Eisenberg et al., 2007; Martinez et al., 2008; Uhler et al., 2011; Schauwers et al., 2004). A full investigation of the effects of very early CI on speech perception will require a larger-scale assessment on a thorough battery of phoneme contrasts. This investigation likely will include multiple sites because the feasibility of recruiting a substantial sample of infants who receive CIs before one year of age at a single CI research site is low.

The paucity of data on early auditory skills in infants and toddlers with HL exposes a considerable gap in our knowledge. How can we determine adequate and appropriate auditory progress for a young child with HL without normative data to guide expectations? One way to estimate the effect of a degraded auditory signal on speech perception is to present a signal that simulates HL or a hearing device to listeners with NH. CI simulations employ spectral reduction techniques, which divide an acoustic signal into frequency bands via multiple bandpass filters while maintaining the temporal envelope changes in speech, have served as successful models of speech perception in adult CI recipients (e.g., Dorman and Loizou, 1997; Eisenberg, Shannon, Martinez, Wygonski, and Boothroyd, 2000; Fu et al., 1998; Shannon, Zeng, Kamath, Wygonski, and Ekelid, 1995). CI simulations also allow researchers to parse the effect of a compromised signal on speech perception without confounding influences of auditory deprivation or cognitive abilities, but few researchers have applied this methodology to a pediatric population (Dorman, Loizou, Kemp, and Kirk, 2000; Eisenberg et al., 2000; Eisenberg, Martinez, Holowecky, and Pogorelsky, 2002; Newman and Chatterjee, 2013; Nittrouer, Lowenstein, and Packer, 2009; Nittrouer and Lowenstein, 2010) and still fewer to infants (Bertoncini, Nazzi, Cabrera, and Lorenzi, 2011; Warner-Czyz, Houston, and Hynan, 2014). Emerging evidence suggests the amount of information infants and toddlers glean from a CI-simulated signal changes over the course of development with a tradeoff among chronologic age, stimulus and response difficulty, and number of channels throughout infancy and toddlerhood.

5 Summary and conclusions

The human auditory system functions fully at birth, but becomes increasingly more sensitive to intensity, frequency, and temporal information during the first 2–3 years of life. During the first year of life, infants develop increasingly refined perceptual acuity that allows them to identify acoustic-phonetic differences that differentiate words. Toddlers undergo a process of learning which acoustic-phonetic features differentiate words and which do not. In infants with HL, intensity, frequency, and temporal resolution is reduced. Reduced auditory resolution may result in a smaller perceptual space in which to form acoustic-phonetic representations of phonemes and words, making them more easily confusable. At the same time, infants with HL may adapt their perceptual space to accommodate the reduced auditory resolution. Much more work is needed to understand how congenital HL affects speech perception and word recognition. Testing NH infants using speech stimuli that simulates hearing loss can supplement studies of speech perception in infants with HL, which are difficult to carry out.

References

Abdala, Carolina & Richard C. Folsom. 1995. The development of freqeuncy resolution in humans as revealed by the auditory brain-stem response recorded with notched-noise masking. *Journal of the Acoustical Society of America* 98. 921–930.

Aslin, Richard N. & David B. Pisoni. 1980. Some developmental processes in speech perception. In Grace H. Yeni-Komshian, James F. Kavanagh, and Charles. A. Ferguson (eds.), *Child phonology*, 2nd edn., volume 2, 67–96. New York: Academic Press.

Bargones, Jill Y., Lynne A. Werner & Marean G. Cameron. 1995. Infant psychometric functions for detection: mechanisms of immature sensitivity. *Journal of the Acoustical Society of America* 98. 99–111.

Barker, Brittan A. & J. Bruce Tomblin. 2004. Bimodal speech perception in infant hearing aid and cochlear implant users. *Archives of Otolaryngology, Head and Neck Surgery* 130 (5). 582–586.

Bergeson, Tonya R., Derek M. Houston & Richard. T. Miyamoto. 2010. Effects of congenital hearing loss and cochlear implantation on audiovisual speech perception in infants and children. *Restorative Neurology and Neuroscience* 28 (2). 157–165.

Bertoncini, Josiane, Thierry Nazzi, Laurianne Cabrera & Christian Lorenzi. 2011. Six-month-old infants discriminate voicing on the basis of temporal envelope cues (L). *Journal of the Acoustical Society of America* 129. 2761–2764.

Best, Catherine T., Gerald W. McRoberts & Nomathemba M. Sithole. 1988. Examination of perceptual reorganization for nonnative speech contrasts: Zulu click discrimination by English-speaking adults and infants. *Journal of Experimental Psychology: Human Perception and Performance* 14. 345–360.

Bortfield, Heather, James L. Morgan, Roberta M. Golinkoff & Karen Rathbun. 2005. Mommy and me: Familiar names help launch babies into speech-stream segmentation. *Psychological Science* 16. 298–304.

Burns, Tracey C., Katherine A. Yoshida, Karen Hill & Janet F. Werker. 2007. The development of phonetic representation in bilingual and monolingual infants. *Applied Psycholinguistics* 28 (3). 455–474.

Cole, Ronald A. & Jola Jakimik. 1980. A model of speech perception. In R. A. Cole (ed.), *Perception and production of fluent speech*, 133–163. Hillsdale, NJ: Erlbaum.

Colletti, Liliana. 2009. Long-term follow-up of infants (4–11 months) fitted with cochlear implants. *Acta Otolaryngologica* 129 (4). 361–366.

Colletti, Liliana, Marco Mandalà & Vittorio Colletti. 2012. Cochlear implants in children younger than 6 months. *Otolaryngology, Head and Neck Surgery* 147. 139–146.

Colletti, Liliana, Marco Mandalà, Leonardo Zoccante, Robert V. Shannon & Vittorio Collett. 2011. Infants versus older children fitted with cochlear implants: performance over 10 years. *International Journal of Pediatric Otorhinolaryngology* 75. 504–509.

Dettman, Shani J., Darren Pinder, Robert J. S. Briggs, Richard C. Dowell & Jaime R. Leigh. 2007. Communication development in children who receive the cochlear implant younger than 12 months: risks versus benefits. *Ear and Hearing* 28 (2 Suppl). 11S–18S.

Dorman, Michael F. & Philip C. Loizou. 1997. Speech intelligibility as a function of the number of channels of stimulation for normal-hearing listeners and patients with cochlear implants. *American Journal of Otology* 18. S113–S114.

Dorman, Michael F., Philip C. Loizou, J. Fitzke & Z. Tu. 1998. The recognition of sentences in noise by normal-hearing listeners using simulations of cochlear-implant signal processors with 6–20 channels. *Journal of the Acoustical Society of America* 104. 3583–3585.

Dorman, Michael F., Philip C. Loizou, L. L. Kemp & Karen I. Kirk. 2000. Word recognition by children listening to speech processed into a small number of channels: data from normal-hearing children and children with cochlear implants. *Ear and Hearing* 21. 590–596.

Eilers, Rebecca E. & Fred D. Minifie. 1975. Fricative discrimination in early infancy. *Journal of Speech and Hearing Research* 18. 158–167.

Eilers, Rebecca E., Wesley R. Wilson & John M. Moore. 1977. Developmental changes in speech discrimination in infants. *Journal of Speech and Hearing Research* 20. 766–780.

Eimas, Peter D. 1974. Auditory and linguistic processing of cues for place of articulation by infants. *Perception and Psychophysics* 16. 513–521.

Eimas, Peter D. 1975. Auditory and phonetic coding of the cues for speech: Discrimination of the [r-l] distinction by young infants. *Perception and Psychophysics* 18. 341–347.

Eimas, Peter. D. & Joanne L. Miller. 1980a. Discrimination of the information for manner of articulation. *Infant Behavior and Development* 3. 367–375.

Eimas, Peter D. & Joanne L. Miller. 1980b. Contextual effects in infant speech perception. *Science* 209. 1140–1141.

Eimas, Peter D., Joanne L. Miller & Peter W. Jusczyk. 1987. On infant speech perception and the acquisition of language. In H. Stevan (ed.), *Categorical perception: The groundwork of cognition*, 161–195. New York: Cambridge University Press.

Eimas, Peter D., Einar R. Siqueland, Peter Jusczyk & James Vigorito. 1971. Speech perception in infants. *Science* 171. 303–306.

Eisele, W. Alan, Richard C. Berry & Thomas H. Shriner. 1975. Infant sucking response patterns as a conjugate function of changes in the sound pressure level of auditory stimuli. *Journal of Speech, Language, and Hearing Research*. 296–307.

Eisenberg, Laurie S., Amy. S. Martinez & Boothroyd, Arthur. 2004. Perception of phonetic contrasts in infants: Development of the VRASPAC. In R. T. Miyamoto (ed.), *Cochlear implants: International congress series* 1273, 364–367. Amsterdam: Elsevier.

Eisenberg, Laurie S., Amy. S. Martinez & Arthur Boothroyd. 2007. Assessing auditory capabilities in young children. *International Journal of Pediatric Otorhinolaryngology* 71. 1339–1350.

Eisenberg, Laurie S., Amy. S. Martinez, Amy Schaefer, Suzanne R. Holowecky & Stephanie Pogorelsky. 2002. Recognition of lexically controlled words and sentences by children with normal hearing and children with cochlear implants. *Ear and Hearing* 23. 450–462.

Eisenberg, Laurie S., Robert V. Shannon, Amy S. Martinez, John Wygonski & Arthur Boothroyd. 2000. Speech recognition with reduced spectral cues as a function of age. *Journal of the Acoustical Society of America* 107. 2704–2710.

Fennell, Christopher T. 2011. Object familiarity enhances infants' use of phonetic detail in novel words. *Infancy* 17 (3). 339–353.

Fennell, Christopher T. & Sandra R. Waxman. 2010. What paradox? Referential cues allow for infant use of phonetic detail in word learning. *Child Development* 81 (5). 1376–1383.

Fennell, Christopher T. & Janet F. Werker. 2003. Early word learners' ability to access phonetic detail in well-known words. *Language and Speech. Special Issue: Phonological acquisition* 46 (2–3). 245–264.

Folsom, Richard C. & Michael K. Wynne. 1987. Auditory brain stem responses from human adults and infants: wave V tuning curves. *Journal of the Acoustical Society of America* 81. 412–417.

Fu, Qian-Jie, Robert V. Shannon & Xiaosong Wang. 1998. Effects of noise and spectral resolution on vowel and consonant recognition: acoustic and electric hearing. *Journal of the Acoustical Society of America* 104. 3586–3596.

Grieco-Calub, Tina M., Jenny R. Saffran & Ruth Y. Litovsky. 2009. Spoken word recognition in toddlers who use cochlear implants. *Journal of Speech, Language, and Hearing Research* 52 (6). 1390–1400.

Holman, Michelle A., Matthew L. Carlson, Colin L. Driscoll, Kendra J. Peterson, Rajanya S. Grim, Douglas P. Sladen et al. 2013. Cochlear implantation in children 12 months of age and younger. *Otology and Neurotology* 34. 251–258.

Holt, Rachel F. & Mario A Svirsky. 2008. An exploratory look at pediatric cochlear implantation: is earliest always best? *Ear and Hearing* 29 (4). 492–1511.

Hoonhorst, Ingrid, Cecile Colin, Emily Markessis, Monique Radeau, Paul, Deltenre & Willy Serniclaes. 2009. French native speakers in the making: from language-general to language-specific voicing boundaries. *Journal of Experimental Child Psychology* 104 (4). 353–366.

Horn, David L., Derek M. Houston & Richard T. Miyamoto. 2007. Speech discrimination skills in deaf infants before and after cochlear implantation. *Audiological Medicine* 5. 232–241.

Houston, Derek M. & Peter W. Jusczyk. 2000. The role of talker-specific information in word segmentation by infants. *Journal of Experimental Psychology: Human Perception and Performance* 26. 1570–1582.

Houston, Derek M. & Richard T. Miyamoto. 2010. Effects of early auditory experience on word learning and speech perception in deaf children with cochlear implants: Implications for sensitive periods of language development. *Otology and Neurotology* 31. 1248–1253.

Houston, Derek M., David B. Pisoni, Karen I. Kirk, Elizabeth A. Ying & Richard T. Miyamoto. 2003. Speech perception skills of deaf infants following cochlear implantation: a first report. *International Journal of Pediatric Otorhinolaryngology* 67. 479–495.

Houston, Derek M., Jessica Stewart, Aaron Moberly, George Hollich & Richard T. Miyamoto. 2012. Word learning in deaf children with cochlear implants: effects of early auditory experience. *Developmental Science* 15. 448–461.

Jesteadt, Walt & Robert C. Bilger. 1974. Intensity and frequency discrimination in one- and two-interval paradigms. *Journal of the Acoustical Society of America* 55. 1266–1276.

Jesteadt, Walt, Craig C. Wier & David M. Green. 1977. Intensity discrimination as a function of frequency and sensation level. *Journal of the Acoustical Society of America* 61. 169–177.

Johnson, Elizabeth K. 2003. *Word segmentation during infancy: The role of subphonemic cues to word boundaries.* Baltimore, MD: The Johns Hopkins University doctoral dissertation.

Jusczyk, Peter W. & Richard N. Aslin. 1995. Infants' detection of the sound patterns of words in fluent speech. *Cognitive Psychology* 29. 1–23.

Jusczyk, Peter W., Elizabeth A. Hohne & Angela Bauman. 1999. Infants' sensitivity to allophonic cues for word segmentation. *Perception and Psychophysics* 61. 1465–1476.

Jusczyk, Peter W., Derek. M. Houston & Mary Newsome. 1999. The beginnings of word segmentation in English-learning infants. *Cognitive Psychology* 39. 159–207.

Kaga, Kimitaka & Yoshisato Tanaka. 1980. Auditory brainstem response and behavioral audiometry. Developmental correlates. *Archives of Otolaryngology* 106. 564–566.

Keefe, Douglas H. & Ellen Levi. 1996. Maturation of the middle and external ears: acoustic power-based responses and reflectance tympanometry. *Ear and Hearing* 17. 361–373.

Kishon-Rabin, Liat, Tammy Harel, Minka Hildesheime & Osnat Segal. 2010. Listening preference for the native language compared to an unfamiliar language in hearing and hearing-impaired infants after cochlear implantation. *Otology and Neurotology* 31. 1275–1280.

Kisilevsky, Barbara S., Sylvia M. J. Hains, C. Ann Brown, Charlotte T. Lee, Bernadette Cowperthwaite, Sherri S. Stutzman, Melissa L. Swansburg, Kang Lee, Xe Xie, Hefeng Huang, Hai-HuiYe, Ke Zhang & Zengping Wang. 2009. Fetal sensitivity to properties of maternal speech and language. *Infant Behavior and Development* 32. 59–71.

Klein, Alan J. 1984. Frequency and age-dependent auditory evoked potential thresholds in infants. *Hearing Research* 16. 291–297.

Kuhl, Patricia K., Karen A. Williams, Francisco Lacerda, Kenneth N. Stevens & Bjorn Lindblom. 1992. Linguistic experience alters phonetic perception in infants by 6 months of age. *Science* 255. 606–608.

Lasky, Robert E., Ann Syrdal-Lasky & Robert E. Klein. 1975. VOT discrimination by four to six and a half month old infants from Spanish environments. *Journal of Experimental Child Psychology* 20 (2). 215–225.

Leigh, Jaime R., Shani J. Dettman, Richard C. Dowell & Robert J. Briggs. 2013. Communication development in children who receive a cochlear implant by 12 months of age. *Otology and Neurotology* 34 (3). 443–450.

Lesinski-Schiedat, Anke, Angelika Illg, Ralf Heermann, Bodo Bertram & Thomas Lenarz. 2004. Paediatric cochlear implantation in the first and in the second year of life: A comparative study. *Cochlear Implants International* 5 (4). 146–159.

Liberman, Alvin M., Katherine S. Harris, Jo Ann Kinney & Harlan L. Lane. 1961. The discrimination of relative-onset time of the components of certain speech and non-speech patterns. *Journal of Experimental Psychology* 61. 379–388.

Lisker, Leigh & Arthur S. Abramson. 1964. A cross language study of voicing in initial stops: Acoustical measurements. *Word* 20. 384–422.

Liu, Liquan & Rene Kager. 2015. Bilingual exposure influences infant VOT perception. *Infant Behavior and Development* 38. 27–36.

Marean, G. Cameron & Lynne A. Werner. 1991. Forward masking functions of 3-month-old infants. *Journal of the Acoustical Society of America* 89 (4B). 1914.

Martinez, Amy, Laurie Eisenberg, Arthur Boothroyd & Leslie Visser-Dumont. 2008. Assessing speech pattern contrast perception in infants: Early results on VRASPAC. *Otology and Neurotology* 29. 183–188.

Matkin, Noel. 1977. Assessment of hearing sensitivity during the preschool years. In Fred Bess (ed.), *Childhood deafness*, 127–134. New York: Grune and Stratton.

Mattys, Sven L., Peter W. Jusczyk, Paul A. Luce & James L. Morgan. 1999. Phonotactic and prosodic effects on word segmentation in infants. *Cognitive Psychology* 38. 465–494.

Maxon, Antonia B. & Irving Hochberg. 1982. Development of psychoacoustic behavior: sensitivity and discrimination. *Ear and Hearing* 3. 301–308.

Moffitt, Alan R. 1973. Intensity discrimination and cardiac reaction in young infants. *Developmental Psychology* 8. 357–359.

Moore, Brian C. 1973a. Frequency difference limens for narrow bands of noise. *Journal of the Acoustical Society of America* 54. 888–896.

Moore, Brian C. 1973b. Frequency difference limens for short-duration tones. *Journal of the Acoustical Society of America* 54. 610–619.

Morrongiello, Barbara A. & Sandra E. Trehub. 1987. Age-related changes in auditory temporal perception. *Journal of Experimental Child Psychology* 44. 413–426.

Narayan, Chandan R., Janet F. Werker & Patrice S. Beddor. 2010. The interaction between acoustic salience and language experience in developmental speech perception: evidence from nasal place discrimination. *Developmental Science* 13 (3). 407–420.

Nazzi, Thierry, Josiane Bertoncini & Jacques Mehler. 1998. Language discrimination by newborns: Toward an understanding of the role of rhythm. *Journal of Experimental Psychology: Human Perception and Performance* 24 (3). 756–766.

Nazzi, Thierry, Galina Iakimova, Josiane Bertoncini, Severine Fredonie & Carmela Alcantara. 2006. Early segmentation of fluent speech by infants acquiring French: Emerging evidence for crosslinguistic differences. *Journal of Memory and Language* 54. 283–299.

Newman, Rochelle & Monita Chatterjee. 2013. Toddlers' recognition of noise-vocoded speech. *Journal of the Acoustical Society of America* 133. 483–494.

Nicholas, Johanna G. & Ann E. Geers. 2013. Spoken language benefits of extending cochlear implant candidacy below 12 months of age. *Otology and Neurotology* 34 (3). 532–538.

Nittrouer, Susan & Joanna H. Lowenstein. 2010. Learning to perceptually organize speech signals in native fashion. *Journal of the Acoustical Society of America* 127. 1624–1635.

Nittrouer, Susan, Joanna H. Lowenstein & Robert R. Packer. 2009. Children discover the spectral skeletons in their native language before the amplitude envelopes. *Journal of Experimental Psychology: Human Perception and Performance* 35. 1245–1253.

Northern, Jerry L. & Marion P Downs. 2002. *Hearing in children*. Baltimore, MD: Lippincott Williams and Wilkins.

Olsho, Lynne W. 1984. Infant frequency discrimination. *Infant behavior and development* 7. 2–35.

Olsho, Lynne W. 1985. Infant auditory perception: Tonal masking. *Infant behavior and development* 7. 27–35.

Olsho, Lynne W., Elizabeth G. Koch, Elizabeth A. Carter, Christopher F. Halpin & Nancy B. Spetner. 1988. Pure-tone sensitivity of human infants. *Journal of the Acoustical Society of America* 84. 1316–1324.

Olsho, Lynne W., Elizabeth G. Koch & Christopher F. Halpin. 1987. Level and age effects in infant frequency discrimination. *Journal of the Acoustical Society of America* 82. 454–464.

Olsho, Lynne W., Celia Schoon, Ron Sakai, Robin Turpin & Vincent Sperduto. 1982. Auditory frequency discrimination in infancy. *Developmental Psychology* 18. 721–726.

Parry, Georgina, C. Hacking, John Bamford & John Day. 2003. Minimal response levels for visual reinforcement audiometry in infants. *International Journal of Audiology* 42. 413–417.

Partanen, Eino, Satu Pakarinen, Teija Kujala & Minna Huotilainen. 2013. Infants' brain responses for speech sounds in fast multifeature MMN paradigm. *Clinical Neurophysiology* 124. 1578–1585.

Robertson, Susie, Deborah von Hapsburg & Jessica S. Hay. 2013. The effect of hearing loss on the perception of infant- and adult-directed speech. *Journal of Speech, Language, and Hearing Research* 56. 1108–1119.

Saffran, Jenny R., Richard N. Aslin & Elissa L. Newport. 1996. Statistical learning by 8-month-old infants. *Science* 274. 1926–1928.

Saffran, Jenny R., Janet F. Werker & Lynne A. Werner. 2006. The infant's auditory world: Hearing, speech, and the beginnings of language. In D. Kuhn, R. S. Siegler, W. Damon, and R. M. Lerner (eds.), *Handbook of child psychology: Cognition, perception, and language*, 6th edn., 58–108. Hoboken, NJ: John Wiley.

Salamy, Alan & Charles M. McKean. 1976. Postnatal development of human brainstem potentials during the first year of life. *Electroencephalography and Clinical Neurophysiology* 40. 418–426.

Sambeth, Anke, Satu Pakarinen, Katja Ruohio, Vineta Fellman, Titia L. van Zuijen, Minna Huotilainen. 2009. Change detection in newborns using a multiple deviant paradigm: A study using magnetoencephalography. *Clinical Neurophysiology* 120. 530–538.

Sato, Yutaka, Yuko Sogabe & Reiko Mazuka. 2010. Discrimination of phonemic vowel length by Japanese infants. *Developmental Psychology* 46 (1). 106–119.

Schauwers, Karen, Steven Gillis, Kristin Daemers, Carina De Beukelaer & Paul J. Govaerts. 2004. Cochlear implantation between 5 and 20 months of age: The onset of babbling and the audiologic outcome. *Otology and Neurotology* 25 (3). 263–270.

Schmale, Rachel & Amanda Seidl. 2009. Accommodating variability in voice and foreign accent: flexibility of early word representations. *Developmental Science* 12 (4). 583–601.

Schneider, Bruce A., Barbara A. Morrongiello & Sandra E. Trehub. 1990. Size of critical band in infants, children, and adults. *Journal of Experimental Psychology: Human Perception and Performance* 16. 642–652.

Schneider, Bruce A., Sandra E. Trehu & D. Bull. 1979. The development of basic auditory processes in infants. *Canadian Journal of Psychology* 33. 306–319.

Schneider, Bruce A., Sandra E. Trehub, Barbara A. Morrongiello & Leigh A. Thorpe. 1989. Developmental changes in masked thresholds. *Journal of the Acoustical Society of America* 86. 1733–1742.

Segal, Osnat & Liat Kishon-Rabin. 2011. Listening preference for child-directed speech versus non-speech stimuli in normal-hearing and hearing-impaired infants after cochlear implantation. *Ear and Hearing* 32. 358–372.

Shannon, Robert V., Fan-Gang Zeng, Vivek Kamath, John Wygonski & Michael Ekelid. 1995. Speech recognition with primarily temporal cues. *Science* 270. 303–304.

Singh, Leher, James L. Morgan & Katherine S. White. 2004. Preference and processing: The role of speech affect in early spoken word recognition. *Journal of Memory and Language* 51 (2). 173–189.

Sinnott, Joan M. & Richard N. Aslin. 1985. Frequency and intensity discrimination in human infants and adults. *Journal of the Acoustical Society of America* 78. 1986–1992.

Spetner, Nancy B. & Lynne W. Olsho. 1990. Auditory frequency resolution in human infancy. *Child Development* 61. 632–652.

Stager, Christine L. & Janet F. Werker. 1997. Infants listen for more phonetic detail in speech perception than in word-learning tasks. *Nature* 388. 381–382.

Steinhardt, Jacinto. 1936. Intensity discrimination in the human eye. *The Journal of General Physiology* 20 (2). 185–209.

Swingley, Daniel. 2015. Two-year-olds interpret novel phonological neighbors as familiar words. *Developmental Psychology* 52 (7). 1011–1023.

Teas, Donald C., Alan J. Klein & Steven J. Kramer. 1982. An analysis of auditory brainstem responses in infants. *Hearing Research* 7. 19–54.

Tharpe, Anne Marie & Daniel H. Ashmead. 2001. A longitudinal investigation of infant auditory sensitivity. *American Journal of Audiology* 10. 104–112.

Trehub, Sandra. & M. Sam Rabinovitch. 1972. Auditory-linguistic sensitivity in early infancy. *Developmental Psychology* 6. 74–77.

Trehub, Sandra E. 1976. The discrimination of foreign speech contrasts by infants and adults. *Child Development*. 466–472.

Trehub, Sandra. E., Bruce A. Schneider, Leigh A. Thorpe & Peter Judge. 1991. Observational measures of auditory sensitivity in early infancy. *Developmental Psychology* 27. 40–49.

Tsao, Feng-Ming, Huei-Mei Liu, & Patricia K. Kuhl. 2006. Perception of native and non-native affricate-fricative contrasts: Cross-language tests on adults and infants. *Journal of the Acoustical Society of America* 120. 2285–2294.

Tsushima, Teruaki, Osamu Takizawa, Midori Sasaki, Satoshi Siraki, Kanae Nishi, Morio Kohno, Paula Menyuk & Catherine Best. 1994. Discrimination of English /r-l/ and /w-y/ by Japanese infants at 6–12 months: Language specific developmental changes in speech perception abilities. In *Proceedings from the 3rd international conference on spoken language processing*, vol. 4, 1695–1698. Yokohama, Japan: The Acoustical Society of Japan.

Uhler, Kristin, Christie Yoshinaga-Itano, Sandra A. Gabbard, Ann M. Rothpletz & Herman Jenkins. 2011. Longitudinal infant speech perception in young cochlear implant users. *Journal of the American Academy of Audiology* 22 (3). 129–142.

van de Weijer, Joost. 1998. *MPI series in psycholingustics: Language input for word discovery* (Vol. 9). Nijmegen, The Netherlands.

Warner-Czyz, Andrea D., Derek M. Houston & Linda S. Hynan. 2014. Vowel discrimination by hearing infants as a function of number of spectral channels. *Journal of the Acoustical Society of America* 135. 3017–3024.

Werker, Janet F. & Chris E. Lalonde. 1988. Cross-language speech perception: Initial capabilities and developmental change. *Developmental Psychology* 24. 624–683.

Werker, Janet F. & Judith E. Pegg. 1992. Infant speech perception and phonological acquisition. In Charles A. Ferguson, Lise Menn, & Carol Stoel-Gammon (eds.), *Phonological development: Models, research, implications*, 285–311. Timonium, MD: York Press.

Werker, Janet F. & Richard C. Tees. 1984. Cross-language speech perception: Evidence for perceptual reorganization during the first year of life. *Infant behavior and development* 7. 49–63.

Werner, Lynne A. 1996. The development of auditory behavior (or what the anatomists and physiologists have to explain). *Ear and Hearing* 17. 438–446.

Werner, Lynne. A. & Jill Y. Bargones. 1992. Psychoacoustic development of human infants. In Carolyn Rovee-Collier & Lewis Lipsitt (eds.), *Advances in infancy research*, 103–145. Norwood, NJ: Ablex.

Werner, Lynne. A. & Kumiko Boike. 2001. Infants' sensitivity to broadband noise. *Journal of the Acoustical Society of America* 109. 2103–2111.

Werner, Lynne. A., Richard C. Folsom & Lisa R. Mancl. 1993. The relationship between auditory brainstem response and behavioral thresholds in normal hearing infants and adults. *Hearing Research* 68. 131–141.

Werner, Lynne A., Folsom, Richard C., & Mancl, Lisa R. 1994. The relationship between auditory brainstem response latencies and behavioral thresholds in normal hearing infants and adults. *Hearing Research* 77. 88–98.

Werner, Lynne. A. & Gillenwater, Jay M. 1990. Pure-tone sensitivity of 2- to 5-week-old infants. *Infant Behavior and Development* 13. 355–375.

Werner, Lynne. A. & Mancl, Lisa R. 1993. Pure-tone thresholds of 1-month-old infants. *Journal of the Acoustical Society of America* 93. 2367.

Werner, Lynne. A., Marean, G. Cameron, Halpin, Christopher F., Spetner, Nancy B., & Gillenwater, Jay M. 1992. Infant auditory temporal acuity: gap detection. *Child Development* 63. 260–272.

Werner, Lynne A. & VandenBos, Gary R. 1993. Developmental psychoacoustics: what infants and children hear. *Hospital and Community Psychiatry* 44. 624–626.

Won, Jong H., Drennan, Ward R., Kang, Robert S., & Rubinstein, Jay T. 2010. Psychoacoustic abilities associated with music perception in cochlear implant users. *Ear and Hearing* 31. 796–805.

Woodward, Julide Z. & Aslin, Richard N. 1990. Segmentation cues in maternal speech to infants. Paper presented at the 7th biennial meeting of the international conference on infant studies. Montreal, Quebec, Canada.

Yoshida, Katherine A., Fennell, Christopher T., Swingley, Daniel, & Werker, Janet F. 2009. Fourteen-month-old infants learn similar-sounding words. *Developmental Science* 12 (3). 412–418.

Outi Bat-El and Avivit Ben-David
3 Developing phonology

1 Introduction

Language is a complex system and its acquisition involves the interaction of various principles, grammatical as well as general cognitive ones. In this paper, we concentrate on universal phonological principles that play a role during the early stages of language production. We examine language acquisition from two angles: (i) the disparity between the adults' target words and the corresponding children's productions, and (ii) the nature of the system governing the children's productions and its development.

Following Tesar and Smolensky (1998), we assume that during every stage of language development the children acquiring language L have a grammar L^m, and that the grammar gradually develops (L^m, L^n, L^o...) until it overlaps (almost entirely) with the adults' grammar L.

The principal reason for the disparity between L (adults) and $L^{m...o}$ (children) is the role of the *markedness constraints* (Battistella 1996, de Lacy 2006, Rice 2007) in early grammar. As the notion of markedness is controversial, we limit our definition to typological markedness, which is often phonetically grounded in acoustic and/or articulatory properties (Hayes et al. 2004). For example, both typological and phonetic factors support the markedness relation $t < \widehat{tf}$ (t is less marked than $\widehat{tf}$). Phonetically, $\widehat{tf}$ involves more articulators than t and is thus articulatorily more complex. Typologically, most languages have t (Hawaiian being a unique exception), but many languages do not have $\widehat{tf}$ (Maddieson 1984). These facts also correlate with the pace of acquisition, as t is acquired long before $\widehat{tf}$.

Markedness constraints are relevant to syllable structure. Typologically, there are languages that have only syllables without a coda (e.g. Hua, Maori), i.e. CV (and V), but there are no languages that have only syllables with codas, i.e. CVC (and VC). Acoustically, consonants in coda position are relatively weak due to the weak acoustic cue in the transition between the coda consonants and the following onset (i.e. from C_i to C_j in $VC_i.C_jV$). Here again, there is a markedness relation CV < CVC, theoretically attributed to the markedness constraint NO CODA, defined below along with two other markedness constraints (see §4).

Outi Bat-El, Tel-Aviv University
Avivit Ben-David, Hadassah Academic College

DOI 10.1515/9781614514909-004

(1) Markedness constraints (Prince and Smolensky 1993/2004)

	Constraint	Child	Target		
a.	NO CODA	pɔ́	pɔ́p	'doll'	(Dutch; Levelt 1994)
	A syllable does not have a coda				
b.	NO COMPLEX ONSET	ké	klé	'key'	(French; Rose 2000)
	A syllable does not have a complex onset				
c.	NO COMPLEX CODA	dʌp	dʒʌ́mp	'jump'	(English; Smith 1973)
	A syllable does not have a complex coda				

Note that markedness does not necessarily correlate with structural complexity. For example, while the syllable V is structurally less complex than the syllable CV, as the former has fewer elements than the latter, the CV syllable is deemed less marked than the V syllable. Also, while children often delete a target segment to comply with a markedness principle, they may also insert a segment for this very same reason. For example, Hebrew-acquiring children delete a consonant in target clusters (e.g. ktaná → taná 'small fm.sg.'), but they sometimes insert a vowel (e.g. ktaná → kataná 'small fm.sg.'). In both cases, the children comply with the NO COMPLEX ONSET constraint (1b), though in the latter case there is additional structure.

In this paper we discuss phonological development with reference to the hierarchical organization of the phonological word:

(2) The phonological word

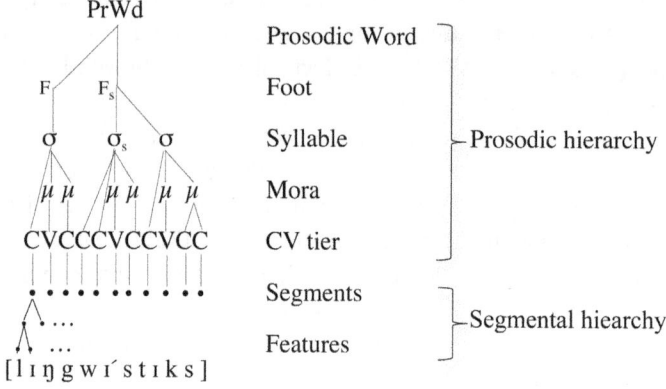

Within the phonological word in (2), we distinguish between the prosodic hierarchy (Selkirk 1982, McCarthy and Prince 1986, Nespor and Vogel 1986) and the segmental hierarchy (Clements 1985, Clements and Hume 1995). We start the discussion with the prosodic word (§2), where we attend to the phonological development in terms of number of syllables; in this context we emphasize the role of the MINIMAL WORD constraint. Below the prosodic word is the foot, which is responsible for the stress pattern (§3); in this context, we argue for the role of the trochaic bias. When we get to the development of the syllable structure (§4), we discuss the role of the constraints No Coda and No Complex and contemplate on a notorious anti-universal phenomenon in the children's productions – the deletion of word initial onsets, in violation of the Onset constraint. At this point, we reach the bottom of the hierarchy and discuss the development of the segments (§5), giving special attention to the development of contrasts. Before the concluding remarks (§7), we present our view on atypical phonological development (§6), arguing that its essence lies in the a-synchronization among layers in the phonological structure in (2).

2 The prosodic word and the Minimal Word constraint

The most studied constraint relevant to the prosodic word is the Minimal Word constraint (McCarthy and Prince 1986), which delimits the minimal and maximal size of the word to a binary foot (two syllables or two moras).[1] Languages use the Minimal Word constraint to demarcate the *minimal* size of the prosodic word, as in Cavineña (Guillaume 2008), where monosyllabic roots undergo epenthesis to reach the disyllabic minimal size (e.g. /kʷa/ → *kʷau* 'go', /he/ → *heu* 'come').[2] Languages also use the Minimal Word constraint to demarcate the *maximal* size of the prosodic word. For example, a typical verb stem in Hebrew and Arabic is limited to two syllables (Bat-El 2011), and 70% of the words in Chinese are nowadays disyllabic (Duanmu 2007, based on He and Li 1987).[3] We also witness active processes of syllable truncation in hypocoristics (e.g. Australian English *Australian* → *Aussie*, *postman* → *postie*), where hypocoristics consist of no more and no less than two syllables (Bat-El 2005).

During the **minimal word stage** (MW-stage), children's productions are limited to a maximal size of two syllables (Demuth 1996, Kehoe 2000, Fikkert 1994, Levelt et al. 2000, Lleó and Demuth 1999), like hypocoristics.

---

[1] Languages differ as to whether their feet are moraic (e.g. Dutch, English, and German) or syllabic (e.g. Greek, Hebrew, and Spanish).
[2] This is true for major lexical items. Function words do not constitute independent prosodic words, unless under emphasis. For example, English definite article [ðə] is hosted by a prosodic word (e.g. {ðəbɔj}_PrWd 'the boy'), unless under emphasis, in which case its size is bimoraic, [ði:], i.e. a minimal word size.
[3] Monosyllabic roots in Chinese often join into a compound to form a disyllabic word (Duanmu 2007). Since the meaning of the compound is semantically identical to that of the root (e.g. *mei* 'coal' + *tan* 'charcoal' → *mei-tan* 'coal'), the trigger of compounding must be the Minimal Word constraint.

(3) Truncation to meet the maximal word size requirement (2 syllables)

Greek (Kappa 2002)			Japanese (Ota 2003)		
Child	Target		Child	Target	
súla	xrisúla	'name'	ʒi:da	dʒido:ʃa	'car'
ɣúti	jaúrti	'yoghurt'	kowa	koɾewa	'this is?'
béla	obréla	'umbrella'	meda	tadaima	'I'm back'
pepés	kanapés	'couch, nom.sg'	pa:ʒe	t͡ʃimpand͡ʒi:	'chimpanzee'

While truncation toward a disyllabic maximum is common in child language, there is little evidence of epenthesis for meeting the minimal disyllabic size (as in the example above from Cavineña). In general, epenthesis is relatively rare in language development (as opposed to deletion), in Dutch (Taelman 2004), Hebrew (Ben-David 2001), as well as in other languages. For example, target monosyllabic words in Hebrew are produced faithfully also during the MW-stage (Ben-David 2001), and the few cases of epenthesis found in Dutch do not show structural improvement in respecting the MINIMAL WORD constraint (Taelman 2004).

The MW-stage is a major stage in the children's prosodic development (Demuth and Fee 1995, Demuth 1996), but not the only one. The gradual development of the prosodic word, syllable by syllable, is demonstrated below for trisyllabic Hebrew target words with different stress patterns (Ben-David 2001, Adam 2002). The stages of development are labeled with reference to the minimal word (MW).[4]

(4) The development of the prosodic word (Hebrew)

	Stage	mataná 'present'	poméla 'pommelo'	múzika 'music'
a.	Sub-MW	na	me / la	mu / ka
b.	Pre-MW	na	méla	múka
c.	MW	taná	méla	múka
d.	Post-MW	mataná	poméla	múzika

When children start producing meaningful words, during the **Sub-MW stage** (4a), they produce mainly monosyllabic words, as in Spanish *bóka* → *bu* 'mouth', *ésta* → *ta* 'this', and *tása* → *tja* 'cup' (Macken 1978). Given this prosodic limitation, the children's production lexicon is limited, containing many homonyms (e.g. *da* for both Hebrew *jaldá* 'a girl' and *todá* 'thank you'). This stage is often too short to be observable in typically developing children, but atypically developing children (see §6), who often stretch their language acquisition over longer periods, provide solid

---

[4] The distinction between stages is, of course, not abrupt, and during every stage there are remaining forms from the earlier stage and new forms from the subsequent stage (see Adam 2002 for intermediate stages). However, the structure characterizing a particular stage is statistically dominant.

evidence for this stage. Adam and Bat-El (2008b) show the difference between two Hebrew-acquiring boys during the same stage of lexical development (150 cumulative attempted words); 86% (159/184) of the words produced by the boy with prolonged phonological development (1;10.02–1;11.13) were monosyllables, as opposed to 22% (20/92) in the typically developing boy (1;05.15–1;05.29).

With time, the number of syllables in the word gradually expands toward the target, and the degree of contrast among the words thus grows as well (see also §4). During the following **Pre-MW stage** (4b), the children start producing disyllabic words, but mostly with penultimate stress, as this is the unmarked stressed pattern (see §3). Only later, during the **MW stage** (4c) discussed above, they produce disyllabic words regardless of the stress pattern of the target word. Truncation continues at later stages for trisyllabic and longer target words (e.g. Greek *fotoɣría* → *kaía* 'photo', *poðílato* → *poðíla* 'bicycle'; Hebrew *televízja* → *evíza* 'television', *taʁnególet* → *tagólet* 'hen').

3 Stress and the trochaic bias

Under the prosodic word node in (2) stands the foot, which is responsible for the stress pattern. Due to its strong acoustic cues, stress is highly accessible and thus plays a major role in language acquisition (Echols and Newport 1992, Archibald 1995), where the perceptual saliency of stress boosts a faithful match between target and output (with relatively few cases of stress shift). Given its relative strength, stress has the power of protecting target syllables from truncation. Therefore, during the development of the prosodic word, when children truncate syllables (see §2), unstressed syllables are truncated, while stressed ones are preserved (Fikkert 1994, Wijnen, Krikhaar and Os 1994, Gerken 1996, Kehoe and Stoel-Gammon1997, Pater 1997, Prieto 2006).

(5) Preservation of stressed syllables and truncation of unstressed ones

Kuwaiti Arabic (Ayyad 2011)			Russian (Zharakova 2005)		
Child	Target		Child	Target	
ðíːf	nəðíːf	'clean'	kápa	kápait	'it is dripping'
snaːn	ʔasnáːn	'teeth'	mʲisʲ	míʃɨ	'mice'
qálə	bərtəqálə	'orange'	bʲáka	sabáka	'dog'
θálləθ	muθálləθ	'triangle'	sʲik	jizík	'tongue'

Children's early productions support the trochaic bias (Allen and Hawkins 1978), showing preference for the typologically unmarked trochaic foot (sw – a **s**trong/ stressed syllable followed by an **w**eak/unstressed/ syllable). As in some of the examples in (5), the syllables surviving truncation form a trochaic foot also when the target word has three or more syllables with penultimate stress (see extensive discussion in Tzakosta 2004). For example, Catalan kəput͡ʃétə 'little hood' is truncated to the trochaic form tétə and not the iambic form *put͡ʃé (Prieto 2006). There are also a few examples where children shift stress to form a trochaic foot; e.g. English kæŋɡəɹú → wáwo 'kangaroo' (Kehoe 1997) and Dutch χi:tá:r → hí:ta: 'guitar' (Fikkert 1994).

We note here the importance of final syllables, which are preserved more often than other unstressed syllables (Echols and Newport 1992, Kehoe 2000, Ben-David 2001, 2014). The trochaic bias cannot explain cases in which trisyllabic targets like télefon are truncated to téfo, rather than téle, though both are equally trochaic. Here again, it is the perceptual saliency of final syllables that protects these target syllables from truncation (Echols and Newport 1992, Albin and Echols 1996).

Much of the evidence supporting the trochaic bias is drawn from languages with a predominantly trochaic stress pattern. In these languages, however, one cannot tease apart universal preference from language-specific frequency. Hebrew, however, provides solid evidence for the trochaic bias (Adam and Bat-El 2008a, 2009, Bat-El 2015) because stress is predominantly final (iambic foot) in the language and yet children still show preference for penultimate stress (the trochaic foot):[5] They have more attempted targets with penultimate stress than with final stress and more productions with penultimate stress than with final stress (see (4b) for pre-MW stage). It should be noted that French-acquiring children do not show a trochaic bias. This is because the stress system in French has no exceptions (always final), and thus children acquire the iambic pattern before the onset of speech (Rose 2000).

The acquisition of stress patterns is a good juncture for a brief discussion on the nature-nurture debate, i.e. whether children acquire language with the aid of universal principles (Chomsky's generative approach) or they attend only to the frequency of patterns in their ambient language (usage-based approach; Tomasello 2001).

When frequency and universal principles converge, as in the case of the trochaic foot in English and Dutch, we cannot settle this dispute. Languages like French, where the non-universal pattern is consistent and exceptionless, cannot help either, since the children acquire the non-universal pattern early, without showing evidence of contemplation. The languages that can settle this dispute are those in which (i) there is no convergence between frequency and the relevant universal principle (unlike English and Dutch), and (ii) the system is irregular and cannot be easily acquired (unlike French). Hebrew stress has these two properties and thus provides solid support for Adam and Bat-El's (2008a, 2009) argument that both universal principles and frequency play a role, in this order. At the onset of speech, when

---

5 About 70% of the noun stems and 95% of the verb stems in Hebrew bear final stress (iambic), with marginal differences between type and token, also in child directed speech (Segal et al. 2008, Adam and Bat-El (2008a, 2009).

children cannot yet figure out the system in their language because of the irregularity in it, they resort to universal principles. Later on, the distributional frequency of the language plays a stronger role and the children start following the crowd.[6]

4 Syllable structure and the ONSET constraint

Following the phonological structure in (2), we now turn to the level below the foot – the syllable. All languages have CV syllables; some even have only CV syllables (e.g. Hua, spoken in New Guinea). Therefore, CV, often called the core syllable, is typologically the least marked syllable. Assuming that phonological structures in the children's productions develop on some markedness scale, from the least to the most marked, we expect the order of acquisition in (6), based on the hierarchy developed in Levelt et al. (2000) for the acquisition of syllable structure in Dutch (curly brackets indicated 'either-or').[7]

(6) Markedness hierarchy of syllable structure
    a.   b.   c.   d.   e.

$$\text{CV} < \begin{Bmatrix} \text{CVC} \\ \text{V} \end{Bmatrix} < \text{VC} < \begin{Bmatrix} \text{CVCC} \\ \text{CCVC} \end{Bmatrix} < \text{CCVCC}$$

This order, which allows a certain degree of (inter- and intra-language) variation, is predicted from the following markedness constraints (Prince and Smolensky 1993/2004):

(7) Syllable structure constraints (partially repeated from (1))
    a. ONSET: A syllable has an onset
    b. NO CODA: A syllable does not have a coda
    c. NO COMPLEX
        i. NO COMPLEX ONSET: A syllable does not have a complex onset
        ii. NO COMPLEX CODA: A syllable does not have a complex coda

---

[6] With a head-turn experiment, Segal and Kishon-Rabin (2012) showed that 80% (24/30) of the 9 months old Hebrew-acquiring infants looked longer at the highly frequent Hebrew weak-strong (iambic) patterns, suggesting, according to the authors, acquisition of the frequent pattern before the onset of speech. This perceptual preference probably plays a certain role in early productions, since otherwise the percentages of trochaic productions would have been much higher and would have lasted longer. That is, perception precedes production, but production does not start at the point where perception arrives but rather tracks back to an earlier point in the developmental path.
[7] In Greek, the syllables V, VC, CCV, and CVC are attested simultaneously (Tzakosta and Kappa 2008).

The least marked CV syllable (6a) obeys all the markedness constraints on syllable structure, by having an onset (respecting ONSET), but not a complex one (respecting NO COMPLEX ONSET), and not having a coda (respecting NO CODA). The CVC and V syllables (6b) violate one constraint each; CVC violates NO CODA and V violates ONSET. In the absence of universal priority between these two constraints, the hierarchy in (6) allows inter-child and inter-language variation. The VC syllable (6c) violates both ONSET and NO CODA, and is thus more marked than CVC and V. The syllables with the complex syllable margins (6d) violate NO COMPLEX, either NO COMPLEX ONSET in CCVC or NO COMPLEX CODA in CVCC. Here again, the absence of universal priority allows variation. However, the CCVCC syllable (6e) is worse than these two due to its cumulative complexity, having both a complex onset and a complex coda.

As predicted, the least marked CV syllable is indeed the first syllable to appear in children's speech. Similarly, the most marked CCVCC syllable is reported to be the last syllable to appear. In between these two edges of the syllable markedness hierarchy there is inter-child and inter-language variation, some predicted by the hierarchy and some not. The variation is demonstrated below with reference to Hebrew vs. Dutch.

In Dutch, the order between CVCC and CCVC syllables is child-specific (Levelt et al. 2000); some children start with complex onsets, thus producing CCVC before CVCC, while others start with complex codas, thus producing CVCC before CCVC. This distinction is not relevant for Hebrew, which hardly has any words with complex codas.

In Hebrew, the order between CVC and V syllables is child-specific (Ben-David 2001). Given the target word *kapít* 'teaspoon', the first stage for all children is the CV syllable *pi*, whereas the second stage allows variation: some children first add a coda (*pi* ⇒ *pit*), thus giving priority to the CVC syllable, while others first add a syllable, starting with its nucleus (*pi* ⇒ *api*), thus giving priority to the V syllable.[8] Notably, such variation is not reported for the acquisition of Dutch, where the CVC syllable is acquired before the V syllable (Levelt et al. 2000); at the stage where children already produce CVC syllables (e.g. *pus* 'cat', *diχt* → *dɪs* 'closed') they add consonants to onsetless target words (e.g. *óto* → *tóto* 'car', *ap* → *pap* 'monkey').

An inter-language variation not predicted by the markedness hierarchy in (6) has to do with the VC syllable (6c). Unlike in Dutch, where the markedness hierarchy is followed (Levelt et al. 2000), in Hebrew the VC syllable is acquired much earlier, along with the CV syllable. However, the production of the VC syllable is often limited to monosyllabic VC target words, due to a constraint HAVE C, requiring at least one consonant in the word (Ben-David 2001). This constraint is universally supported by the important role of consonants (as opposed to vowels) in conveying

---

[8] The arrow ⇒ indicates that the input is the child's production in an earlier stage, while the arrow → indicates a target (adult's) input.

lexical contrast (Nespor et al. 2003, Hochmann et al. 2011). That is, during the stage where target words like *kaf* 'spoon' are produced as *ka*, complying with NO CODA, target words like *af* 'nose' are produced faithfully, complying with HAVE C, which has priority over NO CODA.⁹

HAVE C is a dominant constraint in the speech of typically developing children, but atypically developing children (see §6) often violate it, producing consonant-free words (Tubul-Lavy 2005, Adi-Bensaid 2006, Adi-Bensaid and Tubul-Lavy 2009). The loss of contrast in such cases is pervasive, to the extent that Hebrew target words like *adóm* 'red', *jaʁók* 'green', *gadól* 'big', and *matók* 'sweet' are all produced as *aó*. Although the violation of HAVE C was observed in the speech of atypically developing children, Adi-Bensaid and Bat-El (2004) do not consider it an atypical phenomenon but rather residues of the pre-word babbling stage. The pace of atypical language development is often slow enough to allow observing phenomena that go undetected or are negligible in typical development. We nevertheless do find such productions in typically developing infants who start talking very early, for example, a boy aged 1;6 produced [i] for *dúbi* 'teddy bear' and *ʃuít* 'beans', and [u] for *kadúr* 'ball' and *sus* 'horse'. However, such examples are marginal within and across typically developing children.

Because the syllable types are acquired gradually, when children attempt to produce target words with syllable types not yet acquired, their productions are simplified versions of the adults' words. The most common process of simplification of syllable structure is deletion.

(8) Syllable structure simplification via consonant deletion

	French (Rose 2000)			English (Smith 1973)		
	Child	Target		Child	Target	
NO CODA	pi	pip	'(it) pikes'	baɪ	baɪk	'bike'
	pɪpé	bibít	'bug'	dæpú:	ʃæmpú:	'shampoo'
NO COMPLEX ONSET	ke	kle	'key'	bɛd	brɛd	'bread'
	tatœ́	tʃaktœ́ʁ	'tractor'	mɔ:	smɔl	'small'
NO COMPLEX CODA	pak	paʁk	'park'	wɛp	ʃɛlf	'shelf'
	pɔt	pɔʁt	'door'	dæp	stæmp	'stamp'

Simplification of complex syllable margins (onsets and codas) follows the SONORITY DISPERSION PRINCIPLE (Clements 1990), according to which sonority is maximally

---

9 In some cases a glottal stop is observed in onset position, but this is a sheer phonetic effect. Had the glottal stop in *ʔaf* 'nose' been considered a phonological consonant, we would expect to get *ʔa 'nose' at the stage where we get *ka* for *kaf* 'spoon'. This does not happen in typical development.

dispersed between onset and nucleus and minimally dispersed between nucleus and coda. We assume the fairly standard sonority hierarchy below:

(9) The Sonority Hierarchy

Stops < Affricates < Fricatives < Nasals < Liquids < Glides < Vowels

When children delete one of the consonants to comply with No COMPLEX ONSET, they follow the SONORITY DISPERSION PRINCIPLE and delete the more sonorous consonant in a complex onset.[10]

(10) Complex onset reduction

Hebrew (Bloch 2011)			Polish (Łukaszewicz 2007)			Greek (Kappa 2002)		
Child	Target		Child	Target		Child	Target	
gída	glída	'ice cream'	góva	gwóva	'head'	fúto	frúto	'fruit'
paxím	pʁaxím	'flowers'	mɛ́kɔ	mlɛ́kɔ	'milk'	poí	proí	'morning'
tunót	tmunót	'pictures'	suf	snuf	'dream'	cílo	ksílo	'wood'
ki	ski	'ski'	tɔnt	stɔnt	'from here'	píti	spíti	'house'

Cluster reduction is the most common simplification strategy. There are a few examples of other strategies, such as epenthesis in European Portuguese (*grẽdɨ → kirẽdɨ* 'big', *mõʃtru → mõʃtiru* 'monster'; Freitas 2003) and Hebrew (*ʃnijá → ʃinijá* 'second fm.sg.', *dli → deli* 'bucket'; Ben-David 2001), as well as a handful of vowel-consonant metathesis in Hebrew (*gviná → givná* 'cheese', *psantéʁ → pastéʁ* 'piano'; Ben-David 2001), but these are relatively rare.

There is, however, a notorious anti-markedness phenomenon in language acquisition, where a target syllable with an onset corresponds to an onsetless syllable in the child's productions (Ben-David 2001, 2012, Buckley 2003; see a review in Vihman and Croft 2013). In terms of target-child output correspondence, it seems that children delete an onset, thus violating the universal markedness constraint ONSET for no obvious reason. Onset deletion is not limited to a particular segment (Karni 2012) or to a particular stress pattern, though stressed syllables seem to be better at preserving target structure than unstressed ones (see §6).[11]

---

[10] The SONORITY DISPERSION PRINCIPLE also requires minimal dispersion between nucleus and coda. This, however, does not gain much support in children's productions due to the stronger effect of the relatively high degree of markedness of sonorants (Bat-El 2012).

[11] Out of the three children studied in Karni (2011, 2012), two deleted significantly more onsets in unstressed syllables than in stressed ones, and one the other way around. See also Vihman and Croft (2007) for the role of rhythm in onsetless patterns.

(11) Word initial onset deletion

Hebrew (Karni 2011, 2012)			Finnish (Savinainen-Makkonen 2000)		
Child	Target		Child	Target	
adú	kadúʁ	'ball'	ájja	nálle	'teddy bear'
éve	dévek	'glue'	áippa	váippa	'nappy'
émeʃ	ʃémeʃ	'sun'	ámppu	lámppu	'lamp'
itá	mitá	'bed'	íkko	sísko	'sister'
aʃón	laʃón	'tongue'	éppa	héppa	'horsie'
úki	pinúki	Name	ássin	kássi:n	'into the bag'

Onset deletion in children's productions posits a challenge to markedness-based approaches (Jakobson 1941/68, Stampe 1973/79), including Optimality Theory (Prince and Smolensky 1993/2004), given the typologically and phonetically-based constraint ONSET (7a). The question is then why do children delete consonants in onset position?

The crucial observation is that onsetless syllables corresponding to target syllables with an onset are limited in their distribution, occurring mostly at the beginning of polysyllabic productions.[12] As argued in Ben-David (2001, 2012) and Ben-David and Bat-El (2016), onsetless syllables arise in the course of the development of the prosodic word (see §3), which progresses from the final, often stressed target syllable toward the initial syllable. The first target syllable produced by the child is the final and/or stressed one (e.g. Hebrew *mataná* → *ná* 'present'). The word then gradually grows through the addition of syllables. But the addition of each syllable proceeds in stages – first the nucleus and then the onset (*ná* ⇒ *aná* ⇒ *taná*). It is within this progression, when a nucleus is added but not yet its onset, that a target syllable with an onset is produced without an onset. In terms of adult-child relation, this is manifested as deletion.

The universal principle requiring an onset is violated in the children's speech only under the assumption that there is only one input-output relation in the child's grammar, where the input is the adults' output. While maintaining the view that children match their productions against the adult's target, we also contend to the output-output approach, according to which children match their productions against their earlier productions.

(12) The rise of onsetless syllables (*mataná* 'present')

	Development →				
Input – child	→ná	→aná	→taná	→ataná	
Child's production	ná	aná	taná	ataná	mataná
Input – adult			mataná		

---

12 There are also a few cases where a target consonant is deleted because it has not be acquired yet or is highly marked, and may thus look like onset deletion. E.g. Hebrew *paʁá* → *paá* 'cow', *péʁax* → *péax* 'flower', *ʁóni* → *óni* 'Name' (Ben-David 2001); English *up* 'soup', *it* 'seat' (Smith 1973).

If we take *aná*, for example, and compare it with the target word *mataná*, we see multiple deletions, including onset deletion. However, if we compare *aná* with the child's earlier production, i.e. *ná*, there is an addition of one segment. At early stages of development, children prefer adding one segment at a time (*ná* ⇒ *aná*), even at the cost of violating the markedness constraint requiring an onset. By doing so, they avoid cumulative complexity (Ferguson and Farwell 1975, Waterson 1978, Bat-El 2012), which arises when two segments are added at the same time (*ná* ⇒ *taná*).

In this respect, child language resembles languages that prohibit onsetless syllables everywhere except word/phrase initially; for example Arameic (Mutzafi 2004), Koyra Chiini (Heath 1999), and Luganda (Tucker 1962). Word initial position is known for its important role in word recognition, thus often resisting alternation (Marslen-Wilson and Zwitserlood 1989, Goodglass *et al.* 1997, Beckman 1998, Smith 2002), sometimes at the cost of preserving a weak onset or no onset at all (Bat-El 2014). But while in the adults' language, word initial onsetless syllables are *preserved* due to their *importance* for processing, in child language they *arise* due to the relative *neglect* of the left edge of the word, given the course of development described in (12). The most important edge in the course of acquisition is the right edge, which is even more important than the stressed syllable (Ben-David 2014, Ben-David and Bat-El 2015).

5 Segmental contrast

As in the other phonological units, children's segmental inventory also grows gradually, through the addition of more and more consonants and thus contrastive features. The major contrast in adults' segmental inventories is between consonants and vowels, which carry different aspects of language: consonants play an important role at the lexical level, and vowels are more important at the prosodic and morpho-syntactic levels (Nespor et al. 2003, Nazzi 2005).

Despite this contrast, consonants and vowels share place features during the very early stages of acquisition, when every word has only one place of articulation (Levelt 1994, Fikkert and Levelt 2008; see also Vihman and Keren-Portnoy 2013 for a collection of articles on the whole word approach): [labial] words have labial consonants and round vowels, [dorsal] words have dorsal consonants and back unrounded vowels, and [coronal] words have coronal consonants and front vowels. Gradually, children start producing two places of articulation within the same word (Gierut et al. 1993).

(13) One and two Place features per word

1 Place per word; English (Fudge 1969)			2 Places per word; Dutch (Levelt 1994)			
	Child	Target		Child	Target	
Coronal	ti	'a drink'	Coronal + Labial	tu	stul	'chair'
	den	'again'	Coronal + Dorsal	diχ	diχt	'closed'
Labial	bo	'ball, book'	Labial + Coronal	fut	χut	'good'
	bɔm	'beating a drum'	Labial + Dorsal	puχ	bRuχ	'bridge'
Dorsal	kʌk	'cake, truck'	Dorsal + Coronal	dun	dun	'do'
	kʌgɯ	'doggie'	Dorsal + Labial	pofi	kofi	'coffee'

Segmental development is best characterized by the growth of contrast among features, in line with Rice and Avery's (1995) proposal of contrast enhancement, couched within the theoretical framework of Feature Geometry (Clements 1985, Sage 1986, McCarthy 1988, Clements and Hume 1995). Rice and Avery propose a markedness mechanism built-in within the feature hierarchy, indicating the unmarked feature (in parenthesis) for each node (due to space limitation, we ignore here the acquisition of vowels).

(14) The feature hierarchy (Rice and Avery 1995, Rice 1996)

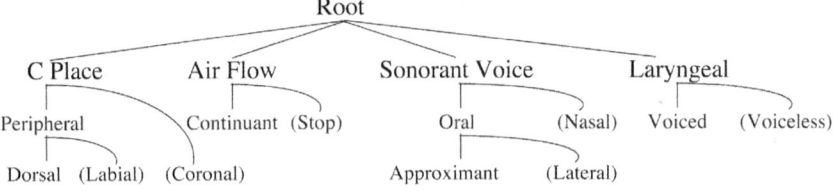

The arguments for this (slightly modified) model are based primarily on assimilation patterns in adult languages; its power of prediction with regard to acquisition is impressive though not complete. The model makes two predictions: (i) between two sister features, the unmarked will be acquired before the marked one; e.g. stops before fricatives (continuant); (ii) before the marked feature is acquired, it will be replaced by its unmarked counterpart; e.g. fricatives will be replaced by stops.

The model makes the correct predictions with regard to obstruents (Air Flow node), since stops are indeed acquired before fricatives, which are replaced by stops (15a). However, the model makes only partially correct predictions with regard to sonorants (Sonorant Voice node). The prediction that nasals are acquired before non-nasal sonorants is born out mostly in atypical development, as in Egnlish mɛ 'yes' (Ingram, 1989) and na 'watch' (Bernhardt and Stemberger 1998). In addition, contrary to the model's prediction, laterals are acquired after approximants, and are often replaced by them (15b).

(15) The acquisition of manner features

a. Fricative → stop			b. Lateral → approximant	
German			English	
(Grijzenhout and Joppen 1998)			(Ferguson and Farwell 1975)	
Child	*Target*		*Child*	*Target*
dúːje	zɔ́nə	'sun'	bæ/baᵘ	'ball'
túːa	ʃúə	'shoe'	ʔokʰu/ʔaʊgʰo	'all gone'
dátɪ	féɛtɪç	'ready'	bowuː	'balloon'

The four organizational nodes in (14) are not in markedness relation with respect to each other. Therefore, the model does not predict an order of acquisition between sonorants (Sonorant Voice) and obstruents (Air Flow). However, assuming that less structure is less marked (Harris 1990), obstruents must be less marked than sonorants.

With regard to place of articulation, it has been argued that Coronal is the least marked (Paradis and Prunet 1991), followed by Labial and then Dorsal. In lines with the view of contrast enhancement, (16) below illustrates the development of place features.

(16) The development of place of articulation (based on (14) above)

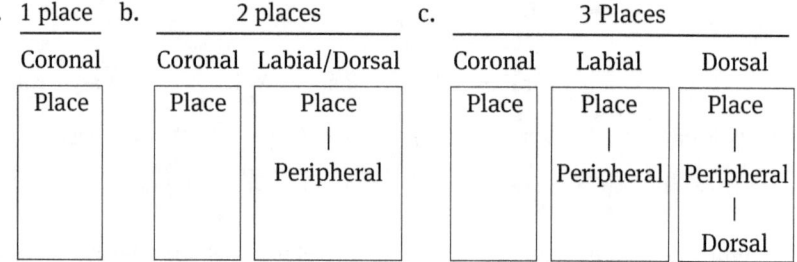

When the contrast is not yet fully developed, children substitute the marked place of articulation for the unmarked one. Substitution can be context-free (17a), but it is often due to consonant harmony (see also §7), i.e. conditioned by a neighboring consonant (17b). Quantitative studies of consonant harmony, such as Tzakosta (2007) for Greek and Gafni (2012a,b) for Hebrew show that coronal, the least marked place of articulation, is the preferred trigger, i.e. children prefer replacing other places of articulation with a coronal.

(17) Place substitution with Coronals

a. Context free		b. Consonant Harmony		
English (Stoel-Gammon 1996)		Hebrew (Gafni 2012a,b)		
Child	Target	Child	Target	
tup	'cup'	nen	ken	'yes'
tɑː	'car'	tot	tov	'good'
bʊt	'book'	til	pil	'elephant'
pɪdi	'piggy'	nanáj	banáj	'builder'
dus	'goose'	natán	katán	'small'
tʰi	'key'	didál	migdál	'tower'
tʊdi	'cookie'	ʃtáid	ʃtáim	'two'

There is evidence for context free substitutions of dorsals with coronals (17a) but not for context free substitution of labials with coronals, nor for the acquisition of coronals before labials. So here again, the model above gains only partial support, as it predicts the acquisition of coronals before labials.

Substitution is often restricted by position within the word, where the rightmost consonant (in syllable coda position) is faithful, while the leftmost consonant (in syllable onset position) is substituted; e.g. tʊk 'cook', tɪk 'kick' (Stoel-Gammon 1996). This follows from the right edge prominence in acquisition. That is, due to the development of the word from right-to-left (see §3), segments at the earlier acquired right edge are more faithful than segments in other positions within the word, in particular the left edge (Dinnsen and Farris-Timble 2008, Ben-David and Bat-El 2015, 2016).

6 Atypical phonological development: Cases of a-synchronization

We view the mental organization of language as a nested complex system, with interactive components, where each component is also a complex system. The phonological word presented in (2) is a complex system, with interaction among the different layers of representation. In typical development, the different layers develop in tandem, thus allowing establishing the baseline for a synchronized development.

Among children with phonological disorders, we distinguish between "prolonged development" and "atypical development". Both types of disorder often (but not always) show delayed development, which may also involve late onset of speech. However, while prolonged development is synchronized, as in typical development, atypical development is often characterized with a-synchronization among layers of representation (Bat-El 2009). A-synchronization arises when the development of one layer of representation in (2) lags behind the others.

A-synchronization between the segmental layer and the prosodic word layer is identified in productions with consonant harmony and context free segmental substitutions. Consonant harmony is a well-studied phenomenon in language acquisition (Vihman 1978, 1996; Stoel-Gammon and Stemberger 1994; Levelt 1994; Goad 1996; Pater 1997; Pater and Werle 2003; Fikkert and Levelt 2008; Tzakosta 2007; Gafni 2012a,b). Consonant harmony, which appears in children's speech regardless of the ambient language, is characterized by many-to-one correspondence between the target word and the child's production, where different target consonants within a word correspond to identical (or similar) consonants in the child's production.

(18) Typical consonant harmony (see also (17b))

	Child	Target	
Dutch	sis	vis	'fish'
(Levelt 1994)	kóχa	kɔ́pjə	'cup'
	pipóto	kipóto	'dump truck'
Greek	póma	stóma	'mouth'
(Tzakosta 2007)	vavó	stavró	'cross Acc.'
	gagónɛ	ðagónɛ	'bite 3rd sg. Pres.'
Hebrew	til	pil	'elephant'
(Gafni 2012a,b)	χáχal	záχal	'caterpillar'
	lalám	ʃalóm	'hello'

Consonant harmony disappears from children's production quite early, before they stop omitting syllables (Grunwell 1982) and before they start producing long words. Therefore, most examples of consonant harmony found in the literature consist of one or two syllables, and occasionally three. In general, the greater the number of syllables in the child's production the fewer instances of consonant harmony found.

While typically developing children rarely produce quadrisyllabic words with consonant harmony, atypically developing children may often do so.[13] As shown in (19a) below (data from Tubul-Lavy 2005), the number of syllables, the stress pattern and the vowels in the children's productions are adult-like, but the forms are nevertheless qualitatively atypical exhibiting surface consonant harmony in quadrisyllabic productions. At the stage where children produce words with four syllables (prosodic word layer) they are expected to have no consonant harmony (segmental layer).

---

[13] See Bat-El (2009) for two other characteristics of typical consonant harmony and how they do not hold in atypical development.

(19) A-synchronization between the segmental layer and prosodic layer (Hebrew)

a. Atypical consonant harmony

Child	Target	
mekikáim	metsiltáim	'cymbals'
elikóke	elikópteʁ	'helicopter'
pepipópe	elikópteʁ	'helicopter'
teledída	televízja	'television'
gaegóe	tarnególet	'hen'
kakuéde	kaduʁégel	'football'
measése	mevaʃélet	'she cooks'

b. Atypical segmental acquisition

Child	Target	
kíka	íma	'mummy'
kóke	ʃmóne	'eight'
kakó	tsaóv	'yellow'
kuká	bubá	'doll'
kakáki	matsáti	'I found'
kakiká	xavitá	'omelet'
kikakáki	miʃkafáim	'glasses'

Although the two datasets in (19) exhibit surface consonant harmony (cf. *pepipópe* (19a) and *kikakáki* (19b)), we claim that the sources are different. The data in (19b) are drawn from a child age 3;0 with severe phonological disorders (assessed by the second author) and a consonant inventory consisting of one consonant only – /k/ (note that typically developing Hebrew-acquiring children produce at least 10 different consonants by the age of 3;00; Ben-David 2015). Thus, what looks like consonant harmony could just as well be non-assimilatory replacement of all consonants with /k/ (see Tzakosta 2007 and Gafni 2012a,b for the problems that arise when distinguishing between assimilatory and non-assimilatory replacements). The data in (19a) seems to be true consonant harmony, because the children's inventory is much richer. For example, the child (age 4:09) who produced *pepipópe* for *elikópter* 'helicopter' (19a), also had productions without harmony (during the same session), which allowed revealing his consonant inventory; e.g. *kubiyó* for *kubiyót* 'building blocks', *axatía* for *avatíax* 'watermelon', *rakéze* for *rakévet* 'train', *axiéli* for *naxliéli* 'wagtail (bird)'.

Turning now to **a-synchronization between the prosodic word layer and the syllable layer**, notice in (19) that most syllables in the children's productions, including the final ones are codaless. More data displaying codaless productions are provided in (20).

(20) A-synchronization between the syllable layer and the prosodic layer (Hebrew)

Child	Target	
uéde	yomulédet	'birthday'
tabaó	tabaót	'rings'
abió	avirón	'airplane'
axatía	avatíax	'watermelon'
aisái	mixnasáim	'pants'
meluléke	meluxléxet	'dirty'

These codaless productions display an a-synchronization between the prosodic word layer and the syllable layer. In typical development of Hebrew, final codas start appearing in monosyllabic productions, and at the latest in disyllabic productions (Ben-David 2001); trisyllabic productions without final target codas are rare and quadrisyllabic productions without final target codas are non-existent. The data in (19) and (20) show again that the development of the prosodic word layer is way ahead of that of the syllable level, i.e. the two did not develop in tandem as expected.

A-synchronization can also be revealed with quantitative data, as in (21) below, where two children with an almost identical pMLU are compared (Ben-David and Veig 2015).[14]

(21) A-synchronization in quantitative terms (% of correct productions)

		Typical development		Atypical development	
	Age	2;01		2;11	
	pMLU	6.68		6.69	
a.	**Prosodic Word**	91%	(64/70)	100%	(66/66)
b.	Final coda	94.3%	(51/54)	70.3%	(38/54)
c.	Non-final coda	66.7%	(17/25)	23.1%	(7/29)
d.	Initial complex onset	75%	(3/4)	17%	(1/6)
e.	Consonants mastered	83%	(15/18)	67%	(12/18)

Here again, it is the prosodic layer (21a) that runs ahead of all other layers in the atypically developing child. On this layer, the atypically developing child fares even better than the typically developing child; the former reaches ceiling while the latter is still omitting syllables. However, on all other layers the atypically developing child is way behind the typically developing one. He omits more final codas (21b) and of course more medial codas (21c); he simplifies more word initial complex onsets (20d) and has mastered fewer consonants (20e).

The data above were drawn from different types of atypical populations, but in all cases one or two layers lag behind the prosodic word level. We have not yet studied the extent at which language-specific structural properties play a role in determining the layers involved in a-synchronization, but our data from Hebrew-acquiring children differ from that presented in Grunwell (1982:48) from an English acquiring child. According to Grunwell's (1982:183) chronology of phonological processes, typically developing English-acquiring children complete the acquisition of

---

[14] Phonological MLU (pMLU) measures the phonological complexity of words. It captures the segmental level by counting the number of correct consonants and the prosodic level by counting the number of total segments in the word, as most prosodic simplifications result in segment omission (Ingram and Ingram 2001).

final codas before complex onsets. However, Grunwell provides data from an atypically developing child (age 8;0) with impoverished codas (only nasals) but with complex onsets consisting of a stop followed by a lateral; that is, the development of the coda seems to lag behind the development of the complex onset.

(22) A-synchronization between syllabic and sub-syllabic layers (English)

Child	Target	
tɬaʔ	trʌk	'track'
plɛʔ	brɛd	'bread'
tɬeɪʔ	greɪps	'grapes'
tɬɔ	klɔz	'claws'
pli	pliz	'please'
plam	pram	'pram'
tɬeɪʔ	greɪps	'grapes'
plaʊn	braʊn	'brown'

Here, the **a-synchronization** is **within the syllable**, between the syllable layer to which onset is directly attached and the sub-syllabic moraic layer to which the coda is attached.[15]

(23) Syllabic and sub-syllabic layers

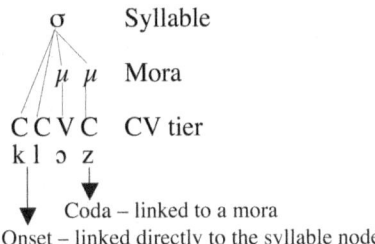

σ   Syllable
μ μ   Mora
C C V C   CV tier
k l ɔ z

Coda – linked to a mora
Onset – linked directly to the syllable node

There are more questions than answers with respect to a-synchronization. For example, do the lower layers always lag behind the higher ones? As a-synchronization is between layers, we predict that the order of acquisition within a layer will always hold; for example, final codas will be acquired before medial codas regardless of the type of population, unless the language does not support this order, as in European Portuguese; Freitas et al. (2001). In this respect we may also inquire regarding the contribution of language specific grammar and frequencies of structures to patterns of a- synchronization.

---

15 See Bernhardt and Stemberger (1998) for an extensive study on atypical development with reference to markedness constraints.

7 Concluding remarks

This paper addressed the acquisition of phonology from two angles: (i) the children's grammar and (ii) the relation between the children's productions and the corresponding attempted targets. Attention has been drawn to markedness constraints, which play a major role in children's grammar, crucially, a greater role than in their ambient language. The different effect of these constraints in the adults' and children's grammars yields different surface forms, and the relation between these surface forms is expressed in terms of phonological processes in language acquisition. For example, cluster simplification in syllable onset position in the child's productions is with reference to the adults' productions. This process is due to the markedness constraint NO COMPLEX ONSET, which is "stronger" in children's grammar than in some adults' grammars (e.g. English, Hebrew). Of course, we do not expect to see cluster simplification in the speech of Japanese-acquiring children, since Japanese does not have complex onsets, meaning that the constraint is "strong" in both adults' and children's grammars.

Markedness constraints assume representations, like the phonological representation of the word (2). This hierarchical representation has been attended in this paper layer by layer, with emphasis on the course of development. The layers are, of course, connected to each other and therefore must develop in tandem. When one layer lags behind another, there is a-synchronization, which characterizes atypical phonological development. Future studies should approach atypical development from this theoretical perspective in order to arrive at the delimitations of synchronization, and the characteristics of a-synchronization.

References

Adam, Galit. 2002. *From variable to optimal grammar: Evidence from language acquisition and language change*. Tel-Aviv University Ph.D. dissertation.

Adam, Galit & Outi Bat-El. 2008a. The trochaic bias is universal: Evidence from Hebrew. In A. Gavarró & M.J. Freitas (eds), *Language acquisition and development: Proceedings of GALA 2007*, 12–24. Newcastle: Cambridge Scholars Publishing.

Adam, Galit & Outi Bat-El. 2008b. Segmental effects on syllable selection: Evidence from Hebrew. In A. Gavarró & M.J. Freitas (eds.), *Language acquisition and development: Proceedings of GALA 2007*, 1–11. Newcastle: Cambridge Scholars Publishing.

Adam, Galit & Outi Bat-El. 2009. When do universal preferences emerge in language development? The acquisition of Hebrew stress. *Brill's Annual of Afroasiatic Languages and Linguistics* 1. 1–28.

Adi-Bensaid, Limor. 2006. *The prosodic development of Hebrew-speaking hearing impaired children*. Tel-Aviv University Ph.D. dissertation.

Adi-Bensaid, Limor & Outi Bat-El. 2004. The development of the prosodic word in the speech of a hearing impaired child with a cochlear implant device. *Journal of Multilingual Communication Disorders* 2. 187–206.

Adi-Bensaid, Limor & Gila Tubul-Lavy. 2009. Consonant-free words: Evidence from Hebrew speaking children with cochlear implants. *Clinical Linguistics and Phonetics* 23. 122–132.

Albin, Drema D. & Cathrine. H. Echols. 1996. Characteristics of stressed and word-final syllables in infant-directed speech: Implications for word-level segmentation. *Infant Behavior and Development* 19. 401–418.

Allen, George D. & Sarah Hawkins. 1978. The development of phonological rhythm. In A. Bell and J.B. Hooper (eds.), *Syllables and segments*. Amsterdam: North-Holland Publishing Company.

Archibald, John. 1995. The acquisition of stress. In John Archibald (ed.), *Phonological acquisition and phonological theory*, 81–109. Hillsdale, NJ: Erlbaum.

Ayyad, Hadeel. 2011. *Phonological development of typically developing Kuwaiti Arabic-speaking preschoolers*. University of British Columbia Ph.D. dissertation.

Battistella, Edwin L. 1996. *The logic of markedness*. Oxford: Oxford University Press.

Bat-El, Outi. 2005. The emergence of the trochaic foot in Hebrew hypocoristics. *Phonology* 22. 1–29.

Bat-El, Outi. 2009. Harmonic domains and synchronization in typically and atypically developing Hebrew-speaking children. *Language Sciences* 31. 117–135.

Bat-El, Outi. 2011. Semitic templates. In M. van Oostendrop, C. Ewen, E. Hume & K. Rice (eds), *Blackwell Companion to Phonology*, 2586–2608. Malden, MA: Wiley-Blackwell.

Bat-El, Outi. 2012. The sonority dispersion principle in the acquisition of Hebrew word final codas. In S. Parker (ed.), *The sonority controversy*, 319–344. Berlin: De Gruyter Mouton.

Bat-El, Outi. 2014. Staying away from the weak left edge: A strengthening strategy. In Bendjaballah, Sabrina, Noam Faust, M. Lahrouchi & Nicola Lampitelli. *The form of structure, the structure of forms*. Amsterdam: John Benjamins.

Bat-El, Outi. 2015. The trochaic bias: Nature or nurture. A paper presented in DGfS 37 workshop *Universal Biases on Phonological Acquisition and Processing*, Leipzig.

Beckman, Jill N. 1998. *Positional faithfulness*. University of Massachusetts, Amherst, Ph.D. dissertation.

Ben-David, Avivit. 2001. *Language acquisition and phonological theory: Universal and variable processes across children and across languages*. Tel-Aviv University Ph.D. dissertation. [in Hebrew].

Ben-David, Avivit. 2012. The development of prosodic structure: Evidence from typical longitudinal data. *Brill's Annual of Afroasiatic Languages and Linguistics* 4. 55–79.

Ben-David, Avivit. 2014. Stress or position: Deciding between prominence and position in prosodic development. A paper presented at the 15th International Clinical Linguistics and Phonetic conference, Stockholm, Sweden.

Ben-David, Avivit. 2015. Norms in Hebrew phonological acquisition. *The Israeli Journal of Language, Speech and Hearing Disorders* 32. 1–15.

Ben-David, Avivit & Outi Bat-El. 2015. Strong vs. strong, but which is stronger? Stressed and final syllables in language acquisition. A paper presented in DGfS 37 workshop Strong vs Weak Prosodic Positions: Possible Variation and Relevance for Grammar, Leipzig.

Ben-David and Rotem Veig. 2015. A-synchronization between the codas and the prosodic word in atypical phonological development. Unpublished manuscript, Hadassah Academic College.

Ben-David Avivit and Outi Bat-El. 2016. Paths and stages in the acquisition of Hebrew phonological word. In R. Berman (ed.), *Acquisition and Development of Hebrew: From Infancy to Adolescence*, 39–68. Amsterdam: John Benjamins.

Bernhardt, Barbara H. & Joseph P. Stemberger. 1998. *Handbook of phonological development from the perspective of constraint-based nonlinear phonology*. San Diego: Academic Press.

Bloch, Tamar. 2011. *Simplification patterns in the acquisition of word initial consonant clusters in Hebrew*. Tel-Aviv University M.A. thesis.

Buckley, Eugene. 2003. Children's unnatural phonology. In P. Nowak and C. Yoquelet (eds), *Proceedings of the Berkeley Linguistics Society* 29. 523–534.

Clements, Nick G. 1985. The geometry of phonological features. *Phonology Yearbook* 2. 225–252.
Clements, Nick G. 1990. The role of the sonority cycle in core syllabification. In John Kingston and Mary Beckman (eds.), *Papers in laboratory phonology I: between the grammar and physics of speech*, 283–333. Cambridge: Cambridge University Press.
Clements, Nick G. & Elizabeth Hume. 1995. The internal organization of speech sounds. In John Goldsmith (ed.), *Handbook of phonological theory*, 245–306. Oxford: Blackwell, Oxford.
Dinnsen, Daniel A. & Ashley W. Farris-Timble. 2008. The prominence paradox. In Daniel A. Dinnsen and Judith Gierut (eds.), *Optimality theory, phonological acquisition, and disorders*, 277–308. London: Equinox.
Duanmu, San. 2007. *The phonology of standard Chinese*. Oxford: Oxford University Press.
Demuth, Katherine. 1996. The prosodic structure of early words. In J. Morgan and K. Demuth (eds.) *Signal to syntax: Bootstrapping from speech to grammar in early acquisition*, 171–184. Mahwah, NJ: Lawrence Erlbaum Associates.
Demuth, Katherine & Jane Fee. 1995. Minimal words in early phonological development. Unpublished manuscript, Brown University and Dalhhousie University.
Echols, Catharine H. & Elissa L. Newport. 1992. The role of stress and position in determining first words. *Language Acquisition* 2. 189–220.
Ferguson, Charles A. & Carol B. Farwell. 1975. Words and sounds in early language acquisition. *Language* 51. 419–439. [Reprint with an appendix in Vihman and Keren-Portnoy 2013, 93–132.]
Fikkert, Paula. 1994. *The acquisition of prosodic structure*. HIL/Leiden University Ph.D. dissertation. The Hague: Holland Academic Graphics.
Fikkert, Paula & Clara Level. 2008. How does place fall into place? The lexicon and emergent constraints in the developing phonological grammar. In Peter Avery, Elan Dresher and Karen Rice (eds.), *Contrast in phonology: Perception and acquisition*, 231–268. Berlin: Mouton de Gruyter.
Freitas, Maria João. 2003. The acquisition of onset clusters in European Portuguese. Probus. *International Journal of Latin and Romance Linguistics* 15. 27–46.
Freitas, João, Matilde Miguel & Isabel Faria. 2001. Interaction between prosody and morphosyntax: Plurals within codas in the acquisition of European Portuguese. In J. Weissenborn & B. Höhle (eds.), *Approaches to bootstrapping* v. 2, 45–57. Amsterdam: John Benjamins.
Fudge, Eric C. 1969. Syllables. *Journal of Linguistics* 5. 253–286.
Gafni, Chen. 2012a. *Consonant harmony in the scope of language development*. Tel-Aviv University M.A. thesis.
Gafni, Chen. 2012b. Child consonant harmony: Identification and properties. *Brill's Annual of Afroasiatic Languages and Linguistics* 4. 30–54.
Gerken, LouAnn. 1994. A metrical template of children's weak syllable omission from multisyllabic words. *Journal of Child Language* 21. 565–584.
Gerken, LouAnn. 1996. Prosodic structure in young children's language production. *Language* 74. 683–712.
Gierut, Judith A., Mi-Hui Cho &Daniel A. Dinnsen. 1993. Geometric accounts of consonant-vowel interactions in developing systems. *Clinical Linguistics and Phonetics* 7. 219–236.
Goad, Heather. 1996. Consonant harmony in child language: An optimality-theoretic account. In S.J. Hannahs and M. Young-Scholten (eds.), *Focus on phonological acquisition*, 113–142. Amsterdam: John Benjamins.
Goodglass, Harold, Arthur Wingfield, Mary R. Hyde, Jean Berko Gleason, Nancy L. Bowles & Roberta E. Gallagher. 1997. The importance of word-initial phonology: Error patterns in prolonged naming efforts by aphasic patients. *Journal of the International Neuropsychological Society*. 128–138.
Grijzenhout, Janet & Sandra Joppen. 1998. *First steps in the acquisition of German phonology: A case study*. SFB 282 Working Paper Nr. 110. Revised version.
Grunwell, Pamela. 1982. *Clinical phonology*. London: Croom Helm.
Guillaume, Antoine. 2008. *A grammar of Caviñea*. Berlin: Mouton de Gruyter.

Harris, John. 1990. Segmental complexity and phonological government. *Phonology* 7. 255–300.
Hayes, Bruce, Robert Kirchner & Donca Steriade. 2004. *Phonetically based phonology*. Cambridge: Cambridge University Press.
He, Kekang & Dakui Li. 1987. *Xiandai Hanyu San Qian Changyong Ci Biao* [*Three thousand most commonly used words in modern Chinese*]. Beijing: Beijing Shifan Daxue Chubanshe.
Heath, Jeffrey. 1999. *A Grammar of Koyra Chiini: The Songhay of Timbuktu*. Berlin; New York: Mouton de Gruyter.
Hochmann, Jean-Rémy, Silvia Benavides-Varela, Marina Nespor &Jacques Mehler. 2011. Consonants and vowels: Different roles in early language acquisition. *Developmental Sciences* 14. 1445–1458.
Ingram, David. 1989. *Phonological disability in children: Studies in disorders of communication*, 2nd edn. London: Cole and Whurr.
Ingram, David & Kelly Ingram. 2001. A whole-word approach to phonological analysis and intervention. *Language, Speech, and Hearing Services in the Schools* 32. 271–283.
Jakobson, Roman. 1941/68. *Child language, aphasia and phonological universals*. The Hague and Paris: Mouton.
Kappa, Ionna. 2000. A longitudinal study on phonological development of the early words. In Marina Mattheoudakis (ed.), *Proceedings of the 14th International Symposium on Theoretical and Applied Linguistics*, 124–133. Thessaloniki: University of Thessaloniki.
Kappa, Ionna. 2002. On the acquisition of syllabic structure in Greek. *Journal of Greek Linguistics* 3. 1–52.
Karni, Noa. 2011. *Chain shift and local constraint conjunction in the acquisition of Hebrew onsets*. Tel Aviv University M.A. thesis.
Karni, Noa. 2012. Minimizing faithfulness violation in the acquisition of Hebrew onset. *Brill's Annual of Afroasiatic Languages and Linguistics* 4. 80–103.
Kehoe, Margaret. 1997. Stress error patterns in English-speaking children's word productions. *Clinical Linguistics and Phonetics* 11. 389–409.
Kehoe, Margaret. 2000. Truncation without shape constraints: The latter stages of prosodic acquisition. *Language Acquisition* 8. 23–67.
Kehoe, Margaret and Carol Stoel-Gammon. 1997. The acquisition of prosodic structure: An investigation of current accounts of children's prosodic development. *Language* 73. 113–144.
de Lacy, Paul. 2006. *Markedness: Reduction and preservation in phonology*. Cambridge: Cambridge University Press.
Lleó, Conxita & Katherine Demuth. 1999. Prosodic constraints on the emergence of grammatical morphemes: Crosslinguistic evidence from Germanic and Romance languages. In Annabel Greenhill, Heather Littlefield and Cheryl Tano (eds.), *Proceedings of the 23rd Annual Boston University Conference on Language Development*, 407–418. Somerville, MA: Cascadilla Press.
Levelt, Clara C. 1994. *On the acquisition of place*. HIL/Leiden University Ph.D. dissertation. The Hauge: Holland Academic Graphics.
Levelt, Clara C., Niels O. Schiller & Willem J. Levelt. 2000. The acquisition of syllable types. *Language Acquisition* 8. 237–264.
Łukaszewicz, Beata. 2007. Reduction in syllable onsets in the acquisition of Polish: Deletion, coalescence, metathesis and gemination. *Journal of Child Language* 34. 53–82.
Macken, Marlys A. 1978. Permitted complexity in phonological development: One child's acquisition of Spanish consonants. *Lingua* 44. 219–253.
Maddieson, Ian. 1984. *Patterns of sounds*. Cambridge: Cambridge University Press.
Marslen-Wilson, William & Pienie Zwitserlood. 1989. Accessing spoken words: The importance of word onset. *Journal of Experimental Psychology* 15. 576–585.
McCarthy, John J. 1988. Feature geometry and dependency: A review. *Phonetica* 43. 84–108.
McCarthy, John J. & Alan Prince. 1986. *Prosodic morphology*. Rutgers Technical Report TR-32. New Brunswick: Rutgers University Center for Cognitive Science.

Mutzafi, Hezi. 2004. *The Jewish neo-Aramaic dialect of Koy Sanjaq (Iraqi Kurdistan)* [Semitica Viva series, Band 32]. Wiesbaden: Harrassowitz Verlag.

Nazzi, Thierry. 2005. Use of phonetic specificity during the acquisition of new words: Differences between consonants and vowels. *Cognition* 98. 13–30.

Nespor, Marina, Marcela Peña & Jacques Mehler. 2003. On the different roles of vowels and consonants in speech processing and language acquisition. *Lingue e Linguaggio* 2. 203–229.

Nespor, Marina & Irene Vogel. 1986. *Prosodic phonology*. Dordrecht: Foris.

Ota, Mitsuhiko. 2003. *The development of prosodic structure in early words: Continuity, divergence and change*. Amsterdam: John Benjamins.

Paradis, Carole & Jean-Francois Prunet. 1991. *The special status of coronals: Internal and external evidence*. San Diego, CA: Academic Press.

Pater, Joe. 1997. Minimal violation and phonological development. *Language Acquisition* 6. 201–253.

Pater, Joe & Adam Werle. 2003. Direction of assimilation in child consonant harmony. *The Canadian Journal of Linguistics* 48. 385–408.

Prieto, Pilar. 2006. The relevance of metrical information in early prosodic word acquisition: A comparison of Catalan and Spanish. *Language and Speech* 49. 231–259.

Prince, Alan & Paul Smolensky. 1993/2004. *Optimality theory: Constraint interaction in generative grammar*. Malden, MA: Blackwell. (Revision of 1993 technical report, Rutgers University Center for Cognitive Science).

Rice, Keren. 1996. Aspects of variability in child language acquisition. In Barbara Bernhardt, John Gilbert and David Ingram (eds.), *Proceedings of the UBC International Conference on Phonological Acquisition*, 1–14. Somerville, MA: Cascadilla.

Rice, Keren. 2007. Markedness in phonology. In Paul de Lacy (ed.), *The Cambridge handbook of phonology*, 79–97. Cambridge: Cambridge University Press.

Rice, Keren & Peter Avery. 1995. Variability in a deterministic model of language acquisition: A Theory of segmental elaboration. In John Archibald (ed.), *Phonological acquisition and phonological theory*, 23–42. Hillsdale, NJ: Erlbaum.

Rose, Yvan. 2000. *Headedness and prosodic licensing in the L1 acquisition of phonology*. McGill University Ph.D. dissertation.

Savinainen-Makkonen, Tuula. 2000. Word initial consonant omissions: A developmental process in children learning Finnish. *First Language* 20. 161–185.

Sage, Elizabeth C. 1986. *The representation of features and relations in non-linear phonology*. MIT Ph.D. dissertation.

Segal, Osnat, Bracha Nir-Sagiv, Liat Kishon-Rabin & Dorit Ravid. 2008. Prosodic patterns in Hebrew child-directed speech. *Journal of Child Language* 29. 239–49.

Segal, Osnat & Liat Kishon-Rabin. 2012. Language-specific influence on the preference of stress patterns in children learning an iambic language (Hebrew). *Journal of Speech, Language, and Hearing Research* 55. 1329–1341.

Selkirk, Elisabeth O. 1982. *The syntax of words*. Cambridge, MA: MIT Press.

Smith, Jennifer L. 2002. *Phonological augmentation in prominent positions*. University of Massachusetts, Amherst, Ph.D. dissertation.

Smith, Neilson V. 1973. *The acquisition of phonology: A case study*. Cambridge: Cambridge University Press.

Stampe, David. 1973/79. *A dissertation in natural phonology*. University of Chicago, New York: Garland Publishing.

Stoel-Gammon, Carol. 1996. On the acquisition of velars in English. In Barbara Handford Bernhardt, J. Gilbert & D. Ingram (eds.), *Proceedings of the UBC International Conference on Phonological Acquisition*, 201–214. Somerville, MA: Cascadilla Press.

Stoel-Gammon, Carol and Joseph Stemberger. 1994. Consonant harmony and phonological underspecification in child speech. In M. Yavas (ed.), *First and second language phonology*, 63–80. San Diego, CA: Singular.

Tesar, Bruce & Paul Smolensky. 1998. The learnability of optimality theory. *Linguistic Inquiry* 29. 229–268.

Taelman, Helena. 2004. *Syllable omissions and additions in Dutch child language: An inquiry into the function of rhythm and the link with innate grammar*. University of Antwerp Ph.D. dissertation.

Tomasello, Michael. 2001. *Constructing a language: A usage-based theory of language acquisition*. Cambridge, MA: Harvard University Press.

Tubul-Lavy, Gila. 2005. *The phonology of Hebrew speaking dyspraxic children*. Tel-Aviv University Ph.D. dissertation. [in Hebrew]

Tucker, Archibald N. 1962. The syllable structure in Luganda: A prosodic approach. *Journal of African Languages* 1. 122–166.

Tzakosta, Marina. 2004. *Multiple parallel grammars in the acquisition of stress in Greek L1*. Leiden University Ph.D. dissertation.

Tzakosta, Marina. 2007. Genetic and environmental effects in L1 phonological acquisition: The case of consonant harmony in Greek child speech. *Journal of Greek Linguistics* 8. 5–30.

Tzakosta, Marina & Ionna Kappa. 2008. Syllable types in child Greek: A developmental account. In A. Gavarró and M.J. Freitas (eds.), *Language acquisition and development: Proceedings of GALA 2007*, 467–471. Newcastle: Cambridge Scholars Publishing.

Vihman, Marilyn. 1978. Consonant harmony: Its scope and function in child language. In J. Greenberg (ed.), *Universals of human language, v. 2: Phonology*, 281–334. Stanford, CA: Stanford University Press.

Vihman, Marilyn. 1996. *Phonological development: The origins of language in the child*. Cambridge, MA: Blackwell.

Vihman, Marilyn & William Croft. 2003. Phonological development: Toward a "radical" templatic phonology. *Linguistics* 45. 683–725.

Vihman, Marilyn M. & Tamar Keren-Portnoy (eds). 2013. *The emergence of phonology: Whole-word approaches and cross-linguistic evidence*. Cambridge: Cambridge University Press.

Waterson, Natalie. 1978. Growth of complexity in phonological development. In N. Waterson and C. Snow (eds.), *The development of communication*, 415–442. Chichester: Wiley.

Wijnen, Frank, Evelien Krikhaar & Els Den Os. 1994. The (non)realization of unstressed elements in children's utterances: Evidence for a rhythmic constraint. *Journal of Child Language* 21. 59–84.

Zharkova, Natalia. 2005. Strategies in the acquisition of segments and syllables in Russian-speaking children. In In Marina Tzakosta, Claartje Levelt & Jeroen van de Weijer (eds.), *Developmental paths in phonological acquisition. Special issue of Leiden Papers in Linguistics* 2.1, 189–213.

I **Linguistic acquisition**

Section 2: Lexical knowledge

Suvi Stolt
4 Early lexicon and the development that precedes and follows it – A developmental view to early lexicon

1 Introduction

Early lexical development begins at the end of the first year by the acquisition of receptive lexicon, and it continues roughly at the age of one year by the development of expressive lexicon. By the end of the second year children have usually acquired the first, basic lexicon of their native language. The development of language is a complex process. In this process children need to acquire the different domains of language (lexicon, phonology, morphology, syntax, pragmatics), and, in addition to this, they also have to find out how the different domains of language ability are interacting with each other. In the literature and in research, the development of different linguistic domains are often viewed separately. However, the purpose of the present chapter is to describe how the early lexical development is tied to the development that precedes it, and how it is tied to the development that follows. This perspective may help to understand what the important building blocks for the development of early lexicon are and how early lexicon growth is connected to later language development. The present chapter is divided into two parts. The first part focuses on the development during the first year and especially on the matter of how the early development is related to the development of early lexicon. The second part concentrates on how the early lexicon is tied to even later development.

2 Early development forms the basis for lexical development

During the first year of life children acquire many abilities which enable the lexical development to begin. Early auditory perception skills are necessary for the development of lexicon and language ability. Early vocalization development makes it possible to control phonation and articulation in an effective and useful manner. Furthermore, motor and cognitive development provide a basis for conceptual development, and lastly, early interactions provide a meaningful context for lexical development and for language development in general.

Suvi Stolt, University of Helsinki

DOI 10.1515/9781614514909-005

Children's auditory perception and discrimination skills develop actively during the first year of life (e.g. Curtin and Hufnagle, 2013). Right after birth, infants prefer to listen human language which is spoken around them, and they also prefer to listen their own mother's voice over other women's voices. Furthermore, infants are capable of discriminating consonant and vowel contrasts, also those not included in their native language, already during the first months of their lives. However, this ability weakens during the first few months of life, and at the end of the first year, children focus more on the contrasts of their own native language (see review in Saffran et al., 2006). By the age of 6–8 months, infants begin to be aware of word boundaries. For example stress, prosodic and rhythmic cues are used when solving the word segmentation problem. Finally, at the end of the first year of life, children are able to recognize familiar words (e.g. Fenson et al., 2007). Early speech perception and discrimination skills have been shown to be associated with later language development. Guttorm et al. (2005) reported that the auditory speech processing skills in newborn babies measured using brain event-related potentials predicted children's receptive language development at 2;5 years of age. There was also a tendency for the association between very early speech discrimination skills and receptive language ability at 5;0 in the same study. On the other hand, Tsao, Liu and Kuhl (2004) reported that the speech discrimination ability measured at 6 months of age was associated with the development of receptive and expressive lexicon measured at 13, 16 and at 24 months of age in a sample of 28 full-term children. Thus, as for example the findings of these two studies demonstrate, early speech discrimination and speech perception skills are connected to later language development and play a role in it.

Regarding the early vocalization development during the first year of life, the following, four developmental stages have been identified (Oller, 2000): *the phonation stage, the primitive articulation stage, the expansion stage* and *the canonical stage*. During these stages children express emerging capacity to control the different properties of speech signals. In the following, the description and the meaning of each stage is described based on the findings of Oller (2000). During the first stage, the phonation stage, children produce crying sounds, vegetative sounds, and, in addition to this, they also produce brief, smooth voicing sounds. These smooth voicing sounds do not have a full vocalic status yet; still, children express the capacity of producing normal phonation when expressing these sounds. During the primitive articulation stage, children begin to move their vocal tract at the same time as the smooth voicing sounds are produced. As a result, the dorsum or back of the tongue comes into contact with the palate and results in a sound called gooing (or cooing). Although the gooing sound is not yet accurately articulated, and although it is produced at the back of the throat only, gooing can be considered as the beginning of articulation. During the third stage, the expansion stage, children begin to vary their vocalizations actively in terms of pitch, duration, amplitude and quality. The resonance of the vowel-sounds that children produce at this stage resembles more and more the full resonance of the vowels of the adult language. In addition, children also begin to produce primitive syllables: a vowel sound is combined with the movement of lips or tongue. Thus, the achievements of this stage are vowel resonance and the ability to articulate consonant sounds. Lastly, during the canonical stage, children are already able to produce well-timed and well-articulated, repeated sequences. These sequences are often produced at the front of the mouth with the help of the lips or the tip of the tongue (e.g. /bababa/ or /dadada/). In other words, infants show that they are capable of producing well-timed articulation. Early vocalization development has at least two important functions (Oller, 2000). Firstly, children practice their vocal control and articulation skills during this developmental period. These skills can then be used later in speech and language. Secondly, early vocalizations are also an important element in the early interactions between a child and a care-taker.

One central task that children have to solve during the process of early lexical development is to find a link between a symbol (i.e. a word) and its referent. In addition, children have to figure out the correct and exact meaning for different symbols, i.e. words. The emerging motor and cognitive skills provide aid for these two important tasks. Significant changes in how a child moves and interacts with the environment take place during the first eighteen months of life. In addition, memory skills and the ability to perceive, analyze and store information also develop actively during infancy. Better motor and cognitive skills provide increasingly sophisticated possibilities for a child to explore and notice more and more specific object features (compare Iverson, 2010). In lexical acquisition this information can be used when mapping meanings to linguistic symbols, words.

The lexicon, and language in general, are not acquired in isolation, but in the early interactions between a caretaker and a child. Roughly by the age of one year, children have acquired the capacity to share and coordinate their attention with a social partner with respect to an event or an object. This *joint attention* skill has been considered fundamental for language acquisition. It helps to recognize the intended referent of the partner – the word-object mapping task is facilitated. Morales et al. (2000) analyzed whether the individual differences in the capacity to follow the attention focus of others (i.e. the skill of responding to joint attention, RJA) were related to vocabulary acquisition. It was found that RJA at 0;6, 0;8, 0;10 and at 1;0 was positively associated with individual differences in the lexicon development during the second year of life.

To conclude, when early vocabulary development begins at the end of the first year, children have already acquired many things which can be taken advantage of in the lexicon acquisition. Early auditory perception and auditory discrimination skills make it possible to segment speech and to concentrate on the meaningful units in the word learning and language acquisition process. Early vocalization development provides a basis for phonation and articulation. As lexical acquisition begins, children can already express well-timed, well-articulated sequences, although these sequences do not have symbolic status yet. Furthermore, increasingly better and more specific motor and cognitive abilities provide children with tools to explore their environment and to derive information on different objects around them. This information can then be taken to the lexical acquisition process. Lastly, the development of attention sharing skills, and especially the capacity to share attention with a social partner, provide a context for the development of lexicon and for the language development: the word-object mapping task becomes easier when the attention focus of the communicative partner can be shared.

3 Early lexical development is connected to the development of grammar

Children acquire their first receptive words usually roughly at the age of 8–9 months, and they say their first words roughly at the age of one year. At two years of age, children have usually acquired the expressive lexicon of approximately 300 words, although the individual variation is high. According to empirical findings, there exists a tight connection between early expressive lexicon growth and the emergence of grammar in children with different target languages at the end of the second year (e.g. Bates and Goodman, 1999; Bates, Dale and Thal, 1995; Caselli, Casadio and Bates, 1999; Conboy and Thal, 2006; Stolt et al., 2009).

One early sign of grammatical development is the emergence of verbs and closed class words (e.g. articles, quantifiers, question words, pronouns, prepositions, particles) to the lexicon. Children usually begin their vocabulary development by the acquisition of early social terms (i.e. onomatopoetic expressions, names of people, early routine words). In addition, nouns are typically acquired very actively when the lexicon size is roughly between 50 and 200 words. On the other hand, verbs and closed class words are rare in small lexicons (<50 words). Children acquire these words slowly, side by side with the growth of lexicon size. Thus, as the lexicon size grows, the number and proportion of verbs and closed class words also grow steadily in relation to lexicon size. Closed class words are acquired even at a slower pace than verbs: when the lexicon size is approximately >400 words, the proportion of verbs in the lexicon is roughly 15–20% and the proportion of closed class words is 8–10%, respectively, in children with different target languages (e.g. Caselli, Casadio and Bates, 1999; Stolt et al., 2009). The acquisition of verbs and closed class words makes it possible for a child to build up sentences, to modify their meanings and to express grammatically specific meanings in a much more effective manner than before.

About at the same time as children begin to acquire verbs and closed class words, they also begin to use word combinations. In English-speaking children, early word combinations have been shown to emerge when the lexicon size is between 50 and 200 words (Bates, Dale and Thal, 1995). A comparable finding has been described in children who acquire Finnish: the mean value of lexicon size was 313 words (min. 33, max. 581) in those children who had begun to use word combinations, and 46 words (min. 5, max. 116) in those children who did not use word combinations in a group of 2-year-old Finnish children in a recent study (Stolt et al., 2009). The difference in the lexicon size between the groups of children who did/did not use words combinations was significant.

The early development of morphological inflections has also been reported to be associated with early expressive lexicon growth. Thordardottir, Weismer and Evans (2002) showed that both Icelandic and English-speaking children acquired verb inflections in relation to the growth of expressive vocabulary size in a group of 2-year-old children. This finding was clear in both language groups although also differences were detected: Icelandic children needed to acquire a higher number of lexical items than English-speaking children before the grammatical regularity could be detected. This difference was interpreted to be due to a larger morphological system of Icelandic when compared to English (Thordardottir, Weismer and Evans, 2002). Furthermore, the emergence of morphological inflections is not associated with the general expressive lexicon size only, but the emergence of nominal/verb inflections has also been shown to be associated with the growth of respective lexicon (i.e. nominal/verb lexicon) at least in children who are acquiring a highly inflected language (Stolt et al., 2009; see also Thordardottir, Weismer and Evans, 2002). Lastly, grammatical complexity has been shown to increase as the size of expressive lexicon increases in children acquiring English and Italian (Caselli, Casadio and Bates, 1999). To conclude, based on the findings of various studies, the different features of early grammatical development are significantly associated with the increase of early expressive lexicon at the end of the second year in children with different target languages, at least in children acquiring languages such as English, Italian, Icelandic and Finnish.

What might explain this tight connection between the early expressive lexicon and the emergence of grammar? At least three different explanations have been offered (Bates and Goodman, 1999). According to the first explanation, *perceptual bootstrapping*, efficient word perception requires some amount of top-down processing: a listener has to compare unclear word forms, which often occur in fluent speech, to the possible word candidates. In the case of small grammatical items such as closed class words and bound inflections, top-down processing is also needed, perhaps even more so than in content words, since closed class words and bound inflections are short and low in stress. Thus, it may be necessary for a child to acquire a certain amount of content words before the acquisition of small grammatical items can begin: content words provide a structure for the perception of closed-class words and bound morphemes which are often produced right before or after a content word (Bates and Goodman, 1999). The second explanation is called *logical bootstrapping*. It has been shown that relational terms such as verbs and adjectives are acquired later than nouns (e.g. Gentner and Boroditsky, 2001). The logical bootstrapping explanation suggests that children cannot acquire relational terms before they have acquired an adequate number of content words which relational terms can relate. According to the third explanation, *syntactic bootstrapping*, children make use of morpho-syntax (word order, morphological cues) to learn the meanings of novel words (Bates and Goodman, 1999; see also summary in Dromi, 1999), and due to this, grammar emerges in close connection with lexicon growth. Although these explanations can offer some reasons for the tight connection between the lexicon and grammar, none is exclusive. Still, they can help to understand the link between the early vocabulary and grammatical growth.

Empirical findings on the tight connection between the expressive lexicon and grammar have questioned earlier theoretical considerations which viewed the lexicon and grammar as separate modules. A question of whether these two language domains develop independently, with different developmental rates and onset times or together, in close contact with each other, has arisen. Different proposals (dual mechanism view, e.g. Pinker, 1991; single mechanism view, e.g. Bates and Goodman, 1999) have been suggested to clarify the emergence of early morphology and grammar. The dual mechanism view suggests that the specific grammatical rule-based mechanism, which is independent of the lexicon, mediates the acquisition of inflectional morphology. The single mechanism view, in contrast, proposes that lexical items are stored, regularities between them are detected and followed by organization. Morphological growth is associated with the development of early vocabulary. The empirical findings described above provide support for the latter proposal in particular.

4 The predictive value of early lexical development

It is not yet clear how far-reaching expectations one may make about the later language development on the basis of early lexicon. The longitudinal studies in different groups of children can provide information on the possible predictive value of early lexical development. Children with very small expressive lexicon size at the end of the second year or at the beginning of the third year have been considered as *late talkers*. The definition of late talker status varies. Perhaps the most widely used definition is based on the specific language milestones (<50 words and/or no word combinations) at the age of two years, but the percentile cutoff values (e.g. the 10th or the 15th percentile) have also been used (Rescorla and Dale, 2013). For clinical purposes, the definition of no true words by 17 months of age has also been proposed (Camarata, 2013). The late onset of word production and a very slow growth of the early expressive lexicon can serve as indicators of a pervasive condition such as autism, global intellectual disability or phonological or receptive language disorder (Camarata, 2013); these conditions usually have long-term effects on the child's development. Therefore it is important to verify that the late onset of word production and/or the slow early lexical development are not part of a wider disability or syndrome (Camarata, 2013). The following risk signs (when appearing together with slow expressive lexical development) for the long-term difficulties have been listed: lack of symbolic play, a low rate of nonverbal communication, few communicative gestures or vocalizations, few consonants in babble, limited response to language, the presence of weak comprehension skills and/or the family history with language delays or reading problems (Paul and Weismer, 2013).

Longitudinal follow-up studies provide important information on the possible predictive value of early lexicon in late-talkers. Rescorla (2013) followed the language development of a group of late talkers whose receptive language ability and cognitive development were age-adequate at intake, up to the age of 17 years. Children had adequate hearing and they came from the middle to high socioeconomic background. The control group, a sample of typically developing children, came from the same socioeconomic background as the children in the late talkers group. The findings showed that the majority of the children in the late talkers group had age-adequate language skills by the age of five years. Still, the late talkers as a group had weaker language skills than the controls through the age of 17 years. In addition, the early vocabulary score was a significant predictor of vocabulary, grammar, verbal memory and reading comprehension at the age of 13 years. At 17, the early vocabulary score explained 17% of the variance in the vocabulary/grammar factor (Rescorla, 2013). Based on the results of this study, and on other studies which have followed the development of late talkers with normal cognitive development, it can be concluded that the majority of the children who are late talkers at an early age and who have no clear reason for their slow early vocabulary development, will attain typical language scores by the age of five years. However, as a group late talkers continue to have lower language scores than the children with typical language development (Rescorla, 2013). The difference in the skills such as auditory perception and auditory processing, verbal working memory, grammatical rule learning, phonological discrimination and word retrieval may explain the differences between the language scores of the late talkers and those of typical development (Rescorla, 2013).

The predictive value of slow early expressive lexical development may be different in children with some kind of developmental risk (e.g. hereditary risk for dyslexia, very preterm birth) when compared to children with no such risk. Lyytinen, Eklund and Lyytinen (2005) followed the language development of a group of children with a hereditary risk for dyslexia and a control group of children with no such risk from birth to 5;5 years of age. In addition, reading and spelling outcomes were measured at eight years of age. The results showed that those late talkers in the at-risk group, who had both weak expressive and receptive language ability at 2 and at 2;5 years of age, performed the weakest of all other children in the study, at 5;5 years of age. In contrast, the late talkers in the control group with an early expressive delay only, did catch up with their peers by the age of 3;5. These children also maintained their age-appropriate language skills at 5;5 (Lyytinen et al., 2005). Furthermore, the typical early language skills did not ascertain fluent reading skills at eight years of age: at-risk children with typical early language development performed significantly more weakly in the reading and spelling tasks at eight years of age than the control children with typical, early language development (Lyytinen et al., 2005).

Prematurely born (born <37 gestational weeks) children have a higher risk for different developmental problems than those born at term. However, the predictive value of very early language development for later language skills has not been studied intensively in prematurely born children. The predictive value of early expressive lexicon size was analyzed in a group of preterm children ((low-birth-weight children; birth weight ≤1500 g; mean gestational age of the group 28 weeks) and their full-term controls in a recent study (Stolt et al., 2014). Lexicon size was measured at the age of two years (the corrected age was used for preterm children, that is, the age calculated from the expected date of delivery, instead of the actual birth date) and language skills were measured again at the age of five years. It was found that the predictive value of small early expressive lexicons differed between the groups: early, small expressive lexicon size predicted significantly later, weak language skills especially in the preterm group, but not in the controls. This study provided information on the predictive value of early expressive language in preterm children, but the possible predictive value of early receptive language development remained open. In another study (Stolt et al., 2016), the predictive value of early receptive language was analyzed in a group of prematurely born (mean gestational age of the group 28 weeks) children and in their full-term controls using the hierarchical linear regression analysis. The findings showed that the receptive language ability measured at two years of age (the corrected age for preterm children) was a significant predictor of language skills at five years of age in preterm children and in controls. When the early expressive lexicon size (measured at two years of age) was added to the model, it did not add any significant information in either of the groups (Stolt et al., 2016).

5 Conclusions

The main focus of the present chapter has been in describing how early lexical development is based on the development that happens during the first year of life, and vice versa, on how early grammar emerges in close association with expressive lexicon growth at the end of the second year of life. One may conclude that lexical development is crucially dependent on the preceding development, and, that lexical development provides a basis for the emergence of grammar. In addition, the predictive value of early lexical development on even later language development has also been considered in different groups of children such as late talkers, children with a hereditary risk for dyslexia, and preterm children. Regarding the predictive value of early vocabulary development one may sum up that in children with no additional risk for later, weak language development the slow early expressive lexicon acquisition has only weak predictive value: many late talkers with no obvious cause for the slow development of early expressive lexicon will catch up with their peers, especially if the early receptive vocabulary acquisition has proceeded in a typical manner. However, the late talking status may still be an indicator for a later relative weakness in linguistic skills (Rescorla and Dale, 2013). Furthermore, if a child has some kind of a risk for language problems (e.g. hereditary risk for dyslexia, very preterm birth), then the predictive value of early lexicon is stronger. In these cases, early receptive language development provides important information on the language development of the children.

References

Bates, Elizabeth, Philip S. Dale & Donna Thal. 1995. Individual differences and their implications for theories of language development. In Paul Fletcher & Brian MacWhinney (eds.), *The handbook of child language*, 96–151. Oxford: Blackwell.

Bates, Elizabeth & Judith C. Goodman. 1999. On the emergence of grammar from the lexicon. In Brian MacWhinney (ed.), *The emergence of language*, 29–80. Mahwah, NJ: Lawrence Erlbaum Associates.

Camarata, Stephen M. 2013. Which late talkers require intervention? Matching child characteristics and risk factors to treatment. In Leslie A. Rescorla & Philip S. Dale (eds.), *Late talkers. Language development, interventions and outcomes*, 303–324. Baltimore: Brookes Publishing Company.

Caselli, Cristina, Paola Casadio & Elizabeth Bates. 1999. A comparison of the transition from first words to grammar in English and Italian. *Journal of Child Language* 26(1). 69–111.

Conboy, Barbara T. & Donna J. Thal. 2006. Ties between the lexicon and grammar: Cross-sectional and longitudinal studies in bilingual children. *Child Development* 77(3). 712–735.

Curtin, Suzanne & Dan Hufnagle. 2013. Speech perception. In Edith L. Bavin (ed.), *The Cambridge handbook of child language*, 107–124. Cambridge: Cambridge University Press.

Dromi, Esther. 1999. Early lexical development. In Martyn D. Barrett (ed.), *The development of language*, 99–131. East Sussex: Psychology Press.

Fenson, Larry, Virginia A. Marchman, Donna J. Thal, Philip S. Dale, J. Steven Reznick & Elizabeth Bates. 2007. *The MacArthur-Bates communicative development inventories user's guide and technical manual*, 2nd edn. Baltimore: Paul. H. Brookes Publishing.

Gentner, Dedre & Lera Boroditsky. 2001. Individuation, relativity, and early word learning. In Melissa Bowerman & Stephen C. Levinson (eds.), *Language acquisition and conceptual development*, 215–256. Cambridge: Cambridge University Press.

Guttorm, Tomi K., Paavo H.T. Leppänen, Anna-Maija Poikkeus, Kenneth M. Eklund, Paula Lyytinen & Heikki Lyytinen. 2005. Brain event-related potentials (ERPs) measured at birth predict later language development in children with and without familial risk for dyslexia. *Cortex* 41(3). 291–303.

Iverson, Jana M. 2010. Developing language in a developing body: the relationship between motor development and language development. *Journal of Child Language* 37. 229–261.

Lyytinen, Paula, Kenneth Eklund & Heikki Lyytinen. 2005. Language development and literacy skills in late-talking toddlers with and without familial risk for dyslexia. *Annals of Dyslexia* 55(2). 166–192.

Morales, Michael, Peter Mundy, Christine E.F. Delgado, Marygrace Yale, Daniel Messinger, Rebecca Neal & Heidi K. Schwartz. 2000. Responding to joint attention across the 6- through 24-month age period and early language acquisition. *Journal of Applied Developmental Psychology* 21(3). 283–298.

Oller, Kimbrough D. 2000. *The emergence of the speech capacity*. Mahwah, NJ: Lawrence Erlbaum Associates.

Paul, Rhea & Susan Ellis Weismer. 2013. Late talking in context: The clinical implications of delayed language development. In Rescorla, Leslie A. & Philip S. Dale (eds.), *Late talkers. Language development, interventions and outcomes*, 203–218. Baltimore: Brookes Publishing Company.

Pinker, Steven. 1991. *Rules of language*. Science 253. 530–535.

Rescorla, Leslie A. 2013. Late-talking toddlers. In Leslie A. Rescorla & Philip S. Dale (eds.), *Late talkers. Language development, interventions and outcomes*, 219–239. Baltimore: Brookes Publishing Company.

Rescorla, Leslie A. & Philip S. Dale. 2013. Where do we stand now? Conclusions and future directions. In Leslie A. Rescorla & Philip S. Dale (eds.), *Late talkers. Language development, interventions and outcomes*, 377–387. Baltimore: Brookes Publishing Company.

Saffran, Jenny R., Janet F. Werker & Lynne A. Werner. 2006. The infant's auditory world: Hearing, speech, and the beginnings of language. In Deanna Kuhn, Williams Damon, Robert Siegler & Richard M. Lerner (eds.), *Handbook of child psychology. Vol. 2, Cognition, perception, and language*, 6th edition, 58–108. New York: John Wiley.

Stolt, Suvi, Leena Haataja, Helena Lapinleimu & Liisa Lehtonen. 2009. Associations between lexicon and grammar at the end of the second year in Finnish children. *Journal of Child Language* 36(4). 779–806.

Stolt, Suvi, Annika Lind, Jaakko Matomäki, Leena Haataja, Helena Lapinleimu & Liisa Lehtonen. 2016. Do the early development of gestures and receptive and expressive language predict language skills at 5;0 in prematurely born very-low-birth-weight children? *Journal of Communication Disorders* 61. 16–28.

Stolt, Suvi, Jaakko Matomäki, Annika Lind, Helena Lapinleimu, Leena Haataja & Liisa Lehtonen. 2014. The prevalence and predictive value of weak language skills in children with very low birth weight – a longitudinal study. *Acta Paeditrica* 103(6). 651–658.

Thordardottir, Elin T., Susan Ellis Weismer & Julia L. Evans. 2002. Continuity in lexical and morphological development in Icelandic and English-speaking 2-year-olds. *First Language* 22, 003–028.

Tsao, Feng-Ming, Huei-Mei Liu & Patricia K. Kuhl. 2004. Speech perception in infancy predicts language development in the second year of life: a longitudinal study. *Child Development* 75(4). 1067–1084.

Li Sheng
5 Typical and atypical lexical development

1 Introduction

Lexical development refers to the growth of vocabulary knowledge in childhood. Words are form-meaning pairings in the child's lexical inventory. This chapter focuses on the development of lexical breadth, delineating the course and rate of the learning of form-meaning pairings by children, and elaborating on factors that facilitate or hamper this learning process.

1.1 Typical course of lexical development

One of the first easily noticed and most celebrated milestones in early lexical development is the production of the first word. Children typically reach this milestone at the end of their first year. By this time, most children have already accumulated several dozen words and phrases in their comprehension repertoire. Between approximately 12 and 18 months of age, children slowly add words to their production repertoire such that by the end of this six-month period, they reach the 50-word mark. It is usually at this point that the speed of lexical learning picks up, giving the impression of a word spurt, or vocabulary explosion. The word spurt refers to a sudden increase in the rate at which new words appear in children's vocabulary. According to Benedict (1979) and Goldfield and Reznick (1990), prior to the word spurt, children add 8 to 11 words per month; but after the spurt, the number shifts to an average of 22 to 37 words per month. Not all children in published longitudinal studies show a word spurt (Nelson, 1973; Goldfield & Reznick, 1990). There is also variation in the age at which children may show the word spurt. The so-called late spurters may not demonstrate a vocabulary spurt until after their productive vocabulary has reached 100 words (Mervis & Bertrand, 1995).

The content of children's first 50 words has been under much scrutiny. Nelson (1973) found that over 60% of children's first 50 words comprise general nominals or common nouns (i.e., ball, milk). The remaining words are dispersed into categories such as specific nominals (i.e., Mommy, Ellie), action words (i.e., go, look), modifiers (i.e., big, all gone), personal social words (i.e., no, please), and grammatical function words (i.e., is, for). Although children's vocabulary composition reflects their perceptual experience, the predominance of nouns in early vocabulary, also known as the noun bias, suggests that certain concepts are easier to acquire than others. Gentner's

Li Sheng, University of Delaware

natural partitions hypothesis (1978) posits that noun meanings are easier to encode than verb meanings because nouns encode familiar entities or things in children's environment whereas verbs encode relational meanings that are less available from direct visual experience and must be figured out from hearing the verb in use.

The use of standardized tools has greatly facilitated the study of early lexical development. Two such tools, the MacArthur-Bates Communicative Developmental Inventory (CDI, Fenson et al., 1993), and the Language Development Survey (LDS, Rescorla, 1989), present a list of words and phrases to parents and caretakers of young children and rely on their judgment to yield estimates of children's receptive and/or expressive vocabulary. Ease of administration and sound psychometric properties have spurred the adaptation of these tools into numerous languages other than English. Using these instruments, large-scale studies across many languages have identified several common patterns that characterize early lexical development in children acquiring distinct languages. First, there are large individual variations in the rate of vocabulary development for every language that has been studied. Using the English CDI and the LDS, studies have found that typically developing children may produce their first word anywhere between 10 and 15 months. At two years of age, children at the top 10th percentile have vocabularies that are 9 times larger than those of children at the bottom 10th percentile (Bates et al., 1994; Rescorla & Achenbach, 2002). Second, girls typically have larger reported vocabulary than boys in early childhood. Third, word comprehension usually precedes word production. The English CDI data show that at 12 months, the average child has just begun to produce their first word but has already acquired a receptive vocabulary of over 50 words. Despite these commonalities, there are cross-language and cross-cultural differences in lexical learning: children sampled in the United States have been reported to have larger vocabulary than children sampled in the UK, Australia, New Zealand, and Greece (Bavin et al., 2008; Hamilton et al., 2000; Papaeliou & Rescorla, 2011; Reese & Read, 2000). These findings may be attributed to a number of potential factors such as the adaptation of the original American CDI to other cultures and languages, cultural differences in parental expectations, children's exposure to daycare settings, or differences in the frequency of occurrence of the CDI words in child-directed speech (Hamilton et al., 2000). Similarly, Mandarin-speaking children from Beijing are reported to have larger vocabulary than Cantonese-speaking children from Hong Kong (Tardif, Fletcher, Liang, & Kaciroti, 2009). According to these authors, being the only-child, being raised in monolingual households, and having higher caregiver education may have conferred advantages on vocabulary learning to the Mandarin-speaking children from Beijing.

Cross-linguistic studies have also investigated differences in vocabulary composition across different languages. Using the Q correlation, a statistical technique that measures the concordance in word use between samples, studies have found moderately high correlation values of 0.51 for US-Greek and 0.56 for US-Korean samples, indicating considerable concordance but also differences in vocabulary composition across countries (Papaeliou & Rescorla, 2011; Rescorla, Lee, Oh, & Kim, 2013). By contrast, the Q correlation between two independent Korean samples was 0.95, indicating almost identical word use in young children who speak the same language. With regard to the noun bias, nouns are found to predominate in the early vocabulary of virtually all languages. But the extent of this bias differs cross-linguistically with languages such as Spanish, Hebrew, French, German, and Italian showing a strong predominance of nouns but Mandarin, Korean, and Dutch showing a weaker noun bias (Bornstein et al., 2004; Choi & Gopnik, 1995; Kauschke & Hofmeister, 2002; Tardif, 1996; Tomasello & Merriman, 1995). The noun bias also tends to peak when children have from 51 to 100 and 101 to 200 words but diminishes in size as vocabulary grows larger (Bornstein et al., 2004).

Beyond the preschool years, parent surveys are no longer used to document vocabulary growth because parents and caretakers cannot keep track of children's vocabulary knowledge. Anglin (1993) systematically sampled words from an English dictionary and asked 1st, 3rd, and 5th graders to define or recognize definitions of the sampled words. The percentage of words known in the sample was then calculated and used to estimate how many of the entries in the entire dictionary the child would know. First-, third-, and fifth-grade children have vocabulary size that approximates 10,000, a little less than 20,000, and almost 40,000 words, respectively, in the recognition of vocabularies (Anglin, 1993). Anglin also divided words into subcategories such as root words (e.g., tree, guard), inflected words (e.g., trees, guarding), and derived words (e.g., guardian, preacher). Derived words increase most substantially over this period, from an average 16% of recognition vocabulary in grade 1 to almost 40% by grade 5. At the same time, root words decrease in percentage from 30% in grade 1 to 19% in grade 5.

More recent studies have utilized a longitudinal design to examine children's vocabulary and reading skills from pre-school to late elementary school years (Song et al., 2015; Verhoeven, van Leeuwe & Vermeer, 2011). In a study of native Mandarin-speaking children, Song et al. (2015) identified three distinct lexical growth patterns, namely high-high (with a large initial vocabulary size and a fast growth rate), low-high (with a small initial vocabulary size and a fast growth rate), and low-low (with a small initial vocabulary size and a slow growth rate). The high-high group had significantly higher vocabulary throughout the age span. The latter two groups were initially comparable in vocabulary size; but differences emerged after school entry and persisted till the end of the sampling period. The higher maternal educational level of the high-high group may have led to a richer learning environment that supported vocabulary and reading skill development. Despite having similar maternal education and nonverbal IQ, the low-high group showed greater phonological awareness than the low-low group as early as age five. This difference became even larger at age six. Superior morphological awareness and rapid naming performance was also identified for the low-high in comparison to the low-low group after school entry. Greater skills in the phonological and morphological domains were hypothesized to be protective factors that enabled the low-high group to catch up in their vocabulary and reading development (Song et al., 2015).

To summarize, during the preschool years, children expand vocabularies rapidly, learning about 5 words per day (Carey, 1978). In school-age years, vocabulary continues to grow quantitatively with an addition of about 12 words per day, 2 to 3 of which are root words (Anglin, 1993; Biemiller & Slonim, 2001). There are qualitative changes during this period in terms of the relative contribution of different word types to total vocabulary knowledge, with derived words quickly gaining prominence in higher grades. By early adulthood, college students are estimated to know between 15,000 and 17,000 root words (D'Anna, Zechmeister, & Hall, 1991; Goulden, Nation, & Read, 1990; Nusbaum, Pisoni, & Davis, 1984). This number increases exponentially when derived words are taken into consideration. Vocabulary growth is closely related to phonological and morphological processing skills (Song et al., 2015). Vocabulary and reading skills also share a reciprocal relationship during the school-age years (Verhoeven et al., 2011).

2 Factors that influence lexical development

Lexical development is influenced by factors that are internal to the child as well as factors external to the child and related to the environmental input. Child-internal factors include age, sex, perceptual abilities such as audition and vision, and cognitive abilities such as attention and memory capacity, and social-pragmatic ability. The effects of age and sex are illustrated in the above description of typical lexical development. The influence of perceptual abilities will be demonstrated through discussions of children who have impairment in the auditory or visual modality. The influence of cognitive abilities will be elucidated by evidence from special populations such as Down syndrome, Specific Language Impairment, or Autism Spectrum Disorders. An important contributor to vocabulary outcomes across typical and atypical populations is the child's verbal memory ability. Verbal memory refers to the capacity to retain newly encountered sound sequences. Verbal memory capacity is related to an individual's current vocabulary size and predicts vocabulary growth over time (Baddeley, 2003; Gathercole, 2006).

Child-external factors are the quantity and quality of linguistic input. These aspects of linguistic input are highly related to the family's socioeconomic status (Hart & Risley, 1995; Hoff, 2003). Higher socioeconomic status is generally associated with greater amount of speech directed to the child, greater maternal responsivity, and greater use of feedback strategies that promote learning (e.g., expansion, reformulation). Variations in linguistic input can also be presented when children have a delayed onset of linguistic input or are exposed to more complex linguistic input. These variations will be illustrated through discussions of two populations at risk for lexical delay, namely, international adoptees and bilingual children.

2.1 Atypical populations

2.1.1 Hearing impairment

Children with hearing impairment (HI) face significant barriers in oral language learning due to limited audition. Vocabulary deficits are related to the degree of HI such that children with mild-to-moderate HI are two-three years behind their normal hearing peers in vocabulary and those with severe-to-profound HI show even greater delays and widened gaps relative to hearing peers over time. However, the impact of severity of HI may be modulated or even offset by other factors. Moeller (2000) presents evidence that age of enrollment into intervention and family involvement, but not severity of hearing loss, predict receptive vocabulary outcomes at age five. Children who enroll in intervention by 11 months had similar vocabulary to their normal hearing peers and achieved significantly greater scores than HI peers who had later ages of enrollment.

School-age children who are hearing-aid users tend to perform more poorly than their normal hearing peers in experimental studies of word learning. Factors that predict word learning performance include chronological age, existing vocabulary knowledge, number of words to be learned, and listening condition. Noise has an adverse effect on word learning in children fitted with hearing aids but not in children with normal hearing (Pittman, 2011). Children with HI require more trials to learn words presented in noise than in quiet but normal hearing children require the same number of trials in both conditions. Given that word learning is slowed in suboptimal listening conditions, the value of each exposure to the new word is diminished. This effect is cumulative, resulting in significantly smaller vocabulary over time. Auditory deprivation not only slows vocabulary learning, but also compromises the integrity of the verbal memory system and the overall linguistic foundation. However, children may demonstrate robust verbal memory and word learning performance in the presence of mild-to-moderate HI (Stiles, McGregor, & Bentler, 2012). These children also outperform children with specific language impairment on measures of working memory and word learning (Hansson, Forsberg, Lofqvist, Maki-Torkko, & Sahlen, 2004).

Advancement in implant technology has motivated investigations of language outcomes in children who receive cochlear implantation. Studies have reported an enduring advantage of early age of implantation on vocabulary outcomes that is seen as early as preschool and maintained into mid-elementary school years. In a sample of 60 children who received implantation by the third birthday, 72% scored within or above one standard deviation of the normative mean on a test of single-word receptive vocabulary at age 10.5 (Geers & Nicholas, 2012). As in other populations, the role of verbal memory in lexical learning is highlighted in recent works that shows a close relationship between the growth trajectory of verbal memory and the growth rate of vocabulary in children with cochlear implant (Kronenberger, Pisoni, Harris, Hoen, Xu, & Miyamoto, 2012).

2.2 Blindness

Despite the lack of access to the visual modality and delay in joint attention skills, blind children appear to acquire their first words at around the same age as sighted children (Bigelow, 1990). There are broad similarities between blind and sighted children in the general categories of words acquired; however, several differences in vocabulary composition and word use are noted. First, blind children are reported to have fewer words for objects that can be seen but not touched (e.g., cloud, flag), and more words for things that can be experienced auditorily (e.g., drum, radio) (Bigelow, 1987). Second, consistent with the role of visual information in learning the extension of object category labels, blind children make fewer generalizations of newly learned words, treating them as names for specific referents rather than labels for categories (Bigelow, 1990; Dunlea, 1989). Third, acquisition of auxiliary verbs (e.g., can, will, do) is reportedly delayed in blind children. Mothers of blind children may be more likely to use direct imperatives (e.g., "Put on your hat") and fewer yes/no questions (e.g., "Can you put on your hat?") than mothers of sighted children, leading to fewer opportunities for blind children to hear these words (Landau & Gleitman, 1985). Finally, when providing verbal definition of familiar objects, blind children refer to tactile and auditory dimensions of the objects more frequently but visual properties less frequently than sighted children (Vinter, Fernandez, Orlandi, & Morgan, 2012). These findings suggest robust vocabulary development in blind children as well as differences in lexical composition and use in line with their unique sensorimotor experiences.

2.3 Down syndrome (DS)

First word production occurs at roughly the same *mental age* (MA) in children with DS and typically developing children (Caselli et al., 1998). At later ages, lexical production deficits have been reported in children with DS relative to MA-matched peers (Chapman, Seung, Schwartz, & Kay-Raining Bird, 1998; Roberts, Price, Barnes, et al., 2007; Roberts, Price, & Malkin, 2007), although other studies have reported that older children and adolescents with DS did not differ from MA-matched peers on vocabulary production (Laws & Bishop, 2003; Ypsilanti, Grouios, Alevriadou, & Tsapkini, 2005). A recent large-scale study with Spanish children with DS (Galeote, Sebastián, Checa, Rey, & Soto, 2011) indicated comparable oral productive vocabulary and superior lexical comprehension and gestural production in the DS group relative to MA-matched peers. The DS group's strengths in lexical comprehension may be due to their greater chronological age and subsequently greater life experiences. In a series of experimental word learning studies, children with DS showed equal or superior word learning performance despite their significantly lower verbal memory capacity than MA peers (Mosse & Jarrold, 2011). These findings suggest that lexical acquisition in DS may not rely as heavily on verbal memory as it does in other populations. Perhaps relatively intact domain-general memory capacity for serial orders and relatively preserved social skills might have facilitated word learning in these children.

2.4 Specific language impairment (SLI)

In children with SLI, production of the first word may be delayed until around 23 months of age and the 50-word milestone may not be reached till 3 years of age (Leonard, 1998). Great individual differences in vocabulary size characterize this population and children with both receptive and expressive vocabulary deficits are more likely to be diagnosed at preschool age than those with expressive vocabulary deficits only (Lahey, 1988). Although vocabulary is a relative strength compared to morphosyntax, children with SLI do score significantly lower on standardized tests of receptive and expressive vocabulary (Sheng & McGregor, 2010a). Deficits in lexical breadth persist into adolescence and remain stable throughout school-age years (McGregor, Oleson, Bahnsen, & Duff, 2013). Studies have examined the relative difficulty of verb learning and use in SLI in comparison to the learning and use of nouns. This literature is still inconclusive with some studies supporting exacerbated difficulties with verbs than nouns but others suggesting equal difficulties with both classes of words (for a review see Sheng & McGregor, 2010b). Verbal memory deficits are highly characteristic of the SLI population (Montgomery, 2002) and there is evidence of a causal link between poor verbal memory and impaired lexical growth in SLI (Gathercole & Baddeley, 1990). In a cross-population study that included children with SLI and MA-matched children with DS, it was found that both groups had smaller verbal memory capacity than typically developing MA-matched peers but that the DS group had higher receptive and expressive vocabulary performance than the SLI group (Laws & Bishop, 2003). However, a longitudinal investigation indicated that although the DS group had an initial advantage in vocabulary size, this was not maintained. The preschool-aged children with SLI improved on vocabulary and verbal memory over time, but the children with DS appeared to plateau in their vocabulary and verbal memory performance within the one-year period (Hicks, Botting, & Conti-Ramsden, 2005).

2.5 Autism spectrum disorder (ASD)

Lexical ability in children with ASD varies from no words to age-appropriate vocabulary size (Ellis Weismer, Lord, & Eisler, 2010). Although lexical ability is significantly delayed in children with ASD, these children do show growth in vocabulary over time (Charman, Drew, Baird, & Baird, 2003; Smith, Mirenda, & Zaidman-Zait, 2007). Others have suggested that lexical development is delayed but not deviant in ASD (Rescorla & Safyer, 2013). For instance, in studies that utilized parent surveys such as the LDS and the CDI, children with ASD show similar percentages of nouns, verbs, and closed-class terms as typical peers matched on vocabulary size (Charman et al., 2003). In laboratory-based novel word learning studies, young children with ASD, just like their typically developing peers, showed a noun bias in that they preferred to interpret a novel word as a noun instead of a verb (Swenson, Kelley, Fein, & Naigles, 2007). However, deviant patterns have also been reported. Among a large sample of preschoolers with ASD, around 30% of the children displayed an atypical profile of raw expressive vocabulary size approaching receptive vocabulary size, a departure from the typical profile in which receptive vocabulary growth is well in advance of expressive vocabulary (Hundry et al., 2010). Children with ASD may also have difficulties learning the meaning of abstract words and mental state terms (Tager-Flusberg & Caronna, 2007). These difficulties may be related to their deficiencies in the use of the social communication context and their difficulties developing a theory of mind (McGregor & Bean, 2010). In general the deficits in lexical learning in ASD are not due to their inability to map form and meaning pairs but rooted in their challenges in the social pragmatic domain.

3 At risk populations

3.1 International adoptees

Internationally adopted (IA) children are unique test cases in the examination of early lexical development for two reasons (Snedeker, Geren, & Shafto, 2012). First, IA children are different from infants learning their first language because they usually have more advanced cognitive ability and sensorimotor skills. At the same time, these children are similar to infants learning their first language because they are likely to be exposed to child-directed speech (i.e., motherese) that have characteristics known to promote language learning. Second, IA children are differentiated from second language learners because they experience an abrupt change in their social environment and total immersion into a novel language. These sudden changes usually result in a complete loss of the birth language and rapid learning of the new language within a short period of time.

Many studies of IA children have utilized parent report instruments such as the CDI and LDS to document their lexical development post adoption. There are several main findings in this literature. First, age of adoption is an important predictor of lexical learning speed and long-term outcomes. Studies have consistently found that initially older adoptees show a faster learning rate than younger ones. This is sometimes followed by deceleration in learning rate among the older adoptees and acceleration among the younger adoptees such that at a comparable age (e.g., 30 months), younger adoptees tend to do better than older adoptees on vocabulary measures (Krakow, Tao, & Roberts, 2005; Snedeker et al., 2012; Tan, Loker, Dedrick, & Marfo, 2012). In other words, longer-term exposure to the new language results in advantages in vocabulary size on the part of the younger adoptees.

Second, in comparison to same-age non-adopted peers, IA children show initial lag in vocabulary size but this gap gradually closes. In fact, receptive vocabulary may approach monolingual normal range within as little as 6 months and expressive vocabulary may reach normal limits within 12 to 24 months (Cohen, Lojkasek, Zadeh, Pugliese, & Kiefer, 2008; Glennen, 2007; Glennen & Masters, 2002). However, aberration from this general pattern has been reported in a small-scale longitudinal study of Chinese adoptees in French-speaking Canada (Gauthier, Genesee, Dubois, & Kasparian, 2013). These children did not show a significant lag behind monolingual norms on the French CDI at 15 months of age with only 5.4 months of French exposure; but a significant delay surfaced at 20 months of age after about 10 months of French exposure. This lag occurred at a point when the monolingual children were demonstrating the word spurt. It may be that a longer exposure period to the new language is required before the IA children demonstrate the word spurt. Longer exposure may also be necessary for these children to acquire phonologically complex words that are more common in older children's lexicon.

Third, there is variation in the physical and cognitive skills of IA children. Estimates of speech language delays among Chinese adoptees vary from 20% (Roberts, Pollack, & Krakow, 2005) to 43% (Miller & Hendrie, 2000). Interestingly, presence and severity of development delay does not seem to be predictive of vocabulary and language outcomes (Glennen, 2005; Tan et al., 2012). The highly resilient language outcomes among IA children may be partially explained by the fact that most IA children are raised in families of relatively high socioeconomic status and that IA children are almost exclusively girls.

Fourth, mothers of IA children are found to talk more, repeat more, and use more re-directive strategies than mothers of non-adoptees from similar socioeconomic background (Gauthier et al., 2013). The increased amount of maternal language input and the mother's active attempts to seek and maintain their children's attention may have served important roles in expediting the children's lexical learning.

3.2 Bilingual children

Bilingual children, both simultaneous and sequential (also termed second language learners), show differences in lexical learning in comparison to monolinguals. It is well-known that bilingual children have smaller single-language vocabulary than their monolingual peers (Bialystok, Luk, Peets, & Yang, 2010; Cobo-Lewis, Pearson, Eilers, & Umbel, 2002). Combined-language measures such as conceptual vocabulary and total vocabulary have been recommended for use when calculating bilingual children's vocabulary size to enable a more fair comparison to monolinguals (Junker & Stockman, 2002; Marchman, Fernald, & Hurtado, 2009; Pearson, Fernández, & Oller, 1993). Conceptual vocabulary takes into account the number of known concepts represented in the child's lexicons; whereas total vocabulary gives credit for every form-meaning pairing regardless of language. As such, these measures are less likely to under-estimate the bilingual child's lexical learning capacity. A recent longitudinal study with Spanish-English bilingual toddlers revealed that the total vocabulary measure yielded mean scores and growth rate that were similar to monolingual peers. The conceptual vocabulary measure yielded scores that were significantly lower and slower-growing than total vocabulary. More importantly, total vocabulary identified the same proportion of bilingual children at risk for language delay (i.e., below the 25th percentile on monolingual norms) as the CDI did for English monolingual controls (Core, Hoff, Rumiche, & Señor, 2013). These results point to the possibility that conceptual measure at this age range may underestimate bilingual children's vocabulary and lead to over-identification of children at risk for language difficulty.

Although the bilingual disadvantage in single-language vocabulary size has been reported in both the receptive and expressive modalities, there has been evidence that this disadvantage may be eliminated in laboratory-based vocabulary comprehension task (Poulin-Dubois, Bialystok, Blaye, Polonia, & Yott, 2013). 16-month-old bilingual infants showed comparable accuracy and reaction time on a computerized L1 vocabulary comprehension task as their monolingual peers; however, the bilingual infants' L1 productive vocabulary was significantly smaller than that of their monolingual peers (Poulin-Dubois et al., 2013). This pattern is not surprising given that we all understand more than we can express; but it does suggest that bilingual children may have a larger receptive-expressive gap than monolinguals. Gibson and colleagues (Gibson, Oller, Jarmulowicz, & Ethington, 2012) noticed this receptive-expressive gap even when standardized vocabulary test scores were used. This is unexpected because standardized test scores control for the inherent differences between receptive and expressive tasks. More specifically, Gibson et al. (2012) found a larger receptive-expressive gap in children's Spanish (L1) than English (L2) and this gap was seen in children with different levels of English exposure. This is puzzling as the sequential bilingual children in Gibson et al.'s study have had more cumulative Spanish exposure than English exposure. It is possible that the recent onset of English exposure may have led to suppression or inhibition of the L1, a mechanism that enables the child to pay more attention to the L2.

Lexical acquisition in typically developing bilingual children is facilitated by cross-language cognates. Cognates are words that are similar in meaning and form across two languages (e.g., the English word elephant and its Spanish translation elefante). Similar to adults, bilingual Spanish-English speaking children demonstrate a cognate advantage in both L1 and L2 receptive and expressive vocabulary tasks (Kelley & Kohnert, 2012; Pérez, Peña, & Bedore, 2010; Sheng, Lam, Cruz & Fulton,

2016). A recent study examined the cognate effect in three groups of Spanish-English bilingual children: typically developing children, children with language impairment, and children who showed risks but did not meet the full-on criteria of language impairment (Grasso, Peña, & Bedore, 2014). The typical group again showed a cognate advantage in an expressive vocabulary task, but the language impaired and at-risk groups did not. In fact, the language impaired group showed the opposite pattern, naming cognates at a lower level of accuracy than non-cognates. This intriguing finding, while still needs replication, suggests that bilingual children with language impairment are not able to utilize words learned in one language to bootstrap the learning of similar form-meaning pairings in the other language. Instead, cognates may cause competition or conflict in the child's lexicon and delay learning.

Lexical acquisition in bilingual children is also affected by properties of the language input. Bowers and Vasilyeva (2011) found that different aspects of preschool teachers' language are correlated with bilingual and monolingual children's receptive vocabulary growth over the duration of a school year. For monolingual children, the teacher's lexical diversity, indexed by the number of different words in a recorded speech sample, was positively correlated with growth; but for the sequential bilingual children, lexical growth was positively correlated with the teachers' total amount of speech (i.e., number of total words) but negatively correlated with sentence complexity (i.e., number of words per utterance).

To summarize, bilingual children show differences from monolinguals in the rate of single-language vocabulary growth, the relative gap between receptive and expressive vocabulary, and the sensitivity to various aspects of the language input. In certain instances, the effect of language impairment may be greater than the effect of bilingualism, resulting in the reversal of the well-documented cognate facilitation effect in language impaired populations.

4 Conclusion

This chapter provides an overview of lexical development from infancy to school-age years. Vocabulary grows fast and continuously during childhood. Lexical learning relies on a coalition of child-internal and child-external factors. Lexical learning is robust in the face of sensory deprivation (i.e., hearing impairment and blindness) and a slightly delayed onset (i.e., international adoptees) when children have relatively intact cognitive skills and a supportive linguistic environment. Cognitive impairment in the form of global intellectual disability, reduced linguistic capacity, and social-pragmatic deficiencies (i.e., Down syndrome, SLI, ASD) appears to have more far-reaching negative effects on the child's lexical learning. Finally, the unique patterns in vocabulary learning among bilingual children with and without language impairment illustrate the effects of a more complex linguistic environment and reduced language learning capacity.

References

Anglin, Jeremy M. 1993. *Vocabulary development: A morphological analysis.* Monographs of the Society for Research in Child Development 58 (10, Serial No. 238).

Baddeley, Alan. 2003. Working memory and language: An overview. *Journal of Communication Disorders* 36. 189–208.

Bates, Elizabeth, Virginia Marchman, Donna Thal, Larry Fenson, Philip Dale, J. Steven Reznick, Judy Reilly & Jeff Hartung. 1994. Development and stylistic variation in the composition of early vocabulary. *Journal of Child Language* 21. 85–123.

Bavin, Edith L., Margot Prior, Sheena Reilly, Lesley Bretherton, Joanne Williams, Patricia Eadie, Yin Barrett & Obioha C. Ukoumunne. 2008. The early language in Victoria study: Predicting vocabulary at age one and two years from gesture and object use. *Journal of Child Language* 35(3). 687–701.

Benedict, Helen. 1979. Early lexical development: Comprehension and production. *Journal of Child Language* 6. 183–200.

Bialystok, Ellen, Gigi Luk, Kathleen F. Peets & Sujin Yang. 2010. Receptive vocabulary differences in monolingual and bilingual children. *Bilingualism: Language and Cognition* 13. 525–531.

Biemiller, Andrew & Naomi Slonim. 2001. Estimating root word vocabulary growth in normative and advantaged populations: Evidence for a common sequence of vocabulary acquisition. *Journal of Educational Psychology* 93. 498–520.

Bigelow, Ann. 1987. Early words of blind children. *Journal of Child Language* 14. 47–56.

Bigelow, Ann. 1990. Relationship between language and thought in young blind children. *Journal of Visual Impairment and Blindness* 84(8). 414–419.

Bornstein, Marc H., Linda R. Cote, Sharone Maital, Kathleen Painter, Sung-Yun Park, Liliana Pascual, Marie-Germaine Pêcheux, Josette Ruel, Paola Venuti & Andre Vyt. 2004. Cross-linguistic analysis of vocabulary in young children: Spanish, Dutch, French, Hebrew, Italian, Korean, and American English. *Child Development* 75(4). 1115–39.

Bowers, Edmond P. & Marina Vasilyeva. 2011. The relation between teacher input and lexical growth of preschoolers. *Applied Psycholinguistics* 32. 221–241.

Carey, Susan. 1978. The child as a word learner. In Morris Halle, Joan Bresnan & George A. Miller (eds.), *Linguistic theory and psychological reality*, 264–293. Cambridge, MA: MIT Press.

Caselli, M. Cristina, Stefano Vicari, Emiddia Longobardi, Laura Lami, Claudia Pizzoli & Giacomo Stella. 1998. Gestures and words in early development of children with Down syndrome. *Journal of Speech, Language, and Hearing Research* 41. 1125–1135.

Chapman, Robin S., Hye-Kyeung Seung, Scott E. Schwartz & Elizabeth Kay-Raining Bird. 1998. Language skills of children and adolescents with Down syndrome: II. Production deficits. *Journal of Speech, Language, and Hearing Research* 41. 861–873.

Charman, Tony, Auriol Drew, Claire Baird & Gillian Baird. 2003. Measuring early language development in pre-school children with autism spectrum disorder using the MacArthur Communicative Development Inventory (Infant Form). *Journal of Child Language* 30. 213–36.

Choi, Soonja & Alison Gopnik. 1995. Early acquisition of verbs in Korean: A cross-linguistic study. *Journal of Child Language* 22(3). 497–529.

Cobo-Lewis, Alan B., Barbara Zurer Pearson, Rebecca E. Eilers & Vivian C. Umbel. 2002. Effects of bilingualism and bilingual education on oral and written English skills: A multifactor study of standardized test outcomes. In D. Kimbrough Oller & Rebecca E. Eilers (eds.), *Language and literacy in bilingual children*, 64–97. Clevedon, UK: Multilingual Matters.

Cohen, Nancy J., Mirek Lojkasek, Zohreh Yaghoub Zadeh, Mirella Pugliese & Heidi Kiefer. 2008. Children adopted from China: A prospective study of their growth and development. *Journal of Child Psychology and Psychiatry* 49. 458–468.

Core, Cynthia, Erika Hoff, Rosario Rumiche & Melissa Señor. 2013. Total and conceptual vocabulary in Spanish-English bilinguals from 22 to 30 months: implications for assessment. *Journal of Speech, Language, and Hearing Research* 56. 1637–1649.

D'Anna, Catherine A., Eugene B. Zechmeister & James W. Hall. 1991. Toward a meaningful definition of vocabulary size. *Journal of Literacy Research* 23. 109–122.

Dunlea, Anne. 1989. *Vision and the emergence of meaning. Blind and sighted children's early language.* Cambridge: Cambridge University Press.

Fenson, Larry, Elizabeth Bates, Philip S. Dale, Virginia A. Marchman, J. Steven Reznick, and Donna J. Thal. 1993. *MacArthur communicative development inventories: User's guide and technical manual.* San Diego, CA: Singular.

Galeote, Miguel, Eugenia Sebastián, Elena Checa, Rocío Rey & Pilar Soto. 2011. The development of vocabulary in Spanish children with Down syndrome: Comprehension, production, and gestures. *Journal of Intellectual and Developmental Disability* 36. 184–196.

Gathercole, Susan E. 2006. Nonword repetition and word learning: The nature of the relationship. *Applied Psycholinguistics* 27. 513–543.

Gathercole, Susan E. & Alan D. Baddeley. 1990. Phonological memory deficits in language disordered children: Is there a causal connection? *Journal of Memory and Language* 29. 336–360.

Gauthier, Karine, Fred Genesee, Marie-Eve Dubois & Kristina Kasparian. 2013. Communication patterns between internationally adopted children and their mothers: Implications for language development. *Applied Psycholinguistics* 34. 337–359.

Gentner, Dedre. 1978. On relational meaning: The acquisition of verb meaning. *Child Development* 49. 988–998.

Geers, Ann E. & Johanna G. Nicholas. 2012. Enduring advantages of early cochlear implantation for spoken language development. *Journal of Speech, Language, and Hearing Research* 56. 643–653.

Gibson, Todd A., D. Kimbrough Oller, Linda Jarmulowicz & Corinna A. Ethington. 2012. The receptive-expressive gap in the vocabulary of young second-language learners: Robustness and possible mechanisms. *Bilingualism: Language & Cognition* 15. 102–116.

Glennen, Sharon. 2005. New arrivals: Speech and language assessment for internationally adopted infants and toddlers within the first months home. *Seminars in Speech and Language* 26(1). 10–21.

Glennen, Sharon L. 2007. Predicting language outcomes for internationally adopted children. *Journal of Speech, Language and Hearing Research* 50. 529–548.

Glennen, Sharon & M. Gay Masters. 2002. Typical and atypical language development in infants and toddlers adopted from Eastern Europe. *American Journal of Speech–Language Pathology* 11. 47–433.

Goldfield, Beverly A. & J. Steven Reznick. 1990. Early lexical acquisition: Rate, content, and the vocabulary spurt. *Journal of Child Language* 17. 171–83.

Goulden, Robin, Paul Nation & John Read. 1990. How large can a receptive vocabulary be? *Applied Linguistics* 11. 341–363.

Grasso, Stephanie Marie, Elizabeth D. Peña & Lisa M. Bedore. 2014. A cross-linguistic comparison of cognate production in bilingual children with and without language impairment. Talk presented at the *14th International Congress for the Study of Child Language*, Amsterdam, The Netherlands.

Hamilton, Antonia, Kim Plunkett & Graham Schafer. 2000. Infant vocabulary development assessed with a British communicative development inventory. *Journal of Child Language* 27. 689–705.

Hansson, Kristina, Jessica Forsberg, Anders Löfqvist, Elina Mäki-Torkko & Birgitta Sahlén. 2004. Working memory and novel word learning in children with hearing impairment and children with specific language impairment. *International Journal of Language and Communication Disorders* 39. 401–422.

Hart, Betty & Todd R. Risley. 1995. *Meaningful differences in the everyday experience of young American children*. Baltimore: Brookes.

Hick, Rachel F., Nicola Botting & Gina Conti-Ramsden. 2005. Short-term memory and vocabulary development in children with Down syndrome and children with specific language impairment. *Developmental Medicine & Child Neurology* 47. 532–538.

Hoff, Erika. 2003. Causes and consequences of SES-related differences in parent-to-child speech. In Bornstein, Marc H. & Robert H. Bradley (eds.), *Socioeconomic status, parenting, and child development*, 147–160. Mahwah, NJ: Erlbaum.

Hudry, Kristelle, Kathy Leadbitter, Kathryn Temple, Vicky Slonims, Helen McConachie, Catherine Aldred, Patricia Howlin & Tony Charman. 2010. Preschoolers with autism show greater impairment in receptive compared with expressive language abilities. *International Journal of Language and Communication Disorders* 45. 681–690.

Junker, Dorte A. & Ida J. Stockman. 2002. Expressive vocabulary of German-English bilingual toddlers. *American Journal of Speech-Language Pathology* 11. 381–394.

Kauschke, Christina & Christoph Hofmeister. 2002. Early lexical development in German: A study on vocabulary growth and vocabulary composition during the second and third year of life. *Journal of Child Language* 29(4). 735–57.

Kelley, Alaina & Kathryn Kohnert. 2012. Is there a cognate advantage for typically developing Spanish-speaking English-language learners? *Language, Speech, and Hearing Services in Schools* 43. 191–204.

Krakow, Rena A., Shannon Tao & Jenny Roberts. 2005. Adoption age effects on English language acquisition: Infants and toddlers from China. *Seminars in Speech and Language* 26(1). 33–43.

Kronenberger, William G., David B. Pisoni, Michael S. Harris, Helena M. Hoen, Huiping Xu & Richard T. Miyamoto. 2012. Profiles of verbal working memory growth predict speech and language development in children with cochlear implants. *Journal of Speech, Language, and Hearing Research* 56(3). 805–825.

Lahey, Margaret. 1988. *Language disorders and language development*. New York: Macmillan.

Landau, Barbara & Lila R. Gleitman. 1985. *Language and experience. Evidence from the blind child*. Cambridge, MA: Harvard University Press.

Laws, Glynis & Dorothy V.M. Bishop. 2003. A comparison of language abilities in adolescents with Down syndrome and children with specific language impairment. *Journal of Speech, Language, and Hearing Research* 46. 1324–1339.

Marchman, Virginia A., Anne Fernald & Nereyda Hurtado. 2009. How vocabulary size in two languages relates to efficiency in spoken word recognition by young Spanish-English bilinguals. *Journal of Child Language* 37. 817–840.

McGregor, Karla K. & Allison Bean. 2012. How children with autism extend new words. *Journal of Speech, Language, and Hearing Research* 55. 70–83.

McGregor, Karla K., Jacob Oleson, Alison Bahnsen & Dawna Duff. 2013. Children with developmental language impairment have vocabulary deficits characterized by limited breadth and depth. *International Journal of Language and Communication Disorders* 48. 307–319.

Mervis, Carolyn B. & Jacquelyn Bertrand. 1995. Early lexical acquisition and the vocabulary spurt: A response to Goldfield & Reznick. *Journal of Child Language* 22. 461–468.

Miller, Laurie C. & Nancy W. Hendrie. 2000. Health of children adopted from China. *Pediatrics*, 105(6). 76–91.

Moeller, Mary Pat. 2000. Early intervention and language development in children who are deaf and hard of hearing. *Pediatrics* 106. e43.

Montgomery, James W. 2002. Understanding the language difficulties of children with specific language impairments: Does verbal working memory matter? *American Journal of Speech Language Pathology* 11. 77–91.

Mosse, Emma K. & Christopher Jarrold. 2012. Evidence for preserved novel word learning in Down syndrome suggests multiple routes to vocabulary acquisition. *Journal of Speech, Language, and Hearing Research* 54. 1137–1152.

Nelson, Katherine. 1973. Structure and strategy in learning to talk. *Monographs of the Society for Research in Child Development* 38 (149).

Nusbaum, Howard C., David B. Pisoni & Christopher K. Davis. 1984. *Sizing up the Hoosier mental lexicon: Measuring the familiarity of 20,000 words. (Research on Speech Perception: Progress Report No. 10)*. Bloomington, IN: Indiana University.

Papaeliou, C.F., & Rescorla, L.A. 2011. Vocabulary development in Greek children: A cross-linguistic comparison using the Language Development Survey. *Journal of Child Language* 38. 861–887.

Pearson, Barbara Zurer, Sylvia C. Fernández & D. Kimbrough Oller. 1993. Lexical development in bilingual infants and toddlers: Comparison to monolingual norms. *Language Learning* 43. 93–120.

Pérez, Anita Méndez, Elizabeth D. Peña & Lisa M. Bedore. 2010. Cognates facilitate word recognition in young Spanish-English bilinguals' test performance. *Early Childhood Services* 4. 55–67.

Pittman, Andrea. 2011. Age-related benefits of digital noise reduction for short-term word learning in children with hearing loss. *Journal of Speech, Language, and Hearing Research* 54. 1448–1463.

Poulin-Dubois, Diane, Ellen Bialystok, Agnes Blaye, Alexandra Polonia & Jessica Yott. 2013. Lexical access and vocabulary development in very young bilinguals. *International Journal of Bilingualism* 17. 57–70.

Reese, Elaine & Stephanie Read. 2000. Predictive validity of the New Zealand MacArthur Communicative Development Inventory: Words and sentences. *Journal of Child Language*, 27(2). 255–66.

Rescorla, Leslie. 1989. The Language Development Survey: A screening tool for delayed language in toddlers. *Journal of Speech and Hearing Disorders* 54. 587–99.

Rescorla, Leslie & Thomas M. Achenbach. 2002. Use of the Language Development Survey (LDS) in a national probability sample of children 18 to 35 months old. *Journal of Speech, Language, and Hearing Research* 45. 733–43.

Rescorla, Leslie, Youn Min Cathy Lee, Kyung Ja Oh & Young Ah Kim. 2013. Lexical development in Korean: Vocabulary size, lexical composition, and late talking. *Journal of Speech, Language, and Hearing Research* 56. 735–747.

Rescorla, Leslie & Paige Safyer. 2013. Lexical composition in children with Autism Spectrum Disorder (ASD). *Journal of Child Language* 40. 47–68.

Roberts, Jenny A., Karen E. Pollock & Rena Krakow. 2005. Continued catch-up and language delay in children adopted from China. *Seminars in Speech and Language* 26. 76–85.

Roberts, Joanne, Johanna Price, Elizabeth Barnes, Lauren Nelson, Margaret Burchinal, Elizabeth A. Hennon, Lauren Moskowitz, Anne Edwards, Cheryl Malkin, Kathleen Anderson, Jan Misenheimer & Stephen R. Hooper. 2007. Receptive vocabulary, expressive vocabulary, and speech production of boys with fragile X syndrome in comparison to boys with Down syndrome. *American Journal on Mental Retardation* 112. 177–193.

Roberts, Joanne E., Johanna Price & Cheryl Malkin. 2007. Language and communication development in Down syndrome. *Mental Retardation and Developmental Disabilities Research Reviews* 13. 26–35.

Sheng, Li, Boji Pak-Wing Lam, Diana Cruz & Aislynn Fulton. 2016. A robust demonstration of the cognate facilitation effect in first language and second language naming. *Journal of Experimental Child Psychology* 141. 229–238.

Sheng, Li & Karla K. McGregor. 2010a. Lexical-semantic organization in children with specific language impairment. *Journal of Speech, Language, and Hearing Research* 53. 146–159.

Sheng, Li & Karla K. McGregor. 2010b. Object and action naming in children with specific language impairment. *Journal of Speech, Language, and Hearing Research* 53. 1704–1719.

Smith, Veronica, Pat Mirenda & Anat Zaidman-Zait. 2007. Predictors of expressive vocabulary growth in children with autism. *Journal of Speech, Language, and Hearing Research* 50. 149–60.

Snedeker, Jesse, Joy Geren & Carissa L. Shafto. 2012. Disentangling the effects of cognitive development and linguistic expertise: A longitudinal study of the acquisition of English in internationally-adopted children. *Cognitive Psychology* 65. 39–76.

Song, Shuang, Mengmeng Su, Cuiping Kang, Hongyun Liu, Yuping Zhang, Catherine McBride-Chang, Twila Tardif, Hong Li, Weilan Liang, Zhixiang Zhang & Hua Shu. 2015. Tracing children's vocabulary development from preschool through the school-age years: an 8-year longitudinal study. *Developmental Science* 18. 119–131.

Stiles, Derek J., Karla K. McGregor & Ruth A. Bentler. 2012. Vocabulary and working memory in children fit with hearing aids. *Journal of Speech, Language, and Hearing Research* 55. 154–167.

Swensen, Lauren D., Elizabeth Kelley, Deborah Fein & Letitia R. Naigles. 2007. Processes of language acquisition in children with autism: Evidence from preferential looking. *Child Development* 78. 542–57.

Tager-Flusberg, Helen & Elizabeth Caronna. 2007. Language disorder: Autism and other pervasive developmental disorders. *Pediatric Clinics of North America* 54. 469–81.

Tan, Tony Xing, Troy Loker, Robert F. Dedrick & Kofi Marfo. 2012. Second-first language acquisition: Analysis of expressive language skills in a sample of girls adopted from China. *Journal of Child Language* 39. 365–382.

Tardif, Twila. 1996. Nouns are not always learned before verbs: Evidence from Mandarin speakers' early vocabularies. *Developmental Psychology* 32. 492–504.

Tardif, Twila, Paul Fletcher, Weilan Liang & Niko Kaciroti. 2009. Early vocabulary development in Mandarin (Putonghua) and Cantonese. *Journal of Child Language* 36. 1115–1144.

Tomasello, Michael & William E. Merriman. 1995. *Acquisition of the verb lexicon*. New York: Academic Press.

Verhoeven, Ludo, Jan van Leeuwe & Anne Vermeer. 2011. Vocabulary growth and reading development across the elementary school years. *Scientific Studies of Reading* 15. 8–25.

Vinter, A., V. Fernandes, O. Orlandi, & P. Morgan. 2012. Verbal definitions of familiar objects in blind children reflect their peculiar perceptual experience. *Child: Care, Health and Development*, 39(6). 856–863.

Weismer, Susan Ellis, Catherine Lord & Amy Esler. 2010. Early language patterns of children on the autism spectrum compared to toddlers with developmental delay. *Journal of Autism and Developmental Disorders* 40. 1259–73.

Ypsilanti, A., Grouios, G., Alevriadou, A., & Tsapkini, K. 2005. Expressive and receptive vocabulary in children with Williams and Down syndromes. *Journal of Intellectual Disability Research* 49. 353–364.

Herbert L. Colston

6 Figurative language acquisition and development

1 Introduction: Types of figurative language

The traditional received view on figurative language acquisition and development in typically developing children has held that full adult-like proficiency in figurative language cognition, predominantly with verbal irony and metaphor, develops relatively late as an ability in children. Metaphor and verbal irony also differ in their developmental progression according to this view, with irony involving seemingly multiple progressive stages of development, but both developing to reasonable mastery by adolescence. Established research looking at other figures has revealed a longer duration of development, continuing through childhood into adolescence and extending even into adulthood (e.g., proverbs and idioms). Work on clinical populations and groups with varying abilities (e.g., reading) also has established the impact of certain conditions, deficits and disorders on figurative language acquisition, although not without controversy (Gernsbacher and Pripas-Kapit, 2012). Autism and its spectrum disorders in particular have been discussed as a contributors to figurative language developmental deficits, especially so for verbal irony, largely through the claim of theory of mind (ToM) deficits.

Research on the development of figurative language comprehension, and to a lesser extent production, has continued steadily over the last couple of decades. This research has expanded as well as challenged some of the claims of the traditional view by exploring in more detail the comprehension and use of a wider array of figurative forms, and the skills and disorders that affect which kinds of figurative language cognition. Research focusing on individual figures has also benefitted from a number of trends, including; cross-linguistic comparisons, close linkages with theoretical work in cognitive linguistics and relevant phenomena in cognitive psychology, new cognitive scientific developments like embodiment, observations of productions, and by questioning the late-development view.

This chapter reviews recent research in figurative language acquisition and development in typical development across an array of figurative forms including metaphor, proverbs, hyperbole, idioms, verbal irony and metonymy, as well as across the full range of relevant age groups. The chapter concludes with some commentary about future directions of figurative language developmental/acquisition research:

Metaphor – Patterns of metaphor and similar figurative development in English-speaking adolescents have been replicated in other languages such as Italian and Swedish (Bigozzi, 2004). Most notably, comprehension of metaphors (i.e., discussion

---

Herbert L. Colston, University of Alberta

of particular target domains, such as HAPPINESS, using terms from other domains, UP, e.g., "Her mood soared"), by the age of 9 years was revealed, and shows overall, although non-linear, increase at least through age 14 years. This work on "aesthetic-poetic sensitivity" in Italian-speaking students also marks an external effect on metaphorical comprehension development, with a flattening of development corresponding to the transition to secondary school, where educational methods tend to stress the development of logical thinking.

Metaphor productions were also observed in Swedish-speaking preschool children (Pramling and Samuelsson, 2007), where the observed early metaphorical language use was argued, in accordance with previous work, to benefit both meta-language skill (Pramling, 2010) as well as sense-making itself (Corts, 2006; Littlemore, 2001), collectively referred to as "communicative and cognitive socialization" (Mauritzson and Saljo, 2003; Saljo, 2000; 2005). For example, a pre-school teacher amusingly responding,

> "How peculiar, an elephant smelling skunk!",
>
> to a child's statement that a smelly elephant,
>
> "… smells skunk",

both invites consideration of the nature of the linguistic metaphor and enables cross-domain conceptual understanding on the children's part.

Various cross-linguistic *differences*, however, have been noted in adults' and children's comprehension of metaphoric language. For example, English and Turkish differ in how they typically handle motion events. English, a satellite-framed language, typically uses the verb in a complex motion event statement to encode manner, reserving a particle or prefix to handle path (e.g., "He crawled into the room"). Turkish, on the other hand, usually uses such verbs to encode path, leaving the manner portion to some subordinated construction (e.g., "He entered the room crawling"). This difference transfers to metaphorical descriptions of motion events that are frequently used to discuss target domains related to paths and movement. Adult English speakers typically use a greater range of manner-encoded verbs in metaphorical statements than adult Turkish speakers (e.g., respectively, "time flashes by", versus, "the future escaped suddenly from my hands"). These differences are robust and have been obtained in corpus and elicitation measurements (Ozcaliskan, 2005).

Most interestingly for purposes here, these metaphorical language differences are also obtained in children around age 4 (Ozcaliskan, 2007). Monolingual English- and Turkish-speaking children (one group around age 4, another around age 5, along with adult groups), were shown picture books and were played audio stories depicting situations where metaphorical statements were made containing motion verbs (e.g., ideas, as if they were objects, departing from a person's mind, for instance a girl forgetting what she was to purchase at a market). The children's comprehension of the statements was measured, and descriptions/explanations of the statements' meanings were collected. Overall comprehension success was fairly good and the same across languages, with the older children better at differentiating nonconventional and conventional descriptions of the metaphorical statements (e.g., time passes but not jumps). Turkish and English speakers differed, however, in their descriptions' details, with Turkish speakers showing less attention to manner of motion as used in the metaphorical statements compared to the children speaking English (e.g., "her thoughts have wondered", compared to "things... escape and go from her mind"). This effect held at all ages.

More recent research has shown that children are sensitive to functional as opposed to perceptual similarity in metaphor-like figurative utterances, preferring for example, "the sun is like an oven", over, "the sun is like an orange", indicating more abstract understandings of the nature of figurative comparisons (Thomas, Van Durren, Purser, Mareschal, Ancari and Karmiloff-Smith, 2010). Such abstract understandings are limited, though, in their inferential chain-complexity, with statements having short chains (e.g., "X has a warm heart") understood progressively better than longer-chained constructions (e.g., "X has a heart that burns", and, "X has a heart that is a stove") respectively (Bosco, Vallana and Bucciaretti, 2012; Bosco, Angeleri, Colle, Sacco and Bara, 2013).

Proverbs – Children's understanding of proverbs (i.e., relatively-fixed, often culturally-based constructions using varieties of figurative methods frequently for extollation, e.g., "Don't count your chickens before they're hatched"), has traditionally been one area supportive of the late development view, with proverb comprehension progressing through later adolescence and even into adulthood. Newer empirical work has shown the development of proverb understanding correlates positively with various linguistic and cognitive skills, including word knowledge, reading proficiency, and analogical reasoning (Nippold, Allen and Kirsch, 2001), as well as academic level (Berman and Ravid, 2010) and overall academic success based on reading/literature and mathematics ability (Nippold, 1998; 2000).

Moreover, gains in proverb comprehension even seem related to life transitions in adolescence (Nippold, 2000). This finding was shown in comparisons between adolescents and young adults in grades 6, 8, 10, 12 and University level. Performance on a written, multiple-choice, "Proverb Comprehension Task" (Nippold, Hegel, Uhden and Bustamante, 1998), revealed the greatest gains in comparisons between 6th and 8th graders, as well as between 12th grade and University level participants – arguably corresponding to transitions between preadolescence and adolescence, and between adolescence and early adulthood.

More recently, mental imagery was shown to be related to concrete proverb comprehension in children but neither adolescents nor adults (Duthrie, Nippold, Billow and Mansfield, 2008). Children ($M = 12$), adolescents ($M = 17$) and adults ($M = 24$) performed a mental imagery task, followed by a proverb comprehension task. Participants provided written descriptions of their mental images of 20 concrete proverbs (e.g., "one bad apple spoils the barrel"). The descriptions were given figurativeness scores by the researchers. For the comprehension task, 20 different concrete proverbs, presented at the end of short vignettes, were read by the participants. Participants then chose which of several possible statements they thought best expressed each proverb's meaning. The two measures were correlated only in the children, although a relationship might have obtained in the other groups with more difficult proverbs (the adolescents and adults had comprehension scores near ceiling, possibly obscuring a relationship with mental imagery).

One study on proverb comprehension development provided evidence that partly challenges the late-development view. Children/adolescents in groups aged 9-, 11-, and 14-years comprehended two kinds of unfamiliar proverbs; "literally true" (e.g., Hungry dogs will eat dirty pudding") and "literally false" (e.g., A growing youth has a wolf in his belly), (Power, Taylor and Nippold, 2001). Although an overall difference was found in comprehension accuracy with the youngest group performing slightly worse than the other groups, there were no differences in performance across the type of proverb. Within each group, comprehension performance was steady across more- and less-figurative proverbs, indicating an early presence of figurative proverbial comprehension skills.

Hyperbole – Hyperbole productions (i.e., overstatements of magnitude or extent of referent topics, e.g., "She always wins") were observed in two studies observing English-speaking preschool children (Varga, 2000), and comparing English-speaking children and adults (Colston, 2007). The Varga study observed widespread hyperbolic language play in children as young as 4 years, as well as a developmental progression through age 5. The emotional impact of hyperbole for speakers and hearers was noted. Also observed were cascading instances of verbal hyperbolic utterances through groups of children.

Hyperbolic productions by younger and older American children and one group of adults, spoken in naturalistic settings were collected in both self-recorded and overhearer-recorded situations in the Colston study (2007). Comparisons of the hyperboles produced by children versus adults, and between younger versus older children, revealed remarkable similarities. Hyperbole was both highly prominent and extraordinarily similar according to measures such as; frequency of numerals, frequency and type of comparison statements (e.g., using "like" or "as"), frequency of inverted hyperboles, rated degree of expectation violation demonstrated by the speakers, ratings of the speaker's surprise, and the distribution of combined hyperboles (e.g., utterances that contained more than one hyperbole, "... she's always late, I don't think she's ever been on time"). Indeed, this study revealed that adults (a separate group not involved in any of the production recordings) were unable to determine which utterances from the production recordings were actually made by children. A subset of the utterances produced by the adults and children were carefully selected to fully represent the two larger pools of utterances, and were then randomly mixed. The separate group of adults then estimated the age of the speaker of each utterance in the subset. The estimated age for the children speakers (actual mean age = 7 years) was 20 years on average. The estimated age for the adult speakers (actual mean age = 23 years) was 25.

Idioms – Recent research on idiom comprehension development focuses on three interconnected but separable directions (i.e., varyingly fixed, often somewhat opaque constructions using varieties of figurative processes, i.e., "bite the bullet" or "spill the beans"). Several studies have further examined the roles that characteristics of idioms themselves play in learning idiomatic phrases, including; familiarity, transparency, decomposability, imagability, definability, syntactic structure and conventionality. Studies have continued investigations of Theory of Mind (ToM) ability and its effect on idiom comprehension. Other work has looked at cognitive and social abilities in children, and their impact on idiomatic cognition.

One study (Nippold and Taylor, 2002) revealed high transparency of idiomatic meaning alone seems sufficient for adolescents (aged 16 years) to comprehend some unfamiliar idiomatic meanings (familiarity refers to how frequently an expression occurs in a language, transparency concerns the extent to which "literal" and figurative meanings of an idiom are similar or related). But for children (aged 11 years), comprehension requires or is especially helped only by a combination of high transparency and high familiarity. Indeed, the transparency ratings on the idioms used in this study did not differ between the two age groups – suggesting that idiomatic transparency can be seen by younger people, and may be a stable quality of idioms, but it may not allow children sufficient means to always successfully comprehend unfamiliar idioms.

A subsequent study investigated more specifically the role of transparency in idiom comprehension, focusing on mental imagery as a concomitant mechanism (Nippold and Duthrie, 2003). This work revisited the "meta semantic hypothesis of figurative understanding", which argues that, beyond exposure to idioms and their contextual support, internal semantic analysis of idiomatic meaning is key to idiom comprehension. For instance, mental imagery may be one specific cognitive process that enables comprehension of transparent idioms. Idioms with high transparency (e.g., "blow off steam") were comprehended more easily by both adults and children (mean age 12 years), and mental images given in response to these idioms were also more detailed compared to opaque idioms (e.g., "bring down the house"). Consider two mental images provided by children for these two idioms respectively, "I see somebody punching a punching bag. I hear the thud of the fists. I feel the freedom of using a punching bag", versus, "A huge explosion that collapses a house".

As regards decomposability, children in all but the oldest of four age groups (second-kindergarteners [mean age = 4.7], third-kindergarteners [M = 5.6], first-graders [M = 6.9] and second-graders [M = 8], as defined by the French school system) found non-decomposable idioms ("expressions in which a no part is used literally", as in, "kick the bucket") harder to comprehend than decomposable expressions (e.g., "lay down the law"). The study (Caillies and Le Sourn-Bissaoui, 2006) also demonstrated that academic learning (indicated by grade) as opposed to verbal competence per se (as measured by McCarthy's [1976] verbal aptitude scale) was better able to predict comprehension of the decomposable idioms. The authors claim that the higher correlation between academic learning and decomposable idiom comprehension is due to word awareness – acquired during kindergarten. Even five-year olds could understand many decomposable idioms quickly when presented in context. The authors do not rule out, however, other contributions from pragmatic knowledge (e.g., knowledge about speakers' beliefs and intentions).

The gradual pattern of idiom comprehension development was mirrored in adolescents' and adults' ability to define idiom meaning, a more difficult skill than comprehension alone (Chan and Marinellie, 2008). Pre-adolescents (M = 10.8 yrs), younger adolescents (M = 13.4 yrs), older adolescents (M = 17.15 yrs), and adults (M = 19.95), rated their familiarity with ten frequently-used idioms, and then wrote short definitions of the idioms. The correctness/completeness of the definitions were then assigned quantitative scores. Idiom familiarity and definitional skill improved generally with age – each was moderately to highly correlated with age, and with each other.

A study by Laval (2003) investigated the roles context and linguistic convention play in idiom comprehension in three groups of French speakers (ages 6, 9 and adult). Conventionality as defined by Laval concerns how readily a person interprets an idiom's idiomatic meaning instead of its possible literal meaning when the latter is warranted. The participants were presented with short cartoon scenarios that created bias toward either literal or idiomatic interpretations of common idioms (e.g., "Here, I'll get even with you"). In this example, a literal bias would involve a girl paying money to a boy pretending to be a salesperson, for candy he'd given her. The idiomatic bias would involve the girl exacting revenge on the boy by punching him for something he'd done to her. The researchers only analyzed cases where the idiomatic interpretations were selected by the participants (e.g., "Flora punches Pablo"). Context helped comprehension across all age groups (e.g., idiomatic interpretations of the idioms occurred more often in idiomatic contexts compared to literal contexts).

Most interesting though, was the age progression of the influence of linguistic convention – indicated when a participant gave the idiomatic (incorrect) meaning for the statements used in the literally-biasing contexts. Linguistic convention was near zero in the 6-year olds. It was higher, but not significantly so, in the 9-year olds. Slightly under half the time, though, the adults selected the incorrect idiomatic answers (e.g., "Flora punches Pablo") when the correct literal ones were called for (e.g., when the statement, "Here, I'll get even with you", was read following the story was about the pretend storekeeper and paying for candy).

Syntactic properties of idiomatic phrases and their effect on development was also investigated. Crutchley (2007) for example, had children (6- to 11-years old) interpret idiomatic verb + particle constructions (e.g., "look up" and "call off") in a forced-choice picture selection task. A predicted frequency effect of the constructions was found, and children's choices of distractor items in the task demonstrated a holistic rather than analytic strategy for comprehension of less-familiar constructions. The authors argued that verb syntax and overall semantic knowledge, along with limited contextual information was used in children's comprehension of the idiomatic expressions. This study, perhaps contrary to Nippold's findings on idioms and proverbs, suggests that children may not always employ de-compositional semantic analyses when comprehending unfamiliar idioms (in addition to contextual analysis and lexical, "big word" idiomatic retrieval). Rather, children may additionally consider syntactic features of verbs embedded in idiomatic expressions.

A different trend in research on idiom development continued investigations of ToM, with one study suggesting that ToM is not universally involved in all idiom comprehension. Five-, 6- and 7-year old children completed multiple ToM tasks, including a second-order false-belief task (Caillies and Le Sourn-Bissaoui, 2008). The children then comprehended decomposable and non-decomposable idioms in context. Only the non-decomposable idiom comprehensions were predicted by performance on the false-belief task. A more recent study replicated this work demonstrating how recursive ToM aids non-decomposable but not decomposable idiom comprehension (Caillies and Le Sourn-Bissaoui, 2013). This work further indicates the intertwined contributions of socio-pragmatic and other cognitive skills particularly in idiomatic figurative language comprehension as well as the differing combinations of these skills required for decomposable versus non-decomposable idioms comprehension.

A study by Cain, Towse and Knight (2009) investigated the pattern of multiple contributing cognitive mechanisms to idiom comprehension, including inferences from context and semantic analysis. Children, aged 7, 8, 9 and 10 were compared against 11- and 12-year olds, and against adults, in two idiom comprehension experiments. Comprehension was measured in a multiple choice task, and the authors manipulated whether idioms were familiar or novel, transparent or opaque, and presented with or without parallel contextual support. The results revealed effects of all variables, even some in the youngest group, lending support to Levorato and Cacciari's (1992) Global Elaboration Model, but extended to younger children. This model claims that figurative competence requires no special ability, procedure or knowledge but rather is explained via general cognitive and linguistic abilities that develop normally in children. The authors argue that young children process language at both a small-grain phrase, and at the discourse level to reach comprehension of figurative meaning, but that these skills are not fully developed in 11- and 12-year-olds. Another study by Le Sourn-Bissaoui, Caillies, Bernard, Delean and Brule (2012) investigated perspective-taking and its effect on idiom comprehension. This work also revealed effects on decomposable idiom comprehension but not un-decomposable ones, on children aged 5 to 7 years in an auditory comprehension task.

2 Verbal irony

Most of the recent research on figurative development/acquisition has been on verbal irony (i.e., a family of figurative forms involving constructions with semantic meanings oppositional or contradictory in some way to referent events, e.g., saying, "Great" about a negative event). This work evaluated effects of social cognition and social function development on verbal irony comprehension, as well as possible cultural differences and neural substrates. It also addressed new theoretical claims and methodologies.

Socio/Cognitive Abilities – For example, one study examined children's ability to incorporate personality trait information into verbal irony comprehension. At age 5, children can understand personality characteristics very well, and their verbal irony understanding is just beginning. To evaluate whether children can incorporate their knowledge of personalities into their emerging ability with verbal irony, Pexman, Glenwright, Hala, Kowbel and Jungen, (2006) first independently evaluated 5–6-year olds' abilities with personalities and verbal irony (experiment 1). They next measured how well children can integrate these domains (experiment 2).

Children were shown video-recorded puppets depicting mean or nice behavior. Children then answered questions about; their behavioral predictions for the puppets, their beliefs about the endurance of the puppets' traits and their estimates of the traits' extremities. Analysis of the answers revealed near-perfect performance at behavior prediction (e.g., "Do you think Betty will help Mark by watering the plants?") and trait endurance (e.g., "Does Betty like helping others?"). Extremity ratings (ranging from "nice" to "mean") were also symmetrically near the extremes of the scale for the corresponding puppets. Children at this age thus have well-developed personality trait knowledge.

Irony comprehension was evaluated by showing neutral-trait puppets interacting with other puppets who either succeeded or failed at some task (e.g., carrying groceries). The neutral-trait puppets would then speak either an ironic criticism (a positive comment about the failure, "You are so careful") or a literal compliment (the same comment spoken about the success). Comprehension was measured with standard belief and intent questions (e.g., "When Linda said, 'You are so careful', did she think Alex was careful or not careful?", and, "When Linda said, 'You are so careful', was Linda trying to be mean or nice?"). Latency to answer the belief question was also recorded (e.g., time from belief question offset to response onset). Results revealed moderate comprehension of ironic criticism (proportion correct on belief and intent questions was .60 and .41 respectively, compared to near-perfect answers for the literal comments). Responses to the belief questions were also significantly slower and more variable for the ironic criticisms.

The second experiment presented children aged 5–6 and 7–8 either congruent puppet comments (e.g., mean puppet says ironic criticism, or nice puppet says literal compliment) or incongruent puppet comments (e.g., mean puppet says literal compliment, or nice puppet says ironic criticism). Results revealed first an age effect – older children had higher comprehension rates than younger children (based on belief and intent questions as in experiment 1). Also, an interaction was found concerning puppet trait and comment type. Ironic criticisms were comprehended better when coming from mean (versus nice) puppets. Literal compliments were comprehended better when coming from nice (versus mean) puppets. Overall, though, comprehension of ironic criticisms was moderate, as in the first experiment.

For the latency measure, younger children were much slower to correctly respond to the ironic criticisms (versus literal compliments), but older children were only slightly slower in their ironic criticism comprehensions. The results thus reveal an early moderate integration of personality information into ironic criticism comprehension, and a significant improvement in this integration from age 5–6 to 7–8.

Filippova and Astington (2008, see also 2010) investigated which specific social and cognitive skills might be required for successful and complete irony comprehension, and whether they are acquired in a particular order. The authors hypothesized that four skills would be acquired in the following order; ability to reject the literal meaning, understanding the actual beliefs held by a speaker, deriving the intention of the speaker, and gleaning the attitude of an ironic speaker. They then measured children aged approximately 5, 7 and 9 years, along with adults, on irony comprehension (with questions addressing ironic utterance meaning, speaker beliefs, speaker's communicative intention, and speaker attitude or motivation). They also measured advanced ToM ability, and skill on standardized language, memory and prosody tests.

Virtually all of these measures correlated with each other, indicating a strong correspondence among irony, ToM and general cognitive and social skills. Most interesting though, was the finding that the order of acquisition of skills described above does seem to hold across development, and they are interdependent. On this view, understanding a speaker's beliefs requires being able to reject that speaker's literal meaning. Knowing the speaker's intention depends on understanding what a speaker believes. Finally, deriving a speaker's attitude toward something requires understanding that speaker's intentions.

Another study looking at the contribution of ToM to irony processing revealed that older children (8–10 years) and adults can inhibit their own contextual knowledge to appropriately comprehend a speaker's ironic intent, compared to younger children (6–7 years) who fail at this task. Second order ToM was also implicated in this difference (Nilsen, Glenwright and Huyder, 2011). Other socio/cognitive abilities such as inferential chain following and mental representation formation were also found to affect both ironic comprehension and production in three groups of children (5:0–5;6, 6;6–7;0, and 8;0–8;6). Results revealed a steady improvement across tasks designed to measure these abilities, coinciding with developments in irony production and comprehension.

Other more recent work focusing more on the pure social aspects of irony cognition has addressed children using irony in response to another person's initial irony. Seven to eleven year-old children responded with irony this way approximately 9% of the time overall, and ironic criticism responses showed an age effect but ironic compliments did not (Whalen and Pexman, 2010). Recchia, Howe, Ross and Alexander (2010) also observed usages of irony in parents interacting with their children (in selected dyads, younger child M = 4;39, older child 6;33) in their homes. Results revealed an age effect of irony comprehension, with differential ironic usage by parental gender – mothers used rhetorical questions in confliction contexts more often than fathers. Fathers in turn used hyperbole, understatement and rhetorical questions in both conflictional and positive contexts.

These social effects of irony in interaction seem mostly driven by children's attempt to achieve the gists in social exchanges rather than more precise social cognition results. Fillipova and Astington (2010) for example showed clear differences between groups of 5, 7 and 9 year-old children and adults, on abilities to assess speaker meaning, belief, intention and motivation, but weaker differences between the groups on socio-communicative aspects of the ironies (e.g., how nice, mean and funny speakers were being). Angeleri and Airenti (2014) corroborated this theme with a demonstration that "shared" knowledge between interlocutors helps young children with joke appreciation and to a lesser extent, irony comprehension (comparing 3;0 and 6;5 year-olds).

Such gist assessment abilities can also be achieved with different strategies. For instance although typically developing children, and those with high-functioning Autism Spectrum Disorder, can demonstrate similar abilities to derive social functions of irony (e.g., determining speaker intent in using ironic criticisms), they do so with different means (Pexman, Rostad, McMorris, Climie, Stowkowy and Glenwright, 2011). This study compared two groups of typically developing children with a group of high-functioning Autism Spectrum Disorder children on an irony comprehension task. The groups were comparable on speaker intent judgements for ironic forms of criticism, but the groups differed on judgment latencies, eye gaze patterns and evaluations of humor. Such differences could also be connected to other processes related to irony processing and assessments of irony social functions, such as empathy for other humans. Children's abilities with respect to empathy are related to even low-level irony processing – irony ability correlates positively with empathic skills in typically developing 8 and 9 year olds, and indeed can be found at the earliest phases of processing (Nicholson, Whalen and Pexman, 2013).

Deriving ironic intent from intonational and contextual content also shows a developmental progression. Lavel (2004) presented 3- and 7-year-old French speaking children with stories ending in sarcastic requests. Requests that were spoken with ironic intonation were interpreted correctly as young as age 3, but context appeared to help children only by age 7. It thus appears that surface marking of ironic intent is beneficial for children before their cognitive ability to incorporate contextual information in deriving ironic intent is fully developed.

Direct Access Evaluation and Eye Tracking – Other work revisited the direct-access versus literal-first theoretical debate concerning verbal irony comprehension with evidence from eye-tracking (Climie and Pexman, 2008). This study compared two groups of children (5–6 years-of-age versus 7–8 years-of-age) and adults, using puppets that made literal (criticism and compliment) and ironic (criticism and compliment) remarks. The puppets would first act out a short vignette with props and other puppets. The puppet speakers were initially presented to the participants as being either neutral, very funny, or very serious. Measures of belief, intent and estimated humorousness of the speaker-puppets, were taken. The latency to respond to the intent question (coded from digital video recordings), and two measures using eye-tracking (first look and total look, described below) were also measured.

The intent question in this study enabled two relevant kinds of eye-tracking analyses. Rather than the usual oral or written intent question (e.g. "Was the speaker trying to be mean or to be nice?"), the present study had participants refer to one of two intent-puppets, one nice (a duck) and the other mean (a shark), to indicate the speaker-puppet's intent. The specific intent question was, "Was (speaker-puppet's name) like the shark or like the duck?" Video recordings of the children allowed detailed analysis of the visual, oral and gestural references to the intent-puppets in the children's responses.

Relevant results on adults revealed accurate appraisal that speakers using ironic criticism intend to be mean, but less accuracy when adults' determined speaker's intent in using ironic compliments. Adults were also accurately able to incorporate personality trait information in assessing speaker intent in using ironic language (e.g., statements made by speakers initially labeled as "funny", were perceived as intended humor more often than statements made by speakers labeled "serious"). These results replicated earlier findings.

Results on children revealed some incorporation of speaker personality when interpreting ironic remarks (rated humor was less when a serious puppet made a comment). Accuracy was not, however, at adult levels. Latency measures showed children taking longer to comprehend ironic criticism compared to every kind of literal comment. The authors claim this is due to more complicated inferencing being required upon hearing ironic remarks. Older children performed all judgments faster relative to younger children.

The eye-tracking data were compelling. Analysis with the first-look data (at which intent-puppet did the participant looked toward initially), provided zero evidence of children first looking at the "literal" intent-puppet during judgments of the speaker-puppets' intent in using ironic speech. Rather, children tended to look first at the "ironic" intent-puppet during judgments on a puppet speaking ironically.

Analysis of the total-look data (the proportion of total decision time spent gazing at the correct intent-puppet) revealed that children incorporated personality trait information when judging speakers' intent. Children looked proportionately longer at correct intent-puppets when speakers were described as being serious, compared to when they were described as being funny or with no traits. The authors interpret this as indicating greater certainty on children's part, in judging the intent of serious speakers. Children did not, though, indicate comparable certainty when "funny" speakers were ironically speaking. The authors judged this finding to indicate children don't associate being funny with being ironic, automatically when doing this task.

Social Functions – Other studies investigated children's abilities concerning the social functions of verbal irony. Children appear to comprehend some, but not always all, of verbal irony's social functions. For example, Hancock, Dunham and Purdy (2000) investigated the social functions of praise and criticism. Children (approximately aged 5–6 years) saw videotaped portrayals of speakers making literal, ironic criticism and ironic compliment remarks after short contextual scenes (e.g., a person brags about being a good basketball player, then misses a shot, and a speaker says, "You really are bad at basketball" [literal], or "You really are good at basketball" [ironic criticism] – ironic compliment would entail the person bragging, *making* the basket and then the speaker saying the negative remark). The children were then asked questions designed to assess their knowledge of first-order belief and speaker intent.

Participants answered the questions nearly perfectly on all literal statements. For ironic statements, results differed depending on the expectations established in the preceding contextual scenes. In the first experiment, all of the contexts established positive expectations (as in the examples above). Here an asymmetry was found in responses to the belief questions – the proportion of correct answers were greater for ironic criticism (47%) than ironic compliments (25%). The intent question produced no asymmetry – proportion of correct answers was at approximately 42%. In a second experiment that had the ironic compliment questions echo explicit negative expectations from the contextual scenes (e.g., the person first complains about being a *bad* basketball player), performance was still lower for all ironic comments compared to literal remarks, but no asymmetries were obtained.

Thus, similar to what is found on adults, ironic criticism (e.g., saying, "nice job" about a failure) is fairly readily comprehended, but ironic praise (e.g., saying, "terrible job" about a success) requires more explicit expectations for the negative outcome that fails to occur (e.g., the performer saying she is terrible at something before she actually succeeds at it). The study also replicates earlier findings of the separability of non-literal meaning detection, versus speaker intent derivation – averaging across all irony conditions, children were better at answering the belief questions (non-literal meaning detection) than the intent ones (speaker intent derivation). This pattern of difference between ironic praise and criticism also holds cross-culturally. Canadian and Czech children (7 and 9 year-olds) and adults showed marked age differences in interpretation of ironic praise, but relatively stable patterns of development in ironic criticism interpretation (Filippova, 2014a). This latter study argued for social and cultural differences in language socialization and irony usage as potential causes of irony interpretation variances cross-culturally.

Tinge Assessment – Other work has looked at children's ability to appreciate the tingeing of criticism and humor in verbal irony use (Harris and Pexman, 2003). Children aged 5–6 and 7–8 years viewed puppets making ironic and literal criticisms, as well as ironic and literal compliments, and answered standard belief and intent questions afterward. Participants also indicated how funny/serious they thought the puppets were, using a visual rating scale. Literal criticisms and compliments were comprehended almost perfectly by both groups. Older children (92%) comprehended more ironic criticisms than younger children (65%), but no difference was found in the groups on their comprehension of ironic compliments, which overall were comprehended less successfully (M = 38%) than ironic criticisms. Children rated literal criticisms as meaner than ironic criticisms, demonstrating children's appreciation of the tinge function of verbal irony. Children also rated literal criticisms as more serious than ironic criticisms, but the mean rating for the ironic criticisms was still near the "serious" end of the scale. Children thus don't appear to be *fully* appreciating the humor function of verbal irony.

Subsequent studies sought to explain the finding of children noting the tinge function of verbal irony, but not its humor function. Pexman, Glenwright, Krol and James (2005) studied two groups of children (M = 7;8, M = 9;7), using pairs of puppets. Pairs were manipulated to be friends, enemies or strangers, and one of the puppets would make a comment to the other after the other puppet had succeeded or failed at something (e.g., performing a flip while on a trampoline). Comments either were literal ("Wow, you are so graceful", after a successful flip, or, "Wow, you are so clumsy," after a failed flip) or they were ironic ("Wow, you are so graceful", after a failed flip, or, "Wow, you are so clumsy", after a successful flip). In addition to standard belief and intent measures, participants indicated how teasing and funny they believed the comments to be, and the degree to which they identified with the puppets (e.g., "which of these puppets acts most like you?").

The belief and intent results generally replicated previous research in that ironic criticisms are comprehended better than ironic compliments. Both ironic remarks are comprehended worse though, than literal remarks. Comprehension of ironic remarks also improved with age. The results with the relationship variable indicated that children did use the relationship between the puppets to comprehend remarks that were literal (e.g., children realized that friends were less likely to criticize one another and more likely to give compliments to one another), but relationship did now show an impact on ironic remarks. The relationship variable also did little to modulate the participants' ratings of humor and teasing functions of ironic remarks. The authors conclude that children at these ages are just starting to share adult-like perceptions of the social functions of verbal irony, possibly because of face concerns, difficulties in representing conflicting emotions, and limited knowledge about social functions of verbal irony.

Pexman and Glenwright (2007) used a puppet paradigm similar to those described above to investigate the progression of appreciation of ironic criticisms versus ironic compliments. Children between years 6 and 10 years seem to achieve a speaker belief understanding before acquiring understandings of a speaker's intent-to-tease and the speaker's attitude, when comprehending ironic criticisms. When comprehending ironic compliments, however, children seem to acquire a speaker-belief and speaker's-intent-to-tease understanding prior to understanding the speaker's attitude. One possibility here is that appreciation of the intent-to-tease comes later with ironic criticisms given their frequent overriding aggressive or insulting motivation, which may shroud the parallel function of teasing more so than in ironic compliments.

Culture and Language – Work with Chinese children has also shown some social function appreciation ability as young as 6 years, as well a progression in the complexity of social function appreciation as development proceeds through age 10 years (Meng and Jijia, 2006; Jijia and Meng, 2005). This work leads to an interesting possibility that cultural differences may play a role in the early development of social language function appreciation with figurative language.

Neural Substrates – An interesting corollary to the social function developmental work has investigated the neural substrates of social function cognition from figurative language (Wang, Lee, Sigman and Dapretto, 2006). Brain activation in social function processing appears to move from frontal regions to posterior occipitotemporal regions as children move toward adulthood. This possibly reflects the automatization of reasoning about mental states in verbal irony comprehension.

Theoretical Developments – Other work has addressed specific theoretical claims. Creusere (2000), for example, evaluated the two fundamental requirements of the Allusional Pretense Theory of verbal irony – pragmatic insincerity and allusion to violated expectations, in experiments on children (the author studied 8-year olds even though verbal irony comprehension has been found in younger children, because the measures used would likely have been too difficult for younger children).

The study gave 8-year olds brief stories depicting situations affording irony (e.g., a man making needless noise while a woman is attempting to speak on the phone). Different versions of ironic remarks were presented, spoken at the end of the stories; true assertions, counterfactual assertions, offerings, questions and statements of thanks (e.g., for the thanks statements, "Thanks a lot for banging the pots while I was on the phone"). Participants were then given questions designed to measure, among other things, knowledge of the speaker's meaning, purpose, speaker sincerity, and 1st-order belief and 2nd-order intention.

Examples of these questions for the noisy man with woman on the phone story are as follows:

> Knowledge of speaker meaning: "Why did Sue say that to Bill?"
>
> Purpose: "What did Sue mean when she said that to Bill?"
>
> Sincerity: "Did Sue appreciate Bill banging the pots?"
>
> 1st-Order Belief: "Did Sue think that Bill was quiet or noisy"
>
> 2nd-Order Intention: "Did Sue want Bill to know what she was thinking?"

Results revealed that responses to both allusion (speaker meaning and purpose) and sincerity questions were significantly better than chance, and were correlated with one another. First-order belief and second-order intention questions also produced responses significantly better than chance. No effect of form of ironic utterance was found on allusion, but the forms differed on insincerity in the following order from least insincere; questions < counterfactual assertions and offerings < true assertions and statements of thanks.

The Hancock, Dunham and Purdy (2000) study described above also sought to evaluate Allusional Pretense's two theoretical tenets and found support for them in children's comprehension of ironic criticism and ironic compliments. Recall the finding of an asymmetry in children's comprehension of ironic criticisms versus ironic compliments in the absence of supportive contexts for the ironic compliments – a result also usually found in adults. But when initial expectations for negative outcomes are provided, then ironic compliments are comprehended as well as ironic criticisms by children (as in adults).

The authors concluded that these results extend the Allusional Pretense account's claims about allusion and pragmatic insincerity to relatively young children. The asymmetry observed replicates findings on adults where, without explicit expectations being established in a context, ironic criticisms can rely on an allusion to generally positive social norms and other expectations. When explicitly negative expectations are established in a context though, ironic compliments achieve the same ease of comprehension as ironic criticisms. Overall, performance at irony comprehension was lower in children, indicating their early stage of experience with irony, but the presence and absence of the asymmetry in their performance as a result of prior explicit expectations, mirrors adult comprehension.

A theoretical debate on the nature of ToM and its basis in irony comprehension also emerged. Papp (2006) argues for instance that the typically found two-tiered system of first- and second-order mind-reading ability is insufficient to describe irony comprehension abilities in people with Autism Spectrum Disorder and in normal development. A case is made to expand current divisions of mind-reading ability to multiple other levels. Other accounts however, are arguing that ToM is needlessly dualistic, and that common-sense descriptions of a person understanding another minds' content, based on language, violate logically distinguished concepts of meaning (Costall, Leudar and Reddy, 2006; Colombino, 2006).

3 Conclusion

Research on typical figurative language development/acquisition has benefitted from adoption of new methodologies, tighter assessments of co-variates of figurative cognition, cross linguistic comparisons and other developments. Further work in this area could achieve greater advancements by attending to trends in other areas of developmental and cognitive research such as multi-modality, embodiment, and others. As one example, a recent study investigated verbal and gestural irony in children aged 3 through 15 years (Pexman, Zdrazilova, McConnachie, Deater-Deckard and Petrill, 2009). This work showed greater usages of gestural irony over verbal, and at relatively early ages (as young as 4 years). Gestural work may thus reveal earlier and perhaps different kinds of ironic cognition and possible underpinnings of ironic thought in children, perhaps younger than what verbal irony can reveal.

Further work on lesser studied forms of figurative language, and mixtures of figurative language might also open new avenues for research. Work on metonymy and its development/acquisition, for instance is relatively limited (although see Waggoner, 2010). Research addressing mixed forms of figurative language, or direct comparisons of multiple kinds of figurative language in parallel, are also fairly rare (see Rundblad and Annaz, 2010; and Van Herwegen, Dimitriou, and Rundblad, 2013 for work comparing metaphor and metonymy, showing relatively earlier development of metonymy).

Other work could focus on tighter comparisons of both production and comprehension on individual figurative forms to see how they relate in their developmental progression, and how that might compare to other relative rates of production/comprehension acquisition. Work looking at the prevalence of figurative production and comprehension in children in real-world settings across different figures could enlighten ideas about cultural and social influences on development. Other understudied influences (e.g. siblings) could also benefit by a focus on measuring prevalences. One last concern might be over measurements that investigate families of figurative forms that might actually differ in their developmental/acquisition progression if treated individually (Wilson, 2014). Filippova (2014b) for instance, notes that different treatments of discourse and situational irony, as well as across production and comprehension, could help reveal different competencies for irony cognition. Potential problems in ecological validity of different methods might also be illuminated with this approach. It might thus behoove researchers to attend to different subtypes of presumed figurative families (e.g., different kinds of metonymy) as well as the validity of different measures, in investigations of figurative development/acquisition to delineate what might be acquired earlier versus later and why.

References

Angeleri, Romina & Gabriella Airenti. 2014. The development of joke and irony understanding: A study with 3- to 6-year-old children. *Canadian Journal of Experimental Psychology/Revue canadienne de psychologie experimentale* 68. 133–146.

Berman, Ruth A. & Dorit Ravid. 2010. Interpretation and recall of proverbs in three school-age populations. *First Language* 30. 155–173.

Bigozzi, Lucia. 2004. Development of reading basic cognitive-linguistics competences in students from 9 to 14 years old. *Ricerche di Psicologia* 27. 101–123.

Bosco, Francesca M., Romina Angeleri, Livia Colle, Katiuscia Sacco & Bruno G. Bara. 2013. Communicative abilities in children: An assessment through different phenomena and expressive means. *Journal of Child Language* 40. 741–778.

Bosco, Francesca, Marianna Vallana & Monica Bucciarelli. 2012. The inferential chain makes the difference between familiar and novel figurative expressions. *Journal of Cognitive Psychology* 24. 525–540.

Caillies, Stephanie & Sandrine Le Sourn-Bissaoui. 2013. Nondecomposable idiom understanding in children: Recursive theory of mind and working memory. *Canadian Journal of Experimental Psychology/Revue canadienne de psychologie experimentale* 67. 108–116.

Caillies, Stephanie & Sandrine Le Sourn-Bissaoui. 2006. Idiom comprehension in French children: A cock-and-bull story. *European Journal of Developmental Psychology* 3. 189–206.

Caillies, Stephanie & Sandrine Le Sourn-Bissaoui. 2008. Children's understanding of idioms and theory of mind development. *Developmental Science* 11. 703–711.

Cain, Kate, Andrea S. Towse & Rachael S. Knight. 2009. The development of idiom comprehension: An investigation of semantic and contextual processing skills. *Journal of Experimental Child Psychology* 102. 280–298.

Chan, Yen-Ling & Sally, A. Marinellie. 2008. Definitions of idioms in preadolescents, adolescents, and adults. *Journal of Psycholinguistic Research* 37. 1–20.

Climie, Emma A. & Penny M. Pexman. 2008. Eye gaze provides a window on children's understanding of verbal irony. *Journal of Cognition and Development* 9. 257–285.

Colombino, Tommaso. 2006. Problems with a relevance-theoretic account of autism. *Theory & Psychology* 16. 169–177.

Colston, Herbert, L. 2007. What figurative language development reveals about the mind. In Andrea C. Schalley & Drew Khlentzos (eds.), *Mental states, volume 2: Language and cognitive structure*, 191–212. Amsterdam: John Benjamins.

Corts, Daniel P. 2006. Factors characterizing bursts of figurative language and gesture in college lectures. *Discourse Studies: An Interdisciplinary Journal for the Study of Text and Talk* 8. 211–233.

Costall, Alan, Ivan Leudar & Vasudevi Reddy. 2006. Failing to see the irony in 'mind-reading'. *Theory & Psychology* 16. 163–167.

Creusere, Marlena. 2000. A developmental test of theoretical perspectives on the understanding of verbal irony: Children's recognition of allusion and pragmatic insincerity. *Metaphor and Symbol* 15. 29–45.

Crutchley, Alison. 2007. Comprehension of idiomatic verb + particle constructions in 6- to 11-year-old children. *First Language* 27. 203–226.

Duthie, Jill K., Marilyn A. Nippold, Jesse L. Billow & Tracy C. Mansfield. 2008. Mental imagery of concrete proverbs: A developmental study of children, adolescents, and adults. *Applied psycholinguistics* 29. 151–173.

Filippova, Eva & Janet Wilde Astington. 2008. Further development in social reasoning revealed in discourse irony understanding. *Child Development* 79. 126–138.

Filippova, Eva & Janet Wilde Astington. 2010. Children's understanding of social-cognitive and social-communicative aspects of discourse irony. *Child Development* 81. 913–928.

Filippova, Eva. 2014a. Developing appreciation of irony in Canadian and Czech discourse. *Journal of Pragmatics* 74. 209–223.

Filippova, Eva. 2014b. Irony production and comprehension. In Danielle Matthews (ed.), *Pragmatic development in first language acquisition*, 261–278. Amsterdam: John Benjamins.

Gernsbacher, Morton Ann & Sarah R. Pripas-Kapit. 2012. Who's missing the point? A commentary on claims that autistic persons have a specific deficit in figurative language comprehension. *Metaphor and Symbol* 27. 93–105.

Hancock, Jeffrey T., Philip J. Dunham & Kelly Purdy. 2000. Children's comprehension of critical and complimentary forms of verbal irony. *Journal of Cognition and Development* 1. 227–248.

Harris, Melanie & Penny M. Pexman. 2003. Children's perceptions of the social functions of verbal irony. *Discourse Processes* 36. 147–165.

Zhang Jijia and Zhang Meng. 2005. The effects of others' expectancy on 6- to 10-year-old children's cognition of different types of irony. *Acta Psychologica Sinica* 37. 767–775.

Laval, Virginie. 2003. Idiom comprehension and metapragmatic knowledge in French children. *Journal of Pragmatics* 35. 723–739.

Laval, Virginie. 2004. Pragmatics and nonliteral language: Children's understanding of sarcastic-requests. *Psychologie Francaise* 49. 177–192.

Le Sourn-Bissaoui, Sandrine, Stephanie Caillies, Stephane Bernard, Michel Deleau & Lauriane Brule. 2012. Children's understanding of ambiguous idioms and conversational perspective-taking. *Journal of Experimental Child Psychology* 112. 437–451.

Levorato, Chiara & Cristina Caccairi. 1992. Children's comprehension and production of idioms: The role of context and familiarity. *Journal of Child Language* 19. 415–433.

Littlemore, Jeannette. 2001. The use of metaphor in university lectures and the problems that it causes for overseas students. *Teaching in Higher Education* 6. 333–349.

Mauritzson, Ulla & Roger Saljo. 2003. "Ja vill va Simba å du ä Nala: Barns kommunikation och koordination av perspektiv i lek [I want to be Simba and you are Nala: children's communication and coordination of perspectives in play]". In Johansson, E. and Pramling Samuelsson, I. (eds.), Förskolan – barns första skola [Preschool: children's first school], 159–196. Lund: Studentlitteratur.

McCarthy Dorothea. 1976. Echelles d'aptitudes pour enfants de McCarthy. Paris: ECPA.

Meng, Zhang & Zhang Jijia. 2006. Effects of intonation on 6 to 10-year-old children's cognition of different types of irony. *Acta Psychologica Sinica* 38. 197–206.

Nicholson, Andrew, Juanita M. Whalen & Penny M. Pexman. 2013. Children's processing of emotion in ironic language. *Frontiers in Psychology* 4. ArtID 691.

Nilsen, Elizabeth S., Melanie Glenwright & Vanessa Huyder. 2011. Children and adults understand that verbal irony interpretation depends on listener knowledge. *Journal of Cognition and Development* 12. 374–409.

Nippold, Marilyn A. 1997. Proverb explanation through the lifespan: A developmental study of adolescents and adults. *Journal of Speech, Language, and Hearing Research* 40. 245–253.

Nippold, Marilyn A. 2000. Language development during the adolescent years: Aspects of pragmatics, syntax and semantics. *Topics in Language Disorders* 20. 15–28.

Nippold, Marilyn A. & Catherine L. Taylor. 2002. Judgments of idiom familiarity and transparency: A comparison of children and adolescents. *Journal of Speech, Language, and Hearing Research* 45. 384–391.

Nippold, Marilyn A. & Jill K. Duthie. 2003. Mental imagery and idiom comprehension: A comparison of school-age children and adults. *Journal of Speech, Language, and Hearing Research* 46. 788–799.

Nippold, Marilyn A., Melissa M. Allen & Dixon I. Kirsch. 2001. Proverb comprehension as a function of reading proficiency in preadolescents. *Language, Speech, and Hearing Services in Schools* 32. 90–100.

Nippold, Marilyn A., S. L. Hegel, L. D. Uhden & S. Bustamante. 1998. Development of proverb comprehension in adolescents: Implication for instruction. *Journal of Children's Communication Development* 19. 49–55.

Ozcaliskan, Seyda. 2005. Metaphor meets typology: Ways of moving metaphorically in English and Turkish. *Cognitive Linguistics* 16. 207–246.

Ozcaliskan, Seyda. 2007. Metaphors we move by: Children's developing understanding of metaphorical motion in typologically distinct language. *Metaphor and Symbol* 22. 147–168.

Papp, Szilvia. 2006. A relevance-theoretic account of the development and deficits of theory of mind in normally developing children and individuals with autism. *Theory & Psychology* 16. 141–161.

Pexman, Penny M., Lenka Zdrazilova, Devon McConnachie, Kirby Deater-Deckard & Stephen A. Petrill. 2009. "That was smooth, mom": Children's production of verbal and gestural irony. *Metaphor and Symbol* 24. 237–248.

Pexman, Penny, M. & Melanie Glenwright. 2007. How do typically developing children grasp the meaning of verbal irony? *Journal of Neurolinguistics* 20. 178–196.

Pexman, Penny M., Melanie Glenwright, Suzanne Hala, Stacey, L. Kowbel & Sara Jungen. 2006. Children's use of trait information in understanding verbal irony. *Metaphor and Symbol* 21. 39–60.

Pexman, Penny M., Melanie Glenwright, Andrea Krol & Tammy James. 2005. An acquired taste: Children's perceptions of humor and teasing in verbal irony. *Discourse Processes* 40. 259–288.

Power, Rachel, Catherine L. Taylor & Marilyn A. Nippold. 2001. Comprehending literally-true versus literally-false proverbs. *Child Language Teaching and Therapy* 17. 1–18.

Pramling, Niklas & Ingrid Samuelsson. 2007. The prosaics of figurative language in preschool: Some observations and suggestions for research. *Early Child Development and Care* 177. 707–717.

Pramling, Niklas. 2010. Unearthing metaphors: Figurativeness in teacher-child talk about soil and related matters. *Early Childhood Education Journal* 38. 57–64.

Recchia, Holly E., Nina Howe, Hildy S. Ross & Stephanie Alexander. 2010. Children's understanding and production of verbal irony in family conversations. *British Journal of Developmental Psychology* 28. 255–274.

Rundblad, Gabriella & Dagmara Annaz. 2010. Development of metaphor and metonymy comprehension: Receptive vocabulary and conceptual knowledge. *British Journal of Developmental Psychology* 28. 547–563.

Saljo, Roger. 2000. *Larande i praktiken: Ett sociokulturellt perspektiv* [Learning in practice: A sociocultural perspective]. Stockholm: Prisma.

Saljo, Roger. 2005. *Larande och kulturella redskap: Om larprocesser och det kollektiva minnet* [Learning and cultural tools: On processes of learning and collective memory]. Stockholm: Norstedts Akademiska.

Spotorno, Nicola & Ira A. Noveck. 2014. When is irony effortful? *Journal of Experimental Psychology: General* 143. 1649–1665.

Thomas, Michael S., Mike C. Van Duuren, Harry R. Purser, Denis Mareschal, Daniel Ansari & Annette Karmiloff-Smith. 2010. The development of metaphorical language comprehension in typical development and in Williams syndrome. *Journal of Experimental Child Psychology* 106. 99–114.

Van Herwegen, Jo, Dagmara Dimitriou & Gabriella Rundblad. 2013. Development of novel metaphor and metonymy comprehension in typically developing children and Williams syndrome. Research in *Developmental Disabilities* 34. 1300–1311.

Varga, Donna. 2000. Hyperbole and humor in children's language play. *Journal of Research in Childhood Education* 14. 142–151.

Waggoner, John E. 2010. Temperature-based metonymies for emotions in children and adults. *Psychological Reports* 106. 233–245.

Wang, Ting, A., Susan S. Lee, Marian Sigman & Mirella Dapretto. 2006. Neural basis of irony comprehension in children with autism: The role of prosody and context. *Brain: A Journal of Neurology* 129. 932–943.

Whalen, Juanita M. & Penny M. Pexman. 2010. How do children respond to verbal irony in face-to-face communication? The development of mode adoption across middle childhood. *Discourse Processes* 47. 363–387.

Fataneh Farnia
7 Figurative language development: Implications for assessment and clinical practice

1 Introduction

This chapter begins with a description of the developmental changes in elements of language and communicative competence throughout childhood and adolescence. It highlights the importance of higher order/figurative language in adolescents' academic achievement, social relationships and ability to connect with peers and adults. The chapter also discusses the neurobiological and cognitive underpinning of higher order/figurative language impairment as well as the overlap of higher order/figurative language impairment with socioemotional difficulties. Factors that may affect the development of this aspect of language in bilinguals and across languages are discussed, as are issues related to identification and treatment of higher order/figurative language impairment.

2 Developmental changes in language

A large body of research has confirmed the distinct developmental qualitative and quantitative changes in modes of communication across ages. This research indicates that while there are individual differences in the level and speed of language acquisition, these skills are acquired in an orderly and predictable pattern. Infants use preverbal means to communicate and around the age of one year, words (holophrases) emerge followed by two word sentences around age 18 months. Between 18 and 24 months, toddlers begin trying to use more complex words (three syllable words) and produce three word sentences. They can follow two-step directions and express some emotions using language. In the preschool years and as children transition to middle childhood and enter the school system, they continue to develop their understanding of semantics in language and to acquire new grammatical structures. They also learn that some words or phrases have multiple meanings (including figurative meanings). In typically developing children, encountering these words and phrases in rich contextual conversational settings contributes to the development of semantic processing strategies. These strategies enable incidental learning through social interactions and are critical for school readiness. The skills acquired also facilitate preschoolers' self-regulation that has a strong association with school

Fataneh Farnia, University of Toronto

readiness and with later academic achievement (Liebermann, Giesbrecht, and Muller 2007).

In order to develop an understanding of the different meanings of a word or phrase children use all the cognitive and linguistic resources available to them and the context of the interaction (Cain, Oakhill, and Elbro 2003). They begin to understand and use more common transparent idiomatic expressions (e.g., *piece of cake, thumbs up, walking on thin ice*) that are somewhat established as fixed lexical units (Bulut and Celik-Yazici 2004; Jackson and Zé Amvela 2007; Norbury 2004). At school entry, well-developed semantic processing strategies help children to gradually understand rules for social communication (pragmatics), which is important for figurative language, form new relationships and adjust to the classroom requirements and routines (Mendez, Fantuzzo, and Cicchetti 2002).

In a study of school age children, Brinton, Fujiki, and Mackey (1985) found that transparent idioms and/or nonliteral expressions such as *lend me a hand* can be understood by over 60% of kindergartners and two third of children in upper elementary grades. However, opaque idioms such as *hit the ceiling* were not understood by any kindergarten and less than half of the upper elementary students. In middle childhood, the increasing appearance of opaque idioms and figurative expressions in oral and textual interactions places heavier demands on cognitive processing skills such as working memory (Im-Bolter, Cohen, and Farnia 2013; Toma and Daum 2006). During this age period, further development of higher order/figurative language is positively associated with a dynamic interplay among cognitive, linguistic and pragmatic skills.

3 Prevalence of language impairment

Language impairment is a heterogeneous disorder and refers to a range of expressive and/or receptive language difficulties that interfere with communication. Prevalence estimates of language impairment in the general population apply to impairments in one or more of the areas of structural language development in preschoolers and children in primary and secondary schools. These areas include phonological processing, oral expression, and listening comprehension. Estimates of the prevalence of language impairment are between 2% and 19% in the preschool population (ASHA 2009). Estimates of the prevalence of communication impairment, including social interactions, written expressions and/or reading comprehension, are between 13% and 19% in children at primary and secondary schools (Harrison et al. 2009; McLeod and McKinnon 2007).

The exact prevalence is difficult to pinpoint, however, because of differences between studies in their criteria for diagnosis of language impairment. Nevertheless, even when less stringent diagnostic criteria have been applied, there are many associations between language impairment and both concurrent and later learning (particularly reading) and psychosocial problems (Beitchman et al. 1996; Brownlie et al. 2004; Catts et al. 2002; Young et al. 2000). These prevalence figures do not differentiate the various aspects of language functioning. Compared to what we know about the prevalence of language impairment in childhood, there are not any estimates of the prevalence of late emerging language impairments that surface only during adolescence (Reed 2005). When longitudinal studies have followed children into adolescence the focus has been on the persistence of the early identified language problems (Conti-Ramsden et al. 2013; Mok et al. 2014; Stothard et al. 1998) rather than on language problems that emerge later.

4 Late emerging language impairment: Higher order/figurative language impairment

In the transition from childhood to adolescence, the demand on skills that are required for verbal reasoning, social interactions, self-expression, self-control and academic achievement increase. There is also a concomitant growth in demands on language complexity and abstractness, understanding nonliteral meanings and linguistic ambiguity in social and textual interactions (Cohen, Farnia, and Im-Bolter 2013).

Language skills development in the middle school years, during the transition from preadolescence to adolescence, is associated with dramatic changes in brain development. In particular, major changes begin to take place in the frontal lobe that controls executive function, the executive planner of the brain that is responsible for guiding and managing interrelated cognitive, emotional, and behavioral functions (Fuster 2002; Sowell et al. 2004). This executive planner is also associated with higher level cognitive functions like reasoning and judgment and supports rule learning at higher levels of abstraction (Badre, Kayser, and D'Esposito 2010; Yurgelun-Todd 2007). The substantial brain maturation in preadolescence and adolescence is characterized by concomitant growth in cognitive capacities and the ability to communicate for a range of purposes and in diverse social settings.

Adolescence is a very important period because the ability to understand the nonliteral meaning in language represented by higher order or figurative language (e.g., metaphor, idioms, sarcasm) becomes essential for learning, academic achievement, and social interactions. Further, competent figurative language skills requires the integration of cognitive, affective, communicative, social, and linguistic information; a task that places heavy demands on an adolescent's growing working memory abilities. Working memory is important not only for processing and memory elements of immediate situations, but also for retrieving relevant knowledge from the past needed to make inferences. The close relationship between cognitive and figurative language skills is evident in activities such as thinking with concepts (e.g., understanding dichotomies: liberalism/conservatism, nature/nurture), thinking critically (e.g., deciding whether you support the Assisted Suicide Law), thinking creatively (e.g., choosing vivid and meaningful words or expression), and thinking hypothetically.

Adolescents with higher order language impairment have shown to have significantly lower levels of working memory (Cohen et al. 2013). Additional evidence comes from a longitudinal study of community and speech-language clinic samples. Four-year old children who were diagnosed with language impairment no longer met the criterion for language impairment when tested 1.5 year later. When tested again in adolescence, 66% of them had significant deficits compared to the comparison group in verbal short-term memory and phonological skills. They also showed problems with inferential reading comprehension, a skill that requires higher order language and abstract thinking skills (Snowling, Bishop, and Stothard 2000).

In adolescence, the demand on language for social communication, interpersonal and social relationships, inferential thinking, understanding and conveying abstract concepts, and understanding of nonliteral meanings and linguistic ambiguity increases (Nippold 2007). Furthermore, adolescence is a time when friendships become more intense and demanding. Normally developing adolescents learn how to talk to teachers and peers, make accurate estimates of others' mental states, and have increased capacity to appreciate the reciprocal nature of relationships. This contributes to the effectiveness of solving problems in emotionally loaded situations. Lack of ability to cope with ambiguity and make inferences pervades social interactions during adolescence. Difficulties with figurative language can undermine adolescents' ability to engage in appropriate interactions with peers and may affect their self-esteem and feelings of self-worth.

5 Higher order/figurative language

Language is a treasure trove is a statement that is deliberately nonliteral and symbolic, but at the same time unique in that a characteristic is being expressed through a figurative and symbolic expression that requires interpretation. Forms of figurative language include idioms, metaphors, proverbs, sarcasm, and others. These forms juxtapose semantic entities that are not related naturally, but do have relevant parts and commonalities (Glucksberg 2003; Glucksberg, Gildea, and Bookin 1982; Lakoff and Johnson 2004) or those that carry vagueness and ambiguity. Although consistently nonliteral, figurative language expressions have varying degrees of relation to literal meanings. In some instances, they are salient (the idiomatic meaning of danger in *walking on thin ice*) and because of frequent exposure are easier for language users to understand and use. More salient forms of figurative language tend to be easily stored in the mental lexicon and are highly accessible compared to less salient forms of figurative language, which do not have a clear representation in the mental lexicon (i.e., are nonsalient), and thus are not readily accessible (the metaphoric meaning of 'being useless if there is not any support' in *authority is a chair*). Therefore, making inferences on the basis of unfamiliar thematic information (e.g., association between *language* and *treasure trove* in the example above) is effortful and requires some contextual cues that can aid comprehension (Giora 2003; Nippold, Moran, and Schwarz 2001).

Adolescents with language impairment are at risk for poor performance in all areas of development (Beitchman et al. 1996; Snowling et al. 2001). More specifically, adolescents with figurative language impairment have difficulty making inferences in their spoken and written language and in paraphrasing or rephrasing with ease. They also sometimes have difficulties in social situations understanding others when meaning is indirect (e.g., teasing, bantering) and expressing themselves clearly when talking about ideas or relationships (Im-Bolter et al. 2013; St Clair et al. 2011). These problems persist into adulthood and put them at greater risk of emotional and behavioral difficulties (Conti-Ramsden et al. 2012; Durkin and Conti-Ramsden 2010; Im-Bolter and Cohen 2007), lower standing in their careers and subsequent lower earnings than their typically developing counterparts (e.g., Beitchman et al. 1996).

5.1 Social and textual discourse

Higher order/figurative language plays an important role in our everyday communications and the ways we think (Gibbs and Beitel 1995). We use figurative language for interpersonal communications and to express emotions and ideas that literal language cannot convey. Figurative language can be found in books, newspapers, reports, and research papers. They are found in oral communications, TV programs, songs, and movies. In daily interactions, figurative language occurs on average about six per minute of speech (Pollio et al. 1977). In a study of classroom teachers' use of language, Lazar and colleagues found that 27% of classroom teachers' utterances included at least one type of figurative language. Moreover, the use of figurative language increased by grade level from 5% in kindergarten to 20% in grade 8 (Lazar et al. 1989). After 4th grade, students encounter 4.08 idioms per minute both in classroom activities and in the curriculum texts (Nippold et al. 2001).

Given the increasing frequency of use of figurative language in adolescence and its protracted period of development it is not surprising that figurative language has been shown to be associated with both academic and cognitive functioning during this period. For example, performance on figurative language tasks (e.g., idiom comprehension) is related to measures of reading comprehension in preadolescents aged 10 to 12 years (Nippold, Allen, and Kirsch 2001; Nippold et al. 2001) and measures of intelligence and academic achievement throughout adolescence (Nippold and Martin 1989).

Moreover, technological advances over the past decades have changed the ways we communicate. The ever-increasing speed of communication over the Internet and social media has had an impact on our everyday language. A host of new words (e.g., *unfriend, emoticons, buzzword, hashtag*) have originated from Internet and social media. In addition to creating new words, we have seen reappropriation of existing words (i.e., giving new meanings to existing words such as viral[1], troll/trolling[2]). Most of these words have characteristics of salient lexical units (e.g., *go viral*– to spread rapidly via the Internet, email, or other media) with special conventional communicative function. Use of ambiguous language that can reasonably be interpreted in more than one way can hamper communication and lead to uncertainty and misinterpretation of discourse. Thus, children and adolescents with higher order language impairment are likely to be at a disadvantage as they fail to engage in the on-line processing of a significant proportion of the information that is being presented to them in the classroom, in daily conversation, or through any textual and visual medium (e.g., books, TV, movies, Internet).

5.2 Academic achievement

Adolescence gives rise to many shifts in cognitive development that contribute to the increasing capacity to understand and use figurative language. At the same time, during this developmental period, academic demands for inferential thinking, understanding abstract concepts, and independent learning increase. These skills require more sophisticated reasoning and problem solving. In particular, the ability to reason about problems that are removed from their physical referent (e.g., algebraic expressions) becomes more common. Similarly, in order to understand a phrase such as *kick the bucket* the adolescent must access figurative understanding that is far removed from the literal meaning of the words.

Successful interpretation and use of figurative communication fosters the flourishing of academic, personal, and professional relationships (Thoma and Daun 2006). In typically developing adolescents, idiom comprehension has been shown to have a positive association with academic achievement (Nippold and Martin 1989). Furthermore, academic achievement during adolescence is heavily reliant on reading and writing skills and the capacity for self-guided study. From the fifth grade onward, reading comprehension is used as an essential tool for learning and this reaches a peak in adolescence when work on independent projects becomes a priority. Moreover, in adolescence reading for factual information (literal comprehension) is overtaken by the need to make inferences from what is read when the language of text is not completely explicit (inferential comprehension). In particular, this deeper comprehension requires the reader to make inferences that bridge elements in the text or otherwise support the coherence needed for comprehension (Perfetti, Landi, and Oakhill 2005). Adolescents with figurative language impairment are unlikely to make inferences from written text and have skilled comprehension monitoring strategies (Levine 1999).

---

[1] Viral: Pertaining to or involving the spreading of information and opinions about a product or service from person to person, especially on the Internet.
[2] trolling: Typically unleashing one or more cynical or sarcastic remarks on an innocent by-stander, because 'it's the internet and, hey, you can'.

5.3 Socioemotional development

The inherent association between linguistic and socioemotional competence has been established in the literature (e.g., Beitchman et al. 1989; Bishop 2003; Cohen et al. 1998; Carpenter and Drabick 2011). There are documented relations between higher order/figurative language impairment and mental health problems (Cohen et al. 2013; Reed 2005) and immature social cognition (Im-Bolter et al. 2013). Prevalence studies indicate an overrepresentation of children and adolescents with language impairment in clinical populations.

One contributing factor may be the overlapping behavioral symptoms of language processing deficits and socioemotional psychopathology such as 'not following directions', 'being distracted', and 'lack of self-regulation' (Redman 2002). Linguistic demands of the self-report tools, used to assess children's and adolescents' personality and socioemotional symptoms, is another potential contributing factor. These tools often include implicit linguistic information and complex syntax. They require interpretation of figurative language and accurate comprehension of temporal adverbs (Webster, Brown-Triolo and Griffith 1999). The high demand linguistic processing involved in these tools may overburden adolescents' information processing ability. Thus, adolescents with poor receptive language skills or with language impairment are more likely to respond impulsively to these questions and report higher levels of emotional and behavioral difficulties (Conti-Ramsden et al. 2013).

To shed light on the interplay between language impairment and mental health of adolescents, Cohen and colleagues (2013) assessed structural and higher order/figurative language of adolescents referred for assessment and treatment of mental health disorders. They found that 45% of adolescents in the clinic-referred sample had at least one type (i.e., receptive, expressive) of unsuspected higher order/figurative language impairment compared to 15% of their counterparts in the comparison group.

Cohen and colleagues (2013) suggest that when figurative language impairment and socioemotional problems coexist, a bilateral treatment approach should be taken to improve the treatment outcomes in children and adolescents with various psychopathologies. By including tests of higher order/figurative language into the standard assessment battery of clinicians and researchers in developmental psychology and psychopathology and neuropsychology, it will be possible to plan and implement interprofessional services.

6 Cognitive and neural correlates of figurative language comprehension

Since the mid-1970s, there has been an interest in figurative language not only in literary studies, but also in educational research. A number of theories and hypotheses have been proposed to delineate and explain the cognitive processes that underlie the comprehension of different types of figurative expressions. These theories address the communicative layers involved in understanding figurative expressions beyond syntax or semantics. They focus on the order in which the shallow and deep layers of figurative expressions are processed.

The comparison theory focuses on the shared properties of the literal and figurative components of an expression. It asserts that when interpreting figurative language expressions, there is an interplay between the literal and figurative meanings (Grice 1975; Searle 1979). That is, there are overlapping features that create the ground of the figurative expression. Where the literal and figurative expressions are denotatively distant (e.g., *Jane is a tiger*), they require sequential processing. In these cases the literal and figurative meanings are mutually exclusive. To interpret the expression one has to first rule out the literal meaning in order to comprehend the figurative alternative. Black (1962) suggested that the overlap between literal and figurative expressions is reciprocal and is represented at both lexical and conceptual levels.

In the 1980s, there was an increasing tendency for developing integrated cognitive-linguistic approaches. These approaches reframed the relationship between literal and figurative language and highlighted the role of cognition in this relationship. The systematic mapping model (Lakoff and Johnson 1980, 1999) asserted that metaphors are at the heart of ordinary everyday language semantics and are characterized by numerous conceptual cross-domain mappings that address literal-metaphoric relationships. That is, more concrete and relatively easy to imagine source domains are mapped onto more abstract and less easy to conceptualize target sources. These conceptualized figurative expressions can be primary, where mappings may be grounded in physical experiences (e.g., *kind heart*) or complex in which literal elements of the source domain are mapped onto the figurative aspects of the target domain (e.g., *His reasoning fell apart*).

Another line of cognitive-language research proposed that the processing and interpretation of the literal and figurative expressions takes place in parallel (Glucksberg and Ksysar 1990). This model suggests that the comprehension process involves inhibiting irrelevant features and drawing attention to the specific relevant features of the expression (Gernsbacher et al. 2001; Glucksberg, Newsome, and Goldvarg 2001). However, in spite of the involvement of the parallel processes, interpretations of the figurative expressions are highly context-dependent (Gibbs 1994). That is, the literal meaning is processed and comprehended first through contextual information (Clark and Lucy 1975; Ortony 1993) and the search for the figurative meaning starts only after the literal meaning is found to be irrelevant or inappropriate.

An increasing body of recent experimental research using brain imaging techniques has shed light on the underlying cognitive mechanisms that drive the development of higher order/figurative language. These new and informative data can help researchers and clinicians to understand the neurological and cognitive processes associated with nonliteral figurative language comprehension and the modes of access to meaning.

Meta-analyses of imaging studies on figurative language processing indicate a consistent pattern of activation of frontal and temporal brain regions mainly in the left hemisphere (e.g., Bohrn, Altmann, and Jacobs 2012; Rapp, Mutschler and Erb 2012; Vartanian 2012). The prefrontal cortex helps to sustain executive functions or capacities required to accomplish a wide range of mental activities. These functions include but are not limited to short-term (e.g., Chao and Knight 1998) and working memory (e.g., Fuster, Bordner and Kroger 2000), inhibitory control of interference and filtering or gating mechanisms for information processing (e.g., Shimamura, Janowsky, and Squire 1990) that are required for comprehending oral and written language including comprehension of figurative expressions.

The prefrontal cortex is also involved in the interpretation of proverbs. Patients with focal left frontal lobe lesions with average IQ, no history of neurological or psychiatric disorders or aphasia performed significantly poorer on a proverb interpretation task than a healthy control group (Murphy et al. 2013). Involvement of the prefrontal cortex in processing and comprehension of idioms was also shown in studies of individuals with Alzheimer's disease and Down syndrome (Papagno and Vallar 2001) and patients with schizophrenia (Titon, Holzman and Levy 2002). In all these latter studies, patients were asked to interpret idioms in an idiom comprehension task. In all the cases patients interpreted the literal meanings first. These patients' inability to give the definition of idioms correlated with their performance on measures of executive function (Romero Lauro et al. 2007; Zempleni et al. 2007).

These findings suggest that to access the figurative meanings the literal meanings should be inhibited/suppressed and the left temporal lobe where the semantic information is stored must be activated. Since inhibition and suppression are associated with prefrontal cortex, it is expected that individuals with prefrontal cortex or left frontal lobe lesions will have impaired processing (Papagno et al. 2003; Papagno et al. 2006) and poor activation of executive functions responsible for complex cognitive control mechanisms.

During adolescence, changes in the prefrontal cortex underlie the development of processing speed and complex cognitive control mechanisms, executive functions. These two main cognitive developments are critical for successful communication. In adolescents with language impairment, mental operations and inference making, performing rapid mental shifts (e.g., Lum, Conti-Ramsden, and Lindell 2007), integrating the input from conversations and formulating quick responses (Brinton, Fujiki, and Powell 1997; Owens, Metz, and Haas 2003) are compromised. In addition, in adolescents with higher order language impairment aspects of executive functions are implicated in poor pragmatic skills, that is, in lack of ability to interact effectively and successfully with peers and adults in social settings (Ryder and Leinonen 2014), incompetent social problem solving (Im-Bolter et al. 2013), difficulty in emotion regulation (e.g., Denckla, Romine, and Reynoth 2004), poor comprehension monitoring and inference making from oral or written text (Booth, Boyle, and Kelly

2010; Hulme and Snowling 2009; Palladino et al. 2001), and poor academic achievement (Latzman et al. 2010).

Taken together, findings from this body of experimental research indicate that in adolescents with higher order figurative language impairment, slow processing of incoming input and difficulties in executive functions compromise the effortless access to the meaning of figurative language. These skills are highly correlated with and essential for interpreting figurative language expressions and higher level thinking. Therefore, they should be considered in the assessment and intervention planning for adolescents with language impairments.

7 Figurative language processing and contextual factors

Adolescents with language problems often fall into two categories. The first category includes adolescents who have a language impairment or some sort of learning disability that affects their development on different grounds. Some of the adolescents in this group may have a long history of language impairment that was identified in childhood and persisted into their adolescence. Others may have late emerging language impairments that involves impairment of higher order figurative language processing. The second category includes adolescents with limited language proficiency. Adolescents with limited language proficiency may be from diverse cultural and linguistic backgrounds, or their language difficulties may be associated with contextual factors such as low socio-economic status and its correlates such as low parental education, poverty, poor health and social disadvantage, or a combination of some or all of these factors. Research has shown that these factors are associated with poor vocabulary, difficulty in organizing thought to express themselves, as well as difficulty in initiating and maintaining social interactions and switching between styles (formal and informal) or situations.

It appears that regardless of the group membership all these adolescents, to a various extent, have difficulty with both receptive and expressive aspects of language (Reed 2005). However, the underlying indicators of these difficulties may be somewhat different for the two groups. For example, indicators of persistent or late emerging language impairment in adolescents include inability to produce narratives without making many errors (Wetherall, Botting, and Conti-Ramsden 2007), consistent poor vocabulary (Stothard et al. 1998), difficulty in joining in social interactions and keeping up with conversations (Brinton and Fujiki 2005), difficulty understanding complex sentences, figurative, nonliteral language (Bishop, Adams, and Rosen 2006), limited working memory capacity and information processing issues (e.g., Montgomery 2005). Whereas, indicators of language difficulties in adolescents with limited language proficiency include limited use of complex long words even though they are aware of their importance and inability to link the words to the situations appropriately. Similar to adolescents with language impairment the adolescents with limited language proficiency have poor narrative skills (Spencer, Clegg, and Stackhouse 2009), and inappropriate register where they have difficulty realizing which mode of register to shift to (e.g., from formal to casual) in certain situations. Thereby, they may be perceived as rude or immature when they are engaged in conversations. (e.g., Payne 2005; Segalowitz 2010).

Aspects of higher order language are largely culture-specific. It is argued that in a language learning context, the interpretation of highly frequent, salient forms of figurative language is easier than the interpretation of the forms that are opaque. That is, the more salient and transparent the figurative expressions, the more likely it is for adolescents with limited language proficiency to rely on the lexical components to interpret their meanings. Conversely, the less transparent and more nonsalient the forms of figurative expressions, the more they will need to rely on contextual cues to interpret meanings (Boers and Demecheleer 2001; Nippold and Martin 1989).

Moreover, it may be difficult to reliably assess figurative language comprehension across multiple language, ethnic, and cultural backgrounds. Research indicates that cross-culturally, children's ability to interpret idioms (e.g., Nippold, Taylor and Baker 1996) and more complex figurative language (e.g., Im-Bolter et al. 2013) improves across development. However, since the frequency and the degree of semantic transparency of figurative language and higher order communication may differ between the target and first languages, these differences directly impact the on-line processing of figurative language.

Nevertheless, it is expected that similar to the native speakers of a given language, as children who learn an additional language get older, they become increasingly exposed to and familiar with figurative expressions through hearing, reading, and using them. They also develop the cognitive abilities needed to flexibly interpret both literal and figurative meaning simultaneously. However, it is unclear whether typical development of these language abilities progresses in the same stages or at the same speed amongst learners from different language, ethnic and cultural backgrounds. It is also unclear how figurative language competence is developed in language learners with language impairment.

It is believed that processes and strategies required to comprehend higher order/figurative language are the same as processes and strategies children use for language comprehension in general (Levorato and Cacciari 1995). These involve understanding of words, phrases and semantic categories in context which, in turn, enable language users to integrate and make meaningful inferences from the oral or written discourse.

8 Assessment, clinical, educational, and research implications

The high degree of overlap between higher order/figurative language impairment and adolescents' poor socioemotional, social cognition, contextual, oral and written discourse and academic outcomes warrants immediate planning for a multifaceted comprehensive assessment of different areas of functioning. Thus, it is important to identify problems as early in the development as possible in order to introduce/offer the most appropriate treatment plans. It is also important to reliably identify the early markers of figurative language impairment and devise interventions targeting deficient language abilities in adolescents.

8.1 Implications for assessment and identification

Adolescents' language development, behaviors and emotions must be understood within a developmental context. This highlights the importance of including a test of higher order/figurative language in the standard assessment battery of school psychologists, clinicians, and researchers in developmental psychology and psychopathology. The comprehensive battery of developmentally-sensitive assessment tools is essential for two related purposes. First, it provides screening of adolescents' language skills that is driven by knowledge of normative expectations and learning outcomes. This is particularly relevant in identifying adolescents with or at-risk for higher order/figurative language problems. Second, a detailed comprehensive assessment must follow to distinguish adolescents with a language impairment from those with a language delay defined as late but typical development (e.g., second language learners) or language difference associated with different geographical, social, cultural and ethnic variations (e.g. dialects). The in-depth follow-up assessment will help to avoid the overidentification of language delayed or language different adolescents as language impaired (see Bland-Stewart 2005). It is worth mentioning that while the cognitive and language profiles of these groups may be different, higher order/figurative language intervention is beneficial to all of them to help to close the gap for some and raise the bar for others.

8.2 Implications for intervention

Demands and complexity of cognitive and language processing, social interactions and academic work increase steadily during adolescence. Without well-designed, multifaceted interprofessional language-based interventions that target all the areas of deficiency, adolescents with language impairments face additional obstacles in keeping up with these increasing demands. Involvement of adolescents in their own intervention planning is crucial. Helping them to become aware of and identify their areas of weakness (i.e., weak metalinguistic and metacognitive skills, inefficient information processing abilities and problem solving skills, and inefficient interpersonal interactions) and determine the priorities and objectives of their intervention plan can increase their buy-in. It will also strengthen their motivation to engage in the intervention (Reed 2005; Fallon et al. 2015).

8.3 Conclusions and implications for future research

Timely identification and treatment of higher order/figurative language impairment is of essence. There are only a handful of individually administered communicative functioning screening tests, dating back to the 1980s and 1990s (Reed 2005). These screening measures do not necessarily test different modalities of higher order/figurative language. There is a lack of standardized screening and assessment measures that reflect present-day language usage and provide present-day norms. This lack of measures that can be used in research and clinical settings to assess higher order/figurative language status may result in many cases left undiagnosed and untreated. A test of figurative language that generates relevant norms for typically developing and various clinical populations of children and adolescents is called for.

References

ASHA. 2009. *Incidence and prevalence of speech, voice, and language disorders in the adults in the United States*: 2008 edition. http://asha.org/research/reports/speech_voice_language.htm

Badre, David, Andrew S. Kayser & Mark D'Esposito. 2010. Frontal cortex and the discovery of abstract action rules. *Neuron* 66 (2). 315–326.

Beitchman, Joseph H., R. Nair, M. Clegg, B. Ferguson & P. G. Patel. 1986. The prevalence of psychiatric disorders in children with speech and language disorders. *Journal of the American Academy of Child and Adolescent Psychiatry* 25 (4). 528–535.

Beitchman, Joseph H., Beth Wilson, E. B. Brownlie, Heather Walters & William Lancee. 1996. Long-term consistency in speech/language profiles: I. developmental and academic outcomes. *Journal of American Academy of Child and Adolescent Psychiatry* 35 (6). 804–814.

Beitchman, Joseph H., E. B. Brownlie, A. Inglis, J. Wild, B. Ferguson & D. Schachter. 1996a. Seven-year follow-up of speech/language impaired and control children: Psychiatric outcome. *Journal of the American Academy of Child and Adolescent Psychiatry*. 37 (8). 961–970.

Bishop, Dorothy V. M., Caroline V. Adams & Stuart Rosen. 2006. Resistance of grammatical impairment to computerised comprehension training in children with specific and non-specific language impairments. *International Journal of Language and Communication Disorders* 41 (1). 19–40.

Bishop, Dorothy V. M. & Andrew Edmundson. 1987. Specific language impairment as a maturational lag: Evidence from longitudinal data on language and motor development. *Developmental Medicine and Child Neurology* 29 (4). 442–459.

Black, Max. 1962. *Models and metaphors*. Ithaca, NY: Cornell University Press.

Bland-Stewart, Linda M. 2005. Difference or deficit in speakers of African-American English? What every clinician should know... and do. *The ASHA Leader* 10 (6). 6–31.

Boers, Frank & Murielle Demecheleer. 2001. Measuring the impact of cross-cultural differences on learners' comprehension of imageable idioms. *English Language Teaching Journal* 55 (3). 255–262.

Bohrn, Isabel C., Ulrike Altmann & Arthur M. Jacobs. 2012. Looking at the brains behind figurative language – A quantitative meta-analysis of neuroimaging studies on metaphor, idiom, and irony processing. *Neuropsychologia* 50 (11). 2669–2683.

Brinton, Bonnie & Martin Fujiki. 2005. Social competence in children with language impairment: making connections. *Seminars in Speech and Language* 26 (3). 151–159.

Brinton, Bonnie, Martin Fujiki & Teresa A. Mackey. 1985. Elementary school age children's comprehension of specific idiomatic expressions. *Journal of Communication Disorders* 18 (4). 250–251.

Brinton, Bonnie, Martin Fujiki & Jann M. Powell. 1997. The ability of children with language impairment to manipulate topic in a structured task. *Language, Speech and Hearing Services in Schools* 28 (1). 3–11.

Brownlie, E. B., Joseph H. Beitchman, Michael Escobar, Arlene Young, Leslie Atkinson, Carla Johnson, Beth Wilson & Lori Douglas. 2004. Early language impairment and young adult delinquent and aggressive behavior. *Journal of Abnormal Child Psychology* 32 (4). 453–467.

Bulut, Türkay & İlkay Çelik-Yazici. 2004. Idiom processing in L2: Through rose-colored glasses. *The Reading Matrix* 4 (2). 105–116.

Cacciari, Cristina & Patrizia Tabossi. 2014. *Idioms: Processing, structure, and interpretation.* New York: Psychology Press.

Cain, Kate, Jane V. Oakhill & Carsten Elbro. 2003. The ability to learn new word meanings from context by school-age children with and without language comprehension difficulties. *Journal of Child Language* 30 (3). 681–694.

Carpenter, Johanna L. & Deborah A. G. Drabick. 2011. Co-occurrence of linguistic and behavioural difficulties in early childhood: a developmental psychopathology perspective. *Early Child Development Care* 181 (8). 1021–1045.

Catts, Hugh W., Marc E. Fey, J. Bruce Tomblin & Xuyang Zhang. 2002. A longitudinal investigation of reading outcomes in children with language impairments. *Journal of Speech, Language, and Hearing Research* 45 (6). 1142–1157.

Chao, Linda L. & Robert T. Knight. 1998. Contribution of human prefrontal cortex to delay performance. *Journal of Cognitive Neuroscience* 10 (2). 167–77.

Cohen, Nancy J., Melanie A. Barwick, Naomi B. Horodezky, Denise D. Vallance & Nancie Im. 1998. Language, achievement, and cognitive processing in psychiatrically disturbed children with previously identified and unsuspected language impairments. *Journal of Child Psychology and Psychiatry* 39 (6). 865–877.

Cohen, Nancy J., Fataneh Farnia & Nancie Im-Bolter. 2013. Higher order language competence and adolescent mental health. *Journal of Child Psychology and Psychiatry* 54 (7). 733–744.

Conti-Ramsden, Gina, Pearl L. H. Mok, Andrew Pickles & Kevin Durkin. 2013. Adolescents with a history of specific language impairment (SLI): Strengths and difficulties in social, emotional and behavioral functioning. *Research in Developmental Disabilities* 34 (11). 4161–4169.

Conti-Ramsden, Gina, Michelle C. St Clair, Andrew Pickles & Kevin Durkin. 2012. Developmental trajectories of verbal and nonverbal skills in individuals with a history of specific language impairment: From childhood to adolescence. *Journal of Speech, Language, and Hearing Research* 55 (6). 1716–1735.

Romine, Cassandra Burns & Cecil R. Reynolds. 2004. Sequential memory: A developmental perspective on its relation to frontal lobe functioning. *Neuropsychology Review* 14 (1). 43–64.

Durkin, Kevin & Gina Conti-Ramsden. 2010. Young people with specific language impairment: A review of social and emotional functioning in adolescence. *Child Language Teaching and Therapy* 26 (2). 105–121.

Fallon Karen A., Lauren A. Katz & Rachel Carlberg. 2015. Balanced intervention for adolescents and adults with language impairment: A clinical framework. *Seminars in Speech and Language* 36 (1). 5–16.

Fuster, Joaquín M. 2002. Frontal lobe and cognitive development. *Journal of Neurocytology* 31 (3-5). 373–385.

Fuster, Joaquín M., Mark Bordner & James K. Kroger. 2000. Cross model and cross-temporal associations in neurons of frontal cortex. *Nature* 405. 347–351.

Gernsbacher, Morton Ann, Boaz Keysar, Rachel R. W. Robertson & Necia K. Werner. 2001. The role of suppression and enhancement in understanding metaphors. *Journal of Memory and Language* 45 (3). 433–450.

Gibbs, Raymond W., Jr. 1994. *The poetics of mind: figurative thought, language, and understanding.* Cambridge: Cambridge University Press.

Gibbs, Raymond W. & Dinara Beitel. 1995. What proverb understanding reveals about how people think. *Psychological Bulletin* 118 (1). 133–154.

Giora, Rachel. 2003. *On our mind: Salience, context and figurative language.* New York: Oxford University Press.

Glucksberg, Sam. 2003. The psycholinguistics of metaphor. *Trends in Cognitive Sciences* 7 (2). 92–96.

Glucksberg, Sam, Patricia Gildea & Howard B. Bookin. 1982. On understanding nonliteral speech: can people ignore metaphors? *Journal of Verbal Learning and Verbal Behavior* 21 (1). 85–98.

Glucksberg, Sam, Mary R. Newsome & Yevgeniya Goldvarg. 2001. Inhibition of the literal: filtering metaphor-irrelevant information during metaphor comprehension. *Metaphor and Symbol* 16 (3–4). 277–298.

Grice, H. Paul. 1975. Logic and conversation. In Peter Cole & Jerry L. Morgan (eds.), *Syntax and semantics 3: Speech acts*, 41–58. New York: Academic Press.

Harrison, Linda. J., Sharynne McLeod, Donna Berthelsen & Sue Walker. 2009. Literacy, numeracy and learning in school-aged children identified as having Speech and language impairment in early childhood. *International Journal of Speech-Language Pathology* 11 (5). 392–403.

Hulme, Charles & Margaret J. Snowling. 2009. *Developmental disorders of language, learning and cognition.* Oxford: Wiley-Blackwell.

Im-Bolter, Nancie & Nancy J. Cohen. 2007. Language impairment and psychiatric comorbidities. *Pediatric Clinics of North America* 54 (3). 525–542.

Im-Bolter, Nancie, Nancy J. Cohen & Fataneh Farnia. 2013. I thought we were good: Social cognition, figurative language, and adolescent psychopathology. *Journal of Child Psychology and Psychiatry* 54 (7). 724–732.

Jackson, Howard & Etienne Zé Amvela. 2007. *Words, meaning and vocabulary; an introduction to modern English lexicology (2nd edition).* New York: Continuum Publishing Group.

Kerbel, Debra & Pam Grunwell. 1997. Idioms in the classroom: An investigation of language unit and mainstream teachers' use of idioms. *Child Language Teacher and Therapy* 13 (1). 113–123.

Lakoff, George & Mark Johnson. 2004. *Metaphors we live by (2nd edition).* Chicago: University of Chicago Press.

Latzman, Robert, Natasha Elkovitch, JohnYoung & Lee Anna Clark. 2010. The contribution of executive functioning to academic achievement among male adolescents. *Journal of Clinical and Experimental Neuropsychology* 32 (5). 455–462.

Lazar, Rhea Tregabov, Genese A. Warr-Leeper, Cynthia Beel Nicholson & Suzanne Johnson. 1989. Elementary school teachers' use of multiple meaning expressions. *Language, Speech, and Hearing Services in Schools* 20. 420–430.

Levine, Melvin D. 1999. *Developmental variation and learning disorders.* Cambridge, MA: Educators Publishing Service.

Levorato, M. Chiara & Cristina Cacciari. 1995. The effects of different tasks on the comprehension and production of idioms in children. *Journal of Experimental Child Psychology* 60 (2). 261–283.

Levorato, M. Chiara. 1999. Idiom comprehension in children: Are the effects of semantic analysability and context separable? *European Journal of Cognitive Psychology* 11 (1). 51–66.

Liebermann, Dana, Gerald F. Giesbrecht & Ulrich Muller. 2007. Cognitive and emotional aspects of self-regulation in preschoolers. *Cognitive Development* 22 (4). 511–529.

Lum, Jarrad, A.G., Gina Conti-Ramsden & Annukka K. Lindell. 2007. The attentional blink reveals sluggish attentional shifting in adolescents with specific language impairment. *Brain and Cognition* 63 (3). 287–295.

Marton, Klara, Luca Campanelli, Naomi Eichorn, Jessica Scheuer & Jungmee Yoon. 2014. Information processing and procative interference in children with and without specific language impairment. *Journal of Speech, Language and Hearing Research* 57 (1). 106–119.

McLeod, Sharynne & David H. McKinnon. 2007. The prevalence of communication disorders compared with other learning needs in 14,500 primary and secondary school students. *International Journal of Language and Communication Disorders* 42 (Suppl 1). 37–59.
Mendez, Julia L., John Fantuzzo & Dante Cicchetti. 2007. Profiles of social competence among low-income African American preschool children. *Child Development* 73 (4). 1085–1100.
Mok, Pearl L. H., Andrew Pickles, Kevin Durkin, Gina Conti-Ramsden. 2014. Longitudinal trajectories of peer relations in children with specific language impairment. *Journal of Child Psychology and Psychiatry and Allied Disciplines* 55 (5). 516–527.
Montgomery, James W. 2005. Effects of input rate and age on real-time language processing of children with specific language impairment. *International Journal of Language and Communication Disorders* 40 (2). 171–188.
Murphy, Patrick, Tim Shallice, Gail Robinson, Sarah E. Macpherson, Martha Turner, Katherine Woollett, Marco Bozzali & Lisa Cipolotti. 2013. Impairment in proverb interpretation following focal frontal lobe lesions. *Neuropsychologia* 51 (11). 2075–2086.
Nippold, Marilyn A. 2007. *Later language development*. Austin, TX: Pro-Ed.
Nippold, Marilyn A., Melissa M. Allen & Dixon I. Kirsch. 2001. Proverb comprehension as a function of reading proficiency in preadolescents. *Language, Speech, and Hearing Services in Schools* 32 (2). 90–100.
Nippold, Marilyn A. & Stephanie Tarrant Martin. 1989. Idiom interpretation in isolation versus context: a developmental study with adolescents. *Journal of Speech and Hearing Research* 32 (1). 59–66.
Nippold, Marilyn A., Catherine Moran & Ilsa E. Schwarz. 2001. Idiom understanding in preadolescents: Synergy in action. *American Journal of Speech-Language Pathology* 10. 169–179.
Norbury, Courtenay Frazier. 2004. Factors supporting idiom comprehension in children with communication disorders. *Journal of Speech, Language, and Hearing Research* 47. 1179–1193.
Ortony, Andrew. 1993. *Metaphor and thought (2nd edn)*. Cambridge: Cambridge University Press.
Owens, Robert E., Dale Evan Metz & Adelaide Haas. 2003. *Introduction to communication disorders: A life span perspective (2nd edn)*. Boston: Allyn & Bacon.
Papagno, Costanza & Giuseppe Vallar. 2001. Understanding metaphors and idioms: A single-case neuropsychological study in a person with Down syndrome. *Journal of the International Neuropsychological Society* 7 (4). 516–528.
Payne, Ruby K. 2005. *A framework for understanding poverty (4th edn)*. Highlands, TX: aha! Process
Perfetti, Charles A., Nicole Landi & Jane Oakhill. 2005. The acquisition of reading comprehension skill. In Margaret J. Snowling & Charles Hulme (eds.), *The science of reading*, 227–247. Oxford: Blackwell.
Pollio, Howard R., Jack M. Barlow, Harold J. Fine & Marilyn R. Pollio. 1977. *Psychology and the poetics of growth: Figurative language in psychology, psychotherapy, and education*. New Jersey: Lawrence Erlbaum Associates.
Rapp, Alexander M., Dirk T. Leube, Michael Erb, Wolfgang Grodd & Tilo T.J. Kircher. 2004. Neural correlates of metaphor processing. *Cognitive Brain Research* 20 (3). 395–402.
Rapp, Alexander M., Dorothee E. Mutschler & Michael Erb. 2012. Where in the brain is nonliteral language? A coordinate-based meta-analysis of functional magnetic resonance imaging studies. *Neuroimage* 63 (1). 600–610
Romero Lauro, Leonor J., Marco Tettamanti, Stefano F. Cappa & Constanza Papagno. 2008. Idiom comprehension: A prefrontal task? *Cerebral Cortex* 18 (1). 162–170.
Ryder, Nuala & Eeva Leinonen. 2014. Pragmatic language development in language impaired and typically developing children: Incorrect answers in context. *Journal of Psycholinguistic Research* 43 (1). 45–58.
Searle, John R. 1979. *Expression and meaning*. Cambridge: Cambridge University Press.
Segalowitz, Norman. 2010. *Cognitive bases of second language fluency*. New York: Routledge.

Shimamura, Arthur P., Jeri S. Janowsky & Larry R. Squire. 1990. Memory for the temporal order of events in patients with frontal lobe lesions and amnesic patients. *Neuropsychologia* 28 (8). 803–813.

Snowling, Margaret J., John W. Adams, Dorothy V. M. Bishop & Susan E. Stothard. 2001. Educational attainments of school leavers with a preschool history of speech-language impairments. *International Journal of Language and Communication Disorders* 36 (2). 173–183.

Sowell, Elizabeth R., Paul M. Thompson, Christiana M. Leonard, Suzanne E. Welcome, Eric Kan & Arthur W. Toga. 2004. Longitudinal mapping of cortical thickness and brain growth in normal children. *Journal of Neuroscience* 24 (38). 8223–8231.

Stothard, Suzanne E., Margaret J. Snowling, Dorothy V. M. Bishop, Barry B. Chipchase & Carole A. Kaplan. 1998. Language-impaired preschoolers: A follow-up into adolescence. *Journal of Speech, Language and Hearing Research* 41 (2). 407–418.

Stringaris Argyris K., Nicholas C. Medford, Vincent Giampietro, Michael J. Brammer & Anthony S. David. 2007. Deriving meaning: Distinct neural mechanisms for metaphoric, literal, and non-meaningful sentences. *Brain and Language* 100 (2). 150–162.

St Clair, Michelle C., Andrew Pickles, Kevin Durkin & Gina Conti-Ramsden. 2011. A longitudinal study of behavioral, emotional and social difficulties in individuals with a history of specific language impairment (SLI). *Journal of Communication Disorders* 44 (2). 186–199.

Thoma, Patrizia & Irene Daun. 2006. Neurocognitive mechanisms of figurative language processing-Evidence from clinical dysfunctions. *Neuroscience and Biobehavioral Reviews*. 30 (8). 1182–1205.

Titone, Debra, Philip S. Holzman & Deborah L. Levy. 2002. Idiom processing in schizophrenia: Literal implausibility saves the day for idiom priming. *Journal of Abnormal Psychology* 111 (2). 313–320.

Vartanian, Oshin. Dissociable neural systems for analogy and metaphor: implications for the neuroscience of creativity. *British Journal of Psychology* 103 (3). 302–316.

Webster, D. D., D. Brown-Triolo & P. L. Griffith, P. L. 1999. Linguistic factors affecting personality assessment of children and adolescents. In Diana Rogers-Adkinson & Penny Lynn Griffith (eds.), *Communication disorders and children with psychiatric and behavioral disorders*, 259–293. San Diego: Singular.

Wetherall, Danielle, Nicola Botting & Gina Conti-Ramsden. 2007. Narrative in adolescent specific language impairment (SLI): a comparison with peers across two different narrative genres: *International Journal of Language and Communication Disorders* 42 (5). 583–605.

Williams, Diane L., Gerald Goldstein & Nancy J. Minshew. 2006. Neuropsychologic functioning in children with autism: further evidence for disordered complex information-processing. *Journal of Child Neuropsychology* 11 (4–5). 279–298.

Yang, Fanpei Gloria, Jerome Fuller, Navid Khodaparast & Daniel C. Krawczyk. 2010. Figurative language processing after traumatic brain injury in adults: A preliminary study. *Neuropsychologia* 48 (7). 1923–1929.

Young, Arlene R., Joeseph H. Beitchman, Carla Johnson, Lori Douglas, Leslie Atkinson, Michael Escobar & Beth M. Wilson. 2002. Young adult academic outcomes in a longitudinal sample of speech/language impaired and control children. *Journal of Child Psychology and Psychiatry* 43 (5). 635–645.

Yurgelun-Todd, Deborah. 2007. Emotional and cognitive changes during adolescence. *Current Opinion in Neurobiology* 17 (2). 251–257.

Zempleni, Monika-Zita, Marco Haverkort, Remco Renken & Laurie A. Stowe. 2007. Evidence for bilateral involvement in idiom comprehension: An fMRI study. *Neuroimage* 23 (3). 596–603.

Britta Biedermann, Nora Fieder and Lyndsey Nickels
8 Spoken word production: Processes and potential breakdown

1 Introduction

The processes of spoken word production have been a focus of interest for decades and this research has been summarised in several reviews (e.g., Friedmann, Biran, & Dotan, 2013; Nickels, 1997, 2001a,b; Wilshire, 2008). However, many questions remain unanswered and consequently spoken word production remains an area of research interest, informed by data from unimpaired and impaired adult language, as well as language development. Several theories of spoken language production have been proposed over the last half century, each differing slightly in levels of representation, processing steps, and activation flow. In this chapter, we focus on four of the most influential theories of spoken language production.

2 Spoken word production in adult speakers

While, in this section, we only discuss four (prominent) models of speech production, we acknowledge that there are other theoretical frameworks (e.g. Harley, 2013; Stemberger, 1985). These theoretical frameworks differ in the extent to which processing is thresholded (complete at one level before proceeding to the next; e.g. Morton, 1985; Levelt, Roelofs & Meyer, 1999) or cascaded (can flow to subsequent levels prior to selection; e.g. Dell, Martin, Saffran, & Gagnon, 1997), feedforward (flows only in one direction, e.g. Levelt et al., 1999) or interactive (flows both forward and backward through the model; e.g. Dell et al., 1997). We refer the reader to Rapp and Goldrick (2000; Goldrick & Rapp, 2002) for detailed discussion of these issues. In addition, the vast majority of theories of spoken word production assume localist representations (i.e. a single node for a single representation), including all of those described here. However, some computational models implement distributed representations, where no single unit codes for any one item or feature, but instead items are represented by a pattern of activation across a whole array of units. To our knowledge there are no models that focus on spoken word production which incorporate distributed representations (but see, Plaut, 2002). Finally, we only address language production in monolingual speakers, and do not discuss models of bi- or multi-lingual speakers (e.g., Green, 1998; Green & Abutalebi, 2013). However, we

Britta Biedermann, Curtin University and Macquarie University
Nora Fieder, Macquarie University and Humboldt Universität
Lyndsey Nickels, Macquarie University

note that the majority of these theories of bi-/multi-lingual language production are relatively underspecified in terms of production processes, instead they (necessarily) focus on the interaction between languages. Hence, it is likely that the underlying processes for producing a word will be similar across monolinguals and bilinguals, but with additional processing constraints for the multilingual speaker.

2.1 The Logogen model

The Logogen model originated as a model of word recognition (e.g. Morton, 1964; 1969) but was later extended to include spoken and written word production (e.g. Kay, Lesser & Coltheart, 1992; Swinburn, Porter & Howard, 2014; Whitworth, Webster & Howard 2014). It has been incredibly influential, and remains one of the few theories that encompasses all modalities of language input and output. It remains particularly widely used in clinical practice, and forms the basis for assessment tools (e.g. Psycholinguistic Assessments of Language Processing in Aphasia (PALPA), Kay, Lesser and Coltheart, 1992; Comprehensive Aphasia Test (CAT), Swinburn, Porter and Howard, 2010), and textbooks guiding assessment and treatment choices (e.g. Whitworth, Webster and Howard, 2014). Consequently, the Logogen model is commonly used as a tool to help localise the nature of the breakdown of language after stroke and (albeit less widely) in developmental language impairment. Here, we concentrate on the components required to utter a spoken word. Figure 1 depicts the example of saying aloud 'dog' within the Logogen model. According to this model, a speaker needs to first activate a conceptual entry from a pre-lexical component called the 'Cognitive System'. Once a concept has been activated, it activates the corresponding entry in the 'Phonological Output Lexicon' (POL)[1], a store of all word forms that the speaker knows. As soon as a word has reached a threshold of activation in the POL, this word (logogen) can then activate the corresponding representation in the next component, the 'Phonological Output Buffer' (originally known as the Response Buffer). It is at this level that the phonemes of a word are activated. The Phonological Output Buffer also serves as a working memory store, holding the phonemes of the target word active until they are required for articulation.

In terms of information flow from one process to the next, the Logogen model only allows for feed forward processing in word production, and no interactive feedback processes are incorporated. It works in a serial and discrete fashion, in the sense that processing at one level is complete before there is activation of the next level. This model does not distinguish between meaning representations (semantics) that are specific to words (lexical-semantics) and those that are more general and include non-linguistic aspects of meaning (conceptual representations; but see

---

[1] In the original Logogen model the representations at this level would have been termed "phonological output logogens", however, here we use the currently more standard terminology.

Butterworth, 1983, and Nickels, 2001a for discussion). Neither does it address the storage and access of grammatical information to do with words (lexical-syntax) such as grammatical number (whether a word is singular or plural), or, in languages where it is required, grammatical gender (e.g., in French whether a noun is feminine and requires a feminine determiner "la chaise" (the chair), or masculine "le bureau" (the desk)). In common with many theories of spoken word production it also does not specify processes subsequent to selection of phonemes (phonological and phonetic encoding), for further discussion see Wilshire, 2008).

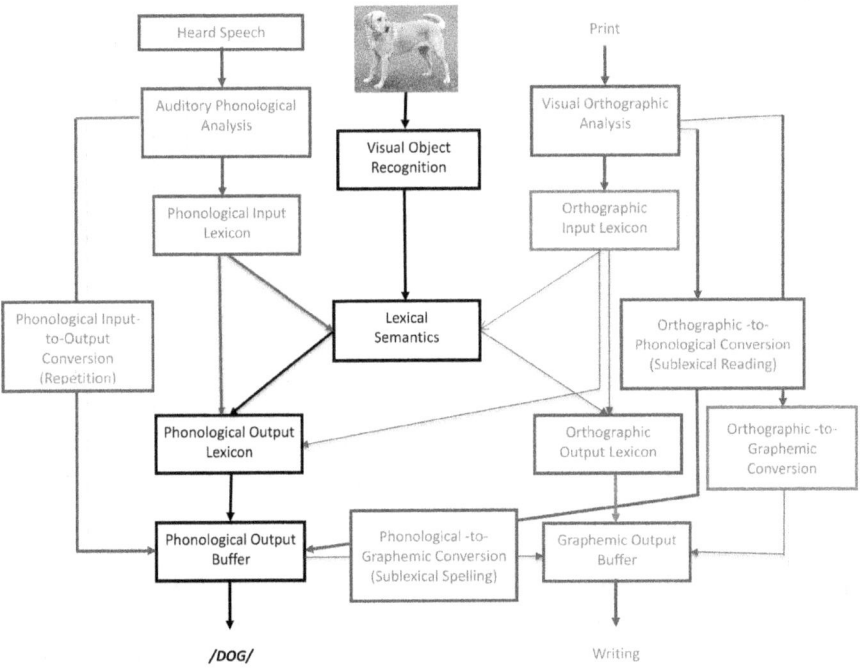

Figure 1: The Logogen model (based on Morton, 1985; Patterson and Shewell, 1987).

2.2 The Two-Step model

The Two-Step model was proposed by Levelt et al. (1999) as an extension of Levelt's (1989) theory of spoken word production and has been implemented computationally in the WEAVER++ model (e.g. Roelofs, 1997; 2014). This model specifically aimed to account for results of experimental (chronometric) studies with unimpaired speakers. Like the Logogen model, this model is strictly serial. Even though it is called the 'Two-Step' model, it differentiates between three significant phases. The first phase involves activation of lexical concepts (at the level we will refer to as lexical semantics). A lexical concept is an information unit that can be mapped directly onto language: it concerns 'meaning that can be packaged into one lexical item, or a lexical phrase'. This 'lexical meaning package' is then mapped onto a lexical-syntactic node (a

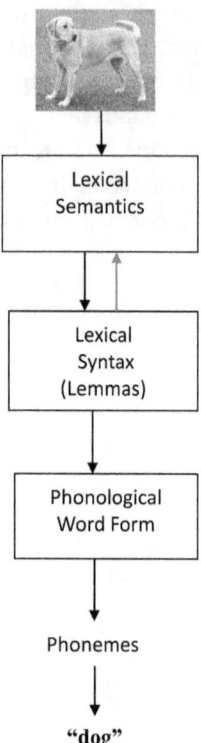

Figure 2: Levelt et al.'s Two-Step model (1999)

lemma). The lemma specifies, for example, whether the lexical item needs to be expressed as a noun, verb or other word class, whether it is being used to refer to a single or multiple object, and therefore needs to be expressed as singular or plural, or to refer to an event in the past, present or future requiring different grammatical tense markers. Other grammatical differences between words are stored at this level as well, for example, many languages, including English, differentiate between 'count' and 'mass' nouns and other languages, including Italian, French, German and Hebrew differentiate between a number of grammatical genders. This level is also known as the *lemma* level (since Kempen & Huijbers, 1983). However, importantly, the definition of what a lemma constituted shifted between Levelt (1989), where it encompassed both lexical semantics and lexical syntax, and Levelt et al. (1999), where it was purely syntactic. According to Levelt et al. (1999), the lexical-semantic and lexical-syntactic levels interact with each other and are therefore active simultaneously. However, only a single lexical-syntactic entry is mapped onto the next level, the phonological word form level: only one selected lexical-syntactic entry activates its corresponding word form. Levelt (1989; 1999) described this processing step as the 'major rift' in lexicalisation, and it also explains the name of his model:

The Two-Step model – the first step refers to all processes prior to lexical-syntactic selection, and the second step refers to everything following, concerning phonological and phonetic processing. The phonological word form level includes information about the internal structure of the word form including, the phonemes, syllabic structure and word stress. After the phonological word form has been selected, its corresponding phonemes will then be activated and selected at the phoneme level, and inserted into syllable frames, which in turn map onto stored articulatory plans for syllables, which are then unpacked prior to articulation (see Figure 2).

2.3 The Interactive Activation model

In contrast to the two previous models, the Interactive Activation model (see Figure 3) was specifically designed to account for speech error data both from unimpaired

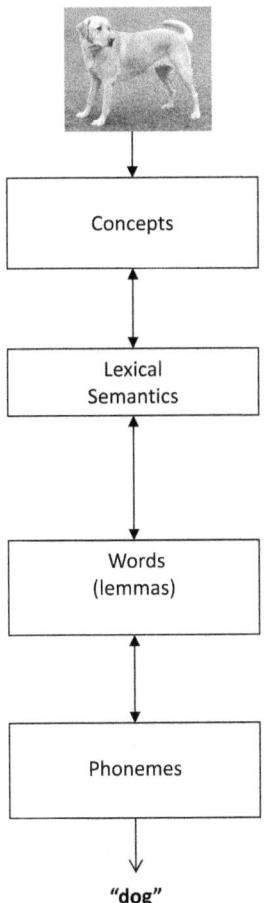

Figure 3: The Interactive Activation Model (based on Dell, Schwartz, Martin, Saffran, & Gagnon, 1997)

participants and those with aphasia. This model was a development of Dell's (1986) earlier, more comprehensive, account of spoken word production. Like Levelt and colleagues, Dell (1986) also proposed a two-step architecture with the first step involving a lexical-semantic level that maps onto a lexical-syntactic level, which, in turn in a second step, maps lexical-syntax onto a word form level and finally a phoneme level. In contrast, Dell et al. (1997) no longer include a word form level with the lexical-syntactic word node level mapping directly onto single phonemes[2].

The major difference between this model and the Logogen and Levelt et al.'s Two-Step model is that it allows both cascading of activation and interactivity between levels. If one lexical node in the network is activated (regardless of at which level), it activates all nodes that it is connected to (at levels above and below). In one activation cycle, each node receives activation and the activation level also decays back towards zero. After a fixed number of activation cycles, the most active node at the word (lexical-syntactic) level is selected and receives a jolt of extra activation which is sent to its phonemes which are selected in turn. The model can be used to simulate impaired performance by reducing the connection strength between levels (semantic connections or phonological connections; Foygel & Dell, 2000).

2.4 The Interactive Network model

Another prominent word production model is the Interactive Network Model (Caramazza, 1997; Caramazza & Miozzo, 1997; 1998), which essentially maps meaning onto form for word production, but without assuming an intervening level of lexical-syntactic processing. This model incorporates cascading feed forward links between levels. First, a lexical-semantic network is activated that represents semantic features, which in turn activates, in parallel, a phonological word form network and an orthographic word form network (only the former is discussed in this review). The phonological word form network activates the word form's corresponding sounds at the phoneme level. The primary activation of lexical-syntax happens via the phonological word form network (see Figure 4). Pre-activation of lexical-syntax via semantics (see the dotted line in Figure 4) is only possible for syntactic features that have semantic content (for example, word category or number), whereas syntactic features such as 'grammatical gender' are semantically empty and can therefore only be activated after activation of the word form. This order of activation makes a strong claim of phonological mediation before syntax can be accessed, an assumption that differs from Levelt's Two-Step model where phonological information and syntactic information are both activated simultaneously (at different levels)[3].

---

[2] Hence, in this theory the word form representation can best be conceived of as the links between the lexical-syntactic word nodes and the individual phonemes.
[3] Although early descriptions of the Two-Step model suggested that phonology was only activated after selection of lexical syntax, Levelt et al. (1999) make it clear that selection of lexical-syntax is not always required prior to activation of phonological form: nodes at the lexical-syntactic level activate both lexical-syntactic diacritics and phonological form simultaneously.

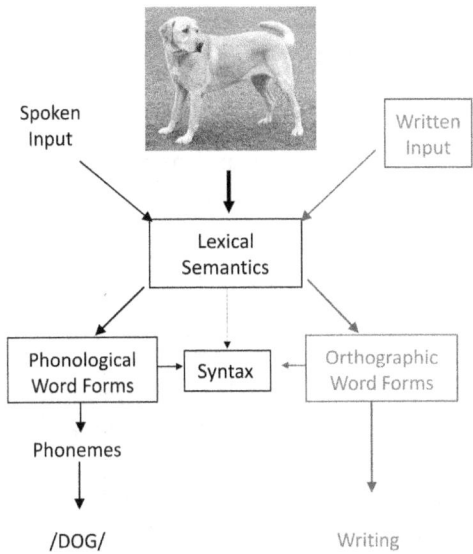

Figure 4: The Independent Network (IN) model (based on Caramazza, 1997; Caramazza & Miozzo, 1998).

2.5 Summary

In sum, Morton's Logogen model is widely used as a clinical tool for interpreting the results of assessments. It is a strictly serial and thresholded model, and does not allow for cascading of activation. It also does not include representation of lexical-syntax. Here, Levelt and colleague's Two-Step model can help out, which is also strictly serial, but incorporates a lexical-syntactic level – some authors have integrated features of both Levelt et al's Two-Step and the Logogen model into a single composite model (e.g.. Biran & Friedmann, 2012; Nickels, 1997). Caramazza's Interactive Network model also includes lexical-syntax but this is activated via the word form, and this model allows cascading of activation from one level to the next. Finally, Dell and colleagues's Interactive Activation model includes both cascading and feedback of activation between all processing levels, and incorporates a lexical-syntactic level.

Overall, each model contributes and highlights different aspects of processing mechanisms, and processing order that are important in spoken word production.

3 Psycholinguistic variables influencing spoken word production

Different stimulus properties have been found to affect picture naming speed and/or accuracy and their effects have been attributed to different levels of processing (for review of effects on latency in participants without language impairments see Alario, Ferrand, Laganaro, New, Frauenfelder, & Segui, 2004; and for effects on accuracy in people with aphasia see, for example, Nickels & Howard, 1995; Howard, Best, Bruce, & Gatehouse, 1995). We focus on those variables that are relevant for spoken word production, but note that other variables are relevant specifically to the processing of pictures in picture naming (e.g., visual complexity, image agreement, name agreement).

3.1 Imageability

The variable *imageability* is commonly attributed to the semantic system. *Imageability* is a variable which reflects a rating of how easy it is to visualise an image from memory. For example, *'market'* is rated as harder to visualise than *'apple'*. In general, items high in imageability are easier (faster or more accurate) to produce than items low in imageabilty (see for example, Kremin, Lorenz, De Wilde, Perrier, Arabia, Labonde & Buitoni, 2003).

3.2 Typicality

Typicality relates to how prototypical an item is in relation to other members of its category (e.g., how well represents 'penguin' the category of birds). Rossiter and Best (2013) obtained typicality ratings from people with aphasia and showed that it was a significant predictor of picture naming accuracy, with generally better performance for typical items. To date this variable has been mostly neglected when controlling for psycholinguistic variables on (spoken) word production (see also Sandberg, Sebastian, & Kiran, 2012).

3.3 Semantic neighbourhood

Semantic neighbourhood density refers to how many items there are that are related in meaning to the target word (although there are a number of different ways that this has been calculated in the literature; e.g., Bormann, 2011; Kittredge, Dell, & Schwartz, 2007; Mirman, 2011). Whether there are facilitatory or inhibitory effects may depend on the semantic relationship (e.g., shared feature (cat-dog); associate (cat-basket)). The locus of these effects is likely to be in the interface between semantic and lexical-syntax processing (or semantics and phonological form if there is no intervening syntactic level as, for example, proposed by Caramazza, 1997).

3.4 Frequency

Frequency is measured from objective counts of how often a word is used in everyday (spoken) language. For example, 'phone' is uttered more frequently than 'abode'. The more frequently a word is used, the faster it is produced and/or the less errors occur. *Frequency* is strongly correlated with *age-of-acquisition and length*. It is generally assumed to have its effects at the level of the lexical system, for spoken word production this would concern the phonological output lexicon. However, the issue is not without debate (see, e.g., Jescheniak & Levelt, 1994) and some authors suggest that frequency affects all levels of processing (see for example, Navarette, Benedetta, Alario, & Costa, 2006; Kittredge, Dell, Verkuilen, & Schwartz, 2008; Knobel, Finkbeiner, & Caramazza, 2008). In theories with interaction between levels, in particular, the effects of frequency may be observed across all levels of processing.

3.5 Age-of-acquisition

Age of Acquisition is strongly correlated with frequency, imageability and word length, and is usually measured as a rating of the age at which a word was first learned. Usually early acquired words are processed faster and are less error prone than words learned late in life. While there has been some debate regarding the locus of age-of-acquisition effects, many researchers suggest it relates to retrieval from the phonological output lexicon (e.g. Alario et al., 2004).

3.6 Phonological neighborhood

Phonological Neighborhood is defined as the number of words which differ from the target by only one phoneme (e.g., mine, pine, mime, mane). The effects of phonological neighbourhood density are complex, with some authors suggesting facilitatory effects (e.g., Baus, Costa & Carreiras, 2008; Mirman, Kittredge, & Dell, 2010) and others (e.g., Sadat, Martin, Costa, & Alario, 2014) suggesting that a dense phonological neighborhood causes inhibition in both unimpaired and impaired spoken word production. Phonological neighbourhood has been hypothesised to have its effects at the phonological word form level, the phoneme level and/or between these levels.

3.7 Word length

Word Length has its effects after the word form has been accessed. Although there is little evidence for an effect of *word length* on picture naming latencies, words with more phonemes are more prone to error than words with fewer phonemes in people with aphasia (Nickels & Howard, 1995; 2004). This has been attributed to impairments of the phonological buffer (that serves as a working memory for meaningful sounds) and/or phonological encoding: activation and maintenance of activation of phonemes, and/or selecting phonemes and/or inserting those phonemes into syllable frames.

4 The impairment of spoken word production

The cognitive neuropsychological approach uses as its core methodology the localisation of language breakdown within cognitive models of language processing, such as those discussed above. This approach not only ensures that we understand the breakdown of language in all its different forms, but also helps us to acknowledge the very many possibilities for language breakdown that can potentially be observed within a given theory (Coltheart, Patterson, & Marshall 1980; Marshall, 1984). In turn, the different patterns of language impairment can help us to understand the limitations of our current theories, and hence can be the basis for further expansion of our theoretical understanding.

4.1 Acquired impairments: Word finding difficulties in adult speakers with aphasia

In this section, we will demonstrate how to localise the source of speech errors in the language production system, although as is noted below it is not a one-to-one correspondence between speech errors and level of impairment (see also, Lorenz & Ziegler, 2009).

We will illustrate this localisation using examples from three people with aphasia following a stroke: GSW (Nickels, unpublished), AER and CI (Nickels, 1992; Nickels & Howard, 1995; 2004). On the same set of pictures, AER, GSW, and CI show approximately the same accuracy in picture naming (AER: 54% correct, GSW 52%, CI 58%). However, importantly, even though accuracy is similar, we cannot conclude that they have the same impairment. Critically, their error responses differ which gives us (partial) insight into their level of breakdown (see Figure 5). AER and GSW produce responses that are related to their targets in meaning (semantic errors; e.g 'trumpet' produced for 'saxophone') or descriptions of the target (e.g., 'a dog's residence' for 'kennel'). In contrast, CI's errors consist mostly of responses which share many of the phonological segments of the target (e.g., producing /ɛləvænt/ for 'elefant').

We will now discuss the origins of these errors, within the architecture derived from the Logogen model as depicted in Figure 1.

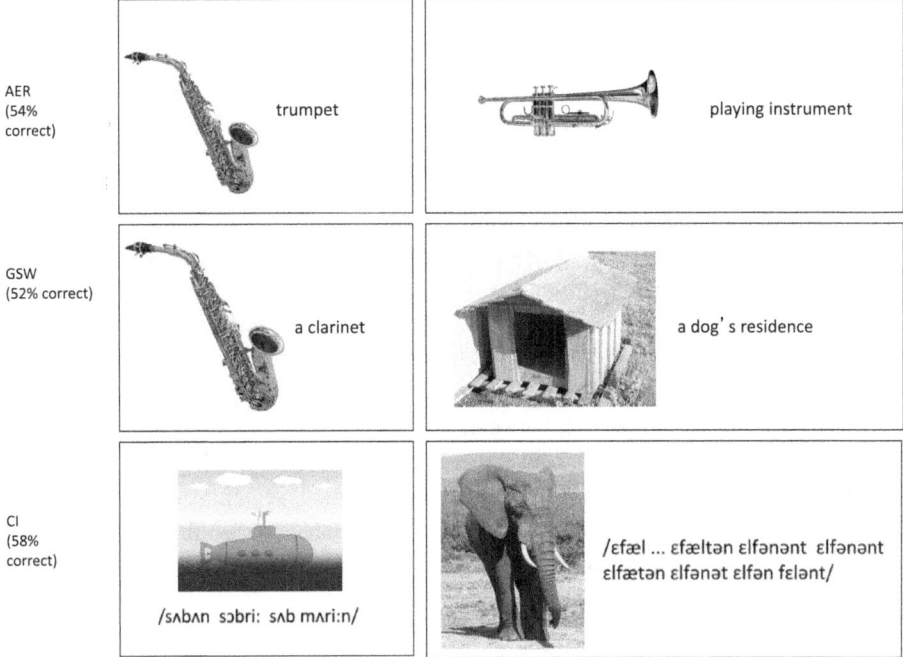

Figure 5: Different picture naming responses of AER, GSW, and CI

4.1.1 Origins of semantic errors

Semantic errors, such as naming a saxophone as a 'trumpet', are common in the spoken word production of many people with aphasia but also occur in the speech errors of unimpaired speakers. Importantly, this type of error can originate from more than one functional location in the process of spoken word production (e.g., Caramazza & Hillis, 1990; Lorenz & Ziegler, 2009): i) an impaired semantic system; ii) the links between the semantic and the phonological levels; iii) the phonological output lexicon (as a framework see Figure 1).

4.1.2 Determining the source of semantic errors?

If the impairment concerns the semantic system directly (e.g., JBR, Warrington & Shallice, 1984; JCU: Howard & Orchard-Lisle, 1984), tasks that use different modalities that use semantic information will all be impaired (e.g., spoken picture naming, written picture naming, spoken and written word-picture matching). However, tasks that do not require semantic processing can be unaffected (in the absence of any additional impairment; e.g., reading aloud of regular words or non-words, auditory repetition). Presenting a phonological cue for a semantically related item might cause the 'wrong' target production. For example, when a picture of a tiger is presented, giving the phoneme /l/ may trigger the response 'lion'.

If the impairment is located in the link between the semantic system and the phonological word form level or at the phonological level itself, then (in the absence of additional impairments) comprehension of spoken and written words will be intact, as will written naming.

However, it is important to note, that not only can semantic errors arise as a result of these different impairments, these impairments can result in different types of error, although semantic errors are the most common: Each of the three possible sources of impairment also can result in 'no responses' and, when the impairment is severe, responses unrelated to the target.

For impairments in the link between the semantic system and the phonological word form level, other errors may have some of the characteristics of 'tip-of-the-tongue' responses: for example, producing a detailed semantic description such as 'it's a wild animal', or 'it has stripes'). Sometimes, depending on the target language, grammatical gender might be available in such a word form search (e.g., for German 'der' ... 'der' ... [Tiger]).

4.1.3 Origins of phonological errors

Responses that share sounds with their targets (e.g., producing /ɛləvænt/ for 'elefant', or 'sheet' for 'sheep') can also arise from different sources: i) the phonological output lexicon, ii) the link from the phonological output lexicon to the phoneme level or buffer, iii) the phoneme system/ buffer itself, and iv) phonetic processes.

4.1.4 Determining the source of phonological errors

With all levels of impairment that result in phonological errors, comprehension and written naming should be unimpaired.

Traditionally, phonological output lexicon impairments have been thought to result in phonological errors (e.g., Nickels, 1997). For example, Kay and Ellis (1987) reported the (now) classic case of EST, who suffered from phonological anomia, showing intact comprehension, but poor spoken output. However, more recently it has been debated whether impairments to the phonological lexicon can result in phonological errors (compare e.g., Nickels, 2001, & Friedmann et al., 2013). It is clear that with this level of impairment, all non-lexical production tasks should be unimpaired (reading aloud of regular words and nonwords, repetition). The phonological errors that arise from this level of impairment will tend to be real words (e.g. 'sheet' for 'sheep').

If the impairment is in the links from word form level to phoneme level or at the phoneme level itself, phoneme deletions, additions, or exchanges are expected and longer words will be particularly impaired. In contrast, metrical structure is generally intact (e.g., syllable number, stress pattern).

If the impairment is at post-phoneme level/ post-buffer, involving phonological and phonetic encoding (e.g. inserting phonemes into syllable plans, retrieving, unpacking and producing syllable patterns), the pattern may be similar to those of a phoneme level/buffer impairment, however, in addition, there may be effects of syllable complexity on performance (e.g., presence vs absence of consonant clusters) and features of apraxia of speech. Theories of spoken word production such as those introduced earlier often not specify these levels of processing. For these types of impairments, we require a model that maps lexical and post-lexical processes onto motor processes (e.g., Hickok, 2012).

4.2 Developmental impairments: Word-finding difficulties in children

While in acquired disorders, problems in spoken word retrieval are described as 'anomia', in the developmental literature they are more commonly called 'word-finding difficulties' (WFD). These impairments are not uncommon in children, and they often co-occur with other language and/or cognitive impairments (Best, 2005, Friedmann et al., 2013): Word finding difficulties are reported to occur in 23% of children with language impairment (Dockrell, Messer, George, & Wilson, 1998) and in 50% of children with learning disabilities (German, 1998). Children produce the similar kinds of errors to those that are observed in acquired anomia.

As is common in developmental fields, often there has been a tendency for WFD to be ascribed to a single underlying impairment. However, it is clear, that like adults different children may have different underlying impairments (e.g., Best, 2005) and adult language production theories may be used for the localisation of underlying impairment(s) of WFD in children, (e.g., Levelt et al. 1989; 1999) as, to date, no detailed developmental theory of lexical access exists (Dockrell & Messer, 2004). In the same way as in adults, WFD can be the result of impairments of both *storage of* or *access to* semantic or phonological representations (Best, 2005; Faust, Dimitrovsky and Davidi, 1997; Kail and Leonard, 1986). In addition to modality-specific accounts, WFD in the context of co-occurring specific language impairments and/or dyslexia have been accounted for by more general underlying deficits, such as impaired auditory processing (e.g., Bishop, 1997; Tallal & Stark, 1981) which are beyond the scope of this review.

Despite the fact that a diagnostic criterion of word finding difficulties has been better comprehension than production, semantic impairments are nevertheless commonly ascribed as an underlying locus of impairment. Children with this level of impairment have difficulties in both language production and comprehension (Best,

2005). A number of studies have argued for a phonological locus of impairment, as children with WFD were found to produce lower proportions of semantic errors (McGregor, 1997), and higher proportions of phonological errors (Dockrell, Messer & George, 2001) compared to controls. Moreover, as noted above, semantic errors can be caused by phonological access problems (McGregor, 1994; Messer & Dockrell, 2006). Evidence for a phonological origin of children's WFD comes from studies which have found an influence of lexical variables (e.g., frequency, phonological neighbourhood density) on naming accuracy and error types (German & Newman, 2004; Newman & German, 2002), single case studies which have found impaired performance on phonologically based tasks (Chiat & Hunt, 1993; Constable, Stackhouse & Wells, 1997), and intervention studies where phonologically based treatment improved word finding by decreasing semantic and/or phonological errors (e.g., Best, 2005; German, 2002; McGregor, 1994).

In sum, there is no single underlying cause of WFD in children: just as in adults with aphasia, individual children have different levels of impairment as is clearly illustrated in the case studies described by Best (2005).

5 Impairment and theory – A reciprocal relationship

Just as theoretical accounts can help us to understand the nature of language impairment(s), language impairments can help us to evaluate the adequacy of our theoretical models and further specify the nature of processing and representation. Here, we use an example from the empirical investigation of lexical-syntactic impairments to inform our understanding of lexical-syntactic processing.

Countability is a grammatical and semantic characteristic which divides nouns into mass nouns (e.g., milk, rice) and count nouns (e.g., chair, cat). Mass nouns are unusual in that they cannot be grammatically pluralised (e.g., cats vs. *rices), combined with numerals (e.g., three cats vs. *three rices) or quantifiers that denumerate (e.g., many cats vs. *many rice). Semantically, count nouns mostly represent individual entities with clear boundaries, while mass nouns often represent substances and aggregates without clear boundaries. There has been debate in the literature regarding whether the difference between mass and count nouns is coded at the level of lexical-syntax or lexical-semantics.

We have used data from people with aphasia to inform this debate (Fieder, Nickels, Biedermann, & Best, 2014; Fieder, Nickels, Biedermann, & Best, 2015). RAP and DEH were more impaired in describing pictures with noun phrases when those phrases required mass nouns (e.g., some rice) compared to when they required count nouns (e.g., a cat) (RAP 67% mass, 90% count; DEH 17% mass, 77% count). Interestingly, neither DEH nor RAP had more difficulties in naming pictures with a mass noun compared to count nouns when a phrase was not required (e.g., rice vs. cat; RAP 81% mass, 72% count; DEH 69% mass, 69% count). This allowed us to conclude that the problem with mass noun phrases was not due to a problem with the representation and processing of the individual mass nouns. We also determined that DEH and RAP did not have a problem with producing the determiners they needed to use to make the phrases – the same determiner could be produced correctly when needed for count noun phrases: For example, producing "*a rice" for "some rice" (mass), but correctly producing "some cats" (count); or producing "*these sugar" for "this sugar" but "this cat" (count) see Figure 6a and 6b). This pattern indicated that the phonological forms of the determiners were accessible.

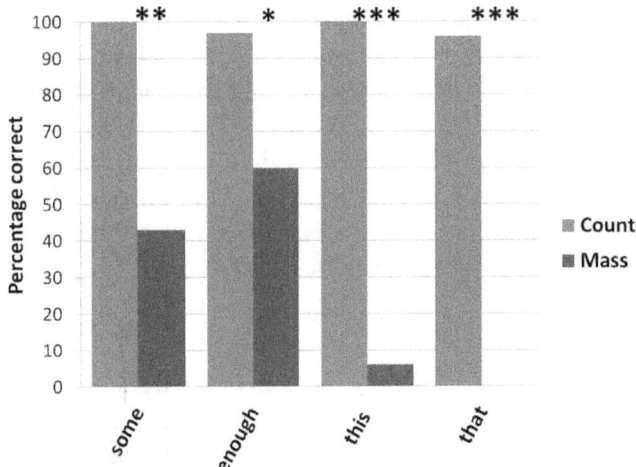

Figure 6a: RAP's determiner accuracy for the determiners which are shared between mass and singular/plural count nouns in the different picture naming tasks with NPs.

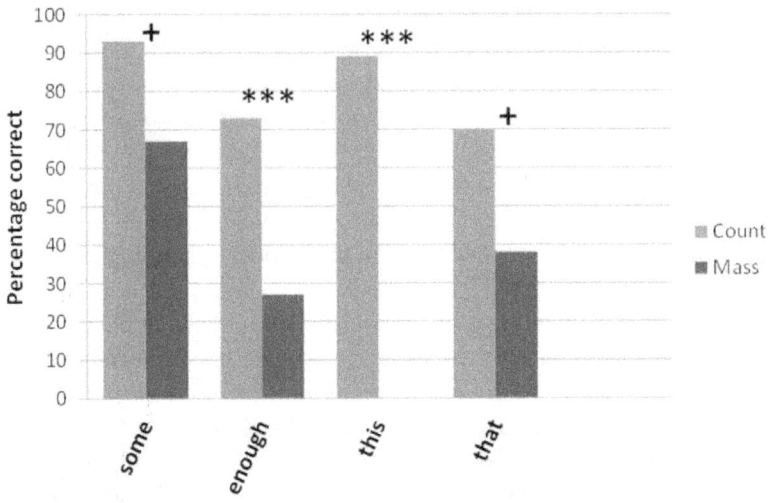

Figure 6b: DEH's determiner accuracy for the determiners which are shared between mass and singular/plural count nouns in the different picture naming tasks with NPs.

To explain these data, where the same words (determiners) can be produced in one context but not another, requires a model which can distinguish between the contexts. Here, the contexts are different only in that one refers to mass nouns and the other to count nouns – which establishes a difference in lexical syntax. Hence, only models that include lexical syntax can account for the data – which is evidence against the Logogen model. Moreover, as in Caramazza et al.'s Independent Network model (Figure 4), lexical syntax is only activated *after* phonology, it is also hard to see how this model can account for the data. However, Levelt et al.'s Two-Step model (Figure 2) and the Dell et al.'s Interactive Activation model (Figure 3) both comprise a lexical-syntactic level which *precedes* activation of phonology, and are therefore consistent with these data (although Dell et al. is not sufficiently specified to unequivocally determine).

In sum, RAP and DEH's mass specific difficulties could be ascribed to an impairment at the lexical-syntactic level. The results provided evidence that countability (whether a noun is mass or count) is specified at a separate lexical-syntactic level and influences the selection of mass noun determiners.

6 Treatment as a tool for theory development

Once again, while localising impairment within theoretical accounts can help guide treatment, Nickels, Kohnen, & Biedermann (2010) highlighted the potential of treatment as a tool to develop and test cognitive theories. One of the major methods used in treatment to inform theory is generalisation, a concept in treatment that refers to improvement of items beyond the treated sets. Generalisation can occur within modality, across items or across modalities. In this section, we will demonstrate how two opposing psycholinguistic theories concerning the representation(s) of homophones (words that sound the same, but have different meanings, such as 'knight' and 'night') can be disentangled with the help of treatment of anomia. For homophones, the Two-Step model (Levelt et al., 1999) and the Interactive Activation model (e.g., Dell, 1990) propose that the two homophonic words share a phonological representation at word form level (see Figure 7a), whereas Caramazza's Interactive Network model proposes each homophone has an independent phonological representation (e.g., Caramazza, 1997) (see Figure 7b).

Our approach, inspired by Blanken (1989), capitalised on the fact that phonological treatment of anomia in aphasia usually results in item-specific improvement which is attributed to improved retrieval of the phonological form from the lexicon (Nickels, 2002). This provided an ideal test basis for examining the representation of homophones: if there are independent word form representations for homophones, then treatment of one homophone ("night") should not improve naming of the other (untreated) homophone ("knight"). If, however, homophones share a phonological

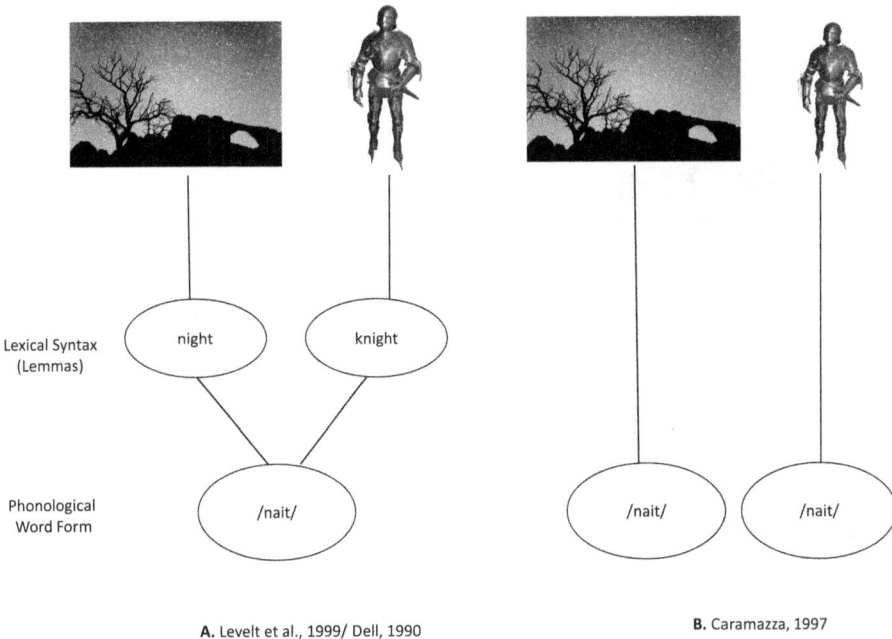

Figure 7: Opposing assumptions about homophone representations

representation, improved naming of one homophone ("night") following treatment should generalise to improved naming of the untreated homophone partner ("knight"). This underlying hypothesis underpinned three experiments with three people with aphasia and breakdown at the phonological word form level. All three experiments used the same paradigm: treatment for spoken picture naming using a phonological cueing hierarchy (one training was carried out in German: Biedermann, Nickels, & Blanken, 2002; and two in Australian English: Biedermann & Nickels, 2008a;b). The picture naming treatment involved the training of only one homophone partner, while the other was never depicted or referred to during treatment. Before and after training, picture naming performance for the treated homophone, the untreated homophone partner, an untreated phonologically related control group, and a semantically related control group was measured. After treatment we found the treated *and* the untreated homophone partner improved in naming performance, while phonologically and semantically related control items did not improve, as was predicted by the shared representation hypothesis. For example, treatment of 'night' improved naming for not only 'night' but also 'knight', but no improvement was observed for 'kite' or 'day' (see Figure 8).

This study illustrates how we can use the effects of treatment of spoken word production impairments to reveal the underlying organisation in our mental lexicon: in this case we found evidence supporting shared phonological representations for

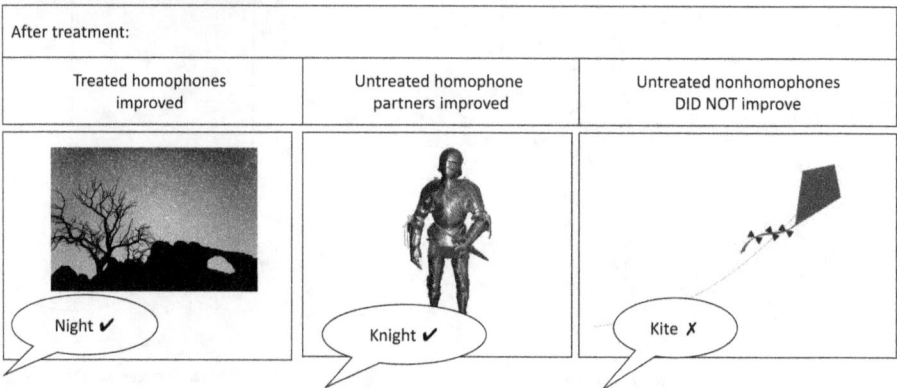

Figure 8: Homophone treatment results (e.g., Biedermann and Nickels, 2008a;b)

homophones, that supports the assumption of Levelt et al.'s Two-Step model (Figure 2) and Dell et al.'s Interactive Activation model (Figure 3), and rejects the independent word form representation view postulated by Caramazza et al.'s Independent Network model (Figure 4). The Logogen model (Figure 1) is agnostic when it comes to shared or independent or shared word form representations in the phonological word form lexicon.

7 Conclusions

This chapter has aimed to highlight the multi-faceted issue of how spoken word production can breakdown. Speech errors that look the same might mask different sources of breakdown, but can be disentangled by careful use of convergent evidence from additional tasks, that enable identification of differences in (the) functional deficit(s). As Marshall (1984) first pointed out, because of the number of different components and connections in the language system, there are many hundreds of different potential combinations of impairment (see also Coltheart, 2001), consequently a syndrome-based approach is inappropriate and we need to work out the precise breakdown for each individual. The underlying theories that are needed to achieve this require an interdisciplinary approach. It requires evidence from psycholinguistic data sets as well as cognitive neuropsychological assessment tools and data sets together to inform our theories of the mental lexicon. It is only with well specified theories that we will be able to truly understand the nature of the impairment in language disorders and, hence, ensure that our treatment is accurately targeted.

References

Alario, F.-Xavier, Ludovic Ferrand, Marina Laganaro, Boris New, Uli Frauenfelder & Juan Segui. 2004. Predictors of picture naming speed. *Behavior Research Methods, Instruments, & Computers* 36 (1). 140–155.
Baus, Cristina, Albert Costa & Manuel Carreiras. 2008. Neighbourhood density and frequency effects in speech production: A case for interactivity. *Language and Cognitive Processes* 23 (6). 866–888.
Best, Wendy. 2005. Investigation of a new intervention for children with word-finding problems. *International Journal of Language and Communication Disorders* 40 (3). 279–318.
Biedermann, Britta, Gerhard Blanken & Lyndsey Nickels. 2002. The representation of homophones: Evidence from remediation. *Aphasiology* 16 (10–11). 1115–1136.
Biedermann, Britta & Lyndsey Nickels. 2008. The representation of homophones: More evidence from the remediation of anomia. *Cortex* 44 (3). 276–293.
Biedermann, Britta & Lyndsey Nickels. 2008. Homographic and heterographic homophones in speech production: Does orthography matter? *Cortex* 44 (6). 683–697.
Biran, Michal & Naama Friedmann. 2012. The representation of lexical-syntactic information: Evidence from syntactic and lexical retrieval impairments in aphasia. *Cortex* 48 (9). 1103–1127.
Bishop, Dorothy. 1997. *Uncommon understanding: Development and disorders of language comprehension in children*. Hove: Psychology Press.
Blanken, Gerhard. 1989. Wortfindungsstörungen und verbales Lernen: Eine Einzelfallstudie. *Neurolinguistik* 2. 107–126.
Bormann, Tobias. 2011. The role of lexical-semantic neighborhood in object naming: Implications for models of lexical access. *Frontiers in psychology* 2. 1–11.
Butterworth, Brian. 1983. Lexical representation. In Brian Butterworth (ed.), *Language production Vol. 2: Development, writing and other language processes*, 257–294. London: Academic Press.
Caramazza, Alfonso. 1997. How many levels of processing are there in lexical access? *Cognitive Neuropsychology* 14 (1). 177–208.
Caramazza, Alfonso & Argye Hillis. 1990. Where do semantic errors come from? *Cortex* 26 (1). 95–122.
Caramazza, Alfonso & Michelle Miozzo. 1997. The relation between syntactic and phonological knowledge in lexical access: Evidence from the 'tip-of-the-tongue' phenomenon. *Cognition* 64 (3). 309–343.
Caramazza, Alfonso & Michelle Miozzo. 1998. More is not always better: A response to Roelofs, Meyer, and Levelt. *Cognition* 69 (2). 231–241.
Chiat, Shula & Jon Hunt. 1993. Connections between phonology and semantics: An exploration of lexical processing in a language-impaired child. *Child Language Teaching and Therapy* 9 (3). 200–213.
Coltheart, Max. 2001. Assumptions and methods in cognitive neuropsychology. In Brenda Rapp (ed.), *The handbook of cognitive neuropsychology*. Hove: Psychology Press.
Coltheart, Max, Karolyn Patterson & John Marshall. 1980. *Deep dyslexia*. Henley-on-Thames: Routledge.

Constable, Alison, Joy Stackhouse & Bill Wells. 1997. Developmental word-finding difficulties and phonological processing: The case of the missing handcuffs. *Applied Psycholinguistics* 18. 507–536.

Dell, Gary. 1986. A spreading-activation theory of retrieval in sentence production. *Psychological Review* 93 (3). 283–321.

Dell, Gary, Myrna Schwartz, Nadine Martin, Eleanor Saffran & Deborah Gagnon. 1997. Lexical access in aphasic and nonaphasic speakers. *Psychological review* 104 (4). 801–838.

Dell, Gary. 1990. Effects of frequency and vocabulary type on phonological speech errors. *Language and Cognitive Processes* 5. 313–349.

Dockrell, Julie & David Messer. 2004. Lexical acquisition in the school years. In Ruth Berman (ed.), *Language development: Psycholinguistic and typological perspectives*, 35–52. New York: John Benjamins.

Dockrell, Julie, David Messer & R. George. 2001. Patterns of naming objects and actions in children with word finding difficulties. *Language and Cognitive Processes* 16 (2–3). 261–286.

Dockrell, Julie, David Messer, R. George & A. Ralli. 2003. Beyond naming patterns in children with WFD-Definitions for nouns and verbs. *Journal of Neurolinguistics* 16. 191–211.

Dockrell, Julie, David Messer, R. George & G. Wilson. 1998. Children with word-finding difficulties – Prevalence, presentation and naming problems. *International Journal of Language and Communication Disorders* 33. 445–454.

Faust, Miriam, Lily Dimitrovsky & Shira Davidi. 1997. Naming difficulties in language disabled children: Preliminary findings with the application of the tip of the tongue paradigm. *Journal of Speech, Language and Hearing Research* 40. 1026–1036.

Fieder, Nora, Lyndsey Nickels, Britta Biedermann & Wendy Best. 2014. From "some butter" to "a butter": An investigation of mass and count representation and processing. *Cognitive Neuropsychology* 31 (4). 313–349.

Fieder, Nora, Lyndsey Nickels, Britta Biedermann & Wendy Best. 2015. How 'some garlic' becomes 'a garlic' or 'some onion': Mass and count processing in aphasia. *Neuropsychologia* 75. 626–645.

Foygel, Dan & Gary Dell. 2000. Models of impaired lexical access in speech production. *Journal of Memory and Language* 43. 182–216.

Friedmann, Naama, Michal Biran & Dror Dotan. 2013. Lexical retrieval and its breakdown in aphasia and developmental language impairments. In Cedric Boeckx & Kleanthes Grohmann (eds.), *The Cambridge handbook of biolinguistics*, 350–374. New York: Cambridge University Press.

German, Diane. 1998. Prevalence estimates for word-finding difficulties in LD students: Implications for assessment/instructional accommodations. Paper presented at the annual meeting of the Learning Disabilities Association, Washington, D.C.

German, Diane. 2002. A phonologically based strategy to improve word-finding abilities in children. *Communication Disorders Quarterly* 23 (4). 179–192.

German, Diane & Rochelle Newman. 2004. The impact of lexical factors on children's word finding errors. *Journal of Speech, Language, and Hearing Research* 47. 624–636.

Goldrick, Matthew & Brenda Rapp. 2002. A restricted interaction account (RIA) of spoken word production: The best of both worlds. *Aphasiology* 16 (1–2). 20–55.

Green, David. 1998. Mental control of the bilingual lexico-semantic system. *Bilingualism: Language and cognition* 1 (02). 67–81.

Green, David & Jubin Abutalebi. 2013. Language control in bilinguals: The adaptive control hypothesis. *Journal of Cognitive Psychology* 25 (5). 515–530.

Harley, Trevor. 2013. *The psychology of language: From data to theory*. New York: Psychology Press.

Hickok, Georgy. 2012. Computational neuroanatomy of speech production. *Nature Reviews Neuroscience* 13 (2). 135–145.

Howard, David, Wendy Best, Carolyn Bruce & Claire Gatehouse. 1995. Operativity and animacy effects in aphasic naming. *International Journal of Language & Communication Disorders* 30 (3). 286–302.

Howard, David & Virginia Orchard-Lisle. 1984. On the origin of semantic errors in naming: Evidence from the case of a global aphasic. *Cognitive Neuropsychology* 1 (2). 163–190.

Jescheniak, Jörg & Willem Levelt. 1994. Word frequency effects in speech production: Retrieval of syntactic information and of phonological form. *Journal of Experimental Psychology: Learning, Memory, and Cognition* 20 (4). 824.

Kail, Robert & Laurence Leonard. 1986. Word-finding abilities in language-impaired children. *ASHA Monographs* 25.

Kay, Janet, Ruth Lesser & Max Coltheart. 1992. *PALPA: Psycholinguistic assessments of language processing in aphasia*. New York: Psychology Press.

Kay, Janet & Andrew Ellis. 1987. A cognitive neuropsychological case study of anomia: Implications for psychological models of word retrieval. *Brain* 110 (3). 613–629.

Kempen, Gerard & Pieter Huijbers. 1983. The lexicalization process in sentence production and naming: Indirect election of words. *Cognition* 14. 185–209.

Kittredge, Audrey, Gary Dell & Myrna Schwartz. 2007. Omissions in aphasic picture naming: Late age-of-acquisition is the culprit, not low semantic density. *Brain and Language* 103 (1). 132–133.

Kittredge, Audrey, Gary Dell, Jay Verkuilen & Myrna Schwartz. 2008. Where is the effect of frequency in word production? Insights from aphasic picture-naming errors. *Cognitive Neuropsychology* 25. 463–492.

Kittredge Audrey, Gary Dell & Myrna Schwartz. 2010. Naming and repetition in aphasia: steps, routes, and frequency effects. *Journal of Memory and Language* 63. 541–559.

Knobel, Mark, Matthew Finkbeiner & Alfonso Caramazza. 2008. The many places of frequency: Evidence for a novel locus of the lexical frequency effect in word production. *Cognitive Neuropsychology* 25 (2). 256–286.

Kremin, Helgard, Antje Lorenz, Martine De Wilde, Danièle Perrier, Caterine Arabia, Emilie Labonde & Claire-Lise Buitoni. 2003. The relative effects of imageability and age-of-acquisition on aphasic misnaming. *Brain and Language* 87 (1). 33–34.

Levelt, Willem. 1989. *Speaking: From intention to articulation*. Cambridge, MA: MIT Press.

Levelt, Willem, Ardi Roelofs & Antje Meyer. 1999. A theory of lexical access in speech production. *Behavioral & Brain Sciences* 22. 1–75.

Lorenz, Antje & Wolfram Ziegler. 2009. Semantic vs. word-form specific techniques in anomia treatment: A multiple single-case study. *Journal of Neurolinguistics* 6. 515–537.

Marshall, John. 1984. Toward a rational taxonomy of the developmental dyslexias. In Rattihalli N. Malatesha & Harry Whitaker (eds.), *Dyslexia: A global issue*, 211–232. The Hague: Martinus Nijhoff.

McGregor, Karla. 1994. Use of phonological information in a word-finding treatment for children. *Journal of Speech, Language, and Hearing Research* 37. 1381–1393.

McGregor, Karla. 1997. The nature of word-finding errors of preschoolers with and without word finding deficits. *Journal of Speech, Language, and Hearing Research* 40. 1232–1244.

Messer, David & Julie Dockrell. 2006. Children's naming and word-finding difficulties: Descriptions and explanations. *Journal of Speech, Language, and Hearing Resea*rch 49. 309–324.

Messer, David, Julie Dockrell & Nicola Murphy. 2004. The relationship between naming and literacy in children with word-finding difficulties. *Journal of Educational Psychology* 96. 462–470.

Mirman, Daniel. 2011. Effects of near and distant semantic neighbors on word production. *Cognitive, Affective, & Behavioral Neuroscience* 11 (1). 32–43.

Mirman, Daniel, Audrey Kittredge & Gary Dell. 2010. Effects of near and distant phonological neighbors on picture naming. In *Proceedings of the 32nd annual conference of the Cognitive Science Society*, 1447–1452.

Morton, John. 1964. A preliminary functional model for language behaviour. *International Journal of Audiology* 3 (2). 216–225.

Morton, John. 1969. Interaction of information in word recognition. *Psychological review* 76 (2). 165–178.

Morton, John. 1979. Facilitation in word recognition: Experiments causing change in the Logogen model. In *Processing of visible language*, Vol. 13, 259–268. New York: Springer US.

Morton, John. 1985. *Naming*. In Ruth Epstein & Stanton P. Newman, *Current perspectives in dysphasia*. Edinburgh: Churchill Livingstone.

Navarrete, Eduardo, Benedetta Basagni, F.-Xavier Alario & Albert Costa. 2006. Does word frequency affect lexical selection in speech production? *The Quarterly Journal of Experimental Psychology* 59 (10). 1681–1690.

Newman, Rochelle & Diane German. 2002. Effects of lexical factors on lexical access among typical language learning children and children with word-finding difficulties. *Language and Speech* 45. 285–317.

Nickels, Lyndsey. 1997. *Spoken word production and its breakdown in aphasia*. Hove: Psychology Press.

Nickels, Lyndsey. 2001a. Spoken word production. In Brenda Rapp (ed.), *The handbook of cognitive neuropsychology*, 291–320. Hove: Psychology Press.

Nickels, Lyndsey. 2001b. Words fail me: Symptoms and causes of naming breakdown in aphasia. In Rita Sloan Berndt (ed.), *Handbook of neuropsychology* (2nd edn., vol. 3), 115–135. Amsterdam: Elsevier Science.

Nickels, Lyndsey. 2002. Therapy for naming disorders: Revisiting, revising and reviewing. *Aphasiology* 16. 935–980.

Nickels, Lyndsey & David Howard. 1995. Aphasic naming: What matters? *Neuropsychologia* 33. 1281–1303.

Nickels, Lyndsey & David Howard. 2004. Dissociating effects of number of phonemes, number of syllables and syllabic complexity on aphasic word production. *Cognitive Neuropsychology* 21. 57–78.

Nickels, Lyndsey, Saskia Kohnen & Britta Biedermann. 2010. An untapped resource: Treatment as a tool for revealing the nature of cognitive processes. *Cognitive Neuropsychology* 27 (7). 539–562.

Patterson, Karolyn & Christina Shewell. 1987. Speak and spell: Dissociations and word-class effects. In Max Coltheart, Guiseppe Satori & Remo Job (eds.), *The cognitive neuropsychology of language*, 273–295. London: Lawrence Erlbaum Associates.

Plaut, David. 2002. Graded modality-specific specialization in semantics: A computational account of optic aphasia. *Cognitive Neuropsychology* 19. 603–639.

Rapp, Brenda, & Matthew Goldrick. 2000. Discreteness and interactivity in spoken word production. *Psychological review* 107 (3). 460.

Roelofs, Ardi. 1997. The WEAVER model of word-form encoding in speech production. *Cognition* 64 (3). 249–284.

Roelofs, Ardi. 2014. A dorsal-pathway account of aphasic language production: The WEAVER++/ARC model. *Cortex* 59. 33–48.

Rossiter, Clare & Wendy Best. 2013. "Penguins don't fly": An investigation into the effect of typicality on picture naming in people with aphasia. *Aphasiology* 27. 784–798.

Sadat, Jasmin, Clara Martin, Albert Costa, A. & F.-Xavier Alario. 2014. Reconciling phonological neighborhood effects in speech production through single trial analysis. *Cognitive psychology* 68. 33–58.

Sandberg, Chaleece, Rajani Sebastian & Swahti Kiran. 2012. Typicality mediates performance during category verification in both ad-hoc and well-defined categories. *Journal of Communication Disorders* 45. 69–83.

Stemberger, Joseph. 1985. An interactive activation model of language production. *Progress in the psychology of language* 1. 143–186.
Swinburn, Kate, Gillian Porter & David Howard. 2004. *CAT: comprehensive aphasia test*. Psychology Press.
Tallal, Paula & Rachel Stark. 1981. Speech acoustic cue discrimination abilities of normally developing and language impaired children. *Journal of the Acoustical Society of America* 69. 568–574.
Warrington, Elisabeth & Tim Shallice. 1984. Category specific semantic impairments. *Brain* 107 (3). 829–853.
Wilshire, Carolyn. 2008. Cognitive neuropsychological approaches to word production in aphasia: Beyond boxes and arrows. *Aphasiology* 22. 1019–1053.
Whitworth, Anne, Janet Webster & David Howard. 2014. *A cognitive neuropsychological approach to assessment and intervention in aphasia: A clinician's guide*. Hove: Psychology Press.

I **Linguistic acquisition**

Section 3: Grammatical constructions

Michael Ramscar, Melody Dye, James Blevins and Harald Baayen
9 Morphological development

1 Introduction

Language, whether spoken or written, is the primary means by which humans communicate. Yet exactly how communication is achieved through language has yet to be explained. This chapter describes our approach to understanding how morphological systems work and what morphological development entails. The approach is rooted in the way minds learn, and is based on clearly and explicitly stated learning mechanisms for which there is a wealth of biological evidence; It is consistent with the principles that govern artificial communication systems (Shannon, 1948); And, unusually, it makes surprising – and successful – predictions about the pattern of morphological development. Because it is rooted in the discriminative principles of learning, the perspective on language our approach offers is very different to the associative, combinatoric view taken by most researchers. However, we believe that this perspective will prove to be of fundamental importance to understanding human communication, and consequently, the challenges facing children with communicative disorders. Accordingly, in this chapter we describe the principles of learning in detail, along with the picture of morphological and linguistic development they give rise to.

2 Language, morphology and development

In thinking about how human communication works, linguists have typically assumed that language facilitates communication by conveying meanings, much as trains convey passengers (Reddy, 1979). Linguistic theories assume that words – and the sub-word units called morphemes – encode units of meaning, such that the word 'units' is composed of two morphemes (the morpheme 'unit' and the morpheme 's'), and the word 'morphemes' is composed of three ('morph,' 'eme' and 's').

From this perspective, the task facing a language learner can be broken down into a three-fold process. It involves learning what the conceptual units of her language are, learning how to associate them with sound units to create morphemes, and figuring out the kinds of morphemes that can be combined to form complex words (along with how sequences of morphemic combinations combine to yield higher-order sequences, such as sentences).

Michael Ramscar and Harald Baayen, Eberhard Karls Universität Tübingen
Melody Dye, University of California at Berkeley
James Blevins, University of Cambridge

Over a century of study has uncovered a number of problems with this approach. Critically, at both a behavioral and neural level, it has been found that learning simply doesn't work in the associative manner that linguistic theories are wont to imagine. What has traditionally been called "associative" learning is not associative at all. Rather, it is a systematic process that serves to discriminate the details of a learner's internal representation of the world (Ramscar et al, 2010).

Further, while humans are perfectly capable of learning to discriminate between events and behaviors, they do so in ways that do not involve the discrete internal representations (i.e., the "units of meaning") that are supposed to provide the stock of combinable elements in combinatorial approaches to language (Wittgenstein, 1953; Ramscar and Port, 2015). Finally, though by no means exhaustively, combinatorial approaches to language describe meanings as being encoded into verbal and written signals by speakers and writers to later be decoded by readers and listeners; However, the process this envisages violates the basic principles of coding theory, as it assumes that the appropriate meanings of words or morphemes with many potential "senses" can be successfully decoded from signals that do not actually code for these senses. (In the case of written English, the available coding resources do not even consistently discriminate different lexical forms from one another, such as the past and present tenses of *read*).

Although most cognitive scientists are familiar with at least some of these problems, most theories of language acquisition and processing remain steadfastly rooted in associative combinatorics, even in the absence of an adequate account of what exactly gets combined, or how the encoding and decoding of meanings is actually supposed to work. In what follows, we describe an account of language learning and processing based on *discrimination learning*. It does not assume that morphemes serve to convey meanings, but rather that they serve to discriminate between meaningful states of affairs in communication. From this perspective, the task facing a language learner is that of learning which potential states of the world morphemes may discriminate, and how the distinctions afforded by morphemes can be used in communication. To illustrate the utility of this approach, we show how it not only provides a satisfactory account of many phenomena associated with morphological development, but also makes surprising (and successful) predictions about the way that patterns of morphological over-generalization develop and recede.

3 How do children learn?

Any account of how children master morphological processing seeks to answer two questions: *what* do children learn, and *how* do they learn it? In the recent past, a great deal of linguistic theorizing has proceeded from *what* to *how*. Perhaps unsurprisingly, these theories have struggled to explain how the *what* of their theoretical postulates are learned. This has, in turn, led to a situation where the psychological bases of many theories of language are opaque, and where claims about "innate mechanisms" abound.

We take the opposite tack: starting from *how* children learn, we consider how this might constrain our conjectures about *what* children learn. One potential benefit of this approach is that our current scientific understanding of learning is far more advanced than that of language. We share many of our basic learning mechanisms with other animals, and in many domains, animal models have proved invaluable in illuminating the biological and neural structures underlying these mechanisms.

Legend has it that Ivan Pavlov's famous discovery – that ringing a bell before giving dogs food later caused the dogs to salivate whenever the bell sounded – was a felicitous accident.[1] Whatever the exact truth of the matter, his discoveries have given rise to a popular idea: That animals learn to "associate" unrelated events according to the frequency with which a stimulus (a bell) and a response (salivation) are paired. Empirically, however, this naïve view of conditioning – as a process that simply tracks co-occurrences – has long been known to be wrong (Rescorla 1988), as have two popular (yet equally false) beliefs about the conditions that produce learning: First, that explicit rewards and punishments are necessary for learning; and second that a co-occurrence between a stimulus and a response is sufficient for learning.

Empirically, mere association cannot account for conditioning. For example, if a group of rats is trained on a schedule of tones and shocks, they will quickly learn to associate the tone and shock, and freeze when later tones sound. However, if rats are exposed to an identical number of tone-shock pairings into which a number of tones that are *not* followed by shocks are interpolated (i.e., *Tone, Tone, Tone-Shock, Tone-Shock, Tone, Tone, Tone, Tone, Tone-Shock, Tone, Tone, Tone, Tone, Tone-Shock…* etc), the rats show a different pattern of learning. As the number of tones not followed by shocks increases, tone-shock associations decrease proportionally (Rescorla, 1968).

Given that the *non*-occurrence of shocks after tones influences the degree to which rats condition to the tones, it follows that learning must comprise more than simple counts of positive co-occurrences of cues with events. To explain how rats learn from the *background rate* of the tones (a phenomena that popular "associative" conceptions of learning cannot explain; Rescorla, 1988), modern theories of learning suppose that in the two situations just described, the "no shock" trials act to alter rats' implicit expectations about the tones. These theories conceive of learning as a process that serves to reduce uncertainty in the predictive mental models that learners construct out of their experience with their environments (Rescorla, 1988). Functionally, learning modulates the value that an organism implicitly assigns to sensory cues as predictors of the events that it experiences. As events unfold, representations of cue values change as a function both of current expectations, and the degree to which

---

[1] The bell is actually a myth (Todes, 2014).

these expectations have led the learner to anticipate (or fail to anticipate) what actually occurs.

Importantly, learning to predict an outcome from one cue has an impact on the uncertainty that drives the learning of other cues. This is best illustrated by *blocking* (Kamin, 1969): If a rat learns it will be shocked upon hearing a tone, and then later a light is paired with the tone, learning about the light as a cue to the shock will be inhibited, because the tone is already fully predictive of the shock. Thus the rat will be unlikely to freeze in response to the light alone.

These and other results demonstrate that rats do not learn simple "associations" between stimuli and responses, but rather learn the degree to which cues are systematically informative about events, a process that discriminates cues that are more informative from cues that are less so (Rescorla, 1988). Since there are invariably far more uninformative coincidences in the environment than informative ones, it follows that expectations that are wrong have more influence on the shape of learning than expectations that are right – which is why discrimination learning is often described as being *error-driven*.

Finally, we should stress that although our rat learning example focused on tones, in principle, *everything* in the local environment could have potentially influenced learning (Rescorla, 1988). However, in the same way that rats learn to discount tones as predictive cues the more they encounter them absent shocks, they also learn to discount other aspects of their environment that have high background rates relative to a relevant outcome. For the sake of simplicity, models and explanations tend to focus solely on potentially informative cues, ignoring cues whose high background rates are likely to render them largely irrelevant in competitive terms. In principle, however, the novelty of a cue is entirely relative, and can only be computed in relation to the other available cues, and a learner's previous experience with them (Rescorla 1988).

Beginning with Rescorla and Wagner (1972), many formal models employing these principles have been devised to fit and predict learning effects. The Rescorla-Wagner learning rule is a discrepancy function that takes the difference between expectation and reality on a given trial, and uses this to update expectations by modifying the values of a set of cues in relation to that outcome. Stated formally, learning occurs whenever the outcome of a given trial fails to match the expectations generated by the available environmental cues. Cue values V_X are updated in proportion to the overall mismatch, which is given by the discrepancy function ΔV. That function takes the difference between the outcome λ and the summed predictive value of all cues present, V_{tot}, and weights it by two parameters, which denote cue salience (α), and learning rate (β).

$$\Delta V_X^{n+1} = \alpha_X \beta (\lambda - V_{tot})$$

Formally, λ represents the maximum predictive value for an outcome. On trials where the outcome occurs, λ is usually set to 1, and on trials when it does not, to 0. The configural value of the cue set is updated as follows:

$$V_{tot} = V_X^n + \Delta V_X^{n+1}$$

As this suggests, learning tracks predictive accuracy. Cue values are strengthened when an outcome's likelihood is underestimated, and weakened when the likelihood is overestimated. Learning is also a zero-sum game. The predictive value 'lost' by one cue, can be subsumed by other cues, leading to competition between cues, and preferential strengthening of the most reliable ones, and discriminatory weakening of others. The trajectory of this competition is shaped both by 'positive evidence' (co-occurrences between cues and predicted events) and 'negative evidence' (the absence of a predicted event following a cue).

While much of the impetus for the development of this kind of learning rule came from behavioral experiments in animals, there is now good evidence for their neurobiological basis in humans (see Schultz, 2006). Learning rules of this type accurately predict patterns of synaptic firing in midbrain dopamine neurons in learning tasks (Waelti, Dickinson, and Schultz, 2001) and have been productively applied to many aspects of human behavior and cognition, such as decision making, executive function, habitual learning, and response selection (Montague, Hyman, and Cohen, 2004), demonstrating considerable predictive and explanatory power.

While for historical reasons the Rescorla-Wagner learning rule is often characterized in associative terms (see e.g. Miller, Barnet, and Grahame 1995, Siegel and Allan 1996), it is important to note that in computational terms, the rule describes a *discriminative* learning mechanism (Ramscar et al, 2010; Ramscar et al, 2013c). Since this learning rule is arguably the best-supported formalism in psychology, with a sizeable – and still growing – body of behavioral evidence arguing in support of its principles (Miller, Barnet, and Grahame 1995; Siegel and Allan 1996; Ramscar, Dye, and McCauley 2013), characterizing learning in discriminative terms can help elucidate the mechanisms that govern neuropsychological development (Ramscar et al, 2010; Ramscar, Dye, and McCauley 2013).

Indeed, adopting this approach has proven useful to both predicting and understanding morphological development as children learn language. Experimental results offer reason to believe that children are exquisitely attuned to the structure of their linguistic environments in precisely the manner predicted by discriminative models (Ramscar et al. 2010, 2011, Ramscar at al 2013a).[2] Indeed, in our research, we have found that these models successfully predict patterns of development in set-size

---

[2] Although Saffran et al (1996) claim that their "statistical learning" results are incompatible with Rescorla-Wagner learning, given a flat cue structure – like a stream of syllables – the model actually asymptotes at cue weights that approximate the transitional probability between each syllable (Ramscar et al, 2010), which behaviorally is what Saffran et al observed in infants.

learning (*subitization*; Ramscar et al., 2011) and rule-understanding in children (Ramscar et al., 2013), as well as changing patterns of performance in simple lexical "association" tasks across the lifespan (Ramscar et al., 2013; Ramscar et al., 2014).

Given this, and given our aim of using *how* learning works to uncover *what* is learned in morphological development, it is worth noting that the logic of discrimination suggests that, far from the "blooming, buzzing confusion" of multiple entities described in much of developmental psychology, a newborn learner is best conceptualized as entering the world with a large, undifferentiated set of cues connected to little or no environmental knowledge. Starting from $N = 1$, the set of (more or less individuated) entities in the learner's representation of the world then begins to expand as perceptible variances and invariances in the environment encourage discrimination learning (James, 1890).

4 What is morphology, and how might it be learned?

4.1 The combinatoric approach

Having established in broad terms *how* children learn, we now turn our attention to *what* they learn. That is, we can now consider whether discriminative learning mechanisms are sufficient to account for morphological development, and if so, how.

We ought to acknowledge here that interest in morphological development extends far beyond the simple concern of understanding, say, plural marking, for its own sake. Over the course of the past quarter century, research on morphological development has been seen "as addressing some of the most important issues in cognitive science" (Seidenberg and Plaut, 2014, p. 1), largely because:

> [Morphology has...] three interesting characteristics. First, it is systematic: Most past tenses are formed by adding the morpheme that is spelled -ed and pronounced as in the examples baked, baited, and bared. Second, it is productive: People can readily generate past tenses for novel forms such as nust-nusted or wug-wugged. Third, it is quasiregular (Seidenberg and McClelland, 1989): There is a main pattern but also irregular forms that deviate from it in differing degrees (e.g., keep-kept, run-ran, go-went). Phenomena such as tense on verbs and number on nouns have been taken as simple, decisive demonstrations that grammatical rules are an essential component of linguistic knowledge (Pinker, 1999). Irregular forms exist outside this system of core linguistic knowledge and are learned and generated by other mechanisms such as memorization and association.

Rumelhart and McClelland's (1986) model offered an alternative view of this last point. Taking the phonological form of a verb's present tense as input, it generated the phonological form of its past tense as output using a uniform procedure for all tenses. It also supported the generation of past tense forms for novel verbs. The model and the various claims made about it caused controversy and launched a debate that has generated an enormous body of research on a range of morphological phenomena.

For our current purposes, however, the agreements in this debate are more relevant than its disagreements: Almost all the participants in this debate accept that the *what* of morphological development is a means of composing and decomposing associative morphemes. Hence, in the case of English plurals, they assume that a child learns a morpheme that associates the concept *mouse* with the word "mouse", an association between the concept *mice* and "mice", an association between the concept *rat* and "rat", and an association between the concept for *sets of objects* (excluding multiple mouses) and a morphemic gesture characterized linguistically as a terminal sibilant on a noun, and often written as +s, etc.

Yet, as we described above, the *what* of the "associative" learning process has actually been found to be discriminative. The "association-tracking" at the heart of the processes imagined in this debate is actually an evolutionary twist on Sherlock Holmes' dictum – "When you have eliminated the impossible, whatever remains, however improbable, must be the truth." When a rat learns to associate a tone with a shock, the "association" is what is left over after learning has systematically weighed every other potential source of information and found it wanting.

Consistent with this picture of learning, researchers studying human categorization have found that at a behavioral and neurological level, human performance is best accounted for by models that don't actually contain pre-established (or even determinable) categories, but instead treat categorization as an active process of discriminating between more or less appropriate category labels (or other affordances and behaviors) in context (see Ramscar and Port, 2015 for a review). Similarly, the non-discrete nature of meanings could be described as the closest thing that philosophy has to offer to a fact (Wittgenstein, 1953; Quine, 1960). All of which indicates that the idea of the "associative morpheme" – a discrete mapping between a discrete unit of meaning and a discrete linguistic unit – is incompatible with what we know about human learning; about the nature of meaning; and about the computational properties of the human categorization system.

What is more, if we accept the message of this evidence, and allow that morphological systems do not involve a discrete set of mappings between a set of units of meaning and the lexical forms of a language, then a significant peculiarity of this debate – and indeed, of the way linguists think about morphology more generally – becomes apparent. In the Rumelhart and McClelland (1986) model and most subsequent models of morphological development, the child is envisioned as learning a combinatorial, transformational rule that (e.g.) adds the English past tense morpheme +ed to a verb stem in order to transform an uninflected form into a past tense form. Accordingly, the model's training set was devised to teach this transformation; uninflected forms are repeatedly turned into past tense forms, as if the learning environment comprised mature speakers going about saying, "*go-went, walk-walked, speak-spoke, talk-talked, etc.*"[3]

However, this characterization of the learning environment is dubious in the extreme. Mature speakers do not wander around giving extensive tutorials on the nature of supposed transformations, saying, "*go-went, walk-walked, etc.*" They talk about what interests them, in context. This means that children rarely, if ever, hear "*go*" then "*went*" in close proximity. Instead, they hear "Wanna *go* see a movie?" on Tuesday, and "Oh no! I forgot to put the trash out before we *went* to the movies last night," on Wednesday.

In other words: 1) Children don't learn in the way envisaged by the combinatoric account of morphology; 2) The units it supposes that they learn are highly implausible; And 3) Children learn morphological systems without ever actually encountering morphemes being used transformatively. Thus it seems possible, perhaps even likely, that a different approach to the conceptualization of morphological processing might yield a better account of *what* develops, as well as *how*.

4.2 The counter-intuitive appeal of discriminative morphology

We begin our formulation of this alternative account by considering the very things that the combinatoric story gets wrong: the nature of learning, human knowledge representation, and the learning environment. As we noted above: learning is discriminative; categorization is an active, context driven process that serves to discriminates between lexomes (and other more or less discrete affordances and behaviors); and children hear lexomes used in contexts that offer precious little evidence for transformations at all.

To illustrate how these constraints might influence what a child actually learns, we take English nominal morphology as an illustrative example, and consider how these factors might give rise to the typical patterns of over-regularization children exhibit while learning the nominal system. A fuller description of this approach, along with code to produce the simulations described below, can be found in Ramscar et al. (2013d).

In English, correct irregular plural marking is particularly difficult to acquire (Ramscar and Dye, 2011), even in comparison to the more commonly studied case of past tense marking. This reflects the nature of the input. Consider verbs: While irregulars are rare as types, they tend to have high token frequencies, such that the 40 most frequent verb forms are all irregular (Davies, 2009). Moreover, in the Reuters

---

[3] Although Rumelhart and McClelland (1986) use a discriminative learning rule analogous to Rescorla-Wagner, they describe their model as a pattern associator, and adopt a combinatoric view of morphology.

Corpus (Rose et al., 2002) just three irregular verbs (*be*, *have*, and *do*) account for fully a quarter of the attested verbs forms, with past tense verb forms outnumbering base or present tense verb forms. Thus, in learning past tense inflection, children are likely to encounter more past inflected than uninflected verb forms, and of these, more irregular than regular past inflections.

Noun plurals are different: Children mainly encounter singular forms, and when they do encounter plurals, they are likely to be regular. In the Reuters Corpus, only around 30% of nouns occur in their plural form, and of these, the overwhelming majority of types and tokens are regular. While this makes the learning problem for plurals substantively more difficult than the past tense, the two problems may not be different in kind; As with the past tense, children's irregular plural production follows a 'U-shaped' developmental trajectory, such that children who have been observed to produce "mice" in one context still frequently produce over-regularized forms such as "mouses" in another (Arnon and Clark, 2011).

Our account of nominal development assumes, first and foremost, that native languages are not learned in formal teacher-pupil settings, but by hearing them used in context. We also assume that lexical and morphological systems are systematically informative, such that the combined value of both positive and negative evidence favor a mapping between the experiences a child has with the class of objects described by a given noun, and the noun itself. For example, a child learning the lexome (or lexical form) "mice", will hear the word used in a way that makes it most informative about mice, or depictions of them, and must learn to associate the appropriate cues in the environment (*mouse-things*) with that lexome (Quine, 1960, Wittgenstein, 1953). Conceptually, this assumption reflects the idea that adult speakers use language in informative ways, and hence, that a *mouse* ought to be more informative about the lexome "mouse", and *mice* more informative about the lexome "mice", than vice versa (otherwise, "mice" could equally mean *mouse*, and "mouse" could equally mean *mice*). Accordingly, when a child is asked to name a picture of *mice*, the child is able to say "mice", because learning has discriminated a set of mappings between the mice-relevant semantic dimensions of the child's experience and the more or less discrete gestural/phonetic form "mice".

At the outset of word learning, all and any kind of *stuff* in the world will seem potentially informative about concrete nouns such as "mouse" and "mice". Thus learning to discriminate the correct cues to each form will involve discriminating the *particular stuff* that is best associated with any given singular and plural form of a noun (e.g., *mousiness* in the case of "mouse" and "mice") from other kinds of stuff. At the same time, learning to discriminate singulars from plurals will require discriminating the specific stuff that best predicts one as opposed to the other (i.e. the presence of *multiple mouse objects* ought to predict "mice", as opposed to a *single mouse object*, which ought to predict "mouse").

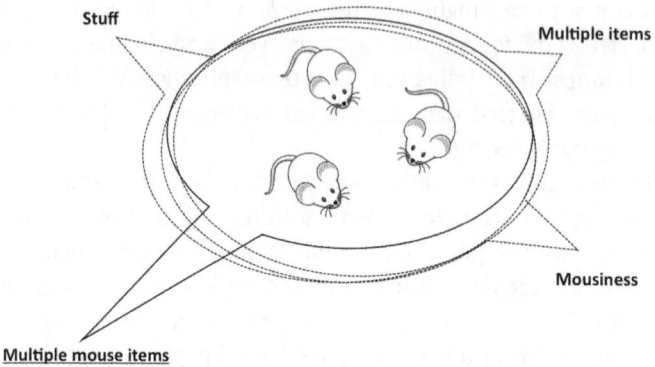

Figure 1: Four semantic-dimensions that will be consistently reinforced by a child's exposure to the word "mice" in the context of mice. (While these dimensions are separated for explanatory clarity, as far as the learning mechanisms are concerned, they could equally be values on continuous perceptual dimensions)

To illustrate how these distributional differences influence the learning of English nominal morphology, Figure 1 depicts four environmental dimensions that will reliably and consistently covary with the irregular plural form "mice." Although these semantic dimensions will co-occur with the word "mice" at the same rate, their covariance with other singular and plural nouns will differ. Because of these differences in background rate, the error associated with each dimension will vary in kind. Accordingly, although early in learning, generic cues like *stuff* will receive positive reinforcement when "mice" is encountered in context, their ubiquity will also cause them to produce a high degree of error. Indeed, compared to more uniquely informative cues, they will occur far more often in contexts in which "mice" is not heard. Thus, the influence of the more generic cues will wane over the course of learning, as learners converge on *multiple mouse-items* as the best cue to "mice."

In learning, error arises as a function of experience, which means that the pattern of reinforcement and unlearning of the semantic dimensions in Figure 1 depends heavily on their distribution in the learning environment. While the set of singular and plural lexomes that are usually classed together and called 'regular' plurals in English are distinguished by a number of subtle differences (such as different sibilant allomorphs), broadly speaking, regular plurals are far less discriminable from one another than irregular plurals, particularly in terms of how they discriminate plurality from singularity. In regular plural lexomes, plurality is uniformly denoted by the presence of some form of final sibilant. By contrast, irregulars employ a variety of means of discriminating singular and plural forms. This guarantees that irregular plural lexomes are, at once, less similar to their singular forms than regular lexomes (e.g., "dog" / "dogs" vs. "child" / "children"), and are also less similar to other irregulars ("foot" / "feet" vs. "child" / "children").

At this point, it is worth expanding a little on what we mean by a lexome: In our model of nominal learning, the challenge is seen as one of learning to discriminate the semantic (and lexical) cues to a system of phonetic and lexical contrasts simultaneously in context (Ramscar, Dye, and Klein, 2013; Ramscar and Port, 2015). As such, the degree to which any given phonetic lexical contrast has itself been discriminated will depend entirely on the current state of the learner.

Having said this, the discrete lexomes described here represent a simplification for descriptive and modeling purposes of what is, in reality, a far more continuous system. The requirements of the modeling task will dictate the specific representations adopted. For instance, it might be helpful for some theoretical purposes to represent the state of the plural system mastered by a young learner as comprising irregular forms, regular stems, and a single lexome marking the regular plural contrast +s, whereas for other purposes, the regular plural contrast might be more appropriately represented by positing different lexomes for each regular plural allomorph. For example, in modeling the adult ability to discriminate and respond to prosodic differences in the stems of regular forms (Baayen et al., 2003, Kemps et al., 2005), well learned regular plural and singular forms might best be modeled as individuated lexomes.

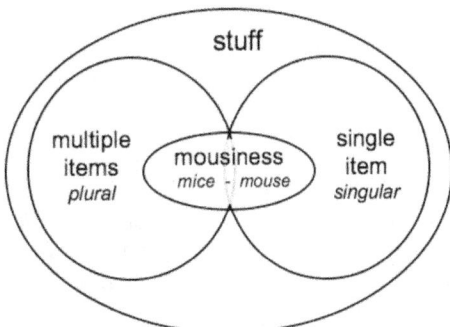

Figure 2: The relative specificity of the four dimensions as cues to plural forms. While the less specific cues (*stuff* and *mousiness*) will receive positive reinforcement early in learning, their ubiquity will cause them to produce more error than the uniquely informative cues. As a result, the influence of the less specific cues will wane as experience grows.

Figure 2 shows how the various potential semantic cues to "mice" overlap relative to a fairly simple set of lexomes – comprising irregular forms, regular stems, and a single lexome marking the regular plural contrast +s – in an idealized young learner. As can be seen, the structure of the lexicon is such that learning to correctly produce "mice" will require unlearning a number of irrelevant semantic cues.

As a child learns from this distribution of lexomes, the semantic dimension *multiple items* will initially be reinforced whenever plural forms are used to talk about any set of objects in context. In this distribution, most noun forms employ largely the same phonetic form to denote kind semantics (e.g., various articulations of "rat" are all strongly associated with rat semantics). It is thus the presence or absence of a terminal sibilant (+s) that discriminates between singularity and plurality when the noun stem is used. This means that initially, whenever a set of objects is to be described, the child's language model will predict that a form should have a final sibilant.

However, this expectation will change over time. Consider: whenever mouse objects are talked about, the relationship between *multiple mouse objects* and "mice" will be reinforced, as well as that between *multiple items* and "mice". This means that in other contexts where plurals are used, *multiple items* will not only lead the child to implicitly expect a final sibilant, it will also cause "mice" to be expected. When the child does not hear "mice", this will lead to error, downgrading the relationship between *multiple items* and "mice" in the child's language model. Similarly, whenever "mice" are talked about, the relationship between *multiple items* and a terminal sibilant will be weakened. Over time this will gradually increase the association between *multiple mouse objects* and "mice" in mice contexts, while decreasing the association between *multiple objects* and "mice" in non-mice contexts. Thus, the distribution of evidence in the linguistic environment will support discrimination of the appropriate cues to "mice".

So far we have discussed what the expectations of a naïve observational learner might be. A key question is how this will be influenced by production. Here we can envisage two scenarios: In the first, production serves to reinforce itself, such that when the noise in a child's underlying model of the world results in her saying "mouses," "mouses" is reinforced as a response. In the second case, production is driven by a child's model of her intended behavior (what she has observed), but it is the *attempts* to perform a behavior that reinforce the underlying model, not whatever noisy behavior emerges from them. Model-based learning, which we adopt here, can explain why practice leads ballroom dancers towards the right steps, rather than reinforcing treading on toes (Gläscher et al., 2010).

Behaviorally, of course, we know English speakers often do go through a period of saying "mouses" in childhood, but as they grow older, they come to produce only the adult form, "mice". In our model, we assume that this reflects an interim state that arises from the distributional properties of the learning environment, and is resolved by further sampling from this distribution. This is, of course, one of the vital advantages of formal models – they generate unambiguous predictions.

Ramscar and Yarlett (2007) present a computational simulation that reinforces a model of the world rather than the overt behavior it would generate, and which predicts that eliciting over-regularized forms from children will actually cause them to over-regularize *less*. In a series of experiments, Ramscar and Yarlett then show that children exhibit the very behavior predicted by the model: When seven-year-old children repeatedly produced the same plurals across blocks of trials, their rates of over-regularization went down in later blocks. This occurred even when children were given positive feedback on the incorrect forms they produced, lending further support to the idea that learning reinforces children's models of the world, rather than their behavior per se.

Ramscar et al (2013d) show that when the challenges facing a child language learner are explicitly set up in the way shown in Figures 1 and 2, the distribution of forms and semantics in English invariably leads to what has been described as "U-shaped" performance in plural production: Mastery of correct irregular forms is preceded by a phase in which both correct and incorrect irregular plurals are produced. Moreover, Ramscar et al show that in this model, the ultimate elimination of interference from sibilant final forms – which give rise to over-regularization – is driven by error caused by the inappropriate expectation of irregular forms when the semantics of *regular* forms are present in a lexical context. That is, the same non-discriminative semantic dimension that causes children to expect a sibilant final form in an irregular context – leading to over-regularization – causes them to erroneously expect irregular forms in regular contexts, gradually causing this non-discriminative dimension a cue to be unlearned as cues to irregulars, thereby reducing over-regularization.

This results in an unambiguous prediction: Engaging children at an appropriate stage of development in a task invoking the semantics of regular forms ought to bring about a reduction in over-regularization. To test this, Ramscar et al first pre-tested children on a task that elicited both regular and irregular plural and singular forms. One group of children then performed a color-related control task, while the other performed a memory task involving the same regular plural forms from the elicitation task along with regular lures. The children were then post tested using the elicitation task.

Predictably, the color task had no effect on over-regularization. However, consistent with the detailed predictions of the model, the younger children tested in the memory condition showed a small but significant *increase* in over-regularization. By contrast, the same exposure to the semantics of regular plural forms brought about a large and significant *decrease* in over-regularization in the older children (Ramscar et al. 2013a), just as the model predicts. In other words, the pattern of children's over-regularization and their retreat from it is exactly as one would predict given the way that children learn, the forms that they learn, and the way that these forms are distributed semantically.

5 The scientific appeal of discrimination learning

Because children reliably go through a period in which they over-regularize, and because they reliably stop over-regularizing without encountering any explicit instruction to do so, it has often been argued that their behavior presents a logical puzzle: Why would they ever stop (Pinker 1984, 2004; Pinker and Prince 1988)?

The models and the results reported here show that the patterns of over-regularization behavior exhibited by developing English speakers are not puzzling. On the contrary, over-regularization is a direct byproduct of the distributional properties of the English language, and in typically developing children, the same processes and circumstances that give rise to the problem ultimately resolve it. Thus, over-regularization is a self-correcting problem, with little need for explicit correction. (Indeed, because learning reinforces children's models of the world, explicit feedback about behavior often has little obvious effect on what children actually learn; Ramscar and Yarlett, 2007.)

In the light of the debate that has surrounded this phenomenon, it seems worth noting that our explanation does not "solve" the puzzle of over-regularization as it has previously been posed. There are two reasons for this: First, because, while this puzzle has frequently been framed as a "logical problem", it is only actually a problem if one ignores some well-established facts about animal learning (Rescorla and Wagner, 1972), or if one assumes that human infants are somehow less capable learners than the animals these principles were derived from – namely, rats (Pinker, 2004).

And second, because once one understands how learning works, it becomes clear that the way the problem has been posed in the past makes little sense. Learning is not a process that "associates" "units" of forms and meanings in the way that morphologists have traditionally imagined (Ramscar and Port, 2015), but is instead a discriminative process in which *systems* of associations are learned implicitly, as a result of the process of dissociating anything and everything else. Learning has evolved to enable humans and other animals to make sense of the world by reducing its dimensionality and complexity in order to highlight what is relevant (Trimmer et al., 2012).

While it is not always easy to intuit exactly how this process allows us to map our semantic model of the world onto the system of forms in a language, it is possible to model this complex process computationally, and thereby gain a richer understanding of it. By contrast, not only does it make little sense from a learning perspective to imagine that language learners are faced with the task of acquiring rules that transform or agglutinate "form units" that map to "meaning units" – as morphologists have traditionally imagined – but, as the numerous claims that have been put forward for this or that aspect of linguistic processing being innate over recent years would seem to attest, conceiving of how this kind of combinatoric system actually works in any kind of detail appears to be all but impossible.

6 Discrimination learning and morphology

It is often assumed that regularity is a desirable or normative goal for morphological systems, and that irregular paradigms represent deviations from the uniform patterns that systems (or their speakers) strive to maintain. Such an assumption is challenged, however, by phenomena like suppletion, in which an inflected stem-change produces a phonologically unrelated allomorph (e.g., "mouse" / "mice"), rendering patterns of form-meaning mappings unpredictable.

A discriminative perspective makes precisely the opposite assumption. In discriminative models, the difference between overtly suppletive forms (such as "mouse" / "mice") and more regular forms (such as "rat" / "rats") is that the former serve to accelerate the rate at which a speakers' representation of a specific form/meaning contrast becomes discriminated from the form classes that express similar contrasts. The logic of these models is that all learning serves to increase the level of suppletion in a system of form-meaning mappings.

From this perspective, suppletive irregular forms (like "mice") are not categorically different types, as morphologists have been wont to imagine, but are merely extreme instances of the system of discriminative contrasts that linguistic communication relies on. Moreover, when one examines language use from this perspective, it is clear that these systematic contrasts are ubiquitous at the sub-phonemic level. Thus for example, while the combinatorial paradigm has long assumed that the forms of language are constructed out of an alphabet of phones (Port and Leary, 2005), numerous studies have made clear how markedly this idealization departs from the empirical truth. For example, the duration and fundamental frequency of the *cap* in "captain" differs systematically from the morphologically unrelated "cap". Moreover, analyses have shown that the nature of linguistic contrasts is such that even so-called homophones – like "time" and "thyme" – appear to be gesturally and acoustically distinct (Gahl, 2008).

The patterns of contrast observed in the lexicon are also observable at a morphological level: Baayen et al. (2003) found that a sample of speakers produced Dutch nouns with a longer mean duration when they occurred as singulars than when they occurred as the stem of the corresponding plural. Kemps et al. (2005) show that speakers are sensitive to these prosodic differences, finding that "acoustic differences exist between uninflected and inflected forms and that listeners are sensitive to them" (Kemps et al. 2005: 441). Plag et al. (2014) observed similar contrasts and sensitivities to them in a study of phonemically identical affixes in English.

It thus follows that from a discriminative perspective, it is the *regularity* in morphological systems that stands in need of explanation. Discrimination learning suggests a solution here as well. Unlike derivational processes, inflectional processes are traditionally assumed to be highly productive, defining uniform paradigms within a given class. Lemma size is thus not expected to vary, except where forms are unavailable due to paradigm 'gaps' or 'defectiveness'. However, corpus studies suggest that this expectation is an idealization. Many potentially available inflected forms are unattested in corpora, and as corpus sizes increase, sampling does not converge on uniformly populated paradigms, but rather reinforces classes and develops longer tails (Blevins et al., 2015).

In order for a collection of partial samples to allow for the generation of unattested forms, the forms that speakers do know must be organized into systematic structures that collectively enable the scope of possible variations to be realized. These structures thus correspond to lexical neigbourhoods, whose effects have been investigated in a wide range of psycholinguistic studies (Baayen et al. 2006; Gahl et al. 2011). From the present perspective, these neighbourhoods are not independent dimensions of lexical organization. Instead they constitute the creative engine of the morphological system, permitting the extrapolation of the full system from partial patterns. Regular paradigms thus enable language users to generate previously unencountered forms in the same way as is captured by our model of plural morphology. Regular forms are not the product of an explicit rule, or of any kind of explicit grammatical knowledge, but rather, they are *implicit* in the distribution of forms and semantics in the language as a system.

7 Discriminative language learning

Traditionally, linguistic and social learning have been painted as being in opposition to "mere associative learning" (e.g., Tomasello, 2003), and most scientists and practitioners likely still believe this to be the case. However, these contrasts ultimately rely on a faulty understanding of what associative learning actually is (Rescorla, 1988). As we have highlighted above, associative learning is in fact a *discriminative* process, and one which is inherently systematic. While the systematicity of learning is simple to state, the explanatory tools it provides are both subtle and powerful.

In illustrative work, Ramscar et al (2013c) have shown that changes across the lifespan in adults' ability to learn the association of arbitrary pairs of words such as *jury* and *eagle* – while at first glance an almost prima facie example of a combinatorial process – are far better predicted and modeled in terms of systematic discrimination learning in the lexicon. For instance, it is well attested empirically that while learning frequently co-occurring pairs (like *lock–door*) differs little with age, learning unlikely pairs like *jury-eagle* becomes increasingly difficult. From a discriminative perspective, the explanation for this is straightforward: The fact that the latter pair only co-occurs rarely causes them to become negatively associated in the lexical system as a whole, and these negative weights increase with experience. Thus, although learning to pair *jury* and *eagle* appears to be a combinatoric process, it turns out that actual behavior in the task is best explained by modeling the lexicon as a densely interconnected system in which all lexical items are related by complex patterns of co-occurrence, and in which learning causes items to become associated or dissociated from one another as a function of experience (i.e., in the same way as morphology was treated in our model above). When paired associate learning is modeled as a task that requires its subjects to reverse the systematic *dissociations* that ordinary experience teaches (i.e., that *jury* is not informative about *eagle*), the changing ability of adults to learn these pairs at various ages can be predicted with surprising accuracy (Ramscar et al 2013c).

By highlighting the systematic nature of language learning, this view of morphological development sheds new and productive light on the many apparent puzzles that arise when the learning of aspects of linguistic systems is considered in isolation. It is because of this systems-level focus that this approach will ultimately yield fruitful methods for understanding how and when language learning goes awry: As Quine (1960) noted, learning language requires that a child master not only the relationship between a system of conventionalized sound and meanings relationships, but also that the child learn how to use this system to communicate. Being able to do so appears to hinge on learning to share subjectivity; the child must somehow learn to comprehend the shared point of view of her community (see also Tomasello, 2003; Wittgenstein, 1953).

Exactly how human infants come to discriminate the "intersubjectively available cues as to what to say and when" (Quine, 1960) is an incredibly complex task. A discriminative account of communication grounded in learning theory allows us to frame questions about the way that children learn the sets of conventionalized cues that underpin languages (Wittgenstein, 1953) in ways that are tractable and amenable to formal description. For example, if communicative conventions – and language – are the product of learning, why is language apparently solely the preserve of humans? What is *special* about human learners?

One part of the answer to this question lies in the difference between the way that the brains of humans and other animals develop, and its impact on learning. Like many other primates, humans are born with immature brains. Birth is followed by synaptogenesis (the proliferation of synapses) followed by an extended pruning period (synaptic elimination). Brain development in humans, however, is markedly different from that of other primates. In monkeys, the postnatal development of the brain occurs at the same rate in all cortical areas. In contrast, human cortical development is uneven: Synaptogenesis in the visual and auditory cortex peaks a few months after birth, while the same developments occur later in the prefrontal cortex, which doesn't fully mature until late adolescence (Ramscar and Gitcho, 2007; Thompson-Schill, Ramscar, and Evangelia, 2009).

One important behavioral consequence of delayed prefrontal development is young children's inability to select behaviors that conflict with prepotent responses (Ramscar, et al. 2013b). In adults, prefrontal control mechanisms bias responses and attention according to goals or context, selectively maintaining task-relevant information and discarding task-irrelevant information (Ramscar and Gitcho, 2007; Thompson-Schill, Ramscar, and Evangelia, 2009). The absence of this capacity in young children can be illustrated by contrasting their performance with that of adults on biased selection tasks, such as guessing the hand an M&M is in. When the hands are biased 25:75, children up to age 5 tend to overmatch, fixating on the high-probability "good" hand. After age 5, however, a probability matching strategy emerges (Derks and Paclisanu, 1967). This is a rare instance in which children's inability to think flexibly is an advantage – probability matching actually reduces the number of M&Ms won.

Another area of learning in which cognitive flexibility may well prove disadvantageous is in the process of learning even a "simple" morphological system like that of English noun inflection. Linguistic knowledge is, in its essence, conventional. In the presence of a linguistic cue, a social animal needs to be able to understand or respond appropriately given the context. For this to happen, linguistic signals, must be both conventionalized and internalized (Wittgenstein, 1953). Learning the system of cues that yields appropriate understanding is far more likely to happen if learners are unable to filter their attention during the course of learning. Given a similar set of cues and labels to learn, young learners will tend to sample the environment in much the same way, and thus are more likely to develop similar expectations regarding the relationship between cues and symbols.

In contrast to children, adults struggle to master linguistic conventions (including English noun morphology; Johnson and Newport, 1989). This may reflect an inevitable handicap brought about by their increased ability to selectively attend and respond to the world and the cues in it. Because development increases the complexity of the human learning architecture, allowing learners to filter their attention in learning, it is likely that it also dramatically reduces the ability to learn conventions by naively sampling in the manner described above (Ramscar and Gitcho, 2007; Thompson-Schill et al., 2009). Put simply, the greater variety there is in what adults attend to during learning, the less conventionality there will be in what adults learn. Conversely, the less that children are able to direct their attention in learning, the more what they learn will be shaped by their immediate physical, social, and linguistic environments, and the more their learning about common regularities in these environments will be conventionalized (see also Finn et al., 2013, 2014; Hudson Kam and Newport, 2005, 2009; Singleton and Newport, 2004).

Although discriminative rules can be used to model some of the brain's learning processes, it is clear that there is far more to learning than error monitoring. Humans, especially adult humans, are not the passive observers of the environment that Rescorla-Wagner idealizes them to be. Our understanding of exactly how attention and learning trade off against one another, and how this affects what gets learned as frontal regions mature is, as yet, in its infancy. However, the learning and control processes we describe are amenable to computational and biological modeling, and progress is being made in this regard (Ramscar et al., 2013c).

To emphasize the point that an idealized model can be useful even when incomplete, consider that Triesch, Teuscher, Deák, and Carlson (2006) have shown how gaze following emerges naturally from discriminative learning mechanisms, provided that a child has access to a caregiver that tends to look at things in a ways the infant finds informative. A model like this is far more likely to lead to an understanding of how social development goes awry, and how it impacts on other aspects of learning, than the many current theories that propose that gaze following is the result of an unspecified innate mechanism. As Box and Draper (1987) famously noted, while models are always wrong in the limit, they can still be very useful.

8 Conclusion

While the studies reviewed here have uniformly concerned themselves with normal language development, the discriminative approach has the potential to provide a raft of new insights into the impaired development that is characteristic of language disorders. Normal developmental trajectories depend both on stable learning processes, and on broad sampling of the linguistic environment. When sampling is impoverished, either because of the surrounding linguistic environment or because of perceptual deficits, such as hearing loss, trajectories may be predictably slowed or impaired. Learning may also be disrupted if the coordinative processes that subsume this type of sampling are in some way compromised (e.g., as a result of idiosyncrasies in attentional mechanisms, in the timing of prefrontal development, or in the social dynamics of parent-child interaction; Gros-Louis, West, and King, 2014; Warlaumont et al. 2014).

By assessing the structure of the linguistic input and the dynamics of the learning process, discriminative models furnish the analytic tools to better investigate and isolate the myriad causes of disordered development. Such analyses can pinpoint where the child is on the learning trajectory (e.g., identifying the difference between younger and older learners based on their errors; Ramscar et al. 2013d) and also suggest possible interventions to help move them along (such as adopting postnominal constructions to facilitate color and number learning, Ramscar et al. 2010; 2011; or highlighting optimal timing dynamics between parent and child in labeling, Yu and Smith, 2012). Many other such other targeted interventions are possible; the space of possible applications has only begun to be explored.

We have sought here to provide an overview of what a discriminative learning approach to language learning looks like, along with the benefits that adopting formal and conceptual models of discriminative learning can bring to our understanding of human development. It is our hope that more of our colleagues will be inspired to consider this approach in the future.

References

Arnon, Inbal, & Eve V. Clark. 2011. Why *brush your teeth* is better than *teeth* – Children's word production is facilitated in familiar sentence-frames. *Language Learning and Development* 7(2). 107–129.

Baayen, R. Harald, Laurie Beth Feldman & Robert Schreuder. 2006. Morphological influences on the recognition of monosyllabic monomorphemic words. *Journal of Memory and Language* 55(2). 290–313.

Baayen, R. Harald, James M. McQueen, Ton Dijkstra & Robert Schreuder. 2003. Frequency effects in regular inflectional morphology: Revisiting Dutch plurals. In Baayen, R. Harald & Robert Schreuder. (eds.), *Morphological structure in language processing*, 355–370. Berlin: Mouton de Gruyter.

Blevins, Jim, Petar Milin, & Michael Ramscar. 2015. Zipfian discrimination. *NetWordS*.

Box, George E.P. & Norman Richard Draper. 1987. *Empirical model-building and response surfaces*. New York: Wiley.

Davies, Mark. 2009. The 385+ million word corpus of contemporary American English (1990-present). *International Journal of Corpus Linguistics* 14. 159–90.

Davis, Matthew H., William D. Marslen-Wilson & M. Gareth Gaskell. 2002. Leading up the lexical garden path: Segmentation and ambiguity in spoken word recognition. *Journal of Experimental Psychology: Human Perception and Performance* 28(1). 218.

Derks, Peter L. & Marianne I. Paclisanu. 1967. Simple strategies in binary prediction by children and adults. *Journal of Experimental Psychology* 73(2). 278–285.

Finn, Amy S., Taraz Lee, Allison Kraus & Carla L. Hudson Kam. 2014. When it hurts (and helps) to try: The role of effort in language learning. *PloS one* 9(7). e101806.

Finn, Amy S., Carla L. Hudson Kam, Marc Ettlinger, Jason Vytlacil & Mark D'Esposito. 2013. Learning language with the wrong neural scaffolding: the cost of neural commitment to sounds. *Frontiers in systems neuroscience*, 7.

Gahl, Susanne. 2008. Time and thyme are not homophones: The effect of lemma frequency on word durations in spontaneous speech. *Language* 84(3). 474–496.

Gahl, Susanne, Yao Yao & Keith Johnson. 2012. Why reduce? Phonological neighborhood density and phonetic reduction in spontaneous speech. *Journal of Memory and Language* 66(4). 789–806.

Gläscher, Jan, Nathaniel Daw, Peter Dayan & John P. O'Doherty. 2010. States versus rewards: dissociable neural prediction error signals underlying model-based and model-free reinforcement learning. *Neuron* 66(4). 585–595.

Gros-Louis, Julie, Meredith J. West & Andrew P. King. 2014. Maternal responsiveness and the development of directed vocalizing in social interactions. *Infancy* 19(4). 385–408.

Hudson Kam, Carla L. & Elissa L. Newport. 2005. Regularizing unpredictable variation: The roles of adult and child learners in language formation and change. *Language Learning and Development* 1. 151–195.

Kam, Carla L. Hudson & Elissa L. Newport. 2009. Getting it right by getting it wrong: When learners change languages. *Cognitive Psychology* 59(1). 30–66.

James, William. 1890. *The principles of psychology*. New York: Henry Holt.

Johnson, Jacqueline S. & Elissa L. Newport. 1989. Critical period effects in second language learning: The influence of maturational state on the acquisition of English as a second language. *Cognitive Psychology* 21. 60–99.

Kamin, Leon J. 1969. Predictability, surprise, attention, and conditioning. *Punishment and Aversive Behaviour*. 279–296.

Kemps, Rachèl JJK, Mirjam Ernestus, Robert Schreuder & R. Harald Baayen. 2005. Prosodic cues for morphological complexity: The case of Dutch plural nouns. *Memory & Cognition* 33(3). 430–446.

Montague, P. Read, Steven E. Hyman & Jonathan D. Cohen. 2004. Computational roles for dopamine in behavioural control. *Nature* 431(7010). 760–767.

Miller, Ralph R., Robert C. Barnet & Nicholas J. Grahame. 1995. Assessment of the Rescorla-Wagner model. *Psychological bulletin* 117(3). 363.

Niv, Yael. 2009. Reinforcement learning in the brain. *Journal of Mathematical Psychology* 53. 139–154.

Pavlov, Ivan. 1927. *Conditioned reflexes: An investigation of the physiological activity of the cerebral cortex*, trs. Gelb Anrep. London: Oxford University Press.

Pinker, Steven. 2004. Clarifying the logical problem of language acquisition. *Journal of Child Language* 31. 949–953.

Port, Robert F. & Adam P. Leary. 2005. Against formal phonology. *Language* 81(4). 927–964.

Plag, Ingo, Julia Homann & Gero Kunter. 2015. Homophony and morphology: The acoustics of word-final S in English. *Journal of Linguistics* 53(1). 181–216.

Quine, W. V. O. 1960. *Word and object*. Cambridge, MA: MIT Press

Reddy, Michael. 1979. The conduit metaphor. *Metaphor and thought* 2. 164–201.

Ramscar, Michael. 2013. Suffixing, prefixing, and the functional order of regularities in meaningful strings. *Psihologija* 46(4). 377–396.

Ramscar Michael & R. Harald Baayen. 2013. Production, comprehension, and synthesis: a communicative perspective on language. *Frontiers in Psychology* 4. 233. doi:10.3389/fpsyg.2013.00233.

Ramscar, Michael & Melody Dye. 2011. Learning language from the input: Why innate constraints can't explain noun compounding. *Cognitive Psychology* 62(1). 1–40.

Ramscar, Michael, Melody Dye, Hanna Muenke Popick & Fiona O'Donnell-McCarthy. 2011. The enigma of number: Why children find the meanings of even small number words hard to learn and how we can help them do better. *PLoS ONE* 6(7). e22501. doi:10.1371/journal.pone.0022501

Ramscar, Michael, Melody Dye, Jessica W. Gustafson & Joseph Klein. 2013. Dual routes to cognitive flexibility: Learning and response conflict resolution in the dimensional change card sort task. *Child Development* 84(4). 1308–23.

Ramscar, Michael, Melody Dye & Joseph Klein. 2013. Children value informativity over logic in word learning. *Psychological Science* 24(6). 1017–1023.

Ramscar, Michael, Melody Dye & Stewart M. McCauley. 2013. Error and expectation in language learning: The curious absence of 'mouses' in adult speech. *Language* 89(4). 670–793.

Ramscar, Michael & Nicole Gitcho. 2007. Developmental change and the nature of learning in childhood. *Trends in cognitive sciences* 11(7). 274–279.

Ramscar, Michael, Peter Hendrix, Bradley Love & R. Harald Baayen. 2013. Learning is not decline: The mental lexicon as a window into cognition across the lifespan. *The Mental Lexicon* 8(3). 450–481.

Ramscar, Michael, Peter Hendrix, Cyrus Shaoul, Petar Milin & R. Harald Baayen. 2014. The myth of cognitive decline: Non-linear dynamics of lifelong learning. *Topics in Cognitive Science* 6. 5–42.

Ramscar, Michael & Robert Port. 2015. Categorization (without categories). In Dawbroska, Ewa & Dagmar Divjak (eds.), *Handbook of cognitive linguistics*, 75–99. Berlin, Boston: De Gruyter Mouton.

Ramscar, Michael & Daniel Yarlett. 2007. Linguistic self-correction in the absence of feedback: A new approach to the logical problem of language acquisition. *Cognitive Science* 31(6). 927–960.

Ramscar, Michael, Daniel Yarlett, Melody Dye, Katie Denny & Kirsten Thorpe. 2010. The effects of feature-label-order and their implications for symbolic learning. *Cognitive Science* 34(6). 909–957.

Rescorla, Robert A. 1968. Probability of shock in the presence and absence of CS in fear conditioning. *Journal of Comparative & Physiological Psychology* 66. 1–5.

Rescorla, Robert A. 1988. Pavlovian conditioning: It's not what you think it is. *American Psychologist* 43(3). 151–160.

Rescorla, Robert A. & Allan R. Wagner. 1972. A theory of Pavlovian conditioning: Variations in the effectiveness of reinforcement and nonreinforcement. In Abraham H. Black & William F. Prokasy (eds.), *Classical conditioning II: Current research and theory*, 64–99. New York: Crofts.

Rose, Tony, Mark Stevenson & Miles Whitehead. 2002. The Reuters Corpus Volume 1-From yesterday's news to tomorrow's language resources. *LREC* 2. 827–832.

Rumelhart, David E. & James L. McClelland. 1986. *On learning the past tenses of English verbs*. California University, San Diego: La Jolla Institute for Cognitive Science.

Saffran, Jenny R., Richard N. Aslin & Elissa L. Newport. 1996. Statistical learning by 8-month-old infants. *Science* 274(5294). 1926–1928.

Schultz, Wolfram. 2006. Behavioral theories and the neurophysiology of reward. *Annual Review of Psychology* 57. 87–115.

Schultz, Wolfram. 2010. Dopamine signals for reward value and risk: basic and recent data. *Behavioral and Brain Functions* 6. 1–9.

Seidenberg, Mark S. & David C. Plaut. 2014. Quasiregularity and its discontents: The legacy of the past tense debate. *Cognitive Science* 38(6). 1190–228.

Seidenberg, Mark S. & James L. McClelland. 1989. A distributed, developmental model of word recognition and naming. *Psychological review* 96(4). 523.

Shannon, Claude Elwood. 1948. A mathematical theory of communication. *Bell Systems Technical Journal* 27(3). 379–423.

Siegel, Shepard & Lorraine G. Allan. 1996. The widespread influence of the Rescorla-Wagner model. *Psychonomic Bulletin & Review* 3(3). 314–321.

Singleton, Jenny L. & Elissa L. Newport. 2004. When learners surpass their models: The acquisition of American Sign Language from inconsistent input. *Cognitive Psychology* 49. 370–407.

Thompson-Schill, Sharon L., Michael Ramscar & Evangelia G. Chrysikou. 2009. Cognition without control when a little frontal lobe goes a long way. *Current Directions in Psychological Science* 18(5). 259–263.

Todes, Daniel P. 2014. *Ivan Pavlov: A Russian life in science*. Oxford: Oxford University Press.

Tomasello, Michael. 2003. *Constructing a language: A usage-based theory of language acquisition*. Cambridge, MA: Harvard University Press.

Tomasello, Michael. 2008. *Origins of human communication*. Cambridge, MA: MIT Press.

Triesch, Jochen, Christof Teuscher, Gedeon O. Deák & Eric Carlson. 2006. Gaze following: Why (not) learn it? *Developmental Science* 9(2). 125–147.

Trimmer, Pete C., John M. McNamara, Alasdair I. Houston & James A.R. Marshall. 2012. Does natural selection favour the Rescorla–Wagner rule? *Journal of Theoretical Biology* 302. 39–52.

Waelti, Pascale, Anthony Dickinson & Wolfram Schultz. 2001. Dopamine responses comply with basic assumptions of formal learning theory. *Nature* 412. 43–48.

Warlaumont, Anne S., Jeffrey A. Richards, Jill Gilkerson & D. Kimbrough Oller. 2014. A social feedback loop for speech development and its reduction in autism. *Psychological Science* 25. 1314–1324.

Wittgenstein, Ludwig. 1953. *Philosophical investigations*. London: Blackwell.

Yu, Chen & Linda B. Smith. 2012. Embodied attention and word learning by toddlers. *Cognition* 125(2). 244–262.

F. Nihan Ketrez
10 Acquisition of an agglutinative language under adverse neonatal conditions

1 Introduction

This study focuses on the grammatical development of preterm (<37 weeks) and low birth weight (<2500 grams) children acquiring Turkish, and compares their developmental pattern in the domain of morphology (utterance and word length) to full term and normal birth weight children. Children who acquire language under adverse neonatal conditions are expected to have delays in their development in general. However, the results of studies on the language development of preterm/low birth weight (Pterm/LBW) versus full term/normal birth weight (Fterm/NBW) children vary. Some find delays in LBW children, some do not. Some find delays only in some areas of language, and some talk about a more general delay. Some observe delays only in extremely LBW children (<1000 grams), while report no delays for others.

Because the preterm birth usually occurs during a critical point in development, especially the brain development, it results in cognitive and neurological problems (Volpe 2001). Severe neurological damages are usually observed in extremely LBW children (<1000) while others experience only some mild delays. MRI studies show that preterm birth and low birth weight affect the architecture of the brain and this may result in brain injury that has long term effects (Martinussen 2005). During the first year of their life, Pterm/LBW children may have problems in their perceptual, motor, and cognitive abilities and these general problems may result in delays in other areas as well. Language is reported to be among them. Those studies that find differences in Pterm/LBW and Fterm/NBW children report that Pterm/LBW children start speaking later, go through the language acquisition milestones slower and are more likely to have language disorders when compared to their Fterm/NBW peers (Bailey and Wolery 1989, Field, Dempsey and Shuman 1981, Siegel 1982, Grunau et al. 1990, McCormick and Schiefelbusch 1990, Byrne et al. 1993, Briscoe et al. 1998, Vohr et al. 1988, Breslau et al. 2000, Sansavini and Guarini 2014, among many others,). Jansson-Verkasalo et al. (2004) report that Finnish-speaking LBW children at age 2;0 had relatively shorter sentences and had significantly lower scores in language tests in general. At age 4;0, children had deficiencies in language comprehension, auditory discrimination and naming. Language delay may be observed even in those children who do not have any other neurological problems (Özbek et al. 2005). Van Noort-van der Speck et al. (2012) observe that preterm infants' scores are lower than

---

F. Nihan Ketrez, İstanbul Bilgi University

DOI 10.1515/9781614514909-011

their full term peers in all the linguistic functions in early childhood. They catch up in adolescence in relatively simpler functions such as receptive vocabulary but they continue to be delayed in more complex linguistic functions such as grammar, phonological working memory, phonological awareness and semantic memory. Guarini et al. (2010) study the language and literacy of preterm Italian-speaking children at age eight and find that their subjects did not have a general delay, when compared to the controls, but have slight difficulties in linguistic abilities (grammar, lexicon, phoneme synthesis and deletion of the first syllable), and more difficulties in reading and writing.

LBW children do not only have disadvantaged biological or cognitive conditions due to their preterm birth. Their social interaction with their primary care givers and other people around them may also be different. They may be less attentive and less demanding of social interaction, and this may result in less attention or a different type of attention by care givers (Sansavini and Guarini 2014). Because parents of preterm infants have to deal with issues related to primary health problems, they may not have much energy and time for activities that could support their children's language development. Preterm children are more likely to spend time at the hospital and intensive care-units, which are not ideal environments for language development because of limitations of social interaction and language use. It is not surprising to observe that the length of hospital stay is inversely associated with language development in Pterm/LBW children (Casiro et al. 1990). Preterm children, especially the extremely low birth ones, are at higher risk for physical problems such as auditory, visual, and motor problems and this potentially affect their social interaction with their peers and adults. Xoinis et al. (2007), for example, lists auditory risks observed in preterm children. Similarly, Mikkola et al. (2005) reports that at age 5, only one fourth of the extremely LBW children are observed to be normally developed. 20% of them had major disabilities. Four percent needed a hearing aid, 30% had ophthalmic problems. Vohr et al. (2000) observed hearing impairment in 11%, and visual impairment in 9% of their cohort of 1151 infants at the age of 18 months. They also report that LBW is related to other chronic diseases. Therefore, LBW children's language acquisition experience may be influenced not only by their neurological condition due to preterm birth but also by the environment that may not be stimulating enough for language development due to their special health conditions.

Despite these disadvantages and potential problems, there are also studies that do not find any developmental differences between Pterm/LBW and Fterm/NBW infants in terms of language around age 2;0–3;0 or later (See, for example, Greenberg and Crnic 1988, Ungerer and Sigman 1983). These studies report that those children who were lagging behind catch up with their peers around age 2;0. Aram et al. (1991) observe that specific language impairment (SLI) is not more frequent in LBW children (defined as 1500 grams or less at birth) around age 8. In their study which is based on 200 randomly selected LBW children, they observe differences in other cognitive areas. Menyuk et al. (1991) find that the differences between preterm and full term children in terms of their reading ability in later years (5–8 years) are not very big but preterm infants are still at higher risk for reading difficulties. In contrast, Barsky and Siegel (1992) do not find any differences in reading scores of preterm and full term infants. Menyuk et al. (1995) studies 28 preterm and 28 term children longitudinally until 3;0 years of age (for a 30 month period) through different types of measures (including a lexical diary, MLU, comprehension and production tests that are used to evaluate children's morphological, syntactic, pragmatic and semantic development) and observe that preterm and full term children are not different in any of the measures that they applied. They attribute this to parents' special attention to their preterm children, among other environmental conditions that help children overcome the challenges of preterm birth.

The differences between the studies which observe a difference between NBW and LBW children and those who cannot find any difference may be due to the differences in methodology, areas of language that were studied, age range of the children, as well as the uncontrolled environmental and biological factors that affect language development. Home environment and how much attention children receive from their care-givers, for example, is difficult to control. It is also important to note that not all LBW children are alike in terms of their physical conditions. Some of these children are also small for gestational age (SGA), so low birth weight is not necessarily due to preterm birth. Being SGA is considered to be a greater risk factor for overall development than LBW and preterm birth (Strauss and Dietz, 1998; Lundgren et al 2001). In SGA children, language is observed to be among the areas that are at risk (Kok, et al. 1998). Moreover, in some studies that focus on preterm birth and low birth weight, multiple-birth infants, who are likely to have low birth weight due to their special prenatal conditions, are included in the analyses together with singleton children. Multiple-birth children are observed to have atypical language development. Although the delay that is observed in their development may be related to their preterm and low birth weight, their atypical development may also be due to psychosocial reasons, such as less direct and mostly distracted linguistic input from their care-givers (Reznick, 1997; Stafford, 1987; Tomasello, Mannle, and Kruger, 1986; Conway et al., 1980; Thorpe, Rutter, and Greenwood, 2003, among others). Therefore having different types of populations under preterm birth or low birth weight may have different and variable results.

A review of previous work on preterm/LBW and full term/NBW children reveal that there are still a lot that we do not know about the development of children in this particular population. One of the gaps in research in this area is the cross-linguistic contributions. Most literature on preterm and LBW children come from European languages and most studies are conducted using standardized tests on large populations of children without going into the details and possible individual differences in each child. In this study, we observe the acquisition of Turkish, a language with rich agglutinative morphology, with the goal of contributing to the cross-linguistic investigation of the development of LBW infants. The data were collected at children's home, through an observation of children's natural interaction with their primary care-givers. It provides us with the opportunity to observe the behavior and language of the child in a more natural context, with the adults who contribute to the linguistic context of development.

Turkish is an agglutinative language in which word formation is mainly realized by suffixation. Verbs are inflected by negation, tense/aspect and modality markers and person/number in the form of an agreement marker that has various paradigms depending on the tense/aspect markers that they follow. The yes/no question marker may be attached to the verb complex, or it appears between the tense/aspect marker and the agreement marker. Passive, causative, reflexive and reciprocal markers are directly attached to the verb stems and are followed by inflectional markers. Although it is possible to attach 10+ suffixes to a stem, as illustrated by the well-known Turkish example in (1), in actual everyday speech, speakers do not usually have words longer than 5–6 morphemes. The example in (2) is a more natural word that could be found in the corpora. It has a passive marker attached to the verb, the abilitative mood marker, negation, progressive (aspect) marker, person agreement, question marker and finally the past tense marker follows.

(1) *Avrupa-lı-laş-tır-a-ma-dık-lar-ımız-dan-mı-ymış-sınız?*
Europe-ATR-DERV:V-CAUS-ABIL-NEG-REL:DIK-PLU-POSS&1P-ABL-QUE-2P
'Are you one of those that we could not Europeanize?'

(2) *oku-n-a-m-ıyor-lar-mı-ydı?*
read-PASS-ABIL-NEG-PROG-3P-QUE-PAST
'could they not be read?'

Nouns can carry relatively less number of inflections but they can still be inflected by the possessive marker, case markers and plural marker. Turkish has accusative, dative, locative, ablative, genitive and instrumental/comitative cases. When nouns appear in the predicate position, they can bear tense/aspect and agreement markers as well. Because there is no phonological realization of the copula, these markers appear on the noun and contribute to the complexity of the noun. All suffixes are attached one after another, undergoing various alternations due to vowel harmony and other phonological changes (e.g., (de)voicing, high vowel omission before vowels).

(3) *anne-ler-i-ni*
anne-PLU-POSS&3S-ACC
'their mother-acc'

(4) anne-si-mi-siniz?
    mother-POSS&3S-QUE-2P
    'are you her/his mother?'

In addition to these, Turkish relative clause and subordinate clause formation are also realized through suffixation. They bear appropriate suffixes (-(y)An, -DIK/-(y)AcAK, or -mA(K)) followed by possessive or case markers when they occur in the object positions. These formations add richness to the structures and increase the number of morphemes in an utterance.

Despite these alternations, Turkish inflectional marking is relatively regular, with a few exceptional irregularities (See for example, Nakipoğlu and Ketrez 2005). Children follow morphological cues to assign grammatical roles (Slobin and Bever 1985) and make assumptions regarding the argument structure of verbs (Göksun, Naigles and Küntay 2008). Normally developing children start producing both nominal and verbal inflection quite early, usually around the one-word stage (Aksu-Koç and Slobin 1985). The number of suffixes that they attach to stems increase by age and reach the MLU of 3,00 or higher by age 2;0–2;6 (Ketrez 1999, Xanthos et al. 2011).

Children's errors that are observed to be in the form of omissions or substitutions are very few in number. Ketrez (2006), for example, reports that the child that is studied longitudinally between 1;3,3–2;0,4 omits the accusative case in only 8% of the obligatory contexts. Because the errors are observed only in the immediately preverbal position, where it is legitimate to omit this marker, they are attributed to the child's overgeneralization of the omission rule in the adult language. Errors observed in other case markers are even less in number.

2 Method

2.1 Participants

Participants of the study were 10 Pterm/LBW (6 male and 4 female) and 10 Fterm/NBW (6 male and 4 female) children. LBW children included 4 low birth weight (LBW), 3 very low birth weight (VLBW) and 3 extremely low birth weight (ELBW) children. LBW children were those whose birth weight was below 2500 grams regardless of their gestational age. VLBW children were those who have a birth weight lower than 1500 grams. ELBW children had a birth weight lower than 1000 grams. The mean birth weight of the LBW group as a whole was 1517 with a range between 495 grams and 2490 grams. The gestational age of the group ranged between 26–34 weeks with a mean of 30 weeks. One child in VLBW group (VLBW-EN) and one child in the ELBW group (ELBW-EL) were SGA (small for gestational age) according to the norms reported for Turkey in Topçu et al. (2014). Table 1 displays the birth weight and gestational age information of children in this category together with information regarding the length of the sessions that were included in the study and total number of utterances. The last column shows the ages of the children during each session.

Table 1: Birth weight, gestational age and recording information of preterm low birth weight (LBW), preterm very low birth (VLBW) and preterm extremely low birth weight (ELBW) children participants

Child	Sex	B.weight (grams)	G.age (weeks)	Length (mins)	Total no. of Utterences	Ages at sessions
LBW-NA	F	2490	34	67	368	1;11,13, 2;0,9, 2;0,28
LBW-AL	M	2300	33	66	231	2;0,7, 2;1,0, 2;1,15
LBW-KU	M	2100	33	43	288	1;11,13, 2,0,11, 2;1
LBW-DU	F	1934	33	69	478	1;11,19, 2;0,26, 2;1,16
VLBW-BE	M	1500	29	40	72	2;0,27, 2;1,17
VLBW-EN	F	1400*	34	65	390	1;11,06, 1;11,23, 2;0,10
VLBW-AY	M	1100	30	58	94	1;11,13, 1;11,27, 2;0,10, 2;0,24
ELBW-EF	M	980	27	63	182	2;0,4, 2;0,17, 2;1,4
ELBW-KA	M	880	26	63	364	1;11,6, 2;0,4, 2;0,19
ELBW-EL	F	495*	26	94	257	1;11,0, 1;11,13, 2;0,7, 2;1,3
Mean		1517	30	62,8	272,4	

(*) Small for gestational age (SGA)

Normal birth weight (NBW) children were observed as a control group. Children were born with birth weights 2500 grams and higher (up to 4200 grams) were considered normal. The NBW children in this study had a birth weight range between 2900 and 3800 grams and their mean birth weight was 3373 grams. Their gestational age ranged between 37–41 weeks with a mean of 38,9 weeks. Table 2 displays the information of the participants as well as the information regarding the recordings.

Table 2: Birth weight, gestational age and recording information of Fullterm/Normal Birth Weight (NBW) children

Child	Sex	B.weight (grams)	G.age (weeks)	Length (minutes)	Total no. Utterances	Ages at sessions
NBW-MI	F	3800	39	85	839	1;11,19, 2;0,5, 2;0,23
NBW-İS	M	2900	37	61	432	1;11,22, 2;0,8, 2;0,28
NBW-ZD	F	3360	41	49	248	2;0,4, 2;1,0
NBW-OZ	M	2900	40	60	201	2;0,4, 2;0,19, 2;1,3
NBW-DR	F	3380	38	63	125	1;11,28, 2;0,4, 2;0, 28
NBW-FI	M	3090	39	63	149	1;11,11, 1;11,23, 2;0,17, 2;1,9
NBW-BE	F	3250	39	56	230	1;11,16, 2;0,2, 2;0,23
NBW-DT	M	3680	38	73	480	1;11,17, 2;0,2, 2;0,17
NBW-TZ	M	3775	40	48	286	2;0,20, 2;1,4
NBW-BA	M	3600	38	58	139	1;11,6, 2;0,4, 2;0,24
Mean		3373	38,9	61,6	312,9	

All participants belonged to middle socio-economic status families living in İstanbul and were recruited when they responded to an ad posted at mailing lists and blogs that were typically followed by mothers. All mothers had at least a high school degree. All, except VLBW-BE, who had 6-year-old twin brothers, did not have any siblings. At the time of the recording, they did not attend kindergarten. They were taken care of either by their stay-at-home mothers, grandmothers, or a full-time nanny. All the participants, including the extremely LBW ones, were normally developing in social interaction, language, and fine motor abilities according to the Turkish adaptation of Denver II Developmental Screening Test (Anlar and Yalaz, 1996). Two participants in the VLBW group (VLBW-AY and VLBW-BE) had delay (questionable scores) only in their gross motor abilities.

2.2 Procedure

Participating children were longitudinally video-recorded at their home for 20–30 minutes, twice a month between 1;1–3;0 as a part of an extensive language development study. The recordings were then transcribed and morphologically coded following the CHILDES conventions (MacWhinney 2000). The sessions that corresponded to the ages 1;11, 2;0 and 2;1 were selected for analysis for this particular study. Number of sessions and total duration of the sessions are seen in the last two columns of Table 1 and Table 2. During the sessions, children played with adults freely. Some material and toys were used to initiate conversations and keep the child engaged in the activity, but they were not in any form of formal testing material.

Four different analyses were run on the merged files of each child using the CLAN program and children's MLU (mean length of utterance) in terms of morphemes (MLUm) and words (MLUw) MLW (mean length of word) and PBF (percentage of base forms) were examined with the goal of documenting the differences between LBW and NBW children's word and utterance sizes. PBF analysis was proposed by Gagarina and Voeikova (2002) as a method of evaluation of the morphological complexity in children's speech. Base forms are the default morphological forms in early language. In Turkish, base forms are proposed to be the uninflected bare forms and PBF score of Turkish CDS is observed to be around 50% (Ketrez and Aksu-Koç 2009).

3 Results and discussion

The birth weights of the participants in the Pterm/LBW (n = 10) and Fterm/NBW (n = 10) groups were 1517 grams (Range: 495–2490, SD: 666,6) and 3373 grams (Range: 2900–3800, SD: 338,7) respectively. Similarly, their gestational ages were 30,5 weeks (Range: 26–34, SD: 3,308) and 38,90 weeks (Range: 37–40, SD: 1,197). Independent

Samples *t*-tests conducted on the birth weights and the gestational ages of the groups confirm that Pterm/LBW and Fterm/NBW children have significantly different birth weights and gestational ages ($t(18) = 5,504$, $p = .031$) and $t(18) = 18,732$, $p = .000$). The rest of the analyses that are reported below are conducted to observe whether the two groups of children have differences in the complexity levels of their utterances and words.

MLUw range of the Preterm/LBW children was 1,00–2,06 with a mean of 1,24 (SD: .101) while the range of NBW children was 1,10–2,28 with a mean of 1,84 (SD: .372). An independent samples *t*-test conducted on MLUw suggested that Fterm/NBW children had significantly longer utterances in terms of the number of words ($t(18) = 3,85$, $p = .001$).

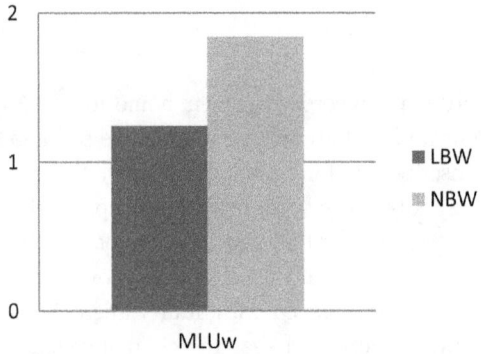

Figure 1: MLUw of LBW and NBW children

The second analysis looked at children's MLU in terms of morphemes. The MLUm range of the children in the LBW group was 1,00–2,85 and their mean was 1,68 (SD: .590). In the NBW children, the lowest MLU was 1,25, the highest was 3,32. Their group mean was 2,28 (SD: .823). So in the LBW group there was a child who had not started inflecting any words yet, while all the children, at least to some extent, inflected words in the NBW group. Moreover, the LBW children never got as high as 3,00 morphemes in average in terms of utterance size. Despite these differences between the individual children in each group, independent samples *t*-test run on the mean scores of the two groups yielded no significant difference between the MLUm of LBW and NBW children ($t(16,329) = 1,866$, $p = .080$). It is important to note that, in the NBW group there were children whose MLUm is smaller than the MLUm of some of the LBW children and it was also the other way around (See Tables 3 and Table 4). There were some LBW children, whose MLU was bigger than some NBW children. It is likely that this variance affected the result and the difference appeared only as a trend.

Table 3: MLUw, MLUm, MLW and PBF of LBW participants

Preterm/Low Birth Weight (LBW) children					
child	b.w.	g.a.	MLUw	MLUm	MLW
LBW-NA	2490	34	1,38	2,09	1,54
LBW-AL	2300	33	1,01	1,06	1,03
LBW-KU	2100	33	1,34	2,03	1,53
LBW-DU	1934	33	2,06	2,85	1,59
VLBW-BE	1500	29	1,21	1,62	1,34
VLBW-EN	1400	34	1,28	2,19	1,74
VLBW-AY	1100	30	1,00	1,00	1,00
ELBW-EF	980	27	1,05	1,50	1,44
ELBW-KA	880	26	1,07	1,22	1,16
ELBW-EL	495	26	1,04	1,32	1,28
Mean	1517	30,5	1,24	1,68	1,36

Table 4: MLUw, MLUm, MLW and PBF of NBW participants

Term/Normal Birth Weight (NBW) children					
child	b.w.	g.a.	MLUw	MLUm	MLW
NBW-MI	3800	39	1,99	3,31	1,70
NBW-İS	2900	37	2,08	3,32	1,72
NBW-ZD	3360	41	1,15	1,77	1,42
NBW-OZ	2900	40	1,70	1,84	1,44
NBW-DR	3380	38	2,27	1,30	1,21
NBW-FI	3090	39	1,40	1,33	1,12
NBW-BE	3250	39	2,28	2,74	1,32
NBW-DT	3680	38	2,10	1,47	1,16
NBW-TZ	3775	40	1,84	3,01	1,76
NBW-BA	3600	38	2,27	2,60	1,76
Mean:	3373,5	38,9	1,84	2,28	1,46

Earlier work on Turkish morphological development reported that a Turkish child's MLUm reached around 3,00 at age 2;0 (Ketrez 1999, Aksu-Koç and Ketrez 2003, Ketrez and Aksu-Koç 2009, among others). In this study, we had three NBW children who reached this MLUm level (NBW-MI, NBW-İS and NBW-TZ). However, the rest of the children, seven out of ten, did not reach 3,00 at 2;0. When these fast developing children are excluded, the MLU of the NBW children becomes 1,84, which is closer to the MLU of LBW children (1,75). Five children, which was half of the NBW children, did not even get as high as 2,0, similar to the LBW children. So the majority of the NBW children were very similar to the LBW children.

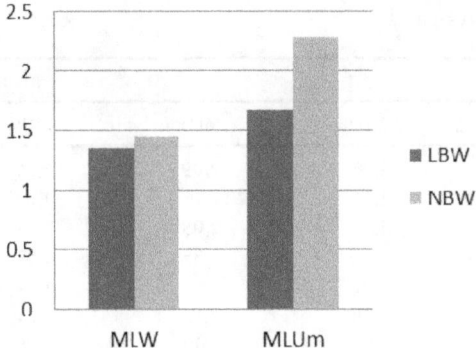

Figure 2: MLUm and MLW of LBW and NBW children

The third analysis conducted on the word size in terms of number of morphemes yielded similar results. MLW of NBW children was 1,46 (SD: .257) with a range of 1,12–1,76, while the MLW of LBW children was 1,36 (SD: .247) with a range of 1,00–1,174. An independent samples t-test conducted on the MLW of two groups revealed that there was no significant difference between the word sizes of the two groups around age 2;0 ($t(18) = .406, p = .851$).

In these analyses that looked at children's utterance and word sizes, those children who were SGA did not perform any worse than the other children. Moreover, VLBW-EN was among the children who had the highest MLUm, MLUw and MLW. In all three analyses, her scores were higher than the group means. The other SGA child, ELBW-EL, had scores below the group means, but she was still not the one with the lowest scores. These results, based on two children, suggest that SGA condition did not appear as a further risk factor in word complexity.

Finally, LBW and NBW children's PBF scores were compared (Table 5). The mean PBF of the LBW group and NBW group were 72,4 (SD: 14,48) and 66,2 (SD: 16,42), respectively, and they range between 52,05–100 (LBW) and 45,11–89,1 (NBW). In both groups the lowest PBF was around the adult level (50%). In the LBW group the highest two PBF belonged to VLBW-AY (100%) and VLBW-AL (95,9%). In the NBW children the highest PBF was 89,1%. So in this final analysis, too, we observed that LBW children did not lag behind their NBW peers (Chi-square (1, $n = 20$) = 0.8415, $p = 0.35$). On the contrary, in the NBW group there were children (E.g., NBW-FI, NBW-DT) who lagged behind some of the LBW children (E.g., VLBW-EN, LBW-DU).

In this analysis, too, SGA children did not appear as the ones with the lowest scores. VLBW-EN appears as the child who had the lowest PBF score (52%). ELBW-EL had a PBF of 75,37%, which was above the group mean, but it was still not the highest one. So, in this analysis too being SGA did not seem to result in an extra challenge for the Pterm/LBW infants.

Table 5: PBF scores of Preterm/LBW and Full term/NBW children

child	b.w.	g.a.	PBF	child	b.w.	g.a.	PBF
LBW-NA	2490	34	63,07	NBW-MI	3800	39	50,60
LBW-AL	2300	33	95,9	NBW-İS	2900	37	52,99
LBW-KU	2100	33	62,82	NBW-ZD	3360	41	62,96
LBW-DU	1934	33	54,77	NBW-OZ	2900	40	69,64
VLBW-BE	1500	29	67,41	NBW-DR	3380	38	84,31
VLBW-EN	1400	34	52,05	NBW-FI	3090	39	89,14
VLBW-AY	1100	30	100	NBW-BE	3250	39	72,42
ELBW-EF	980	27	64,55	NBW-DT	3680	38	84,84
ELBW-KA	880	26	84,55	NBW-TZ	3775	40	50,26
ELBW-EL	495	26	75,37	NBW-BA	3600	38	45,11
Mean	1517	30,5	72,05	Mean:	3373,5	38,9	66,22

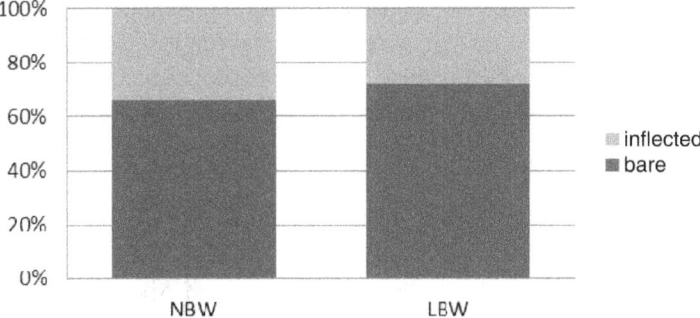

Figure 3: Percentage of Base form (PBF) of LBW and NBW children

In summary, analyses that were conducted on Pterm/LBW and Fterm/NBW children's MLUm, MLW and PBF did not show any differences between the groups in three of the analyses. LBW children were different only in terms of the number of words in an utterance, rather than morphological complexity of words or utterances. This may be attributed to the facilitating impact of the morphological complexity in language development. In cross-linguistic studies conducted on a variety of typologically different languages (see for example Slobin (1985) or Xanthos et al. (2011)), Turkish children appear as the ones who have the most complex morphological development at an early age. Results in the present study show that morphological complexity contributes to the language acquisition of the developmentally disadvantaged preterm/LBW children as well. It appears that the number of words that a child can put together to form sentences can be effected by this neonatal condition, while word size in terms of morphemes is not that vulnerable and is not subject to vary at age 2;0 due to the birth weight or gestational age of children.

4 Conclusion

The results suggested that children who experienced adverse neonatal conditions do not necessarily lag behind their full term and normal birth weight peers in terms of morphological complexity. In terms of the word and utterance sizes in morphemes and PBF, Pterm/LBW and Fterm/NBW children observed here are not different. Pterm/LBW children lag behind only in the number of words in an utterance. These results are consistent with the results in the literature that report differences only in some areas of grammar and contribute to them with novel data from a language that has not yet been explored from this perspective.

It is important to note again that the majority of LBW children in this study were normally developing children. It is likely that they were not very different when compared to NBW children because of this special property. Another crucial property of the participants was that they had educated mothers, and they belonged to middle socio-economic status. So in terms of environmental properties they had advantages, which most probably helped them tackle the adverse neonatal conditions. The results here suggest that LBW and preterm children may have normal language development, at least in the domain of morphological complexity, when they do not have serious neurological defects.

Acknowledgments

This study was supported by a grant from TUBİTAK, Turkish Scientific and Technological Research Council (2011–2014, Grant no.: 111K270, Principle investigator: F. Nihan Ketrez Sözmen)

References

Aksu-Koç, Ayhan & Dan I. Slobin. 1985. Acquisition of Turkish. In Dan I. Slobin (ed.), *Crosslinguistic study of language acquisition*, Vol. 1, 839–878. New Jersey: Lawrence Earlbaum Assoc.

Aksu-Koç, Ayhan & F. Nihan Ketrez. 2003. Early verbal morphology in Turkish: Emergence of inflections. In Dagmar Bittner, Wolfgang U. Dressler & Marianne Kilani-Schoch (eds.), *Mini-paradigms and the emergence of verb morphology*, 27–52. Berlin: Mouton de Gruyter.

Anlar, Banu & Kalbiye Yalaz. 1996. *Denver II Gelişimsel Tarama Testi Türk Çocuklarına Uyarlanması ve Standardizasyonu* [Adaptation to Turkish children and standardization of Denver II Developmental Screening Test]. Hacettepe Çocuk Nörolojisi Gelişimsel Tıp Araştırmaları Grubu, Ankara.

Aram, Dorothy M., Maureen Hack, Suzanne Hawkins, Barbara M. Weissman & Elaine Borawski-Clark. 1991. Very-low-birthweight children and speech and language development. *Journal of Speech and Hearing Research* 34. 1169–1179.

Bailey, Donald B. & Mark Wolery. 1989. *Assessing infants and preschoolers with handicaps*. Columbus, OH: Merrill.

Barsky, Valerie & Linda S. Siegel. 1992. Predicting future cognitive, academic, and behavioral outcomes for very low-birth-weight infants. In Sarah L. Friedman & Marian D. Sigman (eds.), *The psychological development of low birth weight children*, 275–298. Norwood, NJ: Ablex.

Breslau, Naomi, Howard D. Chilcoat, Eric O. Johnson, Patricia Andreski & Victoria C. Lucia. 2000. Neurologic soft signs and low birth weight: Their association and neuropsychiatric implications. *Biological Psychiatry* 47. 71–79.

Briscoe, Josie, Susan E. Gathercole & Neil Marlow. 1998. Short-term memory and language outcomes after extreme prematurity at birth. *Journal of Speech Language and Hearing Research* 41. 654–666.

Byrne, Joseph, Christine Ellsworth, Elizabeth Bowering & Michael Vincer. 1993. Language development in low birth weight infants: The first two years of life. *Journal of Developmental & Behavioral Pediatrics* 14(1). 21–7.

Casiro, Oscar G. Diane M. Moddemann, Richard Stanwick, Vinnie K. Panikkar-Thiessen, Heather Cowan & Mary S. Cheang. 1990. Language development of very low birth weight infants and fullterm controls at 12 months of age. *Early Human Development* 24(1). 64–77.

Conway, Dorice, Hugh Lytton & Fred Pysh. 1980. Twin-Singleton language differences. *Canadian Journal of Behavioral Science* 12(3). 264–271.

Field, Tiffany, Jean Dempsey & H. H. Shuman. 1981. Developmental follow-up of pre-term and post-term infants. In Marian Sigman & Sarah Friedman (eds.), *Preterm birth and psychological development*, 299–312. New York: Academic Press.

Gagarina, Natalia & Maria D. Voeikova. 2002. Early syntax, first lexicon and the acquisition of case forms by two Russian children. In Maria D. Voeikova & Wolfgang U. Dressler (eds.), *Pre- and Protomorphology: Early phases of morphological development in Nouns and Verbs*, 115–133. Munich: Lincom Europa.

Göksun, Tilbe, Letitia Naigles & Aylin Küntay. 2008. Turkish children use morphosyntactic bootstrapping in interpreting verb meaning. *Journal of Child Language* 35. 291–323.

Greenberg, Mark T. & Keith A. Crnic. 1988. Longitudinal predictors of developmental status and social interaction in premature and full-term infants at age two. *Child Development* 59. 554–570.

Grunau Ruth, V.E. Sheila Kearney & Michael Whitfield. 1990. Language development at 3 years in pre-term children of birth weight below 1000g. *British Journal of Disorders of Communication* 25. 173–182.

Guarini, Annalisa, Allesandra Sansavini, Cristina C. Fabbri, Sylvia Savini, Rosina Alessandroni, Giacomo Faldella, & Annette Karmiloff-Smith. 2010. A long-term effects of preterm birth on language and literacy at eight years. *Journal of Child Language* 37(4). 865–885.

Jansson-Verkasalo, Eira, Marita Valkama, Leena Vainionpää, Eija Pääkkö, Eero Ilkko & Matti Lehtihalmes. 2004. Language development in very low birth weight preterm children: A follow-up study. *Folia Phoniatrica Logopaedica* 56. 108–119.

Ketrez, F. Nihan. 1999. *Early verbs and the acquisition of Turkish argument structure*. Unpublished MA Thesis. Boğaziçi University, İstanbul.

Ketrez, F. Nihan. 2006. A case study on the accusative case in Turkish. In Michal T. Martinez, Asier Alcazar & Roberto Mayoral (eds.), *Proceedings of the Thirty-Third Western Conference on Linguistics (WECOL 2004)*. Volume 16. 163–173. Fresno, California: California State University, Fresno Publications.

Ketrez, F. Nihan & Ayhan Aksu-Koç. 2009. Early nominal morphology: Emergence of case and number. In Maria D. Voeikova & Ursula Stephany (eds.), *The development of number and case in the first language acquisition: A cross-linguistic perspective*, 15–48. Berlin: Mouton de Gruyter.

Kok, Joke H. Lya A. den Ouden, Pauline S. Verloove-Vanhorick & Roland Brand. 1998. Outcome of very preterm small for gestational age infants: The first nine years of life. *BJOG: An International Journal of Obstetrics & Gynaecology* 105. 162–168.

Lundgren, Ester Maria, Sven Cnattingius, Björn Jonsson & Torsten Tuvemo. 2001. Intellectual and psychological performance in males born small for gestational age with and without catch-up growth. *Pediatric Research* 50. 91–96.

MacWhinney, Brian. 2000. *The CHILDES Project: Tools for analyzing talk.* Hillsdale, New Jersey: Lawrence Erlbaum Associates, Publishers.

Martinussen, Marit, Bruce Fischl, H. B. Larsson, J. Skranes, S. Kulseng, T. R. Vangberg, T. Vik, A.-M. Brubakk, O. Haraldseth & A. M. Dale. 2005. Cerebral cortex thickness in 15-year-old adolescents with low birth weight measured by an automated MRI-based method. *Brain* 128. 2588–2596.

McCormick, Linda & Richard L. Schiefelbusch. 1990. *Early language intervention: An introduction.* (2nd Ed). Columbus, OH: Merrill.

Menyuk, Paula, Marie Chesnick, Jacqueline Weis Liebergott, Blanche Korngold, Ralph D'Agostino & Albert Belanger. 1991. Predicting reading problems in at risk children. *Journal of Speech and Hearing Research* 34. 893–903.

Menyuk, Paula, Jacqueline Weis Liebergott & Martin C. Schultz. 1995. *Early language development in full-term and premature infants.* Hillsdale, New Jersey: Lawrence Erlbaum Associates, Publishers.

Mikkola, Kaija, Niina Ritari, Viena Tommiska, Teija Salokorpi, Liisa Lehtonen, Outi Tammela, Leena Pääkkönen, Päivi Olsen, Marit Korkman & Vineta Fellman. 2005. Neurodevelopmental outcome at 5 years of age of a national cohort of extremely low birth weight infants who were born in 1996–1997. *Pediatrics* 116(6). 1391–1400.

Nakipoğlu, Mine & F. Nihan Ketrez. 2005. Children's overregularizations and irregularizations of the Turkish aorist. In David Bamman, Tatiana Magnitskaia & Colleen Zaller (eds.), *BUCLD 30: Proceedings of Boston University Conference on Language Development*, Volume 2, 399–410. Somerville, MA: Cascadilla Press.

Özbek, Aylin, Suha Miral, Neslihan Eminağaoğlu & Hasan Özkan. 2005. Development and behavior of non-handicapped preterm children from a developing country. *Pediatrics International* 47(5). 532–40.

Reznick, Steven J. 1997. Intelligence, language, nature and nurture in young twins. In Robert. J. Sternberg & Elena L. Grigorenko (eds.), *Intelligence, heredity and environment*, 483–504. New York: Cambridge University Press.

Sansavini, Alessandra & Annalisa Guarini. 2014. Language development in preterm infants and children. In Patricia Brooks & Vera Kempe (eds), *Encyclopedia of language development.* Thousand Oaks, CA: Sage Publications.

Siegel, Linda. 1982. Reproductive, perinatal and environmental factors in the cognitive and language development of preterm and full-term infants. *Child Development* 53. 963–973.

Slobin, Dan I. (ed.). 1985. *Crosslinguistic study of language acquisition.* New Jersey: Lawrence Earlbaum.

Slobin, Dan I. & Thomas G. Bever. 1982. Children use canonical sentence schemas: A cross-linguistic study of word order and inflection. *Cognition* 12(3). 229–265.

Stafford, Laura. 1987. Maternal input to twin and singleton children: implications for language acquisition. *Human Communication Research* 13. 429–462.

Strauss, Richard S. & William H. Dietz. 1998. Growth and development of term children born with low birth weights: effects of genetic and environmental factors. *Journal of Pediatrics* 133. 67–72.

Thorpe, Karine, Michael Rutter & Rosemary Greenwood. 2003. Twins as a natural experiment to study the causes of mild language delay: II: Family interaction risk factors. *Journal of Child Psychology and Psychiatry and Allied Disciplines* 44. 342–355.

Tomasello, Michael, Sara Mannle & Kruger, C. Ann. 1986. Linguistic environment of 1- to 2-year-old twins. *Developmental Psychology* 22(2). 169–176.

Topçu, Hasan Onur, Ali İrfan Güzel, Emre Özgü, Yunus Yıldız, Salim Erkaya & Dilek Uygur. 2014. Birth weight for gestational age: A reference study in a tertiary referral hospital in the middle region of Turkey. *Journal of the Chinese Medical Association* 77. 578–582.

Ungerer, Judy & Sigman, Marian. 1983. Developmental lags in preterm infants from one to three years of age. *Child development* 54(5). 1217–1228.

Van Noort-van der Spek, Inge, Marie-Christine Franken & Nynke Weisglas-Kuperus. 2012. Language functions in preterm-born children: A systematic review a meta-analysis. *Pediatrics* 129(4). 745–54.

Vohr, Betty R., Cynthia Garcia Coll & William Oh. 1988. Language development of low-birthweight infants at two years. *Developmental Medicine & Child Neurology* 30. 608–615.

Vohr, Betty R., Linda L. Wright, Anna M. Dusick, Lisa Mele, Joel Verter, Jean J. Steichen, Neal P. Simon, Dee C. Wilson, Sue Broyles, Charles R. Bauer, Virginia Delaney-Black, Kimberly A. Yolton, Barry E. Fleisher, Lu-Ann Papile & Michael D. Kaplan. 2000. Neurodevelopmental and functional outcomes of extremely low birth weight infants in the national institute of child health and human development neonatal research network, 1993–1994. *Pediatrics* 105(6). 1216–1226.

Volpe, Joseph J. 2001. *Neurology of the newborn*. Philadelphia: W.B. Saunders Company.

Xanthos, Aris, Sabine Laaha, Steven Gillis, Ursula Stephany, Ayhan Aksu-Koç, Anastasia Christofidou, Natalia Gagarina, Gordana Hrzica, F. Nihan Ketrez, Marianne Kilani-Schoch, Katharina Korecky-Kröll, Kovačević Melita, Klaus Laalo, Marijan Palmović, Barbara Pfeiler, Maria D. Voeikova & Wolfgang U. Dressler. 2011. On the role of morphological richness in the early development of noun and verb inflection. *First Language* 33. 411–433.

Xoinis, Konstantine, Yusnita Weirather, Hareesh Mavoori, Steven Shaha & Lynn M. Iwamoto. 2007. Extremely low birth weight infants are at high risk for auditory neuropathy. *Journal of Perinatology* 27. 718–723.

Batia Seroussi
11 Later morpho-lexical acquisition

1 Introduction

The development of the lexicon is a life-long process that begins in the first year of life and continues across adolescence and adulthood. The trajectory of the developing lexicon is characterized by a multi-dimensional increase both in breadth (for example, in the number of items that it includes) and depth (such as in the number of new senses associated with existing items) (Anglin, 1993; Clark, 1993; Corson, 1995; Deane et al. 2014; Nagy and Anderson, 1984; Nagy and Herman, 1987; Webb and Sasao, 2013) of the vocabulary. A language domain critical to enabling this increase both in quantity and quality of the lexicon is derivational morphology, the lexical as opposed to strictly grammatical branch of morphology concerned with processes of word-formation and the internal structure of words (Aronoff, 1976; Bybee, 1985; Matthews, 1991; Spencer, 1991).

2 Background on derivational morphology

The role of derivational morphology, or the status of morphemes as independent units in the mental lexicon is not unequivocal. One of the central debates related to morphology concerns form-meaning relations in the mental lexicon: the question of whether words are processed as wholes or are decomposed into their component morphemes, and if so, under what circumstances and to what extent. The issue of lexical decomposition involves the two key notions of semantic and phonological transparency. Derived words are considered semantically transparent if they are clearly related in meaning; for example the prefix *re* in words like *redial* and *restart* denotes repetition of *dial* and *start* respectively; in contrast, the morpho-phonologically derived verbs *recover* and *return* represent semantic opacity, since they do not indicate repetition of *covering* or *turning*. The noun *tact* and its associated adjective *tactful* represent phonological transparency since the addition of a suffix does not incur any sound change, in contrast to the relation between the verb *introduce* and the noun *introduction*, where the shift from verb-final *s* to noun-medial *kš* entails a phonological change that renders the relation phonologically opaque. Some researchers claim that words are processed as wholes in the mental lexicon (e.g., Butterworth, 1983) whereas other models propose that words are decomposed into morphemes irrespective of semantic and/or phonological transparency (Taft and Forster, 1976). Most models assume that a decomposition process is more likely to occur in cases of

Batia Seroussi, Levinsky College of Education

semantic and/or phonological transparency, whereas opacity of either or both sources yields more adherence to whole-word representation in the mental lexicon (Chiliant and Caramazza, 1995; Gonnerman, Seidenberg and Andersen, 2007; Marslen-Wilson et al., 1994; Schreuder and Baayen, 1995). Most also agree that decomposition processes are affected by factors such as productivity (Bybee, 1985; Baayen, 1994) and frequency so that they are more likely in case of infrequent words (e.g. *treelet*) (Anglin, 1993; Deacon, Whalen and Kirby, 2011; Hay and Baayen, 2001). Semantic transparency, phonological transparency and frequency play an important role in development as well, as discussed further in the developmental section of this paper.

2.1 Derivational morphology in English

This section provides a brief description of the structure of the lexicon in English, as the language most discussed in the chapter. Derivational morphemes in English include stems – both free stems in the form of independent words and bound stems that cannot occur independently – and affixes, both prefixes and suffixes. For example, the bi-morphemic word *happiness* includes the free stem *happy* and the suffix *-ness*, while the tri-morphemic word *unhappiness* includes the additional prefix *–un*; and the bi-morphemic words *impress* and *express* are constructed from the bound stem *-press* and the prefixes *im-* and *ex-* respectively (Aronoff, 1976; Corson, 1995). Affixes termed "neutral" are those like *-ness* or *–ment* (e.g., *happy / happiness, judge / judgement*), which do not cause phonological change in the corresponding stem, in contrast to non-neutral affixes like*–tion, -ity* (e.g. *connect / connection, serene / serenity*) that entail phonological changes such as stress shift and vowel change in the corresponding stem. The distribution of stems and affixes interacts with the dual sources of the double-layered lexicon of English, native Germanic and Graeco-Latinate (Bar-Ilan and Berman, 2007; Corson, 1995; Goodwin, Gilbert and Cho, 2013; Jarmulowicz and Taran, 2013). The Germanic lexicon is made of mainly everyday, colloquial items typical of spoken usage, whereas the Latinate lexicon is considered on a higher, more literate, register (see Corson, 1995, for a detailed review of the history of the English language). The Germanic-Latinate distinction is crucial not only in terms of register, but also structurally, in derivational morphology: Words of Germanic origin are typically monosyllabic and mono-morphemic, their stems are free and they typically take neutral type affixes (e.g. *calm-calmness*). In contrast, words of Latinate origin are typically polysyllabic and multi-morphemic, their stems are bound and affixation entails phonological changes (e.g., *severe-severity*). An important domain for derivational morphology in English is, thus, the high-register Latinate lexicon, a relatively late acquisition that develops mainly in the school years (Corson, 1995; Tyler and Nagy, 1984; Nagy and Townsend, 2012). It makes sense that this distinction between words of Latinate versus Germanic origin of words should have an important developmental impact, although most research on acquisition of derivational morphology in English fails to address this issue (see Bar-Ilan and Berman, 2007).

3 The acquisition of derivational morphology in English

This section starts with an attempt to disambiguate a variety of relevant terms with a high degree of overlap, at times employed indiscriminately in the literature, such as: morphological knowledge, morphological awareness, and morphological processing (Bowers, Kirby and Deacon, 2010; Kuo and Anderson, 2006). *Morphological awareness*, defined as "awareness of morphemic structures of words and the ability to reflect on and manipulate that structure" (Carlisle, 1995, p. 194), is considered an indicator of a high level of explicit meta-linguistic knowledge, related to both cognitive and linguistic skills (Gombert, 1992; Karmiloff-Smith, 1992). For example, a task such as judgment of whether two words are related (e.g., *happy-happiness*) requires a certain level of meta-linguistic knowledge that increases if participants are also required to explain the relationship. Explanation is more demanding than judgment since it entails access to and deployment of technical terms that are often both specific and abstract (e.g., stem, suffix, adjective) and hence a level of explicitness not necessary in judgment tasks (for a detailed discussion of the interplay between linguistic and meta-linguistic awareness see Carlisle, 1995). Some studies employ the term "morphological awareness" in cases where participants are required to operate at a quite basic level of meta-linguistic awareness, for example, being asked to add the agentive suffix *-er* to nouns, in a quite straightforward and common procedure that reaches ceiling effect relatively early in development (Clark and Hecht, 1982). Other studies, aimed at a more explicit expression morphological awareness, employ a variety of terms, which likewise tend to blur the borderline between different levels and types of morphological knowledge. The present paper attempts to clarify such issues by reviewing a wide range of terms and types of morphological data discussed in the research literature, located at various points along the continuum of from strictly linguistic to clearly metalinguistic knowledge.

3.1 Pioneering studies

Derivational morphology in English is strongly related to later language development, to the school years, and to the written modality (Anglin, 1993; Bar-Ilan and Berman, 2007; Berninger et al., 2010; Corson, 1995; Kieffer and DiFelice Box, 2013; Nagy and Townsend, 2012; Nippold and Sum, 2008; Nir-Sagiv, Bar-Ilan and Berman, 2008). A few pioneering studies, have, however, examined morphological knowledge in preschool children (e.g., Berko, 1958; Clark, 1993; Clark and Berman, 1984; Clark and

Hecht, 1982), demonstrating that English-speaking children pay attention to the internal structure of words long before they enter school. The studies of Clark and her associates on 3- to 6-year-olds found that, whereas children as young as three comprehended the base verb of agents and instruments with the suffix -*er* in more than 80% of the cases, the correct use of the same suffix for agents was 55% and for instruments 42%, gradually increasing to 91% and 72% respectively at age 5 to 6 years. In Berko's (1958) famous "wug" study, children aged 4 to 7 years and adults were asked to manipulate nonce words and to add inflectional and derivational suffixes, for example, to derive adjectives (e.g., *quirky* from the nonce-word *quirk*) or add agentive suffixes (*zibber* to the nonce verb *zib*). Only 11% of the five-year-olds produced the nonce word *zibber*, a task on which adults obtained 100% success, underlining the well-attested difference between processing real words as against nonce words.

Three seminal studies that explored morphological knowledge at school age established an important platform for further research. In chronological order, the first is the developmental study of Tyler and Nagy (1989) on three types of morphological knowledge in children in 4th, 6th and 8th grade: **relational**, defined as the ability to recognize that two words (e.g., *quick* and *quickly*) share a common morpheme, **syntactic** – knowledge of the syntactic properties of each suffix (e.g., that the suffix *ly* denotes an adverb); and **distributional** – the constrainsts on Latinate versus Germanic suffixes (for example, that the suffix *ity* attaches only to Latinate adjectives (e.g. *active* – *activity*) and not to Germanic adjectives (e.g. *good* – *goodity*). In line with their assumptions, they found that relational knowledge was the first to be acquired, followed by syntactic and distributional knowledge respectively; while non-neutral (phonologically opaque) suffixes posed an extra challenge, mainly to the younger age groups, and success was significantly lower on nonce than on real words at all age groups. In a later study, Anglin (1993) presented 1st, 3rd, and 5th graders with words of various degrees of frequency and morphological complexity randomly sampled from Webster's dictionary, revealing that awareness of morphological complexity in general and of affixes in particular increased with age. Success on morphological problem solving – decomposing unknown multi-morphemic words into their component morphemes in order to access their meaning – increased with age, including: precision in segmentation of multi-morphemic words (e.g. *helplessness*) into morphemes (*help, less, ness*) and awareness of the syntactic properties of derivational morphology such that younger children did relatively better with free stems and neutral affixes while older children succeeded in processing bound stems and non-neutral affixes as well. In a third study, Carlisle (1995) took explicit account of the important role of morphological knowledge as a bridge between semantic, phonological, and syntactic knowledge; she also portrayed various facets of morphological knowledge along a continuum of metalinguistic explicitness; and, third, methodologically, the tasks she devised and assigned – such as production of derivatives by adding derivational suffixes in the context of a sentence (e.g., *My uncle is a* ____

(farm)) and the "comes from" task (e.g., *Does the word fabulous comes from fable?*) – to this day constitute a point of reference for studies in the domain.

3.2 Contemporary studies

The bulk of research on derivational morphology in English in the 21st century centers around the school years and relates to various types of knowledge, involving different levels of explicitness. One set of such studies involve priming techniques, which explore the most implicit, sometimes unconscious morphological knowledge, for example, by means of the fragment completion method, in which children are presented with primes of stems and their derivatives (*need, needing, needy*, and the unrelated morphologically *needle*) and asked to complete fragments like *ne___* to form words (Deacon et al., 2010; Feldman et al., 2002; Rabin and Deacon, 2008). Results of these studies and others using different priming paradigms such as sentence completion (McCutchen, Logan and Biangardi-Orpe, 2009) and masked priming (Beyersmann, Castles & Coltheart, 2012; Quémart, Casalis and Colé, 2011) revealed similar trends: morphological priming occurred in the age range of 1st to 8th grade with no differences in amount of priming as a function of age-schooling level, yielding the conclusion that implicit morphological knowledge stabilizes very early in development. Further, in the study of McCutchen et al. significant priming appeared only to morphologically related words (e.g. *planner* and *plan*) but not to phonologically (e.g. *planet* and *plan*) or semantically related pairs (*strategy* and *plan*), a finding that validated the central role of morphology in the developing mental lexicon. The findings of two masked-priming studies performed in Hebrew, a typologically distinct language, (Schiff, Raveh and Fighel, 2012; Schiff, Raveh and Kahta, 2008) yielded results consistent with studies performed in English and French: on the one hand, significant morphological priming effects emerged irrespective of age and, on the other, the impact of phonological and semantic transparency was demonstrated by stronger priming effects to phonologically or semantically transparent targets.

Other, more conscious studies of morphological awareness include: extraction of the stem of a derived words (e.g. *complex* in the word *complexity*), adding suffixes to stems (e.g., completion of the sentence *My father is a farmer* with a derivative of the stem *farm*) (Carlisle, 1995), non-word derivation, or adding suffixes to nonexisting stems (e.g. completion of the sentence *The man is a great tranter* with a derivative of the stem *trant) (Berko, 1958; Mahoney, 1994), judgment whether pairs of words are related or the "comes from" task (e.g., *Are fun and funny related? / Does the word funny come from the word fun? Are corn and corner related? Does the word corner come from corn*) (Carlisle, 1995; Mahoney, 1994; Nagy, Berninger and Abbot, 2006) and analogies (e.g., *run-ran, swim-?*) (Kirby et al., 2012; Ravid and Shiff, 2006). The bulk of such studies were in writing or involved both the written and oral modalities, and only a few studies with schoolchildren were purely oral: Two of these required participants to produce the agentive -*er* suffix – in the 1st grade (Wolter, Wood and D'zatco, 2009) or in the 1st and 3rd grades (Duncan, Casalis and Colé, 2009), while the third investigated reading aloud of morphologically-complex words, part phonologically opaque and part phonologically transparent (Jarmulowicz and Taran, 2007). The main findings of the oral studies were for age-related improvement in morphological abilities and significant correlations between oral morphological skills and literacy achievements.

Mixed modality studies of morphological awareness (for example, the investigator read aloud words that participants were required to write) or studies performed exclusively in writing typically found positive correlations between written language and vocabulary as well as with at least one of the various aspects of literacy – reading accuracy, reading comprehension, and spelling (Apel et al., 2012; Berninger et al., 2010; Carlisle and Stone, 2005; Deacon et al., 2011; Foorman, Petscher and Bishop, 2012; Goodwin et al., 2013; 2014; How and Larkin, 2013; Kieffer and DiFelice Box, 2013; Kieffer and Lesaux, 2012a, b, c; Kirby et al., 2012; Mann and Singson, 2003; McCutchen, Green and Abbot, 2008; Nunes, Bryant and Barros, 2012; Pacton and Deacon, 2008). Yet there is some controversy as to the precise extent and nature of the effects of morphological awareness on literacy as well as on the developmental trajectories that they yield. Thus, while all of the studies that examined the effect of morphological awareness on reading accuracy found positive correlations between the two skills, they revealed different developmental trajectories. Carlisle and Stone (2005), for example, found morphological effects on reading accuracy of isolated words and phonological transparency effects both in 3rd and 6th grades, whereas Foorman et al.'s (2012) study of children between 3rd and 10th grade found a stronger relation between morphological awareness and reading accuracy in their younger age groups of 3rd to 5th grades. The picture with respect to morphological awareness and reading comprehension is even more complex, pointing to a dense, age-dependent network of direct and indirect relations. For example, Apel et al.'s (2012) work with 2nd and 3rd graders found that morphological awareness uniquely contributed to both spelling and word recognition and approached significance in its unique contribution to reading comprehension. Kieffer and colleagues (Kieffer and DiFelice Box, 2013; Kieffer and Lesaux, 2012b, c) found both direct and indirect contribution, via vocabulary size, of morphological awareness to reading comprehension in the 6th grade. In another study of Kirby et al., (2012), morphological awareness predicted reading comprehension significantly in 3rd grade, partially in 2nd grade, and not at all in 1st grade. It seems, thus, that morphology, interfacing as it does with all other domains of language use and structure (Carlisle, 1995; Gonnerman et al., 2007; Kieffer and Lesaux, 2012b; Kuo and Anderson, 2006; McCutchen et al., 2008) has the most pervasive and long lasting effects on reading and writing, a finding that should be borne in mind and whose implications should be considered both in theory and in practice.

Studies on the acquisition of derivational morphology in English have expanded recently beyond monolingual native speakers of English to concern with bilinguals or learners of English as a second language whose native languages differ from English in morphology (Farran, Bingham and Matthews, 2012; Goodwin, et al., 2012; Hayashi and Murphy, 2013; Kieffer and Lesaux 2012a; Kieffer and Lesaux, 2012c; Lam et al., 2012; McBride-Chang et al., 2008; Pasquarella et al., 2011; Ramírez, Chen and Pasquarella, 2013; Saiegh-Haddad and Geva, 2008). Importantly, the bulk of these studies found morphological awareness to be a powerful tool contributing to vocabulary. For example, Saiegh-Haddad and Geva's (2008) study of Arabic-English bilinguals found reciprocal correlations between morphological awareness and reading fluency in both languages. Farran et al. (2012), however, who studied the same populations, found that the correlations were significant only in Arabic, a finding which they interpreted as due to difference in experimental methods between the two studies.

Frequency is a particularly powerful factor in acquisition of derivational morphology in several respects. First, studies that included frequency as an independent variable found that more frequent words were processed more quickly and/or accurately than less frequent words both in the written and oral modalities (Deacon et al., 2011; Goodwin et al., 2012; Jarmulowicz and Taran, 2007; Nippold and Sum, 2008). Second, frequency was found to interact with compositionality, so that infrequent words were more prone to decomposition than their frequent counterparts (Anglin, 1993; Hay and Baayen, 2001, Reichle and Perfetti, 2003). A third facet of frequency relates to form-meaning relations in the mental lexicon since, as noted earlier, the studies of Anglin (1993), Clark and Hecht (1982), and Tyler and Nagy (1989) found success in manipulating nonce words to be significantly lower than with real words. The study of Marinellie and Kneile (2012) likewise underlined the interrelation between frequency and compositionality: Their study requiring 4th graders to read passages with derived pseudo-words with non-existing bases and existing suffixes found morphological awareness to be highly related to the ability to parse and to efficiently read infrequent words. The reading model of Reichle and Perfetti (2003), for example, predicts this phenomenon of greater efficiency in morphological decomposition of infrequent words by skilled readers.

Studies which incorporated phonological transparency as an independent variable found this to be another factor that interacted with morphological awareness, with greater success manifested on morphological awareness tasks in phonologically transparent as against phonologically opaque words (Carlisle and Stone, 2005; Goodwin et al., 2013; Jarmulowicz and Taran, 2007; Mann and Singson, 2003; McCutchen et al., 2008). For example, Goodwin et al.'s (2013) tested 7th and 8th graders' performance on a reading comprehension test, a reading vocabulary test, and a test of accuracy of root and derived word reading. Their study, which controlled for various aspects of frequency as well as for orthographic, phonological, and semantic transparency, used a variety of morphological tasks (including: (a) the "comes from" task, e.g.,

"Does the word *additive* come from *add*? Does the word *altogether* come from *alto*?"; (b) matching existing suffixes to nonce roots, and (c) a sentence-completion task with a correct derivative out of four options) found significant effects on success at word reading for both frequency and phonological transparency as well as of individual variables such as the level of morphological awareness and vocabulary knowledge.

The study of Green et al. (2003) analyzing inflectional and derivational forms in narratives written by 3rd and 4th grades provides a novel, discursive perspective on the free use of morphological structures. They found that amount and accuracy of derived forms in the narratives increased with age, with the following suffixes occurring (in descending order): *-ly* (e.g., *quickly*), *-ed* (e.g., *scared*), *-y* (e.g., *lucky*), *-ing* (e.g., *missing*), *-ful* (e.g., *wonderful*), *-er* (e.g., *teacher*). Rather unexpectedly, the agentive suffix *-er* was the least frequent, in contrast to its early mastery in experimental conditions (Clark and Hecht, 1982). Another central finding in the Green et al. study was that as high as one-third (34%) of the 4th graders did not write even a single derived form. The findings of Corson (1995), Bar-Ilan and Berman (2007), and Nir-Sagiv, Bar-Ilan and Berman (2008) for an increase with age, especially in late adolescence, and use of more Latinate (typically morphologically complex) vocabulary in expository texts compared with a higher ratio of Germanic (typically morphologically simple) vocabulary in oral narratives are very much in line with those of Green et al. For example, Corson (1995) found a significant increase in the use of Latinate vocabulary between 12 and 15 years of age, while Bar-Ilan and Berman found a steady increase in the proportion of Latinate vocabulary between 4th grade, 7th grade, 11th grade, and adults. These findings demonstrate that the locus of derivational morphology is not only in production of derived forms in experimental versus in more naturalistic conditions, but also that both contexts provide important complementary insights into deployment of various types of linguistic structures – in the case in point, more advanced versus more basic types of derivational morphology.

4 Intervention studies

The cumulative evidence on the contribution of morphological knowledge to language / literacy achievements triggered another type of educational studies in the form of intervention studies that investigate improvement in performance as a result of deliberate focus on morphological awareness. Intervention studies differ along various dimensions, including their frequency and duration, group size, and age of participants. The morphological teaching materials employed in such studies are also diverse with respect to degree of explicitness: morphological analysis – recognition and identification of morphemes, on the one hand, and morphological synthesis – combination and production of derived forms, on the other. Several studies focused on students with typical language development (Bowers and Kirby, 2010; Kim, Apel and

Otaiba, 2013; McCutchen et al., 2013) others included populations of low SES status (Apel et al., 2013; Apel and Diehm, 2013; Rámirez, Walton and Roberts, 2014), children with language / literacy difficulties (Goodwin and Ahn, 2010; Kirk and Gillon, 2009; Tsesmeli and Seymour, 2009; Wolter and Green, 2013), and language minority learners (Kieffer and Lesaux, 2012b). For example, Apel and colleagues (Apel et al., 2013; Apel and Diehm, 2013; Kim et al., 2013) demonstrated that morphological intervention is effective as early as in the periods of kindergarten and 1st and 2nd grade, with age groups traditionally considered too young for explicit morphological instruction. Significant direct gains in morphological awareness were found after intervention in the studies of Apel and colleagues, and this effect was stronger for low SES groups, and emerged in addition to literacy gains, which were found to be indirectly related to the morphological skills taught. Ravid and Geiger's (2009) intervention study in Hebrew for 4th graders also found direct gains in the specific morphological skills taught (e.g. task of analogies) and indirect gains in other linguistic skills not taught in the intervention program (e.g. task of producing derived nominals), further indication of the powerful and pervasive effect of morphology on the mental lexicon. These results were corroborated and replicated in other intervention studies cited in papers that performed meta-analyses (Bowers, Kirby and Deacon, 2010; Carlisle, 2010; Goodwin and Ahn, 2010; 2013), leading to improvements in linguistic / literacy skills, typically greater for disadvantaged populations and for younger participants. In the most recent meta-analyses of Goodwin and Ahn (2010, 2013), for example, significant and moderate direct intervention effects were found in morphological knowledge, phonological awareness, vocabulary, decoding and spelling, all of which also contributed indirectly to reading comprehension.

5 Summary and developmental trends

Several developmental generalizations governing the course of acquisition of derivational morphology in English are summarized in what follows. The first is a general developmental principle that applies to derivational morphology as well – comprehension precedes production. Along similar lines, tasks that require more implicit metalinguistic knowledge, typically recognition or identification, achieve success earlier than tasks that require more explicit production of specific labels such as stems, affixes etc. Results of priming studies, which demonstrated robust morphological priming effects irrespective of age, as against the more gradual and age-dependent results of other more explicit studies exemplify this discrepancy.

The second generalization refers to order of acquisition of derivational morphemes. In the course of acquisition of derivational morphology in English stems are more salient and acquired earlier than affixes. A young participant in Anglin's study (1993), for example, who was asked to provide a sentence with the derived noun *stillness* composed a sentence to the stem *still* (*You stand still*) and ignored the suffix *ness*. One reason for this saliency could be phonological, since stems are typically longer and, in English, often take stronger stress, than affixes. Another reason could be semantic, since stems typically convey more concrete "hard-core" semantic meanings (e.g. *still*) than affixes, that are more abstract and express more syntax-dependent categories (e.g. *ness*).

Several factors – phonological, psycholinguistic, semantic, syntactic, and usage variables such as frequency and register – determine the internal order of acquisition within each category of affixes. Free stems are more accessible and early acquired than bound stems that typically pertain to the more advanced Latinate lexicon, a superiority that has phonological grounds as well, since bound stems are typically non-neutral. As for affixes, those that convey one-to-one mapping between form and meaning (Clark, 1993; Clark and Berman, 1984), that is, they convey one typical or most productive meaning are easier to acquire, as in the case of the suffix *-ly* denoting an adverb (e.g. *nice-nicely, strong-strongly*) and only occasionally marking adjectives (e.g., *lonely, friendly*). The study of McCutchen et al. (2003), in which the suffix *ly* was the most prevalent in the written discourse of 3rd and 4th graders, supports this precedence of transparent forms: The negation prefixes, *un* (e.g. *un*believable), *in* (e.g. *in*frequent), *dys* (e.g. *dys*lexic), *il* (e.g. *il*legal), *im* (e.g. *im*possible), *ir* (e.g. *ir*regular) and *non* (e.g. *non-neutral*), exemplify one (meaning)-to-many (forms) mapping: all convey the same meaning, but the distribution of their forms depends on phonological restrictions and involves lexically specific knowledge. The word *cook* represent another violation of one-to-one mapping, as a single form that conveys two different meanings – either as a verb or as an agent noun formed by zero conversion.

Another developmental principle that applies mainly to early language development is sensitivity to productivity, since children first acquire the most common word formation means in their language. For example, Clark and Hecht cite a conversation between 4 year-old Yara and her mother (p. 1), in which Yara asks her mother: "What is this called?", Her mother replies: "A typewriter" and Yara 'corrects' her mother: "No, You're the typewriter. That's a typewrite". This dialogue exemplifies Yara's sensitivity to the productive use of the suffix *er* as agentive, whereas use of this same suffix for instruments is less productive and acquired later. Eventually, conventional forms take over from more transparent forms of expression, as in the example of *animal doctor* being replaced by the conventional *veterinarian*. Yara's 'refusal' to accept the instrument noun "typewriter" derives directly from the clash between the productive but unacceptable form *typewriter* as agentive and the conventional form *typist* or *secretary*.

A fourth developmental property is the superiority of phonological transparency – termed "formal simplicity" by Clark and her associates – in the sense that derivational processes which do not entail phonological change have precedence over ones that incur shifts in stem forms under affixation. For example, neutral, typically Germanic-based, affixes such as *ness* (e.g. *open-openness*), are acquired before their non-neutral affixes typically Latinate counterparts such as *ity* (e.g. *divine-divinity*). This finding is corroborated time and again in every single study that includes phonological transparency as an independent variable, both in early and in later, school-age development and across languages other than English, in cases where affixation involves changes in the syllabic and/or segmental composition of the stem.

A further, highly robust developmental factor is sensitivity to frequency, which both facilitates morphological manipulation and also triggers decomposition strategies. Base frequency, affix frequency and surface frequency have been found to interact (Deacon et al., 2011; Goodwin et al., 2013; Green et al., 2003) in determining the overall effect of frequency on morphological processing.

The marked difference between the results of Berko (1958) as against those of Clark and Hecht (1982) with respect to the agentive suffix *er* (around 90% success in production at the age of 5–6 for real words in the later study, as against only 11% success in applying the same suffix to nonce words in Berko's study) can be explained as due to frequency of use of nonce, non-existent items as against real words. Similar results were found in the study of Tyler and Nagy, where success in assigning the correct suffix for real words ranged between 40–50% in 4th grade and reached almost 100% in 8th grade, while the same task with nonce words elicited a significantly smaller ratio of success, from approximately 10% up to around 55% in 4th and 8th grade respectively. That is, even relatively skilled 8th graders found it difficult to tease apart form and meaning and to assign suffixes to meaningless stems. The discrepancy between processing of real as against nonce words can also be interpreted as indicating dependency between form and meaning, giving support to the idea of a morpheme as a structural unit that bears meaning. Studies show time and again that children achieve only low levels of success in morphological manipulation of items that are devoid of meaning, as in the case of nonce words.

In sum, derivational morphology is typified by its manifold, multi-pronged interrelations with a range of other domains, including literacy, form-meaning dependency, phonological transparency, semantic transparency, frequency, and syntax – all of which highlight the major role it plays as a mediator in the mental lexicon. This interfaced character of derivational morphology suggests that theorists and practitioners alike would do well to acknowledge its impact and to apply its principles as widely as possible – whether for analysis, instruction, diagnosis, and/or treatment.

References

Anglin, Jeremy M. 1993. Vocabulary development: A morphological analysis. *Monographs of the Society for Research in Child Development* 58(10). 1–166.

Apel, Ken, Danielle Brimo, Emily Diehm & Lynda Apel. 2013. Morphological awareness intervention with kindergartners and first- and second-grade students from low socioeconomic status homes: A feasibility study. *Language, Speech and Hearing Services in Schools* 44(2). 161–173.

Apel, Ken & Emily Diehm. 2013. Morphological awareness intervention with kindergarteners and first and second grade students from low SES Homes: A small efficacy study. *Journal of Learning Disabilities* 47(1). 65–75.

Apel, Ken, Elizabeth B. Wilson-Fowler, Danielle Brimo & Nancy A. Perrin. 2012. Metalinguistic contributions to reading and spelling in second and third grade students. *Reading and Writing* 25(6). 1283–1305.
Aronoff, Mark. 1976. *Word formation in generative grammar*. Cambridge, MA: MIT Press.
Baayen, Harald R. 1994. Productivity in language production. *Language and Cognitive Processes* 9(3). 447–469. DOI: 10.1080/01690969408402127
Bar-Ilan, Laly & Ruth A. Berman. 2007. Developing register differentiation: The Latinate-Germanic divide in English. *Linguistics* 45(1). 1–36.
Berko, Jean. 1958. The child's learning of English morphology. *Word* 14 X. 150–177.
Berninger, Virginia. W., Robert D. Abbott, William E. Nagy & Joanne Carlisle. 2010. Growth in phonological, orthographic, and morphological awareness in grades 1 to 6. *Journal of Psycholinguistic Research* 39(2). 141–163.
Beyersmann, Elisabeth, Anne Castles & Max Coltheart. 2012. Morphological processing during visual word recognition in developing readers: Evidence from masked priming. *The Quarterly Journal of Experimental Psychology* 65(7). 1306–1326.
Bowers, Peter N. & John R. Kirby. 2010. Effects of morphological instruction on vocabulary acquisition. *Reading and Writing* 23(5). 515–537.
Bowers, Peter N. John R. Kirby & Hélène S. Deacon. 2010. The effects of morphological instruction on literacy skills: A systematic review of the literature. *Review of Educational Research* 80(2). 144–179.
Bybee, Joan L. 1985. *Morphology: A study of the relation between meaning and form*. Amsterdam: John Benjamins.
Carlisle, Joanne F. 1995. Morphological awareness and early reading achievement. In Laurie Beth Feldman (ed.), *Morphological aspects of language processing*, 189–209. Hillsdale, NJ: Erlbaum.
Carlisle, Joanne F. 2010. Effects of instruction in morphological awareness on literacy achievement: An integrative review. *Reading Research Quarterly* 45(4). 464–487.
Carlisle, Joanne F & Addison C. Stone. 2005. Exploring the role of morphemes in word reading. *Reading Research Quarterly* 40(4). 428–449.
Clark, Eve V. 1993. *The lexicon in acquisition*. Cambridge: Cambridge University Press.
Clark Eve V. & Ruth A. Berman. 1984. Structure and use in the acquisition of word formation. *Language* 60(3). 543–590.
Clark Eve V. & Barbara Frant Hecht. 1982. Learning to coin agent and instrument nouns. *Cognition* 12(1). 1–24.
Corson, David. 1995. *Using English words*. Dordrecht: Kluwer.
Deacon, Hélène S, Emily Campbell & Meredith Tamminga. 2010. Seeing the harm in harmed and harmful: Morphological processing by children in Grades 4, 6, and 8. *Applied Psycholinguistics* 31(4). 759–775.
Deacon, Hélène S, Rachel Whalen & John R. Kirby. 2011. Do children see the danger in dangerous? Grade 4, 6, and 8 children's reading of morphologically complex words. *Applied Psycholinguistics* 32(3). 467–481.
Deane, Paul, René R. Lawless, Chen Li, John Sabatini, Isaac I. Bejar & Tenaha O'Reilly. 2014. Creating vocabulary item types that measure students' depth of semantic knowledge. *ETS Research Report Series* 1. 1–19.
Farran, Lama K., Gary E. Bingham & Mona W. Matthews. 2012. The relationship between language and reading in bilingual English-Arabic children. *Reading and Writing* 25(9). 2153–2181.
Feldman, Laurie B., Jay Rueckl, Kristen DiLiberto, Matthew Pastizzo, & Frank R. Vellutino. 2002. Morphological analysis by child readers as revealed by the fragment completion task. *Psychonomic Bulletin and Review* 9(3). 529–535.

Foorman, Barbara R., Yaacov Petscher & Denise M. Bishop. 2012. The incremental variance of morphological knowledge to reading comprehension in grades 3–10 beyond prior reading comprehension, spelling, and text reading efficiency. *Learning and Individual Differences* 22(6). 792–798.

Goodwin, Amanda P. & Soyeon Ahn. 2010. A meta-analysis of morphological interventions: Effects on literacy achievement of children with literacy difficulties. *Annals of Dyslexia* 60(2). 183–208.

Goodwin, Amanda P. & Soyeon Ahn. 2013. Meta-analysis of morphological interventions in English: Effects on literacy outcomes for school-age children. *Scientific Studies of Reading* 17(4). 257–285.

Goodwin, Amanda P., Jennifer K. Gilbert & Sun-Joo Cho. 2013. Morphological contributions to adolescent word reading: An item response approach. *Reading Research Quarterly* 48(1). 39–60.

Goodwin, Amanda P., Jennifer K. Gilbert, Sun-Joo Cho & Devin M. Kearns. 2014. Probing lexical representations: Simultaneous modeling of word and reader contributions to multidimensional lexical representations. *Journal of Educational Psychology* 106(2). 448–468.

Goodwin, Amanda P., Corinne Huggins, Maria S. Carlo, Diane August & Margarita Calderon. 2012. Minding morphology: How morphological awareness relates to reading for English language learners. *Reading and Writing* 26(9). 1387–1415.

Gombert, Jean Emile. 1992. *Metalinguistic development*. Translated from the French by T. Pownal. Chicago: University of Chicago Press.

Green, Laura, Deborah McCutchen, Catherine Schwiebert, Tom Quinlan, Amy Eva-Wood & J. Juelis. 2003. Morphological development in children's writing. *Journal of Educational Psychology* 95(4). 752–761.

Hay, Jennifer B. & Harald R. Baayen. 2001. Parsing and productivity. In Geert Booij & Jaap van Marle (eds.), *Yearbook of morphology*, 203–235. Dordrecht: Kluwer Academic.

Hayashi, Yuko & Victoria A. Murphy. 2013. On the nature of morphological awareness in Japanese–English bilingual children: A cross-linguistic perspective. *Bilingualism: Language and Cognition* 16(1). 49–67.

Karen How & Rebecca F. Larkin. 2013. Descriptive writing in primary school: How useful are linguistic predictors of reading? *The Journal of Educational Research* 106(5). 360–371.

Jarmulowicz, Linda & Valentina L. Taran. 2007. Exploration of lexical–semantic factors affecting stress production in derived words. *Language, Speech and Hearing Services in Schools* 38(4). 378–389.

Jarmulowicz, Linda & Valentina L. Taran. 2013. Lexical morphology: Structure, process, and development. *Topics in Language Disorders* 33(1). 57–72.

Karmiloff-Smith, Annette. 1992. *Beyond modularity*. Cambridge, MA: MIT Press.

Kieffer, Michael J. & Catherine DiFelice Box. 2013. Derivational morphological awareness, academic vocabulary, and reading comprehension in linguistically diverse sixth graders. *Learning and Individual Differences* 24. 168–175.

Kieffer, Michael J. & Nonie K. Lesaux. 2012a. Development of morphological awareness and vocabulary knowledge in Spanish-speaking language minority learners: A parallel process latent growth curve model. *Applied Psycholinguistics* 33(1). 23–54.

Kieffer, Michael J. & Nonie K. Lesaux. 2012b. Effects of academic language instruction on relational and syntactic aspects of morphological awareness for sixth graders from linguistically diverse backgrounds. *The Elementary School Journal* 112(3). 519–545.

Kieffer, Michael J. & Nonie K. Lesaux. 2012c. Direct and indirect roles of morphological awareness in the English reading comprehension of native English, Spanish, Filipino, and Vietnamese speakers. *Language Learning* 62(4). 1170–1204.

Kim, Young-Suk, Kenn Apel & Stephanie Al Otaiba. 2013. The relation of linguistic awareness and vocabulary to word reading and spelling for first-grade students participating in response to intervention. *Language, Speech, and Hearing Services in Schools* 44(4). 337–347.

Kirby, John R., Hélène S. Deacon, Peter N. Bowers, Leah Izenberg, Lesly Wade-Woolley & Rauno Parrila. 2012. Children's morphological awareness and reading ability. *Reading and Writing* 25(2). 389–410.

Kirk, Cecilia & Gail T. Gillon. 2009. Integrated morphological awareness intervention as a tool for improving literacy. *Language, Speech and Hearing Services in Schools* 40(3). 341.

Kuo, Li-jen & Richard C. Anderson. 2006. Morphological awareness and learning to read: A cross-language perspective. *Educational Psychologist* 41(3). 161–180.

Lam, Katie, Xi Chen, Esther Geva, Yang C. Luo, Yang & Hong Li. 2012. The role of morphological awareness in reading achievement among young Chinese-speaking English language learners: A longitudinal study. *Reading and Writing* 25(8). 1847–1872.

Mahony, Diana L. 1994. Using sensitivity to word structure to explain variance in high school and college level reading ability. *Reading and Writing* 6(1). 19–44.

Mann, Virginia & Maria Singson. 2003. Linking morphological knowledge to English decoding ability: Large effects of little suffixes. In Egbert .M.H. Assink & Dominiek Sandra (eds.), *Reading complex words: Cross-language studies*, 1–25. New York: Kluwer Academic.

Marinellie, Sally A. & Lynn A. Kneile. 2012. Acquiring knowledge of derived nominal and derived adjectives in context. *Language, Speech and Hearing Services in Schools* 43(1). 53–65.

Marslen-Wilson, William, Lorraine K Tyler, Rachelle Waksler & Lianne Older. 1994. Morphology and meaning in the English mental lexicon. *Psychological Review* 101(1). 3–33.

McBride-Chang, Catherine, Twila, Tardif, Cho Jeung-Ryeul, Hua Shu., Paul Fletcher, Stephanie F. Stokes, Anita Wong & Kawai Leung. 2008. What's in a word? Morphological awareness and vocabulary knowledge in three languages. *Applied Psycholinguistics* 29(3). 437–462.

McCutchen, Deborah, Laura Green & Robert D. Abbott. 2008. Children's morphological knowledge: Links to literacy. *Reading Psychology* 29(4). 289–314.

McCutchen, Deborah, Becky Logan & Ulrike Biangardi-Orpe. 2009. Making meaning: Children's sensitivity to morphological information during word reading. *Reading Research Quarterly* 44(4). 360–376.

McCutchen, Deborah, Sara Stull, Sara; Becky Logan Herrera, Sasha Lotas & Sarah Evans. 2013. Putting words to work: Effects of morphological instruction on children's writing. *Journal of Learning Disabilities* 47(1). 86–97.

Matthews, Peter H. 1991. *Morphology* (2nd edition). Cambridge: Cambridge University Press.

Nagy, William E. & Richard C. Anderson. 1984. How many words are there in printed school English? *Reading Research Quarterly* 19(3). 304–330.

Nagy, William E. & Patricia A. Herman. 1987. Breadth and depth of vocabulary knowledge: Implications for acquisition and instruction. In Margaret. G. McKeown and Mary E. Curtis (eds.), *The nature of vocabulary acquisition*, 19–36. Hillsdale, NJ: Erlbaum.

Nagy, William E., Virginia V. Berninger & Robert D. Abbott. 2006. Contributions of morphology beyond phonology to literacy outcomes of upper elementary and middle school students. *Journal of Educational Psychology* 98(1). 134–147.

Nagy, William E. & Dianna Townsend. 2012. Words as tools: Learning academic vocabulary as language acquisition. *Reading Research Quarterly* 47(1). 91–108.

Nelson, Douglas L. & Cathy L. McEvoy. 2000. What is this thing called frequency? *Memory and Cognition* 28(4). 509–522.

Nippold, Marilyn A. & Lei Sun. 2008. Knowledge of morphologically complex words: A developmental study of older children and young adolescents. *Language, Speech and Hearing Services in Schools* 39(3). 365–373.

Nir-Sagiv, Bracha, Laly Bar-Ilan & Ruth A. Berman .2008. Vocabulary development across adolescence: Text-based analyses. In Anat Stavans & Irit Kupferberg (eds.), *Studies in language and language education: Essays in honor of Elite Olshtain*, 47–74. Jerusalem: Magnes Press.

Nunes, Terezinha, Peter Bryant & Rossana Barros. 2012. The development of word recognition and its significance for comprehension and fluency. *Journal of Educational Psychology* 104(4). 959–973.

Pacton, Sébastien & Hélène S. Deacon. 2008. The timing and mechanisms of children's use of morphological information in spelling: A review of evidence from English and French. *Cognitive Development* 23(3). 339–359.

Pasquarella, Adrian, Xi Chen, Katie Lam, Yang C. Luo & Gloria Ramírez. 2011. Cross-language transfer of morphological awareness in Chinese–English bilinguals. *Journal of Research in Reading* 34(1). 23–42.

Quémart, Pauline, Séverine Casalis & Pascal Colé. 2011. The role of form and meaning in the processing of written morphology: A priming study in French developing reader. *Journal of Experimental Child Psychology* 109(4). 478–496.

Rabin, Jennifer Hélène S. Deacon. 2008. The representation of morphologically complex words in the developing lexicon. *Journal of Child Language* 35(2). 1–13.

Ramírez, Gloria, Xi Chen & Adrian Pasquarella. 2013. Cross-linguistic transfer of morphological awareness in Spanish-speaking English language learners: The facilitating effect of cognate knowledge. *Topics in Language Disorders* 33(1). 73–92.

Ramírez, Gloria, Patrick Walton & William Roberts. 2014. Morphological awareness and vocabulary development among kindergarteners with different ability levels. *Journal of Learning Disabilities* 47(1). 54–64.

Ravid, Dorit & Vital Geiger. 2009. Promoting morphological awareness in Hebrew-speaking gradeschoolers: An intervention study using linguistic humor. *First Language* 29(1). 81–112.

Ravid, Dorit and Rachel Schiff. 2006. Roots and patterns in Hebrew language development: Evidence from written morphological analogies. *Reading and Writing* 19(8). 789–818.

Reichle, Erik D & Charles A. Perfetti. 2003. Morphology in word identification: A word-experience model that accounts for morpheme frequency effects. *Scientific Studies of Reading* 7(3). 219–237.

Saiegh-Haddad, Elinor & Geva, Esther. 2008. Morphological awareness, phonological awareness, and reading in English-Arabic bilingual children. *Reading and Writing: An Interdisciplinary Journal* 21(5). 481–504.

Schiff, Rachel, Michal Raveh & Avital Fighel. 2012. The development of the Hebrew mental lexicon: When morphological representations become devoid of their meaning. *Scientific Studies of Reading* 16(5). 383–403.

Schiff, Rachel, Michal Raveh and Shani Kahta. 2008. The developing mental lexicon: Evidence from morphological priming of irregular Hebrew forms. *Reading and Writing* 21(7). 719–743.

Schreuder, Robert & Harald R. Baayen. 1995. Modeling morphological processing. In Laurie B. Feldman (ed.), *Morphological aspects of language processing*, 131–154. Hillsdale, NJ: Lawrence Erlbaum.

Spencer, Andrew. 1991. *Morphological theory: An introduction to word structure in generative grammar*. Oxford & Cambridge, MA: Basil Blackwell.

Taft, Marcus & Kenneth I. Forster. 1976. Lexical storage and retrieval of polymorphemic and polysyllabic words. *Journal of Verbal Learning & Verbal Behavior* 15(6). 607–620.

Tsesmeli, Styliani N. & Philip H.K. Seymour. 2009. The effects of training of morphological structure on spelling derived words by dyslexic adolescents. *British Journal of Psychology* 100(3). 565–592.

Webb, Stuart A. & Yosuke Sasao. 2013. New directions in vocabulary testing. *RELC Journal* 44(3). 263–277.

Wolter, Julie A. & Laura Green. 2013. Morphological awareness intervention in school-age children with language and literacy deficits: A case study. *Topics in Language Disorders* 33(1). 27–41.
Wolter, Julie A, Alexis Wood & Kim W. D'Zatko. 2009. The influence of morphological awareness on the literacy development of first-grade children. *Language, Speech, and Hearing Services in Schools* 40(3). 286–298.

Ruth A. Berman
12 Development of complex syntax: From early clause-combining to text-embedded syntactic packaging

1 Introduction: Domain of inquiry

Concern in this chapter is with acquisition and development of complex syntax in the expression of inter-clausal constructions by typically-developing children and adolescents. In functional linguistic perspective, the domain of "complex syntax" has been variously referred to as "clause-linkage" (Haiman and Thompson1988), "connectivity" (Berman 1998, 2009), "nexus" (Foley and Van Valin 1984), or "syntactic packaging" (Berman and Slobin 1994). In child language studies, it is commonly termed "acquisition of complex sentences", as in Bowerman's (1979) and Limber's (1973) groundbreaking chapters and, more recently, in Diessel's (2004) detailed study of early grammatical development in English and in Lust, Foley, and Dye's (2009) generative approach to the topic. The term *clause-combining* is adopted for present purposes, specifying inter-clause rather than intra-clausal constructions as the focus of concern and in order not to attribute to young preliterate children knowledge of the "sentence", as an abstract, theory-dependent notion that is notoriously difficult to define (Chafe 1994), and which has a particularly dubious status in oral language use (Halliday 1989: 66–67).

The basic unit of analysis in the present context is thus the *clause* as a linguistic construction that contains "a unified predication ... which expresses a single situation (activity, event, state)" (Berman and Slobin 1994: 660), while complex syntax derives from the ability to combine clauses into longer units of syntactically and thematically connected stretches of discourse. This involves the idea of *syntactic packaging* in the sense of "the various ways in which situations can be analyzed into components and encoded in multi-clausal constructions" (*ibid*: 538). A key requirement for two or more clauses to be defined as combined in the boundaries of a given clause package is that semantically and discursively they refer to the same topic, and that they contain a syntactically independent "main clause", to which other clauses in the same package add more information or elaborate on its content (Berman and Nir 2009; Nir 2008). Such relations are illustrated by the personal-experience narrative of a middle-school student in (1) – divided into clauses and clause packages (CPs). Clause types are defined by labels (see legend), embedded

---

Ruth A. Berman, Tel Aviv University

clauses are indicated in angled brackets, and connective conjunctions marked in bold.[1]

(1) Personal experience narrative written by a 7th-grade girl [eg07fnw]

P1	1	One day in second grade my teacher Mrs P gave us a spelling test	MC
	2	to do	CMP-NF
P2	3	A boy <named Ben> just did not know the spelling words	MC
	4	<named Ben>	RC-NF
P3	5	He hid the spelling words	MC
	6	**that** Mrs P gave us	RC
	7	to study during the week	CMP-NF
P4	8	Ben took out his binder	MC
	9	**and** hid his spelling words under the book	CO-SSO
P5	10	Ben got away copying the first few words	MC
	11	**but** the teacher caught him	CO-DS
P6	12	There were still a few more words left in the spelling test	MC
	13	I really did not know	MCJ
	14	**what** he would do next	CMP-Q
P7	15	**When** I was not looking	ADV-pre
	16	Ben started to look at my answers	MC
	17	I think	MCJ
	18	**0** there were about five more words left	CMP
P8	19	I told the teacher	MC
	20	**0** he was copying me	CMP
	21	**so** he ended up sitting by himself	ADV

Legend: **ADV** = Adverbial Clause, **ADV-pre** = Preposed Adverbial, **CMP** = Complement Clause, **CMP-Q** = Indirect Question, **CO** = Coordinate Clause [**DS**=Different Subject, **SS**=Same Subject, **SSE** = Subject Elision], **MC** = Main Clause, **MCJ** = Juxtaposed Main Clause, **NF** = Non-Finite Clause

This written text consists of 21 clauses, divided into 8 packages, whose Main Clauses are connected to the surrounding clauses by (1) overt lexico-syntactic **connectives** in the form of the coordinating conjunctions *and, but* and the subordinating conjunctions *that, what, when*; or (2) by **0** = **zero**: (a) where the conjunction *that* is elided

---

[1] English-language examples are used throughout for reader convenience. The text in (1) is from the data collected by Judy S. Reilly, San Diego State University, in the framework of a cross-linguistic project on Developing Literacy in Different Languages and Different Contexts, Ruth Berman PI (Berman 2008; Berman and Verhoeven 2002). Data from extended texts are taken from this and other research projects with which the author was associated, including the "frogstory" picture-book oral narratives (Berman and Slobin 1994), supplemented by secondary sources including diary studies and longitudinal samples of interactive conversations (e.g., Clark 2009: 229–253; Diessel 2004; French 1986).

in Complement Clauses #18 and #20, (b) where no connective is needed in Non-Finite clauses #2, #4, and #7, or (c) the CP contains two Main Clauses, one Juxtaposed to another as in #13, #17 (Mann and Thompson 1986).[2]

The task of clause-combining presents children with various challenges beyond structural linguistic complexity as analyzed in (1), including: cognitive online processing capacity in packaging different pieces of information into a single stretch of speech output; appropriate lexico-semantic expression of varied thematic relations between situations; and the pragmatic ability to elaborate on a given predication within a single conversational turn. It is thus not surprising that fully proficient command of these abilities manifests a long developmental path in progression "from emergence to mastery" (Berman 2004) – starting with toddlers' early attempts at combining clauses and on to packaging together larger units by schoolchildren and adolescents in extended texts, as outlined in Section 2 below. Different factors that interact with development in command of complex syntax are then briefly reviewed (Section 3), including target language typology, medium of production (speech / writing), discourse genre (interactive, narrative, expository), and language-disordered compared with typically developing populations. The chapter concludes by considering principled issues regarding complex syntax in child language research (Section 4).

2 The developmental path to proficient clause-combining

This section focuses on language production rather than (mainly experimental) comprehension studies (e.g., Crain and Thornton 1998; Friedmann and Novogrodsky 2004; Lidz 2007), based largely on data from research on typically developing English- and Hebrew-speaking children (see endnote 1). Reviewed below are the early period of clause-combining (Section 2.1), complex syntax at late preschool age (2.2), and school-age text-embedded syntactic packaging (2.3).

---

2 Categories of analysis were established in cooperation with Bracha Nir in the framework of a research project on development of clause combining in Hebrew (Berman and Nir 2012). Three features distinguish our analysis of complex syntax from much child language research in the domain: (1) Coordination and Subordination are treated together as related facets of clause-combining; (2) Major clause types are divided into subcategories (e.g., Coordinate Clauses as having same, different, or elided subjects; Complement Clauses as reported statements, direct speech, indirect questions; Relative Clauses as headless, asyndetic, or marked by a relativizer; and (3) each non-Main Clause in a given CP is defined as *contingent on* another, mostly following but also preceding the MC to which it is related, thus circumventing the issue of clausal inter-dependence, as crucial for characterizing the internal "syntactic architecture" of a given CP, but not considered further here.

2.1 Early clause-combining

Age around two years is generally identified as a starting point for complex syntax (e.g., for English – Bowerman 1979; Clark 2009: 229–253; Diessel 2004; for Hebrew – Berman and Lustigman 2014; Dromi and Berman 1986; for French – Sekali 2012), typically once simple-clause construction is well-established, even if not yet fully mastered.

2.1.1 Precursors to fully-blown CC

Two main types of "precursors" pave the way for later-developing autonomous clause-combining (CC) – interactive and structural. *Interactive precursors* rely on supportive contexts, generally provided by adult caretakers as aids to toddlers' early clause-combining. Three main types of support can be identified, from largely affective to more structurally based (Berman and Lustigman 2014): (a) *Affirmations* – encouraging, quite minimal comments that typically come between or even interrupt a sequence of two or more predicates produced by the child, signaling that the interlocutor is there with them, waiting for more to come (e.g., *really, yes of course, that's nice*); (b) *Scaffolding* – interactive prompts that also occur in adult conversational discourse, but here are typically intended to instruct the child, not only to keep the conversation moving (e.g., *and ...? and then? and what happened afterwards?*); and (c) *Co-construction* – a dependent clause constructed by the child is structurally contingent on the input, often in the form of an adult's *why* question that triggers an adverbial clause beginning with *(be)cause* in response or a *what* clause initiating a complement construction – e.g., *what did the teacher say > that she'll help me, what made you mad > that he hit me* (Diessel 2004: 161–163).

A second, *structural, class of precursors* are linguistic constructions that children produce autonomously, in the form of partial, not fully or conventionally marked elements – a phenomenon characteristic of transitional periods in children's shift from one phase of linguistic knowledge and language use to another in general (e.g., Berman 1986; Lustigman, 2013). Three main means can be identified here, the first of which is juvenile, the others accepted in adult language use. (a) *Non-marking, by ungrammatical omission* of required connectives between two clauses produced in a single intonational string, as from English-speaking children aged 1;11 to 2;2 years – with the adverbial *where* lacking in (2a) and (2b) and the relativizer *that* missing in (2c) and (2d).[3]

---

[3] Such omissions are not readily identifiable in English, as a language which allows *that* deletion in a range of complement and relative clause constructions (e.g., *I know he's there, I want the dolly you took*).

(2) a. *I get bigger I have tea*
   b. *That a map gorilla live.*
   c. *This is my doggy cries.*
   d. *There's a tape go around right here.*

Another means of early clause combining is (b) *juxtaposition* of two or more thematically related clauses, without overt marking of the semantic relation between them, as in (3), also from children around age 2 years.

(3) a. *Daddy go doctor, Daddy back sore.*
   b. *You lookit this book. I lookit that book.*
   c. *Car there. Me drive it*
   d. *Let me. I wanna clean.*
   e. *Go on school bus. Later R do that.*

Such unmarked or "asyndetic" CC constitutes *a transitional strategy* en route to fully explicit marking of the syntactico-semantic relations between two or more clauses – analogously to Scollon's (1976) distinction between horizontal vs vertical constructions in the transition from the one-word stage to multi-word combinations. They show that two-year-olds can string together more than a single predicate to express various semantic relations, such as reason in (3a), contrast in (3b), function in (3c), purpose in (3d), and sequentiality in (3e). But these sequences need to be inferred from context, since they are not explicitly marked by an appropriate lexical connective.

A third structural precursor to fully-blown CC are (c) *extended predicates* – strings of two or more verbs or verbal operators, with the first, tensed item typically modal (*want to, have to, need to, try to*) or aspectual (*be going to, start to, go on, stop*), followed by a non-finite infinitive or participle. Such verbal complexes have been labeled variously as "predicate complement constructions" (Bloom, Tackoff, and Lahey 1982), "complement taking verbs" (Diessel 2004), or "complex VPs" (Givón 2009: 129–203).[4] Like juxtaposition or stringing of clauses, these are part of adult grammar, too. However, they are not analyzed as clause-combining but as occurring in the boundaries of a single clause, since they modify a given predication rather than specifying a separate situation or event (Berman and Slobin 1994: 660–882; Dromi and Berman 1986; Vasilyeva, Waterfall, and Huttenlocher 2008). This is phonologically

---

4 Roeper (2007) cites the following examples from a 25-month old English-acquiring child – *I can no eat it, I can no get it, I want cut it the bread, I trying hammer it* – as characterizing the period when "children seem suddenly to explode with long sentences ... where two structures are connected in not quite adult fashion". Interestingly, all reflect this type of construction.

evident in English contractions such as *wanna, hafta, gonna* and morphologically in Hebrew where many of these predicate-initial elements are suppletive verbs or adjectives (e.g., *carix* 'must, have-to' *yaxol* 'can, be-able-to', *asur* 'not-allowed').

With development, around 2 to 3 years of age, such precursors play a less prominent part in children's CC, as follows. While affirmations, scaffoldings, and co-constructions continue to figure in interactive contexts, clause-combining becomes increasingly *autonomous* and less reliant on caretaker input. Other important advances at this stage are that: ungrammatical omissions of required connectives are rarer; juxtaposition of two related clauses is frequently replaced by overt lexico-syntactic connectives; and extended predicates occur in clause- combining contexts, not only in isolated clauses.

2.1.2 Lexico-semantic marking of inter-clausal relations

As noted, use of overt connectives often emerges first by *co-construction* with an interlocutor rather than in autonomous strings of child output, as in (4).

(4) Mother: What did you want to tell me?
    Child: That baby crying.
    Mother: You're right, so he is! Why's he crying?
    Child: Cos can't find his teddy.

Between ages 2 to 3 years, children use more varied and more specific lexical connectives, revealing increased semantic and syntactic complexity. For example, in coordination, children in their early 2s use the conjunction *and* to link together two events or circumstances with no necessary connection (e.g., *Mommy works] and Daddy lives here]])*, followed by expression of temporal sequence, often together with *then* (e.g., *I take off my pants] and get into bath]], We played on the slides] and then rode on the ponies]])*, and later with a resultative meaning (e.g., *he fell] and hurt himself]], Daddy's back hurts] and (so) he went to the doctor]])*.[5] By age three, children also use the coordinating conjunction *but* to express contrast, and various subordinating conjunctions, mainly *that* for Complement and Relative clauses, and marking Adverbial relations by items like *because* for reason, *so* for consequence and, rather later, *if* for conditionals. These developments in English, like their counterparts in other languages, express children's increasingly ability to explicitly connect events in sequence (required for narrative construction) and to associate situations with relevant circumstances in a (still limited) network of semantic relations.

---

5 A square bracket indicates clause boundary, and a double square bracket, the end of an utterance]].

Another advance in this domain, generally between ages 3 to 4, is the wider range of predicating items used in "matrix clauses" introducing Complement Clauses. The early V-V constructions noted above occur with a wider range of verbs (e.g., modals like *try, need, like, prefer* and aspectuals like *continue, manage, used to*), while sentential complements are used in relation to more varied and abstract tensed predicates. Early attention-getting verbs like *look (what I did), see (what happened)* are supplemented by increasingly abstract mental-state verbs: in addition to cognitive predicates like *I know] he's there]], I think] she'll come]]*, children use verbs like *remember, imagine;* they extend basic verbs of saying and telling to additional speech act predicates (e.g., *promise, suggest, expect*) followed, rather later, by epistemic modal verbs like *hope, wish* (see Diessel 2004: 90–105). That is, while Complement clauses are structurally quite straightforward, the range of predicates used to trigger them changes with age. As in language acquisition in general, in development of CC, too, structural advances in syntactic complexity go hand in hand with richer, more abstract lexico-semantic usage.

2.1.3 Relative clauses

Unlike Complement and Adverbial clauses which, with age, show mainly lexico-semantic developments like those noted above, Relative Clauses (RCs) involve primarily structural complexity, since they add clause-level information to a noun occurring in another clause which they serve to modify, functioning analogously to adjectives. Such constructions have been the focus of extensive research (e.g., Sheldon 1979; Kidd 2011), largely in the form of experimental comprehension studies of relative processing difficulty, from two intersecting points of view: What element in the matrix clause is modified – sentence subject (e.g., the boy <who kept his pet frog in a jar> went to sleep that night]]) or object (e.g., *the dog got his head stuck in the jar*] *where the frog was kept*]]) and what element in the RC is deleted or replaced by a relative pronoun (e.g., a subject RC in *the boy who kept his pet frog in a jar* versus an object RC in *the jar (that) the frog was kept in*). Much ink has been spilled to prove that center-embedded RCs modifying the subject are harder to process than ones modifying post-verbal objects that come at the end of the utterance, and that children have more difficulty with object RCs (e.g, *the boy I saw, the boy I played with*) than with subject RCs (e.g., *the boy that saw us, the boy that played with us*). In fact, however, the latter, "center-embedded" types of constructions are extremely rare in production data, as pointed out long ago by Limber (1976), who noted that "in all my data of several thousand utterances of children and adults, only **two** subject NPs showed up – one shaky example from a three-year old and another from an adult" ... From the adult: *Well these buses that I've had today have been really weird* and from the child: *I think that the girl ... that's here ... doesn't ... she doesn't want me to open it*. Besides, current research suggests that other, non-syntactic factors play a role in RC processing – such as the semantic category of the modified (matrix) and embedded (RC-internal), whether animate or inanimate (e.g., *boy ~ jar* versus *girl ~ grandmother*), and whether full nouns or pronouns are at issue (e.g., *the boy (that) the girl saw* versus *the boy (that) she saw*) (Arnon 2010).

Relative Clauses are less common in child speech than Coordinate, Complement, and Adverbial constructions, although even 2-year-olds can express their modifying function by stringing together a clause with a head noun and an associated modifying clause (e.g., *I want watch. Goes tick tock*]]. *That's Mommy foot.] Hurted her.*]] *Where dolly?*] *Granny give me*]]. RC production is documented for different languages mainly from age 3 to 4 years, starting with the "presentational" type (*there was a boy that had a frog*) as a bridge to RCs contingent on clauses with lexical verbs (*I know a boy that has a pet frog*). In general, RCs that require prepositional stranding or pronominalization (e.g., English *the jar he kept the frog in* ~ Hebrew *ha-kad še hu hixzik bo et ha-cfardea* 'the-jar that he kept in-it the-frog', *the girl we bought a present for* ~ *ha-yalda še kaninu la matana* 'the-girl that we-bought for-her (a) present) are late-developing and are often omitted or incur other errors (Dasinger and Toupin 1994; Diessel 2004), occurring at later preschool-age in more abstract contexts such as definitions (Friedmann, Aram, and Novogrodsky, 2011).

In sum, by age 4 years, children acquiring different languages can and do make use of the major means for clause-combining in their language, with several concurrent developments: (1) Coordination serving various semantic functions in use of the basic connective *and*, (2) Complement clauses introduced by a richer, more complex range of verbs, (3) Adverbial clauses associated with Main clauses by more varied temporal and logical relations, and (4) Relative clauses modifying a broader range of nominal referents.

2.2 Consolidation of CC at late preschool age

The period between around 4 to 6 years, with age 5 manifesting "a frontier age psycholinguistically" (Karmiloff-Smith 1986) in CC as in other domains, sees several converging developments: Longer strings of clauses are combined in syntactically more complex constructions to express varied semantic relations. The examples in (5) illustrate expression of *temporal sequentiality* by children asked to describe making cookies and a birthday party (from French 1986), with clause boundaries marked by a bracket, and a double bracket]] indicating utterance boundary or "a separate sentence".

(5) a. *She gots something out*] *to bake muffins with.*]]
    But first she has to buy some things for muffins.]
    (Age 2;11) = 2 utterances, 3 clauses

b. *You know] what I do] is,] I just blow off the candles] and eat it.]
And before I eat it, I just take out all the candles.]*
(Age 4;1) = 2 utterances, 6 clauses

c. *And, um, the person will open it.] And take off, take off the ribbon]
before they open it] and find out] what's inside.]*
(Age 4;3) = 2 utterances, 5 clauses

d. *You make the dough,] eat them,] but only when they're baked].*
(Age 5;4) = 1 utterance, 3 clauses

The younger child's two utterances in (5a) represent largely linear chaining, the first including a nonfinite Adverbial clause of purpose (*to bake muffins with*) and the second an expanded predicate *has to buy*.[6] The 4-year-olds produced longer, more densely packaged strings including Complement clauses, predicate Coordination with same-subject elision (*I blow off the candles and 0 eat it; they open it and 0 find out*), a preposed Adverbial clause (*before I eat it, I take out* …). Importantly, these children already demonstrate an ability for *stacking* one dependent clause after another, as in the Adverbial sequence containing both a Coordinate and Complement clause <u>before</u> they open it] <u>and</u> find out] <u>what's inside</u>]] in (5c) and the Coordinated clauses in (5d) followed by an Adverbial: *make the dough*], *0 eat them*, <u>but only when</u> *they're baked*]. These illustrate advanced CC with varied syntactic constructions, expressing a range of temporal relations, not only sequentiality (typically with *and then*) but also anteriority (*before*) and simultaneity (*open it and find out*).

Other more complex adverbial relations are used to express what French (1986, p. 126) terms "optional pathways" in describing scriptal events, as in (6).

(6) a. *And then we buy some stuff] and then we go home] or go to school]
or go to Stuart's]]*
(Age 4;0)

b. *Well, if they have one here for real] you have to crawl] or roll]
to get the fire out]*
(Age 5;1)

c. *But if you have time] you get your coat on] and run, run, run.]]
But sometimes you don't even have time] to put your shoes on.]]*
(Age 5;6)

---

6 Items like *but, and* in these examples are analyzed as utterance-initial interactive discourse markers rather than as syntactically and semantically motivated connectives linking two clauses (Berman 1996).

The string of four clauses in (6a) is typical of the "chaining" of successive events in narratives of children at this developmental phase, with *and (then)* favored for expressing temporal sequentiality (Berman 1996; Berman and Slobin 1994: 177–180). In contrast, the CC constructions in (5b) and (5c) are both syntactically and semantically complex, since they are introduced by Adverbial clauses of condition (*if they have one here, if you have time*), followed by their consequence(s) (*you have to crawl, you get your coat on*). At this stage, such constructions are confined mainly to so-called "Type 1" present-tense conditionals expressing a contingency that may be realized, while unreal hypotheticals (*if they had one here, if you had had time*) developing later.

Similar age-related differences emerge in non-scriptal narrative sequences, as in (7a) from a 3-year-old versus (7b) from a 5-year-old, translated from accounts of Hebrew-speaking children asked to tell about a quarrel or fight they had been in.

(7) a. *I quarreled with Elad] and I cried.]] He pushed me down] and hit me on the head] and pulled my hair] and he also broke my head.]] And I had blood] and they put iodione on my eye] and then my Daddy came]] his name is Eli] and then they took me to the doctor] and I cried.]] And then they took me to the hospital]].*
(Adi, aged 3;5) 13 clauses, 5 clause packages

b. *Once at the birthday of a kid from my school, I quarreled with a friend of mine] because she didn't want to let me join in their game of one, two, three]]. So I was mad] and I told her] that I'm not friends with her.]] And afterwards she asked me] to be friends] and she agreed] that I'd play with them.]]*
(Orit, aged 5;2) 9 clauses, 3 clause packages

The older girl's account in (7b) illustrates several developments in late preschoolers' narrative connectivity: Her story is more densely packaged together into fewer narrative segments than the younger girl's in (7a); she uses more varied means of inter-clausal linkage, adding to the basic *and (then)* subordinating clauses with *that, because,* and the nonfinite phrase *to be friends*; and she introduces each package with lexico-semantic marking of their relation to what is to come (the double-underlined items *once, so, afterwards*).

A somewhat more staggered development in clause-combining is illustrated in (8), excerpts relating the events of a pictured storybook by children aged 3, 5, and 9 years old respectively (Berman and Slobin 1994: 176–181).

(8) a. *A owl's flying]] Snow in there]] And the boy tried to climb up it]] And he did]] And the dog is going away]] A deer trying, jumping over,] and a dog's running away with the deer]] And the boy on top of the deer]]*
(Age 3;5) 8 clauses, 7 packages

b. _And then_ he put his boot on his head, _and then_ his other boot on his foot]]
And after he went out calling for the frog]] _And then_ the dog fell out _and_ the boy jumped out.]]
(Age 5;8) 5 clauses, 3 packages

c. _Once_ there was a boy] _who_ had a pet frog and a dog]] And _that night_ he was watching it] _and_ <_when_ he went to sleep > the frog got out of his jar] _and_ ran away]] _The next morning_ when he woke up] he saw] _that_ the frog was gone]]
(Age 9;1) 9 clauses, 3 packages

These three excerpts from picturebook narratives reflect a more general developmental trajectory in text-embedded clause-combining: From initial reliance on largely _isolated_ clauses to sequential and some causal _chaining_ of events (with _and then, afterwards, because_), and on to more densely packaged _chunking_ of clauses at school-age. This same progression, shown by different children in different languages, emerges earlier in conversationally-embedded personal experience accounts than in more structured picture-based elicitations (see Section 3.3 below).[7]

2.3 School-age developments

The development of "chunking" by combining several clauses in a single syntactically and semantically related unit of discourse reflects two major developments from middle childhood across adolescence. Quantitatively, more clauses are packaged together in such units, as shown for narrative texts in different languages. In oral picture book accounts, the vast bulk of clauses of the 3-, 4- and 5-year-olds occur as isolated units, by age 9 years, over one-third of all clauses are packaged together with other clauses, and between one half to two-thirds among adults (Berman and Slobin: 541). In written personal-experience narratives, 4th- and 7th-grade schoolchildren combined on average between 2.3 to 2.8 clauses per CP in both English and Hebrew (e.g., the text in (1) above has 21 clauses in 8 CPs), going up to a mean of over 3.5 in English and around 3.0 in Hebrew among adolescents and adults (Berman and Nir 2009).

Another major advance at school-age, most markedly from adolescence, is more qualitative, in the form of several more complex types of syntactic _dependencies_: (a) increased _preposing_ of Adverbial clauses as a means of focusing on background information (as in the last CP in (8c) and Clause #15 in (1) above); (b) _stacking_ of Coordination, so that a single Complement or Relative clause, for example, includes

---

[7] Interestingly, a similar developmental path was early on identified by Pritcher and Prelinger's (1963) study of children's make-believe stories.

two or more Coordinate clauses; and (c) *nesting* of clauses so that one or more subordinate clauses are embedded inside another (as in the clause in angled brackets in (8c)). The excerpts in (9) –, from oral accounts of 9-year-olds – illustrate such dependencies.

(9) a. We went to see our aunt] <u>because</u> she's getting real old] **and** she's going to die pretty soon]]

b. He thought] (<u>that</u>) I wouldn't hit it] <u>and</u> < <u>when</u> I did hit it >] he fell down]].

An even richer set of dependencies is illustrated in (10) below, the middle section of a written personal-experience narrative of a high-school 16-year-old, 51 clauses in length.

(10) CP 1 At my grade school I had a classmate   MC
         2 <u>who</u> was clearly popular
         3 <u>because</u> he was feared
         4 not respected.
         5 <u>or</u> loved
    CP 2 6 <u>Making</u> my daily life and those of many others miserable
         7 was <as it seemed> the highlight of his existence   MC
         8 <as it seemed>
    CP3 9 This classmate <who I had first met in kindergarten>   MC
            retained his malicious streak throughout all of elementary
            and junior high school
         10 <<u>who</u> I first met in kindergarten
         11 <u>until</u> he witnessed.
         12 0 his behavior cause his expulsion from high school
    CP4 13 One morning, <u>as</u> I stood in the schoolyard in the company of friends
         14 <u>while</u> I was enjoying a conversation y with a friend of mine.
         15 he appeared   MC
         16 <u>and</u> entered our conversation as an unwelcome intruder.
         17 <u>and</u> told me
         18 <u>to</u> shut up
         19 <u>and</u> pushed me.
         20 <u>to</u> reinforce his message.

These 20 clauses are chunked together in only four syntactic packages, demonstrating complex structural inter-dependencies, including preposed adverbials (#14), stacking of coordinate and non-finite clauses (#4–5; #16–20), sentence-internal nestings (#8, 10), and use of a non-finite sentential subject (#6).

A related, even more sophisticated type of late school-age development emerges, in non-narrative texts of the kind critical to academic performance, as in (11), an essay written by an 11th-grade boy asked to discuss the topic of interpersonal conflict.

(11) CP1 1 *Conflict is a large problem, particularly in High School* MC
           2 *<u>although</u> it never goes away.*
     CP2   3 *High School is a major focal point of conflict because of the extreme amount of new tension* MC
           4 *<u>that</u> students are confronted with*
     CP3   5 *coming from a sheltered environment with the close supervision and intervention of parents and teachers*
           6 *students are thrust into realization of the so called "real world"* MC
           7 *<u>where</u> you must now make choices*
           8 *<u>and</u> resolve problems on your own*
     CP4   9 *<u>while</u> you are never really on your own*
          10 *this new freedom can give the overwhelming feeling* MC
          11 *<u>of distancing</u> yourself from your parents' control*
     CP5 12 *students are exposed to many new people* MC
          13 *<u>and</u> begin to form social cliques or groups*
          14 *these groups not only follow racial and ethnic lines but also the class bracket* MC-J
          15 *<u>that</u> they are placed in such frames as advanced or remedial*
     CP6 16 *this can have an impact on people because of the exposure or lack of it or jealousy and envy*
     CP7 17 *Peer pressure is one of the main causes of conflict* MC
          18 *<u>which</u> never goes away*
          19 *<u>but that</u> students have a hard time*
          20 *learning to cope with*
     CP8 21 *<u>while</u> conflict is not a necessarily bad thing*
          22 *it does help prepare people for the real world* MC
          23 *<u>which</u> is full of conflict and problems*

At first glance, clause-combining in (10) – with an average of less than 3 clauses per CP – appears less condensed than in the narrative excerpt in (9). Yet the essay illustrates other developments in sophisticated, high-school written syntax. First, clause-combining is supplemented by increased *intra-clause* complexity and density: While the narrative in (9) averages 5.9 words per clauses, the essay in (10) has a mean of 8.8 words per clause – reflecting dense packaging of information within the boundaries of a single predication. Relatedly, complex clause-internal syntactic constructions enhance textual cohesiveness and structural density, such as heavy nominals (e.g., clause #5) – including inside adverbial and other prepositional phrases (e.g., #clauses 16, 17) – and non-finite participials (*coming from, distancing, learning*). Second, the excerpt in (10) reflects more sophisticated and varied use of non-temporal connectives (*although, while* = adversative *whereas, where* as a Relative Clause marker, *which* introducing a Relative Clause that modifies a proposition rather than a noun phrase. Other analyses reveal use of explicit markers specifying relations between text segments (e.g., *for example, in other words, as a result*) as a hallmark of sophisticated clause-combining abilities in expository prose (Katzenberger 2014), further underlining the intimate connection between lexicon and syntax in development of clause combining abilities.

In sum, "complex syntax" involves an intricate interweaving of both intra-clausal and inter-clausal packaging of information, with advanced lexico-semantic and morphological means creating densely cohesive discursive texture. Such expressive skills are beyond the capacities of young children, but by later school-age they prove critical for scholastic success and achievement of linguistic literacy (Berman, submitted; Ravid and Tolchinsky 2002).

3 Factors impinging on clause-combining complex syntax

Several factors beyond the developmental challenges noted in the preceding sections impinge on command of complex syntax. Issues of language typology, discourse genre, medium of expression, and language/learning difficulties are reviewed here briefly, inter alia because there is relatively little research on complex syntax in these areas. With respect to *linguistic typology*, comparison of clause-combining in relating the contents of a picture book showed that the task faced by Turkish-acquiring children differs considerably from that of their peers acquiring a Germanic, Romance, or Semitic language, since they need from the start to use nominalized constructions rather than finite subordinated clauses (Berman and Slobin 1994: 538–554). Second, the study of Dasinger and Toupin (1994) showed that Relative Clauses were far commoner, and occurred at a younger age, among Spanish-speaking children compared with their English-, and German-speaking peers, while Hebrew-speaking's children apparently early command of RCs was largely due to their reliance on verbless copular contexts linked to a main clause by the ubiquitous subordinator *še* 'that' (Dromi and Berman 1986) in constructions that in English, French, or German might take the form of a prepositional phrase (e.g., *the boy looked in the hole that (is) in the tree, the dog ran away from the bees that (are) behind him*).

These findings are supported by data from written personal-experience narratives of schoolchildren, adolescents, and adults, where Spanish texts used finite subordination for packaging together clauses far more extensively and from an earlier age than their Hebrew-speaking counterparts (Berman and Nir 2009). Across development, Hebrew speaker-writers tend to link and intersperse clauses by means of paratactic chaining by coordination; in this, they are more similar to their French- than their English-speaking counterparts – although with age, the latter come to rely increasingly on non-finite participial subordination, whereas Hebrew prose continues to favor coordinating constructions.[8]

Relative *amount* of reliance on subordination appears to differ by language. For example, in the oral picture book stories, the Spanish-speaking 3-year-olds combine clauses in a single syntactic package around 20% of the time, compared with far lower proportions in English and Hebrew. Related differences emerge in average number of clauses combined together in a single syntactic package in these three languages in personal-experience narratives of schoolchildren and adolescents – from a mean of 2.8 to 3.5 in English, compared with only 2.5 to 3.0 in Hebrew, and as high as 3.5 to 5.0 in Spanish.

Moreover, findings from different cross-linguistic samples reflect the impact of target language typology on the constructions *favored* for achieving discursive cohesion through CC, even in languages which share largely similar means of coordination and subordination (Berman, 1998; Nir and Berman 2010). Qualitatively, clause-combining strategies showed language-related developmental trajectories, with specific syntactic constructions playing more or less of a role among children acquiring different languages. For example, advanced CC in English and French (Jisa, 2004) is marked by increased reliance on non-finite subordination in the form of present or past participles (e.g., **learning** *that he was not on the team, J threw a fit; the dog ran as fast as he could,* **chased** *by a swarm of bees*). In contrast, Hebrew favors same-subject coordination for cohesive connectivity (e.g., *he heard he did not make the team* **and** *became very angry, the boy woke up* **and** *didn't find his pet*). In contrast, as noted, the oral narratives of Spanish-speaking preschoolers rely more on Relative Clauses than their peers in other languages; while in Turkish, non-finite (nominalized) subordination is the rule rather than the exception, with one or more nonfinite clauses preceding the final, finite Main Clause, so that Turkish-speaking 3-year-olds will already produce CC strings equivalent to English *leaving the jar] he ran away]], while running] the boy fell down]]*. That is, what appears a highly marked or complex syntactic structure in one language may represent a straightforward, hence early-acquired option for CC in another.

---

8 The structural and/or historical underpinnings of these rhetorical preferences merit separate study, since the four languages share a similar repertoire of clause-combining constructions, by coordination and complement, adverbial, and relative clause subordination. One explanation lies in other typological features of a language that interact in unexpected ways with clause-combining; for example, the fact that Spanish same-subject coordinate and complement clauses require ellipsis of the repeated subject, whereas English, French, and Hebrew respectively allow and require pronominalization, or that Hebrew non-finite participles and gerundives are confined to elevated, literary or journalistic usage.

As against such language-specific syntactic and rhetorical preferences, the developmental path in expressing *semantic* relations between clauses is largely shared across languages. For example, in the temporal domain, usage proceeds from early sequential *and (then)* to co-occurrent *when* and on to more specific simultaneity by *while*, which in turn leads up to even tighter interweaving of different phases in an event by such high-register means as English *in doing so, he* ... or its Hebrew equivalent *be-asoto kax, hu* ... These observations underscore the role of shared semantic and discursive development as a function of age and schooling level, combined with the impact of language-particular structural options available or required for clause-combining complex syntax.

There is relatively little evidence regarding the impact of *medium of expression* (writing or speech) on clause-combining strategies – in contrast to the extensive literature documenting large and significant differences in overall text *length*, with shorter texts constructed in writing than in speech across age-groups from 1st grade to adulthood and across languages in different types of elicitations (Berman and Verhoeven 2002; Silva et al 2010). Thus, the study of Silva et al comparing written and oral narrative retellings of 1st and 2nd grade children showed little difference in syntactic complexity between texts in the two modalities, measured by Hunt's (1965, 1970) "Syntactic Complexity Index", as length and number of subordinate clauses per T-Unit (a terminable unit, defined as a main clause and any subordinated clauses attached to it). Two orthogonal explanations are suggested for this lack of difference: Developmental – the young age and hence lack of experience and proficiency in producing written language of the participants; and methodological – the relatively superficial measure applied to characterize syntactic complexity.[9] A more sensitive breakdown of clause types along lines illustrated in (1) above, measured by clause packages rather than T-units – as in (10) and (11) – reveals several modality-based differences in English and Hebrew narrative texts produced by schoolchildren and adolescents (Berman submitted; Berman and Nir 2007, 2009). On the one hand, in both languages, the oral narratives packaged together on average significantly more clauses in a single syntactic unit of discourse than the written – a finding that appears to run counter to the commonsense idea that written language is more "complex" than spoken, although it accords well with Halliday's (1989) insights as to what in fact constitutes "complexity" in language use. On the other hand, the *type* of clauses differed as a function of mode of production: Spoken texts used three types of clauses significantly more than their written counterparts: (a) *direct speech* in favor of syntactically marked complements, (b) lexico-syntactically unmarked but thematically related *juxtaposed* clauses, and (iii) *parenthetical* comments as asides that interrupt the flow of sequential events. These findings for modality-driven differences in

---

9 The validity of Hunt's T-unit measure as a criterion of syntactic complexity is queried by Berman and Katzenberger 2004; Johansson 2009; Scott 2008.

CC show that narrators construe spoken language usage as a more interactively communicative medium of expression in contrast to the more monitored, syntactically "well-formed" language of writing.

The factor of *discourse genre* is another area that has received relatively little attention in relation to development of clause-combining complex syntax. Studies in different languages show that from middle childhood on, expository essay type texts tend to include more clauses per clause package, and to use more complex types of syntactic dependencies than the less familiar, academically oriented genre of narrative discourse. For example, across age-groups, Relative Clauses were commoner in expository essays than in written narratives produced by the same students in English and Hebrew (Berman and Nir 2007), a finding supported by the Scott and Windsor (2000) study of English-speaking children aged 10 to 12 years, and by research showing that Relative and Adverbial clauses have higher frequency in descriptive than in narrative texts (Scott, 2004). Besides, as noted above, morpho-lexical markers of temporal sequencing typical of narratives (*and then, afterwards, later on*, etc.) are early acquisitions, whereas the type of lexical connectors required to create cohesive texts in non-narrative contexts (e.g., *for example, as a result, in contrast*) emerge far later.

Finally, a few brief words relevant to the theme of this volume, the impact of language/learning disabilities on development of complex syntax. Research pertaining to clause-combining complex syntax all point to considerable deficits in this respect. For example, Bishop and Donlan's (2005) study of 7- to 9-year-old children with SLI compared with their typically developing peers, which included a test requiring repetition of sentences of "increasing length and grammatical complexity", led them to conclude that "use of complex syntax and causal concepts are more important than non-verbal IQ in determining children's event memory". In her analysis of 100-utterance samples of adult-child school-age children's conversations, Marinellie (2004) adapted Miller and Chapman's (2000) C(ommunication)-Unit measure – defined as "an independent clause and any modifiers, such as a dependent clause ... or a main clause plus one additional clause, introduced with *and, but,* or *or* ... referred to as coordinate clauses" – to show that children with SLI produced and combined together fewer complex sentences than their typically developing peers. Other pedagogically and clinically motivated studies generally apply the basically quantitative measures of T-unit length and amount of subordinate clauses in different types of discourse (see endnote 9). These studies, too, conclude that adolescents with various types of disorders attain significantly lower scores than their typically developing peers on such counts (e.g., Nippold, Mansfield, Billow, and Tomblin 2008, 2009), while Ward-Lonergan (2010:160) notes that "higher-level syntactic structures" appear less frequently in the language use of school-age children with language impairments compared to their typically developing peers, where such structures include complex sentences, defined as "a sentence that contains an independent clause and at least one dependent clause".

These findings are supported by more sensitive, linguistically motivated analyses. For example, Friedmann and Novogrodsky (2004) found that Hebrew-speaking SLI children aged 9 to 12 years showed considerable deficits in comprehension and production of relative clauses compared with their normally developing peers. Studies closer to the conception of "clause-combining complex syntax" in the present context include those of Scott and her associates on oral and written text production of English-speaking pre-adolescents (e.g., Scott 2004, 2009; Scott and Windsor, 2002) and of Davidi on written text production of typically developing and language/learning impaired Hebrew-speaking middle-school students (Berman and Davidi, 2014; Davidi, in progress). Their analyses of, respectively, text production and reconstruction in different discourse genres by pre-adolescents with language/learning difficulties compared with their typically developing peers found that, while all participants in both groups could produce a full range of subordinating constructions (complement, adverbial, and relative clauses), the language/learning impaired students tended to produce relatively more isolated clauses rather than combining them in syntactically units. Importantly, only the typically developing students were able to stack and embed such constructions one inside another in densely compacted dependencies of the kind criterial of later developments in syntactic packaging (see Sections 2.2 and 2.3 above.

4 Conclusions and implications of research on developing complex syntax

Several principled issues emerge from the above examination of development of clause-combining complex syntax. First, as in child language research in general, varying approaches have an impact on how researchers characterize children's developmental path in acquisition of "complex sentences". For example, in Kidd's (2011) collection, authors view Relative Clauses as acquired at early preschool-age or as continuing into school-age, depending on varying factors: theoretical perspective, ambient language typology, whether analysis is based on isolated sentences or embedded in discourse, in comprehension and/or production, in strictly structuralist terms (e.g., Friedmann and Novogrodsky 2004) or from a functionalist perspective (Dasinger and Toupin 1994; Diessel and Tomasello 2000). Relatedly, characterizations of the domain of "complex syntax" (Section 1 above) differ when measured in largely quantitative terms of length of (often arbitrarily defined) elements such as T-units and number of subordinate clauses compared with functionally motivated analyses. More fine-grained approaches, for example, detail subtypes of clauses (e.g., coordination with same or different or elided subjects, relative clauses on different types of head nouns), and take into account inter-relations between clauses combined together in a single syntactico-semantic unit of discourse at varied levels and in different types of inter-clausal dependencies. In developmental terms (Section 2), while pioneering research on acquisition of complex syntax in the 1970s focused on early, preschool abilities, current research on later language development into and beyond middle childhood demonstrates that CC, like language acquisition in general, has a lengthy developmental history from initial emergence of linguistic forms to proficient, discourse-motivated command of how to deploy these forms in varied communicative contexts. Finally different factors impinging on development of the domain (Section 3) demonstrate the critical role of clause-combining complex syntax in terms of cross-linguistic comparisons, literacy development and use of more formal written language, in genres other than early-acquired conversational and narrative discourse settings, as well as, perhaps most importantly for the readers of the present volume, in identifying language/learning difficulties at more advanced levels of age-schooling development.

References

Arnon, Inbal. 2010. Re-thinking child difficulty: The effect of NP type on children's processing of relative clauses in Hebrew. *Journal of Child Language* 37. 27–57.

Berman, Ruth A. 1986. A step-by-step model of language learning. In Iris Levin (ed.), *Stage and structure: Re-opening the debate*, 191–219. Norwood, NJ: Ablex.

Berman, Ruth A. 1998. Typological perspectives on connectivity. In Norbert Dittmar & Zvi Penner (eds.), *Issues in the theory of language acquisition*, 203–224. Bern: Peter Lang.

Berman, Ruth A. Form and function in developing narrative abilities: The case of 'and'. In Dan I. Slobin, Julie Gerhardt, Amy Kyratzis & Jiansheng. Guo (eds.), *Social interaction, context, and Language*, 243–68. Mahwah, NJ: Lawrence Erlbaum.

Berman, Ruth A. 2005. Between emergence and mastery: The long developmental route of language acquisition. In *Language development across childhood and adolescence*, 9–34 (Trends in Language Acquisition Research, Vol. 3). Amsterdam: John Benjamins.

Berman, Ruth A. under review. Linguistic literacy and later language development.

Berman, Ruth A. & Irit Katzenberger. 2004. Form and function in introducing narrative and expository texts: A developmental perspective. *Discourse Processes* 38. 57–94.

Berman, Ruth A. & Bracha Nir. 2007. Comparing narrative and expository text construction across adolescence: A developmental paradox. *Discourse Processe* 43 (2). 79–120.

Berman, Ruth A. & Lyle Lustigman. 2014. Emergent clause-combining in adult-child interactional contexts. In Inbal Arnon, Marisa Tice, Chigusa Kurumada & Bruno Estigarribia (eds.), *Language in interaction*. Amsterdam: John Benjamins.

Berman, Ruth A. & Bracha Nir. 2009. Clause-packaging in narratives: A crosslinguistic developmental study. In Jiansheng Guo, Elena Lieven, Sue Ervin-Tripp, Nancy Budwig, Keika Nakamura & Şeyda Özçalişkan (eds.), *Crosslinguistic approaches to the psychology of language: Research in the tradition of Dan I. Slobin*, 119–126. New York: Taylor & Francis.

Berman, Ruth A. & Bracha Nir. 2011. Modality effects on language variation in narrative text construction. Talk given at French Cognitive Linguistics Association (AFLiCo IV), Lyon.

Berman, Ruth A. & Dan I. Slobin. 1994. *Relating events in narrative: A crosslinguistic developmental study*. Hillsdale, NJ: Lawrence Erlbaum.

Bishop, Dorothy & Chris Donlan. 2005. The role of syntax in encoding and recall of pictorial narratives: evidence from specific language impairment. *British Journal of Developmental Psychology* 23. 25–46.

Bloom, Lois, Jo Tackeff & Margaret Lahey. 1984. Learning "to" in complement constructions. *Journal of Child Language* 11. 391–406.

Bowerman, Melissa. 1979. The acquisition of complex sentences. In Paul Fletcher & Michael Garman (eds.), *Language acquisition*, 1st edn, 283–305. Cambridge: Cambridge University Press.

Bybee, Joan & Michael Noonan. 2001. *Complex sentences in grammar and discourse:* Amsterdam: John Benjamins.

Chafe, Wallace L. 1994. *Discourse, consciousness, and time: the flow of language in speech and writing*. Chicago: Chicago University Press.

Clark, Eve V. 2009. *First Language Acquisition*. 2nd ed. Cambridge: Cambridge University Press.

Crain, Stephen & Rosalind Thornton. 1998. *Investigations in Universal Grammar: A guide to experiments in the acquisition of syntax and semantics*. Cambridge, MA: MIT Press.

Dasinger, Lisa & Cecile Toupin. 1994. The development of relative clause functions in narrative. In Ruth A. Berman & Dan I. Slobin, *Relating events in narrative: A crosslinguistic developmental study*, 457–514. Hillsdale, NJ: Lawrence Erlbaum.

Davidi, Orna. In progress. Written reconstruction of informative and poetic texts of typically developing pre-adolescents compared with their language/learning impaired peers. Tel Aviv University dissertation.

Davidi, Orna & Ruth A. Berman. 2014. Writing difficulties of Hebrew-speaking children with language/learning impairments: Insights from text reconstruction. In Barbara Arfé, Julie Dockrell & Virginia Berninger (eds.), *Writing development in children with hearing loss, dyslexia, or oral language problems: Implications for assessment and instruction*. Oxford: Oxford University Press.

Diessel, Holger. 2004. *The acquisition of complex sentences*. Cambridge: Cambridge University Press.

Diessel, Holger & Michael Tomasello. 2000. The development of relative clauses in English. *Cognitive Linguistics* 11. 131–151.

Dromi, Esther & Ruth. A. Berman. 1986. Language-general and language-specific in developing syntax. *Journal of Child Language* 14. 371–387.

Foley, William A. & Robert D. Van Valin. 1984. *Functional syntax and Universal Grammar*. Cambridge: Cambridge University Press.

French, Lucia. 1986. The language of events. In Katherine Nelson (ed.), *Event knowledge: Structure and function in development*, 119–136. Hillsdale, NJ: Lawrence Erlbaum.

Friedmann, Naama and Rona Novogrodsky. 2004. Acquisition of relative clause comprehension in Hebrew: A study of SLI and normal development. *Journal of Child Language* 31. 661–681.

Friedmann, Naama, Dorit Aram & Rona Novogrodsky. 2011. Definitions as a window to the acquisition of relative clauses. *Applied Psycholinguistics* 32. 687–710.

Givón, Talmy. 2009. *The genesis of syntactic complexity*. Amsterdam: John Benjamins.

Haiman, John & Sandra A. Thompson. 1988. *Clause combining in grammar and discourse*. Amsterdam: John Benjamins.

Halliday, Michael A.K. 1989. *Spoken and written language*. Oxford: Oxford University Press.

Hunt, Kellog. 1965. *Grammatical structures written at three grade levels*. Research Report 3. Urbana, IL: National Council of Teachers of English.

Hunt, Kellog. 1970. Recent measures in syntactic development. In Mark Lester (ed.), *Readings in applied transformational grammar*, 179–192. New York: Holt, Rinehart and Winston.

Johansson, Victoria. 2009. *Developmental aspects of text production in writing and speech*. Lund: Travaux de l'Institut de Linguistique de Lund 48.

Karmiloff-Smith, Annette. 1986. Some fundamental aspects of language development after age five. In Paul Fletcher & Michael Garman (eds.), *Language acquisition*, 2nd edn., 455–474. Cambridge: Cambridge University Press.

Katzenberger, Irit. 2004. The development of clause packaging in spoken and written texts. *Journal of Pragmatics* 36. 1921–1948.

Kidd, Evan. 2011. *The acquisition of relative clauses: Processing, typology, and function*. Amsterdam: John Benjamins.

Lidz, Jeffrey. 2007. The abstract nature of syntactic representations: Consequences for a theory of learning. In Erika Hoff & Marilyn Shatz (eds.), *Handbook of language development*, 277–303. London: Blackwell.

Limber, John. 1973. The genesis of complex sentences. In Timothy Moore (ed.), *Cognitive development and the acquisition of language*, 169–186. New York: Academic Press.

Limber, John. 1976. Unravelling competence, performance, and pragmatics in the speech of young children. *Journal of Child Language* 3. 309–318.

Lust, Barbara, Claire Foley & Christina Dye. 2009. The first language acquisition of complex sentences. In Edith Bavin (ed.), *Handbook of child language*, 463–505. Cambridge: Cambridge University Press.

Lustigman, Lyle. 2013. Developing structural specification: Productivity in early Hebrew verb usage. *First Language* 33. 47–67.

Mann, William C. & Sandra A. Thompson. 1986. Relational propositions in discourse. *Discourse Processes* 8. 57–90.

Marinellie, Sally A. 2004. Complex syntax used by school-age children with specific language impairment (SLI) in child-adult conversation. *Journal of Communication Disorders* 37. 517–533.

Miller, Jon F. and Robin S. Chapman. 2000. *SALT: Systematic Analysis of Language Transcripts*. University of Wisconsin-Madison: Waisman Center.

Nippold, Marilyn A., Tracy C. Mansfield, Jessie L. Billow & J. Bruce Tomblin. 2008. Expository discourse in adolescents with language impairments: Examining syntactic development. *American Journal of Speech-Language Pathology* 17. 356–366.

Nippold, Marilyn A., Tracy C. Mansfield, Jessie L. Billow & J. Bruce Tomblin. 2009. Syntactic development in adolescents with a history of language impairments: A follow-up investigation. *American Journal of Speech-Language Pathology* 18. 241–251.

Nir, Bracha. 2008. *Clause packages as constructions in developing narrative discourse*. Tel Aviv: Tel Aviv University dissertation.

Nir, Bracha & Ruth A. Berman. 2010. Complex syntax as a window on contrastive rhetoric. *Journal of Pragmatics* 42. 744–765.

Pitcher, Evelyn G. and Ernst Prelinger. 1963. *Children tell stories: An analysis of fantasy*. New York: International Universities Press.

Ravid, Dorit & Liliana Tolchinsky. 2002. Developing linguistic literacy: A comprehensive model. *Journal of Child Language* 29. 419–448,

Roeper, Thomas. 2007. *The prism of grammar*. Cambridge, MA: Bradford Books.

Scollon, Ron. 1976. *Conversations with a one-year old: A case study of the developmental foundations of syntax*. Honolulu: University Press of Hawaii.

Scott, Cheryl M. 1988. Spoken and written syntax. In Marilyn A. Nippold (ed.), *Later language development: Ages nine through nineteen*, 49–95. Austin, TX: Pro-Ed.

Scott, Cheryl M. 2004. Syntactic ability in children and adolescents with language and learning disabilities. In Ruth A. Berman (ed.), *Language development across childhood and adolescence*, 111–134. Amsterdam: John Benjamins.

Scott, Cheryl M. 2009. Assessing expository texts produced by children and adolescents. In Marilyn A. Nippold & Cheryl M. Scott (eds.), *Expository discourse in children, adolescents, and adults: Development and disorders*, 195–217. New York: Taylor & Francis.

Scott, Cheryl & Jennifer Windsor. 2000. General language performance measures in spoken and written narrative and expository discourse in school-age children with language learning disabilities. *Journal of Speech, Language, and Hearing Research* 43. 324–339.

Sekali, Marie. 2012. The emergence of complex sentences in a French child's language from 0;10 to 4;01: causal adverbial clauses and the concertina effect. *Journal of French Language Studies* 22(1). 115–141.

Sheldon, Amy. 1979. The acquisition of relative clauses in French and English: Implications for language-learning universals. In Fred Eckman (ed.) Current themes in linguistics: Bilingualism, experimental linguistics, and language typologies, 49–70. Washington, DC: International Publications.

Silva, Maria Luisa, Verónica Sánchez Abchi & Ana Borzone. 2010. Subordinated clause usage and assessment of syntactic maturity. *Journal of Writing Research* 2. 47–64.

Vasilyeva, Marina, Heidi Waterfall & Janellen Huttenlocher. 2008. Emergence of syntax: Commonalities and differences across children. *Developmental Science* 11. 84–97.

Ward-Lonergan, Jeannene M. 2010. Expository discourse in school-age children and adolescents with language disorders. In Marilyn A. Nippold and Cheryl M. Scott (eds.), *Expository discourse in children, adolescents, and adults: Development and disorders*, 155–190. New York: Taylor & Francis.

II **Oral and written communication**

Section 4: Communication and discourse

Vanessa Schell and Mark Sabbagh
13 Theory of mind and communication: Developmental perspectives

1 Introduction

Communication is successful when interlocutors come to a mutual understanding about some state of affairs. This goal, though simple, is often achieved through a rich combination of both linguistic and social-cognitive skills. At issue is the fact that the "semantic" meaning of our message rarely carries the full force of our communicative intention. Sometimes this incongruity can be purposeful and rhetorically powerful, as it is in cases of artful uses of devises such as sarcasm and irony. In other situations, our failure to specify our full communicative intention reflects our efficient reliance on pragmatic principles regarding how speakers use language within socio-culturally defined contexts in order to achieve certain communicative ends. This distinction between the semantic and the pragmatic underscores the point that our goals in communicating are about recovering interlocutors' intentions. Utterances provide clues about those intentions, and our skill at both providing and interpreting those clues within their contexts sets certain limits on the extent to which we are successful in a broad range of communicative situations.

These issues have important implications for considering the typical course of communicative development. Although the ability to communicate certainly turns on infants' and young children's developing abilities to perceive, parse, and rapidly analyze communicative percepts (e.g., speech, gesture, sign), gleaning meaning from these percepts requires some understanding of communicators' intentions. In what follows, we will review work showing that many aspects of children's communicative development are affected by a developing understanding of communicative intentions. We will begin by reviewing a large but older literature showing that by the end of the second year, children are skilled at using clues about speakers' communicative intentions to make one of their earliest communicative advances, such as learning to link novel words with objects and actions. We will then review evidence showing that as their social-cognitive understandings mature and allow for more sophisticated understandings of communicative intentions they become better able to interpret and evaluate others' communicative acts and make their own.

2 Theory of mind

Communicative intentions are mental states held by partners in a communicative exchange. Children's abilities to make judgments about communicative intentions,

Vanessa Schell and Mark Sabbagh, Queen's University

then, is part of their "theory of mind" – the term given to the more general suite of cognitive skills and conceptual understandings that guides and limits their abilities to make judgments about other's mental states. More than two decades of research have been focused on characterizing both the timetable of children's theory of mind abilities and the factors that affect their development (see Sabbagh, Benson and Kuhlmeier, 2013, for a recent review). In short, some aspects of theory of mind understanding are present from very early in development, though, the preschool years represent a period of substantial change in children's abilities to explicitly reason about others' mental states. These developments are likely conceptual in nature – although theory of mind is related to advances in vocabulary development, syntactic development, and executive functioning (see Benson and Sabbagh, 2012; Gundel and Johnson, 2013; de Villiers, 2007; and Apperly, 2012), development in any one is not sufficient absent the necessary conceptual understandings.

It is important to note that though it is often talked about as a unitary construct, theory of mind understanding encompasses many component cognitive processes and conceptual understandings (see e.g., Sabbagh, 2004; Schaafsma et al., 2014). Beginning very early in development, children appear to understand that human action is intentional and directed toward internally represented goals (see e.g. see, Baldwin 1993; Wellman 1993). This understanding provides a basis for a broad range of basic distinctions in understanding social action, including the distinction between accidental versus intentional actions (Meltzoff 1995; Carpenter, Akhtar, and Tomasello 1998). Perhaps most important for the present discussion, children's understanding that human action is goal oriented comes to include the idea that different people can have different perceptions or preferences about the world (e.g., Flavell, 1974). As an example, consider a two-sided card that has a picture of a bunny on one side and a boat on the other. If this card is held up with the bunny side facing the child and the boat side facing the adult, infants as young as 24-months old understand that what the child sees is different from what the adult sees (e.g., Masangkay et al. 1974). Infants also appear to understand that two different people can have different likes and dislikes that shape the specific content of their goal-directed behavior (Wellman and Liu 2004; Repacholi and Gopnik 1997).

Though powerful, these early abilities have an important limitation. Specifically, they allow infants to recognize that people can differ in what they see or prefer but not in *how* they see something (Moll and Tomasello 2006). This later understanding begins to emerge between the ages of 3- to 5-years-old. This understanding is generally thought to be symptomatic of a broader shift in children's understanding of how mental states connect with the world (Perner 1991; Wellman, Cross and Watson 2001). In particular, children come to understand that mental states are representations that are formed by experience and ultimately separable in content from the realities they are meant to represent. Although there are many developmental phenomena that go along with this shift, perhaps the most famous is "false belief" understanding (e.g., Wimmer and Perner 1983; Wellman et al. 2001). In a typical false belief task, a doll named Sally places a marble in a basket and leaves the room. While she is gone, another doll named Anne moves the marble to a box. When Sally returns, children are asked where she will look for the marble. Three-year-olds will consistently answer that Sally will look in the new location; whereas 4- and 5-year-olds will answer that she will look in the location that she originally placed. In passing this task, children show that they understand that because of her experiences, Sally can think something that is wrong with respect to some true state of affairs. This realization marks the beginning of children's understanding that mental states are representations and interpretations of the world that can be distinct among individuals in the same moment (i.e., participants watching the story unfold know something that Sally does not) and different from some true state of affairs.

Our goal here is to review how developments in theory of mind from infancy to late childhood can help us to understand the mechanisms that support young children's communicative development as it unfolds in infancy and over the preschool years. We will attempt to trace this trajectory through two broad communicative tasks: 1) making sense *of* others, and 2) making sense *to* others.

3 Making sense of others

3.1 Learning words

For the linguistic novice, making sense of others' communicative acts poses many important challenges. Beyond the important abilities to parse the percepts of other's communicative acts into the relevant analyzable units, one must determine what *meanings* those units have. For the present purposes, we are going to discuss children's early abilities to make sense of novel words. Working out meanings of words requires solving at least two big problems (c.f., Quine 1960). The first is sometimes called the problem of reference or "extension" and involves figuring out what aspect of the world the word is supposed to apply to. The second is the problem of meaning or "intension" and involves determining the specific qualities that the word is used to communicate.

To illustrate the distinction between the problems of extension and intension, consider the situation in which the young word learner first hears the word "cup" in a mealtime context. Solving the problem of extension means identifying the specific thing in the world that the word refers to, among a potentially wide array of candidates (bowl, tray, table, etc.). Then, solving the intension problem involves arriving at the conclusion that the word means the "whole object" rather than some other logically valid possibility, such as some intrinsic or relational characteristic (e.g., it is round, it is on the tray, etc.). The problem is that the language itself is insufficient to solve these problems. There is nothing about simply saying the word "cup" that directs the novice word learner's attention to the cup, nor about the word that specifies that it deserves a "whole object" interpretation. Recognizing this, some researchers turned their attention to understanding the extent to which theory of mind skills that might help make inferences about speakers' referential intentions may be helpful (see Bloom, 2002 for a review).

3.2 Early theory of mind skills help with extension

The way in which early theory of mind understandings of intentional action might help solve the extension problem is through the understanding that 1) speakers' utterances are goal-directed, intentional, and about the world, and 2) clues about those specific goals and intentions can come by considering what the speaker is attending to and perceiving as they make the utterance. Of the many cues that might be informative about speakers' intentions, researchers have spent the most time considering children's use of gaze direction and joint attention to help identify a speaker's likely referential intention. There is some evidence that infants' are especially interested in others' gaze from very early in development (D'Entremont, Hains, and Muir 1997; Butterworth and Jarrett 1991), and will covertly shift their attention in response to shifts in another's gaze direction (Hood, Willen and Driver, 1998). But note that infants' attention to other's gaze direction must be matched with "theory of mind" skills such as perspective taking. This is because infants must recognize that it is the *speaker's* direction of gaze that determines the contents of their intentional states, even if what the speaker is looking at is different from what infants are interested in when the word is heard.

A series of experiments by Dare Baldwin and colleagues demonstrated that just after their first birthday, infants put early theory of mind understandings to work to solve the extension problem. In one experiment (Baldwin 1991), 18-month-olds were given a toy to play with while the experimenter played with a toy in an opaque bucket. Just as the infant was focused on her toy, the experimenter uttered a novel label in a typical labeling phrase (i.e., "Look a modi"). Results showed that after hearing the label, infants disengaged from their object, looked at the experimenter, and followed her gaze to the inside of the bucket. Eventually, the experimenter withdrew the object from the bucket but did not again refer to the object with the novel label. What was perhaps most astonishing about the results was that even though they never heard the label and saw the object at the same time, infants still showed evidence for having mapped the word to the object. Thus, children truly recognized that the speaker was using the word "modi" to refer to the object in the bucket (whatever it ultimately was), even though it could not be seen when the label was provided.

Similarly, in another experiment by Baldwin and colleagues (Baldwin et al. 1996), infants played with toys while sitting with two experimenters. One experimenter sat directly across from the infant, and another sat out of view behind a rice paper screen. In one condition, just as infants were focused on a target toy, the experimenter sitting in view of the infant provided a novel label along with appropriate gaze cues. In another condition, the labels were provided in the same way but by the experimenter who was out of view. Results showed that, though cues such as temporal covariation were similar in both conditions, infants only formed a word-object link when there were intentional cues. These findings provide clear evidence that intentional cues not only help children to solve the extension problem, but also may be children's first choice of strategy in doing so.

Children's abilities to use intentional cues goes beyond the face-to-face interactions that we tend to think of as canonical, and extend to situations in which children are simply "eavesdropping" on others' conversations. Following early work showing that children learn well from overhearing adult conversations, Akhtar, Jipson, and Callanan (2001) developed a paradigm similar to those used by Baldwin in which children were given a toy of their own to play with while two adults talked over a novel object. Just as children were engaged with their own toy, one of the adults labeled the novel object. Just as in the face-to-face interactions, here children disengaged from their own toy and followed the speaker's gaze to determine the target of the speaker's referential intentions.

One could argue that the fact that infants solve the extension problem by checking following the speaker's gaze does not, on its own, demonstrate sensitivity to referential intentions, per se (Sabbagh and Baldwin, 2001). A more reductive possibility is that young children have learned, over time, that the target of the speaker's gaze when the word is used is simply a good predictor of how the word will be used again in the future. Word learning is at least in part a matter of detecting the covariation of words and their referents, and research has shown that children can detect word-referent covariation even when it is presented without overt social cues (Werker et al. 1998; Smith and Yu 2008). Furthermore, recent work with modeling approaches has shown that covariation detection in a non-idealized but naturalistic conversational setting is far more efficient when it has a cue like gaze direction to help draw attention to the aspects of the environment that do indeed covary regularly (Frank, Goodman, and Tenenbaum 2009). Perhaps then, children's use of gaze information is not about intentional understanding, but rather reflects a way in which children might have optimized how they deploy their attention in linguistic interactions in order to prime the covariation detection mechanisms that are critical for early word learning.

Evidence about whether children are sensitive to referential intentions per se, then, might come from work showing that they are sensitive to cues about intentions that extend beyond the use of speaker's gaze direction. Intriguingly, it seems that there is evidence that by their second birthday, children do indeed use a variety of cues to make judgments about speakers' referential intentions. Much of this work comes from Michael Tomasello and colleagues. For instance, in one study (Tomasello, Strosberg, and Akhtar 1996), an experimenter arranged four opaque buckets in front of children and then declared his intention to find a novel object ("I'm going to get the *fep*"). The experimenter then opened each of the buckets in succession, pulling out a novel object each time. His search concluded with the final bucket whereupon removing the toy he said "aha!" and then played with the toy. To an adult, the gloss of the situation is that the experimenter was unsuccessful in finding the toy on the first three tries but successful on the final one, and thus, the final toy must be the target of the novel word. Results showed that 2-year-olds shared this intuition, thereby suggesting that not only do they use gaze direction, but also they can use emotional cues to discern a speaker's referential intentions.

In a similar sort of study, children used these "pragmatic" cues that provide information about referential intentions in order to learn novel verbs. In this study, 2-year-olds observed an experimenter perform a novel action on familiar characters (e.g. using a catapult to throw a doll of the Sesame Street character, Big Bird). While being familiarized with this action, the experimenter did not use a name for the action. Then, the experimenter suggested doing the action with another doll (e.g., "Let's meek Ernie") and produced the prop used previously to perform the nameless action. But, the experimenter pretended not to be able to find the Ernie doll and so the novel action was never performed after hearing the novel word. Of course, pragmatically savvy adults realize that the novel verb, "meek" must be used to refer to the action that was previously performed. In a subsequent comprehension test, when children were asked to "meek" a novel character, they performed the nameless action even though the novel verb never directly accompanied the action (Tomasello and Barton 1994).

Perhaps the most intriguing demonstration of children's abilities to use perspective-taking skills to work out others' referential intentions comes from work by Nameera Akhtar and colleagues (Akhtar, Carpenter, and Tomasello 1996). Various theories of how pragmatics work have as their central idea that people's utterances should be made and interpreted as *relevant* to the current situation. Of course, knowing what is relevant to another person may depend to some degree on one's perspective-taking skills. In a neat demonstration of this, Akhtar and colleagues developed a situation in which children played with 3 novel objects in the presence of their parent and an experimenter. At one point the parent left and in their absence, another novel object was added. Upon re-entering the room, the parents said "Look, a gazzer!" Although there were 4 possible objects that the novel word "gazzer" could have referred to children mapped the label onto the object that was newly introduced. Akhtar and colleagues interpret this as demonstrating that children combine their pragmatic understandings with their perspective-taking skills to infer that the object that was novel to their parent (but not especially novel to the child) must be the referent of the new word. After all, if the parent had meant to refer to one of the other toys, then the parent would have used the label when they had the chance earlier in the procedure.

It is worth noting that this "mentalistic" interpretation of the findings from Akhtar et al. (1998) was not without controversy. In particular, Samuelson and Smith (1999) suggested that the findings could be accounted for with non-mentalistic mechanisms of contextual learning and presented data from a modified procedure that was designed to bolster this claim. Yet, still others subsequently claimed that mentalistic mechanisms were likely operating even in the modified procedure that Samuelson and Smith used. When another group of researchers redesigned the procedure to subvert children's use of mentalistic reasoning (while leaving contextual learning mechanisms free to operate), children did not show good evidence for learning (Diesendruck and Markson 2004).

As theory of mind skills become more sophisticated and include additional understandings, such as desires and beliefs, children appear to put these understandings to work for word learning as well. Saylor et al. (2009) presented 3-year-olds with novel objects and asked which one they wanted to play with. In response to the child's stated preference, the experimenter either expressed a desire towards the same object or to the opposite object. The objects were removed from sight and placed in a box whereupon the experimenter introduced a novel label for one of the objects by asking for the box and expressing her interest in playing with one of the objects (e.g. "I really want to play with the riff, there's a riff in here). Since the new label was provided when the objects were out of sight, children had to use the experimenter earlier desire in order to determine which object she was referring to. Results showed that children consistently mapped the label onto the object that the experimenter previously preferred, even when that desire did not coincide with their own. Impressively, children were able to track the experimenter's changing desires (e.g. Now I want to play with the *dawnoo*) and judge that the new desire and label referred to the second novel object.

Finally, there is some evidence that children are sensitive to the role that a speaker's knowledge might play in shaping their communicative intentions. For instance, Southgate and colleagues (2007) had infants view the location of 2 novel objects being switched to opposite boxes while the experimenter was out of the room. When she returned and labeled one of the boxes with the object in it, 17-month-olds attached the novel label to the other object that was originally in the box she had labeled. This suggests that in order to attach the label to the intended referent, infants used the experimenter's absence to judge that she did not know the objects were switched (Southgate, Chevallier and Csibra 2007). Moreover, when the experimenter was present for the switch, infants judged that she knew which boxes the objects were in, and they attached the label to the object in the box that she labeled. Other work with this age group shows similar evidence of children using what their partner can and cannot see to guide their referential interpretations (Moll and Tomasello, 2006; Buttelman, Carpenter and Tomasello 2009).

This brief review only skims the surface of the work showing that young children are adept at using both cues from the speaker (i.e., gaze direction, emotional information) and contextual knowledge (i.e., what's new to the speaker, what the speaker saw) to make judgments about a speaker's referential intentions. These judgments can help them solve the extension problem inherent in word learning.

3.3 Early theory of mind and learning word meanings

Although limited, there is some evidence that children can use early theory of mind abilities to help figure out the *meanings* of words, per se. One of the most basic distinctions in meaning is whether a novel word is used to refer to an object or to an action. To explore whether children can use contextual cues about referential intentions to make this distinction, Tomasello and colleagues (1995) taught children novel words in two conditions. In one condition, children saw an experimenter carry out multiple nameless actions on a single novel object. In a contrasting condition, children saw the reverse – a single nameless action was performed on multiple novel objects. Following these introductory phases, the experimenter then said "Look, modi!" while performing a novel action with a novel object. Following the "discourse novelty" findings from above when children assumed that speakers were talking about things that were new to them, it feels natural to infer that when different novel actions are being performed on the same object, that the term "modi" must refer to the novel action. In contrast, when it is the object that is changing across the demonstrations, then "modi" must refer to the object. Children showed this pattern of results clearly, thereby suggesting that they could assign meanings in accordance with pragmatic judgments about referential intentions.

A more subtle but equally important distinction in assigning meaning is determining whether a word is intended to refer to the referent as a "whole object" or rather as a "part" of the object. There is some evidence that an appreciation of pragmatics and communicative intentions may be useful for solving this problem as well. At issue is the pragmatic principle of linguistic contrast (Clark 1988, 1990) – children expect different words to have contrasting meanings. Linguistic contrast can help children distinguish between whole-object versus part interpretations of novel terms based upon the labeling context. If some object has a known label (say "mug") and a speaker refers to it with a novel label (say "handle") children following the linguistic contrast principle might assume that because the whole-object already has a perfectly good name, then the speaker must intend something other than the whole-object with their use of the novel term. Insofar as parts are a salient (and also nameless) part of the object, children might assume that the speaker intends to talk about a salient part.

Some research supporting this claim comes from Saylor and colleagues (2002 who showed that children made more individual part interpretations of a novel object when the speaker provided lexical contrast (i.e., "See this boat? What color is the *ziv*?"). What was remarkable about their findings was children used contrast framing to guide part interpretations even when the whole object was as novel as the part (i.e., "See this *blicket*? What color is the *modi*?" Finally, children used contrast when instead of labeling the whole object, the experimenter merely circled the whole object gesturally. Together, these findings show that young children's interpretations of novel words are sensitive to contextual cues that provide information about a speaker's communicative intentions.

3.4 Later theory of mind and non-literal language

From the outset, we have suggested that theory of mind is required when communicative intentions are underspecified by the speaker's utterances. Word learning is such a case because naïve word learners lack the knowledge necessary to interpret the utterance itself, and so must rely on other information to understand what the speaker is trying to say. Another common case in which children must "go beyond" the utterance itself is when interpreting non-literal language. "Non-literal" language refers to utterances for which the implied meaning diverges from the meaning that would normally follow from the conventional semantics stipulated by the terms. Non-literal language is common, comprising approximately 8% of adult conversation (Gibbs 2000) and includes common conversational ploys such as sarcasm, metaphor, hyperbole, understatement, and rhetorical questions.

In the present context, non-literal language is important because making correct interpretations of non-literal language seems to require a suite of relatively complex theory of mind inferences. The bulk of the research has has investigated children's understanding of verbal irony. Verbal irony is a way in which a speaker can indirectly convey an attitude towards a situation by making a counter-factual statement. Say, for example, that two friends are playing hockey together and one shoots and misses the net by a wide margin. Upon seeing the poor performance, the observing friend might pipe up with the comment, "Nice shot!" Clearly, the friend intends not a compliment, but instead a playful critique. Understanding this requires reasoning about theory of mind in a complex way because the beliefs, desires, and intentions that motivate the utterance are distinct in content from the utterance itself.

First, upon hearing an utterance that is incongruent to the context, the child must judge that the speaker does not actually *believe* what he said (e.g. that you took a nice shot). This understanding is based on a later-developing theory of mind understanding that an individual's beliefs may not be (and *need not* be) representative of some objective state of affairs. In this case, the words that are used (i.e., the truth the proposition uttered) may be opposite to the intention being conveyed. It is not until after these understandings have been solidly acquired that children appear to show even a nascent appreciation of verbal irony. For example, Hancock and colleagues (2000) had 5- and 6-year-old children watch videos in which one character claimed to be a good basketball player but then subsequently missed the basket, at which time, a friend uttered either an ironic criticism (e.g. You sure are a good basketball player!) or a literal criticism (You sure are a bad basketball player!). When the friend used a non-literal criticism, half of children claimed that the he did not actually believe that player was good. At this age, upon hearing an utterance that is contrary to the true state of affairs, children begin to appreciate that the incongruity in the statement is not an error but used intentionally, and that the speaker does not actually believe what they have said. By 7 or 8, children become adept at judging that the speaker does not want the addressee to interpret the statement literally but has another meaning in mind (Filippova and Astington, 2008).

Recognizing that the propositional truth of an utterance may mismatch with the speaker's intention is a first step to understanding non-literal language such as verbal irony. To complete the interpretation, the child must identify the *attitude* – that is, the specific communicative intention) that underlies the utterance (e.g. Is the speaker being nice or funny, or critical?). Sometimes, this complex reasoning about others' mental states is called "second-order" theory of mind because one must recognize that not only that others' have mental states, but also that one can have mental states *about* those mental states (e.g., beliefs about beliefs). This emerges between the ages of 5- and 7-years old, which, as suggested above, roughly corresponds to when children begin to figure out the speaker's attitude when interpreting ironic utterances. For example, in a series of studies Pexman and colleagues had school-aged children judge the meanness and humor of ironic and literal criticisms and compliments. For example, children watched a puppet show in which one puppet painted a picture, and in some cases the painting was messy and in others the painting was perfect. When the picture was messy, another puppet used either an ironic criticism (You are an awesome painter) or a literal criticism (You are a horrible painter). When the picture was perfect, the other puppet said either a literal compliment (You are an awesome painter) or an ironic compliment (You are a horrible painter). From as young as 5-years-old, children correctly identified the ironic intentions of the utterances in either case. However, it was not until 9- or 10-years-old that children began to recognize that a speaker was intending to be humorous by using ironic language (Pexman et al. 2005; Dews et al. 1996) and this understanding does not appear adult-like until sometime in adolescence.

These findings raise an important point with respect to the connections between theory of mind and non-literal language more generally. Though theory of mind skills are related to successfully interpreting these non-literal utterances, other cognitive and conceptual processes are also necessary to support the rich interpretations that we make of these kinds of utterances. A number of researchers have noted that social experience and pragmatic knowledge play an important role by providing children with exposure to the contexts in which non-literal language is used. In these interactions children learn when and how non-literal language is appropriately used for rhetorical purposes (Pexman et al. 2009). Nonetheless, theory of mind advances that allow children to reason about the distinction between the canonical interpretation of what is "said" (i.e., literal meaning) and what the speaker *intends* provide the cornerstone for further processing of what a speaker might mean. That is, without a theory of mind that suggests this possibility of a dissociation between literal and intended meaning, non-literal language would be rejected as non-sensical, as is the case with individuals who have brain damage that makes interpreting non-literal language difficult (see e.g., Sabbagh, 1999).

4 Making sense to others

When constructing a message, the main goal of a speaker is to have their audience correctly interpret their intended message. The difficulty in constructing messages is that not all addressees can be guaranteed to understand a given message. Consider this example, if I watch my favorite baseball team win and wish to share this with others, saying "Great game last night!" may be all the information needed for a fellow fan to interpret my meaning. However if I want to make small talk with a stranger, whose knowledge of baseball I am unaware of, I have to include additional information such as the sport and team name to facilitate successful interpretation.

Seminal work by Daniella O'Neil (1996) suggested that even 2-year-olds might vary the information they provide to an addressee. In her work, two-year-olds were introduced to a novel toy, which was then placed into one of two containers upon a high shelf. Half of the time, the child's parent witnessed the toy being placed into the containers and the other half of the time the parent was out of the room or had covered his/her eyes, unaware of the location of the toy. When the parent was not witness to the hiding of the toy, children more often named the toy and its location and made more gestures and looks toward the location in order to enlist the help of the parent to retrieve it. Despite their immature linguistic skills, some of children's earliest messages reflect an appreciation for the knowledge state of their addressee.

Of course, it is not always enough to know that your addressee requires more information; it is arguably more important to determine what information specifically will be necessary for interpreting a novel utterance. To explore this, Matthews and colleagues (2006) showed 2-, 3-, and 4-year-olds video clips of characters acting out different verbs (eating, crying, jumping, and falling over) and asked children to describe what was happening to a confederate. The confederate either sat beside the child and had visual access to the content of the video or sat behind the TV and was unable to see the screen or the child. When the experimenter cannot see the video, a successful description must include information about which character is on the screen and what action he is performing. However, when the experimenter watches the video with the child, descriptions can be simplified as both parties can see the actions for themselves. Three- and 4-year-olds, but not 2-year-olds simplified their descriptions in the side-by-side condition relative to the separated condition. By 4-years-old, pronouns were more common in the side-by-side condition as well. This suggests that by 4, around the time that explicit understandings of theory of mind are in place, children are able to reliably discriminate what kinds of information are or are not likely to be shared, and adjust their conversational contributions appropriately.

Also emerging in the preschool years is children's ability to craft their utterances in a way that reduces potential "referential ambiguity" – instances in which the referent of a given utterance may be ambiguous because multiple possibilities are available. Consider this example, if there are two cups on a table and a friend asks you to "pass the cup", it is ambiguous which is the correct referent. It is clear by his wording (i.e., the use of the definite article "the" instead of the indefinite "a") that he has a specific referent in mind, but it is unclear which one. My friend's communicative failure lies in not recognizing that even though I could see both cups, I did not have the knowledge relevant to identify the cup my friend had in mind. Because of this, more information is required, such as the inclusion of an adjective that would allow the addressee to distinguish the two referents (i.e., the *blue* cup).

Paradigms that test children's sensitivity to referential ambiguity typically use a display case with a number of boxes, some of which are occluded so that if an object was placed in the box, it could only be visible from one side of the display case. In these studies, children have visual access to all of the objects in the boxes whereas the partner seated on the other side, has visual access to only certain toys. On some trials, objects of different kinds are visible to the partner (e.g. cup, car, book) and so the use of bare nouns is sufficient to discriminate the speaker's request. On other trials, two objects of the same kind are visible to the addressee (e.g. two cars) and thus including an adjective is essential to disambiguating the referent and making a successful request. When tested, children begin to make these necessary modifications to ease referential ambiguity after their fourth birthday (Nilsen and Graham 2009; Nadig and Sedivy, 2002). This ability develops rapidly over the early school years –40% of five year olds provided adjectives and this number increased to 75% across the sixth year (Nilsen and Graham 2009; Nadig and Sedivy 2002). In an interesting twist, however, there is some evidence that modifications to ease referential ambiguity can be more prevalent even in 4-year-olds if children are highly motivated to have a successful communication (James, 2002).

These studies we have just mentioned look at young children's abilities to modify their communicative contributions to take into account whether the interlocutor has a particular piece of knowledge. This skill is valuable when one has a good basis for making judgments about another's knowledge (e.g., whether they have or had relevant perceptual access to a scene). However, knowledge states can also be thought of as more "traitlike" in the sense that there are some people who are more knowledgeable than others. For example, general knowledge is likely to vary with age such that a 2-year-old knows less than a preschool, who in turn knows less than a child in grade school, and so on. Adults show awareness of this by modifying both how they talk and what they say when speaking with children; they speak more slowly use simpler language with more varying intonation, and produce shorter utterances to match children's communicative abilities. As above, we argue that recognizing the necessity for these speech modifications rests, at least to some extent, on theory of mind skills that enable one to recognize that the knowledge of an addressee might be different from the speaker's own.

Intriguingly, classic work by Shatz and Gelman (1973) suggest that children communicate differently depending on their addressee's general knowledge characteristics.

An experimenter introduced 4-year-old children to a toy and asked the children to describe what the toy was and how to use it. Later, children were told that they were going to play with a partner and that their partner would really like the toy so the child should tell them all about the toy. Conversational partners were younger children, children of the same age, or adults. Children tended to make their utterances shorter and more simplistic when their partner was younger than themselves. For adults and same aged peers, children used longer utterances. Curious to know whether children adjusted their messages outside of the laboratory, Shatz and Gelman asked mothers to record their 4-year-old talking with a younger playmate. Again, they found that children simplified their messages to reflect the knowledge level of their partner.

Although we have suggested that theory of mind skills should be necessary for children's abilities to shape their conversational contributions in line with their interlocutor's knowledge states, the evidence for a connection between theory of mind and conversational skill has been mostly indirect. One such study by de Rosnay et al. (2013) examined how children's performance on first and second order theory-of-mind tasks predicted their conversational skills in school settings. Five- to eight-year-olds were rated by their teachers on skills such as the ability to pick up on the interlocutors thoughts, emotions, and knowledge state, adapt messages based on communicative partner (e.g. peer vs. principal) and their flexibility in topics. Results indicated that children who performed better on theory of mind tasks were rated as more competent communicators, independent of their language abilities and emotional understanding. Direct evidence of this relationship is limited to work conducted by Reches and colleagues (Reches and Pereira 2007). In their study, 3- to 6-year olds were told where they could find both a treasure chest and, separately, the keys to unlock the chest. Both the chest and the keys were in locations that required a number of steps to find and retrieve them (e.g. the chest was in 1 of 4 red boxes stacked underneath a blanket). Once children were confident in their knowledge of the location they had to direct a same-aged partner who was ignorant of the location to the treasure by providing directions from outside the room with the treasure. Results showed that preschool-aged children who showed competence in separate assessments of theory of mind were better able to consider the perspective of their partner and were more effective at leading their partner to the location of the treasure relative to the children who showed poor understanding of theory of mind. Children with more mature theory of mind abilities were more precise and accurate in their instructions and used more control questions to determine comprehension. When their partner was confused or misunderstood the instruction, these children were faster at assessing misunderstanding, used less ambiguous instructions and were able to reformulate their messages to facilitate understanding.

Together, these findings show that just as theory of mind skills are important for understanding others, theory of mind skills are likely to be important for making oneself understood. Theoretically the tasks seem to require theory of mind skills that allow one to recognize that others' knowledge may be different from one's and modify one's communicative contributions appropriately. Empirically, children begin modify their communicative contributions in line with their interlocutors' mental states around the age of four, which dovetails well with what we know about the developmental trajectory of theory of mind skills. A few studies now have shown a more explicit link that individual differences in theory of mind are connected with this particular kind of conversational competence. Yet, more work needs to be done to establish this association as a causal connection.

5 Autism Spectrum Disorder

If theory-of-mind inferences are important for some aspects of communicative development, then we would expect that individuals who have difficulty with theory of mind should show predictable communicative difficulties. One way to assess this possibility is through studies with individuals with Autism Spectrum Disorder (ASD). Though a number of clinical populations show difficulties with certain aspects of theory of mind understanding (e.g. schizophrenia, ADHD), none appear to be as pronounced or well researched as individuals with ASD. ASD is a heterogenous, neurodevelopmental disorder that is characterized by insistence on sameness and difficulties in language, communication and social interaction. It is now well-established that individuals with ASD have difficulties with theory of mind relative to groups that are matched for general intellectual functioning, and that these difficulties persist even when other cognitive skills are in the typical range (e.g., Baron-Cohen, 1999).

For the present discussion, what is most interesting is that theory of mind deficits appear to affect word extension. For example, recall Baldwin's (1991) finding that children map novel labels to the items that occupy the speaker's attentional focus and not children's own, even when that item is not visible in the scene. Baron-Cohen, Baldwin and Crowson (1997) used the same paradigm with individuals diagnosed with ASD and found a very different pattern. Specifically, when children with ASD heard novel labels while focused on their own object, they attached the novel label onto the object they were fixated on (see also Preissler and Carey, 2005). Thus, theory-of-mind difficulties present in ASD affect at least one of the theory-of-mind based strategies for lexical acquisition.

A similar pattern of deficits is apparent when considering instances in which speakers' communicative intentions are based upon contextual novelty. Following work described above by Tomasello and colleagues, Parish-Morris et al (2007) presented children with an opaque bag with 4 toys inside and announced that an object called a 'parlu" was inside and she wanted to find it. She pulled out 3 objects one at a time and expressed that none of the toys were the correct object. Then the experimenter passed the bag with the remaining toy intended to be the parlu to the child and asked for help in finding it. To interpret her intentions, the child must realize that the parlu is in the bag but none of the objects so far are correct so the last object must be called a parlu. In contrast to the strong performance of a matched control group, children with ASD chose the correct object only 26% of the time.

Finally, it is well-established that individuals with ASD have difficulty with understanding communicative intentions in discourse, particularly as they pertain to non-literal language (see e.g., Sabbagh, 1999; Tager-Flusberg, 2001 for reviews). Although there are many examples, perhaps the most convincing is the early work by Happe (1994) showing how varying levels of theory of mind ability influenced individuals with ASD's interpretation of non-literal language. Individuals were divided into groups based on their performance on theory of mind tasks of false belief and second-order mental states. These individuals were tested on their interpretation of simile, metaphor and irony. All individuals were able to make correct judgments about similes since they make the speaker's intention explicit, usually by using the term "like" (e.g., "Simon had been walking in the snow for hours. His feet were *like* ice."). It is not necessary to go beyond the literal meaning of the statement. In contrast, only those with increasingly advanced theory-of-mind skills could understand metaphor and irony. Both metaphor and irony require the speaker to go beyond non-literal utterance to identify the speaker's underlying message. Since then, evidence for impairments on advanced theory-of-mind tasks have been repeatedly documented in the literature (Beaumont and Sofronoff, 2008; Brent, Rios, Happé, and Charman, 2004; Kaland et al., 2008; Sobel, Capps, and Gopnik, 2005; White et al., 2009) and even in work that demonstrates contexts in which high functioning individuals pass the advanced tasks, they tend to struggle with comprehending the full communicative intent. In fascinating work, Pexman and colleagues (2011) demonstrated that although individuals with ASD may be able to decipher ironic statements, they struggle to appreciate the social function of such communicative devices. Expanding upon her research on the interpretation of irony, typically developing children and children with ASD were compared on their decoding of ironic criticism and compliments. By reducing the verbal demands of the task, Pexman et al. (2011) found that children with high functioning ASD were comparable to typically developing children in accurately identifying what the speaker's intention and actual beliefs were. Where children with ASD's performance diverged was in their identification of the humorous intent of the ironic criticism or compliment, to which the author suggested that children with ASD may be able to comprehend irony, but fail to its understand its communicative purpose.

Although under certain conditions, such as reduced tasks demands, children with ASD are successful on theory of mind tasks there is evidence that they still struggle in everyday interactions, which present complex and dynamic communicative demands. Work by Peterson, Garnett, Kelly, and Atwood (2009) examined how children with ASD's conversational skills were related to their performance on theory-of-mind tasks. Children who passed advanced theory-of-mind tasks were rated as having greater skill in conversations than those who failed, although interestingly, even those who passed the most demanding tasks struggled with their conversational skills when compared to typically developing children.

As suggested above, a number of clinical syndromes besides ASD have been connected with theory of mind impairments, including schizophrenia. Although the research on communication and communicative development is sparse, there is evidence that non-literal language understanding is impaired in these groups as well (e.g. Mo, et al., 2008). Taken together, these findings provide evidence that theory-of-mind skills are a critical component of various aspects of communication and to the extent that their development or use are impaired, there will be predictable effects on the communicative repertoire.

6 Summary

Theory-of-mind skills are important for communicative development throughout childhood. Some theory-of-mind skills are early emerging and we have reviewed research showing that these skills support aspects of lexical development, semantic development, and discourse competence. The preschool-years see major advances in theory-of-mind understanding which sets the stage for more sophisticated inferences about others' communicative intentions, such as the understanding and use of non-literal language. Though the evidence for a connection is theoretically and empirically sound, more work is needed to provide evidence for a causal association between theory of mind understandings and children's communicative development.

References

Akhtar, Nameera, Malinda Carpenter & Michael Tomasello. 1996. The role of discourse novelty in early word learning. *Child Development* 67(2). 635–645.

Akhtar, Nameera, Jennifer Jipson & Maureen A. Callanan. 2001. Learning words through overhearing. *Child development* 72(2). 416–430.

Apperly, Ian. A. 2012. What is "theory of mind"? Concepts, cognitive processes and individual differences. *The Quarterly Journal of Experimental Psychology* 65(5). 825–839.

Astington, Janet W. 1993. *The child's discovery of the mind*. Cambridge, MA: Harvard University Press.

Baldwin, Dare A. 1991. Infants' contribution to the achievement of joint reference. *Child development* 62(5). 874–890.

Baldwin, Dare A. 1993. Early referential understanding: Infants' ability to recognize referential acts for what they are. *Developmental psychology* 29(5). 832.

Baldwin, Dare A., Ellen M. Markman, Brigitte Bill, Renee N. Desjardins, Jane M. Irwin & Glynnis Tidball. 1996. Infants' reliance on a social criterion for establishing word-object relations. *Child development* 67(6). 3135–3153.

Beaumont, Renae & Kate Sofronoff. 2008. A multi-component social skills intervention for children with Asperger syndrome: The junior detective training program. *Journal of Child Psychology and Psychiatry* 49(7). 743–753.

Bloom, Paul. 2002. *How children learn the meanings of words*. Cambridge, MA: MIT press.

Brent, Ella, Patricia Rios, Francesca Happé & Tony Charman. 2004. Performance of children with autism spectrum disorder on advanced theory of mind tasks. *Autism* 8(3). 283–299.

Buttelmann, David, Malinda Carpenter & Michael Tomasello. 2009. Eighteen-month-old infants show false belief understanding in an active helping paradigm. *Cognition* 112(2). 337–342.

Butterworth, George & Nicholas Jarrett. 1991. What minds have in common is space: Spatial mechanisms serving joint visual attention in infancy. *British journal of developmental psychology* 9(1). 55–72.

Carpenter, Malinda, Nameera Akhtar & Michael Tomasello. 1998. Fourteen-through 18-month-old infants differentially imitate intentional and accidental actions. *Infant Behavior and Development* 21(2). 315–330.

Clarke, Eve J. 1988. On the logic of contrast. *Journal of Child Language* 15(2). 317–335.

Clarke, Eve J. 1990. On the pragmatics of contrast. *Journal of Child Language* 17(2). 417–431.

D'Entremont, Barbara, S. M. J Hains & D. W. Muir. 1997. A demonstration of gaze following in 3-to 6-month-olds. *Infant Behavior and Development* 20(4). 569–572.

de Rosnay, Marc, Elian Fink, Sander Begeer, Virginia Slaughter & Candida Peterson. 2014. Talking theory of mind talk: young school-aged children's everyday conversation and understanding of mind and emotion. *Journal of Child Language* 41(05). 1179–1193.

De Villiers, Jill. 2007. The interface of language and theory of mind. *Lingua* 117(11). 1858–1878.

Dews, Shelly, Ellen Winner, Joan Kaplan, Elizabeth Rosenblatt, Malia Hunt, Karen Lim, Angela McGovern, Alison Qualter & Bonnie Smarsh. 1996. Children's understanding of the meaning and functions of verbal irony. *Child Development* 67(6). 3071–3085.

Diesendruck, Gil, Lori Markson, Nameera Akhtar & Ayelet Reudor. 2004. Two-year-olds' sensitivity to speakers' intent: an alternative account of Samuelson and Smith. *Developmental Science* 7(1). 33–41.

Filippova, Eva & Janet Wilde Astington. 2008. Further development in social reasoning revealed in discourse irony understanding. *Child Development* 79(1). 126–138.

Flavell, John H. 1974. The development of inferences about others. In Theodore Mischel (ed.), *Understanding other persons*. Oxford: Blackwell & Mott.

Flavell, John H. & Patricia H Miller. 1998. Social cognition. In William Damon (ed.) *Handbook of child psychology* (Cognition, perception, and language 2), 851–898. New York: Wiley.

Flavell, John H. 1999. Cognitive development: Children's knowledge about the mind. *Annual Review of Psychology* 50. 21–45.

Frank, Michael C., Noah D. Goodman & Joshua B. Tenenbaum. 2009. Using speakers' referential intentions to model early cross-situational word learning. *Psychological Science* 20(5). 578–585.

Gibbs, Raymond W. 2000. Irony in talk among friends. *Metaphor and Symbol* 15(1–2). 5–27.

Gundel, Jeanette. K. & Kaitlin Johnson. 2013. Children's use of referring expressions in spontaneous discourse: Implications for theory of mind development. *Journal of Pragmatics* 56. 43–57.

Hancock, Jeffrey T., Philip J. Dunham & Kelly Purdy. 2000. Children's comprehension of critical and complimentary forms of verbal irony. *Journal of Cognition and Development* 1(2). 227–248.

Happé, Francesca GE. 1993. Communicative competence and theory of mind in autism: A test of relevance theory. *Cognition* 48(2). 101–119.

Harris, Melanie & Penny M. Pexman. 2003. Children's perceptions of the social functions of verbal irony. *Discourse Processes* 36(3). 147–165.

Hood, Bruce M., J. Douglas Willen & Jon Driver. 1998. Adult's eyes trigger shifts of visual attention in human infants. *Psychological Science* 9(2). 131–134.

James, Trudy Lynn. 2001. *Relations between pragmatic development and theory of mind in young children*. Unpublished doctoral dissertation (NQ69161), University of Toronto, Canada.

Kaland, Nils, Kirsten Callesen, Annette Møller-Nielsen, Erik L. Mortensen & Lars Smith. 2008. Performance of children and adolescents with Asperger syndrome or high-functioning autism on advanced theory of mind tasks. *Journal of Autism and Developmental Disorders* 38(6). 1112–1123.

Masangkay, Zenida S., Kathleen A. McCluskey, Curtis W. McIntyre, Judith Sims-Knight, Brian E. Vaughn & John H. Flavell. 1974. The early development of inferences about the visual precepts of others. *Child Development* 45. 357–366.

Matthews, Danielle, Elena Lieven, Anna Theakston & Michael Tomasello. 2006. The effect of perceptual availability and prior discourse on young children's use of referring expressions. *Applied Psycholinguistics* 27(3). 403–422.

Meltzoff, Andrew N. 1995. Understanding the intentions of others: re-enactment of intended acts by 18-month-old children. *Developmental Psychology* 31(5). 838.

Miller, Scott A. 2009. Children's understanding of second-order mental states. *Psychological Bulletin* 135(5). 749.

Mo, Shuliang, Yanjie Su, Raymond C. K. Chan & Jianxin Liu. 2008. Comprehension of metaphor and irony in schizophrenia during remission: the role of theory of mind and IQ. *Psychiatry Research* 157(1). 21–29.

Moll, Henrike & Michael Tomasello. 2006. Level 1 perspective-taking at 24 months of age. *British Journal of Developmental Psychology* 24(3). 603–613.

O'Neill, Daniela K. 1996. Two-year-old children's sensitivity to a parent's knowledge state when making requests. *Child Development* 67(2). 659–677.

Nadig, Aparna S. & Julie C. Sedivy. 2002. Evidence of perspective-taking constraints in children's on-line reference resolution. *Psychological Science* 13(4). 329–336.

Nilsen, Elizabeth S. & Susan A. Graham. 2009. The relations between children's communicative perspective-taking and executive functioning. *Cognitive Psychology* 58(2). 220–249.

Perner, Josef. 1991. *Understanding the representational mind*. Cambridge, MA: MIT Press.

Peterson, Candida, Michelle Garnett, Adrian Kelly & Tony Attwood. 2009. Everyday social and conversation applications of theory-of-mind understanding by children with autism-spectrum disorders or typical development. *European Child & Adolescent Psychiatry* 18(2). 105–115.

Pexman, Penny M. & Melanie Glenwright. 2007. How do typically developing children grasp the meaning of verbal irony? *Journal of Neurolinguistics* 20(2). 178–196.

Pexman, Penny M., Melanie Glenwright, Andrea Krol & Tammy James. 2005. An acquired taste: Children's perceptions of humor and teasing in verbal irony. *Discourse Processes* 40(3). 259–288.

Pexman, Penny M., Lenka Zdrazilova, Devon McConnachie, Kirby Deater-Deckard & Stephen A. Petrill. 2009. "That was smooth, mom": Children's production of verbal and gestural irony. *Metaphor and Symbol* 24(4). 237–248.

Pexman, Penny M., Kristin Rostad, Carly A. McMorris, Emma A. Climie, Jacqueline Stowkowy & Melanie R. Glenwright. 2011. Processing of ironic language in children with high-functioning autism spectrum disorder. *Journal of Autism and Developmental Disorders* 41(8). 1097–1112.

Quine, Willard V.O. 1960. *Word and object*. Cambridge, MA: MIT Press.

Repacholi, Betty M. & Allison Gopnik. 1997. Early reasoning about desires: Evidence from 14-and 18-month-olds. *Developmental Psychology* 33(1). 12.

Resches, Mariela & Miguel Perez Pereira. 2007. Referential communication abilities and theory of mind development in preschool children. *Journal of Child Language* 34(01). 21–52.

Sabbagh, Mark & Dare A. Baldwin. 2001. Learning words from knowledgeable versus ignorant speakers: Links between preschoolers' theory of mind and semantic development. *Child Development* 72(4). 1054–1070.

Samuelson, Larissa K. & Linda B. Smith. 1998. Memory and attention make smart word learning: An alternative account of Akhtar, Carpenter, and Tomasello. *Child Development* 69(1). 94–104.

Saylor, Megan M., Mark A. Sabbagh & Dare A. Baldwin. 2002. Children use whole-part juxtaposition as a pragmatic cue to word meaning. *Developmental Psychology* 38(6). 993.

Shatz, Marilyn & Rochel Gelman. 1973. The development of communication skills: Modifications in the speech of young children as a function of listener. *Monographs of the Society for Research in Child Development*, 1–38.

Smith, Linda B. & Chen Yu. 2008. Infants rapidly learn word-referent mappings via cross-situational statistics. *Cognition* 106(3). 1558–1568.

Sobel, David, Lisa M. Capps & Alison Gopnik. 2005. Ambiguous figure perception and theory of mind understanding in children with autistic spectrum disorders. *British Journal of Developmental Psychology* 23(2). 159–174.

Southgate, Victoria, Atsushi Senju & Gergely Csibra. 2007. Action anticipation through attribution of false belief by 2-year-olds. *Psychological Science* 18(7). 587–592.

Tomasello, Michael & Michael E. Barton. 1994. Learning words in nonostensive contexts. *Developmental Psychology* 30(5). 639.

Tomasello, Michael & Nameera Akhtar. 1995. Two-year-olds use pragmatic cues to differentiate reference to objects and actions. *Cognitive Development* 10(2). 201–224.

Tomasello, Michael, Randi Strosberg & Nameera Akhtar. 1996. Eighteen-month-old children learn words in non-ostensive contexts. *Journal of Child Language* 23(1). 157–176.

Wellman, Henry M. 1990. *The child's theory of mind*. Cambridge, MA: MIT Press.

Wellman, Henry M. 1993. Early understanding of mind: The normal case. In Simon Baron-Cohen, Helen Tager-Flusberg, Donald J. Cohen & Fred R. Volkmar, (eds.), *Understanding other minds: Perspectives from autism*, 10–39, Oxford, New York: Oxford University Press.

Wellman, Henry M, Daivd Cross & Julanne Watson. 2001. Meta-analysis of theory-of-mind development: The truth about false belief. *Child Development* 72(3). 655–684.

Wellman, Henry M. & David. Liu. 2004. Scaling of theory-of-mind tasks. *Child Development* 75(2). 523–541.

Werker, Janet. F., Leslie B. Cohen, Valerie L. Lloyd, Marianella Casasola & Christine L. Stager. 1998. Acquisition of word-object associations by 14-month-old infants. *Developmental Psychology* 34(6). 1289.

White, Sarah, Elizabeth Hill, Fransesca Happé & Uta Frith. 2009. Revisiting the strange stories: revealing mentalizing impairments in autism. *Child Development* 80(4). 1097–1117.

Wimmer, Heinz & Josef Perner. 1983. Beliefs about beliefs: Representation and constraining function of wrong beliefs in young children's understanding of deception. *Cognition* 13(1). 103–128.

Beyza Ş. Ateş and Aylin C. Küntay

14 Socio-pragmatic skills underlying language development: Boundaries between typical and atypical development

1 Introduction

Human infants develop a unique combination of socio-pragmatic skills enabling them to learn language and effective communication from interactions in social engagement with others in the first two years of life. The scope of linguistic pragmatics includes appropriate use of the linguistic code in the direction of requirements or demands of a communicative context and/or partner (Levinson, 1983). However, pragmatic development also includes knowing community- or culture-specific communication rules (Carminol and Sparks, 2014) and appropriately integrating linguistic code with non-linguistic action (Küntay, Nakamura, and Ateş-Şen, 2014). Therefore, prelinguistic infants' communication with others is especially important since it allows us to understand the developmental course of "pure pragmatic" skills that emerge well before and play a key role in the acquisition of linguistic structures (Matthews, 2014).

With such an understanding, the present section focuses on how infants use nonverbal devices such as looks and gestures in order to achieve a successful communication and how then they translate these early emerging pragmatic skills into more advanced forms such as joint engagement and referential interaction. We will cover crosslinguistic and crosscultural work as we believe in the benefits of conducting more comparative work about the role of pragmatics on typical language acquition generally (Küntay et al., 2014), and on atypical communicative development specifically (Norbury, 2014).

The first two parts review past and recent research about the typical and atypical development of nonverbal communicative devices and focus on how use of these devices gives rise to higher order socio-pragmatic understanding including joint attention and referential communication. The last section critically evaluates the present research and proposes future directions for understanding the criteria of (a)typical development of socio-pragmatic skills.

Beyza Ş. Ateş, Koç University
Aylin C. Küntay, Koç University

2 The importance of nonverbal devices in children's socio-pragmatic development

2.1 Understanding the role of eyes

Eyes serve several functions for human interactions such as collecting information about the physical world (Baron-Cohen, Campbell, Karmiloff-Smith, Grant, and Walker, 1995), establishing an affective bond between the infant and the caregiver (Robson, 1967), inferring others' internal states such as their thoughts, intentions, desires, and goals (Baron-Cohen, 1995; Baron-Cohen et al., 1995), and sharing interests about outside entities such as objects and persons (Bakeman and Adamson, 1984). In accordance with the aim of the present chapter, we focus on communicative and referential functions of eyes, which include three important gaze behaviors: mutual gaze, spontaneous gaze following, and gaze alternation.

Newborns have a preference for facelike features rather than blank stimuli (Easterbrook, Kisilevsky, Muir, and Laplante, 1999) or scrambled faces (Goren, Sarty, and Wu, 1975; Morton and Johnson, 1991) and show sensitivity to faces with opened rather than closed eyes (Batki, Baron-Cohen, Wheelwright, Connellan, and Ahluwalia, 2000) and with direct rather than averted eye gaze (Farroni, Csibra, Simin, and Johnson, 2002). In other words, infants are sensitive to communicative potential of eyes beginning from very early ages. Around 2 months, infants begin to preferentially look at the eye region of a speaker's face (Hainline, 1978; Haith, Bergman, and Moore, 1977; Maurer and Salapatek, 1976). By 4 months, they begin to discriminate different directions of eye gaze (Caron, Caron, Robert, and Brooks, 1997; Hains and Muir, 1996; Vecera and Johnson, 1995). However, as they get older, infants' attention shifts from the eye to the mouth region of a speaker. For example, 6-month-old infants divided their looks equally to the eye and mouth region of a person speaking about unfamiliar objects. By 9 months, the infants dominantly looked at the mouth region of the person under the same conditions (Tenenbaum, Shah, Sobel, Malle, and Morgan, 2013). By the middle of the first year of life, they shift their attention from face-to-face or dyadic interactions to object exploration, but they do not share their interest in objects with other people yet (Bakeman and Adamson, 1984). Around the same time, they start to look in the same direction of other people's looks (Butterworth and Grover, 1990; Butterworth and Jarrett, 1991; D'Entremont, Hains, and Muir, 1997; Moll and Tomasello, 2004). For instance, 73% of 3- to 6-month-old infants' first eye turns were in the direction of an adult's 90-degree head-turn towards a puppet (D'Entremont et al., 1997). 6- to 12-month-old infants were able to localize any object in their visual field by following an adult's communicative cues of head turn or eye gaze. However, their localization of the objects beyond their visual field, such as toys behind various barriers scattered around a room, took longer time and occurred between 12 and 18 months (Moll and Tomasello, 2004).

There is an ongoing debate about when children begin to follow a communicator's eye gaze independently from the distance and the visual accessibility of the target, and whether or when children understand that eye gaze signals information about mental states of a communicative partner. In order to answer these questions, researchers use two main paradigms: the "eye status" and the "barriers" paradigms (Moll and Tomasello, 2004). In the "eye status" paradigm (e.g. Brooks and Meltzoff, 2002; Corkum and Moore, 1995; Moore and Corkum, 1998), researchers measure infants' head turn to a distal object following an adult's eye gaze under various communicative conditions such as head and eye turn in the same direction, head and eye turn in the opposite direction, only head turn with the eyes looking straight ahead, only eye turn with the head facing forward, head turn with closed eyes, head turn with open eyes, etc. In the "barriers" paradigm (e.g. Butler, Caron, and Brooks, 2000; Moll and Tomasello, 2004), the researchers examined infants' head turns to an object hidden behind various barriers such as an opaque screen, a dividing wall, a box, a panel, and a drawer, etc. by following an adult's eye gaze.

Studies examining the timing of children's ability to follow another person's eye gaze showed inconsistent results. For example, using the "eye status" paradigm, Corkum and Moore (Corkum and Moore, 1995; Moore and Corkum, 1998) showed that only 18-month-old infants are able to localize a target object based merely on eye gaze (i.e. only the eyes were moving while the head was stable) rather than head and eye cues together (i.e. head and eyes moved in the same direction) or only head cues (i.e. only head moved while the eyes was looking straight ahead). However, using the same paradigm, Caron, Butler, and Brooks (2002) indicated that 14-month-old infants are sensitive to the eye gaze of a communicative partner, especially in the congruent condition where the person's eyes and head were turned towards the same direction rather than in the incongruent condition where the person' head turned while the eyes were directed straight ahead. Brooks and Meltzoff (2002) showed that the infants' sensitivity to the eye status develops even earlier. 10- and 11-month-old infants were more likely to follow an adult's head turn as long as that person's eyes were open rather than closed. The studies using the "barriers" paradigm also pointed out inconsistent results about the timing of children's ability to follow another person's eye gaze. For instance, Butler and colleagues (2000) examined 14- and 18-month-olds' gaze following in three distinct conditions: the screen condition (i.e. an opaque screen obscured where an adult was looking at), the no-screen condition (i.e. there was not a screen obscuring the adult's view), and the window condition (i.e. the screen had a transparent window, which allowed the child to see the adult's view). Only the older group followed the adult's turn relatively more in the no-screen and the window conditions than the screen condition; but the the younger group behaved similarly in all of the three conditions. Consequently, it was suggested that understanding the intentional nature of looking develops between 14 and 18 months of age, but not before. Moll and Tomasello

(2004) also investigated 12- and 18-month-old infants' gaze following in a task requiring them to find various objects hidden behind different barriers in a room, such as a dividing wall, a box, a panel, and a drawer. To determine the locations of the target objects, the angles of the experimenter's head turns changed between 70 and 80 degrees. Both 12- and 18-month-olds were able to follow the experimenter's eye gaze towards the target objects, often even locomoting a short distance in order to see the targets placed out of their visual field.

The inconsistent results probably stem from differences in experimental manipulations. For example, as pointed out by Moll and Tomasello (2004), the experiments where adults look at an object hidden behind various barriers represent infants' natural communicative environments or interactions better than the experiments that present various communicative cues in an unnatural or uncommon manner such as head turns with closed eyes. Infants might find the latter type of situations as unnatural and might not get the communicative message of "this is for you". The inconsistent results might also occur depending on whether other communicative cues (e.g. body posture, head orientation, vocal behavior, etc.) accompany gaze direction or not (Akhtar and Gernsbacher, 2008). Infants at earlier ages in particular might need multiple or converging communicative cues in order to understand that these cues refer to an external entity beyond their egocentric perspective.

Setting aside task variations, we can conclude that children start to follow others' eye gaze between 6 and 12 months for targets inside the children's visual field, and between 12 and 18 months for targets outside the children's visual field. This discrimination is important since the ability to locate a target out of one's visual field needs understanding that the eyes convey some information about one's mental states including intentions, desires, goals, etc. (Baron-Cohen, 1995). The development of this ability around 18 months corresponds to a time when infants show more mastery in joint attentional skills. In other words, they become capable of sharing their interest in objects with other people by coordinating their attention or shifting their looks back and forth between a communicative partner and a specific entity (Bakeman and Adamson, 1984). Also, infants' behavior can be accepted as joint attention only if they and their communicative partner know together that they have a mutual interest in this entity (Tomasello, 1995). Carpenter and Liebal (2011) described this aspect of joint attention as a kind of "mind reading". In short, a joint attentional episode includes three important behaviors: sharing, following, and directing attention (Carpenter, Nagel, Tomasello, Butterworth, and Moore, 1998).

Until this point, we reviewed studies that focus on the role of eyes in following and sharing attention with others. Another device playing an important role especially in directing others' attention to an external entity as well as following and sharing others' attention is declarative gestures – in particular index finger pointing. In the next section, we review studies about children's comprehension and production of declarative gestures.

2.2 Understanding the role of gestures

Around the first birthdays, infants are capable of following one's point to a distal target (e.g. objects on the wall of a room) (Aureli, Perucchini, and Genco, 2009; Camaioni, Perucchini, Bellagamba, and Colonnesi, 2004; Carpenter et al., 1998) and to a target outside their visual field (e.g. occluded behind a barrier) (Liszkowski and Tomasello, 2011; Moll and Tomasello, 2004). Between the first and second birthdays, infants are able to use previously shared attentional frame with an interactant to interpret this person's intention or motivation for pointing an object. (Behne, Carpenter, and Tomasello, 2005; Liebal, Behne, Carpenter, and Tomasello, 2009). For example, while playing a hiding-finding game, infants at 14 months made use of an adult's ostensive pointing to an opaque container with gaze shifts between the child and the container to inform the child about the location of a hidden toy (Aureli et al., 2009; Behne et al., 2005). 18-month-olds made use of an adult's pointing directed to a toy on the floor in a larger activity context where they were tidying up a room by picking up the toys and putting them into a basket. However, in a control condition, the children did not heed the point of a second person entering the room in the middle of the activity (Liebal et al., 2009).

By the end of the first year of life, infants also begin to point by themselves. There are different motives for infants' pointing. They point imperatively for requesting help to obtain an object (e.g. reaching for an object on a shelf, asking for a toy locked inside a transparent box) or to complete an action (e.g. getting on a swing) (Carpenter et al., 1998). They also point declaratively for calling one's attention and interest to an external entity or event (Bates, Camaioni, and Volterra, 1975; Carpenter et al., 1998; Liszkowski, Carpenter, Henning, Striano, and Tomasello, 2004; Liszkowski, Carpenter, Striano, and Tomasello, 2006; Liszkowski, Carpenter, and Tomasello, 2007a; 2007b; 2008). As an example (Liszkowski, 2007a), following 12-month-olds' index finger pointing to a referent, if an adult correctly attended to the referent and shared her interest about the referent with the infants, the infants continued to share attention and interest with the adult by pointing more across the trials. When the adult showed interest but misidentified the referent, the infants tried to redirect the person's attention to the correct referent by repeating their pointing within the same trial. When the adult correctly identified the referent, but did not show positive emotions such as excitement about it, the infants stopped pointing within the trials, overall pointed in fewer trials, and did not attempt to share their attention and interest with the adult anymore. 12-month-olds also pointed to the location of an absent referent (i.e. a puppet popping out a window of a cloth screen) after it was removed from the display, especially for an adult who had previously missed the display of this referent (Liszkowski et al., 2007b). Moreover, when the interlocutor misunderstood their pointing (i.e. saying "Hmm?", "What?", "What's there?", or "Hmm?" in response to the infants' points), 12- and 18-month-olds tried to repair the message by repeating their points and by accompanying their points with vocalizations (Liszkowski, Albrecht, Carpenter, and Tomasello, 2008). As a special kind of declarative pointing, infants are also able to use pointing informatively for providing recipients with the information they want to or need to know (Liszkowski et al., 2006). For instance, 12- and 18-month-olds used informative points in order to show the location of an object to an adult who was searching for it. That is, they pointed more often to the target object searched by the adult than to a distractor object (Liszkowski et al., 2006). The last two motives are deemed especially important because they show that infants understand others as psychological agents with intentional and informational states (Liszkowski et al., 2006). In other words, they achieve "shared intentionality" or a "joint attentional frame" (Liszkowski and Tomasello, 2011; Tomasello, 2006; Tomasello, Carpenter, Call, Behne, and Moll, 2005; Tomasello, Carpenter, and Liszkowski, 2007).

Index finger pointing with declarative functions is proposed to be a human-specific form of communication (Bates, 1979; Bruner, 1981; Levinson, 2006; Liszkowski et al., 2012; Salomo and Liszkowski, 2013; Tomasello, 2008). Non-human primates and dogs are cognitively equipped with and motivated to use only the imperative function of index finger pointing (Gomez, 2007; Hopkins and Leavens, 1998; Povinelli, Bering, and Giambrone, 2003; Tomasello, 2006). Moreover, independent from their cultures, infants from Canada-Nova, China-Shanghai, Indonesia-Bali, Japan-Kyota, Mexico-Tzeltal, Mexico-Yucatan, Nethelands-Nijmegen, Papua New Guinea-Rossel Island, Peru-Montaro, and Turkey-İstanbul started pointing with their index finger around 8 to 15 months (Altınok, 2014; Brown, 2011; Callaghan, Moll, Rakoczy, Warneken, Liszkowski, Behne, and Tomasello, 2011; Carpenter et al., 1998; Liszkowski, Brown, Callaghan, Takada, and de Vos, 2012; Liszkowski et al., 2007a, 2007b; Salomo and Liszkowski, 2013; Savaş, 2014). Furthermore, there is some research indicating that the occurrence of prelinguistic pointing is related to some important milestones in language development, such as the emergence of first words, the vocabulary spurt, and the transition to syntax (Capirci, Iverson, Pizzuto, and Volterra, 1996; Carpenter et al., 1998; Iverson, Capirci, and Caselli, 1994; Iverson and Goldin-Meadow, 2005; Özçalışkan and Goldin-Meadow, 2005; Rowe and Goldin-Meadow, 2009a; 2009b; Rowe, Özçalışkan, and Goldin-Meadow, 2008; see also the metanalysis by Colonnesi, Stams, Koster, and Noom, 2010). For example, between 14 and 22 months, infants increasingly used gestures in combination with their speech in order to supplement their first verbal referential attempts (e.g. one-word sentences such as object labels) or their structurally more complex sentences (e.g. two-word sentences) (Özçalışkan and Goldin-Meadow, 2005). Moreover, the delay of index finger pointing is linked to various developmental problems in infants' communication skills (Bates et al., 1997; Sauer, Levine, Rowe, and Goldin-Meadow, 2010). For instance, 15 out of 22 children who failed to show either declarative pointing or declarative pointing in addition to pretend play behaviors at 18 months were diagnosed with developmental delay without the autism component at 42 months. Moreover, 10 out of 12 children who failed to show all of the three key behaviors of communicative development (i.e. declarative pointing, gaze following, and pretend play) were diagnosed with autism at 42 months (Baron-Cohen et al., 1996). Finally, children diagnosed with autism were less likely to use declarative index finger pointing by themselves and follow another person's pointing to an external entity (Gernsbacher, Stevenson, Khandakar, and Goldsmith, 2008).

Although a vast amount of studies have shown that the appearance of pointing in early childhood is universal, there is also some research showing some important differences in the dominance, form, and emergence of pointing gestures. (Callaghan et al., 2011; Liszkowski et al., 2012; Liszkowski and Tomasello, 2011; Salomo and Liszkowski, 2013; Wilkins, 2003). For example, other forms of pointing such as chin-pointing and lip-pointing are more common than index finger pointing in Barai, Yimas, and Watam of Papua New Guinea (Wilkins, 2003). Age of emergence and frequency of infants' pointing might change depending on maternal education and social-interactional experiences of cultural groups (Callaghan et al., 2011; Liszkowski et al., 2012; Liszkowski and Tomasello, 2011; Salomo and Liszkowski, 2013). For instance, Chinese, Dutch, and Mayan infants' frequency and emergence of pointing diverged from each other depending on the amount of time they spent in triadic joint actions and the amount of pointing in the input provided to them. The Chinese infants were exposed to triadic joint activities and gestural input more frequently than the Dutch infants, and the Dutch infants had more frequent exposure to triadic activities and gestural input than the Mayan infants. In turn, the Chinese infants pointed more than the Dutch infants, and the Dutch infants pointed more than the Mayan infants. Moreover, emergence of index finger pointing by the Mayan infants occurred at a later age than for the Chinese and Dutch infants (Salomo and Liszkowski, 2013). Furthermore, Tzeltan infants in a Mayan community pointed less frequently and the duration of their pointing was shorter than Rossel infants in Papua New Guinea (Brown, 2011). Infants' pointing also showed within-culture differences depending on activity context (Puccini, Hassemer, Salomo, and Liszkowski, 2010) or socio-economic conditions (SES) (Rowe and Goldin-Meadow, 2009a). For example, 12-month-olds pointed significantly more in a situation where they looked at different objects displayed on the walls of a room together with their caregivers than a situation where they and their caregivers played freely with various toys (Puccini et al., 2010). As another example, 14-month-old infants with high SES backgrounds pointed more often in comparison to their peers with low SES backgrounds; this difference was explained by the variation in the frequency of the caregivers' pointing gestures (Rowe and Goldin-Meadow, 2009a).

In sum, by the middle of the second year of life, children become competent users and interpreters of various socio-pragmatic cues such as looks and gestures and start able to coordinate their attention in accordance with others' attention. These newly emerging capacities open the way for successful referential communication. As infants get older, they move from dyadic to triadic interactions. In other words, they spend more time to share their interest in outside entities with a communicative partner rather than just engaging in face-to-face play with an adult or manipulating a toy non-communicatively (Bakeman and Adamson, 1984; Trevarthen and Hubley, 1978). Around 18 months, children have a more active role (rather than just be passive learners) in building coordinated attentional segments with their social partners in referential interaction contexts (Bakeman and Adamson, 1984). Infants' increasing competency in correctly reading various communicative or socio-pragmatic cues and effectively using joint attentional or referential skills is closely related to their competency in understanding a social partner's intentions about external entities and adjusting their behaviors according to the requirements of their communicative partner and conversational context. For instance, following eye gazes and/or pointing gestures of a communicative partner will possibly help infants to find an object hidden within an opaque box or behind a barrier. However, natural conditions are somehow different from the conditions in the experimental studies and children's actual task is beyond matching a novel label with a single referent by following only one modality of communication. In the following section, we present experimental studies that represent the more complex and dynamic nature of referential situations in spontaneous interactions between children and adults.

2.3 Experimental studies representing natural referential interactions

There are two important characteristics of child-parent referential interactions in a natural communicative context. First, there are multiple potential referents in a communicative environment and, in some cases, the infants' focus is on incorrect or non-target referent while the adult is introducing or providing a label for a target object (Harris, Jones, and Grant, 1983; Tomasello and Farrar, 1986). With regard to this point, Baldwin (1991) conducted a study using a "discrepant labeling" paradigm. Children were exposed to one of the two conditions. In the follow-in labeling condition, the experimenter was looking at the referent under the focus of the infant while producing a novel label. In the discrepant labeling condition, the experimenter's and the child's focus was on different referents while the experimenter was producing a label. 16- to 19-month-olds achieved to correctly match the label and the target object under the attention of the experimenter in the discrepant as well as in the follow-in labeling condition. Second, there are multiple communicative cues occurring simultaneously and in some situations, the adults' communicative cues might be vague or might contradict with each other. For example, an adult can suddenly begin to talk about a new referent while still pointing to a previously attended referent (Ateş and Küntay, 2014; 2017). Children seem to solve such ambiguous situations by using various socio-pragmatic cues: For example, Grassmann and Tomasello (2010) examined young 2- and 4-year-old children's responses to an adult's ambiguous verbal and nonverbal referential cues during a playful task where children are allowed to slide various objects through a chute attached into a box. In the novel-familiar condition, the adult verbally asked for a familiar object (e.g. "Give me the **car**") while ostensively pointing to a novel object such as an unusual **yoyo**. In the familiar-familiar condition, the adult asked for a familiar object (i.e. "Give me the **cup**") while ostensively pointing to an incorrect familiar object such as a **car**. The results indicated that both groups of children heavily relied on ostensive pointing rather than object labels in both conditions. Ateş, Kaya, and Küntay (2014) replicated Grassmann and Tomasello's experimental procedure with some modifications. For example, there were two experimenters in two separate rooms. The experimenter in the first room asked the children to play the chute-game after carrying the chosen object to a second experimenter in a separate room. The experimenter in the second room asked the children for the name of the object before allowing them to start playing with the object. Asking for the name of the object after the children's choices allowed us to understand whether the children's verbal responses are consistent with their behavioral responses in referentially ambiguous situations. We confirmed, as in Grassmann and Tomasello (2010), that although the children mostly relied on ostensive pointing rather than verbal labeling in the novel-familiar condition, they followed the two kinds of cues at equal rates in the familiar-familiar condition. Unlike Grassmann and Tomasello's study, in both conditions, the children basically took both objects to the experimenter although they mostly reached the pointed-to object first. Moreover, especially in the novel-familiar condition, there were significant amount of cases where the children produced the novel label heard from the experimenter for the familiar object they had chosen. In other words, for a familiar object, the children produced a novel label (e.g. mota) rather than the real name of the object (i.e. bird), possibly thinking that the familiar object has a second name, such as "mota" as the proper name of the bird. These results altogether suggest that the children seem to solve the ambiguity in both conditions by integrating the cues from verbal and nonverbal modalities of communication. As another example for children's success in overcoming pragmatically ambiguous situations, 12-month-olds correctly identified a target referent (i.e. a toy introduced in the absence of an adult) from an array of objects in response to the adult's ambiguous request (e.g. "Wow! Cool! Can you give me that?") by considering their previous play with that adult (Tomasello and Haberl, 2003). Based on their previous experiences, they were also more likely to map novel words to familiar objects if they decided that the informant was knowledgeable and accurate rather than ignorant and inaccurate (Krogh-Jespersen and Echols, 2012). In other words, if the experimenter's verbal statements implied that she knew the object and if she produced correct labels for the objects presented before the target object, the children were more likely to rely on the information provided by the experimenter. However, 3-year-olds tended to map a novel word to an unfamiliar referent when the speaker gave specific (e.g. the function of the object) rather than general information about the target object (Nilsen, Graham, and Pettigrew, 2009). Therefore, by preschool years, children seem to have capability of using different strategies in order to map a novel label with a specific object by taking some important socio-pragmatic factors into account. By the same age period, between 2 and 5 years, children are also able to detect referentially inappropriate or unexpected situations as long as the infelicity of the situation is apparent to them (Davis and Katsos, 2010; Morisseau, Davies, and Matthews, 2013). For example, 5-year-olds showed sensitivity to both under-informative (e.g. "find the orange" in the presence of more than one orange entities) or over-informative (e.g. "find the cat with a tail" in the presence of only one cat) sentences. In such cases, they demanded clarification, checked the experimenter by verbally reacting or intently looking at the experimenter until she provided a clarification for the situation, and gave late responses to the experimenter's questions (Morisseau et al., 2013). They also rated a speaker's under-informative, but not over-informative, utterances as bad and silly rather than good and sensible in a binary-judgment task, and gave fewer rewards to the speakers who used either over- or under-informative in comparison to optimal utterances. However, as speakers, preschool children are optimally informative as long as there is only one instance of a certain entity. When there is more than one instance, they are usually under-informative (Davis and Katsos, 2010). Moreover, even they reacted to the situations violating their socio-pragmatic expectations, preschool children rarely correct inappropriately informative sentences when they were given a chance to do so in a production task (Morisseau et al., 2013).

Thus, by preschool years, children seem to be capable of detecting pragmatically ambiguous or violated situations and developing various strategies in order to find logical solutions for these situations. However, we do not know yet whether toddlers and preschoolers use similar strategies with adults when they face with or experience relatively more ambiguous communicative situations. In order to answer this question, we need some studies that systematically compare the performance of children with adults under situations with distinct levels of ambiguity.

In the next section, in order to understand underlying factors behind the problems in the development of higher order socio-pragmatic skills such as joint attention and referential communication, we present some studies focusing on the development of basic socio-pragmatic skills including gaze behavior and gestures in children with atypical development.

3 Problems in socio-pragmatic skills of atypical populations

We cover here research about autism spectrum disorder (ASD), taking into account the proposal that children with ASD represents the least favorable example of pragmatic development and social communication (Norbury, 2014). We also present some studies comparing the development of socio-pragmatic skills between the children with ASD and with other disorders such as Specific Language Impairment, William's syndrome, and Down syndrome.

For children with ASD, impairment in joint attentional skills has been explored quite closely (Baron-Cohen et al., 1996; Leekam, Baron-Cohen, Perrett, Milders, and Brown, 1997; Leekam, Hunnisett, and Moore, 1998; Lord, 1995; Loveland and Landry, 1986; Mundy and Newell, 2007; Mundy, Sigman, and Kasari, 1994; Mundy, Sigman, Ungerer, and Sherman, 1986; Sigman, Ruskin, Mervis, and Robinson, 1999). Recent research has attempted to understand these children's problems in joint attentional interactions by separately examining problems in spontaneous gaze following, mutual engagement, and declarative gestures.

One of the markers of atypical development is abnormalities in eye contact. Children with ASD tend to look at their communicative partner's eyes less than typically developing children (Dalton et al., 2005; Klin, Jones, Schultz, Volkmar, and Cohen, 2002). However, there are also studies showing that the overall amount of eye contact of these children does not differ from their typically developing peers (Sigman, Mundy, Ungerer, and Sherman, 1986; Volkmar and Mayers, 1990). Therefore, there is a lot of research dedicated to understanding what the basic problem of autistic-spectrum children is with regard to eye contact (e.g. Baron-Cohen et al., 1995; Dawson, Meltzoff, Osterling, Rinaldi, and Brown, 1998; Senju, Yaguchi, Tojo, and Hasegawa, 2003). Although some researchers suggest that the problem is related to face-processing abilities such as face discrimination and face recognition (Dawson, Webb, and McPartland, 2005; Klin, Sparrow, de Bildt, Cicchetti, Cohen, and Volkmar, 1991), there is other research indicating that these children have intact face-processing skills. For instance, they are able to recognize the identity of a person from upside down photographs (Hobson, Ouston, and Lee, 1988). Moreover, they can correctly identify which direction a person is looking at (Baron-Cohen et al., 1995; Leekam et al., 1997). For instance, school-aged children with autism were able to detect where a person is looking at from the photographs that include either matched or mismatched head and eye direction (Leekam et al., 1997). Moreover, when they were presented a pair of cartoon faces that either was looking away or directly looking at the child and were asked the question of "Which one is looking at you?", they were able to correctly answer this question (Baron et al., 1995). However, these children still performed poorly on tasks that required them to spontaneously follow an adult's eye gaze towards an external entity (Leekam et al., 1997; 1998; Leekam, Lopez, and Moore, 2000).

There are various explanations for these children's problems in spontaneous-gaze following (for extended discussion, see Nation and Penny, 2008). Baron-Cohen and colleagues (1995) proposed that the children with ASD have problems in understanding the fact that eyes convey some information about various mental states such as others' desires, intentions, goals, and thoughts. In a series of experiments that included three groups of children with the same verbal mental age (i.e. children with autism, with mental handicap resulted from an unknown etiology or William's syndrome, and with typical development), Baron and colleagues (1995) found that the children with ASD failed to infer the desire or goal of a character placed at the center of a cardboard from her/his looks at one of the sweets placed at each corner of the same cardboard. Rather, they predicted the character's choice of candy in accordance with their own preferences. The children's impaired performance in these tasks seems not to be resulting from their limitations in understanding graphical representations, since a third experiment showed that these children's egocentric choices were lower when an arrow was used as a cue, in comparison to a face with eyes directed to the target candy. An alternative explanation argues that these children have problems in attention allocation skills (Leekam et al., 2000), in directing their attention to a particular stimulus that is under the focus of their communicative partner. In other words, they have problems in rapidly shifting their attention from one stimulus to another (Courchesne, Chisum, and Townsend, 1994; Courchesne et al., 1994; Pascualvaca, Fantie, Papageorgion, and Mirsky, 1998). For instance, they have difficulty in diverting their attention from an auditory to a visual (Courchesne et al., 1994) or from a central to a peripheral stimulus (Casey, Gordon, Mannheim, and Rumsey, 1993). However, there are other studies showing that the children with autism have intact attention allocation skills (e.g. Kylliainen and Hietanen, 2004; Swettenham, Condie, Campbell, Milne, and Coleman, 2003).

The contradictory findings might be explained by Dawson and colleagues' argument suggesting that the level of impairment in these children's attention allocation skills changes depending on the nature of the stimuli (i.e. social vs. non-social; static vs. moving) (Dawson, 1991; Dawson and Levy, 1989). The problems in their attention allocation skills are more apparent in the presence of social stimuli (e.g. gestures, facial expressions, eye gaze) rather than non-social stimuli because of relatively more complex and unpredictable nature of social stimuli (Dawson, Meltzoff, Osterling, Rinaldi, and Brown, 1998). Social stimuli include information about various mental states such as goals, desires, and thoughts, so that similar social cues might have different meanings depending on distinct communicative situations. Moreover, communicative cues from multiple modalities, which could be consistent or contradictory with each other, possibly create some difficulty for children in processing such multidimensional information. Dawson and colleagues (1998) tested three groups of children (i.e. children with ASD, down syndrome, and typical development) to determine whether they turned towards to either social (i.e. clapping hands, calling children's name) or non-social stimuli (i.e. playing a musical jack-in-the-box, shaking a rattle) and whether they were able to follow an experimenter's looks or points to a toy placed in front or back of them. The results indicated that the orientation error of the children with ASD was greater than the other two groups of children, and the group differences were even greater when the stimuli were social rather than non-social. Moreover, the children with ASD made more errors than the children with Down syndrome or typical development when they needed to follow the attentional flow of another person. There was a significant correlation between these children's performance in following others' attentional shifts and orienting to social stimuli, but not to non-social stimuli. Therefore, the authors concluded that these children's incompetent joint attentional skills such as following gaze shifts of and building mutual engagement with a communicative partner, might be resulting from their failure in visually orientating to social stimuli. However, contradictory findings based on a large amount of research focusing on reflexive attentional cuing have questioned the credibility of Dawson and colleagues' argument. Some studies pointed out that the children with ASD showed the same reflexive orienting response to social (e.g. eye gaze, head turn) and non-social (e.g. arrows) cues, while the others showed that their reflexive orienting response was valid only for non-social cues (for a review, see Nation and Penny, 2008). Based on these findings, Nation and Penny (2008) underscored the fact that the people with ASD show normal reflexive orienting response to social cues in cued-attention tasks, which measure the differences in a participant's reaction time to expected versus unexpected location of a stimulus presented on a computer screen (Posner, 1980) but not in tasks representing naturalistic or spontaneous interactions. Leekam and colleagues (2000, 2006) argue that if the children's performance is affected by the orientation of social stimuli in both situations including natural dyadic and triadic interactions, then Hobson's (1993) I-thou intersubjectivity model suggesting that children's problems in joint attention skills result from difficulties in interpersonal engagement is supported. According to this model, children have problems in neural processes that function in one's understanding the fact that he/she is a separate entity and other people are entities that have a relation with her/him. In fact, these children's incompetencies in creating joint attentional bids with a communicative partner and referring to external entities are based on problems in dyadic interactions. Leekam, Lopez, and Moore (2000) examined both dyadic and triadic interactions of two groups of preschool children: the children with ASD and the ones with developmental delays without an ASD component (e.g. organic disorders, global or specific developmental delays). In order to observe dyadic interactions, the experimenter tried to make eye contact with the child by either merely looking at the child or also verbally calling the child's attention in addition to looking at her. In order to observe triadic interactions, they adapted Corkum and Moore's (1995) "gaze-following" paradigm, which was originally designed to measure typically developing 6- to 12-month-old infants' responses to an experimenter's head turns. This paradigm includes three phases: baseline, training, and testing. In the baseline phase, the children's responses to an experimenter's head turn were measured in the absence of a target object, where the target object was hidden within an opaque box. In the training phase, following the experimenter's head-turn, the target object in the direction of the head turn was activated through a remote control by a second experimenter and became visible to the child. In the testing phase, the target object was activated and became visible depending on the child's correct head turn requiring the child to follow the direction of the first experimenter's head turn. Leekam and colleagues

(2000) suggested that Corkum and Moore's paradigm also works with the same principle of attentional cuing paradigm by Posner (1980), since the appearance of the target object stimulates the peripheral visual field and the children have a chance to predict the location of the target object based on a cue (i.e. the experimenter's head turn). Yet, in comparison to the cued attention tasks, this task represents naturalistic interactions better. In the trials assessing dyadic interactions, overall, the children with autism were less responsive to the experimenter's attempts to make eye contact in comparison to the children with developmental delay. In the gaze-following trials as well, the children with ASD were less responsive to the communicative cues of the experimenter. Only 20% of the children with autism (4 out of 20), but 65% of the children with developmental delay spontaneously followed the gaze direction of the experimenter. From the remaining 80% of the children with autism (16 out of 20), only half of them followed the experimenter's head turn as long as the target object became visible. However, the other half of 80% did not follow the experimenter's head turn at all. They concluded that the problems in both dyadic and triadic interactions might be responsible for impairment in joint attentional skills of children with autism. Moreover, when the same procedure was replicated with a non-human, non-communicating cue such as a toy train that informed the children about the direction of an upcoming target object, both the children with ASD and developmental delay showed worse performance compared to their performance in turning towards the right direction following the human social cue. Therefore, children with ASD seem to have problems in both dyadic and triadic interactions and these problems seem to go beyond the nature of stimuli. Although these findings seem to indirectly support Hobson's argument suggesting that the problems in joint attentional tasks based on difficulties in interpersonal or dyadic interactions, they did not explicitly test whether interpersonal interactions are directly responsible for problems in joint attentional skills.

Leekam and Ramsden's (2006) study focused on this question by investigating whether difficulties of children with ASD in dyadic interactions are specifically associated with impairments in joint attentional skills, but not other communicative skills that do not require joint attentional skills (i.e. behavior regulation). Representing dyadic interactions, they examined how these children responded to an experimenter's vocal (e.g. "Hey! Look at me!" or "Jamie, Look at me!"), and non-vocal (e.g. touching child's hands or waving hand) attempts for building eye contact with the child. In the study, behavior regulation was measured though children's responses to the experimenter's either gestural or verbal requests whereas joint attention skills were measured children's deictic gestures referring to a third-person entity or their responses to the experimenter's communicative attempts about a third person entity. The results showed that the children with ASD responded to the experimenter's referential attempts less than their peers with developmental delays, particularly with regard to vocal attempts. Moreover, the low ability group of children with ASD performed especially lower than the children with developmental delays on the tasks requiring children to use joint attentional skills. Only ASD children's performance indicated an association between dyadic attention and joint attentional skills.

Based on Atkinson, Hood, Wattam-Bell, and Braddick's (1992) research with typically developing 1- and 3-month-old infants, Leekam and colleagues (2000) also argued that the children with ASD might have some problems in pairing their partners' communicative cues with a target in a specific location, especially in the presence of a distractor. In other words, similar to 1-month-olds in Atkinson and colleagues' study, the children with autism might suffer from disengaging from a central stimulus and shifting their attention to a peripheral stimulus when the presentation of the two kinds of stimuli are overlapping. This argument was tested by manipulating the presence of a central stimulus via two different kinds of trials. In the overlap trials, the central stimulus was kept present during the first appearance of the target peripheral object and also during its whole presentation. In the non-overlap trials, the target peripheral object replaced the central stimulus, that is, the central stimulus was unavailable as long as the peripheral object was visible to the child. The results pointed out that the accuracy of the children with autism was the same as that of the children with developmental delays. In fact, low-IQ children with autism were even significantly faster than their peers with developmental delay in disengaging from a central stimulus and shifting their attention to a peripheral one.

As suggested by Luyster and Lord (2009), the inconsistent results in the literature might be due to the differences in the experimental procedures such as display of real objects vs. representations of them (via a computer screen), number of cues affecting the level of the saliency of the target object, or linguistic structure of verbal stimuli. Aketchi and colleagues' (2011) research might provide an answer to this argument: Based on Baldwin's (1991) paradigm, they presented a situation through a computer screen that requires a responder to associate an object to a novel label in accordance with the gaze direction of the speaker in the presence of a distractor. There were two experimental conditions. In the follow-in condition, the speaker looked at the object that the child was looking at and produced a novel label for this object. In the discrepant condition, the speaker looked at and produced a novel label for the other object rather than the one that the child was looking at. The results showed that the children with ASD were more likely to select the object under the speaker's rather than their own focus. Moreover, they looked at the target (i.e. under the focus of the speaker) and the distractor (i.e. under the focus of the child) objects for an equal amount of time, but the children with typical development preferred to look at the target object longer. However, in a second experiment, when the researchers increased the saliency of the target object by jiggling its representation on the screen, the frequency of both groups' selection of the target object and the duration of their looking time at the target object increased in comparison to the first experiment. Therefore, the authors concluded that the failure of the children with ASD results from their inability to discriminate the target object under the focus of the speaker from the competitors. In a more recent experiment, Akechi, Kikuchi, Tojo, Osanai, and

Hasegawa (2013) applied exactly the same procedure but, to represent natural interactions, they added index finger pointing accompanying eye gaze. They found that the performance of the children with ASD was improved in the discrepant learning condition in comparison to their performance in the prior study where the experimenter solely used eye gaze as a communicative cue (See Study 1 in Akechi et al., 2011). Furthermore, parental reports of the children with ASD (Leekam et al., 1998) showed that additional cues accompanying eye gaze such as pointing gestures and attention getters (e.g. "Look!") increased their children's performance in spontaneous gaze following. Therefore, both experimental studies (Aketchi et al., 2000; Akechi et al., 2013; Leekam et al., 2000) and parental reports (Leekam et al., 1998) supported the proposal that the children's performance in the presence of distractors might be enhanced by using multiple communicative cues that signal the target entity.

It is also important to note that the level of impairment in joint engagement and attentional orientation changes depending on the children's chronological and mental age, suggesting that the problems in these skills probably lessen as children get older (Leekam et al., 1998; Leekam et al., 2000; Leekam and Ramsden, 2006; Mundy et al., 1994). Then, one possibility is that the core skills that are necessary for a healthy communication such as gaze following and deictic gestures could be delayed rather than impaired in these populations of children (Camaioni, 1997; Leekam et al., 2000). For example, children with ASD were able to understand and to produce declarative pointing between 3 and 5 years of age (Camaioni et al., 1997) and to follow a recipient's eye gaze between 4 and 5 years of age (Leekam et al., 2000). Moreover, children with ASD spontaneously followed one's head-turn and eye gaze better if they had a relatively higher mental age (over 48 months) (Leekam et al., 1998). However, as the studies reviewed in the previous section have shown, these behaviors develop by the middle of the second year of life in typically developing children. Parental reports also showed that gaze following of children with ASD appeared approximately three years later than their typically developing peers even their performance in the cases where other cues accompanying parents' gaze direction such as head turn and pointing were included (Leekam et al., 1998). Although there are no any longitudinal studies beginning from the preverbal period until the adolescence years, based on the results of the existing studies, one can argue that the gap between the socio-communicative skills of children with ASD and their typically developing peers do not entirely disappear over years. An important question we need to address is why these children show a delay in the development of the core socio-pragmatic skills needed for a healthy and effective communication.

The most empirically defendable reason for this delay seems to us is that the children with atypical development have problems appreciating their partners' communicative cues such as their eye gaze, pointing gesture, mostly in terms of understanding the communicative intention behind these behaviors (Baron-Cohen et al., 1995; Gliga, Elsabbagh, Hudry, Charman, Johnson, and Team, 2012; Leekam et al., 2000; Leekam and Ramsden, 2006). Supporting this argument, Gliga and colleagues (2012) found that children at risk for the development of ASD did not acquire a novel label successfully although they effectively followed the eye gazes of their communicative partner. Therefore, word-learning requires more than solely associating a novel label with a target object via the help of various informative cues. In other words, through paying attention to multiple and salient socio-pragmatic cues, these children need to understand that both they and their communicative partners are intentional agents whose behaviors represent various mental states (Tomasello, 1999).

Another issue we should consider is whether the suggested definitions and measurement methods of the target socio-pragmatic skills are appropriate for different populations with distinct socialization histories. This point brings us to question the validity of suggested definitions and measurement protocols of pragmatic skills accepted as "typical".

4 Boundaries between the definitions of typical and atypical socio-pragmatic skills

Most researchers use gaze alternation as an indicator for the occurrence of higher order socio-pragmatic skills such as joint attention and ignore other channels of communication such as the auditory or tactile modalities. Although observing the visual component of attention is easier or more reliable, there are some cultural communities or communicative situations within the same cultural community where using only visual channel of communication might be misleading or actually might not be a valid measure to examine the development of target socio-pragmatic skills. Therefore, in order to objectively understand which skills or behaviors are predictors or indicators of higher-level socio-pragmatic understanding, we need to adopt a cross-culturally sensitive perspective, which emphasizes the importance of various ethnographic or semi-natural studies bringing up different practices in diverse groups or populations.

An important amount of ethnographic studies has shown that the structure of children's communicative environment and interactions are more variable than the ones in the experimental studies that have been mostly conducted with European samples. For instance, children from different cultures or various communities within the same culture are exposed to different interactional practices (e.g. dyadic vs. polyadic interactions), activity types (e.g. formal, school-like or informal contexts), and communicative partners with changing or different expectations and communicative goals (Akhtar and Gernsbacher, 2008). In some cultures, at least until a certain age, infants are not treated as conversational partners in the European fashion – for example they are not exposed to face-to-face or dyadic interaction as much as their peers in European cultures (Brown, 2011; De Leon, 1999). Infants in the Tzeltal Mayan community are mostly carried in a shawl and rarely set down until the end of the first year of life. They have relatively fewer interlocutors in comparison to their peers in European countries and those interlocutors are mostly unresponsive to their preverbal utterances. The caregivers avoid initiating interactions and eye contact with their babies until the babies are mature enough to initiate interactions with their caregivers by themselves. In fact, they use bodily interactions in order to sooth their infants or keep them calm, only point to external entities such as animals in order to distract their infants from uncomforting internal states. Tzeltal infants do not often attend to others' points, exhibit accompanying eye gaze to their own points, or use eye gaze with a different purpose, to check an interlocutor's attention or interest (Brown, 2011). De Leon's (1999) study also indicated that Zinacantec infants in the Tzotzil Mayan community are wrapped in a skirt and carried on the caregivers' back 70% of the time from birth until 8 months, leaving little opportunity for children to engage in face-to-face, dyadic interactions with others at earlier time points. However, as opposed to European or Western infants, they have more chance to physically contact with their caregivers, which creates a communicative context allowing them to benefit from other nonverbal channels of communication. In fact, caregivers understand the babies' needs from their body movements and specific vocalizations. As an example, infants' deep guttural vocalization is inferred as their desire to urinate. Moreover, there are specific routines that allow Zinacantec children to participate in interactions between adults as proto-speakers or proto-addressees. For instance, beginning from the age of 4 months, caregivers attend to and interpret their babies' gestures and vocalizations and translate these communicative acts to others via "elicitation routines", also called as "elema routines" by Schieffelin (1990). In these interactions, the caregiver formulates what the child tries to say using "say X" frame (e.g. "She said she wanted to pee") while the child actively follows or participates in this interaction. In a sense, the caregivers have a mediator role in order to help their preverbal, nonspeaking youngsters to communicate with others. At the same age period, the caregivers also attempt to build joint attention with their babies through various communicative devices such as rhetorical questions (e.g. "Do you see it?", "Where did you go?"), interactional routines (e.g. greetings, games such as peekaboo, rhymes), and motherese register (i.e. special vocabulary used for only young children) rather than a specific kind of triadic interaction with gaze shifts between the communicative partner and an outside entity. The caregivers and their children in this society share the same visual field by synchronic eye or head movements. For example, when a passerby greeted a caregiver carrying the baby on her lap, the caregiver and the baby synchronically turned their heads and eyes towards that person while the baby was listening the dialogue between the two adults. Therefore, in this interaction, the infant as a "side participant" shared her caregiver's engagement to an outside entity (the passerby). By eight months, these infants are embedded to the interactions between adults by synchronically producing vocalizations and changing their gaze directions and/or body position. By 10 months, when the children become physically more active, close physical interactions between caregiver-child dyads are replaced by long-distance verbal monitoring that mostly includes imperatives, questions, and declaratives. By 2-years-old, when the spoken language emerges, children are accepted as a communicative partner and actively involved in dyadic conversations. If we evaluate from the common (Western) perspective, we might think that the children living in these societies possibly develop delayed or impaired skills in socio-pragmatic aspect of language since they are exposed to prototypical joint attentional frames relatively later (i.e. around the age of 2) than children in Western societies. However, from a cross-culturally comparative perspective, behaviors generally accepted as universal or functional in adult-child interaction such as early joint attentional interactions might reflect a cultural bias of European researchers (Rogoff, 1990).

European researchers have mostly not investigated communicative cases where children's gaze shift from an object to a person is not resulted from sharing intentionality, but rather from their relatively automatic response to the person's specific behavior (Carpenter et al., 1998). Furthermore, most European-based research has not examined the cases where children attend to an entity by using other modalities (e.g. auditory or tactile) rather than the visual modality. For instance, the sound of a bus travelling outside (and remaining outside of the visual field) can draw a child's attention and lead to a conversation between the child and his caregiver about buses, passengers on the bus (Ateş and Küntay, 2014; 2017). Alternatively, children can simultaneously attend to two or more events by using distinct modalities of communication for each event. As an example, they might auditorily attend to an entity (e.g. the sound of a cartoon on tv) while simultaneously visually attend to another entity (e.g. looking at the pictures of a book with their parent). Supporting this argument, there are some empirical studies showing that children are able to learn new skills from an ongoing event not directly addressed to them. For instance, they are able to learn to build new origami figures by watching an adult demonstration addressing their sibling (Correa-Chavez and Rogoff, 2009; Correa-Chavez, Rogoff, and Arauz, 2005) and to learn novel words by overhearing the speech between two adults (Akhtar, 2005; Akhtar, Jipson, and Callanan, 2001; Floor and Akhtar, 2006; Gampe, Liebal, and Tomasello, 2012; Schneidman et al., 2009). Moreover, their learning from overheard situations is robust in the presence of a competing event, such as an unrelated talk between the same-aged peers or a distractor toy (Akhtar, 2005; Correa-Chavez and Rogoff, 2009). Some research showed that children's success in learning from non-addressed, overheard situations was associated with their distinct attentional strategies. For instance, children who are able to follow two or more events at the same time without interrupting their attention for one event for the sake of the other event(s) were more successful in learning new origami figures by watching the interaction between an adult and her addressee (Correa-Chavez and Rogoff, 2009). These differences in attentional strategies are basically attributed to the differences between cultures with regard to child-raring practices and/or goals. For example, in some (usually traditional) cultures, the responsibility to learn belongs to the children, that is, children are expected to learn by themselves through observing and participating in family and community activities and caregivers support their learning only when the children ask for help. In some other (usually European) cultures, adults take the main responsibility to teach their children via structured, child-focused activities that mostly require dyadic or face-to-face interactions (Chavajay and Rogoff, 1999; Correa-Chavez and Rogoff, 2009; Correa-Chavez et al., 2005; Lopez, Correa-Chavez, Rogoff, and Gutierrez, 2010; Rogoff, Correa-Chavez, and Silva, 2011; Silva, Correa-Chavez, and Rogoff, 2010).

Some cross-cultural studies have also indicated that caregivers' responses to their children's socio-communicative cues such as eye gazes, smiles, touches, and vocalizations vary from culture to culture (Fogel, Toda, and Kawai, 1988; Kärtner et al., 2008). For example, Kärtner and colleagues (2008) examined semi-naturalistic interactions between caregiver-child dyads from six cultural communities (i.e. Los Angeles-USA, Berlin-Germany, Beijing-China, Delhi-India, urban and rural Nso-Cameroon) when the infants were 3 months old. They showed that the mothers from Berlin and Los Angeles more frequently responded to their infants' vocalizations using the visual channel of communication (e.g. eye gaze, smile or facial expression with raised eyebrows) than the mothers in other communities. Moreover, the caregivers from rural Nso more often responded to their infants' touches than the ones from other cultural communities except for Los Angeles. The caregivers in Los Angeles were also more responsive to their infants' touches than the caregivers in urban Nso and Berlin. The authors explained these differences by Keller's (2007) proposal that in interdependent cultures, proximal components of parenting (i.e. body contact and body stimulation) have a more significant value while in independent cultures, distal components of parenting (e.g. face-to-face interaction and object play) play a more important role in child raring practices. Murase, Dale, Ogura, Yamashita, and Mahieu (2005) also indicated that typically developing children follow different routes in their referential interactions during a shared book-reading session with their mothers. For example, American children more often labeled the pictures (e.g. "elephant") on the book following their mothers' elaborative questions (e.g. "What is its color?") about these pictures than Japanese children did. However, Japanese children more often labeled the pictures following their mothers' labels for these pictures than American children did. In other words, Japanese children basically used imitation in order to talk about external entities. Moreover, American mothers more frequently followed their children's labeling with elaborative questions than Japanese mothers did. However, Japanese mothers more frequently their children's labels with confirmative utterances showing that they share the fact or idea provided by the children (e.g. "That's right!") than American mothers did. The authors explained the distinct structure of these parent-child interactions through Azuma's (1994) socialization models: American learning basically relies on the instruction model with predefined roles suggesting that adults are mentors while children are learners. However, Japanese learning mostly relies on the osmosis model suggesting that children are responsible to learn new skills through modelling and incidental learning.

Even if we accept that the visual channel of communication is the only or the main route for the establishment of joint attention, according to Carpenter and Liebal's (2011) proposal, people might enter into joint attentional episodes at different levels and therefore use distinct cognitive processes requiring different kinds and combinations of communicative cues or behaviors. For instance, the communicative path for the establishment of a joint attentional episode is quite different from each other in a situation where an adult consciously wants to introduce a referent to a child and in a situation where a referent in a mutual environment simultaneously draws both the adult's and the child's attention by itself because of its salience. In the first situation, at least three types of communicative cues are required in order to get the attention of a communicative partner: "initiation looks", "reference looks", and "sharing looks". Initiation looks signal the initiator's communicative intent and aim to draw the recipient's attention to an entity. These looks are usually accompanied by attention getters and ostensive cues. Reference looks show the initiator's referential intent and are usually accompanied by deictic gestures. Therefore, the first two kinds of looks are one-sided and function to begin a joint attentional episode. However, sharing looks are bidirectional, usually accompanied by a smile and comments and show that two communicative partners finally achive to jointly attend to an external entity. In other words, they occur when the two partners equally participate in the event and mutually share their attention. Thus, in the second situation, sharing looks meaning, "Hey, did you see that?" are sufficient in order to complete the episode automatically initiated by a mutual context (e.g. a loud noise). Accumulated research is mostly about the cases like in the former example where one of the communicative partners has a more dominant role; but mostly ignores the situations like in the second example where both communicative partners have a more equal role in the establishment of a joint attentional episode.

Therefore, it seems better to avoid evaluating the development of children's socio-pragmatic skills as "typical" or "atypical" merely based on a certain combination of a limited range of behaviors. In other words, "shared intentionality" or "knowing something together" might be achieved through distinct combinations and order of verbal/linguistic structures and nonverbal strategies depending on different socio-cultural characteristics of a certain group and distinct levels or types of interaction even within the same group. Based on this argument, one possibility is that children identified as having "atypical" development might follow different routes than their peers identified as having "typical" development about higher-order socio-pragmatic skills. Carpenter and colleagues' (2002) study might be accepted as indirect evidence for this argument: 3- to 4-year-old children with autism produced referential behaviors before developing joint attentional skills. This is a reversed pattern when compared to the typically developing children who achieved joint attentional engagement before the production of their first referential behaviors (Carpenter et al., 1998). That is, when attentional and behavioral skills were examined separately, the order of the occurrence of attentional (i.e. sharing, following, directing attention) and behavioral (i.e. following, directing behavior) skills was the same for both the children with atypical or typical development. However, when attentional and behavioral skills were examined together, 83% of typically developing children in the study of Carpenter and colleagues (1998) showed the following pattern: share attention- follow attention- follow behavior- direct attention- direct behavior. However, 67% of the children with autism exhibited the following pattern: follow behavior- share attention- direct behavior- follow attention- direct attention. They were also less successful in comparison to their peers with developmental delays in the tasks such as "gaze following" and "declarative gestures". However, they were equally successful as their peers having developmental delays in the tasks such as imitative learning, which required children to reproduce a target action modelled by the experimenter. At this point, it is important to touch upon a body of work investigating different intervention methods to close the gaps in socio-pragmatic skills of the children with developmental delays and their typically developing peers. In these intervention studies, teaching joint attentional skills is accepted as a key component for the efficiency of an intervention program since it is accepted as foundational for other social and language skills such as functional and symbolic play and spontaneous speech (Whalen, Schreibman, and Ingersoll, 2006; White et al., 2011). White and colleagues' (2011) systematic review of 27 intervention studies including participants between the ages of 22 months and 10 years old showed that there are at least two groups of intervention studies aiming to improve children's joint attentional skills. In the first group of studies, joint attention is accepted as a collateral variable, meaning that the target skills in the intervention are not basic components of joint attentional skills; but still they are expected to contribute to the development of children's joint attentional skills (e.g. Baker, 2000; Ingersoll and Schreibman, 2006; Vismara and Lyons, 2007; Zercher, Hunt, Schuler, &Webster, 2001). As an example, these studies aimed to change some communicative conditions by incorporating ritualistic themes, reinforcement, and physical prompts into a game or to teach some skills such as liberty to make a selection and imitation. The second group of studies aimed to teach core components of joint attention such as pointing and gaze alternations (e.g. Gulsrud, Kasari, and Paparella, 2007; Jones, 2009; Kasari, Freeman, and Paparella, 2006). White and colleagues showed that, in both types of studies, (at least some) children's joint attentional skills showed improvement at the end of the intervention program (White et al., 2011). These findings suggest that a wider range of skills including imitation rather than only behaviors including looks and points might help children to gain joint attentional skills. However, in these studies the definition of joint attention as the outcome variable is somehow different from each other as well as the behaviors targeted in the intervention. The outcome variables in these interventions included different definitions of joint attention such as coordinated joint attention (i.e. children's active engagement with both an adult and an object) and supported joint attention (i.e. children's passive attention to an adult and an object, usually as a result of parental attempt). Alternatively, they included different sets of joint attentional skills including responses to or initiation of some joint attention behaviors such as pointing, showing, and/or coordinated looks between a person and object. Moreover, intervention studies differed from each other in some other important aspects such as the age of focus group, the cognitive functioning level of participants (e.g. low-, medium-, or high-functioning children), the delivery agent of intervention (e.g. video, parent, or peer), the total number of participants (e.g. single subject or group studies), the density of intervention (e.g. the duration of one session, the number of sessions in a week, and the total length of intervention), the setting of intervention (e.g. clinic, school, or home), and some methodological characteristics (e.g. single subject design, group design, or randomized design) (for a detailed review, see Reichow and Volkmar, 2010). Therefore, we need more systematic studies in order to examine some unanswered questions including 1) Which behaviors or skills should be targeted in order to improve children's joint attentional skills in an intervention study?; 2) Do we need interventions targeting distinct behaviors or skills depending on distinct characteristics of focus groups (e.g. age, cognitive functioning level, family characteristics, etc.)?; and 3) What kind of interventions are more effective for the development of what kind of joint attentional skills?

Some recent studies examining the interactions between child-caregiver dyads showed that the caregiver input provided to children and responses of children to the input have some distinct features for children with developmental delays and their peers with typical development. For instance, in spite of the same amount of speech, the mothers of typically developing children produced more wh- questions in general, and more subject wh- questions than the mothers of children with autism (Goodwin, Fein, and Naigles, 2015). Bedford and colleagues (2013) also indicated that 2-year-old toddlers at a high risk for autism used the adult input differently than their typically developing peers. For instance, they failed to benefit from adult feedback in a word learning task; but their same-age peers efficiently used adult feedback and improved their performance.

These findings altogether seem to support our argument suggesting that the children with atypical development and their parents might give primacy to different mechanisms or modalities of communication.

5 Conclusion

The present review shows that, by the middle of the second year of life, children are competent users of various socio-pragmatic cues (e.g. looks, gestures), which enable them to understand their communicative partner's mental states such as intentions, goals, desires, and thoughts. These newly emerging capacities serve the development of higher-order socio-pragmatic skills such as joint attention and referential communication and help children to adjust their behaviors according to the requirements of a social partner and/or a communicative context. By preschool years, children are also capable of detecting pragmatically inappropriate situations and to find functional solutions to these situations. Research focusing on children with developmental delays, especially with ASD, has shown that these children have the core skills (e.g. spontaneous gaze following, deictic gestures) that are necessary for a healthy communication; but the emergence of these skills is rather delayed when compared with typically developing peers. In spite of different explanations with regard to the reasons for this delay, we think that children with atypical developmental profile have problems in appreciating relevant socio-pragmatic cues regarding their social partners' mental states. Therefore, it seems that they are lacking basic skills of "intention understanding" or "mind reading". However, even research examining typically developing children has important limitations. First, we need more comprehensive research that investigates the role of various communicative cues from different modalities on the establishment of joint attentional episodes between children and their communicative partners. Second, we need to understand whether different communicative cues such as looks, touches, verbal statements are more beneficial at distinct types and/or levels of joint attentional episodes. Third, we need to understand whether there are different routes for the establishment and maintenance of joint attentional episodes during various types of interactions and across different cultural communities or sub-communities within the same culture. Addressing these issues will help us understand whether common and well-established definition and research methods in examining socio-pragmatic skills of children reflect solely Western criteria or are valid to generalize to different groups of children.

The current review also shows that we need more research in order to fill in the gaps in the literature targeting children with atypical development. For instance, to our knowledge, there has not been any research focusing on early periods (before the age of 2) considering the effect of verbal and nonverbal mechanisms and co-speech gestures on the establishment of joint attention in child-parent interactions of atypical populations. Before evaluating socio-pragmatic language development of children with atypical profiles, we also need to consider 1) whether the quantity and quality of the input provided to the children with atypical development are the same as their typically developing peers; 2) If they are not the same, whether the differences in the input provided to the children with atypical development explain between- and within- group differences in the skills previously reviewed; and 3) Even when they are the same, whether children with atypical development benefit to a different extent from the verbal and nonverbal mechanisms in adult input; and 4) Whether these children follow distinct routes in order to develop an understanding that other people have distinct mental and informational states, and therefore to achieve "shared intentionality."

References

Akechi, Hironori, Yukiko Kikuchi, Yoshikuni Tojo, Hiroo Osanai & Toshikazu Hasegawa. 2013. Brief report: Pointing cues facilitate word learning in children with autism spectrum disorder. *Journal of Autism and Developmental Disorders* 43 (1). 230–235.

Akechi, Hironori, Atsushi Senju, Yukiko Kikuchi, Yoshikuni Tojo, Hiroo Osanai & Toshikazu Hasegawa. 2011. Do children with ASD use referential gaze to learn the name of an object? An eye-tracking study. *Research in Autism Spectrum Disorders* 5 (3). 1230–1242.

Akhtar, Nameera. 2005. The robustness of learning through overhearing. *Developmental Science* 8 (2). 199–209.

Akhtar, Nameera & Morton Ann Gernsbacher. 2008. On privileging the role of gaze in infant social cognition. *Child Development Perspectives* 2 (2). 59–65.

Akhtar, Nameera, Jennifer Jipson & Maureen A. Callanan. 2001. Learning words through overhearing. *Child Development* 72 (2). 416–430.

Altınok, Nazlı. 2014. *Predictors and outcomes of pointing behavior in early communicative development: From child-directed interactions to gestures to words*. Istanbul, Turkey: Koç University MA thesis.

Ateş, Beyza, Mustafa Kaya & Aylin C. Küntay. 2014. When referential cues are contradictory: Young children's reliance on ostensively cued pointing vs. lexical labels. Poster presented at *the 1th International Symposium on Brain and Cognitive Science, (ISBCS)*, Boğaziçi University, İstanbul, Turkey, April 2014.

Ateş, Beyza & Aylin C. Küntay. 2014. How do Turkish learners and their caregivers integrate discourse-pragmatic knowledge and gestures in their referential expressions? Paper presented at *19th Biennial International Conference on Infant Studies*, Berlin, Germany, July 2014.

Ateş, B. & Küntay, A. 2017. Referential interactions of Turkish-learning children with their caregivers about non-absent objects: Integration of nonverbal devices and prior discourse. *Journal of Child Language*. 1–26. doi:10.1017/S0305000917000150.

Atkinson, Janette, Bruce Hood, John Wattam-Bell & Oliver Braddick. 1992. Changes in infants' ability to switch visual attention in the first three months of life. *Perception* 21 (5). 643–653.

Aureli, Tiziana, Paola Perucchini & Maria Genco. 2009. Children's understanding of communicative intentions in the middle of the second year of life. *Cognitive Development* 24 (1). 1–12.

Azuma, Hiroshi. 2014. Two modes of cognitive socialization in Japan and the United States. In Patricia M., Greenfield & Rodney R. Cocking (eds.), *Cross-cultural roots of minority child development*, 275–283. New York, NY: Psychology Press.

Bakeman, Roger & Lauren B. Adamson. 1984. Coordinating attention to people and objects in mother-infant and peer-infant interactions. *Child Development* 55 (4). 1278–1289.

Baker, Mary J. 2000. Incorporating the thematic ritualistic behaviors of children with autism into games: Increasing social play interactions with siblings. *Journal of Positive Behavior Interventions* 2 (2). 66–84.

Baldwin, Dare A. 1991. Infants' contribution to the achievement of joint reference. *Child Development* 62 (5). 875–890.

Baron-Cohen, Simon. 1995. *Mindblindness: An essay on autism and theory of mind*. Cambridge, MA: MIT Press.

Baron-Cohen, Simon, Ruth Campbell, Annette Karmiloff-Smith, Julia Grant & Jane Walker. 1995. Are children with autism blind to the mentalistic significance of the eyes? *British Journal of Developmental Psychology* 13 (4). 379–398.

Baron-Cohen, Simon, Dare A. Baldwin & Mary Crowson. 1997. Do children with autism use the speaker's direction of gaze strategy to crack the code of language? *Child Development* 68 (1). 48–57.

Baron-Cohen, Simon, Anthony Cox, Gillian Baird, John Swettenham, Natasha Nightingale, Kate Morgan, Auriol Drew & Tony Charman. 1996. Psychological markers in the detection of autism in infancy in a large population. *British Journal of Psychiatry* 168 (2). 158–163.

Bates, Elizabeth. 1979. *The emergence of symbols: Cognition and communication in infancy*. New York, NY: Academic Press.

Bates, Elizabeth, Luigia Camaioni & Virginia Volterra. 1975. The acquisition of performatives prior to speech. *Merrill-Palmer Quarterly of Behavior and Development* 21 (3). 205–226.

Bates, Elizabeth, Donna Thal, Doris Trauner, Judi Fenson, Dorothy Aram, Julie Eisele & Ruth Nass. 1997. From first words to grammar in children with focal brain injury. *Developmental Neuropsychology* 13 (3). 275–343.

Batki, Anna, Simon Baron-Cohen, Sally Wheelwright, Jennifer Connellan & Jag Ahluwalia. 2000. Is there an innate gaze module? Evidence from human neonates. *Infant Behavior and Development* 23 (2). 223–229.

Bedford, Rachael, Teodora Gliga, Kathryn Frame, Kristelle Hudry, Susie Chandler, Mark H. Johnson & Tony Charman. 2013. Failure to learn from feedback underlies word learning difficulties in toddlers at risk for autism. *Journal of Child Language* 40 (1). 29–46.

Behne, Tanya, Malinda Carpenter & Michael Tomasello. 2005. One-year-olds comprehend the communicative intentions behind gestures in a hiding game. *Developmental Science* 8. 492–499.

Brooks, Rechele & Andrew N. Meltzoff. 2002. The importance of eyes: How infants interpret adult looking behavior. *Developmental Psychology* 38 (6). 958–966.

Brown, Penelope. 2012. The cultural organization of attention. In Alessandro, Duranti, Elinor Ochs & Bambi B. Schieffelin (eds.), *The handbook of language socialization*, 29–55. Malden, MA: Wiley-Blackwell.

Bruner, Jerome. 1981. The social context of language acquisition. *Language and Communication* 1 (2/3). 155–178.

Butler, Samantha C., Albert J. Caron & Rechele Brooks. 2000. Infant understanding of the referential nature of looking. *Journal of Cognition and Development* 1 (4). 359–377.

Butterworth, George & Lesley Grover. 1988. The origins of referential communication in human infancy. In Lev Weiskrantz (ed.), *A Fyssen Foundation Symposium* (Thought without language, 16), 5–24. Oxford: Oxford University Press.

Butterworth, George & Nicholas Jarrett. 1991. What minds have in common is space: Spatial mechanisms serving joint visual attention in infancy. *British Journal of Developmental Psychology* 9 (1). 55–72.

Callaghan, Tara, Henrike Moll, Hannes Rakoczy, Felix Warneken, Ulf Liszkowski, Tanya Behne & Michael Tomasello. 2011. Early social cognition in three cultural contexts. *Monographs of the Society for Research in Child Development* 76 (2). 1–142.

Camaioni, Luigia. 1997. The emergence of intentional communication in ontogeny, phylogeny and pathology. *European Psychologist* 2 (3). 216–225.

Camaioni, Luigia, Paola Perucchini, Francesca Bellagamba & Cristina Colonnesi. 2004. The role of declarative pointing in developing a theory of mind. *Infancy* 5 (3). 291–308.

Camaioni, Luigia, Paola Perucchini, Filippo Muratori & Annarita Milone. 1997. Brief report: A longitudinal examination of the communicative gestures deficit in young children with autism. *Journal of Autism and Developmental Disorders* 27 (6). 715–725.

Capirci, Olga, Jana M. Iverson, Elena Pizzuto & Virginia Volterra. 1996. Gestures and words during the transition to two-word speech. *Journal of Child Language* 23 (3). 645–673.

Carmiol, Ana M. & Alison Sparks. 2014. Narrative development across cultural contexts: Finding the pragmatic in parent-child reminiscing. In Danielle, Matthews (ed.), *Pragmatic development in first language acquisition (TİLAR series)*, 279–294. Amsterdam: John Benjamins.

Caron, Albert J., Samantha Butler & Rechele Brooks. 2002. Gaze following at 12 and 14 months: Do the eyes matter? *British Journal of Developmental Psychology* 20 (2). 225–239.

Caron, Albert J., Rose Caron, Jennifer Roberts & Rechele Brooks. 1997. Infant sensitivity to deviation in dynamic facial-vocal displays: The role of eye regard. *Developmental Psychology* 33 (5). 802–813.

Carpenter, Malinda & Kristin Liebal. 2011. Joint attention, communication & knowing together in infancy. In Axel Seemann (ed.), *Joint attention: New developments in psychology, philosophy of mind & social neuroscience*, 159–181. Cambridge, MA: MIT Press.

Carpenter, Malinda, Katherine Nagell, Michael Tomasello, George Butterworth & Chris Moore. 1998. Social cognition, joint attention & communicative competence from 9 to 15 months of age. *Monographs of the Society for Research in Child Development* 63 (4, Serial No. 255). 1–176.

Carpenter, Malinda, Bruce F. Pennington & Sally J. Rogers. 2002. Interrelations among social-cognitive skills in young children with autism. *Journal of Autism and Developmental Disorders* 32 (2). 91–106.

Casey, B. J., C. T. Gordon, Glenn B. Mannheim & Judith M. Rumsey. 1993. Dysfunctional attention in autistic savants. *Journal of Clinical and Experimental Neuropsychology* 15 (6). 933–946.

Chawarska, Katarzyna, Ami Klin & Fred Volkmar. 2003. Automatic attention cueing through eye movement in 2-year-old children with autism. *Child Development* 74 (4). 1108–1122.

Colonnesi, Cristina, Geert Jan J. M. Stams, Irene Koster & Marc J. Noom. 2010. The relation between pointing and language development: A meta-analysis. *Developmental Review* 30 (4). 352–366.

Corkum, Valerie & Chris Moore. 2014. Development of joint visual attention in infants. In Chris Moore & Philip J. Dunham (eds.), *Joint attention: Its origins and role in development*, 61–84. New York, NY: Psychology Press.

Correa-Chávez, Maricela & Barbara Rogoff. 2009. Children's attention to interactions directed to others: Guatemalan Mayan and European American patterns. *Developmental Psychology* 45 (3). 630–641.

Correa-Chávez, Maricela, Barbara Rogoff & Rebeca Mejía Arauz. 2005. Cultural patterns in attending to two events at once. *Child Development* 76 (3). 664–678.

Courchesne, Eric, Heather Chisum & Jeanne Townsend. 1994. Neural activity-dependent brain changes in development: Implications for psychopathology. *Development and Psychopathology* 6 (4). 697–722.

Courchesne, Eric, Jeanne Townsend, Natacha A. Akshoomoff, Osamu Saitoh, Rachel Yeung-Courchesne, Alan J. Lincoln, Hector E. James, Richard H. Haas, Laura Schreibman & Lily Lau. 1994. Impairment in shifting attention in autistic and cerebellar patients. *Behavioral Neuroscience* 108 (5). 848–865.

Dalton, Kim M., Brendon M. Nacewicz, Tom Johnstone, Hillary S. Schaefer, Morton Ann Gernsbacher, Hill H. Goldsmith, Andrew L. Alexander & Richard J. Davidson. 2005. Gaze fixation and the neural circuitry of face processing in autism. *Nature Neuroscience* 8 (4). 519–526.

Dawson, Geraldine. 1991. A psychobiological perspective on the early socioemotional development of children with autism. In Dante Cicchetti & Sheree Toth (eds.), *Rochester Symposium on Developmental Psychopathology* (Vol. 3), 207–234. Rochester, NY: University of Rochester Press.

Dawson, Geraldine & Arthur Lewy. 1989. Arousal, attention & the social impairments of individuals with autism. In Geraldine Dawson (ed.), *Autism: Nature, diagnosis & treatment*, 49–74. New York, NY: Guilford Press.

Dawson, Geraldine, Andrew N. Meltzoff, Julie Osterling, Julie Rinaldi & Emily Brown. 1998. Children with Autism fail to orient to naturally occurring social stimuli. *Journal of Autism and Developmental Disorders* 28 (6). 479–485.

Dawson, Geraldine, Sara Jane Webb & James McPartland. 2005. Understanding the nature of face processing impairment in autism: Insights from behavioral and electrophysiological studies. *Developmental Neuropsychology* 27 (3). 403–424.

D'Entremont, Barbara, Sylvia M. J. Hains & Darwin W. Muir. 1997. A demonstration of gaze following in 3- to 6-month-olds. *Infant Behavior and Development* 20 (4). 569–572.

Easterbrook, Megan A., Barbara S. Kisilevsky, Darwin W. Muir & David P. Laplante. 1999. Newborns discriminate schematic faces from scrambled faces. *Canadian Journal of Experimental Psychology* 53 (3). 231–241.

Farroni, Teresa, Gergely Csibra, Francesca Simion & Mark H. Johnson. 2002. Eye contact detection in humans from birth. *Proceedings of the National Academy of Sciences of the United States of America* 99 (14). 9602–9605.

Floor, Penelope & Nameera Akhtar. 2006. Can 18-month-old infants learn words by listening in on conversations? *Infancy* 9 (3). 327–339.

Fogel, Alan, Sueko Toda & Masatoshi Kawai. 1988. Mother-infant face-to-face interaction in Japan and the United States: A laboratory comparison using 3-month-old infants. *Developmental Psychology* 24 (3). 398–406.

Gernsbacher, Morton Ann, Jennifer L. Stevenson, Suraiya Khandakar & H. Hill Goldsmith. 2008. Why does joint attention look atypical in autism? *Child Development Perspectives* 2 (1). 38–45.

Gliga, Teodora, Mayada Elsabbagh, Kristelle Hudry, Tony Charman & Mark H. Johnson. 2012. Gaze following, gaze reading and word learning in children at-risk for autism. *Child Development* 83 (3). 926–938.

Goodwin, Anthony, Deborah Fein & Letitia Naigles. 2014. The role of maternal input in the development of *wh*-question comprehension in autism and typical development. *Journal of Child Language* 42 (1). 1–32.

Gomez, Juan-Carlos. 2007. Pointing behaviors in apes and human infants: A balanced interpretation. *Child Development* 78 (3). 729–734.

Goren, Carolyn C., Merrill Sarty & Paul Y. K. Wu. 1975. Visual following and pattern discrimination of face-like stimuli by newborn infants. *Pediatrics* 56 (4). 544–549.

Grassmann, Susanne & Michael Tomasello. 2010. Young children follow pointing over words in interpreting acts of reference. *Developmental Science* 13 (1). 252–263.

Gulsrud, Amanda C., Connie Kasari, Stephanny Freeman & Tanya Paparella. 2007. Brief report: Children with autism's response to novel stimuli while participating in interventions targeting joint attention or symbolic play skills. *Autism* 11 (6). 535–546.

Hainline, Louise. 1978. Developmental changes in visual scanning of face and non-face patterns by infants. *Journal of Experimental Child Psychology* 25 (1). 90–115.

Hains, Sylvia M. J. & Darwin W. Muir. 1996. Infant sensitivity to adult eye direction. *Child Development* 67 (5). 1940–1951.

Haith, Marshall M., Terry Bergman & Michael J. Moore. 1977. Eye contact and face scanning in early infancy. *Science* 198 (4319). 853–855.

Harris, Margaret, David Jones & Julia Grant. 1983. The nonverbal context of mothers' speech to infants. *First Language* 4 (10). 21–30.

Hobson, Peter. 1993. Understanding persons: The role of affect. In Simon Baron-Cohen, Helen Tager-Flusberg & Donald J. Cohen (eds.), *Understanding other minds: Perspectives from autism*, 204–227. Oxford: Oxford University Press.

Hobson, R. Peter, J. Ouston & A. Lee. 1988. What is in a face? The case of autism. *British Journal of Psychology* 79 (4). 441–453.

Hopkins, William D. & David A. Leavens. 1998. Hand use and gestural communication in chimpanzees (*Pan troglodytes*). *Journal of Comparative Psychology* 112 (1). 95–99.

Ingersoll, Brooke & Laura Schreibman. 2006. Teaching reciprocal imitation skills to young children with autism using a naturalistic behavioral approach: Effects on language, pretend play & joint attention. *Journal of Autism and Developmental Disorders* 36 (4). 487–505.

Iverson, Jana M., Olga Capirci & M. Cristina Caselli. 1994. From communication to language in two modalities. *Cognitive Development* 9 (1). 23–43.

Iverson, Jana M. & Susan Goldin-Meadow. 2005. Gesture paves the way for language development. *Psychological Science* 16 (5). 367–371.

Jones, Emily A. 2009. Establishing response and stimulus classes for initiating joint attention in children with autism. *Research in Autism Spectrum Disorders* 3 (2). 375–389.

Kasari, Connie, Stephanny Freeman & Tanya Paparella. 2006. Joint attention and symbolic play in young children with autism: A randomized controlled intervention study. *Journal of Child Psychology and Psychiatry* 47 (6). 611–620.

Kärtner, Joscha, Heidi Keller, Bettina Lamm, Monika Abels, Relindis D. Yovsi, Nandita Chaudhary & Yanjie Su. 2008. Similarities and differences in contingency experiences of 3-month-olds across sociocultural contexts. *Infant Behavior and Development* 31 (3). 488–500.

Keller, Heidi. 2007. *Cultures of infancy*. Mahwah, NJ: Lawrence Erlbaum Associates.

Klin, Ami, Warren Jones, Robert Schultz, Fred Volkmar & Donald Cohen. 2002. Defining and quantifying the social phenotype in autism. *American Journal of Psychiatry* 159 (6). 895–908.

Klin, Ami, Sara S. Sparrow, Annelies de Bildt, Domenic V. Cicchetti, Donald J. Cohen & Fred R. Volkmar. 1999. A normed study of face recognition in autism and related disorders. *Journal of Autism and Developmental Disorders* 29 (6). 499–508.

Küntay, Aylin C., Keiko Nakamura & B. Ateş Şen. 2014. Crosslinguistic and crosscultural approaches to pragmatic development. In Danielle Matthews (ed.), *Pragmatic development in first language acquisition (TiLAR series)*, 317–342. Amsterdam: John Benjamins.

Kylliäinen, Anneli & Jari K. Hietanen. 2004. Attention orienting by another's gaze direction in children with autism. *Journal of Child Psychology and Psychiatry* 45 (3). 435–444.

Leekam, Susan, Simon Baron-Cohen, Dave Perrett, Maarten Milders & Sarah Brown. 1997. Eye-direction detection: A dissociation between geometric and joint attention skills in autism. *British Journal of Developmental Psychology* 15 (1). 77–95.

Leekam, Susan R., Emma Hunnisett & Chris Moore. 1998. Targets and cues: Gaze-following in children with autism. *Journal of Child Psychology and Psychiatry* 39 (7). 951–962.

Leekam, Susan R., Beatriz López & Chris Moore. 2000. Attention and joint attention in preschool children with autism. *Developmental Psychology* 36 (2). 261–273.

Leekam, Susan R. & Christopher A. H. Ramsden. 2006. Dyadic orienting and joint attention in preschool children with autism. *Journal of Autism and Developmental Disorders* 36 (2). 185–197.

León, Lourdes de. 1999. The emergent participant: Interactive patterns of socialization of Tzotzil (Mayan) children. *Journal of Linguistic Anthropology* 8 (2). 131–161.

Levinson, Stephen C. 1983. *Pragmatics*. Cambridge, the U.K.: Cambridge University Press.

Levinson, Stephen C. 2006. On the human "interaction engine". In Nicholas J. Enfield & Stephen C. Levinson (eds.), *Roots of human sociality: Culture, cognition & interaction*, 39–69. London: Berg.

Liebal, Kristin, Tanya Behne, Malinda Carpenter & Michael Tomasello. 2009. Infants use shared experience to interpret pointing gestures. *Developmental Science* 12 (2). 264–271.

Liszkowski, Ulf, Konstanze Albrecht, Malinda Carpenter & Michael Tomasello. 2008. Infants' visual and auditory communication when a partner is or is not visually attending. *Infant Behavior and Development* 31 (2). 157–167.

Liszkowski, Ulf, Penny Brown, Tara Callaghan, Akira Takada & Conny de Vos. 2012. A prelinguistic gestural universal of human communication. *Cognitive Science* 36 (4). 698–713.

Liszkowski, Ulf, Malinda Carpenter, Anne Henning, Tricia Striano & Michael Tomasello. 2004. Twelve month-olds point to share attention and interest. *Developmental Science* 7 (3). 297–307.

Liszkowski, Ulf, Malinda Carpenter, Tricia Striano & Michael Tomasello. 2006. 12- and 18-month-olds point to provide information. *Journal of Cognition and Development* 7 (2). 173–87.

Liszkowski, Ulf, Malinda Carpenter & Michael Tomasello. 2007a. Reference and attitude in infant pointing. *Journal of Child Language* 34 (1). 1–20.

Liszkowski, Ulf, Malinda Carpenter & Michael Tomasello. 2007b. Pointing out new news, old news & absent referents at 12 months of age. *Developmental Science* 10 (2). F1–F7.

Liszkowski, Ulf, Malinda Carpenter & Michael Tomasello. 2008. Twelve-month-olds communicate helpfully and appropriately for knowledgeable and ignorant partners. *Cognition* 108 (3). 732–739.

Liszkowski, Ulf & Michael Tomasello. 2011. Individual differences in social, cognitive & morphological aspects of infant pointing. *Cognitive Development* 26 (1). 16–29.

López, Angélica, Maricela Correa-Chávez, Barbara Rogoff & Kris Gutiérrez. 2010. Attention to instruction directed to another by U.S. Mexican-Heritage children of varying cultural backgrounds. *Developmental Psychology* 46 (3). 593–601.

Lord, Catherine. 1995. Follow-up of two-year-olds referred for possible autism. *Journal of Child Psychology and Psychiatry* 36 (8). 1365–1382.

Loveland, Katherine A. & Susan H. Landry. 1986. Joint attention and language in autism and developmental language delay. *Journal of Autism and Developmental Disorders* 16 (3). 335–349.

Luyster, Rhiannon & Catherine Lord. 2009. Word learning in children with autism spectrum disorders. *Developmental Psychology* 45 (6). 1774–1786.

Matthews, Danielle. 2014. Introduction: An overview of research on pragmatic development. In Danielle Matthews (ed.), *Pragmatic Development in First Language (TİLAR series)*, 1–11. Amsterdam: John Benjamins.

Maurer, Daphne & Philip Salapatek. 1976. Developmental changes in the scanning of faces by young infants. *Child Development* 47 (2). 523–527.

Moll, Henrike & Michael Tomasello. 2004. 12- and 18-month-old infants follow gaze to spaces behind barriers. *Developmental Science* 7 (1). F1–F9.

Moore, Chris & Valerie Corkum. 1998. Infant gaze following based on eye direction. *British Journal of Developmental Psychology* 16 (4). 495–503.

Morton, John & Mark H. Johnson. 1991. Conspec and Conlern: A two-process theory of infant face recognition. *Psychological Review* 98 (2). 164–181.

Mundy, Peter & Lisa Newell. 2007. Attention, joint Attention & social cognition. *Current Directions in Psychological Science* 16 (5). 269–274.

Mundy, Peter, Marian Sigman & Connie Kasari. 1994. Joint attention, developmental level & symptom presentation in autism. *Development and Psychopathology* 6 (3). 389–401.

Mundy, Peter, Marian Sigman, Judy Ungerer & Tracy Sherman. 1986. Defining the social deficits of autism: The contribution of nonverbal communication measures. *Journal of Child Psychology and Psychiatry* 27 (5). 657–669.

Murase, Toshiki, Philip S. Dale, Tamiko Ogura, Yukie Yamashita & Aki Mahieu. 2005. Mother-child conversation during joint picture book reading in Japan and the USA. *First Language* 25 (2). 197–218.

Nation, Kate & Sophia Penny. 2008. Sensitivity to eye gaze in autism: Is it normal? Is it automatic? Is it social? *Development and Psychopathology* 20 (1). 79–97.

Norbury, Frazier Norbury. 2014. Atypical pragmatic development. In Matthews, Danielle (ed.), *Pragmatic development in first language acquisition* 343–361. Amsterdam: John Benjamins.

Özçalışkan, Şeyda & Susan Goldin-Meadow. 2005. Gesture is at the cutting edge of early language development. *Cognition* 96 (3). B101–B113.

Povinelli, Daniel J., Jesse M. Bering & Steve Giambrone. 2003. Chimpanzees' "pointing": Another error of the argument by analogy? In Sotaro Kita (ed.), *Pointing: Where language, culture & cognition meet*, 35–68. Mahwah, N.J.: Lawrence Erlbaum Associates.

Preissler, Melissa Allen & Susan Carey. 2005. The role of inferences about referential intent in word learning: Evidence from autism. *Cognition* 97 (1). B13–B23.

Puccini, Daniel, Mireille Hassemer, Dorothé Salomo & Ulf Liszkowski. 2010. The type of shared activity shapes caregiver and infant communication. *Gesture* 10 (2–3). 279–296.

Pascualvaca, Daisy M., Bryan D. Fantie, Maria Papageorgiou & Allan F. Mirsky. 1998. Attentional capacities in children with autism: Is there a general deficit in shifting focus? *Journal of Autism and Developmental Disorders* 28 (6). 467–478.

Posner, Michael I. 1980. Orienting of attention. *The Quarterly Journal of Experimental Psychology* 32 (1). 3–25.

Reichow, Brian & Fred R. Volkmar. 2010. Social skills interventions for individuals with autism: Evaluation for evidence-based practices within a best evidence synthesis framework. *Journal of Autism and Developmental Disorders* 40 (2). 149–166.

Robson, Kenneth S. 1967. The role of eye-to-eye contact in maternal-infant attachment. *Journal of Child Psychology and Psychiatry* 8 (1). 13–25.

Rogoff, Barbara. 1990. *Apprenticeship in thinking: Cognitive development in social context*. New York, NY: Oxford University Press.

Rogoff, Barbara, Maricela Correa-Chávez & Katie G. Silva. 2011. Cultural variation in children's attention and learning. In Morton Ann Gernsbacher, Richard W. Pew, Leaetta M. Hough & James R. Pomerantz (eds.), *Psychology and the real world: Essays illustrating fundamental contributions to society*, 154–163. New York, NY: Worth Publishers.

Rowe, Meredith L. & Susan Goldin-Meadow. 2009a. Differences in early gesture explain SES disparities in child vocabulary size at school entry. *Science* 323 (5916). 951–953.

Rowe, Meredith L. & Susan Goldin-Meadow. 2009b. Early gesture selectively predicts later language learning. *Developmental Science* 12 (1). 182–187.

Rowe, Meredith L., Şeyda Özçalışkan & Susan Goldin-Meadow. 2008. Learning words by hand: Gestures' role in predicting vocabulary development. *First Language* 28 (2). 182–199.

Salomo, Dorothe & Ulf Liszkowski. 2013. Sociocultural settings influence the emergence of prelinguistic deictic gestures. *Child Development* 84 (4). 1296–1307.

Sauer, Eve, Susan C. Levine & Susan Goldin-Meadow. 2010. Early gesture predicts language delay in children with pre- or perinatal brain lesions. *Child Development* 81 (2). 528–539.

Savaş, Özge. 2014. *The nature of early child-directed interactions in advantaged and disadvantaged households*. Istanbul, Turkey: Koç University MA thesis.

Senju, Atsushi, Kiyoshi Yaguchi, Yoshikuni Tojo & Toshikazu Hasegawa. 2003. Eye contact does not facilitate detection in children with autism. *Cognition* 89 (1). B43–B51.

Shneidman, Laura A., Jennifer Sootsman Buresh, Priya M. Shimpi, Jennifer Knight-Schwarz & Amanda L. Woodward. 2009. Social experience, social attention and word learning in an overhearing paradigm. *Language Learning and Development* 5 (4). 266–281.

Schieffelin, Bambi B. 1990. *The give and take of everyday life: Language, socialization of Kaluli children*. New York, NY: Cambridge University Press.

Sigman, Marian, Ellen Ruskin, Shoshana Arbelle, Rosalie Corona, Cheryl Dissanayake, Michael Espinosa, Norman Kim, Alma López, Cynthia Zierhut, Carolyn B. Mervis & Byron F. Robinson. 1999. Continuity and change in the social competence of children with autism, Down syndrome & developmental delays. *Monographs of the Society for Research in Child Development* 64 (1). 1–139.

Silva, Katie G., Maricela Correa-Chávez & Barbara Rogoff. 2010. Mexican-heritage children's attention and learning from interactions directed to others. *Child Development* 81 (3). 898–912.

Swettenham, John, Samantha Condie, Ruth Campbell, Elizabeth Milne & Mike Coleman. 2003. Does the perception of moving eyes trigger reflexive visual orienting in autism? *Philosophical Transactions of the Royal Society of London Series B: Biological Sciences* 358 (1430) 325–334.

Tenenbaum, Elena J., Rajesh J. Shah, David M. Sobel, Bertram F. Malle & James L. Morgan. 2013. Increased focus on the mouth among infants in the first year of life: A longitudinal eye-tracking study. *Infancy* 18 (4). 534–553.

Tomasello, Michael. 2014. Joint attention as social cognition. In Chris Moore & Philip J. Dunham (eds.), *Joint attention: Its origins and role in development*, 103–130. New York, NY: Psychology Press.

Tomasello, Michael. 1999. *The cultural origins of human cognition*. Cambridge, MA: Harvard University Press.

Tomasello, Michael. 2006. Acquiring linguistic constructions. In Deanna Kuhn & Robert Siegler (eds.), *Handbook of child psychology: Cognition, perception, and language*. New Jersey, the U.S.A: John Wiley & Sons.

Tomasello, Michael. 2008. *Origins of human communication*. Cambridge, MA: MIT Press.

Tomasello, Michael, Malinda Carpenter, Josep Call, Tanya Behne & Henrike Moll. 2005. Understanding and sharing intentions: The origins of cultural cognition. *Behavioral and Brain Sciences* 28 (5). 675–735.

Tomasello, Michael, Malinda Carpenter & Ulf Liszkowski. 2007. A new look at infant pointing. *Child Development* 78 (3). 705–722.

Tomasello, Michael & Michael Jeffrey Farrar. 1986. Joint attention and early language. *Child Development* 57 (6). 1454–1463.
Tomasello, Michael & Katharina Haberl. 2003. Understanding attention: 12- and 18-month-olds know what's new for other persons. *Developmental Psychology* 39 (5). 906–912.
Trevarthen, Colwyn & Penelope Hubley. 1978. Secondary intersubjectivity: Confidence, confiding and acts of meaning in the first year. In Andrew Lock Ed (ed.), *Action, gesture & symbol: The Emergence of Language*, 183–229. New York, NY: Academic Press.
Vecera, Shaun P. & Mark H. Johnson. 1995. Gaze detection and the cortical processing of faces: Evidence from infants and adults. *Visual Cognition* 2 (1). 59–87.
Vismara, Laurie A. & Gregory L. Lyons. 2007. Using perseverative interests to elicit joint attention behaviors in young children with autism: Theoretical and clinical implications for understanding motivation. *Journal of Positive Behavior Interventions* 9 (4). 214–228.
Volkmar, Fred R. & Linda C. Mayes. 1990. Gaze behavior in autism. *Development and Psychopathology* 2 (1). 61–69.
Whalen, Christina, Laura Schreibman & Brooke Ingersoll. 2006. The collateral effects of joint attention training on social initiations, positive affect, imitation & spontaneous speech for young children with autism. *Journal of Autism and Developmental Disorders* 36 (5). 655–664.
White, Pamela J., Mark O'Reilly, William Streusand, Ann Levine, Jeff Sigafoos, Giulio Lancioni, Christina Fragale, Nigel Pierce & Jeannie Aguilar. 2011. Best practices for teaching joint attention: A systematic review of the intervention literature. *Research in Autism Spectrum Disorders* 5 (4). 1283–1295.
Wilkins, David. 2003. Why pointing with the index finger is not a universal (in sociocultural and semiotic terms). In Sotaro, Kita (ed.), *Pointing: Where language, culture & cognition meet*, 171–215. Mahwah, N.J.: Lawrence Erlbaum Associates.
Zercher, Craig, Pam Hunt, Adriana Schuler & Janice Webster. 2001. Increasing join attention, play & language through peer supported play. *Autism* 5 (4). 374–398.

Edy Veneziano
15 Learning conversational skills and learning from conversation

1 Introduction

Fluent speakers master multiple skills and are able to draw on them simultaneously while talking or responding to their interlocutors. They have the necessary phonological, lexical, semantic and grammatical knowledge of their language, as well as pragmatic skills allowing them to keep track of context, of shared knowledge and of past discourse. Children acquire these skills progressively. Conversations with knowledgeable and cooperative partners provide privileged settings where some of these acquisitions can take place.

This chapter examines the relationship between conversation and language development from a double perspective. The first concerns the *conversational skills* that need to be acquired to become a competent speaker in everyday situations; the second perspective concerns the *contribution of conversational functioning* to children's acquisition of lexical and grammatical language knowledge. Although children also learn from speech they hear or overhear, child-adult conversational exchanges constitute optimal experiences for language learners in that they realize several facilitating conditions simultaneously (e.g., Veneziano 2014).

2 Conversational skills

Competent speakers do not need only lexical and grammatical knowledge of their language. They also need the pragmatic knowledge that allows them to use language in socially and culturally adequate ways to communicate effectively and smoothly with others. Some of these skills concern the regulation of the exchange among the interlocutors, such as mastering the implicit rules of turn taking, attracting the interlocutor's attention or responding to the latter's signals. Others relate to what and how things need to be said to best attain the intended communicative goals, or to the inferences that need to be made in order to understand the communicative intentions of the interlocutor: How to initiate or maintain a topic through the unfolding of the conversation, how to make requests likely to be satisfied or to negotiate disagreements, how to ask for or respond to clarifications, or repair breakdowns in mutual understanding, or how to best make contributions that take into account

---
Edy Veneziano, Université Paris Descartes

previous discourse and the knowledge participants share ("common ground", e.g., Clark 1996).

These skills take time to acquire and children grasp them in the practice of everyday communication with expert speakers (e.g., Pan and Snow 1999).

2.1 The underpinnings of conversational skills

The implementation of conversational skills involves mastery of underlying cognitive, socio-cognitive and linguistic abilities.

Cognitively, conversational functioning necessitates high-level representational abilities. On the one hand, children need to relate to language, a representational object that requires attention to both the signifier and the signified components of the verbal sequence. On the other, in conversation, interlocutors need to go back and forth in time to keep track of what has been said in previous discourse and to project towards the possible future contributions of the interlocutor. This information, spread out over time and space, is retrieved and convened simultaneously in thought in order to make adaptive communicative choices at each turn in the conversational exchange. These retroactive and proactive movements can be assumed to underlie even a simple adjacency pair such as the question-answer pair (which, according to Schegloff and Sacks 1973, is a basic unit of conversation). The question is often asked on the basis of past experience with the interlocutor, and with a view on what the interlocutor is able or likely to answer. The answer needs to relate retroactively to the question and is provided with a view on what the questioner might reply in turn, as this is clearly illustrated by the 'turnabout' (Kaye and Charney 1980), that is a turn with the double function of answering the previous question and of soliciting the interlocutor's next turn, as in the following simple example by a 22-month-old boy:

> Example 1 – 22-month-old boy and his mother
>
> Mother$_1$: *Qu'est-ce qu'il mange le garçon?* 'What is the boy eating?'
>
> [pointing to the picture of a boy holding an apple and a pear in a picture book]
>
> Child$_1$: *pomme?* 'apple?'
>
> [turnabout: answer to the previous question and at the same time confirmation request that solicits the next turn from the mother]
>
> Mother$_2$: *oui une pomme* 'yes an apple'

Functioning as an adequate conversational partner also requires socio-cognitive abilities. Conversational exchanges are based on a cooperative principle that is expressed by four maxims (Grice 1975). One of them is the 'maxim of quantity' by which speakers are supposed to be informative, that is, to talk about what interlocutors don't already know and is likely to be of interest to them (e.g., Hausendorf and Quasthoff 1992), while being just as informative as is required, and no more (Grice 1975). To meet these requirements successfully entails identifying and taking into account the intentional and epistemic states of others. It requires a theory of mind, at least at the implicit, *know-how*, level. Indeed, relating to and taking into account the mental states of the interlocutor is essential for choosing what to talk about and for inferring the interlocutor's communicative intentions from his/her speech.

In conversations, speakers also need to make the appropriate linguistic choices that often depend on a close interplay between socio-cognitive and linguistic abilities. Once the alternative possible forms and structures are acquired, the appropriate choice often depends on what has already been said in the preceding turns and on what is in the common ground of the participants. For example, for referring expressions, alternative forms may consist of omission, the use of definite or indefinite articles, demonstratives, clitic pronouns, or lexical terms. The choice among these linguistic expressions depends on the accessibility of the referent for the interlocutor such as, for example, whether the referent is new or was already focused upon in the immediate context or in previous discourse (e.g., Ariel 1988; Gundel, Hedberg, and Zacharski 1993).

2.2 Learning conversational skills

2.2.1 Turn taking

In face-to-face conversations, speakers' contributions are regulated by the alternation of speakers' turns. Turn alternation is probably linked to the difficulty human beings have to process speech while talking. It is interesting to note that the pattern of alternation is realized early in mother-infant interaction and well before caretakers and infants can exchange contents through vocal/verbal interaction. Martin (1981: 58–60) provides examples of turn-taking between a mother and her two-day-old baby in natural interaction.

Mothers are cooperative conversational partners and greatly contribute to the apparent smoothness of turn alternation. However, around 3 months, infants also contribute actively to turn alternation, which becomes the dominant way of interacting (Ginsburg and Kilbourne 1988). Contingency of turn alternation has an impact on the content of the productions. Infants' vocalizations are judged to be more speech-like (Bloom, Russell, and Wassenberg 1987), and mothers talk less about themselves (Murray and Trevarthen 1986) when the partners' turns are contingent to each other than when they are not.

Children's participation in smooth turn taking is facilitated by early one-to-one interactions with caretakers who adjust to the children's timing of responding. Caretakers wait as much as six times longer than they would normally do in conversation with mature speakers before intervening again after a question (e.g. Stivers et al. 2009). With age, children acquire more sophisticated skills that allow them to intervene appropriately and to keep their turn in conversations with competitive peers, where getting and holding the floor is much more complicated (Pan and Snow 1999). They also become able to manage more complex multiparty conversations where children are required to compete not with one but with several interlocutors. In this setting, children need to be able to manage interruptions, resolve overlaps, and, if they wish to continue the conversation, maintain the attention of the different partners (e.g. Casillas 2014).

2.2.2 Be relevant

Conversational exchanges involve more than alternation of turns. Speakers relate to the content of participants' turns. Thus children need to learn how to relate to the interlocutor's verbal or nonverbal turns and to do so in a relevant way. This skill, which is essential for maintaining topics, responding to questions, or addressing requests, needs the ability to decenter from one's own point of view in order to take into account the partner's interventions. As is the case for turn alternation, here too mothers help infants to grasp this essential discourse principle by offering two kinds of support. First, they produce vocal productions that are in the children's repertoire, either in initiation or in response to the infants' vocalizations. In this way, children can relate to the content of their mother's utterances by just producing what they are capable of anyway, thus reducing to a minimum the distance between the infant and the partner's capabilities. These vocal exchanges occur in the first year of life (e.g., Snow 1977) and provide the infants with a clear example of content relatedness between successive turns (Veneziano 1988).

Second, mothers interpret children's vocalizations as if they were meaningful words (e.g., Papousek and Papousek 1989; Veneziano 1988, 2005). Relatedness starts by being explicit and apparent. Mothers interpret what children say, often expanding or recasting it into grammatically well-formed utterances (Cazden 1972; Nelson 1987; Farrar 1990) that incorporate the words used by the children. Children are then likely to continue to relate to the caregiver's intervention, the latter being itself the continuation of the child's previous utterance.

Until about 18 months, children and their mothers are more likely to respond to partner's turns that are themselves related to their own interventions than to partner's turns that initiate a topic. This process results in extended discourse centered on a particular topic (sometimes just one lexical item), giving rise to exchanges of reciprocal imitation (Tomasello, 2003; Veneziano 1988, 2005), as in the following example (from Veneziano 2005):

Example 2 – 16-month-old boy and his mother

[the child is playing with the wheels of a toy truck]

$Child_1$: / 'ʃea: 'u'lɛl/ *xx galgal* 'xx wheel'

$Mother_1$: *maze? galgal?* 'what's that? 'wheel?'

Child₂: /'a'lo/ *galgal* 'wheel' [holding the wheel]

Mother₂: *galgal # galgal galgal* wheel # wheel wheel'

Child₃: /'a'lal/ *galgal* 'wheel' [holding the wheel]

Mother₃: efo *galgal*? hine # hine # hine galgal

'where is (the) wheel? here # here # here is (the) wheel'

During the second and third years, though imitative uptakes of each other's utterances remain an important conversational strategy[1], both children and adults relate more often just to the meaning of the partner's utterance, for example, by answering questions, commenting on propositions or justifying requests after a refusal.

With age, children develop more appropriate and sophisticated linguistic devices to relate cohesively to the partner's interventions as, for example, conjunctive adverbs such as *so, but* and modal expressions like *not sure, absolutely* (Scott 1984).

2.2.3 Be informative

Mothers and their young children talk mostly about what is present in the situation and thus about what is known or readily accessible to both. Here-and-now talk, particularly when held during joint attention, favors early lexical acquisition (e.g., Tomasello and Farrar 1986; Dunham, Dunham, and Curwin 1993). This is not, however, how competent speakers usually use language. Rather, they use it informatively, that is, they use language in a "displaced" way (e.g., Hockett 1958), to talk about objects and events that are absent from the enunciative situation, to recall the past and to talk about the future, to create imaginary events, to make hypotheses, etc. If it is used to talk about present entities and events, language refers to non perceptible aspects such as providing explanations or making one's interlocutor "aware of something of which he was not previously aware" (Lyons 1977: 33). This is another basic conversational skill, implied by Grice's maxim of quantity (Grice 1975). As mentioned earlier, respecting this principle requires an implicit theory of mind.

2.2.4 Informativeness and Theory of Mind

Typically-developing children provide early signs of their implicit knowledge about the mental states of others when, for example, they manage to draw the attention of their interactional partner to the object of their own interest, to follow the partner's

---

[1] Older children may use these vocal/verbal exchanges of reciprocal imitation as devices to maintain contact, particularly in a playful way with peers (e.g., McTear, 1985).

center of attention (e.g., Tomasello 1995), or when, in requesting a hidden object, they adapt their communicative behaviors to the state of knowledge of their interlocutor (depending, for example, on whether the latter has witnessed the hiding of an object or not, O'Neill 1996). At the same period, one-and-a-half to two-year-old children understand what the referent of a nonce word is on the basis of what children consider to be new for the speaker (e.g., Tomasello and Haberl 2003).

In their second year of life typically developing children also start to use language in an informative way. They start talking about internal states, their own and others', referring at first to intentional ('want'), physical (such as being hungry or in pain) and emotional states (such as being scared or angry), and later to epistemic states such as 'know' or 'think' (e.g., Lamb 1991; Shatz 1994; Veneziano 2009). In their second year children also start talking about past events, at first occurring within conversations scaffolded by familiar partners, where they uptake parts of the partner's talk or add original contributions to mostly adult-initiated exchanges. Somewhat later they also initiate references to the past or simple fictional narratives (e.g., Sachs, 1983; Lucariello & Nelson, 1987; Veneziano and Sinclair 1995). At around the same time they also provide early justifications of speech acts such as requests and refusals (for example, the child refuses the help of the mother by saying 'no, *I want to do it by myself*') (e.g., Dunn and Munn 1987; Shatz 1994; Veneziano and Sinclair 1995). It has been shown that justifications affect the course of the exchange. The partner who receives a refusal is more likely to concede when the locutor justifies his/her refusal than when s/he does not (e.g., Dunn and Munn 1987; Veneziano 2001, 2010). At around the same period, children also seem to selectively verbalize aspects of a situation that are subjective and thus supposedly more difficult for their interlocutors to find out. For example, during pretend play, the subjectively-created symbolic transformations are verbalized more often than the 'literal' or the pretend meanings that are more easily accessible to the onlookers (e.g., Veneziano 2002).

The occurrence of these different behaviors at around the same developmental period shows that children start grasping the conversational rule by which speakers provide interlocutors with information that is not readily available to them (Veneziano 2009).

2.2.5 Informativeness and discourse

An additional and more elaborate step in information management is taken when children adapt their linguistic resources to present referents as a function of what has been said in previous discourse or of what is in "common ground" with the interlocutor (e.g. Gundel et al. 1993; Matthews et al. 2006). From 3 years on, children tend to prefer lexical nouns to pronouns, and indefinite to definite articles (for languages such as English and French that make this distinction) when referents are new or not shared by the partners, but it takes several years to attain full proficiency in any context and level of functioning. So, the ability to choose the appropriate forms to introduce, maintain and reintroduce referents in extended discourse such as narratives develops gradually over the school years. Young children overuse pronouns, making it difficult sometimes for a listener to understand what they are talking about. With age, children come to use definite articles and pronouns mostly when the listener has access to the referents, be it in the situation, in previous discourse or in common ground (e.g., Kail and Hickmann 1992), with development continuing through the lifespan (Hendriks, Koster and Hoeks, 2014).

2.2.6 'Repairing' one's utterances in conversation

Another conversational skill – also based on the understanding of others' mental states – is the ability to 'repair' one's utterances, or to ask partners to 'repair' their own, usually after an explicit request by the partner, or when one's original utterance has not attained the intended goal.

In repair sequences the partner can ask a general (*hum?, what?*) or a specific question, questioning part of the utterance. An early strategy to repair is to 'try again', sometimes simply repeating the original verbalization, sometimes pronouncing it differently, or sometimes revising parts of the utterance.

From the third year on, children respond differently to general (*what did you say?*) and to specific queries (*you put what?*), usually providing only the questioned constituent after the latter, and repeating the entire utterance after the former (e.g., Anselmi et al. 1986). Self-repairs also occur. They are observed already in the second year in the case of requests (e.g., Marcos 1991). Children improve their skills in their third and fourth years when they can spontaneously self-repair requests that are ignored or refused by the interlocutor, by repeating them, reformulating them in a more polite or more direct way, or by adding a justification.

3 Conversation and children's acquisition of core language knowledge

Children may learn from the words and language structures they hear or overhear (e.g., Akhtar, Jipson and Callanan, 2001; Gampe, Liebal and Tomasello 2012). Language usages may be thought to provide positive evidence of the lexicon and the grammaticality of utterances, associated or not with 'automatically reinforcing' behaviors, such as positive caregiving (e.g., Novak and Pelaez, 2004). Moreover, the absence of a given construction may well function as indirect evidence for its ungrammaticality (Scholz 2004: 961), from which Gold recognized human learners could profit (Gold 1967: 454).

Conversational exchanges, however, provide the language-learning child with a concentrate of optimal experiences that facilitate the acquisition of an early lexicon and of basic structures and uses of the language.

3.1 Why can children learn in conversations?

When children participate in conversational exchanges they are *highly motivated* to make themselves understood as well as to understand their partners, making them particularly attentive to the utterances of their interlocutors and to the effect that their own utterances have on them. This gives a first edge to conversational exchanges with respect to general input.

In conversations adults and children construct *common ground* (Clark 1996) or shared information. Moreover, caregivers get information on children's production and comprehension abilities, something that can help them to adapt their speech more closely to the children's specificities. And children can adapt their talk by monitoring the effect of their utterances on the caregivers.

In conversation children receive *well-timed interpretations* of their utterances in the form of recasts, expansions, reformulations and corrections[2]. All these different types of caregivers' responses share the property that changes in form (between the child's and the caregiver's utterances) take place while meaning remains invariant.

Finally, because conversations "are more than the sum of their parts" (Clark 1996:318), they have the potential for creating events from which new knowledge can arise. This particular aspect of conversations will be elaborated and illustrated later on.

3.2 Adults' contingent responses to TD and LI children

Adults' recasts, expansions and reformulations provide children with positive evidence – the uptake of the words used by the children in their utterances – as well as negative feedback – the transformation of children's utterances into different, grammatically-well-formed utterances (Chouinard and Clark 2003; Novak and Pelaez 2004; Veneziano 2005). In this favorable context, children have the opportunity to compare their own utterances to those produced by the adult, spot the specific items that don't match, and eventually change their original forms into more appropriate ones (Saxton 2000; Chouinard and Clark 2003; Veneziano 2005, 2014). Corrections

---

[2] Definitions of recasts, expansions, reformulations and corrections vary. In their original use, expansions are utterances that express the adult's interpretation of the child's previous utterance by reproducing one or more of its elements (Cazden, 1972). For example, "*Eve is having lunch*" is an expansion of the child's utterance "*Eve lunch*". A recast adds to that the specific grammatical correction of one or more elements such as articles, possessives, plurals and auxiliaries. For example, 'Yes, *the dog is running*' is a recast of the child's utterance '*dog running*', where both the Noun Phrase (*dog* → *the dog*) and the auxiliary (*running* → *is running*) are recast (Farrar, 1990; Camarata & Nelson, 1992).

can be explicit but also implicit, as when adults reformulate utterances that are not phonologically, lexically or grammatically correct but do not reformulate those that correspond to the conventions of the language (Saxton 1997, 2000; Strapp 1999; Otomo 2001; Chouinard and Clark 2003; Veneziano 2005, 2014). These behaviors were generally observed in western-style societies in caregivers interacting with typically-developing children learning one or more than one language at the same time. The frequency of their occurrence depends also on children's age and level of language development (less so when children are more competent speakers) (e.g., Snow 1995), as well as on the type of activity, with book-reading soliciting the highest number (Rezzonico et al. 2014).

Corrective responses also occur in the speech that caregivers address to their language impaired (LI) children. Some studies report no major differences between caregivers of LI and TD children, matched on language measures (Fey et al. 1999; Proctor-Williams et al. 2001; Rezzonico et al. 2014). If differences in the quantity of expansions or recasts seem to be present, the difference disappears when these behaviors are related to the amount of language produced by the children (Paul and Elwood, 1991). Other studies find however that while parents of LI and young language-delayed children produce similar amounts of linguistic input as parents of typically-developing children, they however provide fewer responses, expansions and recasts (e.g., Conti-Ramsden, Hutcheson, and Grove 1995; Nelson et al. 1995; de Weck 2001; Vigil, Hodges, and Klee 2005; Saxton 2005). Moreover these kinds of responses differ in their function. Mothers of LI children mainly use these responses to request, to assert and to ask children to request and assert, while mothers of TD children use them more to respond, to acknowledge the children's previous utterance and to request clarifications (Conti-Ramsden 1990). These differences are thought to be due to the fact that parents adjust their conversational behavior to their children's abilities, attempting to compensate for their child's more passive role (Whitehurst et al., 1988; Conti-Ramsden 1990; Tannock and Girolametto 1992).

3.3 Effects of contingent responses on language acquisition of TD and LI children

Contingent responses in general were found to be early predictors of later school outcomes in large longitudinal studies (e.g., Walker et al. 1994). Considered more specifically, an adult's corrective responses (such as recasts, expansions and reformulations) were found to have positive effects on the acquisition of different aspects of language. Variation in these responses correlates with children's mean length of utterances (MLU), the elaboration of noun and verb phrases, the use of auxiliaries (Hoff-Ginsberg 1985; Moerk 1990), of copulas and articles (e.g., Farrar 1990, 1992; Hoff-Ginsberg 1985), and the use of grammatical morphemes such as the English plural and the form of the present progressive (-ing) (Farrar 1990).

Training studies have shown positive effects of recasts on the acquisition of verbal morphology and verbal constructions (Nelson 1977; Farrar 1992), as well as on the passive structure (Baker and Nelson 1984). Saxton (1997) found that 5-year-olds were able to learn the irregular past tense of unfamiliar verbs with just 20 corrective reformulations, and Strapp et al. (2008) found that the effectiveness of recasts was dependent on age and on what children still need to learn: 3-year-olds were able to learn only the irregular plural of nonsense nouns, while 5-year-olds also learned the irregular past tense of nonsense verbs.

Results concerning the effect of expansions, recasts or corrective responses on LI children present a mixed picture (cf. the meta-analysis of Law, Garrett, and Nye 2004). Positive effects were found on various morphosyntactic aspects in LI children with expressive difficulties (Camarata and Nelson, 1992; Fey, Cleave, and Long 1993; Camarata, Nelson, and Camarata 1994; Nelson et al. 1996). However LI children seem to need specific conditions for corrective responses to have a positive effect on them. For example, Proctor-Williams et al. (2001), who reported no quantitative differences in the rate of recasts between parents of LI and of TD children, found positive effects of recasts on copulas and articles in TD children but not in LI children. In contrast with the Camarata et al. study (1994) where LI children learned grammatical features from recasts, in the Proctor et al. study the rate of the specific recasts provided by the parents was only one fourth of the rate provided in the Camarata et al. training study. Proctor et al. conclude that children with LI can benefit from recasts in so far as these are produced in much greater quantity than what is typically the case in conversations with TD children. Moreover, with LI children, corrective responses seem to be more effective if their number is spread over sessions (Smith-Lock et al 2013), rather than condensed repeatedly within the same session (Connell and Stone 1992; Leonard et al. 2006). For example, Smith-Lock et al. (2013) found that an intensive grammatical training of 8 sessions within one week, dispensed in a school setting to 5-year-old children, was less effective than the same amount of training spread over a period of 8 weeks. Riches, Tomasello, and Conti-Ramsden (2005) also found that distributed training sessions were more beneficial than massed training sessions for novel verb learning. However, results of studies aiming to determine the optimal frequency, rate and length of intervention in children with language impairment or delay, do not always go in the same direction (see, for example, Barratt, Littlejohns, and Thompson 1992; Proctor-Williams and Fey 2007; Bellon-Harn 2012). And studies concerning the impact of these different kinds of interventions or treatments in everyday clinical practice, an issue of particular concern to practitioners are still sparse (Dollaghan 2007; Cirrin et al. 2010).

In conversations, children are not only recipients of adults' utterances, they are also active participants and their responses to caregivers are just as important. They manifest their abilities to pay attention to adults' utterances and their level of understanding and processing of the latter. In the early stages of language acquisition, children's imitative uptakes of words produced by mothers in conversation are positively correlated with word acquisition (Snow 1987). Although children differ in the extent to which they imitate (Bloom, Hood, and Lightbown 1974; Veneziano 1988, 2005), the majority of their imitations involved words they didn't already use spontaneously (Bloom et al. 1974, Veneziano 2005). In an analysis of the longitudinal data of six Hebrew-acquiring children, Veneziano (2005) showed that words imitated by the children, repeated or reformulated by their mother, or both, were produced in conventional forms at later sessions. Moreover, at later sessions, these productions were recognized as meaningful words by the mother, and solicited comments that advanced the theme of the conversation two to three times more often than words appearing in that session for the first time.

3.4 Conversation as a dyadic phenomenon

Conversations are however more than caregivers' responses to children's utterances and children's responses to caregivers' utterances. They are highly intricate dyadic phenomena where partners are mutually influenced by each other's contributions and act *jointly* to create *sequences of contingent replies*.

The potential relevance of sequences of this kind was already pointed out in early studies of language acquisition (e.g., Slobin 1968; Brown, Cazden, and Bellugi 1969). Recent studies that have taken into account sequences of contingent replies confirm their importance. They found, for example, that children were more likely to continue the topic after expansions, reformulations or recasts by caregivers than after their initiating turns. A similar result was observed for caregivers who were significantly more likely to continue the topic and reformulate children's utterances when the latter were themselves responses to the caregivers' utterances than when they were topic-initiating turns (e.g., Scherer and Olswang 1984; Veneziano, 1988, 2005).

In such a context of mutual responding, children are likely to modify their utterances within the conversational sequence itself. For example, in a longitudinal study of 12- to 19-month-old children acquiring Hebrew, Veneziano (2005, 2014) found that, between 14 and 17 months, children improved their productions in 21% to 50% of the conversational exchanges containing at least two turns by the child, with improvements being more likely to occur if the mother's reformulation was produced in between the child's turns.

Children are likely to modify their initial utterances also after confirmation or clarification requests or after caregivers' misinterpretation of their intentions (Anselmi et al. 1986; Marcos 1991; Chouinard and Clark 2003). Clarification requests may also lead children to revise the grammatical form of their previous utterance, provided they already have some knowledge of the correct grammatical form (Saxton 2000; Saxton, House-Price, and Dawson 2005).

The relevance of *sequences of contingent replies* can also be seen in children's development towards multiword speech. Children's participation in these conversational exchanges provides them with the opportunity to produce sequences of Successive Single-Word Utterances, (SSWUs) which are considered pivotal in the change from single-word to two-word speech (Bloom 1973; Scollon 1979; Veneziano, Sinclair, and Berthoud 1990; Veneziano 2013). An example of SSWU is provided below:

> Example 3 – Simplified example of a SSWU at 20-months (Mother and child look at a picture of children sliding from a waterslide into a swimming pool)
>
> Child$_1$: *children*
>
> Mother$_1$: 'the *children fell* into the water # isn't it?'
>
> Child$_2$: *fell*

In SSWUs, like the one in example 3 above, the child produces two one-word utterances ('children' and 'fell') bearing on the same event. By doing this, children take a first step towards combining the meanings of words, although not yet within a single utterance. SSWUs illustrate well how progress may result from the partners' joint interactional functioning: it is because the mother expands the child's initial utterance 'children' that the child has the opportunity to produce her second utterance 'fell'; and it is because the child can turn herself away from the word produced earlier that she can now focus on a new word contained in the mother's reformulation.

4 Concluding remarks

The relation between conversation and language development was considered first from the point of view of the *conversational skills* that are necessary to become a competent speaker of a language, such as managing turn alternation, topic continuation, contingent responsiveness, using language informatively for one's interlocutor or choosing the appropriate linguistic forms that take into account prior discourse and common ground among the partners. These skills develop with age and are closely linked to progress in language acquisition.

We then looked at the relation from the point of view of the contributions that conversational functioning makes to children's acquisition of language knowledge. We have emphasized that although children may learn from the language they hear or overhear around them, conversations have specific properties that provide children with highly privileged opportunities for learning. In conversations, children are active participants, motivated to understand what is said to them as well as to make themselves understood, and thus likely to attend to what is being said and to the reactions to their own speech. Caregivers, in western societies at least, in general are cooperative partners who often provide contingent responses that interpret and recast children's utterances, and solicit further on-topic contributions from them.

Sequences of contingent replies provide great opportunities for children to compare their production to that of the adult, observe transformations of form with very similar meaning, and possibly make appropriate changes and/or include in their talk new aspects of a situation. As Brown et al. pointed out already in the late sixties, the transformations that utterances undergo 'as they shuttle between persons in conversation' may ultimately provide the 'richest data available to the child for acquiring language' (Brown et al. 1969: 72).

An important variable that shouldn't be underestimated in this process is the way children themselves participate in conversational exchanges, depending on whether they are willing and motivated to contribute and what kinds of contributions they make to the exchange. Do they focus on caregivers' utterances, are they attentive to the specific features considered to help children's improvements and self-corrections? Do they provide evidence that they can see the differences between their own and the adult's productions? Are they motivated to change? And there are also individual variables such as the children's level of language development, their capacity to process and structure language material and their motivation for emulating the adult's speech, which are all sources of individual variation.

The difficulties encountered by language impaired and language delayed children are in line with the idea that children play a very important role in their own learning (e.g. Elbers 1995). These children indeed need more expansions and recasts and repeated training sessions over long stretches of time before they can acquire or improve aspects of their language production (e.g. Smith-Lock et al. 2013; Riches et al. 2005).

Moreover, explanations of language acquisition should not underestimate the fact that conversational exchanges are co-constructed by the turns contributed by each participant and result from what caregivers and children do *together*, each turn opening up new possibilities as well as setting constraints on the choices made by each speaker.

The intricate nature of conversations is well recognized by researchers studying the interaction between parents and their language impaired children. LI children are seen to influence their caregivers and vice-versa, often falling into a sort of 'inadequate feedback loop': children provide inadequate feedback to their caregivers, leading the latter to use a pattern of interactive techniques that may 'be less than optimal for language acquisition.' (Tannock and Girolametto 1992: 54).

Child-directed speech, and the language that children overhear, certainly contain relevant information for language learning children. However, conversational exchanges, and in particular sequences of reciprocal contingent responses and, more generally, of extended discourse may be the best facilitating resource available in the early stages of language acquisition, and at all those critical points where new knowledge is being acquired. Because a great number of facilitating features are co-present in conversational exchanges, children may draw from them what is most suitable and accessible to their individual way for dealing with the appropriation of the language.

References

Akhtar, Nameera, Jennifer Jipson & Maureen A. Callanan. 2001. Learning words through overhearing. *Child Development* 72. 416–430.

Anselmi, Dina, Michael Tomasello & Mary Acunzo. 1986. Young children's responses to neutral and specific contingent queries. *Journal of Child Language* 13. 135–144.

Ariel, Mira. 1988. Referring and accessibility. *Journal of Linguistics* 24. 65–87.

Baker, Nancy D. & Keith E. Nelson. 1984. Recasting and related conversational techniques for triggering syntactic advances in young children. *First Language* 5. 3–22.

Barratt, Jean, Peter Littlejohns & Julie Thompson. 1992. Trial of intensive compared with weekly speech therapy in preschool children. *Archives of Disease in Childhood* 6. 106–108.

Bellon-Harn, Monica L. 2012. Dose frequency: Comparison of language outcomes in preschool children with language impairment. *Child Language Teaching and Therapy* 28. 225–240.

Bloom, Kathleen. 1988. Quality of adult vocalizations affects the quality of infant vocalizations. *Journal of Child Language* 15. 469–480.

Bloom, Lois. 1973. *One word at a time*. The Hague: Mouton & Co.

Bloom, Lois, Lois Hood & Patsy Lightbown. 1974. Imitation in language development: If, when and why. *Cognitive Psychology* 6. 380–420.

Bloom, Kathleen, Ann Russell & Karen Wassenberg. 1987. Turn taking affects the quality of infant vocalizations, *Journal of Child Language* 14. 211–227.

Brown, Roger, Courtney Cazden & Ursula Bellugi. 1969. The child's grammar from I to II. In J. P. Hill (ed.), *Minnesota Symposia in Child Psychology*, Vol. II., 28–73. Minneapolis: University of Minnesota Press.

Camarata, Stephen M. & Keith E. Nelson. 1992. Treatment efficiency as a function of target selection in the remediation of child language. *Clinical Linguistics and Phonetics* 6. 167–178.

Camarata, Stephen M., Keith E. Nelson & Mary N. Camarata. 1994. Comparison of conversational-recasting and imitative procedures for training grammatical structures in children with specific language impairment. *Journal of Speech and Hearing Research* 37. 1414–1423.

Casillas, Marisa. 2014. Turn-taking. In Matthews, Danielle (ed.), *Pragmatic development in first language acquisition*, 53–70. Amsterdam: Benjamins.

Cazden, Courtney B. 1972. *Child language and education*. New York: Holt, Rinehart & Winston.

Chouinard, Michelle M. & Eve V. Clark. 2003. Adult reformulations of child errors as negative evidence. *Journal of Child Language* 30. 637–669.

Cirrin, Frank M., Tracy L. Schooling, Nickola W. Nelson, Sylvia F. Diehl, Perry F. Flynn, Maureen Staskowski, T. Zoann Torrey & Deborah F. Adamczyk. 2010. Evidence-based systematic review: Effects of different service delivery models on communication outcomes for elementary school-age children. *Language, Speech & Hearing Services in Schools* 41. 233–264.

Clark, Herbert H. 1996. *Using Language*. Cambridge: Cambridge University Press.

Connell, Phil J. & C. Addison Stone. 1992. Morpheme learning of children with specific language impairment under controlled instructional conditions. *Journal of Speech and Hearing Research* 35. 844–852.

Conti-Ramsden, Gina. 1990. Maternal recasts and other contingent replies to language impaired children. *Journal of Speech and Hearing Disorders* 55. 262–74.

Conti-Ramsden, Gina, Graeme D. Hutcheson & John Grove. 1995. Contingency and breakdown: Children with SLI and their conversations with mothers and fathers. *Journal of Speech and Hearing Research* 38. 1290–1302.

de Weck, Geneviève. 2001. Stratégies d'étayage d'adultes en interaction avec des enfants normaux et dysphasiques. In Almgren, Margareta, Andoni Barrena, María-José Ezeizabarrena, Itziar Idiazabal & Brian MacWhinney (eds.), *Research on child language acquisition*, 352–386. Somerville, MA: Cascadilla Press.

Dollaghan, Christine A. 2007. *The handbook of evidence-based practice in communication disorders.* Baltimore, MD: Brookes Publishing Co.

Dunn, Judy & Penny Munn. 1987. Development of justification in disputes with mother and sibling. *Developmental Psychology* 23. 791–798.

Dunham, Philip J., Frances Dunham & Ann Curwin. 1993. Joint-attentional states and lexical acquisition at 18 months. *Developmental Psychology* 29. 827–831.

Elbers, Loekie. 1995. Production as a source of input for analysis: evidence from the developmental course of a word blend, *Journal of Child Language* 22. 47–71.

Farrar, Michael Jeffrey. 1990. Discourse and the acquisition of grammatical morphemes. *Journal of Child Language* 17. 607–624.

Farrar, Michael Jeffrey. 1992. Negative evidence and grammatical morpheme acquisition. *Developmental Psychology* 28. 90–98.

Fey, Marc E., Patricia L. Cleave, Steven H. Long & Diana L. Hughes. 1993. Two approaches to the facilitation of grammar in children with language impairment. *Journal of Speech, Language and Hearing Research* 36. 141–157.

Fey, Marc E., Tracy E. Krulik, Diane Frome Loeb & Kerry Proctor-Williams. 1999. Sentence recast use by parents of children with typical language and children with specific language impairment. *American Journal of Speech-Language Pathology* 8. 273–286.

Gampe, Anja, Kristin Liebal & Michael Tomasello. 2012. Eighteen-month-olds learn novel words through overhearing. *First Language* 32. 385–397.

Ginsburg, Gerald P. & Brock K. Kilbourne. 1988. Emergence of vocal alternation in mother-infant interchanges. *Journal of Child Language* 15. 221–235.

Gold, E. Mark. 1967. Language identification in the limit. *Information and Control* 10. 447–474.

Grice, H. Paul. 1975. Logic and conversation. In Peter Cole & Jerry L. Morgan (eds.), *Syntax and Semantics: Speech Acts*, 41–58. New York: Academic Press.

Gundel, Jeanette K., Nancy Hedberg & Ron Zacharski. 1993. Cognitive status and the form of referring expressions in discourse. *Language* 69. 274–307.

Hausendorf, Heiko & Uta M. Quasthoff. 1992. Children's storytelling in adult-child interaction: three dimensions in narrative development. *Journal of Narrative and Life History* 2. 293–306.

Hendriks, Petra, Charlotte Koster & John CJ Hoeks. 2014. Referential choice across the lifespan: why children and elderly adults produce ambiguous pronouns. *Language and Cognitive Processes* 29. 391–407.

Hockett, Charles Francis. 1958. *A course in modern linguistics.* New York: Macmillan.

Hoff-Ginsberg, Erika. 1985. Some contributions of mothers' speech to their children's syntactic growth. *Journal of Child Language* 12. 367–385.

Kail, Michele & Maya Hickmann. 1992. French children's ability to introduce referents in narratives as a function of mutual knowledge. *First Language* 12. 73–94

Kaye, Kenneth & Rosalind Charney. 1980. How mothers maintain 'dialogue' with two-year olds. In David R. Olson (ed.), *The social foundations of language and thought*, 211–230. New York: Norton.

Lamb, Sharon. 1991. Internal state words: Their relation to moral development and to maternal communications about moral development in the second year of life. *First Language* 11. 391–406.

Law, James, Zoe Garrett & Chad Nye. 2004. The efficacy of treatment for children with developmental speech and language delay/disorder: a meta-analysis. *Journal of Speech, Language and Hearing Research* 47. 924–943.

Leonard, Laurence B., Stephen M. Camarata, Monika Pawłowska, Barbara Brown & Mary N. Camarata. 2006. Tense and agreement morphemes in the speech of children with specific language impairment during intervention: Phase II. *Journal of Speech, Language & Hearing Research* 49. 749–770.

Lucariello, Joan & Katherine Nelson. 1987. Remembering and planning talk between mothers and children. *Discourse Processes* 10. 219–235.

Lyons, John. 1977. *Semantics*. Vol. 1. Cambridge: Cambridge University Press.

Marcos, Haydée. 1991. Reformulating requests at 18 months: Gestures, vocalizations & words. *First Language* 11. 361–375.

Martin, John Antony Michael. 1981. *Voice, speech and language in the child: Development and disorder*. Vienna, New York: Springer Verlag.

Matthews, Danielle, Elena Lieven, Anna Theakston & Michael Tomasello. 2006. The effect of perceptual availability and prior discourse on young children's use of referring expressions. *Applied Psycholinguistics* 27. 403–422.

McTear, Michael. 1985. *Children's conversation*. New York: Basil Blackwell.

Moerk, Ernst L. 1990. Three-term contingency patterns in mother-child verbal interactions during first-language acquisition. *Journal of the Experimental Analysis of Behavior* 54. 293–305.

Murray, Lynne & Colwyn Trevarthen. 1986. The infant's role in mother-infant communications. *Journal of Child Language* 13. 15–29.

Nelson, Keith E. 1977. Facilitating children's syntax acquisition. *Developmental Psychology* 13. 101–107.

Nelson, Keith E. 1987. Some observations from the perspective of the rare event cognitive comparison theory of language acquisition. In Keith E. Nelson & Anne van Kleeck (eds.), *Children's language*, Vol. 6. Hillsdale, N.J.: Lawrence Erlbaum.

Nelson, Keith E., Stephen M. Camarata, Janet Welsh, Laura Butkovsky & Mary Camarata. 1996. Effects of imitative and conversational recasting treatment on the acquisition of grammar in children with specific language impairment and younger language-normal children. *Journal of Speech, Language & Hearing Research* 39. 850–859.

Nelson, Keith E., Janet Welsh, Stephen M. Camarata, Laura Butkovsky & Mary Camarata. 1995. Available input for language impaired children and younger children of matched language levels. *First Language* 15. 1–17.

Novak, Gary & Martha Pelaez. 2004. *Child and adolescent development: A behavioral systems approach*. Thousand Oaks, CA: Sage.

O'Neill, Daniela K. 1996. Two-year-old children's sensitivity to a parent's knowledge state when making requests. *Child Development* 67. 659–677.

Otomo, Kiyoshi. 2001. Maternal responses to word approximations in Japanese children's transition to language. *Journal of Child Language* 28. 29–57.

Pan, Barbara A. & Catherine E. Snow. 1999. The development of conversation and discourse skills. In Marrett, Martyn D. Barrett (ed.), *The development of language*, 229–250. Hove: Psychology Press.

Papoušek, Mechthild & Hanuš Papoušek. 1989. Forms and functions of vocal matching in interactions between mothers and their precanonical infants. *First Language* 9. 137–157.

Paul, Rhea & Terril J. Elwood. 1991. Maternal linguistic input to toddlers with slow expressive language development. *Journal of Speech and Hearing Research* 34. 982–88.

Proctor-Williams, Kerry & Marc E. Fey. 2007. Recast density and acquisition of novel irregular past tense verbs. *Journal of Speech, Language and Hearing Research* 50. 1029–1047.

Proctor-Williams, Kerry, Marc E. Fey & Diane Frome Loeb. 2001. Parental recasts and production in copulas and articles by children with specific language impairment and typical language. *American Journal of Speech-Language Pathology* 10. 155–168.

Rezzonico, Stefano, Geneviève de Weck, Anne Salazar Orvig, Christine da Silva Genest & Somayeh Rahmati. 2014. Maternal recasts and activity variations: A comparison of mother–child dyads involving children with and without SLI. *Clinical Linguistics & Phonetics* 28. 223–240.

Riches, Nick G., Michael Tomasello & Gina Conti-Ramsden. 2005. Verb learning in children with SLI: Frequency and spacing effects. *Journal of Speech, Language & Hearing Research* 48. 1397–1411.
Sachs, Jacqueline. 1983. *Talking about the there and then: the emergence of displaced reference in parent-child discourse*. In Keith E. Nelson (ed.), Children's language, Vol. 4, 1–28. Hillsdale, NJ: Erlbaum.
Saxton, Matthew. 1997. The contrast theory of negative input. *Journal of Child Language* 24. 139–61.
Saxton, Matthew. 2000. Negative evidence and negative feedback: Immediate effects on the grammaticality of child speech. *First Language* 20. 221–252.
Saxton, Matthew, C.armel Houston-Price & Natasha Dawson. 2005. The prompt hypothesis: Clarification requests as corrective input for grammatical errors. *Applied Psycholinguistics* 26. 393–414.
Schegloff, Emanuel A. & Harvey Sacks. 1973. Opening up closings. *Semiotica* 8. 289–327.
Scherer, Nancy J. & Lesley B. Olswang. 1984. Role of mothers' expansions in stimulating children's language production. *Journal of Speech, Language & Hearing Research* 27. 387–396.
Scholz, Barbara C. 2004. Gold's theorems and the logical problem of language acquisition. *Journal of Child Language* 31. 959–961.
Scollon, Ronald. 1979. A real early stage: An unzipped condensation of a dissertation on child language. In Schieffelin, Bambi B. & Elinor Ochs (eds.), *Developmental pragmatics*, 215–227. New York: Academic Press.
Scott, Cheryl M. 1984. Adverbial connectivity in conversations of children 6 to 12. *Journal of Child Language* 11. 423–452.
Shatz, Marilyn. 1994. *A toddler's life: Becoming a person*. New York: Oxford University Press.
Slobin, Dan I. 1968. Imitation and grammatical development in children. In Norman S. Endler, Laurence Boulter & Harry Osser (eds.), *Contemporary issues in developmental psychology*, 437–443. New York: Holt, Rinehart & Winston.
Smith-Lock, Karen, Suze Leitão, Lara Lambert, Polly Prior, Anne Dunn, Julia Cronje, Sara Newhouse & Lyndsey Nickels. 2013. Daily or weekly? The role of treatment frequency in the effectiveness of grammar treatment for children with specific language impairment. *International Journal of Speech-Language Pathology* 15 (3). 255–267.
Snow, Catherine E. 1977. The development of conversations between mothers and babies. *Journal of Child Language* 4. 1–22.
Snow, Catherine E. 1987. Imitativeness: A trait or a skill? In Gisela E. Speidel & Keith E. Nelson (eds.), *The many faces of imitation in language learning*, 73–90. New York: Springer Verlag.
Snow, Catherine E. 1995. Issues in the study of input: Fine tuning, universality, individual and developmental differences and necessary causes. In Paul Fletcher & Brian MacWhinney (eds.), *The handbook of child language*, 180–193. Oxford: Blackwell.
Stiversa, Tanya, N. J. Enfield, Penelope Brown, Christina Englert, Makoto Hayashi, Trine Heinemann, Gertie Hoymann, Federico Rossano, Jan Peter de Ruiter, Kyung-Eun Yoon and Stephen C. Levinson. 2009. Universals and cultural variation in turn-taking in conversation. *Proceedings of the National Academy of Science* 106. 10587–10592.
Strapp, Chehalis M. 1999. Mothers', fathers' & siblings' responses to children's language errors: Comparing sources of negative evidence. *Journal of Child Language* 26. 373–391.
Strapp, Chehalis M., Dana M. Bleakney, Augusta L. Helmick & Hayley M. Tonkovich. 2008. Developmental differences in the effects of negative and positive evidence. *First Language* 28. 35–53.
Tannock, Rosemary & Luigi Girolametto. 1992. Reassessing parent focused language intervention programmes. In Steven F. Warren & Joe Ernest Ed Reichle (eds.), *Causes and effects in communication and language intervention*, 49–79. Baltimore: Paul H. Brookes.
Tomasello, Michael. 1995. Joint attention as social cognition. In Chris Moore & Phil Dunham. (eds.), *Joint attention: Its origins and role in development*, 103–130. Hillsdale, NJ: Lawrence Erlbaum.

Tomasello, Michael. 2003. Constructing a language: A usage-based theory of language acquisition. Cambridge, MA: Harvard University Press.

Tomasello, Michael & Michael Jeffrey Farrar. 1986. Joint attention and early language, *Child Development* 57. 1454–1463.

Tomasello, Michael & Katharina Haberl. 2003. Understanding attention: 12- and 18-month-olds know what's new for other persons. *Developmental Psychology* 39. 906–912.

Veneziano, Edy. 1988. Vocal-verbal interaction and the construction of early lexical knowledge. In John L. Locke & Michael D. Smith (eds.), *The emergent lexicon: The child's development of a linguistic vocabulary*, 109–147. New York, N.Y.: Academic Press.

Veneziano, Edy. 2001. Interactional processes in the origins of the explaining capacity. In Keith E. Nelson, Ayhan Aksu-Koc & Carolyn E. Johnson (eds.), *Children's Language, Vol. 10: Developing Narrative and Discourse competence*, 113–141. Mahwah, N.J.: L. Erlbaum.

Veneziano, Edy. 2002. Language in pretense during the second year: What it can tell us about "pretending" in pretense and the "know-how" about the mind. In Robert W. Mitchell (ed.) *Pretense in animals and children*, 58–72. Cambridge, UK: CUP.

Veneziano, Edy. 2005. Effects of conversational functioning on early language acquisition: When both caregivers and children matter. In Barbara Bokus (ed.), *Studies in the psychology of child language*, 47–69. Warsaw, Poland: Matrix.

Veneziano, Edy. 2009. Language and internal states: A long developmental history at different levels of functioning. *Rivista di Psicolinguistica applicata /Journal of Applied Psycholinguistics* IX (3), 9–27.

Veneziano, Edy. 2010. Justifications and their effects in early adult-child interaction: Developmental trends and individual differences. In Rita Zukauskiene (ed.), *Proceedings of the XIV European Conference on Developmental Psychology*, 153–160. Pianoro, Italy: Medimond.

Veneziano, Edy. 2013. A cognitive-pragmatic model for the change from single-word to articulate speech: A constructivist approach. *Journal of Pragmatics* 56. 133–150.

Veneziano, Edy. 2014. Conversation and language acquisition: Unique properties and effects. In Inbal Arnon, Marisa Casillas, Chigusa Kurumada & Bruno Estigarribia (eds.), *Language in interaction: Studies in honor of Eve V. Clark*, 83–100. TILAR Series, John Benjamins.

Veneziano, Edy & Hermina Sinclair. 1995. Functional changes in early child language: the appearance of references to the past and of explanations. *Journal of Child Language* 22. 557–581.

Veneziano, Edy, Hermine Sinclair & Ioanna Berthoud. 1990. From one word to two words: repetition patterns on the way to structured speech. *Journal of Child Language* 17. 633–650.

Vigil, Debra C., Jennifer Hodges & Thomas Klee. 2005. Quantity and quality of parental language input to late-talking toddlers during play. *Child Language Teaching and Therapy* 21. 107–122.

Walker, Dale, Charles Greenwood, Betty Hart & Judith Carta. 1994. Prediction of school outcomes based on early language production and socioeconomic factors. *Child Development* 65. 606–621.

Whitehurst, Grover J., J. E. Fischel, C. J. Lonigan, M. C. Valdez-Menchaca, B. D. DeBaryshe & M. B. Caulfield. 1988. Verbal interaction in families of normal and expressive language-delayed children. *Developmental Psychology* 24. 690–699.

Ayhan Aksu-Koç & Aslı Aktan-Erciyes
16 Narrative Discourse: Developmental Perspectives

1 Introduction

Narrative is a major mode of discourse in everyday life. Through narratives we make sense of our experiences while sharing them with others. In Bruner's terms, we "... negotiate and renegotiate meanings by the mediation of narrative interpretation..." (1990: 67). Narratives – with real or imaginary content – are perspectival in that the same experience or event can be presented in more than one way depending on the context, the audience and the intentions of the narrator for telling it. Yet, there is an ordering of events which makes sense in terms of the goal that precipitated the telling and gives the narrative its form (Bruner 1990; Labov and Waletzky 1967).

A narrative can be defined as the presentation in language of a sequence of temporally and causally connected real or fictional events organized around a theme and motivated by cognitive and affective states of the actors engaged. A well-formed narrative, therefore, has both a *referential* function realized by plot-forwarding eventive clauses informing about the who, where and when of the action, and an *evaluative* function realized by clauses expressing the intentionality behind those actions (Labov and Waletzky 1967), corresponding respectively, to what Bruner (1986) calls the 'plane of action' and the 'plane of consciousness'. A well-formed narrative also rests on the skillful use of *linguistic forms* in functionally appropriate ways to achieve a coherent text expressed in a cohesive fashion (Halliday and Hasan 1976). Linguistic forms range from grammatical morphemes and lexical items to complex syntactic structures, and among the textual functions are temporal and causal connectivity, referentiality, and perspective. A third characteristic of a skillful narrative is its *communicative adequacy* which has to do with the way information is structured and expressed to ensure its processibility and comprehension by the audience (Johnston 2008).

In order to become effective narrators, then, children must have at least three types of knowledge. The first is *conceptual knowledge* comprising two kinds of mental schemes: *scripts* and *story schemas*. Scripts are generalized representations that embody knowledge about types of events that occur in particular contexts (Nelson 1996). *Story schemas*, on the other hand, are cognitive representations of the temporal-causal relations constituting the action structure and its motivating circumstances that confer it with meaning; story schemas form the foundation of

---

Ayhan Aksu-Koç and Aslı Aktan-Erciyes, Boğaziçi University

the *macrostructure* of the story (Mandler 1987; Stein and Glenn 1979, 1982; Trabasso and Rodkin 1994). While scripts are built in everyday experience and provide content for narratives (Nelson 1996; Hudson and Shapiro 1991), the development of story schemas – with the basic form of an *onset, unfolding* and *resolution* – rests on adult-child conversations about past events, storytelling and book reading interactions (Schick and Melzi 2010). The second type of knowledge is linguistic and involves the use of grammatical knowledge for the cohesive expression of units longer than the clause (Bamberg 1987; Berman and Slobin 1994; Hickmann 2003). Children have acquired the basic grammatical structures of their language by the age of 3, what they have to further learn is form-function relations in narrative which entails "(t)he development of the linguistic means to connect events and syntactically 'package' them into coherent structures – at the levels of scene, episode and overall plot" (Berman and Slobin 1994: 2). The third kind of knowledge is *pragmatic*. To ensure communicative adequacy children must decide about the focus and content of what to tell depending on who the audience is, asses their presuppositions and expectations to structure information accordingly, and make appropriate choice of linguistic forms for clear reference (Hickmann 2003). All this requires perspective taking and meta-representational skills covered by what has come to be known as 'theory of mind' (Astington and Baird 2005) as well as use of working memory resources (Arnold and Griffin 2007; Johnston 2008). Narrative competence, therefore, rests on the integration of skills at the conceptual level for coherence, the linguistic level for cohesion and the pragmatic level for social-interactional and communicative appropriateness.

Developmentalists study narrative discourse for a number of reasons. First, narratives present the optimal context for tracing lexical and grammatical development and the changing form-function relations during the preschool and early school years (Berman and Slobin 1994; Hickmann 2003; Johnston 2008). Second, narrative as a universal 'mode of thought' (Bruner 1986) plays a constitutive role in cognitive and social-emotional development, in autobiographical memory and identity formation (Fivush 1991; Nelson 1996; McLean and Pasupathi 2012). Third, narratives constitute a foundation for literacy acquisition because experience with stories gives children the opportunity to encounter new vocabulary and syntactic structures and learn how to comprehend and produce decontextualized language, an important predictor of literacy acquisition and school success (Dickinson and Tabors 2001; Hart and Risley 1995; Peterson 1994; Ravid and Berman 2006; Snow 1991). Finally, narratives provide a context for detection of language development problems related to working memory capacity, decoding and encoding of lexical and morphosyntactic structures, and constraints in socio-cognitive understanding (Bishop and Donlan 2005; Botting et al. 2001, 2002; Johnston 2008; McFadden and Gillam 1996; Norbury and Bishop 2002).

The present chapter presents an overview of the typical course of development of narrative production during the preschool and early school years. In section 2, we briefly address some methodological issues. In section 3, we refer to social-interactional processes as contexts of development (3.1), then we discuss the course of structural developments in personal and fictional narratives (3.2), followed by the quantitative and qualitative changes in expressive skills (3.3), and lastly, changes in referential ability and evaluative language that illustrate developments in the pragmatic component of narratives (3.4). We conclude in section 4 by noting the implications of typical development for communicative disorders.

2 Genre and techniques of elicitation

Studies of narrative development have concentrated mainly on two genres, *personal* and *fictional*, that differ in terms of "the source of knowledge in which the narrative has its origins" (Shiro 2003: 169). Personal narratives are recounts of a real past experience while fictional narratives are either a composition about an imaginary situation or a recall of a previously heard story (McCabe et al. 2008). As Shiro (2003: 165) observes, "Genre determines how a text is organized, which topic is appropriate, what lexical and grammatical choices are acceptable. Moreover, the situational context limits the type of discourse that can be used." It is therefore not surprising that studies of personal and fictional narratives typically use different methodologies and yield somewhat different developmental patterns.

Personal narratives are either spontaneously occasioned in conversation or elicited by use of some minimal verbal input such as a suggested topic or a story stem (Haden, Haine, and Fivush 1997; Ervin-Tripp and Küntay 1997; Miller and Sperry 1988; Peterson and McCabe 1983; Ravid and Berman 2006). Personal narratives have the advantage of being first-person stories which require only a spatio-temporal shift in perspective since the child is at once the protagonist in the past and the narrator in the present. As accounts of personal experience, they present familiar content but depend on the child's memory for these events.

Fictional narratives are commonly elicited by use of an already structured model story presented orally for retelling (Aksu-Koç and Küntay 2002; Liles 1993; Martinot 2000; Merrit and Liles 1987; Ripich and Griffith, 1988; Schneider and Dubé 1997) or generated by visual prompts such as a single picture, a sequence of pictures (Eisenberg et al. 2008; Gagarina et al. 2012; Hickmann 2003; Karmiloff-Smith 1981a; Schneider and Dubé 2005), a wordless picture book (Berman and Slobin 1994; Miller et al. 2006), or a wordless video clip (Shiro 2003; Eaton, Collis, and Lewis 1999). Oral or visual prompts scaffold the child's production because they present a specific content already structured episodically, but these are third-person stories that, in addition to a spatio-temporal shift, require shifting perspective across characters. Oral prompts have the advantage of modeling the linguistic format of the story but depend on memory for retelling, whereas picture sequences that present the plot as it unfolds guide the generation process but without the expressive support. Fictional narratives may also be elicited by use of unstructured techniques such as asking the child directly to tell a story or by using some toy-prompts in play context (Benson 1993; Ilgaz and Aksu-Koç 2005; Nicolopoulou 1997; Ucelli et al. 2005). The task demands are higher in this procedure as both the structuration and the expression of the narrative depends fully on the child's imagination and constructive activity, without any verbal or visual scaffolding or memory of personal experience to serve as content.

In short, personal vs. fictional genres and the elicitation techniques of retelling, generation, and spontaneous production differ in terms of the demands they make on long term and working memory, story schemas and linguistic schemas. Their relative advantages as assessment techniques depend on children's age, familiarity with story content, complexity of the pictures for inference and whether production or comprehension is assessed. From the researcher's point of view, orally or visually generated fictional stories have the advantage of providing a standard against which the structural and/or linguistic characteristics of the narratives of individual children can be compared. Personal experience narratives show variation across individual narrators and pose difficulties for such comparisons and generalizations.

3 Narrative Perspectives and Developmental Trends

Research on narrative development has been conducted from a variety of perspectives (Bamberg 1997). Here, we consider (i) the social-interactionist perspective which focuses on the contexts of narrative development, (ii) the cognitive tradition where the focus is on macrostructural developments, (iii) the linguistic-constructivist approach where attention is on the relations between linguistic form and discourse function, and (iv) the pragmatic perspective which is concerned with communicative adequacy. Crosslinguistic and cultural approaches crosscut these perspectives.

3.1 Social-interactional processes as contexts of development

Considered within an interactive framework, narrating is regarded as an activity generated by participants of the interaction. Changes take place "in terms of linguistic forms as well as in terms of interactive functions that these forms serve" (Bamberg 1997:47). Children acquire narrative skills through social interactions with more competent partners. Scripts and story grammars develop in the preschool years through adult-child conversations (Blum-Kulka and Snow 2002; Minami 2002; Nelson 1996; Uccelli et al. 2005), experience with oral stories and joint book-reading (Justice et al. 2009; Schick and Melzi 2010; Snow and Dickinson 1990), and telling and acting out stories (Nicolopoulou 1997). Social and cultural practices of communication and educational resources available in the child's environment also have determining effects on the nature of the developing skills.

Most research has focused on mother-child interactions and the nature of the language mothers use. Two distinct parental styles have been identified: elaborative and repetitive (Eisenberg 1985; Fivush 2001; Reese, Haden, and Fivush 1993). Elaborative mothers use language enriched with detail, pose open-ended questions, and offer new information that helps the child reconstruct the past event, whereas repetitive mothers insist on eliciting specific information by repeating the question they asked or the information they already provided. Children of elaborative mothers have been observed to produce more informative narratives and to have higher levels of decontextualized language than children of repetitive mothers (Fivush and Fromhoff 1988; Hudson 1990; Leyva et al. 2009; Peterson, Jesso, and McCabe 1999; Schick and Melzi 2010; Snow 1991).

Research has also focused on parent-child interaction during joint book reading. Based on a meta-analysis, Bus, Ijzendoorn and Pellegrini (1995) concluded that joint book reading contributes to general language growth and achievements in emergent literacy by providing an efficient platform for scaffolding. However, findings related to effects on children's narrative skills appear controversial; while some studies report gains in this domain as well (Harkins, Koch, and Michel 1994; Reese et al. 2010; Zevenbergen and Whitehurst 2003), others have not found a positive relationship between shared book reading and narrative skills for either personal or elicited fictional narratives (Sénéchal et al. 2008). Most studies explore the effects of the complexity of the mother's talk by attending to her style of reading, identified as either *didactic* or *narrative* (Haden, Reese, and Fivush 1996). Didactic style of reading is descriptive of objects and characters in the story and emphasizes recall of facts, whereas narrative style of reading expands on the theme, making inferences and predictions and highlighting what is reportable. Again, while some studies have found more complex mother-talk during didactic book sharing (Price et al. 2009), others have observed the narrative style to be more complex, more decontextualized and more abstract, and children's narrative talk, in turn, to be similarly more decontextualized (Haden, Reese, and Fivush 1996; Justice et al. 2002; Nyhout and O'Neil 2013). Overall, the findings show variation in maternal style as a function of the age of the child, and genre of the book read, and familiarity with the book, in addition to what may be a consistent style of the mother.

Parent-child interaction is molded by cultural norms and values, hence cultural differences in social interaction styles also influence narrative building. In general, East Asian mothers have been found to favor a low-elaborative interaction style, limiting the extent to which children are allowed to introduce their own topics compared to Euro-American mothers. Japanese mothers, for example, were observed to request fewer descriptions from their children and to give fewer evaluations than do North American mothers, thereby helping shape children's narratives to take the culturally valued form of short collections of experiences rather than an elaborated one (Minami 2002). Similarly, the interactive style of Chinese mothers was found to be repetitive and not conducive to discussions of opinions and emotions while that of American mothers was elaborative, encouraging children to express themselves in these terms (Wang 2001). These comparisons of Euro-American and East Asian mother-child talk about personal past experiences point to differences in emphasis on children's thoughts, feelings and individuality, as opposed to emphasis on moral values and culturally acceptable behaviors (Minami and McCabe 1995; Mullen and Yi 1995; Luo, Snow, and Chang 2011). Differences in parent-child talk and narrative styles have also been observed between Euro-Americans who promote narratives composed of a sequence of events organized around a single topic, and Afro-American (Curenton and Justice 2004; Heath 1982; Michaels 1981) and Latino subcultures (Carmiol and Sparks 2014) who value narratives composed of a collection of events linked within a general theme. However, the positive relation between mothers' elaborative style and children's narrative skills have not been found to differ across low income White, Hispanic and Afro-American groups, though the amount of elaborativeness may be less than that of middle class groups (Leyva et al. 2009).

3.2 Conceptual-Structural knowledge and narrative coherence: Macrostructure

Developments in the organization of narratives in terms of goals, actions and outcomes have been the major concern in narrative studies of cognitive orientation (Berman and Slobin 1994; Johnston 2008; Peterson and McCabe 1983; Stein and Glenn 1982; Trabasso and Rodkin 1994). Most research has used one of two major analytic frameworks. *High-point analysis* (Labov and Waletzky 1967) proposes that narratives give a chronological description of events that culminate at a problem constituting the high point, a subsequent resolution and a coda. The high-point is the deviation from the normal that makes the story worth telling and includes an evaluation by the narrator. The second framework is the *story grammar* approach (Mandler 1987; Stein and Glenn 1979, 1982) which posits that a story is composed of a setting and one or more episodes that are hierarchically related. An episode is minimally constituted of a problem that initiates the subsequent events (*onset*), attempts at solving the problem (*unfolding*), and the consequences of these attempts (*resolution*). A finer breakdown is into setting, initiating event, internal response, attempt, consequence, and reaction. Both frameworks have been used to analyze children's personal narratives although story grammars have been more commonly used in the analysis of fictional narratives.

In their pioneering work on narrative development, Peterson and McCabe (1983) applied both high-point analysis and story grammar framework to personal narratives of 3- to 9-year-olds. The different analytical frameworks applied to the same genre revealed some interesting differences. High point analysis showed that 3-year-olds produced two event narratives, while 4-year-olds combined more than two events but often out of sequence. Narratives of 5-year-olds were well sequenced but ended prematurely at the climactic event. Six-years and older children told well-formed classic narratives that included information about characters, setting, events leading to the climax and a resolution. The story grammar analysis of the same stories showed that the older children produced coherent narratives with complete or complex episodic structures that included an initiating goal, an attempt to achieve it, and an outcome, whereas narratives of the younger children were pre-episodic. However, 'reactive sequences' – comprising causally linked but unplanned events that are considered pre-episodic in Stein & Glenn's hierarchy – were observed in large numbers across all age groups between 5–9 years, which suggested that these may be a mature type of structure for personal event narratives even if they don't fit the structural schema of an episodically organized narrative. This mismatch between the results of the two analytical frameworks indicated that the structure of personal narratives may not exactly map on to the schema of an episodically organized narrative as fictional narratives do. Using the story grammar framework, Allen et al. (1994) also identified reactive sequences as mature types of structures for personal but not for spontaneous fictional narratives of 4- to 8-year-olds. Comparing the structure of personal narratives of 4;6 year olds from different socio-economic backgrounds, Peterson (1994) observed that high-point analysis revealed differences between groups whereas story grammar analysis did not. Such findings all indicate different routes and pace of development for the two genres, a point we return to shortly.

The most comprehensive work on fictional narratives is the crosslinguistic study by Berman and Slobin and their colleagues (1994) of narratives of English-, German-, Spanish-, Hebrew- and Turkish-speaking 3-, 5-, and 9-year-olds and adults, elicited by use of the wordless picture book *Frog Where are You?* (Mayer, 1969).[1] This work documents the closely intertwined macro- and micro-structural developments in the story grammar tradition.

The macro level analysis of the 'frog stories' in the five languages revealed a progression by age from an actional-eventive, to an episodic, and finally to a global-thematic organization (Berman and Slobin 1994). Narratives of 3-year-olds consisted of picture by picture descriptions with no reference to plot onset, unfolding or resolution, hence no temporally advancing storyline. Utterances linked on a perceptual-spatial basis referred to characters within each picture treated independently

---

[1] The collaborators for the project were, for American English T. Renner, for German M. Bamberg, for Spanish E. Sebastian, for Hebrew R. Berman, and for Turkish A. Aksu-Koç. Since this original study the book *Frog Where are You?* has been used to study the narrative development of children learning a wide variety of languges and has been declared an assessment device by the U.S. Department of Health and Human Services, 2002.

from an actional-eventive perspective. Narratives of 5-year-olds displayed emerging episodic structures with temporal organization and local causal connections. Despite considerable variability, most had an anchor tense, indicating the emergence of a narrative time distinct from the time of speech and perception, and referred to at least two of the three plot components. Nine-year-olds' narratives had complete episodic structures and made reference to upcoming and previous events, showing a transition from temporal-causal to thematic organization. Evaluations in terms of character intentionality that bind plot advancing events evidenced clear differentiation of the narrative and the discourse temporal axes (Aksu-Koç and von Stutterheim 1994). Adult narratives, on the other hand, were thematically organized, included elaborated background circumstances and evaluations, and were expressed in rhetorical style, displaying a global organization around a unified action structure (Berman and Slobin 1994).

Other studies of fictional stories generated with pictorial stimuli point to similar developmental milestones. Five-year-olds' narratives contain more story grammar elements than narratives of younger children. Six- to 7-year-olds include information on setting and characters, and provide evidence for the stabilization of the action structure. Reference to characters' internal states to connect the chronologically ordered events into a goal-directed thematic whole is observed around 8–9 years of age. Referential relations are marked to adapt to different audience conditions with shared vs. non-shared knowledge around 9–10 years, after which children's stories become complex, detailed and structurally coherent (Hickmann 2003; Hudson and Shapiro 1991; Kail and Hickmann 1992; Küntay 2002; Mäkinen 2014; Muñoz et al. 2003; Schneider, Hayward, and Dube 2006; Stein and Glenn, 1982, among others).

The developmental milestones for personal versus fictional narratives indicate that the pace and paths of development in the two genres are somewhat different. Comparisons of personal vs. fictional narratives show more developed levels of performance (e.g. presence of temporal sequence, anchor tense, more episodic components and evaluative comments) in personal than fictional stories before 9–10 years of age (Allen et al. 1994; Hudson and Shapiro 1991). Berman (1995), analyzing studies of narratives of different genres and elicitation techniques, observed that Hebrew-speaking preschool children who produced coherent personal narratives engaged in picture description when telling fictional stories. Shiro (2003) examined the use of evaluations by school age children and found that younger children and children from low socio-economic backgrounds were at a disadvantage when performing fictional than personal narratives. Such differences suggest that children are developing major genre-specific narrative skills early on (Nyhout and O'Neill 2013; Sénéchal et al. 2008; Ucelli et al. 2006). The evidence that progress in the two genres follow different routes at different paces has raised the question of whether one is developmentally prior to the other. Hudson and Shapiro (1991) have argued that accounts of personal experiences which may be first in the form of scripts or descriptive sequences are transformed into stories organized episodically at some point. In this view, personal narratives are one source for the development of story schemas proposed by story grammars. Ervin-Tripp and Küntay's (1997) analysis of personal narratives of 4;6 year olds occasioned by different circumstances in a preschool setting is informative for episodic-structuration-in-the-making in that all included some (if not all) components of a developing narrative organization (a topic, orientation, complicating action, resolution and coda) depending on the adult's probing and conversational scaffolding.

Another line of development proposed to contribute to narrative competence is play (Engels 2005; Feldman 2005; Nelson 1996; Nicolopoulou 1997; Paley 1990; Ucelli et al. 2005). Ucelli et al. (2005) point to early mother-child talk in contexts of fantasy play as a foundation for later fictional narratives. Nicolopoulou (1997) argues that by engaging in the symbolic activities of narrative and play, children actively appropriate the narrative forms and narrative contents that pre-exist in the cultural context. The hypothesis that enacted play narratives promote discursive narratives is based on several premises. Pretense play, just like narratives, requires an organization of events around a plot. Both require operating in the representational medium; however, action is the defining feature of pretense play before it is fully representational (Feldman 2005; Perner 1991; Nelson 1996). Play, therefore, provides the actional context to facilitate plot construction by enabling its simultaneous expression in action and verbalization (Paley 1990). Nicolopoulou (2009) provides evidence from her analyses of spontaneous fictional narratives generated and acted out every day within the preschool setting throughout the course of a year. Her findings indicate the power of this practice by revealing the genesis of gender-typed narratives (Nicolopoulou, Scales, and Weintraub 1994) and the evolution of the concept of character over time (Nicolopoulou and Richner, 2007). Further evidence for the connection between play and narrative comes from studies where 4-year-olds were observed to produce episodically organized fictional narratives in a play context with toys, but pre-episodic narratives in response to a direct verbal instruction to tell a story (Eckler and Weininger 1989; Ilgaz and Aksu-Koç 2005). Such findings support the view that action and objects scaffold both the conceptual organization of the narrative and its expression, and that play provides a second route for the construction of story schemata yielding episodically structured narratives.

To sum up, children start with proto-narratives about personally experienced past events around 2- to 3-years (Miller and Sperry, 1988) and become able to produce different types of episodic compositions that include evaluative as well as referential components by 5- to 6-years of age. Pace of development is slower for fictional narratives where the major development at this age is the temporal-causal episodic organization of events. Narratives with evaluative references to character intentionality are not fully observed before 7- to 8-years. The developmental dip reflected by shorter narratives of a stereotyped format that mention fewer story events observed around 9–10 years (Bamberg 1987; Berman and Slobin 1994; Mäkinen et al.

2014; McCabe and Peterson 1991; Schneider et al. 2006), and explained by Karmiloff-Smith (1981b) with the proposal that 9- to 10-year-olds engage in top-down processing guided by a story schema that has been internalized, can be taken to indicate a basic level of completion of narrative structuration. Skill in producing coherent narratives with a global level organization, however, continues to develop until late childhood and adolescence (Berman and Slobin 1994; Hickmann 2003).

3.3 Linguistic knowledge and narrative cohesion: Microstructure

Developments in macrostructure and microstructure are intertwined; changes in narrative function, semantic content and syntactic context of a form occur concurrently with changes in narrative structure (Berman 2009). The important developments are twofold: increase in productivity and syntactic complexity, and change in form-function relations.

3.3.1 Productivity and syntactic complexity

Recent research with clinical interests has focused on determining indicators of narrative development, both linguistic and structural. The linguistic skills entailed in narrative competence have been identified as two relatively independent dimensions, productivity and syntactic complexity. Productivity is typically measured by two indicators, narrative length and lexical diversity. Length is measured by *number of clauses* and by *number of communicative units* [*C-Unit* (Loban 1976) or *terminal unit, T-Unit* (Hunt 1970)] defined as an independent clause and all its associated modifiers including subordinate clauses. Lexical diversity is measured by *number of different words* (*types*). The best indicators of syntactic complexity are found to be *mean length of C-units, subordinate clause types* (e.g. adverbial, relative, complement) and *clausal density* (mean number of subordinate clauses per C-unit) (Bishop & Donlan 2005; Craig, Washington, and Thompson-Porter 1998; Gillam and Johnston 1992; Heilmann et al. 2010; Justice et al. 2006; Liles et al. 1995; Mäkinen et al. 2014; McFadden and Gillam 1996). It is generally agreed that syntactic complexity captures both age differences and differences between typically developing and developmentally delayed children whereas productivity measures do not always do so. Number of C-units and word tokens are not very informative since with age, children package more information into a C-unit, which results in a decrease in the number of C-units (or main clauses) and an increase in clausal density (Aksu-Koç 1994; Aksu-Koç 2005; Mäkinen et al. 2014), resulting in shorter but more coherently organized and cohesively expressed narratives.

As almost every study of narrative development has shown, productivity and syntactic complexity increase with age. Five-year-olds' narratives differ from younger and older children's, displaying a transitional picture, and significant changes in these dimensions are observed between 5- to 9-years of age (Bamberg 1987; Berman and Slobin 1994; Bishop and Donlan 2005; Johnston 2008; Justice et al. 2006; Peterson and McCabe 1983). Since quantitative measures of productivity and complexity, while necessary, are not sufficient indicators of the well-formedness of a narrative, research has focused on the relations between these indices of expressive skills and macro-structural changes. Findings variously demonstrate that increases in productivity and complexity are correlated with increases in the number of episodic components children incorporate in their stories (Allen et al. 1994; Bishop and Donlan 2006; Fernandez 2013; Heilmann et al. 2010; McFadden and Gillam 1996; Muñoz et al. 2003; Pearce, McCormack, and James 2003). The relations between linguistic and macro-structural variables change with age, however. Heilmann et al. (2010) who found lexical diversity to be the most robust predictor of narrative organization skills for 5- to 7-year-olds proposed that the significant factor for older children 7- to 9-years of age may, however, be syntax. Mäkinen et al. (2014) who found lexical diversity to be the only measure that predicted informativeness of story content for Finnish 4- to 8-year-olds concluded that this is a useful measure of semantic skills as well as productivity. Indeed, in agglutinating languages such as Finnish and Turkish where derivational morphology carries both a syntactic and a semantic load, lexical diversity should be taken as a measure of not only productivity or semantic skills, but also of syntactic complexity.

Strong evidence for the relationship between productivity, syntactic complexity and sophistication of episodic structuring is provided by Liles et al. (1995) who demonstrated that measures of linguistic structure (grammatical use of subordinate clauses, productivity within subordinate clauses) and measures of episodic structure (proportion of episodic components expressed over total number of episodes) obtained from narratives of 7- to 12-year olds loaded on two different factors, indicating independent dimensions. However, the percentage of complete cohesive ties (realized by subordinating structures) was shared by both factors, in line with the view that intersentential cohesion and episode organization overlap. This brings us to a consideration of the development of form-function relations through use of cohesive devices in children's texts.

3.3.2 Relations between linguistic form – discourse function

Cohesion is the qualitative perspective from which relations between narrative structure and microstructural features are examined. Cohesion refers to the degree to which the propositions and character references within a narrative are linguistically connected and information flow across utterances is regulated (Halliday and Hasan 1976; Hickmann 2003; Shapiro and Hudson 1991). The most studied cohesive mechanisms in children's narratives are the use of conjunctions for temporal and causal *connectivity*, which we take up below, and the use of noun phrases, pronouns and ellipsis for *referentiality*, which we discuss under section 3.4.[2]

Berman and Slobin (1994; Berman 2009) documented the close relationship between children's narrative organization skills and advances in their use of grammatical forms (e.g., verb tense, aspect, and voice) and complex syntactic structures (coordinating and subordinating constructions), demonstrating that developments in the use of cohesive devices involves changing relations between linguistic form and discourse function. With age, old forms assume new functions while concurrently new forms are recruited to meet old functions (Slobin 1973). This is most clearly explained by Berman (2009) with an example concerning the changing uses of the conjunction *and* characterized in terms of its position in the utterance, its discourse function and the intention it expresses. In the narratives of 3- and 4-year-olds *and* is used utterance initially, its function is to announce that the narrator has more to say in the same conversational turn, and the intention signaled is 'I have more to say'. In the narratives of 5- and 6-year-olds the position is also clause initial, however the function is to chain events in chronological sequence, and the intention is 'something else / more happened'. In the narratives of 9- and 10-year-olds *and* is text embedded, functions to chunk within a given discourse topic, and the intention conveyed is 'the events or states are related' (Berman 2009: 357–358). The following two examples from the Turkish frog stories (in English translation, Aksu-Koç 1994: 367) illustrate this with the changing use of the temporal adverb *then/later*. In (1) '*Later the boy looks upon waking up, the frog is not there*', '*later/then*' is used to sequence two events in chronological order by a 5-year-old, while in (2) '*Later on, calling the bees he asked their help in order to find his frog*' the same adverb is used by a 9-year-old to link a local event to the general theme, the search for the frog.

Research on the expression of connectivity in children's narratives displays a similar sequence across languages. Three-year-olds who typically produce descriptive sequences with no action structure chain utterances in discourse by use of parallel syntactic constructions in successive clauses and the additive connective '*and*' (Bennett-Kastor 1986; Berman and Slobin 1994; Jisa 1987; Shapiro and Hudson 1991; Peterson and McCabe 1988). By age 5–7, children who can impose a linear organization on events and maintain an anchor tense use temporal adverbs of sequence and simultaneity, causal conjunctions and complement clauses for connectivity, however, mainly at the local level between adjacent utterances (Aksu-Koç and von Stutterheim, 1994; Fernandez 2013; Silva 1991). The expressive devices used by 9- to 10-year-olds are not more diverse but are applied to new functions based on changes in discourse structure. Temporal adverbs used previously to relate successive events, now mark episode boundaries while events within episodes are related

---

[2] Both connectivity and referentiality are discussed with language specific analyses in the individual chapters on English, German, Spanish, Hebrew and Turkish in Berman and Slobin (1994). Here we summarize the overall patterns.

with adverbial and complement clauses (Aksu-Koç and von Stutterheim 1994; Bamberg and Marchman 1991; Berman and Slobin 1994; Vion and Colas 2004, 2005). This means that by using subordination, children can package several related events into syntactically larger units or chunks that are then related with adverbs of sequence or simultaneity at episode boundaries. With increasing awareness of the information needs of the listener, connectives get to be used effectively for background – foreground distinctions (Aksu-Koç and von Stutterheim 1994; Berman and Slobin 1994; Silva 1991). Thus, older children use expressive devices to effect cohesion not only at the intersentential level but across the text, at the thematic level. Adult texts, in addition, show novel narrative organizational functions such as retrospection, prospection, generalizing, summarizing, and rhetorical effects, realized with already available forms (Berman and Slobin 1994).

These developments at the interface of linguistic knowledge and narrative structure demonstrate that what leads to mature narrative competence involves changes in how linguistic forms are deployed for emerging discourse functions, and that changing form-function relations are informative indicators in addition to quantitative measures of syntactic complexity.

3.4 Pragmatic skills and communicative adequacy

Communicative adequacy requires that the narrator conveys the intended information in a way that is easily understood and tracked by the listener. This is achieved by the clear specification of who is doing what, where and when at the *referential* level and why the events are happening the way they do at the *evaluative* level. While referentiality is an important mechanism of text cohesion, evaluations are necessary for text coherence. In terms of their cognitive prerequisites both rest on developments in social cognition, in particular, on the understanding of other minds, be it the listener's or a character's in the story. The research in both domains show that requirements of communicative adequacy in narrative discourse is multidimensional, and competence shows gradual development. We first consider developments in referentiality and then advances in the evaluative function.

3.4.1 Referentiality

Studies of reference in children's narratives examine how characters are *introduced* as new participants in the story, *reintroduced* as participants previously referred to but brought back to focus after intervening discourse, and *maintained* as characters whose identities can be presupposed. These discourse functions require that *new* information is encoded with indefinite constructions, *given* information is encoded with forms high in specificity such as definite nominals, and *presupposed* information with pronouns, either overt or null (Gundel, Hedberg, and Zacharski 1993). In making their referential choices, children need to distinguish between new, given, and presupposed information, update the changing informational status of characters in their mental model of the story as it unfolds, track the changes in the listener's evolving mental model, and map appropriate linguistic forms onto the appropriate discourse functions. Furthermore, they need to use referential devices cohesively not only between utterances but also across the text (Berman, 2009; Hickmann 2003; Johnston 2008; Wong and Johnston 2004). In short, reference in narrative is a cognitively complex function with demands on working memory and perspective taking abilities.

The cognitive prerequisites of referential communication (e.g., joint attention, pointing, awareness of common ground and intention reading) emerge at the end of the first year of life and children show sensitivity to different discourse-pragmatic factors from 2 years onwards (Graf and Davies 2014). The basic referential devices (e.g. determiners, noun phrases, pronouns, nominal ellipsis) have been acquired by age 3 and are used with pragmatic skill at the sentence level in conversational discourse (Miller and Sperry 1988; Rozendaal and Baker 2008; Serratrice 2005; Slobin and Talay 1986, among others) and in early personal narratives (Peterson and Dodsworth 1991; Peterson 1993). These are, however, interactive pieces of discourse where cohesive ties hold between adult-child utterances. Even in their first person narratives children have difficulty in making clear reference, and a lot of ambiguity gets resolved through adult questioning and scaffolding in the context of social interaction (Berman 2009).

Findings from crosslinguistic research converge on the fact that learning to make adequate reference in narrative discourse is a protracted process. For character introduction young children prefer definite forms (Aksu-Koç and Nicolopoulou 2015; Hickman, Kail, and Roland 1996; Kail and Hickmann, 1992). The use of indefinites becomes moderately frequent around 7 years and reaches a consistently high rate as that of adults around 9 to 10 years of age (Hickmann, Kail, and Roland 1996; Kail and Hickmann 1992; Karmiloff-Smith 1981a, 1981b; Küntay 2002; Warden 1981). For the reintroduction function, definite nominals start to be used around 4 years, and increase gradually until age 10. Use of pronominals (overt or null) for character maintenance, on the other hand, is an earlier development, observed at a high rate at all ages (Aksu-Koç and Nicolopoulou 2015; Hickmann and Hendriks 1999; Wong and Johnston 2004; Stephany 1998).

The changes in children's referential strategies are not independent of the changes in their narrative organizational skills. For 3- to 4-year-olds, reference is initially exophoric, pronominal forms are used deictically without any attention to mutual knowledge with the listener. Shift to the discourse internal anaphoric strategy is observed once events get to be sequentially ordered on the temporal axis of narrative around 5 years of age (Berman 2009; Karmiloff-Smith 1981a). However, the tendency to assume mutual knowledge appears to have persistent effects in case of the introduction function. As Kail and Hickmann (1992) note, only 9-year-olds differentiate the situations of shared vs. nonshared knowledge systematically, while younger children use deixis in both cases (Hickmann et al. 1996; Serratrice 2008; Warden 1981).

This developmental trajectory – maintenance first, reintroduction next, and introduction last – has been confirmed by studies in English (Wigglesworth 1990); English, French and German (Hickmann et al. 1996; Hickmann and Hendriks 1999), Italian (Orsolini, Rossi, and Pontecorvo 1996), French (Vion and Colas 1999), Hebrew (Berman and Katzenberger 1998), Turkish (Küntay 2002), Mandarin (Wong and Johnston 2004) and English, Greek and Turkish (Aksu-Koç and Nicolopoulou 2015). However, the pace of development of the form-function relations varies depending on language typology. This is so particularly for the introduction function. Hickmann et al.'s (1996) comparison of English, German, French and Mandarin, and Aksu-Koç and Nicolopoulou's (2015) comparison of English, Greek and Turkish both show that character introductions with indefinite nominals is delayed in Mandarin and Turkish, languages that rely on an optional indefinite marker and global indicators (e.g., word order, case) for the definite-indefinite distinction. Greek, German and French, on the other hand, have grammaticized determiners that agree with nouns, providing morphologically rich local cues that help entrench the definite – indefinite distinction and its function appropriate marking at an earlier age.

There are a number of methodological factors that influence children's referential performance which are informative about the cognitive and processing demands of narrative construction. One of these factors concerns the number of characters in the story (Aksu-Koç and Nicolopoulou 2015; Berman and Katzenberg 1998; Vion and Colas 1999). The presence of a main character, that is, a 'thematic subject' (Karmiloff-Smith 1981b) affects how children use referential forms. In English, French and German, young preschoolers restrict subject pronouns for this referent, organizing their entire narrative around it while using nominals for other characters (Hickmann et al. 1996: Bamberg 1987). Turkish children, on the other hand, reserve the sentence initial subject position for the main character (Aksu-Koç and Tekdemir 2004; Aksu-Koç and Nicolopoulou 2015). The thematic subject strategy provides an external grip on the action structure, but at the expense of linguistic clarity, and may be regarded to be a result of competition for working memory resources between different domains such as conceptual and linguistic structure (Colozzo et al. 2011; Justice et al. 2006; Gillam and Johnston 1992). Another effect of the number of characters on referential choice is seen in the use of forms higher in specificity when there are two main characters in the story. Preschoolers tend to use more nominals than pronominals in two main character compared to one main character stories (Aksu-Koç and Nicolopoulou 2015; Berman and Katzenberger 1998; Serattrice 2008), suggesting the need to be more explicit in the presence of two characters even in contexts when reference would not necessarily be ambiguous. The same phenomena has been observed in adults by Arnold and Griffin (2007) who argue that speaker-internal processes such as competition for attentional resources in the speaker's representation of the discourse may be operative, and by Rosa and Arnold (2011) who provide evidence that speakers first monitor their own mental processes rather than respond to the listeners' needs. As noted above, uses of new information markers are differentiated as a function of mutual knowledge around age 9 (Kail and Hickmann 1992). This late development has been commonly explained by younger children's inability to take into account the informational perspective of the listener. The above findings suggest that this inability may also be explained by the limitations of working memory resources on the child's own representation of discourse.

A second methodological factor concerns the nature of elicitation conditions. Schneider and Dubé (1997, 2005) report that kindergartners in their study displayed a higher level of referential adequacy when retelling orally presented stories than when formulating stories from pictures alone, whereas 7- to 8-year-olds performed equally in both conditions. Shapiro and Hudson (1991) observed that picture sequences incorporating a well-formed story structure with an embedded problem generated more coherently organized and cohesively expressed narratives compared to pictures portraying typical but uneventful events. On the other hand, comparison of retellings by 7- to 11- year-olds of orally presented stories coupled with pictures or a video-clip with those generated on the basis of pictures or a story stem alone has shown similar organizational structures (Berman 1995; Liles 1993). These findings indicate that providing linguistic and/or episodic support reduces task demands in children's referential performance in storytelling and that such support is particularly important for younger children.

Overall, the research on referentiality in narrative indicates that in addition to age and social-cognitive maturity, the structural properties of the referential system of the language being acquired, the structure of the stimuli used to elicit the stories, and the conditions of elicitation play a determining role on the pace of achievement of communicative adequacy in this domain.

3.4.2 The evaluative function

Evaluations contribute to the coherence and communicative adequacy of a narrative by specifying the reasons for the events and their outcomes in terms of the intentional, emotional and belief states of the protagonists, thus rendering them meaningful.

Evaluations are conceptually complex because they require different levels of perspective shifting. As noted in section 2, in personal narratives the child's perspective as the narrator is spatio-temporally displaced from his perspective as an actor in the narrative world. In fictional narratives, in addition to spatio-temporal displacement, the represented perspective of the story character is displaced from the representing perspective of the child as a narrator (Shiro 2003). This requires the capacity for meta-representation, a social-cognitive skill at the core of theory of mind functioning manifest around 4–5 years of age when children coordinate different perspectives and develop a concept of mental agent that enables them to grasp the causal links between reality, mental states and action (Astington and Baird 2005; Nelson 1996; Perner 1991; Tomasello, Kruger, and Ratner 1993). Evaluations are linguistically complex because they are expressed with complement clauses, the necessary syntactic structures for the use of mental state verbs, and with subordinate clauses that are functional in presenting inferred psychological causes. Evidence from research shows gradual growth over the preschool years for the use of these verbs and sentential constructions (Astington and Jenkins 1999; Bartsch and Wellman 1995; Bishop and Donlan 2005; de Villiers 2007; Tager-Flusberg 1997). In short, the underpinnings of the evaluative function in narrative are complex and require an integration of narrative schemas, linguistic schemas and mindreading skills.

Among the indicators analyzed for the evaluative function are references to frames of mind (mental state and emotion terms), character speech (representing events from the character's perspective), hedges on the truth value of assertions, negative qualifiers, causal connectors, onomatopoeia and paralinguistic indicators such as facial expressions, gesture, prosody and stress (Bamberg and Damrad-Frye 1991; Bamberg & Reilly 1996; Küntay and Nakamura 2004). Earliest evaluations have been reported from conversational personal narratives of 2- to 3-year-olds and comprise emotional terms and intensifiers (Miller and Sperry 1988; Umiker-Sebeok 1979). Types of evaluative devices increase with age, showing a wide variety between 4–9 years and a shift from use of character speech at younger ages to explanations by reference to mental states around 5- to 6-years (Chang 2004; Ely and McCabe 1993; Peterson and McCabe 1983; Peterson and Biggs 2001). Analyses of generated fictional narratives such as the 'frog story' in English (Bamberg and Damrad-Frye 1991), Hebrew (Berman and Slobin 1994), Japanese and Turkish (Küntay and Nakamura 2004), Japanese (Nakamura 2009), Colombian Spanish (Fernandez 2013), Walpiri (Bavin 2009) and African American English (Curenton 2011; Curenton and Justice 2004) as well as other fictional narratives (Capps, Losh, and Thurber 2000; Eaton, Collis, and Lewis 1999; Norbury and Bishop 2002; Shapiro and Hudson 1991; Shiro 2003) show a similar developmental trend, though at a slower pace. Overall, it has been observed that 3-year-olds scarcely make any evaluations while 4- and 5-year-olds prefer character speech and occasionally use other evaluative types. Between 7–9 years of age, mental and emotional state words reflecting frames of mind, enrichment expressions and hedges increase in frequency, approaching the pattern displayed by adults. Cultural practices and language specific rhetorical styles have also been found to play a role in this developmental course.

As noted above, the (relatively) late emergence of the evaluative function in fictional narratives has been explained by reference to developments in theory of mind. The social-interactional processes discussed in section 3.1 provide the context of development in this domain as well. Early parental talk elaborating causal and contrastive information about mental states, story-telling, story-reading and conversations with peers, all contribute to understanding others as mental agents (Astington and Baird 2005; Guajardo and Watson 2002; Nelson 2005; Nicolopoulou and Richner 2007; Ratner and Olver 1998; Slaughter, Peterson, and Mckintosh 2007; Symons et al. 2005). Developments in theory of mind, in turn, contribute to narrative skills; after 4 years when ToM skills improve, children's ability to integrate reference to internal states into the action structure of their narratives also improves (Astington and Jenkins 1999; Pelletier and Astington 2004; Wellman and Bartsch 1988). The evidence suggesting both directions of causality indicates that these relations are bidirectional, with direction of influence shifting at different points in development.

Since by age 5 children have developed an understanding of how the mind works, other explanatory factors need to be considered for the low level of reference to intentional, emotional and belief states by 5- and even 7-year-olds. Studies of language impaired children point to processing factors that constrain children's use of syntactic schemas in coordination with story schemas (Bishop and Donlan 2005; Botting 2002; Capps, Losh, and Thurber 2000; Colozzo et al. 2011; Johnston 2008; Justice et al. 2006; Miranda, McCabe, and Bliss 1998; Norbury and Bishop 2002). Studies of typically developing children provide similar evidence. Kindergarteners presented with short wordless videos for story generation (Eaton, Collis, and Lewis 1999) and low-income 8-year-olds presented with oral stories for retelling (Aksu-Koç 2005) were found to offer more evaluative explanations when prompted with questions about character mental states as compared to when they were just asked to tell the story. Such findings indicate that children may have an understanding of the epistemic states of characters but may not readily be able to express them linguistically, either because they are not aware how crucial it is to report them, or due to a competition for working memory between efforts to formulate complex syntax and to maintain a coherent action structure. Evidence from even older children shows that use of mindreading skills may be undermined when the psychological states binding the events of the action structure are too complex, increasing the demands on narrative skills. Both Aksu-Koç and Tekdemir (2004) and Veneziano, Albert, and Martin (2009) observed that even if they had already achieved false belief understanding, 6- to 9-year-olds tended to avoid reference to the false-belief problems embedded in the picture sequences used as elicitation materials while they succeeded in advancing the plotline with a coherent flow of events. Authors of both studies reasoned that the children did not spontaneously take on a mind-oriented approach in storytelling possibly because the task of story construction used up a lot of cognitive and linguistic resources, limiting the ability to apprehend and/or express epistemic states.

In summary, developments in the ability to integrate evaluative statements into event schemas in terms of cause-effect relations gain pace after age 5. This ability is at first closely tied to local relations, but with increasing skill in decontextualization, the eventive and the evaluative components get rearranged hierarchically, relating to the global theme of the narrative (Bamberg and Damrad-Frye 1991). Results of the fine grained qualitative analyses in this body of research finds a most succinct summary in Shiro's (2003) observations that mere frequency of evaluative expressions does not ensure the quality of the narrative, not all kinds of evaluative expressions are equally effective, and evaluatives contribute to narrative coherence only when they combine with referential clauses, making clear reference to cause-effect relations to indicate how motives affect actions.

4 Conclusion

In this overview we focused on the developmental trajectories documented by research for the three major components of narrative competence, conceptual-structural, linguistic-functional and pragmatic-communicative. Evidence showed that personal narratives develop earlier than fictional narratives, and that the two genres follow somewhat different pathways and progress at different paces. However, around 5–7 years children display competence in producing episodically composed narratives and begin to provide a meaningful intentional structure that relates the constitutive events to one another and to a global theme. The integrated use of cognitive, linguistic and theory of mind skills necessary for conceptual coherence, linguistic cohesion and pragmatic adequacy is achieved through a gradual process that extends well into school years, with all nuances not fully stabilized even then.

When clinical concerns are at issue, the use of narrative analysis to evaluate individual children's level of competence is necessary but needs special care. We observed that typically developing children display differences in performance stemming from differences in language typology, genre, method of elicitation and framework of analysis. These differences indicate that children's narrative competence needs to be assessed from multiple perspectives, using different tasks. Research of the last two decades is abundant with evidence showing that depending on the type of impairment, one or the other of the knowledge schemes fall short, revealing trade-offs between conceptual, linguistic and pragmatic complexity due to constraints in processing capacity and socio-cognitive skills. Course of development in typically developing children is informative about which component skills may be vulnerable to deviance or delay. Knowledge of what aspects of the system are acquired at roughly what age is informative about what is easy versus complex and gives a baseline for expectations, a standard for comparison and guidelines for intervention.

References

Aksu-Koç, Ayhan. 1994. Development of linguistic forms: Turkish. In Ruth A. Berman & Dan I. Slobin (eds.), *Relating events in narrative: A crosslinguistic developmental study*, 329–385. Hillsdale, New Jersey: Lawrence Erlbaum.

Aksu-Koç, Ayhan. 2005. Role of the home-context in the relations between narrative abilities and literacy practices. Dorit Ravid & H. Bat-Zeev Shyldkrot (eds.), *Perspectives on language and language development*, 259–278. Dordrecht: Kluwer.

Aksu-Koç, Ayhan & Christiane von Stutterheim. 1994. Temporal relations in narrative: Simultaneity. In Ruth A. Berman & Dan I. Slobin (eds.), *Relating events in narrative: A crosslinguistic developmental study*, 393–455. Hillsdale, New Jersey: Lawrence Erlbaum.

Aksu-Koç, Ayhan & Aylin Küntay. 2002. Causal relations in memory for narrative discourse: Evidence from Turkish. Paper presented at the IX. International Congress for the Study of Child Language, University of Wisconsin, July 2002.

Aksu-Koç, Ayhan & Ageliki Nicolopoulou. 2015. Character reference in young children's narratives: A crosslinguistic comparison of English, Greek, and Turkish. *Lingua* 155, 62–84.

Aksu-Koç, Ayhan & Göklem Tekdemir. 2004. Interplay between narrativity and mindreading: A comparison between Turkish and English. In Sven Strömqvist & Ludo Verhoeven (eds.), *Relating events in narrative, volume 2: Typological and contextual perspectives*, 307–327. Mahwah, New Jersey: Lawrence Erlbaum.

Allen, Marybeth S., Marilyn K. Kertoy, John C. Sherblom & John M. Pettit. 1994. Children's narrative productions: A comparison of personal event and fictional stories. *Applied Psycholinguistics* 15(02), 149–176.

Arnold, Jeanne, E. & Zenzi M. Griffin. 2007. The effect of additional characters on choice of referring expression: Everyone counts. *Journal of Memory and Language* 56(4), 521–536.

Astington, Janet W. & Jodie A. Baird. 2005. Why language matters for theory of mind. In Janet W. Astington & Jodie A. Baird (eds.), *Why language matters for Theory of Mind*, 3–25. Oxford: Oxford University Press.

Astington, Janet W. & Jennifer M. Jenkins. 1999. A longitudinal study of the relation between language and theory-of-mind development. *Developmental Psychology* 35(5), 1311–1320.

Bamberg, Michael. 1987. *The acquisition of narratives: Learning to use language*. Vol. 49. Walter de Gruyter.

Bamberg, Michael. 1997. *Narrative development: Six approaches*. Mahwah, New Jersey: Lawrence Erlbaum.

Bamberg, Michael & Robin Damrad-Frye. 1991. On the ability to provide evaluative comments: Further explorations of children's narrative competencies. *Journal of Child Language* 18(03), 689–710.

Bamberg, Michael & Virginia Marchman. 1991. Binding and unfolding: Towards the linguistic construction of narrative discourse. *Discourse Processes* 14(3), 277–305.

Bamberg, Michael & Judy Reilly. 1996. Of emotion, narrative, and affect: How children discover the relationship between what to say and how to say it. In Dan I. Slobin, Julie Gerhardt, Amy Kyratzis and Jiansheng Guo (eds.), *Social interaction, social context, and language: Essays in honor of Susan Ervin-Tripp*, 329–342. New York/London: Psychology Press.

Bartsch, Karen & Henry M. Wellman. 1995. *Children talk about the mind*. Oxford: Oxford University Press.

Bavin, Edith. 2009. Plot and evaluation: Walpiri children's Frog stories. In Jiansheng Guo, Elena Lieven, Nancy Budwig, Susan Ervin-Tripp, Keiko Nakamura, and Seyda Ozcaliskan (eds.), *Crosslinguistic approaches to the psychology of language: Research in the tradition of Dan Isaac Slobin*, 137–147. New York/London: Psychology Press.

Bennett-Kastor, Tina L. 1986. Cohesion and predication in child narrative. *Journal of Child Language* 13(02), 353–370.

Benson, Margaret S. 1993. The structure of four-and five-year-olds' narratives in pretend play and storytelling. *First Language* 13(38), 203–223.

Berman, Ruth A. 1995. Narrative competence and storytelling performance: How children tell stories in different contexts. *Journal of Narrative and Life History* 5(4), 285–313.

Berman, Ruth A. 2009. Language development in narrative contexts. In Edith Bavin (ed.), *Cambridge handbook of child language*, 354–75. Cambridge: Cambridge University Press.

Berman, Ruth A. & Dan I. Slobin. 1994. Narrative structure. In Ruth A. Berman & Dan I. Slobin (eds.) *Relating events in narrative: A crosslinguistic developmental study*, 39–84. Hillsdale, New Jersey: Lawrence Erlbaum.

Berman, Ruth A. & Irit Katzenberg. 1998. Cognitive and linguistic factors in the development of picture-series narration. *Studi Italiana di Linguistica Teorica ed Applicata* 27, 21–46.

Bishop, Dorothy & Chris Donlan. 2005. The role of syntax in encoding and recall of pictorial narratives: Evidence from specific language impairment. *British Journal of Developmental Psychology* 23(1), 25–46.

Blum-Kulka, Shoshana & Catherine E. Snow. 2002. *Talking to adults: The contribution of multiparty discourse to language acquisition*. Mahwah, New Jersey: Psychology Press.

Botting, Nicola. 2002. Narrative as a tool for the assessment of linguistic and pragmatic impairments. *Child Language Teaching and Therapy* 18, 1–21.

Botting, Nicola, Brian Faragher, Zoe Simkin, Emma Knox & Gina Conti-Ramsden. 2001. Predicting pathways of specific language impairment: what differentiates good and poor outcome? *Journal of Child Psychology and Psychiatry* 42(08), 1013–1020.

Bruner, Jerome S. 1986. *Actual minds, possible worlds*. Cambridge, MA: Harvard University Press.

Bruner, Jerome S. 1990. *Acts of meaning*. Cambridge, MA: Harvard University Press.

Bus, Adriana G., Marinus H. van Ijzendoorn & Anthony D. Pellegrini. 1995. Joint book reading makes for success in learning to read: A meta-analysis on intergenerational transmission of literacy. *Review of Educational Research* 65(1), 1–21.

Capps, Lisa, Molly Losh & Christopher Thurber. 2000. The frog ate the bug and made his mouth sad: Narrative competence in children with autism. *Journal of Abnormal Child Psychology* 28(2), 193–204.

Carmiol, Ana M. & Alison Sparks. 2014. Narrative development across cultural contexts. In Danielle Matthews (ed.), *Pragmatic development in first language acquisition. Trends in language acquisition re*search 10, 279–293.

Chang, Chien-Ju. 2004. Telling stories of experiences: Narrative development of young Chinese children. *Applied Psycholinguistics* 25(01), 83–104.

Colozzo, Paolo, Ronald B. Gillam, Megan Wood, Rebecca D. Schnell & Judith R. Johnston. 2011. Content and form in the narratives of children with Specific Language Impairment. *Journal of Speech, Language and Hearing Research* 54(6), 1609-1627.

Craig, Holly K., Julie A. Washington & Connie Thompson-Porter. 1998. Average C-unit lengths in the discourse of African American children from low-income urban homes. *Journal of Speech, Language, and Hearing Research* 41(2), 433–444.

Curenton, Stephanie M. 2011. Understanding the landscapes of stories: The association between preschoolers' narrative comprehension and production skills and cognitive abilities. *Early Child Development and Care* 181(6), 791–808.

Curenton, Stephanie M. & Laura M. Justice. 2004. African American and Caucasian preschoolers' use of decontextualized language: Literate language features in oral narratives. *Language, Speech, and Hearing Services in Schools* 35(3), 240–253.

de Villiers, Jill. 2007. The interface of language and theory of mind. *Lingua* 117(11), 1858–1878.

Dickinson, David K. & Patton O. Tabors. 2001. *Beginning literacy with language: Young children learning at home and school*. Baltimore, MD: Paul H. Brookes.

Eaton, Judy H., Glyn M. Collis & Vicky A. Lewis. 1999. Evaluative explanations in children's narratives of a video sequence without dialogue. *Journal of Child Language* 26(03), 699–720.

Eckler, Judith A. & Otto Weininger. 1989. Structural parallels between pretend play and narratives. *Developmental Psychology* 25(5), 736–743.

Eisenberg, Ann. 1985. Learning to describe the past. *Discourse Processes* 8, 177–204.

Eisenberg, Sarita L., Teresa A. Ukrainetz, Jennifer R. Hsu, Joan N. Kaderavek, Laura M. Justice & Ronald B. Gillam. 2008. Noun phrase elaboration in children's spoken stories. *Language, Speech, and Hearing Services in Schools* 39(2), 145–157.

Ely, Richard & Allyssa McCabe. 1993. Remembered voices. *Journal of Child Language* 20(03), 671–696.

Engel, Susan. 2005. The narrative worlds of *what is* and *what if*. *Cognitive Development* 20(4), 514–525.

Ervin-Tripp, Susan M. & Aylin Küntay. 1997. The occasioning and structure of conversational stories. *Typological Studies in Language* 34, 133–166.

Feldman, Carol F. 2005. Mimesis: Where play and narrative meet. *Cognitive Development* 20(4), 503–513.

Fernández, Camila. 2013. Mindful storytellers: Emerging pragmatics and theory of mind development. *First Language* 33(1), 20–46.

Fivush, Robyn. 1991. The social construction of personal narratives. *Merrill-Palmer Quarterly* 37, 59–81.

Fivush, Robyn & Fayne A. Fromhoff. 1988. Style and structure in mother-child conversations about the past. *Discourse Processes* 11(3), 337–355.

Gagarina, Natalia, Daleen Klop, Sari Kunnari, Koula Tantele, Taina Välimaa, Ingrida Balčiūnienė, Ute Bohnacker & Joel Walters. 2012. MAIN: Multilingual Assessment Instrument for Narratives. ZASPiL Nr. 56. Berlin.

Gillam, Ronald B. & Judith R. Johnston. 1992. Spoken and written language relationships in language/learning-impaired and normally achieving school-age children. *Journal of Speech, Language, and Hearing Research* 35(6), 1303–1315.

Graf, Eileen, and Catherine Davies. 2014. The production and comprehension of referring expressions. In Danielle Matthews (ed.), *Pragmatic development in first language acquisition. Trends in language acquisition research* 10, 161–181. Amsterdam: John Benjamins.

Guajardo, Nicole R. & Anne C. Watson. 2002. Narrative discourse and theory of mind development. *The Journal of Genetic Psychology* 163(3), 305–325.

Gundel, Jeanette K., Nancy Hedberg & Ron Zacharski. 1993. Cognitive status and the form of referring expressions in discourse. *Language* 69, 274–307.

Haden, Catherine A., Elaine Reese & Robyn Fivush. 1996. Mothers' extratextual comments during storybook reading: Stylistic differences over time and across texts. *Discourse Processes* 21, 135–169.

Haden, Catherine A., Rachel A. Haine & Robyn Fivush. 1997. Developing narrative structure in parent–child reminiscing across the preschool years. *Developmental Psychology* 33(2), 295–07.

Halliday, Michael K. & Ruqaiya Hasan. 1976. *Cohesion in English*. London: Longman.

Harkins, D. A., Koch, P. E., & Michel, G. F. 1994. Listening to maternal story telling affects narrative skill of 5-year-old children. *Journal of Genetic Psychology* 155, 247–257.

Hart, Betty & Todd R. Risley. 1995. *Meaningful differences in the everyday experience of young American children*. Baltimore, MD: Paul H. Brookes.

Heath, Shirley B. 1982. What no bedtime story means: Narrative skills at home and school. *Language in Society* 11(01), 49–76.

Heilmann, John, John F. Miller, Ann Nockerts & Catherine Dunaway. 2010. Properties of the narrative scoring scheme using narrative retells in young school-age children. *American Journal of Speech-Language Pathology* 19(2), 154–166.

Hickmann, Maya. 2003. *Children's discourse: Person, space and time across languages* (Vol. 98). Cambridge: Cambridge University Press.

Hickmann, Maya, Henriëtte Hendriks, Françoise Roland & James Liang. 1996. The marking of new information in children's narratives: a comparison of English, French, German and Mandarin Chinese. *Journal of child language* 23(03), 591–619.

Hickmann, M., Michele Kail & Françoise Roland. 1996. Cohesive anaphoric relations in French children's narratives as a function of mutual knowledge. First language 15, 277–300.

Hickmann, Maya & Henriëtte Hendriks. 1999. Cohesion and anaphora in children's narratives: A comparison of English, French, German, and Mandarin Chinese. *Journal of Child Language* 26(02), 419–452.

Hudson, Judith. A. 1990. The emergence of autobiographic memory in mother–child conversation. In Robyn Fivush & Judith. A. Hudson (eds.), *Knowing and remembering in young children*, 166–196. New York: Cambridge University Press.

Hudson, Judith. A. & Lauran R. Shapiro. 1991. From knowing to telling: The development of children's scripts, stories, and personal narratives. In Allyssa McCabe & Carol Peterson (eds.), *Developing narrative structure*, 89–136. Hillsdale, NJ: Lawrence Erlbaum.

Hunt, Kellogg W. 1970. Syntactic maturity in schoolchildren and adults. *Monographs of the Society for Research in Child Development* 35(1), iii–67.

Ilgaz, Hande & Ayhan Aksu-Koç. 2005. Episodic development in preschool children's play-prompted and direct-elicited narratives. *Cognitive Development* 20(4), 526–544.

Jisa, Harriet. 1987. Sentence connectors in French children's monologue performance. *Journal of Pragmatics* 11(5), 607–621.

Johnston, Judith R. 2008. Narratives: Twenty-five years later. *Topics in Language Disorders* 28(2), 93–98.

Justice, Laura M., Sarah E. Weber, Helen K. Ezell & Roger Bakeman. 2002. A sequential analysis of children's responsiveness to parental print references during shared book-reading interactions. *American Journal of Speech-Language Pathology* 11(1), 30–40.

Justice, Laura M., Ryan P. Bowles, Joan N. Kaderavek, Teresa Ukrainetz, Sarita L. Eisenberg & Ronald B. Gillam. 2006. The index of narrative microstructure: A clinical tool for analyzing school-age children's narrative performances. *American Journal of Speech-Language Pathology* 15(2), 177–191.

Justice, Laura M., Joan N. Kaderavek, Xitao Fan, Amy Sofka & Aileen Hunt. 2009. Accelerating preschoolers' early literacy development through classroom-based teacher–child storybook reading and explicit print referencing. *Language, Speech, and Hearing Services in Schools* 40(1), 67–85.

Kail, Michele & Maya Hickmann. 1992. French children's ability to introduce referents in narratives as a function of mutual knowledge. *First Language* 12(34), 73–94.

Karmiloff-Smith, Annette. 1981a. *A functional approach to child language: A study of determiners and reference*. Vol. 24. Cambridge: Cambridge University Press.

Karmiloff-Smith, Annette. 1981b. The grammatical marking of thematic structure in the development of language production. In Werner Deutsch (ed.), *The child's construction of language*, 121–148. New York: Academic Press.

Küntay, Aylin C. 2002. Development of the expression of indefiniteness: Presenting new referents in Turkish picture-series stories. *Discourse Processes* 33(1), 77–101.

Küntay, Aylin C. & Keiko Nakamura. 2004. Linguistic strategies serving evaluative functions. A comparison between Japanese and Turkish narratives. In Sven Strömqvist & Ludo T. Verhoeven (eds.), *Relating events in narrative, volume 2: Typological and contextual perspectives*, 329–358. Mahwah, NJ: Lawrence Erlbaum.

Labov, William & Joshua Waletzky. 1967. Narrative analysis. Oral versions of personal experience. In June Helm (ed.) *Essays on the verbal and visual arts*, 12–44. Hillsdale, New Jersey: University of Washington Press.

Leyva, Diana, Elaine Reese, Wendy Grolnick & Carrie Price. 2009. Elaboration and autonomy support in low-income mothers' reminiscing: Links to children's autobiographical narratives. *Journal of Cognition and Development* 9(4), 363–389.

Liles, Betty Z. 1993. Narrative discourse in children with language disorders and children with normal language: A critical review of the literature. *Journal of Speech, Language, and Hearing Research* 36(5), 868–882.

Liles, Betty Z., Robert J. Duffy, Donna D. Merritt & Sherry L. Purcell. 1995. Measurement of narrative discourse ability in children with language disorders. *Journal of Speech, Language and Hearing Research* 38(2), 415–425.

Loban, Walter. 1976. Language development kindergarten through age twelve. Urbana, IL: National Council of Teachers of English.

Luo, Ya-Hui, Catherine E. Snow, and Chien-Ju Chang. 2011. Mother-child talk during joint book reading in low-income American and Taiwanese families. *First Language*, 1–18.

Mäkinen, Leanna, Soile Loukusa, Paivi Laukkanen, Eeva Leinonen & Sari Kunnari. 2014. Linguistic and pragmatic aspects of narration in Finnish typically developing children and children with specific language impairment. *Clinical Linguistics & Phonetics* 28(6), 413–427.

Mandler, Jean M. 1987. On the psychological reality of story structure. *Discourse Processes*, 10(1), 1–29.

Martinot, Claire. (2000). Etude comparative des processus de reformulation chez des enfants de 5 a 11 ans. *Langages* 140, 92–121.

Mayer, Mercer. 1969. *Frog, where are you?* New York: Dial Press.

McCabe, Allyssa, Lynn Bliss, Gabriela Barra & Maribeth Bennett. 2008. Comparison of personal versus fictional narratives of children with language impairment. *American Journal of Speech-Language Pathology* 17(2), 194–206.

McCabe, Allyssa, & Carole Peterson. 1991. *Developing narrative structure*. Hillsdale, NJ: Lawrence Erlbaum.

McFadden, Teresa U. & Ronald B. Gillam. 1996. An examination of the quality of narratives produced by children with language disorders. *Language, Speech, and Hearing Services in Schools* 27(1), 48–56.

McLean, Kate C. & Monisha Pasupathi. 2012. Processes of identity development: Where I am and how I got there. *Identity* 12(1), 8–28.

Merritt, Donna Disegna & Betty Z. Liles. 1987. Story grammar ability in children with and without language disorder: Story generation, story retelling, and story comprehension. *Journal of Speech, Language, and Hearing Research* 30(4), 539–552.

Michaels, Sarah. 1981. Sharing time: Children's narrative styles and differential access to literacy. *Language and Society* 10, 423–442.

Miller, Jon F., John Heilmann, J., Ann Nockerts, Aquiles Iglesias, Leah Fabiano & David J. Francis. 2006. Oral language and reading in bilingual children. *Learning Disabilities Research & Practice* 21(1), 30–43.

Miller, Peggy J. & Linda L. Sperry. 1988. Early talk about the past: The origins of conversational stories of personal experience. *Journal of Child Language* 15(02), 293–315.

Minami, Masahiko. 2002. *Culture-specific language styles: The development of oral narrative and literacy*. Published in the series 'Child language and child development', Clevendon: Multilingual Matters.

Minami, Masahiko & Allyssa McCabe. 1995. Rice balls and bear hunts: Japanese and North American family narrative patterns. *Journal of Child Language* 22(02), 423–445.

Miranda, A. Elisabeth, Allyssa McCabe, and Lynn S. Bliss. 1998. Jumping around and leaving things out: A profile of the narrative abilities of children with specific language impairment. *Applied Psycholinguistics* 19 (04), 647–667.

Mullen, Mary K. & Soonhyung Yi. 1995. The cultural context of talk about the past: Implications for the development of autobiographical memory. *Cognitive Development* 10(3), 407–419.

Muñoz, Maria L., Ronald B. Gillam, Elizabeth D. Peña, & Annette Gulley-Faehnle. 2003. Measures of language development in fictional narratives of Latino children. *Language, Speech, and Hearing Services in Schools* 34(4), 332–342.

Nakamura, Keiko. 2009. Language and affect: Japanese children'suse of evaluative expressions in narratives. In Jiansheng Guo, Elena Lieven, Nancy Budwig, Susan Ervin-Tripp, Keiko Nakamura, and Seyda Ozcaliskan (eds.), *Crosslinguistic approaches to the psychology of language: Research in the tradition of Dan Isaac Slobin*, 225–239. New York/London: Psychology Press.

Nelson, Katherine. 1996. *Language in cognitive development. The emergence of the mediated mind*. New York: Cambridge University Press.

Nelson, Katherine. 2005. Language pathways into the community of minds. In Janet W. Astington & Jodie A. Baird (eds.), *Why Language Matters for Theory of Mind*, 26–49. Oxford: Oxford University Press.

Nicolopoulou, Ageliki. 1997. Children and narratives: Toward an interpretive and sociocultural approach. In Michael Bamberg (ed.), *Narrative development: Six approaches*, 179–215. Mahwah, New Jersey: Lawrence Erlbaum.

Nicolopoulou, Ageliki. 2009. Rethinking character representation and its development in children's narratives. In Jiansheng Guo, Elena Lieven, Nancy Budwig, Susan Ervin-Tripp, Keiko Nakamura, and Seyda Ozcaliskan (eds.), *Crosslinguistic approaches to the psychology of language: Research in the tradition of Dan Isaac Slobin*, 241–251. New York/London: Psychology Press.

Nicolopoulou, Ageliki, Barbara Scales, & Jeff Weintraub. 1994. Gender differences and symbolic imagination in the stories of four-year-olds. In Anne H. Dyson & Celia Genishi (eds.), *The need for story: Cultural diversity in classroom and community*, 102–123. Urbana, IL: NCTE.

Nicolopoulou, Ageliki & Elizabeth S. Richner. 2007. From actors to agents to persons: The development of character representation in young children's narratives. *Child Development* 78(2), 412–429.

Norbury, Courtenay F. & Dorothy V. Bishop. 2002. Inferential processing and story recall in children with communication problems: A comparison of specific language impairment, pragmatic language impairment and high-functioning autism. *International Journal of Language & Communication Disorders* 37(3), 227–251.

Nyhout, Angela & Daniela O'Neil. 2013. Mothers' complex talk when sharing books with their toddlers: Book genre matters. *First Language* 33, 115–131.

Orsolini, Margherita, Franca Rossi & Clotilde Pontecorvo. 1996. Re-introduction of referents in Italian children's narratives. *Journal Child Language* 23, 465–486.

Paley, Vivian G. 1991. *The boy who would be a helicopter*. Cambridge, MA: Harvard University Press.

Pearce, Wendy M., Paul F. McCormack & Deborah. G. James. 2003. Exploring the boundaries of SLI: Findings from morphosyntactic and story grammar analyses. *Clinical Linguistics & Phonetics* 17(4-5), 325–334.

Pelletier, Janette & Janet Wilde Astington. 2004. Action, consciousness and theory of mind: Children's ability to coordinate story characters' actions and thoughts. *Early Education and Development* 15(1), 5–22.

Peterson, Carole. 1993. Identifying referents and linking sentences cohesively in narration. *Discourse processes* 16(4), 507–524.

Peterson, Carole. 1994. Narrative skills and social class. *Canadian Journal of Education* 19(3), 251–269.

Peterson, Carole & Allyssa McCabe. 1983. *Developmental psycholinguistics: Three ways of looking at a child's narrative.* New York: Plenum.

Peterson, Carole & Allyssa McCabe. 1988. The connective AND as discourse glue. *First Language* 8(22), 19–28.

Peterson, Carole & Pamela Dodsworth. 1991. A longitudinal analysis of young children's cohesion and noun specification in narratives. *Journal of Child Language* 18(02), 397–415.

Peterson, Carole, Beulah Jesso & Allyssa McCabe. 1999. Encouraging narratives in preschoolers: An intervention study. *Journal of Child Language* 26(01), 49–67.

Peterson, Carole & Marleen Biggs. 2001. "I was really, really, really mad!" Children's use of evaluative devices in narratives about emotional events. *Sex roles* 45(11-12), 801–825.

Perner, Josef. 1991. *Understanding the representational mind.* Cambridge, MA: The MIT Press.

Price, Lisa Hammett, Anne Kleeck, & Carl J. Huberty. 2009. Talk during book sharing between parents and preschool children: A comparison between storybook and expository book conditions. *Reading Research Quarterly* 44(2), 171–194.

Ratner, Nancy K. & Rose R. Olver. 1998. Reading a tale of deception, learning a theory of mind? *Early Childhood Research Quarterly* 13(2), 219–239.

Ravid, Dorit & Ruth A. Berman. 2006. Information density in the development of spoken and written narratives in English and Hebrew. *Discourse Processes* 41(2), 117–149.

Reese, Elaine, Catherine A. Haden & Robyn Fivush. 1993. Mother-child conversations about the past: Relationships of style and memory over time. *Cognitive Development* 8(4), 403–430.

Reese, Elaine, Diana Leyva, Alison Sparks & Wendy Grolnick. 2010. Maternal elaborative reminiscing increases low-income children's narrative skills relative to dialogic reading. *Early Education and Development* 21(3), 318–342.

Ripich, Danielle N. & Penny L. Griffith. 1988. Narrative abilities of children with learning disabilities and nondisabled children: Story structure, cohesion, and propositions. *Journal of Learning Disabilities*, 21(3), 165–173.

Rosa, Elise C. & Jennifer E. Arnold. 2011. The role of attention in choice of referring expressions. In *Proceedings of PRE-Cogsci: Bridging the gap between computational, empirical and theoretical approaches to reference*, 20 July, Boston, MA.

Rozendaal, Margot I. & Anne E. Baker. 2008. A cross-linguistic investigation of the acquisition of the pragmatics of indefinite and definite reference in two-year-olds. *Journal of Child Language* 35(04), 773–807.

Schick, Adina & Gigliana Melzi. 2010. The development of children's oral narratives across contexts. *Early Education and Development* 21(3), 293–317.

Schneider, Phyllis & Rita V. Dubé. 1997. Effect of pictorial versus oral story presentation on children's use of referring expressions in retell. *First Language* 17, 283–302.

Schneider, Phyllis & Rita V. Dubé. 2005. Story presentation effects on children's retell content. *American Journal of Speech-Language Pathology* 14(1), 52–60.

Schneider, Phyllis, Denyse Hayward & Rita V. Dubé. 2006. Storytelling from pictures using the Edmonton narrative norms instrument. *Journal of Speech Language Pathology and Audiology* 30(4), 224–230.

Serratrice, Ludovica. 2005. The role of discourse pragmatics in the acquisition of subjects in Italian. *Applied Psycholinguistics* 26(03), 437–462.

Serratrice, Ludovica. 2008. The role of discourse and perceptual cues in the choice of referential expressions in English preschoolers, school-age children, and adults. *Language Learning and Development* 4(4), 309–332.

Sénéchal, Monique, Stephanie Pagan, Rosemary Lever & Gene P. Ouellette. 2008. Relations among the frequency of shared reading and 4-year-old children's vocabulary, morphological and syntax comprehension, and narrative Skills. *Early Education and Development* 19(1), 27–44.

Shapiro, Lauren R. & Judith A. Hudson. 1991. Tell me a make-believe story: Coherence and cohesion in young children's picture-elicited narratives. *Developmental Psychology* 27(6), 960–974.

Shiro, Martha. 2003. Genre and evaluation in narrative development. *Journal of Child Language* 30(01), 165–195.

Silva, Marlıyn. 1991. Simultaneity in children's narratives: the case of *when, while* and *as*. *Journal of Child Language* 18(3), 641–662.

Slaughter, Virginia, Candida C. Peterson, and Emily Mackintosh. 2007. Mind what mother says: Narrative input and theory of mind in typical children and those on the autism spectrum. *Child development* 78(3), 839–858.

Slobin, Dan I. 1973. Cognitive prerequisites for the development of grammar. In Charles Ferguson & Dan I. Slobin (eds.), *Studies of child language development*, 175–208. New York, NY: Academic Press.

Slobin, Dan I. and Aysegül Talay. 1986. Development of pragmatic use of subject pronouns in Turkish child language. In Ayhan Aksu-Koç & Eser Erguvanlı Taylan (eds.), *Proceedings of the Turkish Linguistic Conference*, pp. 207–228. Istanbul: Boğaziçi University publications.

Snow, Catherine E. 1991. The theoretical basis for relationships between language and literacy in development. *Journal of Research in Childhood Education* 6(1), 5–10.

Snow, Catherine E. & David K. Dickinson. 1990. Social sources of narrative skills at home and at school. *First Language* 10, 87–103.

Stein, Nancy L. & Christine G. Glenn. 1979. An analysis of story comprehension in elementary school children. In Roy O. Freedle (eds.), *New directions in discourse processing: Vol 2. Advances in discourse processes*, 53–120. Norwood, NJ: Ablex.

Stein, Nancy L. & Christine G. Glenn. 1982. Children's concept of time: The development of a story schema. In W. X. Friedman (ed.), *The developmental psychology of time*, 255–282. San Diego, CA: Academic Press.

Stephany, U. 1998. Referent tracking in Greek and German children's narratives. In Ayhan Aksu-Koç, Eser Erguvanlı Taylan, Sumru A. Özsoy & Aylin Küntay (eds.), *Perspectives on Language Acquisition: Selected Papers from the VIIth International Congress for the Study of Child Language*, 277–291. Istanbul: Boğaziçi University Press.

Symons, Douglas K., Candida C. Peterson, Virginia Slaughter, Jackie Roche & Emily Doyle. 2005. Theory of mind and mental state discourse during book reading and story-telling tasks. *British Journal of Developmental Psychology* 23(1), 81–102.

Tager-Flusberg, Helen. 1997. Language acquisition and theory of mind: Contributions from the study of autism. *Research on communication and language disorders: Contributions to theories of language development*, 135–160. Baltimore, MD: Paul Brookes Publishing.

Tomasello, Michael, Ann C. Kruger & Hilary H. Ratner. 1993. Cultural learning. *Behavioral and Brain Sciences* 16(03), 495–511.

Trabasso, Tom & Philip C. Rodkin. 1994. Knowledge of goal/plans: A conceptual basis for narrating Frog, where are you? In Ruth A. Berman & Dan I. Slobin (eds.), *Relating events in narrative: A crosslinguistic developmental study*, 85–106. Hillsdale, New Jersey: Lawrence Erlbaum.

Ucelli, Paola, Lowry Hemphill, Barbara Alexander Pan & Catherine E. Snow. 2005. Conversing with toddlers about the nonpresent: Precursors to narrative development in two genres. In Lawrence Balter & Catherine S. Tamis-LeMonda (eds.), *Child Psychology. A handbook of contemporary issues (2nd edn.)*, 215–237. New York: Psychology Press.

Umiker-Sebeok, D. Jean. 1979. Preschool children's intraconversational narratives. *Journal of Child Language* 6(01), 91–109.

Van Kleeck, Anne, P. H. Van Kleeck, Steven A. Stahl & Eurydice B. Bauer (eds.). 2003. *On reading books to children: Parents and teachers*. Mahwah, NJ: Lawrence Erlbaum.

Veneziano, Edy, Laetitia Albert & Stephanie Martin. 2009. Learning to tell a story of false belief: A study of French-speaking children. *Crosslinguistic approaches to the psychology of language: Research in the tradition of Dan Isaac Slobin*. 277–289. New York: Psychology Press.

Vion, Monique & Annie Colas. 1999. Maintaining and reintroducing referents in French: Cognitive constraints and development of narrative skills. *Journal of Experimental Child Psychology* 72, 32–50.

Vion, Monique & Annie Colas. 2004. On the use of the connective 'and' in oral narration: a study of French-speaking elementary school children. *Journal of child language* 31(2), 399–419.

Vion, Monique & Annie Colas. 2005. Using connectives in oral French narratives: Cognitive constraints and development of narrative skills. *First Language* 25(1), 39–66.

Wang, Qi. 2001. "Did you have fun?": American and Chinese mother–child conversations about shared emotional experiences. *Cognitive Development* 16(2), 693–715.

Warden, David A. 1981. Learning to identify referents. *British Journal of Psychology* 72, 93–99.

Wellman, Henry M. & Karen Bartsch. 1988. Young children's reasoning about beliefs. *Cognition* 30(3), 239–277.

Wigglesworth, Gillian. 1990. Children's narrative acquisition: A study of some aspects of reference and anaphora. *First Language* 10(29), 105–125.

Wong, Anita M. Y. & Judith R. Johnston. 2004. The development of discourse referencing in Cantonese-speaking children. *Journal of Child Language* 31(03), 633–660.

Zevenbergen, Andrea A. & Grover J. Whitehurst. 2003. Dialogic reading: A shared picture book reading intervention for preschoolers. *On reading books to children: Parents and teachers*, 177–200. Mahwah, NJ: Lawrence Erlbaum.

Ageliki Nicolopoulou and Sarah Trapp

17 Narrative interventions for children with language disorders: A review of practices and findings

1 Introduction

The ability to tell stories is a complex and sophisticated skill that requires the coordination of higher-order cognitive, linguistic, and social abilities. It consists of generating or retelling temporally and causally-related events that portray a picture of the social world. In telling stories, children need to possess rich vocabulary and complex sentence structure not only to express their ideas but also to establish character continuity and sentence connectivity. In addition, they also need to show an appreciation of basic story plot structure to help organize their narrations in a coherent way. One such organizational structure (but not the only one, see Nicolopoulou 2008) often used in research is the so called "story grammar," which requires the coordination of story elements in the following way: characters in space and time act in goal-directed ways (they want things and set out to get them) but on the way they encounter obstacles or problems they must solve to achieve their goal. Furthermore, narratives tend to convey events that often the listener has not experienced directly so that the speaker must use only words to convey these happenings without the support of the context where they occurred (Snow 1991). In this respect, successful narration also requires the ability to take the perspective of the listener and their prior knowledge so that the narrator is able to convey the narrated events in a way that can be understood easily by the listener.

Given the complex coordination of lexical, morphosyntactic, and pragmatic elements required for narration, it is not surprising that children with specific language impairments (SLI) show difficulties in producing and comprehending narratives (Leonard 2014). These children have significant language learning difficulties that are not accompanied by substantial cognitive, hearing, oral-motor or other neurological problems (Gillam and Kahmi 2013). Their language difficulties extend to their ability to tell and produce stories so that their narrative abilities seem to develop slower than those of typically developing children (Fey et al. 2004).

Accumulating evidence indicates that the narrations of children with language disorders differ from those of normally developing children in the overall organization of narratives (global or macrostructure) or in the way their sentences are constructed or connected together (local or microstructure) (for further explication of

Ageliki Nicolopoulou, Lehigh University
Sarah Trapp, Teachers College, Columbia University

these terms, see Aksu-Koç and Erciyes, this volume). In terms of macrostructure, their narratives have fewer story grammar elements (Ukrainetz and Gillam 2009) and less developed overall narrative quality (Fey et al. 2004) than those of typically developing age-peers. In terms of microstructure, their narratives have fewer different word types (Vandewalle et al. 2012) and fewer complex sentences (Norbury and Bishop 2003). And while some of these limitations are overcome by second grade by many of these children, several of them resurface by fourth grade (Fey et al. 2004).

Along with narration problems, many children with SLI have literacy problems, poor academic achievement, and/or social and acting-out problems (Bishop and Norbury 2008). It has been argued that because a significant part of classroom instruction, assessment, and interaction occurs in narrative form, especially during the preschool and early elementary years, these children's difficulties with narratives contribute to their literacy and academic problems. Research has convincingly demonstrated that early narrative abilities are an important predictor of successful acquisition of literacy and school success (Griffin et al. 2004; Reese et al. 2010). Furthermore, the inability to express well one's ideas and needs through narration may lead to a sense of frustration and impotence, which in turn leads to acting-out behavior and school disengagement.

Thus, given the significance narratives have on everyday social life and academic achievement, there have been attempts over the years to create narrative intervention programs that promote the narrative abilities of children with language impairments. In the climate of increasing accountability among speech-language pathologists (SLPs) to draw on evidence-based practices, the goal of this chapter is to provide a systematic and critical review of narrative-based interventions for children with SLI. Our aim is to provide an account of the types of interventions used so far, to evaluate their effectiveness in promoting the narrative abilities of this population, and to propose some directions for future research.

2 Setting the stage: Some considerations

To achieve these goals, we conducted a systematic search of electronic databases (Abstracts Web of Science, Academic Search Premier, Cochrane Library, ERIC, Linguistics and Language Behavior Medline via PubMed, PsychInfo, and Psychology and Behavioral Science Collection) by combining the phrase *language disorder* along with close cognates (*language impairment* or *difficulty* and *specific language impairment, disorder,* or *difficulty*) in all possible permutations with *narrative intervention, narrative treatment, narrative therapy, storytelling, telling,* and *retelling*.

We used the following inclusion criteria. First, we included peer-reviewed articles published in journals or other scholarly venues starting from 1990 to 2014 that reported an empirical study. The research design could range from randomized clinical trials or experimental and control groups to single group or single-subject designs that included some statistical analyses, even if minimal. Second, we included narrative interventions, whether story- or book-based, that could be delivered alone or in combination with other intervention activities. Third, these narrative interventions were directed to children with specific language impairment (SLI) or language impairment (LI) and at times to at-risk children for language disorders. We excluded studies that were directed only to children with learning or reading disabilities or just social communicative problems. And fourth, the goal of the intervention was to promote some aspect of the participants' narrative abilities, whether together with other aspects (e.g., vocabulary, grammatical constructions) or not. While we reviewed a large number of articles, only 12 publications met our criteria (see Table 1).

Because a brief systematic review of narrative-based interventions for children with language impairments was published a few years ago (Petersen 2011), we compared our final set of articles with those reviewed in that publication. Our final list included eight articles reviewed by Petersen along with four ones not reviewed by him; and we also excluded two articles reviewed by him that did not meet our criteria (Peña et al. 2006; Tyler and Sandoval 1997). Thus, there is considerable divergence of the articles included in these two reviews. More critically, our review goes beyond Petersen's in that we present the interventions into three broad groups based on the specific intervention used and their organizing questions as well as other activities that help to bring out some key patterns.

To a surprising degree, all intervention studies we reviewed were based on the story grammar approach to narratives. As mentioned before, this means a focus on the basic elements that are assumed to be critical in creating and generating a coherent narration based on the model of the goal-directed activity of the main protagonist: character, the appearance of a problem, attempt(s) to solve it, and resolution. We discerned three somewhat distinct groups or even phases in the narrative interventions we reviewed.

The first phase centers on Klecan-Aker's clinical research. Klecan-Aker and colleagues created and evaluated a story grammar-based intervention that targeted the teaching of story grammar elements for early elementary school-aged children with language disorders (Green and Klecan-Aker 2012; Klecan-Aker, Flahive, and Fleming 1997; Green and Klecan-Aker 2012). The second phase still focused in evaluating similar story grammar interventions but these were directed to younger children, namely preschoolers and kindergarteners who were either delayed or at-risk for language problems (Davies, Schanks, and Davies 2004; Hayward and Schneider 2000; McGregor 2000; and Spencer and Slocum 2010). Given this focus, the teaching of story grammar elements was enriched with child-friendly activities such as using pictures or symbols to help children grasp the abstract nature of the story grammar elements as well as using games to help consolidate these concepts.

Table 1: Overview of narrative-based intervention studies for speech language impairment (SLI) or language delayed (LD) or at-risk children

Study	Children (#, age, language difficulties)	Design	Narrative intervention			Results: Pre- & posttests narrative (& other) measures					
			Duration	Materials	Procedure	Pre- & posttests: Narrative materials (Other narr measures)	Global/ macronarrative structure	Local/ micronarrative structure	Other measures	Generalization attempts
Klecan-Aker (1993)	1 white male; 8;8 yrs Specific Language Impairment	Single subject Pre- & Posttests	12 weeks (1 hr / session; twice per week)	The Expression Connection (Klecan-Aker, 1991) Six Level 5 model stories (with one picture per story) Materials for multiple choice & fill-in-the blanks	Establish child's baseline Teach story grammar elements for next narr Level (from 3–6) Move to higher level only after child applied info to multiple choice & fill-in-the blanks activities	Oral & written spontaneous stories (Profile inspection; no statistical tests)	**Pre < Post** Story complexity	**Pre < Post** # t-units # clauses/t-unit (slightly) **Pre = Post** # words/t-unit # words/clauses	**Pre < Post** Reading comp (slightly) **Pre = Post** Receptive, expressive language	Pre- & posttests stories different from treatment
Klecan-Aker, Flahive & Fleming (1997)	15 students R: 6;2 to 8;9 M: 7;2 Language Learning Disabled	Random group assignment 8 Experimental subjects 7 Control subjects Baseline, intervention, and maintenance periods	12 weeks (30 min / session; 3x per week)	Same as above, except now use of four model stories Sequence cards School handouts Magazine pictures	Same as above	Randomly selected 2 story stimuli from four pictures	**Exp > Control** Story complexity	**Exp > Control** # clauses # words # words/t-unit **Exp = Control** # t-units # clauses/t-unit	N/A	Pre- & posttests stories different from treatment
Green & Klekan-Aker (2012)	24 children R: 6;3 to 9;6 Language Learning Disabled	Single group pre/posttest (No Control)	13 weeks (30 min / session; twice per week)	Same as above, with five model stories	First three weeks teach story grammar elements for Level 3 stories Next three weeks completion of multiple choice & fill-in-the blank activities	Same as above	**Pre < Post** Story complexity	**Pre < Post** # t-units **Pre = Post** # words/t-unit # words/clause # clauses/t-unit	**Pre = Post** Identify nouns, verbs, adjectives, & prepositions in sentences (control measure)	Pre- & posttests stories different from treatment

Study	Children (#, age, language difficulties)	Narrative intervention			Results: Pre- & posttests narrative (& other) measures				Generalization attempts
		Design	Duration	Materials	Procedure	Pre- & posttests: Narrative materials (Other narr measures)	Global/ macronarrative structure	Local/ micronarrative structure	Other measures
Hayward & Schneider (2000)	13 children R: 4;8 to 6;4 M: 5;2 Moderate to severe Language Impairments	Mixed group (No Control) 2 diff baseline & treatment lengths Pre- & Post-test	4–6 weeks (20 min / session; twice per week)	Four similar 5 picture stories From *Oops* (Mercer) Cue cards for story grammar components	Teach story grammar components Match them with story pictures Sort, sequence & identify missing story components Reformulate scrabbled stories Temporal, causal relations & character emotions targeted	Story generation 2 created stories for pre-tests & intervention materials 2 stories for posttests Weekly probes identical to pre-test condition	*Group:* **Pre < Post** Story info units Episode level *Single-Subject:* **Pre < Pro** Story info units (47%) Episode levels (40%)	N/A	N/A	Partial: Pre- & treatment stories same; but not posttest
Davies, Shanks & Davies (2004)	31 children R: 5 to 7 M: 5;11 Language Delayed	Single group design (No Control) Pre- & Post-test	8 weeks (40 min / session; 3x per week)	Stories from familiar classroom stories Colored cue cards for 5 story grammar element (who, where, when, what happened, why) Puppets	SLT taught story grammar elements (1 ½ wks per element) Retold stories Child use cue cards to identify elements Generate own stories with use of puppets & role playing After the 8 weeks, intervention implemented in classroom	RAPT (Renfrew Action Picture Test) RAPT I (info) test RAPT G (grammar) test Bus Story (retelling task)	**Pre < Post** RAPT G Bus Story episode quality # of connectives Connective type	**Pre < Post** RAPT I **Pre = Post** # of C-units Bus Story Info score	N/A	Pre- & posttests stories different from treatment

Study	Children (#, age, language difficulties)	Narrative intervention: Design	Duration	Materials	Procedure	Results: Pre- & posttests narrative (& other) measures: Pre- & posttests: Narrative materials (Other narr measures)	Global/ macronarrative structure	Local/ micronarrative structure	Other measures	Generalization attempts
McGregor (2000)	13 AA Head Start children R: 3;4 to 4;9 Risk for Language Problems	Single-subject experimental treatment design: 2 pairs of tutors & tutees 3 pairs of 3 children (Control group)	8 weeks (20 min / session; ten per week)	20 seven-page long wordless picture-books	Tutors told story to tutee Tutee retold story to tutor Clinician prompted tutors and tutees	Story retelling Novel stories *Corduroy*	**Pre < Post** # of story elements	**Pre < Post** Cohesive elements # of different words # of words MLU	N/A	Generalization probes (untrained stories) during intervention and maintenance phases
Spencer & Slocum (2010)	5 Head Start children R: 4;3 to 5;1 M: 4;6 Language Impaired	Single-subject design Groups of 3–4 children (No Control) Baseline, intervention, and maintenance periods	School year: (20 min / session; daily)	Ten 5 picture novel stories that followed a template Story grammar icons on cards Story games: bingo cards; cubes; sticks	Identify story grammar elements Tell retell stories while other children played story grammar games Tell personal stories while other children played games	*Story retelling* 40 novel assessment stories that followed same template as intervention stories *Story generation* Personal stories based on assessment stories	**Pre < Post** INC score for retell INC score for personal generation (3/5 children)	N/A	N/A	Pre- & posttests stories different from treatment
Gillam, MacFadden & van Kleeck (1995)	8 children R: 9 to 12 M: 10;10 Specific Language Impairment	Nonrandomized two well matched groups Whole language group (4 SLI) Language skills group (4 SLI)	Two school years	*Whole language:* Books *Language skills:* Workbooks	*Whole Language (WL):* Pre-discuss books Read book out loud Discuss book Oral recreate book Alternate book authoring	No narrative baseline Two spoken & two written stories from a selected set of three color photographs (with replacement)	*Contents:* **WL > LS** # of ideas per T-unit & Embedded dyads	*Language form:* **LS > WL** Morphemes per idea units % acceptable grammatical units % of marked relationships	N/A	Posttest stories different from treatment

Study	Children (#, age, language difficulties)	Design	Narrative intervention			Results: Pre- & posttests narrative (& other) measures				
			Duration	Materials	Procedure	Pre- & posttests: Narrative materials (Other narr measures)	Global/ macronarrative structure	Local/ micronarrative structure	Other measures	Generalization attempts
					Write own story Connect books read *Language Skills (LS):* Workbook exercise Sequence reading Spelling lessons Phonological analysis w/SLP					
Swanson, Fey, Mills, & Hood (2005)	10 children R: 6;11 to 8;9 M: 7;10 *Specific Language Impairment*	Single subject design *Goal selection per child:* 3 grammatical and 3 narrative production goals, each addressed every 2 weeks Pre- & Post-tests	6 weeks (50 min / session; 3x per week)	*Story retell:* 26 three picture novel canonical stories *Story generation:* Single complex picture selected from a small set of similar pictures	*Retelling:* Retell story from last session Clinician reads new story Child retell new story Practiced grammatical targets *Story generation:* Was asked to retell story at home	Two sets of 3 pictures ("Blackie" and "Hammie")	Pre < Post Narrative Quality	Pre = Post # of different words DSS (grammatical outcomes) RS subtest of CELF-3 (syntactic structures)	Pre = Post NWR (phono. working memory)	Pre & posttest stories different from treatment

Study	Children (#, age, language difficulties)	Design	Narrative intervention				Results: Pre- & posttests narrative (& other) measures				
			Duration	Materials	Procedure	Pre- & posttests: Narrative materials (Other narr measures)	Global/ macronarrative structure	Local/ micronarrative structure	Other measures	Generalization attempts
Gillam, Gillam & Reece (2012)	24 children R: 6 to 9 *Language Impaired:*	Nonrandomized parallel groups design CLI: 8 LI DLI: 8 LI CON: 8 LI Pre- & Post- tests	CLI & DLI: 6 to 8 weeks (50 min / session; 3x per week) Control: No treatment (tested in summer)	CLI: 4 children's books (3 sessions per book) DLI: No-Glamour series card games	CLI: Listen to book Discuss vocab Retell book Work on gram- matical targets Generate own story DLI: Grammar cards for improving social language & behavior	CELF-4 Test of Narrative Language (TNL) Monitoring Indicators of Scholarly Language (MISL)	*Macrostructure:* CLI = CON DLI = CON *Narr Language Index:* CLI > CON DLI = CON *Narr Compr:* CLI > CON DLI = CON	*Microstructure:* CLI > CON DLI > CON	*Recalling sentences:* CLI > CON DLI = CON *Formulated sentences:* CLI > CON DLI > CON	Pre & posttest stories different from treatment
Gillam, Olszewski et al. (2014)	40 children R:6;6 to 7;4 M: 7 *At-Risk for Language Difficulties*	Experimental group design: 21 Experimental subjects (10 high- & 11 low-risk) 19 Control sub- jects (11 high- & 7 low-risk) Pre- & Post- tests group comparison	Experiment: 6 weeks (30 min / session; 3x per week) Control: Typical instruction	Six wordless picture books (Phase 1: 10 pictures; Phase 2: 15 pictures)	Experiment: Ph 1: Listen to book, discuss vocab & teach story grammar elements Ph 2: Listen to book, elaborate stories, & work on grammatical targets Ph 3: Story generation of complex & ela- borated stories. Plus embedded vocabulary instruction in all phases Control: Typical instruc- tion in reading & writing	Spontaneous narratives produced to a single-scene prompts (selected from 3 single-scene choices)	MISL macro + micro structure into one score (only effect sizes calculated) *MISL:* Experimental = large effect Control = small effect		Criterion referenced vocabulary probe Exp. = large effect Control = negative effect	Pre & posttest stories different from treatment

Study	Children	Design	Narrative intervention			Results: Pre- & posttests narrative (& other) measures				
	(#, age, language difficulties)		Duration	Materials	Procedure	Pre- & posttests: Narrative materials (Other narr measures)	Global/ macronarrative structure	Local/ micronarrative structure	Other measures	Generalization attempts
Petersen, Gillam, Spencer & Gillam. (2010)	3 children R: 6;3 to 8;1 *Neurologically Impaired*	Multiple-baseline, single subject design Baseline, Intervention and Maintenance periods	8 weeks (Ten 60 min sessions)	Pictures from children's books Story grammar icons	Retell stories that correspond to sequential pictures Teach & apply story grammar elements Same as above with single pictures of complex scenes Find missing story elements from recorded stories Generate stories while clinician draws pictures for each story element Retell story with or without drawings	Laminated pictures on construction paper (Picture prompted)	*Pic Prompted:* **Pre < Post** Story grammar Episodic *Verbally Prompted:* **Pre < Post** Story grammar Episodic	*Pic Prompted:* **Pre < Post** Causality # Adverbs # Noun Phrases Pronominal reference cohesion **Pre = Post** Temporal adverbial subordinate clauses *Verbally Prompted:* **Pre = Post** Causal, temporal & adverbial clauses	N/A	Pre & posttest stories different from treatment

The third phase of intervention research also focused on the teaching of story grammar elements, but these were embedded in and extended to a range of meaningful activities. There was a self-conscious effort to articulate the contextualized approach to teaching and using narrative skills; and these researchers also targeted vocabulary and other linguistic skills that children with SLI often lack. This research also focused in comparing contextualized to decontextualized narrative interventions and used somewhat more sophisticated methodology than the bulk of research in the other two phases (Gillam, Gillam, and Reece 2012; Gillam, McFadden, and van Kleeck 1995; Swanson et al. 2005). Finally, while this contextualized intervention research was used with children with SLI, it was also used with children at risk for language problems (Gillam et al. 2014) as well as with children whose language problems are neurologically based (Petersen et al. 2010). We now turn to review these three phases of narrative intervention research.

3 The expression connection program: Klecan-Aker and colleagues

Klecan-Aker was the first researcher to test the efficacy of a narrative intervention program in an article published in 1993. In this and subsequent studies (Green and Klecan-Aker 2012; Klecan-Aker, Flahive, and Fleming 1997), Klecan-Aker and colleagues used a narrative intervention program they developed, the Expression Connection program (Klecan-Aker 1991).

This program aims to promote the oral narrative abilities of children by teaching them to structure their narrations through the use of story grammar elements such as setting, initiating events, action/attempt, consequence, internal response, and consequence or resolution. Specifically, it consists of a narrative elicitation procedure for collecting and analyzing the pre-treatment stories of the participating children that serve as the baseline level, and a structured program for individualized intervention (for details, see Green and Klecan-Aker 2012). The program uses a hierarchically organized model of stories based on the number of story grammar components they contain. Level 1 stories include no story grammar components, Level 3 stories have three story elements (initiating event, action, and consequence), and Level 5 contain all three Level 3 elements, plus one more, and an ending that indicates a clear resolution of the initial problem.

One picture randomly selected from a set of five is used to elicit narratives for baseline and for posttest. After establishing the baseline story level for a child, the intervention program takes place for two or three 30-minutes sessions each week for 12 or 13 weeks. It consists first of teaching the basic terminology regarding the story grammar elements for the story level above the child's baseline level, with Level 3 being the lowest level taught. This information is then applied to multiple-choice and fill-in-the-blank activities. As children progress in consistently making appropriate choices from the multiple-choice format, they advance to the fill-in the blank activities which require greater mastery of the story grammar elements for the child to be correct. When this level is mastered, the clinician proceeds to the next level, repeating the sequence of activities just outlined, until reaching Level 5 stories.

Klecan-Aker and colleagues evaluated the effectiveness of this intervention program in three different studies using school-aged children with SLI: One used a single-case design (Klecan-Aker 1993), one a single group design (Green and Klecan-Aker 2012), and the third a treatment vs no-treatment control design (Klecan-Aker et al. 1997). While the results were encouraging, they were also limited in various ways.

In the first study, Klecan-Aker (1993) tested the efficacy of this narrative intervention program with a single SLI subject, an 8;8 white male second grader. She found that, after the 12-week intervention, both the narrative complexity and number of T-units (sum of simple and complex sentences) for posttest stories increased as compared to the pretest stories. Similar results were found in a second study (Green and Klecan-Aker 2012) using a single-group design to test the impact of this intervention on 24 children (14 males and 10 females, ranging in age from 6;3 to 9;6) with language learning difficulties. The intervention was delivered by an SLP (second author), in groups of 8 children in the classroom for 30 minutes twice weekly. Comparisons of pretest and posttest stories elicited randomly by one of the five pictures contained in the Expression Connection program indicated that stories improved in complexity from Level 2.1 (range 1–3) to Level 4.33 (range 3–5). The stories also improved for overall number of T-units, but not for words per T-units, words per clause, and clauses per T-unit.

Only Klecan-Aker, Flahive, and Fleming (1997) compared this narrative intervention program against a no-treatment control group by testing 8 experimental (4 males and 4 females ranging from 6;6 to 8;9 years) and 7 control children. After a 16-week intervention (30 minutes 3 times per week), the experimental group told significantly more complex stories than the control group. There were also differences favoring the experimental group over the no-treatment, with the experimental group telling longer stories (number of clauses) and more lexically diverse stories (number of words per clauses and number of words per T-units). However, this study – as did the previous two studies – used the same picture to elicit stories for pre- and post-tests and similar ones for training during the intervention. Thus, while the results seem promising, it is unclear whether the gains generalize to broader story-telling abilities or whether the children were simply trained to tell stories that included a larger number of story grammar elements and had greater lexical diversity, but for a highly similar set of materials.

In summary, Klecan-Aker and colleagues were the first to introduce and test a story-grammar based intervention that was initially used by clinicians in private settings and later on in schools. What distinguishes this from other interventions we review below is the highly targeted and repetitive nature of teaching a basic set of story grammar elements without any extra activities. This research provides some suggestive evidence that such an intervention can benefit language impaired school-aged children. However, the evidence is limited as to whether we can attribute the observed improvements to the targeted story grammar intervention since only one small-scale study used a control group. In addition, a nagging question remains as to whether the observed changes generalize beyond the similar materials used here for pretest, posttest, and for training. Thus, while the Expression Connection program seems to provide some clinically positive results, the power of this intervention and its potential generalizability remain uncertain.

4 Enriching story-grammar interventions and applying them to younger children

The next four studies we review (Davies, Schanks, and Davies 2004; Hayward and Schneider 2000; McGregor 2000; and more recently Spencer and Slocum 2010) apply story grammar interventions to a younger group of children – preschoolers and kindergartners. The key question these studies address is whether story-grammar interventions can promote the narrative abilities of younger children who are language impaired, delayed, or at-risk. Because of this focus, they create materials to supplement the teaching of story grammar elements to make them easier for younger children. They also place these interventions in classroom settings and seek the support of teachers (Davies et al. 2004) and peers (McGregor 2000) who are valuable resources in classroom settings.

4.1 Hayward and Schneider 2000

This was the first study to examine whether the oral narratives of preschool or kindergarten children who are language impaired be improved through a targeted story grammar intervention. They tested 13 children ages 4;8 to 6;4 diagnosed with moderate to severe language impairments who were attending a language intensive and narrative enriched early childhood program. These children were taught story grammar components (e.g., character, initiating event, attempt, and consequence) while participating in small intervention groups (2 or 3 children) twice per week, each lasting for 20 minutes. The researchers also enriched the teaching of the story grammar elements by creating child-friendly story grammar activities that included colored cue cards whose color and symbols signaled different story grammar components. For intervention materials, the researchers used two picture books they created that were also used to elicit stories for pretest assessments; two other very similar books were used for posttest assessments. Each of these books consisted of five pictures from the book *Oops* by Mercer Mayer (1977) and focused on Heather the Hippo who encountered a small adventure that involved another animal. After teaching the children the meaning of the cue cards, the researcher-clinician gave them the stories they had created and asked them to identify the story grammar elements using the cue cards; they also supplemented these activities by having the children sort and sequence the story components, identify missing story components, and reformulate scrambled stories.

The results from this study are inconclusive. Posttest scores for both number of story grammar elements (information units) and episode levels (descriptive sequence, action sequence, reactive, abbreviated/incomplete episode, and complete episode) were significantly higher than pretest scores. However, looking at single-subject data and comparing the differences from baseline to the end of the intervention phase, the results were less favorable. Only 57% of the participants showed significant increases in story information units, and 40% in episode levels. Inspecting the data further, only 13% (2) of the children improved on both measures, while 47% (7 children) improved on one of these two measures, and 27% (4 children) did not improve on any of these measures. It is clear then that the story grammar intervention used here benefited fully very few children and partially only half of them. Most critically, the study design cannot isolate the effects of the story grammar intervention from the intensive early childhood curriculum that these children were participating in as the intervention was going on. Further, the generalizability of the benefits observed is questionable as the stories used for posttests materials were very similar, even though not identical, to the pretest and intervention materials. Thus, one cannot conclude with any confidence that preschool and kindergarten language impaired children improved from the story grammar intervention used here.

4.2 Davies, Schanks, and Davies 2004

This study evaluated whether a story grammar intervention program combined with successful enriching elements used with older children can improve the narratives of 5- to 7-year-olds with language delays when delivered in classrooms initially by SLPs and later on by teachers and learning support staff. A total of 31 children with language delays from schools serving high need areas participated in this study. Children worked in small groups and the intervention took place in three 40 minute sessions per week that lasted for 8 weeks. The intervention program aimed to help children recognize the structure of narratives in terms of story grammar elements through the use of five leading questions (who, where, when, what happened, why) and ending. Each of these questions was the intervention focus over the period of one to two weeks; the SLPs also used colored cue cards labeled with corresponding story grammar elements (as did Hayward and Schneider). The children practiced in identifying these elements using a set of stories retold by members of the group. The stories were taken from familiar classroom texts, nursery rhymes, and tales. After the children were confident in using the cue cards, they were asked to generate their own simple stories with the use of puppets and role-playing to help them visualize the recorded stories. They were also asked to think about the way they were using the story grammar questions when listening to their own recorded stories. Thus, a concerted effort was made to apply the story grammar elements to a larger set of stories than researchers have done so far, which may be most helpful to children in identifying the story grammar elements in a wider range of stories.

In a welcome departure from the studies reviewed so far that have used similar stories for both training and for pre- and posttest assessments, the effects of the intervention were measured with two age-standardized tests: the Renfrew Action Picture test (RAPT) and the Bus Story (a story retelling task). Children were pretested just before the start of the intervention and post-tested within a month of its completion. The results were reported in terms of narrative macro- and microstructure. With respect to microstructure, the results were mixed in that only RAPT information showed significant improvements, while Bus story information scores and C-units did not improve. With respect to macrostructure, significant improvements were found for the RAPT grammar and for the Bus story connectives, but not for Bus episode quality. The researchers explained the lack of improvements for the Bus story by the greater cognitive difficulty that this multiple-episode story placed on the children as compared to the RAPT test. However, except for the RAPT and Bus story info, the rest of the Bus measures are not age-adjusted to correct for maturation. Thus, despite the positive and encouraging results, this intervention needs to be replicated using a control group so that we can more confidently attribute the observed effects to the intervention and not to the effects of accumulating language experience as the children get older and participate in richer language experiences.

4.3 McGregor 2000

This small-scale study focused on preschool children who were at risk for language problems and also explored the use of competent peer tutors. Two African American children attending a federally funded preschool program (Head Start) in a major metropolitan area were selected whose language abilities were very low based on the retelling of a familiar book in this classroom (*Corduroy*). These children were matched with two other children in this class who scored well on the retelling of this book and served as their tutors.

The intervention consisted of the tutor selecting one book from the 20 books designed for this study to tell the story to the tutee. The stories depicted an animate character (e.g., a boy or a girl of diverse ethnicity) encountering a simple everyday problem and attempting to solve it, such as losing a shoe or catching a train. A key aspect of this program was that the clinician prompted the tutor's telling and provided feedback on the use of story grammar elements through requesting more information and/or using expansions. Following this, the tutee told the same story to the tutor while the clinician provided similar prompting and feedback as she had previously provided to the tutor. The intervention was delivered in 20-minute sessions for 10 sessions over the period of 8 weeks and consisted of four tutor-tutee turns (i.e., reading four different storybooks) per session.

This single-subject treatment design used an AB plus maintenance format. Multiple children's narrations were elicited using the books created for this intervention during the no-intervention baseline (A) period (baseline probes), the intervention (B) period (the telling of trained books during training probes and of untrained books during generalization probes) and a no-intervention maintenance period (the telling of three trained and three untrained books). Children's narrations were coded for *narrative fluency* (number of different words, the total number of words, mean length of utterances in words) and nine targeted *story elements* that included structural (main character, feeling, setting, complicating action, dialogue, and coda) and cohesive elements (additive, temporal, and causal conjunctions). This AB design was supplemented by an additional control probe to eliminate maturation effects. Children's pre- and post-test narrations for a familiar story book in this classroom, *Corduroy*, were elicited both before and after the intervention from both the intervention and no-intervention groups. Thus, pre- and post-intervention increases in the number of story elements in the no-intervention group was used as a control against which to judge any increase in the story elements used by each member of the intervention group.

The data displayed graphically for each tutee during baseline, intervention, and maintenance phases indicate pre- and post-intervention gains. But it is unclear how confident we can be about these results. A major weakness of this study is that only two tutees took part in the intervention and only those whose language was very low. Just any experience with language could have helped to increase these children's language and narrative abilities. Thus, while this intervention looks promising, it requires replication with a larger group of children that can be compared to a control group.

4.4 Spencer and Slocum 2010

A more recent intervention also targeted at risk preschool children for language problems. Even though this study incorporated a variety of enriching components and activities used in some of the studies just reviewed (Hayward and Schneider 2000; McGregor 2000), the results are also preliminary and they suffer from several of the same limitations we have seen in the bulk of the studies reviewed so far.

Five low-income children (age range: 4;3 to 5;1) enrolled in a federally funded preschool program for poor children (Head Start) participated in this study. These children were identified to be at-risk based on their below average performance on two narrative language tasks, a retell and a narrative of personal experience. The intervention focused on teaching story grammar elements, and the children applied these elements not only to 3rd person stories about realistic preschool activities (as previous studies have done) but also to narratives of personal experience that are the earlier form of storytelling and the most prevalent in everyday interactions (see Aksu-Koç and Erciyes this volume).

For intervention and assessment materials, the researchers created stories about realistic preschool experiences that contained the same number of story grammar elements (character, problem, internal response, action, and consequence) and were similar in length and complexity. A total of 40 assessment and 10 intervention stories were created and only the latter were accompanied by 5 pictures, with each picture depicting one or more story grammar elements. The researchers also developed a number of story grammar games such as bingo, story cubes, story sticks, and story gestures. For baseline assessment, narration was elicited from a story drawn from the pool of assessment stories, personal stories, and book reading. When the intervention started, the daily assessments continued and were followed by the intervention. After two weeks from the end of the intervention, a maintenance story retell and personal experience assessment were collected.

The intervention took place daily outside the classroom for about 20 minutes and continued during the entire school year. Children worked in small groups and each participating child was grouped with classroom students (not part of this study) who had better narrative abilities. The group worked under the support, guidance, and promptings of an adult instructor. The adult modeled telling a story using the set of pictures that corresponded to the day's story, and then identified the story grammar elements by placing story grammar icons at the lower end of each corresponding picture. Two children took turns telling the story, and while each child was narrating the story, two others played one of the story grammar games in relation to the narrated stories. Lastly, the adult went on to elicit personal stories from two other children, and while each child narrated their story, two others played story grammar games in relation to the narrated stories.

Despite the fact that the intervention lasted for the entire school year and that it was used almost daily, the results were not as strong as one may expect. Overall, the five children improved in their retelling skills but not in their generation of personal narratives as measured by the Index of Narrative Complexity scoring system that incorporates several structural elements (character, setting, initiating events, internal response, plans, action/attempts, complications, consequences) and other features of narrative (narrator evaluation, formulaic markers, temporal markers, dialogue, and causal adverbial clauses). Looking more closely at the retelling data, it seems that they benefited mainly the children who, according to the authors "had sufficient language skills before the intervention but lacked knowledge of story structure" (p. 193).

Since we are dealing with a single-subject design, it is important to calculate the strength of the observed changes. Calculating the percent of non-overlapping data points between baseline and intervention phase and using the cutting off points recommended by Wendt (2009), we see that for two of the five children the treatment was highly effective (>90%), for one it was fairly effective (70%–90%), and for two it was questionably effective (50%–70%). In addition, the fact that the assessment materials used were very similar (but not identical) to the intervention materials and the stories used conveyed realistic preschool experiences, it weakens our confidence that the narrative skills acquired through this intervention can generalize to a wide range of storytelling contexts, especially those of storybooks. It is also puzzling why children's narratives of personal experiences did not improve. In short, while the results from this study are promising, they are not as successful as one may expect. Thus, replication is necessary with a larger group of children whose performance is compared to a control group.

4.5 Summary

All four studies reviewed in this section targeted the teaching of story grammar elements and included child-friendly activities such colored cue cards to identify story grammar elements and other games to support the practicing of these concepts. In three of these studies, the researchers generated the stories for testing and intervention materials using a template, while in the fourth one the researchers (Davies et al. 2004) used a wider range of stories (e.g., books, texts, rhymes, personal stories). This is welcome as we suspect it trains children to apply the story grammar model to a broad range of materials, and thus we expect greater generalizability. However, this issue of generalizability remains largely unexplored.

In addressing the question of whether preschool and kindergarten children can benefit from story grammar interventions to promote their narrative abilities, these four studies indicate that the evidence is not strong with respect to preschoolers who are language impaired (Hayward and Schneider 2000), language delayed or at-risk (Davies et al. 2004; McGregor 2000; Spencer and Slocum 2010). None of the studies used a control group so the effect of language experience and maturation to explain increases in narrative production cannot be eliminated, especially since children are now attending preschools and engage in language rich activities. In addition, the single case studies used far too few children, and three out of the four studies did not test generalization effects whether during the intervention or maintenance phase. Thus, given the significance of this research in finding appropriate interventions to prevent language difficulties, better designs are badly needed.

5 Articulating a contextualized story-grammar approach to narrative intervention

The third group of narrative intervention studies we review here self-consciously articulates a contextualized approach and seeks to compare it to a decontectualized approach. This area of research has been headed by Gillam and colleagues with research going back to 1995, but most of it took place in the last decade. But before we can review these studies, we need to explain what Gillam and colleagues mean by contextualized narrative intervention.

Among SLPs, there is a school of thought asserting that the best way to deliver successful interventions to language impaired children is to follow as much as possible the contextualized approach of normal language learning (Ukrainetz 2006). This approach is based on the Vygotksian socio-cultural interactionist view advocating that language is learned when children engage in socially meaningful activities with skilled others who provide them with models and support in the context of genuine communicative interactions. Translating this approach to successful intervention practices, Judith Johnston (1985: 128) has eloquently argued that "the challenge of intervention with the language-disordered child is to simplify the language learning without changing its character. Language learning must remain integrated with intellect, motivated by communication, actively inductive, and self-directed [...] But language learning must also be facilitated in specific, well-calculated ways." This is the case because research has shown that children with language or learning disorders also require explicit skill instruction, as well as drill and practice, to generalize things in new contexts (Gillam et al. 2012). Thus, this approach advocates that the clinician must strive for a balance between the therapeutic and the natural to accelerate the language learning of these children.

Besides articulating the contextualized language or narrative intervention approach, there has been increased interest in contrasting it with a decontextualized approach. As explained recently by Gillam and colleagues (2012), contextualized language interventions (CLI) describe treatment approaches "in which specific teaching steps are used to train multiple linguistic targets or curriculum-related skills within activities that involve rich, meaningful, and coherent references to people, objects, and actions" (2012: 276). Put concretely, clinicians model and elicit target language structures in various curricular activities that show topic continuity and generate a great deal of clinician-child interactions. In contrast, in decontextualized language interventions (DLI) children are taught language skills in discrete, practitioner-directed activities with minimal topic continuity across activities. An example of discrete classroom curricular activities is when children define specific words, followed by an activity where they use past-tense verbs to describe pictures, followed by an activity in which they explain whether two words are similar or different and so on. While each activity may involve burst of interactions between child and practitioner, each topic and interactive context is different and discrete.

5.1 Testing the efficacy of contextualized vs. decontextualized narrative interventions

5.1.1 Gillam, McFadden, and van Kleeck 1995

The first study that introduced this contextualized approach and compared it to a decontextualized one was conducted by R. Gillam, McFadden, and van Kleeck going back to 1995. Specifically, it examined the effects of a whole language approach (viewed as CLI) in relation to a language skills approach (viewed as DLI), each of them used over the period of two years. The research question was whether each approach promoted differentially the oral and written narrative abilities of eight children (ages 9 to 12 years) with specific language disorders, half of which participated in each curricular approach that was part of the classroom they attended. All these children also met with an SLP once or twice each week for 30 minutes.

The whole language intervention approach used children's books that illustrated specific story grammar concepts (e.g., a character or problem), and the bookreading activity supported rich clinician-child interactions that formed the continuity of different aspects of the whole language curriculum. Books were read and discussed including the similarities and differences among them; and children orally recreated the stories with toys and props and later on wrote their own stories. In contrast, children in the language skills intervention approach completed skill exercises in workbooks, sequenced reading and spelling programs, and ditto packets. Phonic decoding skills were taught each day and students completed a group decoding drill.

To test the efficacy of these two approaches, two spoken and two written narratives were elicited from the children as posttests using each time a new set of 3-picture sequences depicting various actions or daily scenes. Results indicated that each intervention approach promoted different language skills with DLI promoting form-based (morphosyntactic) language skills and CLI promoting content-based (semantic) language skills. Specifically, the spoken and written narratives of children who participated in the language skills approach (DLI) had higher scores on morphemes per T-unit, on percentage of grammatically acceptable utterances, and on the number of conjunctions between sentences than children who received the whole language approach (CLI). In contrast, the spoken narratives of children who participated in the whole language approach used more propositions per utterance, greater number of episodes and percent of embedded episodes than children who received DLI. The results were less consistent for the written narratives.

Despite the positive and interesting results, this study suffers from major limitations in that only four subjects participated in each curriculum program, only posttests were obtained, and the study lasted for two academic years, which increases the likelihood that a host of other factors may have affected the results. Furthermore, not only there were no fidelity measures used, but each curricular approach was limited to only one classroom so that the observed differences cannot be separated from the specific qualities of each classroom teacher or other classroom activities that each of them used.

5.1.2 Swanson et al. 2005

This study also offers preliminary and indirect evidence of the positive effects of a contextualized intervention. The researchers evaluated the feasibility of a narrative-based language intervention that combined contextualized activities targeting narration (interactive book-reading activities where adults prompted and guided children towards adult narrative models) with the explicit goal of teaching decontextualized skills targeting grammatical difficulties of specific children (e.g., retelling sentences that contained problem areas for specific children such as negation, present progressive, or coordinating conjunctions).

Ten 7- to 8-year-old children with SLI participated in a 6-week program for 50-min sessions three times per week delivered individually to each child and included both story retell and story generation activities. Pre- and posttest comparisons for individual children based on narrations and conversational samples indicated clinically significant increases for story quality (macrostucture), but not for lexical diversity. In addition, there were no increases for children's knowledge of syntax (the developmental sentence score), even though a great deal of time and effort was spent in having children repeat correct sentences based on children's specific difficulties. Thus, this study provides some evidence for benefits steming from the contextualized aspect of the intervention over the decontextualized one, but the evidence is indirect (both aspects of the intervention were delivered to the same child) and also limited (because of the qualitative nature of the evidence and the small number of participants).

5.1.3 S. Gillam, R. Gillam, and Reece 2012

This study is the closest to a direct comparison between CLI and DLI. However, instead of comparing these two conditions to each other, Gillam and colleagues compared each to a no-treatment condition. It is puzzling why the researchers chose this parallel group design, but it may be due to the small sample size as there were only eight children per condition who ranged from 6;00 to 8;06 years.

The contextualized language intervention (CLI) was structured around commercially available children's books and revolved around multiple classroom activities that shared continuity based on book themes (bedtime and parties). Children were taught story grammar elements through the use of books and were also taught complex vocabulary including the definition of key story grammar terms. Children were also given the opportunity to practice using story elements though retelling model stories but also through constructing their own stories. Thus, while story grammar elements were prominent in this intervention, they were used in conjunction with a host of other activities such as answering comprehension questions, generating inferences, comparing and contrasting characters as well as brainstorming solutions to problems portrayed in the stories.

Children in the decontextualized language intervention (DLI) answered questions and played card games from the No-Glamour series which included a commercially packaged grammar games and situational drill cards designed to improve vocabulary, sentence complexity, and social language. Clinicians engaged the children in each game card for an average of 12 min, and all children took turns participating in all the games and for an approximately equal amount of time. Children using the language cards engaged in many of the same activities as did the children in CLI (e.g., asking and answering questions, listening, using negatives, semantics, and grammar, making inferences, comparing and contrasting, paraphrasing, retelling), but there was no topic continuity across these different activities as each question on each card was on a different topic.

Both interventions took place in a public school in 50-min sessions three times per week for 6 weeks. The interventions were conducted in small groups of 3 to 4 students and were carried out by a certified SLP employed by the public school and by graduate students supervised directly by the SLP. Pre- and posttest measures were obtained assessing memory (Recalling Sentences) and sentence production (Formulated Sentences) and four narrative discourse measures based on the single picture elicitation from the Test of Narrative Language (TNL): Narrative Language Index, Narrative comprehension, Monitoring Indicators of Scholarly Language (MISL) separately for macro- and microstructure (Gillam and Gillam 2013). Another group of eight children similar in age who did not receive treatment and did not attend school because of summer vacation served as the control group.

Results indicated that children in the CLI group did better than children in the control classroom on memory and sentence production as well as on all narrative measures, except in narrative macrostructure. In contrast, children in the DLI group did better than children in the control condition, but only on sentence production and microstructure. Looking at effect sizes, the researchers reported that these were larger for the CLI group than for the DLI group. But effect sizes can neither replace direct comparison of CLI and DLI groups nor can they guarantee that such differences translate to statistical significance between groups.

Interestingly, these results do not dovetail well with the Gillam et al. (1995) findings in that the CLI group had greater effect sizes than the DLI group on almost every measure in this study. This may be the case because the CLI approach also targeted specific linguistic structures that in the original study were reserved for the DLI approach. Another curious finding is that the current CLI approach did not promote macrostructure, which was the strength of the whole language approach in the Gillam et al. study (1995). Thus based on these divergent results as well as on the small sample size, this study needs to be replicated with a larger sample where the two conditions are compared directly to each other.

In sum, the three studies reviewed in this section do not offer strong support that contextualized narrative approaches are better than decontextualized ones in promoting narrative abilities. Thus, whether one of these approaches is more advantageous for children with SLI and language disorders in promoting narrative and language skills, remains an open question.

5.2 Expanding the use of contextualized narrative interventions

5.2.1 S. Gillam et al. 2014

Even though there is not yet strong support that CLI is superior to DLI, this study tested whether CLI may affect differently the performance of low- and high-risk children in promoting not only narrative skills but also vocabulary. Like the previous narrative intervention program used by S. Gillam and colleagues (2012), this program included a mixture of story modeling, story retelling, story generation, and comprehension instruction. It incorporated the explicit teaching of story grammar elements together with opportunities to practice using these elements by retelling and creating stories. It also incorporated vocabulary instruction (8 target words per week) for basic book print concepts, story grammar elements, internal responses, and words specific to the content of the books. Children were encouraged to repeat the vocabulary words as well as use them in discussions about the books and in their own stories. And while narrative books were used, these were carefully controlled in that the researchers used six wordless picture books created for this project.

Specifically, the researchers worked with two classrooms serving children from high poverty areas, resulting in 21 7-year-olds in the experimental group and 19 7-year-olds in the no-treatment control group. About half of the children in the experimental classroom (11) and in the control classroom (12) were high-risk for language difficulties based on their Test of Narrative Language (TNL) performance. The narrative language intervention was provided to all children in the experimental classroom for a total of 30 min, three times per week, over the course of six weeks. Often SLPs delivered the intervention, but occasionally teachers. The comparison classroom received the typical instruction of reading and writing at the same period of time and a graduate student helped the teacher during these periods.

For pre- and posttests, children were asked to tell a story using a single complex picture selected from a small set of three single-scene pictures and different pictures were used for pre- and posttests. These narratives were scored using MISL which measures both macrostructure (character, setting, initiating event, internal response, plan, action/attempt, and consequence) and microstructure (coordinating and subordinating conjunctions, mental/linguistic verbs, adverbs, elaborated noun phrases, grammaticality, and tense). The researchers also created a criterion referenced vocabulary probe to measure students' understanding of the vocabulary used during the intervention.

Because each condition was nested in one classroom resulting in a non-randomized comparison study, only descriptive statistics were provided using pre- posttest measures while also calculating confidence intervals and effect sizes. Thus, these data are preliminary and largely suggestive. It was found that overall only children in the experimental classroom made significant improvements on narrative and vocabulary measures while children in the control classroom did not. Within the experimental classroom, children in the high-risk subgroup showed grater gains in narration than children in the low-risk subgroup, while children in the low-risk showed greater gains in vocabulary than children in the high-risk group. There were no subgroup differences in the control classroom.

In short, this is a promising study that needs to be replicated with a larger sample as it shows that a contextualized approach may be more beneficial to high-risk than low-risk children in promoting narrative abilities while the opposite was true for vocabulary. It is also important that the macro- and microstructure measures be reported separately in light of the Gillam et al. (2012) results which, contrary to Gillam et al. (1995), found that the contextualized approach did not improve narrative macrostructure. However, the narrative measure reported here was a composite of macro- and microstructural elements thus making comparisons with other studies difficult.

5.2.2 Petersen et al. 2010

The last study we review in this group also used a CLI approach. This intervention also used commercially available books and it attempted to promote the narratives of three neuromuscular impaired children whose language impairments tend to be relatively intractable. These children, ranging from 6 to 8 years, each had a different neurological disorder (cerebral palsy, spina bifida, and an unspecified disorder) that resulted in moderate-to-severe receptive and expressive language impairments but had normal nonverbal IQ. The intervention was similar to the contextualized one by S. Gillam et al. (2012, 2014) in that it was based on retelling stories using children's books in a discussion format while also providing children with ample opportunities to create their own stories. It targeted not only story grammar components and episodic structure (macrostructure), but also microstructural elements such as specific linguistic causal structures (*because, so*) and temporal adverbial subordinate clauses (e.g., *when, after, before*). The clinician met with each child for a total of 10 60-minute sessions.

To assess the effects of the intervention, a multiple-baseline single-subject design was used. Participants were asked to generate stories during baseline, intervention, and maintenance (8 months after the intervention). The assessment probes used were picture prompted (tell a story about a picture that had no clear initiating event) and minimally prompted narratives (tell their favorite TV show or their favorite episode in a movie or TV show). The latter prompts were used to assess generalization of narrative skills. Results indicated that all three children showed improvements in their macrostructure (story grammar elements and episodic construct) and microstructure of picture prompted narratives such as causality that was targeted, but also the number of adverbs and noun phrases as well as pronominal reference cohesion that were not targeted. In terms of generalization (minimally prompted narratives), children improved only in macrostructure but not in microstructure elements. And finally in terms of maintenance, the narratives collected from the two children (the third refused) showed positive improvements in both their macrostructure and microstructure elements when compared with their baseline narratives. In short, while these results are very encouraging, especially as they tested school-age children with recalcitrant language impairments, they are also limited in that only a very small number of participants were tested using a single subject design, which while carefully done, can provide only suggestive results as to the efficacy of this contextualized intervention.

5.3 Summary

The five studies reviewed in this section present a range of contextualized narrative interventions that are hypothesized to be more advantageous in promoting narrative and language abilities than decontextualized ones. These contextualized narrative interventions still include the teaching of story grammar elements, but these are now embedded in classroom discussions around children's books, which provide children the opportunity not only to engage in discussions but also to create stories using these elements. In addition, they incorporate the explicit teaching of vocabulary and other key linguistic structures useful in constructing effective narratives that are embedded in bookreading and other classroom activities, thus providing children the opportunity to use these elements in meaningful and engaging contexts. However, despite the great promise of contextualized narrative interventions, there is not yet strong evidence indicating that these interventions are better than decontextualized ones in promoting narrative and language skills. The lack of strong evidence has not stopped researchers in testing whether contextualized approaches work better with low or high at-risk children as well as for children with recalcitrant language difficulties. It is critical, though, that the presumed benefit of contextualized narrative interventions over decontextualized ones be tested with a larger sample and with a rigorous research design.

6 Concluding remarks

Our systematic review of narrative intervention studies over the last 25 years with language disordered children indicates that there is not a single narrative intervention program that has been found to be unequivocally better than others. While in recent years, there is a clear preference for a contextualized narrative approach based on children's books, the jury is still out whether this approach produces better results than a decontextualized skill-based approach. It may well be that both approaches have strengths and limitations, and thus each of them may be better suited for some purposes rather than others; or that some well-considered mixture of both may be necessary given the special learning demands of this population. However, these hypotheses have not been fully investigated. In fact, the tendency seems to be for narrative intervention approaches to incorporate various elements that seem to have worked well in some contexts without adequate evidence that they will work well in others. And while narrative intervention programs have been enriched substantially over the years, there is no clear evidence that one works better than others.

Overall, the various interventions tested produced some positive results, but these were often limited to a few clinical cases. The results indicate that all narrative interventions reviewed so far can promote a greater number of story grammar elements (macrostructure), which was the aspect all of them targeted. There is less clear evidence about promoting microstructural elements such as word diversity or various linguistic structures, some of which were targeted while others were not, and exactly which activities can help promote them. To be able to do that, systematic attention should be placed on the materials used to train and measure the outcomes under consideration. Intervention researchers need to avoid using similar materials for both, which was often the case, since then they are "teaching to the test." But researchers also need to think carefully exactly what narrative abilities they are trying to promote and why, an issue that we return to shortly.

A pervasive problem with the narrative intervention studies conducted so far is a strong preference for single-case or single group designs, which tests only one intervention program and does not compare it against another or a no-treatment control group. Out of the 12 studies reviewed here, only 4 studies (33%) evaluated a narrative intervention treatment against a control group; the rest of them (67%) were either single-case or single group designs. In addition, even the few comparative studies used a small number of participants. Thus, it is clear that a large scale randomized study that compares two or more approaches to each other is sorely needed.

6.1 Types of intervention used: Lack of substantial narrative diversity

Another pattern that this review brings out well is that, despite the seeming variability of the various intervention programs, all of them are based on a single model of narrative development, the story grammar approach. This approach takes as its starting-point a specific paradigmatic model of "story structure," centered on the goal-directed activity of a main protagonist that is held to constitute the basic underlying structure of a wide range of stories so that grasping it forms the backbone of successful narrative comprehension and production. The key elements of this postulated structural model are – with some variations – a main character, a spatio-temporal setting, a problem to be solved (often precipitated by an initiating event and the character's reaction to it), an attempt (or attempts) to solve the problem, and a resolution (sometimes with complications involving unsuccessful attempts to solve the problem, reactions to those by the main character, and a final reaction).

However, a careful analysis of children's spontaneous stories (Nicolopoulou 2008) and also of popular children's picture books that are hypothesized to help children construct the cognitive models necessary for story narration, bring out the limitations of this single model of narrative development. One of us (Nicolopoulou 2008) has argued convincingly that young children's spontaneous stories embody different modes of narrative coherence than the one portrayed by the story grammar approach. Furthermore, undergoing analysis of popular children's books in Nicolopoulou's lab indicates that while some picture books embody the story grammar model (e.g., Meyer, *Frog, where are you?*), many do not. For example, many books for young children include "a theme and variation" or "repetition and variation" structure. They present a series of highly similar but also somewhat divergent scenarios (e.g., Mem Fox, *Harriet you'll drive me wild*) that form either the entire storyline or a large part of it. Other popular books convey a series of problems with the purpose of sharing them – but not solving them (e.g., Viorst, *Alexander and the terrible, horrible, no good, very bad day*), and so on. There are many other organizing narrative frameworks in children's books, but space does not allow us to go into further detail here.

While we recognize that the story grammar model is a pervasive one in the narrative literature, which allows SLPs to provide some initial structure for children who have serious problems with narration, this does not mean that we should be content in using just this model. As we just pointed out, this is not the only model nor the most encompassing one. In fact, there are many other organizational frameworks that our narrative interventions should incorporate if we are truly interested in promoting narrative production and comprehension among language disordered children.

6.2 What is being promoted?

Over the years, what exactly has been promoted has changed slightly but maybe not substantially. As noted, all narrative interventions have focused in one way or another in promoting story-grammar components. Initially, the focus was in promoting some broad aspect of global or macrostructure (number of story grammar elements and level of complexity) while also measuring some local or microstructure aspects (such as lexical diversity in terms of number of different words per utterance unit). In recent years, while how one measures macrostructure has not changed substantially, how one measures microstructure has been supplemented by what is called "literate language," which is the use of causal and temporal subordinating conjunctions, coordinating conjunctions, adverbs, elaborated noun phrases, mental and linguistic verbs, and specific nouns with clearly referenced pronouns causal (Petersen et al.

2010). In addition, the emphasis has been not only in promoting global narrative qualities and measuring the effect of the intervention on macrostructure elements, but also in actively *promoting* microstructure aspects that children with language disorders have difficulties with such as vocabulary or other specific lexical components (e.g., temporal adverbial language or causal temporal conjunctions; see Fey et al. 2004; Griffin et al. 2004). This emphasis is rather new and not well established. We believe that narrative intervention efforts should be guided by research investigating the narrative abilities of children with language disorders. While some mention to this research was made occasionally in introducing interventions, this was often haphazard and not well documented. But without a clear account of the narrative strengths and limitations of these children, it would be difficult to create interventions that dovetail well to their needs (see also Collozzo et al. 2011).

One curious aspect of this research is that only narrative production has been measured over the years as the key outcome measure – but rarely narrative comprehension. We believe that this omission indicates shortsightedness as to what abilities should be targeted and promoted for these children. While it is clearly important to promote the ability of these children to produce well-formed narratives, it is equally important to help them improve their narrative comprehension abilities and thus their ability to listen or read and comprehend texts. Targeting narrative comprehension – and not only production – should help to make clear why we need to create narrative interventions that go beyond the story grammar approach to those that incorporate a greater diversity of underlying narrative frameworks. And while in recent years, there was some mention of including comprehension aspects to the contextualized narrative interventions programs, narrative comprehension measures have not been included as an outcome measure in testing the feasibility of these interventions. In closing, by embracing both narrative production and comprehension as intervention targets and outcome measures should better help these children use their improving narrative skills in promoting their overall academic abilities, which is the ultimate goal of these interventions.

References

Aksu-Koc, Ayhan & Asli Erciyes. in preparation. Narrative discourse: Developmental perspectives. [this volume]

Bishop, Dorothy & Courtenay Norbury. 2008. Speech and language disorders. In Michael Rutter, Dorothy Bishop, Daniel Pine, Stephen Scott, Jim Stevenson, Eric Tylor & Anita Thapar (eds.), *Rutter's child and adolescent psychiatry*, 5th edn, 782–801. Oxford: Blackwell.

Collozzo, Paola, Ronald Gillam, Megan Wood, Rebecca Schnell & Judith Johnston. 2011. Content and form in the narratives of children with specific language impairment. *Journal of Speech, Language, and Hearing Research* 54(6). 1609–1627.

Davies, Peter, Becky Shanks & Karen Davies. 2004. Improving narrative skills in young children with delayed language development. *Educational Review* 56(3). 271–286.

Fey, Marc, Hugh Catts, Kerry Proctor-Williams, Bruce Tomblin, & Xuyang Zhang. 2004. Oral and written story comprehension skills of children with language impairment. *Journal of Speech, Language, and Hearing Research* 47. 1301–1318.

Fox, Mem. *Harriet, you'll drive me wild!* 2000. San Diego: Voyager Books.

Gillam, Ronald, Teresa McFadden & Anne van Kleeck. 1995. Improving the narrative abilities of children with language disorders: Whole language and language skills approaches. In Marc Fey, Jennifer Windsor & Steven Warren (eds.) *Communication intervention for school-age children*, 145–182. Baltimore, MD: Paul H, Brooks.

Gillam, Sandra & Ronald Gillam. 2013. *Monitoring Indicators of Scholarly Language (MISL)*. Logan: Utah State University.

Gillam, Sandra, Ronald Gillam, & Kellie Reece. 2012. Language outcomes of contextualized and decontectualized language intervention: Results of an early efficacy study. *Language, Speech, and Hearing Services in Schools* 43. 276–291.

Gillam, Sandra & Alan Kamhi. 2013. Specific language impairment. In Jack Damico, Nicole Müller & Martin Ball (eds.), *The handbook of language and speech disorders*, 210–226. Malden, MA: Wiley-Blackwell.

Gillam, Sandra, Abbie Olszewski, Jamison Fargo & Ronald Gillam. 2014. Classroom-based narrative and vocabulary instruction: Results of an early-stage, nonrandomized comparison study. *Language, Speech, and Hearing Services in Schools* 45. 204–219.

Green, Laura & Joni Klecan-Aker. 2012. Teaching story grammar components to increase oral narrative ability: A group intervention study. *Child Language Teaching and Therapy* 28(3). 263–276.

Griffin, Teri, Lowry Hemphill, Linda Camp, & Dennis Palmer Wolf. 2004. Oral discourse in the preschool years and later literacy skills. *First Language* 24(2). 123–147.

Hayward, Denyse & Phyllis Schneider. 2000. Effectiveness of teaching story grammar and knowledge to pre-school children with language impairment: An exploratory study. *Child Language Teaching and Therapy* 16(3). 255–284.

Johnston, Judith. 1985. Fit, focus, and functionality: An essay on early language intervention. *Child Language Teaching and Therapy* 1. 125–134.

Klecan-Aker, Joan. 1993. A treatment programme for improving story-telling ability: A case study. *Child Language Teaching and Therapy* 9(2). 105–115.

Klecan-Aker, Joan. 1991. *The expression connection: A structured approach in teaching storytelling to school-age children*. Vero Beach, FL: Speech Bin.

Klecan-Aker, Joan, Lynn Flahive & Sally Fleming. 1997. Teaching storytelling to a group of children with learning disabilities: A look at treatment outcomes. *Contemporary Issues in Communication Science and Disorders* 24. 23–32.

Leonard, Laurence. 2014. *Children with specific language impairment*. Cambridge, MA: MIT Press.

Liles, Betty. 1993. Narrative discourse in children with language disorders and children with normal language: A critical review of the language. *Journal of Speech and Hearing Research* 36(5). 868–882.

McGregor, Karla. 2000. The development and enhancement of narrative skills in a preschool classroom: Towards a solution to clinician-client mismatch. *American Journal of Speech-Language Pathology* 9. 55–71.

Mayer, Mercer. 1969. *Frog, where are you?* New York: Dial Press.

Mayer, Mercer. 1997. *Oops.* New York: Dial Books for Young Readers.

Nicolopoulou, Ageliki. 1997. Children and narratives: Toward an interpretive and sociocultural approach. In Michael Bamberg (ed.), *Narrative Development: Six Approaches*, 179–215. Mahwah, NJ: Erlbaum.

Nicolopoulou, Ageliki. 2008. The elementary forms of narrative coherence in young children's storytelling. *Narrative Inquiry* 18. 299–325.

Norbury, Courtenay & Dorothy Bishop. 2003. Narrative skills of children with communication impairments. *International Journal of Language Communication Disorders* 38(3). 287–313.

Pena, Elizabeth, Ronald Gillam, Melynn Malek, Roxanna Ruiz-Felter, Maria Resendiz, Christine Fiestas & Tracy Sabel. 2006. Dynamic assessment of school-age children's narrative ability: An experimental investigation of classification accuracy. *Journal of Speech, Language, and Hearing Research* 49. 1037–1057.

Petersen, Douglas. 2011. A systematic review of narrative-based language intervention with children who have language impairment. *Communication Disorders Quarterly* 32(4). 207–220.

Petersen, Douglas, Sandra Gillam, Trina Spencer & Ronald Gillam. 2010. The effects of literate narrative intervention on children with neurologically based language impairments: An early stage study. *Journal of Speech, Language, and Hearing Research* 53. 961–981.

Reese, Elaine, Sebastian Suggate, Jennifer Long & Elizabeth Schaughency. 2010. Children's oral narrative and reading skills in the first 3 years of reading instruction. *Reading and Writing* 23. 627–644.

Sénéchal, Monique & Rosemary Lever. 2014. Young children's narrative abilities: Links to syntax comprehension and reading. In Sue Robson & Suzanne Quinn (eds.), *The Routledge international handbook of young children's thinking and understanding*, 96–108. Oxford: Routledge.

Snow, Catherine. 1991. The theoretical basis for relationships between language and literacy in development. *Journal of Research in Childhood Education* 6(1). 5–10.

Spencer, Trina & Timothy Slocum. 2010. The effect of a narrative intervention on storytelling and personal story generation skills of preschoolers with risk factors and narrative language delays. *Journal of Early Intervention* 32(3). 178–199.

Swanson, Lori, Fey Marc, Carrie Mills, & Lynn Hood. 2005. Use of narrative-based language intervention with children who have specific language impairment. *American Journal of Speech-Language Pathology* 14(2). 131–143.

Tyler, Ann & Kathleen Sandoval. 1994. Preschoolers with phonological and language disorders: Treating different linguistic domains. *Language, Speech, and Hearing Services in Schools* 25. 215–234.

Ukrainetz, Teresa & Ronald Gillam. 2009. The expressive elaboration of imaginative narratives by children with specific language impairment. *Journal of Speech, Language and Hearing Research* 52. 883–898.

Ukrainetz, Teresa. 2006. Assessment and intervention within a contextualized skill framework. In Teresa Ukrainetz (ed.) *Contextualized language intervention: Scaffolding PreK-12 literacy achievement*, 7–58. Austin, TX: Pro-Ed.

Vandewalle, Ellen, Bart Boets, Tinne Boons, Pol Ghesquière & Inge Zink. 2012. Oral language and narrative skills in children with specific language impairment with and without literacy delay: A three-year longitudinal study. *Research in Developmental Disabilities* 33. 1857–1870.

Viorst, Judith. 1987. *Alexander and the terrible, horrible, no good, very bad day*. Atheneum Books.

Wendt, Oliver. 2009. Calculating effect sizes for single-subject experimental designs: An overview and comparison. *Ninth Annual Campbell Collaboration Colloquium. Oslo, Norway*.

Julie Radford
18 Helping language learning in inclusive classrooms

1 Introduction

Classrooms are very important settings around the world because they are the sites where children spend a large proportion of their time. As most of the business that is conducted in classrooms is through language, the quality of the interaction is of paramount importance. High quality spoken language is needed for children's learning (of both their native language and curriculum subjects) because it fosters active and empowered pupils. The best possible discourse in classrooms is therefore a major priority in children's early years (DCSF 2008a). The international inclusion agenda has meant that youngsters with special educational needs (SEN) are educated largely in the general education classrooms (Giangreco, Doyle and Suter 2013). The main purpose of this chapter, therefore, is to show how to increase the participation of children with SEN through high quality classroom interaction. In order to meet the interests of readers of this volume, rather than all children with SEN, the focus will be children who have speech, language and communication difficulties or autistic spectrum disorder. Examples will be drawn from several projects that involve children aged between 4–11 years.

1.1 The organisation of classrooms

How classrooms are organised has significant implications for the nature of the talk and the opportunities for children with SEN to actively participate. There are three basic types of organisation: whole class teaching, small group work and one-to-one arrangements for children with significant needs. There are variations and trends in these arrangements across different countries. For example, one-to-one support, through the use of paraprofessionals or teaching assistants (TAs), is more common in the UK and USA than in Germany (Giangreco, Doyle and Suter 2013).

This chapter sets out a framework for inclusive dialogic discourse in order to illustrate practices that assist language learning. It will focus on the contexts for learning that are most supportive for children with SEN: small group and one-to-one with a paraprofessional or teacher assistant (TA). The chapter shows, through detailed illustrative examples from several research projects, how to foster inclusive dialogic discourse and concludes with many recommendations for training and professional

Julie Radford, University College London

development. It will therefore be valuable to all those who support vulnerable children, with particular reference to speech and language therapists/pathologists. The chapter draws on the author's work that has been informed by well-established theories of teaching and learning, rooted in sociocultural theory. It also draws on several studies that have used conversation analysis (CA) of adult-pupil talk which offer a detailed and qualitative approach to analysing discourse.

1.2 What is high quality inclusive discourse?

One of the most dominant and enduring forms of discourse in classrooms, worldwide, is recitation (Alexander 2000). Recitation takes the form of a three-part sequence of turns (called the I-R-E) (Mehan, 1979). The sequence typically begins with a teacher initiating question (I) to which the teacher already knows the answer so the student's response (R) is usually very short. The I-R sequence is most often followed by a teacher evaluation move that assesses the pupil's answer. The third move can perform other work beyond evaluation so it is commonly known as a follow-up turn (F) and IRF sequences are ubiquitous: there are many sequences in the same lesson (Macbeth, 2004). Of major concern is the fact that, when recitation and test-like questioning prevail, children with SEN are at risk of minimal participation (Hardman, Smith, and Wall 2005). This problem is at odds with the current inclusion agenda and, worryingly, has not been adequately attended to in either policy or the professional development of education staff. There is evidence that recitation-like teaching modes benefit mainstream pupils, for example in literacy and mathematics lessons (Smith et al. 2004). However, a major concern in the UK is that they disadvantage children with SEN and speech and language difficulties in particular (DCSF 2008b). The reasons are obvious: recitation places heavy demands on the listener in terms of the amount of oral information to process which, for children with any type of difficulty with language learning, can have serious consequences.

In the quest to define high quality classroom discourse, many scholars have stressed the urgency of finding alternatives to recitation (Burns and Myhill 2004; Mercer and Littleton 2007; Skidmore 2006). A well-regarded alternative is dialogic teaching because it addresses the issues associated with minimal participation. Dialogic teaching is characterised by several distinctive features that are useful for both whole class interaction as well as small group work: interactions must be *purposeful, cumulative, collective, supportive* and *reciprocal* (Alexander 2008). The collective principle means that children and adults talk together so adults need to orchestrate how children participate, including how they take turns (Rojas-Drummond et al. 2013). The reciprocal, supportive and cumulative principles are very important because they are all concerned with how ideas are jointly constructed and negotiated: in reciprocal talk children are encouraged to share ideas and listen to each other;

supportive talk means being able to offer ideas freely; cumulative talk entails children building on their own and each others' ideas (Alexander 2008). Finally, classroom discourse needs to be purposeful in the sense that talk should be planned with specific goals in view; these could be educational or therapeutic objectives related to language learning. From these examples it is clear that the principles refer to both the children's verbal activity as well as that of the teacher.

In addition to the above principles, scaffolding is a key theory to explain the high quality classroom discourse that takes place in small groups and one-to-one settings. Scaffolding has its origins in the sociocultural theory of Vygotsky (1981). The theory proposes that, through social interaction with others at the intermental level, young children develop higher mental functions such as thinking and reasoning (Edwards and Mercer 1989). To be effective, such social exchanges must lie within children's 'zone of proximal development' (ZPD), that is, the area between what they can accomplish on their own as opposed to what they can do with the help of more capable others, such as parents (Vygotsky 1978). The ZPD has been developed further and taken from parent-child interaction and usefully applied to educational contexts, especially for children with special educational needs.

An extensive review of scaffolding research concluded that three fundamental principles were commonly found across studies (Van de Pol, Volman, and Beishuizen 2010). The key characteristics are: *contingency, fading* and *transfer of responsibility*. Contingency refers to how support is adjusted in the moment, either tailored to the learner's current level of performance or (ideally) to a slightly higher level. An example of such a move would be to use a diagnostic question such as 'What do you think x means?' to ascertain the student's current level of understanding. After listening carefully to the child's response, if the adult pitches the next turn at a slightly higher level, it is possible to claim that she or he is interacting contingently.

The other two principles of scaffolding, fading and transfer of responsibility, are closely interrelated. In the case of fading, the adult would gradually withdraw the scaffold by decreasing support for the student and withdrawing it altogether when it is no longer needed (Van de Pol, Volman, and Beishuizen 2010). How and when to fade within a sequence of discourse is clearly a sensitive matter for adults, as it rests on their appreciation of the learner's competence in given tasks. If fading is successful, responsibility will be transferred to the student.

Based on the above principles of scaffolding and dialogic teaching, the chapter now sets out a framework for language learning through high quality interactions. First, there will be an exploration of how adults and children construct ideas together (topic). The next section illustrates how adults deal with children's errors (repair) and will compare the implications of correction strategies versus prompting children to self-repair. Scaffolding strategies will be explored in more detail in one-to-one and small group work and introduce the useful device of heuristic scaffolding. The final part of the chapter shows strategies for supporting children with word finding difficulties. Throughout the chapter examples will be shown from both literacy and mathematics lessons.

2 Constructing topic together

How topic is generated is at the heart of all classroom interaction. To facilitate language learning, ideas must be jointly constructed by the adult and child together. Studies that use conversation analysis (CA) show that 'topic' does not mean *what* is talked about (e.g. holidays, friends) but, instead, *how* it is jointly constructed over a sequence of turns. As mentioned, in the classroom this typically means a question-answer sequence such as a teacher initiation (I) and a child response (R). However, a much richer interpretation of the I-R sequence is needed to gauge if it fits the dialogic principles. Essentially, the adult question must be authentic and make a genuine enquiry to solicit the child's ideas or opinions. One way of doing this in informal, conversational talk is through a 'topic elicitor' (Radford and Tarplee 2000). This typically takes the form of a child-oriented question such as 'What did you do at the week-end?' If the child replies with an item of news such as 'I went to the beach', the adult can topicalise this in the follow-up (F) turn with a phrase such as 'really?' and pursue the child's topic with a further child-oriented question such as 'What did you do there?'.

Whilst such an exchange may be useful in the playground and occasional talk in lessons, classrooms do not usually provide many opportunities for informal conversation. However, during a study of specialist activities for children with specific language difficulties, we found a teacher who built into her timetable a daily 'speaking book' activity (Radford, Ireson, and Mahon 2006). In this task, the adult and child share a visual resource in the form of a book. Several pictures have been stuck into the book, selected mainly by the child about experiences at home or at school, e.g. holidays, pets, the school play, etc. The pair typically discusses one picture at a time, each page representing a potentially different topic for talk. The technique that the adult uses in Extracts 1 and 2 is a statement that starts with 'Tell me…'. What is noteworthy here is not the grammatical design; in extract 2, 'Can you tell me about..?' is, in fact, a closed question. The important feature is that these turns work as 'topic elicitors' because the child treats them as an opportunity to supply news, ideas or opinions.

Extract 1: Topic elicitors

1 Adult   Oka::y (.) right (.) what do you want to look at first.
2 Child   This one.
3   (points at photograph)
4 Adult   This one **tell me about this one**.
5 Child   We were mice in the play and we bobbed up and down.

Extract 2: Topic elicitor

1 Adult **Tell me about this one**.
2 Child Uhh there's a girl, and she's crying, because her brother is killed.
3 Adult Can you **tell me about the girl**?

When a topic elicitor successfully elicits news or opinions from the child, the adult is able to pursue the child's ideas, as seen in example 2, with further elicitors. The notable feature about these strategies is that they are oriented to the child's ideas and are not therefore pursuing the adult's agenda.

Literacy lessons also lend themselves to dialogic exchanges that involve collaborative topic generation and are therefore very helpful for language learning. One example of a small group task is to construct a story together. The extract shown here is taken from a lesson led by a specialist teacher who has a postgraduate qualification in teaching children with language impairments (Radford, Ireson and Mahon 2006). She works on a daily basis with a small group of eight children, aged 5–6 years old, who mainly have expressive language difficulties. In this activity, the teacher skilfully elicits the children's own ideas though 'topic invitations'. The key point is that she is asking the children to make all of the decisions, including how to open the story, the characters, the setting, the plot, the ending and the title e.g. 'What should we call our story?'. She draws each of their ideas onto a flipchart, thus demonstrating the collective principle of generating a story together. The following extract shows one of the strategies that she employs. In example (3) the group has already responded to the question 'Who should be in our story?' with offering the idea of a 'cheetah', thus deciding the key character. In line 1, the adult uses a topic invitation: 'Where does it live?'. The response to this question is a proposal that the setting of the story is a 'house'. What is also notable about this extract is that the child volunteers further information at line 6 regarding the number of the house ('forty four'). Volunteering of ideas by children in classrooms is rare, which is testament to this teacher's skill in creating a supportive culture for writing the story. The extract also illustrates how she accepts the children's ideas by reformulating them as a narrative and drawing them onto the flipchart.

Extract 3: Topic invitation

1   Adult One day, there was a cheetah. **Where does it live?**
2   Child In a house
3   Adult In a house?
4   Child (nods)
5   Adult Cheetah lives in a house?
6   Child Forty four
7   Adult A house called forty four. Okay, here comes the house. One day
8   (draws the house)
9   there was a cheetah, lived in a house, number, forty four
10   (draws roof and door) (writes 44)

One of the notable features of topic invitations is that they are usually designed as 'Wh'-type questions. In addition, they commonly feature the pronoun 'we' ('What/who should we..?') which emphasises the collective nature of the task: it is the joint responsibility of the group to generate the ideas needed for the story. In order for the activity to be effective, however, it needs to be repeated regularly, especially with young children. The example is nonetheless impressive, given that these children are as young as five and have specific language difficulties. This example fits the reciprocal principle very well because the children need to listen to each others' ideas, and also the supportive principle because ideas are freely offered without fear of a negative response to an incorrect answer. The task also satisfies the requirements to be cumulative since everyone's contributions are necessary to build the story.

3 Responding to children's errors and misunderstandings

Children with speech, language and communication difficulties inevitably make many linguistic errors, both grammatical and lexical, during their classroom interactions. In addition, their turns frequently lack clarity, especially when complex curriculum concepts are being discussed. There are two ways of interpreting this: on the one hand, their use of language presents a challenge to staff and peers who have difficulty understanding them; on the other hand, their errors and misunderstandings could provide valuable opportunities for language learning. This paper makes the case for the latter perspective because the turn following the child's 'error', according to scaffolding theory, provides a contingent opportunity for supplying a linguistic model that the child will notice.

Conversation analysts use the term 'repair' for sequences of talk that deal with any types of trouble in an interaction (Schegloff 2007). There are different types of repairs, depending on who makes the 'error' and who does the repairing. For the purpose of supporting language learning, there are two notable types of repair sequences: a) other-initiated other-repairs (OIOR), where the adult carries out the repair or correction, and b) other-initiated self-repairs (OISR) where the adult prompts the child to self-repair. However, the implications for learning are very different because, in using OIORs, adults retain a high level of control which means that they are not transferring responsibility to the child for thinking about how to reformulate their language (Radford, Ireson, and Mahon 2012). By contrast, in using OISRs, the adult is not supplying the answer, thus the child is prompted to think about how to reformulate their grammar and/or semantics. We now present some examples and discuss their implications for the child's active participation.

Extract 4, through use of an OIOR in line 3, shows how the adult makes a grammatical correction during an exchange about a picture. The adult's first question uses the past tense, so when the child gives an answer in the present tense, the adult accepts the meaning of the child's response but changes the erroneous verb form from 'don't' to 'didn't'. The child displays an agreement in line 4 with 'yeah' but this could be a response to the meaning of the adult's turn, as opposed to acknowledging the correction of form. Indeed, the child does not repeat the adult's correction.

Extract 4: OIOR as grammatical correction

(talk about a picture book)
1. Adult: What did they do in the story?
2. Child: They **don't** know what to play.
3. Adult: They **didn't** know what to play, did they?
4. Child: Yeah, but I know what the problem,
5. Adult: Mm?

Extract 5: OIOR as semantic correction

(talk about a familiar reading book that includes pictures)
1. Adult: Here is a mountain see me ssss
2. Child: (0.4) uhhm **snow**
3. Adult: Good try. see me **ski**
4. Child: Ski,

Extract 5 is also an OIOR but it is different in so far as it involves a semantic error on the part of the child. The adult and child are looking at a picture of a person skiing in the snow. The adult cues the child with the first sound of the word: 'ssss'. The child says 'snow' which is a potentially correct answer, grammatically and semantically, but the adult is following the written text which says 'ski'. After giving encouragement ('good try'), she corrects the child by saying 'ski'. The child repeats this in the following turn which shows that she has made good use of the adult's model.

In order for a correction sequence to help language learning in the classroom, several conditions must be satisfied (Radford 2010). First of all, the corrective turn of the adult must be in the adjacent F turn, following the child's error or unclear turn. In this way, any correction provides a model that ideally contrasts with the child's version. Secondly, the design of the corrective turn must be pitched carefully, as a semantic or grammatical upgrade. When these conditions are met, the repair fits the important scaffolding principle of contingency. Different types of repairs are helpful for children with specific language difficulties, depending on the child's error. For example, a grammatical error would be followed by a reformulation of the grammatical model.

In a study of repair in small group activities for children with specific speech and language difficulties, grammatical corrections were rarely taken up (Radford, Ireson and Mahon 2012). Indeed, out of 99 OIORs, the children self-repaired their grammar in only three cases. In spite of the lack of take-up, the repair nonetheless offers a potentially valuable linguistic model (of the past tense in Extract 4). By contrast, semantic upgrades of lexical items were frequently taken up by the children (as in Extract 5). The fact that the lexical item was used by the child provides good evidence of the effectiveness of the correction. One of the explanations for the lack of take-up of grammatical recasts is that the correction is embedded rather than exposed. An embedded correction lacks saliency since it is prosodically unstressed. Radford, Ireson and Mahon (2012) make the case that further conditions are necessary to ensure that recasts are noticed. These include: a) placement of the contrastive repair at the end of the corrective turn and b) contrastive stress (loudness) on the repair to expose the model.

As mentioned, one of the main problems of correction, and therefore explicit modelling in response to errors, is that the adult retains a high level of control over the interaction. In some lesson contexts this can be unhelpful because it reduces children's involvement and responsibility for finding the answer on their own.

Other-initiated self-repairs are better for supporting learner independence because the correction is withheld by the adult. Extract 6 shows a teaching assistant (TA) leading a small group reading session. Lines 2 and 3 show the children reading along with her, word by word. Most of the children read the final word 'clothes' correctly, but Mike says 'washing'. In the next turn the TA could have given an outright correction but, instead, she withholds giving him the answer. At line 5 she provides explicit feedback about the precise trouble ('not washing') and prompts Mike with the first sounds ('cl') to find the answer on his own. This is successful because he is then able to self-repair his error. This is good practice by the TA because she encouraged Mike to be independent and think for the answer without over-reliance on her support.

Extract 6: Other-initiated self-repair

```
1   TA      Now with your pointy fingers. Ok we're going to read together.
2           [time, for, all, the, dirty, clothes so
3   Group   [time, for, all, the, dirty, [clothes
4   Mike                                  [washing
5   TA      Not washing it begins with a cl so its, [clothes
6   Mike                                            [clothes
[= overlapped speech
```

4 Supporting TAs to use scaffolding

The growth of TAs around the world in recent years has been astonishing. They are currently being used in many countries as a significant workforce for inclusion (Giangreco, Doyle and Suter 2013). What is most surprising is that they mainly play a pedagogical role in supporting children with significant needs, despite the fact that their training is very different from that of the teacher (Blatchford, Russell, and Webster 2012). Children with speech, language and communication difficulties are frequently at an advantage in this respect because they may be supported directly, or indirectly in a consultative capacity, by a speech and language therapist/pathologist. Therapists may therefore be in a position to advise the teacher about the role of the TA and relevant talk strategies. Although direct therapy, delivered by therapists or their specialist assistants, is arguably the most efficacious, children can make some gains in expressive language skills when similar programmes are delivered by school staff (McCartney et al. 2011). However, the authors note that, in order to be effective, such interventions need to be carefully monitored through on-going training and support.

Therefore, as trainers of TAs, how should therapists prioritise their limited resources when working in schools? Scaffolding is a helpful theory to underpin the work of TAs because one of primary concerns in relation to their support is that the child becomes dependent on the adult. Therapists can help TAs understand the scaffolding principles of fading and transfer of responsibility. Heuristic scaffolding has been shown to be particularly effective in mathematics and literacy lessons because it concerns how children use learning strategies to solve problems (Radford et al. 2014). Heuristic is defined by the Cambridge online dictionary (2012) as: 'a method of teaching, allowing students to learn by discovering things themselves, learning from their own experiences rather than by telling them'. The purpose of heuristic scaffolding is to empower students by developing their awareness of relevant approaches to problem-solving (Holton and Clarke 2006).

The following examples illustrate three heuristic strategies known as models, questions and prompts. First of all, extract 7 shows a model (in line 7) that affords the highest level of support of the three strategies. This sequence takes place 10 minutes into a mathematics lesson when the students are working on problems set by the teacher. The TA is supporting individuals and small groups in turn when they need help, paying particular attention to those with special educational needs. It is not uncommon for the children to ask the TA questions when they are experiencing difficulty.

Extract 7: Heuristic model (high support)

1	TA	It is well done, yeah, 34 it definitely is, isn't it?
2	Rob	What is the model?
3	TA	Model, model? What do you think that is?
4	Rob	Mode?
5	TA	Yes. What is mode anyway?
6	Rob	Uhh
→ 7	TA	**Mode (.) most. It sounds similar, doesn't it?**
8	Rob	Yeah. Most, so that would be eighteen.
9	TA	Yes it would.

Rob, in line 2, asks the TA about the *'model'* which is an error, given that his current mathematics problem concerns finding the 'mode'. The TA puts responsibility back to Rob in asking what he thinks it is, thus withholding giving the definition herself. In the next turn, Rob self-corrects to *'mode'* which the TA confirms and puts the question, again, back to him. Line 6 is troublesome in so far as Rob does not supply the TA with an answer. At this point the TA has different options: one possibility is to give Rob the full answer straightaway, for him to repeat, but this would risk closing down his active involvement. Instead, she models a mnemonic strategy, which includes a phonological clue, to help him recall the answer (line 7). Rob repeats her clue and successfully supplies the correct answer. It is notable that the TA creates several opportunities for Rob to take responsibility. The heuristic model can be potentially used by him to self-scaffold, in order to attempt to tackle the problem independently in the future, when she is not there. Heuristic models afford relatively high support by the adult because she is telling him the strategy as opposed to getting him to recall it. In this extract it is used in the context of repair when the student is stuck and needs additional help. In terms of scaffolding principles, the extract amply demonstrates contingency in action but not, in itself, transfer of responsibility.

In Extract 8, the arrowed turn demonstrates the TA's use of a heuristic question. Such a question nominates a learning strategy whilst simultaneously asking the child to recall part of it. As such, a heuristic question lies in the negotiated zone between the scaffolder and the learner. The sequence is taken from the same mathematics lesson as Extract 7.

Extract 8: Heuristic question (mid support)

```
    1  TA     Ok, so what would the mode be from that list?
    2  Scott  What's the mode mean again?
→   3  TA     Mode. Mode, what does it sound like?
    4         (1.0)
    5  TA     Mode (.) it sounds like (.) most? Mode yes?
    6  Scott  Oh all right. Most common.
    7  TA     Yes.
    8  Scott  It would be (.) five.
    9  TA     Yes, well done.
```

The TA begins this episode by asking Scott a question about the mode. As he is in trouble because he is unable to give the required answer, he initiates a repair by asking her for a definition. The TA has the option next of supplying an explanation but, instead, opts to return a question to Scott, thus increasing his responsibility for thinking about the answer. The question is heuristic because it concerns a learning strategy that could help Scott remember the answer on his own. The TA allows him some thinking time to recall the clue but, as his response is unforthcoming, she supplies the model of the hint herself in line 5. At this point the clueing is sufficient for Scott to recall the rest of the strategy as he is able to say *'most common'*. In terms of scaffolding, this sequence shows how support is adjusted over time. The TA first of all uses a lower level device (a heuristic question) and when this fails, she contingently adjusts her support to a higher level (a heuristic model). Yet, even the model affords Scott a degree of independence because it is a partial clue that requires him to retrieve the full definition. The sequence is exemplary practice if the pedagogical goal is to foster student independence, as it clearly operates very differently from supplying the answer immediately.

The third type of heuristic scaffolding, illustrated in Extract 9, gives the child even more responsibility than the earlier examples. Rather than articulating a model of the strategy, or nominating the technique, the TA requires Josh to recall it entirely on his own. The exchange takes place in the second half of the mathematics lesson, referred to earlier, when a new problem is being discussed concerning finding the 'range'.

Extract 9: Heuristic prompt (low support)

	1	TA	Oh well done. You've done your mode.
	2		So what would your range be?
	3	Josh	For what?
	4	TA	For fitness.
	5		(0.3)
→	6	TA	**How do you find your range?**
	7	Josh	Get the biggest number.
	8	TA	Yep.
	9	Josh	And divide by the smallest number.
	10	TA	That's not your range
	11		(0.2)
→	12		**From the biggest number:::**
	13	Josh	Divide by the smallest number.
	14	TA	Not divide.
	15	Josh	Take away.
	16	TA	Yes, that's the one. Well done.

Having completed the 'mode' problem, the TA moves on to ask Josh about the 'range'. Josh (line 3) clarifies the specific question that is being discussed, that is, the range of students' fitness scores. The first problem arises at line 5 where there is a silence which the TA treats as Josh being unable to select a score. In the next turn, the simplest solution would be for her to tell him the answer but that would increase Josh's dependence on her. Instead, the question that she uses equates with a heuristic prompt because it invites him to tell her the working out method. This is a low-assistance move as it is designed as an open question, which affords him maximum responsibility for thinking of the answer. Indeed, it is pitched contingently because Josh is able to state the first part of the working out procedure: *'Get the biggest number'*. The TA treats this as a partial response, offering confirmation, but allowing him to continue at line 9: *'And divide by the smallest number'*. Josh has, in fact, attempted to verbalise a heuristic device that he could use to self-scaffold in the future. There is only one problem, which is *'divide'*. The TA recognises this issue and gives him very clear feedback that his verb is incorrect. She pauses for a moment, where he could self-repair, but he does not. At line 12, she repeats his idea from line 7 but does not complete the sentence grammatically, stretching the final sound in anticipation of his completion: *'number:::'*. Designed in this way, the turn works heuristically, prompting Josh to complete the sentence by self-correcting his error, *'divide'*. Josh fulfils the job of completing the sentence but he fails to self-repair his error. It takes one more feedback move from the TA before he arrives at the correct answer. Despite the child's difficulties in this extract, it is notable how the TA persists in using low level strategies that afford transfer of responsibility to the learner. Indeed, it is evident that Josh has been actively involved and that there is a positive outcome for him.

Heuristic strategies operate on a continuum of support to transfer responsibility to the learner. Figure 1 shows the hierarchical relationship between the three types of techniques, according to the degree of support afforded by the TA: heuristic models, questions and prompts. Prompts offer a low level of assistance, and therefore maximum for the learner, questions give medium support. Models offer the highest level of support and are necessary when the student is in difficulty and needs to be told the learning strategy. For a fuller analysis of possible heuristic strategies and their relative strength to assist the learner contingently, see Radford et al. (2014).

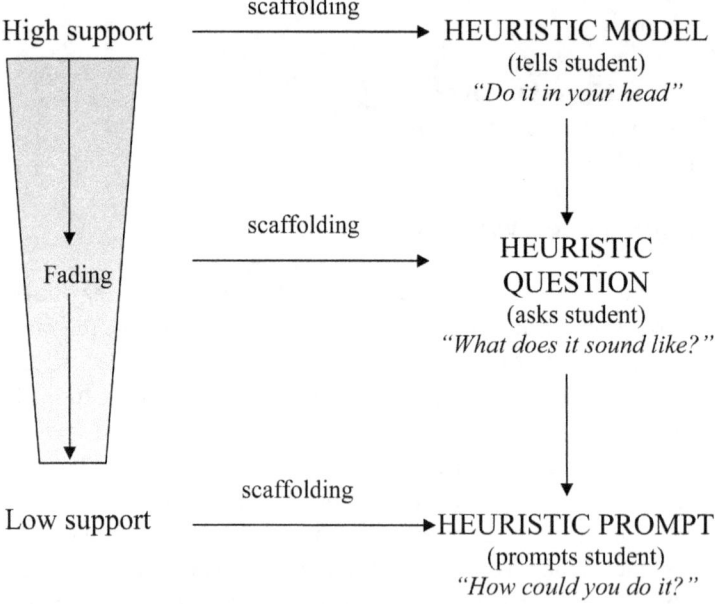

Figure 1: Hierarchy of heuristic scaffolding

5 Children with word-finding difficulties

As has been shown, many valuable language learning opportunities can be offered via contingent talk in small group work. Yet, there are some children who have significant speech and language difficulties that require individualised programmes in classrooms, with strategies tailored to suit their needs. A fairly common example is children who exhibit word finding difficulties. During classroom discourse, such children may have difficulty in answering the teacher or TA's questions and in initiating dialogue with adults and peers. A typical exchange might include silences, search behaviours such as 'uhh' and dysfluencies (Radford 2009). Recalling the dialogic principle of *purposeful*, it is important that all members of classroom staff are equipped with planned responses to support these children's interactions.

Whilst much is known about general strategies to support youngsters with word finding difficulties, little research has explored their actual interactions during classroom learning experiences. A recent study that used CA has shown how a range of supportive devices work on a moment-by-moment basis to evoke the active participation of the child (Radford 2010b). These include the adult use of prompts, hints and models. These strategies operate on a hierarchy of support, depending on the degree of independence offered to the student to find the word themselves.

Extract 10: prompting and hinting

```
    1  Adult  … and then what was this one?
    2  Child  We went to (2.6) uh:: (3.6)
→   3  Adult  [(places pen tip on photo
       Child  [ (1.2)
    4  Adult  Who's this?
    5  Child  Santa
```

First, extract 10 shows that a verbal hint can be useful to increase support after a non-verbal gesture has not helped. When the adult asks a question about a picture of a trip to see Santa, the child begins her news telling but audibly searches for the correct word. Instead of giving her a model of the vocabulary (a high level of support), the teacher prompts her by pointing at the picture with a pen. The child's silence at line 3 is interpreted by the adult as a difficulty in responding so she increases her support contingently by offering a verbal prompt 'Who's this?'. This strategy also withholds the answer which affords the child with the opportunity to self-repair.

Extract 11: hinting and supplying a model

1	Adult	You've got another picture with an astronaut haven't you.
2	Dean	Yeah
3	Adult	D'you think that's the same one?
4	Dean	Yeah, trying to get to uh: (0.2) it.
5	Adult	**Trying to get to what?**
6	Dean	Trying to get to like that, that
7		*(points at picture)*
8	Adult	**To that planet?**
9	Dean	That planet

Extract 11 demonstrates that the next best strategy after a hint, when a child continues to be in difficulty, is to give an actual model of the elusive word. In describing a picture of an astronaut at line 4, Dean fails to find the word 'planet'. His teacher's following question repeats his actual words up to the point of difficulty. This turn works as a hint as it specifically pinpoints the next word (a noun) but withholds the answer. Dean's problems in retrieving the word continue so the adult finally supplies him with a model (line 8). In terms of scaffolding theory, the three strategies here are related, models offering the most help and non-verbal prompts the least assistance. In order to increase the independence of the learner, models should therefore be avoided as a first offer of support because learners are not prompted to think for themselves. However, when the previous strategies have failed, they may be helpful to reduce the child's anxiety.

6 Conclusion

The complex language that is used in inclusive classrooms can be disabling for children who have speech, language and communication difficulties. There is therefore an urgent need to create a language learning environment where the child will succeed in their interactions and avoid failure. This chapter has set out a framework for providing effective language learning opportunities in our classrooms. Evidence has been presented to show how a range of curriculum activities can be adapted in order to optimise the learning of language in small groups. The chapter has shown how high quality, adapted dialogue can be used during everyday curriculum activities such as mathematics and literacy. There are important implications of this framework for the professional development of school-based staff who support children with speech, language and communication difficulties on a daily basis.

First of all, the use of oral strategies needs to be underpinned by a good understanding of dialogic discourse and the key principles of scaffolding: contingency, fading and transfer of responsibility. Open topic elicitors and topic invitations have a major role to play in fostering the active participation of students to offer their ideas and opinions. When children make grammatical or semantic errors, a first strategy (to promote independence) is the use of other-initiated self-repairs in the form of a prompt. Corrections can also be helpful but they need to be pitched in the learner's zone of next linguistic development and marked in such a way that the child notices the contrast between their error and the correction. Heuristic scaffolding is particularly important because it develops students' awareness of their own approaches to solving a problem. Heuristic strategies include models, questions and prompts and they have relative strength to assist the learner. Finally, for children with word finding difficulties, scaffolding strategies include prompting to offer the least assistance, hints to supply a mid level of support and finally, models of the word or phrase to give the child the answer when they are struggling and in need of most help. It must be acknowledged, however, that the research so far on these intervention strategies has been observational and exploratory. Future studies might therefore be designed to examine whether or not these discourse strategies make a difference to pupil outcomes (academic or social).

Earlier work by the author has shown that classroom-based teaching assistants can make effective use of the aforementioned strategies. Speech and language therapists/pathologists have a crucial role to play in this respect because of their unique expertise in how language learning can be supported.

References

Alexander, Robin. 2008. *Towards dialogic teaching: Rethinking classroom talk.* (4th edn.) Dialogos.
Alexander, Robin. 2000. *Culture and pedagogy: International comparisons in primary education.* Oxford: Blackwell.
Blatchford, Peter, Anthony Russell & Rob Webster. 2012. *Reassessing the impact of teaching assistants: How research challenges practice and policy.* Oxon, UK: Routledge.
Burns, Chris & Debra Myhill. 2004. Interactive or inactive? A consideration of the nature of interaction in whole class teaching. *Cambridge Journal of Education* 34. 35–50.
Cambridge Dictionaries Online. http://dictionary.cambridge.org/dictionary/british/heuristic (accessed 9 may 2012)
DCSF. 2008a. *Every child a talker: Guidance for early language lead practitioners.* London: DCSF.
DCSF. 2008b. *The Bercow report: A review of services for children and young people (0–19) with speech, language and communication needs.* Nottingham: DCSF Publications.
Edwards, Derek & Neil Mercer. 1987. *Common knowledge: The development of understanding in the classroom.* London: Routledge.
Giangreco, Michael, Mary Doyle & Jesse Suter. 2013. Teacher assistants in inclusive classrooms. In Lani Florian (ed.), *The SAGE handbook of special education*, 2nd edn. 691–702. London: Sage.
Hardman, Frank, Fay Smith & Kate Wall. 2005. Teacher-pupil dialogue with pupils with special educational needs in the National Literacy Strategy. *Educational Review* 57. 299–316.
Holton, Derek & David Clarke. 2006. Scaffolding and metacognition. *International Journal of Mathematical Education in Science and Technology* 37. 127–143.

Macbeth, Douglas. 2004. The relevance of repair for classroom correction. *Language in Society* 33. 703–736.

McCartney, Elspeth, James Boyle, Sue Ellis, Susan Bannatyne & Mary Turnball. 2011. Indirect language therapy for children with persistent language impairment in mainstream primary schools: Outcomes from a cohort intervention. *International Journal of Language and Communication Disorders* 46. 74–82.

McDermott, Ray & Herve Varenne. 1996. Culture development disability. In Richard Jessor Anne Colby & Richard A. Shweder (eds.), *Ethnography and Human Development*, 101–126. Chicago: University of Chicago Press.

Mehan, Hugh. 1979. What time is it, Denise? Asking known information questions in classroom discourse. *Theory into Practice* 18. 285–294.

Mercer, Neil & Karen Littleton. 2007. *Dialogue and the development of children's thinking: A sociocultural approach.* London: Routledge.

Radford, Julie. 2009. Word searches: On the use of verbal and non-verbal resources during classroom talk. *Clinical Linguistics and Phonetics* 23. 598–610.

Radford, Julie. 2010a. Practices of other-initiated repair and correction in SSLD classroom discourse. *Applied Linguistics* 31. 25–44.

Radford, Julie. 2010b. Adult participation in children's word searches: On the use of prompting, hinting and candidate offers. *Clinical Linguistics and Phonetics* 24. 83–100.

Radford, Julie, Paula Bosanquet, Rob Webster, Peter Blatchford & Christine Rubie-Davies. 2014. Fostering learner independence through heuristic scaffolding: A valuable role for teaching assistants. *International Journal of Educational Research* 63. 116–126.

Radford, Julie, Judy Ireson & Merle Mahon. 2006. Triadic dialogue in oral communication tasks: What are the implications for language learning? *Language and Education* 20. 191–210.

Radford, Julie, Judy Ireson & Merle Mahon. 2012. The organisation of repair in SSLD classroom discourse: How to expose the trouble source. *Journal of Interactional Research in Communication Disorders* 3. 143–165.

Radford, Julie & Clare Tarplee. 2000. The management of conversational topic by a ten-year-old child with pragmatic difficulties. *Clinical Linguistics and Phonetics* 14. 387–403.

Rojas-Drummond, Sylvia, Omar Torreblanca, Haydee Pedraza, Maricela Velez & Kissy Guzman. 2013. Dialogic scaffolding: Enhancing learning and understanding in collaborative contexts. *Learning, Culture and Social Interaction* 2. 11–21.

Schegloff, Emmanuel. 2007. *Sequence organisation in interaction: A primer in conversation analysis.* Cambridge: Cambridge University Press.

Skidmore, David. 2006. Pedagogy and Dialogue. *Cambridge Journal of Education* 36(4). 503–514.

Smith, Fay, Frank Hardman, Kate Wall & Maria Mroz. 2004. Interactive whole class teaching in the national Literacy and Numeracy Strategies. *British Educational Research Journal* 30(3). 395–411.

Van de Pol, Janneke, Monique Volman & Jos Beishuizen. 2010. Scaffolding in teacher-student interaction: A decade of research. *Educational Psychology Review* 22. 271–296.

Vygotsky, Lev Semenovich. 1978. *Mind in society: The development of higher psychological processes.* Cambridge, MA: Harvard University Press.

Vygotsky, Lev Semenovich. 1981. The genesis of higher mental functions. In James V. Wertsch (ed.), *The concept of activity in Soviet psychology*, 144–188. Armonk, NY: Sharpe.

II **Oral and written communication**

Section 5: Linguistic literacy

David R. Olson
19 What is literacy? And what is a literate disability?

1 Introduction

What is literacy, indeed! In this chapter I will address some of the conceptual issues involved in defining literate competence and, indirectly, literate disorders. I will leave to others the task of reviewing the extensive research on such specific aspects of literacy as word and letter recognition or those of comprehension and composition, the sites where important forms of learning are required. Rather I will try to set out the network of competencies relevant to defining literacy by addressing what one learns in becoming literate and the traps one may fall into on the way.

Literacy is a set of personal skills embedded in a set of social practices (Scribner and Cole, 1981). One learns the skills in order to engage in such social practices as reading a book, writing a message or mastering a discipline. Those more general social practices give motive and meaning to the acts of reading and writing. Failure to recognize those practices and the purposes they serve in attempts at teaching reading may make learning impossible. Learners have to understand the point of the enterprise.

Literacy is a social competence that allows one to communicate with others through the use of visual signs, a simple alternative to orally communicating with others. Even when the other is not present, writing like speaking ordinarily serves some social purpose such as providing a warning, providing information or simply, as we say, "keeping in touch". Some of us object to "Twitter" because it involves writing with no one in mind!

To read a text is first and foremost to recover the meaning, which in a tradition extending from William James to E. B. Huey (1910) and into the present, has been identified with the communicative intention, the audience-directed purpose of the writer; failure to recognize that intention is the mark of communication failure. Young children asked "Can you stand up?" simply stand up. Older children may reply "Yes" and remain sitting. Like the younger children the older children recognize the intention of the speaker as a request to stand up but noting the ambiguity of the expression, they may interpret it as a request for information about their ability and jokingly reply "Yes". Grasping the meaning is grasping the communicative intentions of a speaker or writer. We may call this concept of meaning, following Grice (1989) the *speaker's meaning*. Grice went on to distinguish that more general speaker's meaning from what he called *sentence meaning*, the meaning more closely associated

---

David R. Olson, University of Toronto

with the linguistic form. Linguistic form remains relatively implicit in speech, attention normally falling on the intended meaning. In my own writing (Olson, 1977) I made a similar distinction between *utterance* and *text* associating the sentence meaning primarily with written texts. Writing, I claimed, tended to make sentence meaning more explicit. An awareness of sentence meaning is of particular relevance to learning to read and again to learning to read complex texts. Both call attention to the linguistic form, as we shall see.

Reading is particularly problematic when the text is autonomous or "unsponsored" (Harris, 2009), that is cut off from the writer and available to undefined bodies of readers. Such is the case of most written texts and especially those used for teaching the subject matter of the school. Reading for information, as in the case of school texts, leaves the author's purpose largely undefined allowing readers to bring their own purposes to the text. Failure to detect the author's purpose or alternatively, failure to construct one's own purpose, makes reading difficult if not impossible. To read for meaning or comprehension requires that one construct or imagine a suitable context in terms of which the text is to be interpreted. Failure to detect the intended context or to imagine an invalid context in arriving at a meaning is one kind of reading failure. Even for a text fixed by writing the possible contexts are almost infinite leaving the reader is with many interpretive possibilities (Derrida, 1988). Visual analogies abound; Picasso use bicycle handlebars to represent bull's horns. Failure to resolve these contextual possibilities may result in reading the "sentence meaning" without recovering a possible intended "speaker's" or writer's meaning, the most common kind of reading failure.

2 Defining reading

Definitions serve a purpose. "All the world's a stage" seems a somewhat grand claim but defining the world as a stage helps us the distance that world by viewing it through a proscenium arch. Similarly, defining reading broadly as in the expression "Reading the book of nature" may seem at best a metaphor but it helps us to see that reading applies to more than print and may lead us to approach nature in a descriptively prosaic way as it appears to have done in the Early Modern Period (Olson 1994). So too literacy may be seen in very general terms as a kind of competence with representations ranging from ritual, to art, and to literature. Or it may be seen more narrowly as the ability to read and produce documents that represent by visible marks what one could express in ordinary oral speech.

Although both oral and graphic modes may involve sharing a social intention, those by means of *graphic* signs communicate in a distinctive way. So while it is not incorrect to say that we "read" the clouds for information about the weather we modern readers would insist that the clouds were not put there to inform us about the weather – there was no intention – so it is not "true" writing; the term *reading* in this case is metaphorical. And while we may say we "read" pictures in the attempt to recover what the artist intended to communicate, we would still insist that it is not "true" reading as the written marks and symbols do not correspond to or *represent* any specific conventional linguistic form that expresses that intention. Neither of these assumptions are universal and children fail to clearly distinguish what is "good for reading" (Ferreiro, 1985) they will continue to be puzzled about the relation between form and meaning, between what is "said" and what is "meant" (Olson, 1994). Thus we arrive at a more austere definition of reading: *Reading is the ability to recover the communicative intentions of a writer through recovering the linguistic form the author uses to convey that intention.* Thus it is misleading to simply claim that "reading is grasping meaning" in that the claim fails to indicate the means whereby that meaning is grasped. It is the route to the meaning, the visual marks, a graphic code for speakable utterances, that is the defining feature of writing. Neither clouds nor pictures nor diagrams have this central definitive feature of writing systems, namely, the representation of meaning by means of visual marks that in turn represent the linguistic form that is originally and most commonly expressed through speech.

One of the enduring controversies that the above definition attempts to resolve is whether the signs of writing index linguistic forms or index meaning directly. The above definition implies that in reading the route to meaning is indirect and involves the recovery of the underlying linguistic form that is, the grammar and morphemes (words) of the language. But it does not exclude the possibility of recovering the underlying linguistic form without recovering details of the phonological form. Some writing systems, Chinese, Japanese and Hebrew among them, are composed primarily of signs representing morphemes, word-like units of meaning, along with signs that represent units of sound, phonemes (Ravid, 2012; Downing and Leong, 1982). Other writing systems are composed of graphemes that correspond more systematically to phonemes. But that does not prevent a skilled reader from treating single letters, such as the plural /s/ as a morphemic sign or clusters of letters as representing a morpheme such as *photo* in *photography* (Nunes and Bryant, 2009). Hence, it is possible that can one read at least some expressions without pronouncing the words to oneself. Many readers, myself included, imagine the voice of the author, hearing the sounds including the rising intonation at the end of a question, even when reading silently and certainly without moving my lips. What I have denied is that one can grasp a meaning or an intention directly without detecting either the linguistic form or the sound structure represented by the alphabet. But it remains possible that a reader may recover the linguistic form of the expression without necessarily recovering the details of the phonology. Much depends on the level of skill of the reader, the purpose of the reading, and the nature of the text.

The history of writing systems of the world (Daniels, 2009) shows that the writing systems evolved to the point that they could successfully represent by graphic signs anything that could be said. No writing system is perfect in that none capture stress and intonation, important clues in spoken language, features that may be approximated through such visual devices as punctuation and variations in typeface. Indeed, that is a definition of a writing system or script, namely, a system of visual signs that specify or represent anything that could be said. Learning how these signs work to represent an oral expression whether in reading or in writing may be thought of as *basic literacy*. *Advanced literacy* goes beyond basic literacy in that literacy is also a window to the literate practices of the larger society in that it is through reading and writing that one has access to the specialized knowledge of government, the economy and the literature and science of the larger society. To acquire such specialized knowledge makes special demands on the reader and on his or her literate competence. The ability to read and write such documents require *interpretive* and *composition* activities that are tied to particular domains of specialized knowledge and to specialized way of using language. Specialized ways of using written language for such purposes are described as written *genres* and the knowledge expressed as *disciplinary knowledge*.

3 Defining literacy

The acquisition of basic literacy has long been studied in terms of learning to read. But since the 1980s it has become more common to treat reading as an aspect of the larger topic of literacy. The name change reflects a growing awareness that reading and writing are not only mental competencies but social practices that one engages in with others past or present. Learning to be literate is like learning a language. It is in a sense sharing knowledge of a system analogous to playing chess or bridge in that it introduces one to a special club with both insiders and outsiders. The traditional practice of segregating children on the basis of their level of reading ability, putting the best readers into one group and labeling them for example as the "Bluebirds", while assigning the poorest readers to another group for example the "Robins" (as was common in my time) is now discouraged, appropriately so, because it accentuates the inclusive and exclusive properties of becoming part of the community of readers. Learning to read is an important occasion for persons to learn to share a social practice organized around a set of shared rules and conventions. Becoming a reader is perhaps the most important graduation a child may ever experience.

The name change from reading to literacy, as mentioned, is meant to acknowledge that reading as a skill is deeply embedded in the ordinary practices of oral communication, most obviously in reading aloud. It is meant to highlight the relations between previously distinguished aspects of communication, not only between the oral and the written but also between reading and writing, between decoding and comprehending and the like. At the same time it has lead to research that indicates just how these processes are related.

Take for example the relation between the oral and the written. Writing systems map one to the other in the sense that what is written can be read aloud and anything said can be transcribed. But the traffic is not all in one direction; writing is not just recording what is said. Speech competence itself comes to be shaped, through learning, to reflect the standards set by writing, thus we are asked to speak in whole sentences even if ordinary oral discourse often lacks such grammatical proprieties. And writing comes to reflect the voice of the idealized speaker. The relations between speaking and writing are so deep and so dynamic that some collapse speaking, writing, hearing speaking, into one more general competence described as *whole language*. However, while recognizing their interdependence it is equally important to distinguish them as the most important aspect of learning to read is precisely learning just how those forms of competence are related.

4 From utterance to text: The problem of mapping writing to speech

Just as the oral and the written are deeply interactive, so too are the relations between oral and written *words*, oral and written *sentences* and most profoundly oral sound and the graphic symbols representing them, namely, between phonemes and the letters of the alphabet. Mapping these relations is never simply one-way. This is at the heart of learning to read and has required important changes in the theory of reading.

Until recently thinking about writing has carried forward Aristotle's claim for an ordered hierarchy from thought to writing. Humans are said to have ideas, ideas may be shared through talk and talk may be transcribed through writing. All of these assumptions have come under scrutiny.

First, ideas are not innocent cognitive states but rather cognitive states structured by language. Some go so far as to claim that ideas are "sentences in the head" that is to have a thought or idea is to organize an experience into the categories available in a language. Without denying that babies like other mammals learn from their experience, it is widely agreed, following Wittgenstein's (1956) arguments against a private language, that to entertain a thought or a belief it is necessary to have a language. Language is not simply the social verbal form for *sharing* beliefs, it is an essential ingredient of belief and intentions.

As an aside, it may be worth mentioning why conditioning is not belief formation; the latter requires a language that goes beyond mere associations. Similarly, learning to read is not a matter of associating a label with an object "A is for apple"; written signs are representations of verbally articulated beliefs. Reading difficulties, consequently, cannot be treated simply in terms of training associations. It is rather a matter of forming appropriate beliefs about the relations between written signs and graphic signs, sentences for expressions, word signs for words and letters for phonemes. Children are easily confused as to what the visual signs represent.

Secondly, reading a word is not simply finding the graphic equivalent of an oral word. The problem is that oral speech does not present itself to consciousness as a string of discrete items called words. Indeed young children's first concept of a word is as a piece of writing (Reid, 1966). To find a mapping from oral to written words a learner must first find the units across which an identity can be established. On the one side the utterance must be dissolved into a string of isolatable items, oral words, and on the other the printed string of marks must be broken up into the smaller cluster of letters that are bounded on each side by a space, the written word. Considerable research evidence going back to Piaget (1959; Vernon and Ferreiro, 1999) has shown that acquiring a concept of a word is an important achievement not only because of word recognition but because of the difficulties of focusing on the language and then analyzing the stream of speech into discernable elements. If when reading to young children one asks "Where does it say 'My porridge is too hot'?" they tend to respond by pointing to the picture of the hot porridge rather than to the text (Olson, 2009). What may be seen as a reading failure is better understood as the acquisition of a shared metalanguage for talking about language and about writing. Once isolated as a word, an important part of learning to read, the word itself becomes not only an object for reading but also an object for study. That opens the door to definition, the attempt to define words in terms of other words – a skill much prized by IQ tests – but also to synonymy, homophony, antonymy. Reflection on language is what we call rationality (Olson, 2012).

Third, learning to read and write is not simply learning to transcribe the sounds of language again for the reason that the elements to be transcribed or represented, in this case phonemes, those elements of sound into which a spoken work can be analyzed, are not available as discrete objects of consciousness so that letters can be associated with them. Phonemes and graphemes interact; they provide the meaning for each other. One must learn to hear speech in a particular way in order to hear the phonemes in a spoken word. Only then can one learn to represent them by graphemes. *Phonological awareness* is a matter of becoming aware of those specific sound properties of speech that may then be represented by letters. Thus learning letters in itself is not sufficient for representing sounds and words. Letter knowledge is not simply learning to discriminate shapes, rather it is learning to recognize those shapes as representing the phonemes that learners can detect in their own and others spoken words. Much unprofitable debate is given to advocates for the priority of learning to recognize words as opposed to grasping meaning. The real issue is the relation between the graphic forms and the oral forms. The critical issue is learning to analyze and conceptualize the spoken form in a manner appropriate to mapping their relations to written words and letters.

Reading and writing have long been considered distinct processes and the relation between reading words and spelling them is seen as involving distinctive processes. However, important research has shown that reading and spelling are highly interactive. Learning to spell directs attention to the phonological properties of the spoken word, the very phonological properties that are represented by specific letters and letter combinations (Vernon and Ferreiro, 1999). Awareness of spelling informs readers of where to look for distinctive information for word identification. The point is that reading and writing must be seen as interdependent. Phonological confusions are appropriately addressed through learning to spell.

To summarize, the development of literate competence is made complex by the fact that both ends of the mapping, the visual marks and the spoken utterance, have to be readjusted in order to carry out the required mapping. The development of literate competence requires that one learn a set of distinctive marks, primarily the letters of the alphabet, collections of such letters into words, and ordered sets of words into sentences. On the other side, the oral competence has to be reorganized into units that can be put into relation with those written marks. Just as much learning goes into learning to analyze what is spoken into the required units – phonemes, morphemes, words and sentences – as goes into learning the visual signs themselves.

5 Implications of literacy

Literacy learning is important not only because it allows us to communicate across space and time. It is equally important for how it make a learner conscious of properties of language that would otherwise remain implicit and transparent. Literacy learning is, therefore, metarepresentational knowledge, learning to talk and think about language. Whereas concepts like *ask, say,* and *tell* are part of ordinary oral discourse, concepts like *word, mean, phoneme, letter, sentence, define, synonym, metaphor* are distinctive of and essential to talking and thinking about reading and literacy. Writing is a device not only for communication but for thinking about language and for high levels of thinking generally (Olson, 2012).

Advanced literacy is that level of competence involved in reading, interpreting, criticizing, summarizing as well as composing and editing written texts. Such high levels of competence are not only the outcomes of extended education they are the competencies required for participation in many of the enterprises of a modern bureaucratic society. The importance of "bookish" knowledge is often minimized by progressive reformers who correctly note the difficulties learners have in dealing with extended texts. But some then go on, incorrectly, to suggest that there are alternative media or means of instruction that can achieve those traditionally carried by literacy. It is important to acknowledge that the ability to understand and compose extended prosaic texts play a central and inescapable role in abstract knowledge and modes of thinking.

6 From teaching to therapy

Much has been written about the "medicalization" of routine psychological functions, calling normal rowdiness "hyperactivity" and offering prescriptions, for example. The same danger lies in calling the systematic errors that occur in learning to read "learning disabilities" to be diagnosed and treated. Indeed, I suspect that there are few literacy disabilities, only incomplete learning. It is unlikely, but possible, that there are children above seven years who are simply incapable of forming meta-linguistic concepts such as word, phoneme/sound, or sentence although admittedly such concepts require extensive teaching and require conceptual change on the part of the learner. Learning to read and write is the progressive mastery of concepts and rules for their application. Reading difficulties may often be traced to particular gaps in knowledge and confusions as to the task involved. Reading difficulties may reflect the absence of needed conceptual distinctions – between sounds, letters, words, meanings and the like. Conceptual confusions may be addressed through teaching, making clear what is required at each stage of the learning process (Valtin, 2013). Teachers and reading experts are skilled in tracing these failures to their source. One may question whether or not such gaps in knowledge are appropriately thought of as disabilities. Absence of knowledge is ignorance, a gap that may be filled by providing information. Absence of ability is a "disability" implying not only a lack of knowledge but a lack of a basic resource for acquiring that knowledge. Thus, a disability may require extensive rehabilitation. No doubt such serious disabilities do occur. However, reading ability is a kind of knowledge along with the rules for applying that knowledge. Reading difficulties should first be traced to these possible misunderstandings and only then to a presumably absent skill requiring remediation. Teaching of reading requires the sharing of a mutual frame of reference that allows for mutual understanding between teacher and learner so that they can work together to resolve those misunderstandings. A medicalized diagnosis and treatment model may inadvertently by-pass the conditions for optimal learning.

7 Conclusion

In acquiring literate competence, specifically in learning to read, children explore and revise a number of hypotheses about both about the linguistic properties of their own and other's speech and about what the graphic signs represent whether morphemes, words, syllables or phonemes or entire utterances. Acquiring the critical concepts and the rules relating them require both grasping the principles involved and extended practice in deploying them systematically. Teaching involves both recognizing learner's difficulties and helping learners overcome them. Diagnosis and therapy are called when failure persists in the face of appropriate occasions for learning. Honoring this rule would greatly reduce the number of children labeled as dyslexic.

Thus many of the systematic difficulties that are subsequently interpreted as disorders have their bases in the more routine failures in acquiring literate competence. Failure to recognize common words may be a result not of disability but of failure to abstract those common words from the stream of speech. Learning literacy requires that learners grasp important conceptual distinctions that are normally addressed by teaching or an improved literacy curriculum. On the other hand, the diagnosis and treatment of reading failure may be relevant and important if it provides access to more intensive help in learning how to read and write. Even then, one must avoid distinctions that marginalize poor readers by assigning them to a marginal reading group, the "Robins".

References

Daniels, Peter T. 2009. Grammatology. In David R. Olson & Nancy Torrance (eds.), *The Cambridge handbook of literacy*, 25–45. Cambridge: Cambridge University Press.
Derrida, Jacques. 1988. *Limited inc.* Evanston, IL: Northwestern University Press.
Downing, John & Che Kan Leong. 1982. *Psychology of reading.* New York: Macmillan.
Ferreiro, Emilia. 1985. Literacy development: A psychogenetic perspective. In David R. Olson, Nancy Torrance & Angela Hildyard (eds.), *Literacy, language & learning*, 217–228. Cambridge: Cambridge University Press.
Grice, Paul. 1989. *Studies in the ways with words.* Cambridge, MA: Harvard University Press.
Harris, Roy. 2009. *Rationality and the literate mind.* London: Routledge.
Huey, Edmund Burke. 1910. *The psychology and pedagogy of reading.* New York: Macmillan.
Nunes, Terezinha & Peter Bryant. 2009. *Children's reading and spelling: Beyond the first steps.* Oxford: Wiley-Blackwell.
Olson, David R. 1977. From utterance to text: The bias of language in speech and writing. *Harvard Educational Review* 47(3). 257–281.
Olson, David R. 1994. *The world on paper.* Cambridge: Cambridge University Press.
Olson, David R. 2009. A theory of reading/writing: From literacy to literature. *Writing Systems Research* 1(1). 51–64.
Olson, David R. 2012. Literacy, rationality and logic: The historical and developmental origins of logical discourse. *Written Language & Literacy* 15(2). 153–164.
Piaget, Jean. 1959. *The language and thought of the child.* London: Routledge & Kegan Paul.
Ravid, Dorit. 2012. *Spelling morphology: The Psycholinguistics of Hebrew spelling.* New York: Springer.
Reid, Jessie. 1966. Learning to think about reading. *Educational Research* 9(1). 56–62.
Scribner, Sylvia & Michael Cole. 1981. The psychology of literacy. Cambridge, MA: Harvard University Press.
Valtin, Renate. 2013. About the dubious role of phonological awareness in the discussion of literacy policies. In Kenneth S. Goodman, Robert C. Calfee & Yetta M. Goodman (eds.), *Whose knowledge counts in government literacy policies? Why Expertise Matters*, 94–109. London: Routledge.
Vernon, Sofia & Emilia Ferreiro. 1999. Writing development: A neglected variable in the consideration of phonological awareness. *Harvard Educational Review* 64(4). 395–415.
Wittgenstein, Ludwig. 1956. *Philosophical investigations* (trans. G. E. M. Anscomb). Oxford: Blackwell.

Dorit Aram
20 Promoting early literacy of children from low socioeconomic backgrounds in preschool and at home

1 Introduction

One of the keys to academic success is a solid starting point. In fact, a body of research on continuity during the transition from preschool to school has emphasized the role of early literacy skills as chief predictors of later achievements. Acknowledging the environment's strong impact on children's early literacy encourages comprehensive intervention planning. This chapter describes studies that assessed the effectiveness of home-based and preschool-based early interventions in promoting major literacy components among children from families of a low socioeconomic status (SES).

Early literacy refers to children's knowledge regarding spoken and written language prior to formal schooling. It includes skills and knowledge that are precursors to conventional forms of reading and writing. Researchers agree that the major components that establish early literacy are oral language skills, phonological awareness, print awareness, and early writing (Whitehurst and Lonigan 2002). *Oral language* refers to the ability to produce or comprehend spoken language, including vocabulary, morphology, and grammar. *Phonological awareness* is sensitivity to the sound structure of words and ability to manipulate sounds within words. *Print awareness* refers to children's alphabetic skills of recognizing and naming letters as well as their orthographic awareness – familiarity with the conventions of print (e.g., directionality, differences between letters and numbers). *Early writing* refers to children's first representations of spoken language via written symbols (e.g., by writing letters and spelling words) and the understanding of letter-sound mappings (that written letters stand for sounds). Together, these early literacy components are the building blocks of later academic achievements.

Vast evidence has pointed to the existence of a continuum of children's literacy achievements, extending from the early years through the school years, as manifested in diverse components. For example, Bartl-Pokorny et al. (2013) found that vocabulary during the second year of life predicts reading comprehension at age 13. Likewise, Whitehurst and Lonigan (2002) showed that preschool children's phonological awareness and alphabetic skills predicted their reading and writing in second grade. This continuity in literacy achievements has been found across languages as diverse as

Dorit Aram, Tel Aviv University

Finnish (Lepola, Poskiparta, Laakonen, and Niemi 2005), Flemish (Bossaert, Douemn, Buyse, and Verschueren 2011), Chinese (Zhang, Tardiff, Shu, Li, Liu, McBride-Chang, Liang, and Zhang 2013), English (Piasta, Pescher, and Justice 2012), Hebrew (Aram 2005), Arabic, (Aram, Korat, and Hassona-Arafat 2013), and French (Costa, Perndry, Soria, Pulgar, Cusin, and Dellatolas 2013).

To identify the best early predictors of literacy acquisition, the National Early Literacy Panel (NELP 2008) conducted a meta-analysis of 299 articles that assessed the predictive relations between early literacy components at the end of kindergarten and children's later decoding, spelling, and reading comprehension in first or second grade. Generally, the best predictors were alphabetic knowledge, phonological awareness, and early writing. Complex early oral language skills such as grammar, expressive vocabulary (definitions), and listening comprehension also showed strong relationships with later decoding and reading comprehension.

Early literacy develops in real life settings through positive interactions with significant others. Children who are trying to develop literacy are engaged in difficult cognitive work, and the quality of the support that they receive makes a vital contribution to their success (Neuman and Dickinson 2002). Ample evidence indicates an association between low SES background and children's educational trajectory, where children from low SES families experience less effective literacy interactions (e.g. conversations, shard book reading, writing interactions) than children from higher SES families (e.g., Berliner, 2006; Duncan and Murnane 2011; Klein and Yablon 2008). The Organization for Economic Co-operation and Development study (OECD 2010), based on the 2009 Programme for International Student Assessment (PISA) test results, determined that on a reading comprehension test, a student from an advantaged SES scores 88 points higher, on average, than his/her peer from a low SES, a gap that equals two grade levels. The discrepancy in literacy achievements between children from lower and higher SES is already salient in preschool (e.g., Snow, Burns, and Griffin 1998).

Literacy can be a source of transformation in societies because it is a capability – a "substantive freedom" – by which persons can exert choices to achieve alternative combinations of functioning (Sen 1999). Reviews of early education interventions have documented that intensive interventions render positive effects on the early development of children from a low SES (e.g., Barnett and Hustedt 2003). In a foreword to a handbook on early childhood intervention, Zigler ([2000]: xii) wrote:

> Now that we have a clearer picture of general intervention efficacy, the major task is to identify which interventions work best and how these results are achieved, as well as which components of interventions are most essential to achieve maximum benefit. This latter question is critical, given the limited funding with which most interventions must be mounted and sustained.

Following Zigler's recommendation, the current chapter aims to present a series of preschool-based and home-based early literacy interventions for low SES populations, to explore which interventions work best and which components predict the maximum benefit to children's early literacy. In light of the diversity in early literacy programs and the fact that only few have been found effective (Dickinson, Freiber, and Barnes 2011), this chapter focuses on the specific benefits for children's literacy of two sets of major adult-child literacy activities: shared book reading (three studies) and joint writing (three studies). Specifically, this chapter inquires which intervention components in each joint activity are most fruitful for promoting early literacy skills.

The empirical studies reported here investigated adult-child interventions that were conducted in Israel by my literacy research team[1] in the two main environmental contexts for young children's literacy development – in the children's homes and preschools. Most of the children in Israel attend preschool from the age of 3 years, for six days per week, usually for six hours a day.

2 Shared book reading

Reading books to young children is widely recognized as an important adult-child early literacy activity (van Kleeck and Stahl 2003). Children who are exposed to frequent storybook reading surpass their counterparts consistently on vocabulary, and in some reports also on alphabetic skills (e.g., Sénéchal 2006). However, the contribution of storybook reading to children's vocabulary depends on the adults' reading style. "Interactive" reading, which includes engagement of children in discourse surrounding the text, was found to enhance children's progress more than regular straightforward reading (Mol, Bus, de Jong, and Smeets 2008). Nevertheless, many adults – including preschool teachers and parents from different SES backgrounds – mainly read books to children while only infrequently attempting to involve the children in discourse (e.g. Aram, Bergman Deitcher, Sabag Shushan, and Ziv, 2017; Smadja, and Aram 2013, 2015). Various causes may underlie the prevalence of this less effective practice. Adults may think that the book "tells" the story and that there is no need to elaborate further. They may be unaware of young children's limited vocabulary, restricted listening comprehension, and partial understanding of story grammar. Adults may also have limited skills for involving children in discourse; for example, perhaps they do not know how to ask questions or do not allow children enough time to process the questions and form their replies. Finally, perhaps adults just do not see the opportunity that books offer to converse with children and further introduce them to their social world and culture.

Most research on shared reading interventions has measured their impact on *oral language* skills (mainly vocabulary), whereas fewer studies examined their impact on

---

[1] Some of these studies were done in collaboration with the late Prof. Iris Levin who was among the pioneers in this field in Israel and became one of the world's leading experts, known for her prolific and insightful work on emergent literacy in Hebrew and Arabic.

other skills like *print awareness* (*alphabet knowledge, early reading*), *phonological awareness*, and *early writing*. For example, out of the 19 studies in a meta-analysis assessing the impact of shared reading interventions on children's early literacy skills (NELP 2008), a full 16 focused on *oral language* skills, whereas only 2 studies focused on *phonological awareness* and *alphabet knowledge*, and only 1 study focused on *writing*. The meta-analysis results indicated that shared book-reading interventions have a substantial impact on children's *oral language* and *print knowledge* skills but not on their *phonological awareness* or *alphabetic knowledge*. The one study examining *early writing* as an outcome reported a moderate impact (NELP 2008). Yet, the NELP report authors underscored that shared book-reading intervention studies have insufficiently assessed the programs' effects on literacy measures other than *oral language*.

To narrow this gap in the empirical literature, the current chapter describes the impact of a series of shared reading interventions on a wide range of early literacy skills extending beyond *oral language* for children from low SES families who may be considered at risk for lower early literacy. Moreover, to deepen and generalize our understanding regarding the impact of shared book-reading interventions on children's development, these studies were implemented by different mediators (students, teachers, and parents), in different settings (preschool and home), while stressing different shared reading components (plot and print).

2.1 Preschool-based shared book-reading interventions: Which components should be stressed?

Two intervention studies on shared book reading that our research team conducted in preschools (Aram 2006; Aram and Biron 2004) aimed to identify which mediating activities adults prefer during shared book reading. We intended to reveal the shared book reading's components that would be most fruitful in promoting a variety of early literacy skills. Both studies were implemented in preschools located in a low SES town in central Israel that contains a high percentage of multi-problem families characterized by domestic violence, economic distress, poor health, single parenthood, and so on (Center for Socioeconomic Research 2000). The interventions (supported by the Price-Brody Initiative) were established to help foster early literacy in these young children at risk for a poor educational trajectory.

2.1.1 Focus on plot

In the first study, our aim was to promote children's literacy skills during shared book reading that focused on the plot via rich conversations and creative activities

(Aram and Biron 2004). In the intervention, master's students worked in two preschools with small groups of 4–6 children twice weekly over the school year, reading a total of 11 storybooks with the preschoolers and conducting activities focusing on each story's subjects and plot. About six sessions (lasting ~20–30 min.) were devoted to each book. In each session, the student read the book aloud twice, verified that all of the children understood the plot, and discussed central concepts and ideas via group discussions, arts and crafts (e.g., drawing, clay sculpting), and drama activities. The central concepts varied widely, including topics like fears, friendship, and animals. The student employed interactive reading techniques such as praising and encouraging children to contribute to the conversation, asking open-ended questions, re-voicing children's words, and expanding on children's ideas.

Participants in Study 1 were 85 low SES preschoolers aged 3–5 years, consisting of 42 children in the intervention group and 43 in a control group. The control group consisted of two preschools in the same neighborhood who continued their activities according to the national curricula. Preschoolers' literacy was assessed in the preschools before and after intervention. We assessed children's *oral language* – vocabulary; *phonological awareness* (identifying alliterations and rhymes); *print awareness* – orthographic awareness (selecting a Hebrew word vs. a non-word) and letter knowledge; and word *writing* (writing two pairs or words: Words in each pair differed in their phonological length).

All the children showed progress from pretest to posttest on all the literacy measures. Children who participated in the shared book reading intervention showed greater progress than children in the control group on *phonological awareness* (alliterations, rhymes) and on *print awareness* with regard to orthographic knowledge (selecting a Hebrew word vs. a non-word and explaining their choice, e.g., "This is not a word in Hebrew because it has English in it"). However, they did not show significantly better gains in *oral language* (receptive vocabulary), *print awareness* with regard to letter knowledge, or *early writing* skills (according to Levin and Bus, 2003).

In light of the limited benefits found for this shared reading intervention alongside its ineffectiveness for *oral language*, the letter knowledge component of *print awareness*, and *early writing*, the intervention underwent refinement to focus on the book's vocabulary and include direct reference to print. It was then implemented the following year in the same town with different participants.

2.1.2 Focus on plot and print

This time, four preschool teachers conducted the intervention themselves. Teachers have implemented programs in only a few shared book-reading intervention studies (see Wasik, Bond, and Hindman 2006). However, programs implemented by teachers may offer greater productivity due to their potential for generalization, whereas researcher-operated interventions may not necessarily be transferable to classrooms.

Thus, the second shared book-reading design conducted interventions utilizing the classroom teachers as mediators.

Participants in Study 2 were 78 preschoolers aged 3–5 years (37 in the intervention group, 41 in the control group) from the same low SES Israeli town (Aram 2006). The children in the four control preschools continued "business as usual" in their classroom curriculum. In the intervention group, trained teachers used a year-long biweekly intervention schedule, reading a total of 10 storybooks with the preschoolers in small groups (4–5 children per group). The teachers read the books, verifying that children understood the plot and using interactive reading techniques. Based on previous studies (Justice and Ezell 2002; Ukrainetz, Cooney, Dyer, Kysar, and Harris 2000), in addition to focusing on each story's central concepts like print directionality, identification of title and of words) (Justice and Ezell 2002) and phonological awareness (Ukrainetz, Cooney, Dyer, Kysar, and Harris 2000) during shared reading, in addition to focusing on each story's central concepts, the teacher systematically drew the children's attention to the storybook's print through activities like talking broadly about each book's title with reference to the print, identifying words that appeared frequently in the book (e.g., main characters' names), naming letters in words, and stressing rhymes or other play-on-word instances. In the last session of the unit on each book, teachers invited children to tell the story by themselves as a group, following the pictures. Unlike the first study, where creative activities (crafts, drama, etc.) were at heart of the program, this time they were only offered as an optional after-session activity.

Preschoolers' literacy (*oral language* – vocabulary, *phonological awareness*, *print awareness* – letter knowledge, and *early writing* – name and word writing) was assessed in the preschools before and after intervention. Results showed the positive impact of this preschool-based teacher-mediated shared reading intervention for low SES children, with its dual focus on plot and print. It yielded more significant gains not only on children's *phonological awareness* (alliteration and rhymes) but also on their *oral language* (vocabulary), *print awareness* (alphabetic knowledge), and *early writing* (name writing), compared to their counterparts in the control group.

From these preschool-based studies, we learned that an efficient shared book-reading intervention must include two components: explicit reference to both the plot and the print. The adult in the interaction should indeed refer to the plot and help children understand its meaning and flow but must also discuss the book's vocabulary and systematically draw children's attention to the book's print. Moreover, children must be active participants in the shared book-reading interaction. With this knowledge, we next attempted to design a productive shared book-reading intervention in the homes of children from low SES families.

2.2 Home-based shared book reading

The next shared reading study targeted parents, assuming that parents hold primary responsibility for their children's wellbeing and development (Britto, Brooks-Gunn, and Griffin 2006). Parents are motivated to promote their children's present and future welfare. Guiding parents in mediating their children's learning may broaden their conception of parental roles, at least with respect to schooling. Encouraging parents from a low SES population to take on the role of learning mediator to their children is an ambitious endeavor because of these parents' relatively limited educational resources and their competing duties and stressors.

In light of our prior preschool-based intervention outcomes, in Study 3 mothers were coached to refer to both plot and print via interactive reading. To help mothers relate systematically to the plot component, we stressed reference to story grammar – the narrative's basic structure identifying the protagonist, the problem(s) s/he faces, the solution(s) attempted and reached, and the lesson to be drawn from the story. We assumed that clear reference to story grammar in addition to the other components (plot and print) might deepen the child's processing and understanding of the story, as a cohesive, large unit of text (van Kleeck 2008) and thus might widen the intervention's effect on various early literacy skills.

Study 3 (supported by the Israel Academy of Sciences and Humanities) was conducted in a town whose residents are mainly of low Socio-Economic-Status (Levin and Aram 2012). Participants were 61 mother-child dyads from low SES families (34 in the intervention group and 27 in the control group). Children were aged 5–6 years (mean: 5;5 years; months). Children for the intervention and the control groups were recruited from the same preschools, and mothers in the control participated in a shared book-reading workshop at the end of the study.

In the intervention group, mothers participated in a workshop on effective shared book reading prior to the intervention. During the 7-week intervention, a research assistant visited the family each week, bringing a new storybook to read as well as written guidelines for the shared interaction. The research assistant taught the mother how to read each book to her child three times during that week. On each of the seven selected books, printed stickers were affixed to different pages, proposing comments for the mothers to voice or questions for the mother to ask her child before, during, and after book reading. Mothers were coached to use the proposed questions sensitively, by adjusting the questions to their child's needs. Open-ended questions focusing on text comprehension or on word meaning were frequent. A few questions connected the story to the child's experiences. Other questions and comments referred to the print (e.g., noticing repeating words, asking about the initial letter of a word) and to the story grammar (e.g., stating who is the main character, asking about her goal).

Videotapes of shared book-reading interactions after the intervention showed that mothers in the intervention group tripled the number of times they initiated dialogues with their children compared to before the intervention, thereby greatly increasing their children's participation in the discourse during reading. Still, despite our efforts to encourage these mothers to refer to print and story grammar during their shared reading experiences, mothers hardly did so, and as seen next, children in the intervention group did not progress more than children in the control group on alphabetic skills (except for letter isolation).

Children's literacy was assessed in the preschools before and after intervention and at a follow-up interval 2.5 months later on *oral language* skills (vocabulary, providing definitions, sentence comprehension, story comprehension), *phonological awareness* (isolating initial sounds in words), *print awareness* (alphabetic skills like naming letters, isolating the first letter in words), and *early writing* (word writing). Findings showed that immediately after completing the parent-mediated intervention, children in the intervention group outperformed their peers in the control group only on the receptive vocabulary test (*oral language*) and on *phonological awareness*. However, 2.5 months later, they outperformed their peers on *phonological awareness*, high level *oral language* measures (sentence and story comprehension), and *print awareness* (letter isolation). Interestingly, as mentioned above, although we directly coached mothers to discuss the written language with their children during shared reading, they had difficulty complying and, as a result, the intervention mostly promoted the children's *oral language skills*.

2.3 What can we learn from these shared book-reading interventions?

Our series of research studies on young children from low SES backgrounds showed that shared book-reading interventions are productive in fostering literacy both in preschools and at home. They are productive across ages, with both younger (3–5-year-olds) and older (5–6-year-olds) children benefiting from them. Overall, these book-reading interventions contributed well to *oral language* and *phonological awareness* but contributed less well to *print awareness* (alphabetic skills) and *early writing*. In the preschools, when we specifically coached teacher mediators to refer to print during shared reading (Study 2), the teachers complied and the children progressed on both *oral language* skills and on *print awareness* (basic alphabetic skills). Weaker gains were shown when the intervention focused only on the book's central concepts without direct focus on print (Study 1).

At home, mothers from low SES backgrounds learned to read books more interactively, and their children's *oral language* competencies progressed (Study 3). This is very important because vocabulary and listening comprehension are strong predictors of reading comprehension. Yet, children's *print awareness* (alphabetic skills) and *early writing* were hardly impacted by the mother-mediated shared reading intervention. We attribute these findings to the fact that mothers had difficulty referring to print despite our research team's guidance and encouragement. Perhaps relating to print seemed less natural or too complex to these mothers from a low SES background, who often had only a high school education level, compared to the preschool teachers in Study 2 who did succeed in referring to print when mediating the shared book intervention. In addition, perhaps children's storybooks, with their colorful illustrations, frequent use of humor, and simple appealing themes may pull these mothers toward referring more to the plot and less the print. Indeed, there is evidence that young children's (3–6-year-olds) eye fixation on print is rare during storybook reading (Evans and Saint-Aubin 2005).

Considering that perhaps book reading may less naturally lend itself to adults' references to print and promotion of *print awareness* and *early writing*, we explored the effects of a second line of interventions where adults may help mediate the alphabetic code for children through joint writing activities. We expected this second direction of intervention, through adult-child writing, to provide what storybook-reading interventions could not effectively provide: promotion of children's *print awareness* (alphabet knowledge), and *early writing* competencies.

3 Adult-child joint writing

Children in Western society live in a print-rich environment, with vast exposure to commercial and public signs; texts appearing on television, computers, and games; and books and written materials provided in their educational settings. Young children's attempts to write begin long before they understand the alphabetic principle – the understanding that letters represent sounds (e.g., Neumann, Hood, and Neumann 2008; Neumann et al. 2009). Naturally, in early educational settings and at home, adults join young children's interest in the written world and support them when they initially scribble and then attempt to write letters, words, and names on labels, notes, lists, greeting cards, signs, reminders, and so on (e.g., Hall 2000; Neumann et al. 2009; Neumann and Neumann 2010; Saracho 2000).

Children enjoy writing, but they need adults' help to gradually learn the process of translating the spoken word to written symbols (Shatil, Share, and Levin 2000). In contrast with the vast research on storybook reading, adult-child joint writing and its relations with children's early literacy and later literacy achievements have received much less research attention (Aram and Levin 2011). Nevertheless, a line of studies did explore the effects of adult writing support on children's early literacy. Higher-level support, which encourages children to independently and carefully go through the writing process from the segmentation of the word into its sounds, through the connection of the sounds to letter names, until producing the letters on paper, have consistently been linked with children's *print awareness* and *early writing* skills across varied orthographies (e.g., Aram and Levin 2001 in Hebrew; Lin et al. 2009 in Chinese; and Bindman, Worzalla, Hindman, Aram, and Morrison 2014 and Bindman, Skibbe, Hindman, Aram, and Morrison 2014 in English). Furthermore, adults' writing mediation predicted children's reading and writing in school (Aram and Levin 2004 in Hebrew; Aram et al. 2013 in Arabic).

For the last decade or more, in many preschools across the world including Israel, children have been encouraged to write (Ministry of Education 2006). Nevertheless, few studies have focused on enhancing writing at this young age and on pinpointing what young children might gain from learning to write (but see Martins and Silva 2006; Ouellette and Sénéchal 2008). Ouellette and Sénéchal (2008) conducted a 4-week training study guiding kindergartners in how to improve their invented writing. The writing intervention showed greater benefits to children's *phonological awareness*, *print awareness* (orthographic awareness), and recognition of *printed words* than did a control group trained using phonological activities or involved in drawing.

Piasta and Wagner (2010) criticized early literacy interventions where children practice *print awareness* (letter knowledge) and *phonological awareness* separately, for their lack of emphasis on letter-sound relationships. Acknowledging the potential value of writing activities as a communicative literacy activity that specifically focuses on letter-sound relationships, we initiated a series of interventions where adults mediated the writing of children from low SES backgrounds. We aimed to study the particular benefits of preschool-based and home-based writing interventions for young children, which have been less investigated empirically than shared reading interventions in these settings.

3.1 Preschool-based writing intervention: When to begin?

Interventions focusing on alphabetic skill training are usually implemented to target children aged 5–7 years. Yet, early literacy interventions for younger children generally refrain from including alphabetic skills or writing components (e.g., Karweit and Wasik 1996). We undertook a study to explore the extent to which young children aged 3–5 years may gain from a writing intervention in their preschool (Aram 2006). Moreover, we wanted to examine if differences might emerge between children aged 4–5 years and their younger classmates aged 3–4 years attending the same preschool settings.

Six preschools from a low SES town participated in Study 4 (supported by the Price-Brody Initiative). Three preschools took part in the intervention group, and three other preschools (the control group) continued with their regular curricula. Each preschool served about 35 children in two age groups: 3–4-year-olds and 4–5-year-olds. During a year-long program, each of the six preschool teachers worked with a small group of 4–6 children for about 30 minutes twice weekly. The groups were assembled homogeneously according to their level of early literacy skills. The teacher mediated writing by focusing on letters, words' phonological segments, and letter-sound mappings. In line with the spirit of preschool pedagogical thinking, groups practiced literacy related play activities within children's Zone of Proximal Development (Vygotsky 1980). In general, children were first taught to recognize their written name and the written names of their friends. Gradually, they were explicitly taught letter-name and letter-sound correspondences, word segmentation, and encoding skills, mostly using the group participants' names and names of friends outside the group as words for practice. Later, they started writing functional print (e.g., a roster of their classmates' telephone numbers). Inasmuch as younger children (3–4-year-olds) may not yet have the necessary fine motor coordination to write with a pencil, especially at the beginning of the year, we encouraged all children in the intervention group to practice writing and forming letter shapes in diverse ways: using stamps, stickers, magnetized letters, newspaper cuttings, pencils, and crayons.

All participants were assessed for a range of literacy skills before and after the intervention. The pretest versus posttest comparison showed that children who received the intervention progressed significantly more than children in the control group on *phonological awareness*, *print awareness* (orthographic awareness, letter knowledge), and *early writing* (of names and words). They did not outperform the control group on *oral language* skills. Interestingly, the younger children progressed more than their older peers on phonological awareness, letter knowledge, and name writing.

So, when to begin writing interventions? This study's results revealed that children as young as 3 years of age benefited significantly from the writing intervention. The younger children (3–4-year-olds) benefited as much as their older peers (4–5-year-olds) on all early literacy measures, and they even benefited more on phonological awareness, letter knowledge, and name writing. These results correspond with Whitehurst et al.'s (1999) claim that younger children are at a more sensitive period for literacy development. Study 4 confirmed that preschool educators can work with young 3–4-year-old children from low SES on writing activities within a developmentally appropriate framework, and that such activities are indeed fruitful in promoting children's *print awareness* and *early writing*.

Guidance on writing refers to the level of support that caregivers provide to children while writing words, thereby teaching them about the written system. Acknowledging the importance of joint writing with young children from low SES, we decided to deepen our understanding regarding writing development, with a focus on identifying optimally efficient feedback to give children during adults' writing guidance.

3.2 Preschool-based writing interventions: The merits of different feedback

When guiding a child to write, many adults dictate letters to children or display a model to copy, paying less attention to children's understanding of the encoding process (e.g., Worzalla et al. 2014). We wondered if such feedback is the most fruitful in helping children understand the writing encoding process. Moreover, some educators and parents believe that children construct their own knowledge about writing by autonomously exploring ways in which to write (e.g., Bissex 1980). If that is the case, then the role of caregiver's feedback would be viewed as minor. Thus, in Study 5, we wanted to compare the effectiveness of three types of feedback for promoting children's literacy: dictating and displaying letters, explaining the encoding process and displaying letters, or merely encouraging children to write. We also assessed how children's initial literacy skills and self-regulation skills might affect their learning pace.

Study 5 was executed by research assistants in ten preschools in a low SES town and was supported by the Israel Academy of Sciences and Humanities (Levin and Aram 2013). In each preschool, we implemented three writing interventions with different feedback and a control group. Participants were 197 children aged 5–6 years from low SES divided into four groups: 50 in the process-product mediation group (encoding), 48 in the product mediation group (dictation), 51 in the no mediation group (mere encouragement), and 48 in the no intervention (control) group that continued its regular curriculum without intervention. In each of the three intervention groups, children practiced writing five words twice weekly for 16 weeks, before and after receiving different feedback from the researcher. The three interventions all followed the same spell-feedback-spell practice sequence for all 5 words in each session.

In the *process-product mediation* group, the feedback focused on the word's phonological segmentation and the letters to write. After the child spelled each word, the researcher showed how she encodes that word by segmenting the word into sounds. For each sound, the researcher matched the sound with a letter name aloud, chose the correct magnetic letter from a magnetized letter bank containing all the letters, said its name, and placed that letter on a line. She continued this process until the word was displayed. Then she said the whole word twice, returned the magnetic letters randomly to the board, and asked the child to write the word again. In the *product mediation* group, the feedback focused on dictating the spelling of a word by naming each required letter. After the child spelled each word, the researcher showed how she spells that word: The researcher chose the correct magnetic letter from the letter bank, named it, placed that letter on a line, and continued until the word was displayed. Then she said the whole word twice, returned the magnetic letters randomly to the board, and asked the child to write the word again. In the *no mediation* intervention group, children did not receive any feedback but were merely encouraged to spell the five words. For each word, the researcher asked the child to spell using the magnetized letters. When the child said that s/he had finished writing the word, the researcher returned the magnetic letters randomly to the board and asked the child to write the word again without providing any feedback.

Children's literacy was assessed before and after the intervention, including: *print awareness* – letter naming and recognition, *phonological awareness*, *early writing* – spelling, and *early reading* – decoding. *Process-product* mediation proved to be most effective in promoting children's literacy achievements, beyond the effects of children's baseline levels for self-regulation and early literacy skills. Importantly, the common writing practice used by parents and teachers of dictating letters without explicating the encoding process did not lead to significant gains.

The results of this preschool-based joint writing intervention study were very informative. Beyond showing this activity's productivity for promoting *print awareness* and *early writing* in children from a low SES background, this study pinpointed the best adult intervention practice: helping children go through the whole process of segmenting a word into its sounds and matching each sound with its letter aloud. Adults' feedback should expose children not only to the correct product but also to the spelling's underlying process. Furthermore, we learned that dictating letters or practicing writing without any feedback are almost ineffective in promoting children's *print awareness* or *early writing*. Based on these preschool-based results, we next designed a pioneering home literacy intervention that focused on parent-child joint writing in families from a low SES.

3.3 Home-based writing intervention: Teaching mothers to write with their children

To the best of our knowledge, prior to our study, home literacy interventions among low SES families had centered on shared book reading without attempting to encourage and teach parents to write with their preschool-age children. Respecting parents' importance in promoting their young children's development, in Study 6 we aimed to teach parents to mediate writing to their children and thus promote their children's various early literacy skills (Aram and Levin 2014). We examined whether an intervention program that coached mothers in how to guide their children's writing could improve maternal *writing guidance* – the level of support that mothers provided to children in writing words, thereby teaching them about the written system.

Participants in Study 6 (supported by the Israel Academy of Sciences and Humanities) were 69 children (aged 5–6 years) from a low SES town and their mothers: 37 in the writing mediation intervention group and 32 in the control group that received a visuo-motor skills mediation intervention. Mothers in both groups were asked to engage their child for about 30 minutes three times per week, for 7 weeks, in appealing educational activities designed by the researchers. Each week, a research assistant visited each family in both groups, bringing new games and activities and coaching mothers to perform the week's tasks.

In the writing mediation group, mothers received instruction in how to promote their children's early literacy skills by scaffolding children's word writing. Objectives were to promote children's: comprehension of the alphabetic principle, letter knowledge, awareness of phonology, and word spelling. Mothers were coached to guide their children's word writing at the highest possible level of independence, by encouraging the child to segment words into phonemic sounds, to connect sounds with letters representing those sounds, to retrieve the required letters' shapes, and then to print them. Mothers received coaching in how to write with their children and play with them three times that week using games to practice letter knowledge, phonological awareness, and word spelling (e.g., writing words that start with the same sound, writing a shopping list, writing a telephone contact list).

In the visuo-motor skills mediation control group, mothers received coaching in how to engage their children three times that week to enhance fine visual-motor skills – by scaffolding children in activities of drawing, painting, cutting, gluing, following lines, coloring, and so on.

Children's literacy was assessed before and after the intervention, including *print awareness* (e.g., alphabetic skills, word reading), *phonological awareness, early writing* (e.g., word spelling), and *oral language* (e.g., receptive vocabulary, expressive vocabulary). In addition, mother-child dyads were videotaped during joint writing at home at three intervals: before and after the intervention and 2.5 months later. Results showed that the joint writing intervention contributed more than the visuo-motor skills control group to enhancing children's *print awareness, phonological awareness*, and *early writing*, beyond the effects of age and of children's baseline literacy scores. However, neither group showed significant gains in *oral language* skills. Analyses of mother-child writing interactions revealed that mothers in the intervention group learned to guide writing at a very high level, significantly higher than mothers in the control group.

3.4 What can we learn from these joint writing interventions?

In contrast with traditional practices that teach reading before spelling and that perceive spelling as an activity that supports reading, Chomsky (1971) proposed that children should be taught first to write and then to read. Indeed, the three writing-based studies presented in the second part of this chapter seem to indicate that writing activities appear to be at least as important as reading activities, if not more. These studies illustrated the productivity of involving young children in writing experiences, in the educational setting and at home, for promoting children's *print awareness* (alphabetic skills, word recognition), *phonological awareness*, and *early writing*.

These promising findings show that even mothers from a low SES background can learn to mediate their children's writing if they receive coaching, and that such maternal mediation at home is beneficial for advancing children's literacy. Furthermore, we found that preschool teachers can work with young children on writing skills, fitting these activities into their everyday demanding agenda, and that integration of such activities into the developmentally appropriate education framework is indeed fruitful for promoting young children's literacy.

When teachers and parents ask how to mediate writing to young children and what feedback to give children in preschool and at home, our research provides some important insight. To optimally foster children's writing, adults should explain and demonstrate the multistep processes of sound-to-grapheme mapping involved in the spelling of a word, along with the display of the correct spelling product. Our writing intervention program coached mothers and teachers to guide writing at the highest possible level. This entails starting with an expectation of the highest autonomy in spelling from the child but gradually lowering expectations if the child fails to follow the adult's guidance, trying to adapt the guidance to the child's knowledge. For example, when inviting the child to write the word "table," the mother might ask "What sound do you hear at the beginning of the word? Which letter stands for *t*?" If the child does not know, she may give a hint (e.g. "it's like the first letter in your sister's name Tamar"). Only then, if the child still does not know, will she tell him the letter name. Then she will continue to adapt her guidance to the child's knowledge about the letter's shape.

Parents, teachers, and policy makers must all take note of three important implications of joint writing research: First of all, writing guidance at the highest possible level appears to be a crucial factor. In previous studies where tutors guided writing (Martins and Silva 2006; Ouellette and Sénéchal 2008), guidance was provided at one level ahead of the child's own spelling. This is probably why children's literacy improvement was limited. In our writing interventions, children's literacy skills progressed dramatically. This implies that limiting guidance to a level close to that of the child's own writing may not be the most fruitful guidance. Second, merely dictating letters to young children does not appear to enhance their understanding of the writing process. Third, simply encouraging children to write, without giving them feedback, is also inefficient for advancing children's writing in particular and early literacy in general.

These findings hold particular implications for the low-SES population. Evidence suggests that children who start school lagging behind their counterparts on *print awareness* (alphabetic skills) and *phonological awareness* are likely to remain behind, especially if they are from a low SES family (Whitehurst and Lonigan 2002). A good start – obtainable both at home and in the preschool – is likely to help young children develop more efficient early literacy skills.

4 Conclusion and general discussion

Promoting early childhood development is one of the most important tasks a country can undertake to ensure its citizens' future health and wellbeing. Emotional, social, and academic abilities are formed during early childhood and influence the individual throughout the lifetime. Thus, investing in the early years to enhance early child development can improve outcomes in multiple domains, and it represents a sound economic investment (Heckman 2007).

This chapter presented a series of early literacy intervention studies conducted in the homes and in the early educational settings of Hebrew-speaking children from low SES families in Israel, who are especially deserving of such economic investment because they are at risk for lower educational trajectories. In these interventions focusing on two major adult-child literacy activities – shared book reading and joint writing – teachers and parents were encouraged to read to their children and write with them in more efficient ways to facilitate different literacy skills. Overall, shared book reading was found to promote *oral language* skills (e.g., vocabulary, comprehension), whereas writing with children was found to promote *print awareness, phonological awareness,* and *early writing*. Thus, the two sets of activities clearly appear to offer complementary contributions to children's literacy development.

Our conclusion coincides with Sénéchal and LeFevre's (2002) ideas regarding the home literacy model. They suggested that the major parental activity that promotes *print awareness* is teaching literacy skills like letter knowledge, grapho-phonemic mappings, and word writing, whereas the major parent-child joint activity that promotes *oral language* is storybook reading. The studies presented in this chapter indeed show that shared reading and joint writing promote different early literacy skills and can be promoted by adults both at home and at preschool.

Importantly, there was no evidence that the effectiveness of the writing interventions was influenced by the children's age or developmental level. That is, the impact of such interventions emerged regardless of whether the children were 3 or 5 years old. This contradicts what teachers and parents commonly think about writing activities – that they are relevant only in the school years. Regrettably, this misconception often prevents adults today from actively exposing young children and encouraging them to engage in writing activities (e.g., writing notes, lists, words).

Once adults recognize the importance of both joint reading and joint writing activities, they need to consider the "how" of introducing such tasks in order to maximize effectiveness. As our research review has shown, important features of both shared book reading and writing mediation have been pinpointed that can significantly improve these activities' effectiveness. Therefore, it is crucial for parents and teachers to receive coaching in the best ways to write with young children and read books with them. Moreover, when it comes to books, beyond the frequency and nature of shared book reading, it is vital to choose the most appropriate books (Aram, Bergman Deitcher, & Adar, forthcoming; Bergman Deitcher, Aram, & Adar, 2017). Helping parents and teachers select the right children's books can lead to more meaningful and frequent shared book-reading experiences.

The preschool and the home are different environments with different agendas. While preschools focus more on teaching and learning, homes first and foremost provide parenting and emotional care. Consequently, literacy should be taught in preschool through a well-planned curriculum, whereas at home it may be integrated into everyday communication, daily games, and chores that promote a close caregiver-child relationship and provide entertainment. Parents must receive coaching in how to construct effective yet appealing early literacy activities (shared book reading and joint writing) within their daily interactions with their children.

It seems that parents, at least those we investigated who lacked higher education, failed to guide their children to refer to print when reading storybooks, even when coached systematically to do so. However, these parents were able to effectively guide their children to increase print awareness while engaging in the joint writing activities. It seems that mothers from low SES perceive alphabetic activities as school-related (Ninio 1979) and do not integrate them into home or leisure activities with their children, unless they are explicitly taught how to do so. Importantly, these findings suggest that home-based interventions should carefully integrate both components, shared reading and writing. Shared book reading can focus on the plot, which contributes to children's *oral language*, but can also focus on the book's socioemotional themes. Indeed, the plots of children's storybooks often deal with interpersonal and affective topics, and parents from low SES backgrounds who were coached to exploit these contents during shared reading successfully learned to discuss sociocognitive and socioemotional situations with particular relevance to their young children's lives (Aram, Fine, and Ziv 2013).

Unfortunately, despite the extensive merits identified for adult-child joint writing, parents and teachers continue to show considerably more awareness about the importance of shared book reading. The significant adults in young children's lives, both at home and in preschool, must become more sensitive to sporadic occurrences of writing interaction and at the same time must initiate more writing activities, specifically while explaining and demonstrating the encoding processes.

Yet, it seems that curricular reforms alone are insufficient to enhance teachers' sensitivity. The Ministry of Education's 2006 national early literacy curriculum began to encourage preschool teachers to practice writing with their students. Indeed, teachers recently reported that, since the curriculum's implementation, they have increased their writing activities with children; yet, relative to other literacy activities (e.g., shared book reading), the writing activities' frequency continues to remain lower (Sverdlov, Aram, and Levin 2014). Hence, preschool teachers clearly need support and coaching to execute a deep change in integrating everyday writing practices into their preschool settings. Our current challenge is to find ways to convince them of writing activities' benefits, particularly for the low SES population.

Considering preschool teachers' role as vital agents for reducing children's developmental disparities that already begin at this early age, provision of support to teachers may help them meet the many challenges of implementation. Yet, the education system alone cannot cope with the societal problems that come about as a result of socioeconomic and ethnocultural differences. Thus, a dual approach should be undertaken, where in addition to teachers as change agents, parents are also considered to be responsible, capable partners. Together, they can make a difference in promoting these at-risk children's early literacy – to furnish the better early foundation shown to be an important key to later academic success.

References

Aram, Dorit. 2005. The continuity in children's literacy achievements: A longitudinal perspective from kindergarten to second grade. *First Language* 25. 259–289.

Aram, Dorit. 2006. Early literacy interventions: The relative roles of storybook reading, alphabetic skills activities, and their combination. *Reading and Writing: An Interdisciplinary Journal* 19.

Aram, Dorit, & Iris Levin. 2001. Mother-child joint writing in low SES: Socio-cultural factors, maternal mediation and emergent literacy. *Cognitive Development* 16. 831–852.

Aram, Dorit & Shira Biron. 2004. Joint storybook reading and joint writing interventions among low SES Israeli preschoolers: Differential contribution to early literacy. *Early Childhood Research Quarterly* 19. 588–610.

Aram, Dorit & Iris Levin. 2004. The role of maternal mediation of writing to kindergartners in promoting literacy in school: A longitudinal perspective. *Reading and Writing: An Interdisciplinary Journal* 17. 387–409.

Aram, Dorit. Deborah Bergman Deitcher, & Gali Adar (forthcoming). Understanding parents' support for complexity in children's books. *Reading Horizons*.

Aram, Dorit, Ofra Korat & Safieh Hassona-Arafat. 2013. The contribution of early home literacy activities to reading and writing in Arabic in first grade. *Reading and Writing: An Interdisciplinary Journal* 26. 1517–153.

Aram, Dorit, Yaara Fine & Margalit Ziv. 2013. Enhancing parent-child shared book reading interactions: Promoting references to the book's plot and socio-cognitive themes. *Early Childhood Research Quarterly* 28. 111–122.

Aram, Dorit & Iris Levin. 2011. Home support of children in the writing process: Contributions to early literacy. In Susan B Neuman & David K. Dickinson (eds.), *Handbook of early literacy* (Vol. 3), 189–199. NY: Guilford.

Aram, Dorit & Iris Levin. 2014. Mother-child joint writing as a learning activity. In Joan Perera, Melina Aparici, Elisa Rosado & Nayme Salas (eds.), *Literacy studies. Perspectives from cognitive neurosciences, linguistics, psychology and education*, 29–45. New York: Springer.

Aram, Dorit, Deborah Bergman Deitcher, Tami Sabag- Shushan & Margalit Ziv. 2017. Shared book reading interactions within families from low socioeconomic backgrounds and children's social understanding and prosocial behavior. *Journal of Cognitive Education and Psychology* 16. 157–177.

Arcavi, Abraham & Neomy Mandel-Levy. 2014. *Education for all and for each and every one in the Israeli education system*. Jerusalem: The Israel Academy of Sciences and Humanities.

Bartl-Pokorny, Katrin D., Peter B. Marschik, Steffi Sachse, Vanessa A. Green, Dajie Zhang, Larah Van Der Meer, Thomas Wolin & Christa Einspieler. 2013. Tracking development from early speech-language acquisition to reading skills at age 13. *Developmental Neurorehabilitation* 16(3). 188–195.

Barnett, W. Stevan & Jason T. Hustedt. 2003. Preschool: The most important grade. *Educational Leadership* 60. 54–57.

Ben David, Dan & Xaim Bleix. 2013. Poverty and inequality in Israel: Longitudinal development comparing to the OECD. In Dan Ben David (ed.), *The state of the country: Society, economics, and policy 2013*, 17–68. Jerusalem: Taub Center. (Hebrew).

Bergman Deitcher, Deborah, Dorit Aram, and Gali Adar. 2017. Book selection for shared reading: Parents' considerations and researchers' views. *Journal of Early Childhood Literacy*. DOI: 10.1177/1468798417718236.

Berliner, David. 2006. Our impoverished view of educational reform. *Teachers' College Record* 108(6). 949–995.

Bindman, Samantha W., Lori E. Skibbe, Annemarie H. Hindman, Dorit Aram & Frederick J. Morrison. 2014. Parental writing support and preschoolers' early literacy, language, and fine motor skills. *Early Childhood Research Quarterly* 29. 614–624.

Bissex, Glenda 1980. *GNYS AT WRK: A child learns to read and write*. Cambridge, MA: Harvard University Press.

Bossaert, Goele, Sarah Doumen, Evelien Buyse & Karine Verschueren. 2011. Predicting children's academic achievement after the transition to first grade: A two-year longitudinal study. *Journal of Applied Developmental Psychology* 32. 47–57.

Britto, Pia R., Jeanne Brooks-Gunn & Terri M. Griffin. 2006. Maternal reading and teaching patterns: Associations with school readiness in low-income African-American families. *Reading Research Quarterly* 41. 68–89.

Center for Socioeconomic Research. 2000 (February). *Statistical data about Jaffa* (Studies and Surveys Report No. 69). Tel Aviv: Author. (Hebrew).

Costa, Hugo Câmara, Hervé Perdry, Carmen Soria, Salomé Pulgar, Françoise Cusin & Georges Dellatolas. 2013. Emergent literacy skills, behavior problems and familial antecedents of reading difficulties: A follow-up study of reading achievement from kindergarten to fifth grade. *Research in Developmental Disabilities* 34. 1018–1035.

Dickinson, David K., Jill B. Freiberg & Erica Barnes. 2011. Why are so few interventions really effective? A call for fine-grained research methodology. In Susan B. Neuman & David K. Dickinson (eds.), *Handbook of early literacy research* (Vol. III), 337–357. New York: Guilford Press.

Duncan, Greg & Richard Murnane. 2011. Introduction: The American dream, then and now. In Duncan Greg & Richard Murnane (eds.), *Whither opportunity? Rising inequality, schools, and children's life chances*, 3–26. New York: Russell Sage.

Evans, Mary-Ann, & Jane Saint-Aubin. 2005. What children are looking at during shared storybook reading. *Psychological Science* 16. 913–920.

Hall, Nigel. 2000. Interactive writing with young children. *Childhood Education* 76. 358–364.

Hayes, Andrew, F. 2012. PROCESS: A versatile computational tool for observed variable mediation, moderation, and conditional process modeling [White paper]. Retrieved from http://www.afhayes.com/public/process2012.pdf. (Accessed 1 June 2016).

Justice, Laura M. & Helen K. Ezell. 2002. Use of storybook reading to increase print awareness in at-risk children. *American Journal of Speech-Language Pathology* 11. 17–29.

Klein, Pnina & Yaacov Yablon. 2008. *Mi-mechkar la-asya be-hinuch la-gil ha-rach* [From research to practice in early childhood education]. Jerusalem: Israel Academy of Science and Humanities [Hebrew].

Karweit, Nancy & Barbara. A. Wasik. 1996. The effects of story reading programs on literacy and language development of disadvantaged preschoolers. *Journal of Education for Students Placed at Risk* 4. 319–348.

Levin, Iris & Dorit Aram. 2013. Promoting early literacy via practicing invented spelling: A comparison of different mediation routines. *Reading Research Quarterly* 48. 1–16.

Levin, Iris & Dorit Aram. 2012. Mother–child joint writing and storybook reading and their effects on kindergartners' literacy: An intervention study. *Reading and Writing: An Interdisciplinary Journal* 25. 217–249.

Levin, Iris & Adriana G. Bus. 2003. How is emergent writing based on drawing? Analyses of children's products and their sorting by children and mothers. *Developmental Psychology* 39. 891.

Lepola, Janne, Elisa Poskiparta, Eero Laakkonen & Pekka Niemi. 2005. Development of and relationship between phonological and motivational processes and naming speed in predicting word recognition in Grade 1. *Scientific Studies of Reading* 9. 367–399.

Lin, Dan, Cathrine McBride-Chang, Dorit Aram, Iris Levin, Rebecca M. Cheung, Yonne Y. Chow & Liliane Tolchinsky. 2009. Maternal mediation of writing in Chinese children. *Language and Cognitive Processes* 24. 1286–1311.

Martins, Mararida, & Cristina Silva. 2006. The impact of invented spelling on phonemic awareness. *Learning and Instruction* 16. 41–56.

Ministry of Education. 2006. *Tochnit limudim "Tashtih likrat kria ve-ktiva ba-gan"* [National curriculum: A foundation towards reading and writing in preschool]. Jerusalem: Author [Hebrew].

Mol, Suzanne E., Adriana G. Bus, Maria T. de Jong & Daisy J.H. Smeets. 2008. Added value of dialogic parent-child book reading: A meta-analysis. *Early Education and Development* 19. 7–26.

NELP. 2008. *Developing early literacy*. Report of the National early literacy panel.

Neuman, Susan B. & David K. Dickinson. 2002. *Handbook of early literacy development*. New York: Guilford Press.

Neuman Susan B, Ellen H. Newman & Julia Dwyer. 2011. Educational effects of a vocabulary intervention on preschoolers' word knowledge and conceptual development: A cluster-randomized trial. *Reading Research Quarterly* 46. 249–272.

Neumann, Michelle M., Michelle Hood & David L. Neumann. 2008. The scaffolding of emergent literacy skills in the home environment: A case study. *Early Childhood Educational Journal* 36. 313–319.

Neumann, Michelle & David Neumann. 2010. Parental strategies to scaffold emergent writing skills in the pre-school child within the home environment. *Early Years: An international Journal of Research and Development* 30. 79–94.

Ninio, Anat. 1979. The naive theory of the infant and other maternal attitudes in two subgroups in Israel. *Child Development* 50. 976–980.

OECD. 2010. *PISA 2009 Framework: Key Competencies in Reading, Mathematics and Science*. Paris: OECD Publishing.

Ouellette, Gene & Monique Sénéchal. 2008. Pathways to literacy: A study of invented spelling and its role in learning to read. *Child Development* 79. 899–913.

Piasta, Shayne B., Yaayov Petscher & Laura M. Justice. 2012. How many letters should preschoolers in public programs know? The diagnostic efficiency of various preschool letter-naming benchmarks for predicting first-grade literacy achievement. *Journal of Educational Psychology* 104. 945–958.

Piasta, Shayne B. & Richard K. Wagner. 2010. Learning letter names and sounds: Effects of instruction, letter type, and phonological processing skill. *Journal of Experimental Child Psychology* 105. 324–344.

Saracho, Olivia N. 2000. Literacy development in the family context. *Early Child Development and Care* 163. 107–114.

Sen, Amartya. 1999. *Development as freedom*. New Delhi: Oxford University Press.

Sénéchal, Monique. 2006. Testing the home literacy model: Parent involvement in kindergarten is differentially related to grade 4 reading comprehension, fluency, spelling, and reading for pleasure. *Scientific Studies of Reading* 10. 59–87.

Sénéchal, Monique & Lefevre Jo-Ann. 2002. Parental involvement in the development of children's reading skill: A five-year longitudinal study. *Child Development* 73. 445–460.

Shatil, Evelin, David C. Share & Iris Levin. 2000. On the contribution of kindergarten writing to grade 1 literacy: A longitudinal study in Hebrew. *Applied Psycholinguistics* 21. 1–21.

Skibbe, Lori E., Samantha W. Bindman, Annemarie H. Hindman, Dorit Aram & Frederick J. Morrison. 2013. Longitudinal relations between parental writing support and preschoolers' language and literacy skills. *Reading Research Quarterly* 48(4). 387–401.

Snow, Catherine E., M. Susan Burns & Peg Griffin. 1998. Introduction. In Catherine E. Snow, M. Susan Burns & Peg Griffin (eds.), *Preventing reading difficulties in young children*, 17–41. Washington, DC: National Academy Press.

Sverdlov, Aviva, Dorit Aram & Iris Levin. 2014. Kindergarten teachers' literacy beliefs and self-reported practices: On the heels of a new national literacy curriculum. *Teaching and Teacher Education*, 39, 44–55.

Ukrainetz, Teresa A., Margaret. H. Cooney, Sara K. Dyer, Aimee J. Kysar & Trina J. Harris. 2000. An investigation into teaching phonemic for awareness through shared reading and writing. *Early Childhood Research Quarterly* 15. 331–355.

van Kleeck, Anne & Steven Stahl. 2003. Preface. In Anne van Kleeck, Steven Stahl & Eurydice B. Bauer (eds.), *On reading books to children*, vii-xiii. Mahwah, NJ: Lawrence Erlbaum.

van Kleeck, Anne. 2008. Providing preschool foundations for later reading comprehension: The importance of and ideas for targeting inferencing in story-book sharing interventions. http://onlinelibrary 642.wiley.com/doi/10.1002/pits.20314. (Accessed 1 June 2016).

Vygotsky, Lev S. 1980. *Mind in society: The development of higher psychological processes*. Harvard University Press.

Wasik, Barbara A., Mary-Alice Bond & Anne-Marie Hindman. 2006. The effects of a language and literacy intervention on Head Start children and teachers. *Journal of Educational Psychology* 98. 63–74. http://psycnet.apa.org/journals/edu/98/1/63. (Accessed 1 June 2016).

Whitehurst, Grover. J & Lonigan, Christopher, J. 2002. Emergent literacy: Development from prereaders to readers. In Susan B. Neuman & David K. Dickinson (eds.), *Handbook of early literacy development*, 11–29. New York: Guilford Press.

Zhang Yuping, Tardif Twila, Shu Hua, Li Hong, Liu Hongyun, Catherine McBride-Chang, Liang Weilan & Zhang Zhixiang. 2013. Phonological skills and vocabulary knowledge mediate socioeconomic status effects in predicting reading outcomes for Chinese children. *Developmental Psychology* 49. 665–671. http://psycnet.apa.org/journals/dev/49/4/665.

Zigler, Edward. 2000. Foreword. In Jack Shonkoff, & Samuel Meisels (eds.), *Handbook of early childhood intervention*, xi–xv. Cambridge: Cambridge University Press.

Ziv, Margalit, Marie-Lyne Smadja & Dorit Aram. 2013. Mothers' mental-state discourse with preschoolers during storybook reading and wordless storybook telling. *Early Childhood Research Quarterly* 28(1). 177–186. doi:10.1016/j.ecresq.2012.05.005

Ziv, Margalit, Marie-Lyne Smadja & Dorit Aram. 2015. Preschool teachers' reference to theory of mind topics during different contexts of shared book reading. *Teaching and Teacher Education* 45. 14–24. doi:10.1016/j.tate.2014.08.009

David L. Share
21 Foundations for a universal model of learning to read

1 Introduction

Until quite recently, written language was either ignored by linguists (e.g., Bloomfield 1933; Chomsky 1968; Saussure 1916) or denigrated as unworthy of scholarly attention (see, for discussion, Ravid 2012 and Sampson 1985) – a mere shadowy reflection of spoken language, the proper focus for linguistic enquiry. While it is true that spoken language divides humans from the other animals, it is *written* language and the literacy it affords, that divides humanity itself; separating cultures, communities and individuals from one another. And the world over, poverty and disempowerment go hand in hand with illiteracy and semi-literacy.

The foundations of literacy, of course, are the basic reading and writing skills taught on entry to formal schooling around the world and which remain the primordial *raison d'etre* of this institution. Literacy learning is unquestionably much more than the foundational word reading skills discussed here, but it is nothing without them. And the key to these foundations has remained unchanged since the invention of writing; the near-instantaneous access to the meanings locked in the symbol strings of the written text. Speed is the quintessence of reading expertise (LaBerge and Samuels 1974; Perfetti 1985). The skilled reader sails effortlessly through some four to five words per second (Rayner 1998); a single familiar word is read as quickly as a single letter (Cattell 1885). This process is not only fast but unstoppable. Highway road-signs and billboards are designed to exploit this inescapable aspect of skilled reading – even at high speeds, the driver need only glance at the print and the message is home. Even when a printed word or phrase is flashed so briefly that the reader is not even aware of having seen anything – not even a blur, the brain will dutifully register the message (Forster and Davis 1984). More than any other factor, it's the pace and effortlessness of reading coupled, of course, with the wide availability of writing media that has transformed a technology that was once the preserve of an elite few, largely remote from the everyday lives of the populace, into one of the most remarkable and ubiquitous technological and cultural tools that humankind has yet developed.

But how does this remarkable feat come to be? It does not come "for free" (Liberman 1992) but takes time, effort and practice – years of daily practice in fact. Like other skills, it rarely develops spontaneously simply by seeing and hearing others read, like spoken language, although the desire (or lack thereof) to join the

---

David L.Share, Haifa University

community of readers/writers springs from the same source. For much of humanity, however, reading is not fluent, but reluctant, halting and laborious. In many developing countries, illiteracy or semi-literacy is endemic. Even in the most literate societies in the world, substantial numbers of individuals struggle to learn to read (Shaywitz and Shaywitz 1998; Snowling 2000).

Few topics have fired such debate and acrimony for so long as the question of how to teach children to read (Adams 1990; Chall 1967; Cronin 2015; Goodman 1989; Strauss and Altwerger 2007); and still, dissatisfaction with general levels of literacy attainment abounds and debate over methods continues unabated (Buckingham, Wheldall, and Beamont-Wheldall 2013; Cronin 2015; Seidenberg 2013; Tunmer et al. 2013).

A science of reading must be anchored in an appreciation of the diversity yet unity (DeFrancis 1989) of languages and writing systems and the social-cultural-historical context of literacy learning. The 7000 or so living languages in the world today (Ethnologue 2014) are not all English-like (Christiansen and Chater 2015; Evans and Levinson 2009), nor is the majority of the world learning to read a European alphabet (Daniels and Bright 1996) or even a writing system that can be said to consist of "letters" (Daniels 2017). Ethnocentrism is a normal and natural facet of human nature, but in reading science, it blinds researchers to the dangers of applying models developed on a single language or writing system to the rest of humanity (Frost 2012; Share 2008a). There has been growing concern among social scientists (Harari 2014; Henrich, Heine and Norenzayan 2010), linguists (Evans and Levinson 2009; Gaur 1995; Rogers 2005; Sampson 1985) and reading researchers (Feitelson 1988; Frost 2012; Share 2008a; Wimmer and Landerl 1997) that conclusions from studies conducted on highly educated populations from affluent European cultures may have limited applicability across humanity. Reading research, in particular, has been overwhelmingly dominated by work on English, which appears to be an outlier among European alphabets (Seymour, Aro and Erskine 2003; Share 2008a; Ziegler and Goswami 2005). I have argued that because spelling–sound relations are so complex in English orthography, much of reading research has been confined to a narrow Anglocentric research agenda addressing theoretical and applied issues with only limited relevance for a universal science of reading and literacy, and although this situation is now beginning to change (see, for example, Eviatar and Share 2013; McCardle 2012; Nag and Perfetti 2014; Nag and Snowling 2011; Saiegh-Haddad and Joshi 2014) the theories and models currently being used to frame work elsewhere are still understandably entrenched in Anglocentric and Eurocentric/alphabetocentric thinking (Share 2014).

The following essay offers some guidelines for constructing a general theory of learning to read, one that seeks universals yet embraces the enormous diversity among languages and writing systems around the globe. There is much in common – our biological heritage and limited-capacity processing system – but fundamental differences exist as well owing to language and writing system diversity.

I begin by first asking *who* should be collaborating in this enterprise. Which disciplines should inform a theory of learning to read? While educators have the primary, but not sole charge, to provide children with the tools needed for literacy acquisition, it is equally clear that no single discipline has right-of-way and that a complete science of reading requires multiple interlocking levels of explanation that can only come via genuine disciplinary cross-talk. The various disciplinary insights should complement rather than compete against one another.

2 Marking out the construction site

A complete and truly panoramic science of reading, one that speaks to all languages and orthographies in all social settings, past and present, must be founded on four disciplines; cognitive science, linguistics, graphonomy (the study of writing systems) and socio-cultural-historical studies.

2.1 Biological constraints

The anatomical and functional architecture of the human brain places severe constraints on the ability of the human reading system to process temporally sequenced information such as audible and visible language (Baddeley 1986 2012; Christiansen and Chater 2015; LaBerge and Samuels 1974; Perfetti 1985). These limitations of human information processing are the product of biological constraints shaped by evolution (Christiansen and Chater in press; DeHaene 2009) – principally attention and memory.

The functional anatomy of the human eye was designed to navigate a three-dimensional terrestrial world, hence has had to adapt ("exapt") to the peculiarly 2-dimensional world of print. The human fovea allows only one-and-a-bit words to be seen with acuity (Rayner 1998), thereby dictating more or less word-by-word reading. This creates a "moving-window" of vision as the fovea flicks from word to word in a "skipping-spotlight" fashion quite unlike most eye movements in the natural world.[1] And contrary to the claims of many commercial schemes for speed reading, humans are not capable of reading whole phrases or lines. If humans possessed the panoramic visual acuity of diurnal raptors such as eagles, the story would be very different, although we are blissfully unaware of our visual lacunae. This strange skipping-spotlight information uptake also dictates that writing systems the world over must cram distinct units of meaning (e.g., Chinese characters, English

---

[1] This fact is often overlooked by test designers and experimental psychologists aiming to assess visual processing and visual memory whose measures often rely on this uniquely "literate" pattern of eye movements.

words, Korean syllable blocks) into small densely packed blocks occupying no more than around 2 degrees of visual angle. Furthermore, these visual-orthographic "bites" must include sufficient visual variety to accommodate unique combinations of letters, kana, and character components necessary for the tens of thousands of basic units of meaning (morphemes) that make up the hundreds of thousands of unique words in a language. Indeed, the number of distinctive features (lines, curves) for a morpheme or word in English may be very similar to the number of strokes in a Chinese character. Consideration of the structure of the eye and vocal tract together with the limited-capacity processing capabilities of the human brain explains the logic of the dual patterning or combinatorial structure of spoken and written language, namely, that a finite number of meaningless units (such as phonemes or letters) are combined and recombined to create a potentially infinite number of unique words (Hockett 1950; Sandler et al. 2002). Only combinations of a limited repertoire of simple (and easily formed for writing) shapes (curved or straight lines in alphabets, strokes in Chinese) allows virtually limitless permutations of these building blocks.

2.2 Cognitive science

This sequential word by word uptake (and sometimes letter by letter for the novice) places an enormous burden on the speed of information processing and the temporary storage of information in working memory. Like spoken language, written language obliges immediate "now-or-never" processing which is only possible when larger, meaning-bearing chunks are unitized (Christiansen and Chater 2015; Frazier and Rayner 1986). If word reading is too slow, older material will be lost or submerged under a deluge of new incoming material. Word reading must not only be very fast but sufficiently effortless to the point that we can not only identify each meaning-bearing unit (morphemes or words), its context-specific meaning, but also integrate words both within and across phrases and texts (Oakhill, Cain and Elbro 2015) while constructing a mental model of the text as a whole (Kintsch 1988 2012) *and* monitoring our own understanding of the text. Human attentional limitations allow us to perform only one cognitive activity at a time unless a second activity is highly routinized or "automatized". Reading is an exemplary case of multi-tasking only by virtue of the automatization of word reading. The question I address here is how is it possible for the non-literate brain to accomplish this remarkable feat?

2.3 Linguistics

Writing systems must encode (more correctly "encipher") language, not meaning or concepts. A non-linguistic concept-based semasiography has never been created except in very restricted communicative contexts, never achieving the full expressive power of human language (Coulmas 1989, Daniels, 2017; DeFrancis 1989; Rogers

2005; Shankweiler 2012). This is the reason that, in contrast to numerical systems such as Arabic numerals which directly symbolize numerical concepts (compare the digit 2 which is not language-dependent to *two*, *due*, or שתיים), there can never be a "universal" writing system (unless, of course, all the world speaks one and the same language). All writing, therefore, represents a particular language, thus the study of language is crucial for a true science of reading. Each orthography gives expression to the particular phonology, morphology, semantics/pragmatics and syntax of its parent language. The profound difficulties learning to read in a language (or even dialect) that is not the child's own native tongue attests to the importance of understanding the linguistic bedrock of literacy. Even for children learning to read their native tongue, there are often significant differences between the language of written text and the spoken vernacular in lexis, syntax, morphology and even phonology: All scripts are, to some degree diglossic. Learning to read is learning new forms of language even for the native speaker.

2.4 Writing systems

Although writing represents language, it is not merely a reflection of language (Olson 1977; 1994). It is an additional and unique dimension of language learning in its own right because writing systems, like spoken languages, differ in many ways (see Share and Daniels 2014), and these differences have a profound influence on the course of reading acquisition (Frost 2012; Perfetti and Harris 2013; Seymour et al. 2003; Ziegler and Goswami 2005). Orthography is not a constant in the literacy learning equation. The choice (or invention) of an orthography for unwritten or endangered languages is an issue for the majority of the world's languages. Reform of existing orthographies and even the case of swapping one orthography for another in times of social upheaval are by no means rare events. Even in affluent societies with a long tradition of literacy, the sense of immutability associated with the written word is illusory (Scragg 1978). Although written language is inherently more conservative than spoken language, it too is a living breathing organism that ceases to change only when it becomes extinct. Every writing system must adapt to the ever-changing needs of its users, their culture and technology of communication. The notion of *the* ideal or optimal orthography is also a myth (Share 2012) especially the common but pernicious belief that the alphabet is a universally superior system (see Share 2014). In short, an understanding of variation in writing system architectures is essential to a theory of learning to read.

2.5 Social-cultural-historical studies

Because writing is a cultural creation, constrained by biology, not a built-in biological fact of human brain architecture, the social, cultural and historical context of reading, writing and literacy is also fundamental to understanding the broader context of learning to read. Whether the exclusive preserve of an elite designed to disempower other sectors of a society (Gee 2014) or to empower the masses. The social-cultural-historical backdrop to reading and more generally literacy, unfortunately, is beyond the scope of this short essay and this author's expertise, and hence cannot be given the consideration it deserves.

3 What does it mean to acknowledge that reading is a skill?

Writing has been hailed as the greatest technological/cultural innovation in the history of humankind. In the history of our species it is an extremely recent but profoundly transforming technology. Because it has no evolutionary base, it is in a sense "unnatural" (Gough and Hillinger 1980). Unlike biologically primary abilities such as auditory localization or depth perception where there is little variation across populations, learning to read is biologically secondary and like other learned skills, such as playing golf or the flute, is characterized by enormous diversity. Unfortunately, the history of psychological research into reading has seen a strong tradition of inquiry concerned with establishing universals of human behavior. Most experimental psychologists share the belief that the main goal of reading research is to develop theories that describe the *fundamental* and *invariant* phenomena of reading across orthographies (see, e.g., Frost 2012). Elucidation of the cognitive operations common to all readers, and, more generally, to human cognition, has always topped the agenda: Variability and individual differences are of minor concern, often denigrated as the "noise" or "error variance" in the system.

Reading is a very recent cultural innovation, a technology, yet one so remarkably successful and transforming that it now has attained the status of a universal desiratum – guarded jealously by those who wished to disempower sectors such as American slaves or women. In the two million years or so of human evolution, a mere five millennia since the advent of writing represents little more than the blink of an eye. Biologically, the brain of homo sapiens is no different than it was some 50,000–60,000 years ago, hence writing and reading have no roots in evolution. Reading piggybacks on structures evolved for other purposes (DeHaene 2009). Neuro-plasticity makes reading and writing possible by "recycling" structures for new functions such as reading (DeHaene 2009; Rapp 2015). The brain does not come "wired" to read, so reading doesn't come "naturally": it requires explicit instruction and plenty of practice like all skills.

To say that reading is a learned skill requiring explicit instruction does not mean that teachers teach children to read – they only teach children how to teach themselves by providing the infrastructure – the logic or systematicity of the writing system. Even in Indic akshara-based writing systems (see Nag 2007) and Chinese (Anderson et al. 2013; Li and McBride 2013) which are popularly regarded as systems that can only be learned via massive akshara-after-akshara, character-after-character memorization, it has been shown that the more successful readers understand the underlying combinatorial logic and are applying it independently and productively to expand and refine their word reading skill.

4 Learning to read: A universal old/new framework

The central claim of this essay is that there exists a fundamental and universal dualism in printed word learning that applies to all words in all possible orthographies. Ironically, it is probably Saussure ([1922] 1983) – a linguist with little regard for reading or literacy who, according to Coltheart (2005), articulated the first dualist conception of reading. *"We read in two ways; the new or unknown word is scanned letter after letter, but a common word is taken in at a glance"* (translated 1983: 34). The emphasis here is on new/unfamiliar versus familiar words. Unfortunately, like most early 20th century linguists, Saussure promptly dismissed the topic of written language as unworthy of attention by scholars of language.

One of the first modern cognitivist formulations of the dualist or dual "route" idea (Forster and Chambers 1973) adopted this same approach. Forster and Chambers discussed two alternative ways to pronounce printed words

> *First, the pronunciation could be computed by application of a set of grapheme-phoneme rules, or letter-sound correspondence rules. This coding can be carried out independently of any consideration of the meaning or familiarity of the letter sequence... Alternatively, the pronunciation may be determined by searching long-term memory for stored information about how to pronounce familiar letter sequences, obtaining the necessary information by a direct dictionary look-up, instead of rule application. Obviously, this procedure would work only for familiar words.* (p. 627)

Both Saussure and Forster and Chambers emphasized *familiarity* and the distinction between a sequential letter by letter process in the case of unfamiliar words versus a holistic one-step process for familiar words. Both appear to focus on the skilled reader.

4.1 Unfamiliar-to-familiar/novice-to-expert dualism

I pick up the thread by placing the unfamiliar/familiar dualism in a developmental context, emphasizing the transition from unfamiliar-*to*-familiar and not merely unfamiliar *and* familiar. My point of departure is the observation that *every* printed word is, at one point, unfamiliar, even a child's own name. Thus, the reader must possess some means of independently identifying words/morphemes encountered for the first time. I maintain that this is true for *every* orthography; alphabets, abjads, abugidas/alphasyllabaries, syllabaries and morpho-syllabaries including Chinese (Anderson et al. 2003 2013) and Japanese Kanji (Joyce 2011). The need for a way to identify novel printed words is crucial for the novice and expert reader alike because most words have very low frequencies of occurrence and are rarely, if ever, seen in print even by skilled readers[2]. On the other hand, the reader must eventually be able to achieve a high degree of unitization or "chunking" either of letter strings, aksharas, stroke patterns or character compounds to enable the rapid, parallel, and near-effortless recognition of familiar words and morphemes perceived as whole units via a direct memory-retrieval mechanism (Anderson et al. 2013; Kwok and Ellis 2015; LaBerge and Samuels 1974; Logan 1988 1997; Perfetti 1985). I now elaborate.

The overarching goal of this unfamiliar-to-familiar development is speed and effortlessness (often termed "automaticity"[3]) – the quintessence of reading skill (LaBerge and Samuels 1974; Perfetti 1985). Speed is the most discriminating marker of developmental and individual differences across writing systems (Breznitz 2006; Share 2008a; Wolf and Katzir-Cohen 2001), and, furthermore, the *sine qua non* of rapid, silent (private) reading – the greatest virtue of the technology of writing and the literate cultures it engenders.

How is this accomplished?

Following in the footsteps of many leading theories (Coltheart et al 1993 2001; Ehri 1979, 2005; Forster 1976; Forster and Chambers 1973), I argue simply that readers gradually build a visual word recognition system (often labeled a *reading* or *sight vocabulary* by educators, or *orthographic lexicon* by psycholinguists) word by word (or, more probably, morpheme by morpheme). This instance-based (Logan 1988) or item-based learning (Share 1995) proceeds one item at a time – it is not a stage-oriented model (see Share 1995) because separate morphemes necessarily have distinct visual forms (as elaborated below), thus each must be individually learned as an unique visual configuration of the limited set of letters (in phonemic scripts), aksharas in Brahmi-derived Indic-based scripts or character combinations in morphosyllabaries (Shu, Chen, Anderson, Wu and Xuan 2003; Shu et al. 2003) which constitute the building blocks of the orthography. It is attention to *orthographic detail* that systematically maps onto sound (the English letter <t> almost always symbolizes the sound /t/, or meaning (the word-final past tense morpheme <ed> which sacrifices phonological transparency for morphemic transparency) and the string <soft> consistently indicates a common morpheme at the price of phonological inconsistency (<soft>/<soften>). Similarly, the semantic radical denoting 'tree' 木 consistently signals morphemes

---

[2] Even in the case of monosyllabic English words, it seems likely that the skilled reader is familiar with only around half of the 8000 items (Treiman 1993). The fact that word frequencies appear to follow a power law (also called Zipf's law) in which a small proportion of words are very common but many, indeed most, words are quite rare.

[3] This popular term is highly problematic owing to disagreements regarding its definition and operationalization, see, for example, Stanovich 1990; Moors and de Houwers 2006).

with meanings related to the concept 'tree' and the phonetic /ma/ (operating on the rebus principle) reliably symbolizes the sound of a number of homophones with unrelated meanings. Because these connections between symbols and sounds or meanings are *systematic* and non-arbitrary, they are both productive (can be applied to new cases (both pre-existing but unfamiliar to the reader/writer and newly invented items) with the same symbols for both reading and writing and reproducible (can often be regenerated if forgotten). This non-abitrary "bonding" (Ehri 1979) of graphs to units of sound and meaning ensures well-secured and durable connections between orthography and sound as well as orthography and meaning (as elaborated in the lexical quality hypothesis, Perfetti 2007; Perfetti and Hart 2002). In the absence of combinatoriality as in the hypothetical case of a pure logography, or the common reality of the curious pre-literate child as yet unaware of the combinatoriality of print, each word or morpheme must be learned anew and memorized as best as possible with the aid of mnemonics. This is true logographic "reading" (Ehri 1979; Ferreiro and Teberosky 1979; Frith 1980; Harris and Coltheart 1986; Marsh et al. 1979) epitomized in attempts to read, or write by producing referential elements (in the case of writing) such as enlarged letters for writing <elephant>, or using the color red for <tomato>). It is here that truly non-orthographic *visual memory* abilities sometimes come into play, (see Yin and McBride 2015). Almost immediately, however, this strategy runs into the unavoidable difficulties generating unique "clues" for each word (the two "eyes" in the word <look>, the "tail" at the end of the word <dog> which rapidly leads them up a blind and very short alley (Ehri 1979; Frith 1980; Gough and Roper-Schneider 1980; Marsh et al. 1979; Share and Gur 1999). This unsystematic non-combinatorial rote learning is little different from trying to memorize thousands of phone numbers – a feat few are capable of. These observations explain why no writing system, not even Chinese, contains more than a handful of pictograms (e.g., 木 'tree') or ideograms (e.g., 二 'two') that directly convey meaning.

The compilation of unitized words and morphemes does not occur in one go, one phase, or one stage of reading but begins at the very outset of reading development (in many cases with a child's name) and continuing throughout the entire reading lifespan. Like the power law of word frequency, encounters with novel printed words decline steadily over the years but probably never cease simply because most words are rare, appearing once or twice (if ever) in a million words of running text (Carroll, Davies and Richman 1971).

4.2 Word identification for unfamiliar words; word recognition for familiar words

I reserve the term *word identification* for the initial process of determining the identity of an unfamiliar word – working out a match between the written word and a known spoken word. This is, for the most part, a conscious problem-solving task because the printed word rarely supplies (nor need supply) exhaustive and unambiguous phonological information owing to stress (présent/presént), homography (wind/wind), but above all, the "distance" between the spoken word in the reader's dialect and the "careful" or canonical form in print that is typically idealized as the "correct" pronunciation but is actually one of a family of pronunciations both synchronically and diachronically (Elbro and Arnbak 1996). When ambiguity exists owing to an unpredictable ("irregular") or incomplete spelling or to imperfect mastery of the relevant spelling-sound relations, the reader must resort to supra-lexical factors, primarily semantic and syntactic context to resolve the ambiguity (Pritchard, Coltheart, Marinus, and Castles 2015; Share 1995; Tunmer 2014).

Word identification is not only deciphering (or writing) a new word but also *establishing* the unitized representations – primarily orthographic because it obliges attention to the separate elements in the word (letter identity and order for linear scripts) or, in the case of non-linear aksharic or morpho-syllabic scripts, separate strokes or features and their spatially ordered arrangement). The universal basis of this word learning process is the use of mapping between spelling and sound or spelling and meaning at the sub-lexical level (phonemes, sub-syllables, morae, syllables or morphemes). This provides a self-teaching mechanism based on a *finite* (and therefore learnable) number of elements that empowers the reader to identify a potentially infinite number of words *on his/her own* in the course of independent day-to-day reading (Hockett 1950; Sandler et al. 2002; Shankweiler 2014). This is the same combinatoriality or "particulate" principle common to human language and other hierarchical systems such as DNA. The genius of human language is infinite expression achieved via finite means. Neither contextual guessing alone, nor direct instruction furnish these means by themselves although both have important *supplementary* roles in the growing print lexicon (Share 1995).

The decipherability/learnability of a script is fundamental and universal. It does not depend on mechanistic all-or-none rules, but is approximative and probabilistic for at least two reasons. Even if it were possible to list all the grapheme-phoneme correspondence (GPC) "rules" for a given orthography (we now have a complete computational set in English (Coltheart et al. 2001; Pritchard et al. 2015; Ziegler, Perry and Zorzi 2014) but which only cover the subset of monosyllabic words painting a misleadingly rosy picture of decipherability in English but which completely overlooks morphology. The pronunciation of polysyllabic words is a very different story, and depends a great deal on morphology (Venezky 1970). Few orthographies are fully transparent phonologically because of the need for morphemic transparency and the fact that from the moment an orthography is created it begins to age, as pronunciations typically change faster than writing systems. Even Korean, hailed as the most perfect alphabet makes concessions for the sake of morphological clarity at the expense of phonological transparency. No orthography is fully transparent; it only needs to be sufficiently transparent. Not only is stress often unmarked, but tone too (most of the world's languages have tone, Roberts 2011), and homography exists in almost all orthographies to some extent (it is is endemic in Semitic abjads, Saiegh-Haddad 2014; Share in press). This creates a degree of ambiguity in almost every script invoking the need for a good vocabulary with many well-specified representations, that is, lexical quality (de Jong and Elbro 2011; Perfetti 2007). Additional sources of information (regarding pronunciation, meaning, and syntax) are needed to *supplement* (not *supplant*) deciphering processes. For longer words, working memory constraints are likely to degrade or distort the integrity of the decoded elements (when deciphering long polysyllabic words, many children are liable to alter the deciphered string). For less phonologically transparent orthographies (e.g., English, Danish, unpointed Hebrew and Arabic, Thai, Chinese) the role of these lexical and supra-lexical factors will be greater (Anderson et al. 2003; McBride et al. 2011; Ricketts, Nation and Bishop 2007; Share 2017; Wang et al. 2011). The point is that no "regular" script ever delivers an idealized complete and unambiguous end-product – all scripts are (phonologically) irregular to some degree – Chinese is merely furthest along the continuum of phonological opacity.

4.2.1 Two ways to learn new words; Writing, not just reading

There appear to be two main ways to learn new words; deciphering from orthography to phonology (with varying degrees of lexical and contextual support) and writing (Chen and Pasquarella 2017; Wu, Li, and Anderson 1999). The self-teaching role of letter-sound translation (deciphering in phoneme-based writing systems – abjads and alphabets) has been discussed at length in Share 2008b 2011). The role of writing in orthographic learning is less well-researched and less consistent, however, the bulk of this work suggests that the motor-kinesthetic production of letters, one after each other in linear scripts, like the strict order of stroke formation in morpho-syllabaries makes an important contribution to orthographic learning (Cunningham and Stanovich 1990; Hulme 1983; Kalindi et al. 2015; Longchamp et al. 2008; Monk, Hulme and Ives 1987; Shachar-Yames and Share 2008; Shoham-Zilberman 2011; Tan, Spinks, Eden, Perfetti and Siok 2005). According to Wu et al., the typical routine for learning characters in mainland China involves pronouncing the new character, discriminating it from other characters, writing it "in the air", rehearsing the correct order of strokes, analyzing the structure, and explaining the meaning (Wu et al. 1999, p. 578). Furthermore, the national curriculum stipulates that, from Grade 3, children are expected to learn new words *independently* and new characters from Grade 5 (p. 578). These observations also suggest why whole-word, look-and-say instruction is futile because it does not oblige attention to orthographic *detail*, that is, to letter level or feature-level orthographic information. This also reaffirms, yet again, the fact that no pure word-based writing system (logography) has ever existed in either ancient or modern times (DeFrancis 1989; Gelb 1952; Joyce 2011; Unger and DeFrancis 1995): it would simply be unlearnable and unproductive (Mattingly 1985).

In contrast to initial word *identification*, I reserve the term *recognition* for the *re*-cognition of a familiar or partly familiar word. The heart of this process is orthographic, that is, recognition of elements with systematic links to sound and meaning as opposed to the non-systematic visual-logographic cues used by pre-literates. This instant recognition of familiar (unitized) morpheme-specific or word-specific configurations of orthographic constituents (linear or non-linear) is accompanied and assisted by the universal activation of phonology and meaning (Perfetti 2003). The distinction between word identification and word recognition, however, is not a dichotomy, but more akin to a graded continuum of orthographic learning (as manifest in spelling development), although for normal readers (but not disabled readers (Ehri and Saltmarsh 1995; Reitsma 1983; Share and Shalev 2004) this learning process is rapid and robust (Share 2004 2008b).

Ultimately, and perhaps ironically, all accomplished readers do eventually build up something like a mental logography (or rather morphography), namely, a large store of whole-morpheme or whole-word units (see Pritchard et al. in press; Ziegler et al. 2014) each a unique combination of letters, aksharas or characters recognized via direct one-step retrieval from memory. In this respect, there is no difference between learning to read an alphabet – even a highly regular one, and Chinese characters or Japanese Kanji because each must necessarily have a unique word-specific or morpheme-specific visual configuration which may amount to no more than a single dot.

Summarizing the main unfamiliar-to-familiar argument, I suggest that word identification processes trigger a process of item by item construction of a lexicon of unitized orthographic representations each fused into a recognizable chunk or unit that systematically and reproducibly links up to meaningful units of sound or meaning (probably at multiple hierarchical levels) thereby permitting rapid accurate and near-effortless recognition. As already noted earlier, this is not a stage or phase of reading development but an incremental and ongoing process which begins from the moment the learner starts to appreciate the logic of the writing system and systematically connect signs with sounds and meaning.

5 Dual nature of writing

This basic and universal "unfamiliar-to-familiar" dualism (seen from an item-based perspective) or "novice-to-expert" dualism (from the reader's perspective) also converges with the dual nature of an efficient orthography. Specifically, an efficient script represents a compromise between the competing needs of the novice and the expert reader (Rogers 1995; Venezky 2007). This orthographic dualism might be termed the "learnability/unitizability" criterion.

5.1 Learnability/decipherability for the novice

An effective orthography must provide the reader with a means for deciphering (often mistakenly referred to as "decoding") and/or learning (i.e., memorizing) new words independently (Share 1995, 2008a). This applies equally to the newcomer to the world of print and to the skilled reader who is also encountering many new words. Furthermore, and this is crucial to skill learning in all domains, this deciphering/learning process must lay the foundations for rapid, direct-retrieval mechanisms. This is possible only if the learning process capitalizes on the combinatorial structure of the writing system (systematic orthography-phonology or orthography-meaning correspondence). Even in Chinese, characters that directly represent meanings (pictographs – 木 'tree', ideographs 上 'above', 三 'three') constitute only a tiny fraction of the Chinese character corpus (Shu, Anderson et al. 2003; Taylor and Taylor 1995). The overwhelming majority of Chinese words are compounds containing elements indicating meaning (around 200 semantic radicals) and 800+ phonetic components. Even when Chinese is taught without the support of supplementary alphabetic scripts such as pinyin (as in Hong Kong), the combination of semantic and phonetic information (and, sometimes, semantic and semantic information, e.g., 木 'tree', 森 'forest') has been shown to be productive for the novice (see Anderson, Li, Ku, Shu and Wu 2003; Chan and Seigel 2001; Cheung, McBride-Chang and Chow 2006; Ho and Bryant 1997; Shu, Anderson, and Wu 2003). Of course, in mainland China, alphabetic pinyin would appear to be a self-teaching mechanism *par excellence* although it remains to be established whether the fact that pinyin adhere to a different (alphabetic) logic and do not necessarily draw attention to the combinatorial structure of Chinese characters helps or hinders memorization of the characters.

This "do-it-yourself" or "self-teaching" function of orthographic learnability (Jorm and Share 1983; Share 1995, 2008b, 2011) supplies an economical means for identifying/learning new words and establishing the detailed orthographic representations on which rapid, fully-unitized skilled word recognition is founded.

5.2 Unitizability for the expert

A successful script must also answer to the needs of the expert-to-be by providing distinctive morpheme-specific (or word-specific) orthographic configurations required for unitizing and automatizing skilled word recognition. Ideally, each morpheme should have one and only one representation (morpheme "constancy") without showing morphophonemic variation (e.g., *soft/soften*), with different morphemes represented differently (morpheme "distinctiveness") (e.g., *two, too, to*) (Rogers 1995). A script that maintains morpheme "constancy" – the same morpheme always spelled the same way, may help readers derive meanings of novel morphologically related words, but it may be morpheme *distinctiveness* which is crucial for the unitization of word recognition. In other words, it's not that the w in *two* is essential for revealing morphemic relatedness (e.g., *twelve, twice, twilight*) – a highly doubtful assumption for the young reader, but that this etymological quirk provides unique spellings for potentially confusable homophones (*too/two/to*). Historically, conscious efforts were often made by spelling reformers to avoid homophones becoming homographs and thereby minimize ambiguity (Carney 1994, chapter 7; Scragg 1974, chapter 4).

Historically, the morphemic principle, essential for unitizability, often takes precedence over the competing learnability principle (Daniels and Bright 1996; Perfetti 2003; Venezky 2007; but see Serbo-Croatian, Lukatela, Carello, Shankweiler and Liberman 1995). Letter-form constancy (something that only became possible with printing), spelling constancy and word separation, may all be important factors in the unitization process (Saenger 1991).

A script that caters primarily to the needs of skilled readers, such as pre-communist Chinese characters (and in many respects English orthography, see Chomsky and Halle 1968), will pose major (but not insurmountable) challenges for novices. Conversely, a script that provides maximum learnability (or decipherability) for novices, the highly regularized pedographies in English such as *i.t.a.* (Chasnoff 1968), Korean hangul, or Japanese kana, will often fail (as a stand-alone script) to meet the needs of skilled readers, primarily owing to the failure to distinguish homophonic morphemes. Purely phonemic scripts such as pinyin and Zhu-Yin-Fu-Hao, as well as syllabic/moraic scripts such as Japanese kana appear to be remarkably easy to learn to decipher (e.g., Mason, Anderson, Omura, Uchida and Imai 1989; McCarthy 1995; Taylor and Taylor 1995), but if extensive homophony exists in the spoken language, such scripts will violate the morphemic distinctiveness principle and prove impracticable without supplementary morpheme-based characters (as in the case of Japanese Kanji) which provide more direct links to morpheme identity). By the same token, i.t.a was never destined to supplant conventional English orthography because it ignores the morphemic principle. Conversely, primarily morphemic scripts such as Chinese characters which serve the literacy needs of a privileged few very well but require the novice to invest extraordinary amounts of time and effort (Hoosain 1995; Shu et al., 2003; Taylor and Taylor 1995) appear to be more easily acquired by the novice (and the general populace) when supplemented by decipherable phonemic scripts such as pinyin (Siok and Fletcher 2001; Taylor and Taylor 1995).

5.3 Many orthographies have dual versions

Catering to the divergent needs of novices and experts, many scripts have dual versions – a maximally phonologically transparent version taught to beginners, and a more morphemically accommodating version (but often less phonologically transparent) for skilled readers. Among these are the pointed (fully vocalized) and unpointed (incompletely vocalized) variants of Hebrew (Ravid 2006; Share in press), Arabic (Henik-Rotkin and Saiegh-Haddad 2014), and Farsi (Baluch and Besner 1991). For example, unpointed Hebrew (the standard form used for newspapers, books, magazines etc. aimed at adult readers) includes a number of vowel letters (AHVY or matres lectionis) that provide a minimal (incomplete and inconsistent) representation of vowels. A second, historically later-developing system of vowel signs was developed in post-exilic times when Hebrew was disappearing as a spoken language) and today is retained to teach children to read (Share in press). This system of diacritic-style signs (dots and dashes) provides complete and consistent vowel representation turning a phonologically (primarily vocalically) opaque script into a highly transparent one with near-perfect one-to-one correspondence between signs and sounds. This system is rapidly mastered by the beginning reader (Feitelson 1988; Share, in press; Shatil and Share 2003) but quickly becomes superfluous as the developing reader relies increasingly on higher-order morphological and lexical knowledge to supply the missing vowel information (Bar-On and Ravid 2011; Frost 1995; Share & Bar-On, 2017). By Grades 2 and 3, vowel points are typically discarded, barely noticed by the maturing reader. A similar situation exists in Arabic with the three long vowel letters representing (in this case consistently) all three long vowels in Arabic in one-to-one fashion (Saiegh-Haddad and Henkin-Roitfarb 2014). For the beginning reader, the three short vowels are also indicated by diacritic-style vowel signs which are later dropped. In mainland China, decipherability is maximized for the beginning reader by an auxiliary system of Roman alphabetic letters, *pinyin*, which is first taught in the first 10 weeks of school, then used to assist the learning of Chinese characters (Liu 1978; Shu et al. 2003; Siok and Fletcher 2001; Taylor and Taylor 1995). As in the case of Hebrew vowel signs, pinyin is gradually faded out (Wu et al. 1999) and eventually forgotten.

In Japan, the highly consistent and rapidly acquired moraic kana are used (*furigana*) to teach the morpho-syllabic Kanji which are often misclassified as logographic[4]. Kana, appear (like diacritics) above the kanji character a number of times before being dropped on the assumption that the assistance is no longer needed.

English, too, has a long history of script innovations designed to boost phonological transparency for the beginning reader. These include diacritical marks (e.g., ā "long" vowel; ă "short" vowel), phonetically simplified spellings such as i.t.a., and beginning texts restricted to vocabulary with regular spellings, Dr. Seuss being the most well-known. The research on these materials consistently shows that beginning readers learn to decode more quickly than traditional orthography (see, e.g., Chasnoff 1968), but soon lose any advantages when the child is required to make the transition to Standard English orthography.

---

[4] Most kanji are compounds (like Chinese compounds) which combine a semantic radical with a phonetic element that provides either an unambiguous pronunciation or useful partial information (Joyce 2011).

The dual nature of writing systems is also brought to light in situations where pronunciation precision is paramount especially in religious contexts such as oral recitation of sacred texts, post-exilic Hebrew vowels, and liturgical works in languages no longer spoken. For example, the Avesta, the sacred book of the Zoroastrian religion, adopted a fully vocalized, 51-character alphabet long after the Avestan language (an Iranian language) became extinct. When Islam spread to non-Arabic-speaking countries, more precision was needed for correctly pronouncing sacred texts hence diacritics were added to distinguish different consonants and for short vowels. For the same reasons, the pitch accent was added to Greek during Hellenistic times by Alexandrian scholars when many non-Greek speaking peoples (following Alexander's conquests) began learning Greek.

6 Conclusions

In this brief chapter, I have attempted to sketch some of the essential ingredients of a universal theory of reading acquisition, one that seeks to highlight the commonalities while embracing the diversity of languages and writing systems. A universal theory of learning to read needs to take into account the full range of spoken language and writing system diversity. I have also stressed the importance of taking into consideration insights from neurobiology, cognitive science, linguistics and writing systems research in order to gain a deeper understanding of one of the most complex and influential skills that we ask of the developing child. Cross-talk between these (and other) disciplines is essential for this enterprise. Too often, disciplines compete for prominence rather than seeking complementary, interlocking levels of explanation.

I propose a dual psycholinguistic framework that not only has a long and venerable history but also converges with linguists' insights into the "dual patterning" (combinatoriality) of spoken language (Hockett 1950; Sandler et al. 2002) as well as the dual nature of an efficient orthography serving the needs of both the novice for *decipherability/learnability* (via phonological transparency) and the expert for unitization (via morphemic transparency). Richard Venezky (1970) pointed out some decades ago that sound (phonology) *and* meaning (morphology) "share leading roles" in English orthography. I suggest that this is a universal of learning to read. Specifically, I build on the *unfamiliar-to-familiar* dualism outlined earlier in Share (2008a) which highlights the developmental transition (common to all human skill learning) from slow, deliberating, step-by-step, unskilled performance to rapid, unitized, one-step skilled processing.

I do not presume to offer a first-draft universal model – we know too little at this point about learning to read in non-European, non-alphabetic writing systems, and we are still captive of the Anglocentric and Eurocentric/alphabetic research agenda in ways we are only now beginning to appreciate (see Share 2014). I would venture to propose, nonetheless, some general features of a universal model of learning to read that may be useful when construction work actually commences.

I propose several broad features of learning to read around the globe. Here I draw inspiration from the groundbreaking work of Linnea Ehri and others on learning to read in English. I see four phases; a pre-literate visual-logographic phase, a cipher-learning phase in which children learn the combinatorial building blocks of their writing system via explicit instruction – letters, aksharas, syllabograms, or characters. This cipher-learning phase can be extremely rapid (e.g., 10 weeks are allotted in mainland China to master pinyin) or very long – years for complex aksharas, and Chinese characters and Japanese Kanji (see Nag's 'contained-extensive' notion) which supplies the "tools of the trade" with which children may commence work building their orthographic knowledge base, namely word-specific and/or morpheme-specific connections.

From the moment children begin learning the building blocks, lexicalization of the learning/deciphering process begins, at least for some children (Anderson et al. 2013; Share 1995; Snowling and Nag 2007). Thus, the growing volume of print exposure together with growing print knowledge and word identification capabilities lead to increasingly refined and sophisticated knowledge of the orthography and orthography-phonology and orthography-meaning connections. This operates is a reciprocal fashion (see Ziegler et al. 2014).

Over the years a unitized orthographic lexicon develops (probably at multiple hierarchical levels, Perfetti 1992, including letters/morphemes/words, strokes/stroke patterns/semantic/phonetic components/characters/words) as well as the speed and efficiency that epitomizes skilled reading.

Finally, and back to biology, the speed of reading across the worlds' writing systems probably does not vary appreciably although this hypothesis remains to be tested.

References

Adams, Marilyn J. 1990. *Beginning to read*. Cambridge, MA: Bradford.
Anderson, Richard C., Yu-Min Ku, Wenling Li, Xi Chen, Xinchun Wu & Shu Hua. 2013. Learning to see patterns in Chinese characters. *Scientific Studies of Reading* 17. 41–56.
Anderson, Richard C., Wenling Li, Yu-Min Ku, Shu Hua & Ningning Wu. 2003. Use of partial information in reading Chinese characters. *Journal of Educational Psychology* 95. 52–57.
Baddeley, Alan. 1986. Working memory, reading and dyslexia. *Advances in Psychology* 34. 141–152.
Baddeley, Alan. 2012. Working memory: theories, models, and controversies. *Annual Review of Psychology* 63. 1–29.
Baluch, Bahman & Derek Besner. 1991. Strategic use of lexical and nonlexical routines in visual word recognition: Evidence from oral reading in Persian. *Journal of Experimental Psychology: Learning, Memory and Cognition* 17. 644–652.
Bar-On, Amalia & Dorit Ravid. 2011. Morphological analysis in learning to read pseudowords in Hebrew. *Applied Psycholinguistics* 32. 553–581.
Bloomfield, Leonard. 1933. *Language*. Oxford, England: Holt.
Buckingham, Jennifer, Kevin Wheldall & Robyn Beaman-Wheldall. 2013. Why Jaydon can't read: The triumph of ideology over evidence. *Policy* 29. 21–32.

Breznitz, Zvia. 2006. *Fluency in reading: Synchronization of processes.* Mahwah, NJ: Erlbaum.
Carney, Edward. 1994. *A survey of English spelling.* London: Routledge.
Carroll, John Bissell, Peter Davies & Barry Richman. 1971. *The American heritage word frequency book.* Boston: Houghton Mifflin.
Cattell, James M. 1886. The time it takes to see and name objects. *Mind* 11. 63–65.
Chall, Jeanne S. 1967. *Learning to read: The great debate.* New York: McGraw-Hill.
Chasnoff, Robert E. 1968. Two alphabets: A follow-up. *The Elementary School Journal.* 251–257.
Chen, Becky X. & Adrian Pasquarella. in press. Learning to read Chinese. To appear in Ludo Verhoeven and Charles A. Perfetti (eds.), *Reading acquisition: Cross-linguistic and cross-script perspectives.* Cambridge: Cambridge University Press.
Cheung, Him, Catherine McBride-Chang & Bonnie W. Y. Chow. 2006. Reading Chinese. In Malatesha R. Joshi and P. G. Aaron (eds.), *Handbook of orthography and literacy,* 421–438. Mahwah, NJ: Erlbaum.
Chomsky, Noam. 1968. Remarks on nominalization. *Readings in English transformational grammar.*
Chomsky, Noam & Morris Halle. 1968. *The sound pattern of English.* New York: Harper and Row.
Christiansen, Morten H. & Nick Chater. 2015. The now-or-never bottleneck: A fundamental constraint on language. *Behavioral and Brain Sciences* 38.
Coltheart, Max. 1978. Lexical access in simple reading tasks. In Geoffrey Underwood (ed.), *Strategies of information processing,* 151–216. London: Academic Press.
Coltheart, Max, Brent Curtis, Paul Atkins & Micheal Haller. 1993. Models of reading aloud: Dual-route and parallel-distributed-processing approaches. *Psychological review* 100 (4). 589.
Coltheart, Max, Kathleen Rastle, Conrad Perry, Robyn Langdon & Johannes Ziegler. 2001. DRC: a dual route cascaded model of visual word recognition and reading aloud. *Psychological review* 108 (1). 204.
Coulmas, Florian. 1989. *The writing systems of the world.* B. Blackwell.
Cronin, Virginia. 2015. Have we been wrong about phonics? *General Med* 3 (2). 1–4.
Cunningham, Anne E. & Keith E. Stanovich. 1990. Early spelling acquisition: Writing beats the computer. *Journal of Educational Psychology* 82 (1). 159.
Daniels, Peter, T. 2017. *An exploration in writing systems.* Sheffield, England: Equinox.
Daniels, Peter T. & William Bright. 1996. *The world's writing systems.* New York: Oxford University Press.
de Boer Bart, Wendy Sandler & Simon Kirby. 2012. New perspectives on duality of patterning: Introduction to the special issue. *Language and Cognition* 4. 251–259.
DeFrancis, John. 1989. *Visible speech: The diverse oneness of writing systems.* Honolulu, HI: University of Hawaii Press.
DeHaene, Stanislas. 2009. *Reading in the brain.* New York: Penguin.
de Saussure, Ferdinand. 1915. *Course in general linguistics.* Chicago: Open Court.
Ehri, Linnea C. 1979. Linguistic insight: Threshold of reading acquisition. In T. Gary Waller and G. MacKinnon (eds.), *Reading research: Advances in research and theory* 1, 63–114. New York: Academic Press.
Ehri, Linnea C. 2005. Development of sightword reading: Phases and findings. In Margaret J. Snowling and Charles Hulme (eds.), *The science of reading: A handbook,* 135–154. Malden, MA: Blackwell.
Ehri Linnea C. & Jill Saltmarsh. 1995. Beginning readers outperform older disabled readers in learning to read words by sight. *Reading and Writing* 7 (3). 295–326.
Elbro, Carsten & Elisabeth Arnbak. 1996. The role of morpheme recognition and morphological awareness in dyslexia. *Annals of dyslexia* 46 (1). 209–240.
Elbro Carsten, Peter F. de Jong, Daphne Houter & Anne-Mette Nielsen. 2012. From spelling pronunciation to lexical access: A second step in word decoding? *Scientific Studies of Reading* 16. 341–359.

Evans, Nicholas & Stephen C. Levinson. 2009. The myth of language universals: language diversity and its importance for cognitive science. *Behavioral and Brain Sciences* 32. 429–492.

Eviatar, Zohar & David L. Share. 2013. Processing Semitic writing systems: Introduction to a special issue of writing systems research. *Writing Systems Research* 5. 131–133.

Feitelson, Dina. 1988. *Facts and fads in beginning reading: A cross-language perspective*. Westport, CT: Ablex Publishing.

Ferreiro, Emilia & Ana Teberosky. 1982. *Literacy before schooling*. Portsmouth, NH: Heinemann Educational Books Inc.

Frazier, Lyn & Keith Rayner. 1987. Resolution of syntactic category ambiguities: Eye movements in parsing lexically ambiguous sentences. *Journal of Memory and Language* 26. 505–526.

Frith, Uta. (ed.). 1980. *Cognitive processes in spelling*. London: Academic Press.

Frost, Ram. 1995. Phonological computation and missing vowels: Mapping lexical involvement in reading. *Journal of Experimental Psychology: Learning, Memory, and Cognition* 21. 398–408.

Frost, Ram. 2012. Towards a universal model of reading. *Behavioral and Brain Sciences* 35. 263–279. doi:10.1017/S0140525X11001841

Forster, Kenneth I. 1976. Accessing the mental lexicon. *New approaches to language mechanisms* 30. 231–256.

Forster, Kenneth I. & Susan M. Chambers. 1973. Lexical access and naming time. *Journal of Verbal Learning and Verbal Behavior* 12. 627–635.

Forster, Kenneth I. & Chris Davis. 1984. Repetition priming and frequency attenuation in lexical access. *Journal of experimental psychology: Learning, memory, and cognition* 10 (4). 680.

Gaur, Albertine. 1995. Scripts and writing systems: A historical perspective. In Insup Taylor and David R. Olson (eds.), *Scripts and literacy*, 19–30. Dordrecht: Kluwer Academic.

Gee, James P. 2015. *Literacy and education*. London: Routledge.

Gelb, Ignace J. 1952. *A study of writing*. Chicago: University of Chicago Press.

Goodman, Kenneth S. 1989. Whole-language research: Foundations and development. *The Elementary School Journal* 90. 207–220.

Gough, Philip B. 1983. Context, form, and interaction. *Eye movements in reading* 331. 358.

Gough, Philip B. & Michael L. Hillinger. 1980. Learning to read: An unnatural act. *Annals of Dyslexia* 30 (1). 179–196.

Harris, Margaret & Max Coltheart. 1986. *Language processing in children and adults: An introduction*. London: Routledge and Kegan Paul.

Henrich, Joseph, Steven J. Heine & Ara Norenzayan. 2010. The weirdest people in the world? *Behavioral and Brain Sciences* 33. 61–135.

Ho, Connie Suk-Han & Peter Bryant. 1997. Learning to read Chinese beyond the logographic phase. *Reading Research Quarterly* 32. 276–289.

Hockett, Charles. 1960. The origin of speech. *Scientific American* 203 (3). 89–96.

Hoosain, Rumjahn. 1995. Sound and meaning of scripts. In Insup Taylor and David R. Olson (eds.), *Scripts and literacy: Reading and learning to read alphabets, syllabaries, and characters*, 131–144. New York: Kluwer.

Hulme, Charles. 1983. *Reading retardation and multisensory teaching*. London: Routledge and Kegan Paul.

Hulme, Charles, Andrew Monk & Sarah Ives. 1987. Some experimental studies of multi-sensory teaching: The effects of manual tracing on children's paired-associate learning. *British Journal of Developmental Psychology* 5 (4). 299–307.

Jorm, Anthony F. & David L.Share. 1983. Phonological recoding and reading acquisition. *Applied Psycholinguistics* 4. 103–147.

Joyce, Terry. 2011. The significance of the morphographic principle for the classification of writing systems. In Susanne R Borgwaldt & Terry Joyce (eds.), *Typology of writing systems* 51, 62–84. John Benjamins Publishing.

Kalindi, Sylvia Chanda, Catherine McBride, Xiuhong Tong, Natalie Lok Yee Wong, Kien Hoa Kevin Chung & Chia-Ying Lee. 2015. Beyond phonological and morphological processing: Pure copying as a marker of dyslexia in Chinese but not poor reading of English. *Annals of Dyslexia*. 1–16.

Kintsch, Walter. 1988. The role of knowledge in discourse comprehension: A construction integration model. *Psychological Review* 95. 163–182.

Kintsch, Walter. 2012. Psychological models of reading comprehension and their implications for assessment. In John P. Sabatini, Elizabeth Albro and Tenaha O'Reilly (eds.), *Measuring up: Advances in how we assess reading ability*, 21–38.

Kwok, Rosa Kit Wan & Andrew W. Ellis. 2015. Visual word learning in skilled readers of English. *The Quarterly Journal of Experimental Psychology* 68 (2). 326–349.

LaBerge, David and Jay S Samuels. 1974. Toward a theory of automatic information processing in reading. *Cognitive Psychology* 6. 293–323.

Lewis, M. Paul, Gary F. Simons & Charles D. Fennig (eds.). 2015. Ethnologue: Languages of the world, 18th edn. Dallas: SIL International.

Liberman, Alvin M. 1992. The relation of speech to reading and writing. In Ram Frost and Leonard Katz (eds.), *Orthography, phonology, morphology, and meaning*, 167–178. Amsterdam: Elsevier.

Liu, Stella S. F. 1978. Decoding and comprehension in reading Chinese. In Dina Feitelson (ed.), *Cross-cultural perspectives on reading and reading research*, 144–156. Newark, DE: International Reading Association.

Logan, Gordon D. 1988. Toward an instance theory of automatization. *Psychological Review* 95. 492–527.

Logan, Gordon D. 1997. Automaticity and reading: Perspectives from the instance theory of automatization. *Reading and Writing Quarterly* 13. 123–146.

Longcamp, Marieke, Marie-Thérèse Zerbato-Poudou & Jean-Luc Velay. 2005. The influence of writing practice on letter recognition in preschool children: a comparison between handwriting and typing. *Acta psychologica* 119 (1). 67–79.

Lukatela, Katerina, Claudia Carello, Donald Shankweiler & Isabelle Y. Liberman. 1995. Phonological awareness in illiterates: observations from Serbo-Croatian. *Applied Psycholinguistics* 16 (4). 463–488.

Marsh, George, M. Friedman, V. Welch & P. Desberg. 1981. A cognitive-developmental theory of reading acquisition. *Reading research: Advances in theory and practice* 3. 199–221.

Mason, Jana M., Richard C. Anderson, Akimichi Omura, Nobuko Uchida & Mutsumi Imai. 1989. Learning to read in Japan. *Journal of Curriculum Studies* 21. 389–407.

Mattingly, Ignatius G. 1985. Did orthographies evolve? *Remedial and Special Education* 6 (6). 18–23.

McBride-Chang, Catherine, Fanny Lam, Catherine Lam, Becky Chan, Cathy Y. C. Fong, Terry T. Y. Wong & Simpson W. L. Wong. 2011. Early predictors of dyslexia in Chinese children: Familial history of dyslexia, language delay, and cognitive profiles. *Journal of Child Psychology and Psychiatry* 52 (2). 204–211.

McCardle, Peggy, Brett Miller, Jun R. Lee & Ovid J. Tzeng. 2011. *Dyslexia across languages: Orthography and the brain-gene-behavior link*. Baltimore: Paul H Brookes Publishing.

McCarthy, Suzanne. 1995. The Cree syllabary and the writing system riddle: a paradigm in crisis. In Insup Taylor and David R. Olson (eds), *Scripts and Literacy*, 59–75. Dordrecht: Kluwer. doi:10.1007/978-94-011-1162-1_5.

Moors, Agnes & Jan De Houwer. 2006. Automaticity: A conceptual and theoretical analysis. *Psychological Bulletin* 132. 297–326.

Morten H. Christiansen & Nick Chater. 2015. The now-or-never bottleneck: A fundamental constraint on language. *Behavioral and Brain Sciences*. 1–52.

Nag Sonali. 2007. Early reading in Kannada: the pace of acquisition of orthographic knowledge and phonemic awareness. *Journal of Research in Reading* 30. 7–22.

Nag, Sonali & Charles A. Perfetti. 2014. Reading and writing: insights from the alphasyllabaries of South and Southeast Asia. *Writing Systems Research* 6 (1). 1–9.
Nag, Sonali & Maggie J. Snowling. 2011. Cognitive profiles of poor readers of Kannada. *Reading and Writing* 24 (6). 657–676.
Oakhill, Jane, Kate Cain & Carsten Elbro. 2014. *Understanding and teaching reading comprehension: a handbook.* Routledge.
Olson, David. 1977. From utterance to text: The bias of language in speech and writing. *Harvard educational review* 47 (3). 257–281.
Olson, David R. 1994. *The world on paper.* Cambridge, England: Cambridge University Press.
Perfetti, Charles A. 1985. *Reading ability.* New York: Oxford University Press.
Perfetti, Charles A. 1992. The representation problem in reading acquisition. In Philip. B. Gough, Linnea C. Ehri and Rebecca Treiman (eds.), *Reading acquisition*, 145–174. Hillsdale, NJ: Erlbaum.
Perfetti, Charles A. 2003. The universal grammar of reading. *Scientific Studies of Reading* 7. 3–24.
Perfetti, Charles A. 2007. Reading ability: Lexical quality to comprehension. *Scientific Studies of Reading* 11 (4). 357–383.
Perfetti, Charles. A & Lindsay N. Harris. 2013. Universal reading processes are modulated by language and writing system. *Language Learning and Development* 9. 296–316.
Perfetti, Charles A. & Lesley Hart. 2002. The lexical quality hypothesis. *Precursors of Functional Literacy* 11. 67–86.
Pritchard Stephen C., Max Coltheart, Eva Marinus & Anne Castles. 2015. A computational model of the self-teaching hypothesis based on the dual-route cascaded model of reading. Unpublished doctoral dissertation, Macquarie University, NSW, Australia.
Ravid, Dorit. 2006. Hebrew orthography and literacy. In R. Malatesha Joshi and P. G. Aaron (eds.), *Handbook of orthography and literacy*, 339–364. Mahwah, NJ: Erlbaum.
Ravid, Dorit. 2012. *Spelling morphology: The psycholinguistics of Hebrew spelling.* New York: Springer.
Rayner, Keith. 1998. Eye movements in reading and information processing: 20 years of research. *Psychological Bulletin* 124 (3). 372.
Reitsma, Pieter. 1983. Printed word learning in beginning readers. *Journal of Experimental Child Psychology* 36 (2). 321–339.
Ricketts, Jessie, Kate Nation & Dorothy V. M. Bishop. 2007. Vocabulary is important for some, but not all reading skills. *Scientific Studies of Reading* 11. 235–25.
Roberts, Dave. 2011. A tone orthography typology. *Written Language and Literacy* 14. 82–108.
Rogers, Henry. 1995. Optimal orthographies. In Insup Taylor and David R. Olson (eds.), *Scripts and literacy: Reading and learning to read alphabets, syllabaries, and characters*, 31–44. New York: Kluwer.
Rogers, Henry. 2005. *Writing systems: A linguistic approach.* Malden, MA: Blackwell.
Saenger, Paul. 1991. The separation of words and the physiology of reading. In David R. Olson and Nancy Torrance (eds.), *Literacy and orality* 198–214. New York: Cambridge University Press.
Saiegh-Haddad, Elinor & Roni Henkin-Roitfarb. 2014. The structure of Arabic language and orthography. In Elinor Saiegh-Haddad and Malatesha Joshi (eds.), *Handbook of Arabic literacy*, 3–28. Springer Netherlands.
Saiegh-Haddad, Elinor and Malatesha Joshi. 2014. *Handbook of Arabic literacy and orthography.* New York: Springer.
Sampson, Geoffrey. 1985. *Writing systems.* Stanford: Stanford University Press.
Scragg, Donald George. 1974. *A history of English spelling* 3. New York: Manchester University Press.
Seidenberg, Mark S. 2013. The science of reading and its educational implications. *Language Learning and Development* 9. 331–360.
Seymour, Philip H. K., Mikko Aro & Jane M. Erskine. 2003. Foundation literacy acquisition in European orthographies. *British Journal of Psychology* 94. 143–174.

Shahar-Yames, Daphna & David L. Share. 2008. Spelling as a self-teaching mechanism in orthographic learning. *Journal of research in reading* 31 (1). 22–39.

Shankweiler, Donald. 2012. Reading and phonological processing. In Vilayanur S. Ramachandran (ed.), *The Encyclopedia of human behavior* 3, 249–256. New York: Academic Press.

Share, David L. 1995. Phonological recoding and self-teaching: Sine qua non of reading acquisition. *Cognition* 55. 151–218. doi:10.1016/0010-0277(94)00645-2.

Share, David L. 2004. Orthographic learning at a glance: On the time course and developmental onset of self-teaching. *Journal of Experimental Child Psychology* 87. 267–298.

Share, David L. 2008a. On the Anglocentricities of current reading research and practice: The perils of over-reliance on an "outlier" orthography. *Psychological Bulletin* 134. 584–615.

Share, D. L. 2008b. Orthographic learning, phonology and the self-teaching hypothesis. In Robert Kail (ed.), *Advances in child development and behavior* 36. 31–82. Amsterdam: Elsevier.

Share, David L. 2012. Frost and fogs, or sunny skies? Orthography, reading, and misplaced optimism. *Behavioral and Brain Sciences* 35. 307–308.

Share, David L. 2014. Alphabetism in reading science. *Frontiers in Psychology* 5, 752. doi:10.3389/fpsyg.2014.00752.

Share, David. L. in press. Learning to read Hebrew. To appear in Ludo Verhoeven and Charles A. Perfetti (eds.), *Reading acquisition: Cross-linguistic and cross-script perspectives*. Cambridge: Cambridge University Press.

Share, D. L. & Bar-On, A. 2017. Learning to read a Semitic Abjad: The Triplex model of Hebrew reading development. *Journal of Learning Disabilities*. Doi: 10.1177/0022219417718198

Share, David L. & Talya Gur. 1999. How reading begins: A study of preschoolers' print identification strategies. *Cognition and Instruction* 17 (2). 177–213.

Share, David L. & Talya Gur. in preparation. When less is more: When declining decoding skill signals progress in reading.

Share, David L & Peter T Daniels. 2015. Aksharas, alphasyllabaries, abugidas, alphabets and orthographic depth: Reflections on Rimzhim, Katz and Fowler (2014).*Writing Systems Research*, 1–15.

Share, David L & Carmit Shalev. 2004. Self-teaching in normal and disabled readers. *Reading and Writing* 17. 769–800.

Shatil, Evelyn & David L. Share. 2003. Cognitive antecedents of early reading ability: A test of the modularity hypothesis. *Journal of Experimental Child Psychology* 86. 1–31.

Shaywitz Sally E. & Bennett A. Shaywitz. 2005. Dyslexia (specific reading disability), Biological Psychiatry 57. 1301–1309.

Shu, Hua, Richard C. Anderson & Ningning Wu. 2000. Phonetic awareness: Knowledge of orthography-phonology relationships in the character acquisition of Chinese children. *Journal of Educational Psychology* 92. 56–62.

Shu, Hua, Xi Chen, Richard C. Anderson, Ningning Wu & Yue Xuan. 2003. Properties of school Chinese: Implications for learning to read. *Child Development* 74. 27–47.

Siok, Wai Ting & Paul Fletcher. 2001. The role of phonological awareness and visual-orthographic skills in Chinese reading acquisition. *Developmental Psychology* 37. 886–899.

Snowling, Margaret. J. 2000. *Dyslexia*. Blackwell.

Stanovich, Keith E. 1990. Concepts in developmental theories of reading skill: Cognitive resources, automaticity, and modularity. *Developmental Review* 10. 72–100.

Strauss, Steven L. & Bess Altwerger. 2007. The logographic nature of English alphabetics and the fallacy of direct intensive phonics instruction. *Journal of Early Childhood Literacy* 7. 299–319.

Stuart, Morag & Max Coltheart. 1988. Does reading develop in a sequence of stages? *Cognition* 30. 139–181.

Tan, Li Hai, John A. Spinks, Guinevere F. Eden, Charles A. Perfetti & Wai Ting Siok. 2005. Reading depends on writing, in Chinese. *Proceedings of the National Academy of Sciences of the United States of America* 102 (24). 8781–8785.

Taylor, Insup & Martin M. Taylor. 1995. *Writing and literacy in Chinese, Korean, and Japanese*. Amsterdam: John Benjamins.

Treiman, Rebecca. 1993. *Beginning to spell: A study of first-grade children*. New York: Oxford University Press.

Tunmer, William. E. 2014. How cognitive science has provided the theoretical basis for resolving the 'great debate' over reading methods in alphabetic orthographies. In Saths Cooper and Kopano Ratele (eds.), *Psychology Serving Humanity: Proceedings of the 30th International Congress of Psychology 2. Majority World Psychology*. New York: Psychology Press.

Tunmer, William E., Tom Nicolson, Keith T. Greaney, Jane E. Prochnow, James E. Chapman & Alison W. Arrow. 2013. PIRLS before swine. *New Zealand Journal of Educational Studies* 43. 105–119.

Unger, J. Marshall & John DeFrancis. 1995. Logographic and semasiographic writing systems: A critique of Sampson's classification. In Insup Taylor and David R. Olson (eds.), *Scripts and literacy*, 45–58. Dordrecht: Kluwer Academic.

Venezky, Richard. L. 1970. *The structure of English orthography* 82. The Hague: Mouton.

Venezky, Richard L. 2007. In search of the perfect orthography. *Written Language and Literacy* 7. 139–163.

Wang, Hua-Chen, Anne Castles, Lyndsey Nickels & Kate Nation. 2012. Context effects on orthographic learning of regular and irregular words. *Journal of Experimental Child Psychology* 109. 39–57.

Wimmer, Heinz & Karin Landerl. 1997. How learning to spell German differs from learning to spell English. *Learning to spell: Research, theory, and practice across languages*. 81–96.

Wolf, Maryanne & Tami Katzir-Cohen. 2001. Reading fluency and its intervention. *Scientific Studies of Reading* 5. 211–238.

Wu, Xinchun, Wenling Li & Richard C. Anderson. 1999. Reading instruction in China. *Journal of Curriculum Studies* 31. 571–586.

Yin, Li & Catherine McBride. 2015. Chinese kindergartners learn to read characters analytically. *Psychological Science* 26. 424–432.

Ziegler, Johannes C. & Usha Goswami. 2005. Reading acquisition, developmental dyslexia and skilled reading across languages: a psycholinguistic grainsize theory. *Psychological Bulletin* 131. 3–29. doi:10.1037/0033- 2909.131.1.3.

Ziegler, Johannes C., Conrad Perry, &Marco Zorzi. 2014. Modelling reading development through phonological decoding and self-teaching: implications for dyslexia. *Philosophical Transactions of the Royal Society of London B: Biological Sciences* 369.

Zilberman Shoam Behira. 2011. *On the contribution of handwritten spelling to orthographic learning*. Haifa: University of Haifa Unpublished doctoral dissertation.

Séverine Casalis
22 Acquisition of spelling: Normal and impaired/disordered populations

1 Introduction

Research on spelling development has indicated that children use a variety of strategies to spell words. The strategies used strongly depend on the writing system. In the present chapter, I will focus on alphabetical scripts. In this case, letters are the smallest units that spellers have to plan to produce. However, letters are often included in larger units – from grapheme to morpheme and words, through other multi-letter groups – which define several strategies. In alphabetical writing, the consistency of spelling-to-sound relationships has been found to partly determine the relative frequency of use of available strategies in reading aloud (Ziegler and Goswami, 2005). However, even in transparent orthographies, spelling cannot be entirely predicted by sound-to-spelling conversion. Consequently, other language unit may be helpful. Therefore, it is important to examine not only the unit size that children are able to handle when spelling at different stages in reading acquisition, but also how linguistic awareness is connected to spelling achievement. This relationship might be particularly relevant in design of remedial interventions for children with spelling difficulties. The present chapter will review three levels of linguistic processing at work in alphabetical systems: phonological processing, graphotactic processing, and morphological processing, with a particular focus on the last of these three.

2 Normal development

2.1 Dual-route processing and phonological coding

Classical dual-route approaches suggest that children employ two main procedures when spelling: the use of phoneme-to-grapheme correspondences (hereafter PGC), known as the phonological sublexical route, and whole word form retrieval, known as the lexical route (Barry, 1994). Young children rely mostly on the phonological sublexical route, since, although their reading skills are not yet developed and they therefore have not yet had the opportunity to store lexical orthographic forms, they have nevertheless begun to learn some PGC (Sprenger-Charolles, Siegel, Béchennec, and Serniclaes, 2003). It should be observed that this procedure does not produce

---

Séverine Casalis, Université de Lille 3

the correct spelling of many words. For example, in French orthography, PGC can be relied upon for the correct spelling of about 50% of words (Ziegler, Jacobs, and Stone, 1996). English orthography is known to be highly inconsistent, with some vowels being spelled several ways: for example, /ou/ is spelled in 13 different ways in English (Barry, 1994). Even orthographies that are described as highly consistent for reading – that is with simple phoneme-to-grapheme matching, such as Italian or German – contain spelling inconsistencies. Thus, we have, first, to consider that in order to spell correctly children always have to do more than a PGC, and second, to elucidate how orthographic inconsistency affects the use of alternative strategies.

In studies based on the dual-route model, the sublexical route is assessed through pseudoword spelling (Alegria and Mousty, 1996). The complexity of PGC is examined through effects of grapheme complexity (at least two letters for one phoneme, such as /I:/ :"ea"), the use of contextual rules (e.g., how context modifies letter pronunciation, for example /s/ can be spelled "s", or "c" but only before some vowels in the latter case), and inconsistency in PGC (i.e., the availability of multiple ways to spell a given phoneme). The lexical orthographic procedure has been examined through frequency effects.

As an indication of the relevance of phonological information in spelling, children have been found to spell consonants appearing in an unstressed syllable less accurately than consonants appearing in a stressed syllable (Treiman, Berch, and Weatherton, 1993). It has also been found that children make more errors in consonant clusters (Treiman, 1991), and that first and last phonemes are spelled more accurately than middle phonemes (Treiman et al., 1993). Evidence thus suggests that spelling accuracy is sensitive to phonological constraints.

Studies on the development of sublexical and orthographic lexical routes have indicated that children are highly sensitive to phonological information beginning very early on, with marked effects of regularity (Sprenger-Charolles and Casalis, 1995). Some studies have even failed to find evidence of any frequency effect at all at the first stage of spelling acquisition, suggesting a complete absence of lexical processing (Alegria and Mousty, 1996). With increasing skills, children display greater frequency effects and are more prone to take contextual constraints into account. In general, the findings of studies based on the dual-route conception suggest that the use of the orthographic lexical route increases over the course of reading and spelling acquisition, although it does not replace the sublexical route, as phonological effects continue to be present late in spelling development. Moreover, most of these studies have concluded that the two routes do not develop independently (Sprenger-Charolles, Siegel, and Bonnet, 1998, Sprenger-Charolles et al., 2003, Alegria and Mousty, 1996).

Finally, phonological skills have been shown to be a major determinant of spelling achievement. Phonological awareness, defined as the ability to deliberately manipulate phonological segments, has been found to be one of the two foundations of spelling acquisition, the other being letter knowledge (Treiman, 1993). Indeed, children's ability to segment speech in order to map phonological units onto letters is a crucial key to early spelling skills. Given that alphabetical scripts differ in the consistency of PGC, one can wonder whether phonological awareness contributes similarly to spelling acquisition in different languages. Recent studies have indeed indicated that phonological awareness, and to a lesser extent rapid naming, are the strongest determinants of spelling achievement across several European orthographies even though their weight slightly changes across languages (Moll, Ramus et al., 2014).

The orthographic depth hypothesis (Frost, 1994, see also Ziegler and Goswami, 2005) suggests that differences in orthographic depth lead to differences in the processing of written words. Readers in languages with a shallow orthography are expected to rely mostly on phonological information, as it is easily available, whereas deep orthographies encourage readers to use broader units. While this issue has been widely examined in reading and, to certain extent, reading acquisition, less is known with regard to spelling acquisition. Comparisons between English and Austrian young spellers showed that English children performed worse in spelling matched words (Wimmer and Landerl, 1997). However, these effects were here restricted to words. Given that spelling of the vowels in the English words is less consistent than in the German words (e.g. br*ea*d vs Br*o*t), the English children's less accurate word spelling is directly attributable to this inconsistency. Orthographic depth also seems to have a broader impact on spelling acquisition. Juul and Sigurdsson (2005) compared the spelling performance of Icelandic (learning a shallow orthography) and Danish (learning a deep orthography) children matched on first-consonant spelling performance. The Danish children had more difficulty spelling double consonants and consonant clusters than the Icelandic children, a difference that cannot be directly explained by any inconsistency of PGCs in the particular words used in the comparison. It thus seems that children learning to spell in a shallow orthography have less difficulty mastering PGC than children learning in a deep orthography. In addition, the development of both sublexical and lexical spelling procedures has been found to be delayed in deep orthographies as compared to shallow orthographies, such as for example French (deep orthography) vs. Spanish (shallow orthography) (Carrillo and Alegria, 2014). This pattern refutes the Orthographic Depth Hypothesis and its suggestion that the size of units at stake adapts to the sound-to-spelling consistency of the language. On the contrary, the development of the lexical/orthographic route is also delayed in children learning to spell in a deep orthography.

2.2 The influence of distributional properties

Recent research has indicated that other factors besides the use of PGC and whole-word retrieval are relevant in understanding how children learn to spell words. As mentioned earlier, phonological information is not enough to spell words. This is true for a number of reasons: first, phonemes, particularly vowels, may be spelled using several graphemes; second, some letters are doubled; third, some letters are silent. It is noteworthy that letters are not randomly distributed in a given language (e.g., "w" is frequently followed by "h" in English orthography), and that such orthographic regularities sometimes have no phonological counterparts.

Interestingly, children seem to be sensitive to the distributional properties of the letters even before they start learning to read and to spell. Pollo, Kessler and Treiman (2009) found that spellings of "prephonological" children are, to some respects, consistent with the written language that they are exposed to. As such, there is no universal pattern of early spelling production; rather, these productions reflect specific patterns in the written forms of particular languages, and therefore differ across languages. Evidence has been presented that more advanced spellers, such as second to sixth graders, make use of distributional properties. For example, Pacton, Fayol and Perruchet (2005) found in a pseudoword dictation task that children were more prone to spell the sound /o/ with "eau" after a "v" rather than a "k", conforming to the actual pattern in French orthography. A similar pattern was found in word spelling in Spanish: children more often spelled the sound /b/ with the letter "v" before the letter "I" than "u" and inversely with the letter "b" before the letter "u" rather than "I", conforming to bigram frequencies (Carrillo and Alegria, 2014)

Many studies have given evidence of children's learning about aspects of orthography which have no phonological counterpart. It turns out that orthographic knowledge cannot be reduced to phonological coding and, although the development of orthographic skills is correlated with that of phonological skills, a portion of these skills develop as an independent part of the reading and spelling system.

2.3 The role of morphological information

Considering morphology, it is noteworthy that the spelling of the root mostly remains consistent across derivations. This so-called root consistency principle might be helpful for children when spelling: even without knowledge the spelling of a derived word itself, they may be able to deduce it based on knowledge of the spelling of the root and the suffix. Morphological information is also helpful in suffix spelling. For example, in French, the sound /Et/ is frequent at the end of words and can be spelled in several ways ("ette", "ète", "aite"); it sometimes corresponds to a suffix. The suffix "ette" means "little" for feminine words. It can thus be guessed that all the final letters of a word ending with /Et/ is spelled "ette" in any case where this morpheme carries the suffix meaning "little." Note that many non-suffixed French words end with "ette," and that there are also many other spellings of the sound /Et/ that are not morphologically motivated (e.g., "ète" at the end of *athlète* [athlete] or "aite" at the end of *retraite* [retirement]). However, although morphology is not involved in several words, it may help to a certain extent. The question is therefore whether children use this information – and, most importantly, when they are able to use it during the course of spelling acquisition.

Studies conducted in both English and French have evidenced that children are sensitive to morphological information when they have to spell words. The impact of morphology on spelling performance was apparent in Carlisle's (1988) study, as children wrote derived forms correctly in cases where they spelled the root correctly (see also Deacon and Bryant, 2005). Sénéchal (2000) examined a specific difficulty in French word spelling, namely, the silent final consonant. Senechal (2000) had children spell several categories of words. Among them, a "morphological" condition (where the final letter is audible in derived form, such as in *laid/laideur* [ugly/ugliness]) was contrasted to a lexical condition, with a silent final letter and where either the word has no derived form (e.g., *brebis* [ewe]) or the final letter is changed in the derived form (e.g., *sirop* [syrup], *siroter* [to sip]). Critically, Grade 2 and Grade 4 children found it easier to spell the words in the morphological condition than in the lexical condition. Note that the morphological advantage could also be explained as an orthographic effect. Since the root is present in all the derived forms, it is encountered more frequently than simple words as opaque. Therefore, it remains possible that the performance advantage with words in the morphological condition over lexical words is orthographic in nature. A way to control for this, then, is to use similar "roots" for both derived and opaque words. Deacon and Dhooge (2006) compared children's spelling of morphologically complex words, here derived forms such as *rocky*, to their spelling of control words such as *rocket*. Even though an identical clue was provided (*rock*), rather than one that was specific to the morphological condition, the authors found that the derived forms were spelled more accurately than control words. This clearly suggests that young children are sensitive to the root morpheme during spelling.

Besides the case of silent final letters, other specific spelling difficulties have been examined. For example, a typical difficulty in French spelling is attributable to graphemic complexity: that is, the common situation where a given phoneme can be spelled in several ways. Casalis, Deacon, and Pacton (2011) compared the spelling of complex graphemes in both derived and simple words (e.g., ba*ig*nade [bathing] vs. bed*ai*ne [paunch]). The spelling of the complex grapheme was more likely to be accurate when it was included in the derived form rather than a non-derived form.

Given the importance of phonological coding in spelling, it is important to examine the extent to which phonology modulates these morphological effects. Carlisle (1987) asked young and older children to spell roots and derived forms in two conditions: in the first, the root included in the derived form was phonologically modified as compared to the root pronounced in isolation (e.g., *heal-health*), while in the second case, there was no phonological change (e.g., *warm-warmth*). Although the study evidenced a link between spelling performance with root and derived forms, spelling was less accurate when there was a phonological change. However, this difference was not apparent in Deacon and Bryant's (2005) study, where children aged 7 and 9 showed similar benefits in spelling in cases of phonological change (e.g., *objection*) or none (e.g., *illness*).

Beyond the question of interactions between phonology and morphology in spelling, it is also important to examine how morphological information interacts with graphotactic information. As mentioned above, the distributional properties of letters affect spelling accuracy: in other words, spelling has been found to be guided by graphotactic properties. Pacton et al (2005) asked participants in three age groups (8-year-olds, 11-year-olds, and adults) to spell pseudowords. Their experiments focused on the spelling of two specific word endings, namely, /Et/ and /O/, both of which have the property of multiple potential spellings. In addition, /Et/ and /o/ correspond to the suffixes "ette", and "eau", respectively feminine and masculine suffixes meaning "little". In graphotactic terms, these word endings are more frequent in some environments and less so in others: for example, /O/ is frequently spelled "eau" after /v/, and never after /k/. Pseudowords were presented in three different context conditions: in isolation, in a neutral sentence context, or in a sentence context suggesting that the word ending was indeed a suffix (e.g., "a little /vitar/ is a /vitaro/"). The results showed that children used a variety of spellings for inconsistent graphemes, indicating that they were aware of the diversity of spelling. Moreover, their productions reflected sensitivity to distributional properties: /ET/ was more frequently spelled "ette" after /v/ rather than /k/, for example. Second, the children's sensitivity to morphological information was also reflected by the fact that the spelling "eau" and "ette" appeared more frequently in the morphological sentence context. The critical comparison was between different spellings that share the property of being inferable on the basis of morphological information, but that differ in terms of graphotactic probability. Indeed, there was no trend toward disappearance, or even a reduction, in the effect of graphotactic regularities in any group in the morphological sentence context. This suggests that the use of morphological information is also limited by graphotactic information.

Overall, there are a number of indications that children make use of morphological information when spelling. A critical question is therefore whether there is a connection between children's morphological awareness and their use of morphological information in spelling. Morphological awareness has been defined as the ability to manipulate morpheme units (Carlisle and Nomanbhoy, 1993). It may be assessed though several tasks. In sentence production task, children have to complete a sentence with a derived form, given the base (e.g., a man who runs is a … *runner.*). In the analogy task, children are provided with a morphologically related pair as a model and are required to supply the second word in a new pair, given the first (e.g., play-player, run-? answer: *runner*). Developmental studies have indicated that, contrary to phonemic awareness, which develops very quickly during the early stages of reading acquisition, morphological awareness develops progressively over the course of primary and secondary education (Berninger, Abbott, Nagy, and Carlisle, 2010). The issue, then, is to examine to what extent morphological awareness is associated with performance in spelling morphologically complex words.

Sénéchal (2000) examined the connection between morphological awareness scores and spelling in French-speaking children in Grades 2 to 4. She found that morphological awareness scores contributed to children's spelling of derived words only, and not to that of regular (words that can be spelled using only PGC) or deep words (words containing a silent final letter which cannot be guessed using a morphological strategy). Therefore, Sénéchal argued, the contribution of morphological awareness to spelling is specific: it contributes only when morphological knowledge is necessary, rather than generally enhancing the spelling of all words. Casalis, Deacon, and Pacton (2011) obtained a slightly different pattern. Morphological awareness was correlated with spelling performance, but the connection was not specific to derived words, as it was correlated with spelling of both derived and nonderived words. However, when considering the morphological awareness score on some items only (those whose derived form cannot be found by adding a suffix but necessitate a phonological change, such as in five/ fifth) a specific connection between morphological awareness and the spelling of derived words appeared in Grade 4. These results suggest that morphological awareness may play a general role in early spelling development, as well as making a more specific contribution to the spelling of morphologically complex words in older children.

3 Impaired – disordered development

Impaired spelling development should be understood in the context of literacy and language development more generally. It is noteworthy, for example, that children with developmental dyslexia show difficulties not only with reading but also with spelling. Similarly, children who have experienced language disorders may have significantly impaired literacy acquisition, including spelling acquisition. Other children, in contrast, despite being exempt from other language and reading impairments, nevertheless display specific difficulties with spelling. In what follows I will consider these three cases successively.

3.1 Children with dyslexia

Although the reading skills of dyslexic children have been extensively described, less is known about their spelling skills. Persons with dyslexia are known to have systematic difficulties with spelling. Indeed, spelling difficulties generally persist as one of the major impairments remaining in young adults with highly compensated dyslexia, such as university students who have overcome most of their reading difficulties (Tops, Callen, Bijn, and Brysbaert, 2014). But significant questions about developmental dyslexia and spelling remain. First, do children with dyslexia show greater difficulties in spelling than would be expected from their reading skills? Second, is their spelling characterized by specific strategies, or is their spelling similar to that of younger reading level-matched children?

Whether dyslexics exhibit more severe spelling than reading disabilities is an important theoretical question. After all, dyslexia is identified through reading disabilities and not spelling impairment. Note that the DSM (V) includes spelling in the definition of dyslexia. It is thus theoretically possible for dyslexics to display various patterns of spelling achievement. This question is directly related to the issue of the connection between reading and spelling skills. While this issue will be examined in the case of unexpectedly poor spellers (see below), one can wonder whether dyslexia has a stronger impact on spelling than on reading. To examine this question, the spelling performance of children with dyslexia should be compared to that of children matched on reading level. If the performance of participants with dyslexia is similar to that of younger reading level-matched children, it can be concluded that spelling achievement is in line with reading achievement in dyslexia. Inversely, if the performance of participants with dyslexia is worse than that of reading level-matched children, we can conclude that spelling is more strongly impaired than reading in dyslexia. Children with dyslexia have been found to have worse spelling performance than reading-level matched controls on both word and pseudoword spelling (Casalis, 2014; Plisson, Daigle, and Montessinos-Gelet, 2013). It thus appears that dyslexia affects spelling performance more strongly than reading performance. One possible explanation of this discrepancy is that compensation strategies are more readily available in reading than in spelling, such as, for example, anticipations and whole-word recognition. The second question is whether participants with dyslexia use specific strategies, or differ more globally in the procedure involved in spelling. This question has been examined using two different designs, based on either reading-level matching or spelling-level matching. Alegria and Mousty (1996) found children with dyslexia to make less use of contextual information in applying rules for phoneme-to-grapheme conversion than reading level-matched controls. Casalis (2014) also used a reading level match design (see above). In that study, children were asked to spell words and pseudowords and no interaction was found between groups and item type: participants with dyslexia were equally impaired in both the retrieval of orthographic information (for words) and phoneme-to-grapheme correspondences (for pseudowords). In English, Bruck and Treiman (1990) used a spelling level-match design and investigated the spelling of word-initial consonant clusters. Children with dyslexia failed to spell the second consonant in clusters, as did the normal readers/spellers, but were even more impaired when spelling pseudowords. However, other studies have failed to evidence any difference between groups, with children with dyslexia and spelling level-matched controls making similar proportions of phonologically motivated spelling errors (Bourassa and Treiman, 2003).

The importance of the particular language studied in investigations into spelling patterns in dyslexia was recently pointed out in a cross-language study (Giannouli and Pavlidis, 2014). Because English orthography is particularly opaque, its use could lead to an overestimation of the importance of phonological skills in other orthographies. Giannouli and Pavlidis compared the spelling errors of 58 English-speaking participants with dyslexia and 58 Greek-speaking participants with dyslexia. The English-speaking dyslexics made more phonological errors, while the Greek-speaking participants made more grammatical and visual errors. In another study, Dutch-speaking adolescents with dyslexia were found to produce more phonological errors than orthographic or grammatical errors (Tops et al., 2014). A recent study examining the predictors of reading in dyslexia across six languages found that while the determinants of spelling are similar across languages, more complex orthography exacerbates dyslexia (Landerl, Ramus, Moll, et al., 2013). It therefore appears that spelling errors differ slightly across languages in participants with dyslexia.

While there is evidence that children with dyslexia have some difficulties in learning and applying phonological rules for spelling, less is known about their ability to use morphological information in spelling. Studies conducted in both English (Bourassa and Treiman, 2008) and Greek (Seymour and Tsemelsi, 2006) comparing dyslexics to both chronological age-matched and spelling age-matched children found that children with dyslexia showed a similar sensitivity to morphological information as reading-age matched children, and performed worse than chronological age-matched children. This pattern reflects the reciprocal connection between learning to spell and the development of morphological knowledge. However, a recent study conducted in Greek evidenced some slight differences between dyslexics and matched controls in the spelling of morphologically complex items. On the whole, however, their pattern of responses did not strongly differ from that of spelling age-matched children (Diamanti, Goulandris, Stuart, and Campbell, 2014).

3.2 Children with specific language impairment

The way that children with specific language impairment (SLI) learn to read and spell has been recently investigated. In general, children with SLI are found to be strongly delayed in both reading and spelling (van Weerdenburg, Verhoeven, Bosman, and van Balkom, 2011). A deficit in phonological spelling has been documented (Brizzola, Gasperini, Pfanner, Cristofani, Casalini, and Chilosi, 2011). A critical question is whether participants with SLI display specific spelling patterns or are differentially sensitive to particular units. In spite of a delay in spelling acquisition, similar effects are seen in children with SLI as in typically developing children, with less accurate grapheme spelling at the middle and the end of the word, and a strong length effect, with more errors in long words than in short ones (Cordewener,

Bosman, and Verhoeven, 2012). Larkin, Williams, and Blaggan (2013) compared the performance of children with SLI to that of spelling-age matched children on three spelling skills: phonological, orthographic, and morphological. Children with SLI performed worse at phonological spelling, but produced the same number of orthographically legal spellings as the control groups (chronological age and spelling age). They also performed similarly to the spelling age control group on morphological spelling.

The above studies underline the relevance of morphological structure and developing spellers' sensitivity to it. Given their difficulties in language processing, children with SLI might be expected to be less sensitive to the morphological structure of words. To investigate this issue, Deacon, Cleave, Baylis, Fraser, Ingram, and Perlmutter (2014) asked children with SLI and typically developing children to spell a letter string (e.g., *win*) in three conditions: embedded in an inflected form (*wins*), in a derived form (*winner*) or in a control word (*wink*). The children spelled the letter string more accurately when it was embedded in an inflected or a derived form, and this advantage over control words was observed in both SLI and TD groups matched on spelling age, suggesting that children with SLI do not lack sensitivity to morphological structure when spelling. Overall, the spelling of children with SLI mostly are in line with their language difficulties.

3.3 Unexpected poor spellers with well-developed reading skills

Reading and spelling achievement are closely related, with a correlation coefficient ranging from .60 to .80 between reading and spelling (Ehri, 1997). However, dissociations have sometimes been described, with either good spelling skills in combination with poor reading skills (Wimmer and Mayringer, 2002) or good reading skills combined with poor spelling skills (Frith, 1980). Frith observed a group of unexpected poor spellers (good readers). Analysis of errors showed that these good readers spelled phonetically. One hypothesis is that children in this category of poor spellers exhibit mild phonological deficits. On this view, they have developed enough phonological skills to acquire some partial orthographic knowledge, but that knowledge is insufficient to allow them to acquire whole lexical orthographic representations. In order to examine the prevalence of this group, Fayol, Zorman, and Lété (2009) tested 1,453 fifth graders on reading, spelling, and phonological skills. Fifty-eight participants (4% of the sample) performed above the 70th percentile for reading and below the 30th percentile for spelling, thus displaying a dissociation between reading and spelling. However, the precise cause of their specific spelling difficulties remains to be explored in more detail.

Overall, spelling difficulties are most closely linked to phonological skills, but are not limited to this impairment: morphological processing is also impaired. For these reasons, interventional studies should emphasize both phonological and morphological processing.

4 Interventional studies

4.1 Orthographic training

In normal readers and spellers, orthographic knowledge is acquired, at least in part, through a self-teaching mechanism. Share (1995) described this mechanism, stating that each successful decoding of a word reinforces the corresponding lexical orthographic representation. However, in some transparent orthographies such as German, many children with dyslexia who have developed phonological skills nevertheless show impaired spelling performance (Landerl and Wimmer, 2008). According to Landerl and Wimmer, children with dyslexia are less able to self-teach. It thus seems important to develop alternative intervention programs which aim to allow children with dyslexia to learn through alternative mechanisms.

Ise, Schulte, and Korne (2010) proposed a training program for German children with dyslexia based on teaching both explicit spelling rules (e.g., when a consonant should be doubled) and strategies on how to use these rules when spelling. This training was given to children in Grades 5 and 6. Although only a few children received the training, the results revealed significant beneficial effects on spelling scores. It is important to underline that, at least in the shallow orthography of German, training on explicit spelling rules was more effective than training on phonological skills.

4.2 Morphological intervention

As mentioned above, morphological information may be particularly helpful in spelling as it may help in retrieving the orthographic patterns of different members of a given morphological family. Thus, given the root consistency principle, children's spelling of derived forms should be facilitated if they are able to connect the derived form to the base. Nunes, Bryant, and Olsson (2003) tested whether the spelling skills of young developing readers and spellers can be improved by administering different training programs to groups of 7- and 8-year-old children. The study included five training groups: morphological only, morphological with writing, phonological only, phonological with writing, and control. While the morphological and phonological training methods were found to be more effective when associated to training in writing in general, a specific spelling benefit was identified with the morphological training combined with writing.

Children with dyslexia have been found to have a higher error rate with derived words than chronological age controls, particularly because derived words are long and infrequent. At the same time, children with dyslexia have been found to develop greater morphological awareness than phonological awareness, although they performance worse on both types of measures than chronological age-matched children (Casalis, Colé and Sopo, 2004). This suggests that it might be possible to help them rely on this relatively more developed form of awareness in spelling. Arnbak and

Elbro (2000) conducted the first study on the training of morphological awareness in children with dyslexia. Sixty children with dyslexia aged 10 to 12 took part in the study. All received remedial training including phonological awareness, letter-to-sound knowledge, reading, and spelling. The experimental group additionally received training in both derivational and inflectional morphology. The results showed that the post-test performance of the group that received additional training in morphology was superior to that of the control group in both morphological awareness and the spelling of compound and derived words. Based on these positive results, Tsemesli and Seymour (2008) administered a training program in morphology combining oral instruction with written materials to a group of 9 boys (mean age: 13.87 years). A chronological age-matched group and a spelling level-matched group also received the training. The study was based on the word-pair paradigm (a base and a derived word). A particular set of suffixes was targeted in the study, and trained systematically under two conditions: no change (e.g., *luck-lucky*) and an orthographic condition (e.g, *noise-noisy*). The dyslexic and spelling level control groups benefited from the training; the chronological age group also showed benefits, but to a lesser extent. Morphological training effects were stronger on the spelling of derived and compound words than on base words. The dyslexic group improved more on the no-change items. In order to test how learning generalizes, authors compared taught items to untaught items at post-test, and found improvement with both categories of items. Finally, the durability of training effects was assessed by a second post-test administered two months after the completion of the study. The effect was found to be durable in the dyslexic group, at least for adjectives.

5 Conclusion

Developing spelling skills requires relying on several aspects of language. Some of these aspects are specific to the written modality, such as distributional orthographic properties, while others are connected to spoken language, such as phonological and morphological skills. Models of spelling development should therefore integrate these connections. Both phonological and morphological skills have a reciprocal relationship with spelling development. For this reason, the precise extent to which these skills account for and/or depend on spelling acquisition remains to be analyzed. Because spelling difficulties are considered to be closely related to reading difficulties, they have been less specifically studied. However, evidence suggests that spelling difficulties in dyslexia are greater than reading difficulties, and that they remain even after reading difficulties have been overcome. Recent studies on spelling development have considerably developed and have focused on distributional and morphological properties of spelling. These recent findings indicate a need for models of spelling to set aside the classical dual-route approach in order to integrate other relevant dimensions of language, such as morphology, and some spelling-specific knowledge, such as sensitivity to distributional properties.

References

Alegria, Jesus and Philippe Mousty. 1996. The development of spelling procedures in French-speaking, normal and reading-disabled children: Effects of frequency and lexicality. *Journal of Experimental Child Psychology* 63 (2). 312–338.

Arnbak, E. and C. Elbro. 2000. The effects of morphological awareness training on the reading and spelling skills of young dyslexics. *Scandinavian Journal of Educational Research* 44 (3). 229–251.

Barry, C. 1994. Spelling routes (or roots or rutes). In Gordon DA Brown, and Nick C. Ellis (eds.), *Handbook of spelling: Theory, process and intervention*, 27–49. Chichester, UK: Wiley.

Berninger, Virginia W., Robert D. Abbott, William Nagy, and Joanne Carlisle. 2010. Growth in phonological, orthographic, and morphological awareness in grades 1 to 6. *Journal of Psycholinguistic Research* 39 (2). 141–163.

Bourassa, D., and R. Treiman. 2003. Spelling in children with dyslexia: Analyses from the Treiman-Bourassa Early Spelling Test. *Scientific Studies of Reading* 7 (4). 309–333.

Bourassa, D. C. and R. Treiman. 2008. Morphological constancy in spelling: A comparison of children with dyslexia and typically developing children. *Dyslexia: An International Journal of Research and Practice* 14 (3). 155–169.

Brizzolara, D., F. Gasperini, L. Pfanner, P. Cristofani, C. Casalini, and A. M. Chilosi. 2011. Long-term reading and spelling outcome in Italian adolescents with a history of specific language impairment. *Cortex* 47 (8). 955–973.

Bruck, M. and R. Treiman. 1990. Phonological awareness and spelling in normal children and dyslexics: The case of initial consonant clusters. *Journal of Experimental Child Psychology* 50 (1). 156–178.

Carlisle, Joanne F. 1987. The use of morphological knowledge in spelling derived forms by learning-disabled and normal students. *Annals of Dyslexia* 37. 90–108.

Carlisle, Joanne F. 1988. Knowledge of derivational morphology and spelling ability in fourth, sixth, and eighth graders. *Applied Psycholinguistics* 9 (3). 247–266.

Carlisle, Joanne F., and Diana M. Nomanbhoy. 1993. Phonological and morphological awareness in first graders. *Applied Psycholinguistics* 14. 177–195.

Carrillo, María Soledad and Jesús Alegría. 2014. The development of children's sensitivity to bigram frequencies when spelling in Spanish, a transparent writing system. *Reading and Writing* 27 (3). 571–590.

Casalis, Séverine. 2014. Written spelling in French children with dyslexia. In Barbara Arfé, Julie Dockrell & Virginia Berninger (eds), *Writing development and instruction in children with hearing, speech and oral difficulties*, 201–213. NY: Oxford University Press.

Casalis, Séverine, Helene Deacon & Sébastien Pacton. 2011. How specific is the connection between morphological awareness and spelling? A study of French children. *Applied Psycholinguistics* 32 (3). 499–511.

Casalis, Séverine, Pascale Colé, & Delphine Sopo. 2004. Morphological awareness in developmental dyslexia. *Annals of Dyslexia* 54 (1). 114–138.

Cordewener, Kim, Anna Bosman & Ludo Verhoeven. 2012. Characteristics of early spelling of children with Specific Language Impairment. *Journal of Communication Disorders* 45 (3). 212–222.

Deacon, Helene, Patricia Cleave, Julia Baylis, Jillian Fraser, Elizabeth Ingram, Signy Perlmutter. 2014. The representation of roots in the spelling of children with specific language impairment. *Journal of Learning Disabilities* 47 (1). 13–21.

Deacon, Helene & Peter Bryant, 2005. The strength of children's knowledge of the role of root morphemes in the spelling of derived words. *Journal of Child Language* 32 (2). 375–389.

Deacon, Helene & Sarah Dhooge. 2010. Developmental stability and changes in the impact of root consistency on children's spelling. *Reading and Writing* 23 (9). 1055–1069.

Diamanti, Vassiliki, Nata Goulandris, Morag, Stuart, Ruth Campbell. 2014. Spelling of derivational and inflectional suffixes by Greek-speaking children with and without dyslexia. *Reading and Writing* 27 (2). 337–358.

Ehri, Linnea. 1997. Learning to read and learning to spell are one and the same, almost. In Charles Perfetti, Laurence Rieben & Michel Fayol (eds.), *Learning to spell: Research, theory, and practice across languages*, 237–269. Mahwah, NJ: Lawrence Erlbaum.

Fayol, Michel, Michel Zorman & Bernard Lété. 2009. Unexpectedly good spellers too. Associations and dissociations in reading and spelling French. *British Journal of Educational Psychology* 6. 63–75.

Frith, Uta. 1980. Unexpected spelling problems. In U. Frith (ed.), *Cognitive processes in spelling*, 495–515. London: Academic Press.

Frost, Ram. 1994. Prelexical and postlexical strategies in reading: Evidence from a deep and a shallow orthography. *Journal of Experimental Psychology: Learning, Memory, and Cognition* 20. 1–16.

Giannouli, Vicky & George Pavlidis. 2014. What can spelling errors tell us about the causes and treatment of dyslexia? *Support for Learning* 29 (3). 244–260.

Ise, Elena & Gerd Schulte-Körne. 2010. Spelling deficits in dyslexia: Evaluation of an orthographic spelling training. *Annals of Dyslexia* 60 (1). 18–39.

Juul Holder & Baldur Sigurdsson. 2005. Orthography as a handicap? A direct comparison of spelling acquisition in Danish and Icelandic. *Scandinavian Journal of Psychology* 46 (3). 263–272.

Landerl, Karin & Heinz Wimmer. 2008. Development of word reading fluency and spelling in a consistent orthography: An 8-year follow-up. *Journal of Educational Psychology* 100 (1). 150–161.

Landerl, Karin, Frank Ramus, Kristina Moll, Heikki Lyytinen, Paavo H. T. Leppänen, Kaisa Lohvansuu & Gerd Schulte-Körne. 2013. Predictors of developmental dyslexia in European orthographies with varying complexity. *Journal of Child Psychology and Psychiatry* 54 (6). 686–694.

Larkin, Rebecca, Gareth Williams & Samarita Blaggan. 2013. Delay or deficit? Spelling processes in children with specific language impairment. *Journal of Communication Disorders* 46 (5–6). 401–412.

Moll, Kristina, Frank Ramus, Jürgen Bartling, Jennifer Bruder, Sarah Kunze, Nina Neuhoff & Karin Landerl. 2014. Cognitive mechanisms underlying reading and spelling development in five European orthographies. *Learning and Instruction* 29. 65–77.

Nunes, Terezinha, Peter Bryant & Jenny Olsson. 2003. Learning morphological and phonological spelling rules: An intervention study. *Scientific Studies of Reading* 7 (3). 289–307.

Pacton, Sébastien, Michel Fayol & Pierre Perruchet. 2005. Children's implicit learning of graphotactic and morphological regularities. *Child Development* 76 (2). 324–339.

Plisson, Annie, Daniel Daigle & Isabelle Montésinos-Gelet. 2013. The spelling skills of French-speaking dyslexic children. *Dyslexia: An International Journal of Research and Practice* 19 (2). 76–91.

Pollo, Tatiana, Brett Kessler & Rebecca Treiman. 2009. Statistical patterns in children's early writing. *Journal of Experimental Child Psychology* 104 (4). 410–426.

Sénéchal, Monique. 2000. Morphological effects in children's spelling of French words. *Canadian Journal of Experimental Psychology/Revue Canadienne de Psychologie Expérimentale* 54 (2). 76–86.

Share, David. 1995. Phonological recoding and self-teaching: Sine qua non of reading acquisition. *Cognition* 55 (2). 151–218.

Sprenger-Charolles, Liliane & Séverine Casalis. 1995. Reading and spelling acquisition in French first graders: Longitudinal evidence. *Reading and Writing: An Interdisciplinary Journal* 7 (1). 39–63.

Sprenger-Charolles, Liliane, Linda Siegel, Daniele Béchennec & Willy Serniclaes. 2003. Development of phonological and orthographic processing in reading aloud, in silent reading, and in spelling: A four-year longitudinal study. *Journal of Experimental Child Psychology* 84 (3). 194–217.

Sprenger-Charolles, Liliane, Linda Siegel & Philippe Bonnet. 1998. Reading and spelling acquisition in French: The role of phonological mediation and orthographic factors. *Journal of Experimental Child Psychology* 68 (2). 134–165.

Tops, Wims, Maaike Callens, Evi Bijn & Marc Brysbaert. 2014. Spelling in adolescents with dyslexia: Errors and modes of assessment. *Journal of Learning Disabilities* 47 (4). 295–306.

Treiman, Rebecca. 1991. Children's spelling errors on syllable-initial consonant clusters. *Journal of Educational Psychology* 83 (3). 346–360.

Treiman, Rebecca. 1993. *Beginning to spell: A study of first-grade children*. New York: Oxford University Press.

Treiman, Rebecca, Denise Berch & Sarah Weatherston. 1993. Children's use of phoneme-grapheme correspondences in spelling: Roles of position and stress. *Journal of Educational Psychology* 85 (3). 466–477.

Tsesmeli, Styliani & Philip Seymour. 2006. Derivational morphology and spelling in dyslexia. *Reading and Writing* 19 (6). 587–625.

Tsesmeli, Styliani & Philip Seymour. 2008. The effects of training of morphological structure on spelling derived words by dyslexic adolescents. *British Journal of Psychology* 100. 565–592.

van Weerdenburg Marjolijn, Ludo Verhoeven, Anna Bosman, Hans van Balkom. 2011. Predicting word decoding and word spelling development in children with Specific Language Impairment. *Journal of Communication Disorders* 44 (3). 392–411.

Wimmer, Heinz & Karin Landerl. 1997. How learning to spell German differs from learning to spell English. In Charles Perfetti, Laurence Rieben & Michel Fayol (eds.), *Learning to spell: Research, theory, and practice across languages*, 81–96. Mahwah, NJ: Lawrence Erlbaum.

Wimmer, Heinz & Heinz. 2002. Dysfluent reading in the absence of spelling difficulties: A specific disability in regular orthographies. *Journal of Educational Psychology* 94 (2). 272–277.

Ziegler, Johannes & Usha Goswami. 2005. Reading acquisition, developmental dyslexia, and skilled reading across languages: A psycholinguistic grain size theory. *Psychological Bulletin* 131 (1). 3–29.

Ziegler, Johannes, A. M. Jacobs & Gregory O. Stone. 1996. Statistical analysis of the bidirectional inconsistency of spelling and sound in French. *Behavior Research Methods, Instruments, & Computers* 28. 504–515.

Dominiek Sandra
23 The role of morphology in reading and writing

1 Do morphemes affect spelling performance?

1.1 Introduction: Evidence from children's literacy development

Insight into the internal structure of words, at different levels of linguistic description (phonology, morphology) is not self-evident. Numerous studies (see Adams, 1990) have reported that many children have difficulties realizing that the continuous sound stream of a spoken word can be segmented into phonemes. There is nothing in the acoustic signal of *cat* that suggests the presence of the three sounds /k/, /a/, and /t/. On the contrary, our perception suggests there is only one sound: the continuous sound string /kat/. When learning to read we are *taught* that spoken words can be segmented into smaller sound units, which are mapped onto letters. Phonemic awareness is the result of a tedious learning process. What about morphological awareness?

Rebecca Treiman was probably the first to investigate children's morphological awareness. Treiman, Cassar, and Zukowski (1994) studied spelling performance in children between five and eight years old. They compared two word types in which the phoneme /t/ is realized as the sound [d] in American English: monomorphemic words (*duty*) and multimorphemic words (*dirty*). These are matched word pairs: as the /r/ is not pronounced in American English the two items in the example shared the sound ending [dI]. Crucially, the [d] sound (spelled as *t*) marked the end of a stem[1] morpheme in the word *dirty* but not in the monomorphemic word *duty*. Children made significantly fewer errors on derivations. The authors argued that this outcome is evidence that very young children have already developed a sense of morphological awareness and use their knowledge of the stem spelling (*dirt* ends in the letter *t*) to spell the derivation. As this morphological cue is absent in monomorphemic words these words cause more spelling errors.

Cassar and Treiman (1997) focused on the same contrast (monomorphemic vs multimorphemic words) but a different spelling issue: the spelling of word-final consonant clusters. Young spellers often leave out the first of two consecutive consonants. The researchers showed that fewer omission errors were made on morphologically complex words (*canned*) than on matched monomorphemic words (*brand*) that are matched on their final two sounds. Apparently, children's morphological awareness enabled them to use the stem's spelling, resulting in fewer omission errors.

---

[1] The terms 'root' and 'stem' are not consistently used in the psycholinguistic literature on morphology. We will use the term 'stem' throughout the text.

Dominiek Sandra, University of Antwerp

However, there is a possible confound. In both studies the two word types differed in two respects: (a) the critical letter occurred in stem-final position in the multimorphemic words only but (b) the orthographic pattern of the stem also had a higher frequency than the corresponding orthographic pattern in the monomorphemic words (as it recurs in several words). Treiman and co-workers might have found an effect of orthographic frequency rather than morphological awareness.

Deacon and Bryant (2006) controlled for this possible confound. Using item pairs like *rocket-rocked* and *turnip-turning* they matched the two word types on the orthographic frequency of the critical part. The effect survived: children were still better able to spell the multimorphemic words than their controls, supporting Treiman and colleagues' conclusions.

Experiments on French children confirmed the results in English. These studies capitalized on a property that is characteristic for French: word-final letters are often silent, i.e., not pronounced. For instance, even though the French word *gallop* ('gallop') ends in the letter *p*, that letter is not pronounced. However, when a suffix is attached to the word, turning it into the stem of a suffixed derivation, the letter is pronounced. For instance, the sound [p] is heard in the derived verb *galloper* ('to gallop'). Thus one can find out that the letter should also be spelled in *gallop*. Hence, French spellers can solve the problem of silent letters by attaching a derivational suffix to the target word. If the pronunciation of that derivation reveals the identity of a silent stem-final letter, that letter must also be spelled when the stem occurs in isolation.

Sénéchal (2000) and Sénéchal, Basque, and Leclaire (2006) made use of this property to test whether children appeal to this strategy. Good spellers did. They obtained higher scores on 'silent letter' words when these words could be spelled by relying on the above morphological strategy (*gallop*) than when this was not possible (*tabac*, 'tabacco'). They also explicitly reported that they applied this strategy. The fact that morphological awareness was the causal factor was demonstrated with a task tapping into the children's sensitivity to morphological relations. Children who performed well in applying the morphological transformation represented by a given word pair (e.g., *gris-grise*, 'grey'; masculine-feminine) to other words, i.e., those who were sensitive to morphological relationships, also obtained the highest scores when having to spell 'silent letter' words with morphological relatives (*gallop*).

Casalis, Deacon and Pacton (2011) followed the reverse rationale. They used words whose spelling mismatched the spelling predicted by this strategy. For instance, the French word *numéro* ('number') should be misspelled as *numérot* when applying the morphological strategy. Indeed, the derived verb *numéroter* ('to assign numbers to'), in which a [t] sound can be heard, suggests that a *t* must be spelled when the stem occurs without a suffix. Good spellers made these overgeneralization errors, indicating their use of the morphological strategy. In many cases the strategy is helpful but in some cases it is detrimental. The findings that good spellers are more successful in spelling silent letters but also incorrectly spell non-occurring silent letters both reveal its use. Thus the Casalis et al. study confirmed the conclusion of all experiments discussed above.

1.2 Evidence from experienced spellers

Clearly, when even young children's morphological awareness plays a role in spelling, experienced spellers should be quite capable of appealing to their awareness of morphological relationships when spelling multimorphemic words. However, the question is whether they always do so. In the present section I will discuss findings indicating that sometimes the spelling of *inflected* forms does not result from a process that concatenates stem and suffix but from a process that retrieves the stored inflected form in the mental lexicon. The experiments addressed the question whether experienced spellers spell (some types of) inflected words by relying on a compositional route (morpheme assembly) or by relying on a direct route (whole-word form retrieval).

The work I will discuss pertains to *inflected* forms only and is restricted to *homophonous* word forms, which have the same pronunciation as another inflected form but a different morphological structure. It would be unwise to generalize the conclusions beyond this clearly circumscribed set of words.

In Dutch one is confronted with a remarkable spelling problem, which must seem like an incomprehensible paradox to speakers of another language. The rules for spelling regularly inflected verb forms are simple and clear-cut. For instance, a verb's 1st person singular present tense is formed by spelling the stem and adding no suffix letter, whereas the 3rd person singular present tense is formed by adding the suffix letter *t* to the stem. These rules are derived from the spoken language. No suffix is heard in the 1st person singular (e.g., *werken, ik werk;* 'to work', 'I work'), whereas the suffix <t> is heard in the 3rd person singular (e.g., *hij werkt;* 'he works'). This distinction in Dutch is comparable to the distinction between a zero suffix and the <s> suffix in the 1st and 3rd person present tense of English verbs. If all 3rd person verb forms in Dutch could be spelled by simply listening to their final sound (as in *werkt*) there would be no problem. This is the case in English, where a spelling problem for these verb forms indeed does not exist. However, the 1st and 3rd person singular present tense forms of a subset of Dutch verbs are homophones. For instance, the verb forms in *ik word* ('I become') and *hij wordt* ('he becomes') have the same pronunciation [wort] but a different spelling. These forms represent a minority: 5.25% of all verbs and 8.42% of all 1st and 3rd person singular present tenses (Sandra and Van Abbenyen, 2009).

The spelling of Dutch verb forms is governed by a morphographic principle: the orthography reflects a word's constituent morphemes rather than its pronunciation, i.e., the suffix <t> is spelled as the letter *t*, even when the morpheme cannot be heard. A simple rationale underlies this spelling principle: if one hears a <t> suffix in forms like *hij werkt*, this means that there is a morphological marker for the 3rd person singular present tense (realized as the sound [t] in pronunciation and the letter *t* in spelling). As this marker is linked to the syntactic properties of the verb form (3rd person singular present tense), pronunciation does not matter and, hence, the morpheme should be spelled for all verb forms with these syntactic properties.

No one will deny the consistency behind such a spelling rule. At the same time, no one will deny (a) that homophonous verb forms, in which the combination of the stem-final letter and the suffix letter (*dt*) and the stem-final letter itself (*d*) sound the same, require either syntactic analysis (identification of the grammatical subject) or an analogy with the spelling of a verb form without a stem-final /d/ to correctly spell the final sound (e.g., *hij wordt* because of *hij werkt*), (b) that such a process is time-consuming and (c) that such a process is abstract, hence a potential stumbling-block. This is why the descriptively simple spelling rules for Dutch verb forms cause many errors, even in the spelling of experienced writers. The important question is whether these errors occur randomly or reveal a pattern that sheds light on lexical processing and storage. At this point the problem becomes interesting.

Sandra, Frisson, and Daems (1999) set out from the hypothesis that two memory systems might be at work when spelling a verb form with a homophone in its inflectional paradigm: (a) working-memory, in which the preceding words of the sentence are temporarily stored and has to be searched in order to identify the verb form's grammatical subject and (b) the mental lexicon, which might contain representations of the full forms, i.e., morphologically unanalyzed forms, of the two homophones (e.g., *word* and *wordt*). They predicted that the easy accessibility of the higher-frequency homophone would cause more homophone intrusions on the lower-frequency form than vice versa. They also predicted that this effect would be most outspoken in conditions of time pressure, especially when the distance between the grammatical subject and the verb form is relatively large (distance being defined as the number of intervening words), i.e., when there may be insufficient time to identify the subject in working memory. The outcome of the experiment confirmed these predictions. When participants were given a dictation under time pressure, they made significantly more intrusion errors on the lower-frequency homophone and the difference in error rates was larger when the verb form and its subject were separated by four words than when they were adjacent. Subsequent experiments (e.g., Sandra and Van Abbenyen, 2009) confirmed this effect of homophone dominance and also demonstrated that homophonous adjectives and substantives helped determine which homophone spelling was the dominant one.

Importantly, Sandra (2010) reported evidence that this effect could not be reduced to a recency effect, i.e., spellers' tendency to write down the last homophonic form they had read or written. Indeed, there is a high probability that this *is* the higher-frequency homophone, for the simple reason that this form has a high occurrence frequency. Participants showed chance performance when they had to choose which of the two homophones they had read some minutes ago in a series of short text passages, rejecting the prediction of the recency hypothesis. However, their responses reflected the frequency relationship between the homophones. Very often they thought to have read the higher-frequency homophone when in fact they had been presented with the lower-frequency one (a mistake that was made much more often than the reverse one). The finding that the pattern of false memories could be explained in terms of the frequency relation between the two homophones confirms the homophone dominance effect and its interpretation: both homophones are stored in the mental lexion.

Largy, Fayol, and Lemaire (1996) observed a similar phenomenon in French, although their homophones did not belong to the same (verb) paradigm. Their critical items were verb-noun homophones, i.e., crossed grammatical classes. In sentences like *Le chimiste prend des liquides. Il les filtre.* ('The chemist takes liquids. He filters them.') they found errors like *filtres*, which are the plural form of the noun rather than the singular form of the verb (*filtre*, 'filters'). As in the case of Dutch verb forms, these homophone intrusions were frequency-sensitive: intrusion errors were more likely when the noun was more frequent than the target i.e., the verb form. A dual-task technique was required to elicit the errors, i.e., participants had to remember the sentence and then write it down while simultaneously counting a series of clicks. This imposed a heavy burden on working memory resources. The need to use a dual-task paradigm to for eliciting the errors in French might reflect the fact that French spellers, in contrast to spellers of Dutch, are much better trained in spelling silent letters and, hence, are used to make quick grammatical analyses of this kind (recall the small percentage of homophonous verb forms in Dutch).

The Dutch and French experiments show that when experienced spellers have to spell a homophonous verb form but do not have sufficient working memory resources to finish the grammatical analysis in time, they tend to spell the most frequent homophone from the same (Dutch) or a different (French) inflectional paradigm (Sandra and Fayol, 2003). Limitations on working memory allow our mental lexicon to cause homophone intrusions. Any factor that causes a failure to finish the syntactic analysis, whether it be time-pressure, a dual-task technique that consumes most working memory resources, distance to the grammatical subject, or sheer negligence (i.e., no concentration and, hence, little activity in working memory), will enhance the probability of a homophone intrusion, especially when the target form is the lower-frequency homophone. This homophone dominance effect suggests that spellers' mental lexicon contains a representation of two morphologically unanalyzed forms, even though these forms are regular and can be made on the fly. Our mental lexicon seems to store every word form it encounters, even when there is no need to do so. This is not what one would expect from a linguistic perspective.

Note that the effect of homophone dominance may be related to the importance of morphology in the language. Gills and Ravid (2006) compared Dutch and Hebrew children's (grades 1–6) sensitivity to morphology when spelling words with homophonous segments like the ones described above. When the spelling of these segments was cued by morpho-syntactic information (e.g., grammatical properties of the subject, presence of an auxiliary, past tense context) Hebrew children scored much better than their Dutch peers. According to the authors, this is due to the fact that Hebrew makes an abundant use of morphology whereas Dutch does not. Even though Gillis and Ravid studied children whereas the above experiments concerned experienced spellers, their conclusion is quite plausible. Typologically different languages that differ considerably in their reliance on morphology may yield different types of spellers. Hebrew spellers (even young children) are familiar with the importance of morphology and, hence, naturally rely on this knowledge to spell homophonous segments. In contrast, Dutch spellers (even experienced writers) are insufficiently familiar with the role of morphology and, hence, experience problems when having to spell homophonous segments whose spelling is determined by the word's morphological structure.

2 Do morphemes affect reading performance?

In the present section we will focus on the question whether the morphological structure of words plays a role in visual word recognition. Two issues will be addressed: (a) Do morphemes play a role in the process of *lexical access*, i.e., is there a prelexical process that segments letter strings into constituent morphemes for the purpose of achieving access to the lexical representation of the presented word? (b) Do morphemes play a role in the *mental lexicon*, i.e., in the way lexical representations of morphologically complex words are internally structured and/or interconnected? We will concentrate on the processing of derived words because most researchers have focused on these words.

2.1 Do morphemes play a role in the process of lexical access?

Taft and Forster (1975) initiated this line of research. In their seminal paper on the processing of prefixed words they used *bound stems* as a method for probing the nature of the access representations of prefixed words. In a lexical decision task ("Is the presented stimulus a word or a non-word?") they contrasted nonwords of the type *juvenate*, derived from the derivation *rejuvenate* (real stems, although they only occur as bound stems), to nonwords of the type *pertoire*, derived from the mono-morphemic word *repertoire* (pseudo-stems). Their participants were significantly slower to respond "no" to *juvenate* items than to *pertoire* items. This difference remained significant when an illegal prefix was put before the stem (*dejuvenate* vs. *depertoire*), i.e., indicating that the effect was not due to participants' uncertainty whether *juvenate* items were real words or not.

Taft and Forster interpreted their findings as evidence for a prelexical morphological decomposition process and a stem-based lexical access procedure. The lexical processor finds an entry to the mental lexicon for real (bound) stems like *juvenate* but not for pseudo-stems like *pertoire*. They called this prelexical decomposition device "prefix stripping". Prefix stripping is possible in a language like English because these affixes represent a limited set, each occurring with a high token frequency. The latter properties make it possible to quickly check whether the orthographic pattern in word-initial position matches the spelling of a prefix. For instance, whenever the letter string *re* is encountered at a word beginning it can be removed as a potential prefix. Note that this prefix stripping process can only output a *potential* stem, i.e., a letter string that may or may not be an access key to the mental lexicon. Whether it effectively is one can only be known after attempting lexical access with this letter string. Indeed, the morphological status of a letter sequence is by definition unknown at a processing stage where the mental lexicon has not been accessed yet. This is why prelexical prefix stripping will err on words like *repertoire*, as it is blind to lexical knowledge when stripping off the *re* part and subsequenty attempting to achieve lexical access with the remaining letter string. The failure to access the lexicon, in contrast to the successful access attempt after prefix stripping words like *rejuvenate*, explains why Taft and Forster's participants found it easier to give a faster "no"-response to *pertoire* nonwords than to *juvenate* nonwords, i.e., the existence of an access key to the mental lexicon for the latter items suggested a 'word' response whereas a 'nonword' response was required. This decision conflict delayed reaction times.

Apart from the use of bound stems, other techniques have been used to make the same point. *Frequency manipulation* is one of them. It has long been known that high-frequency words are recognized faster than low-frequency ones. Two types of accounts have been proposed for this robust effect: either high-frequency words encounter their access codes earlier in a frequency-ordered access file (Forster, 1976) or they have a higher resting level of activation, such that they need less sensory stimulation to achieve threshold activation and, hence, recognition (Morton, 1969; McClelland and Rumelhart, 1981). If frequency is a determinant of the accessibility of lexical representations, it can be used as a diagnostic for testing hypotheses about the nature of access representations for derived words. More particularly, if derived words are accessed through their stem, access to these words should be faster when they contain a high-frequency stem than a low-frequency stem (everything else being equal). This is indeed what has been found in languages as, for instance, English (Andrews 1986; Bradley, 1979), Italian (Burani and Caramazza, 1987), French (Colé, Beauvillain and Ségui, 1989) and Dutch (Schreuder and Baayen, 1997). However, the effect of stem frequency is more consistently found for suffixed derivations than for prefixed derivations, which Colé et al attribute to a process of lexical access that is driven by left to right processing of the letter string[2].

Stem frequency effects for derivations seem to be sensitive to list composition, which suggests that they are not the result of a mandatory process. For instance, Andrews (1986) only obtained an effect of stem frequency when she included compound words in a lexical decision task. In a paper that puts stem-frequency effects in an entirely different perspective Baayen, Wurm and Aycock (2007) showed that it

---

[2] Note that this dissociation is at odds with Taft and Forster's claim that there is a prelexical prefix stripping mechanism.

is actually hard to find an effect of stem frequency, even when using a set of low-frequency derivations, which most models would expect to produce the strongest effect of stem frequency. They failed to find this effect in three of the four experimental tasks that had to be performed on these items (visual and auditory lexical decision and naming). They did find a small effect of stem frequency when analyzing the reaction times for some 8,000 words in the English Lexicon Project (Balota et al. 2007) but found the effect to be facilitatory only in the lower range of surface frequencies, suggesting that their experiments lacked the necessary power for obtaining a significant stem frequency effect. The authors argued on information-theoretical grounds that the effect of stem frequency should be considerably smaller than the effect of surface frequency, i.e., the frequency of the derivation. Moreover, they estimated that 1,000 items are required to find a stem frequency effect in one out of two experiments designed to detect such an effect, i.e., an effect of stem frequency in derived words is very elusive. Note that this may be due to Baayen et al.'s use of the regression technique, i.e., sampling items across the entire frequency range. The probability of finding an effect of stem frequency is arguably larger in experiments with a factorial design (e.g., derivations with low-frequency vs. high-frequency stems), as was the case in the earlier studies. If so, this would indicate that the effect of stem frequency is not linear and that only extreme comparisons can reveal its (tiny) effect in traditional experiments with some twenty items in each frequency category.

It is important to keep in mind that a demonstration that the stem plays a role in lexical processing, suggesting the existence of a morphological decomposition process, does not imply that the whole word lacks its own representation in the mental lexicon. As a matter of fact, many studies have used the frequency technique to demonstrate that these words do have whole-word representations. An effect of surface frequency, i.e., the frequency of the derivation itself, has often been demonstrated in experiments that matched conditions on stem-frequency (see references above) or in regression studies in which stem-frequency was put under statistical control (Baayen et al., 2007). The existence of both frequency effects can be interpreted in two ways: either the stem acts as the access code to the whole-word representation of the derivation, giving rise to two loci of frequency effects (e.g., Taft, 1979), or the word is processed along two lexical processing routes, a decomposition route and a whole-word route, the fastest one leading to word recognition. This has been suggested in race type models (cf. Schreuder and Baayen, 1997).

Priming has been another popular technique to test hypotheses about the nature of lexical access. Priming is a technique in which two words are presented with a certain time difference between their onsets (possibly 0 ms, i.e., simultaneous presentation) to find out whether processing the first (the prime) has an effect on processing the second (the target). Both words may be presented in the same modality (visual or auditory), so-called intra-modal priming, or they may be presented in different modalities (auditory and visual, usually with auditory primes and visual targets), so-called cross-modal priming. If the prime facilitates responses to the target, i.e., faster and/or more accurate responses, the conclusion is that target processing benefits from the prime's presentation because the same mental representation is accessed during prime and target processing.

In the early years of research on the mental lexicon Murrell and Morton (1974) already demonstrated that a three-minutes' study of a short list of printed words (primes) facilitated the later recognition of morphologically related target words in a tachistoscopic identification task (i.e., inflected or derived words of the same stem; *car-cars; sings-singer*). Even stronger facilitation was obtained for identical word repetition (*car-car*). Importantly, however, no facilitation was found when prime and target shared an orthographic pattern in word-initial position that did not function as a morpheme (*car-card*). The authors concluded that the priming effect did not depend on orthographic overlap but hinged on the repetition of the stem. They argued that the stem morpheme of inflected and derived words acts as a functional unit in word recognition, which later researchers would refer to as the word's lexical access unit. Stanners, Neisser, Hernon and Hall (1979) reported the same effects with intra-modal visual priming and a different experimental procedure, i.e., the presentation of both prime and target as lexical decision trials separated by a large number of intervening trials (the so-called long-lag priming paradigm).

However, authors soon began to worry that priming effects caused by words that can be consciously perceived (and are often responded to in the same task as the target words) may not be informative on the process of lexical access, especially when several minutes or even days intervene between prime and target. In a seminal paper Forster and Davis (1984) argued that the long-lasting facilitation effect of primes on targets raises a serious problem from a 'logical' point of view. If this facilitation is indeed due to the fact that the prime increases the accessibility of the target's lexical representation, word repetition across the life span should eventually result in the disappearance of one of the most well-known and robust effects in the word recognition literature: the word frequency effect. This follows from the fact that the repetition of a low-frequency word in a long-lag priming experiment is much stronger than the repetition of a high-frequency word, a phenomenon that is known as the 'frequency attenuation effect' (Scarborough, Cortese and Scarborough, 1977). Hence, after a sufficient number of repetitions of a low-frequency word the impact on that word's access representation would be equally large as the effect of the many more repetitions of a high-frequency word. As words obviously recur in the course of our experience with written texts (their repetition probability being a direct function of their frequency) the word frequency effect would soon be washed out. However, as mentioned above this effect is one of the most reliable findings in visual word recognition experiments. Hence, the frequency attenuation effect suggests that priming with a long temporal interval between prime and target is uninformative with respect to lexical processing and, hence, also with respect to the role of morphology at the level of lexical access.

Forster and Davis suggested that the frequency attenuation effect does not reflect properties of the mental lexicon but rather the operation of episodic memory, i.e., a memory system in which we store personal experiences, e.g., what we ate this morning but also when and where we encountered a word and (in the case of an experiment) how we responded to it. Infrequent experiences, like seeing a low-frequency word, are salient and hence easier to retrieve from episodic memory when re-experiencing the event. This would explain why long-lag priming causes stronger repetition effects for low-frequency words than for high-frequency ones.

Forster and Davis demonstrated that a *visual masked priming* technique, which makes the prime inaccessible to conscious perception and is, hence, unlikely to result in the creation of an episodic memory trace of the prime, resulted in equal repetition effects (i.e., facilitation) for high-frequency and low-frequency primes. In this technique a lowercase prime word is presented for a very limited prime duration (usually between 50 and 60 ms) and is preceded by a much longer lasting forward mask (i.e., a series of hash marks, presented for 500 ms) and followed by an uppercase target (in this case: the repeated prime word) for 500 ms or until the participant's response (e.g., ##### – table – TABLE). In contrast, when using the same words in the long-lag priming paradigm they did find the typical frequency by repetition interaction. According to Forster and Davis, their finding that masked repetition priming did not interact with frequency demonstrated that the stronger repetition effect for low-frequency words in an unmasked priming paradigm was due to participants' conscious awareness of the prime, suggesting the involvement of episodic memory. Importantly, they demonstrated that their masked repetition effects were not due to orthographic overlap between prime and target but to the repetition of the same lexical item: they did not find a masked repetition effect for nonwords, which have no lexical representation, and obtained no priming with form primes differing in only one letter from their target (e.g., *lack-LOCK*).

The authors concluded that the identical masked repetition effect for high-frequency and low-frequency words reflected facilitation at the level of lexical access, and that this facilitation is identical for all words. Hence, it is insensitive to word frequency. More particularly, they attributed the effect to the temporary and short-lived increased accessibility of a word's access representation, as the result of the prime having accessed this representation just before the target. In contrast with the long-lived effect of clearly visible primes in the long-lag priming paradigm, the short-lived nature of this effect can easily be reconciled with the robust frequency effect in language users, i.e., the problem caused by the frequency attenuation effect no longer exists as masked primes do not give rise to this problematic effect. Accordingly, Forster and Davis concluded that their masked priming technique is much better suited for studying the process of lexical access than the long-lag priming technique.

The next step is to apply this technique to the question at hand: are derived words prelexically decomposed and is their stem used for lexical access? Longtin, Segui and Hallé (2003) reasoned that an automatic process of prelexical decomposition should cause faster lexical decisions on a stem when the masked prime is a derivation consisting of that stem and a suffix. They also reasoned that such a prelexical process should be insensitive to any lexical property of the prime. The lexicon being 'higher up' in the processing sequence, such a process has no access to these properties. Accordingly, the semantic status of the masked derivation should not influence the priming effect. Hence, equally large priming effects are expected for semantically transparent derivations (*gaufrette-GAUFRE;* 'wafer'-'waffle') and opaque ones (*fauvette-FAUVE;* 'warbler'-'wildcat'). Furthermore, even the morphological status of the prime should not affect the size of the priming effect: a target that is a real stem in the prime should show no larger priming effect than a target that is a pseudo-stem. From the perspective of a process of blind prelexical decomposition, any letter sequence that matches the spelling of a stem and is followed by the orthographic pattern of a suffix is bound to access the representation corresponding to the spelling pattern of this possible stem, whether it is a real stem in the input word or not (*baguette-BAGUE;* 'little stick' and 'typical French bread'-'ring'). To exclude an account in terms of orthographic priming, they included a condition in which the prime also contained the target in word-initial position but could not even be a potential morpheme, i.e., on the basis of a superficial orthographic analysis the prime could not be analyzed as the concatenation of the orthographic patterns of a stem and a suffix (*abricot-ABRI;* 'apricot'-'shelter').

They observed significant and equally large facilitation effects for the first three conditions and an inhibition effect for the orthographic condition. Longtin et al. concluded that a prelexical process of blind morphological decomposition segments each letter string that consists of a (potential) suffix into its 'morphemic' constituents. Note that this rationale is the same as the one followed by Taft and Forster when proposing a prelexical prefix stripping process on the basis of their findings with bound stem nonwords. Hence, Longtin et al.'s account explains the nature of a process of prelexical decomposition. This process causes automatic access to the (pseudo-)stem's lexical representation in any word whose orthographic structure can be described as a *superficial* morphological structure of stem + suffix (e.g., *gaufrette, fauvette, baguette*), i.e., purely on the basis of the spelling of these 'morphemes'. In other words, the process of prelexical morphological decomposition is blind to the word's true morphological structure.

The authors are careful to mention that their design does not allow them to answer the question whether prelexical morpological decomposition requires (a) a complete surface morphological structure (as suggested above), i.e., the concatenation of two orthographic patterns that match the spelling of a stem and a suffix, respectively or (b) only a word-final letter string matching a suffix spelling (would *silhouette* be decomposed because the final letter sequence ette is a potential suffix, even though *silhou* is not a French stem?). Nor do their data license the conclusion that all word-final letter strings that have the orthographic appearance of a suffix trigger an attempt at morphological decomposition. Possibly, a high degree of suffix productivity and, hence, (type and/or token) frequency is required for prelexical decomposition to occur. Finally, morphological decomposition might be restricted to languages with many morphologically complex words. Longtin et al mention that about 70% of French words are morphologically complex.

Blind morphological decomposition will sometimes yield a hypothetical stem that causes inappropriate lexical access (pseudo-derivations) or is useless for word recognition (opaque derivations). The Longtin et al data cannot tell us whether this causes a delay in word recognition. This is the case in a sequential processing model, in which a useless access attempt upon blind decomposition is followed by an access attempt based on the whole letter string (cf. Taft and Forster, 1975). This would not be the case in a parallel (race) model, in which lexical access is simultaneously attempted by means of a morphological decomposition and a whole-word access process. Due to this parallel processing, there would be no delay in the recognition of opaque or pseudo-derivations. Schreuder and Baayen's (1995) Morphological Race Model – in which a decomposition route and a whole-word route operate in parallel – is an example of such a model. Note that both sequential and parallel models predict Longtin et al.'s priming effects.

Longtin and Meunier (2005) found that the size of the priming effect does not depend on the lexical status of the prime either. Existing word primes (*rapidement*, 'rapid') and pseudo-word primes containing the same stems (*rapidifier*, 'quickify') caused equally large facilitation. Nor does the priming effect depend on the interpretability of a pseudo-word prime. Possible but non-interpretable pseudo-words (*sportation*, 'sport' + inappropriate suffix) caused equally much facilitation as interpretable ones (*rapidifier*). These findings emphasize the prelexical nature of the process. A prelexical process is purely form-driven and has no access to any lexical or supralexical (semantic) information – unless there is top-down feedback from the lexicon, which the data disconfirm. The only requirement seems to be that the word-final letter string matches the spelling of an existing suffix, which is a purely formal characteristic of the input. Possibly, a potential stem in word initial position is required as well (see above). This also explains why a pseudo-word caused no facilitation when the final letter pattern did not match a suffix spelling, even though its initial letter pattern corresponded to the spelling of an existing stem: primes like *rapiduit* ('rapid' + non-suffix) did not facilitate targets like *rapide*, as the pattern *uit* does not match the spelling of a French suffix. Recall that the orthographic control condition in Longtin et al.'s (2003) study (*baguette-BAGUE*) converges with this conclusion.

Rastle and colleagues obtained similar findings in English, using the same masked priming technique. Rastle, Davis and New (2004) used a very similar manipulation as Longtin et al. They compared the effects of three types of masked (pseudo-)derived primes on (pseudo-)stem targets: (a) derivations with a semantic relationship to their stem (*cleaner-CLEAN*), (b) pseudo-derivations, whose orthographic structure could be segmented into the letter patterns of a stem and a suffix, although these letter strings had no morphemic status in the prime (*corner-CORN*), and (c) monomorphemic control words, whose initial letter pattern matched the spelling of a stem but whose following letters did not match the orthographic pattern of a suffix (*brothel-BROTH*). They found reliable and equally large facilitation effects for the first two prime types but no facilitation for the third one. The authors drew the same conclusion as Longtin and colleagues: a prelexical process segments the prime whenever the word-final orthographic pattern matches the spelling of a suffix. They suggest that this segmentation might be driven by co-occurrence frequencies of letters, like digraph frequencies, which is a low-level orthographic factor. Such frequencies are high within morphemes but low when the digraph straddles the morpheme boundary. Such a 'trough pattern' in the orthographic structure of the word might cause the word to spontaneously 'fall apart' into its (pseudo-)morphemes (Seidenberg, 1987).

According to Rastle et al. this outcome "introduces a functional departure from the standard view of morphology, according to which the decomposition of polymorphemic words is governed by semantic transparency (Marslen-Wilson et al., 1994)." (p. 1093) They do admit that morpho-semantic relationships may play a role at later processing stages, i.e., may determine the way in which words are interconnected in the mental lexicon (at the post-access level).

McCormick, Brysbaert and Rastle (2009) confirmed the prelexical view, reporting equally large masked priming effects for high-frequency and low-frequency English word primes as well as for non-word primes. The fact that masked high-frequency derivations facilitated stem recognition offers strong support for the prelexical decomposition hypothesis, as it is often believed that high-frequency words are not decomposed but recognized as a whole (or that the decomposition process proceeds more slowly than the process of whole-word based access). These findings corroborate the statements by Longtin et al. and Rastle et al. that a blind prelexical process decomposes *all* derivations and derivation-like non-words, i.e., acts on a superficial morphological structure of the orthographic input.

Morphological priming effects in the absence of an effect of semantic transparency have also been reported for a non-alphabetic language, more particularly, Hebrew. In contrast to a language like English (and, to a lesser extent, French), Hebrew is a morphologically rich language. A single stem[3] typically gives rise to a whole family of morphologically related words. Hence, Hebrew speakers naturally acquire the ability to quickly perceive morphological relationships. At the same time, Hebrew differs from many other languages in that morphemes are not concatenated but interlaced, i.e., a vowel pattern is inserted into a consonantal (stem) skeleton. For instance, the vowel pattern CaCoC (where C stands for 'consonant') can be inserted into the consonantal pattern G-D-L ("grow") to yield GaDoL ('big'; example taken from Schiff, Raveh and Fighel, 2012).

In a series of publications Frost and coworkers used the masked priming paradigm to investigate the roles of the consonantal stem and the vowel pattern, the two morphemes that are combined to form a Hebrew word. The findings reported by Frost, Forster and Deutsch (1997) demonstrated that the vowel pattern of nouns (when repeated in primes and targets with different stems) did not cause facilitation.

---

[3] In Hebrew the term 'root' is more appropriate than the term 'stem', i.e., it refers to the form that lies at the basis of an entire inflectional paradigm. For the sake of consistency and to avoid confusion for the reader, I will continue using the term 'stem', even though it is linguistically not correct. Please bear this remark in mind while reading a summary of the Hebrew experiments.

On the other hand, the consonantal stem pattern (presented as a masked prime of three consecutive consonants, i.e., a sequence without intervening vowels) did reliably prime a noun target derived from the same stem. No such priming was obtained when the consonantal prime was semantically but not morphologically related to the target, i.e., when the consonantal stems differed. Another indication that the priming effect was mediated by the shared stem and not by semantic overlap (not even in conjunction with identical stems) was the finding that derived word primes sharing their stem with the subsequent derivational target significantly facilitated target responses, irrespective of whether the two words were semantically related or not (in the latter case, the derived prime was semantically opaque). Finally, and importantly, the finding that the illegal combination of an existing stem and an existing vowel pattern did not facilitate responses to derived targets with the same stem indicates that the extraction of a stem only causes facilitation when that stem is co-activated by a lexical representation of the whole word, i.e., there seems to be an interaction between decomposition-based access to the stem and whole-word based access to the stem.

Deutsch, Frost and Forster's (1998) findings for verb forms, which are also composed of a stem consonantal skeleton and a vowel pattern, differed from those for nouns. Both repetition of the vowel pattern, i.e., using different stems in prime and target, and repetition of the stem, i.e., using different vowel patterns, caused significant priming. Moreover, primes that were illegal combinations of existing stems and vowel patterns facilitated responses to targets with the same vowel pattern. These results suggest that both the stem and the vowel pattern are automatically extracted at a prelexical level and cause access to their representations, without the necessity of co-activation in the prime's whole-word representation (as in the case of nouns).

Frost, Deutsch and Forster (2000) found that the vowel pattern of verb forms only primes the target when both words contain the typical three-consonant structure of a stem. Weak verbs, which lack one consonant in some of their conjugations, do not yield facilitation due to the repetition of the vowel pattern when the prime lacks one of the stem's consonants. This facilitation failure occurred both when the target consisted of a canonical three-consonant stem or of an atypical two-consonant stem (thus matching the phonological structure of the prime). Remarkably, adding a random consonant to a weak verb form prime to create a pseudoword consisting of an existing vowel pattern and a stem that does not exist but conforms to the canonical stem structure did cause facilitation on verb form targets with the same vowel pattern and a canonical stem. Apparently, the presence of a three-consonant pattern and an interlaced vowel pattern suffices to trigger an automatic decomposition process, whether the stem exists or not. Apparently, the decomposition process operates on an abstract orthographic structure to segment the word into its (potential) morphemes and, hence, has no access to lexical knowledge, i.e., the knowledge whether the three-consonant structure is an existing morpheme in Hebrew or not. The authors conclude that a process of prelexical morphological decomposition is operational in Hebrew, both in the nominal and the verbal system, but that the vowel pattern is only relevant for lexical processing in the verbal system whereas the stem plays a role in the processing of both noun and verb forms. They also argue that the importance of the stem causes the emergence of connections among words sharing that stem in the mental lexicon.

Schiff, Raveh, and Fighel (2012) found the same pattern in seventh-grade children (about 12 years): semantically opaque and transparent derivations primed their stems equally in a masked priming paradigm. However, fourth-graders (about 9 years) showed an effect of semantic transparency, suggesting that it takes some time before Hebrew language users realize that morphology is a highly productive mechanism in their language, independently of semantics.

The Hebrew experiments suggest that words in this morphologically rich language, which is moreover characterized by a non-linear morphology, are automatically stem decomposed into their stem and vowel pattern. The stem plays a crucial role in the lexical processing of all words whereas the vowel pattern only seems to matter in the processing of verb forms. Furthermore, this decomposition process appears to be as blind to semantics as in French and English (see above). Noun derivations that primed semantically related noun targets (with the same stem) yielded an equal facilitation effect as noun derivations that were semantically unrelated to their targets. In the case of verb forms the process is also blind to the prime's lexical status: pseudoverbs consisting of an existing stem and vowel pattern primed existing verbs with the same vowel pattern. In the case of nouns this was not the case: pseudonouns consisting of an existing stem and vowel pattern did not prime existing nouns derived from the same stem. It is likely that such pseudonouns also automatically trigger morphological decomposition but that the interaction between the full-form lexical representations and the activated stems is not the same for verb forms and noun forms. The blind nature of the decomposition effect is particularly underscored by the finding that inflected verb forms with a non-canonical stem structure (lacking one consonant because they belong to the inflectional paradigm of weak verbs) only prime a verb target with a canonical stem structure when a random consonant is added, such that the prime consists of a non-existing but canonical consonantal skeleton of a stem and a vowel pattern, thus suggesting a legal morphological structure. Hence, the decomposition process appears to be triggered by abstract characteristics of the orthographic input and is blind to both lexical and semantic knowledge. This conclusion converges nicely with the conclusion from masked priming experiments in Indo-European languages, which strongly suggest the existence of a blind, purely form-driven (hence, entirely bottom-up) process of morphological decomposition.

Despite the many demonstrations that early morphological decomposition is blind to semantic properties of the word, there have been occasional indications that semantics can affect early lexical processing, even in masked priming. Diependaele, Sandra and Grainger (2007) compared the priming effects of a set of visually presented transparent derivations and a set of opaque derivations and pseudo-derivations on a (pseudo-)stem target. Targets were presented auditorily (cross-modal priming) or visually (intra-modal priming). The authors found significant priming of the transparent primes on both auditory and visual targets and weak priming for the pseudo-derived primes on visual targets only. Using the technique of incremental priming, in which primes are presented for different durations (20, 40, and 60 ms), both derived prime types facilitated the auditory or visual processing of the target. However, the effect appeared sooner for the transparent words, and when it appeared for the opaque ones the effect of the transparent primes was larger.

In conclusion: at the prelexical level, a word's morphological structure appears to play an important role. Derivations (at least suffixed derivations) seem to trigger a process of blind morphological decomposition, i.e., a letter string is automatically segmented into *potential* morphological constituents when it can *exhaustively* be parsed into the *spelling patterns* of a stem and affix (apparently, abstract spelling patterns in a language like Hebrew). The findings that the process is blind to the word's semantic transparency indicates that it takes place at the prelexical level, i.e., before the mental lexicon has been accessed. Demonstrations that the process is blind to a word's morphological status, for instance, to differences between true derivations and pseudo-derivations of the *corner* type lead to the same conclusion. Each letter string that looks like the concatenation of a stem and affix is automatically decomposed into these constituent units. Interestingly, these conclusions seem to apply equally to languages like French and English (Indo-European languages) and languages like Hebrew (Semitic languages), which rely on entirely different mechanisms for creating morphologically complex words or word forms, i.e., morpheme sequencing (concatenation) vs. morpheme interlacing.

2.2 Do morphemes play a role at the lexical level?

Since the work by Taft and Forster (Taft and Forster, 1975, 1976; Taft, 1979) many experiments have addressed the question whether lexical *access* is mediated by morphemes rather than whole-word representations. This emphasis on the role of morphology at the access level also permeates the experiments addressing the role of morphology through the use of the masked priming technique (cf. above). However, there have also been attempts to find out whether morphological structure is an organizing factor *within the mental lexicon* itself.

One of the most cited papers in this respect is the study by Marslen-Wilson et al. (1994). Using the technique of *cross-modal priming*, in which clearly perceptible auditory primes were immediately followed by visual targets, they found a significant priming effect of semantically transparent derivations on their stem (e.g., *departure-depart*) but not of semantically opaque derivations (e.g., *department-depart*). Cross-modal priming is a technique that is supposed to probe representations that are independent of a particular sensory modality, and, hence, are stored in the mental lexicon itself (so-called central representations instead of access representations). The rationale behind the technique is the following: if auditory primes affect the processing of visual targets, this suggests that the effect takes place at a modality-independent, abstract representational level. The above-mentioned study by Gonnerman, Seidenberg and Andersen (2007) also made use of cross-modal priming. These authors did not find that priming effects were restricted to fully semantically transparent derivations, suggesting a dichotomy between transparent and opaque derivations, but observed *graded* priming effects. They attributed this to the fact that the mapping of morphemic forms to their meanings across a set of words is not entirely consistent but only *more or less systematic*, varying along a continuum that stretches from fully transparent to fully opaque derivations. Thus there are degrees of semantic transparency across derivations with the same stem, and the degree of gradedness depends on the systematicity in the morpheme-mediated form-meaning mappings. This systematicity is encoded in the mental lexicon in the form of connection weights between input units (forms), hidden units, and output units (meanings), an architecture that naturally causes *graded* effects. According to Gonnerman et al. morphemes should not be conceived as stable building blocks of words, with their own representations in the mental lexicon, but rather as emergent properties of the way in which a particular letter sequence is mapped onto semantic properties, i.e., the specific connectivity structure between the orthographic and semantic levels (through the mediation of a hidden layer). In this connectionist view, morphemes do not exist as 'tangible' units; they are reifications of emergent properties of the processing architecture.

Several studies have made use of unmasked *intra-modal visual priming*, using visual primes and targets. In these experiments the prime, which did not require a response, was presented immediately before the target but was clearly perceptible. Note that this paradigm differs from the long-distance priming paradigm that was used by Stanners et al. (1979) and strongly criticized by Forster and Davis (1984, see above). As the prime immediately precedes the target it is assumed that this technique taps into lexical processing. However, in contrast to the masked priming technique this method is supposed not to probe prelexical processing. Indeed, as claimed by Rastle and colleagues (2004) the major difference between primes that are presented below recognition threshold and primes that can be consciously perceived is that the former trigger automatic processes at the prelexical level, which are purely form-driven and impermeable to semantic influences, whereas the latter trigger processes that involve the activation of lexical connections and semantic integration. Hence, masked primes can shed light on the role of morphological structure at the level of prelexical processing, whereas visible primes can reveal whether and how morphology is important at the level of lexical storage.

Whereas Marslen-Wilson et al.'s experiments in English indicated a strong role of semantic transparency, their priming effects being restricted to semantically transparent derivations, experiments in German revealed a different picture. Work by Smolka and co-workers (Smolka, Komlósi and Rösler, 2009; Smolka, Preller and Eulitz, 2014) indicated that semantic transparency does not affect the magnitude of morphological priming in German prefixed derivations[4]. Transparent and opaque derived verbs facilitated responses to their stem equally much. These priming effects were larger than the effect caused by morphologically unrelated verbs with the same degree of semantic relatedness. At the same time, control primes that were matched on form overlap inhibited target processing. Hence, it appears that the morphological effects cannot be reduced to the combined effects of form and meaning overlap. Smolka argues that German, which belongs to the same language group as English, i.e., it is a Germanic language, behaves like Hebrew, which is a Semitic language, because it makes abundant use of morphology. In contrast to English, German has a rich inflectional morphology and makes use of prefixes and suffixes that are highly productive. According to Smolka this explains why German language users do not rely on semantic transparency when *storing* derivations in their mental lexicon. They are so familiar with derivational processes that they automatically decompose these words, irrespective of a particular derivation's semantic transparency. Thus they resemble Hebrew speakers, who automatically decompose derivations because their language makes an abundant use of derivational structures.

Schreuder and Baayen (1997) used a different technique to demonstrate that morphology is an organizing factor in the mental lexicon. This importance of morphology results in clusters of morphologically related words (i.e., including derivations and compounds but not inflected word forms). They referred to such a cluster as the *morphological family* of a stem. Rather than using derivations in combination with a priming technique they used morphologically *simple* words and investigated how the recognition of these words is affected by their relations to morphologically complex words in which they occur as a morpheme. It can be argued that this technique is less vulnerable to criticism than the unmasked priming technique, which has sometimes been criticized for tapping into automatic but also attentional processes. Note that the reference here does not concern the long-lag priming paradigm, which is likely contaminated by episodic effects. The problem in the present context is the risk of tapping into conscious processes rather than the intended level of automatic processes. This vulnerability was, for instance, demonstrated in the area of semantic priming. Neely (1977) showed that, besides an effect of automatic spreading activation between associatively related words (during the first 250 ms), two other processes are operational, depending on the onset asynchrony between prime and target and properties of the stimulus list: an attention-guided expectancy process (when the target appears later than 250 ms after prime onset) and a process that attempts to semantically integrate the target and the prime. The intervention of the latter two processes may contaminate the priming effect, and, hence, lead to incorrect conclusions on the underlying processing machinery and lexical architecture.

---

4 Note that Marslen-Wilson et al. also used prefixed words. It is interesting to note that many experiments on prelexical morphological decomposition made use of suffixed words (with the exception of Taft and Forster's, 1975, use of bound stems from prefixed derivations), whereas many experiments on the role of morphology in the mental lexicon itself used prefixed derivations.

In their experiments Schreuder and Baayen (1977) showed that lexical decisions to *unprimed monomorphemic* words in Dutch are faster when these words have many derivations and compounds than when they have few (see also Bertram, Baayen and Schreuder, 2000; de Jong, Schreuder and Baayen, 2002; Krott, Schreuder and Baayen, 2002). Importantly, this is an effect of *type frequency*, not token frequency. The *number* of derivations and compounds significantly affect word recognition speed. In contrast, the summed frequencies of all members in the morphological family do not affect the word recognition speed of the simplex words. Interestingly, the family size effect became stronger when the semantically opaque members were removed from the family (Schreuder and Baayen, 1977; Bertram, Baayen and Schreuder, 2000). The fact that type frequency rather than token frequency is the causal factor behind the effect and that semantic transparancy plays a role strongly suggests that the effect sheds light on the internal structure of the mental lexicon. More particularly, it seems to indicate that a stem and all words whose form and meaning have been derived or compounded from that stem's form and meaning, i.e., semantically transparent derivations and compounds, form a morphological family in our memory for words. Apparently, when being presented with the monomorphemic stem, this morphological family is co-activated and, thus, affects the word's recognition speed. Since Schreuder and Baayen's seminal work, family size has been added as a new important variable to the shortlist of important factors in the study of questions pertaining to the mental lexicon. For instance, many studies control for morphological family size when matching the items in different conditions.

This family size effect has been demonstrated in Dutch (Schreuder and Baayen, 1997; De Jong, Schreuder and Baayen, 2000), English (De Jong, Feldman, Schreuder, Pastizzo and Baayen, 2002), and German (Lüdeling and de Jong, 2002), all of which are Germanic languages, which are characterized by a *linear* morphological system, i.e., stems and affixes being concatenated like beads on a string. However, Moscoso del Prado Martín, Bertram, Häikiö, Schreuder and Baayen (2004) demonstrated that morphological family size also affects word recognition speed in Finnish and Hebrew, two languages that do not belong to the Indo-European group and are themselves typologically different as well. As noted above, Hebrew does not have a linear morphology, unlike Germanic languages, but makes use of a consonantal stem 'skeleton' and a vowel pattern for the affix that is inserted into the consonantal stem, yielding a string of *interlaced* morphemes. Although the morphological dimension is pervasive in Hebrew, giving rise to morphologically related words for the large majority of words (see above), a single word does not usually have as many morphologically related words as in, for instance, Dutch (with its frequent use of compounding). Nevertheless, Hebrew readers also exhibit a family size effect. As mentioned above, the effect has also been found in Finnish, where each stem can give rise to extremely many morphological descendants, due to the *agglutinative* nature of this language's morphology (i.e., which involves stringing together, for instance, many suffixes to a stem, each expressing a particular linguistic function). The robust finding of the morphological family size effect across a variety of typologically different languages obviously attests to the crucial importance of morphological families in the mental lexicon, i.e., a convincing demonstration that morphological structure is a major organizing principle of the mental lexicon.

As mentioned above, a word's morphological family size effect seems to reflect the existence in the mental lexicon of a cluster of semantically coherent words that share their stem (e.g., *throw, thrower, throwball*). This might suggest that lexical connections between stem morphemes and derivations/compounds containing these stems are restricted to complex words that are semantically transparent. However, this seems to be at odds with other findings. These were obtained with different experimental techniques than the one used by Baayen and Schreuder and their co-workers, who measured the effect of family size on the word that sits at the centre of the family. Experimental techniques that are supposed to probe the lexical, i.e., post-access, level suggest that languages with a very productive morphology are indifferent to semantic transparency at the lexical level, for instance Hebrew (Bentin and Feldman, 1990) and German (Smolka et al., 2009, 2014).

At this point one can only speculate why this should be the case. One possibility is that intramodal or even cross-modal priming with a sufficiently long prime-target onset asynchrony on the one hand and Baayen and Schreuder's technique for measuring family size, i.e., where morphologically related words are not presented (a very indirect and, hence, strategically uncontaminated technique) on the other hand, reveal two different aspects of the internal organisation of the mental lexicon. The priming paradigm might shed light on the internal structure of a lexical representation itself, i.e., whether the word representation is internally segmented in terms of its constituent morphemes. In contrast, the effect of family size might reflect the interconnectivity among lexical representations on the basis of their morpho-semantic relatedness. Note that, in such an account, the morphological productivity of the language would determine whether a lexical representation is internally structured in terms of its morphemes or not. This would explain the aforementioned dissociation observed by Smolka and co-workers between languages like German and Hebrew on the one hand (morphologically rich) and languages like Dutch and English on the other hand (morphologically poor). In contrast, semantic transparency would be the determinant of the morphological family size effect in all languages. Several experimental findings strongly suggest that the latter statement is correct. First, removing the semantically opaque family members from the family strengthens the effect (Schreuder and Baayen, 1997; Bertram et al., 2002). Second, although the total number of words that are morphologically related to Hebrew homonyms (words derived from a consonantal stem with two different meanings) does not affect reaction times, the number of these words that are semantically related to the stem meaning in the target word causes a facilitatory effect. This is the classical family size effect. In line with this finding the number of words that are semantically related to the other stem meaning causes an inhibitory effect (Moscoso del Prado

Martín, Deutsch, Frost, Schreuder, De Jong and Baayen, 2005). Third, Moscoso del Prado Martín et al. (2005) found that reaction times in a visual lexical decision task in Hebrew can be predicted by the family size of the Hebrew target's Dutch translation equivalent (after controlling for word frequency and length) and vice versa. This, too, strongly suggests that these two typologically languages use morphology in a highly similar way to organize conceptual space. Finally, Lüdeling and de Jong (2002) found an effect of morphological family size in German.

3 Conclusion

The morphological make-up of words is an important structural aspect of the lexicon of (probably all) languages. This is not surprising. When encountering a novel concept that is related to a familiar one, it is easier to refer to it by using a known word that refers to a related and already familiar concept, and combine this word with one or more morphemes rather than coining a phonologically novel word. This enhances communicative efficiency and learnability. Different languages differ in the way they make use of morphology to coin new words. They differ in their productivity with respect to derivation and compounding. For instance, Dutch is highly productive at the level of compounding but less at the level of creating derivations (although some affixes are highly productive). In contrast, Hebrew is highly productive at the level of creating derivations (each consonantal stem is combined with different vowel patterns to produce different words) but less productive at the level of compounding (Berman and Clark, 1989).

The purpose of this paper was to provide a review of the literature on the role of morphology in (a) spelling and (b) reading, more particularly, visual word recognition. In the spelling domain most research has been done on the spelling of bi-morphemic words with inflectional relations (although not exclusively). In contrast, in the study of visual word recognition most research has focused on the processing of derived words (although, again, not exclusively). In my review of the spelling literature I have focused to a large extent on the question how soon children rely on the morphological structure of words in their spelling attempts. I have also described research investigating why a morpheme-based spelling system can cause unexpected spelling problems, more particularly, what happens when descriptively simple syntax-based spelling rules for morphemes must be applied under time-pressure. In my review of the role of morphology in visual word recognition I have especially focused on the recognition process of derived words. In this section I have made a clear distinction between the role of morphology at the prelexical, access level and at the level of the mental lexicon itself.

Many experiments, in different languages, have shown that young children quickly catch on to the morphological structure of words and use it to spell these words. The words used in these experiments could all be spelled without contextual support; even inflected word forms were forms whose spelling was not determined by their syntactic context (e.g., past tense forms). At the same time, other experiments (both in Dutch and French) have focused on experienced spellers and their spelling of regularly inflected words whose spelling does depend on the syntactic context. These experiments have consistently shown that experienced spellers sometimes run into trouble when having to spell inflected word forms, even though their spelling is governed by straightforward morpho-syntactic rules. The spelling problem does not apply across the board but is restricted to regular verb forms that have a homophone in their inflectional paradigm. The time-consuming nature of retrieving the word that is syntactically related to the spelling of the verb form and the time that is subsequently needed to apply the spelling rule creates a spelling trap. In the absence of an output of the rule-governed process the high-frequency form, which is quickly retrieved from the mental lexicon, often causes a homophone intrusion when the low-frequency form is the target. This occurs more often than an intrusion of the less accessible low-frequency homophone when the high-frequency form is the target. The conclusion of this review on the role of morphology on spelling is that, already very early on in literacy development, morphological relationships facilitate the spelling of derivations and inflected forms that can be spelled out of context. However, when morphology is needed to syntactically disambiguate regularly inflected forms with identical pronunciations, more particularly, when a suffix reflects the syntactic dependency relation between the verb form and another word in the sentence, even highly experienced spellers can and do fall prey to spelling errors. This difference might be due to different degrees of difficulty to spell (a) the final letter of the stem (former findings) and (b) the letter of an inflectional suffix (latter findings).

Research on the role of morphology in visual word recognition has focused on two questions. (a) Is morphology used in order to achieve access to the mental lexicon, i.e., at the prelexical level? (b) Is morphology used for representing morphologically complex words in the mental lexicon and creating connections among the lexical representations of morphologically related words? Several techniques have been used to address the former question, but the masked priming technique, with derived word primes and stem targets, has been the most popular one. The overwhelming evidence, coming from different languages, both Indo-European ones (English, French) and Semitic ones (Hebrew), indicates that any derived word that is fully analyzable as stem + affix (almost all studies focus on suffixes), is automatically decomposed (even though the presence of the orthographic pattern of a suffix in word-final position might suffice). This process of morphological decomposition is blind to both the semantic transparency (transparent vs. opaque) and the morphological status (true derivation vs. pseudo-derivation) of the word, and is, hence, purely form-driven, i.e., a prime example of bottom-up processing. The conclusion from these experiments seems to be that an automatic process of morphological decomposition is active at the prelexical level.

Morphological structure also appears to play a role at the lexical level, i.e., the level of lexical representations and the connections between these representations. The use of visible primes that are presented immediately before the target (but with a sufficiently short prime-target asynchrony, cf. Forster and Davis, 1984) suggests that the lexical representation of many derivations is internally stuctured in terms of their stem and affix. However, the morphological richness of a language seems to determine whether such an internal structure is also used for semantically opaque derivations. In languages with a rich morphology, like Hebrew and German, the experimental evidence suggests that the lexical representation of a derived word represents its morphological structure, irrespective of its semantic transparency. However, when a language does not make abundant use of derivational affixes, only semantically transparent derivations seem to be represented in terms of their morphemes. In contrast, the effect of morphological family size, which has been shown to be a semantic effect in several studies by Baayen and co-workers, turns up in all languages studied thus far, whether they are morphologically rich or not and irrespective of their typological properties. This effect apparently reflects the existence of networks of morpho-semantically related words, which seem to populate the mental lexicon in all languages.

We finish this chapter with the conclusion that morphological structure plays a considerable role in both spelling and reading (visual word recognition), at different levels of processing (prelexical vs. postlexical) and representation (within and between lexical representations), and in interaction with other linguistic factors (phonology, i.e., homophones, and semantics, i.e., transparent vs. opaque words). Morphology leaves its stamp on spelling and reading from the beginning of a child's literacy skills until the stage when language users have become expert spellers and readers.

References

Adams, Marylin. 1990. *Beginning to read: Thinking and learning about print.* Cambridge, MA: MIT Press.
Andrews, Sally. 1986. Morphological influences on lexical access: Lexical or nonlexical effects? *Journal of Memory and Language* 25(6). 726–740.
Baayen, Harald, Lee Wurm & Joanna Aycock. 2007. Lexical dynamics for low-frequency complex words. A regression study across tasks and modalities. *The Mental Lexicon* 2(3). 419–463.
Balota, David, Melvin Yap, Michael Cortese, Keitch Hutchison, Brett Kessler, Bjorn Loftis, James Neely, Douglas Nelson, Greg Simpson & Rebecca Treiman. 2007. The English lexicon project. *Behavior Research Methods* 39(3). 445–459.
Bentin, Shlomo & Laurie Feldman. 1990. The contribution of morphological and semantic relatedness to repetition priming at short and long lags: evidence from Hebrew. *Quarterly Journal of Experimental Psychology A* 42(4). 693–711
Berman, Ruth & Eve Clark. Learning to use compounds for contrast. *First Language* 9(27). 247–270.
Bertram, Raymond, Harald Baayen & Robert Schreuder. 2000. Effects of family size for complex words. *Journal of Memory and Language* 42(3). 390–405.

Bradley, Dianne. 1979. Lexical representation of derivational relations. In Aronoff, Mark and Mary Louise Kean (eds.), *Juncture*, 37–55. Cambridge, MA: MIT Press.

Burani, Cristina & Alfonso Caramazza. 1987. Representation and processing of derived words. *Language and Cognitive Processes* 2(3–4). 217–227.

Casalis, Séverine, Hélène Deacon Sébastien Pacton. 2011. How specific is the connection between morphological awareness and spelling? A study of French children. *Applied Psycholinguistics* 32(3). 499–511.

Cassar, Marie & Rebecca Treiman. 1997. The beginnings of orthographic knowledge: Children's knowledge of double letters in words. *Journal of Educational Psychology* 89(4). 631–644.

Colé, Pascale, Cécile Beauvillain & Juan Segui. 1989. On the representation, and processing of prefixed and suffixed derived words: a differential frequency effect. *Journal of Memory and Language* 28(1). 1–13.

De Jong, Nivja, Robert Schreuder & Harald Baayen. 2000. The morphological family size effect and morphology. *Language and Cognitive Processes* 15(4–5). 329–365.

De Jong, Nivja, Laurie Feldman, Robert Schreuder, Matthew Pastizzo & Harald Baayen. 2002. The processing and representation of Dutch and English compounds: peripheral morphological, and central orthographic effects. *Brain and Language* 81(1–3). 555–567.

Deacon, Hélène & Peter Bryant. 2006. This turnip's not for turning: children's morphological awareness and their use of stem morphemes in spelling. *British Journal of Developmental Psychology* 24(3). 567–575.

Deutsch, Avital, Ram Frost & Kenneth Forster. 1998. Verbs and nouns are organized and accessed differently in the mental lexicon: evidence from Hebrew. *Journal of Experimental Psychology Learning Memory and Cognition* 24(5). 1238–1255.

Diependaele, Kevin, Dominiek Sandra & Jonathan Grainger. 2007. Masked cross-modal priming: unravelling morpho-orthographic and morpho-semantic influences in early word recognition. *Language and Cognitive Processes* 20(1–2). 75–114.

Forster, Kenneth. 1976. Accessing the mental lexicon. In Wales, Roger and Edward Walker (eds.), *New approaches to language mechanisms*, 257–287. Amsterdam: North-Holland.

Forster, Kenneth & Chris Davis. 1984. Repetition priming and frequency attenuation in lexical access. *Journal of Experimental Psychology: Learning, Memory and Cognition* 10(4). 680–698.

Frost, Ram, Kenneth Forster & Avital Deutsch. 1997. What can we learn from the morphology of Hebrew? A masked priming investigation of morphological representation. *Journal of Experimental Psychology: Learning, Memory, and Cognition* 23(4). 829–856.

Frost, Ram, Avital Deutsch & Kenneth Forster. 2000. Decomposing morphologically complex words in a nonlinear morphology. *Journal of Experimental Psychology: Learning, Memory, and Cognition* 26(3). 751–65.

Gillis, Steven & Dorit Ravid. 2006. Typological effects on spelling development: A crosslinguistic study of Hebrew and Dutch. *Journal of Child Language* 33(3). 621–659.

Giraudo, Hélène & Jonathan Grainger. 2000. Effects of prime word frequency and cumulative stem frequency in masked morphological priming. *Language and Cognitive Processes* 15(4–5). 421–444.

Gonnerman, Laura, Mark Seidenberg & Elaine Andersen. 2007. Graded semantic and phonological similarity effects in priming: Evidence for a distributed connectionist approach to morphology. *Journal of Experimental Psychology: General* 136(2). 323–345.

Krott, Andrea, Robert Schreuder & Harald Baayen. 2002. Linking elements in Dutch noun-noun compounds: Constituent families as analogical predictors for response latencies. *Brain and Language* 81(1–3). 708–722.

Largy, Pierre, Michel Fayol & Patrick Lemaire. 1996. The homophone effect in written French: The case of verb-noun inflection errors. *Language and Cognitive Processes* 11(3). 217–255.

Longtin, Catherine-Marie & Fanny Meunier. 2005. Morphological decomposition in early visual word processing. *Journal of Memory and Language* 53(1). 26–41.

Longtin, Catherine-Marie, Juan Segui & Pierre Hallé. 2003. Morphological priming without morphological relationship. *Cognitive Processes* 18(3). 313–334.

Lüdeling, Anke & Nivja de Jong. 2002. German particle verbs and word formation. In Nicole Dehé, Ray Jackendoff, Andrew McIntyre & Silke Urban (eds.) *Verb-Particle Explorations*, 315–333. Berlin/New York: Mouton de Gruyter.

Marslen-Wilson, William, Lorraine Tyler, Rachelle Waksler & Lianne Older. 1994. Morphology and meaning in the English mental lexicon. *Psychological Review* 101(1). 3–33.

McCormick, Samantha, Marc Brysbaert & Kathleen Rastle. 2009. Is morphological decomposition limited to low-frequency words? *The Quarterly Journal of Experimental Psychology* 62(9). 1706–1715.

McClelland, James & David Rumelhart. 1981. An interactive activation model of context effects in letter perception: I. An account of basic findings. *Psychological Review* 88(5). 375–407.

Moscoso del Prado Martín, Fermín, Raymond Bertram, Tuomo Häikiö, Robert Schreuder & Harald Baayen. 2004. Morphological family size in a morphologically rich language: The case of Finnish compared with Dutch and Hebrew. *Journal of Experimental Psychology: Learning, Memory, and Cognition* 30(6). 1271–1278.

Moscoso del Prado Martín, Fermin, Avital Deutsch, Ram Frost, Robert Schreuder, Nivja De Jong & Harald Baayen. 2005. Changing places: A cross-language perspective on frequency and family size in Dutch and Hebrew. *Journal of Memory and Language* 53(4). 496–512.

Murrell, Graham & John Morton. 1974. Word recognition and morphemic structure. *Journal of Experimental Psychology* 102(6). 963–968.

Neely, James. 1977. Semantic priming and retrieval from lexical memory: roles of inhibitionless spreading activation and limited-capacity attention. *Journal of Experimental Psychology: General* 106(3). 226–254.

Rastle, Kathleen, Matthew Davis & Boris New. 2004. The broth in my brother's brothel: Morpho-orthographic segmentation in visual word recognition. *Psychonomic Bulletin and Review* 11(6). 1090–1098.

Sandra, Dominiek & Lien Van Abbenyen. 2009. Frequency and analogical effects in the spelling of full-form and sublexical homophonous patterns by 12 year-old children. *The Mental Lexicon* 4(2). 239–274.

Sandra, Dominiek, Steven Frisson & Frans Daems. 1999. Why simple verb forms can be so difficult to spell: the influence of homophone frequency and distance in Dutch. *Brain and language* 68(1–2). 277–283.

Sandra, Dominiek & Michel Fayol. 2003. Spelling errors with a view on the mental lexicon: frequency and proximity effects in misspelling homophonous regular verb forms in Dutch and French. In Harald Baayen & Robert Schreuder (eds.), *Morphological structure in language processing*, 485–514. Berlin: Mouton De Gruyter.

Sandra, Dominiek. 2010. Homophone dominance at the whole-word and sub-word levels: spelling errors suggest full-form storage of regularly inflected verb forms. *Language and speech* 53(3). 405–444.

Scarborough, Don, Charles Cortese & Hollis Scarborough. 1977. Frequency and repetition effects in lexical memory. *Journal of Experimental Psychology: Human Perception and Performance* 3(1). 1–17.

Schiff, Rachel, Michal Raveh & Avital Fighel. 2012. The development of the Hebrew mental lexicon: when morphological representations become devoid of their meaning. *Scientific Studies of Reading* 16(5). 383–403.

Schreuder, Robert & Harald Baayen. 1997. How simplex complex words can be. *Journal of Memory and Language* 37(1). 118–139.

Schreuder, Robert & Harald Baayen. 1995. Modeling morphological processing. In Laurie Feldman (ed.), *Morphological aspects of language processing*, 131–154. Hillsdale, NJ: Erlbaum Press.

Seidenberg, Mark. 1987. Sublexical structures in visual word recognition: access units or orthographic redundancy? In Max Coltheart (ed.), *Attention and performance XII: The psychology of reading*, 245–263. London: Erlbaum.

Sénéchal, Monique. 2000. Morphological effects in children's spelling of French words. *Canadian Journal of Experimental Psychology* 54(2). 76–86.

Sénéchal, Monique, Michelle Basque & Tina Leclaire. 2006. Morphological knowledge as revealed in children's spelling accuracy and reports of spelling strategies. *Journal of Experimental Child Psychology* 95(4). 231–254.

Smolka, Eva, Sarolta Komlósi & Frank Rösler. 2009. When semantics means less than morphology: The processing of German prefixed verbs. *Language and Cognitive Processes* 24(3). 337–375.

Eva Smolka, Katrin Preller & Carsten Eulitz. 2014. 'Verstehen' ('understand') primes 'stehen' ('stand'): Morphological structure overrides semantic compositionality in the lexical representation of German complex verbs. *Journal of Memory and Language* 72(1). 16–36.

Stanners, Robert, James Neiser, William Hernon & Roger Hall. 1979. Memory representation for morphologically related words. *Journal of Verbal Learning and Verbal Behavior* 18(4). 399–412.

Taft, Marcus & Kenneth Forster. 1975. Lexical storage and retrieval of prefixed words. *Journal of Verbal Learning and Verbal Behavior* 14(6). 638–647.

Taft, Marcus and Kenneth Forster. 1976. Lexical storage and retrieval of polymorphemic and polysyllabic words. *Journal of Verbal Learning and Verbal Behavior* 15(6). 607–620.

Taft, Marcus. 1979. Recognition of affixed words and the word frequency effect. *Memory and Cognition* 7(4). 263–272.

Treiman, Rebecca, Marie Cassar & Andrea Zukowski. 1994. What types of linguistic information do children use in spelling? The case of flaps. *Child Development* 65(5). 1318–1337.

Julia Schindler and Tobias Richter
24 Reading comprehension: Individual differences, disorders, and underlying cognitive processes

1 Introduction

Reading comprehension is one of the preconditions for a successful educational development. Therefore, one of the most important goals of the educational system is the early identification of poor readers and the development of individual intervention and remediation programs to help them overcome their reading difficulties. But, under what conditions is a reader considered to be a poor reader? Usually, poor readers are diagnosed with specific reading disability (developmental dyslexia) when they show below age-average reading comprehension in the absence of any other cognitive deficit and adverse environmental factors (American Psychiatric Association 2013; World Health Organization 2010). Thus, only readers performing substantially worse on standardized reading tests than expected levels based on their general level of cognitive functioning are considered to be dyslexic. To date, this discrepancy model of dyslexia is widely used by educators and researchers to identify poor readers and assign them to specific training and remediation programs.

Despite the widespread use of the discrepancy model, diagnosing a reader as dyslexic provides no information about individual underlying causes of poor reading comprehension nor the kind and the extent of required intervention. Even worse, the operational definition of a separate category of dyslectic readers according to the discrepancy model requires the use of cut-off values that, besides lacking a substantial rationale, exclude poor readers from intervention programs who show a broader range of cognitive disabilities.

In this chapter, we will focus on reading-specific cognitive processes as sources for reading difficulties, excluding such possible sources as working memory, general knowledge, visual, attentional, or neurological deficits (for a review on potential causes of dyslexia that are not specific to reading see Vellutino et al. 2004; Vidyasagar and Pammer 2010). We will first discuss the traditional definition of dyslexia based on the discrepancy model and its problems. We argue that a more fruitful approach to characterize poor readers and their individual needs for reading intervention would be to examine reading comprehension deficits in a manner that is consistent with the cognitive processes that constitute reading comprehension rather than to simply diagnose a reader as dyslexic or not. Thus, our goal is to provide an overview

Julia Schindler and Tobias Richter, University of Würzburg of the cognitive processes underlying reading comprehension at the word, sentence, and text level and delineate why and how deficits in these processes can contribute to a low level of reading comprehension. We emphasize that identifying the specific origin of reading difficulties is essential to being able to assign poor readers to an appropriate intervention program.

2 Diagnostic criteria of dyslexia and their problems

Estimates of developmental dyslexia prevalence range from 10 to 15%, depending on the exact operational definition (Vellutino et al. 2004). These numbers render dyslexia one of the most prevalent learning disorders. According to the International Classification of Diseases (ICD-10), dyslexic readers manifest "a specific and significant impairment in the development of reading skills that is not solely accounted for by mental age, visual acuity problems, or inadequate schooling" (F81.0, World Health Organization 2010). The term dyslexia is nonexistent in the fifth edition of the Diagnostic and Statistical Manual of Mental Disorders (DSM-5, American Psychiatric Association 2013). Instead, the manual contains a similar definition of Specific Learning Disorder with reading difficulties as the further specification. Thus, dyslexic readers exhibit severe difficulties in the acquisition of basic reading and spelling skills in the absence of a general learning deficit (Rack, Snowling, and Olson 1992; Vellutino et al. 2004). Schools, remediation programs, and researchers following this definition rely primarily on two skill criteria to identify dyslexic readers: Reading skills that are significantly worse than would be expected based on (1) a reader's chronological age and (2) a reader's cognitive abilities or mental age (often operationalized by measures of intelligence). Thus, readers with at least an average IQ ($\geq$80–90; Siegel 1988) who perform unexpectedly poorly on reading tasks as compared to their peer's performance are considered dyslexic. These readers are usually distinguished from another group of poor readers called *general backward readers* (Rutter and Yule 1975) or *garden-variety poor readers* (Stanovich 1988) who also fail to acquire age appropriate reading skills, but in contrast to dyslexic readers, they are additionally characterized by a broader range of cognitive deficits accompanied by a low IQ ($\leq$80). This is also known as the aptitude-achievement discrepancy, which indicates that a dyslexics' ability to read (achievement) diverges from their expected levels based on their intellectual capacity (aptitude). The discrepancy model is largely based on the work by Yule et al. (1974) who found considerably more poor readers (a "hump") at the lower end of the reading skill distribution of readers than would have been statistically expected assuming a normal distribution. Yule et al. and Rutter and Yule (1975) assume that a subgroup of the poor readers must be qualitatively different from the normally developing poor readers because of a specific reading deficit. Furthermore, Yule (1973) claimed that the future prospects concerning reading development are significantly worse for dyslexic than for backward readers and conclude that the distinction between these two groups of readers is both meaningful and beneficial for remediation.

These conclusions, however, have been extensively challenged in recent years. Two major arguments against the usefulness of the dyslexia definition in identifying and characterizing poor readers have been advanced. The first and most important objection is that dyslexia, defined as unexpectedly low reading achievement despite normally developing cognitive skills, lacks diagnostic value with respect to the kind of underlying deficit and required intervention. One specific unitary deficit in poor readers is a misconception. Instead, the sources of individual reading deficits are multifaceted and heterogeneous. Several reading-related cognitive component skills may be impaired in poor readers to different degrees. Therefore, each deficit requires a specific intervention that addresses the specific impaired reading-related process and its degree of severity (Coltheart and Jackson 1998).

The second objection concerns the assumption of a discrete group of dyslexic readers that differ qualitatively from a group of general backward readers. Stanovich (2005), one of the most emphatic opponents of the discrepancy criterion, maintained that the literature lacks evidence showing that dyslexic and general backward readers process reading-related information in a different manner. Siegel (1988) and Stanovich and Siegel (1994) measured the performance of poor readers with high IQ scores on several tasks that tapped cognitive reading-specific skills and compared it with the performance of readers with lower IQ scores. The children in both studies were presented with a battery of reading-related tasks, for example, word and non-word reading, spelling, phonological recoding, grammatical closure, and sentence repetition, and they were also presented with tasks assessing skills that are less specific to reading such as working memory capacity. Both studies consistently indicated that the distinction of good vs. poor readers strongly predicted children's performance on reading-specific tasks, whereas IQ scores (high vs. low) did not (see also Vellutino, Scanlon, and Lyon 2000 and a meta-analysis by Stuebing et al. 2002). Hence, several authors (e.g. Shaywitz et al. 1992; Stanovich 1988) have argued that dyslexic readers represent the lower end of a continuous distribution of readers rather than a discrete category. If readers vary gradually on a continuum of reading ability and if this reading ability is independent of IQ, then setting an arbitrary IQ-based cut-off between dyslexic and general backward readers has no basis. However, despite these findings, the distinction between dyslexic and general backward readers on the basis of IQ scores is still widely used. Consequently, children classified as poor but not dyslexic readers are often excluded from research and interventional programs based on an arbitrary cut-off criterion (Catts, Hogan, and Fey 2003; Shaywitz et al. 1992; Stanovich 1988). Instead, as Siegel emphasizes, identifying the impaired component processes of reading and the particular form and extent of the deficit would be far more helpful, including determining the appropriate strategy for enhancing the deficient processes (see also Catts et al. 2003).

In view of these findings, we argue for a cognitive-psychological approach to reading comprehension difficulties. Rather than defining a group of dyslexics on the basis of questionable criteria, a more fruitful approach would be to examine the reading difficulties in terms of the underlying cognitive processes and to determine the extent to which these component processes are impaired and the appropriate strategy for improving the mastery of these processes. The aim of the following sections is to provide an overview of the possible sources of difficulties in reading comprehension based on the structure of reading comprehension cognitive-component skills. Diagnostic tools designed to identify individual needs for training and intervention in poor readers must be conceived according to this underlying structure.

3 What causes poor reading comprehension?

Cognitive-psychological research on reading comprehension has identified a number of cognitive processes at the word, sentence, and text level that contribute to reading comprehension (Müller and Richter 2014; Perfetti 2001; Richter and Christmann 2009). First, readers must recognize the written word forms of a text. According to dual-route models of visual word recognition, readers accomplish this task via two different routes (Coltheart et al. 2001). To be able to recognize unknown or infrequent word forms, readers use a *non-lexical*, rule-based phonological route by translating the word letter-by-letter into a phonemic representation (phonological recoding). The phonemic representation is subsequently mapped on to an entry in the mental lexicon. When processing familiar and highly frequent word forms, readers use an orthographic or *lexical* route by which word forms are recognized holistically and mapped directly on to an entry in the mental lexicon (for evidence supporting the dual route cascaded model of visual word recognition – DRC, see e.g. Paap and Noel 1991; Ziegler, Perry, and Coltheart 2000). In addition to visual word recognition, readers need to retrieve its meaning from the mental lexicon. At the sentence level, they must integrate the word forms syntactically and semantically. Finally, in text and discourse comprehension, several sentences need to be integrated into a coherent mental model of the text by establishing local and global coherence relations between adjacent and distant sentences (McNamara and Magliano 2009; Van Dijk and Kintsch 1983). This multi-level structure of component skills implies that reading comprehension succeeds to the extent that readers master all of the cognitive processes involved in reading efficiently. Individual differences in these processes are potential sources of individual differences in reading comprehension skills. Hence, deficits in the mastery of these processes potentially cause specific types of reading difficulties.

3.1 Individual differences at the word level

The majority of studies investigating possible causes of poor reading comprehension have focused on word-level processes. Word-level processes seem to be a reasonable starting point, because the ability to recognize written word forms is clearly crucial for reading comprehension. The importance of word-level processes for individual differences in reading comprehension is expressed very clearly in the *simple view of reading* (SVR, Gough and Tunmer 1986; Hoover and Gough 1990), which assumes reading comprehension (R) to be the product of two types of cognitive abilities, the general ability to comprehend language (C) and the ability to decode written word forms (D):

$$R = D \times C$$

The multiplicative combination of D and C implies that good decoding skills and good general comprehension skills are each necessary but not sufficient to bring about good reading comprehension. Instead, reading comprehension is impaired when only one of the two abilities is low. According to the simple view of reading, decoding is the only process that distinguishes reading from listening comprehension. Consequently, visual word recognition is a prominent candidate when looking for possible sources of reading difficulties.

Another general theoretical approach that emphasizes the role of word recognition processes in reading comprehension is Perfetti's (1985) *verbal efficiency hypothesis*, which states that efficient word recognition constitutes the fundament of successful reading comprehension. The underlying idea is that efficient (i.e. rapid and reliable) word-recognition processes save cognitive resources, which are then available for higher cognitive processing, such as sentence and text level processing. The verbal efficiency hypothesis was further refined into the *lexical quality hypothesis* by Perfetti and Hart (2001, 2002; see also Perfetti 2010), which emphasizes that the quality of the representations of word forms, including the stability and interconnectedness of their constituents (phonological, orthographic, morphological, and semantic components), is the basis for good reading comprehension.

3.1.1 Individual differences in phonological recoding

Most explanatory approaches of dyslexia and of poor reading comprehension in beginning readers agree that a likely source of reading disability is a deficit in phonological recoding. This idea is appealing from a developmental point of view. Phonological recoding skills are the key to the acquisition of reading skills, because word forms are still unknown to beginning readers and need to be recoded letter-by-letter (Coltheart et al. 2001; see also the developmental model by Frith 1985). As a consequence, deficient phonological recoding hinders the child to read the majority of written word forms and impairs all further stages of reading development. Deficits in phonological recoding may be caused by deficits in general phonological processing. Stanovich (1988) and Stanovich and Siegel (1994) compared the performance of poor and skilled readers on several tasks accessing phonological skills in written and auditory modality. They found that all poor readers in their studies, in contrast to skilled readers, exhibited severe problems with tasks, such as regular and exception word naming, non-word naming, and rhyme production. Based on his findings, Stanovich (1988) created the *phonological-core variable-differences model*, which states that poor readers primarily suffer from a deficit in phonological processing skills that prevents them from the acquisition of age-appropriate reading abilities. Evidence in favor of this assumption comes from various sources. For example, Snowling (1980) found that poor dyslexic readers, in contrast to skilled readers, had difficulties recognizing an auditorily presented word in its written form and exhibited the same difficulties in the reverse order. Because this task required grapheme-phoneme-conversion in both directions, Snowling concluded that the poor readers had difficulties in mapping sounds on letters and letters on sounds. Griffith and Snowling (2001) investigated whether the phonological deficit of poor readers is due to deficient phonological representations or to a deficit in retrieving the phonological information. They found that 11- to 12-year-old poor readers with the diagnosis of dyslexia performed worse than good readers of the same age in rapid-naming and non-word reading tasks that required the retrieval of phonological information. However, in an auditory word-gating task, no differences were found between good and poor readers on the amount of phonetic input they needed to identify a spoken word. The authors concluded that the deficit of poor readers is due to deficient retrieval processes rather than deficient phonological representations. This interpretation was further supported by more recent studies by Ramus et al. (2013) and Dickie, Ota, and Clark (2013). Their results indicate that phonological deficits in poor readers are not due to deficient phonological representations but rather to poor skills in assessing or manipulating them. However, using a similar word-gating paradigm to the one used by Griffith and Snowling, Boada and Pennington (2006) found evidence for deficient implicit phonological representations in poor readers rather than deficient phonological retrieval processes. In contrast to the findings by Griffith and Snowling, the poor readers in the study by Boada and Pennington needed more phonetic input to correctly recognize the first letter in a word than the chronological age-control group and more phonetic input to correctly recognize the whole word than the chronological age-control group and the reading age-control group. The authors concluded that poor readers have more "immature phonological representations" (2006: 177) than their age and reading peers.

A number of longitudinal and training studies provided evidence to support the assumption of a causal relationship between phonological deficits and poor reading abilities (Rack et al. 1992; Vellutino et al. 2004). These studies demonstrated that children's phonological skills in kindergarten predict reading comprehension in primary school (e.g. Bradley and Bryant 1983; Scanlon and Vellutino 1996). Moreover, interventions strengthening the phonological awareness in kindergarten and at the beginning of primary school were shown to have a positive impact on later reading comprehension skills (e.g. Bradley & Bryant 1983; for a meta-analysis, see Bus and van IJzendoorn 1999). Some studies suggest that phonological deficits persist even in adults with childhood diagnosis of dyslexia (e.g. Ransby and Swanson 2003; Wilson and Lesaux 2001). However, Castles and Coltheart (2004) emphasized that extant studies providing evidence in favor of a causal relationship between phonological skills and reading skills should be interpreted with caution. They criticized that most of these studies merely show a correlational relationship rather than a causal one and are circular in their argumentation. They also claimed that most longitudinal and training studies fail to meet the necessary criteria to unequivocally ascribe success in reading acquisition to good phonological awareness skills or to phonological awareness trainings. They stated that in terms of a causal relationship, for example, phonological awareness trainings should improve reading skills specifically, i.e. "only reading-related skills" (2004: 76) should benefit from the training. Another claim is that there must be no letter-sound knowledge at all prior to phonological awareness training to not confound training effects with "implicit reinforcement of pre-existing reading skills" (2004: 99). Given that most studies fail to meet these and other critical criteria, Castles and Coltheart concluded that the causal relationship between phonological skills and reading performance still needs to be replicated in future research. However, Hulme et al. (2005) criticized Castles and Coltheart's (2004) "conception of causation [as] overly narrow" (2005: 360). They argued that effects of phonological skills on reading development might be moderated or mediated by other reading-related skills such as letter-sound knowledge, but these influences do not preclude the importance of phonological skills in reading acquisition and development.

Remarkably, the close relationships of phonological deficits and poor reading comprehension are cross-linguistically evident in poor readers of languages other than English. Wimmer (1996) and Ziegler et al. (2003) found that 9- to 13-year-old dyslexic readers in German completed non-word reading tasks as slowly as English dyslexic readers (and more slowly compared to word reading tasks). However, German dyslexic readers performed with notably higher accuracy on non-word reading tasks compared to English dyslexic readers of the same age. The authors attribute the higher accuracy of German dyslexic readers to the transparent orthography of German. The grapheme-phoneme-conversion rules are highly consistent in the German language. Thus, phonological recoding is much easier in German compared to languages with an opaque orthography such as English and is therefore acquired earlier (Wimmer and Goswami 1994). As a result, even dyslexic readers in German have little difficulties reading non-words accurately, but they lack the necessary automaticity to read non-words with little cognitive effort as indicated by long reading times. Wimmer concluded that the deficit underlying poor reading performance is a phonological deficit in both languages (see also Mayringer and Wimmer 2000), but this deficit is somewhat differently expressed in German than in English poor readers.

A possible objection concerning the generalizability of previous findings is that many investigations concentrated on beginning readers. Beginning readers are bound to rely primarily on the non-lexical phonological recoding route when recognizing words, because most written word forms are unknown for them. Hence, for beginning readers, most of the variance in reading comprehension skills is not surprisingly explained by phonological recoding skills. However, more experienced readers increasingly make use of the more efficient (lexical) route of orthographical decoding, depending on the size, quality, and accessibility of their sight vocabulary (Frith 1985). Thus, orthographical decoding skills during the primary school years become an increasingly important source of individual differences in reading comprehension (although phonological recoding skills remain a strong and unique predictor even in Grade 4, Knoepke et al. 2014).

3.1.2 Individual differences in orthographical decoding

Several studies suggest that a deficit in orthographical decoding, also called surface dyslexia, can cause severe reading comprehension problems as well. Castles and Coltheart (1993) disentangled both types of word recognition deficits using non-word and exception-word reading. Because phonological recoding skills are required for non-word reading and orthographical decoding skills are required for exception-word reading, poor readers with a phonological deficit should exhibit difficulties reading non-words but less difficulties reading exception words. In contrast, poor readers with a deficient orthographical decoding route should exhibit difficulties reading exception words but fewer difficulties reading non-words. This pattern of double dissociation was obtained in two experiments. In the first experiment, Castles and Coltheart (Exp. 1) investigated 8- to 14-year-old dyslexic readers' performance on non-word and exception-word reading tasks and found that 85% of the dyslexic readers showed the expected double dissociation. Either their non-word reading skills were significantly poorer than would be expected based on their exception-word reading performance (55%) or their exception-word reading performance was significantly poorer than would be expected based on their non-word reading performance (30%). Thirty four percent of the dyslexic readers even performed poorly on just one of the tasks, whereas they exhibited no difficulties at all with the other task. In their second experiment (Exp. 2), Castles and Coltheart found that readers performing poorly on exception-word reading had no problems comprehending spoken exception words, ruling out an alternative explanation in terms of general language deficits (similar results were obtained by Manis et al. 1996).

Some evidence exists showing that the prevalence of the two types of deficits depends on language-specific differences. As noted earlier, several studies suggested that dyslexic readers' phonological recoding is slow but reliable in transparent orthographies such as German, in contrast to opaque orthographies such as English (e.g. Mayringer and Wimmer 2000; Wimmer 1996; Ziegler et al. 2003). Complementing these findings, more recent studies indicated that dyslexic readers' orthographical decoding route is more likely to be deficient in transparent orthographies (e.g. Martens and de Jong 2006; Zoccolotti et al. 2005). The *word-length effect* has been used to investigate this deficit. When recognizing words via the non-lexical, phonological recoding route, i.e. by means of grapheme-to-phoneme-conversion, the length of written-word forms is positively related to the time it takes to recognize the word. However, when words are recognized via the orthographical decoding route, whole word forms are directly mapped on to their respective lexical entries, and word length has no impact on word recognition times. In a word-naming study based on this logic, Zoccolotti et al. (2005) found that skilled Italian readers' sensitivity to word length decreased from Grade 1 to Grade 2, suggesting a shift from phonological recoding to orthographical decoding. In contrast, dyslexic third graders were as sensitive to word length during word and non-word naming as first graders indicating that they still primarily relied on phonological recoding. Similar results were obtained in Dutch by Martens and de Jong (2006) and in German by Ziegler et al. (2003; for additional evidence suggesting a strong relationship between orthographical decoding skills and text comprehension in German primary school children, see Knoepke et al. 2014).

These findings clearly indicate that conceptualizing dyslexia as a purely phonological deficit fails to explain the variety of poor readers. At least two types of word recognition deficits exist, a more phonologically-based and a more orthographically-based deficit that can underlie reading comprehension problems (e.g. Castles and Coltheart 1993; Manis et al. 1996). This distinction has implications for remediation and intervention programs. The assumption that phonological or grapheme-phoneme-conversion trainings suggested by phonological-core deficit models of dyslexia would work equally well for all poor readers is unreasonable. Instead, testing poor readers on a broader range of word-recognition skills is essential to determine their specific training needs.

Dual-route models make important contributions to the description and explanation of visual word recognition processes, their acquisition and development, various types of word recognition deficits, and language-specific differences with respect to opacity and transparency, but other theoretical approaches of visual word recognition also exist that reject the idea of two functionally distinct routes. Instead they model word recognition in a single information-processing network as in, for example, the *parallel-distributed-processing* (PDP) model (Seidenberg and McClelland 1989) or the *connectionist triangle model* (Plaut et al. 1996). These models explain and predict the various types of deficits in visual word recognition by impaired distributed representations or "computational resource limitations" (e.g. Manis et al. 1996: 189), by impaired network pathways (e.g. Plaut 1999), or by impairment of neurological areas involved in the network responsible for reading (e.g. Woollams 2014). In many cases, these models make similar predictions as dual route models. Thus, deciding among these different approaches is difficult based on the available evidence.

Dual-route models of visual word recognition have been designed to explain reading acquisition, development, and disorders in Indo-European languages with alphabetic scripts such as German, English, and Spanish. Consequently, this approach is probably not suitable to fully explain word recognition processes and thus the relationships between visual word recognition and reading comprehension skills in languages with non-alphabetic scripts such as Chinese and Japanese (for a more detailed discussion on universal principles of visual word recognition, see e.g. Frost 2012).

3.1.3 Individual differences in the quality of and access to meaning representations

The retrieval of word meanings is an additional word-level source of reading comprehension problems. Understanding the meanings of its words is fundamental for understanding what a text is about, suggesting that individual differences in the mastery of this process are a proximal predictor of reading comprehension problems (Richter et al. 2013). According to Perfetti and Hart's *lexical quality hypothesis* (2001, 2002; Perfetti 2007), lexical representations comprise not only formal properties of words (such as the word's phonology or orthography) but also meaning representations. Moreover, the overall quality of a lexical representation depends on the qualities of these components and their interconnectedness. If one of them is not (fully) specified, the lexical representation is lower in quality. A substantial amount of low-quality lexical representations will hamper reading comprehension (Perfetti and Hart 2001, 2002).

In a study with adult readers of varying reading comprehension skills, Perfetti and Hart (2001) demonstrated that the skilled and poor readers differed in the quality of their meaning representations. The participants were presented with written word pairs such as *king – royalty* (2001: 76) and were required to decide whether the words were semantically related. The word pairs appeared word-by-word with differing interstimulus intervals and contained either a homophone, such as *night* (homophonic meaning: knight) in *night – royalty* (2001: 76), or no homophone. The authors expected skilled readers to make faster decisions and to show an earlier interference effect for homophones compared to poor readers. They reasoned that skilled readers have faster access to word meanings because of their superior meaning representations. In line with this assumption, they observed faster decision times and earlier interference effects in the presence of homophones for skilled compared to poor readers.

In a cross-sectional study with primary school children from Grade 1 to 4, Richter et al. (2013) directly tested the assumption that the quality of meaning representations is a proximal predictor of reading comprehension at the text level. The children were presented with tasks accessing the quality of their phonological representations (phonological comparison task), their orthographical representations (lexical decision task), and their meaning representation (semantic verification task), as well as their reading comprehension skills at the text level (ELFE 1–6, Lenhard and Schneider 2006). The results indicate that the overall quality of the children's lexical representations and the efficiency of access to these representations explained a substantial amount of variance in their reading skills. Moreover, the effect of the quality of phonological and orthographical representations on reading comprehension was found to be mediated by the quality of meaning representations. Notably, individual differences in the quality of meaning representations accounted for a substantial amount of variance in reading comprehension that could not be explained by variance in word recognition skills (Richter et al. 2013). A study by Nation and Snowling (1998) suggests a similar conclusion by showing that semantic deficits can explain word recognition and reading comprehension problems in poor readers with normal phonological recoding skills.

Nation and Snowling (1999) used a priming paradigm to demonstrate qualitative differences in the abstract semantic knowledge of children classified as good vs. poor readers. In a priming experiment, the good readers made faster lexical decisions on target words (e.g. *cat*) when a prime of the same category (*dog*, 1999: B1) preceded the target words than when they were preceded by an unrelated word. However, poor readers' responses were primed by preceding category members only when prime and target words were highly associated. In contrast, both good and poor readers showed comparable priming effects when prime and target words were functionally related (e.g. *shampoo – hair*, 1999: B1). The authors assumed that the poor readers primarily possessed an event-based semantic word knowledge, whereas the better readers had already built abstract semantic representations.

In sum, a number of studies using different methods and focusing on different age groups indicate that a low quality and accessibility of word-meaning representations can cause reading comprehension problems in addition to the deteriorating effects of deficits in phonological recoding and orthographical decoding.

3.2 Individual differences beyond the word level

The explanatory approaches of poor reading comprehension skills discussed in the previous sections attribute poor reading abilities primarily to word-level skills. Word-level processes are clearly a major source of reading comprehension difficulties, but the existence of readers who show poor reading comprehension despite adequate word reading skills suggests that cognitive processes beyond the word level must be considered to better understand reading comprehension difficulties (e.g. Cain et al. 2001; Nation and Snowling 1998, Exp. 2, 1999; Stothard and Hulme 1992). Several studies have demonstrated, in accordance with the simple view of reading, that a substantial amount of variance in reading comprehension can be explained by individual differences in general language (listening) comprehension (Catts et al. 2003; Johnston and Kirby 2006; Joshi and Aaron 2000; Kendeou, Savage, and van den Broek 2009; Knoepke et al. 2013; Ransby and Swanson 2003). These language comprehension skills comprise several component skills at the sentence and text level. In the following section, we will discuss studies that examined the potential impact of some of these component skills on reading comprehension problems. The studies included children with adequate word recognition but impaired comprehension skills or they controlled for phonological or word-recognition skills statistically to investigate the unique contribution of sentence- and text-level skills to individual differences in reading comprehension.

3.2.1 Individual differences in syntactic and semantic integration processes

To comprehend a sentence, simply decoding the words of the sentence and retrieving their meanings is not sufficient. The reader must integrate the individual word meanings into a coherent mental representation of the sentence according to its specific syntactic and semantic structure (e.g. Müller and Richter 2014; Richter and Christmann 2009). For example, the sentence *Katie sues Robert* contains exactly the same words as the sentence, *Robert sues Katie*. Based on the word meanings alone, a reader cannot determine the prosecutor and the respondent in the sentence. However, the syntactic structure of transitive English main clauses (subject-verb-object) reveals that in the first sentence *Katie* is the prosecutor and in the second sentence she is the respondent. In addition to the syntactic structure, a reader can also use the semantic context of a sentence to resolve, for example, syntactic or semantic ambiguities. In the sentence, *the bug has been killed/removed*, the interpretation of *bug* as either an insect or a technical error depends entirely on the semantic context of the sentence (insect: *killed*; technical error: *removed*).

Ample evidence exists showing a relationship between individual differences in syntactic and semantic integration processes and reading comprehension. For example, poor syntactic awareness, i.e. a reader's "ability to reflect upon and to manipulate aspects of the internal grammatical structure of sentences" (Tunmer, Nesdale, and Wright 1987: 25) and deficient processes of semantic integration can result in reading difficulties in some poor readers. Byrne (1981) found a positive relationship between syntactic awareness and reading comprehension in poor vs. good beginning readers. In an act-out-task, the children were presented with spoken sentences, which were the same length but differed in grammatical structure complexity. In addition, children worked on a picture-choice task with spoken sentences varying in plausibility containing center-embedded relative clauses. Pictures matching plausible sentences were easy to find with the aid of the semantic context of the sentence, but pictures matching less plausible sentences required the aid of syntactic knowledge for their correct identification. The poor readers' performance on the syntactically more complex sentences in the act-out task and on the less plausible sentences in the picture-choice-task was inferior to the good readers' performance on these sentences. In contrast, the between-group performances were comparable for the less complex and plausible sentences. Similarly, Tunmer et al. (1987) found that older poor readers were less able to correct spoken sentences containing morphological or word-order violations or to supply a missing word in an auditory presented sentence compared to younger skilled readers of the same reading level. Poor readers also seem to have difficulties restructuring the words of a scrambled sentence back into their correct order (Nation and Snowling 2000) and to perform poorly on Bishop's (1983) test for the reception of grammar (TROG; Stothard and Hulme 1992). In a longitudinal study with French children from Kindergarten to Grade 2, Casalis and Louis-Alexandre (2000) found that morpho-syntactic skills in Kindergarten, such as the ability to inflect nouns for gender or verbs for tense form, are predictive of sentence comprehension at the end of Grade 2. Plaza and Cohen (2003) demonstrated that syntactic awareness operationalized by a grammatical judgment and correction task was predictive of reading and spelling skills in French primary school children at the end of Grade 1. Moreover, syntactic awareness accounted for unique variance in reading and spelling even when phonological awareness, naming speed, and auditory memory were statically controlled. These studies suggest that individual differences in syntactic awareness and syntactic integration skills explain unique variance in reading comprehension and that deficient syntactic skills might cause reading difficulties.

In a reading time study with adult readers, Graesser, Hoffmann, and Clark (1980) found that the syntactic complexity and the semantic complexity of sentences (independent from each other) had a greater retarding impact on slow readers compared to fast readers. Considering that the slower readers are likely to have lower reading skills, this finding suggests that poor readers need to invest a greater amount of cognitive resources to comprehend syntactically and semantically complex sentences. Investigating semantic integration skills, Hannon and Daneman (2004) found that less skilled readers tend to invest less cognitive effort in the establishment of coherence relations within a sentence in favor of establishing more global coherence relations. They presented poor and skilled readers with short texts containing a semantic anomalous term in the final sentence of the text, such as *Amanda was bouncing all over because of too many tranquilizers/sedatives/tranquilizing sedatives/tranquilizing stimulants* (2004: 197). Poor readers were less likely to detect anomalies than skilled readers and they were less likely in particular to detect anomalies in internally incoherent noun phrases (e.g. *tranquilizing stimulants*) compared to internally coherent noun phrases (e.g. *tranquilizing sedatives*), indicating a rather shallow semantic processing of the meaning of noun phrases and sentences in poor readers.

Semantic information, in particular the semantic context of a sentence, can also be beneficial for poor readers with deficits in word-level processes, because the context helps these readers to recognize the words and infer their meaning. This explanation is the basic assumption of the *interactive-compensatory model* proposed by Stanovich (1980). The model is based on evidence from a number of inventive experiments that compared the word-recognition performance of good vs. poor readers under different contextual manipulations (see also West and Stanovich 1978). These experiments consistently revealed that the performance of the poor readers depended more heavily on the presence of a facilitating sentence context, whereas the good readers relied on their superior word-recognition skills rather than the sentence context. In a similar vein, Gernsbacher and Faust (1991, Exp. 4) demonstrated that poor readers extensively use a restricting semantic context when it facilitates word recognition (for similar results for dyslexic readers, see Nation and Snowling 1998, Exp. 2). Van der Schoot et al. (2009) found in an eye-tracking study (Exp. 1) and in a self-paced reading study (Exp. 2) that poor 10- to 12-year-old Dutch readers used prior contextual information as effectively as skilled readers to resolve lexical ambiguities. However, in contrast to skilled readers, poor readers were less likely to correct an initial incorrect interpretation of an ambiguous word, indicating less efficient comprehension monitoring in poor readers.

Importantly, Gernsbacher and Faust (1991, Exp. 1) showed that poor readers have difficulties to suppress context-inappropriate meanings. The task was to judge the semantic relatedness of a sentence and a word that was presented after the final word of the sentence (e.g. *He had a lot of patients*). Poor readers showed a substantial and long-lasting interference effect in rejecting a probe word (*calm*) when it did not fit the sentence but was semantically related to a homophone of the final word (*patience*). In contrast, good readers exhibited this interference effect only when the probe word was presented immediately after the sentence. These results suggest an effective and rapid suppression of inappropriate word meanings by good but not poor readers.

In sum, the findings of the reported studies suggest that efficient syntactic and semantic integration processes are an important prerequisite for good text comprehension. If these processes are ineffective or deficient, the overall reading ability may be adversely affected.

3.2.2 Individual differences in inference making and comprehension monitoring

Text comprehension goes beyond the sentence level by requiring the integration of information provided by several sentences into a coherent mental representation. According to Johnson-Laird (1981) and Van Dijk and Kintsch (1983), this mental representation consists of two qualitatively distinct levels. Readers need to construct a coherent representation of the semantic structure of the text (*propositional text base*), and they need to integrate text information and prior knowledge to build a *mental model* (Johnson-Laird 1981) or *situation model* (Van Dijk and Kintsch 1983) of the circumstances described in a text. Thus, constructing a situation model (mental model) is essential for comprehending the text, and it requires several closely related cognitive activities, such as linking the contents of adjacent and distant sentences

(Singer et al. 1992), using prior knowledge for drawing inferences (Graesser, Singer, and Trabasso 1994), predicting upcoming text (Van Berkum et al. 2005), monitoring the plausibility of the text content (Isberner and Richter 2013), and monitoring the comprehension process (Nation 2005). The key question is whether individual differences in these processes explain unique variance in overall reading comprehension in addition to readers' word recognition skills. In a longitudinal study, Oakhill, Cain, and Bryant (2003) and Cain, Oakhill, and Bryant (2004) focused on the unique contribution of inference skills and individual differences in comprehension monitoring to reading comprehension. Inference skills can be defined as the ability to derive information from the text context and from world knowledge to enrich the mental representation of the text. Comprehension monitoring skills can be defined as the metacognitive ability to monitor the comprehension process and to detect comprehension problems as well as inconsistencies with the text or with prior knowledge (Baker 1989). Oakhill et al. (2003) and Cain et al. (2004) presented children with several tasks that assessed inference-making skills, comprehension-monitoring skills, verbal ability, working memory skills, and overall text comprehension. The ability to draw inferences and to monitor their comprehension process explained unique variance in reading comprehension even when verbal ability and single word recognition abilities were statistically controlled. These relationships were found in beginning readers aged 7 to 8 years (Oakhill et al. 2003) and also in older readers until the age of 11 (Cain et al. 2004). Although a substantial amount of variance in reading comprehension was explained by working memory capacity, this general cognitive ability failed to fully explain the effects of inference making and comprehension monitoring on reading comprehension. Instead, both higher-order cognitive component skills of text comprehension accounted for a unique portion of variance in children's reading comprehension. In accordance with these findings, Van der Schoot et al. (2009) demonstrated that poor readers were less able to monitor their comprehension process than skilled readers. In contrast to good comprehenders, poor readers' reading times on disambiguating information that followed a lexically ambiguous word were the same as when the information preceded the word. Moreover, they made more errors responding to comprehension questions when a lexically ambiguous word with a biased (not intended) meaning preceded the disambiguating region. The authors concluded that the poor readers are less likely to detect an interpretation error (as indicated by the lack of reading time increase on the disambiguating information) and to repair it (indicated by lower response accuracy).

The impact of inference skills on text comprehension has received ample attention in research. Bridging inferences that connect two pieces of information in a text, such as anaphoric (e.g. Garnham and Oakhill 1985) and causal inferences (e.g. Singer et al. 1992), are especially important for constructing a coherent situation model. Cain and Oakhill (1999) and Cain et al. (2001) focused on individual differences in such text-connecting inferences and elaborative or gap-filling inferences, which refer to processes of "incorporating information outside of the text, i.e. general knowledge, with information in the text to fill in missing details" (Cain et al. 2001: 490). Seven- to 8-year-old children read short text passages and answered questions requiring the identification of literal assertions in the text, making text-connecting inferences, and gap-filling inferences. Cain and Oakhill (1999) found that poor readers drew fewer inferences of both types than good readers, whereas both groups performed equally well on literal assertions. To rule out the possibility that the poor readers' inferior performance on the inference questions was due to a lack of necessary background knowledge, Cain et al. (2001) replicated the findings holding background knowledge constant. In this study, they provided children with background knowledge about a fictional planet named *Gan* to ensure that all children had the same background. As in the Cain and Oakhill study, the poor readers had significantly more difficulties drawing text-connecting and gap-filling inferences than the good readers. Moreover, poor readers' performance on the inference questions could not be attributed to a lack of background knowledge.

These findings consistently suggest that word-level, sentence-level, and text-level skills independently contribute to text comprehension variance. Oakhill et al. (2003) emphasized that determining the exact causes of reading difficulties and considering this individual pattern of deficits when planning remediation and intervention programs for poor readers is essential. Ideally, educators should take care to tailor such programs as accurately as possible to the needs and deficits of the individual reader. To accomplish this, the gross screening instruments that are typically used for diagnosing reading difficulties need to be augmented with more discriminative psychological tests that assess component skills of reading comprehension. One promising way to assess these skills is to measure the efficiency of the specific component processes of reading comprehension by using reaction-time measures in combination with well-defined reading tasks and test items that are constructed according to (psycho-)linguistic criteria (for an example, see the German-speaking test battery ProDi-L, Richter et al. 2017).

4 Conclusion

This chapter discussed several problems concerning the common definition of dyslexia and its diagnostic value in identifying poor readers and their individual needs for training and intervention. In particular, we emphasized that the diagnosis of dyslexia bears no information about the cause of the individual reading deficit or the kind and extent of intervention that is required. Furthermore, we argued that the distinction between dyslexic and general backward readers based on the wide-spread discrepancy model of dyslexia is not empirically useful. One argument against the discrepancy model is that poor readers classified as dyslexic according to the discrepancy model perform the same on reading-related tasks as poor readers with a more general cognitive deficit. Consequently, both groups require the same reading intervention. In that respect, a cognitive perspective on reading difficulties that examines component processes of reading at the word-, the sentence-, and the text level is far more promising. Even readers in the same age group differ greatly in the extent that they accurately and efficiently master these cognitive processes at all three levels. We argued that individual differences in word-, sentence- and text-level processes contribute uniquely to individual differences in reading comprehension. Against this background, we conclude that the potential causes for reading difficulties are multifaceted and heterogeneous. An important practical implication of this conclusion is that the success of intervention and remediation programs depends heavily on the identification of the specific type of cognitive deficit that causes reading difficulties in the poor reader.

Acknowledgments

The work on this chapter was supported by the German Federal Ministry of Research and Education (BMBF, grants 01GJ0986 and 01GJ1402B).

References

American Psychiatric Association. 2013. *Diagnostic and statistical manual of mental disorders, 5th edn. (DSM-V)*. Washington, DC: American Psychiatric Publications.
Baker, Linda. 1989. Metacognition, comprehension monitoring and the adult reader. *Educational Psychology Review* 1(1). 3–38.
Boada, Richard & Bruce F. Pennington. 2006. Deficient implicit phonological representations in children with dyslexia. *Journal of Experimenta Child Psychology* 95(3). 153–193.
Bishop, Dorothy V. M. 1983. The test for reception of grammar. Manchester: University of Manchester.
Bradley, Lynette & Peter E. Bryant. 1983. Categorizing sounds and learning to read: A causal connection. *Nature* 301(5899). 419–421.
Bus, Adriana G. & Marinus H. van IJzendoorn. 1999. Phonological awareness and early reading: A meta-analysis of experimental training studies. *Journal of Educational Psychology* 91(3). 403–414.
Byrne, Brian. 1981. Deficient syntactic control in poor readers: Is a weak phonetic memory code responsible? *Applied Psycholinguistics* 2(3). 201–212.
Cain, Kate & Jane V. Oakhill. 1999. Inference making ability and its relation to comprehension failure in young children. *Reading and Writing: An Interdisciplinary Journal* 11(5–6). 489–503.
Cain, Kate, Jane V. Oakhill, Marcia A. Barnes & Peter E. Bryant. 2001. Comprehension skill, inference-making ability, and their relation to knowledge. *Memory & Cognition* 29(6). 850–859.
Cain, Kate, Jane V. Oakhill & Peter E. Bryant. 2004. Children's reading comprehension ability: Concurrent predictions by working memory, verbal ability, and components skills. *Journal of Educational Psychology* 96(1). 31–42.

Casalis, Séverine & Marie-France Louis-Alexandre. 2000. Morphological analysis, phonological analysis and learning to read French: A longitudinal study. *Reading and Writing* 12(3). 303–335.

Castles, Anne & Max Coltheart. 1993. Varieties of developmental dyslexia. *Cognition* 47(2). 149–180.

Castles, Anne & Max Coltheart. 2004. Is there a causal link from phonological awareness to success in learning to read? *Cognition* 91(1). 77–111.

Catts, Hugh W. Tiffany Hogan & Marc E. Fey. 2003. Subgrouping poor readers on the basis of individual differences in reading-related abilities. *Journal of Learning Disabilities* 36(2). 151–164.

Coltheart, Max & Nancy E. Jackson. 1998. Defining dyslexia. *Child Psychology & Psychiatry Review* 3(1). 12–16.

Coltheart, Max, Kathleen Rastle, Conrad Perry, Robyn Langdon & Johannes Ziegler. 2001. DRC: A dual route cascaded model of visual word recognition and reading aloud. *Psychological Review* 108(1). 204–256.

Dickie, Catherine, Mitsuhiko Ota & Ann Clark. 2013. Revisiting the phonological deficit in dyslexia: Are implicit nonorthographic representations impaired? *Applied Psycholinguistics* 34(4). 649–672.

Frith, Uta. 1985. Beneath the surface of developmental dyslexia. In Karalyn Patterson, John C. Marshall & Max Coltheart (eds.), *Surface dyslexia: Neuropsychological and cognitive studies of phonological reading*, 301–330. London: Erlbaum.

Frost, Ram. 2012. Towards a universal model of reading. *Behavioral and Brain Sciences* 35(5). 263–329.

Gernsbacher, Morton A. & Mark E. Faust. 1991. The mechanism of suppression: A component of general comprehension skill. *Journal of Experimental Psychology: Learning, Memory, and Cognition* 17(2). 245–262.

Gough, Philip B. & William E. Tunmer. 1986. Decoding, reading, and reading disability. *Remedial and Special Education* 7(1). 6–10.

Garnham, Alan & Jane V. Oakhill. 1985. On-line resolution of anaphoric pronouns: Effects of inference making and verb semantics. *British Journal of Psychology* 76(3). 385–393.

Graesser, Arthur C. Nicholas L. Hoffman & Leslie F. Clark. 1980. Structural components of reading time. *Journal of Verbal Learning and Verbal Behavior* 19(2). 135–151.

Graesser, Arthur C. Murray Singer & Tom Trabasso. 1994. Constructing inferences during narrative text comprehension. *Psychological Review* 101(3). 371–395.

Griffiths, Yvonne M. & Margaret J. Snowling. 2001. Auditory word identification and phonological skills in dyslexic and average readers. *Applied Psycholinguistics* 22(3). 419–439.

Hannon, Brenda & Meredyth Daneman. 2004. Shallow semantic processing of text: An individual-differences account. *Discourse Processes* 37(3). 187–204.

Hoover, Wesley A. & Philip B. Gough. 1990. The simple view of reading. *Reading and Writing: An Interdisciplinary Journal* 2(2). 127–160.

Hulme, Charles, Margaret Snowling, Marketa Caravolas & Julia Carroll. 2005. Phonological skills are (probably) one cause of success in learning to read: A comment on Castles and Coltheart. *Scientific Studies of Reading* 9(4). 351–365.

Johnson-Laird, Philip N. 1981. Comprehension as the construction of mental models. *Philosophical Transactions of the Royal Society, Series B* 295(1077). 353–374.

Johnston, Timothy C. & John R. Kirby. 2006. The contribution of naming speed to the simple view of reading. *Reading and Writing* 19(4). 339–361.

Joshi, R. Malatesha & P. G. Aaron. 2000. The component model of reading: Simple view of reading made a little more complex. *Reading Psychology* 21(2). 85–97.

Kendeou, Panayiota, Robert Savage & Paul van den Broek. 2009. Revisiting the simple view of reading. *British Journal of Educational Psychology* 79(2). 353–370.

Knoepke, Julia, Tobias Richter, Maj-Britt Isberner, Johannes Naumann & Yvonne Neeb. 2014. Phonological recoding, orthographic decoding, and comprehension skills during reading acquisition. *Zeitschrift für Erziehungswissenschaft* 17(3). 447–471.

Knoepke, Julia, Tobias Richter, Maj-Britt Isberner, Yvonne Neeb & Johannes Naumann. 2013. Leseverstehen = Hörverstehen X Dekodieren? Ein Stringenter Test der Simple View of Reading bei Deutschsprachigen Grundschulkindern [Reading comprehension = listening comprehension X decoding? A stringent test of the simple view of reading in German primary school children]. In Angelika Redder & Sabine Weinert (eds.), *Sprachförderung und Sprachdiagnostik: Interdisziplinäre Perspektiven*, 256–276. Münster: Waxmann.

Lenhard, Wolfgang & Wolfgang Schneider. 2005. *ELFE 1–6: Ein Leseverständnistest für Erst- bis Sechstklässler* [ELFE 1–6: A reading comprehension test for grades one to six]. Göttingen: Hogrefe.

Manis, Franklin R. Mark S. Seidenberg, Lisa M. Doi, Catherine McBride-Chang & Alan Petersen. 1996. On the bases of two subtypes of developmental dyslexia. *Cognition* 58(2). 157–195.

Martens, Vanessa E. G. & Peter F. de Jong. (2006). The effect of word length on lexical decision in dyslexic and normal reading children. *Brain and Language* 98(2). 140–149.

Mayringer, Heinz & Heinz Wimmer. 2000. Pseudoname learning by German-speaking children with dyslexia: Evidence for a phonological learning deficit. *Journal of Experimental Child Psychology* 75(2). 116–133.

McNamara, Danielle S. & Joseph P. Magliano. 2009. Towards a comprehensive model of comprehension. In Brian Ross (ed.), *The psychology of learning and motivation, vol. 51*, 297–28. New York: Elsevier.

Müller, Bettina & Tobias Richter. 2014. Lesekompetenz [Reading competence]. In Joachim Grabowski (ed.), *Sinn und Unsinn von Kompetenzen: Fähigkeitskonzepte im Bereich von Sprache, Medien und Kultur*, 29–49. Opladen: Budrich.

Nation, Kate. 2005. Children's reading comprehension difficulties. In Margaret. J. Snowling & Charles Hulme (eds.), *The science of reading: A handbook*, 248–265. Oxford: Blackwell.

Nation, Kate & Margaret J. Snowling. 1998. Individual differences in contextual facilitation: Evidence from dyslexia and poor reading comprehension. *Child Development* 69(4). 996–1011.

Nation, Kate & Margaret J. Snowling. 1999. Developmental differences in sensitivity to semantic relations among good and poor comprehenders: Evidence from semantic priming. *Cognition* 70(1). B1–B13.

Nation, Kate & Margaret J. Snowling. 2000. Factors influencing syntactic awareness skills in normal readers and poor comprehenders. *Applied Psycholinguistics* 21(2). 229–241.

Oakhill, Jane V. Kate Cain & Peter E. Bryant. 2003. The dissociation of word reading and text comprehension: Evidence from component skills. *Language and Cognitive Processes* 18(4). 443–468.

Paap, Kenneth R. & Ronald W. Noel. 1991. Dual route models of print to sound: Still a good horse race. *Psychological Research* 53(1). 13–24.

Perfetti, Charles A. 1985. *Reading ability*. New York: Oxford University Press.

Perfetti, Charles A. 2001. Reading skills. In Neil J. Smelser & Paul B. Baltes (eds.), *International encyclopedia of the social & behavioral science*, 12800–12805. Oxford: Pergamon.

Perfetti, Charles A. 2007. Reading ability: Lexical quality to comprehension. *Scientific Studies of Reading* 11(4). 357–383.

Perfetti, Charles A. 2010. Decoding, vocabulary, and comprehension. The golden triangle of reading skill. In Margaret G. McKeown & Linda Kucan (eds.), *Bringing reading research to life: Essays in honor of Isabel Beck*, 291–303. New York: Guilford.

Perfetti, Charles A. & Lesley Hart. 2001. The lexical bases of comprehension skill. In David S. Gorfien (ed.), *On the consequences of meaning selection: Perspectives on resolving lexical ambiguity*, 67–86. Washington, DC: American Psychological Association.

Perfetti, Charles A. & Lesley Hart. 2002. The lexical quality hypothesis. In Ludo Vehoeven. Carsten Elbro & Pieter Reitsma (eds.), *Precursors of functional literacy*, 189–213. Amsterdam: John Benjamins.

Plaut, David C. James L. McClelland, Mark S. Seidenberg & Karalyn Patterson. 1996. Understanding normal and impaired word reading: Computational principles in quasi-regular domains. *Psychological Review* 103(1). 56–115.

Plaut, David C. 1999. A connectionist approach to word reading and acquired dyslexia: Extension to sequential processing. *Cognitive Science* 23(4). 543–568.

Plaza, Monique & Henri Cohen. 2003. The interaction between phonological processing, syntactic awareness, and naming speed in the reading and spelling performance of first-grade children. *Brain and Cognition* 53(2). 287–92.

Rack, John P. Margaret J. Snowling & Richard K. Olson. 1992. The nonword reading deficit in developmental dyslexia: A review. *Reading Research Quarterly* 27(1). 29–53.

Ramus, Franck, Chloe R. Marshall, Stuart Rosen & Heather K. J. van der Lely. 2013. Phonological deficits in specific language impairment and developmental dyslexia: Towards a multidimensional model. *Brain* 136(2). 630–45.

Ransby, Marilyn. J. & Lee H. Swanson. 2003. Reading comprehension skills of young adults with childhood diagnosis of dyslexia. *Journal of Learning Disabilities* 36(6). 538–555.

Richter, Tobias & Ursula Christmann. 2009. Lesekompetenz: Prozessebenen und Interindividuelle Unterschiede [Reading competence: Levels of processing and individual differences]. In Norbert Groeben & Bettina Hurrelmann (eds.), *Lesekompetenz: Bedingungen, Dimensionen, Funktionen*, 3rd edn, 25–58. Weinheim: Juventa.

Richter, Tobias, Maj-Britt Isberner, Johannes Naumann & Yvonne Neeb. 2013. Lexical quality and reading comprehension in primary school children. *Scientific Studies of Reading* 17(6). 415–434.

Richter, Tobias, Johannes Naumann, Maj-Britt Isberner, Yvonne Neeb & Julia Knoepke. 2017. *ProDi-L: Prozessbezogene Diagnostik des Leseverstehens bei Grundschulkindern* [Process-based assessment of reading skills in primary school children] [Computerized test]. Göttingen: Hogrefe.

Rutter, Michael & William Yule. 1975. The concept of specific reading retardation. *Journal of Child Psychology and Psychiatry* 16(3). 181–197.

Scanlon, Donna M. & Frank R. Vellutino. 1996. Prerequisite skills, early instruction, and success in first-grade reading: Selected results from a longitudinal study. *Mental Retardation and Developmental Disabilities Research Reviews* 2(1). 54–63.

Seidenberg, Mark S. & James L. McClelland. 1989. A distributed, developmental model of word recognition and naming. *Psychological Review* 96(4). 523–568.

Shaywitz, Sally E. Michael D. Escobar, Bennett A. Shaywitz, Jack M. Fletcher & Robert Makuch. 1992. Evidence that dyslexia may represent the lower tail of a normal distribution of reading ability. *The New England Journal of Medicine* 326(3). 145–150.

Siegel, Linda S. 1988. Evidence that IQ scores are irrelevant to the definition and analysis of reading disability. *Canadian Journal of Psychology* 42(2). 201–215.

Singer, Murray, Michael Halldorson, Jeffrey C. Lear & Peter Andrusiak. 1992. Validation of causal bridging inferences. *Journal of Memory and Language* 31(4). 507–524.

Snowling, Margaret J. 1980. The development of grapheme-phoneme correspondence in normal and dyslexic readers. *Journal of Experimental Child Psychology* 29(2). 294–305.

Stanovich, Keith E. 1980. Toward an interactive-compensatory model of individual differences in the development of reading fluency. *Reading Research Quarterly* 16(1). 32–71.

Stanovich, Keith E. 1988. Explaining the differences between the dyslexic and the garden-variety poor reader: The phonological-core variable-difference model. *Journal of Learning Disabilities* 21(10). 590–604.

Stanovich, Keith E. 2005. The future of a mistake: Will discrepancy measurement continue to make the learning disabilities field a pseudoscience? *Learning Disability Quarterly* 28(2). 103–106.

Stanovich, Keith E. & Linda S. Siegel. 1994. Phenotypic performance profile of children with reading disabilities: A regression-based test of the phonological-core variable-difference model. *Journal of Educational Psychology* 86(1). 24–53.

Stothard, Susan E. & Charles Hulme. 1992 Reading comprehension difficulties. The role of language comprehension and working memory skills. *Reading and Writing: An Interdisciplinary Journal* 4(3). 245–256.

Stuebing, Karla K. Jack M. Fletcher, Josette M. LeDoux, Reid G. Lyon, Sally E. Shaywitz & Bennett A. Shaywitz. 2002. Validity of IQ-discrepancy classifications of reading disabilities: A meta-analysis. *American Educational Research Journal* 39(2). 469–518.

Tunmer, William E. Andrew R. Nesdale & Douglas A. Wright. 1987. Syntactic awareness and reading acquisition. *British Journal of Developmental Psychology* 5(1). 25–34.

Van Berkum, Jos J. A. Colin M. Brown, Pienie Zwitserlood, Valesca Kooijman & Peter Hagoort. 2005. Anticipating upcoming words in discourse: Evidence from ERPs and reading times. *Journal of Experimental Psychology: Learning, Memory & Cognition* 31(3). 443–467.

Van der Schoot, Menno, Alain L. Vasbinder, Tako M. Horsley, Albert Reijntjes & Ernest C. D. M. van Lieshout. 2009. Lexical ambiguity resolution in good and poor comprehenders: An eye fixation and self-paced reading study in primary school children. *Journal of Educational Psychology* 101(1). 21–36.

Van Dijk, Teun A. & Walter Kintsch. 1983. *Strategies of discourse comprehension*. New York: Academic Press.

Vellutino, Frank R. Jack M. Fletcher, Margaret J. Snowling & Donna M. Scanlon. 2004. Specific reading disability (dyslexia): What have we learned in the past four decades? *Journal of Child Psychology and Psychiatry* 45(1). 2–40.

Vellutino, Frank R. Donna M. Scanlon & Reid G. Lyon. 2000. Differentiating between difficult-to-remediate and readily remediated poor readers. More evidence against the IQ-achievement discrepancy definition of reading disability. *Journal of Learning Disabilities* 33(3). 223–238.

Vidyasagar, Trichur R. & Kristen Pammer. 2010. Dyslexia: A deficit in visuo-spatial attention, not in phonological processing. *Trends in Cognitive Sciences* 14(2). 57–63.

West, Richard F. & Keith E. Stanovich. 1978. Automatic contextual facilitation in readers of three ages. *Child Development* 49(3). 717–727.

Wilson, Alexander M. & Nonnie K. Lesaux. 2001. Persistence of phonological processing deficits in college students with dyslexia who have age-appropriate reading skills. *Journal of Learning Disabilities* 34(5). 394–400.

Wimmer, Heinz. 1996. The nonword reading deficit in developmental dyslexia: Evidence from children learning to read German. *Journal of Experimental Child Psychology* 61(1). 80–90.

Wimmer, Heinz & Usha Goswami. 1994. The influence of orthographic consistency on reading development: Word recognition in English and German children. *Cognition* 51(1). 91–103.

Woollams, Anna M. 2014. Connectionist neuropsychology: Uncovering ultimate causes of acquired dyslexia. *Philosophical Transactions of the Royal Society B* 369(1634). 1–12.

World Health Organization. 2010. *International Classification of Diseases (ICD-10 online)*. http://apps.who.int/classifications/icd10/browse/2010/en (accessed 19 September 2014).

Yule, William. 1973. Differential prognosis of reading backwardness and specific reading retardation. *British Journal of Educational Psychology* 43(3). 244–248.

Yule, William, Michael Rutter, Michael Berger & James Thompson. 1974. Over- and under-achievement in reading: Distribution in the general population. *British Journal of Educational Psychology* 44(1). 1–12.

Ziegler, Johannes. C. Conrad Perry & Max Coltheart. 2000. The DRC model of visual word recognition and reading aloud: An extension to German. *European Journal of Cognitive Psychology* 12(3). 413–430.

Ziegler, Johannes C. Conrad Perry, Anna Ma-Wyatt, Diana Ladner & Gerd Schulte-Körne. 2003. Developmental dyslexia in different languages: Language-specific or universal? *Journal of Experimental Child Psychology* 86(3). 169–193.

Zoccolotti, Pierluigi, Maria De Luca, Enrico Di Pace, Filippo Gasperini, Anna Judica & Donatella Spinelli. 2005. Word length effect in early reading and in developmental dyslexia. *Brain and Language* 93(3). 369–373.

Liliana Tolchinsky and Naymé Salas
25 Grammar for writing and grammar in writing

1 Introduction

The contribution of grammar to writing quality is a controversial issue. On the one hand, grammatical competence seems essential to writing development. From the early school years onwards, writers are capable of producing stretches of text, but the ease with which such linguistic output can be described in terms of abstract grammatical units – phrases, sentences, complex sentences – might be a distinctive feature of mature writers (Linell, 2004). Therefore, the writer's skill in producing arrangements of linguistic units of different size and monitoring their grammaticality should be a fundamental source of variation in the development of writing competence. Moreover, the grammatical features of a text should be highly influential on the perception of its quality. On the other hand, many educationalists and researchers of written composition coincide with Elbow (1981) in that nothing helps children's writing so much as learning to ignore grammar (p. 169). In addition, psycholinguists have failed to find a consistent relation between the grammatical features of a text, such as clause length or phrase complexity, and its global quality (Berman and Nir 2007).

In this chapter we mediate this controversy by providing an overview of existing evidence on the role of grammar in writing development research. Drawing from published work in several languages, we review what previous studies have found about the link between the writer's grammatical competence and the process of learning to write; that is, we focus on grammar *for* writing. In addition, we also review research that has striven to find links between the grammatical features and the perceived quality of written texts; in this way, we also focus on the role of grammar *in* writing. Our general goal is to determine the impact of grammar on what is considered good writing as it appears in the revised literature.

Some terminological clarifications are in order. This chapter is concerned with the role of grammar in the development of *writing as a discourse modality*, rather than as a notational system (Ravid and Tolchinsky, 2002). Although the writer's linguistic knowledge is clearly involved in understanding notational aspects of writing – e.g., how phonology relates to the graphic elements of the writing system – it is mostly in writing as a special kind of discourse that specific grammatical competence is involved.

Liliana Tolchinsky, Universitat de Barcelona
Naymé Salas, Universitat Autònoma de Barcelona

DOI 10.1515/9781614514909-026

Throughout the chapter we take *grammatical competence* to encompass knowledge of the internal structure of words (morphology), and the internal composition of clauses and inter-clausal relationships (syntax). We focus on the way linguistic units of different levels and complexity are added and linked together to form a written text, rather than on the lexical realization of particular units. While we assume that lexico-grammatical and text-semantic features are essential for forming the semantic units that form written discourse (Halliday 1977), evidence for the link between lexical features (e.g., lexical density, lexical variety) and writing is relatively consistent and robust (e.g., Malvern, Richards, Chipere, and Durán (2004); McNamara, Crossley, and McCarthy (2010); Olinghouse and Leaird 2009). In contrast, we claim that the evidence for the specific contribution of morphology and syntax to writing is usually weak and often contradictory.

The chapter is organized into two main sections. In the first one, we review findings on how and to what extent writers' grammatical competence has been associated with their writing skills (grammar for writing). When examining grammar for writing, we describe the ways in which (good) writing has been defined and we look at studies where the relationship between independent measures of morphological and/or syntactic competence were taken as explanatory variables of writing quality. In the second section, we review prior studies' claims on how the grammatical (i.e., morphosyntactic) features of written texts have been found to be associated with their perceived quality (grammar in writing). When examining previous findings on grammar in writing, then, we are interested in the extent to which the grammatical make up of any given text is predictive of its quality, as perceived by independent raters (e.g., educators). As will be evident in what follows, this approach has yielded multifaceted, rather than straightforward, answers to the issue, given that both the way in which writers apply their knowledge of grammar and the way that grammatical features impact readers' perceptions of text quality, depend on other key factors of text composition.

2 Grammar *for* writing

Most psycholinguists would agree that simple-clause syntax is more or less in place around age three years (Clark 2009; Tomasello 2003). Moreover, children raised in literate contexts show an early awareness of the linguistic features of written language. When 4- to 5-year-olds, who do not yet know how to spell, are asked to dictate to an adult stories that are meant to be written, they deploy certain linguistic forms typical of writing, and avoid others that are typical of colloquial spoken language indicating they grasp some of the rhetorical features of the written, as opposed to the spoken, modality (Blanche Benveniste 1982). However, constructing a text is more than aligning simple clauses or being aware of linguistic forms typical of literate language. Written discourse requires a distinct use of grammar (e.g., Biber 1988; Chafe 1982;

Chafe and Renkema 1993; Halliday 1987; Miller and Weinert 1998). Among other skills, it requires unambiguous introduction and maintenance of referents, command of interclausal connectivity, and knowledge of text macrostructures (Van Dijk 1980); that is, of the organization and global coherence that allows the reader to see the text as a semantic unit.

Written composition is thus a difficult task, in which multiple demands need to be paid attention to and be coordinated efficiently (Alamargot and Chanquoy 2001). The writer must integrate local or microstructural decisions – such as vocabulary, phrase- and clause-internal structure, or interclausal linkage – into the macro-organization of the text. Proficient writers are guided by their knowledge about the topic and by genre-specific writing plans stored in long-term memory. They also take into account the task environment (e.g., what has already been written, mode of transcription, the writing prompt), the needs of their audience, and they set themselves substantive and rhetorical goals, against which they can evaluate the text they produce (Hayes 2012). In other words, these *holistic concerns* (Langacker 1989) aid proficient writers to compose their texts.

In contrast, local decisions made by less experienced writers in the course of composing a text are rarely motivated by holistic concerns (Berman and Nir 2009). They typically entertain quite simplistic writing plans, in which they essentially write ideas as they retrieve them from memory, without factoring in rhetorical issues, audience needs, or general writing goals (e.g., Bereiter and Scardamalia 1987; Berninger, Fuller, and Whitacker 1996; Hayes 2011). The much needed interplay between global-level macrostructural goals and local decisions is a challenge that takes a long time to achieve.

The differences between proficient and inexperienced writers are best illustrated by studies that investigated the process of written composition. As a rule, writers do not compose a text all at once but build it up in "bursts": short periods of writing without interruptions (Hayes 2009, 2012). These bursts, which may be taken to represent the units of writing from a process viewpoint, increase in length with age and, more generally, as a function of expertise with writing. More proficient writers tend to produce bursts averaging 10 to 12 words, while the bursts of middle school writers may consist of only 6 to 7 words (Dockrell and Connelly 2015; Kaufer, Hayes, and Flower 1986), and those of children in the early elementary school years average just 1 to 2 words, with long pauses between them (Castillo and Tolchinsky in prep.). These changes in writing bursts reflect the nature of the underlying writing processes and strategies. In this sense, a recent study revealed that 9- to 10-year-olds planned at the clause level, but that older subjects planned at the level of groups of clauses (Ailhaud, Chenu, and Jisa 2016). Planning over multiple clauses is likely to enable the writer to interact with other elements of the writing process and the task environment (Hayes and Flower, 1980). In short, research on the processing units of writing strongly suggests that immature writers construct their texts bottom up, with minimal top-down control[1], pointing to a connection between their grammatical competence and the quality of their texts.

2.1 Estimating grammatical competence

Several measures have been used to obtain independent measures of writers' grammatical competence. Most measures and tasks tap into morphological and syntactic competence simultaneously, even though researchers often refer to the task as measuring one or the other, depending on the skill which they are targeting.[2] The *morphological awareness* – inspired by the seminal study by Berko (1958) – typically requires transforming or completing a given phrase or sentence orally delivered, with the transformation/completion requiring a target morpheme (e.g., Kent, Wanzek, Petscher, Al Otaiba and Kim; Kim, Al Otaiba, Puranik, Folsom, Greulich, & Wagner 2011; Kim, Al Otaiba, Folsom, Greulich, and Puranik 2014; Muter, Hulme, Snowling, and Stevenson. 2004; Salas and Caravolas, submitted). The sentence provides a context such that the production of the morpheme is obligatory to comply with a grammatical rule, as in subject-verb or determiner-noun agreement. *Sentence imitation* tasks are used to estimate syntactic, rather than morphological, skills, requiring participants to repeat verbatim an orally delivered sentence (e.g., Abbott and Berninger 1993; Berninger, Yates, Cartwright, Rutberg, Remy, & Abbott, 1992; Kent et al. 2014). Sentences that constitute the input to the task usually vary in length and in the complexity of the targeted grammatical construction, on the assumption that they will reflect "a child's familiarity with grammatical markers and word order" (Puranik and AlOtaiba 2012: 1532), since repeating a sentence involves syntactic parsing (Martin and Romani 1994). *Word-order* tasks are another approach to assessing syntax, which entails asking participants to put words or sentence fragments in the right order (e.g., Babayiğit and Stainthorp 2010; Yeung, Ho, Chan, Chung 2012) or to correct sentences with word-order violations (e.g., Muter et al. 2004; Tunmer 1989). In *receptive grammar* tests, participants are required to identify which of a set of pictures best matches a sentence delivered orally (e.g., Bishop 2003). Finally, in *grammaticality judgment* tasks participants must use their linguistic intuition to decide whether a sentence is in keeping with the grammatical rules of their language or not (e.g., Olinghouse 2008). In all cases, the tasks used to assess writers' grammatical competence use decontextualized linguistic constructions casted in isolate sentences. Therefore, they

---

[1] Our conceptualization of bottom-up processes is based on Karmiloff-Smith (1986), who considers bottom-up processing as procedural or data-driven, in contrast to later developing processes that impose top-down organizational strategies/control on bottom-up component parts.

[2] Note, however, that the previous assertion is highly dependent on language typology, since the relative overlap between morphology and syntax should differ considerably for predominantly isolating languages (e.g., Chinese) and highly inflectional or agglutinating languages (e.g., Romance languages, Turkish).

are questionable in terms of their potential to capture the type of grammatical skills concerned with the production of coherent, communicatively-effective written texts; that is, discourse-level grammatical skills.

2.2 What is (good) writing?

Establishing the quality of written products is a complex enterprise, as demonstrated by the varying manners in which the notion of text quality has been operationalized in relevant research. Some studies have assessed writing in terms of *spelling accuracy*, either by the number of words spelled correctly (e.g., Berninger et al. 1998; Lerkkanen, et al. 2004) or the number of correct word sequences (e.g., Videen, Deno, and Marston 1982). Such studies are typically concerned with early writing development, where transcription skills (in this case, spelling) are assumed to severely constrain the composition process (Berninger and Amtmann 2003; Berninger and Swanson 1994; Juel, Griffith, and Gough 1986). Other studies apply one or more measures of *written productivity* in the sense of the amount of text produced, typically measured in number of words, clauses/sentences, or ideas (e.g., Berninger et al. 1992; Kim et al., 2014; Puranik and AlOtaiba 2012). Relying on overall productivity as a proxy for text quality may be justified to the extent that strong associations have been found between the amount of text produced and other measures of text quality (e.g., Berman and Nir 2009; Lee et al. 2010; Salas et al. in press). This association is, however, problematic, as it contradicts the general wisdom that "more is not always better".

Other scholars have chosen to determine text quality by having expert raters (teachers, writing scholars, trained students) evaluate writing skills by assigning a *holistic score* to written products (e.g., Juel et al. 1986; Malvern, Richards, Chipere, and Duran 2004; Uccelli, Dobbs, and Scott 2013). Holistic scoring may be carried out with more or less explicit instructions to raters, who are sometimes given sample texts (e.g., Juel et al. 1986) or detailed scoring criteria (e.g., Connelly et al. 2012; Graham 1990; Juel et al. 1986), but what they all have in common is that a single score is obtained for each text.

A major problem with holistic scoring is that it is inherently subjective and exposed to biases (Charney 1984). For this reason, *multi-feature studies* have been introduced into research on writing development, as a means of obtaining multiple unbiased measures of several aspects of the written products, in the hopes that, in combination, they may capture text quality. Work in this line of research strives to ascertain the compositionality of writing, studying the way in which observable text features and writing skills are interrelated, forming distinct dimensions of writing skills (e.g., Puranik, Lombardino and Altmann 2008; Wagner et al. 2011). In a similar vein, there are studies in educational contexts, known as Curriculum-Based Measures (CBM), which aim at identifying the most valid, reliable, and easy-to-obtain text features to establish the quality of written productions (see McMaster and Espin 2007 for a review).

Another line of research on later language development has evaluated text quality in terms of genre-dependent constraints of *structural well-formedness* and pragmatic appropriateness (Berman and Nir 2007, 2009: 5). Well-formed texts integrate top-down and bottom-up processing (Berman and Nir-Sagiv 2004; Kupersmitt 2006), but a good piece of discourse should go beyond the conventionalized forms of genre to also reflect individual rhetorical style and expressiveness (Slobin 1977).

Finally, a small number of studies have attempted to determine text quality identifying discourse-embedded linguistic constructions as markers of genre appropriateness, usually without taking into account overall text organization (e.g., Tolchinsky and Rosado 2005; but see Berman and Nir-Sagiv 2007 for a welcome exception).

In sum, the quality of written texts has been established in a myriad of ways, which include quantitative and qualitative measures, holistic and analytical, text-embedded or rater-based. Therefore, when discussing findings from studies that examined the explanatory power of grammatical competence on text quality, it seems imperative to take into account how such quality has been determined.

2.3 Relationships between grammatical competence and writing

Very few studies have looked at the direct influence of grammatical competence on writing quality, while some have considered grammar only as part of a more general measure of oral language competence (e.g., Abbott and Berninger 1993; Berninger, Cartwright, Yates, Swanson, and Abbott 1994; Kim et al. 2011), making it impossible to assess the specific role of grammar on writing. Among the studies that found grammatical competence to be associated with writing performance, Olinghouse (2008) reported that a grammaticality judgment task administered to American 3rd graders predicted ratings of text quality. Low to moderate correlations were also reported by Kim et al. (2011) between measures of written productivity (number of words, sentences, and ideas) and measures of receptive grammar and sentence imitation (rs range: .24 to .38).

A number of studies, however, contradicted the above-mentioned findings not having found evidence for a connection between writers' grammatical and written composition skills. For example, Berninger et al. (1992) found that a measure of sentence-level syntax (repeating sentences of increasing structural complexity) did not contribute to explaining variance in the number of words or clauses produced in two writing tasks, elicited in a narrative and an expository frame. Nor did a composite variable of morphosyntactic awareness emerge as a significant predictor of early written productivity skills in English or Spanish (Salas and Caravolas submitted). Moreover, despite the overwhelming evidence for continued problems with writing among SLI children (e.g., Dockrell, Lindsay, and Connelly 2009), no consistent relationship has been found to date between measures of grammatical competence and written outcomes among these populations (e.g., Bishop and Clarkson, 2003; Mackie and Dockrell 2004).

To complicate things further, measures of grammatical competence have been found to be associated in unexpected ways with writing outcomes. In a study on the early development of writing in Turkish – an agglutinative language with an extremely rich morphology – Babayiğit and Stainthorp (2010) found a measure of grade 1 morphological awareness to be a reliable predictor of grade 2 written vocabulary and content, but it was unrelated to a measure that assessed written grammar (specifically, they measured the use of connectors, of tense, and grammatical errors, p. 564).

Thus, despite the strong reasons why grammatical competence would be expected to impinge on writing development, no robust empirical evidence has been obtained, to date, to support them. Our review of the studies that examined the relationship between grammatical competence and writing quality shows that most of them have failed to find a consistent connection between the two.

3 Grammar *in* writing

In this section we look at the grammar-writing relationship from another viewpoint. We focus on the grammar of written discourse; that is, we concentrate on the grammatical make up of any given text. The linguistic expressions in a text are usually opposed to its thematic content or overall organization. Nevertheless, several studies have looked at the microstructural characteristics of texts to see how they relate to macrostructural features such as overall text organization or text quality. Specifically, we review studies that examined the association between grammatical complexity and text quality.

3.1 Text-embedded grammar

The degree of grammatical complexity in a text fulfills rhetorical aims (Langacker 1997; Nir and Berman 2010; Matthiessen and Thompson 1988). First, complex constructions condense information. Chunking ideas in a single unit enables readers/writers to process them simultaneously in a more integrated way (Chafe 1994). However, complex constructions posit higher demands on reading, especially for less skilled readers (Just and Carpenter 1992); thus, writers must learn to find a balance between the amount of condensed ideas and ease of processing. Second, complex constructions provide a means of cohesion (Halliday and Hasan 1976; Sanders and Pander Maat 2006), and function as a suitable device for event construal; that is, they allow readers/writers to look at an event from different perspectives (Langacker 2010). Finally, the use of complex grammar obeys one of Slobin's (1977) charges for effective communication: to be "rhetorical", in the sense of being maximally expressive, since "languages must provide means for expressing notions and for compacting semantic content." (187).

Different measures of grammatical complexity have been proposed as likely indicators of writing development and/or overall text quality (e.g., Hunt 1965). Broadly speaking, a complex grammatical construction is a unit of a different level than its component parts (Huddleston and Pullum 2002). Measures of complexity often involve computing the number of lower-level units (e.g., words) included in higher-level units: phrases, clauses, or discourse-level units. Therefore, they reflect the *syntactic density* within a given unit; that is, how much information is packed into the boundaries of a single clause (Berman and Nir 2009).

Phrase-level length, in words, is a consistent indicator of grammatical complexity, both developmentally and cross-linguistically. It involves computing the average number of words per NP, Prepositional Phrase (PP) or Verb Phrase (VP). For example, the direct object NP in (1) is less grammatically complex than the same construction in (2), because it contains fewer words.

(1) They started to draw <u>pictures</u>.

(2) They started to draw <u>large and funny-looking pictures of kittens</u>.

NP complexity constitutes a powerful diagnostic of text production skills as it has been shown to increase with age and schooling experience in English, Hebrew, French, and Spanish (e.g., Mazur-Palandre, Fayol, and Jisa 2011, for French; Ravid and Berman 2010, for Hebrew; Ravid, van Hell, Rosado, and Zamora 2002, for Hebrew, Dutch, Spanish, and English; Salas 2010 for Spanish).

Clause length, computed as the mean number of words per clause, has been extensively used as an indicator of the grammatical complexity of the text (Beers and Nagy 2011; Berman and Verhoeven 2002; Chafe 1982; Hunt 1970; Ravid 2004), and is associated with the literate register (Chafe and Danielewicz 1987). Its value in developmental research on writing is, however, contradictory, with some studies reporting significant increases in mean clause length as a function of age (e.g., Berman and Ravid 2009), and others reporting plateaus as early as mid-elementary school (e.g., Tolchinsky, Aparici, and Salas submitted).

Another class of text-based measures of grammatical complexity is made up of variations of syntactic packaging, defined as the ability to combine two or more related predications into a single stretch of discourse. This notion, which has been found to be a critical feature of text construction development in oral narratives (Berman and Slobin 1994), underlies different proposals aimed at defining units of discourse analysis encompassing groups of syntactically linked clauses. One of the most frequently used measures of this kind is the *Terminal Unit* (T-Unit), which consists of a main clause and its associated dependent clauses. It was proposed by Hunt (1965, 1970), who reported that the average number of clauses per T-Unit increases with age in written discourse. An alternative form of syntactic packaging is the *clause package* (CP, Nir 2008). A CP consists of a number of clauses linked syntactically, but also thematically and discursively, by different kinds of connectivity devices (Aparici 2010; Aparici, Tolchinsky, and Rosado 2000; Cahana-Amitay and Berman 1999). The scope of a CP lies between the clause and the thematic, topic-based notion of discourse constituent, hence between local linguistic expression and global text organization (Berman 2008). CPs differ from T-Units in that the latter are exclusively based on syntactic criteria, while CPs are defined on the basis of syntactic, thematic and discursive criteria. For example, the two first juxtaposed clauses in (3) would be considered part of the same CP because they are co-referential and thematically linked, whereas they would be considered as two different T-Units because there is no explicit syntactic link between the first and the second clause.

(3) We were siting in a bar drinking something. We were deciding where to go next Saturday.

The level of complexity of these units of discourse can be established in quantitative terms, by computing the number of words or clauses per T-Unit or CP and also in qualitative terms, by identifying the kind of clausal linkage within a CP. For example, CPs in which clauses are linked only by juxtaposition or coordination are less complex than CPs formed by subordinate clauses. Both quantitative and qualitative approaches have shown that T-Units and CPs increase in complexity with age (Aparici 2010; Berman and Nir 2009; Hunt 1965; Nir and Berman 2010), while language- and learning-impaired populations produce units of less complexity as opposed to controls (Leadholm and Miller 1992; Scott and Windsor 2000).

To sum up, computing the syntagmatic density of various linguistic units and the quality of their linkage have been the most favored approaches to estimate the degree of grammatical complexity in written texts. In addition, grammatical complexity has been found to increase with age and schooling. As we shall see next, these measures have been used to ascertain the relationship between the grammatical features of texts and their quality[3].

3.2 Relationships between text-embedded grammar and writing quality

Most research on writing quality has assumed a functional motivation to the grammatical constructions and categories used in texts, which is why measures of grammatical

---

[3] It is beyond the scope of the chapter to discuss the differences between measures of syntactic density and those that assess the degree of nesting or embeddedness (e.g., Ravid and Berman 2010). Suffice it to say that density measures imply more embedded structures (Beers and Nagy 2011; Berman 2009; Davidi 2015); thus, they can be taken as indices of syntactic *embededness*. Moreover, no significant differences were found when grammatical density measures were directly compared with measures of subordination and levels of embedding (Szmrecsányi 2004).

complexity are typically considered a valuable feature of written texts. In this section, we review studies that examined grammatical complexity and its association with or influence on text quality.

A number of studies have found direct associations between grammatical complexity measures and text quality or macro-structural scores. For example, McNamara et al. (2010) found that a measure of grammatical complexity (number of words before the main verb) was one of the three most predictive indices of the quality of essays produced by college students. Similarly, a developmental study by Crowhurst (1983) also showed that argumentative essays with high grammatical complexity scores received significantly higher quality ratings than essays with low grammatical complexity. However, the association between complexity and quality was found only at grades 10 and 12. In a study with younger writers, Wagner et al. (2011) analyzed writing samples of 1st and 4th grade students. Their confirmatory factor analyses showed that a complexity factor (estimated using mean T-Unit length and syntactic density measures) correlated with a macro-organization factor (estimated via a score evaluating the use of topic sentence, and the number and ordering of ideas) in grade 1 ($r = .38$), but not in grade 4 ($r = .07$). Finally, a longitudinal study with Turkish-speaking children found that the content quality of children's 2nd grade written narratives correlated strongly ($r = .59$) with a "structure" score, which evaluated grammatical complexity (Babayiğit and Stainthorp 2010). These findings seem to indicate that the relationship between grammatical features and text quality varies considerably as a function of age and schooling experience.

The grammar-writing association seems to also depend on discourse genre and on the specific measure of complexity used. For example, Beers and Nagy (2009) asked 7th and 8th grade children to complete a story that had been partially written, and to produce a persuasive essay in response to a question. To prevent differences as a function of keyboarding skill, the students dictated while a typist transcribed the texts. Text quality was established by two independent raters, who had to follow specified criteria, including (a) the writer's focus on the topic; (b) supporting details and elaboration; (c) use of effective language; and (d) word-choice, tone, and voice. The authors found that grammatical complexity, measured in words per clause, correlated positively with text quality for essays, but not for narratives. In contrast, when grammatical complexity was measured as T-Unit length, the authors found it to be positively correlated with narrative quality, but negatively with essay quality.

In contrast, other studies found a total disconnect between text quality and grammatical complexity. Berman and Nir-Sagiv (2007, 2009) examined both local linguistic expression (clause length, NP complexity, and syntactic density) and global text quality in gradeschool, junior-high, and high-school students. Here, "global" quality should not be confused with "holistic" quality, since it was evaluated applying a four-level evaluative schema, to both narratives and expository texts, based on three dimensions: (1) cognitive representation, (2) discourse structure and (3) informative content. The general goal of the bespoke rubric was to assess macro-structural well-formedness and overall proficiency in achieving genre-specific rhetorical aims. Thus, the lowest level was credited to narrative texts that relied exclusively on event-description, contained only basic narrative episodes and did not deviate from genre-canonic features and to expository texts that relied on top-down generalities without integrating bottom-up specifications, while they introduced new pieces of information without elaboration or a proper contextualization. In contrast, the highest level of global text quality was attributed to texts that achieved a "creative synthesis" of top-down and bottom-up elements of discourse, integrating both core and satellite elements and rhetorical deviations from canonical genre features. Their results revealed a marked effect of genre in the grammatical make up of the texts. Participants used more subordination, passive voice, and heavier noun phrases in expository texts than in narrative texts. Most important to our argument, there were no significant correlations between local grammatical features and global text quality. Grammatical complexity and global text organization both increased as a function of age and schooling experience, but there was dissociation between them across age groups and genres (Berman and Nir 2009: 434).

Altogether, the findings reviewed above indicate that the contribution of grammatical features to writing quality changes with age and is heavily constrained by genre. However, even when attention to genre has been considered, no straightforward grammar-writing quality (or local-global) relationships have been attested. Therefore, the degree of grammatical complexity per se may not be a suitable marker of writing quality (Crowhurst 1983). Rather, what seems to matter is the use of grammatical constructions in interaction with the communicative context and purpose, since "Grammar is not just about rules, it is about choices and flexibility of expression" (Rimmer 2008). In the next section we review studies that aimed to characterize the ways in which specific grammatical features serve discourse functions.

3.3 Grammar to serve the purposes of discourse genres

A fundamental tenet of genre-based approaches to writing development is that they take into account the extent to which bottom-up categories, at the phrase and clause level, function as diagnostic of genre adequacy. *Genre* refers to the text types that fulfill particular functions, as defined by sociocultural norms and conventions (Halliday and Hasan 1985). It is a dimension of coherence, because it reflects speaker/writer's expectations as to what should be written.

For example, narratives have people, actions, and objects as their protagonists and they describe events, whereas expository texts are centered on an idea or 'theme', and they must construct that theme in the addressee's mind (Britton 1994; Havelock 1986; Katzenberg 2004). In other words, "while narrative discourse is agent-oriented and, furthermore, deals with the actions of particular agents, expository discourse lacks this agent orientation and deals more with generalities" (Longacre 1996: 245).

Within this line of studies it is assumed that writers' awareness of the function served by a given genre mobilizes them to make use of the grammatical options that are best suited to the function in question. Thus, genre awareness allows writers to make grammatical choices that are consistent with the functions of discourse genres, as well as to convey their discourse stance (Berman, Ragnarsdóttir, and Strömqvist 2002). For instance, writers vary in their use of depersonalization devices – e.g., passive voice, non-referential uses of personal pronouns, etc. – as a function of genre. These devices are more typical of expository texts, since they require a more "detached" stance than narrative texts. Agency alternation is thus a genre feature that accounts for variations between narrative and expository writing (Jisa and Tolchinsky 2009; Rosado, Salas, Aparici, and Tolchinsky 2014). Similarly, writers use more complex NPs in expository than in mathematical texts, but conditional constructions are more characteristic of the latter (Ravid, Dromi, and Kotler 2010). This is because expository texts require referents to be clearly identified in order to build a thematic structure in the addressee's mind, which may be achieved by increasing NP complexity, whereas *if*-clauses are crucial to express a mathematical argument.

Genre awareness emerges early on and is evident in the grammatical choices that children make in composing different types of text. Six-year-olds produce very different texts when asked to tell the story of *Hansel and Gretel*, and when asked to describe the witch's house. Verb tense and mood differed markedly between narratives and descriptions in Hebrew (Sandbank 2002) and, across languages and age groups, writers compose narratives predominantly using past tense forms, deictic and anaphoric personal pronouns, and light NP subjects. In contrast, they prefer the timeless present and irrealis mood, impersonal pronouns, heavy NP subjects, and abundance of modals when composing expository texts (Ragnarsdóttir, Aparici, Cahana-Amitay, van Hell, and Viguié 2002; Ravid et al. 2002; Reilly et al. 2002).

It should be noted, however, that while young children are usually familiar with some grammatical constructions of narratives and descriptions, their use of grammar in these text types sometimes differs from adult-like use. For example, Salas (2010) found that the type of NP realization in first-person narratives (lexical vs. pronominal NPs) did not differ as a function of age. However, on closer inspection, while most lexical NP realizations in the adults' texts had been used to identify new referents, many of the children's lexical NPs consisted of unnecessary repetitions. In addition, the grammar of other genres, such as expository texts – and of most school and academic text genres – has been found to have a protracted development that may last well into adolescence (e.g., Rosado et al. 2014; Salas 2010; Schleppegrell, 2001).

In sum, discourse genres motivate the use of specific grammatical constructions (Rosado et al. 2014) and determine the nature of the associations between grammatical constructions and complexity (Beers and Nagy 2011). The communicative purposes on which each discourse genre specializes demand a subtle but distinct configuration of the grammatical repertoire essential for writing. Moreover, some sensitivity to such demands appears to be attained very early on, although mastery of the grammatical make up of some discourse genres takes years of training and experience.

4 Concluding remarks: grammar and writing quality

In this chapter we have reviewed studies that aimed to identify aspects of writers' grammatical competence that explain differences in the quality of their writing, as well as grammatical features of written texts that have an influence on their perceived levels of quality. We agree with Rimmer's (2008) contention that "The importance of grammar to writing is hardly controversial but the exact relationship between the two has proved hard to formulate" (31). Certainly, the studies surveyed above produced inconsistent results. We attribute this inconsistency to two main issues with this kind of research: (1) previous studies may have tested the contribution of grammatical competence on too diverse definitions of writing quality; and (2) they may have assessed a type of grammatical competence not directly related to text production. While grammaticality judgments, sentence imitation, and knowledge of receptive grammar may be useful to estimate knowledge of clause-level grammar, they might not be valid measures to relate to written composition skills.

On the other hand, fine-grained analyses of written text grammar showed that the local decisions that writers must make to construct their texts – types of grammatical construction, internal structuring of clauses, clause combining – are not necessarily linked with their quality. While it is true that overall grammatical complexity increases with school level paralleled with an improvement in overall text quality, the grammar-writing relationship is not straightforward; rather it is motivated by genre, thus highly dependent on the specificities of the communicative purposes to be fulfilled.

From the viewpoint of grammar for writing, only an assessment of genre-based grammatical competence is likely to be predictive of writing skill at the global or macrostructural level; similarly, only a specific combination of text-embedded grammatical features will be predictive of text quality. This avenue of research, however, is at its infancy. The ultimate goal is to go "beyond well-formedness" (Berman and Nir 2009) and the conventionalized forms that define canonical text types, even to transgress the barriers of genre (Galeano 2013[4]), as most good writers do. We still

---

[4] "Por suerte creo que estoy fuera de los géneros. Y eso es el resultado de muchos años de trabajo en que fui descubriendo que lo mío era una síntesis de diferentes géneros. Una tentativa de síntesis para recuperar la unidad perdida del lenguaje humano".

need to discover which grammatical features are relevant to the task of good writing, and which allow writers to achieve personal style and maximal expressiveness, while observing the communicative purposes of different types of texts.

References

Abbott, R. D. & V. W. Berninger. 1993. Structural equation modeling of relationships among developmental skills and writing skills in primary-and intermediate-grade writers. *Journal of Educational Psychology* 85(3). 478–508.

Ailhaud, E., F. Chenu & H. Jisa. In planning. A developmental perspective on the units of written French.

Aparici, M. 2010. El desarrollo de la conectividad discursiva en diferentes géneros y modalidades de producción. Universitat Autónoma de Barcelona.

Aparici, M., J. Perera, E. Rosado & L. Tolchinsky. 2000. Developing literacy across genres, modalities and languages. (International Literacy Project, Working papers, 3. Barcelona: Institute of Educational Sciences. University of Barcelona.

Alamargot, D. & L. Chanquoy. 2001. *Through the models of writing*. Dordrecht: Kluwer.

Babayiğit, S. & R. Stainthorp. 2010. Component processes of early reading, spelling, and narrative writing skills in Turkish: a longitudinal study. *Reading and Writing: An Interdisciplinary Journal* 23. 539–568.

Beers, S. F. & W. Nagy. 2009. Syntactic complexity as a predictor of adolescent writing quality: Which measures? Which genre? *Reading and Writing: An Interdisciplinary Journal* 22. 185–20.

Beers, S. F. & W. Nagy. 2011. Writing development in four genres from grades three to seven: Syntactic complexity and genre differentiation. *Reading and Writing: An Interdisciplinary Journal* 24. 183–202.

Bereiter, C. & M. Scardamalia. 1987. The psychology of written composition. Hillsdale, NJ: Lawrence Erlbaum Associates.

Berko, J. 1958. The child's learning of English morphology. *Word* 14. 150–177.

Berman, R. A. 1996. Form and function in developing narrative abilities: The case of 'and'. In D. Slobin, J. Gerhardt, A. Kyratzis & J. Guo (eds.), *Social interaction, context, and language: Essays in honor of Susan Ervin-Tripp*, 343–367. Mahwah, NJ: Lawrence Erlbaum.

Berman, R. A. 2008. The psycholinguistics of text construction. *Journal of Child Language* 35. 735–771.

Berman, R. A. & B. Nir-Sagiv. 2007. Comparing narrative and expository text construction across adolescence: A developmental paradox. *Discourse processes* 43(2). 79–120.

Berman, R. A. & D. I. Slobin. 1994. *Relating events in narrative: A crosslinguistic developmental study* (Vol. 1). New York: Psychology Press.

Berman, R. A. & L. Verhoeven. 2002. Cross-linguistic perspectives on the development of text-production abilities: Speech and writing. *Written Language & Literacy* 5(1). 1–43.

Berman R. A. & B. Nir. 2004. Linguistic indicators of inter-genre differentiation in later language development. *Journal of Child Language* 31. 334–380.

Berman, R.A. & B. Nir. 2009. Cognitive and linguistic factors in evaluating expository text quality: Global versus local? In V. Evans & S. Pourcel (eds.), *New directions in cognitive linguistics*, 421–440. Amsterdam: John Benjamins.

Berman, R. A. & D. Ravid. 2009. Becoming a literate language user: Oral and written text construction across adolescence. In D.R. Olson & N. Torrance (eds.), *Cambridge handbook of literacy*, 92–111. Cambridge: Cambridge University Press.

Berman, R., H. Ragnarsdottir & S. Stromqvist. 2002. Discourse stance. *Written Language and Literacy* 5(2). 255–289.
Berninger, V.W. & D. Amtmann. 2003. Preventing written expression disabilities through early and continuing assessment and intervention for handwriting and /or spelling problem: Research into practice. In H. Lee Swanson, K. Harris, & S. Graham (eds.), *Handbook of learning disabilities*. New York: Guilford Press.
Berninger, V. W. & H. L. Swanson. 1994. Modifying Hayes and Flower's model of skilled writing to explain beginning and developing writing. *Advances in cognition and educational practice* 2. 57–81.
Berninger, V. W., A. C. Cartwright, C. M. Yates, H. L. Swanson & R. D. Abbott. 1994. Developmental skills related to writing and reading acquisition in the intermediate grades. *Reading and Writing: An Interdisciplinary Journal* 6(2). 161–196.
Berninger, V. W., F. Fuller & D. Whitaker. 1996. A process model of writing development across the life span. *Educational Psychology Review* 8(3). 193–218.
Berninger, V. W., K. Vaughan, R. D. Abbott, A. Brooks, S. P. Abbott, L. Rogan & S. Graham. 1998. Early intervention for spelling problems: Teaching functional spelling units of varying size with a multiple-connections framework. *Journal of Educational Psychology* 90(4). 587–605.
Berninger, V., C. Yates, A. Cartwright, J. Rutberg, E. Remy & R. Abbott. 1992. Lower-level developmental skills in beginning writing. *Reading and Writing: An Interdisciplinary Journal* 4(3). 257–280.
Biber, D. 1988. *Variation across speech and writing*. Cambridge: Cambridge University Press.
Bishop, D. V. & B. Clarkson. 2003. Written language as a window in to residual language deficits: A study of children with persistent and residual speech and language impairments. *Cortex* 39(2). 215–237.
Blanche Benveniste, C. 1982. La escritura del lenguaje dominguero. In Ferreiro (Ed.) *Nuevas perspectivas sobre los procesos de lectura y escritura*, 195–212. Buenos Aires: Siglo XXI.
Britton, B. K. 1994. Understanding expository text: Building mental structure to induce insights. In M. A. Gernsbacher (ed.), *Handbook of psycholinguistics*, 641–674. New York: Academic Press.
Cahana-Amitay, D. & R. Berman. 1999. Initial ideas on L(onger) units. Working Papers in Developing Literacy across Genres, Modalities, and Languages, Vol 3.
Castillo, C. & L. Tolchinsky. (in prep.) The impact of writing process on the quality of written product.
Chafe, W. & J. Danielewicz. 1987. Properties of spoken and written language. In R. Horowitz & S. J. Samuels (eds), *Comprehending oral and written language*, 83–113. San Diego: Academic Press.
Chafe, W. 1982. Integration and involvement in speaking, writing, and oral literature. In D. Tannen (ed.), *Spoken and written language: Exploring orality and literacy*, 35–53. Norwood, NJ: Ablex.
Chafe, W. 1994. *Discourse, consciousness, and time: The flow and displacement of conscious experience in speaking and writing*. Chicago, IL: University of Chicago Press.
Charney, D. 1984. The validity of using holistic scoring to evaluate writing: A critical overview. *Research in the Teaching of English*, 65–81.
Clark, E. V. 2009. *First language acquisition* (2nd edn). Cambridge: Cambridge University Press.
Connelly, V., J. E. Dockrell, K. Walter & S. Critten. 2012. Predicting the quality of composition and written language bursts from oral language, spelling, and handwriting skills in children with and without specific language impairment. *Written Communication* 29(3). 278–302.
Crowhurst, M. 1983. Syntactic complexity and writing quality: A review. *Canadian Journal of Education/Revue canadienne de l'éducation* 8. 1–16
Dockrell, J. E. & V. Connelly. 2015. The role of oral language in underpinning the text generation difficulties in children with specific language impairment. *Journal of Research in Reading* 38. 18–34.
Dockrell, J. E., G. Lindsay & V. Connelly. 2009. The impact of specific language impairment on adolescents' written text. *Exceptional children* 75(4). 427–446.

Elbow, P. 1981. *Writing with power: Techniques for mastering the writing process.* New York: Oxford.
Galeano E. 2013. *Punto Final,* January 25, 2013. 775.
Graham, S. 1990. The role of production factors in learning disabled students' compositions. *Journal of Educational Psychology* 82(4). 781.
Halliday, M.A.K. 1977. Text as semantic choice in social context. In T.A. van Dyck & J. Petofi (eds.), *Grammars and descriptions.* Berlin: De Gruyter.
Halliday, M.A.K. 1987. Spoken and written modes of meaning. In R. Horowitz & S. J. Samuels (eds.) *Comprehending oral and written language,* 55–82. New York: Academic Press.
Halliday, M. A. K. & R. Hasan. 1976. *Cohesion in English.* London: Longman.
Havelock E. 1986. *The muse learns to write: Reflections on orality and literacy from antiquity to the present.* New Haven: Yale University Press
Hayes, J. R. 2011. Kinds of knowledge-telling: Modeling early writing development. *Journal of Writing Research* 3(2). 73–92.
Hayes, J. R. 2012. Modeling and remodeling writing. *Written Communication* 29(3). 369–388.
Hayes, J. R. & L. S. Flower. 1980. Identifying the organization of writing processes. *Cognitive processes in writing.* 3–30.
Huddleston, R. & G. K. Pullum. 2002. *The Cambridge grammar of the English language.* Cambridge: Cambridge University Press.
Hunt, K. 1965. *Grammatical structures written at three grade levels.* NCTE Research Report No. 3. Champaign, IL: National Council of Teachers of English.
Hunt, K. W. 1970. Syntactic maturity in schoolchildren and adults. *Monographs of the society for research in child development,* iii–67.
Jisa, H. & L. Tolchinsky. 2009. Developing a depersonalized stance through linguistic means in typologically different languages: Written expository discourse. *Written Language & Literacy* 12(1). 1–25.
Juel, C., Griffith, P. L. & P. B. Gough. 1986. Acquisition of literacy: A longitudinal study of children in first and second grade. *Journal of Educational Psychology* 78(4). 243.
Katzenberger, I. (2004). Development of clause-package marking in written and spoken expository texts. *Journal of Pragmatics* 36. 1921–1948.
Kaufer, D. S., Hayes, J. R. & Flower, L. S. 1986. Composing written sentences. *Research in the Teaching of English* 20(2). 121–140.
Kent, S., J. Wanzek, Y. Petscher, S. Al Otaiba & Y. S. Kim. 2014. Writing fluency and quality in kindergarten and first grade: the role of attention, reading, transcription, and oral language. *Reading and Writing: An Interdisciplinary Journal* 27(7). 1163–1188.
Kim, Y. S., S. Al Otaiba, J. S. Folsom, L. Greulich & C. Puranik. 2014. Evaluating the dimensionality of first-grade written composition. *Journal of Speech, Language, and Hearing Research* 57(1). 199–211.
Kim, Y. S., S. Al Otaiba, C. Puranik, J. S. Folsom, L. Greulich, & R. K. Wagner. 2011. Componential skills of beginning writing: An exploratory study. *Learning and individual differences* 21(5). 517–525.
Kupersmitt, J. 2006. *Developing text-embedded linguistic temporality in three languages.* Bar-Ilan University, doctoral dissertation.
Langacker, R. W. 2010. Conceptualization, symbolization, and grammar. *International Journal of Cognitive Linguistics* 1(1). 31–64.
Langacker, R. W. 1986. An introduction to cognitive grammar. *Cognitive science* 10. 1–40.
Leadholm, B. & J. Miller. 1992. *Language sample analysis: The Wisconsin guide.* Milwaukee, WS: Wisconsin Department of Instruction.
Lerkkanen, M. K., H. Rasku-Puttonen, K. Aunola & J. E. Nurmi. 2004. The developmental dynamics of literacy skills during the first grade. *Educational Psychology* 24(6). 793–810.

Longacre, R. E. 1996. *The grammar of discourse*. Springer Science & Business Media.
Mackie, C. & J. E. Dockrell. 2004. The nature of written language deficits in children with SLI. *Journal of Speech, Language and Hearing Research* 47(6). 1469.
Malvern, D., B. J. Richards, N. Chipere & P. Durán. 2004. *Lexical diversity and language development*. New York: Palgrave McMillan.
Martin, R. C. & C. Romani. 1994. Verbal working memory and sentence comprehension: A multiple-components view. *Neuropsychology* 8(4). 506.
Matthiessen, C. & S. A. Thompson. 1988. The structure of discourse and 'subordination'. In J. Haiman, & S. A. Thompson (eds.), *Clause combining in grammar and discourse*, 275–330. Amsterdam: John Benjamins.
Mazur Palandre, A., M. Fayol & H. Jisa. 2011. Information flow across modalities and text types. In V. W. Berninger (ed.), *Past, present, and future contributions of cognitive writing research to cognitive psychology*. New York: Psychology Press/Taylor Francis Group.
McMaster, K. & C. Espin. 2007. Technical features of curriculum-based measurement in writing a literature review. *The Journal of Special Education* 41(2). 68–84.
McNamara, D. S., S. A. Crossley & P. M. McCarthy. 2010. Linguistic features of writing quality. *Written Communication* 27(1). 57–86.
Muter, V., C. Hulme, M. J. Snowling & J. Stevenson. 2004. Phonemes, rimes, vocabulary, and grammatical skills as foundations of early reading development: evidence from a longitudinal study. *Developmental Psychology* 40(5). 665–681.
Nir, B. 2008. Clause packages as constructions in developing discourse. Tel Aviv University doctoral dissertation.
Nir, B. & R. A. Berman. 2010. Complex syntax as a window on contrastive rhetoric. *Journal of Pragmatics* 42(3). 744–765.
Olinghouse, N. G. 2008. Student-and instruction-level predictors of narrative writing in third-grade students. *Reading and Writing: An Interdisciplinary Journal* 21(1–2). 3–26.
Olinghouse, N. G. & J. T. Leaird. 2009. The relationship between measures of vocabulary and narrative writing quality in second-and fourth-grade students. *Reading and Writing* 22(5). 545–565.
Puranik, C. S. & S. Al Otaiba. 2012. Examining the contribution of handwriting and spelling to written expression in kindergarten children. *Reading and Writing: An Interdisciplinary Journal* 25(7). 1523–1546.
Puranik, C. S., L. J. Lombardino & L. J. Altmann. 2008. Assessing the microstructure of written language using a retelling paradigm. *American Journal of Speech-Language Pathology* 17(2). 107.
Ragnarsdóttir, H., M. Aparici, D. Cahana-Amitay, J. van Hell & A. Viguié. 2002. Verbal structure and content in written discourse: Expository and narrative texts. *Written Language & Literacy* 5(1). 95–126.
Ravid, D. 2004. Emergence of linguistic complexity in written expository texts: Evidence from later language acquisition. In D. Ravid & H. Bat-Zeev Shyldkrot (eds.), *Perspectives on language and language development*, 337–355. Dordrecht: Kluwer.
Ravid, D. & R. A. Berman. 2010. Developing noun phrase complexity at school age: A text-embedded cross-linguistic analysis. *First Language* 30(1). 3–26.
Ravid, D., & L. Tolchinsky. 2002. Developing linguistic literacy: A comprehensive model. *Journal of child language* 29(02). 417–447.
Ravid, D., J. G. van Hell, E. Rosado & A. Zamora. 2002. Subject NP patterning in the development of text production: Speech and writing. *Written Language & Literacy* 5(1). 69–93.
Ravid, D., E. Dromi, & P. Kotler. 2010. Linguistic complexity in school-age text production: Expository versus mathematical discourse. In Marylin Nippold and Cheryl M. Scott (eds.), *Expository discourse in children, adolescents, and adults: Development and disorders*, 125–157. New York: Psychology Press.

Reilly, J., J. Bernicot, T. Olive, M. Favart, B. Wulfeck & A. Appelbaum. 2014. Written narratives from French and English speaking children with Language Impairment. In B. Arfé, J. Dockrell & V. Berninger (eds.), *Handbook of writing development and instruction in children with hearing, speech and oral language difficulties.* Oxford: Oxford University Press.

Rimmer, W. 2008. Putting grammatical complexity in context. *Literacy* 42(1). 29–35.

Rosado, E., N. Salas, M. Aparici & L. Tolchinsky. 2014. Production and judgment of linguistic devices for attaining a detached stance in Spanish and Catalan. *Journal of Pragmatics* 60. 36–53.

Salas, N. 2010. *Developmental and discursive underpinnings in the expression of Spanish noun phrases.* University of Barcelona, Spain, unpublished masters' dissertation.

Salas, N. Llauradó, A., Castillo, C., Taulé, M., Martí, M.A. 2016. Linguistic correlates of text quality from childhood to adulthood. In J. Perera, M. Aparici, E. Rosado and N. Salas, Written and spoken language development across the lifespan. *Essays in honour of Liliana Tolchinsky*, 307–326. Springer.

Salas, N. & Caravolas, M. submitted. Early development of writing: A cross-linguistic, longitudinal study.

Sandbank, A. 2002. The interplay between the written language and writing conventions in writing texts. In L. Tolchinsky (ed.), *Developmental aspects of learning to write*, 55–76. Dordrecht: Kluwer.

Sanders, T. & H. Pander Maat. 2006. Cohesion and coherence: Linguistic approaches. In K. Brown (ed.), *Encyclopedia of language and linguistics*, vol. 2, 591–595. Amsterdam: Elsevier.

Schleppegrell, M. J. 2001. Challenges in language teacher training. In G. Bräuer (ed.), *Pedagogy of language learning in higher education: An introduction*, 237–252. Westport, CT: Ablex Publishing.

Scott, C.M. & J. Windsor. 2000. General language performance measures in spoken and written narrative and expository discourse of school-age children with language learning disabilities. *Journal of Speech, Language, and Hearing Research* 43.

Slobin, D. I. 1977. Language change in childhood and in history. In J. Macnamara (ed.), *Language learning and thought*, 185–214. New York: Academic Press.

Tolchinsky, L., M. Aparici & N. Salas. submitted. The development of syntactic complexity in Spanish narratives.

Tolchinsky, L. & E. Rosado. 2005. The effect of literacy, text type, and modality on the use of grammatical means for agency alternation in Spanish. *Journal of Pragmatics* 37(2). 209–237.

Tomasello M. 2003. *Constructing a language: A usage-based theory of language acquisition.* Harvard University Press.

Tunmer, W. E. 1989. The role of language-related factors in reading disability. In D Shankweiler & I. Y. Liberman (eds.), *Phonology and reading disability: Solving the puzzle*, 91–131. Ann Arbor: University of Michigan Press.

Uccelli, Paola, Christina L. Dobbs & Jessica Scott. 2013. Mastering academic language: Organization and stance in the persuasive writing of high school students. *Written Communication* 30(1). 36–62.

Van Dijk, T. A. 1980. *Macrostructures. An interdisciplinary study of global structures in discourse. Cognition and interaction.* Hillsdale, NJ: Lawrence Erlbaum.

Videen, J., S. L. Deno & D. Marston. 1982. *Correct word sequences: A valid indicator of proficiency in written expression* (Vol. IRLD-RR-84). University of Minnesota, Institute for Research on Learning Disabilities.

Wagner, Richard K., Cynthia S. Puranik, Barbara Foorman, Elizabeth Foster, Laura Gehron Wilson, Erika Tschinkel & Patricia Thatcher Kantor. 2011. Modeling the development of written language. *Reading and Writing: An Interdisciplinary Journal* 24(2). 203–220.

Yeung, Pui-Sze, Connie Suk-Han Ho, David Wai-Ock Chan & Kevin Kien-Hoa Chung. 2013. Modeling the relationships between cognitive-linguistic skills and writing in Chinese among elementary grades students. *Reading and Writing: An Interdisciplinary Journal* 26(7). 1195–1221.

III **Environmental effects**

Section 6: Socio-economic status

Adriana Weisleder and Virginia A. Marchman

26 How socioeconomic differences in early language environments shape children's language development

1 Introduction

The goal of this chapter is to review ways in which environmental conditions that are associated with socioeconomic status (SES) shape the development of children's language proficiency. An extensive body of research has shown that language development varies as a function of family SES, and that these developmental differences arise – at least in part – from differences in the quantity and quality of parents' verbal interactions with their children. In this chapter we present additional evidence that richer language experience also sharpens infants' skill in processing speech in real time, which in turn facilitates further language learning. In this way, SES-related differences in early language experience give rise to a developmental cascade, with long-term consequences for children's educational and vocational outcomes.

This chapter is organized in four sections. The first section reviews research documenting SES differences in children's language development trajectories. We then examine distal and proximal environmental processes by which SES shapes language development. In section two, we discuss two theoretical models linking SES to child development more generally: the family stress model and the family investment model. Section three then examines the specific role of language experience. We review research showing that the quantity and quality of communicative interactions children experience predict language growth both between and within SES groups. The fourth section discusses processing skills that mediate the uptake of linguistic input and thereby, support language learning. In this section, we examine recent findings showing that richer language experience strengthens infants' language-processing efficiency, a critical skill that has been shown to facilitate language growth. We conclude by discussing how differences in early language experience can have cascading consequences for children's later learning.

2 SES-related differences in early language development

Children who come from families with higher incomes and education have more advanced language skills, on average, than children from less advantaged socio-economic backgrounds. Differences between higher- and lower-SES children have

Adriana Weisleder, Northwestern University
Virginia A. Marchman, Stanford University

been found on measures of language comprehension and production using a variety of different methods, including parent report, spontaneous speech, standardized tests, and measures of language processing (Arriaga, Fenson, Cronan, and Pethick, 1998; Farkas and Beron, 2004; Fernald, Marchman, and Weisleder, 2013; Hart and Risley, 1995). These differences emerge early in infancy and widen over time. By the time of kindergarten entry, children from low-income backgrounds in the United States (U.S.) exhibit language skills that are more than a full standard deviation below their higher-income peers (Lee and Burkam, 2002).

Hart and Risley (1995) conducted one of the most detailed studies investigating trajectories of early vocabulary development in children from different socioeconomic groups. They followed 42 children and their families from 10 to 36 months, collecting monthly recordings of language interactions in the home. Analysis of these recordings revealed differences in vocabulary development between children of professional, working class, and poverty-level families that were noticeable from almost the beginning of speech, and increased over time. By three years of age, children from higher-SES homes had a mean cumulative vocabulary of over 1,000 words, while the mean for lower-SES children was close to 500.

More recent studies with larger and more representative samples have confirmed that SES-differences in vocabulary emerge very early in childhood (Farkas and Beron, 2004; Morgan, Farkas, Hillemeier, Hammer, and Maczuga, 2015; Rowe, Raudenbush, and Goldin-Meadow, 2012). Using a large U.S. dataset of children's scores on the Peabody Picture Vocabulary Test (PPVT; Dunn and Dunn, 1997), Farkas and Beron (2004) examined trajectories of vocabulary knowledge from 3 to 13 years. They found significant race and SES differences in children's vocabulary size that had developed prior to 36 months. Another analysis using a population-based sample found that children from higher SES households had higher parent-reported vocabularies by 24 months: children in the highest income quintile had vocabularies that were half a standard deviation higher than those in the lowest income quintile (Morgan et al., 2015). In another study, SES was found to be a predictor of children's vocabulary and gesture use as early as 14 months, and to predict linear growth in vocabulary between 14 and 46 months (Rowe et al., 2012).

Differences in vocabulary size have been reported between children of college-educated and high school-educated mothers, demonstrating links between SES and language within a middle-class sample (Hoff, 2003). At the other extreme, research with a very low income population in Madagascar revealed differences in preschool children's receptive vocabulary that were associated with family wealth and maternal education (Fernald, Weber, Galasso, and Ratsifandrihamanana, 2011). These studies suggest that SES gradients in language development are present across the socioeconomic spectrum, with the magnitude of the SES-related gaps depending on the range of SES in the sample studied.

SES differences have also been observed in children's grammatical development. Children from higher SES families score higher on measures of grammar on standardized tests (Morisset, Barnard, Greenberg, Booth, and Spieker, 1990; Nelson,

Welsh, Vance Trup, and Greenberg, 2011), produce more complex sentences and use a greater variety of syntactic structures in spontaneous speech (Dollaghan et al., 1999; Huttenlocher, Vasilyeva, Cymerman, and Levine, 2002; Vasilyeva, Waterfall, and Huttenlocher, 2008), and perform significantly better on measures of receptive syntax than children from lower-SES families (Huttenlocher et al., 2002).

In addition to SES-related differences in vocabulary and grammar, recent studies have revealed disparities in children's efficiency in interpreting spoken language (Fernald et al., 2013; Bergelson and Swingley, 2013). Using real-time measures of language comprehension, Fernald et al., (2013) showed that by the age of 18 months, children from higher-SES families were faster and more accurate in identifying the referents of familiar words than children from lower-SES families. This study revealed a 6-month gap in language comprehension skill between higher- and lower-SES children that was already well established by the age of 24 months. These findings have now been replicated with a population of Spanish-speaking families living in Mexico and the United States, showing that Spanish-learning children from higher-SES backgrounds have higher vocabularies and are faster in spoken word recognition than those from lower-SES backgrounds (Weisleder, Marchman, Otero and Fernald, 2017. We return to these studies in Section 4, proposing that these language-processing skills may mediate links between children's early experiences and later vocabulary outcomes.

In sum, these studies show that significant differences between children from higher- and lower-SES families can be observed in measures of language knowledge, language use, and language-processing skill beginning in early infancy. What is crucial here is that these SES-differences are identifiable at the earliest phases of learning and may play a critical role in establishing trajectories of language growth. Studies show that most of the SES effect on vocabulary occurs prior to 36 months and then remains relatively stable throughout the school years, and that the rate of vocabulary growth during this period predicts later vocabulary and school-aged language and cognitive outcomes (Farkas and Beron, 2004; Hart and Risley, 1995; Rowe et al., 2012).

Moreover, there is increasing evidence that early language skills have important consequences for academic achievement (Durham, Farkas, Hammer, Tomblin, and Catts, 2007; Hart and Risley, 1995). Children's language skills at age 2 years uniquely predict academic and behavioral functioning in kindergarten (Gardner-Neblett and Iruka, 2015; Morgan et al., 2015) as well as language and literacy achievement up to elementary school (Lee, 2010; Walker, Greenwood, Hart, and Carta, 1994). In addition, oral language skills at kindergarten entry strongly predict later literacy and overall school success (Dickinson, Golinkoff, and Hirsh-Pasek, 2010; Scarborough, 2001; Snow, Burns, and Griffin, 1998). Given increasing evidence that kindergarten readiness skills are related to educational attainment and adult wealth, these findings suggest that oral language skill is a key variable in the inter-generational transmission of SES (Chetty, Hendren, Kline, Saez, and Turner, 2014; Duncan et al., 2007; Durham et al., 2007).

But what is it about SES that leads to disparities in language skills? Many experiential factors associated with living in poverty are known to affect children's physical, cognitive and social-emotional development – including the physical environment, access to adequate nutrition, and availability of social and emotional support (Bradley and Corwyn, 2002; Engle and Black, 2008). Can we assume that the same factors that have been linked to SES disparities in child development more broadly also account for differences in the domain of language?

The answer to this question depends in part on one's perspective on the nature of language skills. Linguistic ability can be defined narrowly – referring only to a set of abstract computational principles that are unique to human language and distinct from other mechanisms – or more broadly – encompassing the sensory-motor, cognitive, and social skills that underlie communication more generally. To the extent that language development is part of an integrative learning system linked to children's perceptual, cognitive and social-emotional capacities, understanding the mechanisms guiding early language development requires an exploration of factors that affect children's communicative competence broadly defined.

At the same time, communicative development requires learning information that is unique to language, making it distinct in many ways from the development of other socio-cognitive abilities. To advance in language development, children must learn the sounds and words of their native language, the specific ways in which these words are combined, and how these combinations of words are used in different contexts to express particular meanings. Moreover, in order to participate in conversations, children must learn to understand language in real time, as words and sentences fly by, and to respond effectively to those bids for interaction. Thus, outlining the sources of individual differences in language outcomes requires an understanding of broad environmental factors that affect children's cognitive and socio-emotional development, as well as of properties of the language environment that play a more direct role in language-learning.

In the following two sections, we first review the literature on the effects of SES on child development more broadly, and then ask how specific characteristics of parent-child communicative interactions might support language development.

3 How family processes shape children's early environments and development

SES has profound effects on children's lives and outcomes. Aspects of the physical environment, such as sanitation, noise level, and exposure to toxins and dangerous conditions, differ dramatically in lower- and higher-SES families (Evans, 2004; Shonkoff et al., 2012). SES also affects families' access to adequate nutrition and health care, and to social and psychological support (Bradley and Corwyn, 2002; Engle and Black, 2008). There is compelling evidence that these risk factors impact children's cognitive, social-emotional, and physical well-being (Bradley and Corwyn, 2002; Evans, 2006). In addition, there is increasing evidence that a large fraction of the effect of SES on child development is mediated by family processes – including parental mental health, parenting beliefs and behaviors, and family interactions. In particular, differences in parenting – including maternal sensitivity and cognitive stimulation – have been found to account for up to 50% of the relationship between SES and children's pre-academic outcomes (Brooks-Gunn and Markman, 2005; Waldfogel and Washbrook, 2011).

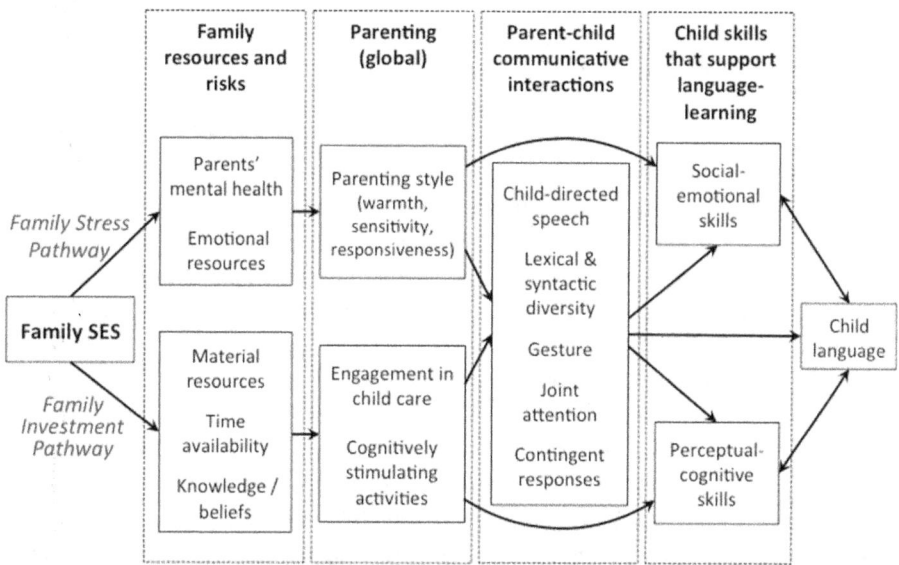

Figure 1: Conceptual model linking family socioeconomic status (SES) with children's language outcomes via its effects on family resources and risks, global aspects of parenting, parent-child communicative interactions, and child skills that support language-learning

Figure 1 provides an overview of two prominent models that have been proposed to explain how family processes mediate the relation between SES and child outcomes: the *Family Stress Model* and the *Family Investment Model* (Linver, Brooks-Gunn, and Kohen, 2002). Here, we build on these models to show how SES might affect children's language development in particular. We propose that SES differences in family resources and risks (leftmost panel) affect children's language outcomes via their influence on global aspects of parenting (mid-left panel) and specific properties of parent-child communicative interactions (mid-right panel), as well as via the effects of these interactions on socio-emotional and perceptual-cognitive skills that support language-learning (right panel). Note that while the family stress and family investment models each emphasize a different causal pathway, these pathways are not mutually exclusive, and could both be operating simultaneously.

The Family Stress model (upper stream in Figure 1) proposes that a key pathway by which poverty affects children's development is through its impact on parental mental health. Economic hardship – such as experiencing unstable income or job loss – can have negative effects on parents' emotional well-being, which influences parenting practices and the quality of parent-child interactions (Conger et al., 1992; McLoyd, 1990). Parents who are overwhelmed with the pressures of poverty are less able to meet the emotional and cognitive needs of their children, which can result in behavioral and developmental problems.

Studies have demonstrated the impact of economic hardship on parental depression and stress, which in turn diminishes parents' ability to provide warm and responsive parenting (McLoyd, 1990; Shonkoff et al., 2012). Parents who are depressed or under greater stress tend to respond less sensitively to their children, to use more harsh and controlling parenting, and to provide less adequate social and cognitive stimulation (Conger, McCarty, Yang, Lahey, and Kropp, 1984; Linver et al., 2002; Stein, Malmberg, Sylva, Barnes, and Leach, 2008). This reduction in parental nurturance and involvement can lead to lower social competence for children and adolescents, to more internalizing and externalizing behaviors, and to reduced language and cognitive development (Anthony et al., 2005; Conger et al., 1992; Kaplan et al., 2014; Stein et al., 2008). Parents' use of negative control strategies, which include high levels of prohibitions and commands, has also been associated with poor language outcomes, with effects evident as early as toddlerhood (Hart and Risley, 1995; Taylor, Donovan, Miles, and Leavitt, 2009).

The Family Investment model postulates a second possible pathway through which SES shapes child development (lower stream in Figure 1), which focuses on families' ability to invest in their children's intellectual development and education (Foster, 2002; Haveman, Wolfe, and Spaulding, 1991). Family investments can take the form of money or time investments. Having a higher income enables families to provide more educationally-enhancing materials and experiences for their children. Children from more affluent families have greater access to books and educational toys, and participate in more enriching activities outside of school, such as music lessons and summer camps (Bradley, Corwyn, McAdoo, and Coll, 2001; Waldfogel, 2012).

Higher-SES parents also spend more time in child-care than lower-SES parents, and spend more of this time engaging in developmentally-enriching activities (Guryan, Hurst, and Kearney, 2008; Phillips, 2011). College-educated mothers spend around two more hours per week caring for their children than non-college educated mothers; they also spend more time reading to their children and less time watching television with them (Sayer, Bianchi, and Robinson, 2004).

Differences in the activities that parents and children engage in contribute to differences in children's language-learning environments. Studies have shown that bookreading interactions promote higher quantity and quality of child-directed speech – including more lexical diversity, grammatical complexity, and episodes of joint attention (Gilkerson, Richards, and Topping, 2015; Hoff-Ginsberg, 1991; Soderstrom and Wittebolle, 2013; Yont, Snow, and Vernon-Feagans, 2003). Consistent with this, the frequency of parental engagement in enriching activities with their children is related to differences in child development, and has been shown to mediate relations between family SES and children's cognitive and language outcomes (Boyce, Gillam, Innocenti, Cook, and Ortiz, 2013; Lugo-Gil and Tamis-LeMonda, 2008; Tomopoulos et al., 2006; Waldfogel and Washbrook, 2011).

Though differences in parental investment have traditionally been attributed to differential access to resources (Foster, 2002), differences in how parents spend time with their children may also stem from differences in parental beliefs (Kohn, 1963). In her ethnographic study of social class and parenting styles, Lareau (2003) characterized middle-class and working-class parents as conforming to different cultural logics of childrearing. According to Lareau, middle-class parents view childrearing as "concerted cultivation", in which their role as parents involves transmitting skills and knowledge to their children. Middle class parents thus engage with their children in activities thought to develop their interests and talents. In contrast, working-class parents believe in the "accomplishment of natural growth" – the idea that as long as they provide love and basic care, their children will grow and thrive. As a result, working-class children participate in many fewer organized activities than middle-class children, but have more free time to develop ties within their extended family. Quantitative studies have provided evidence that supports this link between parental beliefs about child development and their provision of cognitive stimulation in the home (Benasich and Brooks-Gunn, 1996).

Research has also found that parents from different sociocultural groups have different beliefs about the role they play in children's communicative development. In her ethnographic study of two different working-class communities in the southeastern United States, Heath (1983) observed differences in parents' verbal interactions with infants that were based on parental beliefs about children as communicative partners. Parents in an African American community, who rarely spoke with their babies or responded to child utterances, held beliefs that adults cannot make babies talk and that children will 'come to know' on their own. Parents in a Caucasian community displayed beliefs that emphasized the role of parents in teaching their children to do and say the right thing; accordingly, they spoke with their babies often and labeled objects for their children. In a more recent study with an urban sample, Rowe (2008) found that parents' knowledge and beliefs about child development mediated the relation between SES and the amount and quality of caregiver speech to children.

Thus, family circumstances associated with SES, such as parental stress and depression, availability of time and resources, and beliefs, can lead to differences in global aspects of parenting, which in turn contribute to disparities in child development. We now turn to a discussion of how these factors may also shape specific aspects of parent-child communicative interactions that directly affect language learning.

4 How language experience shapes language development

One of the most significant differences in the early experiences of lower- and higher-SES children is the amount and nature of the language input they experience. Hart and Risley (1995) estimated that by 36 months, children from high-SES families had heard 30 million more words directed to them than those growing up in poverty, a stunning difference that predicted important long-term outcomes. Other studies have shown that in interactions with their children, higher-SES mothers gesture more, use more diverse vocabulary and more complex syntax, ask more questions and use fewer directives, and respond more contingently to their infants' vocalizations than do lower SES mothers (Hart and Risley, 1995; Hoff-Ginsberg, 1998; Huttenlocher, Waterfall, Vasilyeva, Vevea, and Hedges, 2010; Rowe and Goldin-Meadow, 2009; Rowe, 2012). These differences in the quantity and quality of language input have been shown to predict differences in children's lexical and grammatical development, both between- and within-SES groups (Hirsh-Pasek et al., 2015; Hoff, 2003; Huttenlocher, Haight, Bryk, Seltzer, and Lyons, 1991; Huttenlocher et al., 2010; Pan, Rowe, Singer, and Snow, 2005; Rowe and Goldin-Meadow, 2009).

How is it that exposure to higher quantity and quality of language input promotes children's language development? One explanation for how exposure to child-directed speech is associated with faster vocabulary growth is that more language from caregivers provides children with more models to learn from as they begin to build a lexicon. Children who hear more speech from their caregivers are exposed to more different words and to more instances of those words in a variety of linguistic and extralinguistic contexts. Thus, they have more opportunities to learn new word forms as well as more information to figure out the meanings of these words (Hoff and Naigles, 2002).

There is compelling evidence that sheer amount of exposure is an important factor in vocabulary development. Children who are exposed to more speech from their parents exhibit faster growth in vocabulary than children with less exposure (Hart and Risley, 1995; Huttenlocher et al., 1991). In addition, studies have found that content words that appear more frequently in child-directed speech are learned earlier than less frequently encountered words (Goodman, Dale, and Li, 2008; Huttenlocher et al., 1991; Roy, Frank, DeCamp, Miller, and Roy, 2015).

The role of frequency in shaping learning has also been demonstrated in experimental studies. In a laboratory task that varied the frequency of novel words presented to children, frequently presented words were more likely to be learned than infrequently presented words (Schwartz and Terrell, 1983). Similar frequency effects have been observed in children with language disorders and in second-language learners. A study with children with specific language impairment (SLI) found that novel words that were presented ten times each resulted in better word learning and retention than those that were presented three times each (Rice, Oetting, Marquis, Bode, and Pae, 1994).

While the sheer amount of exposure is clearly important, there is evidence that the diversity of caregiver speech is also related to children's vocabulary and syntactic development. The number of different words caregivers use predicts children's early vocabulary competence and rate of vocabulary growth (Hoff and Naigles, 2002; Pan et al., 2005; Rowe, 2012). Rowe (2012) found that after controlling for SES, quantity of child-directed speech, and children's previous vocabulary skill, parents' use of diverse and sophisticated vocabulary with their toddlers predicted later vocabulary ability. Hart and Risley (1995) also reported that the number of different nouns and modifiers that parents used per hour was strongly correlated with children's language accomplishments at age three. In addition, the degree of syntactic diversity in caregiver speech is related to children's lexical and syntactic growth. Studies have shown that the number of different syntactic structures caregivers use in interaction with their children predicts the use of more syntactic forms in children's later productions (Huttenlocher et al., 2010).

In addition to frequency and diversity, the kinds of linguistic environments in which words are encountered also affect vocabulary learning. Words heard in isolation, in utterance-final position, and in shorter sentences tend to be learned earlier, possibly because these contexts simplify segmentation (Brent and Siskind, 2001; Naigles and Hoff-Ginsberg, 1998; Roy et al., 2015). Verbs that are heard in more diverse syntactic environments are also learned earlier than those that are heard just as frequently but in fewer syntactic environments (De Villiers, 1985; Naigles and Hoff-Ginsberg, 1998). Given that linguistic context can offer cues to a word's grammatical role (Redington, Chater, and Finch, 1998; Weisleder and Waxman, 2010), exposure to a word in multiple syntactic environments may help children in accurately inferring its meaning.

Studies have also found that children whose mothers produce longer and more complex utterances have more advanced syntactic skills (Hoff-Ginsberg, 1998; Huttenlocher et al., 2002). Huttenlocher and colleagues found that parents who used a higher frequency and proportion of multi-clause sentences had children who also used a higher proportion of multi-clause sentences in their spontaneous speech at home and in school. Moreover, they found that the proportion of multi-clause utterances in parents' speech was related to children's *comprehension* of complex sentences, suggesting that exposure to complex speech influences children's ability to understand and process more complex syntactic structures.

In addition to differences in the quantity and quality of child-directed speech, the number of gestures adults use in communication with their infants is also related to children's vocabulary size (Rowe and Goldin-Meadow, 2009; Rowe, Ozcaliskan, and Goldin-Meadow, 2008). A study with low-income U.S. mothers found that the number of maternal pointing gestures predicted growth in children's productive vocabularies from 14 to 36 months (Pan et al., 2005). Moreover, Rowe and Goldin-Meadow (2009) found that controlling for SES and parental word types, the number of different gestures parents used was related to infants' gesture use at 14 months, which in turn predicted vocabulary size at school entry. This suggests that parent gesture may complement parental speech in promoting the development of vocabulary.

Another explanation for how exposure to language input promotes language development emphasizes socio-pragmatic aspects of conversation, such as joint attention and maternal responsiveness (Akhtar and Tomasello, 2000; Tamis-LeMonda, Bornstein, and Baumwell, 2001). This view emphasizes the role of the interactive context, suggesting that language learning will be most productive in situations in which an adult's communicative intentions can be inferred (Baldwin, 1995; Tomasello, 2003). Consistent with this view, studies have shown that while exposure to speech directed to the child is positively related to lexical development, speech that is overheard by the child is not associated with vocabulary size (Shneidman, Arroyo, Levine, and Goldin-Meadow, 2013; Weisleder and Fernald, 2013). Moreover, the use of 'parentese' (Fernald and Kuhl, 1987) during one-on-one interactions between adults and infants appears to be particularly beneficial to infants' speech development (Ramírez-Esparza, García-Sierra, and Kuhl, 2014).

Also in support of this view, studies have shown that provision of prompt, contingent and appropriate responses to children's communicative attempts are associated with infants' language growth (Gros-Louis, West, and King, 2014; McGillion et al., 2013; Rollins, 2003; Tamis-LeMonda et al., 2001). Children of more responsive mothers have been found to reach language milestones earlier than children of less responsive mothers (Tamis-LeMonda et al., 2001). In a study of British mothers and their 9-month-old infants, maternal utterances that were both semantically appropriate and temporally linked to infants' vocalizations were related to infants' expressive vocabulary at 18 months (McGillion et al., 2013). Another study found that mothers' sensitive responses to their infants' mother-directed vocalizations predicted infants' productive vocabulary and gesture at 15 months, as well as an increase in infants' production of developmentally advanced vocalizations (Gros-Louis et al., 2014). In addition to these observational studies, experimental studies of infants' vocal development have shown that social feedback that is contingent on infants' vocalizations leads to an increase in infants' production of more phonologically advanced vocalizations (Goldstein, King, and West, 2003; Goldstein and Schwade, 2008).

Parents who respond often to their child's vocalizations also tend to provide more input that is contingent on the child's focus of attention. Hart and Risley (1995) observed that when parents responded to their infants' vocalizations they tended to elaborate on a child-chosen topic, while in initiations they tended to shift the child's attention to a new topic. This is important because speech that is semantically contingent is easier for the child to interpret. Studies have shown that the degree of semantic contingency in caregiver speech predicts children's language gains (Barnes, Gutfreund, Satterly, and Wells, 1983; McGillion et al., 2013), and experimental studies have demonstrated that recast-sentences facilitate children's learning of grammatical structures (Baker and Nelson, 1984; Nelson, Carskaddon, and Bonvillian, 1973). Studies have also shown that it is easier for children to learn new object labels when the speaker follows in on the infant's focus of attention (Tomasello and Todd, 1983), and children who spend more time in joint attention with their mothers have more advanced vocabularies than children who spend less time in episodes of joint attention (Akhtar, Dunham, and Dunham, 1991; Tomasello and Farrar, 1986). Together, these studies suggest that caregiver speech that follows the child's attentional focus and is contingent on the child's previous vocalizations is especially conducive to language learning.

5 Processing skills that mediate the uptake of linguistic input

The previous two sections described how differences in children's family environments and in early language experiences are related to differences in language knowledge, but another possibility is that these experiences also shape the underlying information-processing skills that facilitate language learning. Some researchers have explored how infants' emerging ability to process social information – such as eye gaze, expression of emotion, and ability to share attention – underlie children's language growth (Akhtar and Tomasello, 2000; Brooks and Meltzoff, 2005). Many important questions remain regarding environmental factors associated with SES that might shape these abilities; however, a complete discussion of this important pathway is outside the scope of this chapter.

Instead, we focus here on a growing body of research showing that infants' speech-processing skills support access to linguistic information during real-time language comprehension, and thereby affect their ability to learn language from the input. We then propose that these processing skills are themselves shaped by early language experience (Hurtado, Marchman, and Fernald, 2008; Weisleder and Fernald, 2013, 2014).

A number of studies have shown that variability in early speech processing explains differences in children's language development (Benasich and Tallal, 2002; Singh, Reznick, and Xuehua, 2012; Tsao, Liu, and Kuhl, 2004; Vouloumanos and Curtin, 2014). Infants' rapid auditory processing skill at 7.5 months predicts later vocabulary size (Benasich and Tallal, 2002), suggesting that this skill may constrain infants' ability to learn from incoming speech. Studies have also shown that early speech perception and segmentation skills are related to concurrent and later language outcomes (for a review, see Cristia, Seidl, Junge, Soderstrom, and Hagoort, 2013). In particular, infants' discrimination of phonetic contrasts in their native language – but not their discrimination of nonnative contrasts – is related to vocabulary size during the second year and to more advanced language skills in the third year (Kuhl, Conboy, Padden, Nelson, and Pruitt, 2005; Tsao et al., 2004). This suggests that infants' attunement to language-specific contrasts, and reduced sensitivity to non-native contrasts, is a positive predictor of language growth.

While these studies have focused on infants' abilities to process sounds independent of their meaning, research by Anne Fernald and colleagues has sought to understand how children learn to make sense of spoken language from moment to moment. The "looking-while-listening" (LWL) paradigm (Fernald, Zangl, Portillo, and Marchman, 2008) is an experimental procedure for monitoring the time course of spoken language comprehension by young language learners. In the LWL task, infants look at pairs of images while listening to speech naming one of the pictures, and their gaze patterns are video-recorded as the sentence unfolds. Using this paradigm, studies have shown that infants' speed and accuracy in processing familiar words and identifying their referents in the visual scene increases substantially over the second year (Fernald, Pinto, Swingley, Weinberg, and McRoberts, 1998; Hurtado, Marchman, and Fernald, 2007). In addition, individual differences in children's efficiency in real-time language processing relates to gains in other areas of linguistic competence: children who are faster and more accurate in recognizing familiar words in fluent speech are also more advanced in lexical and grammatical development, and exhibit faster growth in vocabulary over the second year (Fernald, Perfors, and Marchman, 2006). Furthermore, children's speed of spoken word recognition accounts for unique variance in standardized tests of expressive language, IQ, and working memory at 8 years of age, showing that processing speed in infancy predicts long-term language and cognitive outcomes (Marchman and Fernald, 2008). Similar relations have been found in late-talking infants at risk for later language delay (Fernald and Marchman, 2012), and in children born preterm (Marchman, Adams, Loi, Fernald and Feldman, 2015). Thus, studies have shown links between early processing speed and later language proficiency in distinct populations of children facing special challenges in language learning, underscoring the broad and fundamental significance of these developmental relations.

But where do individual differences in language processing efficiency come from? Some studies have explored the genetic bases of variation in language outcomes, with particular emphasis on the finding that persistent language disorders are more concentrated in some families than others (e.g., Dale, Price, Bishop, and Plomin, 2003). While it is clear that both environmental and genetic factors must both make major contributions to children's outcomes, a recent emphasis has been to understand how and why environmental factors impact learning, especially in vulnerable sub-populations of children known to be at risk for academic difficulties, such as children from families low in socioeconomic status (Bishop, 2006; Hoff, 2013).

Research by Fernald and colleagues asked whether children's early experience with language shapes critical processing skills in two different studies. In a first study, Hurtado, Marchman, and Fernald (2008) recorded 27 low-SES Latina mothers and their infants in a laboratory play session at 18 months. The children were also tested longitudinally at 18 and 24 months in real-time processing of familiar nouns, and parental report of vocabulary was collected. The study showed that children of mothers who talked more and used more varied language had larger vocabularies at 24 months. But the new and more interesting finding was that features of maternal talk also predicted children's skill in lexical processing: infants who heard more and more varied speech were faster in spoken word recognition at 24 months, indicating that caregiver talk is related not only to children's vocabularies but also to their efficiency in real-time language processing.

In a more recent study, this research was extended in two important ways (Weisleder and Fernald, 2013): First, rather than relying on short samples of mothers' speech in dyadic interactions with infants, we collected more extensive and representative recordings of infants' language environments during a 10-hour day at home, capturing children's interactions with different family members in diverse settings and activities. Second, we used unobtrusive technology to record families in their natural home environments, minimizing artifacts introduced by the presence of an observer or by parents' reactions to an unfamiliar laboratory setting.

We tested 29 children from low-SES Spanish-speaking families. To measure the amount of adult speech children were routinely exposed to, audio-recordings were made during a typical day at home when the child was 19 months old. These audio-recordings were made using a LENA™ digital language processor (DLP; www.lenafoundation.org), a device that is placed in the chest pocket of specialized clothing worn by the child and is designed to record the audio environment surrounding the child for up to 16 hours (Ford, Baer, Xu, Yapanel, and Gray, 2009). LENA (Language ENvironment Analysis) software provided estimates of different components of the infant's language environment, including the number of adult word tokens potentially accessible to the child and the number of speech-like vocalizations produced by the child (Oller et al., 2010; Xu et al., 2008). Native Spanish-speaking coders then listened to the recordings in order to differentiate between speech directed to the target child and speech directed to other adults or children nearby, allowing us to examine the contributions of "child-directed speech" and "overheard speech" independently. Children's language-processing efficiency was assessed at 19 and 24 months in the LWL procedure, and parental report of vocabulary was collected at 24 months.

We found striking variability among these low-SES families in the total amount of speech directed to infants – ranging from more than 12,000 words to fewer than 700 words over a 10-hour day – and these differences in child-directed speech were related to later vocabulary. Exposure to child-directed speech also predicted children's language-processing efficiency at 24 months, as assessed in the LWL task. Importantly, this link remained significant when controlling for infants' earlier processing skill and concurrent vocabulary, suggesting a specific relation between exposure to child-directed speech and infants' gains in processing efficiency from 19 to 24 months.

We then used mediation analysis to examine whether differences in processing skill helped explain the relation between child-directed speech and later vocabulary knowledge. We found that processing efficiency at 19 months mediated the link between child-directed speech and 24-month vocabulary. This suggests that a critical step in the path from early language experience to later vocabulary knowledge is the influence of language exposure on infants' speech-processing efficiency. We propose that infants who hear more talk have more opportunities to exercise skills such as segmenting speech and accessing lexical representations that are vital to word learning. As a result, infants with more exposure to child-directed speech are faster and more accurate to orient to familiar words in real time, enabling them to learn new words more quickly and facilitating vocabulary growth.

6 Conclusions

In this chapter, we reviewed an extensive body of research examining how SES shapes children's early environments, leading to differences in language development between children from higher- and lower-SES backgrounds. We examined two pathways by which SES can lead to differences in parenting, broadly speaking, and in children's opportunities for learning language more specifically. We then examined how these differences in children's language-learning experiences affect not only the development of vocabulary and grammar, but also shape processing skills that support language learning. By examining both broad environmental factors that influence children's cognitive, social, and emotional development, as well as specific properties of the language environment that play a more direct role in language-learning, we have moved closer to understanding the mechanisms underlying the relation between SES and the development of verbal proficiency.

One central insight emerging from this research is that SES influences language development through multiple and mutually influential pathways. A long history of research has identified features of parent-child interactions that provide important supports for language learning. Our ongoing studies are continuing to explore the hypothesis that engaging in verbal interactions with caregivers also provides opportunities for exercise in interpreting language, tuning perceptual and attentional capacities that enable more efficient processing of the speech stream. In this way, exposure to child-directed speech enhances the efficiency with which children learn the fine-grained regularities of their native language and which form the foundation for continued lexical and grammatical growth. We hope that such insights will continue to inform other studies exploring variation in the language-learning trajectories of children from diverse populations who may experience different kinds of learning environments, as well as in children who may be at increased risk for language delays.

References

Akhtar, Nameera, Frances Dunham & Philip J. Dunham. 1991. Directive interactions and early vocabulary development: The role of joint attentional focus. *Journal of Child Language* 18(1). 41–49.

Akhtar, Nameera, & Tomasello, Michael. 2000. The social nature of words and word learning. In Roberta Micknick Golinkoff & Kathryn Hirsh-Pasek (eds.), *Becoming a word learner: A debate on lexical acquisition*. Oxford: Oxford University Press.

Laura Gutermuth Anthony, Bruno J. Anthony, Denise N. Glanville, Daniel Q. Naiman, Christine Waanders & Stephanie Shaffer. 2005. The relationships between parenting stress, parenting behaviour and preschoolers' social competence and behaviour problems in the classroom. *Infant and Child Development* 14(2). 133–154.

Arriaga, Rose I. Larry Fenson, Terry Cronan & Stephen J. Pethick. 1998. Scores on the MacArthur Communicative Development Inventory of children from low and middle-income families. *Applied Psycholinguistics* 19(02). 209.

Baker, Nancy D. & Keith E. Nelson. 1984. Recasting and related conversational techniques for triggering syntactic advances by young children. *First Language* 5(13). 3–21.

Baldwin, Dare A. 1995. Understanding the link between joint attention and language. In Chris Moore & Philip J. Dunham (eds.), *Joint attention: Its origins and role in development*. Hillsdale, NJ: Lawrence Erlbaum.

Barnes, Sally, Mary Gutfreund, David Satterly & Gordon Wells. 1983. Characteristics of adult speech which predict children's language development. *Journal of Child Language* 10(01). 65–84.

Benasich, April Ann & Jeanne Brooks-Gunn. 1996. Maternal attitudes and knowledge of child-rearing: Associations with family and child outcomes. *Child Development* 67(3). 1186–1205.

Benasich, April Ann & Paula Tallal. 2002. Infant discrimination of rapid auditory cues predicts later language impairment. *Behavioural Brain Research* 136(1). 31–49.

Bergelson, Elika & Daniel Swingley. 2013. Young toddlers' word comprehension is flexible and efficient. *PloS One* 8(8). e73359.

Bishop, Dorothy V.M. 2006. What causes specific language impairment in children? *Current Directions in Psychological Science: A Journal of the American Psychological Society* 15(5). 217–221.

Boyce, Lisa K. Sandra L. Gillam, Mark S. Innocenti, Gina A. Cook & Eduardo Ortiz. 2013. An examination of language input and vocabulary development of young Latino dual language learners living in poverty. *First Language* 33(6). 572–593.

Bradley, Robert H. & Corwyn, F. Robert. 2002. Socioeconomic status and child development. *Annual Review of Psychology* 53. 371–399.

Bradley, Robert H. Robert F. Corwyn, Harriette Pipes McAdoo & Cynthia García Coll. 2001. The home environments of children in the United States Part I: Variations by age, ethnicity, and poverty status. *Child Development* 72(6). 1844–1867.

Brent, Michael R. & Jeffrey Mark Siskind. 2001. The role of exposure to isolated words in early vocabulary development. *Cognition* 81(2). B33–44.

Brooks, Rechele & Andrew N. Meltzoff. 2005. The development of gaze following and its relation to language. *Developmental Science* 8(6). 535–43.

Brooks-Gunn, Jeanne & Lisa B. Markman. 2005. The contribution of parenting to ethnic and racial gaps in school readiness. *The Future of Children* 15(1). 139–68.

Nathaniel, Hendren, Turner Nicholas, Kline Patrick, Saez Emmanuel & Chetty Raj. 2014. Is the United States still a land of opportunity? Recent trends in intergenerational mobility. *The American Economic Review* 104(5). 141–147.

Conger, Rand D. Katherine J. Conger, Glen H. Elder, Frederick O. Lorenz, Ronald L. Simons & Les B. Whitbeck. 1999. A family process model of economic hardship and adjustment of early adolescent boys. *Child Development* 63(3). 526–41.

Conger, Rand D. John A. McCarty, Raymond K. Yang, Benjamin B. Lahey & Joseph P. Kropp. 1984. Perception of child, child-rearing values, and emotional distress as mediating links between environmental stressors and observed maternal behavior. *Child Development* 55(6). 2234–2247.

Alejandrina, Cristia, Amanda Seidl, Caroline Junge, Melanie Soderstrom & Peter Hagoort. 2013. Predicting individual variation in language from infant speech perception measures. *Child Development* 85(4). 1330–45.

Dale, Philip S. Thomas S. Price, Dorothy V.M. Bishop, & Robert Plomin. 2003. Outcomes of Early Language Delay: I. Predicting Persistent and Transient Language Difficulties at 3 and 4 Years. *Journal of Speech, Language, and Hearing Research* 46(3). 544–560.

De Villiers, Jill G. 1985. Learning how to use verbs: Lexical coding and the influence of the input. *Journal of Child Language* 12(03). 587–595.

Dickinson David K. Roberta M. Golinkoff & Kathy Hirsh-Pasek. 2010. Speaking Out for Language: Why Language Is Central to Reading Development. *Educational Researcher* 39(4). 305–310.

Dollaghan Christine A. Thomas F. Campbell, Jack L. Paradise, Heidi M. Feldman, Janine E. Janosky, Dayna N. Pitcairn, & Marcia Kurs-Lasky. 1999. Maternal education and measures of early speech and language. *Journal of Speech, Language and Hearing Research* 42(6). 1432–1443.

Duncan, Greg J., Chantelle J. Dowsett, Amy Claessens, Katherine Magnuson, Aletha C. Huston, Pamela Klebanov, Linda S. Pagani Leon Feinstein, Mimi Engel, Jeanne Brooks-Gunn, Holly Sexton, Kathryn Duckworth & Crista Japel. 2007. School readiness and later achievement. *Developmental Psychology* 43(6). 1428–1446.

Dunn, Lloyd M., Leota M. Dunn, Stephan Bulheller & Hartmut Hacker. 1997. *Peabody Picture Vocabulary Test (3rd edn.)*. Circle Pines, MN: American Guidance Service.

Durham, Rachel E. George Farkas, Carol Scheffner, Bruce Hammer, J. Tomblin & Hugh W. Catts. 2007. Kindergarten oral language skill: A key variable in the intergenerational transmission of socioeconomic status. *Research in Social Stratification and Mobility* 25(4). 294–305.

Engle, Patrice L. & Maureen M. Black. 2008. The effect of poverty on child development and educational outcomes. *Annals of the New York Academy of Sciences* 1136. 243–256.

Evans, Gary W. 2004. The environment of childhood poverty. *American Psychologist* 59(2). 77–92.

Evans, Gary W. 2006. Child development and the physical environment. *Annual Review of Psychology* 57. 423–451.

Farkasa, George & Kurt Beron. 2004. The detailed age trajectory of oral vocabulary knowledge: Differences by class and race. *Social Science Research* 33(3). 464–497.

Fernald, Anne & Patricia Kuhl. 1987. Acoustic determinants of infant preference for motherese speech. *Infant Behavior and Development* 10(3). 279–293.

Fernald, Anne & Virginia A. Marchman. 2012. Individual differences in lexical processing at 18 months predict vocabulary growth in typically developing and late-talking toddlers. *Child Development* 83(1). 203–222.

Fernald, Anne, Virginia A. Marchman & Adriana Weisleder. 2013. SES differences in language processing skill and vocabulary are evident at 18 months. *Developmental Science* 16(2). 234–248.

Fernald, Anne, Amy Perfors & Virginia A. Marchman. 2006. Picking up speed in understanding: Speech processing efficiency and vocabulary growth across the 2nd year. *Developmental Psychology* 42(1). 98–116.

Fernald, Anne, John P. Pinto, Daniel Swingley, Amy Weinbergy & Gerald W. McRoberts. 1998. Rapid gains in speed of verbal processing by infants in the 2nd year. *Psychological Science* 9(3). 228–231.

Fernald, Anne, Renate Zangl, Ana L. Portillo & Virginia A. Marchman. 2008. Looking while listening: Using eye movements to monitor spoken language comprehension by infants and young children. In Irina A. Sekerina, Eva M. Fernández & Harald Clahsen (Eds.), *Developmental psycholinguistics: On-line methods in children's language processing*, 97–135. Philadelphia: John Benjamins Pub.

Fernald, Lia C.H. Ann Weber, Emanuela Galasso & Lisy Ratsifandrihamanana. 2011. Socioeconomic gradients and child development in a very low income population: Evidence from Madagascar. *Developmental Science* 14(4). 832–47.

Ford, Michael, Charles T. Baer, Dongxin Xu, Umit Yapanel & Sharmi Gray. 2009. *The LENA Language Environment Analysis System: Audio Specifications of the DLP-0121.*

Foster, Michael E. 2002. How economists think about family resources and child development. *Child Development* 73(6). 1904–1914.

Gardner-Neblett, Nicole & Iheoma U. Iruka. 2015. Oral narrative skills: Explaining the language-emergent literacy link by race/ethnicity and SES. *Developmental Psychology* 51(7). 889–904.

Gilkerson, Jill, Jeffrey A. Richards & Keith J. Topping. 2015. The impact of book reading in the early years on parent-child language interaction. *Journal of Early Childhood Literacy* 17(1). 1–19.

Goldstein, Michael H. Andrew P. King & Meredith J. West. 2003. Social interaction shapes babbling: Testing parallels between birdsong and speech. *Proceedings of the National Academy of Sciences of the United States of America* 100(13). 8030–8035.

Goldstein, Michael H. & Jennifer A. Schwade. 2008. Social feedback to infants' babbling facilitates rapid phonological learning. *Psychological Science* 19(5). 515–523.

Goodman, Judith C. Philip S. Dale & Ping Li. 2008. Does frequency count? Parental input and the acquisition of vocabulary. *Journal of Child Language* 35(3). 515–531.

Gros-Louis, Julie, Meredith J. West & Andrew P. King. 2014. Maternal responsiveness and the development of directed vocalizing in social interactions. *Infancy* 19(4). 385–408.

Guryan, Jonathan, Erik Hurst & Melissa Kearney. 2008. Parental education and parental time with children. *Journal of Economic Perspectives* 22(3). 23–46.

Hart, Betty & Todd R. Risley. 1995. *Meaningful differences in the everyday experience of young American children.* Baltimore, MD: Brookes Publishing Co.

Haveman, Robert, Barbara Wolfe & James Spaulding. 1991. Childhood events and circumstances influencing high school completion. *Demography* 28(l). 133–157.

Heath, Brice Shirley. 1983. *Ways with words: Language, life, and work in communities and classrooms.* Cambridge: Cambridge University Press.

Hirsh-Pasek, Kathy, Lauren B. Adamson, Roger Bakeman, Margaret Tresch Owen, Roberta Michnick Golinkoff, Amy Pace, Paula KS Yust & Katharine Suma. 2015. The contribution of early communication quality to low-income children's language success. *Psychological Science* 26(7). 1071–1083.

Hoff Erika. 2003. The specificity of environmental influence: Socioeconomic status affects early vocabulary development via maternal speech. *Child Development* 74(5). 1368–1378.

Hoff Erika. 2013. Interpreting the early language trajectories of children from low-SES and language minority homes: Implications for closing achievement gaps. *Developmental Psychology* 49. 1–4.

Hoff, Erika & Letitia Naigles. 2002. How children use input to acquire a lexicon. *Child Development* 73. 418–433.

Hoff-Ginsberg, Erika. 1991. Mother-child conversation in different social classes and communicative settings. *Child Development* 62. 782–796.

Hoff-Ginsberg, Erika. 1998. The relation of birth order and socioeconomic status to children's language experience and language development. *Applied Psycholinguistics* 19(04). 603–629.

Hurtado, Nereyda, Virginia A. Marchman & Anne Fernald. 2007. Spoken word recognition by Latino children learning Spanish as their first language. *Journal of Child Language* 33. 227–249.

Hurtado, Nereyda, Virginia A. Marchman, & Anne Fernald. 2008. Does input influence uptake? Links between maternal talk, processing speed and vocabulary size in Spanish-learning children. *Developmental Science* 11(6). F31–F39.

Huttenlocher, Janellen, Wendy Haight, Anthony Bryk, Michael Seltzer & Thomas Lyons. 1991. Early vocabulary growth: Relation to language input and gender. *Developmental Psychology* 27(2). 236–248.

Hutttenlocher, Janellen, Marina Vasilyeva, Elina Cymerman & Susan Levine. 2002. Language input and child syntax. *Cognitive Psychology* 45(3). 337–374.

Huttenlocher, Janellen, Heidi Waterfall, Marina Vasilyeva, Jack Vevea & Larry V. Hedges. V. 2010. Sources of variability in children's language growth. *Cognitive Psychology* 61(4). 343–65.

Kaplan, Peter S. Christina M. Danko, Kevin D. Everhart, Andres Diaz, Ryan M. Asherin, JoAnn M. Vogeli & Shiva M. Fekri. 2014. Maternal depression and expressive communication in one-year-old infants. *Infant Behavior & Development* 37(3). 398–405.

Kohn, Melvin L. 1963. Social Class and parent-child relationships: An interpretation. *American Journal of Sociology* 68(4). 471–480.

Kuhl, Patricia K. Barbara T. Conboy, Denise Padden, Tobey Nelson & Jessica Pruitt. 2005. Speech perception and later language development: Implications for the "Critical Period." *Language, Learning and Development* 1(3–4). 237–264.

Lareau, Annette. 2003. *Unequal childhoods: Class, race, and family life*. Berkeley: University of California Press.

Lee, Joanne. 2010. Size matters: Early vocabulary as a predictor of language and literacy competence. *Applied Psycholinguistics* 32(01). 69–92.

Lee, Valerie E. & David T. Burkam. 2002. *Inequality at the starting gate: Social background differences in achievement as children begin school*. Washington, DC: Economic Policy Institute.

Linver, Miriam R. Jeanne Brooks-Gunn & Dafna E. Kohen. 2002. Family processes as pathways from income to young children's development. *Developmental Psychology* 38(5). 719–734.

Lugo-Gil, Julieta & Catherine S. Tamis-LeMonda. 2008. Family resources and parenting quality: Links to children's cognitive development across the first 3 years. *Child Development* 79(4). 1065–1085.

Marchman, Virginia A., Katherine A. Adams, Elizabeth C. Loi, Anne Fernald & Heidi M. Feldman. 2015. Early language processing efficiency predicts later receptive vocabulary outcomes in children born preterm. *Child Neuropsychology* 22(6). 649–665.

Marchman, Virginia A. & Anne Fernald. 2008. Speed of word recognition and vocabulary knowledge in infancy predict cognitive and language outcomes in later childhood. *Developmental Science* 11(3). F9–F16.

McGillion, Michelle L. Jane S. Herbert, Julian M. Pine, Tamar Keren-Portnoy, Marilyn M. Vihman & Danielle E. Matthews. 2013. Supporting early vocabulary development: What sort of responsiveness matters? *IEEE Transactions on Autonomous Mental Development* 5(3). 240–248.

McLoyd, Vonnie C. 1990. The impact of economic hardship on black families and children: Psychological distress, parenting, and socioemotional development. *Child Development* 61(2). 311–46.

Morgan, Paul L., George Farkas, Marianne M. Hillemeier, Carol Scheffner Hammer & Steve Maczuga. 2015. 24-month-old children with larger oral vocabularies display greater academic and behavioral functioning at kindergarten entry. *Child Development* 86. 1351–1370.

Morisset, Colleen E. Kathryn E. Barnard, Mark T. Greenberg, Cathryn L. Booth & Susan J. Spieker. 1990. Environmental influences on early language development: The context of social risk. *Development and Psychopathology* 2. 127–149.

Naigles, Letitia R. & Erika Hoff-Ginsberg. 1998. Why are some verbs learned before other verbs? Effects of input frequency and structure on children's early verb use. *Journal of Child Language* 25(01). 95–120.

Nelson, Keith E. Gaye Carskaddon & John D. Bonvillian. 1973. Syntax acquisition: Impact of experimental variation in adult verbal interaction with the child. *Child Development* 44(3). 497–504.

Nelson, Keith E. Janet A. Welsh, Elisabeth M. Vance Trup & Mark T. Greenberg. 2011. Language delays of impoverished preschool children in relation to early academic and emotion recognition skills. *First Language* 31(2). 164–194.

Oller, Kimbrough D., P. Niyogi, S. Gray, J. A. Richards, J. Gilkerson, D. Xu, U. Yapanel & S. F. Warren. 2010. Automated vocal analysis of naturalistic recordings from children with autism, language delay, and typical development. *Proceedings of the National Academy of Sciences of the United States of America* 107(30). 13354–13359.

Pan, Barbara Alexander, Meredith L. Rowe, Judith D. Singer & Catherine E. Snow. 2005. Maternal correlates of growth in toddler vocabulary production in low-income families. *Child Development* 76. 763–82.

Phillips, Meredith. 2011. Parenting, time use, and disparities in academic outcomes. In Greg J. Duncan & Richard J. Murnane (Eds.), *Whither opportunity? Rising inequality, schools, and children's life chances*, 207–228. New York, USA: Russell Sage Foundation.

Ramírez-Esparza, Nairán, Adrián García-Sierra & Patricia K. Kuhl. 2014. Look who's talking: Speech style and social context in language input to infants are linked to concurrent and future speech development. *Developmental Science* 17(6). 880–891.

Redington, Martin, Nick Chater & Steven Finch. 1998. Distributional information: A powerful cue for acquiring syntactic categories. *Cognitive Science* 22. 425–469.

Rice, Mabel L. Janna B. Oetting, Janet Marquis, John Bode & Soyeong Pae. 1994. Frequency of input effects on word comprehension of children with specific language impairment. *Journal of Speech Language and Hearing Research* 37(1). 106.

Rollins, Pamela Rosenthal. 2003. Caregivers' contingent comments to 9-month-old infants: Relationships with later language. *Applied Psycholinguistics* 24(02). 221–234.

Rowe, Meredith L. 2012. A longitudinal investigation of the role of quantity and quality of child-directed speech in vocabulary development. *Child Development* 83(5). 1762–1774.

Rowe, Meredith L. & Susan Goldin-Meadow. 2009. Differences in early gesture explain SES disparities in child vocabulary size at school entry. *Science* 323. 951–953.

Rowe, Meredith L. Şeyda Özçalışkan & Susan Goldin-Meadow. 2008. Learning words by hand: Gesture's role in predicting vocabulary development. *First Language* 28(2). 182–199.

Rowe, Meredith L. Stephen W. Raudenbush & Susan Goldin-Meadow. 2012. The pace of vocabulary growth helps predict later vocabulary skill. *Child Development* 83(2). 508–525.

Roy, Brandon C. Michael C. Frank, Philip DeCamp, Matthew Miller & Deb Roy. 2015. Predicting the birth of a spoken word. *Proceedings of the National Academy of Sciences* 112(41). 12663–12668.

Sayer, Liana C. Suzanne M. Bianchi & John P. Robinson. 2004. Are parents investing less in children? Trends in mothers' and fathers' time with children. *American Journal of Sociology* 110(1). 1–43.

Scarborough, Hollis S. 2001. Connecting early language and literacy to later reading (dis)abilities: Evidence, theory, and practice. In Susan B. Neuman & David K. Dickinson (Eds.), *The handbook of early literacy research*, 97–110. New York: Guilford Press.

Schwartz, Richard G. & Brenda Y. Terrell. 1983. The role of input frequency in lexical acquisition. *Journal of Child Language* 10. 57–64.

Shneidman, Laura A. Michelle E. Arroyo, Susan C. Levine & Susan Goldin-Meadow. 2013. What counts as effective input for word learning? *Journal of Child Language* 40. 672–686.

Shonkoff, Jack P. Andrew S. Garner, Benjamin S. Siegel, Mary I. Dobbins, Marian F. Earls, Laura McGuinn, John Pascoe & David L. Wood. 2012. The lifelong effects of early childhood adversity and toxic stress. *Pediatrics* 129(1). e232–e246.

Singh, Leher, Steven J. Reznick & Liang Xuehua. 2012. Infant word segmentation and childhood vocabulary development: A longitudinal analysis. *Developmental Science* 15(4). 482–495.

Snow, Catherine E. Susan M. Burns & Peg Griffin. 1998. *Preventing reading difficulties in young children*. Washington, DC: National Academy Press.

Soderstrom, Melanie & Kelsey Wittebolle. 2013. When do caregivers talk? The influences of activity and time of day on caregiver speech and child vocalizations in two childcare environments. *PloS One* 8(11). e80646.

Stein, Alan, L-E. Malmberg, Kathy Sylva, Jacqueline Barnes & Penelope Leach. 2008. The influence of maternal depression, caregiving, and socioeconomic status in the post-natal year on children's language development. *Child: Care, Health and Development* 34(5). 603–612.

Tamis-LeMonda, Catherine S. Marc H. Bornstein & Lisa Baumwell. 2001. Maternal responsiveness and children's achievement of language milestones. *Child Development* 72(3). 748–767.

Taylor, Nicole, Wilberta Donovan, Sally Miles, and Lewis Leavitt. 2009. Maternal control strategies, maternal language usage and children's language usage at two years. *Journal of Child Language* 36. 381–404.

Tomasello, Micharl. 2003. *Constructing a language: A usage-based theory of language acquisition*. Cambridge, MA: Harvard University Press.

Tomasello, Michael & Michael Jeffrey Farrar. 1986. Joint attention and early language. *Child Development* 57(6). 1454–1463.

Tomasello, Michael & Jody Todd. 1983. Joint attention and lexical acquisition style. *First Language* 4(12). 197–211.

Tomopoulos, Suzy, Benard P. Dreyer, Catherine Tamis-LeMonda, Virginia Flynn, Irene Rovira, Wendy Tineo & Alan L. Mendelsohn. 2006. Books, toys, parent-child interaction, and development in young Latino children. *Ambulatory Pediatrics* 6(2). 72–78.

Tsao, Feng-Ming, Huei-Mei Liu & Patricia K. Kuhl. 2004. Speech perception in infancy predicts language development in the second year of life: A longitudinal study. *Child Development* 75(4). 1067–1084.

Vasilyeva, Marina, Heidi Waterfall & Janellen Huttenlocher. 2008. Emergence of syntax: commonalities and differences across children. *Developmental Science* 11(1). 84–97.

Vouloumanos, Athena & Suzanne Curtin. 2014. Foundational tuning: How infants' attention to speech predicts language development. *Cognitive Science* 38(8). 1675–1686.

Waldfogel, Jane. 2012. The role of out-of-school factors in the literacy problem. *The future of children*, 22(2). 39–54.

Waldfogel, Jane & Elizabeth Washbrook. 2011. Early years policy. *Child Development Research* 2011.

Walker, Dale, Charles Greenwood, Betty Hart & Judith Carta. 1994. Prediction of school outcomes based on early language production and socioeconomic factors. *Child Development* 65(2). 606–621.

Weisleder, Adriana & Anne Fernald. 2013. Talking to children matters: Early language experience strengthens processing and builds vocabulary. *Psychological Science* 24(11). 2143–52.

Weisleder, Adriana & Anne Fernald. 2014. Social environments shape children's language experiences, strengthening language processing and building vocabulary. In Inbal Arnon, Marisa Casillas, Chigusa Kurumada & Bruno Estigarribia (Eds.), *Language in Interaction: Studies in honor of Eve V. Clark*, 29–49. Philadelphia: John Benjamins Publishing Co.

Weisleder, Adriana, V.A. Marchman, N. Otero & A. Fernald. 2017. Early language experience mediates SES-differences in language-processing skill and vocabulary in Spanish-learning children. International Congress for the Study of Child Language (IASCL), Lyon, France.

Weisleder, Adriana & Sandra R. Waxman. 2010. What's in the input? Frequent frames in child-directed speech offer distributional cues to grammatical categories in Spanish and English. *Journal of Child Language* 37(5). 1089–1108.

Xu, Dongxin, Umit H. Yapanel, Sharmistha S. Gray, Jill Gilkerson, Jeffrey A. Richards & John HL Hansen. 2008. Signal processing for young child speech language development. In *Workshop on Child, Computer and Interaction*. P. 20. Chania, Crete: Greece.

Yont, Kristine M., Catherine E. Snow & Lynne Vernon-Feagans. 2003. The role of context in mother–child interactions: An analysis of communicative intents expressed during toy play and book reading with 12-month-olds. *Journal of Pragmatics* 35(3). 435–454.

Kylie Schibli, Nina Hedayati, Hannah Hobbs, Amina Sheik-Ahmed and Amedeo D'Angiulli
27 Cognition and language in different socioeconomic and environmental settings

1 Introduction

During recent years, research has demonstrated that socioeconomic status (SES) should be recognized as a central determinant when studying cognitive abilities and neurodevelopment in children (Schibli and D'Angiulli 2013) but in the scientific literature, poverty, rather than SES, is generally discussed as a confounding variable (Lipina and Posner 2012). SES can be broken down into a variety of dimensions, including: education, occupation, and income. Bradley and Corwyn (2002) claim that SES is best defined as an individual's personal capital, which includes three subcomponents: financial capital or material resources; human capital, defined as non-material resources such as education; and social capital defined by social, professional or neighborhood connections. The definition of SES ranges across studies; for example, some researchers focus solely on human capital (such as the mother's education level) while others incorporate a more contextual definition by trying to incorporate all three subcomponents. Noble et al. (2005) included occupation, and ratio of income to needs in their analysis of SES; whereas, Hackman and Farah (2009) suggested SES is a compound of material wealth involving family income, and non-economic characteristics (i.e. education or prestige).

Historically, poverty is defined as absolute or relative. Absolute poverty is a fixed variable, involving a set threshold for amount of annual income, known as the line of poverty. An individual is considered of low socioeconomic status if their annual revenue falls under the poverty line. Absolute poverty is usually associated with a lack of access to basic needs of survival (i.e. clean drinking water, nutritious food, and adequate shelter). Relative poverty is more dynamic, and is based on a social standard of living. Relative poverty involves judgments of an individual's lifestyle and resources in comparison to the social norms (Foster 1998). Although SES is often defined using the three common measures of education, occupation, and income; it is a multi-factorial construct and can differ across individuals and neighborhoods.

In developmental studies, a child's SES is often measured by that of their parents. A mother's lifestyle has a large effect on her child, both prenatally and in the early years after birth (Lipina and Posner 2012). A lack of support and access to

---

Kylie Schibli, Nina Hedayati, Hannah Hobbs, Amina Sheik-Ahmed and Amedeo D'Angiulli, Carleton University

nutritionally balanced foods, compounded by the stresses associated with poverty, may influence maternal health which may lead to pre-mature births, low birth weight, fetal alcohol syndrome or other developmental disorders (Bradley and Corwyn 2002). Mothers from lower socioeconomic status have limited access to resources and support which may put their child's later development and cognitive abilities at risk.

Bradley and Corwyn (2002) argue that cognitive performance and achievement begin with the home and neighborhood environment. Low SES has been linked with less cognitive stimulation and lowered expectations and guidance for learning from parents and teachers. Low SES may result in limited access to direct and indirect learning opportunities such as reading materials, field trips or educational games. There is a higher rate of school absences among these neighborhoods as children become bored or frustrated with their education. Furthermore, the parents' level of education has been proposed as the single most predictive value of the socioeconomic effects on children's cognitive outcomes (Noble et al. 2005). Noble et al. (2005) discovered that kindergarten children's performance on a series of executive function and language tasks correlated with their parents' level of education in isolation of parental occupation and income-to-needs ratio. It is possible that parents with a higher level of education are more actively involved with their child's achievement in the school setting and are less intimidated to discuss their child's progress with teachers. As Nisbett (2009) puts it, the set of behaviors in higher-level SES parents and families fit a "cognitive culture" of interaction and exploration of the world to promote proactive knowledge-based social and communication skills. However, this seems an adaptive parental response to the environment where the children are being raised (i.e., more authoritarian approach to ensure children's safety) and should not be interpreted moralistically as demonstrating "bad" parenting in low SES families.

Outside of the home, the stigma associated with poverty may negatively influence teachers' response to low SES children, resulting in a lack of attention and positive reinforcement (Rosenthal and Jacobson 1968). This may result in a higher rate of school failure, and behavioral problems. Children from low SES communities are more likely to make poor choices as they are not receiving the same caliber of supervision and mentorship. The factors associated with living in a disadvantaged neighborhood, such as overcrowding, low social cohesion, and less child supervision, may lead to stress. This stress may cause diminished self-esteem and a loss of control over one's emotions. Physiologically, stress can rewire brain structures that are responsible for brain plasticity, neurogenesis, and memory (Lipina and Posner 2012).

Early stress associated with SES has been shown to cause lasting epigenetic modifications, leading to a changes in gene expression (Hackman, Farah, and Meany 2010). Systems including the prefrontal cortex, hippocampus, the amygdala and the hypothalamic-pituitary-adrenal (HPA) axis, are all associated with memory, executive function, and coping with stressful situations or aversive stimuli. Under stress these systems are shown to have a discrepancy in neural connectivity and white matter (Lipina and Posner 2012). The loss of connection may impair hippocampal functions in episodic, declarative, contextual, and spatial memory. This may alter the ability to process new information and make appropriate decisions when faced with unfamiliar challenges. Prenatally and during infancy individuals are sensitive to their home environment and may be influenced by maternal stress, which may lead to complications later in life (Tehranifar et al. 2013).

In recent years developmental neuroscientists have examined children's executive function and language development through the use of behavioral, functional, and structural neuroimaging measures. This chapter outlines current findings in the area of developmental neuroscience related to language and cognitive development across the socioeconomic gradient. There are thousands of studies dealing with SES in relation to child and human development, for obvious space limitations our review is selective in that focuses on developmental studies that relate to neuroscience data. In addition, language and communication is examined from a framework that integrates them within the whole neurocognitive system. As a quick preview, the empirical evidence from neuroscience suggests that the pathways through which poverty and low SES affect language and communication may not be direct, rather, they reflect changes in more general neurocognitive systems.

1.1 Language in different socioeconomic and environmental settings

Environmental settings and socioeconomic status (SES) play crucial roles in shaping the outcome of language development. These factors influence different language constructs including phonological awareness, vocabulary, syntax/grammar, and discourse development. The level of these language constructs are later associated with the progress and/or hindrance of a number of cognitive abilities, academic performance, and social mobility.

1.1.1 Phonological awareness

Phonological awareness (PA) is a fundamental language construct that predicts the trajectory of successful reading skills. PA is defined as the ability to identify words that rhyme, make new words, count syllables and separate the beginning and endings of words, and recognize each phoneme in a word (Yopp and Yopp 2000). Both environment and SES influence the development of phonological awareness. In comparison to middle and high SES, poor phonological awareness and consequently poor reading skills are generally associated with children from lower SES backgrounds (Sices et al. 2007). These children appear to have more difficulty during a phonemic deletion task, where removing a phoneme from a nonsense item would create a real word (Nittrouer 1996). The size of the disparity between low SES and mid SES appears to be increasing from the ages of 2 to 5 years (Hoff 2012). Children of high SES backgrounds are exposed to an advantaged environment as parents recognize the phonological difficulties, and provide the resources necessary to overcome them. Less advantaged parents are less likely to recognize phonological difficulties, and have more difficulty accessing the necessary resources (Noble et al. 2006).

Neuroanatomical differences have been reported linking the disparity in SES and PA. Noble et al. (2006) reported that children of higher SES backgrounds with poor phonological awareness skills had increased right perisylvian function during a reading task. This increased brain region activity during childhood may have contributed to improved reading abilities as adults. The improvement in reading throughout development may be due to an increase in literacy exposure in higher SES environments. This perisylvian function, however, did not translate over to low SES counterparts. In addition, low SES has been linked to the extent to which the left inferior frontal gyrus is activated during a language task in young children. This specifies the decrease in specialization of language function in the left hemisphere in children of low SES backgrounds. In addition, the development of a strong phonological awareness nurtured by child parent/environment interaction is correlated with the maturation of Broca's area (D'Angiulli et al. 2012). In a study with 5-year old children performing a rhyming task, Raizada et al. (2008) found that high SES was strongly correlated with degree of hemispheric specialization in Broca's area, as measured by left-minus-right fMRI activation.

1.1.2 Vocabulary

During the early years of development, the correlation between SES and vocabulary size becomes inherently evident. In one study, the average vocabulary size of 3-year-old children from high SES was more than double the size of their low SES counterparts (Hart and Risely 1995). Families from the higher SES group had professional careers, whereas the lower SES families were relying on welfare subsidies. Research has repeatedly demonstrated that this major discrepancy observed in vocabulary size is in fact representative of the difference in children from high SES and those of low SES. Previous research has indicated that the relation between SES and child vocabulary is mediated by the way in which parents talk to their children (Rowe et al. 2009).

Parents from higher SES possess an enriched vocabulary and tend to speak more often with their children, using more complex syntax (Rowe et al. 2009). This optimizes the chance that children are exposed to a variety of words. It can be assumed that parental vocabulary is conducive to the trajectory of children's vocabulary reservoir. A study conducted in China by Hoff and Tian (2005) demonstrated that although SES was predictive of five percent of language development, since SES is associated with maternal vocabulary, maternal vocabulary served as the mediating variable between SES and language. Instructing low SES mothers and early childhood educators to guide preschoolers' language skills during book reading improves early literacy and expressive vocabulary (Whitehurst et al. 1994). Alternatively, in Israeli Arabic-speaking children's families, the home literacy environment (i.e. books and writing materials) and SES level were associated with emergent literacy skills not maternal involvement (Korat et al. 2013).

1.1.3 Grammar and syntax

According to Noble et al. (2005), SES predicts only five percent variance in receptive grammar skills. Development of grammatical skills is largely associated with variability in the complexity of the speech children hear during development (Zhang et al. 2008). A study on U.S. mothers demonstrated that mothers from high SES backgrounds spoke more often, used lengthier sentences, and an enriched vocabulary when speaking with their children (Hoff-Ginsberg 1991). Children of high SES mothers developed language at a faster rate than their counterparts of mid SES mothers (Zhang et al. 2008). Syntax much like grammar demonstrates a direct relationship between early syntactic input from parent and later enhanced ability of child. Children 22 and 42 months of age produce syntax for complex sentences (Vasilyeva et al. 2008). SES, however, only predicts roughly 15% variance in productive syntax skills and no SES differences are found for simple sentences. The reason SES does not appear to make stronger contributions to syntax could be explained by Vasilyeva et al.'s (2008) study design, where SES groups were differentiated in terms of parental education. Two of the groups were fairly similar such that they both included post-secondary education in their classifications. One group included the completion of a four-year-college program and the other included the completion of a post-graduate program. If a clearer distinction was made between SES groups, it may have been possible that SES variable could have predicted more of the syntactic variance.

1.1.4 Discourse development

Discourse development will be discussed here in terms of babbling, the emergence of language, private speech, nonverbal, and verbal communication. The SES background of bilingual and monolingual infants does not appear to affect the development of precursors to speech, such as canonical babbling, which is the ability to produce well-formed syllables (Oller et al. 1997). Thus, coming from an economically disadvantaged background does not appear to delay speech development. Moreover, SES did not appear to predict late language emergence (LLE) in a study with 1776 two-year old children (Zubrik et al. 2007). Instead, significant predictors of LLE were a family history of LLE, being male, and early neurobiological growth. Although SES does not predict canonical babbling or LLE at a young age, SES does appear to play a role in a child's preschool years.

Quay and Blaney's (2002) study demonstrated that SES and age can influence private speech, nonverbal, and verbal communication in middle and lower SES preschool children. Talking to oneself during private speech in order to direct one's actions decreased from ages 4 to 5 in middle SES preschoolers, but did not change for lower SES preschoolers. As children become more confident in their abilities, they tend to use less private speech and direct their actions through silent thoughts (i.e. inner speech). Lower SES children displayed more nonverbal communication than their middle SES counterparts at both ages 4 and 5. Additionally, the lower SES children showed an increase in nonverbal communication, whereas, the middle SES children showed a decrease between ages 4 and 5. Verbal communication increased between ages 4 and 5 in both SES groups; however, the increase was greater for the middle SES group than the lower SES group.

Quay and Blaney (2002) offer the following explanation for their results: As lower SES children get older, they want to express themselves more by using verbal communication; however, since their language capabilities might not be at the same level as middle SES children, these lower SES children will engage in more non-verbal communication to express their message.

2 Neurocognition in different socioeconomic and environmental settings

Executive function involves higher order processing skills that allow us to monitor and regulate our thoughts and behavior. A prominent perspective is that the social and environmental factors associated with poverty lead to stress which interferes with cognitive function (Mani et al. 2013); whereas an alternative approach is that IQ tests and mainstream schooling show a bias towards a particular contextual upbringing impeding the ability of all children to succeed (D'Angiulli et al. 2012). The majority of studies demonstrating these findings have relied on behavioral measures; however, there has been increased interest in determining the neural mechanisms associated with these differences. Here we review research aimed at exploring neurocognitive differences in the executive function network, including: selective attention, inhibitory control, and working memory.

2.1 Selective attention and inhibitory control

Selective attention refers to the ability to divert and narrow one's focus to important information, and is increasingly necessary for children as they are continually exposed to multiple sources of stimulation. The neural mechanisms of attention are thought to reside in a communication network involving the cingulate, frontal, and parietal cortical regions referred to as the cingulo-frontal-parietal (CFP) cognitive network (see, Table 1; Bush 2011). Closely related with selective attention is inhibitory control. Inhibitory control refers to the ability to override an automatic response by actively suppressing attention to distracting information (van der Molen 2000). Therefore, selective attention and inhibitory control are not mutually exclusive and often occur simultaneously.

Development of inhibitory control is thought to follow maturation of the frontal lobes improving over time. The frontal lobes are the last region of the brain to fully develop with myelinization not complete until early adulthood. Inhibitory control is often tested using cognitive tasks involving conflict resolution, such as the Stroop task (Stroop 1935) which involves the suppression of a familiar response to the written word – reading. In this task, the individual is told to state the color the word is written in and ignore the meaning of the word. Areas of the brain activated during tasks that measure inhibition include the anterior cingulate cortex (ACC), and the dorsolateral prefrontal cortex (DLPFC) (see Table 1; Berger 2011).

Attention tasks have been designed to target brain response in these cortical areas, with a reduction in activation and an inability to perform the task observed in individuals who have neuronal damage or lesions in these regions (du Boisgueheneuc et al. 2006). The event-related potential (ERP) technique provides a means to examine the timing and degree of neuronal activation during task participation.

ERPs refer to a change in brain activity following a sensory stimulus, which can be internal (i.e. the initiation of a thought) or external (i.e. the presentation of a visual image). This non-invasive technique is known for its accuracy with timing allowing a measure for when processing takes place (Picton et al. 2000). Studies exploring the neurocognitive differences in children from lower SES backgrounds have applied this technique.

Selective attention tasks usually involve a visual or auditory target stimulus where children are asked to press a button in response to its presentation, and to withhold their response when presented with distracting stimuli. For example, Stevens, Lauinger, and Neville (2009) had children listen to two competing stories and asked that they attend to one while ignoring the other. ERP analysis demonstrated that children of mothers with a lower education level (suggested to correspond with lower SES) paid equal attention to both stories; whereas children of mothers with a higher education level (intended to represent higher SES) paid more attention to the attended story. The authors posit that this finding suggests children from lower SES may have more difficulty filtering out irrelevant information during early neuronal processing. Yet, when children were asked questions relating to the attended story, both groups were capable of answering the questions correctly to the same degree. Despite differences in brain response, behavioral performance was comparable between both groups. D'Angiulli et al., (2008, 2012) used a similar paradigm with a more comprehensive definition of SES, and obtained similar results.

Children were asked to respond to a tone by pressing a button while ignoring three similar tones. SES was determined based on a variety of parental and environmental measures, including: family income, residential quality, marital status, parental education level and occupation. ERP analysis demonstrated that children from the lower SES group paid similar attention to both types of information in contrast to the higher SES group which narrowed their focus to the relevant information. Again, performance on the task was comparable between the two groups with children showing similar response time and accuracy. Children completed self-reports on boredom to the task and provided saliva samples which were used to identify stress levels before, during, and after task participation (D'Angiulli et al. 2012). They discovered that although children from lower SES backgrounds generally had higher cortisol concentration (i.e. stress hormone) this was not related to reactivity to the task. Also, children reported similar degrees of boredom across the two groups. This would suggest that although children from different socioeconomic backgrounds show different neuronal activation, this cannot be attributed to perceived stress or emotional/motivational reactions to the task. Is it possible that these differences in brain response reflect an adaptation to the child's social environment?

Neuroplasticity is widely recognized, and it is accepted that our social and physical environment influences changes made to our brain. Children growing up in disadvantaged neighborhoods are encouraged to be vigilant and aware of their surroundings, as they may pose a threat to their safety. For some children, growing up in poverty means chaotic and unpredictable living environments (Evans et al. 2005) and witnessing community violence (Patchin 2006). These neural differences can be viewed as an adaptive response to contextual experience and provide evidence on how environment shapes the brain. Behavioral studies indicate that children from lower SES adopt a more impulsive cognitive style which may impact their ability to absorb and reflect on new information (Arán-Filippetti and Richaud de Minzi 2012). Interestingly, when children from middle SES backgrounds were provided inconsistent reinforcement in a response task, they used similar strategies as children from lower SES, providing evidence for the effect of social experience (Bresnahan and Blum 1971).

That children from lower SES backgrounds perform similarly to their more affluent counterparts on selective attention tasks suggests that they can effectively identify and respond to critical information despite attending to all sensory input. These findings suggest that children from lower SES backgrounds have learned to pay attention to everything in their surroundings which one would expect might impede their ability to complete cognitive tasks aimed at filtering out distracting information. However, despite this difference in brain activation during selective attention tasks, these children have not shown an inability to perform successfully (D'Angiulli et al. 2008, 2012; Stevens et al. 2009). ERP analysis does not allow for the examination of structural changes. An attempt to investigate the neurocognitive profile of SES has led to research examining the structural changes of the brain using techniques such as magnetic resonance imaging (MRI).

MRI is a neuroimaging technique that measures the radiation emitted from hydrogen atoms in response to a strong magnetic field. This technique allows the observation of density differences in neuron and axon-rich brain areas and spatial resolution at millimeter scale.

Lawson et al. (2013) examined the relationship between SES and prefrontal cortical thickness using MRI. They examined ten regions in the prefrontal cortex and discovered that two were significantly related to SES: (1) the right anterior cingulate gyrus, and (2) the left superior frontal gyrus. Parental education significantly predicted cortical thickness in both regions, whereas family income did not. Anterior cingulate regions are associated with functions in a variety of domains, including: motor and pain response, cognition and attention, and autonomic activity in response to emotions (Pujol et al. 2002). The left superior frontal gyrus is implicated in working memory, particularly in spatial modalities (du Boisgueheneuc et al. 2006). Differences in structure do not necessarily equate with function, therefore, these findings must be viewed critically. Although, there appears to be a relationship between SES and working memory with children from higher SES often outperforming children from lower SES backgrounds.

2.2 Working memory

Working memory (WM) involves the synthesis of information from sensory memory with information from long term memory in order to create and transform that information into something new. It is believed that WM involves the visuospatial sketchpad, which is designed to make sense of visual and spatial information, and the phonological loop, which is responsible for holding auditory information. It is especially important for academic achievement as children must actively retain information and construct ideas to learn language, reasoning and problem solving. Therefore, the brain regions responsible for this executive function are diverse but activation is found predominately in the DLPFC, and the posterior parietal cortex (see Table 1; Berger 2011). WM is often targeted with tasks assessing memory span. For example, individuals might be asked to recall a series of numbers or the order of a visual presentation.

Farah et al. (2006) discovered that children from middle SES performed significantly better than children from lower SES on a series of tasks targeting WM, memory and language. The authors linked performance on cognitive tasks with areas of the brain commonly known to be activated during task completion and proposed that children growing up in low SES environments have different brain functioning in the lateral prefrontal cortex (working memory), medial temporal (memory), and the left perisylvian (language). According to the authors, the differences in cognitive function reflect differences in brain function that can be directly related to SES disparities. Interpretations need to be examined cautiously as behavioral performance does not necessarily equate with neuronal activation or function..

Poverty is associated with elevated levels of stress hormones (Cohen, Doyle, and Baum 2006) which has been shown to negatively impact memory in both human and animal research. (i.e., Sterlemann et al. 2010; Cerqueira et al. 2007). Although, differently than in animal models, research with humans is mostly correlational in nature, and therefore cannot be used to suggest a causal SES-cognition relationships, Evans and Schamberg (2009) discovered that longer periods of chronic poverty in childhood were associated with reductions in working memory in young adulthood as shown in performance on a sequential memory span test. Furthermore, the relationship was mediated by chronic stress measured through a variety of biological markers of physiological response, including: resting blood pressure, urine for testing epinephrine, norepinephrine and cortisol concentration, and body mass index. The impact of stress has been linked with mental health concerns in adolescence, which is apparent at both ends of the socioeconomic spectrum: low (Goodman et al. 2005) and high SES (Ansary and Luthar 2009). Symptoms associated with anxiety and depression make learning new information especially challenging, and may directly impact WM.

Table 1: Associated type of executive function involved in neurocognitive system communication

Executive function	Neurocognitive system
(Selective) attention[a]	ACC
	PFC
	PC
Inhibitory control[b]	ACC
	DLPFC
Working memory[b]	PPC
	DLPFC

Note: ACC = anterior cingulate cortex; PFC = prefrontal cortex; DLPFC = dorsolateral prefrontal cortex; PC = parietal cortex; PPC = posterior parietal cortex. Adapted from
[a] Bush, George. 2011. Cingulate, frontal, and parietal cortical dysfunction in attention-deficit/hyperactivity disorder. *Biological Psychiatry* 69(12). p. 1160–1167.
[b] Berger, Andrea. 2011. *Self-regulation: Brain, cognition, and development*. Washington, DC: American Psychological Association.

2.3 Linking language and cognition in development

Socioeconomic status (SES) influences language and cognitive outcomes. SES can be measured in terms of maternal education. Children with low maternal education as opposed to children with high maternal education performed worse on linguistic components of a study, including the Test of Silent Word Reading Fluency (TOSWRF), Test of Word Reading Efficiency (TOWRE), and basic reading (Skoe, Krizman and Kraus 2013). These children also performed worse on auditory working memory. Additionally, the low maternal education group had noisier and more variable Auditory Brainstem Responses (ABRs), which can be measured during passive listening tasks. The auditory brainstem bridges the ear's cochlea with the brain's cerebral cortex by acting as a communication hub. Differences in auditory neural acuity may likely be due to environmental influences in childhood and not due to hearing loss or ear infections, since all participants had normal hearing thresholds regardless of which group they fell in. Environmental influences could include more television watching for the low SES children, such that these children passively intake more sound from their environment (Evans 2004) and children from low SES backgrounds tend to be exposed to more noise pollution (Kohlhuber, Mielck, Weiland and Bolte 2006), which increases the quantity of irrelevant auditory input.

After adjusting for several variables, parental education appeared to have a linear positive correlation with the surface area of many brain regions (Table 2), which have been linked to language, reading, and executive functions (Noble et al. 2015). Furthermore, family income showed a logarithmic positive correlation with the surface area of several brain regions (Table 2; Noble et al. 2015), which play a role in language and executive functions. The latter study is the largest source of empirical data relating brain structures and functions across SES gradient. The findings are critical in that they are the most straightforward evidence that the effects of SES on neural systems that are directly associated with language and communication are also associated with more domain general neurocognitive systems.

However, Raizada et al. (2008) found that socioeconomic status positively correlated with activation in the left inferior frontal gyrus (IFG) during an auditory rhyme-judgment task in five-year-old preschool children. The IFG is a brain region involved in language, more specifically word retrieval and verbal fluency (Hirshorn and Thompson-Schill 2006). Differences corresponding to variations in SES have also been detected in vocabulary, phonological awareness, and syntax during various developmental stages, with evidence showing the disparities in the left perisylvian/language system (see Whitehurst 1997 for a review).

In a study on kindergarten children from a variety of socioeconomic backgrounds, Noble et al. (2005) had children complete a series of tasks to examine five brain systems: The left perisylvian/language system, prefrontal/executive system, the medial temporal/memory system, the parietal/spatial cognitive system, and the occipitotemporal/visual cognitive system. They discovered the prefrontal/executive system and the left perisylvian/language system were highly correlated with the effects of SES, where children from low SES families had poorer performance than their middle SES counterparts on most tested tasks that tax these systems (see Table 3). The other neurocognitive systems studied were not found to be associated with SES.

Furthermore, a study involving children aged 3 to 8 years found that children from low SES backgrounds had more difficulty suppressing distracting stimuli on a selective attention task. The authors indicate that this difficulty could transfer to challenges in language development later in life as language requires the ability to attend to specific verbal stimuli (Lipina and Posner 2012). Thus, SES differences in multiple neurocognitive systems may exist, however it appears to be most apparent in tasks targeting the left perisylvian/language and prefrontal/executive systems.

A similar study with first grade children demonstrated that the left perisylvian/language system continues to be highly associated with SES (Noble, McCandliss, and Farah 2007). Disproportionate SES disparities were found in the left perisylvian/language and medial temporal/memory systems with smaller, yet significant disparities in the lateral/prefrontal/working memory system and marginally significant disparities in the anterior cingulate/cognitive control system (see Table 4; Farah et al. 2006). The trend showed lower SES children performed more poorly than middle SES children on tasks that target these systems.. The authors note that language function is not restricted to one brain region but rather a system that relies on the left perisylvian region, an area that includes the left prefrontal cortex (Farah et al. 2006). They suggest that these neurocognitive differences do not imply that these differences in brain function are the result of either genetic or environmental causes. These results provide evidence for correlates of SES, which could include several environmental factors that may influence brain development. Nevertheless, there is no conclusive evidence of whether the causes of the differences are genetic or environmental.

It has been proposed that children from lower SES backgrounds might experience a greater effect when exposed to similar risk factors as children from higher SES in the school setting since they may be showing language development delays prior to kindergarten (Stanton-Chapman et al. 2004). It appears that as the number of risk factors increases, the negative effects of social disadvantage on literacy development and corresponding later academic achievement may be amplified in preschool children from low SES backgrounds (D'Angiulli et al. 2009).

These findings support the need for early childhood interventions that focus on promoting children's early language and cognitive development. Differences between children from variable SES backgrounds appear to be most prevalent in brain areas that are responsible for executive function and language skills. Several studies have focused specifically on behavioral measures which do not necessarily link with neuronal deficits. Contrastingly, others have implied that differences in neuronal activation suggest a disparity in lower SES children despite similar task performance. A contextual understanding of the individual child's experience is instrumental when designing effective interventions.

Table 2: SES in terms of parental education and family income accounting for brain surface area differences

Left hemisphere	Right Hemisphere	Both Hemispheres (Bilateral)
Parental education		
left superior, middle and inferior temporal gyri	middle temporal gyrus	fusiform gyrus
inferior frontal gyrus	inferior temporal gyrus	temporal pole
medial orbito-frontal region	supramarginal gyrus	insula
precuneus	middle and superior frontal gyri	superior and medial frontal gyri
		cingulate cortex
		inferior parietal cortex
		lateral occipital cortex
		postcentral gyrus
Family income		
	right occipital cortex	inferior temporal cortex
	superior frontal cortex	insula
	precuneus cortex	inferior frontal gyrus
		medial prefrontal cortex
		inferior cingulate cortex

Note: p < .05, FDR corrected for all regions listed. Adapted from Noble, Kimberly G., Suzanne M. Houston, Natalie H. Brito, Hauke Bartsch, Eric Kan, Joshua M. Kuperman, Natacha Akshoomoff, David G. Amaral, Cinnamon S. Bloss, Ondrej Libiger, Nicholas J. Schork, Sarah S. Murray, B. J. Casey, Linda Chang, Thomas M. Ernst, Jean A. Frazier, Jeffrey R. Gruen, David N. Kennedy, Peter Van Zijl, Stewart Mostofsky, Walter E. Kaufmann, Tal Kenet, Anders M. Dale, Terry L. Jernigan and Elizabeth R. Sowell. 2015. Family income, parental education and brain structure in children and adolescents. *Nature Neuroscience* 18(5). 773–778.

Table 3: Influence of SES on neurocognitive systems: Effect sizes

System	Effects r(58)
Left perisylvian/language	0.45***
Prefrontal/executive system	0.35**
Medial temporal/memory	0.02[a]
Occipitotemporal/visual cognition	0.23
Parietal/spatial cognition	0.24

Note: **p < .01. ***p < .0001. Effect size degrees of freedom shown in parentheses.
[a] No trend was found for the effects of SES on memory. Adapted from Noble, Kimberly G., M. Frank Norman and Martha J. Farah. 2005. Neurocognitive correlates of socioeconomic status in kindergarten children. *Developmental Science* 8(1). 74–87.

Table 4: Pattern showing comparable ses disparity sizes in various neurocognitive systems

language and memory >>	working memory >	cognitive control >	pattern vision and spatial cognition
LP and MTC	PFC/LC	ACC	OCT and PC

Note: LP = left perisylvian; MTC = medial temporal cortex; PFC = prefrontal cortex; LC = lateral cortex; ACC = anterior cingulate cortex; OCT = occipitotemporal; PC = parietal cortex. Adapted from Farah, Martha J., David M. Shera, Jessica H. Savage, Laura Betancourt, Joan M. Giannetta, Nancy L. Brodsky, Elsa K. Malmud and Hallam Hurt. 2006. Childhood poverty: Specific associations with neurocognitive development. *Brain Research* 1110(1). 166–174.

3 Conclusions

The most important neural plasticity changes occur during early development, with a proliferation of connections to frontal and parietal areas during early life. Differentiation of attention networks begin in the early years demonstrating the importance of supporting and guiding preschool children's learning and cognitive development. Consequently, investing in the early years may level out the playing field and reduce the income achievement gap by providing children from lower SES opportunities similar to those available to higher SES counterparts.

The ability to regulate emotions and behavior, in addition to planning and executing goals is essential for school success. Children from lower SES are believed to have fewer opportunities to practice these skills as they are more likely to experience chaotic, overcrowded, and noisy living environments (Evans et al. 2005); a lack of educational materials within the home and neighborhood (Bradley and Corwyn 2002); a lack of parental investment in regards to academic activities (Hango 2007); poverty-related stress leading to psychological problems (DeCarlo Santiago, Wadsworth, and Stump 2011); social stigma (Robinson, McIntyre, and Officer 2005); lowered expectations from teachers (Rosenthal and Jacobson 1968); and negative personal attribution beliefs (Dweck 1975; Sorić 2009). Furthermore, there has been support for the role of self-regulation skills in promoting resilience among low income youth (Buckner, Mezzacappa, and Beardslee 2003, 2009).

Community-based interventions have the potential to overcome social barriers by incorporating strategies that address the needs of families from that particular neighborhood, and empower children to reach their full potential. Successful interventions, such as The Perry Preschool Project (Schweinhart and Weikart 1980) and The Carolina Abecedarian Project (Barnett and Masse 2007) incorporated social early childhood education programs and health assessments for vulnerable populations. The effect of these interventions lasted into adulthood as children who had received the intensive early education were more likely to enter college and hold a full-time position for an extended period of time when compared with a control group (Campbell et al. 2012). However, these types of interventions have the potential to stigmatize already marginalized populations by targeting specific groups.

Differences in children's neurocognitive development represent the influence of environment and experience, which may be either adaptive or detrimental. Interventions should reflect the needs of children by exploring the ecological factors influencing development while being sensitive to the cultural and ethnic backgrounds of families (Ungar 2011). Governments have the ability to improve children's outcomes by implementing public policy that supports families and increases social capital (sense of trust within a society). Good governance and a trusting society where citizens have the freedom to influence public policy and governments are transparent and devoid of corruption, have been found to promote wealth and reduce social inequality leading to improved health outcomes (Bezo, Maggi, and Roberts 2012).

References

Ansary, Nadia S. & Suniya S. Luthar. 2009. Distress and academic achievement among adolescents of affluence: A study of externalizing and internalizing problem behaviors and school performance. *Development and Psychopathology* 21(1). 319–341.

Arán-Filippetti, Vanessa & Maria C. Richaud de Minzi. 2012. A structural analysis of executive functions and socioeconomic status in school-age children: cognitive factors as effect mediators. *The Journal of Genetic Psychology* 173(4). 393–416.

Barnett, W. Steven & Leonard N. Masse. 2007. Comparative benefit-cost analysis of the Abecedarian program and its policy implications. *Economics of Education Review* 26. 113–125.

Berger, Andrea. 2011. *Self-regulation: Brain, cognition, and development.* Washington, DC: American Psychological Association.

Bezo, Brent, Stefania Maggi & William L. Roberts. 2012. The rights and freedoms gradient of health: Evidence from a cross-national study. *Frontiers in Psychology* 3. 441.

Bradley, Robert H. & Robert F. Corwyn. 2002. Socioeconomic status and child development. *Annual review of psychology* 53(1). 371–399.

Bresnahan, Jean L. & William L. Blum. 1971. Chaotic reinforcement. *Developmental Psychology* 4(1). 89–92.

Brooks-Gunn, Jeanne, Pamela K. Klebanov & Greg J. Duncan. 1996. Ethnic differences in children's intelligence test scores: Role of economic deprivation, home environment, and maternal characteristics. *Child Development* 67(2). 396–408.

Buckner, John C., Enrico Mezzacappa & William R. Beardslee. 2003. Characteristics of resilient youths living in poverty: The role of self-regulatory processes. *Development and Psychopathology* 15. 139–162.

Buckner, John C., Enrico Mezzacappa & William R. Beardslee. 2009. Self-regulation and its relations to adaptive functioning in low incomes youths. *American Journal of Orthopsychiatry* 79(1). 19–30.

Bush, George. 2011. Cingulate, frontal, and parietal cortical dysfunction in attention-deficit/hyperactivity disorder. *Biological Psychiatry* 69(12). 1160–1167.

Campbell, Frances A., Elizabeth P. Pungello, Margaret Burchinal, Kirsten Kainz,Yi Pan, Barbara H. Wasik, Joseph J. Sparling, Oscar A. Barbarin & Craig T. Ramey. 2012. Adult outcomes as a function of an early childhood educational program: An Abecedarian project follow-up. *Developmental Psychology* 48(4). 1033–1043.

Cerqueira, João J., François Mailliet, Osborne F. X. Almeida, Thérèse M. Jay & Nuno Sousa. 2007. The prefrontal cortex as a key target of the maladaptive response to stress. *The Journal of Neuroscience* 27(11). 2781–2787.

Cohen, Sheldon, William J. Doyle & Andrew Baum. 2006. Socioeconomic status is associated with stress hormones. *Psychosomatic Medicine* 68. 414–420.

D'Angiulli, Amedeo, Anthony Herdman, David Stapells & Clyde Hertzman. 2008. Children's event-related potentials of auditory selective attention vary with their socioeconomic status. *Neuropsychology* 22(3). 293–300.

D'Angiulli, Amedeo, William Warburton, Susan Dahinten & Clyde Hertzman. 2009. Population-level associations between preschool vulnerability and grade-four basic skills. *PLoS ONE*, 4(11) e7692.

D'Angiulli, Amedeo, Patricia M. Van Roon, Joanne Weinberg, Tim F. Oberlander, Ruth E. Grunau, Clyde Hertzman & Stefania Maggi. 2012. Frontal EEG/ERP correlates of attentional processes, cortisol and motivational states in adolescents from lower and higher socioeconomic status. *Frontiers in Human Neuroscience* 6 (November). 306.

DeCarlo Santiago Catherina, Martha E. Wadsworth & Jessica Stump. 2011. Socioeconomic status, neighborhood disadvantage, and poverty-related stress: Prospective effects on psychological syndromes among diverse low-income families. *Journal of Economic Psychology* 32. 218–230.

Du Boisgueheneuc, Foucaud, Richard Levy, Emmanuelle Volle, Magali Seassau, Hughes Duffau, Serge Kinkingnehun, Yves Samson, Sandy Zhang & Bruno Dubois. 2006. Functions of the left superior frontal gyrus in humans: A lesion study. *Brain: A Journal of Neurology* 129(Pt 12). 3315–3328.

Duncan, Greg J., W. Jean Yeung, Jeanne Brooks-Gunn & Judith R. Smith. 1998. How much does childhood poverty affect the life chances of children? *American Sociological Review* 63(3). 406–423.

Dweck, Carol S. 1975. The role of expectations and attributions in the alleviation of learned helplessness. *Journal of Personality and Social Psychology* 31(4). 674–685.

Evans, Gary W. 2004. The environment of childhood poverty. *American Psychologist* 59(20). 77–92.

Evans, Gary W., Carrie Gonnella, Lyscha A. Marcynyszyn, Lauren Gentile & Nicholas Salpekar. 2005. The role of chaos in poverty and children's socioemotional adjustment 16(7). 1–7.

Evans, Gary W. & Jennifer Rosenbaum. 2008. Self-regulation and the income-achievement gap. *Early Childhood Research Quarterly* 23. 504–514.

Evans, Gary W. & Michelle A. Schamberg. 2009. Childhood poverty, chronic stress, and adult working memory. *Proceedings of the National Academy of Sciences* 106(19). 6545–6549.

Farah, Martha J., David M. Shera, Jessica H. Savage, Laura Betancourt, Joan M. Giannetta, Nancy L. Brodsky, Elsa K. Malmud & Hallam Hurt. 2006. Childhood poverty: Specific associations with neurocognitive development. *Brain Research* 1110(1). 166–174.

Fitzpatrick, Caroline, Rachel D. McKinnon, Clancy B. Blair & Michael T. Willoughby. 2014. Do preschool executive function skills explain the school readiness gap between advantaged and disadvantaged children? *Learning and Instruction* 30. 25–31.

Foster, James E. 1998. Absolute versus relative poverty. *American Economic Review* 88(2). 335–341.

Goodman, Elizabeth, Bruce S. McEwen, Lawrence M. Dolan, Tara Schafer-Kalkhoff & Nancy E. Adler. 2005. Social disadvantage and adolescent stress. *Journal of Adolescent Health* 37(6). 484–492.

Hackman, Daniel A., Martha J. Farah, and Michael J. Meaney, (2010). Socioeconomic status and the brain: mechanistic insights from human and animal research. Nature Reviews. Vol. 11, 651–659

Hackman, Daniel A. & Martha J. Farah. 2009. Socioeconomic status and the developing brain. *Trends in cognitive sciences* 13(2). 65–73.

Hango, Darcy. 2007. Parental investment in childhood and educational qualifications: Can greater parental involvement mediate the effects of socioeconomic disadvantage? *Social Science Research* 36(4). 1371–1390.

Hart, Betty & Todd R. Risely. 1995. *Meaningful Differences in the Everyday Experiences of American Children*. Baltimore: Brookes Publishing.

Hirshorn, Elizabeth A. & Sharon L. Thompson-Schill. 2006. Role of the left inferior frontal gyrus in covert word retrieval: Neural correlates of switching during verbal fluency. *Neuropsychologia* 44(12). 2547–2557.

Hoff-Ginsberg, Erika. 1991. Mother–child conversation in different social classes and communicative settings. *Child Development* 62(4). 782–796.

Hoff, Erika & Chunyan Tian. 2005. Socioeconomic status and cultural influences on language. *Journal of Communication Disorders* 38(4). 271–278.

Hoff, Erika. 2012. Interpreting the early language trajectories of children from low SES and language minority homes: Implications for closing achievement gaps. *Developmental psychology* 49(1). 4–14.

Kohlhuber, Martina, Andreas Mielck, Stephan K. Weiland & Gabriele Bolte. 2006. Social inequality in perceived environmental exposures in relation to housing conditions in Germany. *Environmental Research* 101(2). 246–255.

Korat, Ofra, Safieh H. Arafat, Dorit Aram & Pnina Klein. 2013. Book reading mediation, SES, home literacy environment, and children's literacy: Evidence from Arabic-speaking families. *First Language* 33(2). 132–154.

Lawson, Gwendolyn M., Jeffrey T. Duda, Brian B. Avants, Jue Wu & Martha J. Farah. 2013. Associations between children's socioeconomic status and prefrontal cortical thickness. *Developmental Science* 16(5). 641–652.

Lipina, Sebastián J. & Michael I. Posner. 2012. The impact of poverty on the development of brain networks. *Frontiers in Human Neuroscience* 6 (August). 238.

Luthar, Suniya. S. & Shawn J. Latendresse. 2005. Children of the affluent: Challenges to well-being. *Current Directions in Psychological Science* 14(1). 49–53.

Mani, Anandi, Sendhil Mullainathan, Eldar Shafir & Jiaying Zhao. 2013. Poverty impedes cognitive function. *Science* (New York, N.Y.) 341(6149). 976–980.

Moreno, Sylvain, Ellen Bialystok, Raluca Barac, E. Glenn Schellenberg, Nocholas J. Cepeda & Tom Chau. 2011. Short-term music training enhances verbal intelligence and executive function. *Psychological Science* 22(11). 1425–1433.

Nisbett, Richard E. 2009. *Intelligence and how to get it: Why schools and culture count*. New York: Northon & Company Inc.

Nittrouer, Susan. 1996. The relationship between speech perception and phonemic awareness: Evidence from low-SES children and children with chronic OM. *Journal of Speech & Hearing Research* 39(5). 1059–1070.

Noble, Kimberly G., Bruce D. McCandliss & Martha J. Farah. 2007. Socioeconomic gradients predict individual differences in neurocognitive abilities. *Developmental Science* 10(4). 464–480.

Noble, Kimberly G., Suzanne M. Houston, Natalie H. Brito, Hauke Bartsch, Eric Kan, Joshua M. Kuperman, Natacha Akshoomoff, David G. Amaral, Cinnamon S. Bloss, Ondrej Libiger, Nicholas J. Schork, Sarah S. Murray, B. J. Casey, Linda Chang, Thomas M. Ernst, Jean A. Frazier, Jeffrey R. Gruen, David N. Kennedy, Peter Van Zijl, Stewart Mostofsky, Walter E. Kaufmann, Tal Kenet, Anders M. Dale, Terry L. Jernigan & Elizabeth R. Sowell. 2015. Family income, parental education and brain structure in children and adolescents. *Nature Neuroscience* 18(5). 773–778.

Noble, Kimberly G., M. Frank Norman & Martha J. Farah. 2005. Neurocognitive correlates of socioeconomic status in kindergarten children. *Developmental Science* 8(1). 74–87.

Noble, Kimberly G., Michael E. Wolmetz, Lisa G. Ochs, Martha J. Farah & Bruce D. McCandliss. 2006. Brain-behavior relationships in reading acquisition are modulated by socioeconomic factors. *Developmental Science* 9(6). 642–654.

Oller, D. Kimbrough, Rebecca E. Eilers, Richard Urbano, & Alan B. Cobo-Lewis. 1997. Development of precursors to speech in infants exposed to two languages. *Journal of Child Language* 24(2). 407–425.

Patchin, Justin W., Beth M. Huebner, John D McCluskey, Sean P. Varano & Timothy S. Bynum. 2006. Exposure to community violence and childhood delinquency. *Crime & Delinquency* 52(2). 307–332.

Picton, T. W., S. Bentin, P. Berg, E. Donchin, S. A. Hillyard, R. Johnson, G. A. Miller, W. Ritter, D. S. Ruchkin, M. D. Rugg & M. J. Taylor. 2000. Guidelines for using human event-related potentials to study cognition: recording standards and publication criteria. *Psychophysiology* 37(2). 127–152.

Pujol, Jesús, Anna López, Joan Deus, Narcís Cardoner, Julio Vallejo, Antoni Capdevila & Tomás Paus. 2002. Anatomical variability of the anterior cingulate gyrus and basic dimensions of human personality. *NeuroImage* 15(4). 847–855.

Quay, Lorene & Robert L. Blaney. 1992. Verbal communication, nonverbal communication, and private speech in lower and middle socioeconomic status preschool children. *The Journal of Genetic Psychology* 153(2). 129–138.

Raizada, Rajeev D. S., Todd L. Richards, Andrew Meltzoff & Patricia K. Kuhla. 2008. Socioeconomic status predicts hemispheric specialisation of the left inferior frontal gyrus in young children. *NeuroImage* 40. 1392–1401.

Robinson, Lynne M., Lynn McIntyre & Suzanne Officer. 2005. Welfare babies: Poor children's experiences informing healthy peer relationships in Canada. *Health Promotion International* 20(4). 342–350.

Rosenthal, Robert & Lenore Jacobson. 1968. Pygmalion in the classroom. *The Urban Review* 3(1). 16–20.

Rowe, Meredith L. & Susan Goldin-Meadow. 2009. Differences in early gesture explain SES disparities in child vocabulary size at school entry. *Science* 323(5916). 951–953.

Schibli, Kylie & Amedeo D'Angiulli. 2013. The social emotional developmental and cognitive neuroscience of socioeconomic gradients: Laboratory, population, cross-cultural and community developmental approaches. *Frontiers in human neuroscience* 7.

Schweinhart, Lawrence J. & David P. Weikart. 1980. *Young children grow up: The effects of the Perry Preschool Program on youths through age 15*. Ypsilanti, MI: The High/Scope Educational Research Foundation.

Sices, Laura, Hudson G. Taylor, Lisa Freebairn, Amy Hansen & Barbara Lewis. 2007. Relationship between speech-sound disorders and early literacy skills in preschool-age children: Impact of comorbid language impairment. *Journal of Developmental and Behavioral Pediatrics* 28(6). 438–447.

Siegler, Robert S. & Martha Wagner Alibali, M W. 2005. *Children's thinking* (4th edn.). Upper Saddle River, NJ: Prentice Hall.

Skoe, Erika, Jennifer Krizman & Nina Kraus. 2013. The impoverished brain: Disparities in maternal education affect the neural response to sound. *Journal of Neuroscience* 33(44). 17221–17231.

Sorić, Izabela. 2009. Regulatory styles, causal attributions and academic achievement. *School Psychology International* 30(4). 403–420.

Stanton-Chapman, Tina L., Derek A. Chapman, Ann P. Kaiser & Terry B. Hancock. 2004. Cumulative risk and low-income children's language development. *Topics in Early Childhood Special Education* 24(4). 227–237.

Sterlemann, Vera, Gerhard Rammes, Miriam Wolf, Claudia Liebl, Karin Ganea, Marianne B. Müller M. B. & Mathias V. Schmidt. 2010. Chronic social stress during adolescence induces cognitive impairment in aged mice. *Hippocampus* 20. 540–549.

Stevens, Courtney, Brittni Lauinger & Helen Neville. 2009. Differences in the neural mechanisms of selective attention in children from different socioeconomic backgrounds: an event-related brain potential study. *Developmental Science* 12(4). 634–646.

Stroop, J Ridley. 1935. Studies of interference in serial verbal reactions. *Journal of Experimental Psychology* 18(6). 643–662.

Tehranifar, Parisa, Hui-Chen Wu, Xiaozhou Fan, Julie D. Flom, Jennifer S. Ferris, Yoon Hee Cho, Karina Gonzalez, Regina M. Santella, and Mary Beth Terry. 2013. Early life socioeconomic factors and genomic DNA methylation in mid-life. *Epigenetics* 8(1). 23–27.

Ungar, Michael. 2011. The social ecology of resilience: addressing context and cultural ambiguity of a nascent construct. *American Journal of Orthopsychiatry* 81(1). 1–17.

Van der Molen, M. W. 2000. Developmental changes in inhibitory processing: evidence from psychophysiological measures. *Biological Psychology* 54(1–3). 207–239.

Vasilyeva, Marina, Heidi Waterfall & Janellen Huttenlocher. 2008. Emergence of syntax: Commonalities and differences across children. *Developmental Science* 11(1). 84–97.

Whitehurst, Grover J., David S. Arnold, Jeffrey N. Epstein, Andrea L. Angell, Meagan Smith & Janet E. Fischel. 1994. A picture book reading intervention in day care and home for children from low-income families. *Developmental Psychology* 30(5). 679–689.

Whitehurst, Grover J. 1997. Language processes in context: Language learning in children reared in poverty. In Lauren B. Adamson & MaryAnn Romski (eds.), *Research on communication and language disorders: Contribution to theories of language development*, 233–266. Baltimore, USA: Brookes.

Yopp, Hallie K. & Ruth Helen Yopp. 2000. Supporting phonemic awareness development in the classroom. *The Reading Teacher* 54. 130–143.

Zhang, Yiwen, Xingming Jin, Xiaoming Shen, Jinming Zhang, Erika Hoff. 2008. Correlates of early language development in Chinese children. *International Journal of Behavioral Development* 32(2). 1–000.

Zubrik, Stephen R., Catherine L. Taylor, Mabel L. Rice, David W. Slegers. 2007. Late language emergence at 24 Months: An epidemiological study of prevalence, predictors, and covariates. *Journal of Speech, Language, and Hearing Research* 50(6). 1562–1592.

Carolyn Letts
28 Language disorder versus language difference: The impact of socio-economic status

1 Introduction

1.1 Why might socio-economic status be important?

Concerns have been raised in the UK and further afield in recent years that children growing up under conditions of social deprivation are seriously disadvantaged in terms of their language acquisition, leading to further disadvantage in literacy development and wider educational progress. In the UK, reports such as the 'Links between Speech Language and Communication Difficulties' produced by the All Party Parliamentary Group on Speech, Language and Communication Difficulties (Royal College of Speech and Language Therapists 2013) and 'Getting in early: primary schools and early intervention', published by the Centre for Policy Studies and the Smith Institute (Gross, 2008), have emphasised the impact of low socio-economic status (SES) on whole cohorts of children. A special issue of the European Journal of Applied Linguistics, published in early 2014, is devoted to issues around language support in preschool settings, and links low proficiency in the school language to both migrant status and low SES (Michel and Kuiken 2014). In response to these concerns, there have been a number of wide-ranging initiatives to support and enrich language development in preschool educational settings.

This issue first began to gain momentum in the UK in the early 2000s with the publication of a study by Locke and colleagues carried out in four nurseries in Sheffield, situated in low SES neighbourhoods (Locke, Ginsborg, and Peers 2002) Children aged between 3;01 and 4;08 (n = 223) were assessed on a standardised test of language development, the CELF-Preschool (Peers, Lloyd, and Foster 2000). They were found to have depressed receptive and expressive language abilities when compared with the standardisation sample of the test (reprentative of the whole of the UK), and if standard cut-off criteria are applied, more of the children than would be expected fell into the category of language delayed or disordered. Other studies investigating links between SES and aspects of language development have been carried out both before and after this date, but at this point SES began to be considered as a potential risk factor for language impairment. General cognitive skills of the Sheffield participants were also assessed but were found to be in line with the rest of the population, suggesting that it was specifically in the area of language development that these children were falling behind. With this growing awareness

---

Carolyn Letts, Newcastle University

came a series of government and charity initiatives to improve educational and linguistic outcomes for children from low SES backgrounds, many aimed at pre-school nursery provision. More details regarding these can be found in Mroz and Letts (2014).

Work from the field of sociolinguistics however has traditionally maintained that perceived differences in language development between children from different social backgrounds represent the normal language variation which will be found in any wider community of people who speak the same language. This goes beyond obvious differences in vocabulary and structure as reflected in different dialects to also subsume differences in interaction styles between adults and children and cultural beliefs about how to interact with children (for example Ochs 1983 compares such patterns in Samoan culture with typical 'Western' patterns). Language as used in educational settings will tend to emulate the language used within families where the parents are highly educated and from the majority culture. Children arriving in school with a different linguistic background will inevitably be disadvantaged by these differences in that they will be unfamiliar with usages and interaction styles deployed within the school setting; however they will have normally developing language. The arguments were encapsulated in the seminal debate in the 1970s between Basil Bernstein who maintained that families from low SES backgrounds talked using a 'restricted code' (Bernstein 1971), and William Labov who provided evidence of highly sophisticated linguistic skills in low SES black teenagers when talking in a familiar context (Labov 1972).

In similar vein, two important studies were published in the UK in the 1980s which were among the first to take advantage of radio microphone technology and the development of computer support for data analysis. Wells and his team conducted in depth analysis of family interactions and language acquisition in a sample of children, stratified for social class, in Bristol, UK. He indicated that any differences in language development related to social class were far outweighed by individual differences among the children, with sometimes quite marked differences between children within the same family (Wells 1986). Tizard et al. (1983) looked at interactions between working- and middle class girls and their mothers or teachers, in the home and in nursery. They found that use of language for complex purposes (for example explaining, reasoning, problem solving) was more frequent for the middle class children and their mothers. However, for the working class children there was a much greater discrepancy in their use of this sort of language when home was compared to nursery. Use was greater in the home, suggesting some inhibition in using language freely in the nursery setting. All the working class girls and their mothers demonstrated use of language for each of the categories of complex purposes on at least one occasion.

Much more recently, Grainger (2013) has taken a critical look at government commissioned reports on links between social deprivation and language and literacy development and concludes that the evidence for this from robust research studies is limited. She notes that the language used to describe effects of SES may involve medical terms such as diagnosis and impairment which has the effect of "pathologisation of working-class children's language patterns" (Grainger 2013: 99). Furthermore some claims that have been made appear to be based on anecdotal comments by teachers.

1.2 Environmental effects of language input versus risk factors

Before discussing the evidence for any link between child language impairment and socio-economic factors, it is important to be clear on the nature of the studies that have been carried out. Many studies looking at links between SES and language development have selected samples of children who to all intents and purposes are developing language in a typical fashion, that is to say that any children known to have a diagnosed difficulty with language have been excluded. Hart and Risley for example did a comparison of vocabulary development and parent-child interaction styles of typically developing children from three groups: professional, working class and parents on welfare (Hart and Risley 1995). Furthermore, the measures used were based on spontaneous recorded conversational samples, and the three groups were compared with each other and not with any wider population standard. Concern arises however when the measures used in this sort of study, even with typically developing samples, are those that are widely used for identification of children with language impairment and indeed have been designed for this purpose. The Locke, Ginsborg, and Peers (2002) study relied exclusively on a standardised test of this sort and found that larger than expected numbers of children had scores that would indicate some sort of language delay or disorder. The ways in which standardised test scores are interpreted by clinicians and researchers working with language impaired children varies. For researchers in specific language impairment (SLI) for example, studies which group together children considered to be disordered typically use a cut-off point of >1.25 SD below the mean as a criterion for the impaired group (see Reilly at al. 2014 for a description and critique of the diagnostic term SLI). Clinicians who work with individual children will use a variety of assessment procedures in addition to standardised testing, and recognise that testing has limitations: at the individual level the child's performance may be affected by how they feel on the day of testing, environmental distractions and so forth, and on a wider level the test is only suitable if the individual child being tested comes from a similar demographic background to those in the standardisation sample (see Lidz 2003 for further information on assessment procedures). So there are a number of important issues to consider when interpreting the findings of studies like those of Locke at al, including: comparability of the standardisation sample and the children in the study; whether any cut-off point used is realistic and valid; and, whether results are a true reflection of the child's language development or whether in fact different types of assessment or measurement would reveal a less worrying picture.

An alternative type of study compares children identified as having a problem with language development, with those considered to be typically developing, and looks for correlations between impairment and a variety of risk factors. A correlation does not of course suggest causation (in either direction); however for long established correlations such as that between smoking and lung cancer, or obesity and heart disease, few would argue that there is no causative link. In these cases, the behaviour or pre-existing condition is considered to increase the individual's chance of developing the disease. The situation with SES and language impairment however is much less easy to interpret; while correlations may exist between SES and language impairments, as is discussed below the way in which this operates is unclear, and also causation could operate in both directions. Low SES may well increase risk of language impairment but language impairment, especially operating through successive generations, is also likely to increase the risk of living in deprivation.

2 The evidence

2.1 Measuring language development and socio-economic status

Both 'language development' and 'SES' are complex constructs which may be measured in different ways. Language, if a linguistic framework is used, is composed of several different levels, including vocabulary, sentence structure and morphology, and this can be extended out further to include levels of phonology and pragmatics. All components are important, but any particular measurement method may focus on a number or only one of these, for example many studies investigating the relationship between language and SES have measured vocabulary. Furthermore, language acquisition at all linguistic levels can be measured in different ways. At one extreme, researchers may examine spontaneous conversation, usually between child and adult, and use analysis techniques to draw conclusions about the language the child is using. This can be a laborious process as data needs to be recorded and transcribed first, so it may be advantageous to manipulate the context or use test 'probes' to elicit specific targets. Taken to the opposite extreme, a standardised test procedure may be used which involves elicited responses throughout and permits comparison with a wider norming population. It is important to consider the context and methods for collecting data on language development as these in themselves may differentially affect the outcome for children from different SES backgrounds.

Methods also vary for measuring SES and there is a range of possible variables that could be considered here including family income, parental employment or occupation, parental education and characteristics of the neighbourhood in which the family live. Social 'class' as derived from parental occupation alone is no longer widely used as an indicator of SES because of shifting patterns of employment (and unemployment) over time both for individuals and within the wider society. Two indicators of SES commonly used currently are level of maternal education, expressed as number of years in education or the highest qualification achieved, and composite measures of neighbourhood characteristics derived from census data. For a fuller discussion of ways of measuring language acquisition and SES, please see Letts et al. (2013).

2.2 Evidence for links between social background and language development

A number of studies exploring this link have been conducted since the Bernstein-Labov debate and the early research mentioned in section 1.1. The seminal study by Hart and Risley (1995) found marked differences in the range of vocabulary used expressively by children according to the three family social groupings, professional, working class and on welfare. Vocabulary was measured by analysing spontaneous recorded output from children within the home. A link between SES and vocabulary development was also found in studies by Qi et al. (2006) and Horton-Ikard and Weismer (2007); both these studies looked at the vocabulary of low SES African-American children in the USA and used vocabulary tests. On the other hand, Black, Peppe, and Gibbon (2008) failed to find any association between receptive vocabulary as measured by a standardised test and SES in a sample (n = 76) of Edinburgh children. Studies that look at syntactic development are similarly contradictory, although there appears to be a general pattern of more complex syntactic structures being less advanced in children with low SES. McIntosh et al. (2007) found low performance in children from low SES backgrounds on a range of language test items, but this was particularly apparent with items requiring complex language such as explanation. Vasilyeva, Waterfall, and Huttenlocher (2008) looked at videotaped language samples from 45 children aged between 1;10 and 3;06 and found no effect for SES on simple sentences, but did find an effect for development of complex sentences.

Results have already been reported above for the study by Locke, Ginsborg, and Peers (2002) that looked at performance of children from low SES backgrounds on a standardised test. A similar study carried out by Law, McBean, and Rush (2011) involved a sample of 138 children aged 5–12 years attending a primary school in Scotland and known to live an area of social deprivation. The children underwent a number of standardised language assessments. Performance was poor on the CELF-IV UK (Semel, Wiig, and Sekord 2006), a version of the test used by Locke, Ginsborg and Peers but developed and standardised for school-age children; mean scores on this test were 1SD below the national mean. Mean scores for tests of receptive vocabulary and narrative were however within normal limits. Letts et al. (2013) looked at scores from the standardisation sample for the New Reynell Developmental Language Scales (Edwards Letts and Sinka 2011) in relation to maternal education and ranking on an index of social deprivation for the postcode of the school or nursery site where the data was collected. A modest effect was found for maternal education and language comprehension and production for children whose mothers had only the statutory minimum years of education. For social deprivation, a modest effect was found only for the Production Scale of the test.

2.3 Links between SES and language delay or disorder

The studies discussed so far have all looked at the relationship between SES and language acquisition in children considered to be typically developing. In the course of this research, some studies have found more children than might be expected to have a language delay, in that they are considerably behind the majority of peers of the same age; these studies have typically used standardised tests to measure language development and to draw these conclusions.

An alternative approach is to start with children who appear to have a language delay or disorder and to make comparisons with children whose language development is within the typical range. Given the concern regarding impact of SES, it is interesting to see to what extent children who have a diagnosed impairment are also socially disadvantaged. Large cohort studies that have tracked children from birth have the capacity to measure the relationship between the risk factors discussed in section 1.2 above and language impairment. One such study that is beginning to yield such information is the Early Language in Victoria Study (ELVS) conducted in Australia. Reilly et al. (2007) and Reilly et al. (2010) used multivariate regression models to calculate the amount of variance contributed by a number of predictors (or potential risk factors) to language outcomes for children at age 2 and at age 4. They are able to report longitudinal outcomes for around 1600+ children who took part in the ELVS study. The outcome measures for language used at age 2 (reported in Reilly et al. 2007) are the Words and Sentences version of the MacArthur-Bates Communicative Development Inventory (CDI: Fenson, Dale, and Reznik 1993), and the Communication and Symbolic Behavior Scales (CSBS: Wetherby and Prizant 2002), the latter having also been carried out when the children were 12 months old. Children were classified as late talkers at age 2 if they performed below the 10th percentile for vocabulary on the CDI. Predictors included level of maternal education and SES as reflected in census data, but also history of speech and language problems within the family, gender, child health factors such a perinatal problems, and maternal vocabulary level. The child's earlier performance on the CSBS (i.e. at 12 months) was also entered into the model.

Reilly et al. (2010) report on the children's progress at age 4 years using a standardised test of language development, and relating performance to the same set of predictors as those reported for the 2 year olds. Children at this age were categorised as low language status if they performed >1.25 SD below the mean on a standardised test and as specific language impaired (SLI) if they fell into this group but nevertheless had non-verbal IQ scores within the normal range.

Maternal education level was a predictor of poor language outcome at both ages and neighbourhood SES was related to this at age 4; however other predictors, notably genetic factors as indicated by family history of speech and language impairment were found to be equally or more important. A high degree of variance was also accounted for by earlier language performance. Reilly et al. (2010) note that SES measures have limited value as predictors of low language status and SLI. Furthermore the researchers note that the various risk factors looked at for the two year olds "seem unlikely to be helpful in screening for early language delay" (Reilly et al. 2009: 344). The increasing importance of SES factors between ages 2 and 4 years lead the researchers to conclude that SES may exert an increasing influence between these ages.

3 Variables that mediate between SES and language acquisition

3.1 Evidence from language input in the home

The evidence so far discussed suggests that there may be a link between social deprivation and poor language development but that this effect is not consistently reported across different studies. Furthermore, although there are more children with language delay and/or disorder to be found within low SES groups, there is no evidence that social deprivation is a direct cause of these problems and indeed even the direction of any effect is unclear. One potential way of explaining these results is to look at factors known to have a more direct effect on language acquisition and which may themselves be associated more with families living in social deprivation than with others. Hart and Risley (1995) for example found that the quantity of language and number of different vocabulary items directed at children from their three social groupings differed significantly, with the children of families on welfare having the least input. Shneidman et al. (2013) found that quantity of vocabulary directed at children at age 2;06 reliably predicted the children's vocabulary use at age 3;06. It did not matter who talked directly to the children, so living in extended households where different adults interacted with children did not make any difference; the children did not however learn from overheard speech.

Parents in families living in disadvantaged circumstances may have less opportunity to spend time talking to their children if working long hours and may themselves have low vocabulary levels especially if having undergone fewer years of education. Furthermore they may have restricted access to quality child care where rich input is provided and limited resources to expose children to novel experiences, and therefore novel vocabulary, through family outings and so forth. This suggestion is supported by a recent study by Song, Spier, and Tamis-Lemondam (2014) who examined the influence of maternal lexical diversity of the mother talking to her child on lexical diversity in the child's speech at age two, and predictively, on lexical diversity in the child's speech at age 3.00. The mother-child dyads all came from low income families and the data consisted of videotaped interactions. Considerable variation in maternal vocabulary was found, but there was a consistent relationship between quantity and diversity of input and the child's vocabulary at both ages. Roulstone et al. (2011) report similar outcomes in a study based on a large dataset, the Avon Longitudinal Study of Parents and Children (ALSPAC). Here children's vocabulary and production of simple sentences at age 2 years, plus factors in the child's early communication environment were considered in relation to school readiness at 5 years. Important aspects of the child's early communicative environment included such things as parental teaching activities, frequency of library visits and toys available to the child as well as the mother's sense of wellbeing and the extent to which she felt supported.

Harrison and McLeod (2010) working with another large longitudinal data set, the Longitudinal Study of Australian Children (LSAC), supply further evidence supporting the importance of mediating factors. They consider four language outcome measures at age 4–5 years: parental concern about the child's expressive language; parental concern about the child's receptive language; performance on a standardised measure of receptive vocabulary; and, use of speech and language therapy services. They comment that SES factors considered in isolation have only a small effect on these outcomes, especially in comparison with neurobiological factors that are intrinsic to the child. In their study, sex of child, ongoing hearing problems and child temperament were found to be important intrinsic variables. However two non-intrinsic factors were found to be important, these being access to a supportive home learning environment and psychological wellbeing of the mother; both of these are vulnerable in situations of social deprivation.

3.2 Features of interaction within the home

Qualitative aspects of interaction between parents and children have also been considered in terms of SES. Hart and Risley (1995) observed that parents in their more advantaged groups gave their children more choices when talking with them, actively listened to the child's contributions and used talk as a means in itself to be sociable. Parents in families on welfare tended to talk less about child-initiated topics and used more imperatives and prohibitions. Later studies by Hoff (2003) and Rowe (2008) report similar findings. Hart and Risley go on to suggest that parents are actively transmitting cultural values though their language and interactive styles and that professional parents "seemed to be preparing their children to participate in a culture concerned with symbols and analytic problem solving" (1995:133). It is important to be aware however that adult-child interaction is culturally determined. For example, Zhan (2010) notes that Javanese mothers use questions with their children but then provide answers themselves rather than waiting for the child to try. Carter et al. (2005) point out that in many cultures children are not accustomed to answering questions to which the adult already knows the answer, something that is a feature of most language tests. So the effects being seen here may reflect the degree to which social and cultural backgrounds prepare the child for educational settings and the sorts of tasks and assessments they are likely to be asked to undertake in these settings. This will of course include formal assessments of language development.

3.3 Insights from second language learning in children

When looking for environmental effects which may mediate between SES and language acquisition, it can be useful to look at studies which track the second language development of children acquiring an additional language through naturalistic exposure. Social conditions for children in this situation can be highly variable. Although often associated with social disadvantage this is by no means always the case; children may be part of long-established ethnic communities that do not experience social deprivation or may be children of 'elite bilinguals' whose parents have professional or business careers which mean they move from country to country. Recently arrived groups however often live in relative poverty and this may include parents who have been highly educated in their country of origin. Furthermore these groups may have very high aspirations for their children to do well in education in the new country. This means that the kinds of factors outlined above will be less closely linked to current SES. Interaction patterns between parent and child will also reflect the kinds of cultural differences outlined above. Studies are beginning to emerge that explore the influence of various factors on successful second language acquisition, measuring second language vocabulary as an outcome.

Scheele and Leseman (2010) report on second language (L2, here Dutch) vocabulary skills for two groups of immigrant children at age 3, Moroccan-Dutch and Turkish-Dutch, as well as comparing Dutch vocabulary for these groups to a group of monolingual Dutch-speaking children. Differences in vocabulary were found to relate to input in the home, specifically activities such as reading with the child. The immigrant children received less Dutch input than the monolingual children in the home, as would be expected, but also received less first language (L1) input. The relationship between L1 input and SES was not significant, and that between L2 input and SES was significant only for one of the immigrant groups (Moroccan-Dutch). So it would seem that vocabulary development here is related to child-rearing practices and activities within the home rather than SES per se. A more recent study by Prevoo et al. (2014) found similar results for older children (mean age 6;01 years), but that the amount of input in the L2 was lower in families with lower SES backgrounds as measured by income and years of education of the parents. The authors recommend that educators should be aware that "children from low-SES families receive less host language input" (963). Rydland, Grover, and Lawrence (2014) looked at trajectories of vocabulary development between ages 5 and 10 in 26 Turkish immigrant children in Norway. They found that maternal education predicted L2 vocabulary growth during this period, but also that teacher-led talk, peer talk and concentration of co-ethnic population in the neighbourhood had an impact on L2 vocabulary level at the preschool stage and that these differences were maintained across subsequent years of the study.

3.4 Influences from outside the home

The findings of the study by Rydland, Grover, and Lawrence (2014) suggest that negative influences on language development resulting from limited home input, which may itself be related to family SES, may be mitigated by external influences, especially in the preschool or nursery environment. There is now some limited further evidence that this may be the case. Letts et al. (2013) found an interaction between age and years of maternal education in their analysis of children's performance on the NRDLS Production Scale in the standardisation sample. The effect of maternal education disappeared with children above around age 3;06. This is a cross-sectional study so it is hard to draw any firm conclusions, but it is possible that preschool education had a compensatory effect for the older children. A report on receptive vocabulary development in children attending nurseries in a large multi-site academy in Northumberland (Jones et al. 2013) found that children attending campuses in areas of low SES had significantly poorer understanding of vocabulary on entry to nursery than those from higher SES backgrounds. However, these children began to close the gap in ability over the course of the two year longitudinal study, with those who had the poorest understanding at the beginning making the greatest progress. Nursery staff had received training in providing an enriched language environment.

4 Conclusions

So where does this leave us regarding the relationship between SES and child language acquisition and impairment? There is evidence for correlations between SES and language acquisition, although a majority of studies have focused on vocabulary acquisition rather than other levels of language. SES factors such as maternal education and neighbourhood disadvantage appear to have a potential negative effect on acquisition of the sort of language skills necessary to participate in education, at least in 'Western' societies. However the influence of SES in this area is arguably indirect with direct influences coming from lack of resources that would stimulate wide ranging vocabulary acquisition and provide experience with language styles important for academic purposes, plus differences in styles of parent-child interaction. These factors may frequently be associated with poverty, but it should not be assumed that they are present universally in situations of social deprivation; many children living in such conditions are not adversely affected, especially if the adults around them are determined to give them the best experiences possible within the constraints imposed by these conditions. There is also emerging evidence that effects of deprivation can be compensated by language-rich preschool education.

Furthermore there is no clear evidence that social deprivation is a causative factor in language impairment. There is considerable dispute over the nature of language impairment and especially specific language impairment (see Reilly et al. 2014, for example), but most agree that if an impairment is diagnosed, there are always features intrinsic to the child, such as poor or slow to develop auditory- and linguistic processing. These difficulties may be exacerbated by the environment and also certain SES groups are likely to contain more adults with impairment who may pass on their difficulties to their children. However, language impairment is evident across all social backgrounds.

For the professional with responsibility for children with language impairment, it will be important to consider carefully any environmental influences that may be reinforcing the difficulties the child already has, such as poor input. However assumptions should not be made that input is impoverished just on the grounds of a low SES background; not only is this potentially alienating to the family and therefore damaging to the child's progress, but such assumptions also carry the risk of misdirection of resources to address a problem that does not exist.

Professionals should also consider the assessment tools used to identify and assess children with potential impairment and should never rely solely on standardised tests, given the social and cultural issues with testing that have been outlined in this chapter. A detailed profile needs to be drawn up, based on a range of formal assessment procedures, language samples and observations, plus information regarding the child's medical history and social background; this should include the concerns of family members and teachers. Professionals such as speech and language therapists will also be called upon to advise on preschool education programmes and are well-placed to do so. Currently such input is more likely to be requested for nurseries situated in areas of social deprivation.

References

All Party Parliamentary Group on Speech and Language Difficulties. 2013. The links between speech, language and communication needs and social disadvantage. London: Royal College of Speech and Language Therapists.
Bernstein, Basil. 1971. *Class, codes and control Vol 1: Theoretical studies towards a sociology of language*. London: Routledge & Kegan Paul.
Black, Esther, Sue Peppé & Fiona Gibbon. 2008. The relationship between socio-economic status and lexical development. *Clinical Linguistics and Phonetics* 22(4–5). 259–265.

Carter, Julie A. Janet A. Lees, Gladys M. Murira, Joseph Gona, Brian GR Neville & Charles RJC Newton. 2005. Issues in the development of cross-cultural assessments of speech and language for children. *International Journal of Language & Communication Disorders* 40(3). 385–401.

Edwards, Susan, Carolyn Letts & Indra Sinka. 2011. *The new Reynell developmental language scales*. London: GL-Assessment.

Fenson, L., P. S. Dale & J. S. Reznik. 1993. The MacArthur communicative developmental inventories: Users guide and technical manual. San Diego: Singular Publishing Group.

Grainger, Karen. 2013. 'The daily grunt': Middle class bias and vested interests in the 'Getting in Early' and 'Why can't They Read?' reports. *Language and Education* 27(2). 99–109.

Gross, Jean. (Ed.). 2008. *Getting in early: Primary schools and early intervention*. London: Centre for Policy Studies and The Smith Institute.

Harrison, Linda J. & Sharynne McLeod. 2010. Risk and protective factors associated with speech and language impairment in a nationally representative sample of 4- and 5-year-old children. *Journal of Speech, Language and Hearing Research* 53(2). 508–529.

Hart, Betty, & Todd R. Risley. 1995. *Meaningful differences in the everyday experiences of young American children*. Baltimore: Paul Brookes.

Hoff, Erika. 2003. The specificity of environmental influence: Socioeconomic status affects early vocabulary development via maternal speech. *Child Development* 74(5). 1368–1378.

Horton-Ikard, RaMonda & Susan Ellis Weismer. 2007. A preliminary examination of vocabulary and word learning in African American toddlers from middle and low socioeconomic status homes. *American Journal of Speech-Language Pathology* 16(4). 381–392.

Jones, K., H. Stringer, C. Robinson, M. Hinson & D. Nicholson. 2013. Partnership working to support the development of children's speech and language skills in the early years foundation stage. Report from Knowledge Transfer Partnership project prepared for Northumberland Church of England Academy. (Unpublished, copies available from helen.stringer@newcastle.ac.uk.)

Labov, William. 1972. The logic of non-standard English. In Pier Paolo Giglioli (ed.), *Language and social context*, 179–215. Harmondsworth: Penguin.

Law, James, Kirsty McBean & Robert Rush. 2011. Communication skills in a population of primary school-aged children raised in an area of pronounced social disadvantage. *International Journal of Language & Communication Disorders* 46(6). 657–664.

Letts, Carolyn, Susan Edwards, Indra Sinka, Blanca Schaefer & Wendy Gibbons. 2013. Socio-economic status and language acquisition: Children's performance on the new Reynell Developmental Language Scales. *International Journal of Language & Communication Disorders* 48(2). 131–143.

Lidz, Carol S. 2003. *Early childhood assessment*. New Jersey: Wiley.

Locke, Ann, Jane Ginsborg, & Ian Peers. 2002. Development and disadvantage: Implications for the early years and beyond. *International Journal of Language & Communication Disorders* 37(1). 3–16.

McIntosh, Beth, Sharon Crosbie, Alison Holm, Barbara Dodd & Sian Thomas. 2007. Enhancing the phonological awareness and language skills of socially disadvantaged preschoolers: An interdisciplinary programme. *Child Language Teaching and Therapy* 23(3). 267–286.

Michel, Marije C. & Folkert Kuiken. 2014. Language at preschool in Europe: Early years professionals in the spotlight. *European Journal of Applied Linguistics* 2(1). 1–26.

Mroz, M & C. Letts. 2014. Early years education, language and social background: A decade of changing policy and practice. *European Journal of Applied Linguistics* 2(1). 79–100.

Ochs, Elinor. 1983. Cultural dimensions of language acquisition. In Elinor Ochs & Bambi B. Schieffelin (eds.), *Acquiring conversational competence*, 185–191. London: Routledge and Kegan Paul.

Peers, I, P. Lloyd & C. Foster. 2000. *Clinical evaluation of language fundamentals – preschool UK*. London: Psychological Corporation.

Prevoo, Mariëlle JL. Maike Malda, Judi Mesman, Rosanneke A.G. Emmen, Nihal Yeniad, Marinus H. van Ijzendoorn & Mariëlle Linting. 2014. Predicting ethnic minority children's vocabulary from socioeconomic status, maternal language and home reading input: Different pathways for host and ethnic language. *Journal of Child Language* 41(5). 963–984.

Qi, Cathy Huaqing, Ann P. Kaiser, Stephanie Milan & Terry Hancock. 2006. Language performance of low-income African American and European American preschool children on the PPVT-III. *Language, Speech and Hearing Services in the Schools* 37(1). 5–16.

Reilly, Sheena, Edith L. Bavin, Lesley Bretherton, Laura Conway, Patricia Eadie, Eileen Cini, Margot Prior, Obioha C. Ukoumunne & Melissa Wake. 2009. The Early Language in Victoria Study ELVS: A prospective, longitudinal study of communication skills and expressive vocabulary development at 8, 12 and 24 months. *International Journal of Speech-Language Pathology* 11(5). 344–357.

Reilly, Sheena, Bruce Tomblin, James Law, Cristina McKean, Fiona K. Mensah, Angela Morgan, Sharon Goldfeld, Jan M. Nicholson & Melissa Wake. 2014. Specific language impairment: A convenient label for whom? *International Journal of Language & Communication Disorders* 49(4). 416–451.

Reilly, Sheena, Melissa Wake, Obioha C. Ukoumunne, Edith Bavin, Margot Prior, Eileen Cini, Laura Conway, Patricia Eadie & Lesley Bretherton. 2010. Predicting language outcomes at 4 years of age: Findings from early language in Victoria study. *Pediatrics* 126(6).

Reilly, Sheena, Melissa Wake, Edith L. Bavin, Margot Prior, Joanne Williams, Lesley Bretherton, Patricia Eadie, Yin Barrett & Obioha C. Ukoumunne. 2007. Predicting language at 2 years of age: A prospective community study. *Pediatrics* 120(6).

Roulstone, Sue, James Law, Robert Rush, Judy Clegg &Tim Peters. 2011. *Investigating the role of language in children's early educational outcomes*. Project Report: UK Department of Education, Bristol.

Rowe, Meredith L. 2008. Relation of socioeconomic status, knowledge of child development and vocabulary skill. *Journal of Child Language* 35(1). 185–205.

Rydland, Veslemøy, Vibeke Grøver & Joshua Lawrence. 2014. The second language trajectories of Turkish immigrant children in Norway from ages five to ten: The role of preschool talk exposure, maternal education and co-ethnic concentration in the neighborhood. *Journal of Child Language* 41(2). 352–381.

Scheele, Anna F. Paul P.M. Leseman & Aziza Y. Mayo. 2010. The home environment of monolingual and bilingual children and their language proficiency. *Applied Psycholinguistics* 31(1). 117–140.

Semel, Eleanor Messing, Elisabeth H. Wiig & Wayne Secord. 2006. *Clinical evaluation of language fundamentals (CELF IV)*. London: Psychological Corporation.

Shneidman, Laura A. Michelle E. Arroyo, Susan C. Levine & Susan Goldin-Meadow. 2013. What counts as effective input for word learning? *Journal of Child Language* 40(03). 672–686.

Song, Lulu, Elizabeth T. Spier & Catherine S. Tamis-Lemonda. 2014. Reciprocal influences between maternal language and children's language and cognitive development in low-income families. *Journal of Child Language* 41(2). 305–326.

Tizard, Barbara, Martin Hughes, Helen Carmichael & Gill Pinkerton. 1983. Language and social class: Is verbal deprivation a myth? *Journal of Child Psychology and Psychiatry* 24(4). 533–542.

Vasilyeva, Marina, Heidi Waterfall & Janellen Huttenlocher. 2008. Emergence of syntax: Commonalities and differences across children. *Developmental Science* 11(1). 84–97.

Wells, Gordon. 1986. *The meaning makers: Children learning language and using language to learn*. Portsmouth, NH: Heinemann Educational Books Inc.

Wetherby, Amy M. & Barry M. Prizant. 2002. *Communication and symbolic behavior scales*. Baltimore, MD: Paul H. Brookes Publishing.

Zhan, Changjuan. 2010. Acquisition of communicative competence. *Journal of Language Teaching and Research* 1(1). 50–52.

III Environmental effects

Section 7: Multilingualism

Annick De Houwer
29 Input, context and early child bilingualism: Implications for clinical practice

1 Introduction

On a global scale, there are likely more children developing bilingually than monolingually (Kohnert 2010). Children become bilingual in a large variety of settings and situations (De Houwer 2009). This variability is of fundamental importance in the understanding of early bilingual development and in the assessment of whether bilingual children are developing as can be expected (De Houwer 2011), or, instead, are experiencing "systemic" (Gathercole 2013a) difficulties with learning language and thus show up a "core language deficit" (Hasson, Camilleri, Jones, Smith and Dodd 2013).

A core problem with language learning will affect all languages a child is exposed to. Deep-seated language learning difficulties may be the result of other problems such as a hearing impairment or they may not be easily attributable to any specific underlying cause (Specific Language Impairment, e.g., Paradis 2010).

This chapter focuses on bilingual children's development, positions that development in the language learning contexts children find themselves in, and suggests a global procedure for screening for possible systemic language learning problems in bilingual children. It fully endorses Article 29, division (c) of the United Nations Convention on the Rights of the Child, stating that the States who are parties to the Convention agree that children's education shall be directed to "The development of respect for the child's parents, his or her own cultural identity, language and values, for the national values of the country in which the child is living, the country from which he or she may originate, and for civilizations different from his or her own" (http://www.ohchr.org/Documents/ProfessionalInterest/crc.pdf, accessed July 2017). This perspective implies that all languages spoken to bilingual children are to be supported. After all, growing up bilingually usually is nobody's express choice but rather the result of important life events such as moving to another country or having parents with different language backgrounds (De Houwer 1999). The sadly still common advice on the part of professionals dealing with young children that parents should stop speaking a home language to children that is not used at (pre)school reflects a lack of respect for children's cultural backgrounds and thus goes against the UN Convention. In addition to home language(s) support being a human rights issue, young bilingual children's well-being is promoted if they are proficient in two languages (Collins, Toppelberg, Suárez-Orozco, O'Connor and

Annick De Houwer, Universität Erfurt

Nieto-Castañon 2011; Han 2010). This is because children's bilingual context involves social connections with important people such as parents, siblings, other relatives, friends and teachers who communicate in linguistically different ways. Children's well-being is hampered if their communicative skills limit themselves to communication with only a portion of those important people (De Houwer 2015a). Furthermore, early well-developed proficiency in a first language promotes linguistic development in a second (Lust, Flynn, Blume, Park, Kang, Yang and Kim 2014).

This chapter concerns children under formal schooling age (normally, under age 5 or 6) who have been learning two spoken languages. The research evidence on children exposed to three or more languages is so far quite limited; however, the facts surrounding the learning of multiple languages appear quite similar to those surrounding the learning of two. Space limitations preclude discussion of the complexities involved when children who are reared bilingually stutter (Shenker 2013) or have known impairments such as hearing loss (Crowe and McLeod 2014), Autism Spectrum Disorder (Kay-Raining Bird, Lamond and Holden 2011) or Down syndrome (Trudeau, Kay-Raining Bird, Sutton and Cleave 2011). It should be clear from the outset that being raised in a bilingual environment is not a cause of language impairment or disorder.

2 Different pathways for early bilingual development

There is a great variety of settings in which young children acquire two languages, and a concurrently great variety of pathways that children take in their bilingual language learning. Yet, a basic difference exists between children raised with two languages from birth (Bilingual First Language Acquisition or BFLA; De Houwer 1990) and children under age 6 who start off hearing a single language (L1) to which at some later time a second one (L2) is added (Early Second Language Acquisition or ESLA; De Houwer 1990; Letts 1991). BFLA children are acquiring two first languages termed language Alpha and language A (Wölck 1987/1988). Typically, BFLA children hear their two languages in the home. ESLA children first acquire their L1 in the home and typically start to hear their L2 through child care or preschool. The precise age at which the L2 starts to be regularly heard varies considerably from child to child. Two large-scale surveys offering empirical data on language input to young children suggest that BFLA occurs about three times as often as ESLA (De Houwer 2007; Winsler, Burchinal, Tien, Peisner-Feinberg, Espinosa, Castro, LaForett, Kim and De Feyter 2014).

BFLA and ESLA children have a fundamentally different experience with language learning. In BFLA, large linguistic variation in the input is present from the outset, and children have been used to people speaking in fundamentally different ways from birth (De Houwer 2006). BFLA children gradually learn to understand two languages at the same time, and can gradually learn to make sense of their bilingual world in an environment that supports their early understanding through specific infant-directed speech embedded in familiar contexts (De Houwer 2009). By the time they are into their second year, they understand words in two languages. This is a fundamental, specifically bilingual milestone (De Houwer 2012, 2014). Understanding translation equivalents, that is, words in both input languages that largely mean the same thing, such as German "Mond" and English "moon", is a very early development as well (De Houwer, Bornstein and De Coster 2006). BFLA infants fast develop a large comprehension vocabulary repertoire: At 13 months they understand as many words as monolingual peers do only 4 months later (De Houwer, Bornstein and Putnick 2014). De Houwer's (2010) comparison of young BFLA children's vocabulary scores to monolingual percentile-based norms in each of two languages confirms this early bilingual advantage.

The ESLA experience is quite different. For hitherto monolingual children, receiving structurally complex input in an unfamiliar language comes as an initial shock: suddenly they can no longer make sense of what people are saying. In addition, except for international adoptees, most ESLA children meet up with a new language in a group setting, with little one-to-one scaffolding-type child directed speech. This does not contribute to children's well-being (De Houwer 2015b): as several studies reviewed in De Houwer (2017) indicate, the first few months in an institutional setting where they understand nothing and are not understood when they communicate verbally is a very upsetting experience for young children that can have far-reaching effects on their psychosocial behavior. It will take some time before ESLA children start to fully understand the new language. Just how much time is hard to predict: much depends on when children started to hear the L2, and on a multitude of other factors. Typically developing ESLA children with first regular exposure to the L2 starting at age three show great increases in L2 comprehension after one year (Hammer, Lawrence and Miccio 2008; Leseman 2000). By age 5, the same ESLA children's levels of L2 vocabulary comprehension are still well below age-matched monolingual children's, though (Hammer et al. 2008). Indeed, compared to children with continuous exposure to English from birth, ESLA children with English as L2 do less well on standardized English vocabulary comprehension tests normed for monolingual English-speaking peers (Bialystok, Luk, Peets and Yang 2010). Given that lexical learning largely depends on input frequency (Hart and Risley 1995), and given that ESLA children have far less total exposure to their L2 than monolingual children to their L1, these results are to be expected. Fortunately, children can rapidly learn more words through increased exposure. Reading offers major advantages here (Nagy and Scott 2004).

Most BFLA families want children to learn to understand and speak two languages from the beginning. There are emotional and cultural connections with both, and children are usually expected to speak both languages at home in function of sociolinguistic variables such as addressee and topic of conversation. In ESLA families there is generally much more of an emotional and cultural connection with children's L1 than with the L2 that children are learning through day-care or preschool, and children will be expected to speak the L1 at home, not the L2. The L2 will be expected in the institutional setting.

However, children often do not live up to parents' and educators' expectations in terms of the language(s) they choose to speak. BFLA children usually start out saying words in both languages as toddlers, but in about a quarter of BFLA families, children stop speaking the home language that is not used at (pre)school soon after they start attending (pre)school (De Houwer 2007, 2009). This implies that in parent-child conversations, each participant speaks another language. These language-incongruent parent-child conversations are not optimal for communication and family dynamics, and often have negative consequences for child and family well-being (De Houwer 2015a).

Once ESLA children develop some speaking proficiency in the L2 they may start to speak it at home as well, in addition to the L1. It is rare that ESLA children completely stop speaking the L1: Only 3% of families that exclusively speak an L1 other than the school language at home have school-aged children who do not speak the L1 (De Houwer 2007).

Early childhood educators often expect children to speak the L2 very soon (Bligh 2014). Such expectations are unrealistic: children need time to learn to speak an L2. Although very little published evidence is available, upon entry into an institutional setting where the L1 is not used many ESLA children first spend some time taking in the new language and dealing with their lack of comprehension (Gibbons 1985). There is great variability amongst ESLA children in how long it takes them to start speaking the L2 at rudimentary levels. Ranges are between no time at all to more than a year (compare Clarke 1999; Sun, de Bot and Steinkrauss 2015; Thompson 2000). Shyness explains some of the variability between children (Keller, Troesch and Grob 2013). Educators can develop several strategies to engage ESLA children in such a way that they become more motivated and able to actually start speaking in the L2 (Deiner 2012; Tabors 2008). Programs to actively show respect and appreciation of children's home language(s) will make both BFLA and ESLA children feel better about themselves and preschool (Chumak-Horbatsch 2012; De Houwer 2015b).

The next section formulates some generalizations regarding key developments in BFLA and ESLA children's speech production.

3 Speech production in BFLA and ESLA

Like monolingual children, BFLA children say their first words between 8 and 15 months of age. BFLA children who are not producing words in any language by age 16 months should be assessed for undiagnosed impairments. Little is known about the early monolingual language development of ESLA-children-to-be. They are usually only studied once their L2 exposure has commenced.

In contrast to most ESLA children, BFLA children start saying words in each of their two languages in early toddlerhood. On average, BFLA toddlers produce as many different words as monolingual peers (De Houwer et al. 2014). However, some individual bilingual toddlers produce more than double the number of words than same-aged top-performing monolinguals (De Houwer et al. 2014), confirming that bilingualism does not lead to lexical delay, as is often erroneously assumed. Lexical norms developed for monolingual children can be used for very young BFLA children to help determine whether a particular child is developing as expected (De Houwer 2010).

For each language separately, the combined evidence for BFLA points to a high degree of similarity with monolingual children in overall language development (De Houwer 2014; Serratrice 2012). Structurally, BFLA children develop each of their languages like basically separate morphosyntactic systems (thus confirming the Separate Development Hypothesis, see De Houwer 1990, 2009). Compared to monolinguals, no delays are to be expected for BFLA children: *in at least one of their languages*, typically developing BFLA children reach similar language development milestones and show the same kind of wide variation as same-aged monolinguals (De Houwer 2009, 2012). Thus suspected delays should not be attributed to bilingualism and left unattended, but should be investigated as they would for monolingual children (Toppelberg, Medrano, Morgens and Nieto-Castañon 2002). Similar levels of development cannot, however, be expected for both languages: uneven development is part of typical development not only in BFLA but also in ESLA (see further point 4. below).

Studies tracking speech production in ESLA usually are limited to children's L2. As regards the L2, developmental trajectories are variable and unpredictable. However, some generalizations can be made. Many ESLA children start speaking the L2 using set formulas and single words (Hakuta 1974; Wong Fillmore 1976; Meisel 2008). With time, ESLA children start to produce sentences that gradually increase in length and complexity. Once ESLA children are able to form sentences in the new L2, they often use morphosyntactic structures in their L2 that do not appear in the speech of children who have heard that language from birth (Fantini 1985; Li Wei 2011; Meisel 2008; Zdorenko and Paradis 2007). While some of these morphosyntactic structures show influence from ESLA children's L1 (Schwartz, Minkov, Dieser, Protassova, Moin and Polinsky 2015), others do not (Granfeldt, Schlyter and Kihlstedt 2007). Cross-linguistic influence has also been reported for L2 phonology (Hambly, Wren, McLeod and Roulstone 2013). The many variations of different L1s and L2s vastly complicate any attempts at predicting speech patterns for a specific L2.

For very young children, there is little information on how fast they generally learn to speak an L2 with some degree of fluency but again there appears to be a great deal of variability. In one of the rare longitudinal linguistically oriented studies on ESLA, Nap-Kolhoff (2010) shows that it takes some preschool-aged children up to two years to learn to speak an L2 to the extent that an unfamiliar adult can understand them. The variability in starting to actually speak the L2 and the level of interactive support in the new L2 likely impact the rates at which ESLA children develop high L2 proficiency, but sufficient empirical data are so far lacking. Various additional factors can account for the variability in the development of L2 speaking skills, such as length of time of exposure combined with the age at which young children first are regularly exposed to the L2 (Schwartz and Rovner 2014), child temperament (Sun et al. 2014), levels of L1 proficiency (Winsler, Kim and Richard 2014), input frequency in the new L2 (compare Sun et al. 2014 and Lin and Johnson 2016), and the language that children choose to speak to key individuals (Hammer, Komaroff, Rodriguez, Lopez, Scarpino and Goldstein 2012).

Both BFLA (Lanza 1997) and ESLA (McClure 1981) children may use mixed utterances, that is, utterances combining words from two languages. This is normal and not to be taken as a sign of language impairment or delay.

4 Uneven development: Implications for assessment

Uneven development refers to the commonly observed fact that bilingual children typically do not perform equally in their two languages (De Houwer 2009). This applies to one particular moment in time and to children's development over time. One language may develop faster than the other, then slow down, and the other language may then "take over". Uneven development shows up both in comprehension and in production. Young bilingual children may be stronger in one language for one particular domain but stronger in the other language for another (see De Houwer and Bornstein (2015) for early word comprehension and production). In the realm of vocabulary, it is well-known that bilingual children know some things only in a single language, and others in two (Conboy and Thal 2006; De Houwer et al. 2006). Both BFLA (De Houwer 2009) and ESLA (Snow and Hoefnagel-Höhle 1978) children may suffer from fast attrition of one of their languages, that is, their levels of proficiency may stagnate or go down. This attrition commonly starts to take place in the first year of children's child care or preschool attendance. ESLA children's rate of learning to understand new words in the L1 may decrease as they start to attend preschool in an L2; a similar effect may obtain for the language that BFLA children are not exposed to at school. The extent to which attrition of speaking skills in the non-school language will occur cannot be predicted, but much depends on continued rich spoken language exposure in the home (Hammer, Lawrence, Rodriguez, Davison and Miccio 2011; MacLeod, Fabiano-Smith, Boegner-Pagé and Fontolliet 2013). Developing reading skills in the language not heard at school will be of major benefit to counteracting the attrition of comprehension skills.

Different language profiles resulting from uneven development and the greater variety of forms to be learned in bilingual settings (De Houwer 2006) lead to extremely wide variation amongst bilingual children in their overall linguistic proficiency (Kohnert 2010). The universality of uneven development in early bilingual development has important implications for language assessment, some of which are only briefly highlighted here (for fuller treatments, see e.g. Cruz-Ferreira 2010; Gathercole 2013b; Howell and Van Borsel 2011; Kohnert 2013; Letts and Sinka 2013; McLeod and Goldstein 2012; Paradis, Genesee and Crago 2011; Schulz and Tracy 2011; Sharp and Gathercole 2013).

Assessment should take into account both languages that bilingual children are acquiring (e.g., Hasson et al. 2013). Just considering single language abilities may give a distorted view, especially if the language children are assessed in what happens to be the child's generally weaker language. However, we are far from having culturally appropriate assessment instruments available in all the world's languages, and then there is the issue of SLPs' knowledge of those languages. The challenges are enormous (Battle 2012; McLeod and Verdon 2014; Verdon, McLeod and Wong 2014).

Assessment involves a comparison to some sort of standard. Often monolingual norms are used. These are based on the continuous increase of proficiency in all domains of a single language over time. In a bilingual setting, young children cannot be expected to continuously increase in proficiency in all domains in each of two languages over time. Furthermore, as many contributions in Gathercole (2013b) explain, there is no reason why bilinguals should perform like monolinguals. However, regulations for clinical practice often only allow for the use of standardized assessment methods with monolingual norms. In some cases this may be appropriate, but children's learning contexts need to be taken into account. BFLA children can be expected to typically develop quite well in several domains in the (pre)school language. For assessing this language, monolingual norms may well be appropriate, since these are also based on children's continuing input to a language from birth. The language that BFLA children hear markedly less often can likely not be compared to monolingual norms. For ESLA children the picture is more diffuse. For children's L1, monolingual norms may be appropriate if there has been continued rich exposure in the L1. There may be a period of time in which children start to hesitatingly use the L2 and where this coincides with a slow-down in L1 development. This is quite normal but an improvement in the L2 should soon be noticeable. In order to assess whether there is a fundamental problem with learning language monolingual norms are not generally usable for ESLA children's L2.

For assessing language in developing bilinguals, Kohnert (2010) recommends the use of multiple measures, in both languages, at different points in time. It should always be taken into account that bilingual children first and foremost need to be able to communicate in different circumstances to the extent that people speaking different languages understand them, even if children are not speaking according to monolingual norms.

Quite fundamentally, the assessment of bilingual preschool children needs to take into account language exposure patterns (De Houwer 2011; Gathercole, Thomas,

Roberts, Hughes and Hughes 2013). Before a full assessment is invested in, however, bilingual children should be screened for potential language learning problems. Also in such screening, language exposure should be given a central role. The general expectations for the two fundamentally different bilingual exposure contexts (BFLA and ESLA) form the background for the screening protocol described below (modified from De Houwer 1998). The protocol heavily relies on information gained from parents (cf. McLaughlin, Blanchard and Osanai 1995).

5 Step-by-step protocol for screening bilingually raised children for possible systemic language learning problems

The protocol here pays attention to children's overall use of one vs. two languages. It is intended for bilingual preschool-age children without any known impairments who understand and speak at least one language (the absence of language comprehension and/or speech in preschool children points to severe developmental problems). Its goal is to help SLPs decide whether a particular bilingual child has special needs, i.e., needs to be followed up or needs to be fully assessed for systemic language learnings problems. The protocol represents a principled approach that may be very difficult to actually put into practice because of the many complexities involving measurement and comparison to expectations. Ideally, screening for possible systemic language learning problems should take place very early for all children. For ESLA children especially, though, screening should ideally take place before they have started to know much of their new L2: At that time, complicating factors like L1 attrition have normally not yet set in, and children can in principle be evaluated like monolingual children.

Step 1 relies on interviewing children's parents and preschool staff. Its focus is on the totality of speech addressed to children in face-to-face conversation and is needed to determine whether children grew up in a BFLA vs. an ESLA setting.

STEP 1. Characterisation of the language input setting
1.1. Which language(s) does the child currently hear at home from caregivers and older siblings?
1.2. Which languages do other people (including other children) currently regularly speak to the child?
1.3. At what age did regular (nearly daily) input to the child in each of these languages start?

Steps 2 and 3 below are intended for BFLA children with regular input to two languages at home (and possibly to one of them at preschool) and for ESLA children who heard an L1 at home since birth and have been regularly exposed to an L2 in a full immersion setting through child care or preschool for at least 6 months prior to evaluation. This protocol is not intended for international adoptees or children who for other reasons no longer receive input in an L1.

Step 2 can partly be realized on the basis of parent and staff report, but steps 2.2. BFLA and 2.4. ESLA normally require SLP testing. Often, though, tools will be lacking to carry out formal testing. In this case parents and staff need to be relied on to help evaluate whether children show any comprehension deficits.

STEP 2. Assessment of the child's language comprehension

2.1. BFLA
Does the child understand two languages?
- YES: go to 2.2. BFLA
- NO: reconsider the child's categorization as BFLA

2.1. ESLA
Does the child understand the L1 but not the L2?
- YES: work with preschool staff to increase L2 support (Deiner 2012). Repeat this procedure after 6 months. Go to 2.4. ESLA
- NO: go to 2.2. ESLA

2.2. BFLA
Does the level of comprehension globally match that of monolingual peers for at least one language?
- YES: go to 3.1. BFLA
- NO: unexpected and needs explanation (just like for monolinguals*)

2.2. ESLA
Does the child understand the L2 but not the L1?
- YES: severe L1 attrition is unexpected and needs explanation and action. Go to 2.4. ESLA
- NO: go to 2.3. ESLA

2.3. ESLA
Does the child understand two languages?
- YES: go to 2.4. ESLA

2.4. ESLA
Is the child's total comprehension (either in just L1, just L2, or in both languages combined) at the level expected for monolingual peers?
- YES: go to 3.1. ESLA
- NO: unexpected and needs explanation (just like for monolinguals*)

* needed: e.g., a thorough screening of the child's hearing, possibly other medical tests, a thorough assessment of the home input situation to see if there are enough language learning opportunities

If there are no language comprehension issues, go on to Step 3, which assesses language production. Parent and staff report will again be useful sources of information. "Speaking a language" in Step 3 refers to the ability to produce sentences rather than just single words.

STEP 3. Assessment of the child's language production

3.1. BFLA
Does the child speak two languages?
- YES: go to 3.3. BFLA
- NO: go to 3.2. BFLA

3.1. ESLA
Does the child understand and speak the L1 but not (or barely) the L2?
- YES: work with preschool to increase L2 support (Deiner 2012). Repeat this procedure after 6 months**. Go to 3.4. ESLA
- NO: go to 3.2. ESLA

3.2. BFLA
Is the single language that the child speaks the language used at preschool?
- YES: work with parents to (re-)activate the child's use of the non-school home language if they so wish (Kohnert, Yim, Nett, Kan and Duran 2005). Go to 3.3. BFLA
- NO: unexpected. The child may be unduly shy. There may be selective mutism (Toppelberg, Tabors Coggins, Lum and Burger 2005). Go to 3.3. BFLA

3.2. ESLA
Does the child understand and speak the L2 but not (or barely) the L1?
- YES: unexpected. Work with parents to counteract L1 attrition (Kohnert et al. 2005). Go to 3.5. ESLA
- NO: go to 3.3. ESLA

3.3. BFLA
Does the level of language production match that of monolingual peers for at least one language?
- YES: no sign of language learning problems
- NO: unexpected and needs explanation (just like for monolinguals*)

3.3. ESLA
Does the child speak two languages?
- YES: go to 3.6. ESLA

3.4. ESLA
Does the level of L1 language production match that of monolingual peers?
- YES: no sign of language learning problems
- NO: unexpected and needs explanation (just like for monolinguals*)

3.5. ESLA
Does the child fluently communicate in the L2?
- YES: no sign of language learning problems; follow up after 12 months to monitor progress
- NO: expected in the first 18 months after first regular L2 exposure; follow up after 6 months to monitor progress

3.6. ESLA
Does the child fluently communicate in at least one language?
- YES: no sign of language learning problems; follow up after 12 months to monitor progress
- NO: *first exposure to L2 up to 18 months ago:* L1 attrition may have started but L2 development still needs to really "take off". Work with parents and preschool to increase input support for L1 and L2 (Kohnert et al. 2005; Deiner 2012).

Follow up after 6 months. Screen for hearing problems.

first exposure to L2 more than 18 months ago: thorough further assessment necessary*

* there may be undiagnosed impairments such as Specific Language Impairment, hearing impairment (in spite of adequate comprehension), psychiatric disorders, and so on

** if after 12 months of rich L2 input and opportunities to use it the child still does not attempt to say sentences in the L2 selective mutism may be an issue (Toppelberg et al. 2005) or there are issues at preschool (Bligh 2014; Chumak-Horbatsch 2012)

6 In conclusion

There is substantial research evidence available about the typical developmental paths that young BFLA children take in each of their languages. In contrast, the paucity of detailed linguistically oriented longitudinal studies of ESLA and the vast heterogeneity within ESLA mean that we know far less about typical ESLA developmental trajectories and that these are harder to identify, or, indeed, may not exist. This is a major hindrance for evaluations of ESLA children's language profiles. Fortunately, recent years have seen a surge in clinically oriented research involving young bilingual children. This has focused a lot on ESLA children. There has also been a tremendous recent increase in attention to issues pertaining to assessment for multilingual clients. The realization that bilingual children's language learning settings need to be taken into account in clinical practice is nearly universally represented in this recent work. Yet that is often not translated into practical guidance. Hopefully the protocol presented here can help practicioners to take bilingual children's language learning settings into account and thus better serve this underserved population.

References

Battle, Dolores (ed.). 2012. *Communication disorders in multicultural and international populations* (4th ed.). St. Louis, MI: Elsevier.
Bialystok, Ellen, Gigi Luk, Kathleen Peets & Sujin Yang. 2010. Receptive vocabulary differences in monolingual and bilingual children. *Bilingualism: Language and Cognition* 13. 525–531.
Bligh, Caroline. 2014. *The silent experiences of young bilingual learners. A sociocultural study into the silent period*. Rotterdam: SensePublishers.
Chumak-Horbatsch, Roma. 2012. *Linguistically appropriate practice: A guide for working with young immigrant children*. Toronto: University of Toronto Press.
Clarke, Priscilla. 1999. Investigating second language acquisition in preschools: A longitudinal study of four Vietnamese-speaking children's acquisition of English in a bilingual preschool. *International Journal of Early Years Education* 7. 17–24.
Collins, Brian, Claudio Toppelberg, Carola Suárez-Orozco, Erin O'Connor & Alfonso Nieto-Castañon. 2011. Cross-sectional associations of Spanish and English competence and well-being in Latino children of immigrants in kindergarten. *International Journal of the Sociology of Language* 208. 5–24.
Conboy, Barbara & Donna Thal. 2006. Ties between the lexicon and grammar: Cross-sectional and longitudinal studies of bilingual toddlers. *Child Development* 77. 712–735.
Crowe, Kathryn & Sharynne McLeod. 2014. A systematic review of cross-linguistic and multilingual speech and language outcomes for children with hearing loss. *International Journal of Bilingualism and Bilingual Education* 17. 287–309.
Cruz-Ferreira, Madalena (ed.). 2010. *Multilingual norms*. Frankfurt: Peter Lang.
De Houwer, Annick. 1990. *The acquisition of two language from birth: A case study*. Cambridge: Cambridge University Press.

De Houwer, Annick. 1998. Jonge meertalig opgroeiende kinderen en mogelijke taalleerproblemen: enkele aandachtspunten voor de logopedische praktijk [Young children raised bilingually and potential language learning problems: a few pointers for clinical practice]. *Logopedie [Logopedics]* 1. 9–17.

De Houwer, Annick. 1999. *Two or more languages in early childhood: some general points and some practical recommendations.* ERIC digest. EDO-FL-99-03, ERIC Clearinghouse on Languages and Linguistics, Washington: Center for Applied Linguistics http://www.cal.org/resource-center/briefs-digests/digests/(offset)/105 (accessed July 2017)

De Houwer, Annick. 2006. Bilingual development in the early years. In Keith Brown (ed.), *Encyclopedia of language and linguistics, 2nd Edition*, 781–787. Oxford: Elsevier.

De Houwer, Annick. 2007. Parental language input patterns and children's bilingual use. *Applied Psycholinguistics* 28. 411–424.

De Houwer, Annick. 2009. *Bilingual first language acquisition.* Bristol: Multilingual Matters.

De Houwer, Annick. 2010. Assessing lexical development in Bilingual First Language Acquisition: What can we learn from monolingual norms? In Madalena Cruz-Ferreira (ed.), *Multilingual norms*, 279–322. Frankfurt: Peter Lang.

De Houwer, Annick. 2011. Language input environments and language development in bilingual acquisition. *Applied Linguistics Review* 2. 221–240.

De Houwer, Annick. 2012. Milestones in bilingual children's language development. In *Encyclopedia of Language and Literacy Development*, 1–8. London, Canada: Western Ontario University.

De Houwer, Annick. 2014. Bilingual language development. In Patricia Brooks & Vere Kempe (eds.), *Encyclopedia of language development*, 49–56. Thousand Oaks: Sage.

De Houwer, Annick. 2015a. Harmonious bilingual development: young families' well-being in language contact situations. *International Journal of Bilingualism* 19. 169–184.

De Houwer, Annick. 2015b. Integration und Interkulturalität in Kindertagesstätten und in Kindergärten: Die Rolle der Nichtumgebungssprache für das Wohlbefinden von Kleinkindern. In Fabienne Becker-Stoll, Christa Kieferle, Eva Reichert-Garschhammer & Monika Wertfein (eds.), *Inklusion und Partizipation. Vielfalt als Chance und Anspruch*, 113–125. Göttingen: Vandenhoeck & Ruprecht.

De Houwer, Annick. 2017. Minority language parenting in Europe and children's well-being. In Natasha Cabrera & Birgit Leyendecker (eds.), *Handbook of positive development in minority children and youth*, 231–246. Berlin: Springer.

De Houwer, Annick & Marc Bornstein. 2015. Balance patterns in early bilingual acquisition: A longitudinal study of word comprehension and production. In Carmen Silva-Corvalán & Jeanine Treffers-Daller (eds.), *Operationalising and measuring language dominance*, 134–155. Cambridge: Cambridge University Press.

De Houwer, Annick, Marc Bornstein & Sandrine De Coster. 2006. Early understanding of two words for the same thing: A CDI study of lexical comprehension in infant bilinguals. *International Journal of Bilingualism* 10. 331–348.

De Houwer, Annick, Marc Bornstein & Diane Putnick. 2014. A bilingual-monolingual comparison of young children's vocabulary size: Evidence from comprehension and production. *Applied Psycholinguistics* 35. 1189–1211 (first published online January 28, 2013)

Deiner, Penny. 2012. *Inclusive early childhood education: Development, resources, and practice.* Boston: Cengage Learning.

Fantini, Alvino. 1985. *Language acquisition of a bilingual child: a sociolinguistic perspective (to age ten).* Clevedon: Multilingual Matters.

Gathercole, Virginia. 2013a. Assessment of multi-tasking wonders: Music, Olympics, and language. In Virginia Gathercole (ed.), *Issues in the assessment of bilinguals*, 1–19. Bristol: Multilingual Matters.

Gathercole, Virginia (ed.). 2013b. *Solutions for the assessment of bilinguals.* Bristol: Multilingual Matters.

Gathercole, Virginia, Enli Thomas, Emily Roberts, Catrin Hughes & Emma Hughes. 2013. Why assessment needs to take exposure into account: Vocabulary and grammatical abilities in bilingual children. In Virginia Gathercole (ed.), *Issues in the assessment of bilinguals*, 20–55. Bristol: Multilingual Matters.

Gibbons, John. 1985. The silent period: An examination. *Language Learning* 35. 255–267.

Granfeldt, Jonas, Suzanne Schlyter & Maria Kihlstedt. 2007. French as cL2, 2L1 and L1 in pre-school children. In Jonas Granfeldt (ed.), *Studies in Romance bilingual acquisition – Age of onset and development of French and Spanish*, 7–42. Lund: Lunds Universitets Språk- och Litteraturcentrum.

Hakuta, Kenji. 1974. A report on the development of the grammatical morphemes in a Japanese girl learning English as a second language. *Working Papers on Bilingualism* 4. 18–44.

Hambly, Helen, Yvonne Wren, Sharynne McLeod & Sue Roulstone. 2013. The influence of bilingualism on speech production: A systematic review. *International Journal of Language and Communication Disorders* 48. 1–24.

Hammer, Carol, Frank Lawrence & Adele Miccio. 2008. Exposure to English before and after entry in to Head Start: Bilingual childrens's receptive language growth in Spanish and English. *International Journal of Bilingual Education and Bilingualism* 11. 30–55.

Hammer, Carol, Frank Lawrence, Barbara Rodriguez, Megan Davison & Adele Miccio. 2011. Changes in language usage of Puerto Rican mothers and their children: Do gender and timing of exposure to English matter? *Applied Psycholinguistics* 32. 275–297.

Hammer, Carol, Eugene Komaroff, Barbara Rodriguez, Lisa Lopez, Shelley Scarpino & Brian Goldstein. 2012. Predicting Spanish-English bilingual children's language abilities. *Journal of Speech-Language-Hearing Research* 55. 1251–1264.

Han, Wen-Jui. 2010. Bilingualism and socioemotional well-being. *Children & Youth Services Review* 32. 720–731.

Hart, Betty & Todd Risley. 1995. *Meaningful differences in the everyday experiences of young American children*. Baltimore: Paul Brookes.

Hasson, Natalie, Bernard Camilleri, Caroline Jones, Jodie Smith & Barbara Dodd. 2013. Discriminating disorder from difference using dynamic assessment with bilingual children. *Child Language Teaching and Therapy* 29. 57–75.

Howell, Pete & John Van Borsel (eds.). 2011. *Multilingual aspects of fluency disorders*. Bristol: Multilingual Matters.

Kay-Raining Bird, Elizabeth, Erin Lamond & Jeanette Holden. 2011. A survey of bilingualism in Autism Spectrum Disorders. *International Journal of Language & Communication Disorders* 47. 52–64.

Keller, Karin, Larissa Troesch & Alexander Grob. 2013. Shyness as a risk factor for local language skills of immigrant preschoolers. *Journal of Applied Developmental Psychology* 34. 328–335.

Kohnert, Kathryn. 2010. Bilingual children with primary language impairment: Issues, evidence and implications for clinical actions. *Journal of Communication Disorders* 43. 456–473.

Kohnert, Kathryn. 2013. *Language disorders in bilingual children and adults. Second edition.* San Diego: Plural Publishing.

Kohnert, Kathryn, Dongsun Yim, Kelly Nett, Pui Fong Kan & Lilian Duran. 2005. Intervention with linguistically diverse preschool children: A focus on developing home language(s). *Language, Speech, and Hearing Services in Schools* 36. 251–263.

Lanza, Elizabeth. 1997. *Language mixing in infant bilingualism: A sociolinguistic perspective.* Oxford: Clarendon Press.

Letts, Carolyn. 1991. Early second language acquisition: A comparison of the linguistic output of a preschool child acquiring English as a second language with that of a monolingual peer. *International Journal of Language and Communication Disorders* 26. 219–234.

Letts, Carolyn & Indra Sinka. 2013. Research and practice in working with children who are bilingual or have English as an additional language and who have language and communication needs. *Child Language Teaching and Therapy* 29. 7–9.

Leseman, Paul. 2000. Bilingual vocabulary development of Turkish preschoolers in the Netherlands. *Journal of Multilingual and Multicultural Development* 21. 93–112.

Lin, Lu-Chun & Cynthia Johnson. 2016. Mandarin-English bilingual vocabulary development in an English-immersion preschool: How does it compare with monolingual development? *International Journal of Bilingualism* 20. 173–189.

Li Wei. 2011. The early acquisition of English as a second language: The case of young Chinese learners of English in Britain. In Annick De Houwer & Antje Wilton (eds.), *English in Europe today: Educational and sociocultural perspectives*, 105–122. Amsterdam/Philadelphia: John Benjamins.

Lust, Barbara, Suzanne Flynn, María Blume, Seong Won Park, Carissa Kang, Sujin Yang & Ah-Young Kim. 2014. Assessing child bilingualism: Direct assessment of bilingual syntax amends caretaker report. *International Journal of Bilingualism*. (accessed September 2014).

MacLeod, Andrea, Leah Fabiano-Smith, Sarah Boegner-Pagé & Salomé Fontolliet. 2013. Simultaneous bilingual language acquisition: The role of parental input on receptive vocabulary development. *Child Language Teaching and Therapy* 29. 131–142.

McLeod, Sharynne & Brian Goldstein (eds.). 2012. *Multilingual aspects of speech sound disorders in children*. Bristol: Multilingual Matters.

McLeod, Sharynne & Sarah Verdon. 2014. A review of 30 speech assessments in 19 languages other than English. *American Journal of Speech-Language Pathology* 23. 708–723.

McLaughlin, Barry, Antoinette Blanchard & Yuka Osanai. 1995. *Assessing language development in bilingual preschool children*. NCBE Program Information Guide Series No. 22. Washington, D.C.: National Clearinghouse for Bilingual Education.

McClure, Erica. 1981. Formal and functional aspects of the code-switched discourse of bilingual children. In Richard Durán (ed.), *Latino language and communicative behavior*, 69–94. Norwood: Ablex Publishers.

Meisel, Jürgen. 2008. Child Second Language Acquisition or Successive First Language Acquisition? In Belma Haznedar & Elena Gavruseva (eds.), *Current trends in child second language acquisition: A generative perspective*, 55–80. Amsterdam/ Philadelphia: John Benjamins.

Nagy, Wiliam & Judith Scott. 2004. Vocabulary processes. Reprinted in Robert Ruddell & Norman Unrau (eds.), *Theoretical models and processes of reading, Fifth edition*, 574–593. Newark, DE: International Reading Association.

Nap-Kolhoff, Elma. 2010. *Second language acquisition in early childhood: A longitudinal multiple case study of Turkish-Dutch children*. Utrecht: Netherlands Graduate School of Linguistics LOT.

Paradis, Johanne. 2010. The interface between bilingual development and specific language impairment. *Applied Psycholinguistics* 31. 3–28.

Paradis, Johanne, Fred Genesee & Martha Crago. 2011. *Dual language development and disorders: A handbook on bilingualism and second language learning (2nd edition)*. Baltimore, MD: Brookes.

Schulz, Petra & Rosemarie Tracy. 2011. *LiSe-DaZ. Linguistische Sprachstandserhebung – Deutsch als Zweitsprache*. (In Verbindung mit der Baden-Württemberg Stiftung). Göttingen: Hogrefe.

Schwartz, Mila, Miriam Minkov, Elena Dieser, Ekaterina Protassova, Victor Moin & Maria Polinsky. 2015. Acquisition of Russian gender agreement by monolingual and bilingual children. *International Journal of Bilingualism* 19. 726–752.

Schwartz, Mila & Hadas Rovner. 2015. The acquisition of definiteness in Hebrew (L2) by bilingual preschool children (Russian-L1): A longitudinal multiple-case study. *International Journal of Bilingualism* 19. 548–571.

Serratrice, Ludovica. 2012. The bilingual child. In Tej Bhatia & William Ritchie (eds.), *The handbook of bilingualism and multilingualism*, 87–108. Oxford: Blackwell.

Sharp, Kathryn & Virginia Gathercole. 2013. Can a novel word repetition task be a language-neutral assessment tool? Evidence from Welsh–English bilingual children. *Child Language Teaching and Therapy* 29. 77–89.

Shenker, Rosalee. 2013. When young children who stutter are also bilingual: Some thoughts about assessment and treatment. *Perspectives on Communication Disorders and Sciences in Culturally and Linguistically Diverse Populations* 20. 15–23.

Snow, Catherine & Marian Hoefnagel-Höhle. 1978. The critical period for language acquisition: Evidence from second language learning. *Child Development* 49. 1114–1128.

Sun, He, Kees de Bot & Rasmus Steinkrauss. 2015. A multiple case study on the effects of temperamental traits in Chinese preschoolers learning English. *International Journal of Bilingualism* 19. 703–725.

Tabors, Patton. 2008. *One child, two languages (second edition). A guide for early childhood educators of children learning English as a second language.* Baltimore: Paul Brookes.

Thompson, Linda. 2000. *Young bilingual children in nursery school.* Clevedon: Multilingual Matters.

Toppelberg, Claudio, Laura Medrano, Liana Morgens & Alfonso Nieto-Castañon. 2002. Bilingual children referred for psychiatric services: associations of language disorders, language skills, and psychopathology. *Journal of the American Academy of Child & Adolescent Psychiatry* 41. 712–722.

Toppelberg, Claudio, Patton Tabors, Alissa Coggins, Kirk Lum & Claudia Burger. 2005. Differential diagnosis of selective mutism in bilingual children. *Journal of the American Academy of Child and Adolescent Psychiatry* 44. 592–595.

Trudeau, Natacha, Elizabeth Kay-Raining Bird, Ann Sutton & Patricia Cleave. 2011. Développement lexical chez les enfants bilingues ayant Trisomie 21. *Enfance* 3. 383–404.

Verdon, Sarah, Sharynne McLeod & Sandie Wong. 2015. Reconceptualising practice with multilingual children with speech sound disorders: People, practicalities, and policy. *International Journal of Language and Communication Disorders* 50. 48–62.

Winsler, Adam, Margaret Burchinal, Hsiao-Chuan Tien, Ellen Peisner-Feinberg, Linda Espinosa, Dina Castro, Doré LaForett, Yoon Kim & Jessica De Feyter. 2014. Early developmental skills of diverse dual language learners: The roles of home language use, cultural heritage, maternal immigration, and sociodemographics. *Early Childhood Research Quarterly* 29. 750–764.

Winsler, Adam, Yoon Kim & Erin Richard. 2014. Socio-emotional skills, behavior problems, and Spanish competence predict the acquisition of English among English language learners in poverty. *Developmental Psychology* 50. 2242–2254.

Wölck, Wolfgang. 1987/1988. Types of natural bilingual behavior: a review and revision. *The Bilingual Review/La Revista Bilingüe* 14. 3–16.

Wong-Fillmore, Lily. 1976. *The second time around: Cognitive and social strategies in second language acquisition.* Stanford University doctoral dissertation. Ann Arbor, MI: Xerox University Microfilms.

Zdorenko, Tatiana & Johanne Paradis. 2007. The role of the first language in child second language acquisition of articles. In Alyona Belikova, Luisa Meroni & Mari Umeda (eds.), *Galana 2: Proceedings of the Conference on Generative Approaches to Language Acquisition North America* 2, 483–490. Somerville, MA: Cascadilla Proceedings Project.

Sharon Armon-Lotem
30 SLI in bilingual development: How do we approach assessment?

1 Introduction

Children with specific language impairment (SLI) and children with bilingual typical language development (biTLD) present similarities in their linguistic performance. As a result, a new area of study has developed whose aim is to disentangle the effects of SLI and bilingualism in bilingual children with SLI (biSLI). By definition, a child is diagnosed with biSLI if language impairment is manifested in both languages. Yet, in many cases, diagnostic tools are not available in one of the child's languages, usually the home language. The present chapter reviews evidence showing that:
a. there is no cumulative effect for bilingualism and SLI,
b. bilingualism and SLI can be disentangled with well-designed tasks, and
c. error patterns are different in bilingualism and SLI.

This chapter brings state-of-the-art information on the diagnosis of children with biSLI, discussing the use of parents' questionnaires to assess the home language, as well as the use of a variety of tools to assess linguistic abilities in both the home language (usually the first language, L1), and, more important, in the societal language (usually the second language, L2). The tools include spontaneous speech and narrative analysis, tasks to assess receptive and expressive vocabulary, and non-word repetition and sentence repetition tasks.

2 Between bilingualism and SLI

Waves of migration throughout the world have led to an increase in the number of children growing up using more than one language, typically using one language at home and a different one at school. Some of these children acquire both languages simultaneously from birth (simultaneous bilinguals), whereas others acquire one language at home and acquire the second one when they begin preschool around the age of three, or often later (sequential bilinguals).

Bilingual children with typical language development (TLD) and children with SLI present misleading similarities in their linguistic performance and thus pose a

---
Sharon Armon-Lotem, Bar-Ilan University

DOI 10.1515/9781614514909-031

diagnostic dilemma (Bedore & Pena, 2008; Paradis, 2010). These similarities are more profound in sequential bilingual children and are manifested across linguistic domains. Deficits in verb and noun morphology are often markers of SLI in monolinguals, with variations between languages in the type and degree of the deficit. Yet difficulties in these same domains are found among sequential bilingual children. Thus, for example, Rice and Wexler (1996) identified tense (or rather its absence) as a clinical marker for SLI, but Paradis and Crago (2000) showed that this marker cannot be used for sequential bilingual children, who tend to err on tense as well even if they do not have SLI. Similarly, Clahsen, Bartke and Goellner (1997) identified omission of nominal agreement as a potential marker of SLI in German, but Clahsen and Hong (1995) found the same difficulty among L2 learners. This similarity extends to other areas of morphosyntax, such as the omission of cases, determiners, and clitics observed among children with SLI (e.g., Lukács, Kas and Leonard, 2013; Polite, Leonard, and Roberts, 2011; and Jakubowicz, Nash, Rigaut, & Gerard, 1998, respectively), but also among sequential bilingual children due to bidirectional transfer (e.g., Meir & Armon-Lotem, 2015; Schwartz & Rovner, 2014; and White, 1996, respectively).

Regarding the lexical abilities of the two populations, two of the earliest indicators of SLI are a restricted lexicon at or after the age of two (Leonard and Deevy, 2004) and extensive use of general purpose words (mostly verbs but also deictic pronouns) to allow communication when difficulties in lexical access arise (Warlaumont and Jarmulowicz, 2012). Yet, when biTLD children are assessed in one of their languages, their lexicon is also often significantly smaller than that of monolingual children with TLD (Bialystok, Luk, Peets, and Yang, 2010; Marchman, Fernald, and Hurtado, 2009), and they too revert to using general purpose words as a strategy for coping with a smaller lexicon (Walters, 2005).

Another domain in which a similarity between children with SLI and sequential bilinguals has been observed is in their ability to tell stories. When telling a story, the speaker is expected to adhere to the rules of *story grammar*, which yields the story's macrostructure. The story grammar governs the sequencing of events in the narrative, beginning with the setting, then moving on to an initiating event, followed by different goals, attempts to achieve them, possible outcomes, and finally ending with a resolution (Berman & Slobin, 1994). The speaker's linguistic knowledge yields the story's microstructure: The speaker is expected to adhere to the rules of the language, using rich vocabulary and forming grammatical sentences that are coherently related to each other through proper referencing. Analysis of microstructure focuses on the linguistic features of the text, from length of utterance and variability in the lexicon to morphological and syntactic competence, often measured by errors.

Monolingual children with SLI find it difficult to tell a coherent story (Miranda, McCabe, & Bliss, 1998; Reilly, Losh, Bellugi, & Wulfeck, 2004). Their narratives tend to show major weaknesses in microstructure that reflect their language deficit (Norbury & Bishop, 2003). These weaknesses are manifested in, for example, a shorter mean length of utterance, a smaller number of different words, morphological and syntactic errors, and referencing through the use of pronouns and null elements without previous anchoring in a full noun phrase. The difficulties observed in microstructure are the reason that narratives are often included in assessment tools. Yet, sequential bilingual children who are assessed in their L2 also show some weaknesses in the microstructure of narratives, because microstructure knowledge requires knowledge of their second language. Thus, in terms of microstructure, sequential bilingual children might perform like monolingual children with SLI, manifesting similar morphological and syntactic errors.

In terms of macrostructure, studies provide conflicting evidence for monolingual children with SLI. For example, Soodla and Kikas (2010) found that children with lower language competence produced significantly fewer story information units, but other studies did not find such differences (Gagarina et al., 2012). Such children's narratives might have weaknesses in microstructure (e.g., be shorter, make use of general purpose verbs, lack coherent references, and manifest morphosyntactic limitations), but their macrostructure is less affected by the impairment. Regarding macrostructure, bilinguals perform like monolinguals. Because macrostructure knowledge is not language-specific, bilingual children can rely on knowledge of story grammar in their first language when telling a story in the second language.

The similarities between biTLD children and monolingual children with SLI that are demonstrated above led to a proliferation of studies asking whether bilingualism and SLI are two of a kind, that is, whether children with SLI acquire their language as if they were bilingual children acquiring their second language. However, it was soon shown that the similarities were only superficial. Paradis and Crago (2004) pointed out that the domains of error (i.e., the grammatical categories that are affected by the impairment or the bilingual situation) are similar, but the nature of the errors within the domains is different. Thus, for example, they found that children with SLI omit auxiliary verbs, whereas biTLD children substitute them with other auxiliaries. Likewise, Armon-Lotem (2014) showed that children with SLI omit prepositions in phrasal verbs, yielding sentences such as "the boy laughed the girl," whereas biTLD children might substitute for the prepositions due to influence of the other language (as in "the boy laughed on the girl"), but will not omit them. Along the same lines, Roeper, Ramos, Seymour, and Abdul-Karim (2001) found that children with SLI omit what they term "relational prepositions," which are "predictable from the verb" (p. 393); Armon-Lotem, Danon, and Walters (2008) showed that biTLD children substitute these same prepositions with other prepositions. Thus, the difficulty in disentangling the two conditions when the number of errors is similar disappears when a qualitative analysis is applied.

A developmental perspective on the linguistic difficulties observed among bilingual children and monolingual children with SLI shows different acquisition trajectories in these two populations. Hamann and Belletti (2006) showed that the initial similarity disappeared once bilingual children became more proficient. Moreover, there are domains in which these two populations are largely dissimilar. Two such domains that are often tested in language assessments are complex syntax and phonological memory. These two domains are impaired among children with SLI but not among bilingual children (Thordardottir & Brandeker, 2013), and thus hold promise for overcoming the obstacles of the superficial similarity mentioned above when testing for SLI.

3 Bilingual children with SLI

So far, this chapter has addressed the linguistic profiles of children with SLI compared to those of sequential bilingual children. But what if a child is born with SLI into a bilingual family, or migrates with parents at a young age, becoming a sequential bilingual? Because SLI is impairment in acquiring language – any language – a bilingual child with SLI will, by definition, manifest the impairment in both languages. That is, a child with biSLI is expected to show atypical language development in both languages. The characteristics of the impairment might differ between the two languages, reflecting the nature of each language. Thus, for example, inflections will be missing to a greater extent in the L1 English than in the L2 Hebrew of an English–Hebrew child with biSLI, because inflections are more salient in Hebrew and are thus affected less by SLI in Hebrew. Håkansson and Nettelbladt (1993), who studied Arabic–Swedish bilingual children in one of the first studies of biSLI, observed that whereas most bilingual children show typical language development in one language or both, some struggle with both languages. Moreover, whereas those who manifest typical development in at least one language show typical progress, children who struggle with both languages typically do not grow out of their difficulty (Håkansson, Salameh, & Nettelbladt, 2003).

The growing number of studies of children with biSLI makes it possible to start generating a profile of typical bilingual development versus impaired bilingual development. Typical bilingual language development is influenced by bidirectional interference across the two languages (for L1 on L2, see, e.g., Blom, Paradis, & Sorenson Duncan [2012]; for L2 on L1 see, e.g., Kwon & Han [2008]), as well as by bilingual language processing as the two languages compete with each other (Walters, 2005). Typical bilingual language development is further influenced by *exposure variables*. Exposure variables include age of onset (AoO) for each language and length of exposure (LoE) to each language, as well as the quantity and quality of exposure during this period, that is, how much linguistic input the child receives in each of the languages and how linguistically rich and native-like this input is. Marinis and Chondrogianni (2011) argue that socioeconomic status (SES) should be considered in addition to the other exposure variables, because SES affects the quantity and quality of the linguistic input the child receives.

Morphological and lexical substitutions due to code interference and code switching, as well as circumlocutions and syntactic code interference, are all normal bilingual features. For example, a Polish–English speaking child who omits articles in English, saying, for example, "I have dog," is demonstrating the interference of Polish, which has no overt article. Similarly, a Russian–Hebrew speaking child who uses feminine subject-verb agreement when talking in Hebrew about monkeys (which are masculine in Hebrew and feminine in Russian) is applying the Russian lexical gender of monkeys within a Hebrew sentence. In contrast, a Polish–English speaking child who finds it difficult to understand an utterance like "this is the girl that the queen kissed," or a Russian–Arabic child who uses singular subject-verb agreement when plural subject-verb agreement is required (i.e., omits the plural morphology) are likely to be at risk of having language impairment, because these features are represented the same way in both languages. Distinguishing between errors that stem from the bilingual situation and those that are possible markers of SLI requires knowledge of the child's two languages.

It is not enough, however, to know both languages. Generating a profile of typical bilingual development versus impaired bilingual development in order to be able to diagnose risk for SLI requires utmost caution because typical bilingual development is itself subject to great variability due to the impact of exposure variables. Variance in age of L2 onset, length of L2 exposure, and quantity and quality of exposure all affect bilingual language development, yielding great heterogeneity. Thus, for example, Thordardottir (2014), in a study of English–French bilingual children, argued that exposure to a language for 50% of the time every day is enough for a bilingual child to reach a typical monolingual profile in each of the languages. Paradis (2011) found that in addition to length of exposure, the degree of success in L2 depends on the type of L1. For example, inflectional morphology marking person or tense is better acquired in the L2 if the L1 has inflectional morphology (e.g., Spanish) than if it does not have inflections (e.g., Chinese).

While it is recommended to use both languages to assess a bilingual child for language impairment (e.g., Thordardottir, 2015), in many cases, diagnostic tools are not available in one of the child's languages, usually the home language. Thus, children are often diagnosed only in the societal language using monolingual norms, because bilingual norms in the societal language are rarely available. Using monolingual norms in the societal language is bound to lead to overdiagnosis. The generation of bilingual norms is challenging, because one must take into consideration the great variance in this population due to the differential impact of the exposure variables as well as the various L1s. Moreover, tools designed specifically for bilingual children are sparse, because the many different combinations of L1 and L2 might lead to different developmental profiles. Thus, for example, Gagarina, Klassert and Topaj's (2010) *Russian language proficiency test for multilingual children* with norms from Russian–German bilinguals, cannot be used to assess the Russian of Russian–Hebrew bilinguals due to differences between German and Hebrew. For example, in

Russian, when a noun is used in a sentence, it is marked overtly by case to indicate its syntactic role, e.g., nominative for subject or accusative for object. These roles are marked by case in German as well, but not in Hebrew. The absence of cases in L2 Hebrew has a strong impact on the use (or rather misuse) of cases in L1 Russian, leading to lower scores on the *Russian language proficiency test* for multilingual children compared to those found for Russian–German bilinguals (Meir & Armon-Lotem, 2015).

Despite the above-mentioned difficulties, the assessment dilemma can be addressed. Parents can be used as agents for assessing the home language, and a variety of language evaluation tools have been developed in recent years to address the problem of assessment in one language only (as mentioned, usually the societal language) without falling into the pitfalls of bidirectional influence and limited exposure. The rest of this chapter briefly describes some of these tools: parental questionnaires as a window to the home language, spontaneous speech and narrative analysis that can shed light on a broad range of linguistic abilities, and more targeted tasks such as those assessing phonological memory (nonword repetition), receptive and expressive vocabulary, and syntactic abilities (sentence repetition tasks). These tools can be used to assess the linguistic abilities of bilingual children, and can help in diagnosing bilingual children who are at risk for language impairment.

4 Parental questionnaires

Parental questionnaires are sometimes used to assess children's abilities. Psychologists use the BRIEF (Gioia, Isquith, Guy, & Kenworthy, 2000) to assess ADHD, and the ABC (Oro, Navarro-Calvillo, & Esmer, 2014) is part of the battery used to assess children on the autistic spectrum. In the study of early language acquisition, the MacArthur–Bates Communicative Development Inventory (CDI; Fenson et al., 2007) is widely used to assess lexical development. These tools have been found to be highly reliable and strongly correlated with children's psychological and psycholinguistic profiles (e.g., Conti-Ramsden, Simkin, & Pickles, 2006). Several proposals have been made over the years for a parental questionnaire that would fill the gap created by the limited access of health and education professionals to the home language of bilingual children (e.g., Parra, Hoff, & Core, 2011; Rescorla & Alley, 2001; Thordardottir, Rothenberg, Rivard, & Naves, 2006; Unsworth, 2013). A review by Li, Sepanski, and Zhao (2006) of 41 questionnaires used with parents of bilingual children identified the most frequent questions that addressed the child's linguistic history. Some of the questions pertained to factual information such as length of residence, age of L2 exposure, as well as length of L2 exposure, length of L2 instruction, and languages spoken at home, whereas others required assessment of the child's speaking, reading, and writing abilities. These are often assessed by asking for details of the child's daily routine and the role of each of the caretakers, and by inquiring about different literacy related activities, in order to evaluate the exact quantity and quality of the linguistic input in both languages. To these questions, Paradis, Emmerzael, and Sorenson Duncan (2010) added two informational questions, one about family history and one regarding parental concerns, and showed that parental assessments of children's linguistic abilities in the home language are a strong predictor of whether or not a child is at risk for SLI.

The two questionnaires developed at Paradis's lab, the Alberta Language and Development Questionnaire (ALDEQ; Paradis et al., 2010) and the Alberta Language Environment Questionnaire (ALEQ; Paradis, 2011), were meticulously designed to explore parental knowledge and enable distinguishing between bilingual children with and without SLI. The ALDEQ has four sections: (a) early milestones, (b) current first language abilities, (c) behavior patterns and activity preferences, and (d) family history. The parents of 170 bilingual children (30 with SLI) with L2 English and a variety of home languages were interviewed using the ALDEQ in order to validate it. Of the four sections, the early milestones section emerged as the strongest discriminator, and the current L1 abilities section as the second-strongest. The ALEQ elicits background information on the child's linguistic environment at home and outside. It includes more factual questions than the ALDEQ about age of arrival, AoO of L2, parents' education, and the child's educational setting. It also includes qualitative questions assessing the proficiency of usage of both languages by the child, the parents, and siblings, both at home and outside, as well as assessing the quantity and quality of linguistic input received by the child in child-directed speech. These variables were correlated with the children's performance in their L2, English, showing that child internal factors, such as short-term memory, are better predictors of vocabulary size and knowledge of verbal morphology than maternal education and whether the home language is morphologically rich (e.g., Spanish) or morphologically poor (e.g., Chinese). That is, a child's linguistic aptitude is the best predictor for success in L2 acquisition. Yet, among children with high linguistic aptitude, i.e., with no language impairment, maternal education and home environment are predictors of success (Paradis, 2011).

Subsequent to these questionnaires, the Parents' Bilingual Questionnaire (PABIQ) in Europe (Tuller, 2015) and the Bilingual Parents' Questionnaire (BIPAQ) in Israel (Abutbul-Oz, Armon-Lotem, & Walters, 2012) were designed to accommodate Paradis's findings and generate a tool to aid in diagnosing SLI in a variety of bilingual settings, with different combinations of L1 and L2. These two questionnaires incorporate the questions from the ALEQ and ALDEQ that were found in previous studies and in several pilot studies to be the best indicators of developmental risk for SLI in bilingual children, as well as some new questions on the exposure to each language. The immediate goal for these adaptations was to enable members of COST Action IS0804, *Language Impairment in a Multilingual Society: Linguistic patterns and the road to assessment* (www.bi-sli.org) to identify children at risk for language impairment in over 30 European countries with different combinations of L1 and L2. Tuller

(2015) reported that piloting and testing included bilinguals with typical language development and bilinguals with SLI, focusing on particular L1–L2 combinations (e.g., Arabic–French, English–Hebrew, Russian–Greek, and Turkish–German), as well as on groups of children with same L2 and a variety of L1s (e.g., L1 English, Arabic, Spanish, Bosnian, Vietnamese, Turkish, Kurdish, Moroccan, Urdu, and L2 Danish).

Of special interest for this chapter is a clinical trial of BIPAQ conducted in Israel with 50 children in order to explore the test's reliability when used by speech and language therapists (SLTs) in the clinic (Abutbul-Oz & Armon-Lotem, 2013). SLTs were asked to assess bilingual children with L2 Hebrew and a variety of L1s who were referred to clinical evaluation due to observed delays in language acquisition. The children were assessed twice: once at first arrival and once post-treatment after at least six months. The SLTs were allowed to use whatever tool was available for them before and after treatment and were asked to write a brief explanation of their diagnosis of the child. Once a child was assessed with SLI upon arrival, the parents were asked to complete the BIPAQ reporting developmental milestones and concerns, L1 abilities, and L2 abilities as assessed by them, and a score was assigned to each child. The post-treatment assessments showed that half of the children no longer had L2 difficulties, so they were not assessed with SLI anymore – a finding that in itself indicates that bilingual children are overdiagnosed with SLI. A comparison of clinicians' post-treatment evaluations of children as having or nor having SLI with BIPAQ scores at the onset of treatment revealed a statistically significant correlation between the post-treatment assessment and the pre-treatment BIPAQ scores. The best predictors of SLI were questions that targeted L1 development and frustration with L1 use. Moreover, the BIPAQ scores of children who were not diagnosed with SLI post-treatment were similar to those of bilingual children who were never referred to the clinic with a risk for SLI.

These studies show the importance of accessing L1, and offer means to do so. In the following sections, the focus shifts to the L2, usually the societal language. Note that some of the tools can be adapted for assessment of the home language, often the L1, if knowledge of this language is at the SLT's disposal.

5 Analysis of spontaneous speech and narratives

Spontaneous samples are widely used in the study of child language, as well as for language assessment in the absence of normed clinical tools. In principle, a spontaneous sample should be collected in both languages of a bilingual child, but this is only valuable if the health or education professional knows the home language of the child and is able to analyze the spontaneous sample to assess the child's abilities in this language. Narratives are another way of collecting a language sample, in a more controlled manner that allows a more comprehensive assessment. For the purposes of the present chapter, only assessment of speech in the societal language is considered.

Spontaneous samples should preferably be collected by a native speaker of the language in which the sample is collected, and with whom the child is familiar. In the absence of such a person, a familiarization period is important to ensure that the sample truly represents the abilities of the child, and is not influenced by an unfamiliar setting or interlocutor. A valuable alternative for an adult native speaker is a child from the same school, as it has been shown that peer talk is as successful at revealing features of a child's spoken language as a conversation with an adult (Cekaite, Blum-Kulka, Grøver, & Teubal, 2014).

Another recommendation to ensure a sample of high quality is to lead the conversation to topics familiar to the child, preferably from the school environment, due to the lexicon available to bilingual children in each language. A study of 80 Russian–Hebrew bilingual children who were engaged in play sessions involving cooking and playground situations showed richer production in the home language in the cooking sessions and richer production in the societal language in the playground sessions (Walters, personal communication). Similarly, a CDI study of 40 English–Hebrew bilingual toddlers showed that they produced more home-related words (for clothing, body parts, and furniture) in English, their home language, and more "outside-related" words (such as words for vehicles, toys, outside, places, people, and games) in Hebrew, the societal language (Armon-Lotem & Ohana, 2017). Thus, an L2 sample which focuses on home activities might not reveal the full abilities of the child in the L2.

A second way to elicit a rich language sample is by eliciting a narrative. This can be done by asking children to talk about an experience they had, such as a fight (Ravid & Berman, 2009), a film they saw, a story that is frequently read at school (Yochana, 2014), or a picture, a set of pictures, or a picture book (such as the frequently-used booklet by Mercer Mayer [2003] *Frog, where are you?*, when it is culturally adequate [Berman and Slobin, 1994]). The impact of a culturally adequate tool is demonstrated, for example, by Fiestas and Pena (2004) who found similar levels of productivity in the narratives of Spanish–English bilingual children ages 4–7 in both languages. Yet, the children had more code interference from L1 Spanish when telling a story from the story book *Frog, where are you?* than when describing a static picture. They further argued that even the content of a picture or picture book should be culturally adequate, for example, using a picture of a traditional Mexican–American family birthday party to elicit narrative in L1 Spanish yielded richer narrative.

Another debate is whether better elicitation is gained from telling or retelling tasks. For example, Guttierez-Clellen (2002) found that retelling is more difficult for children with SLI because it challenges their memory abilities and not just their linguistic abilities. But Hayward, Gillam, and Lien (2007) found that children with SLI actually do better on a retelling than a telling task, including more elements when they are familiar with the story, suggesting that modeling helps them produce a narrative. An advantage for retelling is also found among bilingual children with typical language development (TLD), who include more content in a retelling task than in a telling task (Kunnari & Välimaa, 2014).

Once a sample is obtained, the question of analysis arises. Whereas narratives allow one to analyze macrostructure (e.g., Berman & Slobin, 1994; Labov & Waletzky, 1967; Mandler & Johnson, 1977), there is no consensus on the value of such analysis for disentangling bilingualism from SLI. Soodla and Kikas (2010) found that the quality of macrostructure of narratives produced by Estonian children with SLI was the same as that observed in age-matched peers. For bilingual children, Tsimpli, Peristeri, and Andreou (2014) as well as Altman, Armon-Lotem, Fichman, and Walters (2016) showed that bilingual children with and without SLI produce narratives of the same complexity in terms of macrostructure. In contrast, all studies of narratives of monolingual and bilingual children with SLI show that analysis of microstructure is highly revealing of their linguistic difficulties. Bilingual children with SLI produce significantly shorter utterances and clauses than biTLD children. Moreover, their vocabulary is less varied, as is evident in their repeated use of the same words, yielding a high type-token ratio (indicating the use of the same token many times). These phenomena reflect the reduced complexity of sentences and the restricted lexicon. The limited lexicon is also evident in the use of general-purpose verbs, and in the extensive use of pronouns where a full noun phrase is required, for example, "he" instead of "the boy" when introducing new participants. This leads to reduced coherence of the text, which is worsened by the omission of pronouns in both subject and object position. The reduced complexity of clauses is further manifested by omissions of functional elements and inflections.

The error analysis should take into consideration the bilingual situation by differentiating between errors caused by crosslinguistic influence, such as the omission of the indefinite article in L2 French of a child whose L1 Arabic does not mark indefinite articles, and those caused by the impairment, such as an omission of the definite article in L2 by a child when the L1 makes use of definite articles. Such analysis can also be applied to spontaneous samples.

6 Receptive and expressive vocabulary

The discussion of spontaneous elicitation and narratives addressed expressive vocabulary, that is, word production, but not receptive vocabulary, that is, word comprehension. That discussion explored some of the implications of the unique properties of the bilingual lexicon, such as the use of general purpose words and pronouns, which are also found in the speech of children with SLI. That discussion addressed the productivity of the lexicon, and its size in terms of type-token ratio, but not the impact bilingualism and SLI might have on comprehension. Moreover, in both spontaneous samples and in narratives, there is no control of the tested lexical items. Thus, these methods show what the child knows, but do not show what the child has not yet acquired.

Many studies show that bilingual children exhibit a smaller vocabulary when tested in only one of their languages (Bialystok et al., 2010; Pearson, Fernandez, & Oller, 1995; Umbel, Pearson, Fernández, & Oller, 1992). Thus, testing in a single language with no access to the other can lead to misdiagnosis. For example, Ben-Oved and Armon-Lotem (2016) found that Amharic–Hebrew preschool children scored more than three SDs below the monolingual mean on the SHEMESH naming task for Hebrew (Biran & Friedmann, 2004; 2005). Although this might reflect their low SES, it was found that their performance was similar to that of Russian–Hebrew bilinguals of mid-high SES on the Hebrew adaptation of Kauschke's Noun–Verb naming task (2007).

Other studies further argue that testing in one language does not reflect the full lexical capacity of a bilingual child, whereas testing in both languages does. Oller, Pearson, and Cobo-Lewis (2007) suggest that although bilingual children know fewer words in each language than their monolingual peers, if the vocabulary is taken together as a whole, it is equal to or greater in size than that of monolingual children. These authors maintain that the vocabulary in each language is smaller because bilingual children must divide the time allotted to language learning across two languages. Also, it is possible that the words can be distributed across two languages (Pearson, 1998) because, as mentioned, certain words occur in contexts in which the children only use one of their languages. Bilingual children rarely learn their two languages in similar contexts (Yan & Nicoladis, 2009), so their vocabulary items can be distributed across their two languages (Pearson, 1998). Schelletter (2005) found that vocabulary acquisition of bilingual children often starts with words which are cognates, that is, they are similar in form across the two languages, and that with vocabulary growth, the proportion of cognates declines.

Using Rescorla's (1989) Language Development Survey, Junker and Stockman (2002) found that German–English speaking toddlers' conceptual vocabulary, that is, the total number of concepts known in both languages, was similar to that of monolingual peers with over 40% overlap between the words in the two languages. The conceptual vocabulary of bilingual children has been repeatedly found to be within the monolingual range (e.g., Pearson, Fernandez, & Oller, 1993). However, this has been found to be more typical when the two languages of the child are not balanced, that is, when the child is dominant in one of the languages (Thordordottir et al. 2006).

Moreover, lexical knowledge is probably the component of linguistic knowledge that is the most sensitive to exposure variables. Chondrogianni & Marinis (2011) showed that almost 50% of the performance of bilingual Turkish–English children on vocabulary tests was predicted by a combination of AoO and LoE. This finding implies that bilingual children's vocabulary develops with greater exposure. Armon-Lotem et al. (2011) showed that bilingual children's low scores on standardized tests in Hebrew stemmed mostly from the vocabulary subpart, in which children did not reach the monolingual mean even after four years of exposure to Hebrew; in other subparts the monolingual mean was reached within two years. A study of Welsh–English bilingual children (Gathercole, Thomas, Roberts, Hughes, & Hughes, 2013) further showed that the language used at home has strong impact at a younger age which diminishes with age as the children move into the educational system.

These observations might suggest that vocabulary size is not the best measure for identifying children with SLI within the bilingual population. However, a delay in the acquisition of vocabulary leading to a vocabulary of less than 50 words at the age of two is still considered a strong predictor of SLI (Leonard, 1998). Thus, the question is how not to throw out the baby with the bathwater. How can we assess vocabulary without falling into the partial vocabulary pitfall? Two possible solutions are offered here: one for younger children when vocabulary size is often the single warning sign for SLI, and another for older children when assessment of vocabulary size is valuable more as a measure of potential academic success than as an indicator of risk for SLI.

Earlier in this chapter, when discussing the value of background questionnaires, we addressed the role of parents as agents of the home language who can inform us about the child's ability in the first language. Parents can similarly be enlisted to report their child's vocabulary abilities. Although assessment tools might not be available in the home language, a vocabulary checklist, such as the MacArthur–Bates Communicative Development Inventory (CDI; Fenson et al., 2007), is available in many languages with age-appropriate norms (Jørgensen, Dale, Bleses, & Fenson, 2010) and can be used by both parents and SLTs with minor adaptation in any language if norms are not required. Such adaptation obviously requires the mediation of a speaker of the home language and an understanding of cultural diversity. Gatt, O'Toole, & Haman (2015) addressed these issues, showing the value of bilingual use of the CDI, as well as the value of both total vocabulary score on the CDI and total conceptual vocabulary scores on the CDI in assessment of children who receive bilingual input (but see Patterson and Pearson [2004] and Thoradordottir et al. [2006] for an extensive debate). Gatt et al. also stress the importance of including information from background questionnaires in evaluating the outcome of the CDI. Notably, the CDI is designed for assessing expressive vocabulary, but has a special value when also used for assessing receptive vocabulary, because a gap between the two is more typical of biTLD children, whereas bilingual children at risk for SLI usually show limitations in both (Maital, Dromi, Sagi, & Bornstein, 2000; Armon-Lotem & Ohana, 2017).

While the CDI is informative up to the age of three and as such applies mostly to simultaneous or early sequential bilinguals, controlled tasks targeting receptive vocabulary (picture selection) and expressive vocabulary (naming) are frequently used in preschool years and are thus relevant for sequential bilinguals whose L2 onset begins at preschool. For this population, vocabulary assessment is valuable for intervention rather than as a diagnostic tool. Assessing both languages can serve as a useful predictor of future academic success. Available research targets language-specific pairs but is not necessarily sensitive to the unique features of the bilingual lexicon, such as the role of cognates at the onset of L2 vocabulary acquisition (Schelletter, 2005), circumlocutions as a communicative means (Ambert, 1986), and the use of code switching (Walters, 2005). Moreover, the nature of the errors in elicited vocabulary tasks differs for biTLD children, who make semantic errors and use circumlocutions, and for children with SLI, who make more phonological errors and revert more often to the "don't know" response (Lahey & Edwards, 1999; Simonsen, 2002).

One of the weaknesses of the available vocabulary tests lies in the lack of comparability between tests in different languages and the focus on nouns only, rather than including verbs, which are acquired later. Very few tests target verbs as well (for tests that do, see, e.g., Kauschke, 2007 and Kambanaros, Grohmann, Michaelides, & Theodorou, 2014). Carefully constructed tasks in which both nouns and verbs are tested across the two languages, both for comprehension and production, are the most desirable for sequential bilinguals in order to reveal the full picture (see Haman, Łuniewska, & Pomiechowska, 2015). For example, Kambanaros et al. found a significant difference between action (verbs) and object (nouns) naming in bilectal children who spoke both Cypriot Greek and Modern Greek. Similarly, Jeuk (2003) found that Turkish–German preschoolers had a higher proportion of nouns in their lexicon than monolinguals. Kambanaros et al. further found that the noun-verb gap was larger among the preschoolers (3–5 year olds) than among first graders (6–7 year olds), suggesting that with age, children begin to resolve the processing dilemmas related to the conceptual differences between the two grammatical word classes. Because the gap between nouns and verbs is more significant for children with SLI than for children with TLD (e.g., Andreu, Sanz-Torrent, & Guardia-Olmos, 2012), testing verbs as well as nouns can single out those bilingual children who have SLI.

What emerges from this short review is the value of testing both nouns and verbs, because verbs are more sensitive to language impairment in both expressive and receptive mode in both languages. Nonetheless, this review also highlights the difficulty of using such testing of lexical knowledge to diagnose bilingual children with SLI, due to the high sensitivity of lexical knowledge to exposure variables. The next two sections explore two types of assessments that can be used to test aspects of bilingual development that are less sensitive to exposure variables: nonword repetition (NWR), that tests phonological memory and phonological processing, and sentence repetition (SRep), that tests syntactic knowledge.

7 Nonword repetition

Nonword repetition (NWR) tasks test the ability of a child to repeat wordlike strings of phonemes that often have a certain resemblance to words of the target language (i.e., the language of testing). The strings can either make use of the target language morphology (targetlike), as in *hampent* with English as the language of testing

(Gathercole & Baddeley, 1996), or be less similar to that language (non-targetlike), e.g., utilizing sound combinations that are less frequent in the target language and avoiding any morphological resemblance, as in *tervak* with English as the language of testing (Dollaghan & Campbell, 1998). The ability to repeat nonwords is influenced by the phonological complexity of the strings and their similarity to the target language, but even more so by the linguistic aptitude of the child. More specifically, it has been claimed that NWR targets phonological memory, and, when items are similar to the target language, also familiarity with the morphological properties of that language. Prosodic patterning, phonological complexity, and morphophonology are language-specific and their knowledge has been found to be related to the size of the lexicon (Gathercole, Service, Hitch, Adams, & Martin, 1999).

There are two major types of NWR tasks: The first type is tasks using pseudowords, that is, words that are relatively similar to the target language and which are often derived from them by changing a consonant or two (e.g., the Children's Test of Nonword Repetition [CNRep], Gathercole & Baddeley, 1996). The second type is tasks that move away from the target language and use more universal nonwords, often composed of longer strings of consonants and vowels (e.g., the Nonword Repetition Test [NRT], Dollaghan & Campbell, 1998). While both of these types share the use of the phonemes of the target language, their demands on phonological memory are different: the former measures short-term and long-term phonological memory as well as knowledge of the morphophonology of the target language, whereas the latter measures short-term phonological memory only.

NWR is used in screening tools for language impairment (e.g., van der Lely, Adlof, Hogan, & Ellis-Weismer, 2007) and learning disabilities (Catts, Adlof, Hogan, & Ellis-Weismer, 2005) because it is a good predictor of language and reading difficulties (Baird, Slonims, Simonoff, & Dworzynski, 2011). In the bilingual context, morphophonological characteristics of nonwords might be a disadvantage if the child still has limited morphophonological knowledge of the target language. Yet, if non-targetlike items are used, it has the potential advantage of being indifferent to knowledge of the target language and can thus serve as a measure of linguistic aptitude among bilinguals a well. Furthermore, the early experience of acquiring a second language, which involves learning many unfamiliar words of a morphophonological structure which is different from the L1, might make this task less intimidating to the child compared to other measures of language. Finally, as a measure of working memory, NWR is expected to be less sensitive to background variables such as SES (Engel, Santos, & Gathercole, 2008; Roy & Chiat, 2013).

The potential usefulness of NWR led researchers to perform a range of studies on the performance of bilingual children on NWR, with the goal of identifying a measure that would tease apart bilingualism and SLI (Girbau & Schwartz, 2007; Gutiérrez-Clellen & Simon-Cereijido, 2010). For example, Summers, Bohman, Gillam, Peña, & Bedore (2010) tested Spanish–English bilingual children aged 4;6–6;5 using nonwords of low wordlikeness (i.e., that were less targetlike), but that followed the phonotactic constraints of each language, and found consistent superior performance on the Spanish test. The superior performance of Spanish–English bilingual children on the Spanish test was explained by the lesser complexity of Spanish phonotactics with multisyllabic words comprised of CV combinations only. Likewise, Messer, Leseman, Boom, & Mayo (2010) found that Dutch monolingual four-year-olds outperformed Turkish–Dutch bilingual children on a Dutch NWR test, but the effects of phonotactic probability did not differ between groups, and Engel de Abreu (2011) reported a gap in NWR performance between bilingual children who spoke Luxembourgish as one of their languages and a monolingual group matched on other memory measures. Sharp and Gathercole (2013) attributed the bilingual effect to exposure variables, such as the language spoken at home. Testing Welsh–English bilingual children with varying levels of exposure to L1 Welsh, the authors reported the effect of language exposure: Children who were exposed only to English at home revealed lower performance rates on the repetition of single consonants and clusters that are unique to Welsh.

However, other researchers did not find a difference between bilingual and monolingual children on NWR tests. Lee and Gorman (2012) studied NWR in four groups of children with typical language development: monolingual English, Korean–English bilingual, Chinese–English bilingual, and Spanish–English bilingual children, and did not find a group effect for overall accuracy: The three bilingual groups performed similar to the monolingual English children. Similarly, Armon-Lotem and Chiat (2012) found that Russian–Hebrew preschool children performed as well as their monolingual peers in both languages.

Exploring the use of NWR for children with biSLI, Windsor, Kohnert, Lobitz, and Pham (2010) compared the performance of English-only and sequential Spanish–English children aged 6;0–11;6, with and without language impairment, in both Spanish and English. They found contributions of both experience and aptitude: the English-only groups outperformed their bilingual counterparts in English; the typically developing bilingual group overlapped with the English-only language-impaired group in English, and bilingual children with language impairment performed significantly below their typically developing counterparts in both English and Spanish. Again, prosodic structuring of the Spanish items made them more wordlike (and thus easier to repeat) for the English-only group, yielding the same advantage that was found for familiar segmental phonology in the English test. Moreover, Thordardottir and Brandeker's (2013) study of simultaneous French–English children showed that NWR was less affected by exposure patterns in this population and could distinguish bilinguals with SLI from those with TLD. They further noted that phonological complexity as measured by length affected only children with SLI but not children with TLD. A similar observation was made by Gutiérrez-Clellen & Simon-Cereijido (2010) for Spanish–English children with SLI, who scored significantly lower on NWR than their peers with TLD. However, in this later study many of the biTLD children did not obtain a passing score in even one language, showing performance lower than monolinguals.

The above studies suggest that while bilingualism might yield lower performance on NWR, bilingual children with SLI still show lower performance compared to their peers with TLD. Yet, in some L1–L2 combinations, with some NWR tasks, the gap between bilinguals and monolinguals narrows and bilinguals with SLI perform lower than both groups. In other tasks, monolingual children outperform bilingual children, and both groups outperform bilingual children with SLI. This diversity of the findings suggests that NWR with monolingual norms cannot serve as a diagnostic tool on its own, even if used in both languages (but see Chiat's [2015] proposal for a quasi-universal test). This is where sentence repetition comes in.

8 Sentence repetition

Sentence repetition (SRep) has been identified as the most sensitive and specific tool for screening SLI in monolingual children (Conti-Ramsden, Botting, & Faragher, 2001; Alloway & Gathercole, 2005). In SRep tasks, children are asked to repeat verbatim a series of sentences they have heard. Of all of the assessment tools that currently exist to assess children's language development, SRep is the most comprehensive in that it can address a variety of linguistic levels, from phonological memory to vocabulary, morphology, and syntax. The target sentences in a SRep task vary in their complexity from simple clauses to coordinate clauses, questions, and relative clauses, using structures that are known to be difficult for children with SLI. SRep requires processing the input, storing it, generating the output, and matching it with the stored input. The sentences can be of equal length to control for the impact of short-term memory (e.g., Friedmann & Lavi, 2006), or of varied length (e.g., Marinis & Armon-Lotem, 2015).

The question that arose for researchers was whether SRep is also a good task for diagnosing biSLI. On the negative side, some aspects tested by SRep might be challenging for bilingual children, either due to the bilingual restricted lexicon in the tested language or, especially for sequential bilinguals, due to being in the process of acquiring the second language. On the positive side, beyond testing phonological memory, vocabulary, and morphology, a unique feature of SRep tasks is that they challenge the syntactic abilities of the child, and the degree of syntactic difficulty can be manipulated to match different age groups. Compared to other aspects of language such as morphology or lexicon, syntactic complexity is least affected by bilingualism. Sequential bilinguals transfer complex structures from L1 to L2, generating complex sentences as soon as they have the relevant vocabulary (see, for example Schwartz, 2004). This does not mean that they use these structures flawlessly in their L2, but it does mean that the acquisition of syntax in L2 is much faster than that of other linguistic domains.

Studies of the impact of internal and external (exposure) variables on biTLD children's performance on SRep tasks show that SRep tasks are less sensitive than lexical measures to LoE and AoO (Thordardottir & Brandeker, 2013), but are affected by language dominance, that is, by whether the child is stronger (dominant) in the tested language or in the other language (Verhoeven, Steenge, & van Balkom, 2012). SES was found to have a limited impact, and only among younger children (Campbell, Dollaghan, Needleman, & Janosky, 1997; Roy & Chiat, 2013). Chiat et al. (2013) reported that Russian–German bilingual preschoolers whose mothers had education beyond high school outperformed those whose mothers were less educated, which indicated that SES affects success on SRep tasks. However, this has also been reported for monolingual children (Roy & Chiat, 2013); SES, as mentioned earlier in this chapter, impacts the quantity and quality of linguistic input, with low SES slowing and delaying the acquisition process (Schiff & Ravid, 2012).

The fact that the effect of SES on SRep performance is the same in monolingual and bilingual children argues for SRep being an appropriate task for bilingual children. Indeed, studies of exposure variables in bilingual acquisition show that simultaneous bilingual children score within monolingual norms on SRep regardless of the relative amount of exposure to each language (Thordardottir & Brandeker 2013). Sequential bilinguals with two years of exposure to the L2 also perform within the monolingual norm (e.g., Armon-Lotem, Walters, & Gagarina, 2011, for Russian–Hebrew and Russian–German). Yet, some studies suggest that language dominance matters. Gutierrez-Clellen, Restrepo, and Simón-Cereijido (2006) found that Spanish–English bilinguals who are dominant in Spanish perform like monolinguals on SRep tasks, but those who are dominant in English do not. Verhoeven et al. (2012), likewise, report dominance effect. Moreover, Chiat et al. (2013) found AoO and LoE effects for some bilingual groups (Russian–Hebrew) but not others (Turkish–English and Russian–German).

Chiat et al. (2013) suggested, however, that despite the impact of AoO and LoE, and the possible effects of dominance, bilingual children are able to reach monolingual norms faster with SRep than with other tasks, making it a better diagnostic tool. There is evidence that this is the case, especially when the vocabulary demands of the SRep task are low. Chiat et al., who compared the use of different sentence repetition tasks within different bilingual groups with TLD, observed the impact of lexical complexity on biTLD children's ability to repeat sentences. They found that 70% of a group of seven-year-old Turkish–English children tested with the Sentence Recall subtest of the Clinical Evaluation of Language Fundamentals III (CELF–3; Semel, Wiig & Secord, 2000) scored more than two SDs below the monolingual mean. In contrast, fewer than 5% of Russian–Hebrew, English–Hebrew, and Russian–German children, tested with two other tasks (the Goralnik Screening Test [Goralnik, 1995] for Hebrew and Sprachstandscreening für das Vorschulalter [Grimm, 2003] for German) scored more than two SDs below the monolingual mean (Chiat et al.). While the three tasks vary in many aspects, what the two latter tasks share, and where they diverge from CELF–3, is in the choice of vocabulary. The vocabulary in the Hebrew and German tests focuses on simple everyday activities, but the CELF–3 focuses on academically oriented activities and protagonists. Notably, all three tasks include long sentences and target complex structures such as passives and relative clauses.

Because syntactic complexity does not affect bilinguals' ability in SRep, but vocabulary does, Chiat et al. (2013) recommend using sentences that are syntactically age-adequate, but with a more restricted vocabulary. A series of such tasks have been developed under the umbrella of LITMUS–SRep (Marinis & Armon-Lotem, 2015), which has been adapted to over 20 languages. This tool targets syntactic complexity without taxing lexical access. It makes use of syntactic structures such as questions and relative clauses, which have been found to be impaired among children with SLI, but not among biTLD children, as well as morphosyntactic elements, such as verb inflection, prepositions, and clitic pronouns, which yield different error patterns in the two populations, as reported above. In a study of Arabic–French six-year-old children (Tuller, Abboud, Ferré, Fleckstein, Prévost, Dos Santos, Scheidnes, & Zebib, 2015) in Lebanon and France, it was found that SRep distinguished bilinguals with TLD from those with SLI in both settings, despite major sociolinguistic differences. Tuller et al. further identified specific structures as more sensitive to the impairment than others, including passives, topicalization, and relative clauses, on which bilingual children with TLD scored almost at ceiling and bilingual children with SLI scored very low. Likewise, a study of Russian–Hebrew bilinguals (Armon-Lotem & Meir, 2016) showed that SRep had over 80% accuracy in both L1 and L2, when LoE was taken into account; LoE seems to impact the performance of children with TLD, but not of those with SLI. This suggests that SRep is a good test that can be used either in L1 or L2 to test for SLI. Similar to other studies, the gap was mostly significant for questions, relative clauses and conditionals. To sum up, of the various tests available for diagnosing SLI in bilingual children SRep is the most promising.

9 Conclusion

Although the study of SLI in bilingual children is still ongoing, as is reflected in this chapter, we can draw several conclusions from what is already known:
a. Bilingualism and SLI do not show cumulative effects, as tests of morphology indicate.
b. Bilingualism and SLI can be disentangled when well-designed tasks are used, as is evident from the SRep tasks.
c. Bilingualism and SLI show distinctive error patterns, as is evident from children's lexical and morphological errors.

Whether bilingualism offers a partial compensation for SLI is still an open question. Some studies do point to such effects whereas others are more neutral. This chapter did not address the potential compensatory value of bilingualism in terms of cognitive abilities. Although there has been a wide range of studies of executive functions in bilingual children with TLD, this is still under investigation for children with biSLI. In no way can bilingualism replace therapy for children with biSLI, but it is safe to argue that there is no empirical evidence that the presence of input in more than one language has a detrimental effect on biSLI children's language development. Nor is there a basis to recommend using a single language with a bilingual child (biTLD or biSLI), as long as both languages are supported.

References

Abutbul-Oz, H. & S. Armon-Lotem. 2013. *The use of the Bilingual Parents Questionnaire (BIPAQ) in a clinical setting*. Unpublished manuscript, English Department (Linguistics), Bar Ilan University, Ramat Gan, Israel.

Abutbul-Oz, H., S. Armon-Lotem & J. Walters. 2012. Bilingual Parents Questionnaire (BIPAQ). Unpublished instrument. English Department, Bar Ilan University, Ramat Gan, Israel.

Alloway, T. P. & S. E Gathercol. 2005. The role of sentence recall in reading and language skills of children with learning difficulties. *Learning and Individual Differences* 15(4). 271–282.

Altman, C., S. Armon-Lotem, S. Fichman & J. Walters. 2016. Macrostructure, microstructure and mental state terms in the narratives of English-Hebrew bilingual preschool children with and without SLI. *Applied Psycholinguistics* 37(1), 165–193.

Ambert, A. N. 1986. Identifying language disorders in Spanish-speakers. In A. C. Willig & H. F. Greenberg (eds.), *Bilingualism and learning disability: Policy and practice for teachers and administrators*, 15–33. New York: American Library.

Andreu, L., M. Sanz-Torrent & J. Guardia-Olmos. 2012. Auditory word recognition of nouns and verbs in children with Specific Language Impairment (SLI). *Journal of Communication Disorders* 45(1). 20–34.

Armon-Lotem, S. 2014. Between L2 and SLI: Inflections and prepositions in the Hebrew of bilingual children with TLD and monolingual children with SLI. *Journal of Child Language* 41(1). 1–31.

Armon-Lotem, S. & N. Meir. 2016. Diagnostic accuracy of repetition tasks for the identification of specific language impairment (SLI) in bilingual children: evidence from Russian and Hebrew. *International Journal of Language and Communication Disorders* 51(6). 715–731.

Armon-Lotem, S. & O. Ohana. 2017. A CDI study of bilingual English-Hebrew children – frequency of exposure as a major source of variation. *International Journal of Bilingual Education and Bilingualism* 20(2). 201–217.

Armon-Lotem, S. & S. Chiat. 2012. How do sequential bilingual children perform on non-word repetition tasks? In A. K. Biller, E. Y. Chung, & A. E. Kimball (eds.), *Proceedings of the 36th Annual Boston University Conference on Language Development*, 53–62. Somerville, MA: Cascadilla Press.

Armon-Lotem, S., G. Danon & J. Walters. 2008. The use of prepositions by bilingual SLI children: The relative contribution of representation and processing. In A. Gavarró & M. João Freitas (eds.), *Language acquisition and development: Proceedings of GALA 2007*, 41–46. Cambridge: Cambridge Scholars Press.

Armon-Lotem, S., J. Walters & N. Gagarina. 2011. The impact of internal and external factors on linguistic performance in the home language and in L2 among Russian–Hebrew and Russian–German preschool children. *Linguistic Approaches to Bilingualism* 3. 291–317.

Baird, G., V. Slonims, E. Simonoff & K. Dworzynski. 2011. Impairment in non-word repetition: A marker for language impairment or reading impairment? *Developmental Medicine and Child Neurology* 53. 711–716.

Bedore, L. M. & E. D. Pena. 2008. Assessment of bilingual children for identification of language impairment: Current findings and implications for practice. *International Journal of Bilingual Education & Bilingualism* 11. 1–29.

Ben-Oved, S. H. & S. Armon-Lotem. 2016. Ethnolinguistic identity and lexical knowledge among children from Amharic-speaking families. *Israel Studies in Language and Society* 8 (1–2). 238–275.

Berman, R. A. & D. I. Slobin. 1994. *Relating events in narrative: A crosslinguistic developmental study*. Hillsdale, NJ: Lawrence Erlbaum.

Bialystok, E., G. Luk, K. F. Peets & S. Yang. 2010. Receptive vocabulary differences in monolingual and bilingual children. *Bilingualism: Language and Cognition* 13(4). 525–531.

Biran, M. & N. Friedmann. 2004. *Naming of 100 nouns*. Unpublished instrument. School of Education, Tel Aviv University.

Biran, M. & N. Friedmann. 2005. From phonological paraphasias to the structure of the phonological output lexicon. *Language and Cognitive Processes* 20. 589–616.

Blom, E., J. Paradis & T. S. Duncan. 2012. Effects of input properties, vocabulary size, and L1 on the development of third person singular –s in Child L2 English. *Language Learning* 62. 965–994.

Campbell, T., C. Dollaghan, H. Needleman & J. Janosky. 1997. Reducing bias in language assessment: Processing-dependent measures. *Journal of Speech, Language, and Hearing Research* 40. 519–525.

Catts, H., S. Adlof, T. Hogan & S. Ellis-Weismer. 2005. Are specific language impairment and dyslexia distinct disorders? *Journal of Speech Language and Hearing Research* 48. 1378–1396.

Cekaite, A., S. Blum-Kulka, V. Grøver & E. Teubal. 2014. *Children's peer talk: Learning from each other*. Cambridge: Cambridge University Press.

Chiat, S. 2015. Nonword repetition. In S. Armon-Lotem, J. de Jong & N. Meir (eds.), *Assessing multilingual children: Disentangling bilingualism from language impairment*, 125–150. Bristol, UK: Multilingual Matters.

Chiat, S., S. Armon-Lotem, T. Marinis, K. Polisenska, P. Roy & B. Seeff-Gabriel. 2013. Assessment of language abilities in sequential bilingual children: The potential of sentence imitation tasks. In V. C. Mueller Gathercole (ed.), *Bilinguals and assessment: State of the art guide to issues and solutions from around the world*, 56–89. Bristol, UK: Multilingual Matters.

Chondrogianni, V. & T. Marinis. 2011. Differential effects of internal and external factors on the development of vocabulary, morphology and complex syntax in successive bilingual children. *Linguistic Approaches to Bilingualism* 1(3). 223–248.

Clahsen, H., S. Bartke & S. Goellner. 1997. Formal features in impaired grammars: A comparison of English and German SLI children. *Journal of Neurolinguistics* 10. 151–171.

Clahsen, H. & U. Hong. 1995. Agreement and null subjects in German L2 development: New evidence from reaction-time experiments. *Second Language Research* 11(1). 57–87.

Conti-Ramsden, G., N. Botting & B. Faragher. 2001. Psycholinguistic markers for specific language impairment. *Journal of Child Psychology and Psychiatry* 6. 741–748.

Conti-Ramsden, G., Z. Simkin & A. Pickles. 2006. Estimating familial loading in SLI: A comparison of direct assessment versus parental interview. *Journal of Speech, Language, and Hearing Research* 49. 88–101.

Dollaghan, C. & T. F. Campbell. 1998. Nonword repetition and child language impairment. *Journal of Speech, Language, and Hearing Research* 41. 1136–1146.

Engel, P. M. J., F. H. Santos & S. E. Gathercole. 2008. Are working memory measures free of socioeconomic influence? *Journal of Speech, Language, and Hearing Research* 51. 1580–1587.

Engel de Abreu, P. M. J. 2011. Working memory in multilingual children: Is there a bilingual effect? *Memory* 19. 529–537.

Fenson, L., V. A. Marchman, D. J. Thal, P. Dale, J. S. Reznick & E. Bates. 2007. *MacArthur–Bates communicative development inventories: User's guide and technical manual* (2nd ed.). Baltimore: Brookes.

Fiestas, C. E. & E. D. Peña. 2004. Narrative discourse in bilingual children: Language and task effects. *Language, Speech, and Hearing Services in Schools* 35. 155–168.

Friedmann, N. & H. Lavi. 2006. On the order of acquisition of A-movement, Wh-movement and V-C movement. In A. Belletti, E. Bennati, C. Chesi, E. Di Domenico & I. Ferrari (eds.), *Language acquisition and development*, 211–217. Newcastle, UK: Cambridge Scholars Press.

Gagarina, N., A. Klassert & N. Topaj. 2010. Russian language proficiency test for multilingual children. *ZAS Papers in Linguistics 54*. Berlin: Zentrum für Allgemeine Sprachwissenschaft.

Gagarina, Natalia, Daleen Klop, Sari Kunnari, Koula Tantele, Taina Välimaa, Ingrida Balčiūnienė, Ute Bohnacker & Joel Walters. 2012. MAIN: Multilingual assessment instrument for narratives. Berlin: Zentrum für Allgemeine Sprachwissenschaft

Gathercole, S. E. & A. D. Baddeley. 1996. *The children's test of nonword repetition*. London: Psychological Corporation.

Gathercole, V. C. Mueller, E. M. Thomas, E. Roberts, C. Hughes & E. K. Hughes. 2013. Bilingual norming for vocabulary and grammatical abilities in bilingual children. In V.C. Mueller Gathercole (ed.), *Bilinguals and assessment: State of the art guide to issues and solutions from around the world*, 20–55. Clevedon, UK: Multilingual Matters.

Gathercole, S. E., E. Service, G. J. Hitch, A.-M. Adams & A. J. Martin. 1999. Phonological short-term memory and vocabulary development: Further evidence on the nature of the relationship. *Applied Cognitive Psychology* 13. 65–77.

Gatt, D., C. O'Toole & E. Haman. 2015. Using parental report to assess early lexical production in children exposed to more than one language. In S. Armon-Lotem, J. de Jong & N. Meir (eds.), *Assessing multilingual children: Disentangling bilingualism from language impairment*, 151–195. Bristol: Multilingual Matters

Gioia, G. A., P. K. Isquith, S. C. Guy & L. Kenworthy. 2000. *BRIEF: Behavior Rating Inventory of Executive Function: Professional Manual*. Lutz, FL: Psychological Assessment Resources.

Girbau, D. & R. G. Schwartz. 2007. Non-word repetition in Spanish-speaking children with Specific Language Impairment (SLI). *International Journal of Language and Communication Disorders* 42. 59–75.

Goralnik, E. 1995. *Goralnik Diagnostic Test*. Even Yehuda, Israel: Matan.

Grimm, H. 2003. *Sprachstandscreening für das Vorschulalter*. Göttingen/Bern/Toronto/Seattle: Hogrefe.

Gutierrez-Clellen, V. F. 2002. Narratives in two languages: Assessing performance of bilingual children. *Linguistics and Education* 13(2). 175–197.

Gutiérrez-Clellen, V. F., A. M. Restrepo & G. Simón-Cereijido. 2006. Evaluating the discriminant accuracy of a grammatical measure with Spanish-speaking children. *Journal of Speech, Language, and Hearing Research* 49. 1209–1223.

Gutiérrez-Clellen, V. F. & G. Simon-Cereijido. 2010. Using nonword repetition tasks for the identification of language impairment in Spanish–English-speaking children: Does the language of assessment matter? *Learning Disabilities Research & Practice* 25. 48–58.

Håkansson, G. & U. Nettelbladt. 1993. Developmental sequences in L1 (normal and impaired) and L2 acquisition of Swedish. *International Journal of Applied Linguistics* 3. 131–157.

Håkansson, G., E-K. Salameh & U. Nettelbladt. 2003. Measuring language proficiency in bilingual children: Swedish–Arabic bilingual children with and without language impairment. *Linguistics* 41(2). 255–288.

Haman, E., M. Łuniewska & B. Pomiechowska. 2015. Designing cross-linguistic lexical tasks (clt) for bilingual preschool children. In S. Armon-Lotem, J. de Jong & N. Meir (eds.), *Assessing multilingual children: Disentangling bilingualism from language impairment*, 196–241. Bristol: Multilingual Matters.

Hamann, C. & A. Belletti. 2006. Developmental patterns in the acquisition of complement clitic pronouns: Comparing different acquisition modes with an emphasis on French. *Rivista di Grammatica Generativa* 31. 39–78.

Hayward, D.V., R. B. Gillam & P. Lien. 2007. Retelling a script-based story: Do children with and without language impairments focus on script and story elements? *American Journal of Speech-Language Pathology* 16. 235–245

Jakubowicz, C., L. Nash, C. Rigaut & C.-L. Gerard. 1998. Determiners and clitic pronouns in French-speaking children with SLI. *Language Acquisition* 7. 113–160.

Jeuk, S. 2003. *Erste Schritte in der Zweitsprache Deutsch. Eine empirische Untersuchung zum Zweitspracherwerb türkischer Migrantenkinder in Kindertageseinrichtungen*. Freiburg im Breisgau: Fillibach-Verlag.

Jørgensen, R. N., P. Dale, D. Bleses & L. Fenson. 2010. CLEX: A cross-linguistic lexical norms database. *Journal of Child Language* 37(2). 419–428.

Junker, D. A., & I. J. Stockman. 2002. Expressive vocabulary of German–English bilingual toddlers. *American Journal of Speech-Language Pathology* 11(4). 381–394.

Kambanaros, M., K. K. Grohmann, M. Michaelides & E. Theodorou. 2014. On the nature of verb-noun dissociation in bilectal SLI: A psycholinguistics perspective from Greek. *Bilingualism: Language and Cognition* 17. 169–188.

Kauschke, C. 2007. *Erwerb und Verarbeitung von Nomen und Verben*. Tübingen: Niemeyer. http://www.christina-kauschke.de/Publikationen-de.html

Kunnari, S. & T. Välimaa. 2014. Story content in the narratives of mono- and bilingual Finnish-speaking children. Paper presented at meeting of International Congress for the Study of Child Language (IASCL), Amsterdam.

Kwon, E. Y. & Z-H. Han. 2008. Language transfer in child SLA: A longitudinal case study of a sequential bilingual. In J. Philp, R. Oliver & A. Mackey (eds.), *Second language acquisition and the younger learner: Child's play?* 303–332. Amsterdam: John Benjamins.

Labov, W. & J. Waletzky. 1967. Narrative analysis. In J. Helm (ed.), *Essays on the verbal and visual arts*, 12–44. Seattle: University of Washington Press.

Lahey, M. & J. Edwards. 1999. Naming errors of children with specific language impairment. *Journal of Speech and Hearing Research* 42. 195–205.

Lee. S.-A. S. & B. K. Gorman. 2013. Nonword repetition performance and related factors in children representing four linguistic groups. *International Journal of Bilingualism* 17(4). 479–495.

Leonard, L. B. 1998. *Children with specific language impairment*. Cambridge, MA: MIT Press.

Leonard, L. B. & P. Deevy. 2004. Lexical deficits in specific language impairment. In L. Verhoeven & H. van Balkom (eds.), *Classification of developmental language disorders*, 209–233. Mahwah, NJ: Lawrence Erlbaum.

Li, P., Sepanski, S. & X. Zhao. 2006. Language history questionnaire: A web-based interface for bilingual research. *Behavior Research Methods* 38(2). 202–210.

Lukács, Á., B. Kas & L. Leonard. 2013. Case marking in Hungarian children with specific language impairment. *First Language* 33(4). 331–353.

Maital, S. L., E. Dromi, A. Sagi & M. H. Bornstein. 2000. The Hebrew Communicative Development Inventory: Language-specific properties and cross-linguistic generalizations. *Journal of Child Language* 27. 43–67.

Mandler, G. & N. Johnson. 1977. Remembrance of things parsed: Story structure and recall. *Cognitive Psychology* 9. 111–151.

Marchman, V. A., A. Fernald & N. Hurtado. 2009. How vocabulary size in two languages relates to efficiency in spoken word recognition by young Spanish–English bilinguals. *Journal of Child Language* 37(4). 817–840.

Marinis, T. & S. Armon-Lotem. 2015. Sentence repetition. In S. Armon-Lotem, J. de Jong & N. Meir (eds.), *Assessing multilingual children: Disentangling bilingualism from language impairment*, 95–123. Bristol, UK: Multilingual Matters.

Marinis, T. & V. Chondrogianni. 2011. Comprehension of reflexives and pronouns in sequential bilingual children: do they pattern similarly to L1 children, L2 adults, or children with specific language impairment? *Journal of Neurolinguistics* 2(2). 202–212.

Mayer, M. 2003. *Frog, where are you?* New York: Dial Books (Original work published 1969).

Meir, N. & S. Armon-Lotem. 2015. Disentangling bilingualism from SLI in Heritage Russian: The impact of L2 properties and length of exposure to the L2. In C. Hamman & E. Ruigendijk (eds.), *Language acquisition and development: Proceedings of GALA 2013*, 299–314. Cambridge: Cambridge Scholars.

Messer, M. H., P. P. M. Leseman, J. Boom & A.Y. Mayo. 2010. Phonotactic probability effect in non-word recall and its relationship with vocabulary in monolingual and bilingual preschoolers. *Journal of Experimental Child Psychology* 10. 306–323.

Miranda, A., A. McCabe & L. Bliss. 1998. Jumping around and leaving things out: a profile of the narrative abilities of children with Specific Language Impairment. *Applied Psycholinguistics* 19(4). 247–267.

Norbury, C. F. & D. V. Bishop. 2003. Narrative skills of children with communication impairments. *International Journal of Language Communication Disorder* 38(3). 287–313.

Oller, D. K., B. Z. Pearson & A. B. Cobo-Lewis. 2007. Profile effects in early bilingual language and literacy. *Applied Psycholinguistics* 28(2). 191–230.

Oro, A. B., M. E. Navarro-Calvillo & C. Esmer. 2014. Autistic Behavior Checklist (ABC) and its applications. In V. B. Patel, V. R. Preedy & C. R. Martin (eds.), *Comprehensive guide to autism*, 2787–2798. New York: Springer.

Paradis, J. 2010. The interface between bilingual development and specific language impairment. *Applied Psycholinguistics* 31. 227–252.

Paradis, J. 2011. Individual differences in child English second language acquisition: Comparing child-internal and child-external factors. *Linguistic Approaches to Bilingualism* 1(3). 213–237.

Paradis, J. & M. Crago. 2000. Tense and temporality: Similarities and differences between language-impaired and second-language children. *Journal of Speech, Language and Hearing Research* 43(4). 834–848.

Paradis, J. & M. Crago. 2004. Comparing L2 and SLI grammars in French: Focus on DP. In P. Prévost & J. Paradis (eds.), *The acquisition of French in different contexts: Focus on functional categories*, 89–108 Amsterdam: John Benjamins.

Paradis, J., K. Emmerzael & T. Sorenson Duncan. 2010. Assessment of English language learners: Using parent report on first language development. *Journal of Communication Disorders* 43. 474–497.

Parra, M., E. Hoff & C. Core. 2011. Relations among language exposure, phonological memory, and language development in Spanish-English bilingually developing 2-year-olds. *Journal of Experimental Child Psychology* 108. 113–125.

Patterson, J. & B. Z. Pearson. 2004. Bilingual lexical development: Influences, contexts, and processes. In G. Goldstein (ed.), *Bilingual language development and disorders in Spanish-English speakers*, 77–104. Baltimore, MD: Brookes.

Pearson, B. Z. 1998. Assessing lexical development in bilingual babies and toddlers. *International Journal of Bilingualism* 2. 347–372.

Pearson, B. Z., S. C. Fernández & D. K. Oller. 1993. Lexical development in bilingual infants and toddlers: Comparison to monolingual norms. *Language Learning* 43. 93–120.

Pearson, B. Z., S. Fernandez & D. K. Oller. 1995. Cross-language synonyms in the lexicons of bilingual infants: One language or two? *Journal of Child Language* 22. 345–368.

Polite, E. J., L. B. Leonard & F. D. Roberts. 2011. The use of definite and indefinite articles by children with specific language impairment. *International Journal of Speech Language Pathology* 13(4). 291–300.

Ravid, D. & R. A. Berman. 2009. Developing linguistic register across text types: The case of Modern Hebrew. *Pragmatics and Cognition* 17. 108–145.

Reilly, J., M. Losh, U. Bellugi & B. Wulfeck. 2004. "Frog, where are you?" Narratives in children with specific language impairment, early focal brain injury and Williams Syndrome. In B. Wulfeck & J. Reilly (eds.), Plasticity and development: Language in atypical children [Special issue]. *Brain & Language* 88. 229–247.

Rescorla, L. 1989. The Language Development Survey: A screening tool for delayed language in toddlers. *Journal of Speech and Hearing Disorder* 54. 587–599.

Rescorla, L. & A. Alley. 2001. Validation of the Language Development Survey (LDS). *Journal of Speech, Language, and Hearing Research* 44. 434–445.

Rice, M. L. & K. Wexler. 1996. Toward tense as a clinical marker of specific language impairment in English-speaking children. *Journal of Speech, Language, and Hearing Research* 39. 1239–1257.

Roeper, T., E. Ramos, H. Seymour & L. Abdul-Karim. 2001. Language disorders as a window on universal grammar: An abstract theory of agreement for IP, DP and V-PP. *Brain and Language* 77(3). 378–397.

Roy, P. & S. Chiat. 2013. Teasing apart disadvantage from disorder: The case of poor language. In C. R. Marshall (ed.), *Current issues in developmental disorders*, 125–150. Hove, East Sussex, UK: Psychology Press.

Schelletter, C. 2005. Bilingual children's lexical development: Factors affecting the acquisition of nouns and verbs and their translation equivalents. In J. Cohen, K. T. McAlister, K. Rolstad & J. MacSwan (eds.), *ISB4: Proceedings of the 4th international symposium on bilingualism*, 2095–2103. Somerville, MA: Cascadilla Press.

Schiff, D. & D. Ravid. 2012. Linguistic processing in Hebrew-speaking children from low- and high-SES backgrounds. *Reading & Writing* 25. 1427–1448.

Schwartz, B. D. 2004. On child L2 development of syntax and morphology. *Lingue e Linguaggio* 3(1). 97–132.

Schwartz, M. & H. Rovner. 2015. The acquisition of definiteness in Hebrew (L2) by bilingual preschool children (Russian-L1): A longitudinal multiple-case study. *International Journal of Bilingualism* 19(5). 548–571.

Semel, E., E. Wiig & W. Secord. 2000. *Clinical Evaluation of Language Fundamentals (CELF-IIIUK)* (3rd ed.). London: Psychological Corporation.

Sharp, K. M. & V. C. M Gathercole. 2013. Can a novel word repetition task be a language-neutral assessment tool? Evidence from Welsh–English bilingual children. *Child Language Teaching and Therapy* 29. 77–89.

Simonsen, A. 2002. Naming amongst 6 year old children. *Working Papers* 50. 79–84. Lund University, Sweden.

Soodla, P. & E. Kikas. 2010. Macrostructure in the narratives of Estonian children with typical development and language impairment. *Journal of Speech, Language, and Hearing Research* 53(5). 1321–1333.

Summers, C., T. M. Bohman, R. B Gillam, E. D. Peña & L. M. Bedore. 2010. Bilingual performance on nonword repetition in Spanish and English. *International Journal of Language and Communication Disorder* 45. 480–493.

Thordardottir, E. 2014. The relationship between bilingual exposure and morphosyntactic development. *International Journal of Speech-Language Pathology* 17(2). 97–114.

Thordardottir, E. 2015. Proposed diagnostic procedures for use in bilingual and cross-linguistic contexts. In S. Armon-Lotem, J. de Jong & N. Meir (eds.), *Assessing multilingual children: Disentangling bilingualism from language impairment*, 331–358. Bristol, UK: Multilingual Matters.

Thordardottir E. & M. Brandeker. 2013. The effect of bilingual exposure versus language impairment on nonword repetition and sentence imitation scores. *Journal of Communication Disorders* 46(1). 1–16.

Thordardottir, E., A. Rothenberg, M. E. Rivard & R. Naves. 2006. Bilingual assessment: Can overall proficiency be estimated from separate assessment of two languages? *Journal of Multilingual Communication Disorders* 4. 1–21.

Tsimpli, I., E. Peristeri & M. Andreou. 2014. *Narrative production in monolingual and bilingual children with Specific Language Impairment*. Paper presented at meeting of International Congress for the Study of Child Language (IASCL), Amsterdam.

Tuller, L. 2015. Clinical use of parental questionnaires in multilingual contexts. In S. Armon-Lotem, J. de Jong & N. Meir (eds.), *Assessing multilingual children: Disentangling bilingualism from language impairment*, 301–330. Bristol, UK: Multilingual Matters.

Tuller, L., Abboud, L., Ferré, S., Fleckstein, A., Prévost, P., Dos Santos, C., Scheidnes, M. & R. Zebib. 2015. Specific Language Impairment and Bilingualism: Assembling the Pieces. In Cornelia Hamann & Esther Ruigendijk (eds.), *Language Acquisition and Development. Proceedings of GALA 2013*, 533–567. Newcastle: Cambridge Scholars Press.

Umbel, V. M., B. Z. Pearson, M. C. Fernandez & D. K. Oller. 1992. Measuring bilingual children's receptive vocabularies. *Child Development* 63. 1012–1020.

Unsworth, S. 2013. Assessing the role of current and cumulative exposure in simultaneous bilingual acquisition: The case of Dutch gender. *Bilingualism: Language and Cognition* 16. 86–110.

van der Lely, H. K. J., S. Adlof, T. Hogan & A. Ellis-Weismer. 2007. *The Grammar and Phonology Screening (GAPS) test*. London: Stass Publications.

Verhoeven, Ludo, Judit Steenge & Hans van Balkom. 2005. Linguistic transfer in bilingual children with specific language impairment. *International Journal of Language & Communication Disorders* 47 (2). 176–183.

Walters, J. 2005. *Bilingualism: The sociopragmatic-psycholinguistic interface*. Hillsdale, NJ: Lawrence Erlbaum.

Warlaumont, A. S. & L. Jarmulowicz. 2012. Caregivers' suffix frequencies and suffix acquisition by language impaired, late talking, and typically developing children. *Journal of Child Language* 39. 1017–1042.

White, L. 1996. Clitics in child L2 French. In H. Clahsen (ed.), *Generative approaches to first and second language acquisition*, 335–368. Amsterdam: John Benjamins.

Windsor, J., K. Kohnert, K. F. Lobitz & G. T. Pham. 2010. Cross-language nonword repetition by bilingual and monolingual children. *American Journal of Speech-Language Pathology* 19. 298–310.

Yan, S. & E. Nicoladis, 2009. Finding le mot juste: Differences between bilingual and monolingual children's lexical access in comprehension and production. *Bilingualism: Language and Cognition* 12. 323–323.

Yochana, M. 2014. *Narrative abilities in English-Hebrew bilingual preschool children*. Ramat Gan, Israel: Bar Ilan University unpublished doctoral thesis.

C. Patrick Proctor and Rebecca Louick
31 Development of vocabulary knowledge and its relationship with reading comprehension among emergent bilingual children: An overview

1 Introduction

There is no question that vocabulary knowledge is a fundamental component of reading comprehension and its development. Studies dating back to the early 20th century demonstrate the correlational link between vocabulary and reading comprehension (Whipple 1925; Pearson, Hiebert, and Kamil 2007), and any 21st century researcher who seeks to articulate a model of reading comprehension must take into account processes of vocabulary knowledge as an essential predictor of reading performance. Indeed, Laufer (1997) makes the rather universal claim that "[n]o text comprehension is possible, either in one's native language, or in a foreign language, without understanding the text's vocabulary" (20).

However, the vast majority of what we know about vocabulary knowledge, its development, and its relationship with reading comprehension, derives from literature that has targeted predominantly monolingual populations, or from second language acquisition research among older learners of foreign languages (see, e.g., Coady and Huckin 1997; Meara 2009). As a field, far less is known about bilingual children[1]. While there is an emerging consensus on effective approaches for teaching vocabulary to bilingual learners (notably in English; see Baker et al. 2014; Graves, August, and Mancilla-Martinez 2013), it has only been in these recent years of the 21st century that researchers have begun to ask questions about the nature of vocabulary development and its relationship with reading comprehension among bilingual children.

While there do indeed exist robust models of bilingual education, notably in Europe, researchers of bilingual children tend to invoke a *grand narrative* (see Bloome, Carter, Christian, and Madrid 2008) that articulates the need for children to become proficient readers and writers of the dominant social language (e.g., English, Dutch,

---

[1] In this review, we use the term *bilingual* to capture a population of learners who speak a language at home that is typically not the language of schooling instruction. Other terms used in the research include *limited English proficient, English as an additional language, emergent bilingual, English learner, English language learner,* and *language minority.*

C. Patrick Proctor and Rebecca Louick, Boston College

Norwegian, German, per studies located for this literature review) in order to be successful actors in society. Be that as it may, researchers have a wider range of questions that might be asked with respect to vocabulary development and its relationship to reading comprehension when it comes to working with bilingual children. Notably, bilinguals, unlike their monolingual counterparts, speak a language that is typically different from that of the language of literacy instruction that occurs in schools. Thus, as a research community, we can ask a broader range of questions about vocabulary development and reading comprehension. Specifically, working with bilinguals expands the possibilities for research as follows:

1) Studies that focus on students from various home language backgrounds;
2) Studies that examine the development of vocabulary and/or reading solely in the language of schooling (L2 only);
3) Studies that include the development of vocabulary and/or reading in the home language for cross-linguistic analysis (L1–L2);
4) Studies that examine the development of bilinguals' reading and/or vocabulary in the language of schooling compared with a monolingual sample (Comparison).

Multiple language backgrounds, points of comparison with monolinguals, and the inclusion of the home language distinguish studies with bilingual children from those with exclusively monolingual populations.

Given these complexities, we set out to review the literature on vocabulary and its relationship with reading comprehension among bilingual learners from the earliest exposures to schooling (around 4 years of age) through the end of secondary education (around 18 years of age). This review begins with a brief theoretical orientation to vocabulary knowledge, its development, and its relationship with reading comprehension. We then describe a literature review process that included two components: Peer-reviewed studies of vocabulary development among bilingual learners and peer-reviewed studies that examine the developmental role of vocabulary in predicting reading comprehension.

2 Theoretical orientations to vocabulary and reading comprehension

Vocabulary knowledge is complex, and its relationship with reading comprehension, while consistently strong among monolingual populations (see Pearson et al. 2007), is not so clearly understood. This is largely due to the fact that correlations reveal little about the processes through which vocabulary and reading comprehension affect one another.

2.1 Vocabulary knowledge is a large problem space

Knowing a word's meaning is not as simple as it may seem, and putting it into context within a reading paradigm helps to articulate why. We know that learning to take graphic information and convert it to linguistic form (i.e., to *decode*) is a necessary, but insufficient dimension of the reading process. Depending on the orthography of a given language, the nature of decoding varies, but what characterizes decoding, particularly in alphabetic orthographies, is a finite set of sound-symbol relationships that are relatively easy to learn over shorter spans of developmental time (Paris 2005). As such, Snow and Kim (2007) suggest that decoding skills reside within a small *problem space*, one which, from an instructional perspective, is relatively easy to address. Indeed evidence from many reading studies with bilingual children has converged on the conclusion that, barring atypical development, bilinguals tend to perform on par with their monolingual counterparts with respect to decoding (Mancilla-Martinez and Lesaux 2010; Nakamoto, Lindsey, and Manis 2007; Roberts, Mohammed, and Vaughn 2010; Droop and Verhoeven 2003; Verhoeven 2000).

There is, however, an inverse relationship between how constrained a literacy skill is, and the relative size of the problem space. Decoding is constrained and thus a relatively small problem space. Vocabulary, by contrast, is far less constrained, in part because it takes both expressive (through speaking and writing) and receptive (through listening and reading) forms. Further, while there is arguably a finite number of words for any given language, the range of any lexicon is vast, as evidenced by early vocabulary research documenting the English word learning demands that students encounter when they begin school (approximately 3,000 new words per year; Nagy and Anderson 1984). Thus, while decoding plays a fundamental role in predicting reading comprehension (i.e., in its absence, comprehension is impossible; Hoover and Gough 1990), vocabulary knowledge is far less constrained and a much larger problem space.

Simply knowing a lot of vocabulary words (i.e., breadth), however, is insufficient for facile text comprehension. How well one knows different words (i.e., depth) is also crucial, and perhaps the most comprehensive framework for understanding depth of vocabulary knowledge was articulated by Nagy and Scott (2000). In their conception, five distinct dimensions characterize vocabulary knowledge. First, the dimension of *incrementality* indicates that word meanings are not learned upon a single initial exposure, but rather that word knowledge becomes more in-depth as a function of each use or encounter with a given word, across various contexts. The second dimension, *polysemy*, recognizes that words "are inherently flexible" (Nagy and Scott 2000: 271) and thus have multiple meanings that vary across context and use. Third, *multidimensionality* represents the reality that word meanings vary depending on the nature of their contexts of use. For example, an eight-year-old girl might know how to identify sarcasm when she hears it from her brother, but when she goes to tell her mother about it, she notes that her brother had just "been sarcasm". The fourth dimension is *interrelatedness* and refers to conceptual networks that exist among various words (e.g., relatedness between *cat, meow, feline,* and *claws*). Finally, *heterogeneity* suggests that words have varying functions for different contexts, which has led some researchers to focus, for example, on the role of academic vocabulary as types of words most suitable for instruction in a schooling context (see, e.g., Kieffer and Stahl in press; Nagy and Townsend 2012).

2.2 Assessing vocabulary

From a theoretical perspective, we conceptualize vocabulary knowledge as deep, encompassing at least five dimensions of complexity beyond simply knowing a single meaning for a word. Yet, in operationalizing vocabulary, literacy researchers often rely on discrete and decontextualized tasks that treat vocabulary as a construct separate from its role in reading comprehension (e.g., verbal analogies, synonymns/ antonyms, picture naming or identification). While vocabulary skills are more often assessed receptively (Pearson et al. 2007), they are also assessed expressively, yet in either case, it is common that the items chosen for assessment are selective (as opposed to comprehensive), that is, a set of words chosen without explanation by the test designer. Items are selected likely under some presumption of Nagy and Scott's (2000) *interrelatedness* dimension of vocabulary knowledge. For example, if a student can say "ball" upon seeing a picture of a ball, then an assumption is made that the student is also likely to know other semantically related words that occur with a similar frequency (perhaps *bounce* or *roll*; see Read 2000 for a comprehensive overview of the *discrete-embedded, context-dependent – context-independent*, and *selective-comprehensive* continuua as they apply to second language vocabulary learning).

Decisions to operationalize vocabulary in such a way are clearly related to a need for speed of assessment, both from a research and a diagnostic perspective. Further, these types of assessments are far easier to standardize with a traditional norming sample of children, to whose performance the assessed student will be compared. Despite the practicality of such approaches, we are left wondering exactly what is being measured with such approaches to vocabulary assessment. Indeed, the approach treats vocabulary as a more constrained skill (like decoding), which may have the effect of de-emphasizing the size of the problem space with respect to instruction. Pearson et al. (2007) further caution that, in assessing bilingual children with such measures, the research and instructional communities ought to recognize "special considerations" in assessing vocabulary.

2.3 Vocabulary and reading comprehension

There is no question that vocabulary is associated with comprehension. We have ample evidence from cross-sectional studies among monolingual and bilingual populations to this end, yet we still lack a clear understanding about specifically how the relationship functions. Anderson and Freebody (1985) suggested three hypotheses as to why. The first is that learning new words improves comprehension (*instrumentalist*). Second, general verbal ability accounts for both vocabulary knowledge and comprehension performance (*verbal aptitude*). Finally, vocabulary and comprehension are influenced by how much one knows about a given topic or concept (*knowledge*).

Recent multi-component interventions conducted with bilingual populations in upper elementary and middle school have shown some success in affecting outcomes for both vocabulary learning and reading comprehension (for a review, see Lesaux, Kieffer, Kelley and Harris 2014). However, the interventions described in these studies tend to adopt instructional approaches that derive from all three hypotheses, which sheds little light on the specific drivers of the notable correlations between vocabulary and reading.

3 Purpose and research questions

We have established that vocabulary is a crucial dimension of reading comprehension, irrespective of the language in which one reads or one's language background. However, vocabulary theory is often at odds with its operationalization. Still, even with less-than-optimal indicators of vocabulary, a good deal of research indicates that vocabulary's associations with reading comprehension tend to be strong for both monolingual and bilingual populations. While the extant research with monolinguals is robust, associations between vocabulary and comprehension among bilingual populations have, until recently, been reported primarily through cross-sectional research. Thus, we know far less about the confluence of recent findings on bilinguals' vocabulary development as a point of exploration on its own, nor do we have a strong sense of how vocabulary contributes to the development of reading comprehension among bilingual populations. The purpose of this thematic literature review is to explore both of these dimensions and to identify trends in outcomes as well as future avenues for research. Given the uniqueness of bilingual populations to the study of vocabulary and reading comprehension, we sought to understand the nature of identified studies as well as to overview their findings. We asked two basic research questions:

1. What are the characteristics of each set of identified studies with respect to participants (language background and age/grade ranges) and analyses (intra- or cross-linguistic and comparative or non-comparative)?
2. Using the characteristics established in RQ1, what patterns emerge among findings from each set of identified studies?

To answer RQ 1, we made an initial pass through all identified studies and developed summary tables that provide basic information with respect to participants and types analyses (Tables 1 and 2), which serve as a descriptive overview. To answer RQ2, we took a qualitative, rather than a quantitative, approach, which makes our analyses intuitive and reliant on our judgments rather than on objective quantitative findings (Ford-Connors and Paratore 2014; Shanahan, 2010). We sought out patterns that emerged from the data, using the categories derived from RQ1 as start codes for employing a traditional grounded approach identifying trends and themes in the data (Miles and Huberman 1994).

4 Methods

Our review of the literature was designed to capture two sets of studies. The first set were studies with bilingual children that focused on the nature of vocabulary development, with or without taking into account associations with reading comprehension. The second set were studies that assessed reading comprehension and also sought to understand the role of vocabulary knowledge in predicting comprehension. For the set of vocabulary development studies, an article was considered appropriate for consideration if the researcher(s) assessed what was called "vocabulary" using the same indicator(s) on at least two measurement occasions. For the set of vocabulary → reading comprehension studies, an article was considered appropriate for consideration if the researcher(s) assessed "reading comprehension" on at least one measurement occasion and also included an operationalized indicator of "vocabulary". The study had to be developmental in some sense, which included early vocabulary performance or growth in vocabulary as it predicted growth in reading comprehension and/or later reading comprehension. Articles were excluded if: a) they were case studies; b) they did not report on bilingual learners between the ages of 4 and 18; c) they reported on the results of an intervention; d) the focus was on the impact of particular teacher or parental actions on student vocabulary.

We conducted an extensive database search using multiple descriptors to capture the broadest range of candidate studies, aggregating searches from *Proquest Education*, *PsycInfo*, and *ERIC* databases, and limiting our search to peer reviewed articles and book chapters published since 2000. To conduct the vocabulary search, we included the following terms (with number of results in parentheses): "vocabulary" and either "language minority" (912 results), "English as an additional language" (193 results), or "English language learner" (431 results). We also searched for "vocabulary development" with "bilingual" (1067 results) and "vocabulary growth" with "bilingual" (345 results).

In conducting the reading comprehension search, terms included "vocabulary development," "reading comprehension," and either "language minority" (197 results), "English as an additional language" (32 results), "English language learner" (158 results) or "bilingual" (452 results). Once all results had been cross-checked for repeated findings, we were left with a total of 309 candidate articles that were considered closely to see if they met the search criteria described above.

Once all articles had been reviewed, we were left with a total of 32 peer-reviewed articles that met all criteria for the vocabulary development section, and a total of 27 peer-reviewed articles that met all criteria for the vocabulary → reading comprehension section. These articles were then reviewed with the goal of answering the proposed research questions that guided the study.

5 Results

Results are reported in two sections. The first summarizes findings from the vocabulary development studies, and the second reports on findings from the vocabulary → reading comprehension studies.

5.1 Vocabulary development studies

Of the 28 identified studies, Table 1 shows that 22 focused on English as the L2. Among the remaining studies, the L2s were Dutch (3), German (1), Greek (1) and Hebrew (1). A wide variety of home languages were represented across these studies. Fourteen included students who spoke Spanish at home and English at school (in 10 of these, Spanish was the only L1). Seven studies included Chinese-English bilinguals (including 4 with Cantonese speakers and 3 with Mandarin speakers); 3 included Turkish-Dutch bilinguals and 1 Turkish-German bilinguals. The remaining 5 studies targeted bilinguals with a variety of home languages, including Punjabi, Tamil, Portuguese, Gujerati, Albanian, and Russian, among others.

Sixteen studies began when children were ages typically associated with prekindergarten or kindergarten (i.e. 4.5 years). Five studies began in first grade (approximately age 6), 3 began in second grade, and one each began in fourth, fifth, and sixth grades. Eight studies reported data collected over two consecutive school years. Eleven studies targeted three consecutive school years, 2 covered four consecutive years, and 4 were five or more years in duration. One study assessed students in 2nd grade and again in 5th grade. The majority (16) were intralinguistic, focusing on vocabulary in the L2 only while 12 studies considered cross-linguistic relationships. Sixteen studies compared a bilingual sample with a comparison group of monolinguals, though five of these used national norms instead of a sampled comparison group. Next, we describe four broad themes that emerged from the review.

Table 1: Overview of vocabulary growth studies, including languages spoken, age/grade levels, and presence of a monolingual comparison group.

Article	L1	L2	Ages/Grades	Languages	Comparison
Collins et al. (2014)	Spanish	English	K-2	L1–L2	No
Davison et al. (2011)	Spanish	English	Preschool-grade 1	L1–L2	No
Droop & Verhoeven (2003)	Turkish, Moroccan Arabic, Berber	Dutch	3rd/4th Grade	L2 only	Yes
Farnia & Geva (2011)	Punjabi, Tamil, Portuguese	English	Ages 6–11	L2 only	Yes
Geva & Farnia (2012)	Punjabi, Gujarati, Tamil, Cantonese, Portuguese, "other languages"	English	2nd and 5th Grades	L2 only	Yes
Golberg et al. (2008)	Korean, Mandarin, Cantonese, Spanish, Romanian, Arabic, Japanese, Farsi	English	Ages 5–7	L2 only	Yes[a]
Hammer et al. (2008)	Spanish	English	PreK-K	L1–L2	No
Hemsley et al. (2013)	Samoan	English	PreK-K	L1–L2	Yes
Hutchinson et al. (2003)	Gujerati, Urdu, Punjabi, Bengali, Pushto	English	Early to mid elementary	L2 only	Yes
Jackson et al. (2014)	Spanish	English	PreK- 2nd Grade	L1–L2	No
Jean & Geva (2009)	Cantonese, Portuguese, Punjabi, Hindi, Gujerati, Urdu, Tamil, Sinhalese	English	Grades 5–7	L2 only	Yes
Kieffer & Lesaux (2012)	Spanish	English	Ages 10-13	L2 only	Yes[a]
Kieffer & Vukovic (2013)	Mostly Spanish (85%), some Arabic, French & Punjabi	English	Grades 1–4	L2 only	Yes
Lam et al. (2012)	Chinese	English	K – 2nd Grade	L2 only	No
Lawrence (2012)	Spanish, "other"	English	Grades 6–8	L2 only	Yes
Limbird et al. (2014)	Turkish	German	Grades 1–3	L2 only	Yes
Mancilla-Martinez & Lesaux (2010)	Spanish	English	Ages 4.5-11	L1–L2	Yes[a]
Mancilla-Martinez & Lesaux (2011)	Spanish	English	Ages 4.5-11	L1–L2	Yes[a]
Pendergast et al. (2015)	Spanish	English	Pre-K	L1–L2	No
Prevoo et al. (2015)	Turkish	Dutch	Ages 5–9	L1–L2	No
Rojas & Iglesias (2013)	Spanish	English	Ages 5–8	L1–L2	No
Schwartz & Katzir (2012)	Russian	Hebrew	Ages 7–9	L2 only	Yes
Sheng, Lu, & Kan (2011)	Mandarin	English	Ages 3–8	L1–L2	No
Sheng (2014)	Mandarin	English	Ages 4–8	L1–L2	No
Simos et al. (2014)	Albanian	Greek	Grades 2–4	L2 only	Yes
Uccelli & Paez (2007)	Spanish	English	K to 1st Grade	L1–L2	Yes[a]
Uchikoshi (2014)	Spanish, Cantonese	English	Ages 5–8	L1–L2	No

Note.[a] – Comparisons made with data obtained from a monolingual norming sample, rather than a monolingual sample selected for the study

5.1.1 Relationship of L2 vocabulary level to L2 vocabulary growth rate

A good deal of intralinguistic research has focused on how beginning levels of vocabulary knowledge influence growth in vocabulary over time. Hammer, Lawrence and colleagues reported mixed findings regarding Spanish-English bilinguals in U.S. Head Start programs. In their two studies (each lasting two years), students were identified as those who spoke English at home (Home English Communication, HEC) and those who spoke English only at school (School English Communication, SEC). Hammer, Lawrence, and Miccio (2008) reported that SEC students' English receptive vocabulary levels grew faster than those of HEC students; however, in a similar study, Davison, Hammer and Lawrence (2011) found that the English receptive vocabularies of HEC and SEC students grew at similar rates. In both studies, beginning vocabulary levels for SEC students were significantly lower than their HEC counterparts.

The majority of studies pursuing similar questions found that the less L2 vocabulary knowledge bilingual students had initially, the faster their L2 vocabulary grew. Sheng (2014) followed two groups of Mandarin-English bilingual children for 16 months (1 group beginning at 4 years old, the other at 6). The younger children, who had less English vocabulary knowledge, had faster receptive and expressive vocabulary growth rates than their older peers. Three other articles reported similar findings. Rojas and Iglesias (2013) followed a group of Spanish-speaking ELLs in the U.S. for three years (starting at age 5), measuring expressive vocabulary. Bilinguals who began at higher vocabulary levels tended to have slower rates of growth than peers who began with lower vocabulary. Similarly, in a study following Spanish-speaking students in the U.S. from age 4.5 to age 11, Mancilla-Martinez and Lesaux (2010, 2011) found that students who started out with higher English expressive vocabulary scores had significantly slower rates of growth than those starting out with lower scores.

5.1.2 Comparing bilinguals' L2 vocabulary growth with monolinguals

Related to the above, a good deal of comparative work has examined the growth rates of bilingual learners with monolingual populations. Some of this work has documented bilinguals' L2 vocabulary growth outpacing their monolingual age-mates (Collins, O'Connor, Suárez-Orozco, Nieto-Castañon, and Toppelberg 2014; Golberg, Paradis and Crago 2008; Jackson, Schatschneider and Leacox 2014; Hemsley, Holm and Dodd 2013; Kieffer and Lesaux 2012; Lawrence 2012; Schwartz and Katzir 2011; Simos, Sideridis, Mouzaki, Chatzidaki, and Tzevelekou 2014), while other work finds no significant differences in rates of growth (Hutchinson et al. 2012; Jean and Geva 2009; Limbird et al. 2014; Kieffer & Vukovic 2013). In all cases, however, bilingual children begin with significantly lower levels of vocabulary.

Working with 5-year-old Canadian students who spoke a variety of home languages, Golberg and colleagues (2008) found that students' English receptive vocabulary growth rate was fast enough to nearly meet monolingual norms by the end of the two-year study. Jackson et al. (2014) followed preschool-age, Spanish-speaking ELLs through second grade, assessing receptive vocabulary in both English and Spanish. Students' English receptive vocabulary increased rapidly enough to lessen the gap between their scores, and those of monolingual peers. Collins et al. (2014) reported similar findings among the Spanish-speaking ELLs they followed from kindergarten to second grade.

However, other studies revealed less emphatic results. Schwartz and Katzir (2011) compared the Hebrew vocabulary growth rates of Russian-Hebrew bilinguals with a group of monolingual, Hebrew-speaking peers. Charting growth from the beginning of second through the third grade, bilingual students outpaced their monolingual peers, however, the degree to which the initial gap lessened depended on type of vocabulary measured. Russian speakers demonstrated persistent lags in L2 receptive vocabulary, but their expressive vocabulary grew more quickly and ultimately closed the gap with their monolingual peers. Assessing the expressive and receptive vocabulary of emerging bilinguals with L1 Samoan and monolingual English speakers in Australia, Hemsley et al. (2013) found "progressively less difference" (814) between scores of the two groups during their first 18 months of school (starting at a mean age of 4.9 years). Similarly, during a 2-year study period beginning in the second grade, Simos and colleagues (2014) found that students with L1 Albanian and L2 Greek started out with receptive language scores 1 standard deviation (SD) lower than their L1 Greek peers, but narrowed that difference to .64 SD points by the end of the study.

Similar results have been obtained in the middle grades. Kieffer and Lesaux (2012) followed Spanish-speaking language-minority (LM) learners from ages 10–13, comparing their vocabulary growth rates to national norms. Among their sample, the average growth rate over the entire study period was faster than that of the average monolingual speaker from one grade level to the next ($d = 0.57$). Lawrence (2012) looked at the impact of "summer setback" (1113) on the vocabulary development of bilingual and monolingual sixth and seventh graders, finding that bilingual students had steeper receptive vocabulary growth rates during the school year than did peers who spoke only English at home.

Four studies, with diverse samples, reported that the L2 vocabulary starting points (like the studies above) were significantly lower for bilinguals than for monolinguals, however, growth rates were statistically comparable between the groups. Limbird et al. (2014) followed Turkish-German bilingual and German monolingual children from grades 1 to 3 in Germany, and found comparable expressive German vocabulary growth patterns. Kieffer and Vukovic (2013) worked with a group of English-speaking students in the U.S. from Grade 1 to Grade 4, finding parallel growth trajectories for bilinguals and monolinguals, with monolinguals significantly above bilinguals (both groups performed significantly below national norms). In England, Hutchinson et al. (2003) reported comparable findings of parallel growth and unequal starting points for a composite measure of receptive and expressive vocabulary. Repeated measures ANOVAs revealed effects of group and time, but not group X time interactions from the second through fourth years of school. Finally, Jean and Geva (2009) assessed the receptive and expressive vocabularies of bilingual and monolingual students in Canada for two years, starting in grade 5. Again, bilingual students displayed consistently lower vocabulary scores than the monolingual group, both with comparable rates of vocabulary growth.

5.1.3 How vocabulary grows over time for bilinguals

Among two groups of Mandarin-English bilingual children over two years (the younger cohort from the ages of 3 to 5, the older from the ages of 6 to 8), Sheng, Lu and Kan (2011) found that children demonstrated rapid growth in English, but not Mandarin. Similarly, Pendergast et al. (2015) found that, among Spanish-English bilingual students, Spanish language skills did not change during the pre-K year, while English vocabulary skills grew considerably.

Given such quick L2 growth rates for younger children, researchers have also investigated questions about whether or not L2 vocabulary growth rates change as children get older. Some research reports that L2 vocabulary growth rates start out at a given slope but decelerate over time (Farnia and Geva 2011; Goldberg et al. 2008; Mancilla-Martinez and Lesaux 2011). Mancilla-Martinez and Lesaux (2011) reported a curvilinear growth trajectory in both English and Spanish expressive vocabulary from ages 4.5 through 11. The deceleration rate was the same in both languages, but the vocabulary growth rate began deceleration at age 10 in English, and age 8 in Spanish. Measuring receptive vocabulary, Farnia and Geva (2011) had similar results in their 6-year study beginning at age 6. English vocabulary growth rates began to level off in the upper elementary years, though this plateau was not unique to bilingual students. Indeed, deceleration was slower for bilinguals than for monolinguals. Goldberg et al. (2008) also found deceleration in expressive L2 vocabulary following students from ages 5 through 7.

By contrast, four studies reported linear vocabulary growth rates for bilingual children during periods of study. Rojas and Iglesias (2013) found that the English expressive vocabulary of five-year-old Spanish-speaking ELLs grew at a consistent rate over the three-year study period. Kieffer and Lesaux (2012) found linear growth in English receptive vocabulary among Spanish-English bilinguals from ages 10–13. Kieffer and Vukovic (2013) reported linear receptive vocabulary growth among their sample of bilingual learners from grades 1 to 4. Finally, while Golberg et al. (2008) found that expressive vocabulary growth decelerated over time, they also reported that English receptive vocabulary growth was linear.

There is a lack of pattern in the data with respect to whether one type of vocabulary knowledge is more likely to decelerate versus another. Golberg et al. (2008) argued that deceleration in their study "was most likely an artifact of our measure and not indicative of the general trend in ESL expressive vocabulary development" (56). Rojas and Iglesias (2013) further argued that "methodological differences across studies of ELLs' language growth... make it difficult to compare findings across studies" (642). Despite inconclusive findings with respect to L2 vocabulary growth rates among bilingual learners, one inescapable conclusion from the combined studies is that starting points of vocabulary knowledge are almost universally lower for bilingual learners as compared with their monolingual counterparts (or national norms).

5.1.4 Associations between L1 vocabulary and L2 vocabulary growth

There were L1–L2 studies, spanning various age groups and first languages, that investigated relationships between students' L1 vocabulary (starting points and/or growth rates), and L2 vocabulary growth rate. Working with children with L1 Turkish and L2 Dutch, beginning at age 5–6 and measuring vocabulary growth in both languages over a three-year span, Prevoo, Malda, Emmen, Yeniad and Mesman (2015) did not find a significant relationship between Turkish vocabulary knowledge at Time 1, 2 or 3, and Dutch vocabulary growth over the three- year period. However, studies of children who spoke other languages produced different findings. Two studies of Spanish-English bilinguals (Jackson et al., 2014; Pendergast, Bingham, and Patton-Terry, 2015) found that students were able to transfer their Spanish language skills to English vocabulary development. Pendergast et al. (2015) reported a similar finding in a study of vocabulary growth during the Pre-K year. Jackson et al. (2014) followed Spanish-English bilinguals from pre-kindergarten to second grade, and found that students with stronger Spanish receptive vocabulary in pre-kindergarten demonstrated greater growth in English receptive vocabulary. Also working with Spanish-English bilinguals, this time following them from kindergarten to second grade, Collins et al. (2014) proposed a series of dual language profiles based on the students' language competencies in both L1 and L2. They found that students who were in the limited proficiency group for both languages in kindergarten were most likely to remain in that group in second grade, or to move to the borderline group (meaning that their vocabulary improved, but not enough to be within 1 standard deviation of the monolingual norm). However, when the researchers considered whether students had changed dual language profiles by second grade or remained in the one they had belonged to before, those students who were proficient only in either English or Spanish in kindergarten were most likely to become dual-language proficient by the end of second grade.

Hemsley et al. (2013) reported vocabulary acquisition of four word types in Samoan-English bilinguals: cognates, matched nouns, phrasal nouns, and holonyms.

Students had the most difficulty acquiring L2 phrasal nouns and holonyms, which the researchers deemed to be the most conceptually and phonologically different between languages. However, L2 cognates and matched nouns were more easily acquired, prompting Hemsley et al. (2013) to argue that the degree to which L1 knowledge impacts L2 growth depends upon the type of word being learned. Specifically, "words that require a conceptual shift from L1 take longer to consolidate and strengthen within the L2 lexicon" (799).

5.2 Vocabulary → Reading comprehension studies

Table 2 shows that 27 studies were identified for this section, and of those, 22 were studies focused on L2 English. Two studies targeted L2 Dutch, with 1 L2 German, 1 L2 French, and 1 L2 Norwegian. A wide variety of home languages were represented across these studies, but fully 15 studies targeted students who spoke Spanish in the home and English at school. Chinese-English bilinguals were the focus of 2 studies (one in Hong Kong, Li et al. 2012; the other in Canada, Lam et al., 2012), Turkish-German and Urdu-Norwegian bilinguals were subjects in 2 others. The remaining 7 studies focused on bilingual samples with a variety of home languages (Arabic, Cantonese, English, French, Gujarati, Moroccan, Portuguese, Tamil, and Turkish, among others).

Most all studies were conducted at the elementary school levels. Eight studies began when children were enrolled in Pre-kindergarten or Kindergarten (Mancilla-Martinez and Lesaux, 2010 reported ages beginning at 4.5 years), 8 beginning in the first grade, 5 beginning in second grade (Li et al. 2012 reported ages, beginning at 8 years), 3 beginning in third grade, and 2 beginning in fourth grade. One study, which used a cohort sequential design, included students beginning in second, third, and fourth grade (Silverman et al. 2015). Two studies (Neufeld et al. 2006; Proctor et al. 2012) reported on data collected over a single school year. Nine studies targeted two consecutive school years, 8 covered three consecutive years, 5 worked with students over four years, 3 studies ranged more than five years in duration (Kieffer 2012; Mancilla-Martinez and Lesaux 2010; Nakamoto et al. 2007). Fifteen studies focused on reading and vocabulary in the L2, while twelve, in some form or another, targeted cross-linguistic relationships. Sixteen of the studies compared a bilingual sample with a comparison group of monolinguals, though two of these (Lesaux et al. 2010 and Mancilla-Martinez and Lesaux 2010) used national norms as a point of comparison, and one (Nakamoto et al. 2012) followed 3 groups of Spanish-English bilinguals who were enrolled in 3 different instructional programs.

Table 2: Overview of vocabulary → reading comprehension studies, including languages spoken, age/grade levels, and presence of a monolingual comparison group.

Article	L1	L2	Ages/Grades	Languages	Comparison
Burgoyne et al. (2011)	Punjabi, Urdu, Gujarati, Pushto, Bengali	English	3rd–4th school years	L2 only	Yes
Carlisle et al. (1999)	Spanish	English	1st–3rd Grades	L1–L2	No
Davison et al. (2011)	Spanish	English	Pre-K–1st Grade	L1–L2	Yes
Droop & Verhoeven (2003)	Turkish, Moroccan, Arabic, Berber	Dutch	3rd–4th Grade	L2 only	Yes
Erdos et al. (2014)	English	French	K–1st Grade	L2 only	No
Farnia & Geva (2013)	Gujarati, Tamil, Cantonese	English	4th–6th Grade	L2 only	Yes
Fitzgerald et al. (2015)	Spanish	English	1st–3rd Grades	L2 only	No
Geva & Farnia (2012)	Punjabi, Gujarati, Tamil, Cantonese, Portuguese, and "other languages"	English	2nd and 5th Grades	L2 only	Yes
Gottardo & Mueller (2009)	Spanish	English	1st–2nd Grade	L1–L2	No
Hutchinson et al. (2003)	Gujerati, Urdu, Panjabi, Bengali, Pushto	English	2nd–4th School Years	L2 only	Yes
Kieffer (2012)	Spanish	English	K–8th Grade	L1–L2	No
Kieffer & Vukovic (2013)	Mostly Spanish (85%), some Arabic, French & Punjabi	English	Grades 1–4	L2 only	Yes
Lam et al. (2012)	Chinese	English	K–3rd Grade	L1–L2	No
Lervag & Aukrust (2010)	Urdu	Norwegian	Grades 2–3	L2 only	Yes
Lesaux et al. (2010)	Spanish	English	4th–5th Grade	L1–L2	Yes[a]
Li et al. (2012)	Chinese	English	Ages 8 and 10	L1–L2	No
Limbird et al. (2014)	Turkish	German	1st–3rd Grade	L2 only	Yes
Lindsey et al. (2003)	Spanish	English	K–1st Grade	L1–L2	No
Mancilla-Martinez & Lesaux (2010)	Spanish	English	Ages 4.5–11	L1–L2	Yes
Manis et al. (2004)	Spanish	English	K–2nd Grade	L1–L2	No
Nakamoto et al. (2007)	Spanish	English	1st–6th Grade	L2 only	No
Nakamoto et al. (2008)	Spanish	English	3rd–6th Grade	L1–L2	No
Nakamoto et al. (2012)	Spanish	English	K–3rd Grade	L1–L2	No[b]
Neufeld et al. (2006)	Spanish	English	1st Grade	L2 only	Yes
Proctor et al. (2012)	Spanish	English	2nd–4th Grade	L1–L2	Yes
Silverman et al. (2015)	Spanish	English	2nd–5th Grade	L2 only	Yes
Verhoeven (2000)	Turkish, Arabic, "other"	Dutch	1st–2nd Grade	L2 only	Yes

Note: [a] = Comparisons made with data obtained from a monolingual norming sample, rather than a monolingual sample selected for the study.
[b] = all students were bilingual, but enrolled in 3 different language program models, which were compared with one another

5.2.1 Associations between vocabulary and static reading comprehension

Not surprisingly, virtually all studies reviewed reported strong intralinguistic associations between early vocabulary knowledge and later reading comprehension. Only 3 studies did not find such associations. Lam et al. (2012) worked with two cohorts of Chinese-English bilingual children in kindergarten (n = 46) and first grade (n = 34), testing the children in English only at two time points spaced one year apart (in first and second grades) on a measure of receptive vocabulary, alongside controls that included time 1 reading comprehension, word reading, phonological awareness, and derivational and compound morphological awareness. For the younger cohort, time 1 word reading emerged as the only significant predictor of reading comprehension while for the older cohort, time 1 reading comprehension and derivational morphological awareness were significant predictors of later reading comprehension.

While Li et al. (2012) did find that English receptive vocabulary at age 8 was a significant predictor of English reading comprehension at age 10 net other predictors in their model (SES, phonological awareness, RAN, word reading and vocabulary in Chinese and English word reading and vocabulary), the authors conversely found that Chinese vocabulary was not associated with Chinese reading comprehension, which gave way to Chinese word reading and English reading (positive associations) and English word reading (negative) serving as significant predictors. Manis et al. (2004) worked with 251 Spanish-English bilinguals in Kindergarten through second grade. The authors found that vocabulary knowledge (a composite variable combined with a sentence recall task), measured in kindergarten (Spanish) and first grade (English) significantly predicted second grade reading comprehension within languages, English vocabulary only accounted for 2 percent of variation in English reading as compared with 11.2 percent of variation in Spanish reading explained by Spanish vocabulary.

Cross-linguistically, a good number of studies have investigated whether early vocabulary knowledge in one language predicts reading comprehension in another (Erdos et al. 2014; Gottardo and Mueller, 2009; Kieffer 2012; Lesaux et al. 2010; Li et al. 2012; Lindsey et al. 2003; Mancilla-Martinez and Lesaux 2010; Manis et al., 2004; Nakamoto et al. 2008; Nakamoto et al. 2012; Proctor et al. 2012). Many of these studies simply report null cross-linguistic relationships (Erdos et al. 2014; Gottardo and Mueller, 2009; Lesaux et al. 2010; Lindsey et al. 2003; Mancilla-Martinez and Lesaux 2010; Nakamoto et al. 2012; Proctor et al. 2012), however a few have noted some L1–L2 relationships.

Kieffer (2012) found that kindergarten vocabulary knowledge (a composite variable derived from expressive vocabulary, listening comprehension, and story retelling) was a significant predictor of third grade English reading comprehension, but proved non-significant once kindergarten English vocabulary knowledge was entered into the predictive model. Li et al. (2012) found that, controlling for age 8 Chinese reading comprehension and receptive vocabulary knowledge, Chinese expressive vocabulary at age 8 was a significant predictor of age 10 English reading comprehension. Manis et al. (2004) found that Spanish vocabulary knowledge (composite score using expressive vocabulary and sentence recall) in kindergarten had a direct relationship with second grade English reading, and explained 2 percent additional variance. No effects of English vocabulary on Spanish reading were detected. Finally, Nakamoto et al. (2008) determined that third grade Spanish vocabulary knowledge (latent construct with expressive vocabulary, listening comprehension, and sentence recall) did not directly predict 6th grade English reading comprehension, but that for stronger English decoders, Spanish vocabulary did explain a small (1%) but significant percentage of variance in English reading. Thus, while effects have been detected in cross-linguistic studies, they tend to be modest at best, and suggest that L1 vocabulary is more likely to predict L2 reading, while L2 vocabulary was not shown to be associated with L1 reading comprehension in the 5 studies which investigated that question (Li et al. 2012; Lindsey et al. 2003; Manis et al. 2004; Nakamoto et al. 2008, 2012).

5.2.2 Associations between vocabulary and growth in reading comprehension

Other intra- and cross-linguistic studies have addressed the role of early vocabulary knowledge as it predicts growth in reading comprehension (Farnia and Geva 2013; Fitzgerald, Amendum, Relyea and Garcia 2015; Kieffer 2012; Lervag and Aukrust 2010; Nakamoto et al. 2007; Neufeld et al. 2006; Proctor et al. 2012; Silverman et al. 2015). Intralinguistic studies of reading comprehension growth are notable in that they are less common and findings are variable. In two studies, vocabulary knowledge emerged as a negative predictor of comprehension (Nakamoto et al. 2007, Silverman et al. 2015). Nakamoto et al. (2007) found that lower vocabulary scores were associated with stronger initial linear growth in first through fourth grade, but then also with higher rates of deceleration in fifth and sixth grade. Studying the reading comprehension growth rates of bilingual learners with L1 Spanish and L2 English, Silverman et al. (2015) found that students whose vocabulary breadth scores were lower in second grade outpaced their peers in terms of comprehension growth over the course of the two-year study.

By contrast, Lervag and Aukrust (2010) found that vocabulary showed a positive association with linear reading comprehension growth among a sample of 288 Norwegian students, 90 of whom were Urdu-Norwegian bilinguals in second through third grade. Farnia and Geva (2013) worked with 400 bilingual (multiple language backgrounds) and 153 English-speaking students in grades 1–6 in Canada. They found that vocabulary knowledge was only significant in its interaction with syntactic knowledge as it predicted linear rates of growth in comprehension (though not quadratic growth, which characterized the nature of comprehension change over time). The effect was compounded, such that higher vocabulary and syntax begat stronger comprehension outcomes over time. In three other studies, however, early vocabulary performance was not associated with reading growth (Fitzgerald et al. 2015; Kieffer 2012; Neufeld et al. 2006; Proctor et al. 2012).

Cross-lingusitically, studies are rarer still, with only two addressing issues of L1 (Spanish) vocabulary predicting L2 (English) reading comprehension growth, and both with null results. Kieffer (2012) examined the role of kindergarten vocabulary (a composite score, described previously) on third through eighth grade comprehension growth among 295 bilingual children while Proctor et al. (2012) examined the role of expressive Spanish vocabulary as it predicted Fall – Spring English reading comprehension change over one academic year for a group of 129 second, third, and fourth grade students. While associations were positive, neither study revealed significant relationships.

5.2.3 Is vocabulary knowledge more important for bilingual learners?

A recurrent theme among some comparative studies is the finding (and thus the broader contention) that vocabulary knowledge is "more relevant in the prediction of bilinguals' than monolinguals' reading comprehension" (Limbird et al. 2014: 951; Droop and Verhoeven 2003; Verhoeven, 2000). Other comparative research provides both confirmatory and some contradictory evidence for this contention.

Burgoyne et al. (2011), in an English-language study, worked with 78 students, 39 of whom were monolingual, and 39 who were bilingual (multiple language backgrounds: 2) in their third and fourth years of schooling. The authors gathered both expressive and receptive measures of vocabulary growth from Year 3 to Year 4, and assessed the effects of reading accuracy, listening comprehension, and vocabulary knowledge. Hierarchical regression modeling, with Year 3 variables predicting Year 4 reading comprehension indicated that, for monolinguals, listening comprehension was a significant predictor reading while vocabulary was not. By contrast, vocabulary was the salient predictor of reading comprehension for the bilingual group. Hutchinson et al. (2003) recorded similar findings with a comparable sample of bilingual and monolingual learners, in which expressive vocabulary was a significant predictor among bilinguals of year 4 reading comprehension (B = .3, p = .02), controlling for year 2 reading comprehension. Such was not the case for the monolinguals (B = –.05, p = .69). Relatedly, Kieffer and Vukovic (2013), in their comparative study with 1st through third grade students noted increasing correlations between expressive vocabulary and reading over time, from .12 in 1st grade to .43 in 4th grade for monolinguals. However, for bilinguals, correlations remained consistent across all grades (.49, .50, .40, .41).

In work with Turkish and Moroccan students learning to read in Dutch, Verhoeven (2000) and Droop and Verhoeven (2003) conducted studies in first and second grades, and in third and fourth grades, respectively. Verhoeven (2000) worked with 1154 children (959 monolingual, 195 bilingual), assessing receptive vocabulary at 4 time points (middle and end of Years 1 and 2), and reading comprehension at 3 time points (end year 1, mid and end year 2). Findings revealed that early receptive vocabulary was as a far stronger predictor of later reading comprehension for the bilingual group (B = .63) than for the monolingual group (B = .43). Droop and Verhoeven (2003) had similar findings among a group of students assessed at the beginning and end of grade 3, and at the end of grade 4. End of third grade vocabulary was significantly associated with fourth grade reading, but differentially as a function of language status (.19 for monolinguals vs. .29 for bilinguals). Similar findings have been shown with Turkish-German bilinguals, in which Limbird et al. (2014) used latent variable structural equation modeling to show that word decoding and phonological awareness from second grade most strongly predicted third grade reading, with the path from vocabulary to comprehension emerging as significant only for the bilingual group.

Only two comparison studies described results where differences between groups were negligible (Lervag and Aukrust 2014; Neufeld et al. 2006). In only one instance were inverse results obtained (Geva and Farnia 2012) in which Grade 2 vocabulary predicted Grade 5 reading more strongly for the monolinguals (B = .22, $p < .01$) than for bilinguals (B = .164, $p < .01$). However, significance testing was undertaken only in two of the comparison studies (Limbird et al. 2014; Verhoeven 2000), in which structural equation modeling indicated that models of reading comprehension were better fitting when the bilingual and monolingual samples were separated for analysis.

6 Conclusion and discussion

In this review, we focused on developmental studies with bilingual populations that targeted: 1) vocabulary as an outcome; and 2) the developmental associations between vocabulary and reading comprehension. In general, our review suggests that there is a need for considerably more research in these domains, particularly among children learning L2s that are other than English. Indeed, of the 50 studies reviewed, 40 targeted English as the L2 outcome of interest. Thus, much like early studies of vocabulary and comprehension that targeted monolingual populations and generalized results to bilingual learners, the study of bilingual learners is English-dominant and more research is needed in non-English languages.

Also adding to the need for more research is the fact that findings are not entirely conclusive, particularly in the realm of vocabulary development. In general, results suggest that children who start with lower levels of vocabulary tend to grow at stronger rates than those with higher levels. However, when one disaggregates this analysis by language status (i.e., bilingual vs. monolingual) the picture is less clear. Even though it was almost universally true that bilinguals started out with lower levels of vocabulary as compared with their monolingual counterparts, it was not always the case that their trajectories of growth were steeper than those of their monolingual counterparts. In those cases where trajectories were different, it was rare for vocabulary gaps to be closed over time. This finding takes on added meaning when considering it in connection with the rather compelling finding that vocabulary may play a stronger role in predicting comprehension for bilingual populations. While our analysis reveals a trend, meta-analytic work is necessary to determine if vocabulary knowledge is, indeed, a stronger predictor of reading for bilingual learners. If so, it is imperative to consider ways by which to leverage vocabulary development for bilingual children in school settings.

Studies that specifically examined cross-linguistic effects were rare in the vocabulary group, and relatively common in the vocabulary → reading comprehension group of studies. In both cases, however, cross-linguistic findings were very small. This finding can be interpreted within the framework of the sizes of the problem spaces that vocabulary and comprehension occupy. Both vocabulary and comprehension represent large domains of learning, and given the size of these spaces, there is less likelihood of overlap across languages, particularly if the languages are not orthographically or etymologically related. For example, a Spanish-English bilingual may be able to make sense of the word *rapid* by noting is orthographic and phonological similarity with *rápido*. Cognates such as these represent one of the clearest dimensions of vocabulary overlap, but are non-existent between, for example, Mandarin and Dutch. By contrast, cross-lingusitic research has been most robustly documented with respect to smaller problem spaces, like decoding skills between orthographically comparable languages (see Bialystok, Luk, and Kwan 2005) and script-universal processes like fluency irrespective of orthography (see Pasquarella, Chen, Gottardo, and Geva 2015). More detailed developmental research ought to consider dimensions of vocabulary as they are more and less robust to cross-lingusitic transfer (e.g., Hemsley et al. 2013; see also Ordoñez, Carlo, Snow, and McLaughlin 2002). Work in this domain would go a long way toward addressing Pearson et al.'s (2007) suggestion of "special considerations" in assessing vocabulary among bilingual learners.

In conclusion, researchers in the 21st century have helped to build an emergent foundation on how vocabulary develops and its relationship to reading comprehension. However, much still remains to be learned, particularly given paradox between the vast linguistic heterogeneity of bilingual populations alongside the relative homogeneity of English outcomes being studied in the extant research.

References

Anderson, Richard C. & Peter Freebody. 1985. Vocabulary knowledge. In H. Singer & R.B. Ruddell (eds.), *Theoretical models and processes of reading*, 3rd edn, 343–371. Newark, DE: International Reading Association.

Baker, S., N. Lesaux, M. Jayanthi, J. Dimino, C. P. Proctor, J. Morris, R. Gersten, K. Haymond, M. J. Kieffer, S. Linan-Thompson & R. Newman-Gonchar. 2014. Teaching academic content and literacy to English learners in elementary and middle school (NCEE 2014–4012). Washington, DC: National Center for Education Evaluation and Regional Assistance (NCEE), Institute of Education Sciences, U.S. Department of Education. http://ies.ed.gov/ncee/wwc/publications_reviews.aspx.

Bialystok, Ellen, Gigi Luk & Ernest Kwan. 2005. Bilingualism, biliteracy, and learning to read: Interactions among languages and writing systems. *Scientific Studies of Reading* 9. 43–61.

Bloome, David, Stephanie Power Carter, Beth Morton Christian, Samara Madrid, Sheila Otto, Nora Shuart-Faris, and Mandy Smith. 2008. *Discourse analysis in classrooms: Approaches to language and literacy research*. New York: Teachers College Press.

Burgoyne, K., H.E. Whiteley & J. M. Hutchinson. 2011. The development of comprehension and reading-related skills in children learning English as an additional language and their monolingual, English-speaking peers. *British Journal of Educational Psychology* 81. 344–354.

Carlisle, Joanne F., Margaret Beeman, Lyle Hull Davis & Galila Spharim. 1999. Relationship of metalinguistic capabilities and reading achievement for children who are becoming bilingual. *Applied Psycholinguistics* 20. 459–478.

Coady, James & Thomas Huckin. 1997. *Second Language vocabulary acquisition: A rationale for pedagogy*. Cambridge: Cambridge University Press.

Collins, Erin E., Carola Suárez-Orozco, Alfonso Nieto-Castañon & Claudio O. Toppelberg. 2014. Dual language profiles of Latino children of immigrants: Stability and change over the early school years. *Applied Psycholinguistics* 35. 581–620.

Davison, Megan Dunn, Carol Hammer & Frank R. Lawrence. 2011. Associations between preschool language and first grade reading outcomes in bilingual children. *Journal of Communication Disorders* 44. 444–458.

Droop, Mienke & Ludo Verhoeven. 2003. Language proficiency and reading ability in first- and second-language learners. *Reading Research Quarterly* 38(1). 78–103.

Erdos, Caroline, Fred Genesee, Robert Savage & Corinne Haigh. 2014. Predicting risk for oral and written language learning difficulties in students educated in a second language. *Applied Psycholinguistics* 35. 371–398.

Farnia, Fataneh & Esther Geva. 2011. Cognitive correlates of vocabulary growth in English language learners. *Applied Psycholinguistics* 32. 711–738.

Farnia, Fataneh & Esther Geva. 2013. Growth and predictors of change in English language learners' reading comprehension. *Journal of Research in Reading* 36(4). 389–421.

Fitzgerald, Jill, Steven J. Amendum, Jackie Eunjung Relyea & Sandra G. Garcia. 2015. Is overall oral English ability related to young Latinos' English reading growth? *Reading & Writing Quarterly* 31(1). 68–95.

Geva, Esther & Fataneh Farnia. 2012. Developmental changes in the nature of language proficiency and reading fluency paint a more complex view of reading comprehension in ELL and EL1. *Reading and Writing* 25. 1819–1845.

Golberg, Heather, Johanne Paradis & Martha Crago. 2008. Lexical acquisition over time in minority first language children learning English as a second language. *Applied Psycholinguistics* 29. 41–65.

Gottardo, Alexandra & Julie Mueller. 2009. Are first- and second-language factors related in predicting second-language reading comprehension? A study of Spanish-speaking children acquiring English as a second language from first to second grade. *Journal of Educational Psychology* 101(2). 330–344.

Graves, Michael F., Diane August & Jeannette Mancilla-Martinez. 2013. *Teaching vocabulary to English language learners*. New York: Teachers College Press.

Hammer, Carol Scheffner, Frank R. Lawrence & Adele W. Miccio. 2008. Exposure to English before and after entry into Head Start: Bilingual children's receptive language growth in Spanish and English. *International Journal of Bilingual Education and Bilingualism* 11(1). 30–56.

Hemsley, Gayle, Alison Holm & Barbara Dodd. 2013. Conceptual distance and word learning: Patterns of acquisition in Samoan-English bilingual children. *Journal of Child Language* 40(4). 799–820.

Hoover, Wesley A. & Philip B. Gough. 1990. The simple view of reading. *Reading and Writing* 2(2). 127–160.

Hutchinson, Jane M., Helen E. Whiteley, Chris D. Smith & Liz Connors. 2003. The developmental progression of comprehension-related skills in children learning EAL. *Journal of Research in Reading* 26(1). 19–32.

Jackson, Carla W., Christopher Schatschneider & Lindsey Leacox. 2014. Longitudinal analysis of receptive vocabulary growth in young Spanish English-speaking children from migrant families. *Language, Speech, and Hearing Services in Schools* 45. 40–51.

Jean, Maureen & Esther Geva. 2009. The development of vocabulary in English as a second language children and its role in predicting word recognition ability. *Applied Psycholinguistics* 30. 153–185.

Kieffer, Michael J. 2012. Early oral language and later reading development in Spanish-speaking English language learners: Evidence from a nine-year longitudinal study. *Journal of Applied Developmental Psychology* 33. 146–157.

Kieffer, Michael J. & Nonie K. Lesaux. 2012. Development of morphological awareness and vocabulary knowledge in Spanish-speaking language minority learners: A parallel process latent growth curve model. *Applied Psycholinguistics* 33. 23–54.

Kieffer, Michael J. and Katherine D. Stahl. 2016. Complexities of individual difference in vocabulary knowledge: Implications for research, assessment, and instruction. In P. Afflerbach, *Handbook of individual differences in reading: Reader, text and context*, 120–137. New York: Routledge.

Kieffer, Michael J. & Rose K. Vukovic. 2013. Growth in reading-related skills of language minority learners and their classmates: More evidence for early identification and intervention. *Reading and Writing* 26. 1159–1194.

Lam, Katie, Xi Chen, Esther Geva, Yang C. Luo & Hong Li. 2012. The role of morphological awareness in reading achievement among young Chinese-speaking English language learners: A longitudinal study. *Reading and Writing* 25. 1847–1872.

Lawrence, Joshua Fahey. 2012. English vocabulary trajectories of students whose parents speak a language other than English: Steep trajectories and sharp summer setback. *Reading and Writing* 25. 1113–1141.

Lervåg, Arne & Vibeke Grøver Aukrust. 2010. Vocabulary knowledge is a critical determinant of the difference in reading comprehension growth between first and second language learners. *The Journal of Child Psychology and Psychiatry* 51(5). 612–620.

Lesaux, Nonie K., Michael J. Kieffer, S. Elisabeth Faller & Joan G. Kelley. 2010. The effectiveness and ease of implementation of an academic vocabulary intervention for linguistically diverse students in urban middle schools. *Reading Research Quarterly* 45(2). 196–228.

Lesaux, Nonie K., Michael J. Kieffer, Joan G. Kelley & Julie Russ Harris. 2004. Effects of academic vocabulary instruction for linguistically diverse adolescents: Evidence from a randomized field trial. *American Educational Research Journal*.

Li, Tong, Catherine McBride-Chang, Anita Wong & Hua Shu. 2012. Longitudinal predictors of spelling and reading comprehension in Chinese as an L1 and English as an L2 in Hong Kong Chinese children. *Journal of Educational Psychology* 104(2). 286–301.

Limbird, Christina K., Jessica T. Maluch, Camilla Rjosk, Petra Stanat & Hans Merkens. 2014. Differential growth patterns in emerging reading skills of Turkish-German bilingual and German monolingual primary school students. *Reading and Writing* 27(5). 945–968.

Lindsey, Kim A., Franklin R. Manis & Caroline E. Bailey. 2003. Prediction of first-grade reading in Spanish-speaking English-language learners. *Journal of Educational Psychology* 95(3). 482–494.

Mancilla-Martinez, Jeannette & Nonie K. Lesaux. 2010. Predictors of reading comprehension for struggling readers: The case of Spanish-speaking language minority learners. *Journal of Educational Psychology* 102(3). 701–711.

Manis, Franklin R., Kim A. Lindsey & Caroline E. Bailey. 2004. Development of reading in grades K-2 in Spanish-speaking English-language learners. *Learning Disabilities Research & Practice* 19(4). 214–224.

Meara, Paul. 2009. *Connected words: Word associations and second language vocabulary acquisition*. Amsterdam: John Benjamins.

Miles, Matthew B, & A. M. Huberman. 1994. *Qualitative data analysis: An expanded sourcebook*. Sage.

Nagy, William E. & Richard C. Anderson. 1984. How many words are there in printed school English? *Reading Research Quarterly* 19(3). 304–330.

Nagy, William E. & Judith A. Scott. 2000. Vocabulary processes. In M. L. Kamil, P. B. Mosenthal, P. D. Pearson, & R. Barr (eds.), *Handbook of reading research*, vol. III, 269–284. Mahwah, NJ: Lawrence Erlbaum Associates.

Nagy, William & Dianna Townsend. 2012. Words as tools: Learning academic vocabulary as language acquisition. *Reading Research Quarterly* 47(1). 91–108.

Nakamoto, Jonathan, Kim A. Lindsey & Franklin R. Manis. 2007. A longitudinal analysis of English language learners' word decoding and reading comprehension. *Reading and Writing* 20. 691–719.

Nakamoto, Jonathan, Kim A. Lindsey & Franklin R. Manis. 2008. A cross-linguistic investigation of English language learners' reading comprehension in English and Spanish. *Scientific Study of Reading* 12(4). 351–371.

Nakamoto, Jonathan, Kim A. Lindsey & Franklin R. Manis. 2012. Development of reading skills from K-3 in Spanish-speaking English language learners following three programs of instruction. *Reading and Writing* 25. 537–567.

Neufeld, Paul, Steven J. Amendum, Jill Fitzgerald & Karren M. Guthrie. 2006. First-grade Latino students' English-reading growth in all-English classrooms. *Reading Research and Instruction* 46(1). 23–52.

Paris, Scott G. 2005. Reinterpreting the development of reading skills. *Reading Research Quarterly* 40(2). 184–202.

Pasquarella, Adrian, Xi Chen, Alexandra Gottardo & Esther Geva. 2015. Cross-language transfer of word reading accuracy and word reading fluency in Spanish-English and Chinese-English bilinguals: Script-universal and script-specific processes. *Journal of Educational Psychology* 107(1). 96–110.

Pendergast, Meghan, Gary Bingham & Nicole Patton-Terry. 2015. Examining the relationship between emergent literacy skills and invented spelling in prekindergarten Spanish-speaking dual language learners. *Early Education and Development* 26(2). 264–285. http://doi.org/10.1080/10409289.2015.991083

Prevoo, Mariëlle J. L., Maike Malda, Rosanneke A.G. Emmen, Nihal Yeniad, & Judi Mesman. 2015. A context-dependent view on the linguistic interdependence hypothesis: Language use and SES as potential moderators. *Language Learning* 65(2). 449–469.

Proctor, C. Patrick, Bridget Dalton, Paola Uccelli, Gina Biancarosa, Elaine Mo, Catherine Snow & Sabina Neugebauer. 2011. Improving comprehension online (ICON): Effects of deep vocabulary instruction with bilingual and monolingual fifth graders. *Reading and Writing: An Interdisciplinary Journal* 24. 517–544.

Proctor, C. Patrick, Rebecca D. Silverman, Jeffrey R. Harring & Christine Montecillo. 2012. The role of vocabulary depth in predicting reading comprehension among English monolingual and Spanish-English bilingual children in elementary school. *Reading and Writing* 25. 1635–1644.

Roberts, Greg, Sarojani S. Mohammed & Sharon Vaughn. 2010. Reading achievement across three language groups: Growth estimates for overall reading and reading subskills obtained with the early childhood longitudinal survey. *Journal of Educational Psychology* 102(3). 668–686.

Sheng, Li, Ying Lu & Pui Fong Kan. 2011. Lexical development in Mandarin-English bilingual children. *Bilingualism: Language and Cognition* 14(4). 579–587.

Sheng, Li. 2014. Lexical-semantic skills in bilingual children who are becoming English-dominant: A longitudinal study. *Bilingualism: Language and Cognition* 17(3). 556–571.

Silverman, Rebecca D., C. Patrick Proctor, Jeffrey R. Harring, Anna M. Hartranft, Brie Doyle & Sarah B. Zelinke. 2015. Language skills and reading comprehension in English monolingual and Spanish–English bilingual children in grades 2–5. *Reading and Writing*. http://doi.org/10.1007/s11145-015-9575-y

Simos, Pangiotis G., Georgios D. Sideridis, Angeliki Mouzaki, Aspasia Chatzidaki & Maria Tzevelekou. 2014. Vocabulary growth in second language among immigrant school-aged children in Greece. *Applied Psycholinguistics* 35(03). 621–647. http://doi.org/10.1017/S0142716412000525

Snow, Catherine E. & Yong-Suk Kim. 2007. Large problem spaces: The challenge of vocabulary for english language learners. In R. K. Wagner, A. E. Muse & K. Tannenbarm (eds.), *Vocabulary acquisition: Implications for reading comprehension*, 123–139. New York: Guilford Press.

Uccelli, Paola & Mariela M. Páez. 2007. Narrative and vocabulary development of bilingual children from kindergarten to first grade: Developmental changes and association among English and Spanish skills. *Language, Speech & Hearing Services in Schools* 38(3). 225–236.

Uchikoshi, Yuuko. 2014. Development of vocabulary in Spanish-speaking and Cantonese-speaking English language learners. 2014. *Applied Psycholinguistics* 35. 119–153.

Verhoeven, Ludo T. 1994. Transfer in bilingual development: The linguistic interdependence hypothesis revisited. *Language Learning* 44(3). 381–415.

Verhoeven, Ludo. 2000. Components in early second language reading and spelling. *Scientific Studies of Reading* 4(4). 313–330.

Whipple, Guy (ed.). 1925. *The 24th Yearbook of the National Society for the Study of Education: Report of the National Committee on Reading*. Bloomington, IL: Public School Publishing.

Susan Gass
32 Factors affecting second language acquisition: Successes and nonsuccesses

1 Introduction

Second language learning is a multi-faceted field that covers a range of subdisciplines. For example, researchers have investigated the phenomenon of learning a second language (L2) from a formal linguistic perspective, from a sociocultural perspective, from a neurolinguistic perspective, and from a psycholinguistic perspective, to name a few of the approaches that scholars have taken. In addition, to these theoretical orientations, numerous topics that influence second or foreign language[1] learning have been investigated including, aptitude, attitude, age-related effects, motivation, affect, and language transfer, to name a few. This chapter presents an overview of ways to account for 1) why it is difficult to learn a second language and 2) why it is that learning generally falls short of complete mastery of the target language. The literature referred to in this chapter is focused on adults who have learned their native language and who are then learning another language. Other contexts of learning (e.g., heritage language learning – learning the language of one's home environment or the language of ancestry or bilingual learning – learning two languages simultaneously are not covered in this chapter)[2]. For a fuller array of topics and more in depth treatment, the interested reader is referred to Gass and Mackey (2013).When addressing the fundamental question of how second languages are learned, at least in the context of adult (i.e., post-pubescent) learning, there are two assumptions that can be made: 1) the learner has a full-formed grammar of their L1 and 2) input is the *sine qua non* of learning. How these two factors figure into scholarly approaches differs on the basis of one's theoretical orientation.

The chapter is organized as follows. In the first section, I consider Universal Grammar, a formal approach to learning, that is, where a focus on the forms acquired is the primary concern. This is followed by research on processing and addresses how language learners are constrained by limitations on their ability to process information. The third part of the chapter deals with areas that are outside of a learner's

---

[1] Second language learning refers to learning a language in the environment in which it is spoken (learning French in France, Italian in Italy). Foreign language learning refers to learning a language in the environment where the surrounding language is the native language (an English speaker learning Italian or Spanish in the U.S.).
[2] The interested reader is referred to the discussion in Gass and Glew (2008, in press) for ways different terminology (e.g., SLA, bilingualism) has been used.

Susan Gass, Michigan State University

control and how these also impact final outcomes[3]. Finally, the chapter touches on limitations on L2 learning caused by physical limitations (hearing), focusing on the acquisition of sign language and on learning by hearing-impaired individuals.

FORMAL APPROACHES

Formal approaches to L2 learning investigate language form with the goal of understanding the linguistic system (known as a learner language or interlanguage) that learners have acquired at any point in time. The theoretical linguistic perspective most commonly considered is *Universal Grammar* (UG), the most well-known of generative theories. Underlying this approach to L2 learning is the idea that language learning (both first and second) involves (to greater or lesser degrees) innateness. Whether innateness involves principles that are specific to language learning or whether innateness involves principles that are relevant for all types of learning is a matter of debate (see the discussion on emergentism/usage based approaches in O'Grady, (2001, 2008, 2013) and in O'Grady, Kwak, Lee, and Lee (2011). This will be further dealt with in the section on input below.

The Universal Grammar approach, the focus of this section, is of the first type and sets out to specify the principles that constrain and therefore facilitate language learning. Because first languages are learned relatively quickly and because first language (L1) learning is generally successful, there must be some underlying innate language properties that guide first language learning. The phenomenon of fast and successful acquisition is not in dispute for L1 learning. Within the UG view, there is an assumption that language is a highly complex and abstract system and the learning of that system relies on something other than the input that a learner (child or adult) receives. UG represents an innate language faculty that constrains the possibility of what language is, thereby reducing the burden on a child. An example from White (1989) serves to exemplify what is meant. Consider the possibilities in 1–2 of using either *want to* or *wanna*.

(1) Who do you want to see?

(2) Who do you wanna see?

Further consider 3–4 where *wanna* is not possible (*indicates an ungrammatical sentence).

(3) Who do you want to feed the dog?

(4) *Who do you wanna feed the dog?

---

[3] There are many areas that could be covered in this chapter including motivaton, affect (e.g., anxiety, culture/language shock), and aptitude. The decision to eliminate these topics reflects a conscious choice to only deal with topics over which learners have little/no control (e.g., issues of processing, issues of innateness, issues of input, and age).

White argues UG principles are necessary to account for this distribution; input alone does not provide appropriate information. In 1, the meaning is *You want to see X* and in 3 the meaning is *You want X to feed the dog*. In (3), but not in (1), the question is about an element (X) that is placed between *want* and *to*, effectively blocking contraction. In (1), *want* and *to* are adjacent, thereby allowing contraction given that no intervening element blocks it. The blocking of contractions when the elements are not adjacent stems from underlying principles and cannot be discerned readily from the input alone. On the other hand, O'Grady, Nakamura, and Ito (2008) counter this explanation and argue from a usage-based perspective that it is a matter of processing and not a matter of UG.

Another important construct from child language learning is what is referred to as *evidence* of which there are essentially two types: positive and negative. The first refers to the language the learner is exposed to (input) and the second refers to information about the language that informs the learner that the language form she or he has used is incorrect. It is well known that in child language learning negative evidence (or information about well-formedness) is not a sufficient explanation in that correction does not occur regularly and when it does occur, the child is often more focused on meaning and does not react to form correction, carrying on using the original form.

When it comes to adult L2 learning, the situation is less clear. Not only is there an innate language system that may have guided second language learners through the learning of their L1, there is also an intact language system in play. In other words, learning a new language is in some sense more complex than learning a first language as multiple systems have to be taken into account. Basic questions are the following: 1) Does the innate language faculty that children use in constructing their native language grammars remain operative in second language acquisition? And 2) What is the starting point of acquisition? The L1 or an innate system? Or, is it data from exposure to the L2? Over the years, there have been opposing views, one which argues that child and adult language learning are fundamentally different (e.g., Bley-Vroman, 1989, 2009), and one that argues that the innate language faculty is operative in both L1 and L2 learning. Arguments in favor of the idea that the two learning processes are different, known as the *Fundamental Difference Hypothesis*, point to well-accepted differences in outcomes (child language learning in normal circumstances is complete; adult L2 learning is not). This is supported by the pervasive phenomenon of fossilization (Han, 2014; Long, 2007). Second, as noted above, the starting point is different in that L2 learners have a fully-developed linguistic system at the outset (see discussion below). A third argument relates to personal and social factors that come into play. For example, motivation and attitude toward the target language and target language community may influence the extent to which language learning is successful. This is not the case for child language learning where motivation, for example, is not a relevant factor. The claim is that adult L2 learners do not have access to UG. Instead, what learners know of language universals is constructed through their native language (NL) and not through direct access to UG. Bley-Vroman (2009) introduces an interesting construct, that of *patches*. This refers to the areas of our L1 that we may be unsure of, possibly stemming from differences between actual use and prescriptive grammar. Included in this category might be the *lie/lay* distinction in English. English native speakers (NSs) often hesitate when needing to produce utterances with these vocabulary or grammatical uncertainties. NSs have few patches, whereas language learners have many. Bley-Vroman argues that this may be a quantitative difference, although not a fundamentally different one.

A UG approach to language learning takes the opposite view and argues that L2 learners do have access to UG and that UG, in fact, constrains L2 grammars (White, 2003). An important question concerns the relationship between the L1 and UG. There is not unanimity on the interface of these two systems (and more systems when multiple languages are known). Suffice it to say that positions vary along the lines of which of the two languages serves as the base. Meisel (2011), however, argues that there are three possible knowledge sources that influence learning and can be argued to be the starting point: 1) L2 input, 2) UG, and 3) L1. One position is that L1 is the starting point with full access to UG when the L1 is insufficient. This assumes that L1 and L2 learning are different and also accounts for incomplete knowledge of the L2 as the end result. Other positions advocate a starting point as an intact innate language faculty which serves as the starting point for learning. L1 and L2 learning are fundamentally the same and the endpoint and the paths taken should be the same for both. Differences in the end result are based on performance issues rather than knowledge issues (competence), as discussed below. (See Meisel, 2011, for a review of these various positions).

Another way of looking at acquisition, while still maintaining the basic roles of UG and the L1, is to differentiate between lexical and functional categories. Briefly, lexical categories are nouns, adjectives, verbs, and adverbs. Functional categories serve particular functions (e.g., articles, possessives, plurals, tense markers, case markings, gender markers, complementizers [*if, whether, that*]). Functional categories represent a fixed set of words in a language, whereas lexical categories can be added to frequently, for example, with new technology (blogs, email, twitter, motherboard).

If one accepts the difference between these two types of linguistic categories, one can postulate that the learning of functional categories may not be L1 dependent and, instead, come from the input. Consider grammatical gender or grammatical categories as examples. English does not have grammatical gender so there is nothing from the L1 that will guide a learner in learning a language with grammatical gender or there is nothing, for example, that will guide an English speaker in learning the various categories in Bantu languages (Spinner 2013; Spinner and Thomas, 2014).

Current research is concerned with such questions as: is lexical learning the starting point for learning with the learning of functional categories being much later? Some have argued that only those features that are available to L2 learners are those in the L1 (e.g., Hawkins and Chan, 1997). As a result, there is a syntactic deficit in the L2 linguistic representation. Others (e.g., Prévost and White, 2000) have argued that there is no syntactic deficit; rather, the issue is a mapping one, namely the inability to map intact representations onto L2 surface morphology (see Lardiere, 2012). Slabakova (2013) points out that while there is no consensus on the starting point of acquisition, research emphases and approaches have moved beyond this particular debate.

Slabakova, in trying to account for differences in learning success of different parts of language, proposed the *Bottleneck Hypothesis* (2012). The bottleneck is in the acquisition of inflectional morphology and formal features. Slabakova points out that "inflectional morphemes carry the features that are responsible for syntactic and semantic differences among languages of the world, so it is logical that once these morphemes and their features are acquired, the other linguistic properties (word order, interpretation, etc.) would follow smoothly" (2012, p. 140).

With regard to article acquisition, Ionin, Ko, and Wexler (2004) propose the *Fluctuation Hypothesis* to account for article acquisition. According to Ionin, et al., this hypothesis states that "L2 learners have full access to UG principles and parameter-settings" and "L2 learners fluctuate between different parameter-settings until the input leads them to set the parameter to the appropriate value" (p. 16).

Yet another view is that of Sorace's *Interface Hypothesis* (2011). When learning structures that involve an interface between syntax and another cognitive domain (syntax-semantics, syntax-pragmatics, and syntax lexical-semantics interfaces), one encounters greater difficulty than when acquiring non-interface structures. This accounts for the lack of success that most learners have in reaching native-competence in an L2. But, not all interfaces are created equal, with some (e.g., syntax-pragmatics) resulting in greater non-convergence with L1 grammars (i.e., less success) than others (e.g., syntax-semantics). This may be due either to less automatic processing (L2 learners have knowledge representations that are less developed than those of a native speaker) or to "less efficient access to these representations" (2011, p. 17).

In general, L1 and L2 are both similar and different. Constraints on acquisition based on UG features guide acquisition and may lead to successes. On the other hand, L1 and L2 convergences and conflicts also guide acquisition and result in interlanguage grammars that reflect both UG and L1 (or other L2s) features.

Because of the highly complex nature of learner languages and because of their ever-changing nature, it is not surprising to find little conclusive evidence of why L2 learning is in part successful and why it is not (why do French learners of English continue to say *I am eating slowly my dinner* even in late stages of learning?). Formal linguistic approaches provide a theoretical basis to help tease apart the various factors involved. Ongoing debates reflect definitional aspects (what is meant by starting point?) and issues of falsification (e.g., how does one account for theoretical predictions not being realized?).

In sum, within the general formal framework known as Universal Grammar, we have seen a number of hypotheses proposed that relate to how second languages are learned and why, in most cases, learning does not have the same result as primary language learning. In particular, we examined the Fundamental Difference Hypothesis which states that learning a first and a second are fundamentally different processes.

We have also seen numerous other explanations put forward, such as issues relating to 1) the starting point, 2) the role of the L1, 3) inflectional morphology (Bottleneck Hypothesis), 4) lexical versus functional categories, 5) the interface between syntax and other cognitive domains (Interface Hypothesis), and 6) specific category accesses (articles, as in the Fluctuation Hypothesis). We next consider one more basic issue to an understanding of second language learning and that has to do with differences in knowledge types, namely, implicit and explicit.

2 Knowledge types

The distinction between implicit and explicit knowledge relies on awareness of language with the former characterized by a lack of awareness of what one knows and the latter by conscious knowledge (see DeKeyser, 2003; N. Ellis, 2005; Godfroid et al. 2015). How knowledge of one type or the other comes to be may depend, in part, on the learning context (natural versus classroom). It is clear that native and fluent speakers of a language have implicit knowledge of language and use language on a daily basis without awareness of how they are using language. With specific reference to success and non-success, the ability that learners have to access and use implicit knowledge may be a major factor. Thus, part of understanding how second languages are learned is an understanding of what can and cannot be learned implicitly. For example, Leung and Williams (2012) found that some form-meaning connections (e.g., animacy) can be learned implicitly, whereas others cannot be so readily learned implicitly (in their case learning a form that dealt with the relative size of objects).

3 Processing approaches

Another significant area of research can be found in the area of processing. A layperson's view of language learning involves learning vocabulary items, learning how to pronounce words, and learning how to string words together. As noted in the previous section, in this view the constraints on learning are due primarily to learners' abilities and inabilities to acquire the grammar of the language given the facts of their native language or constraints imposed by an innate language faculty. However, learning a language also involves processing language in real time. As discussed in the previous section, differences in outcomes can be attributed to a different knowledge base (i.e., competence) between the L1 and the L2. Another way to think about outcomes is to consider processing differences. One possibility is that the processing mechanisms in place are the same, but that the cognitive burden of processing an L2 results in what appears to be different modes of processing. A second way to think about this is that processing an L1 is fundamentally different than processing an L2.

According to the Shallow Structure Hypothesis (Clahsen and Felser (2006a, b, in press), L2 learners have less detailed syntactic representations making comprehension difficult and often incomplete. Because learners' syntactic representations are not complete, they rely on other parts of language (e.g., lexical, pragmatic) to facilitate comprehension. In other words, L2 processing tends to rely on meanings rather than on structures (see also Felser and Roberts, 2007). Opponents make the argument that learners do have access to the same structural representations as native speakers (Omaki and Schultz, 2011; Aldwayan, Fiorentino, and Gabriele, 2010). An intermediary position comes from Sorace (2006). In her view, shallow processing may be limited to less proficient learners and not include so-called near-native speakers whose syntactic representations are native-like.

Another contributing factor to learner success (or lack thereof) is the ability/inability of non-native speakers (NNS) to parse a string of sounds or even words on a printed page, which reflects the computation of syntactic structures. Recent research has begun to investigate this through a variety of methods, but one prominent methodology is eye-tracking (see special issue 2013 of *Studies in Second Language Acquisition*). Eye-trackers measures eye gaze during reading or watching something. As Godfroid et al. (2015) note, "the point of gaze serves as an index of overt attention (Wright and Ward, 2008) that can be used to make inferences about participants' corresponding covert attentional processing, or mental focus" (p. 273). This assumes that there is an eye-mind link (Reichle, Pollatsek, and Rayner 2006, 2012); where one focuses one's gaze reflects thought processes. Research using this methodology involves presenting individuals (learners or NSs) with ambiguous or ungrammatical sentences and measuring eye movements. When individuals spend longer on particular words or go back to reread certain parts of a sentence, this constitutes evidence for sensitivity to that particular part of a sentence. For example, if someone were to read the following sentence: *The man walked to the store because she thought it was a nice day*, presumably there would be some hesitation and possibly rereading once an individual (NS or learner) came to the word "she". This would be evidence of sensitivity to a mismatch between the noun phrase 'the man' and the pronominal form 'she' which refers to the noun phrase subject. Keating (2009) looked at gender agreement in Spanish and found that native and advanced learners of Spanish were able to detect incongruous noun-adjective agreement (looking longer and looking back [regressing] to a previous word), but that L2 learners were able to detect incorrect agreement only when the noun adjective pairs were adjacent, but not across syntactic boundaries. Spinner, Gass, and Behney (2013a, b) similarly investigated gender agreement, this time using Italian as the foreign language. They used eye-tracking to understand what learners look for to determine gender, finding that learners used article gender as well as noun endings in making this determination.

According to Processability Theory (Pienemann, 1999, 2007; Pienemann and Keßler, 2012) production and comprehension of second language forms can take place only if those forms can be handled by the linguistic processor. If one can understand how the processor works, we can make predictions about how learning progresses. Essential to this approach is a Processability Hierarchy which informs the processor as it checks grammatical information with a sentence. If one utters a sentence in a language with noun-adjective agreement, the processor will check to see if the various parts of a sentence match (agreement of nouns and adjectives and other parts of a sentence where gender must agree – for example, some past participles). If a learner has not developed appropriate procedures (e.g., procedures for monitoring relevant grammatical elements), matching cannot take place.

Spinner (2013) in a series of studies investigated Processability Theory from the perspectives of production and reception. Using a trajectory of ESL involving a sequence of development that includes past, possessive, plural, objective pronoun, possessive pronoun, adverb, Wh-copula, copula, verbs with particles (e.g., *turn off*), 3rd singular, auxiliary, and tag questions. ESL learners were presented with production (one-on-one conversation) and receptive (audio grammaticality judgment test) tasks. What she found was that Processability Theory predicted the order of emergence in a production task, but did not predict the order in a receptive task. She suggests "that the acquisition of processing procedures may proceed differently in production than in reception (p. 734).

In what follows, I deal briefly with two constructs that have recently entered the second language literature: 1) attention and 2) working memory.

3.1 Attention

In 2001, Schmidt in a discussion of the *noticing hypothesis* claimed that attention "appears necessary for understanding nearly every aspect of second and foreign language learning" (p. 6). Underlying this hypothesis is the idea of noticing a gap. Schmidt and Frota (1986) suggested that "a second language learner will begin to acquire the target like form if and only if it is present in **comprehended input** and 'noticed' in the normal sense of the word, that is consciously" (p. 311, emphasis added). The idea presented here is that learning requires a learner to be actively involved or attending to L2 forms in order for learning to take place (see Robinson, Mackey, Gass, and Schmidt, 2012 for an overview). While most believe that attention and noticing are important constructs, it is important to note that there is a debate that centers around how much and the type of attention necessary for learning (Godfroid, Boers, and Housen, 2013) and what the prerequisites are for learning. Gass, Svetics, and Lemelin (2003) investigated the construct of attention from the perspective of different parts of the grammar (lexicon, morphosyntax, syntax). Learners were placed into a focused attention group or into a non-focused attention group. Learning occurred in attention and non-focused attentioned conditions. However, there was a difference in learning depending on the part of language on which attention was focused. Focused attention was most beneficial for syntax and least for the lexicon. Additionally focused attention had a greater effect in early stages of learning. A possible explanation comes from the fact that with a greater knowledge of language may come a greater ability to self-focus one's attention.

Awareness is another related construct that appears in the literature in tandem with attention. Leow and his colleagues (Leow, 2001; Rosa and Leow, 2004) showed an association between awareness of a form and the learning of that form. Mere noticing was less important than awareness at the level of understanding. Noticing in and of itself is a complex construct, as noted by Godfroid, Boers, and Housen (2013) who provide an overview of the constructs of *noticing, attention*, and *awareness*. A question that is central to research in this area is the determination of noticing: How do we know if something has been noticed? Research methodologies and techniques have become more sophisticated over the years. Eye-tracking methodology is one measure that has been used to understand when something has been noticed. As noted above, the assumption is that eye movements reflect moment-to-moment processing. Godfroid, Boers, and Housen, (2013, p. 489) state "... overt attention (as manifested by the exact eye location) and covert attention (mental focus) are tightly linked." Recent studies come from Godfroid, Boers, and Housen (2013) and Spinner, Gass, and Behney (2013a, b) who used eye-tracking methodology to determine noticing for vocabulary acquisition in the former and gender agreement in the latter.

One cannot ignore the important concept of working memory (WM) as a factor that impacts learning across individuals, yielding greater and lesser successes. A basic assumption is that individuals vary in their ability to carry out simple and complex tasks, such as those governed by WM (e.g., remembering a sequence of telephone number digits long enough to dial them).

According to Williams (2012, p. 427), WM "refers to a temporary storage system that lies at the core of complex cognition....WM can be regarded as a system that is used for the temporary maintenance of task-relevant information while performing cognitive tasks." Briefly, there are two components of WM: 1) storage and 2) manipulation of information. The most commonly used model in SLA research is that of Baddeley and Hitch (1974) who posited two systems (see also Baddeley, 2003a, 2003b): the phonological loop and the visuo-spatial sketch pad. A frequent real-life task is the need to remember something when one does not have anything other than memory to rely on (e.g., remembering an address, phone number, shopping list). In this instance, one uses the storage part of WM, The central executive is the overall controller and coordinator; it focuses attention on some things, inhibits others, and is the manager when multi-tasking is involved.

Conway, Kane, Bunting, Hambrick, Wilhelm, and Engle (2005) see working memory as "a multicomponent system responsible for active maintenance of information in the face of ongoing processing and/or distraction" (p. 770). One's ability to maintain information is the result of domain-specific storage (with processes of rehearsal) and "domain-general executive attention" (p. 770). With L2 learning, there are numerous competing demands, for example, watching a video, listening, and even reading (when captions or subtitles are involved), as discussed in an eye-tracking study by Gass, Winke, and Ahn (2015). In these siuations, an individual's working memory capacity (WMC) might be expected to come into play.

In general, "WM is a multi-component system comprising domain-specific storage systems and a domain-general executive component (Williams, 2012, p. 428)." Williams goes on to say that the differences in the models can be seen in the way Baddeley's model emphasizes storage, whereas as Conway et al. emphasize the executive functioning of WM. Given the fundamental importance of WM in carrying out cognitive tasks, one would imagine that differences in successful learning of an L2 (a complex cognitive task) might be impacted by individual differences in working memory capacity[4]. Phonological short term memory capacity has been shown to impact vocabulary and syntax. Papagno and Vallar (1992) and Service and Craik (1993) found a relationship between phonological short term memory capacity and the ability to repeat known and novel words. Similar results have been found in Service and Kohonen (1995) and Williams and Lovatt (2003). Although it is to be noted that in naturalistic language learning situations (as opposed to laboratory studies), the results are not so clear-cut (see, for example, Masoura and Gathercole, 2005 and French and O'Brien, 2008). WMC has also been linked to general oral fluency (O'Brien, Segalowitz, Freed, and Collentine, 2007) and to general language performance (Kormos and Sáfár, 2008).

Grammar is another area where WMC is related to learning. This is due to the fact that when learning a second language, we receive input that we must maintain actively in memory (storage) in order to determine meaning and syntactic analysis (manipulation). It is likely that the better an individual is at doing this, the better s/he is at learning a second language. Evidence from this comes from laboratory studies (N. Ellis and Schmidt, 1997; Williams and Lovatt, 2003) using an artificial language and an immersion program study (French and O'Brien, 2008).

Finally, Gass, Winke, and Ahn (2015) found evidence of video-based comprehension and WMC. In their study, participants watched a video with captions and were

---

[4] Despite the importance of methodological issues, a discussion of how one determines WMC (either the language of the test or the specific methodology used) is beyond the scope of this chapter (see Gass & Lee, 2011 and Conway et al., 2005).

therefore subjected to two forms of visual input (pictures from video and captions) and oral input. They found that L2 learners with high WMC performed better on a free recall test than those with low WMC (see also Alptekin and Erçetin, 2011). In other words, high WMC individuals were better able to handle the competing demands of watching, listening, and reading.

4 Input and age

In the previous sections, discussions surrounding success and non-success have emphasized linguistic and psycholingusitic issues, that is knowledge and processing. In this section, I consider other topics in the field that have been used to account for why there is differential success in learning a second language: reduced input and age. Before embarking on that discussion, I bring in what are referred to as usage-based models of language learning. In some sense this could be categorized as a formal approach (it deals with language form), but I have opted to include it in this section because meaning and use are crucial to an understanding of this concept. It differs significantly from UG in that it is not a theory that relies on innatism. Rather, it is highly input-dependent. In its simplest form, it relies on extracting patterns from the input which, in turn, is heavily dependent on the effect of frequency on development. Linguistic structures emerge from the patterns of the input and not from an innate language faculty.

4.1 Input

Throughout this chapter, input has been assumed as an essential part of language learning; without it language learning cannot take place. In a foreign language environment, it is clear that input is limited and full exposure to a language is not possible. For example, in a classroom context, one does not hear a range of vocabulary or even grammatical structures (see Muñoz, 2008). For usage-based accounts in which frequency of occurrence guides learners into making linguistic generalizations, reduced exposure to language is an issue that can account for reduced success (see Slabakova, 2013 for a discussion of input and usage-based interpretations).

An issue that has not received much attention has to do with orthographic differences (Hamada and Koda, 2008) and the resultant effect on input. Winke Gass, and Sydorenko (2013) found that orthographic differences (e.g., English speakers learning Spanish versus English speakers learning Chinese) yielded comprehension and vocabulary-learning differences when engaged in a video-based listening activity with and without captions. The order in which videos were watched (captioned video prior to non-captioned video or vice versa) made a difference depending on the L2. L2 learners learning languages with scripts close to English (Spanish, Russian) benefit more from watching first a video without captions followed by watching the same video with captions. On the other hand, where script differences were more profound (Arabic and Chinese), the reverse order yielded better vocabulary learning and greater comprehension. Even in a situation where there is reduced input (e.g., a classroom), an ideal situation for literate adults is to have multi-modal input. When the script is different, a processing burden results with learners not having the benefit of input from the written source. Thus, input in classroom contexts is limited not only in that there is limited exposure to the L2, but even when exposure exists, not all second languages are the same, with writing systems causing limited access in some instances.

4.2 Age differences

The issue of ultimate success based on the age of initial exposure and learning to a second language has continued across the ages (see Herschensohn, 2007; Montrul, 2008). It is a significant theoretical as well as applied issue given the perceived importance of early language programs, although DeKeyser (2012, p. 455) notes that "'earlier is better' when it comes to L2 learning, does not necessarily imply that 'earlier teaching is better'". As Andringa (2014) puts it "[o]ne of the most fundamental issues in the field of SLA concerns the (non) existence of a critical period for language learning: Can late second language learners ever achieve nativelike levels of mastery in the L2?" (p. 566). As with other areas of L2 research, the jury is still out, with arguments on both sides of the issue.

The debate is often softened to include the following variations: age affects learning or there is a sensitive period for language learning such that late learning is less likely (as opposed to not being possible). Still other approaches maintain that late learning is possible, but the underlying mechanisms of getting to that final point are different (e.g., explicit learning takes over in late learning because the ability to learn implicitly atrophies (DeKeyser, 2000; see also DeKeyser, 2012, for a useful review of critical period research).

In what follows, I highlight a few seminal studies that have investigated these issues. Johnson and Newport's (1989, 1991) considered age of arrival in light of ultimate proficiency. These studies suggest that age (16 in their studies) effects indeed affect ultimate learning. Coppietiers (1987) in his study on intuitions found that native and near-native speakers of French have different intuitions about French even though the latter are virtually indistinguishable from native speakers in performance. Birdsong's (1992) study was similar to that of Coppieters in that he investigated judgments of near-native speakers, finding that some learners performed within the same range as native speakers.

In a more recent study, Abrahamsson and Hyltenstam (2009) argue that many of the previous studies in which it is suggested that late learners can achieve nativelike competence are problematic in two ways: 1) the structures investigated are too basic and do not allow for a more sophisticated investigation of L2 knowledge and/ or 2) data have not been analyzed in sufficient detail. In their study, Abrahamsson and Hyltenstam investigated late learners of Swedish (native speakers of Spanish) whose age of arrival in a Swedish context was between 1 and 47 years. They first identified participants who were judged by NSs of Swedish listeners to be NSs of Swedish. Only a small number who started after age 12 were perceived to be NSs of Swedish, whereas a majority of those before that age were judged to be NSs of Swedish. A further look at those who were judged to be NSs through cognitively demanding and complex tasks revealed that none performed within the same range as NSs of Swedish. Their strong conclusion is that "nativelike ultimate attainment of a second language is, in principle, never attained by adult learners and, furthermore, is much less common among child learners than has previously been assumed" (p. 250). There are other studies, such as Montrul and Slabakova (2003), White and Genesee (1996), and van Boxtel, Bongaerts, and Coppen (2005) where nativelike attainment of complex structures by late learners was indeed possible.

DeKeyser, Alfi-Shabtay, and Ravid (2010) collected data from speakers of the same native language (Russian) learning two second languages in different contexts (English in the U.S. and Hebrew in Israel). Despite the different languages being learned (English is morphology poor; Hebrew is morphology rich), the results paralleled one another. In learning grammar, there is a decline in ability to learn language based on age (until age 18). After that, aptitude is a better predictor and age can be factored out as a predictor variable. In other words, as in other studies, there is a rapid decline until a plateau is reached (the age of plateau differs from study to study). One can conclude from this study that the critical period hypothesis is supported.

Another consideration relates to the domain of language under investigation. In an interesting study Granena and Long (2013) found different correlations between age of arrival in a context of a second language on the one hand and phonology, lexicon and morphosyntax, on the other. In particular, in a study of Chinese advanced speakers of Spanish, Granena and Long investigated attainment based on age of arrival in three areas: 1) pronunciation, 2) lexical and collocational knowledge, and 3) syntax and morphosyntax. Their results showed that the decline in performance (as a function of age of arrival) was greatest for phonology, next for lexical and collocational knowledge and the last for syntax. When compared to their native speaker control group, none of the learners performed in the native speaker range for a) pronunciation, when they arrived after five, b) lexis and collocation after 9, and c) morphosyntax after 12.

They also investigated length of residence as a factor, finding that it did relate to lexicon and collocations, but not to pronunciation and morphosyntax. Finally, they considered the role of aptitude as a factor in predicting success of learning. Aptitude was not a factor in the youngest-arriving groups, but did play a role in L2 learners arriving in the target language environment between the ages of 16 and 29, but only for pronunciation and lexis/collocation, not for morphosyntax. The authors conclude that there is not a single sensitive period for language learning; rather, there are multiple sensitive periods depending on language domain. This is certainly consistent with other studies that have looked at differences in language domains for perceptions of feedback (Mackey, Gass and McDonough, 2000) and for the role of attention (Gass et al, 2003).

There are numerous reasons why there is a lack of agreement amongst studies. For example, different measures are used to determine nativelike competence, different structures are used, different statistical analyses are applied to data, native speaker variation is excluded (DeKeyser, 2013), and different language domains are investigated. An important variable highlighted in Andringa (2014) is the comparison group. Who is a native speaker? In a review of the literature, Andringa found that in general there is little information about who the native speaker controls are against whom learners are being measured. In his study, Andringa found that there were differences depending on whether the sample was representative or non-representative, the latter being highly educated speakers: "the incidence NNSs falling within the NS range is affected by the selection of the NSs" (p. 591). There is no definitive answer to any of these questions that may account for why results differ. However, it is something that must be included in any consideration of whether there is a critical period or not.

5 Learning sign language and learning an L2 by hearing impaired

The term second-modality acquisition (M2A) is commonly used to refer to SLA of sign language. The questions posed are quite similar to those asked in the L2 literature. And, some of the same theoretical perspectives are taken in this area of research. One area of divergence is the Cognitive Phonolgy model by Rosen (2004) in which non-linguistic issues are explored. In particular, he proposes two error sources: inaccurate perception of sign formulation and poor motor dexterity. In contrast, Chen Pichler (2011) has argued for inclusion of language-specific features such as markedness and transfer in models of M2A.

Two studies point to language differences (ultimate attainment) and processing differences. An interesting study by Thompson, Emmorey and Kluender (2009) used an eye-tracker to investigate eye movements as a way of articulating complex agreement of verbs, but not all verbs. The construct of agreement was able to be learned by late proficient learners, but the subtleties (only used for a subset of verbs) was not learned. Although, sign language data are not frequently used to support arguments of critical age, it is clear that this study suggests that proficient signers are not able to reach native-like abilities.

Considering how learning takes place and how learners process visual information, Emmorey, Thompson and Colvin (2009) compared eye gazes of native signers and hearing beginner signers of American Sign Language. An eye-tracker was used to determine eye gaze while the participants watched native signers perform two narratives (a story and a spatial description). Although both groups fixated primarily on the signer's face, learners often looked at the signer's mouth (as opposed to eyes) and hands. The authors attribute these differences not to difficulty with linguistic complexity or processing but to the need for beginning signers to attend to mouthing.

Berent (2009) argues that there are parallels between hearing-impaired and non-hearing impaired SLA. The constraints available through UG in non-hearing impaired SLA also appear to hold for second-modality acquisition. From a totally different perspective comes a study by Schönström (2014) who examined handwritten data from deaf learners of Swedish as an L2 within the framework of Processability Theory. She was interested in written development of an L2 by hearing and non-hearing individuals. Her data, from 11- and 16-year-old children, show that both groups of learners follow similar trajectories predicted by Processability Theory. Thus, this study shows how data from hearing-impaired individuals can be used to support theoretical linguistic constructs. More important for the purposes of this chapter is that developmental paths are similar and, hence, are not the source of differential successes between hearing and non-hearing learners of an L2.

6 Conclusion

This chapter has looked at differential successes in L2 learning. In so doing, it has considered only those areas that impact learning over which learners do not have the ability to monitor or change in any significant way. Namely, we have considered linguistic principles, processing constraints, and input. And, we have also considered issues that are part of an individual's profile (e.g., working memory, age). Finally, we have gone outside of what might be referred to as 'mainstream' SLA to include learning of an L2 by hearing-impaired individuals. We acknowledge that this summary has been selective in what it was able to cover. Nonetheless, it has highlighted some of the main areas of L2 research that impact ultimate success of learning.

References

Abrahamsson, N. & K. Hyltenstam. 2009. Age of onset and nativelikeness in a second language: Listener perception versus linguistic scrutiny. *Language Learning* 59. 249–306.

Aldwayan, S., R. Fiorentino & A. Gabriele. 2010. Evidence of syntactic constraints in the processing of *wh*-movement: A study of Najdi Arabic learners of English. In B. VanPatten & J. Jegerski (eds.), *Research in second language processing and parsing*, 65–86. Amsterdam: John Benjamins.

Alptekin, C. & G. Erçetin. 2011. The effects of working memory capacity and content familiarity on literal and inferential comprehension in L2 reading. TESOL Quarterly 45 (2). 235–266.

Andringa, S. 2014. The use of native speaker norms in critical period hypothesis research. *Studies in Second Language Acquisition* 36. 565–596.

Baddeley, A.D. 2003a. Working memory and language: An overview. *Journal of Communication Disorders* 36. 189–208.

Baddeley, A.D. 2003b. Working memory: Looking back and looking forward. *Neuroscience* 4. 29–839.

Baddeley, A.D., & Hitch, G. 1974. Working memory. In G. H. Bower (ed.), *The psychology of learning and motivation*, 47–90. New York: Academic Press.

Berent, Gerald P. 2009. The interlanguage development of deaf and hearing learners of L2 English: Parallelism via Minimalism. In W. Ritchie & T. Bhatia (eds.). *The new handbook of second language acquisition*, 523–543. Bingley, UK: Emerald Group.

Birdsong, D. 1992. Ultimate attainment in second language acquisition. *Language* 68. 706–755.

Bley-Vroman, R. 2009. The evolving context of the fundamental difference hypothesis. *Studies in Second Language Acquisition* 31. 175–198.

Bley–Vroman, R. 1989. What is the logical problem of foreign language learning? In S. Gass & J. Schachter (eds.), *Linguistic perspectives on second language acquisition*, 41–68. Cambridge: Cambridge University Press.

Chen Pichler, D. 2011. Sources of handshape error in first-time signers of ASL. In D. Napoli & G. Mathur (eds.) *Deaf around the world*, 96–121. Oxford: Oxford University Press.

Clahsen, H. & C. Felser. 2006a. Grammatical processing in language learners. *Applied Psycholinguistics* 27 (1). 3–42.

Clahsen, H. & C. Felser. 2006b. Continuity and shallow structures in language processing: A reply to our commentators. *Applied Psycholinguistics* 27 (1). 107–126.

Clahsen, H. & Felser, C. in press. Some notes on the Shallow Structure Hypothesis. *Studies in Second Language Acquisition*. doi.org/10.1017/S027222631170002504.

Conway, A., M. Kane, M. Bunting, D. Z. Hambrick, O. Wilhelm & R.W. Engle. 2005. Working memory span tasks: A methodological review and user's guide. *Psychonomic Bulletin & Review*, 12. 769–786.

Coppieters, R. 1987. Competence differences between native and non-native speakers. *Language* 63. 544–573.

DeKeyser, R. 2000. The robustness of critical period effects in second language acquisition. *Studies in Second Language Acquisition* 22. 499–533.

DeKeyser, R. 2003. Implicit and explicit learning. In C. Doughty & M. H. Long (eds.), *The handbook of second language acquisition*, 313–347. Oxford: Blackwell.

DeKeyser, R. 2012. Age effects in second language learning. In S. Gass. & A. Mackey (eds.), *The Routledge handbook of second language acquisition*, 442–460. New York: Routledge.

DeKeyser, R. 2013. Age effects in second language learning: Stepping stones toward better understanding. *Language Learning* 63. 52–67.

DeKeyser, R., I. Alfi-Shabtay & D. Ravid. 2010. Cross-linguistic evidence for the nature of age effects in second language acquisition. *Applied Psycholinguistics* 31. 413–438.

Ellis, N. 2005. At the interface: Dynamic interactions of explicit and implicit language knowledge. *Studies in Second Language Acquisition* 27. 305–352.

Ellis, N. & R. Schmidt. 1997. Morphology and longer distance dependencies: Laboratory research illuminating the A in SLA. *Studies in Second Language Acquisition* 19. 145–171.

Emmorey, K., R. Thompson & R. Colvin. 2009. Eye gaze during comprehension of American Sign Language by native and beginning signers. *Journal of Deaf Studies and Deaf Education* 14. 237–243.

Felser, C. & L. Roberts. 2007. Processing *wh*-dependencies in a second language: A cross-modal priming study. *Second Language Research* 23. 9–36.
French, L. M. & I. O'Brien. 2008. Phonological memory and children's second language grammar learning. *Applied Psycholinguistics* 29. 463–487.
Gass, S. & M. Glew. 2008. Second language acquisition and bilingualism. In J. Altarriba & R. Heredia (eds.), *An introduction to bilingualism: Principles and processes*, 265–294. New York: Psychology Press.
Gass, S. & J. Lee. 2011. Working memory capacity, inhibitory control, and proficiency in a second langauge. In M. Schmid & W. Lowie (eds.), *Modeling bilingualism: From structure to chaos*, 59–84. Amsterdam: John Benjamins.
Gass, S. & A. Mackey. 2013. *The Routledge handbook of second language acquisition*. New York: Routledge.
Gass, S., I. Svetics & S. Lemelin. 2003. Differential effects of attention. *Language Learning* 53. 497–545.
Gass, S., P. Winke & J. Ahn. 2015. Multimodal processing and cognitive load in the context of captions: An eye-tracking study. Paper presented at AAAL 2015.
Godfroid, A., F. Boers & A. Housen. 2013. An eye for words: Gauging the role of attention in L2 vocabulary acquisition by means of eye-tracking. *Studies in Second Language Acquisition* 35. 483–517.
Godfroid, A., S. Loewen, S. Jung, J.-H. Park, S. Gass & R. Ellis. 2015. Timed and untimed grammaticality judgments measure distinct types of knowledge: Evidence from eye-movement patterns. *Studies in Second Language Acquisition* 37.
Granena, G. & M. Long. 2013. Age of onset, length of residence, language aptitude and ultimate L2 attainment in three linguistic domains. *Second Language Research* 23. 311–343.
Hamada, M. & K. Koda. 2008. Influence of first language orthographic experience on second language decoding and word learning. *Language Learning* 58. 1–31.
Han, Z.-H. 2014. From Julie to Wes to Alberto: Revisiting the construct of fossilization. In Z. Han & E. Tarone (eds.), Interlanguage: Forty years later. Amsterdam: John Benjamins.
Hawkins, R. and C. Y.-H. Chan. 1997. The partial availability of Universal Grammar in second language acquisition: The 'failed functional features hypothesis'. *Second Language Research* 13. 187–226.
Herschensohn, J. 2007. *Language development and age*. New York: Cambridge University Press.
Ionin, T., H. Ko & K. Wexler. 2004. Article semantics in L2 acquisition: The role of specificity, *Language Acquisition* 12. 3–69.
Johnson, J. & E. Newport. 1989. Critical period effects in second language learning: The influence of maturational state on the acquisition of ESL. *Cognitive Psychology* 21. 60–99.
Johnson, J. & E. Newport. 1991. Critical period effects on universal properties of language: The status of subjacency in the acquisition of a second language. *Cognition* 39. 215–258.
Keating, G. 2009. Sensitivity to violations of gender agreement in native and nonnative Spanish: An eye-movement investigation. *Language Learning* 59. 503–535.
Kormos, J. & A. Sáfár. 2008. Phonological short-term memory and foreign language performance in intensive language learning. *Bilingualism: Language and Cognition* 11. 261–271.
Lardiere, D. 2012. Linguistic approaches to second language morphosyntax. In S. Gass & A. Mackey (eds.), *The Routledge handbook of second language acquisition*, 106–126. New York: Routledge.
Leung, J. & J. Williams. 2012. Constraints on implicit learning of grammatical form-meaning connections. *Language Learning* 62. 634–662.
Long, M. H. 2007. *Problems in SLA*. Mahwah, NJ: Lawrence Erlbaum Associates.
Mackey, A., S. Gass & K. McDonough. 2000. How do learners perceive implicit negative feedback? In *Studies in Second Language Acquisition* 22. 471–497.

Masoura, E.V. & S. E. Gathercole. 2005. Contrasting contributions of phonological short-term memory and long-term knowledge to vocabulary learning in a foreign language. *Memory* 13. 422–429.

Meisel, J. 2011. *First and second language acquisition*. Cambridge: Cambridge University Press.

Montrul, S. 2008. *Incomplete acquisition in bilingualism: Re-examining the age factor*. Amsterdam: John Benjamins.

Montrul, S. & R. Slabakova. 2003. Competence similarities between native and near-native speakers: An investigation of the preterite/imperfect contrast in Spanish. *Studies in Second Language Acquisition* 25. 351–398.

Muñoz, C. 2008. Symmetries and asymmetries of age effects in naturalistic and instructed L2 learning. *Applied Linguistics* 29. 578–596.

O'Brien, I., N. Segalowitz, B. Freed & J. Collentine. 2007. Phonological memory predicts second language oral fluency gains in adults. *Studies in Second Language Acquisition* 29. 557–582.

O'Grady, W. 2001. Toward a new nativism. *Studies in Second Language Acquisition* 21. 621–633.

O'Grady, W. 2008. The emergentist program. *Lingua* 118. 447–464.

O'Grady, W. 2013. The illusion of language acquisition. *Linguistic approaches to bilingualism* 3. 253–285.

O'Grady, W., H.-Y. Kwak, M. Lee & O.-S. Lee. 2011. An emergentist perspectiveson partial language acquisition. *Studies in Second Language Acquisition* 33. 323–345.

O'Grady, W., M. Nakamura & Y. Ito. 2008. *Want-to* contraction in second langauge acquisition: An emergentist approach. *Lingua* 118. 478–498.

Omaki, A. & B. Schultz. 2011. Filler-gap dependencies and island constraints in second language sentence processing. *Studies in Second Language Acquisition* 33. 563–588.

Papagno, C. & G. Vallar. 1992. Phonological short-term memory and the learning of novel words: The effect of phonological similarity and item length. *Quarterly Journal of Experimental Psychology* 44A. 47–67.

Pienemann, M. 1999. *Language processing and second language development: Processability theory*. Amsterdam: John Benjamins.

Pienemann, M. 2007. Processability theory. In B. Van Patten & J. Williams (eds.), *Theories in second language acquisition: An introduction*, 137–154. Mahwah, NJ: Lawrence Erlbaum Associates.

Pienemann, M. & J-U. Keβler. 2012. Processability theory. In S. Gass & A. Mackey (eds.), *The Routledge handbook of second language acquisition*, 228–246. New York: Routledge.

Prévost, P. & L. White. 2000. Missing surface inflection or impairment in second language acquisition? Evidence from tense and agreement. *Second Language Research* 16. 103–133.

Reichle, E. D., A. Pollatsek & K. Rayner. 2012. Using E-Z Reader to simulate eye movements in non-reading tasks: A unified framework for understanding the eye-mind link. *Psychological Review* 119. 155–185.

Reichle, E., A. Pollatsek & K. Rayner. 2006. E-Z Reader: A cognitive-control, serial-attention model of eye-movement behavior during reading. *Cognitive Systems Research* 7. 4–22.

Robinson, P., A. Mackey, S. Gass & R. Schmidt. 2012. Attention and awareness in second language acquisition. In S. Gass & A. Mackey (eds.), *The Routledge handbook of second language acquisition*, 247–267. New York: Routledge.

Rosa, E. & R. Leow. 2004. Awareness, different learning conditions, and L2 development. *Applied Psycholinguistics* 25. 269–292.

Rosen, R. 2004. Beginning L2 production errors in ASL lexical phonology: A cognitive phonology model. *Sign Language & Linguistics* 7. 31–61.

Schmidt, R. 2001. Attention. In P. Robinson (ed.), *Cognition and second language instruction*, 3–32. Cambridge: Cambridge University Press.

Schmidt, R. & S. Frota. 1986. Developing basic conversational ability in a second language: A case study of an adult learner of Portuguese. In R. Day (ed.), *Talking to learn: Conversation in second language acquisition*, 237–326. Rowley, MA: Newbury House.

Schönström, K. 2014. Visual acquisition of Swedish in deaf children: An L2 processability approach. *Linguistic Approaches to Bilingualism* 4. 61–88.

Service, E. & F. Craik. 1993. Differences between young and older adults in learning a foreign vocabulary. *Journal of Memory and Language* 32. 608–623.

Service, E. & V. Kohonen. 1995. Is the relation between phonological memory and foreign language learning accounted for by vocabulary acquisition? *Applied Psycholinguistics* 16. 155–172.

Slabakova, R. 2012. L2 semantics. In S. Gass & A. Mackey (eds.), *The handbook of second language acquisition*, 127–146. New York: Routledge.

Slabakova, R. 2013. Adult second language acquisition: A selective overview with a focus on the learner linguistic system. *Linguistic Approaches to Bilingualism* 3. 48–72.

Sorace, A. 2006. Possible manifestations of shallow processing in advanced second language speakers. *Applied Psycholinguistics* 27. 88–91.

Sorace, A. 2011. Pinning down the concept of "interface" in bilingualism. *Linguistic Approaches to Bilingualism* 1. 1–34.

Spinner, P. 2013. The L2 acquisition of number and gender in Swahili: A feature reassembly approach. *Second Language Research* 29. 455–479.

Spinner, P. & J. Thomas. 2014. Morphophonological and semantic cues in the L2 acquisition of Swahili gender. *International Review of Applied Linguistics* 52 (3).

Spinner, P., S. Gass & J. Behney. 2013a. Ecological validity in eye-tracking: An empirical study. *Studies in Second Language Acquisition* 35 (2). 389–415.

Spinner, P., S. Gass & J. Behney. 2013b. Coming eye-to-eye with attention. In J. Bergsleithner and S. Frota, *Studies in honor of Richard Schmidt*, 235–254. Honolulu: NFLRC Press.

Thompson, R. L., K. Emmorey & R. Kluender. 2009. Learning to look: The acquisition of eye gaze agreement during the production of ASL verbs. *Bilingualism: Language and Cognition* 12. 393–409.

van Boxtel, S., T. Bongaerts & P. Coppen. 2005. Native-like attainment of dummy subjects in Dutch and the role of the L1. *International Review of Applied Linguistics in Language Teaching* 43. 355–380.

White, L. 1989. *Universal Grammar and second language acquisition*. Amsterdam: John Benjamins.

White, L. 2003. *Second language acquisition and Universal Grammar*. Cambridge: Cambridge University Press.

White, L. & F. Genesee. 1996. How native is near-native? The issue of ultimate attainment in adult second language acquisition. *Second Language Research* 12. 233–265.

Williams, J. & P. Lovatt. 2003. Phonological memory and rule learning. *Language Learning* 53. 67–121.

Winke, P., S. Gass & T. Sydorenko. 2013. Factors influencing the use of captions by foreign language learners: An eye-tracking study. *The Modern Language Journal* 97. 254–275.

Wright, R. D. & L. M. Ward. 2008. *Orienting of attention*. New York: Oxford University Press.

IV Language and communication disorders

Section 8: Developmental and neurological disorders

IV. Language and communication disorders

Section B. Developmental and radiological diagnosis

Jan de Jong
33 The changing profile of Specific Language Impairment

1 Introduction

Language disorders in children have a longish scientific prehistory, starting in the 19th century (for an overview, see Leonard, 2014). In *La Consultation* (1928), part of the novel cycle *Les Thibault* by the French writer Roger Martin du Gard, Antoine, a medical doctor, is about to meet a little boy 'five or six years old, talking like a toddler, in monosyllables. It seems as if he cannot pronounce certain sounds. But when you tell him to say his little prayer, he bends his knees and says the Our Father, from beginning to end, articulating almost flawlessly! And he seems pretty intelligent' (my translation from the Dutch edition). Later on Antoine is paging through old volumes of the *Revue de Neurologie* to find the 'famous discussion from 1908 about *aphasie*'. That discussion (actually in the *Revue Neurologique* of the same year) was about the localisation of aphasia. It is significant that Antoine browsed through a debate on what we would now call acquired language disorders. The concept of a developmental language disorder with no apparent focal lesion was not yet seen as different from the concept of (adult) aphasia. Antoine would have assumed that these symptoms had a similar anatomical background. Nowadays, terminology that refers to aphasia (or dysphasia) in children is out of favour, precisely due to the lack of evidence for visible brain damage in these children. The most common label now, Specific Language Impairment (SLI), is agnostic where the cause of language impairment is concerned.

SLI has traditionally been defined as a language disorder that appears in the absence of low nonverbal intelligence, of diminished hearing sensitivity, of structural oral anomalies and of primary problems with social interaction (Leonard, 2014: 15). Criteria for measuring each of these other conditions are called *exclusion* criteria. Such exclusion criteria, however, are debatable, as Bishop (2014) argues in depth. She describes SLI as a condition with 'unexplained language problems', to highlight the fact that even if language impairment is accompanied by symptoms of another clinical condition, the latter condition does not explain the language impairment. Criteria for *inclusion* (i.e. measures of the language problem itself) differ. Often statistical criteria are used (for test performance, as measured in standard deviations from the mean of the population). The values for these criteria (e.g. –1,25, –1.5, –2.0 SD) are also dependent on the purpose and practical use of the definition; distribution of services for children with language impairment may be a factor. The more

---

Jan de Jong, University of Bergen & University of Amsterdam

DOI 10.1515/9781614514909-034

inclusive a definition, the more children qualify for these services. Apart from performance on standardized tests, children with SLI are characterised by their linguistic symptoms as they occur in spontaneous speech. These symptoms are the focus of the current chapter.

Recently, I revisited a language sample I recorded of a boy with SLI, who at the time was 8;1 years old. The sample showed several features that are typical of the spontaneous output of language-impaired children. Utterances were incomplete, and not only in contexts where ellipsis is allowed. Arguments were omitted, as well as prepositions, determiners. Substitutions occurred, of prepositions, determiners and pronouns. Verbs were sometimes omitted and when they were present, there were inflectional errors: wrong tense, agreement errors, root infinitives. In addition, lexical errors were made that had consequences for syntax (e.g. using the wrong conjunction or particle or substituting a 'light verb' for a lexical one, leading to shortcomings in argument structure). When a subordinate clause was attempted, the utterance would not be completed or the word order would be incorrect. In short, a mixed picture of ungrammaticality, incompleteness and low complexity.

This mixed picture has not always been in full view. Since SLI became a topic of research interest among, primarily, linguists, its symptom profile has changed. The impairment itself of course has not, but when the symptoms of SLI are described nowadays, the resulting picture will be different from one sketched a couple of decades ago. This is true for scientific research, not so much for clinical practice, but we will see that research has influenced clinical practice.

Early studies on SLI (often including case studies) made an inventory of a broad range of grammatical symptoms. In fact it was considered necessary in those pioneering days to write a full grammar to represent the child's linguistic output. However, since then, research has identified a number of key features of the disorder – often called clinical markers – that have come to draw almost exclusive attention in research. These markers originated in a research tradition that sought to pinpoint the linguistic locus of the grammatical problems involved in SLI. Such studies depended as much on linguistic theory as on empirical data. Theoretical linguistics and the linguistic study of typical language acquisition sometimes set the agenda for research on SLI. The result of this process was that the profile of SLI became narrower. As a consequence SLI is now sometimes seen as a problem with, to take just one example, inflectional morphology. In this chapter, the fruits of the latter line of research will be reviewed.

However, it will also be shown that the current profile might be too narrow. First of all, several symptoms that cannot be easily explained using current explanatory accounts are underexposed. Secondly, theoretical accounts of SLI are still strongly influenced by research on a limited set of languages; in particular SLI symptoms in English have been very influential in the formulation of linguistic explanations. Over the past two or three decades the range of languages investigated has increased, almost exponentially (for an up to date survey, see Leonard, 2014). The impact of this research on other languages is significant but it has yet to lead to alternative accounts of SLI, or adaptations of existing ones, that can explain the symptoms of SLI within a more diverse set of languages.

In an instructive chapter entitled 'Defining SLI', De Villiers (2003:427) made a list of 'decisions' to be made in order to establish what SLI is. They can also be read as a research agenda: the answers to the following questions reflect different, competing positions. According to De Villiers, what we need to know is:

(1) do children with SLI form a separate group, or do they constitute the lower performance on a normal curve? (2) is the cause of the disorder linguistic or not?; (3) are the problems in SLI homogeneous or heterogeneous? (4) is the grammar deficient or intact (but late in maturing)?

Together these questions summarise the common themes of SLI research. I have omitted the hierarchy that is part of De Villiers' schema here (if yes, the next question is...) and will refer to some of the questions separately underneath.

Summing up, the present chapter will take a broad view of SLI while also showing how a more narrow view can give us valuable insights. A caveat: in this chapter I will focus on the grammatical domain, while of course children with SLI also have difficulties in other domains; the disorder is multidimensional. The reason is that the changes in the profile of SLI to be described here, changes that are due to theoretical considerations, have primarily been visible in the grammatical dimension of the profile. In addition to the linguistic explanations that I will refer to in this chapter there are several important accounts of grammatical problems that find non-grammatical sources for the very same difficulties. However, dealing as I will with the grammatical profile of SLI and how it has changed over time, they are not the primary focus of the chapter.

2 A look back at early studies on SLI: The broad picture

Early studies on the grammatical symptoms of SLI were strongly inspired by Chomsky's model of grammar. They involved, following Chomsky's seminal early books (1957, 1965), fine-grained analyses of phrase structure, transformations and morphology in the language production of children with SLI.

In Menyuk's (1964) study, for example, the frequency of occurrence of 28 individual transformations was calculated in a group of 10 children with SLI (or, in Menyuk's terms, children using 'infantile speech') and 10 age-matched typically developing (TD) children. In addition, an inventory was made of the use of (38) 'restricted forms' ('sentences which deviated from complete grammaticalness'). As predicted, the transformations were used more by the TD group but no difference reached significance. As for the restricted forms, there was a difference in the nature of the errors: omissions were mainly identified with the SLI group and substitutions and redundancies with the TD group. The only exception was SLI children's substitution of prepositions. Focusing individually on one three-year old with language delay, Menyuk also observed pronoun case errors and omission of progressive marker *–ing*. Menyuk concluded from her study that 'infantile speech' was a misnomer, in that the oldest children with SLI did not resemble the youngest TD children. The impaired children 'generated their sentences with transformations that involve the fewest numbers of operations and with restricted forms which seem to be early approximations to completed rules' (Menyuk, 1964:118). In short, derivational complexity was low in these children and rules were not fully substantiated.

Morehead and Ingram (1976) partially disconfirmed Menyuk's findings – that have been taken to suggest a qualitative difference between the children with SLI and the TD children – by substituting language matching for chronological age matching. Just like in Menyuk's study, their analysis focused on phrase structure (briefly), on transformations (distinguishing frequent and infrequent types) and on resulting 'construction types'. Using language matching, they found that findings changed substantially. In conclusion, the authors denied that there was a pattern of deviance in SLI – there were more similarities than differences between children with SLI and their language-matched peers.

To end this brief retrospective, I want to refer to an interesting case study from the same era, by Weiner (1974). The case was that of a language-delayed adolescent, age 16;0. Highlighted errors were omissions of plural markings on nouns, prepositions, auxiliary *be*, and past tense marking on regular verbs. The selectional restrictions of some prepositions were not observed by the child. Weiner also pointed at the inconsistent linguistic behaviour in this boy: "The alternation between well-formed and poorly formed constructions seen in Art's use of base structure and morphological rules is also evident in his transformational constructions" (Weiner, 1974: 207). The latter conclusion anticipates a later observation, by Bishop (1994), that children with SLI show variable behaviour: they do not make errors across the board.

These studies are important for two reasons. Firstly, in writing grammars for the subjects involved, they introduced an inclusive approach to the description of symptom areas and aimed to demonstrate how linguistic tools could be used to define the profile of language impairment (an intention explicitly echoed by Clahsen, 2008). It was felt that a comprehensive investigation of the grammar of the language-impaired child was warranted. As a consequence, the list of constructions described as affected by SLI is longer than in most current studies. Secondly, the Morehead and Ingram study was extremely influential in promoting the use of language age matching, based on Mean Length of Utterance (MLU), as a tool for the identification of the specific domains that are affected in SLI. In that sense, this study that itself represented a comprehensive approach paved the way for a narrower profile of SLI. After all, as a consequence, features that were delayed (that is, for which children with SLI performed below chronological age peers only) but not 'deviant' (i.e. features for which children with SLI fall short even of *language*-matched peers) were not seen as worthy of being the focus of research anymore.

3 In search of key linguistic symptoms: The picture narrows

Following Morehead and Ingram's procedure for identifying weaknesses in the grammar of children with SLI, now defined as those domains where performance by children with SLI is weaker than in younger, language-matched children, researchers assembled a list of syntactic and morphological loci of impairment. An early example is found in Johnston and Schery (1976), who explored 14 grammatical morphemes taken from Brown (1973). Language-impaired children reached the conventional level of mastery – 90% use of a morpheme in obligatory contexts – later than typically developing children, but the acquisition order of the morphemes was similar. Johnston and Schery (1976:257) concluded that children with SLI 'were found to differ from normal children in the rate at which they moved from the first use of a morphological rule to its consistent general application'.

Fletcher and Ingham (1995:611), reviewing the literature on SLI, listed the grammatical categories that proved problematic for SLI children with English as their native language: plural *-s*; 3rd person *-s*; past tense *-ed*; auxiliary *be*; determiner *the/a*; infinitive particle *to*; case-marked pronouns.

Compared to the studies referred to previously, it is clear that phrase structure and transformations were not considered part of the linguistic profile anymore, but grammatical (bound and free-standing) morphemes emphatically were. A methodological reason for the focus on grammatical morphology may be that the analysis of morphology allows for unambiguous identification of errors/omissions, because obligatory contexts can be identified. The overwhelming majority of group studies now address linguistic elements that have obligatory contexts. A similar analysis cannot be done for most transformations. As a consequence, the outcome of this research tradition seems to be that phrase structure is intact, but morphology is not. The implication is that this finding may also be an artefact of the analytical procedure most often used.

4 Can symptoms be explained in a unified way?

Once a core set of grammatical features was defined – mostly related to bound morphemes – for which deficiencies were strongly identified with SLI, the search began for what these features had in common, linguistically.

An early example is found in two studies co-authored by Leonard. Eyer and Leonard (1995), who took as their starting point an account of normal acquisition by Radford (1990), who claimed that early child grammars have no functional categories (i.e. the Determiner, Inflection and Complementizer Phrases – DP, IP and CP), but only lexical categories (like noun and verb). Eyer and Leonard tested the hypothesis that the grammars of children with SLI continued to lack functional categories for an extended period. After all, functional categories dominated the list of vulnerable domains. Their hypothesis was not confirmed: even though the children made errors or omitted members of functional categories, there was sufficient evidence of the presence of these categories in the data to reject this explanation of the linguistic shortcomings of children with SLI. In another study, Loeb and Leonard (1991) investigated linguistic phenomena that are associated with the IP, notably verb inflection and subject case marking. By hypothesis, if the problem is in the IP, both should be affected. A correlation between verb inflection and case marking was indeed found in this study (a similar pattern was found by Wexler, Schuetze and Rice, 1998). In addition to the empirical findings, these studies were methodologically important, in that their authors proposed a subset of symptoms that was linguistically coherent and attempted to define a linguistic locus for the children's difficulties.

Another influential study, one that has inspired lively polemics on the nature of SLI, was written by Gopnik (1991). In a case study she described a boy whose linguistic output was characterized by a general lack of grammatical markers. Gopnik labeled this condition 'feature blindness', because the boy's grammar seemed to show no evidence whatsoever of knowledge of grammatical features. Further limiting the symptom profile, Gopnik drew a sharp contrast with another component of grammar, verb argument structure, which she claimed to be intact in her subject. In addition to presenting a radical claim about the fault lines in SLI children's grammar, this study proposed an important dissociation. Functional categories were to be affected in SLI, lexical categories were not. Subsequent research found little support for Gopnik's claims (see Bishop, 1994, who tested the hypothesis in detail), but even if it is obsolete, it is a striking example of how theory and symptoms can meet.

Many subsequent studies focused on verb morphology in particular. A broad consensus on deficient verb morphology as a clinical marker made the symptom profile of SLI even narrower. Neither functional categories nor grammatical features in general were the locus of the problem; the problem was to be located more specifically in verb inflection and, within inflection, in the marking of tense and/or agreement. The explanations for these problems differed. Rice, Wexler and Cleave (1995) found the core problem of English-speaking children with SLI in the extended use of root infinitives that were in optional alternation with inflected verbs (the Extended Optional Infinitive hypothesis; extended, because it refers to a phenomenon commonly found in *younger* TD children). In a later version of their explanation, the possibility was recognized that agreement could also be affected (Wexler et al., 1998). Although Wexler et al. allowed for the possibility of agreement to be affected, they mainly used that to explain subject case errors. 'Bad agreement' (that is, the occurrence of unambiguous agreement errors) was still considered rare. Because case marking is associated with verb inflection, erroneous subject case marking constituted a predictable symptom within this account (cf. Loeb and Leonard, 1991). Attention to agreement was not new: as the locus of a hypothesized key problem in SLI it had already been identified by Clahsen (1989; see also Clahsen et al., 1997; Clahsen, 2008). Clahsen, however, considered agreement relationships – not just between subjects and nouns, but also within noun (or determiner) phrases – the particular domain where the underlying difficulty was to be found.

Among the linguistic explanations referred to above, but also others, there are noticeable differences in how the problem with verb morphology is characterized, in terms of the measure of (ab)normality and in the nature of the damage done. To illustrate, some of the terms that have been used over time are: feature blindness, deficient grammar, missing agreement, agreement deficit, extended optional infinitive, vulnerable markers, rule deficit, representational deficit. These terms in different ways answer one of de Villiers' questions: is the grammar deficient or intact (but late in maturing)? The answers clearly differ: some terms suggest a clear dichotomy between children with SLI and TD children, others suggest that the difference is more continuous. However, another of De Villiers' questions seems to have been given a clear answer: all these accounts claim that the problem in SLI is homogeneous and selectively affects a distinct linguistic domain – sometimes quite narrow, sometimes more broad, but never totally inclusive. After all, symptoms are described here in clusters that are linguistically coherent.

The main contribution of the research referred to in this section is that they present a unified account of separate symptoms in SLI. The ambition of the authors is to define the underlying grammatical problem.

5 From linguistic theories on SLI to assessment

Theoretical views of what language impairment is have also influenced clinical practice. This shows most clearly in the instruments employed for diagnosis.

Crystal (1982) presented an argument for the clinical use of analysis of spontaneous language. He proposed to use language profiles, like LARSP (Crystal, Fletcher and Garman, 1981), rather than (or in addition to) standardized tests, when assessing children's language skills. While tests 'make a radical selection of the possibilities available in the linguistic domain being tested', profiles are intended to create a comprehensive picture of the child's output. 'The motivation for this principle (of comprehensiveness, JdJ) is simply that, in the present state of our knowledge, there is no systematic way of deciding in advance which bits of the data to omit from consideration, without losing information of possible significance for subsequent assessment and remediation (...) the present state of our knowledge of linguistic disability does not allow us to arrive at a theoretically 'correct' number of categories which will guarantee maximum usefulness of a profile chart'. (Crystal, 1982:4–5).

I quote Crystal at length here, because we can observe an interesting change in approaches to language assessment. It seems that there is a tidal wave: from standardized testing (using omnibus tests) to spontaneous language data analysed by profile methods and subsequently, as we will see, back to language tests, but now with a specific linguistic focus. Contra Crystal, there are currently several researchers who would claim that the 'present state of knowledge' now justifies (i) omission of some of the linguistic ingredients of language assessment and (ii) limitation of diagnostic assessment to discrete linguistic hallmarks of SLI. This development is inspired by the increased focus on a limited set of symptoms within a so-called 'clinical marker approach' (Rice and Wexler, 2001).

Within this rationale, symptoms that are not clinical markers tend to be considered as derivative (that is, secondary to core symptoms) or marginal ('data to omit'). This new development has been translated into assessment tools that are devoted to the identification of said key symptoms. A prime example is the *Test of Early Grammatical Impairment* (TEGI; Rice and Wexler, 2001), which focuses on verb inflection – tense and finiteness. The writers recognise the tradition of assessing 'a wide range of language competencies', but argue that 'grammatical morphology has obligatory properties that enhance the clinician's ability to identify affected children' (Rice and Wexler, 2001:1–2). High sensitivity is claimed for the markers that are measured by TEGI and in general criterion-referenced tests for such markers may be a way out of the dependence on statistical measures for language impairment (Bishop, 2014). The clinical marker approach postulates that the usual 'bell-shaped distribution' for skills measured by language tests is replaced by a bimodal distribution for the linguistic marker concerned (Rice and Wexler, 2001:4–6; their illustration concerns a 'hypothesized distribution' of children). Meanwhile, it is important to note that TEGI is, of course, designed to measure performance in English only, so results cannot be generalized to other languages. For those languages that also have an optional infinitive stage (for some languages, instead of an infinitive, there may be another – optional – default form; see Paradis and Crago, 2001), it has yet to be established that the distribution is similarly bimodal (after all, optionality rates differ widely between languages).

A similarly selective approach was taken by Van der Lely (2000), who created a 'Verb Agreement and Tense Test' as well as tests for passive and active sentences and for pronominal reference. Her tests were based on her own theory of SLI, according to which dependency relations in grammar (e.g. subject-verb agreement, the relationship between a verb and its arguments) are most impaired in SLI (the theory postulated a Representational Deficit for Dependent Relationships, RDDR; Van der Lely, 1994).

Underlying the Diagnostic Evaluation of Variation (DELV) test (Seymour, Roeper and de Villiers, 2005) is also a concept of what impairment constitutes. The test was designed to avoid the bias against African-American English that is part of many assessment tools. The TEGI is an example of that: 3rd singular –s marking is not part of African-American English, so targeting it in a test penalizes children whose first language that is. One ambition of the DELV is to target 'underlying linguistic principles', 'as ways to diagnose disorder that would not confuse its signs with surface differences due to dialect.' (Pearson, 2004:14). In that sense, it also constitutes a hypothesis about what is implicated in SLI. Selected elements of DELV are: *Wh*-Questions, understanding of *wh*-movement; understanding of passive sentence construction, including movement of linguistic elements (e.g., subject, object) and hidden/implied properties in passive sentence construction; expressive use of articles. Apart from the linguistic principles that they follow, the hypothesis is that these linguistic components are not dialect- (or even language-) specific.

6 SLI: domains that are 'out of focus'

In the previous sections, it has become clear that the focus of research interest has narrowed down, in particular to verb inflection. This development was supported by research in which primarily weaknesses in verb inflection were identified as a clinical marker. As a consequence, theoretical explanations of grammatical problems have also addressed this domain primarily, with some notable exceptions (e.g. Van der Lely, 1994).

To what extent is this a problem? First of all, one should consider what the aim is of the analysis, whether theoretical or diagnostic and, if diagnostic, whether it concerns screening for language problems or in-depth diagnosis. When screening is the aim, ecological validity is not an issue: the goal is to reliably select the children with SLI and not to make a comprehensive description of their symptoms; only sensitivity and specificity count. When diagnosis and, in a wider sense, clinical intervention is addressed, it is important that the measure used is also ecologically valid. While verb inflection can be a solid index for screening in a language in which verb inflection is vulnerable, it may be only one among many of the linguistic domains a speech-language pathologist will address in intervention. We will review some of the other domains underneath.

An important problem with the clinical markers identified so far is their lack of cross-linguistic validity. To quote Leonard (2014) (and it is significant that this quote is found verbatim in the first (1998) edition of his book as well: no changes here): 'if there is a universal feature of SLI, apart from generally slow and poor language learning, it is well hidden'. In the absence of a universal marker, areas of vulnerability 'will vary from language type to language type' (Leonard, 2014: 150). For a full review of symptoms of SLI in other languages, I refer the reader to Leonard's book. Here I will focus on some examples of symptoms that led (or should lead) to explanatory rationales that differ from those formulated for SLI in English. I should add here that existing theories on SLI are often quite explicit about the (lack of) generality of their predictions. The Extended Optional Infinitive Hypothesis, for instance, by definition only concerns languages that have a developmental stage during which finiteness marking is optional.

Some domains will be itemized here that have drawn less attention in SLI research and, more particularly, that do not feature in linguistic accounts of SLI, either because they are considered marginal or unaffected by the impairment or because they are mostly important to languages that have been less studied.

Case morphology: In the previous sections, verb morphology featured as a vulnerable domain in SLI. However, in many languages, verb inflection is acquired quite early. In those languages, it may not pose a major challenge for children with SLI, while simultaneously noun morphology does. This is true in particular for case marking on nouns. A prime example of this dissociation is found in data from Turkish (Acarlar and Johnston, 2011; also see chapters in Topbaş and Yavaş, 2010). Verb inflection was hardly affected in Acarlar and Johnston's subjects with developmental disorders, but case marking was (while the children in this study did not fit the exclusionary definition of SLI, their difficulties resemble those of children with SLI in other studies). The authors explain this finding by pointing at the salient (i.e. utterance-final) position of the verb in Turkish (although word order is free, Subject Object Verb is the canonical order), whereas the position of the (object) noun is most often medial. Case marking difficulties were also found for other languages, for instance for accusative marking in Hebrew (Dromi, Leonard and Shteiman, 1993).

Argument structure: An overlooked domain that is less language-specific is that of the 'context' of verbs. In an important article, Rice (1991) argued that verbs, not just verb inflection, are a deserving topic of investigation in SLI. Rice showed that problems with verbs could be at the basis of many subsequent language difficulties in SLI. She identifies some of the factors that make verb learning challenging for language-impaired children: they occur in a sentence frame that determines (part of) their meaning, so children must know about these frames, together with the verb lemma; verb argument structures must be learned, but also the possibility of alternating between argument structures; verb learning depends on a combination of semantic and syntactic bootstrapping, for both of which children with SLI may lack sufficient resources. Summarising, according to Rice's chapter verbs are pivotal in the difficulties encountered by language-impaired children.

Rice's chapter reads as an agenda for future research on SLI. Subsequently, however, research on argument structure was a road seldom travelled. Rice herself published some studies that addressed in particular low diversity of verbs and the predominance of General All Purpose (GAP) verbs in the repertoire of children with SLI (Rice and Bode, 1993; Watkins, Rice and Moltz, 1993). A recent chapter by de Jong and Fletcher (2014) provides a review of studies on argument structure in SLI.

Though few in number, together they suggest that argument structure is a vulnerable area in language impairment (recent exemplary studies are: Ebbels, van der Lely and Dockrell, 2007; Murphy, 2012). This conclusion is reminiscent of earlier studies on SLI, where argument structure (or phrase structure) was included in more comprehensive analyses.

Prepositions: Argument structure can be said to be on the interface of semantics and syntax. The same is true for prepositions. While they may be used for lexical purposes (as in locative phrases), they also serve grammatical functions, as in prepositional datives (Grela, Rashiti and Soares, 2005). A similar distinction between grammar and lexicon is found in the same lexical items being used as either verb particles or as spatial prepositions (Juhasz and Grela, 2008; Watkins and Rice, 2001). In both cases the grammatical use of a preposition is more vulnerable than the lexical use. Also, prepositions may be used free or in a restricted way, i.e. selected by the verb. Armon-Lotem (2014), in a study on bilingual children, found that 'restricted' use was more vulnerable than free use.

Word order: English has a rather rigid word order, without verb movement. In V2 languages, on the other hand, the inflected verb has to move to second position (hence V2). In those languages, children have to acquire the correct form and position of the verb in tandem. In some of these languages, word order itself constitutes a problem area in SLI. For instance, research on Swedish showed that children with SLI, in a context where subject and verb must be inverted (VS order instead of SV), erroneously maintained the canonical SV order. They also violated placement restrictions for negations (Hanson, Nettelbladt and Leonard, 2000). Similar errors were found for Afrikaans (Southwood, 2007) and Dutch (de Jong, 1999).

Morpho-phonology: The theories referred to in the previous sections, mostly oriented towards English and German, suggested that problems with grammatical morphology originate in the grammar. However, it might be claimed that the same errors can be defined along different fault lines. Additional data from other languages point in that direction. One set of theories not yet mentioned are the Sparse Morphology hypothesis (Leonard, Sabbadini, Leonard and Volterra, 1987) and the Surface hypothesis (Leonard, 1989). They claim, respectively, that (in particular) grammatical morphemes are vulnerable when a language has sparse (or non-uniform) morphology and/or when the linguistic elements are non-salient. While these explanations target grammatical morphology, they suggest that the difficulties in SLI accumulate once a linguistic element lacks salient surface characteristics and/or is part of a sparse morphological paradigm. These hypotheses originated in cross-linguistic comparisons and they find natural test cases in languages in which the symptoms of SLI are newly explored. In each of these languages linguistic markers can be defined in terms of their saliency and the richness of their paradigm, regardless of the word class. After all, the rationale is not limited to particular grammatical morphemes.

The list of domains that may be affected in SLI as presented above is far from conclusive. Other symptom areas are found in different languages, for instance the production of object clitics in Romance languages like French (Paradis, Crago and Genesee, 2006), and of aspectual markers in Cantonese (Fletcher, Leonard, Wong and Stokes (2005). As can be observed when perusing such studies, each of these symptoms, to be understood, requires a sufficient knowledge of the typological characteristics of the language. The list will certainly become longer, once SLI is studied in (even) more languages.

7 Conclusion

Bishop (2014: 387), in addressing the clinical identification of children with SLI, considers the limitations of the common use of statistical measures for that purpose: '(...) a statistical cut-off will still select a specific proportion, such as the bottom 10%. We can only avoid this by identifying an absolute anchor point for impairment'. Bishop refers to Rice (2000), who, in Bishop's words, 'argued against purely statistical criteria, maintaining that some key differences between impaired and unimpaired children are not readily assessed on tests that generate normal distributions of scores' (Bishop, 2014:387). Obviously, an anchor point is a clinical marker, to be measured by a criterion-referenced test. While this might supply a way out of purely statistical reasoning, Leonard's (2014) conclusion ('universal feature (...) well hidden') suggests that if there is an anchor point, it will not be a universal one. Nevertheless, given the fact that SLI has grammatical symptoms in all languages investigated so far, the search for a common underlying problem that surfaces in a different way across languages will continue.

References

Acarlar, Funda & Judith Johnston. 2011. Acquisition of Turkish grammatical morphology by children with developmental disorders. *International Journal of Language and Communication Disorders* 46 (4). 728–738.

Armon-Lotem, Sharon. 2014. Between L2 and SLI: inflections and prepositions in the Hebrew of bilingual children with TLD and monolingual children with SLI. *Journal of Child Language* 41 (1). 3–33.

Bishop, Dorothy. 1994. Grammatical errors in specific language impairment: competence or performance limitations? *Applied Psycholinguistics* 15 (4). 507–549.

Bishop, Dorothy. 2014. Ten questions about terminology for children with unexplained language problems. *International Journal of Language and Communication Disorders* 49 (4). 381–415.

Brown, Roger. 1973. *A first language. The early stages*. Cambridge, MA: Harvard University Press.

Chomsky, Noam. 1957. *Syntactic structures*. Den Haag: Mouton & Co.

Chomsky, Noam. 1965. *Aspects of the theory of syntax*. Cambridge, MA: MIT Press.

Clahsen, Harald. 1989. The grammatical characterisation of developmental dysphasia. *Linguistics* 27 (5). 897–920.

Clahsen, Harald. 2008. Chomskyan syntactic theory and language disorders. In Martin J. Ball, Michael R. Perkins, Nicole Mueller & Sara Howard (eds.), *The Handbook of Clinical Linguistics*, 165–183. Blackwell: Oxford.

Clahsen, Harald, Susanne Bartke & Sandra Göllner. 1997. Formal features in impaired grammars: A comparison of English and German SLI children. *Journal of Neurolinguistics* 10 (2–3). 151–171.

Crystal, David. 1982. *Profiling linguistic disability.* London: Whurr.

Crystal, David, Paul Fletcher & Michael Garman. 1981. *The grammatical analysis of language disability.* 2nd edition. London: Whurr.

de Villiers, Jill. 2003. Defining SLI: A linguistic perspective. In Y. Levy & J. Schaffer (eds.), *Language competence across populations: Toward a definition of specific language impairment*, 425–447. Mahwah, NJ: Erlbaum.

Dromi, Esther, Laurence B. Leonard & Michal Shteiman. 1993. The grammatical morphology of Hebrew-speaking children with specific language impairment: Some competing hypotheses. *Journal of Speech and Hearing Research* 36 (4). 760–771.

Ebbels, Susan H., Heather K.J. van der Lely & Julie E. Dockrell. 2007. Intervention for verb argument structure in children with persistent SLI: a randomized control trial. *Journal of Speech, Language and Hearing Research* 50 (5). 1330–1349.

Eyer, Julia A. & Laurence B. Leonard. 1995. Functional categories and specific language impairment: a case study. *Language Acquisition* 4 (3). 177–203.

Fletcher, Paul. 2009. Syntax in child language disorders. In R.G. Schwartz (ed.), *Handbook of child language disorders*, 388–405. New York and Hove: Psychology Press.

Fletcher, Paul & Richard Ingham. 1995. Grammatical impairment. In Paul Fletcher & Brian MacWhinney (Eds.), *The handbook of child language*, 603–622. Oxford: Blackwell.

Fletcher, Paul, Laurence B. Leonard, Stephanie Stokes & Anita M.-Y. Wong. 2005. The expression of aspect in Cantonese-speaking children with specific language impairment. *Journal of Speech Language and Hearing Research* 48 (3). 621–6.

Gopnik, Myrna. 1990. Feature blindness: A case study. *Language Acquisition* 1 (2). 139–164.

Grela, Bernard, Lula Rashiti & Monica Soares. 2005. Dative prepositions in children with specific language impairment. *Applied Psycholinguistics* 25 (4). 467–480.

Hansson, Kristina, Ulrika Nettelbladt, & Laurence B. Leonard. 2000. Specific Language Impairment in Swedish: The status of verb morphology and word order. *Journal of Speech, Language, and Hearing Research* 43 (4). 848–864.

Johnston, Judith & Teris Schery. 1976. The use of grammatical morphemes by children with communication disorders. In D.M. Morehead & A.E. Morehead (eds.), *Normal and deficient child language*, 239–258. Baltimore: University Park Press.

Jong, Jan de. 1999. *Specific language impairment in Dutch: inflectional morphology and argument structure*. Groningen: University of Groningen dissertation.

Jong, Jan de & Paul Fletcher. 2014. Argument structure and Specific Language Impairment: Retrospect and prospect. In J. Hoeksema & D. Gilbers (eds.), *Black book. A Festschrift for Frans Zwarts*, 218–228. Groningen: University of Groningen. http://www.let.rug.nl/~hoeksema/jp.pdf (accessed 16 June 2016).

Juhasz, Corinne R. & Bernard Grela. 2008. Verb particle errors in preschool children with Specific Language Impairment. *Contemporary Issues in Communication Sciences and Disorders* 35 (spring). 76–83.

Leonard, Laurence B. 1989. Language learnability and specific language impairment in children. *Applied Psycholinguistics* 10 (2). 179–202.

Leonard, Laurence B. 2014. *Children with specific language impairment. Second Edition*. Cambridge, MA: MIT Press.

Leonard, Leonard B., Letizia Sabbadini, Jeanette S. Leonard & Virginia Volterra. 1987. Specific language impairment in children: a cross-linguistic study. *Brain and Language* 32 (2). 233–252.

Loeb, Diane Frome & Laurence B. Leonard. 1991. Subject case marking and verb morphology in normally-developing and specifically language impaired children. *Journal of Speech and Hearing Research* 34 (2). 340–346.

Martin du Gard, Roger. 1928. *Les Thibault. Quatrieme partie. La consultation*. Paris: Librairie Gallimard.

Menyuk, Paula. 1964. Comparison of grammar of children with functionally deviant and normal speech. *Journal of Speech and Hearing Research* 7 (2). 109–121.

Morehead, Donald M. & David Ingram. 1973. The development of base syntax in normal and linguistically deviant children. *Journal of Speech and Hearing Research* 16 (3). 330–352.

Murphy, Carol-Anne. 2012. *Profiles and characteristics of sentence production difficulties in children with Specific Language Impairment*. Newcastle: Newcastle University dissertation.

Paradis, Johanne & Martha Crago. 2001. The morphosyntax of Specific Language Impairment in French: Evidence for an Extended Optional Default Account. *Language Acquisition* 9 (4). 269–300.

Paradis, Johanne, Martha Crago & Fred Genesee. 2005/2006. Domain-general versus domain-specific accounts of specific language impairment: Evidence from bilingual children's acquisition of object pronouns. *Language Acquisition* 13 (1). 33–62.

Pearson, Barbara Zurer. 2004. Theoretical and empirical bases for dialect-neutral language assessment: Contributions from theoretical and applied linguistics to communication disorders. *Seminars in Speech and Language* 25 (1). 13–26.

Radford, Andrew. 1990. *Syntactic theory and the acquisition of English syntax*. Oxford: Blackwell.

Rice, Mabel L. 1991. Children with specific language impairment: toward a model of teachability. In Norman A. Krasnegor, Duane M. Rumbaugh, Richard L. Schiefelbusch & Michael Studdert-Kennedy (eds.), *Biological and behavioral determinants of language development*, 447–480. Hillsdale, NJ: Erlbaum.

Rice, Mabel L. 2000. Grammatical symptoms of specific language impairment. In Dorothy Bishop and Laurence B. Leonard (eds.), *Speech and Language Impairments in Children: Causes, Characteristics, Intervention and Outcome*, 17–34. Hove: Psychology Press.

Rice, Mabel L. & John. V. Bode. 1993. GAPs in the lexicon of children with specific language impairment. *First Language* 13. 113–132

Rice, Mabel L. & Kenneth Wexler. 2001. *Test of early grammatical impairment*. San Antonio, TX: The Psychological Corporation.

Rice, Mabel L., Kenneth Wexler & Patricia L. Cleave. 1995. Specific language impairment as a period of extended optional infinitive. *Journal of Speech and Hearing Research* 38 (4). 850–863.

Seymour, Harry N., Thomas Roeper, & Jill G. de Villiers, J. G. 2005. *DELV-NR (Diagnostic Evaluation of Language Variation) Norm-Referenced Test*. San Antonio TX: The Psychological Corporation.

Southwood, Frenette. 2007. *Specific language impairment in Afrikaans: Providing a Minimalist account for problems with grammatical features and word order*. Nijmegen: Radboud University Nijmegen dissertation. https://www.lotpublications.nl/specific-language-impairment-in-afrikaans-specific-language-impairment-in-afrikaans-providing-a-minimalist-account-for-problems-with-grammatical-feature-and-word-order

Topbaş, Seyhun & Mehmet Yavaş (eds.). 2010. *Communication disorders in Turkish in monolingual and multilingual settings*. Clevedon: Multilingual Matters.

Van der Lely, Heather K.J. 1994. Canonical linking rules: forward versus reverse linking in normally developing and specifically language-impaired children. *Cognition* 51 (1). 29–72.

Watkins, Ruth V. & Mabel L. Rice. 1991. Verb particle and preposition acquisition in language-impaired preschoolers. *Journal of Speech and Hearing Research* 34 (5). 1130–1141.

Watkins, Ruth V., Mabel L. Rice & Candace C. Moltz. 1993. Verb use by language-impaired and normally developing children. *First Language* 13. 133–144.

Weiner, Paul S. 1974. A language-delayed child at adolescence. *Journal of Speech and Hearing Disorders* 39 (2). 202–12.

Wexler, Kenneth, Carson T. Schütze & Mabel L. Rice. 1998. Subject case in children with SLI and unaffected normal controls: evidence for the Agr/Tns omission model. *Language Acquisition* 7 (2–4). 317–344.

Lara R. Polse, Samantha M. Engel and Judy S. Reilly
34 Neuroplasticity and development: Discourse in children with perinatal stroke and children with language impairment

1 Introduction

For most children the acquisition of their native language appears to be effortless, and by age five, they have mastered much of the grammar of their language, however for a subset of children, language development does not follow the typical path. For some of these atypically developing children, there is a known etiology underlying problems with language development, while in others, the cause is unclear. In this chapter we focus on two groups of children with atypical language development: children with unilateral Perinatal Stroke (PS) and children with Language Impairment (LI). These two groups are intriguing to compare as children with PS have frank brain injury, in some cases to the very brain structures that underlie language processes in typical brains, yet by school age, children with unilateral focal brain injury often perform within the normal range on a variety of language tasks. In contrast, children with LI show no obvious brain anomalies; they are diagnosed at school age because they demonstrate marked and persistent difficulty with language relative to typically developing peers. Comparing the language trajectories of these two groups – one with frank brain injury, but relatively resilient language development, and the other with no clear identifiable brain abnormality, but significant delay and difficulty in language – allows us to consider questions of neural and behavioral plasticity for language and the complementary issue of neural specialization. In this chapter, we discuss discourse and narrative performance in children with PS and LI across a wide age range with the broad goal of better understanding neuroplasticity and development for language.

1.1 The adult model

Before we go on to present the developmental profiles, a brief description of the adult brain organization for language will inform our discussion. Arising from work of Paul Broca and Carl Wernicke almost a century and a half ago, we know that for more than 90% of adults, spoken language is mediated by a left hemisphere fronto-temporal neural network (Rasmussen and Milner 1977). Since their groundbreaking

Lara R. Polse, Samantha M. Engel and Judy S. Reilly, University of California, San Diego and San Diego State University

work in the 1860's, studies of neuropsychological patients speaking hundreds of languages as diverse as English, Italian, Bulgarian, Taiwanese and American Sign Language have confirmed and fine-tuned the original findings of Broca and Wernicke (Goodglass 1993; Menn, Obler and Miceli 1990). Broadly, adults with left frontal lobe lesions typically demonstrate problems with lexical retrieval, morphology and syntactic production; those with left posterior injury typically show more severe comprehension impairments. In contrast, adults with right hemisphere strokes typically exhibit good comprehension and production of language at the sentence level, but exhibit problems with discourse cohesion and non-literal language, e.g., sarcasm, humor and irony (Brownell et al. 1990; Joanette, Goulet and Hannequin 1990; Kaplan et al. 1990; Winner et al. 1998). More recently, functional neuroimaging studies have begun to elucidate the complexity of this network (e.g., Bookheimer 2002; Hickok and Poeppel 2007; Price 2010).

1.2 Children with Perinatal Stroke

Children with Perinatal Stroke (PS) represent a rare group of children (approximately 1 in every 4,000 live births) who have sustained a lesion (as the result of an infarct or hemorrhage) during the last trimester of gestation up until 28 days postnatally (Lynch, Hirtz, DeVeber, and Nelson 2002; Lynch and Nelson 2001). Unlike children with LI who show no obvious neurological impairment, children with PS have a frank neural injury, with discernible extent and severity through the use of neuroimaging technology. One might expect, based on the neurological profiles of these two groups alone, and the consistent findings from research into language following unilateral stroke in adults, that children with PS (especially those with left hemisphere injury) would fare much worse in language development relative to their peers with LI. However, investigations into the language profiles of children from both populations from early childhood through adolescence indicate that there exists a more complex relationship between structural brain development and language function.

It is well documented that children who experience a stroke very early in life show a remarkable level of resilience to the stroke, and their cognitive functioning (including language) is significantly less impacted relative to adults with homologous late-onset strokes (see Stiles et al. 2012 for a comprehensive review). This ability to adapt and reorganize early in life (which diminishes systematically with age) has been attributed to Neuroplasticity – the highly plastic nature of the brain – early in development. While it is clear that the results of a perinatal stroke are indeed attenuated relative to adults with late-onset stroke, a closer look at language development in children with PS from infancy through late adolescence uncovers subtle differences between children with left and those with right hemisphere injury relative to their typically developing peers. These findings indicate that a more elaborate explanation of neuroplasticity in the wake of an early stroke is warranted, but first requires a brief discussion of the long-standing debate regarding the brain's initial state for acquiring language.

The initial state of the brain, whether it is a complexly programmed system that needs only to mature, or a *tabula rasa* (Locke 1689) – a blank slate completely formed through experiences with the world – has been debated for centuries. A strong nativist view of neurolinguistic development (e.g. Chomsky 1959; Fodor 1983) would predict that children with a lesion to left hemisphere language centers of the brain would not develop language similar to their typically developing peers, as the structures that are prewired to support language are damaged and any alternative pathways would result in aberrant language performance. On the other hand, the hemispheric equipotentiality view (e.g. Lenneberg 1967) would predict that if the injury to the left hemisphere language centers occurs sufficiently early, such that the brain can exploit the early plasticity of the brain for language, both hemispheres will be equally suited for supporting language. Thus, according to this view, language in children with injury to either hemisphere should be comparable to one another, as well as comparable to typically developing children. Very few modern neurolinguists subscribe to the strongest versions of either of these theories; rather they are viewed as endpoints on a spectrum with regard to the extent and limits to neuroplasticity following a very early neural injury.

1.3 Children with Language Impairment

Children with Language Impairment (LI) represent a group of children who demonstrate significant impairments in language skills that cannot be accounted for by a neurological or sensory impairment, or by a developmental disorder. Compared to the rarity of children with PS, LI is a relatively common disorder estimated to affect about seven percent of kindergarten children in the U.S. (Tomblin et al. 1997). Children with LI are identified through the use of exclusionary criteria: they fall 1.5 to 2 standard deviations below the mean on standardized measures of language while performing within the normal range on measures of nonverbal intelligence.

Despite the absence of any frank neurological damage, the language profiles of children with LI have been compared to those of adults with Broca's aphasia following left hemisphere brain injury. While language functions are the most commonly studied domain in this population, children with LI also demonstrate deficits in non-linguistic areas, for example visuo-spatial skills (Hick, Botting and Conti-Ramsden 2005), working memory (Archibald and Gathercole 2006; Montgomery 2003), and musical processing (Jentschke et al. 2008) suggesting a broader, rather than specifically linguistic, profile of deficit. And finally, while the language skills of children with LI do change and develop with age, it is unclear whether these children ever completely "catch up" to their typically developing peers. In fact, as adolescents and adults, children with LI are at a greater risk for lower academic achievement and socioemotional difficulties (Conti-Ramsden and Durkin 2014; Reed 2005).

Given the lack of clear neurological evidence to explain the language difficulties observed in children with LI, many theoretical explanations have been proposed to account for the low language performance observed in this clinical group. Some theoretical accounts posit that LI stems from a deficit that is specific to the language domain. Within these accounts, the locus of the deficit ranges: some theories point to syntax or grammar and others to phonological processing (Rice and Wexler 1996; Van der Lely 1998; Leonard 1998). Other accounts propose a domain general deficit, such as processing limitations or deficits in the working memory system (Joanisse and Seidenberg 1998; Kail, 1994; Lum, Gelgic and Conti-Ramsden 2010; Ullman 2004). With these profiles in mind, the following sections provide brief reviews of previous research into language development for children with Perinatal Stroke and children with Language Impairment.

2 Language development in children with PS and children with LI

Typically, children produce their first recognizable word at around 12 months of age. About six months before this, however, children use vocalizations to gain attention, engage in interactions, and practice verbalizing through canonical babbling. When compared to typically developing infants, ten-month-old infants with PS show a delay in the onset of both of these early markers for language – babbling and first words – regardless of whether the stroke was in the right or in the left hemisphere. Importantly, the *developmental trajectory* is similar across TD and PS groups; those who babble earlier also speak earlier and vice versa, indicating a delayed rather than an aberrant language development trajectory for toddlers with PS (Marchman, Miller & Bates 1991).

During the preschool years children begin to understand and use more complex language, stringing words into sentences and sentences into stories. Using a parental report form (MacArthur Bates Communicative Developmental Inventory, Fenson, et al. 1993) and transcribed free-play sessions, Bates and colleagues (1997) found that toddlers and preschoolers with PS showed an overall delay in language onset and first word combinations relative to typically developing children. That is, regardless of lesion site, the group was delayed in early language acquisition milestones. Within this broad delay, they noted some site-specific deficits: in comprehension, those with right posterior injury fared the worst, and in word production and spontaneous speech, those with left posterior injury produced the fewest words and simplest sentences. Other studies of early language in the PS group have reported similar findings: an overall language delay when compared to typically developing toddlers, with the left hemisphere lesion (LHL) group more impaired than those with right hemisphere lesion (RHL) (e.g. Chilosi et al. 2005; Feldman 2005; Vicari et al. 1999).

Unlike children with PS, who are typically diagnosed at birth, or shortly thereafter when parents notice effects of the lesion, children are not diagnosed as having Language Impairment until about five years of age (Bishop and Edmundson 1987; Johnson et al. 1999; Stothard et al. 1998). However, retrospective studies into the early language development of children who are later diagnosed with LI indicate that early developmental milestones such as producing first words and combining words are achieved later than their same age peers (Paul 1996; Rescorla and Lee 2000). At this point in development, these children fall into the group known as "Late Talkers." Late Talkers are toddlers whose productive vocabulary falls below the 10th percentile of productive vocabulary of typically developing children. Research into language development of Late Talkers shows smaller vocabulary sizes and overall less productive speech than their same age peers (Rescorla and Alley 2001). Late Talkers are considered to be "at risk" for being diagnosed with Language Impairment in elementary school (Ellis and Thal 2008; Rescorla 2002; Thal et al. 2004). Thus, tracking the language profile of late talking toddlers provides a glimpse into early language development of children with LI, even though only a subset of these young children will receive a diagnosis of Language Impairment when they reach school age.

In a longitudinal study of early language and discourse development, Thal and colleagues (2004) compared a group of children identified as late-talkers (LT) between 20 and 27 months of age and a group of children with perinatal stroke (PS) using free speech samples. At three years of age, children who were LT and PS used significantly fewer lexical types and tokens than the TD controls, and their grammatical proficiency scores, as measured by the Index of Productive Syntax (IPSYN) (Scarborough 1990), were lower than their TD peers. In the PS group, no differences were found between children with left and right hemisphere involvement. In the LT group, IPSYN scores were lower for children who had delayed comprehension and production than those with delayed production only when production and comprehension were measured at 20–27 months. Both LT and PS groups showed greater variability relative to TD controls in grammatical proficiency, with variability of the PS group exceeding that of LT. An analysis of morphological errors showed that those of the PS and LT groups were similar in quality to the controls; differences were in frequency of occurrence. Thus, in the early stages of language development, children with PS and LI show similar profiles. Both groups begin life as "late-talkers" and their early language development, while delayed and more variable, follows a similar developmental trajectory to that of typically developing children.

2.1 Narrative development

Whereas the preschool years are principally devoted to the acquisition of particular linguistic structures, by age five, children have mastered the vast majority of the morphology and syntax of their native language. However, using these structures flexibly for diverse discourse genres requires extensive practice and time; for example, the ability to construct a clear and cogent narrative develops well into adolescence (Berman and Slobin 1994) even though narratives are common, and frequently occur during dinner-table conversation. Narratives reflect a canonical structure which includes a setting, a problem, the protagonist's response, his or her attempts to resolve the problem, and finally a resolution. While younger children often include the problem and some attempts at its resolution in their stories, the inclusion of a setting is a later-developed skill (Tolchinsky 2004). The setting, which introduces the characters, the time, place, or situation, is critical for the listener, as it establishes the context in which the story will unfold.

As such, narratives draw not only on linguistic, but also cognitive and social skills, and they offer a rich context to investigate both linguistic proficiency (micro-structural aspects) as well as discourse and pragmatic abilities (macro-structural aspects). Micro-structural measures provide information about the form of language and may include lexical diversity, syntactic complexity, story length and morphological accuracy, among other measures. Macro-structural measures provide information about the content of language and may include, for example, story structure, event sequencing, and topic maintenance. Narratives can be elicited in a variety of contexts, including those with or without picture support and across a variety of types and modalities, for example personal or fictional narratives and written or spoken narratives.

2.1.1 Narrative studies of children with PS

Reilly, Bates and Marchman (1998) conducted a narrative study in children with Perinatal Stroke using the wordless picture book, *Frog, Where are you?* (Mayer 1969). Overall, the stories from the PS group (n = 31) were generally shorter than those of the TD group (n = 31), and it was only in the youngest children (ages 4–6) that site-specific differences were evident in morphological proficiency. Specifically, and in line with the Bates and colleagues' (2001) study, those youngsters with posterior left hemisphere injury made more errors than the rest of the PS group, although as a whole the younger children with PS made more errors than their TD peers. On all other measures (lexical, syntactic and discourse level indices), there were no significant differences in the performance of those with left or right hemisphere injury. However, the PS group made more errors and used less complex syntax then the control group until age 10 when their performance on these measures was comparable to controls. Reilly and colleagues also conducted a more qualitative analysis of all the stories from the seven and eight year old children. The stories scoring the highest for plot, elaboration, theme, and reference included only one story from the PS group and the rest of the highest-scoring stories were from controls, while those scoring in the lowest group on these measures included only one TD story; the remaining were from the PS group. Overall, the stories from the children with PS were more impoverished than those of their TD age mates.

A complementary study looking at narratives in children with PS was conducted by Demir, Levine and Goldin-Meadow (2010). They collected stories from five-and-six-year-old children by providing the children with "story stems" which the children were to complete. In analyzing their results, they found no effects for side, site or size of lesion. However, consistent with the performance of this age group in the study by Reilly and colleagues, the PS group (n = 11) scored lower than the controls (n=20) on measures of narrative length and complexity, as well as in the use of subordinate clauses and vocabulary (word types). Interestingly, these same children scored in the normal range on standardized tests of vocabulary and syntax. Such performance discrepancies suggest again, that context plays a stronger role for the PS group than for their TD controls, and that their mastery of morphosyntax is more fragile than it is for age matched controls. In addition, such findings suggest that to understand the language abilities in these children, it is critical to look at performance across a variety of contexts.

2.1.2 Narratives studies of children with LI

The narrative abilities of children with LI differ from children with typical language development at both the micro and macro level. At the micro level, they demonstrate the same deficits identified in non-narrative tasks, specifically, in utterance length, morphological errors, complex syntax, and lexical diversity (Liles 1985; Reilly et al. 2004; Koutsoftas and Gray 2014; Kadaverak and Sulzby 2000; McFadden and Gillam 1996). Children with LI also demonstrate difficulty at the macro-level as reflected in fewer informational units, propositions, story grammar units and difficulty with cohesion and event sequencing (Liles 1985, 1987; Miranda, McCabe and Bliss 1998; Paul 1996; Reilly et al. 2004). An example of difficulty in the macrostructure of narratives comes from Miranda, McCabe and Bliss' (1998) findings that children with LI (n = 10) expanded their personal narratives by adding irrelevant or tangential information often through the use of script-like endings, for example describing routines or listing events unrelated to the story's main theme. The authors identified what they called a "leap-frogging pattern" in the LI group, where events were not ordered chronologically. The LI group also had a higher frequency of unspecified elements, for example the use of *"something"* for a specific referent or omitted referents (e.g. *John went* with no location specified).

In contrast to children's difficulty with linguistic forms, evidence for difficulty at the macro-level is not consistent across the literature: findings from some studies suggest that children with LI perform similarly to children with typical language development in terms of thematic maintenance and inclusion of key events (Boudreau and Hedberg 1999; Reilly et al. 2004). Because task demands vary widely depending on the type of narratives elicited, it is possible that children with LI have less difficulty at the macro-level of narratives when task demands are lower, for example when picture support or modeling is provided. Support for the effect of increasing task demands comes from Boudreau's (2007) finding that children's performance at both the micro- and macro-levels decreased with stories that were complex (both linguistically and structurally) compared to simple stories.

Reilly and colleagues (2004) compared the spoken narratives from a picture book of children with LI (n = 44) and children with PS (n = 52) ages 4–12. Consistent with the findings from Thal and colleagues (2004), children with LI and PS said less than the TD controls, resulting in shorter stories overall. In terms of morphological errors, children with PS and LI performed poorly compared to their TD peers between ages 4–9. By ages 10–12 however, children with PS had caught up to their TD peers while children with LI still lagged behind. A similar pattern was found for use of complex syntax: children with PS followed the normal developmental trajectory at a slower rate and between ages 10–12 performed within the normal range. Children with LI also showed improvement with age but were still below normal performance at age 12. Across all measures, children with PS performed better than those with LI and both groups were delayed compared to the TD control group. By age 12 however, children with PS performed within the normal range on all morphosyntactic measures while children with LI still demonstrated significant delays.

In summary, in narrative development, both clinical groups (PS and LI) look similar at an early age (both falling below the performance of typically developing children) and both groups show improvement over time. However, by about age 10–12, on a narrative task, children with PS tell superior narratives in terms of structure and content relative to children with LI. In the following section, we consider these developmental trends of narrative performance in older children and adolescents of these two groups.

2.1.3 Narratives of older children with PS and LI

Given that performance changes over development and with the demands of a given task, we now will consider the language profiles of these two groups as the children get older and as task demands increase. Narratives from school age children and adolescents allow us to investigate the nature and extent of neuroplasticity for language as these children age, and as brain plasticity diminishes. It allows us to consider issues of change over time as well as performance under increased task demands. Reilly and colleagues collected data on a more challenging narrative task from a sample of older children with PS and LI, ages 7–16. These data were originally presented separately (Reilly, Wasserman and Applebaum 2012; Reilly et al. 2013); here we consider them side by side.

Reilly, Wasserman and Appelbaum (2012) compared spoken personal narratives of typically developing children (n = 60) and children with right and left PS (n = 35) ages 7–16. Similar to previous studies of narratives in children with PS, the results indicate that children with right and children with left hemisphere injury do not differ statistically as a group on measures of morphological or narrative processing (e.g. Reilly et al., 2004). However, even though there is no statistical difference between groups of children with right and those with left hemisphere lesions, only the children with a lesion to the left hemisphere lagged behind their typically developing peers on both macro and micro-level structural elements. This step-like pattern of deficit (LHL > RHL > TD), where only LHL and TD are statistically different from one another, elucidates differences between the two groups *relative to typically developing peers*. This pattern of results provides support for a theory in which there exists an initial left hemisphere bias for language that re-emerges late in elementary school and in adolescence. Reilly and colleagues (2013) compared spoken personal narratives of French and English speaking typically developing children (French speaking TD n = 31, English speaking TD = 60) and children with LI (French speaking LI n = 17, English speaking LI n = 32) aged 7–16. Consistent with previous studies of narratives of children with LI, the English speaking LI children told significantly shorter stories, made significantly more morphological errors, and used less complex syntax than their TD counterparts.

The studies described above employed the same narrative prompt and the same age range and so allow an opportunity to consider what a direct comparison of PS and LI would yield. What we see across these studies is persistent similarities between the language performance of the LI and LHL groups despite such different underlying neural anatomy. Although the LI and LHL groups were significantly different from the TD groups in both studies, the RHL group was not statistically significantly different from either the TD or LHL group. This pattern demonstrates that there is not a neat divide between "typical" and "atypical."

Additionally, while both children with LI and children with LHL have been compared to adults with Broca's aphasia, neither group produced narratives that were similar to that which would be expected from an adult with a late-acquired left hemisphere lesion (i.e. halting, disfluent speech characterized by content nouns yet devoid of syntax), and the distinctive adult right and left hemisphere language profiles did not emerge in these studies. Specifically, according to the adult model, individuals with left hemisphere injury (especially to frontotemporal regions) would be expected to show concomitant deficits in grammatical processing and those with injury to the right hemisphere would be expected to demonstrate more errors of metalinguistic processing, sequencing, and narrative structure. These results do not mirror the adult pattern: children with lesions in right hemisphere regions performed better than (though not significantly different from) children with left hemisphere lesions on measures of morphology *and* narrative structure.

3 Discussion

When viewed within a broad developmental context, the studies discussed here suggest that initially children with PS fall below their typically developing peers on the acquisition of early language milestones, and indeed children with LHL may be especially at risk for delayed language onset. In the preschool and elementary years, children with PS continue to talk less and make more errors than their typically developing peers, but the right/left differences appear to have resolved by school age. In the early elementary school years, children with PS have caught up to their typically developing peers in casual conversational language; and hemisphere and population differences have all but disappeared. Later in childhood and adolescence, in more complex language tasks, subtle hemispheric differences re-emerge, as children with LHL show more language difficulties than children with RHL. This pattern of results may be attributed to neurodevelopmental changes in the brain resulting from the complex relationship between neuroanatomy, language proficiency, and lateralization and specification for language as individuals develop and acquire their native tongue. Moreover, when we include the additional population (children with Language Impairment) to this interpretation of results, we are obliged to consider additional factors to understand why children with no apparent brain tissue damage and children with lesions to the left hemisphere structures typically involved in language processing consistently demonstrate the most similar patterns of behavioral results.

The importance of individual variability, which is consistently reported in studies of children with PS and LI, must not be overlooked. Each individual's experience and interaction with the environment shapes his or her language development, as well as his or her unique functional neuroanatomy to support language. This is true for every individual, but especially for those with either frank or "hidden" structural and functional brain abnormalities such as children with PS and LI respectively. While children with LI do not show the same obvious neural insult as children with PS, there is some evidence from neuroimaging research to indicate children with LI have subtle differences in brain structures that put them at greater risk for developing LI or dyslexia (Leonard et al. 2005). Other studies point to differences in *functional* neuroanatomy and report differences in children with LI. Functional neuroimaging studies report anomalous activity of the left hemisphere in response to speech sounds and language (Badcock et al. 2012; de Guibert et al. 2011; Helenius et al. 2009, 2014; Hugdahl et al. 2004; Pihko et al. 2008 (speech); Weismer et al. 2005 (language)), as well as differences in lateralization for language, observed by functional transcranial Doppler ultrasonography (fTCD) (Whitehouse and Bishop 2008). Differences in structural and functional neural anatomy lead to different routes to language proficiency, and result in increases in individual variability, as well as different patterns of language development.

Another more specific aspect of functional neuroanatomy to consider is the protracted process of lateralization for language that typically developing children experience during all of childhood and into adolescence, which includes long periods of more bilateral distribution of language networks relative to adults. Either a frank insult to one hemisphere or subtle differences in hemispheric responses to speech and language would disrupt this complex process, albeit in different ways. Children with LHL, show an initial delay in language acquisition, but then experience a period of language development similar to TD children. Importantly, this period of relative proficiency is during elementary school, and this is the developmental period in which typically developing children rely heavily on bilateral language networks. This period of bilaterally supported language processing gradually transitions as language processing lateralizes to the left hemisphere, as a consequence of both language development and maturation (e.g. Booth et al. 2003; Brown et al. 2005; Holland et al. 2001; Schlaggar et al. 2002; Schmithorst, Holland and Plante 2007; Szaflarski et al. 2006). Thus, children with an insult to one side of the brain have the opportunity to exploit this natural time of bilaterality for language to strengthen their (putatively) unaffected hemisphere for language. Children with LI, on the other hand, who show subtle abnormal neural anatomy in both hemispheres during the time when children recruit bilateral neural circuitry to support language, do not have the same opportunity to use a "healthy" hemisphere to form strong language networks during this period. Interestingly, as the discussed studies suggest, in the early adolescent years, when older TD children begin to lateralize to predominantly left-hemisphere language structures (similar to the adult profile), subtle deficits in children with a lesion to those left hemisphere structures re-emerge. For children with LI, however, who never had the opportunity to utilize and strengthen healthy functional neuroanatomy for language, the language deficits observed in the elementary school years persist into adolescence.

4 Conclusions

In conclusion, children with Perinatal Stroke and children with Language Impairment both demonstrate subtle deficits in discourse at the micro (grammatical elements) and macro (setting components) levels relative to their typically developing peers, but neither group performs similarly to adults with Broca's aphasia. Furthermore, there seems to exist a step-like pattern of deficit such that children with injury to the left hemisphere and children with Language Impairment perform worse than (though not statistically different from) children with injury to the right hemisphere, and children with injury to the right hemisphere perform worse than (though not statistically different from) typically developing children. Children with Language Impairment and left hemisphere lesions perform more poorly than typically developing children. These studies support a theory which postulates some initial left hemisphere bias for language, which re-emerges in late adolescence, and also partially supports a theory which emphasizes the importance of the lateralization process for language in typical development: As children with PS have a putatively healthy hemisphere, they have the opportunity to exploit the natural period of bilaterality for language, thus strengthening language networks in one (healthy) hemisphere; children with LI, on the other hand, who have been shown to have abnormal lateralization for language, may not have a "healthy" hemisphere in which to form strong language networks, resulting in weaker neural circuitry underlying language overall. The discourse research reviewed in this chapter suggests that while children with PS exploit the natural developmental period of bilateral language distribution to support language processing in simple, conversational contexts in the elementary school years, this alternative developmental process has limits. Older participants with left hemisphere stroke show deficits in more complex linguistic contexts. Children with Perinatal Stroke and children with Language Impairment have contrastive neural profiles yet comparative language profiles. Considering research from these two populations in a broad range of ages and on more complex discourse tasks provides an overview of language function and development of these two groups, as well as insight into the extents and limits to neuroplasticity for language.

Acknowledgments

This project was supported in part by National Institutes of Health Grants NINDS/NIMH P50 NS22343 and NIH/NIDCD Training Grant DC000041. We are very grateful to the participants and their families for their participation in this research and members of the Developmental Laboratory for Language and Cognition (San Diego State University) and staff from the Project for Cognitive and Neural Development, San Diego.

References

Archibald, Lisa M. D. & Susan E. Gathercole. 2006. Short-term and working memory in specific language impairment. *International Journal of Language & Communication Disorders* 41(6). 675–693.

Badcock, Nicholas A. Dorothy V.M. Bishop, Mervyn J. Hardiman, Johanna G. Barry & Kate E. Watkins. 2012. Co-localisation of abnormal brain structure and function in specific language impairment. *Brain & Language* 120(3). 310–320.

Bates, Elizabeth, Judy Reilly, Beverly Wulfeck, Nina Dronkers, Meiti Opie, Judith Fenson, Sarah Kriz, Rita Jeffries, LaRae Miller & Kathyrn Herbst. 2001. Differential effects of unilateral lesions on language production in children and adults. *Brain and Language* 79. 223–265.
Bates, Elizabeth, Donna Thal, Doris Trauner, Judith Fenson, Dorothy Aram, Julie Eisele & Ruth Nass. 1997. From first words to grammar in children with focal brain injury. *Developmental Neuropsychology* 13. 275–344.
Berman, Ruth A. & Dan Isaac Slobin. 1994. *Relating events in narrative: A crosslinguistic developmental study*. Hillsdale, NJ: Lawrence Erlbaum Associates.
Bishop, Dorothy V. M. & Andrew Edmundson. 1987. Language-Impaired 4-Year-Olds: Distinguishing transient from persistent impairment. *Journal of Speech and Hearing Disorders* 52(2). 156–173.
Bookheimer, Susan. 2002. Functional MRI of language: New approaches to understanding the cortical organization of semantic processing. *Annual Review of Neuroscience* 25. 151–188.
Boudreau, Donna M. 2007. Narrative abilities in children with language impairments. In Rhea Paul (ed.), *Language disorders from a developmental perspective*, 331–356. Mahwah, NJ: Lawrence Erlbaum Associates.
Boudreau, Donna M. & Natalie L. Hedberg. 1999. A Comparison of early literacy skills in children with specific language impairment and their typically developing peers. *American Journal of Speech-Language Pathology* 8(3). 249–260.
Brown Timothy T. Heather M. Lugar, Rebecca S. Coalson, Fran M. Miezin, Steven E. Petersen & Bradley L. Schlaggar. 2005. Developmental changes in human cerebral functional organization for word generation. *Cerebral Cortex* 15(3). 275–90.
Brownell, Hiram H. Tracy L. Simpson, Amy M. Bihrle, Heather H. Potter & Howard Gardner. 1990. Appreciation of metaphoric alternative word meanings by left and right brain-damaged patients. *Neuropsychologia* 28(4). 375–383.
Chilosi, Anna M. C. Pecini, Paola Cipriani, P. Brovedani, D. Brizzolara, G. Ferretti, L. Pfanner & Giovanni Cioni. 2005. Atypical language lateralization and early linguistic development in children with focal brain lesions. *Developmental Medicine & Child Neurology* 47(11). 725–730.
Chomsky, Noam. 1959. A review of BF Skinner's Verbal Behavior. *Language* 35(1). 26–58.
Demir, Özlem E. Susan C. Levine & Susan Goldin-Meadow. 2010. Narrative skill in children with early unilateral brain injury: A possible limit to functional plasticity. *Developmental Science* 13(4). 636–647.
Ellis, Erica & Donna Thal. 2008. Early language delay and risk for language impairment. *Perspectives on Language Learning and Education* 15(3). 93–100.
Feldman, Heidi M. 2005. Language learning with an injured brain. *Language Learning and Development* 1(3–4). 265–288.
Fenson, Larry, Steven Resznick, Donna Thal, Elizabeth Bates, Jeff Hartung, Stephen Pethick & Judy Reilly. 1993. *The MacArthur communicative developmental inventory*. San Diego: Singular Publishing Group, Inc.
Fodor, Jerry A. 1983. *The modularity of mind: An essay on faculty psychology*. Boston, MA: MIT press.
Goodglass, Harold. 1993. *Understanding Aphasia*. San Diego: Academic Press.
Guibert, Clement de, Camille Maumet, Pierre Jannin, Jean-Christophe Ferré, Catherine Tréguier, Christian Barillot, Elisabeth Le Rumeur, Catherine Allaire & Arnaud Biraben. 2011. Abnormal functional lateralization and activity of language brain areas in typical specific language impairment (developmental dysphasia). *Brain: A Journal Of Neurology* 134(10). 3044–3058.
Helenius, Päivi, Tiina Parviainen, Ritva Paetau & Riitta Salmelin. 2009. Neural processing of spoken words in specific language impairment and dyslexia. *Brain* 132(7). 1918–1927.
Hick, Rachel, Nicola Botting & Gina Conti-Ramsden. 2005. Cognitive abilities in children with specific language impairment: Consideration of visuo-spatial skills. *International Journal of Language & Communication Disorders* 40(2). 137–149.

Hickok, Gregory & David Poeppel. 2007. The cortical organization of speech processing. *Nature Reviews Neuroscience* 8(5). 393–402.

Holland, Scott K. Elena Plante, Anna Weber Byars, Richard H. Strawsburg, Vince J. Schmithorst & William S. Ball. 2001. Normal fMRI brain activation patterns in children performing a verb generation task. *Neuroimage* 14(4). 837–843.

Holland, Scott K. Jennifer Vannest, Marc Mecoli, Lisa M. Jacola, Jan Mendelt Tillema, Prasanna R. Karunanayaka, Vincent J. Schmithorst, Weihong Yuan, Elena Plante & Anna Weber Byars. 2007. Functional MRI of language lateralization during development in children. *International Journal of Audiology* 46(9). 533–551.

Hugdahl, Kenneth, Hilde Gundersen, Cecilie Brekke, Tormod Thomsen, Lars Morten Rimol, Lars Ersland & Jussi Niemi. 2004. fMRI Brain Activation in a Finnish Family With Specific Language Impairment Compared With a Normal Control Group. *Journal Of Speech, Language, and Hearing Research* 47(1). 162–172.

Jentschke, Sebastian, Stefan Koelsch, Stephan Sallat & Angela D. Friederici. 2008. Children with specific language impairment also show impairment of music-syntactic processing. *Journal of Cognitive Neuroscience* 20(11). 1940–1951.

Joanette, Yves, Pierre Goulet & Didier Hannequin. 1990. *Right-hemisphere and verbal communication*. New York: Springer-Verlag.

Joanisse, Marc F. & Mark S. Seidenberg. 1998. Specific language impairment: A deficit in grammar or processing? *Trends in Cognitive Sciences* 2(7). 240–247.

Johnson, Carla J. Joseph H. Beitchman, Arlene Young, Michael Escobar, Leslie Atkinson, Beth Wilson, E.B. Brownlie, Lori Douglas, Nathan Taback, Isabel Lam & Min Wang. 1999. Fourteen-Year Follow-Up of Children With and Without Speech/Language Impairments Speech/Language Stability and Outcomes. *Journal of Speech, Language, and Hearing Research* 42(3). 744–760.

Kail, Robert. 1994. A method for studying the generalized slowing hypothesis in children with specific language impairment. *Journal of Speech and Hearing Research* 37. 418–421.

Kaplan, Joan, Hiram Brownell, Janet Jacobs & Howard Gardner. 1990. The effects of right-hemisphere damage on the pragmatic interpretation of conversational remarks. *Brain and Language* 38(2). 315–333.

Koutsoftas, Anthony D. & Shelley Gray. 2014. Comparison of narrative and expository writing in students with and without language-learning disabilities. *Language, Speech and Hearing Services in Schools* 43(4). 395–409.

Lenneberg, Eric H. 1967. *Biological foundations of language*. New York: Wiley.

Leonard, Christiana, Linda J. Lomardino, Sally Ann Giess & Wayne M. King. 2005. Behavioral and anatomical distinctions between dyslexia and SLI. In Hugh W. Catts & Alan G. Kamhi (eds.), *The Connections Between Language and Reading Disabilities*, 155–172. Mahwah, NJ: Lawrence Erlbaum.

Leonard, Lawrence B. 1998. *Children with specific language impairment*. Cambridge, MA: MIT Press.

Liles, Betty Z. 1985. Cohesion in the narratives of normal and language-disordered children. *Journal of Speech, Language, and Hearing Research* 28(1). 123–133.

Liles, Betty Z. 1987. Episode organization and cohesive conjunctives in narratives of children with and without language disorder. *Journal of Speech, Language, and Hearing Research* 30(2). 185–196.

Locke, John. 1689. *An essay concerning human understanding*.

Lynch, John Kylan, Deborah G. Hirtz, Gabrielle DeVeber & Karin B. Nelson. 2002. Report of the national institute of neurological disorders and stroke workshop on perinatal and childhood stroke. *Pediatrics* 109(1). 116–123.

Lynch, John Kylan & Karin B. Nelson. 2001. Epidemiology of perinatal stroke. *Current Opinion in Pediatrics* 13(6). 499–505.

Marchman, Virginia A. Ruth Miller & Elizabeth A. Bates. 1991. Babble and first words in children with focal brain injury. *Applied Psycholinguistics* 12(1). 1–22.

Marinis, Theodoros & Heather K. Van der Lely. 2007. On-line processing of wh-questions in children with G-SLI and typically developing children. *International Journal of Language & Communication Disorders* 42(5). 557–582.

Mayer, Mercer. 1969. *Frog, where are you?*. New York: Dial Press.

Mcfadden, Teresa Ukrainetz & Ronald B. Gillam. 1996. An examination of the quality of narratives produced by children with language disorders. *Language, Speech, and Hearing Services in Schools* 27(1). 48–56.

Menn, Lisa, Loraine K. Obler & Gabriele Miceli (eds.). 1990. *Agrammatic aphasia: A cross-language narrative sourcebook* (vol. 2). Meppel, Netherlands: John Benjamins Publishing.

Miranda, Elisabeth A. Allysa McCabe & Lynn S. Bliss. 1998. Jumping around and leaving things out: A profile of the narrative abilities of children with specific language impairment. *Applied Psycholinguistics* 19(4). 647–667.

Montgomery, James W. 2003. Working memory and comprehension in children with specific language impairment: what we know so far. *Journal of Communication Disorders* 36(3). 221–231.

Paul, Rhea. 1996. Clinical implications of the natural history of slow expressive development. *American Journal of Speech-Language Pathology* 5(2). 5–21.

Pihko, Elina, Teija Kujala, Annika Mickos, Paavo Alku, Roger Byring & Marit Korkman. 2008. Language impairment is reflected in auditory evoked fields. *International Journal Of Psychophysiology* 68(2). 161–169.

Price, Cathy J. 2010. The anatomy of language: a review of 100 fMRI studies published in 2009. *Annals of the New York Academy of Sciences* 1191(1). 62–88.

Rasmussen, Theordore & Brenda Milner. 1977. The role of early left-brain injury in determining lateralization of cerebral speech functions. *Annals of the New York Academy of Sciences* 299(1). 355–369.

Reed, Vicki A. 2005. Adolescents with language impairment. In Vicki A. Reed (ed.), *An introduction to children with language disorders*, 3rd edition, 168–219. Boston, MA: Pearson.

Reilly, Judy S. Elizabeth Bates & Virginia Marchman. 1998. Narrative discourse in children with early focal brain injury. *Brain and Language* 61. 335– 375.

Reilly, Judy, Molly Losh, Ursula Bellugi & Beverly Wulfeck. 2004. "Frog, where are you?" Narratives in children with specific language impairment, early focal brain injury, and Williams syndrome. *Brain and Language* 88(2). 229–47.

Reilly, Judy S. Sophie Wasserman & Mark Appelbaum. 2012. Later language development in narratives in children with perinatal stroke. *Developmental Science* 16(1). 67–83.

Rescorla, Leslie & Amie Alley. 2001. Validation of the Language Development Survey (LDS): A parent report tool for identifying language delay in toddlers. *Journal of Speech, Language, and Hearing Research* 44. 434–445.

Rescorla, Leslie & Eliza Lee. 2000. Language impairment in young children. In Shonkoff, Jack P. & Samuel J. Meisels (eds.), *Handbook of early language impairment in children*, 1–55. Albany, NY: Delmar.

Rice, Mabel L. & Kenneth Wexler. 1996. Toward tense as a clinical marker of specific language impairment in English-speaking children. *Journal of Speech and Hearing Research* 39. 1239–1257.

Scarborough, Hollis S. 1990. Index of productive syntax. *Applied Psycholinguistics* 11. 1–22.

Schlaggar, Bradley L. Timothy T. Brown, Heather M. Lugar, Kristina M. Visscher, Francis M. Miezin & Steven E. Petersen. 2002. Functional neuroanatomical differences between adults and school-age children in the processing of single words. *Science* 296(5572). 1476–1479.

Stiles, Joan, Judy S. Reilly, Susan C. Levine, Doris A. Trauner & Ruth Nass. 2012. *Neural plasticity and cognitive development: Insights from children with perinatal brain injury.* New York, NY: Oxford University Press.

Stothard, Susan E. Margaret J. Snowling, Dorothy V. M. Bishop, Barry B. Chipchase & Carole A. Kaplan. 1998. Language-impaired preschoolers: A follow-up into adolescence. *Journal of Speech, Language, and Hearing Research* 41(2). 407–418.

Szaflarski, Jerzy P. Scott K. Holland, Vincent J. Schmithorst & Anna W. Byars. 2006. fMRI study of language lateralization in children and adults. *Human brain mapping* 27(3). 202–212.

Thal, Donna J. Judy Reilly, Laura Seibert, Rita Jeffries & Judith Fenson. 2004. Language development in children at risk for language impairment: Cross-population comparisons. *Brain and Language* 88(2). 167–79.

Tolchinsky, Liliana. 2004. The nature and scope of later language development. In Ruth A. Berman (ed.), *Language development across childhood and adolescence*, 233–247. Amsterdam: John Benjamins Publishing.

Tomblin, J. Bruce, Nancy L. Records, Paula Buckwalter, Xuyang Zhang, Elaine Smith & Marlea O'Brien. 1997. Prevalence of specific language impairment in kindergarten children. *Journal of Speech, Language, and Hearing Research* 40. 1245–1260.

Ullman, Michael T. 2004. Contributions of memory circuits to language: The declarative/procedural model. *Cognition* 92. 231–270.

Van der Lely, Heather K. 1998. SLI in children: Movement, economy and deficits in the computational syntactic system. *Language Acquisition* 72. 161–192.

Vicari, Stefano, A. Albertoni, Anna M. Chilosi, Paola Cipriani, Giovanni Cioni & Elizabeth Bates. 1999. Plasticity and reorganization during language development in children with early brain injury. Project in cognitive and neural development – technical report. Center for Research in Language, University of California, San Diego (CND-9901).

Weismer, Susan Ellis, Elena Plante, Maura Jones & Bruce J. Tomblin. 2005. A functional magnetic resonance imaging investigation of verbal working memory in adolescents with specific language impairment. *Journal of Speech, Language & Hearing Research* 48(2). 405–425.

Whitehouse, Andrew J. O. & Dorothy V. M. Bishop. 2008. Cerebral dominance for language function in adults with specific language impairment or autism. *Brain* 131(12). 3193–3200.

Winner, Elena, Hiram Brownell, Francesca Happé, Ari Blum & Donna Pincus. 1998. Distinguishing lies from jokes: Theory of mind deficits and discourse interpretation in right hemisphere brain-damaged patients. *Brain and Language* 62(1). 89–106.

Naama Friedmann and Max Coltheart

35 Types of developmental dyslexia

1 Introduction

To the best of our knowledge, the first person to suggest that there are different types of developmental dyslexia was the educational psychologist Helmer Myklebust. In Myklebust (1965), he suggested that some dyslexic children have difficulty in learning to read because they "could not acquire the auditory equivalents of the appearances of the letters" (p. 30: Myklebust referred to this condition as "auditory dyslexia"), whilst for other dyslexic children the problem is "the inability to mentally visualize letters and sounds" (p. 23: Johnson and Myklebust, 1967, referred to this condition as "visual dyslexia"). These ideas were taken up by the pediatric neurologist Elena Boder (see for example Boder, 1968, 1969, 1970, 1971, 1973).

She developed a diagnostic screening test based on the distinction between auditory and visual dyslexia and this allowed her to characterize these two subtypes in a little more detail. She proposed (see e.g. Boder, 1973) that some dyslexic children, when attempting to read aloud words that are not in their sight vocabularies, are typically unable to do so because they are "unable to sound out and blend the component letters and syllables of a word" (p. 688). This is Myklebust's auditory dyslexia. Boder referred to it as "dysphonetic dyslexia". These days the form of developmental dyslexia in which there is a specific difficulty in reading aloud unfamiliar letter strings is called "developmental phonological dyslexia".

A second group identified by Boder (1973) were those dyslexic children who are "analytic readers" and read "by ear", "through a process of phonetic analysis and synthesis, sounding out familiar as well as unfamiliar combinations of letters, rather than by whole-word gestalts... [they] can often read the word list by phonetic analysis up to or near [their] grade level, missing out only words that cannot be decoded phonetically" (that is, irregular words). This is Myklebust's visual dyslexia. Boder referred to it as "dyseidetic dyslexia". These days the form of developmental dyslexia in which there is a specific difficulty in reading irregular words aloud is called "developmental surface dyslexia".

At the same time as these early ventures into the subtyping of developmental dyslexia were proceeding, work on subtyping of acquired dyslexia, dyslexia following brain damage, was also beginning to develop. Marshall and Newcombe (1966) offered a detailed description of one such dyslexia type, acquired deep dyslexia, the identifying symptom of which was the frequent occurrence of semantic errors in

---

Naama Friedmann, Tel Aviv University
Max Coltheart, Macquarie University

reading aloud single words. This work was developed further by Marshall and Newcombe (1973), who described the characteristics of three types of acquired dyslexia: as well as deep dyslexia, there was visual dyslexia (which was not the same as the visual dyslexia described by Myklebust and Boder: see below for further discussion of visual dyslexia), and there was a form of acquired dyslexia in which the patient can no longer recognize many formerly familiar words and so can only read them aloud by sounding them out, a process which will fail for irregular words. This is Myklebust's "visual dyslexia" and Boder's "dyseidetic dyslexia", but Marshall and Newcombe (1973) introduced the term "surface dyslexia" for this condition, and that became the standard term. As for the acquired analogue of Myklebust's "auditory dyslexia" and Boder's "dysphonetic dyslexia" – a specific loss of the ability to read aloud unfamiliar letter strings such as nonwords – this was first described by Beauvois and Dérouesné (1979; Dérouesné and Beauvois, 1979) and referred to as "phonological alexia", a term that soon became "phonological dyslexia".

The unification of these originally separate and parallel endeavours – the subtyping of developmental dyslexias and the subtyping of acquired dyslexia – was obviously desirable. Such unification was the aim of a NATO conference held at Maratea, Italy, in October 1982, and published as a book "Dyslexia: A global issue", edited by Malatesha and Whitaker (1984). The two critical papers here are by John Marshall: one was entitled "Towards a rational taxonomy of the developmental dyslexias" (Marshall, 1984a) and the other "Towards a rational taxonomy of the acquired dyslexias" (Marshall, 1984b).

The key point made in these two papers was that both developmental and acquired types of reading disorder need to be interpreted in relation to a model of intact adult skilled reading. Such a model defines the various components of the reading system that children must learn if they are to become skilled readers; and it defines the various components of the reading system any one of which can be individually impaired. Such selective impairment can either be caused by a developmental disorder, or by brain damage, after the relevant component of the reading process has already been fully acquired. Both developmental and acquired disorders produce some particular patterns of preserved and impaired reading abilities – that is, some specific types of acquired dyslexia. So any such model can be used to interpret both developmental and acquired dyslexias; and in addition such models are invaluable for the development of rational assessment procedures and for the design of rational treatment regimes.

Furthermore, the identification and characterisation of various types of dyslexia, in turn, provide constraints for the cognitive model of reading and suggest modifications to it. One example of a fruitful interaction between the reading model and dyslexias can be seen in the case of the functions of the orthographic-visual analyser. In 1977, Shallice and Warrington described a patient who had migrations of letters between words when he was reading words that were presented one next to the other. This dyslexia was later termed (in Shallice and Warrington's 1980 chapter) "attentional dyslexia". One important characteristic of these migrations between words was that letters that migrated to the other word still kept their original position within the word (i.e., the final letter migrates to the final position in the other word, etc.). This finding not only sheds light on the characterisation of this dyslexia but also informs the cognitive theory of the first stage of word reading, because it implies that the function that encodes the position of letters within the word and the function that binds a letter to the word it appears in are separate. And this is indeed how the functions of the orthographic-visual analyser were portrayed since then. Ellis and Young (1988), for example, described the orthographic-visual analyser as involving, in addition to letter identification, two separate functions of position encoding: letter position within words and letter-to-word binding.

The next step of interaction between developmental dyslexia and the reading model came from the other direction, of the model informing dyslexia research. Friedmann and Gvion (2001, and Friedmann and Rahamim, 2007) reasoned that if a function of letter position encoding exists and is a separate function, a dyslexia should exist that results from a selective deficit to this function. Using words that would be sensitive for this kind of impairment, those in which letter position errors create other existing words, they were able to identify this dyslexia, now called "letter position dyslexia", in both acquired and developmental cases. Without the insights from dyslexia, we would not know that the two functions are separate; without the model, this letter position dyslexia may not have been sought for and identified, and relevant treatment would not be developed.

2 Model of word reading

Thus, before we can describe the types of developmental dyslexia, each resulting from an impairment in a different component of the reading model, we start by describing the various components of the dual route model for single word reading, the model that is, of all existing reading models, currently most able to explain and predict known types of dyslexia.

Figure 1 depicts the dual route model. According to this model, the first stage that a written word undergoes is early analysis in the orthographic-visual analysis system. This early stage is responsible for the identification of the letters, the encoding of the position of each letter within the word, and binding of letters to words (Coltheart, 1981; Ellis, 1993; Ellis, Flude, and Young, 1987; Ellis and Young, 1988; Humphreys, Evett, and Quinlan, 1990; Peressotti and Grainger, 1995).

The abstract letter identification stage involves identifying the letter. In this stage, a a a a A A 𝒜 ﬡ will all be stripped of their font and size and be identified as the same abstract letter, still without its sound or name. Letter identity is not enough: to read a word like *clam*, for example, the abstract identities of the letters within it would not suffice, because this might lead to reading it as "calm". Therefore, another important function in the early analysis that needs to be performed before access to

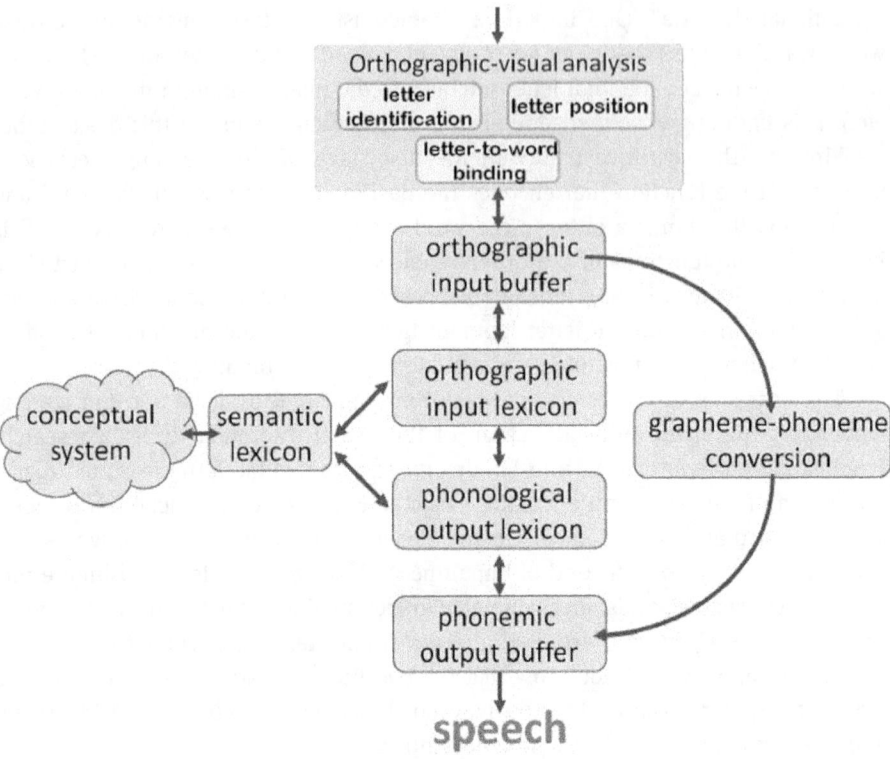

Figure 1: The dual route model for single word reading

the lexicon is letter position encoding. This process encodes the positions of letters in the word, relative to the first and final letter positions.

Reading usually does not involve only a single word, but rather a word in the context of other words. Therefore, another function that is required for correct reading is attenuating the words around the target word, and binding letters with words, allowing for the identification of the letters as part of a specific word.

The output of the orthographic-visual analysis processes is then held in an orthographic short-term store, the orthographic input buffer, until this information can be fully processed by the following components. As a short term memory store, this buffer is sensitive to word length.

Another process that takes place in the pre-lexical stage of word reading, possibly in the orthographic input buffer, is morphological decomposition (Taft, 2015): Words are stored in the orthographic input lexicon decomposed to their stems (for example, the lexicon includes an entry for *bird* and not for *birds*). Therefore, for the words to be identified in the lexicon, they have to be served to the lexicon in a way that it can find them – that is, in a decomposed way. Thus, prior to access to the orthographic input lexicon, morphologically complex words like "birds", "walked", or "ferries" are decomposed to their morphological constituents. The stems (*bird*, *walk*, *ferry*) then activate the relevant entries in the orthographic lexicon, whereas the morphological affixes activate their corresponding entry in a separate morphological output store (probably at the stage of the phonological output buffer, Dotan and Friedmann, 2015), and their relevant meaning, if they have a transparent meaning component (*-s* in *birds* has a transparent plural meaning, whereas *–ment* in *government* is less transparent).

The information in the orthographic buffer is then fed into two routes: the lexical and the sublexical routes. The lexical route allows for quick and accurate reading of known written words; the sublexical route allows reading letter strings that are not part of the lexicons (unfamiliar words or nonwords).

The lexical route starts with the orthographic input lexicon. This lexicon holds entries for words whose written form is known to the reader. It does not contain the meaning or sounds of the words, but it does hold pointers to these representations. This orthographic lexicon is organized by the written frequency of the words, and therefore accessing a more frequent word is faster. This means both that the identification of frequent words as words is faster and also that reading them aloud is faster (compared to words that have similar orthographic and phonological properties but lower frequencies).

To access the phonological form of a written word, the information then flows in the lexical route from the orthographic input lexicon to the phonological output lexicon. The phonological output lexicon holds the phonological information about the sounds of the spoken words the reader knows. It contains information about the consonants and vowels of the word, stress position (in languages where stress is determined lexically), and number of syllables. The direct connection between the orthographic input lexicon and the phonological output lexicon allows the reader to make accurate conversion from a written word to its phonological form in a relatively fast way.

The final stage of the lexical route, which is shared with the sublexical route, is the phonological output buffer. This buffer is a phonological short term component that has two roles: holding the phonological information until it has been fully produced, and assembling units into larger units. The most straightforward units it assembles are the phonemes that arrive from the phonological output lexicon (or from the sublexical route). In this case, phonemes are assembled to create a word. But it is also responsible for assembling other types of building blocks: it unites affixes with their stems to reconstitute morphologically complex words, it assembles number words to create multi-digit numbers, and possibly also assembles syntactic phrases, including the function words within them (Dotan and Friedmann, 2015). The lexical route also includes another branch, which connects the orthographic input lexicon to the conceptual-semantic system. This sub-route allows for the comprehension of written words. The orthographic input lexicon activates the relevant entry in the semantic lexicon, which in turn activates the corresponding concept in the conceptual system. The conceptual system is the a-modal storage of concepts that allows not only for the comprehension of written words, but also for understanding pictures, objects, and heard words. The semantic lexicon is a storage of words, rather than concepts, in which words are organized by their semantic features. (According to some conceptualizations of this lexicon, it does not store words like other lexicons, but rather serves as a hub with pointers from each entry to its phonological, orthographic, and conceptual representations).

Whereas the lexical route is efficient and accurate in reading known words, it is helpless when it comes to words that do not exist in one of the lexicons. In this case, with non-existing words like "lexicof", a different path of reading aloud is required. This different path is provided by the sublexical route, in which reading proceeds via grapheme-to-phoneme conversion. Letters are parsed into graphemes, letters or groups of letters that are the written form of a phoneme. For example, the letters *s* and *h* in "shell" would be parsed as one grapheme, to be converted to a single phoneme, and the same with the double *l* in this word. After this parsing, grapheme-to-phoneme rules are applied sequentially (possibly with separate conversion of consonants and vowels), and the resulting phonemes are gathered in the phonological output buffer, and assembled there to create the full string of a nonword or a new word.

Skilled readers read via all these routes: reading aloud proceeds via the sublexical and lexical-phonological routes, and access to the conceptual-semantic system in the lexical-semantic sub-route is activated for comprehension. However, if the target is a known existing word, reading aloud via the lexical-phonological route is typically quicker than via the sublexical route, and hence the spoken word is principally the result of processing via the lexical route. When the target does not exist in the reader's lexicon, the word is read only via the sublexical route. When the word does exist in the orthographic and phonological lexica, but has low frequency, it will take time to activate its representation in these two lexica, and hence, it might be that it would be read in the same pace through the lexical and sublexical routes, in which case the phonological output buffer would have to deal with results of the two routes together. This would not be problematic when the two routes provide the same output, but when one provides a certain output and the other provides a different output, this may lead to a clash in the phonological output buffer, which may cause delay in reading aloud. This would be the case, for example, in a word like *castles*. The well-informed lexical route would read it with a silent *t*, but the sublexical route would pronounce the *t*.

It seems that the semantic sub-route only partially participates in this party: it is used for comprehension, and for selecting the relevant reading of a heterophonic homograph in sentence context (as in "I shed some *tears* because I found some *tears* in my purple shirt") but it is not a natural route for reading aloud. As we will see below, it is used to read aloud only as a last resort, when there is no other available route.

3 Types of developmental dyslexia

Dyslexias are selective deficits in the various components of the reading model that we have just described, or in the connections between these components. A deficit in each component or connection gives rise to a different pattern of reading difficulty, characterised by different error types and different words that pose most difficulty for the reader. Dyslexias are roughly divided into *peripheral dyslexias*, reading impairments that result from deficits in the orthographic-visual analysis stage, and *central dyslexias*, which are reading impairments in the later stages of the lexical and sublexical routes. We will start by describing the developmental peripheral dyslexias that are currently known, and then proceed to describe the developmental central dyslexias.

3.1 Letter position dyslexia

Encoding of the relative position of letters within the word is one of the functions of the early stage of reading, the orthographic-visual analyzer. Individuals who have a deficit in this function can still identify the letters correctly, but fail to encode the order of the letters within the word. This dyslexia is called *letter position dyslexia* (LPD), and its cardinal symptom is migrations of letters within words. Developmental LPD has been reported for Hebrew, Arabic, English, and has also been identified in Italian and Turkish (for Hebrew: Friedmann, Dotan, and Rahamim, 2010; Friedmann and Gvion, 2005; Friedmann, Gvion, and Nisim, 2015; Friedmann and Rahamim, 2007, 2014; Keidar and Friedmann, 2011; Khentov-Kraus and Friedmann, 2011; Arabic: Friedmann and Haddad-Hanna, 2012, 2014; English: Kohnen et al., 2012; Kezilas et al., 2014; Italian: Luzzatti et al., 2011; Turkish: Güven and Friedmann, 2014). In these languages, the main characteristics of LPD are similar: individuals with LPD tend to transpose letters within words, mainly the middle letters, whereas the first and final letters hardly ever lose their positions. Other properties of LPD are that migration errors occur with both consonants and vowel letters and in both root letters and affixes, and adjacent letters transpose more often than non-adjacent ones. Errors occur in both words and nonwords, and more errors occur when the target word (or nonword) is migratable, namely, when the letter position error creates an existing word. Thus, words like *cloud* (which can be read as "could"), *fried* (fired) and *dairy* (diary) are more difficult in LPD than *clown*, *cried*, and *fairy*; and nonwords like *talbe*, *setps*, and *snig* are harder than nonwords in which a transposition does not create a word. The probability of making a migration error is affected by the relative frequency of the target word and its migration counterpart: there is a higher probability that a child will read *loin* as "lion" than vice versa.

Consider what can account for the lexicality and frequency effects on migration rates in LPD: If the letter position information that arrives from the orthographic-visual analyzer is underspecified for the order of the middle letters, then the input to the orthographic input lexicon would activate an entry that is matching the partial information. In the case of a word like *form*, input that says: "*f* in the beginning, *m* in the end, and in the middle *o* and *r* in some order" would activate both *form* and *from*, and allow for a transposition error to occur. If the target word is *frog* it will only activate *frog*, as, regrettably, the word *forg* does not exist. A similar explanation holds for nonwords: when a nonword like *talbe* is presented, a visual analyser in which letter position encoding is impaired would provide the lexicon information of the identities of the letters, without information about the order of the middle letters. This would activate "table" in the orthographic input lexicon. In contrast, a non-migratable word like *nalbe* would not activate any word in the lexicon, and would hence be read via the sublexical route, which, being sequential, would stand a better chance of correct encoding of letter order. Explaining the effect of frequency follows a similar line: if the word *salt* arrives in the lexicon as "*s* in the beginning, *t* in the end, and in the middle *a* and *l* in some order", because *salt* is much more frequent than *slat* (which means, before you run to your dictionary, a long, thin, flat piece of material), it will be accessed first, and the result will be correct reading (even though the letter positions were not encoded correctly). In contrast, when the word *slat* is presented, again the lexicon would retrieve the more frequent "salt", giving rise to a transposition error.

Another related type of error that individuals with LPD make is omission of doubled letters: for example, they may read *drivers* as "divers", and *baby* as "bay". To account for these errors in individuals with impaired letter position encoding, consider the two *r*'s in *drivers*: they are identical in all properties except for their position within the word. Therefore, a person who cannot encode letter positions would be unable to distinguish between the two instances of *r*, and may omit one of them.

Importantly, not all individuals who make transpositions in reading aloud, such as reading *skate* as "stake", have a reading deficit. Individuals with a deficit in the phonological output buffer may also produce somewhat similar errors when reading aloud. Thus, it is necessary to distinguish between these two possible sources of errors. Distinguishing between them can be done by testing reading without oral production, and testing word and nonword production in tasks that do not involve written input. If the deficit is indeed LPD, a problem in the early stage of reading input, it would also apply to reading tasks that do not involve spoken output but not to spoken output that does not involve reading. Conversely, individuals whose phonological output buffer is impaired would make errors in reading only when they read aloud, would not make errors in silent reading, and would make errors in speaking, even though this involves no written input. Thus, individuals with LPD perform well on word and nonword repetition and in other speech production tasks, and perform poorly on written lexical decision (is *forg* a word?), on written same-different decision task with migratable words (are the two words in the pair *clam* – *calm* the same?), on written word-to-picture matching (is the word *flies* related to a picture of flies or to a picture of files?), and on semantic matching between written words (is *trail* related to a court or to a hike?).

Studies of LPD have also found that text reading is not the best way to identify and diagnose LPD: take, for example, the sentence "Yogurt, feta cheese, and milk are dairy products" even if the letter position encoding fails to encode the order of the letters in "dairy" correctly, semantic considerations may inhibit "diary" in this context, and boost the activation level of "dairy". And indeed, studies that tested migration errors in migratable words presented as single words and in text found that LPD participants make fewer errors when these words are embedded in text (Friedmann and Rahamim, 2007).

Another point relates to whether transpositions result from a general visual problem. In fact, many children with LPD receive the title "impaired eye convergence". Had it been a general visual problem, we would expect them to show the same difficulty in reading numbers and sequences of symbols. However, they do not. In fact, it is very rare to find a person with LPD who also makes migration errors in symbol sequences or numbers (Friedmann, Dotan, and Rahamim, 2010). LPD also does not stem from general attentional disorders. There are children and adults with severe selective attention difficulties whose reading is migration-free, and there are individuals with LPD with no attentional problems (Lukov et al., 2015). Relatedly, Ritalin (Methylphenidate), which is prescribed to individuals with attention disorders and reduces the symptoms of attention deficits in some, has no effect on migrations in reading (Keidar and Friedmann, 2011).

Once diagnosed, LPD can be efficiently treated. For example, Friedmann and Rahamim (2014) found that when children with LPD read while tracing the words letter-by-letter with their finger, the rate of migration errors they make is significantly reduced. Interestingly, colouring each letter in a different colour does not help and may even increase the number of migrations: in this case, the children not only need to bind two features – a letter to its position. They also need to bind another feature – colour – with the letter and with its position.

Knowing the characteristics of this dyslexia is crucial for diagnosing it (and consequently, for treating it efficiently). Without this knowledge, it is easy to miss this dyslexia in some languages. Take for instance the children with LPD reported by Kohnen et al. (2012): they experienced considerable difficulty in reading and their parents and/or teachers were concerned about their reading. However, standard reading tests, which do not include migratable words, failed to detect any difficulty, and classified them as normal readers. It was only once these children were asked to read migratable words – words in which migration of middle letters creates another existing word, that their dyslexia was revealed and diagnosed, and consequently, treated.

This property of LPD, whereby middle-migratable words are the ones that expose the dyslexia, gives rise to cross-linguistic differences in the liability of this dyslexia to be detected. In languages and orthographies in which there are many migratable words (as is the case in Hebrew, for example), LPD will be relatively easily noticed.

In other languages, such as English, a special list of migratable words is needed to detect and diagnose it. Another property of orthographies that interacts with the manifestation of dyslexia in various orthographies is the existence of position-dependent allographs: in Arabic, for example, the same letter takes a different form in different positions within the word. This property has been shown to interact with LPD: letters almost never migrate when their migration would change their allograph (Friedmann and Haddad-Hanna, 2012, 2014). As a result, fewer letter position errors occur in Arabic than in, for example, Hebrew. For diagnosis purposes, this means that in these languages, migratable words in which migration does not change letter form should be presented.

3.2 Attentional dyslexia

A different type of letter migration occurs in a different type of dyslexia, *attentional dyslexia*. In this dyslexia, letters migrate between neighbouring words, but are correctly identified and keep their original relative position within the word. For example, the word pair *cane love* can be read as "lane love" or even "lane cove". Almost all migrations between words preserve the relative position of the migrating letter within the word so that, for example, the final letter in one word migrates into the same position, the final position, in the other word. This indicates that between-word position encoding can be impaired while within-word position encoding remains intact. This point can be seen also in the double dissociation that is found between LPD and attentional dyslexia: there are individuals with LPD without attentional dyslexia, who make letter migrations within words but not between words, and individuals who show the opposite pattern, with letters migrating between, but not within, words (Friedmann, Kerbel, and Shvimer, 2010; Friedmann and Rahamim, 2007; Lukov et al., 2015).

Letter migrations between words occur both horizontally and vertically, namely, letters can migrate from a word that is to the left or to the right or above or below the target word. So far, developmental attentional dyslexia has been reported in Hebrew, Arabic, and English (Friedmann, Kerbel, and Shvimer, 2010; Friedmann and Haddad-Hanna, 2014; Rayner et al., 1989), and it was also detected in Italian and Turkish.

As in LPD, the lexicality of the error response affects the probability that letters will migrate between words: migrations are more likely to occur in attentional dyslexia when the result of migration is an existing word, (both when the target is a word pair and when it is a nonword pair). Other effects relate to the length of the target word and to how similar the two words are: longer words are more liable to migrations between them, and words that differ in only one letter are less liable to migrations than words that differ in more letters. Different positions within the word have different susceptibility to between-word migrations: final letters migrate more than the other letters in the word, and more migrations occur from the first to the second word than vice versa.

Except for migrations between words in which a letter substitutes another letter in the same position in the other word (*light fate* → "fight late"), individuals with attentional dyslexia also make intrusion and elbowing errors, in which a letter migrates to the other word but the letter that has been in the same position in the other word stays. An example for intrusion is, when presented with the pair *light fate*, the *f* migrates to the first position, without deleting the letter that was there, creating "flight late" (or "flight fate"). Letters may also migrate from a word that has recently been viewed and has already disappeared (although this happens to a lesser degree than the migrations from words still seen in the vicinity of the target word). Such "ghost" migrations may be caused by abnormal refresh of the representations of words in the orthographic buffer.

One other type of error that frequently occurs in attentional dyslexia is the omission of one of the instances of a letter that appeared in the same position in the two words (such as reading the word pair *clay plan* as "clay pan"). The reason attentional dyslexics make such omissions can be understood in a way similar to the omission of doubled letters in LPD. In the pair *clay plan*, for example, the only difference between the two *l*'s is the words they belong to. Otherwise, they are identical: they have the same abstract identity and the same within-word position. Individuals with attentional dyslexia fail to bind letters to words, and hence miss the only feature distinguishing between the two letters. Hence, they cannot know that there are two instances of *l*, and they may omit one (Friedmann, Kerbel, and Shvimer, 2010).

Interestingly, migrations between words were also reported in normal reading: already in 1977, Allport discovered that when skilled readers read two (or four) words in very short presentation times, followed by a graphemic mask, they usually manage to identify the letters and their relative position within the words, but still make errors of letter migrations between words (see also Shallice and McGill, 1978; Ellis and Marshall, 1978; Mozer, 1983; and McClelland, and Mozer, 1986). Whereas the phenomenon is superficially similar to the migrations we see in attentional dyslexia, the origins of these migrations are different: in attentional dyslexia they are the result of a failure in the orthographic-visual analyzer in letter-to-word binding, whereas in skilled reading they are the result of two words arriving together in the orthographic input lexicon, activating the letters of the two words, and therefore also words that are composed from these letters (Davis and Coltheart, 2002; Friedmann, Kerbel, and Shvimer, 2010; Shetreet and Friedmann, 2011).

Despite a tempting conclusion to be drawn from its name, attentional dyslexia, like LPD, is not related to a general visuo-spatial attentional deficit. Individuals with attention deficits may show completely normal and migration-free reading, and individuals with attentional dyslexia may have no attention deficits (Lukov et al., 2015). And here too, Ritalin, which improves attention disorders symptoms in individuals with attention disorders, does not affect reading in attentional dyslexia and does not reduce between-word migrations (Keidar and Friedmann, 2011). These considerations makes the name that Shallice and Warrington (1980) selected for this dyslexia slightly confusing (but considering how cumbersome "letter-to-word-binding dyslexia" is, the name remains).

This dyslexia is a wonderful example for how important it is to diagnose each individual with reading difficulties and identify the exact type of developmental dyslexia. Once we know that a child or an adult has trouble reading because "the letters on the page are jumping", as one of our patients described it, helping them is straightforward. Given that the errors originate in neighboring words, once the other words in the area are covered, error rates are magically reduced. In a study of various treatment directions and manipulations on text presentation, Shvimer, Kerbel, and Friedmann (2009) found that reading with a "reading window" – a piece of cardboard with a word-sized window cut in its middle – reduced the general rate of between-word errors in a group of individuals with developmental attentional dyslexia from 31% to 14%, and the rate of between-word migrations dropped from 13% to a mere 4% errors.

What are the predictions for the effect of different orthographies on the manifestation of developmental attentional dyslexia? Again – like in LPD – migratability and letter forms should play a crucial role in this dyslexia: in languages in which the orthographic and morphological structure create a high probability that between-word migrations would create existing words, attentional dyslexia will be more easily detected. If a language has different letter forms when the letters appear after different letters (as is the case in Arabic, for example), some migrations may be blocked, and as a result the between-word migrations rate would be reduced.

3.3 Letter identity dyslexia

Letter identity dyslexia is a deficit in the orthographic-visual analysis, in the function responsible for creating abstract letter identities. It is not a visual deficit, as readers with this dyslexia can still match similar non-orthographic forms, visually match two instances of the same letter in different sizes, and copy letters correctly. However, readers with letter identity dyslexia cannot access the abstract identity of letters from their visual form, so they cannot name a letter, identify a written letter according to its name or sound, or match letters in different cases (Aa). A detailed study of a boy with this type of dyslexia is presented in Brunsdon, Coltheart, and Nickels (2006). This failure to identify letters might result in incorrect identification of letters in isolation, in substitution or omissions of letters within words and non-words, and in "don't know" responses.

Because of the scarcity of reports on this type of developmental dyslexia, it remains to be seen whether *associative visual letter agnosia* is the same type of dyslexia or a separate entity. Associative visual letter agnosia is a difficulty in identifying letters from sight, with preserved ability to identify letters from motion (moving the finger on the lines of the written letter) or touch (for example, holding and feeling the various sides of a plastic form of the letter or a letter-shaped cookie, or having the letter written on the palm of the hand). It currently seems that the main difference between letter agnosia and letter identity dyslexia is that letter agnosia only affects access from the visual modality into the orthographic-visual analyser, but abstract letter identity, if accessed through another modality, is preserved. Letter identity dyslexia, on the other hand, is a deficit in abstract letter identity.

3.4 Neglect dyslexia

Neglect dyslexia has gained considerable attention in the literature of acquired dyslexia, where it has been thoroughly studied with a large number of individuals in several languages (see Vallar, Burani, and Arduino, 2010 for a review). Developmental left neglect dyslexia has been reported only in Hebrew (Friedmann and Nachman-Katz, 2004; Nachman-Katz and Friedmann, 2007, 2008, 2009, 2010) and Arabic (Friedmann and Haddad-Hanna, 2014). Developmental right neglect dyslexia has been identified in Turkish (Güven and Friedmann, 2014). Hemi-spatial neglect relates to the phenomenon of difficulty to report or attend to stimuli on one side of the visual field, typically, the left side. Neglect dyslexia refers to a similar difficulty in reading. Several types of neglect dyslexia are known from the literature on acquired neglect dyslexia. One classification refers to the level at which the neglect occurs: at the word level, where letters on the neglected side of the word are omitted, substituted, or added, and at the sentence or text level, where whole words on the neglected side of the sentence are omitted. It seems that neglect dyslexia at the sentence or text level is part of the effects of visuo-spatial neglect (Haywood and Coltheart, 2001), whereas neglect dyslexia at the word level may be an orthographic-specific deficit, independent of general visuo-spatial attention. Neglect dyslexia is further classified by the side that is neglected, with far more occurrences of left neglect than right neglect.

The only pattern that has been described so far for developmental neglect dyslexia is neglect dyslexia at the word level (neglexia). Readers with neglect dyslexia at the word level neglect one side of the word, typically the left side. Neglecting one side of a word results in omissions, substitutions, or additions of letters on that side of the word, which occur more frequently when the result is an existing word. Because this deficit is at the early, prelexical stage, written word comprehension and lexical decision on written nonwords are affected by neglexia (so that *rice* may be taken to be frozen water, and *gice* may be judged as an existing word).

Developmental neglexia can be orthographic-specific, affecting only letter strings but not symbol strings, and even not number sequences. A dramatic demonstration of the selectivity if neglexia to orthographic material was provided by Friedmann and Nachman-Katz (2008): they presented to children with neglexia sequences in leet characters (Perea, Duñabeitia, and Carreiras, 2008), i.e., characters that can be perceived either as numbers or as letters: For example, 7109179 in Hebrew is "professor"; 816 8055 can be read in English, with some effort, as "big boss". The children with neglexia made neglect errors when instructed to read these words in a word list, but when the same list of stimuli was presented with the instruction "please read these numbers", they made almost no neglect errors.

Data from acquired neglexia indicate that the neglected side of the word is more sensitive to neglect errors when it is part of an affix, and is almost never omitted when it is part of the base or root (Reznick and Friedmann, 2009). It is still unknown if readers with developmental neglexia, whose reading acquisition is marred by their neglexia, develop the normal morphological abilities necessary for morphological decomposition. If they do, they might show the same morphological effect as individuals with acquired neglexia on neglect errors.

Once developmental neglect dyslexia is identified, it can be treated effectively. Nachman-Katz and Friedmann (2010) evaluated different treatment directions, and found that manipulations on the text that attract attention to the left of the word may reduce neglect errors in reading considerably. The group of 20 participants with developmental neglexia who made 42% neglect errors in reading words without any manipulation made only 20% such errors when they traced the word letter-by-letter with their left hand index finger, 23% neglect errors when they tapped with their left finger to the left of the word, 27% when a small blinking lamp was placed to the left of the word they read, and 28% when a coloured vertical line was placed to the left of the word. Vertical presentation of the target words and presentation of the word with a double space between the letters were also useful, reducing error rates from 42% in normal presentation to 30% and 21%, respectively.

Such effects on reading can also assist the distinction between errors on the left that result from limitation of the orthographic input buffer and neglexia. Vertical presentation, tapping with the finger to the left of the word and adding symbols to the left of the word should not affect the reading of a reader with a limited buffer, but do affect reading in neglexia.

The way reading in neglexia may interact with orthography relates, like the dyslexias we described before, to the chances that a relevant error would create an existing word. Thus, languages with dense orthographic neighbourhoods, in which a substitution, omission, or addition of letters on the left of the word has a high probability of creating another existing word would give rise to more neglect errors. The reading direction also affects the manifestation of neglexia, as in languages read from left to right, left neglexia would affect the beginning of words, and in right-to-left languages it would affect their ends. Reading direction may also affect the rate of errors in another way: if, as is typically the case, shifting of attention to the left is impaired, reading in right-to-left orthographies may be more impaired than reading in left-to-right ones.

3.5 Visual dyslexia/orthographic input buffer dyslexia

Visual dyslexia was originally defined, in Marshall and Newcombe's (1973) article and later, as a deficit in the orthographic-visual analysis stage that causes reading the target word as a visually similar word, with errors of substitutions, omissions, migrations, and additions of letters. Marshall and Newcombe themselves said that "There are, no doubt, subtypes of visual dyslexia corresponding to the specific nature of the visual impairment". And indeed, there are. As we have seen already, there are types of dyslexia that result from selective deficits in the orthographic-visual analyser and present specific types of errors (such as letter position errors in LPD, between-word migrations in attentional dyslexia, letter substitutions in letter identity dyslexia), we suggest that a reading impairment should be classified as visual dyslexia only if it cannot be accounted for by a specific deficit in the orthographic-visual analyser such as letter position dyslexia, attentional dyslexia, letter identity dyslexia, or neglexia.

Visual dyslexia, which is distinct from these other impairments of the orthographic-visual analyser, is a deficit in the output of the orthographic-visual analyser. As a result, this dyslexia affects all functions of the orthographic-visual analyser: letter identification, letter position within the word, and letter-to-word binding. Therefore, it involves letter identity errors and letter migrations within and between words.

Distinguishing between visual dyslexia and a selective impairment in each of the functions of the orthographic-visual analyser is easy: visual dyslexia can be distinguished from letter identity dyslexia in that letter identity dyslexia only involves letter substitutions and omissions, but not letter migrations within and between words. Similarly, visual dyslexia can be distinguished from LPD (it involves also letter substitutions and omissions, and letter migrations between words, and not just letter migrations within words), from attentional dyslexia (as it involves also letter substitutions and omissions and letter migrations within words, and not just between-word migrations), and from neglexia (errors occur on all sides of the word, not only on one side).

A somewhat harder task is to distinguish between visual dyslexia and an impairment that affects several functions of the orthographic-visual analyser together. There are not many reports of this type of developmental dyslexia, but it seems that the pattern of errors is slightly different: unlike in LPD, migrations within words in visual dyslexia occur in exterior letters as well as in middle letters (visual dyslexia will see errors like was-saw, letter position dyslexia will not).

Furthermore, it is still an open question whether visual dyslexia and *graphemic buffer dyslexia* are the same dyslexia. Graphemic buffer dyslexia is characterized by all types of errors that we described above for visual dyslexia, it is affected by length, with significantly more errors in longer than in shorter words, and morphological affixes show increased vulnerability: when presented with a morphologically complex word, individuals with graphemic buffer dyslexia often keep the base or the root and omit or substitute the morphological affixes (Sternberg and Friedmann, 2007, 2009). It is also the case that whereas they make letter substitutions and omissions in reading words (and nonwords), they identify single letters correctly.

Like in cases of transposition within and between words, when an individual makes errors that are typical for visual dyslexia or graphemic buffer dyslexia, it is important to make sure that the errors indeed result from an input deficit and do not result from a phonological output deficit. To do so, one should look at reading without oral output and spoken production without written input.

3.6 Surface dyslexia

So far, we have described dyslexias that result from an impairment in the orthographic-visual analysis stage. We now move to describe central developmental dyslexias: impairments in later stages of reading, in the lexical and sublexical routes.

Surface dyslexia is a deficit in the lexical route, which forces the reader to read words aloud via the sublexical route, through grapheme-to-phoneme conversion instead of through the lexical route. Such reading causes several types of problems in reading. Firstly, individuals with surface dyslexia make regularisation errors in reading aloud. This is evident in their reading of irregular words such as *stomach*, *receipt*, or *comb*, which include a silent letter, or a letter that is converted to a phoneme that is different from the phoneme that the grapheme-to-phoneme conversion rules dictate. Surface dyslexia may also affect their reading of words that allow for ambiguous conversion to phonology, such as *bear* (which may be read via the grapheme-to-phoneme conversion route as "beer"). Words that have ambiguous conversion typically include poly-phonic graphemes that can be converted in two or more ways into phonemes. Such words are mainly problematic in surface dyslexia when the poly-phonic graphemes are converted, in the specific word, into the less frequent phoneme (like the letter *i*, which is pronounced one way in *kid* and another way in *kind*). Sublexical reading may also be problematic in words with more than one syllable in languages in which stress is lexically determined and not marked orthographically, and in languages in which not all vowels are specified in the orthography, as is the case in Hebrew and Arabic.

The accurate oral reading of such irregular and unpredictable words requires access to lexical, word-specific knowledge. Such information is stored in the lexical route, in the orthographic input lexicon, so when reading aloud via this lexicon is impossible, these words are liable to be read incorrectly. In contrast, regular words for which there is only one possible reading via the sublexical route, which leads to the correct pronunciation, are read correctly, even if they are infrequent.

Individuals who have pure surface dyslexia, where only the lexical route is impaired, have intact sublexical route, and they are therefore able to read nonwords normally (see Castles, Bates, and Coltheart, 2006, for a discussion of the notion of pure dyslexias).

Surface dyslexia affects not only the accuracy of reading aloud: at least for some individuals with surface dyslexia, those whose orthographic input lexicon is impaired, comprehension is also affected. Consider how comprehension can be achieved via the sublexical route. Take for example the written form *taksi*: this is probably not an entry in your orthographic input lexicon, but you can nevertheless understand it. The way in which the comprehension of such items proceeds is via the sublexical route, which generates a nonword in the phonological output buffer based on grapheme-to-phoneme conversion. The phoneme sequence in the phonological output buffer is then produced in inner speech and thus can access the conceptual-semantic system through the phonological input components, the phonological input buffer and the phonological input lexicon. This is the route that individuals with surface dyslexia use to understand words they read that they cannot recognize orthographically: orthographic-visual analyser, grapheme-to-phoneme conversion, phonological output buffer, phonological input buffer, phonological input lexicon, semantic lexicon, conceptual system.

Now, this long and winding road could achieve correct comprehension of words like *dog* or *paper*, but would be dubious once the word is homophonic. Consider, for example, reading a homophonic word like *wail*. Individuals who read it via the sublexical route and then understand it through the input phonological route would not be able to distinguish *wail* from *whale* and hence have difficulties understanding such homophones. Similarly, *which* and *witch*, which sound the same when read via the sublexical route, can only be distinguished on the basis of their separate entries in the orthographic input lexicon, so an individual with an impaired orthographic input lexicon would not be able to distinguish between them.

A class of words that are specifically difficult for readers with surface dyslexia are words that, when read via the grapheme-to-phoneme conversion route, can result in another existing word. We call these words "*potentiophones*". Many individuals with developmental surface dyslexia develop a tendency to monitor their production and try to produce only existing words. This tendency may also be supported by feedback from the phonological output lexicon, which is only provided to responses that are words that exist in the phonological output lexicon. This tendency is definitely useful for avoiding errors in reading words like *listen, sword, stomach, build,* and *door*, but what about words like *bear, now,* and *none*? In these cases, reading via the sublexical route might end up with other existing words that sound like "beer", "know", and "known".

Finally, beside the problems in accuracy and in comprehension, surface dyslexia results in slower-than-normal reading. Even in cases in which reading via the sublexical route results in an accurate oral reading of the word, as is the case with words like *sport, dog,* and *mark*, the process of sequentially converting each letter into its corresponding phoneme in the sublexical route is slower than reading the whole word via the lexical route (Spinelli et al., 1997; Zoccolotti et al., 1999).

Surface dyslexia is defined as a deficit in the lexical route. The lexical route is a multi-component route, and a deficit in each of these components or in the connections between them can yield surface dyslexia. Importantly, whereas all the deficits in the lexical route result in reading aloud via the sublexical route and hence in inaccurate and slow reading aloud, each of these deficits gives rise to a different pattern of surface dyslexia (Friedmann and Lukov, 2008; Gvion & Friedmann, 2016). Let's consider the possible loci of deficit in the lexical route that would cause a reader to read aloud via the sublexical route: one is the orthographic input lexicon (or the access to it from the orthographic-visual analyser). In this case, not only reading aloud would be affected but also lexical decision of pseudohomophones (the reader will have difficulty determining whether *anser* is a word or not). They will also have difficulties in the comprehension of homophones and potentiophones (and hence will not know whether *whether* is a question word or something that has to do with rain and temperature). Another possibility is that the orthographic input lexicon itself is intact, but its output connections to the semantic lexicon and to the phonological output lexicon are impaired. In this case, lexical decision will be fine but comprehension of homophones will be impaired. Another type of surface dyslexia is interlexical surface dyslexia, where the connection between the orthographic input lexicon and the phonological output lexicon is impaired. In this case both lexical decision and homophone comprehension will be fine, and only reading aloud would be affected. Finally, a deficit in the phonological output lexicon would also force the reader to read aloud via the sublexical route but no problems are expected in lexical decision or homophone comprehension. In the case of phonological output lexicon deficit, word production is impaired not only in the context of reading, but also in naming and in spontaneous speech.

These different types of surface dyslexia dictate different treatment approaches. In the case of interlexical surface dyslexia, it would probably be enough to recommend to the child to stop reading aloud (and to his teachers to stop asking him to read aloud). When the orthographic input lexicon is impaired, one may work on filling the lexicon by repeated exposure to words, by intensive reading (a recommendation that most children with developmental dyslexia do not like to hear), and by linking the written form of the word with its phonological form (for example, looking at the book while a parent is reading and pointing to the word they read while uttering it). Alongside the attempts to rehabilitate the impaired lexical route, treatment can also aim to strengthen the grapheme-to-phoneme conversion rules, including the second tier (multiletter) rules and explicit teaching of morphological orthographic rules.

The properties of surface dyslexia, indicating its sensitivity to homophonicity and regularity, dictate its interactions with various orthographies: Languages with no homophonic letters have better chances of being read correctly, even via the sublexical route. In contrast, readers with surface dyslexia who read languages with many degrees of freedom in reading via the sublexical route: poly-phonic letters, underrepresentation of vowels and stress pattern, and silent letters are liable to make many more errors in reading. In languages with predictable grapheme-to-phoneme conversion like Italian, it is often stress position and reading rate that are the most sensitive markers for surface dyslexia (Zoccolotti et al., 1999).

3.7 Phonological dyslexia

Phonological dyslexia is the mirror image of surface dyslexia: here, the sublexical route is impaired, and reading can only proceed via the lexical route. The defining symptom of phonological dyslexia is the difficulty in reading nonwords, which appears alongside correct reading of words that are stored in the orthographic input lexicon.

Individuals with phonological dyslexia cannot read new words, only words that are already in their orthographic input lexicon (and phonological output lexicon). As one can imagine, this may pose a critical problem for children who have this dyslexia before they begin reading: in their case – every written word is a new word, and no word can be read through the lexical route. These individuals with developmental phonological dyslexia take much longer to learn to read. They usually start mastering reading in second or third grade, when they start having enough whole words in their orthographic input lexicon to allow them to read. They usually encounter this severe difficulty again when they learn to read in a new language.

Such pattern is a result of a deficit in the sublexical route, and it can result from impairments at various points in this route. The most basic type of phonological dyslexia (though it seems not to be the most frequent type) is a deficit in the conversion of single letters into phonemes.

Such impairment would be evident not only in reading nonwords, but also when single letters are presented. Individuals with this type of phonological dyslexia, letter-to-phoneme *conversion phonological dyslexia*, fail even when they try to sound out single letters.

A different type of phonological dyslexia, *multiletter phonological dyslexia*, involves the more complex rules of conversion, which apply to more than a single letter. Such multiletter or context-sensitive rules in English would be for example the rule that dictates how to pronounce the "sh" in *ship* and the "ch" in *chip*; the rule that dictates the way *a* is pronounced in *mate*, which is different from the way it is pronounced in *mat*; and the way the pronunciation of *c* is affected by the following vowel, as in *city* and *cell* versus *care*, *core*, and *cure*. Multiletter phonological dyslexia does not affect the pronunciation of single letters, but can be detected when multiletter graphemes are read. Such multiletter deficit can either result from a deficient parsing of letters into multiletter graphemes or from a deficient conversion of multiletter graphemes (or letters within certain multi-letter contexts) into phonemes. These two sources for multiletter phonological dyslexia may be very difficult to discern, especially in the case of developmental dyslexia (see Marshall and

Newcombe, 1973, for a description of letter-to-phoneme conversion and multiletter phonological dyslexias).

Yet another type of phonological dyslexia, which is a relatively frequent one, is a deficit that does not affect the conversion itself but rather the next stage, in which the phonemes that are the products of the conversion are stored for a short time and assembled into a whole word or a nonword (see e.g., Temple and Marshall, 1983; and Campbell and Butterworth, 1985, for case studies of two young women with developmental phonological dyslexia that probably resulted from such a deficit). The component that is responsible for receiving the output of the conversion, blending it and holding it until its production is complete, is the phonological output buffer. In the case of *phonological-output-buffer-phonological-dyslexia,* no errors are expected in reading single letters or single graphemes. The deficit shows a clear length effect, with longer words and nonwords showing more errors than shorter ones. This type of phonological dyslexia affects nonwords more gravely than words because whereas words can get boosted by activation from the phonological output lexicon, nonwords cannot. Thus, for example, reading aloud of a long nonword such as *elomatod* may crash and give rise to omissions, substitutions, and transpositions of some of the phonemes, but the same reader may still read correctly *elevator,* a word with the same structure and the same number of phonemes. This is because once these phonemes arrive at the phonological output buffer, they activate the corresponding entry in the phonological output lexicon, which, in turn, resonates and reciprocates by adding activation to the existing word (see the double-sided arrow in Figure 1).

Because the phonological output buffer is responsible not only for assembling phonemes of nonwords, but also for assembling morphologically complex words, individuals with phonological output buffer phonological dyslexia often show a deficit in reading morphologically complex words, often omitting or substituting the non-base morphemes. Importantly, because the phonological output buffer is part of the speech production system, and not only responsible for reading, individuals with phonological buffer dyslexia show difficulties with long nonwords and morphologically complex words not only when they read them, but also when they repeat or spontaneously say them (Dotan and Friedmann, 2015).[1]

Therefore, to distinguish between the different types of phonological dyslexia and understand why a child has difficulties reading nonwords, one should not only ask the child to read words and nonwords but also test single letter reading, multi-letter rule knowledge, and repetition of long nonwords.

---

[1] In some languages and in some cases, several responses are possible readings of a nonword: this is the case with a nonword like *knuint* in English, multi-syllable nonwords in which the stress position is not specified, and with most nonwords in which the vowels are not fully specified in languages like Hebrew and Arabic. In these cases, any of the possible conversions would count as correct reading of the nonword, whereas consonant substitutions and omissions that violate grapheme-to-phoneme conversion rules, for example, would count as incorrect reading.

Treatment of the different types of phonological dyslexia should be different: for conversion phonological dyslexia, treatment should focus on explicit teaching of letter-to-phoneme conversion rules. For multi-letter phonological dyslexia, treatment should focus on explicit teaching of multi-letter conversion rules. Individuals with phonological output buffer dyslexia, on the other hand, may benefit from breaking the target word into smaller units, such as syllables or consonant-vowel units, when reading. At the same time, individuals with all types of phonological dyslexia would benefit from enriching their lexicons, which will allow them to read more words via the unimpaired lexical route.

3.8 Vowel letter dyslexia

The sublexical route can also be affected selectively. *Vowel dyslexia* results from a specific deficit in the sublexical route that selectively impairs the way the sublexical route processes vowels (Khentov-Kraus and Friedmann, 2011). Individuals with vowel dyslexia omit, substitute, transpose, and add vowel letters. Thus, the word *bit* can be read as "bat", "but" or even "boat". These errors occur in reading, without parallel errors in speech production, and they affect vowel *letters* rather than vowel phonemes.

Because it is a deficit in the sublexical route, individuals whose only dyslexia is vowel dyslexia have difficulties only when they read nonwords and new words, but they can still read correctly via the lexical route. If, however, the reader has both vowel dyslexia and surface dyslexia, then he will be forced to read even existing words via the sublexical route, and will therefore make vowel errors also in real words.

This developmental dyslexia has been reported so far for Hebrew, Arabic, Italian, and Turkish, and it occurs more frequently in words in which a vowel letter error results in an existing word. As a result it is more prominent in orthographies that allow for vowel letter omissions or transpositions, such as Hebrew and Arabic, in which words can include sequences of consonants, and in orthographies with dense orthographic neighbourhoods.

We discussed before the interaction between letter form and letter position errors: in letter position dyslexia, letter transpositions do not occur if they change letter forms. The story is different in the case of vowel dyslexia, as it affects a stage that is beyond the orthographic-visual analyser: in both Hebrew and Arabic, an error in the grapheme-to-phoneme conversion that places a vowel in an incorrect position, occurs at a stage that is no longer sensitive to the form of the letter, and vowel errors can occur even when they cause a change in letter form.

Additional selective deficits in converting certain features in the sublexical route have been reported for acquired dyslexia, and have been witnessed also in developmental cases, but not yet reported in detail. Such dyslexias are for example the selective deficit in the voicing feature (*dyzlegzia*, Gvion and Friedmann, 2010), and a deficit in the nasality feature (*nasalexia*, Gvion and Friedmann, 2012).

3.9 Deep dyslexia

The main characteristic of *deep dyslexia*, which is its defining feature, is the production of semantic errors in reading, such as reading the written word *lime* as "lemon" or "sour". Other error types that are common in deep dyslexia are morphological (reading *played* as "play", *birds* as "bird", and *smiles* as "smiling"), and visual errors (*clay* as "play", *owl* as "own" and *gum* as "game"). Cases of developmental deep dyslexia have been reported by Johnston (1983), Siegel (1985), Stuart and Howard (1995), and Temple (1988, 1997) for English, and by Friedmann and Haddad-Hanna (2014) for Arabic.

Within the dual route model, this reading pattern was interpreted as multiple lesions in both the sublexical grapheme-to-phoneme conversion route and in the direct lexical route between the orthographic input lexicon and the phonological output lexicon, which force the reader to read via meaning (Ellis and Young, 1988).

This double deficit gives rise to grading of difficulty of various types of words. Basically, words that can be read correctly via their meaning (possibly via visual imagery of the target word) would be the words that are most accurately read by individuals with deep dyslexia. Reading of nonwords, on the other hand, is very severely impaired. When children with deep dyslexia are asked to read nonwords, they either declare that they cannot read these words or lexicalise them – reading them as similar existing words (reading *diger* as "tiger", for example).

Other words that are difficult to imagine, such as function words and abstract words are also affected. When asked to read function words, individuals with deep dyslexia substitute the target word for another function word, substitute it with a visually similar concrete word, or just say that these are words they cannot read. For the same reason, imageability plays a crucial role in reading accuracy in this dyslexia, with imageable and concrete words being read better than abstract words (Coltheart, 1980; Coltheart, Patterson, and Marshall, 1987; Marshall and Newcombe, 1973).

Morphologically complex words are also very difficult to read in this developmental dyslexia, and individuals with this dyslexia substitute or omit morphological affixes when they read morphologically complex words. This could be a result of the imageability effect (try to visually imagine *smiled*. The –ed just vanishes in the process), and it could also result from the process of reading in this dyslexia. Recall that words in the lexicons are represented by their bases, stems or roots, whereas the morphological affixes may be read through a direct route from the orthographic input buffer to the phonological output buffer. If this is the case, and the direct route is impaired, reading of affixes can be severely compromised, whereas the bases can be read better.

This type of dyslexia is especially difficult in its developmental form, because filling the orthographic lexicon and establishing its connection to the phonological output lexicon and the conceptual-semantic system are very difficult given that the deficit in the sublexical route and between the lexicons is present in the time of reading acquisition. A further difficulty relates to the fact that as in acquired deep dyslexia, individuals with developmental deep dyslexia often also show syntactic deficits, and hence, find it harder to rely on sentence context to read words correctly.

Several points of interaction are imaginable between developmental deep dyslexia and the orthography that the reader reads in. Given the specific difficulty in morphologically complex words, languages in which words are more morphologically complex are expected to be more difficult to read. Another interesting interaction was reported in the case of diglossic languages.

In Arabic, for example, the situation is that the spoken language is different from the written, standard language in all respects: syntactically, lexically, morphologically, and phonologically. As a result, reading via naming, in which a child sees a word, understands it, and then names it based on its meaning or visual image, creates a situation in which words written in standard Arabic are read in the spoken vernacular (for example, the developmental deep dyslexic boy FA, reported in Friedmann and Haddad-Hanna, 2014, read the standard Arabic word *dar*, house, as "bet", its spoken counterpart, and *tabib*, a medical doctor in Standard Arabic, as "daktor".

4 Access to semantics dyslexia

Dyslexia can also appear in a somewhat surprising form, whereby reading is fluent and accurate. This is the case of *access to semantics dyslexia*, sometimes termed "direct dyslexia". Individuals with this dyslexia can read aloud all kinds of words, including irregular words, low frequency words, function words, and morphologically complex words. They can also read nonwords and new words accurately. However, they cannot understand written words, even those they can read aloud correctly. The correct reading aloud indicates that the lexical route between the orthographic input lexicon and the phonological output lexicon is preserved in these individuals and so is the sublexical route (Castles, Crichton, and Prior, 2010). This pattern can stem either from a deficit in the access from the orthographic input lexicon to the semantic lexicon or from a deficit in the conceptual/semantic system itself. If the deficit is in the conceptual/semantic system, either in the semantic lexicon or in the conceptual system, we would probably not call it dyslexia, but rather a semantic deficit. In this case, these individuals would also have trouble understanding words they hear, and not only words they read. A semantic deficit would also involve impairments in speech production, with semantic errors, in the case of a semantic lexicon impairment, or unrelated words, in the case of a deficit in the conceptual system (Howard and Gatehouse, 2006; Nickels, 1995, 1997; Nickels and Howard, 1994; Friedmann, Biran, and Dotan, 2013).

A deficit that is more specific to reading, and that would more comfortably fit into the label "dyslexia", is a disconnection between the orthographic input lexicon and the semantic lexicon. Such deficit does not affect reading aloud of single words or nonwords, and does not affect the comprehension of heard words or the production of words. It does, however, affect the comprehension of written words. If the reader does not understand the words he reads, this may also cause incorrect prosody in reading sentences aloud, and incorrect reading aloud of heterophonic homographs. Think, for example, about reading a sentence like "I shed some *tears* because I found some *tears* in my purple shirt" – access to semantics is required in order to select the correct reading of each heterophonic homograph and hence, such sentences are expected to be read incorrectly in semantic access dyslexia.

Clearly, such dyslexia can result in what educators call "reading comprehension difficulties" – when comprehension of single written words fail, one can be sure that the comprehension of sentences and texts would fail as well. Notice, however, the opposite is not true: not all children who have problems in the comprehension of sentences and text have semantic access dyslexia. In fact, in most cases it is their syntactic ability that is impaired, causing impaired comprehension of the sentences with complex syntactic structures (Friedmann and Novogrodsky, 2007; Szterman and Friedmann, 2014). Limited vocabulary can also give rise to reading comprehension difficulties, and so do general attention deficits that prevent the readers from focusing on the text they are reading.

One final note: whereas some researchers call this dyslexia "hyperlexia", we do not recommend using this term. After all, it is not that reading is too good in these individuals; it is their comprehension that is too poor.

5 A note about the relative frequencies of the various types of developmental dyslexia

As we have seen, different types of dyslexia have different properties. Specifically, they are sensitive to different aspects of the presented stimuli. Letter position dyslexia, for example, is manifested mainly in migratable words, namely, words in which a letter position error creates another existing word. Individuals with attentional dyslexia make errors only when several words are presented together. Individuals with surface dyslexia make errors on words that, when read via the sublexical route, can be read in several ways, and are most prone to make errors on words that, when read via grapheme-to-phoneme conversion, can create other existing words. Individuals with phonological output buffer dyslexia can read existing short words well, but have difficulties reading long words, nonwords, and morphologically complex words, etc. This has far-reaching implications for the diagnosis of the various types of dyslexia: if the relevant stimuli for a certain type of dyslexia are not presented, this dyslexia can be missed. A test without migratable words may miss letter position dyslexia, a test that only presents single words in isolation (or word pairs that do not allow for letters that migrate between them to create other existing words) may miss attentional dyslexia, a test with only regular words may miss surface dyslexia, and a test with short, morphologically simple, existing words will miss phonological buffer dyslexia. Additionally, if only reading rate is scored but not error types, certain dyslexias will be missed and it will be impossible to detect them, and, given that reading rate can only yield the distinction between slow and quick, there will be no way to detect the 19 types of dyslexia. (Additionally, slow reading rate does not necessarily indicate dyslexia, as it can result from various general cognitive problems, from attentional difficulties, articulation problems, and more). The current situation is that most standard tests do not include the relevant stimuli to detect all kinds of dyslexia, and are therefore not sensitive to many of the dyslexia types. Typically, they include regular and irregular words, and nonwords. This would allow for the detection of surface dyslexia and phonological dyslexia (without identifying the specific subtypes of these dyslexias), but not the other types of dyslexia. As a result, we usually do not know how frequent the other types of dyslexia are, and this makes it impossible to make any statements about the relative incidences of the different forms of developmental dyslexia.

We do have some insights from Hebrew, where a test that is sensitive to the various types of dyslexia, including the peripheral ones (Tiltan, Friedmann and Gvion, 2003), has been administered in the past 15 years, and some data has accumulated as to the relative frequency of the various types of dyslexia in Hebrew. An analysis of the reading of 465 individuals with developmental dyslexia (Friedmann & Khentov-Krauss, 2016) showed that the most frequent dyslexia in Hebrew is surface dyslexia, followed by letter position dyslexia and vowel letter dyslexia, and the fourth most common developmental dyslexia is attentional dyslexia. Dyslexias that occurred in lower frequencies were (in order of frequency): left neglect dyslexia, visual dyslexia, phonological output buffer dyslexia, dyzlegzia, deep dyslexia, and letter agnosia.

A recent study (Lukov et al., 2014) that tested the attentional abilities and dissociations between attention disorders and dyslexias reported on 83 participants with dyslexia who were tested with the Tiltan battery, and their types of dyslexia were identified accordingly and reported. They showed a similar distribution, where letter position dyslexia is the most frequent dyslexia, followed by surface dyslexia, vowel letter dyslexia, and attentional dyslexia (which occurred in similar rates). To know more about the distribution of types of dyslexia in other languages, tests that are sensitive to the various types of dyslexia should be developed and administered to a large number of participants with dyslexia.

6 Conclusion

The classification of types of developmental dyslexia has theoretical, as well as clinical and educational implications.

One of the most important theoretical implications regards the source of developmental dyslexia. When one considers the multi-faceted nature of developmental dyslexia, and the fact that impairments in different components of the reading process give rise to dyslexias with completely different properties and error types, it becomes evident that one source cannot account for all kinds of developmental dyslexia. Therefore, dyslexia cannot be a deficit in phonological abilities (as claimed by, e.g., Snowling, 1998, but see Coltheart and Jackson, 1998, in the same dyslexia forum), because many types of dyslexia are unrelated to phonology. Examining the various types of dyslexia, one can see that only dyslexias that affect the phonological stages, predominantly certain types of phonological dyslexia, may be related to phonology (see Blomert and Willems, 2010; Castles and Coltheart, 2004, and Castles and Friedmann, 2014, for discussions of this hypothesis). Similarly, dyslexia does not necessarily come with a lexical retrieval deficit (cf. Wolf and Bowers, 1999, for a review). Surface dyslexia that arises from a deficit in the phonological output lexicon does, but most other dyslexias, such as those that result from a deficit in the orthographic-visual analyser, and even other subtypes of surface dyslexia (see Zoccolotti et al., 1999; Friedmann and Lukov, 2008), do not. It is also impossible to determine that developmental dyslexia is a visual deficit (e.g., Stein and Walsh, 1997; Bosse et al., 2007), for two reasons – one is that not all dyslexias result from an orthographic-visual analyzer impairment. Phonological and surface dyslexias, for example, do not. Namely, whereas visual impairments can impede reading, not all dyslexias result from visual impairments. Moreover, even the dyslexias that result from an orthographic-visual analyzer impairment do not result from a visual or attentional impairment. It is often the case that the impairment is selective to orthographic material and does not apply to reading numbers and symbol sequences (Friedmann et al., 2010; Lukov et al., 2015).

Another theoretical contribution of the study of types of dyslexia is its contribution to understanding the cognitive model of reading. The interaction between neuropsychology of reading impairment and the characterization of the reading process is fruitful for both sides. For example, identifying the selective deficit in vowel reading in the sublexical route sheds light on the grapheme-to-phoneme conversion process, suggesting a separate treatment for vowel and consonant letters. In the other direction, letter position dyslexia was identified because the cognitive reading model assumed a letter position encoding function and the prediction for a selective deficit in letter position encoding drove the search for individuals with such a dyslexia.

Finally, the different sources of the various types of dyslexia dictate different treatment directions and different approaches for reading instruction to each of them. Reading with a reading window strikingly improves reading in attentional dyslexia, but does not affect reading in surface dyslexia, deep dyslexia, phonological dyslexia, or letter position dyslexia. Silent reading is a recommended path for individuals with interlexical surface dyslexia but not for those whose surface dyslexia results from a deficit in the orthographic input lexicon. Knowing the different ways the reading process can break down and understanding the properties of each type of dyslexia allows the development and application of focused treatment directions that are tailored to the specific errors and source of each type of developmental dyslexia.

Louis Pasteur once remarked "In the fields of observation chance favors only the prepared mind." (Pasteur, 1854). This is nowhere truer than in the study of developmental dyslexia. In discussing his reported cases of developmental dyslexia, Hinshelwood (1900) observed "I have but little doubt that these are by no means so rare as the absence of recorded cases would lead us to infer. Their rarity is, I think, accounted for by the fact that when they do occur they are not recognised. It is a matter of the highest importance to recognise the cause and the true nature of this difficulty in learning to read which is experienced by these children, otherwise they may be harshly treated as imbeciles or incorrigibles and either neglected or flogged for a defect for which they are in no wise responsible. The recognition of the true character of the difficulty will lead the parents and teachers of these children to deal with them in the proper way, not by harsh and severe treatment, but by attempting to overcome the difficulty by patient and persistent training."

With a mind prepared to identify and diagnose the various types of developmental dyslexia that we already know, and to detect new types of dyslexia that can result from impairments in the reading process that we have not encountered yet, we will be able to help such children and adults with developmental dyslexia, as well as advance the theoretical knowledge in this field.

References

Allport, D. Alan. 1977. On knowing the meaning of words we are unable to report: The effects of visual masking. In S. Dornic (ed.), *Attention and performance VI*, 505–533. Hillsdale, NJ: Erlbaum.

Beauvois, Marie-France & J. Dérouesné. 1979. Phonological alexia: Three dissociations. *Journal of Neurology, Neurosurgery and Psychiatry* 42 (12). 1115–1124.

Blomert, Leo & Gonny Willems. 2010. Is there a causal link from a phonological awareness deficit to reading failure in children at familial risk for dyslexia? *Dyslexia* 16. 300–317.

Boder, Elena. 1968. Developmental dyslexia: A diagnostic screening procedure based on three characteristic patterns of reading and spelling. A preliminary report. In Malcolm P. Douglas (ed.), *Claremont Reading Conference, 32nd Yearbook* 173. Claremont, CA: Claremont University Center.

Boder, Elena. 1969. Developmental dyslexia: A diagnostic screening procedure based on reading and spelling patterns. *Intervention in School and Clinic* 4. 285–287.

Boder, Elena. 1970. Developmental dyslexia: A new diagnostic approach based on the identification of three subtypes. *Journal of School Health* 40. 289–290.

Boder, Elena. 1971. Developmental dyslexia: Prevailing diagnostic concepts and a new diagnostic approach. In Helmer R. Myklebust (ed.), *Progress in learning disabilities, Vol. 2*, 293. New York: Grune and Stratton.

Boder, Elena. 1973. Developmental dyslexia: A diagnostic approach based on three atypical reading-spelling patterns. *Developmental Medicine and Child Neurology* 15. 663–687.

Bosse, Marie-Line, Marie Josèphe Tainturier & Sylviane Valdois. 2007. Developmental dyslexia: the visual attention span deficit hypothesis. *Cognition* 104. 198–230.

Brunsdon, Ruth, Max Coltheart & Lyndsey Nickels. 2006. Severe developmental letter processing impairment: A treatment case study. *Cognitive Neuropsychology* 23. 795–821.

Campbell, Ruth & Brian Butterworth. 1985. Phonological dyslexia and dysgraphia in a highly literate subject: A developmental case with associated deficits of phonemic processing and awareness. *The Quarterly Journal of Experimental Psychology Section A: Human Experimental Psychology* 37 (3). 435–475.

Castles, Anne, Timothy Bates & Max Coltheart. 2006. John Marshall and the developmental dyslexias. *Aphasiology* 20 (9). 871–892.

Castles, Anne & Max Coltheart. 2004. Is there a causal link from phonological awareness to success in learning to read? *Cognition* 91. 77–111.

Castles, Anne, Alison Crichton & Margot Prior. 2010. Developmental dissociations between lexical reading and comprehension: Evidence from two cases of hyperlexia. *Cortex* 46 (10). 1238–1247.

Castles, Anne & Naama Friedmann. 2014. Developmental dyslexia and the phonological deficit hypothesis. *Mind and Language* 29 (3). 270–285.

Coltheart, Max. 1980. Deep dyslexia: A review of the syndrome. In Max Coltheart, Karalyn Patterson & John C. Marshall (eds.), *Deep dyslexia*, 22–47. New York: Routledge & Kegan Paul.

Coltheart, Max. 1981. Disorders of reading and their implications for models of normal reading. *Visible Language* 15. 245–286.

Coltheart, Max & Nancy Ewald Jackson. 1998. Defining dyslexia. *Child Psychology and Psychiatry Review* 3 (1). 12–16.

Coltheart, M., Patterson, K., & Marshall, J. 1987. Deep dyslexia since 1980. In Max Coltheart, Karalyn Patterson & John C. Marshall (eds.), *Deep dyslexia*, 407–451. London: Routledge & Kegan Paul. (Original work published 1980.)

Davis, Colin J. & Max Coltheart. 2002. Paying attention to reading errors in acquired dyslexia. *Trends in Cognitive Sciences* 6. 359–361.

Dérouesné, J. & Marie-France Beauvois. 1979. Phonological processing in reading: Data from alexia. *Journal of Neurology, Neurosurgery & Psychiatry* 42 (12). 1125–1132.

Dotan, Dror & Naama Friedmann. 2015. Steps towards understanding the phonological output buffer and its role in the production of numbers, morphemes, and function words. *Cortex* 63. 317–351.

Ellis, Andrew W. 1993. *Reading, writing, and dyslexia: A cognitive analysis* (2nd edn.) London: Erlbaum.

Ellis, Andrew W., Brenda M. Flude & Andrew W. Young. 1987. "Neglect dyslexia" and the early visual processing of letters in words and nonwords. *Cognitive Neuropsychology* 4. 439–463.

Ellis, Andrew W. & John C. Marshall. 1978. Semantic errors or statistical flukes? A note on Allport's "On knowing the meaning of words we are unable to report." *Quarterly Journal of Experimental Psychology* 30. 569–575.

Ellis, Andrew W. & Andrew W. Young. 1988. *Human cognitive neuropsychology*. Hove: Erlbaum.

Friedmann, Naama, Michal Biran & Dror Dotan. 2013. Lexical retrieval and breakdown in aphasia and developmental language impairment. In Cedric Boeckx & Kleanthes K. Grohmann (eds.), *The Cambridge handbook of biolinguistics*, 350–374. Cambridge, UK: Cambridge University Press.

Friedmann, Naama & Aviah Gvion. 2001. Letter position dyslexia. *Cognitive Neuropsychology* 18. 673–696.

Friedmann, Naama & Aviah Gvion. 2005. Letter form as a constraint for errors in neglect dyslexia and letter position dyslexia. *Behavioural Neurology* 16. 145–158.

Friedmann, Naama, Aviah Gvion & Roni Nisim. 2015. Insights from developmental and acquired letter position dyslexia on morphological decomposition in reading. *Frontiers in Human Neuroscience* 9 (143).

Friedmann, Naama & Manar Haddad-Hanna. 2012. Letter position dyslexia in Arabic: From form to position. *Behavioural Neurology* 25 (3). 193–203.

Friedmann, Naama & Manar Haddad-Hanna. 2014. Types of developmental dyslexia in Arabic. In Elinor Saiegh-Haddad & R. Malatesha Joshi (eds.), *Handbook of Arabic literacy: Insights and perspectives. Language and Literacy Series*, 119–152. The Netherlands: Springer.

Friedmann, Naama & Lilach Khentov-Kraus. 2016, February. The distribution of developmental dyslexias in Hebrew. Presented at the 3rd Conference on Cognition Research of the Israeli Society for Cognitive Psychology. Akko, Israel.

Friedmann, Naama & Limor Lukov. 2008. Developmental surface dyslexias. *Cortex* 44 (9). 1146–1160.

Friedmann, Naama & Ivana Nachman-Katz. 2004. Developmental neglect dyslexia in Hebrew reading child. *Cortex* 40. 301–313.

Friedmann, Naama & Rama Novogrodsky. 2007. Is the movement deficit in syntactic SLI related to traces or to thematic role transfer? *Brain and Language* 101. 50–63.

Friedmann, Naama & Einav Rahamim. 2007. Developmental letter position dyslexia. *Journal of Neuropsychology* 1. 201–236.

Friedmann, Naama & Einav Rahamim. 2014. What can reduce letter migrations in letter position dyslexia? *Journal of Research in Reading* 37 (3). 297–315.

Friedmann, Naama, Dror Dotan & Einav Rahamim. 2010. Is the visual analyzer orthographic-specific? Reading words and numbers in letter position dyslexia. *Cortex* 46. 982–1004.

Friedmann, Naama, Noa Kerbel & Lilach Shvimer. 2010. Developmental attentional dyslexia. *Cortex* 46. 1216–1237.

Güven, Selçuk & Naama Friedmann. 2014. *Types of developmental dyslexia in Turkish*. Unpublished ms. Tel Aviv University and DILKOM, Eskisehir.

Gvion, Aviah & Naama Friedmann. 2010. Dyscravia: Voicing substitution dysgraphia. *Neuropsychologia* 48. 1935–1947.

Gvion, Aviah & Naama Friedmann. 2012. Nasalexia: when bat xen becomes man xed, and marak taim becomes barak naim. Paper presented at the 48th annual conference of the Israeli Speech Hearing and Language Association, Tel Aviv.

Gvion, Aviah & Naama Friedmann. 2016. A principled relation between reading and naming in acquired and developmental anomia: Surface dyslexia following impairment in the phonological output lexicon. *Frontiers in Psychology: Language Sciences* 7 (340). 1–16. doi: 10.3389/fpsyg.2016.00340.

Haywood, Marina & Max Coltheart. 2001. Neglect dyslexia with a stimulus-centered deficit and without visuospatial neglect. *Cognitive Neuropsychology* 18. 577–615.

Hinshelwood, James. 1896. Word-blindness and visual memory. *The Lancet* 147. 196.

Hinshelwood, James. 1900. Congenital word-blindness. *The Lancet* 155. 1506–1508.

Howard, David & Claire Gatehouse. 2006. Distinguishing semantic and lexical word retrieval deficits in people with aphasia. *Aphasiology* 20. 921–950.

Humphreys, Glyn W., Lindsay J. Evett & Philip T. Quinlan. 1990. Orthographic processing in visual word identification. *Cognitive Psychology* 22. 517–560.

Johnston, Rhona S. 1983. Developmental deep dyslexia? *Cortex* 19 (1). 133–139.

Johnson, Doris J. & Helmer R. Myklebust. 1967. *Learning disabilities: Educational principles and practices*. New York: Grune & Stratton.

Keidar, Rakefer, & Naama Friedmann. 2011. Does methylphenidate help readers with letter position dyslexia and attentional dyslexia? *Language and Brain* 10. 195–214.

Kezilas, Yvette, Saskia Kohnen, Meredith McKague & Anne Castles. 2014. The locus of impairment in English developmental letter position dyslexia. *Frontiers in Human Neuroscience* 8 (356). 1–14.

Khentov-Kraus, Lilach & Naama Friedmann. 2011. Dyslexia in vowel letters. *Language and Brain* 10. 65–106.

Kohnen, Saskia, Lyndsey Nickels, Anne Castles, Naama Friedmann & Genevieve McArthur. 2012. When 'slime' becomes 'smile': Developmental letter position dyslexia in English. *Neuropsychologia* 50 (14). 3681–3692.

Lukov, Limor, Naama Friedmann, Lilach Shalev, Lilach Khentov-Kraus, Nir Shalev, Rakefet Lorber & Revital Guggenheim. 2015. Dissociations between developmental dyslexias and attention deficits. *Frontiers in Psychology* 5. 1–18.

Luzzatti, Claudio, Paola Angelelli & Naama Friedmann. 2011. *Types of developmental dyslexia in Italian*. Unpublished Ms., Università degli Studi di Milano-Bicocca, Milano, Tel Aviv University, Tel Aviv, and Universita di Bari, Bari.

Marshall, John C. 1984a. Toward a rational taxonomy of the acquired dyslexias. In Rattihalli N. Malatesha & Harry Whitaker (eds.), *Dyslexia: A global issue*, 211–232. The Hague: Martinus Nijhoff.

Marshall, John C. 1984b. Toward a rational taxonomy of the developmental dyslexias. In Rattihalli N. Malatesha & Harry Whitaker (eds.), *Dyslexia: A global issue*, 45–58. The Hague: Martinus Nijhoff.

Marshall, John C. & Freda Newcombe. 1966. Syntactic and semantic errors in paralexia. *Neuropsychologia* 4. 169–176.

Marshall, John C. & Freda Newcombe. 1973. Patterns of paralexia: A psycholinguistic approach. *Journal of Psycholinguistics Research* 2. 175–199.

McClelland, James L. & Michael C. Mozer. 1986. Perceptual interactions in two-word displays: Familiarity and similarity effects. *Journal of Experimental Psychology: Human Perception and Performance* 12. 18–35.

Mozer, Michael C. 1983. Letter migration in word perception. *Journal of Experimental Psychology: Human Perception and Performance* 9. 531–546.

Myklebust, Helmer R. 1965. *Development and disorders of written language: Picture story language test*. New York: Grune and Stratton.

Nachman-Katz, Ivana & Naama Friedmann. 2007. Developmental neglect dyslexia: Characteristics and directions for treatment. *Language and Brain* 6. 75–90. (In Hebrew).

Nachman-Katz, Ivana & Naama Friedmann. 2008. Developmental neglect dyslexia and its effect on number reading. *Language and Brain* 7. 83–96. (In Hebrew)

Nachman-Katz, Ivana & Naama Friedmann. 2009. Writing words in developmental neglect dyslexia. *Language and Brain* 9, 119–141. (In Hebrew).

Nachman-Katz, Ivana & Naama Friedmann. 2010. An empirical evaluation of treatment directions for developmental neglect dyslexia. *Procedia Social and Behavioral Sciences* 6. 248–249.

Nickels, Lyndsey. 1997. *Spoken word production and its breakdown in aphasia*. Hove: Psychology Press.

Nickels, Lyndsey. 1995. Getting it right – Using aphasic naming errors to evaluate theoretical models of spoken word recognition. *Language and Cognitive Processes* 10. 13–45.

Nickels, Lyndsey & David Howard. 1994. A frequent occurrence – factors affecting the production of semantic errors in aphasic naming. *Cognitive Neuropsychology* 11. 289–320.

Pasteur, Louis. 1854/1954. The spirit of science. In H. Peterson (Ed.), *A treasury of the world's great speeches*. New York: Simon And Schuster.

Perea, Manuel, Jon Andoni Duñabeitia & Manuel Carreiras. 2008. R34D1NG W0RD5 W1TH NUMB3R5. *Journal of Experimental Psychology: Human Perception and Performance* 34. 237–241.

Peressotti, Francesca & Jonathan Grainger. 1995. Letter position coding in random consonant arrays. *Perception and Psychophysics* 57. 875–890.

Rayner, Keith, Loraa A. Murphy, John M. Henderson & Alexander Pollatsek. 1989. Selective attentional dyslexia. *Cognitive Neuropsychology* 6. 357–378.

Reznick, Julia & Naama Friedmann. 2009. Morphological decomposition in the early stages of orthographic-visual analysis: Evidence from neglexia. *Language and Brain* 8. 31–61. (In Hebrew)

Shallice, Tim. 1981. Neurological impairment of cognitive processes. *British Medical Bulletin* 37 (2). 187–192.

Shallice, Tim & Janina McGill. 1978. The origins of mixed errors. In J. Requin (ed.), *Attention and Performance VII*, 193–208. Hillsdale, NJ: Erlbaum.

Shallice, Tim & Elizabeth K. Warrington. 1977. The possible role of selective attention in acquired dyslexia. *Neuropsychologia* 15. 31–41.

Shallice, Tim & Elizabeth K. Warrington. 1980. Single and multiple component central dyslexic syndromes. In Max Coltheart, Karalyn Patterson & John C. Marshall (eds.), *Deep dyslexia*, London: Routledge & Kegan Paul.

Shetreet, Einat & Naama Friedmann. 2011. Induced letter migrations between words and what they reveal about the orthographic-visual analyzer. *Neuropsychologia* 49 (3). 339–351.

Shvimer, Lilach, Noa Kerbel & Naama Friedmann. 2009. An empirical evaluation of various treatment directions in developmental attentional dyslexia. *Language and Brain* 8. 87–118. (in Hebrew)

Siegel, Linda S. 1985. Deep dyslexia in childhood? *Brain and Language* 26. 16–27.

Snowling, Margaret. 1998. Dyslexia as a phonological deficit: Evidence and implications. *Child Psychology and Psychiatry Review* 3 (1). 4–11.

Spinelli, Donatella, Paola Angelelli, Maria De Luca, Enrico Di Pace, Anna Judica & Pierluigi Zoccolotti. 1997. Developmental surface dyslexia is not associated with deficits in the transient visual system. *NeuroReport* 8 (8). 1807–1812.

Sternberg, Terri & Naama Friedmann. 2007. Developmental graphemic buffer dyslexia. *Language and Brain* 6. 91–96. (In Hebrew)

Sternberg, Terri & Naama Friedmann. 2009. Are there separate graphemic buffers for reading and writing? *Language and Brain* 9. 105–117. (In Hebrew)

Stuart, Morag, and David Howard. 1995. KJ: A developmental deep dyslexia. *Cognitive Neuropsychology* 12. 793–824.

Stein, John & Vincent Walsh. 1997. To see but not to read: the magnocellular theory of dyslexia. *Trends in Neuroscience* 20. 147–152.

Szterman, Ronit & Naama Friedmann. 2014. Relative clause reading in hearing impairment: Different profiles of syntactic impairment. *Frontiers in Psychology: Language Sciences* 5 (1229) 1–16.

Taft, Marcus. 2015. The nature of lexical representation in visual word recognition. In Alexander Pollatsek & Rebecca Treiman (eds.), *Oxford handbook of reading*. New York: Oxford University Press.

Temple, Christine M. 1988. Red is read but eye is blue: A case study of developmental dyslexia and follow-up report. *Brain and Language* 34. 13–37.

Temple, Christine M. 1997. *Developmental cognitive neuropsychology*. Hove: Psychology Press.

Temple, Christine M. & John C. Marshall. 1983. A case study of developmental phonological dyslexia. *British Journal of Psychology* 74 (4). 517–535.

Vallar, Giuseppe, Cristina Burani & Lisa S. Arduino. 2010. Neglect dyslexia: A review of the neuropsychological literature. *Experimental Brain Research* 206. 219–235.

Wolf, Maryanne, and Patricia Greig Bowers. 1999. The double-deficit hypothesis for the developmental dyslexias. *Journal of Educational Psychology* 91. 415–438.

Zoccolotti, Pierluigi, Maria De Luca, Enrico Di Pace, Anna Judica, Marco Orlandi & Donatella Spinelli. 1999. Markers of developmental surface dyslexia in a language (Italian) with high grapheme–phoneme correspondence. *Applied Psycholinguistics* 20. 191–216.

Rachel Schiff, Eli Vakil, Yafit Gabay and Shani Kahta
36 Implicit learning in developmental dyslexia as demonstrated by the Serial Reaction Time (SRT) and the Artificial Grammar Learning (AGL) tasks

1 Introduction

Developmental Dyslexia (DD) is characterized by non-fluent word identification and poor spelling performance, which are not the result of sensory impairments, impairments in intelligence, or inadequate educational experience (American Psychiatric Association, 2013; Pennington, 2009). Despite extensive research, the underlying biological and cognitive causes of DD remain under debate, depending on the criteria used to assess the severity of reading difficulty (Fletcher, 2009).

Three major theoretical frameworks were identified in a recent review of more than 1500 references on DD (Démonet et al., 2004). The mainstream hypothesis, i.e. *The Phonological Deficit Hypothesis* (Snowling, 2000), implicates a deficit of direct access to, and manipulation of, phonemic language units retrieved from the long-term declarative memory. This account has been supported by numerous studies which indicate a phonological deficit in DD (Vellutino et al., 2004). However, individuals with DD exhibit difficulties which are not restricted to the language domain. For example, they may also suffer from motor procedural learning impairments (Folia et al., 2008) as well as sensory processing deficits (Stein and Talcott, 1999). The major limitation of the *Phonological Deficit Hypothesis* is its inability to account for these additional impairments. Supporters of this account acknowledge the co-occurrence of these additional impairments along with the phonological deficit but do not see them as playing a casual role in the etiology of DD (Ramus et al., 2003). Nevertheless, the wide range of DD difficulties has led researchers to search for other, more basic deficits than reading which may underlie DD (Nicolson and Fawcett, 1990; Stein and Walsh, 1997).

The *Magnocellular Theory* of DD is unique in its ability to account for all other manifestations of DD (Stein and Walsh, 1997). This account is based on the observation that there are two visual pathways leading information from the eyes to the visual cortex: the magnocellular/parvocellular systems. The magnocellular system is thought to transmit visual and auditory information quickly, whereas the parvocellular system is more important for details. According to the *Magnocellular Theory*, the magnocellular pathway is selectively disrupted in individuals with DD, leading

---

Rachel Schiff, Eli Vakil, Yafit Gabay and Shani Kahta, Bar-Ilan university

DOI 10.1515/9781614514909-037

to visual/auditory perceptual deficits as well as difficulties in visuospatial attention via the posterior parietal cortex (see also Vidyasagar, 1999). Support for this account comes from studies which demonstrated impaired performance of DD individuals on a variety of tasks which tap magnocellular functions (for reviews see Laycock and Crewther, 2008; Stein, 2001) as well as from studies which demonstrated a direct link between reading and magnocellular dorsal stream measures (Kevan and Pammer, 2009). Nevertheless, the validity of this account is still hotly debated, mainly due to nonspecific or irreducible findings (for example, Amitay, Ben-Yehudah, Banai, and Ahissar, 2002; Stuart, McAnally, and Castles, 2001). Furthermore, the proportion of individuals with DD that exhibit motor and sensory disorders is relatively low in relation to phonological deficits (Ramus et al., 2003).

Finally, according to *the Automaticity Deficit Hypothesis* (Nicolson and Fawcett, 1990) which was later modified to the *Cerebellum Deficit Hypothesis (R. I. Nicolson, Fawcett, and Dean, 2001)*, DD children will suffer from problems in fluency for any skill that should become automatic through extensive practice. This hypothesis accounts neatly for the problems in acquiring phonological skills, in reading, in spelling, and in writing. In terms of behavior, that means that a process can be characterized as automatic, if it is executed fluently, less influenced by cognitive demands, and more resistant to interference. According to this framework, for most skills, individuals with DD learn to mask their incomplete automatization by a process of 'conscious compensation', thereby achieving apparently near-normal performance, at the expense of greater effort (*the Conscious Compensation Hypothesis*; R. I. Nicolson and Fawcett, 1994). The brain region candidate which has been proposed by Nicolson and Fawcett to underlie the cognitive automatization deficit was the cerebellum, leading to difficulties in the acquisition and automatizing of cognitive and motor skills. This framework was recently modified to its current form, *Specific Procedural Learning Difficulties (R. I. Nicolson and Fawcett, 2011)* according to which DD arises specifically from impaired performance of the procedural learning system for language. This defect stems from damage to one of the brain areas related to this system (such as the prefrontal cortex around Broca's area, the parietal cortex and sub-cortical structures including the basal ganglia and the cerebellum).

In this paper, we assume the third theory that claims that people with DD are impaired in implicit learning (Nicolson and Fawcett, 1990). Implicit learning refers to a learning process by which we acquire knowledge of the regularities of the learning environment in a passive way, and possibly without awareness (Pothos, 2007). We show that reading impairments in DD mainly reflect a deficit in general capacity for statistical learning. In other words, individuals with DD have difficulty picking up and assimilating the statistical properties and systematic patterns of a structured environment. The current paper demonstrates the deficient general capacity for statistical learning in individuals with DD using two implicit sequence learning paradigms: the Serial Reaction Time (SRT), and Artificial Grammar Learning (AGL). Our aim is to show that the pattern of findings that emerges from studies investigating dyslexic performance on implicit skill learning (as reflected in the SRT) and implicit sequence learning (as reflected in the AGL) helps us identify the nature of deficits that underlies DD.

2 Implicit learning

The term "implicit learning" refers to the unconscious acquisition of new information. It is defined as an unintentional and automatic process that results in knowledge that is difficult to verbalize completely (Reber, 1967). It is typically used to characterize situations where a person learns about the structure of a complex stimulus without necessarily intending to do so (Berry and Dienes, 1993; Reber, 1967). Studies examining implicit learning found that participants were able to abstract and recognize generalized regularities and patterns in presented stimuli without explicit knowledge about these regularities. It has been suggested that this ability may be a prerequisite for acquiring language (Brown, 1973; Pinker, 1994) and for learning linguistic skills such as reading and writing, since this ability is needed for building a system of linguistic categories and 'rules' or generalizations. Since these linguistic skills exhibit much regularity, it is conceivable that contact with such a system will induce implicit learning (Gombert, 2003).

It has already been shown that children are able to detect patterns in real or artificial languages at a very early age by using distributional information such as transitional probabilities. The detection of such distributional patterns may result in skills as diverse as phonetic categorization in infants aged 0:6 (Maye, Werker, and Gerken, 2002), syntactic category formation in children aged 6:1 (Gerken, Wilson, and Lewis, 2005), and sensitivity to lexical orthographic regularities that have not been explicitly taught (Gombert, 2003; Habib, 2000). This pattern sensitivity depends partly on a sequential analysis of distributional information, such as the number of occurrences of elements or the sequential co-occurrence relations among them. The importance of implicit learning to reading is bolstered by connectionist modeling simulations of reading. According to connectionist models (Harm and Seidenberg, 1999; Seidenberg and McClelland, 1989), some initial orthography- phonology connections may be 'taught' explicitly. However, the majority of such learning occurs through coincidence detection of probabilistic properties in the input, and is thus implicit (Sperling, Lu, and Manis, 2004).

Some researchers claim that a deficit in implicit learning may lead to difficulty in learning to read often displayed among individuals with DD (Bennett, et al., 2008; Folia, et al., 2008; Gabay et al., 2012; Pavlidou, Kelly, and Williams, 2010). According to this view, dyslexia is associated with a deficit in extracting statistical regularities from transient input, and affects language as well as other domains (Kerkhoff, De Bree, De Klerk, and Wijnen, 2013). Individuals with DD may have difficulties in acquiring a variety of language skills such as reading, writing, spelling, as well as reading sub-skills such as word identification and phonological decoding (Vellutino, Fletcher, Snowling, and Scanlon, 2004). Studies investigating implicit learning among individuals with DD suggested that this weakness in implicit learning may be narrowed down to paradigms that involve sequential processing (Bennett, et al., 2008; Folia, et al., 2008; Howard, Howard, Japikse, and Eden, 2006; Menghini, Hagberg, Caltagirone, Petrosini, and Vicari, 2006; Russeler, Gerth, and Monte, 2006; Stoodley, Harrison, and Stein, 2006).

3 The Serial Reaction Time (SRT)

A commonly-used task for studying skill learning is the Serial Reaction Time task – SRT (Nissen and Bullemer, 1987). In this task, participants are presented with a visual stimulus in one of several discrete locations and are requested to make a rapid key press corresponding to the stimulus location. Unknown to the participants, the stimuli appear in a repeated sequence and learning of the sequence is indicated by a decreased reaction time across blocks or as a difference between reaction time to sequence and random (or a different sequence) blocks (Seger, 1998). There is a clear evidence of learning irrespective of the participants' conscious awareness to the repeated sequence.

The process of skill acquisition begins with the first exposure to the task, known as acquisition phase or fast learning phase. This phase requires a training interval involving repeated engagement with the procedure being learned (Rattoni and Escobar, 2000), and is accompanied by fast improvements in performance that can be seen within seconds to minutes. The improvements during initial task practice follow a curve and performance gradually reaches an asymptote (i.e., power function). At the brain level, this phase is presumably too fast for extensive structural change, which involve the synthesis of new proteins and the formation of new synapses. Instead, disinhibition or "unmasking" of already existing cortical connections may be the common mechanism underlying acquisition (Walker, 2005). This phase actually reflects the creation of a fragile and unstable mental representation for the task.

A slow learning phase is believed to evolve following successful completion of acquisition, in which slow improvements in performance may be seen within hours or days. This phase involves a consolidation process, a process whereby a newly formed memory becomes increasingly less susceptible to interference (Walker, 2005). Consolidation in the procedural domain relates to two behavioral stages: (1) *Consolidation-based stabilization (CBS)* and, (2) *Consolidation-based enhancement (CBE)*. CBS can be described as a reduction in the fragility of a memory trace after the acquisition of a novel skill (Robertson, Pascual-Leone, and Miall, 2004), which can be seen in the loss of an acquired skill, if an individual immediately attempts to acquire a skill in another task. However, if time elapses between the acquisition of the first skill and training in the second, the amount of interference decreases

(Goedert and Wilingham, 2002). This process, in which memory traces become more stable, takes place within six hours following the initial acquisition. At this stage, behavioral performance is maintained and is not improved. Nonetheless, different patterns of regional brain activation can be developed, indicating a change in the neural representation of the skill (Shadmehr and Holocomb, 1997). Further behavioral improvement can be seen in an additional stage named CBE. During this stage, additional learning takes place in the absence of any further rehearsal or experience. These additional improvements are named *offline learning* and are accompanied by synaptic and structural changes in the brain. Offline learning occurs after a period of night sleep, although additional offline enhancement may occur within several days. Furthermore, it appears that offline learning depends on the amount of practice being given during the entailment practice (Hauptman, Reinhart, Brandt, and Karni, 2005). Following consolidation, the learned skill reaches automaticity (Stickgold and Walker, 2005). In this context, automaticity refers to a shift from controlled performance to a more efficient performance (i.e., is faster, less variable, less vulnerable to interference and with fewer errors) with reduced demands on attention (Shiffrin and Schneider, 1977) and a corresponding shift in brain networks that support performance (Jueptner and Weiller, 1998).

One of the advantages of the SRT task is that several sequence-learning measures could be extracted from it. First is learning rate, which is reflected in reduction in reaction time (RT) across training blocks when the same sequence is presented repeatedly. In addition to the sequence-specific learning, this measure reflects a more generalized skill learning (e.g., mapping the specific response to the specific stimulus position) (Ferraro, Balota, and Connor, 1993; Knopman and Nissen, 1987). Second is indirect sequence learning measured as the increase in RT when a block with a random or different sequence is presented compared to the previous repeated sequence.

The SRT task has been studied extensively in DD in order to examine motor procedural learning. Several studies have revealed impairment in sequence learning among adults with DD as measured by the SRT task (Howard, Howard, Japikse, and Eden, 2006; Menghini, Hagberg, Caltagirone, Petrosini, and Vicari, 2006). These studies point to a deficit in the acquisition stage of sequence learning in DD individuals. This online deficit may be attributed to differences in the processes involved in sequence learning. These processes include the "reaction-time-task learning", as defined by Knopman and Nissen (1987). This process is regarded as related to proficiency in execution of the SRT task (e.g., mapping the specific response to the specific stimulus position). It is argued that individuals with DD failed to show significant decrease in RT during the first session, since they were impaired in general learning ability. Therefore, the practice given to them is not sufficient to produce a reduction in reaction time during the initial stage of learning. This suggests that DD stems mainly from a deficit in the procedural learning system.

In a study that was designed to examine whether this impaired acquisition was attributed to a lack of automatization, Gabay, Schiff and Vakil (2012a) tested a skill learning task in DD and normal readers using a dual task paradigm. The impact of dual task costs on participants' performance was used as an indication of automaticity. Participants completed a sequence-learning task over a first session (acquisition) and a second session 24 hours later (consolidation,) when half of them are under a full attention condition and another half is under a divided attention condition. Results showed delayed acquisition of the motor skill in the DD group compared to normal readers. This study highlights that the differential effect of divided attention on acquisition and consolidation of procedural skill in DD and normal readers, supports the automaticity deficit hypothesis in DD.

Investigating implicit learning among individuals with dyslexia, who are characterized by language learning difficulties, raises the question whether the nature of the stimuli in the learning process might be an influential factor in the process of sequence learning. The study by Simoës-Perlant and Largy (2011) is the first to examine the effect of the nature of the SRT stimuli on performance of dyslexic children by manipulating the items being tracked, rendering them linguistic or nonlinguistic. Their results revealed sensitivity to the nature of the target in sequence learning among children with dyslexia, pointing to differences in the evolution of the response times according to the item being tracked. Their findings suggest that sequence learning among individuals with DD is related to the nature of stimuli rather than an indication of a more general deficit in procedural learning.

Another interesting study exploring the nature of the stimuli by Gabay, Schiff and Vakil (2012b) focused on letter names and motor sequence learning in participants with DD and control participants. Both groups completed the SRT task which enabled the assessment of learning of letter names and motor sequences independently of each other. Results showed that control participants learned both the letter names as well as the motor sequence. In contrast, individuals with DD were impaired in learning the letter names sequence and showed a reliable transfer of the motor sequence. While previous studies established that motor sequence learning is impaired in DD, finding of the abovementioned study indicate dissociation between letter names and motor sequence learning in individuals with DD. Specifically, it was found that both groups showed transfer when spatial locations and manual responses followed a repeated sequence. In contrast, only controls showed a reliable transfer when the letter names sequences followed a repeated pattern, while the DD group failed to show this expected increase. These results indicate that individuals with DD have greater difficulty in the procedural learning of letter names sequences. This impairment may be largely a direct consequence of an underlying dysfunction of the procedural learning system of language.

Data as to implicit learning efficiency or inefficiency among dyslexic children and adults is not yet complete. More studies using different age groups, modalities, and tasks are required for a substantiation of the specific procedural learning difficulties as the core deficit of DD. Another often used implicit learning task is AGL. Important differences of the two tasks concern the motor requirements and the postulated role of the cerebellum for learning.

4 Artificial Grammar Learning (AGL)

AGL examines the learning of symbol sequences generated by a finite state language (Pothos, 2007; Reber, 1967, 1993). A finite state language is a set of rules that indicate which symbol sequences are legal, or grammatical (G), as opposed to illegal, or non-grammatical (NG). In a typical AGL experiment, participants are first presented with a subset of the G sequences as letter strings in a training part, and are asked to observe them, but no other information is provided about the nature of the strings or about what would be required of them. They are then told that the strings they see are all complied to form a set of rules and are asked to identify the novel legal ones, in a set that contains both legal and illegal strings. The extensively replicated finding is that participants can identify the new G sequences with above chance accuracy, while they are largely unable to fully articulate the knowledge on which they based their decisions (Pothos and Kirk, 1994).

Research using the AGL paradigm among children with DD reveals a significantly lower performance among dyslexic than among typically developing readers (Pavlidou et al., 2009; Pavlidou and Williams, 2010; Pavlidou, Kelly, and Williams, 2010; Pavlidou and Williams, 2014). Children with DD are consistently found impaired in their implicit learning abilities, when the complexity of the learning situation is increased and irrespective of the implicit task in use and the stimulus characteristics. For example, Pavlidou et al. (2010) explored implicit learning in a group of TD and DD primary school children nine to twelve years of age using an AGL task. Performance was calculated using two measures of performance: a perfect free recall (PFR) score and a grammaticality judgment score. Findings showed that children with DD, compared to TD children, failed to show implicit learning irrespective of the substring characteristics. This poor performance of reading impaired children on the AGL task raise the hypothesis that implicit learning deficits may not be limited to sequence learning but could also extend to learning mechanisms that abstract rules and could account for some of the reading problems encountered in DD.

Indeed, Pavlidou and Williams (2014) addressed this hypothesis of rule abstraction by testing TD and children with DD on a transfer task, in which the testing items were composed of a different shape set than the one used to create the training set, but the grammar rules remained the same. Their assumption was that if children are deeply learning a grammar, then they should be able to transfer this learning to a novel setting, and this would strengthen the claim that AGL learning requires the abstraction of rules alongside the acquisition of item specific knowledge. Their experiments show that implicit learning is impaired in children with DD regardless of the type of task and/or the stimulus characteristics, as they have difficulties in abstracting higher-order information across complex stimuli.

Studies with adult participants yield contradictory findings. While some studies found no deficit in AGL tasks (Photos and Kirk, 2004; Rüsseler, Gerth and Munte,

2006), Kahta and Schiff (2016) found a lower performance among dyslexic readers than among typically developing TD adults. The performance of adults with DD and TD readers was compared for endorsement rates and for classification rates. Findings showed that while the TD group exceeded chance level in both the transfer and the non-transfer conditions, the DD group exceeded chance level under the non-transfer condition, but failed to do so under the transfer condition, endorsing a borderline classification rate of 56% of the strings. This finding strengthens the conclusion that individuals with DD rely more heavily on surface characteristics of the stimuli, with no evidence of undergoing abstractive processing (Kahta and Schiff, 2016).

Methodological differences might account for the discrepancy between the findings as AGL experiments vary in the level of the grammar system complexity used. In an extensive meta-analysis study, Schiff and Katan (2014) demonstrated the effect of grammar complexity on performance, so that much of the discrepancy in the results of the different AGL studies can be explained by taking into consideration the complexity of the grammar used. By computerizing Bollt and Jones's (2000) technique of calculating topological entropy (TE), a quantitative measure of AGL charts' complexity, Schiff and Katan (2014) examined the association between grammar systems' TE and learners' AGL task performance. Using the automated matrix-lift-action method (Bollt and Jones, 2000), they assigned a TE value for each of these 10 previously used AGL systems and examined its correlation with learners' task performance. The meta-regression analysis showed a significant correlation, demonstrating that the complexity effect transcended the different settings and conditions in which the categorization task was performed. The results reinforced the importance of using this new automated tool to uniformly measure grammar systems' complexity when experimenting with and evaluating the findings of AGL studies.

For example, a study by Katan, Kahta, Sasson and Schiff (2016) investigated performance on two AGL tasks of different complexity levels among dyslexic readers, age matched and reading level matched controls. Results indicate that individuals with dyslexia have a deficiency in AGL tasks especially at the highest complexity grammar system. These findings clearly point to the importance of taking the complexity of the grammar system into account when experimenting with the AGL task, as it can have an impact on the results, particularly in special populations.

It should also be noted that thus far the studies exploring implicit learning processes among adults with DD have focused on the visual modality, while disregarding the auditory modality. Research indicates that individuals with DD exhibit poor access, memorization and manipulation of phonological information (Blachman, 2000; Bradley and Bryant, 1983; Snowling, 2000; Vellutino et al. 2004), and that they have a deficit in their sensitivity to the sequence of auditory stimuli (Tallal, 1980). In a study by Kahta and Schiff (2016), the researchers investigated implicit sequential learning processes among adults with DD using the AGL task. Findings show that individuals with DD failed to reach above chance level in the auditory tasks, whereas when processing visual stimuli they exceeded chance level although to a lesser extent than typically developing readers. This deficit exists for visual as well as auditory stimuli and appears to be more salient in learning auditory sequences. This discrepancy may be related to the specific characteristics of auditory input that might hinder the performance of individuals with DD. Hence, it is difficult to draw a conclusion regarding implicit learning processes among individuals with DD based on the available information. More studies into the auditory modality would complement the evidence available and provide greater insight about the important implicit processes in individuals with DD.

5 Conclusion

To summarize, the present paper observed deficient implicit learning of dyslexic individuals in two widely used implicit learning paradigms. The studies reviewed in it lend support to the notion that DD is associated with an implicit learning dysfunction. Furthermore, reading impairments in DD mainly reflect a deficient in general capacity for statistical learning, hence individuals with DD have difficulty picking up and assimilating the statistical properties and systematic patterns of a structured environment. This poor performance of reading impaired children on the SRT and AGL tasks supports the hypothesis that implicit learning deficits may not be limited to implicit skill learning but could also extend to statistical learning mechanisms that could account for some of the reading problems encountered in DD. The studies included in this paper measured implicit learning using the SRT and AGL tasks. More research is needed to assess the performance of individuals with DD on implicit learning tasks using the abovementioned and other paradigms. We wish to emphasize the importance of studying not only initial learning, but also memory consolidation and transfer abilities in implicit learning of individuals with DD in order to obtain a deeper understanding of learning and memory functions in affected children. Such knowledge would potentially be of great importance to the development of effective clinical strategies.

References

American Psychiatric Association. 2013. *Diagnostic and statistical manual of mental disorders (5th ed.)*. Arlington, VA: American Psychiatric Publishing.

Amitay, Sygal, Meray Ahissar & Israel Nelken. 2002. Auditory processing deficits in reading disabled adults. *Journal of the Association for Research in Otolaryngology* 3. 302–320.

Bennett, Ilana J., Jennifer C. Romano, James H. Howard Jr. & Darlene V. Howard. 2008. Two forms of implicit learning in young adults with dyslexia. *Annals of the New York Academy of Sciences* 1145. 184–198.

Berry, Dianne & Zoltan Paul Dienes. 1993. *Implicit learning: Theoretical and empirical issues*. Hillsdale, NJ, England Lawrence Erlbaum Associates.

Blachman, Benita A. 2000. Phonological awareness. In Michael L Kamil, Peter B. Mosenthal, P. Pearson & Rebecca Ed Barr (eds.), *Handbook of reading research Vol III*, 483–502. Mahwah, NJ: Lawrance Erlbaum Associates.

Bollt, Erik M. & Michael A. Jones. 2000. The complexity of artificial grammars. *Nonlinear Dynamics, Psychology & Life Science* 4. 153–168.

Bradley, Lynette & Peter E. Bryant. 1983. Categorizing sounds and learning to read: A causal connection. *Nature* 301. 419–421.

Brown, Roger. 1973. *A first language: The early stages*. London: George Allen.

Démonet, Jean-François, Margot J. Taylor & Yves Chaix. 2004. Developmental dyslexia. *The Lancet* 363. 1451–1460.

Ferraro, F. Richard, David A. Balota & Lisa T. Connor. 1993. Implicit memory and the formation of new associations in nondemented Parkinson's disease individuals and individuals with senile dementia of the Alzheimer type: A serial reaction time (SRT) investigation. *Brain and Cognition* 21. 163–180.

Fletcher, Jack M. 2009. Dyslexia: The evolution of a scientific concept. *Journal of the International Neuropsychological Society* 15. 501–508.

Folia, Vasiliki, Julia Uddén, Christian Forkstam, Martin Ingvar, Peter Hagoort & Karl Magnus Petersson. 2008. Implicit learning and dyslexia. *Annals of the New York Academy of Sciences* 1145. 132–150.

Gabay, Yafit, Rachel Schiff & Eli Vakil. 2012a. Dissociation between the procedural learning of letter names and motor sequences in developmental dyslexia. *Neuropsychologia* 50(10). 2435–2441.

Gabay, Yafit, Rachel Schiff & Eli Vakil. 2012b. Attentional requirements during acquisition and consolidation of a skill in normal readers and developmental dyslexics. *Neuropsychology* 26. 744–57.

Gerken, Louann, Rachel Wilson & William Lewis. 2005. Infants can use distributional cues to form syntactic categories. *Journal of Child Language* 32. 249–268.

Goedert, Kelly M. & Daniel B. Willingham. 2002. Patterns of Interference in Sequence Learning and Prism Adaptation Inconsistent with the Consolidation Hypothesis. *Learning and Memory* 9. 279–292.

Gombert, Jean-Emile. 2003. Implicit and explicit learning to read: Implication as for subtypes of dyslexia. *Current Psychology Letters. Behaviour, Brain and Cognition* 10.

Habib, Michel. 2000. The neurological basis of developmental dyslexia: An overview and working hypothesis. *Brain* 123. 2373–2399.

Harm, Michael W. & Mark S. Seidenberg. Phonology, reading acquisition, and dyslexia: insights from connectionist models. 1999. *Psychological Review* 106. 491.

Hauptmann, Björn, Eva Reinhart, Stephan A. Brandt & Avi Karni. 2005. The predictive value of the leveling off of within-session performance for procedural memory consolidation. *Cognitive Brain Research* 24. 181–189.

Howard, James H., Darlene V. Howard, Karin C. Japikse & Guinevere F. Eden. 2006. Dyslexics are impaired on implicit higher-order sequence learning, but not on implicit spatial context learning. *Neuropsychologia* 44. 1131–1144.

Jueptner, Markus & Cornelius Weiller. 1998. A review of differences between basal ganglia and cerebellar control of movements as revealed by functional imaging studies. *Brain* 121. 1437–1449.

Kahta, S. & Schiff, R. 2016. Implicit learning deficit among adults with developmental dyslexia: Evidence from the AGL study. *Annals of Dyslexia* 66. 235–50.

Katan, P., Kahta, S., Sasson, A. & Schiff, R. 2016. Performance of children with developmental dyslexia on high and low topological entropy artificial grammar learning task. *Annals of dyslexia*, 1–17.

Kerkhoff, Annemarie, Elise De Bree, Maartje De Klerk & Frank Wijnen. 2013. Non-adjacent dependency learning in infants at familial risk of dyslexia. *Journal of Child Language* 40. 11–28.

Kevan, Alison & Kristen Pammer. 2009. Predicting early reading skills from pre-reading measures of dorsal stream functioning. *Neuropsychologia* 47. 3174–3181.

Knopman, David S. & Mary Jo Nissen. 1987. Implicit learning in patients with probable Alzheimer's disease. *Neurology* 37. 874–788.

Laycock, Robin, Crewther, S.G., Crewther, D.P. 2008. The advantage in being magnocellular: A few more remarks on attention and the magnocellular system. *Neuroscience & Biobehavioral Reviews* 32. 363–373.

Stein, John. 2001. The sensory basis of reading problems. *Developmental Neuropsychology* 20. 509–534.

Maye, Jessica, Janet F. Werker & LouAnn Gerken. 2002. Infant sensitivity to distributional information can affect phonetic discrimination. *Cognition* 82. B101–B111.

Menghini, Deny, Gisela E. Hagberg, Carlo Caltagirone, Laura Petrosini & Stefano Vicari. 2006. Implicit learning deficits in dyslexic adults: An fMRI study. *Neuroimage* 33. 1218–1226.

Nicolson, Roderick I. & Angela J. Fawcett. 2011. Dyslexia, dysgraphia, procedural learning and the cerebellum. *Cortex* 47. 117–127.

Nicolson, Roderick I., Angela J. Fawcett & Paul Dean. 2001. Developmental dyslexia: The cerebellar deficit hypothesis. *Trends in Neuroscience* 24. 508–511.

Nicolson, Roderick I. & Angela J. Fawcett. 1990. Automaticity: A new framework for dyslexia research? *Cognition* 35. 159–182.

Nissen, Mary Jo & Peter Bullemer. 1987. Attentional requirements of learning: evidence from performance measures. *Cognitive Psychology* 19. 1–32.

Pavlidou, Elpis V. & Joanne M. Williams. 2010. Developmental dyslexia and implicit 24 learning: Evidence from an AGL transfer study. *Procedia Social and Behavioral 25 Sciences* 2. 3289–3296.

Pavlidou, Elpis V. & Joanne M. Williams. 2014. Implicit Learning and reading: Insights from typical children and children with developmental dyslexia using the artificial grammar learning (AGL) paradigm. *Research in Developmental Disabilities* 35. 1457–1472.

Pavlidou, Elpis V., Joanne M. Williams & Louise M. Kelly. 2009. Artificial Grammar Learning in children with and without developmental dyslexia. *Annals of Dyslexia* 59. 55–77.

Pavlidou, Elpis V., Louise M. Kelly & Joanne M. Williams. 2010. Do children with developmental dyslexia have impairments in implicit learning? *Dyslexia* 16. 143–161.

Pennington, Bruce F. 2009. *Diagnosing learning disorders: A neuropsychological framework*. 2nd ed. New York: Guilford Press.

Perlant, Aurélie Simoës & Pierre Largy. 2011. Are implicit learning abilities sensitive to the type of material to be processed? Study on typical readers and children with dyslexia. *Journal of Research in Reading* 34. 298–314.

Pinker, Steven. 1994. *The language instinct*. New York: William Morrow.

Pothos, Emmanuel M. & Jane Kirk. 2004. Investigating learning deficits associated with dyslexia. *Dyslexia* 10. 61–76.

Pothos, Emmanuel M. 2007. Theories of artificial grammar learning. *Psychological Bulletin* 133. 227–244.

Ramus, Franck. 2003. Developmental dyslexia: specific phonological deficit or general sensorimotor dysfunction? *Current Opinion in Neurobiology* 13. 212–218.

Rattoni, Federico Bermudes & Martha Escobar. 2000. Neurobiology of learning. In Kurt Pawlik & Mark R. Rosenzweig (eds.), *International handbook of psychology*, 136–150. London: Sage Publications.

Reber, Arthur S. 1967. Implicit learning of artificial grammars. *Journal of Verbal Learning and Verbal Behavior* 6. 855–863.

Reber, Arthur S. 1993. *Implicit learning: An essay on the cognitive unconscious*: New York: Oxford University Press.

Robertson, Edwin M., Alvaro Pascual-Leone & R. Chris Miall. 2004. Current concepts in procedural consolidation. *Nature Review Neuroscience* 5. 576–582.

Rüsseler, Jascha, Ivonne Gerth & Thomas F. Münte. 2006. Implicit learning is intact in adult developmental dyslexic readers: evidence from the serial reaction time task and artificial grammar learning. *Journal of Clinical and Experimental Neuropsychology* 28. 808–827.

Schiff, Rachel & Pesia Katan. 2014. Does Complexity Matter? Meta-Analysis of Learner Performance in Artificial Grammar Tasks. *Frontiers in Psychology* 5.

Seger, Carol A. 1998. Multiple forms of implicit learning. In Michael A. Stadler & Peter A. Frensch (eds.), *Handbook of implicit learning*, 295–320. Thousand Oaks, CA: Sage Publications.

Seidenberg, Mark S. & James L. McClelland. 1989. A distributed, developmental model of word recognition and naming. *Psychological Review* 96. 523–568.

Shadmehr, Reza & Henry H. Holcomb. 1997. Neural correlates of motor memory consolidation. *Science* 8. 821–850.

Shiffrin, Richard M. & Walter Schneider. 1977. Controlled and automatic human information processing: II. Perceptual learning, automatic attending and a general theory. *Psychological Review* 84. 127–190.

Snowling, Margaret J. 2000. *Dyslexia*, 2nd edition. Oxford: Blackwell.

Sperling, Anne J., Zhong-Lin Lu & Franklin R. Manis. 2004. Slower implicit categorical learning in adult poor readers. *Annals of Dyslexia* 54. 281–303.

Stein, John & Joel Talcott. 1999. Impaired neuronal timing in developmental dyslexia: The magnocellular hypothesis. *Dyslexia: An International Journal of Research & Practice* 5. 59–77.

Stein, John & Vincent Walsh. 1997. To see but not to read: The magnocellular theory of dyslexia. *Trends in Neurosciences* 20. 147–152.

Stickgold, Robert & Matthew P. Walker. 2005. Memory consolidation and reconsolidation: What is the role of sleep? *Trends in Neuroscience* 28. 408–415.

Stoodley, Catherine J., Angela J. Fawcett, Roderick I. Nicolson & John F. Stein. 2006. Balancing and pointing tasks in dyslexic and control adults. *Dyslexia* 12. 276–288.

Tallal, Paula. 1980. Auditory temporal perception, phonics, and reading disabilities in children. *Brain and Language* 9. 182–198.

Stuart, Geoffrey W., Ken I. McAnally & Anne Castles. 2001. Can contrast sensitivity functions in dyslexia be explained by inattention rather than a magnocellular deficit? *Vision Research* 41. 3205–3211.

Vellutino, Frank R., Jack M. Fletcher, Margaret J. Snowling & Donna M. Scanlon. 2004. Specific reading disability (dyslexia): what have we learned in the past four decades? *Journal of Child Psychology and Psychiatry and Allied Disciplines* 45. 2–40.

Walker, Matthew P. 2005. A refined model of sleep and the time course of memory formation. *Behavioral and Brain Sciences* 28. 51–64.

Steven Gillis

37 Speech and language in congenitally deaf children with a cochlear implant

1 Introduction

1.1 Congenital hearing loss and cochlear implants

Approximately 3 out of 1,000 neonates suffer from hearing loss. A severe-to-profound (>70 dBHL) bilateral hearing loss is detected in approximately 1 neonate per 1,000 births. Thus, the incidence of hearing loss is relatively high as a congenital deficit. In addition, hearing loss can be progressive after birth, can have a delayed onset or can be caused by exogenous factors early in life, which means that the estimated prevalence of hearing deficits in the early years will be higher than the 1/1000 of babies with congenital hearing impairment (Kral & O'Donoghue 2010). It is estimated that two-thirds of the children with hearing loss show the deficit at birth (Mahdieh et al. 2012). In any case, until the 80ies of the previous century, babies with a severe-to-profound sensorineural hearing loss could be fitted an acoustic hearing aid – which did not address their cochlear malfunctioning – in order to assist their residual hearing as well as possible. But it was not until the advent of cochlear implants (CI) that their hearing loss could be reduced to areas between 20 and 40 dBHL, which represents a "mild" hearing loss.

A cochlear implant is an electronic device that functions as a sensory aid, converting mechanical energy into coded electrical pulses that directly stimulate the auditory nerve fibers, bypassing damaged or missing hair cells in the cochlea. Part of the CI is surgically inserted into the cochlea and the mastoid, and the remaining part is worn externally. The external components consist of a microphone, a signal processor, and a transmitter coil. The microphone receives acoustic signals and converts them into an analog electrical signal that is sent to the processor, which converts the signal into an electrical or digital pattern that is transmitted to the internal part by means of the two coils (the external transmitter coil and the internal receiver coil) through the skin. The internal part then stimulates the electrodes in the cochlea. The electrodes are thus able to deliver electrical stimulation to excite the cochlear neurons of the auditory nerve.

This description pertains to "conventional" cochlear implants: direct electrical stimulation of the auditory nerve. However even in cases of severe hearing deficit, residual hearing may remain, most of the time in the lower frequencies, which may still be amply stimulated by an acoustic hearing aid. That is why a new generation of

---

Steven Gillis, University of Antwerp

devices combines a cochlear implant for high frequency hearing loss and acoustic hearing aid in the same ear for sustaining low frequency hearing. This type of cochlear implant is referred to as a hybrid cochlear implant or as combined electric and acoustic stimulation (EAS, James et al. 2006). Also other types of implantable hearing devices are marketed now, such as several kinds of implantable middle ear devices and brainstem implants for those cases in which conventional hearing aids or cochlear implants are not suited: at present a cochlear implant is the best solution for individuals with a well-functioning auditory nerve but with a malfunctioning cochlea (Möller 2006).

2 Early detection of hearing loss

Early auditory experience is quintessential for developing speech and spoken language skills (Jusczyk 1997, Oller 2000). For this reason impaired hearing should be detected as early as possible so that rehabilitation can start at a very young age (Yoshinago-Itano 2004, Yoshinago-Itano et al. 1998). The purpose of newborn hearing screening is to test babies' hearing in the first few days after birth, or at least within the first months of life. There are objective methods for screening neural responses to sound stimuli. These electrophysiological measures detect automated auditory brainstem responses (AABR) or otoacoustic emissions (OAE) invoked by sound stimuli (usually clicks). Nowadays OAE and AABR can routinely be measured and are absolutely non-invasive: babies can easily sleep through the procedure of the hearing test.

Screening programs which aim to reach every single neonate using OAE and AABR have been implemented in various countries. For instance, in the USA the *EHDI* program[1] (*Early Hearing Detection and Intervention*) aims to identify every newborn with a permanent hearing loss before 3 months of age and to provide "timely and appropriate intervention services before 6 months of age". In Flanders, the northern part of Belgium, the governmental child well-being organisation *Kind & Gezin* launched a UNHSP (Universal Neonatal Hearing Screening Program) in 1998 (De Raeve 2006, Desloovere et al. 2013). The impact of this program was impressive: the age at which babies were diagnosed with a hearing loss decreased from 12 months – before the program had started – to 1 month. Consequently the age at first intervention decreased from 13 to 2 months, the first hearing aids were fitted at 3 months, and a growing number of cochlear implantations took place during the first and second year of life (De Raeve & Wouters 2013). As such, early detection is but a first, though indispensible, step in a long chain of rehabilitation steps. The Flemish example shows, for instance, that each year approximately 96% of all neonates are screened. Moreover, by integrating screening, diagnosis, early intervention and rehabilitation in one program (via a well-defined cooperation protocol between different

---

[1] http://www.infanthearing.org/states_home/index.html, accessed 15/12/2014.

caregivers and health services), it became a unique project with long-term effects: referral for a cochlear implant assessment can be accomplished before the age of nine months (Philips et al. 2009). Children eligible for it receive a CI on average between 14 and 16 months of age, and even before their first birthday. In the preschool population (i.e., between approximately two and six years of age) 94% of the children with a profound hearing loss had received a cochlear implant in 2010, and 25% of them were wearing bilateral implants (De Raeve & Lichtert 2012). Of the children with cochlear implants (and no additional disabilities), 85%–90% eventually enter mainstream education (De Raeve 2014, De Raeve & Lichtert 2012, Desloovere et al. 2013, Van Kerschaver et al. 2007).

This description of UNHSP pertains to the region of Flanders, the Dutch speaking part of Belgium. Elsewhere the situation may not be identical, for instance, in the French speaking part of Belgium, UNHSP started only in 2007 (Vos et al. 2014), but most developed countries have started screening programs (Nikolopoulos 2015).

Thus, in the end, early detection and proper rehabilitation of hearing impairment has a positive effect on speech perception and production, and language development (Geers 2006, Yoshinago-Itano et al. 1998), but also on a further broad spectrum of aspects of an individual's personal, social, educational, and professional life (Hoffman et al. 2014, Kochkin 2010, Quittner et al. 2004).

3 Cochlear implant candidacy and audiological outcome

In the early days of pediatric cochlear implantation, candidacy requirements included an unaided pure-tone average of 90 dBHL or more, and aided thresholds of 60 dBHL or higher, and in addition absence of speech discrimination and word-recognition with well-fitted hearings aids. But the guidelines for CI candidacy have developed over the years (Geers 2006). For instance, currently in the USA FDA guidelines[2] permit implantation in children above two years of age with severe hearing loss, i.e., a hearing loss of 70 dBHL or higher. For children in their second year of life, profound deafness, i.e., a hearing loss of at least 90dBHL, is the criterion. Moreover several centers in the USA provide cochlear implants to children in their first year of life "'off-label' when there is strong evidence that an infant is profoundly deaf and not progressing in his or her speech and hearing development with hearing aids." (Houston et al. 2012: 459). In this respect there is variation in the selection criteria that hold in different countries[3].

---

[2] http://www.nidcd.nih.gov/health/hearing/pages/coch.aspx
[3] For instance, in Belgium the official reimbursement criteria (by social security) since 2006 are (1) pure tone average thresholds of 85 dB HL or greater at 500, 1000, and 2000 Hz; (2) threshold of peak V in brainstem auditory evoked potentials at 90 dB HL or higher; (3) little or no benefit from hearing aids (De Raeve & Wouters 2013).

Most implant users' thresholds lower to 20 to 40 dBHL across all frequencies, i.e. a mild hearing loss. This implies that the implant enables detection of virtually all speech sounds and provides a hearing sensitivity and functionality superior to that obtained with conventional acoustic hearing aids. A sensorineural hearing loss is characterized by an elevated threshold on pure-tone audiometry and by a lower frequency resolution. A good frequency resolving power of the cochlea is essential for normal speech and language development: hearing impaired individuals not only fail to hear many sounds, if they do hear them, they often fail to discriminate them. Conventional hearing aids amplify sounds, but they do not improve the frequency discrimination. That is, a hearing impaired individual will perceive sound better with a hearing aid, without necessarily understanding better what is said. Cochlear implants by contrast not only amplify sound but they also aim at a (partial) restoration of the frequency resolution of the cochlea. This is the major advantage of a cochlear implant over a hearing aid in cases where the hearing loss is severe-to-profound and the cochlear tuning is deficient. It is, however, wise to keep in mind that given this remarkable advantage, cochlear implants still have their limitations: they do not restore normal hearing, outcomes vary among patients, and are very dependent on the actual fitting of the device, and performance is still considerably degraded by ambient noise (O'Donoghue 2013).

4 Deaf children with a cochlear implant: A "moving target"

Studies of spoken language developmental in deaf children with a cochlear implant started appearing in the last decades of the previous century and since then the population has received a growing interest judging from the sheer number of scientific writings. Trying to grasp the gist of children's speech and language development is not trivial since the population can be characterized as "a moving target", to use the words of Geers (2006). Moreover studies employ different methodologies so that research findings are not always easily comparable.

In this section we will review some of the intricacies of this population: on the one hand, cochlear implantation is a fairly recent technological innovation, and new developments are announced regularly. These developments are manifold, for instance, new hardware for the device or innovations in its speech processor. Innovations also concern the age at which children are eligible for implantation: the age when the intervention is allowed to occur has lowered substantially over the past decades. In the USA cochlear implants have been FDA-approved for use in eligible children beginning at 12 months of age since 2000. But in the same year the first child under the age of 6 months received her implant in Belgium. Thus a number of changes have occurred – technological innovations, changes in the eligibility of the pediatric cochlear implant users, etc. – which makes the sample of CI children reported on in the literature "an ever moving target". On the other hand, these changes and developments have occurred simultaneously, which constitutes another aspect of this "moving target": it is difficult to determine the impact of each one of them separately on young children's speech and language development.

Cochlear implant technology has evolved tremendously in the last three decades. For instance, the algorithms that process the incoming speech signals have provided much more details in consecutive generations of devices. The speech extraction schemes in the early implants presented only limited spectral information (fundamental frequency, first two formants) providing ample support for lip reading but were only a very restricted aid to speech perception (Clark et al. 1983, Dowell et al. 1985). More sophisticated strategies developed later provided more information, especially in the higher frequencies, leading to better speech perception (Clark 1989). In the mid-90ies, the introduction of the bandpass filtering principles led to even further enhancements in representing speech features and in a higher rate. These improvements in the speech processing algorithms each led to improvements in speech perception (Sarant 2012). A development in the last decade aims to make use of the (low-frequency) residual hearing of the implantees. For this purpose electrical stimulation is combined with acoustic stimulation, leading again to improved speech perception (Campbell et al. 2013).

Another telling example concerns the number of electrodes in the CI device. The first children were implanted in Melbourne in 1980 with the single channel House cochlear implant (Eisenberg & House 1982). In 1985 the first children received a multichannel CI, and nowadays implants are used with up to 24 channels.

Hence, much more information can be analyzed by the speech processor, and increasingly more information can be transmitted. As these developments enhance speech perception, they also have a vast impact on children's language and speech production (Geers 2006, Peng et al. 2004, Sarant 2012). But this implies a "moving target": research findings that were obtained in children equipped with devices with older generation technology should be cautiously compared with findings in children using newer generation technology. Due to i.a. improved technology the latter have access to more and higher quality information from the device, and hence their understanding and production of speech can be expected to be superior (Geers & Nicholas 2013).

But there is more to it than only technological advances. In two recent studies, the speech intelligibility of 63 CI users was investigated (Montag et al. 2014, Ruffin et al. 2013). Their experience with the device varied from 8 to 18 years, with a mean of 12 years, and they had all received their implant before the age of 7. Systematic differences were found in the group of participants: CI users who used their implant longer appeared to be less intelligible than those with a shorter period of device experience. More specifically, they observed age cohort effects: participants with more than 15 years of CI use were less intelligible than participants with 7 to 9 years of experience. At first sight, this is a surprising finding, since it could be expected that the more experience a CI user has the better the performance would be. Looking for an explanation of this seemingly counterintuitive finding, Montag et al. (2014) found that the duration of CI use strongly correlated with the chronological year in which the implantation took place. Over the past decades the medical and audiological criteria for CI candidacy and age of implantation have changed significantly. It appeared that, indeed, the participants with more years of device experience were also implanted at an older age. Hence, the age cohort effect apparently reflected the decrease in the age at which hearing impaired children were implanted. In other words, the participants' age at implantation was a significant predictor of their long-term speech intelligibility scores, and the higher age at implantation in the older cohort accounted for the relationship between age cohort and language intelligibility outcome. Thus, changes in the clinical practice over the years – a demographic variable – have an impact on the language outcomes in CI users.

In addition to this "moving target" there is also a "vanishing target". The ultimate aim of auditory restoration is for children with a cochlear implant to (eventually) reach a level of speech and language comparable to that of normally hearing peers. This implies that researchers compare spoken language of implanted children with a matched group of normally hearing children. But from another perspective, children with a cochlear implant have a severe-to-profound hearing loss, and, hence, researchers want to find out if their speech and language performance is comparable or better than that of a matched group of children with comparable auditory characteristics (aided and unaided thresholds) wearing acoustic hearing aids. However testing comparable groups of cochlear implant and hearing aid users has become increasingly difficult because the number of available profoundly deaf hearing aid users who do not elect to receive a cochlear implant is becoming smaller and smaller, and thus they constitute a "vanishing target" (Geers 2006). However from previous research it can be concluded that on average children with a CI have more effective speech and language skills than children with similar hearing loss wearing acoustic (or tactile) hearing aids (Svirsky et al. 2000).

5 Characteristics of spoken language development

5.1 Development assessed with standardized tests

Bearing in mind that children with a cochlear implant constitute "a moving target", the published results of language and speech assessments should be evaluated with care (Montag et al. 2014). The studies reported in the literature take – broadly speaking – two different methodological strands: administrating standardized tests and analyzing (spontaneous) speech samples. Standardized tests such as the *Reynell Developmental Language Scales (RDLS)* or *the Peabody Picture Vocabulary Test (PPVT)* are used to evaluate children's expressive and/or receptive language abilities. One of the advantages of such standardized tests is that they allow to determine the *language age* of children. For instance, a language age of 3 years means that the child has the language skills equivalent with those of typically developing three-year-olds. If the language age differs from the chronological age, then the *language quotient* (i.e., language age divided by chronological age) provides an estimate of the delay or the advance of the child's linguistic abilities. In order to estimate the relative progress over time, the rate of development is computed by dividing the change in the language age by the change in chronological age over a particular period of time.

In a large-scale study of 188 children with a cochlear implant, Niparko et al. (2010) investigated children's progress in spoken language comprehension and production with the RDLS. The children were implanted before the age of five, and were tested every six months for a period of three years starting when their device was activated. Three age groups participated: (1) a group implanted before 18 months (N = 72), (2) a group implanted between 18 and 36 months (N = 64), and (3) a group implanted after 36 months (N = 52). Several important findings are reported. In comprehension as well as in production, children with a CI make considerable progress, but on average the developmental trajectories were significantly slower compared with normally hearing peers. But this *average* picture hides an important characteristic of the population of implanted children that has also been remarked by many other investigators: the trajectories are markedly more variable in the CI group in comparison with normally hearing children. This means that there is more variation between CI children than between NH children. Part of the variation comes from the different ages at which the children received their CI. In the youngest group (implanted before 18 months) the developmental trajectories for comprehension and production were significantly steeper than in the two other groups. The increase of the children's abilities in the youngest group was even comparable to that of the normally hearing control group, but the increase in the two other groups was slower than that of normally hearing children. This means that for the youngest implanted children the gap with the normally hearing ones did not widen, while for the later implanted ones, the gap did not become narrower. But since the hearing impaired children already started at a much lower level, even the youngest implanted children still had a delay at the endpoint of the study, i.e., three years after implantation. In order to illustrate what this entails: the expressive level of normally hearing children age 2.3 years is attained by the youngest group of CI children at the age of 3.4 years, by the children implanted between 18 and 36 months at 4.5 years, and by the even later implanted children at 5.2 years.

Variation between children's language abilities at a particular age are a well-documented phenomenon: also in the group of normally hearing children, the RDLS scores differed. But a second main finding of Niparko et al. (2010), also reported in many other studies, is that the variation within a group of CI children is significantly larger. Language and speech outcomes differ more considerably from child to child.

This variation has an important implication: some CI children do exhibit scores comparable to age matched hearing peers, while others still show a marked language delay even after many years of device use. Boons et al. (2012a) report on a large scale study of 288 children who were tested 1, 2, and 3 years after they received a CI (mean age at CI: 2;02, SD = 1;11). Two standardized tests were administered, viz. the RLDS for receptive language skills and the SELT (Schlichting Developmental Language Test) assessing expressive language skills at the word and sentence level. Huge variation in performance was attested: some children scored age appropriately, even beyond what could be expected given their chronological age. On the other side approximately one out of four children "[...] failed to develop a language level comparable with half of their chronological age [...]" (Boons et al. 2012a: 632). Thus, after three years of device use the gaps in language development between implanted children and their NH peers were not eliminated yet (Boons et al. 2012a, Niparko et al. 2010).

What language levels can be expected after an extended period of device use? Do children with CI eventually catch up with their NH peers? Geers & Nicholas (2013) report on a longitudinal study involving 60 children implanted at a mean age of 22.7 months (SD = 7.7). These children were tested at the age of 4.5 years (Nicholas & Geers 2006) and again when they were approximately 10.5 years of age and had on average used their devices for 8.6 years. A number of tests were administered assessing both receptive and productive language development at the word and sentence level. Over half of the sample achieved scores within the average range for NH peers, and 73% of the children implanted before 18 months scored within that range. There were differences between tests. Measured as the percentage of children ranging within or above 1SD from the normative mean, the following percentages are reported: 82% for expressive vocabulary, 72% for receptive vocabulary, 77% for expressive language, 52% for receptive language, and 68% for a overall language score. This suggests that a majority of the implanted children have caught up with their hearing age mates for both expressive and receptive vocabulary and expressive language (including syntax), but that this is the case in a far lesser extend for receptive language measures. Listening to language, processing it, and comprehending it, appears to be much harder for CI children than producing words and sentences.

A finer assessment of the language development profiles after a prolonged use of early CI was targeted by Duchesne et al. (2009). They used the RDLS and showed that after six years of implant use, more than half of the CI children had receptive and expressive age-appropriate language skills at the word level, while less than 50% of the same group of children had receptive and expressive age-appropriate language skills at sentence level. Even though other standardized tests were used, similar outcomes were found in for instance Caselli et al. (2012), Geerset al. (2003), Schorret al. (2008) and Young & Killen (2002). Moreover Duchesne et al. (2009) identified four developmental profiles: (1) lexical and grammatical language components are within normal limits in comprehension as well as in production; (2) delayed development across domains; (3) Normal lexical abilities but a receptive grammatical delay (productive grammar was not assessed), and (4) idiosyncratic discrepancies across domains.

5.2 Development assessed by analyses of spontaneous speech

Studies of children's spontaneous speech or elicited speech in well-targeted experiments, provide an opportunity to analyze in more detail the language and speech of children with a cochlear implant and to unravel non typical phenomena and error patterns.

After implantation a burst in children's speech and language development is witnessed: growth curve analyses show a steep increase of the acquisition curve. In early implanted children the slope is even comparable to that of normally hearing children (Connor et al. 2006, Tomblin et al. 2005, 2008). This profile is independent of the age at implantation, but with later ages at implantation the slope of the curve becomes less and less steep, and, hence, the gap between development in NH and CI children becomes larger.

The onset of canonical babbling is a well-documented example. In NH children, the onset of canonical babbling is expected to occur between approximately 6 and 11 months of age (Molemans et al. 2012, Oller 2000). Children with severe-to-profound hearing loss show marked delays for babbling onset (Koopmans-van Beinum et al. 2001, Nathani et al. 2007), some do not even babble at all (Oller & Eilers 1988). After cochlear implantation children typically start babbling within a few months after the activation of their device. They need on average 4 months of auditory exposure for babbling to take off (Colletti et al. 2005, Ertmer & Mellon 2001, Moeller et al. 2007, Moore & Bass-Ringdahl 2002, Schauwers et al. 2008, Schramm et al. 2009, Wright et al. 2002). Hence CI children need less time to reach this milestone in vocal development than NH children. However, even when implanted very early in life, babbling onset in CI children is delayed in terms of chronological age, and with later ages at implantation, the delay becomes even more important.

Except for being delayed in babbling onset, does speech and language development proceed as in normally hearing infants? The general picture that emerges is that, at a very general level, development in both groups runs parallel but looking in more detail at particular phenomena reveals discrepancies. The latter will be exemplified by looking at studies of (1) children's prelexical babbling development, (2) the development of production accuracy, and (3) morpho-syntactic development.

5.3 Prelexical vocal development

Most published reports assessing the prelexical vocal repertoire in young, early implanted CI children indicate substantial progress after a limited amount of aided hearing experience and even close-to-normal patterns of speech (Anderson et al.

2004, Colletti et al. 2005, Ertmer & Mellon 2001, Schauwers et al. 2004). But detailed analyses of children's babbling show that at the segmental as well as at the suprasegmental level there are marked differences between children with CI and NH children. Looking at which consonants are used in canonical babbles (e.g., [baba], [mama]) it appears that children with CI use markedly more stops than NH children (Schauwers et al. 2008). They seem to make the difference in sonority between the syllable initial consonant and the vowel as large as possible (stops are the least sonorous segments, vowels the most sonorous). At the suprasegmental level, although the length of the babbles is not significantly different (Molemans 2011), CI children's babbles show significantly less variation: reduplicated babbles in which a syllable is repeated (e.g., [baba]) predominate in CI children, while in NH variegated babbles with non-identical syllables (e.g., [bama], [papu]) are significantly more frequent viewed over the entire babbling period. Thus the babbles of CI children are more repetitive as a majority of them consist of a mere repetition of the same syllable.

Thus, soon after they receive their CI, very early implanted children show a burst in their vocal development: they start to produce canonical babbles and their development seems to follow that of normally hearing children. But when homing in on specific details of those babbled utterances, particular discrepancies can be remarked, such as a predominant use of stops and an overall more repetitive structure.

5.4 Phonetic and phonemic accuracy of word productions

As a second example, the segmental accuracy of words is discussed. Segmental accuracy refers to the overall accuracy of children's pronunciation of words: how many phonemes are produced correctly (i.e., phonemic accuracy, which is to be distinguished from phonetic accuracy). For English-speaking children with CI, accuracy is reported to increase with longer implant use (Blamey et al. 2001, Eriks-Brophy et al. 2013, Tobey et al. 2003, Tomblin et al. 2008). After four years of implant use, overall phonemic accuracy is 62.9% (Tomblin et al. 2008). Accuracy increases after six years of implant use to 76.28% according to Tomblin et al. (2008) and approximately 86% according to Blamey et al. (2001). In Blamey et al. (2001) mean age at implantation was 3;9 (SD = 0;11) and in Tomblin et al. (2008) mean age at implantation was 4;6 (SD = 2;1).

In children implanted at an earlier age, viz. on average 1;5, segmental accuracy is shown to be significantly higher in NH children than in children with CI. At age 3;6 and after on average two years of device use, the percentage of phonemes correct is 83% for NH children and 53% for children with CI (Ertmer et al. 2012). At age 4;0, the same trend emerges in the accuracy of word initial consonants in a short sentence repetition task. For NH children of that age, all initial consonants except fricatives and affricates (86% accuracy) reach ceiling accuracy, while for children with CI initial consonant accuracy is only 62% (Ertmer & Goffman 2011). 72% of the hearing impaired children reached average scores at age 5;0 (Eriks-Brophy et al. 2013) and thus seem to have caught up with their NH peers.

In a recent study, Faes, Gillis & Gillis (2016) investigated phonemic accuracy in children acquiring Dutch, implanted at a median age of 1;0. The material consisted of spontaneous speech samples drawn from mother-child conversations. The children were studied up till age 5 (with up to 4;6 years of device use at that age). They found that the accuracy of children with CI is lower than the accuracy of NH age-matched peers during the first year after CI activation. The delay remained significant when assessed at the age of 3 and 4, but the distance between the accuracy scores of the NH and CI children became smaller. Eventually at age 5, the children with CI reached a phonemic accuracy score that was similar to that of their NH peers.

Thus for phonemic accuracy, children with CI seem to catch up gradually with NH peers (Faes et al. 2016). But looking at the fine phonetic detail of the children's consonant and vowel productions indicates that there still remain important differences with the speech of NH children. For instance, Verhoeven et al. (2016) assessed the vowel productions of the CI children also studied by Faes et al. (2016). They found that at the age of 6, after approximately 5 years of device use, the vowel space of the CI children was significantly smaller than that of the NH age-matched peers. This suggests that CI children pronounce their vowels much more centralized and less differentiated than NH children. Comparable results are reported for vowel productions in Croatian (Liker et al. 2007), Greek (Nicolaidis et al. 2007), and German (Neumeyer et al. 2010), although results are not always equivocal (see Baudonck et al. 2011).

5.5 Morpho-synatctic development

Analyses of morphological and syntactic development in children's (spontaneous) speech are rather scarce. In general, the development of CI children's inflection is found to lag behind compared to NH peers. For instance for German, Szagun (2001) showed that inflectional morphology of CI children is less advanced compared to NH children. More precisely, case and gender marking of articles and noun plurals are less accurate in CI children. With respect to nominal plurals, NH children are found to make errors, children with CI make very similar errors, but in addition CI children frequently do not mark plurals, and therefore avoid error making (Szagun 2001). Likewise, Laaha et al. (2015) showed that Dutch and German CI children produce significantly more singular nouns compared to age-matched NH peers in a plural elicitation task. Whereas CI children have difficulties with the inflection of nouns and articles, no differences with respect to verbal morphology in German are found (Szagun 2001). For English, Guo et al. (2013) showed that tense marking is less accurate in CI children as compared to NH peers up to five years of implant use. Hammer (2010) replicated these findings for Dutch speaking children: CI children are delayed with respect to verb morphology, subject-verb agreement and past tense marking. Nevertheless, they appear to have caught up for nominal and verbal morphology by age seven (Hammer 2010).

The richness of the inflectional paradigms of nouns and verbs, i.e., how many different forms of a stem or root occur in the children's language, shows a development from a delay to age appropriate richness. Early implanted children with CI acquiring Dutch start out with significantly poorer verbal and nominal paradigms, but after approximately three years of device use, at a chronological age of 5 years, they appear to have caught up with NH peers (Faes et al. 2015).

In studies of children's spontaneous speech, a similar relative developmental pace of lexical and grammatical development is found as in studies using standardized tests: the delay of CI children covers a shorter period for lexical development as compared to grammatical development, as measured by MLU (Moreno-Torres & Torres 2008). But early implanted CI children are found to catch up with their NH peers when studying their spontaneous speech (Faes et al. 2015, Nicholas & Geers 2007, Tribushinina et al. 2013).

6 Factors affecting spoken language development

What are the factors affecting spoken language development in severe-to-profound congenitally hearing-impaired children? What are the predictors of successful language acquisition and development after cochlear implantation? In the literature several factors have been identified that appear to affect the eventual success of a cochlear implant intervention in severe-to-profound hearing impaired children (Boons et al. 2012a, Cosetti & Waltzman 2012, Geers 2006). Three sets of factors will be described in this section: (1) factors related to the children's audiological condition, such as their pre-operative hearing, (2) factors related to a child's individual condition, such as the presence of additional disabilities or the child's nonverbal cognitive functioning, and (3) environmental factors, such as the socioeconomic background of the child's family.

Given the important inter-individual variation in the spoken language outcomes of CI device users, a central question in research concerns why particular children perform well while others perform less well? This question pertains to short-term effects (e.g., what makes a baby implanted at 12 months of age babble after one month of exposure to sound and another one only after six months?) as well as long-term effects (e.g., why do particular children communicate at age-appropriate levels much earlier than others, and why do some children with a CI remain language delayed?). Essentially the answers to these questions are similar to the answers that are provided for individual variation in language acquisition and development in typically developing children: characteristics of the language learning child and characteristics of the child's environment determine the path of spoken language development. But in comparison to typically developing children there are additional factors, viz. factors related to their auditory condition, such as the causes of their hearing impairment, the various steps in the intervention, the follow-up history after the intervention.

7 Audiology related factors

7.1 Age at identification of hearing impairment

Undoubtedly one of the main predictors of successful spoken language acquisition is the age at which a hearing loss is detected and the severity of the hearing deficit is determined. Very early identification is a crucial milestone in rehabilitation since it triggers – under optimal conditions – a number of further steps: once a baby is diagnosed with a hearing deficit, further steps can be taken such as fitting acoustic hearing aids, monitoring the gain in hearing these may bring about, and may be eventually cochlear implantation. But the surgical procedure is only one step in a chain of events that should be instigated if necessary by early detection of a hearing deficit. Newborn hearing screening programs are the ultimate tool in this respect, and hence, the success of language acquisition in hearing-impaired children depends on them (Yoshinaga-Itano 2004, 2006).

7.2 Preoperative hearing levels

Most studies agree that the degree of hearing loss established upon identification of a hearing deficit has an important impact on speech perception, speech intelligibility, receptive and productive language development after cochlear implantation. Less hearing loss is a predictor of better outcomes (Artières et al. 2009, Holt & Svirsky 2008, Szagun 2001, but see Nicholas & Geers 2006).

7.3 Age at fitting of hearing aids

Early identification of hearing loss has been identified as a factor that contributes to better language and speech outcomes after cochlear implantation. But quite a few studies found that an earlier age of hearing aids fitting – the first step after identification of a hearing loss in the rehabilitation process in most audiological centers – was also a significant predictor of better outcomes: children whose hearing loss was identified within the first six months and who received hearing aids, showed superior language skills when compared to children who were identified later (Artières et al. 2009) and showed better overall speech intelligibility at later ages (Holt & Svirsky 2008, Nicholas & Geers 2006).

7.4 Age at implantation

The age at implantation is an important predictor of language acquisition and development. Children implanted at an earlier age fare better than children implanted later. This appears as a robust and undisputed finding in the literature on CI children's receptive and expressive language development (i.a. Artieres et al. 2009, Connor et al. 2006, Dettman et al. 2007, Geers et al. 2009, Geers & Nicholas 2013, Holt & Svirsky 2008, Nicholas & Geers 2008, Niparko et al. 2010).

Several reasons motivate this finding. First of all, during the first year of life children's perceptual abilities develop enormously: they "home in" on the ambient language, adapting their discrimination and categorization of speech sounds to the language they hear, use the suprasegmentals of the language to segment words and utterances from the speech stream (Jusczyk 1997). Moreover, their speech production attains a number of important milestones during the first few years of life, such as the onset of canonical babbling and the production of the first words. These are not only important milestones in speech production and perception, in the early years also the relationship between the auditory and the articulatory world are established, allowing children to connect their speech-motor programs with the sounds they hear (Redford 2015). Given their poor auditory abilities, severe-to-profound hearing impaired children do not have sufficient auditory stimulation to go through all these important developments during the first years of life, so that early implantation is called for.

A second important reason that motivates early implantation is that the absence of sound input during the first few years of life can result in irreversible changes to the auditory cortex. The developing auditory system is maximally plastic at birth, and this plasticity decreases with age. There appears to be a sensitive period for neural development that is crucial for spoken language development. This limited window of opportunity is maximal in the first 3.5 years, decreases dramatically after 7 years and may be completely closed by 12 years (Gilley et al. 2008, Kral & Sharma 2011, Sharma et al. 2004, 2005). Hence, it is of prime importance that this window of opportunity is not missed.

What is the optimal age window for implantation? The benefits of fitting a CI under the age of 2 have been documented extensively (Anderson et al. 2004, Boons et al. 2012a, Hammes et al. 2002, Svirsky et al. 2004). Currently the question whether implantation in the first year of life has any beneficial effects on children's language and speech, and if so, whether these effects are lasting, are under investigation. At present, the evidence is mixed. Some studies report no advantage or just a limited or a non-lasting advantage of implantation during the first year of life (Colletti et al. 2011, Holt & Svirsky 2008, Lesinski-Schiedat et al. 2004, Vlastarakos et al. 2010). The most elaborate study up till now investigated 35 children implanted before 12 months of age and 85 children implanted before 24 months, three years post implantation (Leigh et al. 2013). The results are mixed: on some measures significant differences between the two groups are reported, while on other measures the difference did not reach significance. For instance, on speech production (viz. percentage phonemes correct) there was no significant difference between the two groups. Both perform significantly poorer than normally hearing peers. But on receptive vocabulary (measured with the PPVT), the youngest implanted children score significantly better than the older implanted ones. Implantation in the first year of life leads to age appropriate receptive vocabulary skills, while later implantation leads to a significant lasting delay after three years of device experience.

7.5 Duration of device use

In addition to the age at implantation, the length of device use appears to have a crucial impact on children's linguistic functioning. For instance, Geers & Nicholas (2013) studied children who had received a CI between their first and third birthdays. At 4.5 years of age they found a significant effect of length of device use: everything else being equal, longer hearing experience resulted in more advanced language production and comprehension. However, this effect appeared to have faded out by 10.5 years of age.

Whether age at implantation or length of device use are the most decisive factors in predicting language outcomes in children who received a CI is still a matter of debate. Geers & Nicholas (2013) found that children with a more advanced level of language use at 4.5 were also more advanced at 10.5 years, and these were the children who were implanted at the earliest ages. Thus, Geers & Nicholas (2013) report a lasting effect of the age of implantation: the age at which children gain access to spoken language through their first implant still has an effect on their linguistic functioning at 10.5 years of age, with younger implanted children still outperforming later implanted ones.

However, Szagun & Stumper (2012) note that whereas age at implantation has been treated as a major influence on the language development of children with CIs, the amount of variance that it actually explains is small (see also Geers et al. 2009; Tomblin et al. 2005). Moreover, their research indicates that instead of age at implantation, length of device use is a more determining factor: a lasting effect of the length of children's robust auditory experience was detected, while the effect of age at implantation was not significant.

7.6 Bilateral (or contralateral) cochlear implant

In the early days of cochlear implantation, children received a single implant: unilateral implantation. Nowadays bilateral implantation – a device in both ears – seems to have become standard practice in many implant centers around the world.

Children with a unilateral implant exhibit excellent speech perception abilities in optimal conditions, such as a quiet room, but their listening abilities become far less accurate under more natural conditions: a noisy background is often reported to hamper interaction, soft or whispered speech are not accurately captured, and locating a speaker in a conversational setting is often difficult. Hence, on the one hand children with a unilateral CI exhibit levels of speech and language development that they would never have obtained with a (acoustic) hearing aid, and many studies in the past have shown that they can reach age appropriate linguistic functioning. But, on the other hand, many children with a unilateral CI have been reported to show delays in language and speech development (Geers 2002, Tobey et al. 2003).

Bilateral implantation has significant positive effects over the unilateral condition on speech perception in quiet and in noise and on sound-source localization (Vincent et al. 2012). The impact on children's receptive and expressive language development is less clear. Some studies report no beneficial effects of bilateral implantation (Niparko et al. 2010, Nittrouer & Chapman 2009). Others found a marked improvement of particular aspects of language comprehension and/or production (Boons et al. 2012a, 2012b, Sarant et al. 2014, Sparreboom et al. 2015). For instance, children with bilateral implants show significantly faster rates of receptive vocabulary development (measured by standardized tests such as the Peabody Picture Vocabulary Test – PPVT) than children in the unilateral condition (the magnitude of the effect was moderated by the child's age at activation, Boons et al. 2012b, Sarant et al. 2014). This faster vocabulary acquisition may be explained by the fact that because bilateral children's hearing is more robust to noise, their ability to learn incidentally (by overhearing) is superior to that of unilaterally implanted children.

Bilateral implantation brings up the question whether the devices should be implanted *simultaneously* or *sequentially*, and whether this has an effect, and more importantly for the present chapter, which mode of operation results in better spoken language performance. The research results are not equivocal. For instance, Sparrenboom et al. (2015) did not find a significant effect of the duration of first or only implant use on receptive vocabulary in children who received their first implant on average at 1;08 and their second on average at 5;01, with a mean inter-implant delay of 3;4 and tested when they were 10 years of age (average 10;8). But Boons et al. (2012b) report that a shorter interval between both implantations was related to higher standard scores: children who underwent a simultaneous cochlear implantation performed better than children who underwent two sequential cochlear implantations. This issue certainly needs further scrutiny.

7.7 Unimodal versus bimodal stimulation

The issue of unimodal versus bimodal stimulation is fairly complicated. On the one hand, in the case of unilateral implantation, the issue is: should auditory stimulation with an acoustic hearing aid in the non-implanted ear, be continued after a cochlear implant, i.e. an implant on one ear and a hearing aid on the other? Does it result in beneficial effects? The answer provided by Nittrouer & Chapman (2009), based on a review of the literature and on their own empirical research, can be briefly summarized as follows: children who had bimodal stimulation at any point in their lives fare better than children who never had bimodal stimulation.

With the introduction of hybrid cochlear implants, bimodal stimulation can also mean bimodal implantation (or combined electric and acoustic stimulation). The impact of this type of device on children's language and speech development is still unclear due to the fact that bimodal implants are a recent innovation. But it may be expected that due to better perception of the low frequencies, children's speech may considerably improve: their vowel production quality may improve and their production of intonation at the word and sentence level is also expected to ameliorate. However, to the best of our knowledge, studies investigating these aspects of speech production contrasting children with a unimodal and a bimodal implant are lacking at present.

7.8 Device placement, fitting and audiological rehabilitation

Several factors related to the actual implantation, the consecutive fitting of the device and the audiological rehabilitation program after device switch on, have only been sparsely dealt with in the literature, while at the same time they may have an important impact on later language and speech outcomes (Nicholas & Geers 2006). In a large scale study involving 188 participants implanted in 6 large implant centers situated in different regions of the United States, the RLDS were administered to all children. In reporting the results of the study, implant center was mentioned as one of the predicting variables: "Center was found to be significantly associated with different rates of increase in comprehension scores." (Niparko et al. 2010: 1504) This means that the language outcomes of children implanted in one place differ from children treated in another one. The reasons for this disparity can be manyfold, but are hardly touched upon in the relevant literature. One factor is the device placement and fitting: the electrodes can be completely inserted or only partially, thus, insertion depth is a relevant parameter. In addition, fitting of the device after it was brought in place, amounts to programming the speech processor for optimal (speech) perception. This process results in a unique program, or "map" for each individual cochlear implant user. Even in adults this "cochlear parametrisation is a difficult and long task, with results ranging from perfect blind speech recognition to patients who cannot make anything out of their implant and just turn it off" (Bourgeois-République et al. 2004: 296). It can readily be inferred that in the case of small children fitting is an even more challenging task with highly variable success, a task that largely depends on "the skill of the audiologist" (Nicholas & Geers 2006: 276).

After device switch on, most children enter into an intensive speech and language training program. Since different audiological centers may follow different rehabilitation schemes, also this factor may contribute to the outcomes found in children implanted in different centers.

8 Child related factors

8.1 Nonverbal cognitive abilities

Nonverbal cognitive ability is a significant predictor of language development in typically developing children as well as in children with an atypical profile, such as SLI, Specific Language Impairment (Botting 2005). Also in the population of severe-to-profound hearing-impaired children with a cochlear implant, nonverbal cognitive abilities are a strong predictor of language (Boons et al. 2012a, b, Geers et al. 2008, Sarant et al. 2014).

8.2 Cause of deafness

The cause of congenital hearing impairment can be classified into three broad categories: (1) a genetic cause (e.g., mutation of the connexin 26 gene) represents ca. 40% of the cases, (2) infectious causes, such as cytomegalovirus or other viral infections, represent 30% of the cases, and (3) an unknown cause is concluded in the remaining 30%. In the genetic category, a further distinction can be made between syndromic deafness, such as Usher syndrome, Alport syndrome, Waardenburg syndrome, etc. About 400 syndromes have an associated hearing loss (Krall & O'Donoghue 2010). Syndromic deafness accounts for approximately 30% of the cases, the remaining 70% is nonsyndromic.

The exact impact of the cause of hearing impairment on the speech and language outcomes of cochlear implantation is not well understood. In a number of studies the outcome of an implantation is compared in children with cytomegalovirus (CMV) infection and children with presumed genetically determined deafness as the presumed cause of their hearing loss. Ramirez Inscoe & Nikolopoulos (2004) report on 16 children with CMV: in comparison with connexin children, they tended to perform more poorly. However, in a more recent study, Philips et al. (2014) show that when the CMV group is further subdivided into those with a normal MRI scan and those with an abnormal MRI scan, the former perform equally well as the connexin children, or even slightly better, while the latter seem to catch up for speech perception, but not for speech production. More research in this area is definitely required.

8.3 Gender

For receptive and productive language measures, boys score lower than girls at 5 years of age, but this effect fades out and was no longer evident when children are tested at 8 years of age (Geers et al. 2009, Sarant et al. 2014). This result is in agreement with other research showing that the gap in language ability between boys and girls in early life closes with increasing age (Ely 2005).

8.4 Additional disabilities

Approximately 30 to 50% of the children with severe-to-profound hearing loss suffer from additional disabilities, such as autistic spectrum disorders, behavioral difficulties, cognitive difficulties, oro-facial disorders, visual impairment, vocal tract anomalies, or a combination of these additional difficulties. A direct comparison of 67 CI children with and 104 CI children without additional disabilities revealed that five years after implantation, additional disabilities have a negative impact on the children's overall speech intelligibility (Nikolopoulos et al. 2008). More specifically, 70% of the children with additional disabilities had developed connected speech intelligibility, while this was 96% for the children without additional disabilities. Moreover, only a small portion of the former group was intelligible for unfamiliar adult listeners. This implies that this group of hearing impaired children need special attention after implantation since additional disabilities appear to be negative predictive factors for the eventual outcome (Beer et al. 2012, Gérard et al. 2010).

9 Environmentally related factors

9.1 Communication modality

Most infants who are deaf or hard of hearing are born into hearing families (an estimated 96%, Mitchel & Karchmer 2004). This poses a problem of communication modality in the family: oral communication is the obvious mode for hearing parents, but with a deaf child the need for signing in combination with oral language (so called total communication) is also an option. The influence of communication modality on speech and language outcomes is difficult to assess (Kirk et al. 2002) but evidence points out that children living in environments that strongly emphasize oral language tend to have better speech and language outcomes (Boons et al. 2012a, Geers et al. 2003, Johnson & Goswami 2010, Kirk et al. 2002, but see McDonald Conner et al. 2000). In a similar vein, children who attend mainstream education (from earlier on) have a better spoken language development than children in special schools (Geers et al. 2003).

9.2 Family related factors

A number of family related factors have been shown to play a role in the success of CI children's rehabilitation: socioeconomic status (SES), maternal education level, the involvement of the family in therapy, parenting style, family size. These factors are related to a certain extend, as for instance SES is determined by education level.

Not surprisingly, high levels of parental involvement have a positive impact on children's language development. For instance, joint picture book reading is a well-known source of vocabulary development (Fletcher & Reese 2005, Vernon-Feagans et al. 2008). Sarrant et al. (2014) found a similar effect in children with CI: the time parents spent reading to their children significantly affected their vocabulary and language scores. Interestingly, the amount of time children spent watching a screen had a negative effect on those scores.

The influence of SES is well known from studies of NH children (Hart & Risley 1995): higher SES families tend to provide their children a qualitatively and quantitatively richer linguistic environment. They talk more, provide more vocabulary, more complex language structures, and in so doing present children more and better opportunities to pick up language. Children's language development tends to benefit from this richer input as judged, for instance, by their richer receptive and expressive vocabularies (Hoff 2003, Rowe 2008). A similar facilitative role is played by SES in the case of CI children (Niparko et al. 2010, Sarant et al. 2014).

The precise effect of these family related factors on CI children's linguistic development is not straightforward since there may well be many mediating factors (Frush Holt et al. 2012). One factor that plays a role is maternal language input: how much input does the child receive? And how finely tuned is the input to the language level of the child? Mothers of young CI children from mid-to-high SES provide equal amounts of speech and they appear to be even more responsive contingently upon their children's utterances in comparison with mid-to-high SES mothers of NH peers (Vanormelingen et al. 2015). In a follow-up study, Vanormelingen and colleagues compared interactions of the same group of mid-to-high SES NH and CI children with the interaction behaviour of mothers of low SES during the first two years of life. They found that mothers in the latter group were not only significantly less talkative, they were also less responsive to their children's vocal efforts. Even more dramatically: these mothers became even less talkative and less responsive over time. The effects on the children's vocal development was noticed early in life: their onset of babbling was seriously delayed in almost half of the participating children (Vanormelingen & Gillis in prep). Szagun & Stumper (2012) investigated mother infant dyads with different educational backgrounds (classified according to the number of years of schooling) and established that educational level correlated significantly with measures such as MLU (mean length of utterance) and number of expansions (expanding an incorrect child utterances "that boat" to "yes, that's a boat"). Higher educational level meant higher MLU and more expansions, and these characteristics of maternal language input implied faster linguistic growth in their implanted children: a richer vocabulary (more word types), more complex language (higher MLU), and higher scores for inflectional morphology 30 months after implantation. Hence, these authors conclude that the CI children's "home linguistic environment", or their experience with language, largely determines their progress in language acquisition.

10 Conclusion

Since the introduction of cochlear implants, severe-to-profound hearing-impaired children are given access to auditory information. The device permits them to develop speech and language skills that surpass those of children with comparable hearing deficits equipped with acoustic hearing aids. In this sense cochlear implantation is a successful innovation. Although implanted children start with an initial delay in spoken language, a quite significant group eventually reaches age appropriate levels of linguistic functioning. But the individual variation is also quite significant: while some children do catch up with their normally hearing peers, others do not achieve much language comprehension and production even after five years of device use (Barnard et al. 2015).

At present the individual variation in linguistic outcomes of cochlear implant recipients remains poorly explained. In the literature various factors have been proposed as determinants of the success of the intervention, but there are many factors that have been identified as predictors, and it proves to be very difficult to control them all in a single study. Moreover, cochlear implant users are a constantly "moving target", which complicates the identification of factors to which successful language development can be attributed and that account for individual variation in the outcomes.

Finally not until very recently the underlying consequences of early auditory deprivation and the consequences of "electrical hearing" for speech perception and production and language comprehension and production are under scrutiny (Houston et al. 2012). Much more research is needed to substantiate recent claims that children with CI pay less attention to speech than their normally hearing peers, have significantly reduced working memory capacity, and hence seem less well equipped for acquiring new words and developing grammar. Consequently our understanding of the neurocognitive underpinnings of these psycholinguistic processes are even less well developed and are in need of further investigation.

References

Anderson, I., V. Weichbold, P.S.C. D'Haese, J. Szuchnik, M. Sainz Quevedo, J. Martin, W. Shehata Dielern & L. Phillips. 2004. Cochlear implantation in children under the age of two – what do the outcomes show us? *International Journal of Pediatric Otorhinolaryngology* 68. 425–431.

Artières, F., A. Vieu, M. Mondain, A. Uziel & F. Venail. 2009. Impact of early cochlear implantation on the linguistic development of the deaf child. *Otology & Neurotology* 30 (6). 736–742.

Barnard, J. M., L. M. Fisher, K. C. Johnson, L. S. Eisenberg, N.-Y. Wang, A. L. Quittner, C. M. Carson, J. K. Niparko, The CDaCI Investigative Team 2015. A prospective longitudinal study of U.S. children unable to achieve open-set speech recognition 5 years after cochlear implantation. *Otology & Neurotology* 36 (6). 985–992.

Baudonck, N., K. Van Lierde, I. Dhooge & P. Corthals. 2011. A comparison of vowel productions in prelingually deaf children using cochlear implants, severe hearing-impaired children using conventional hearing aids and normal-hearing children. *Folia Phoniatrica et Logopaedica* 63. 154–160.

Beer, J., M. Harris, W. Kronenberger, R. Frush Holt & D. Pisoni. 2012. Auditory skills, language development, and adaptive behavior of children with cochlear implants and additional disabilities. *International Journal of Audiology* 51. 491–498.

Blamey, P., J. Sarant, L. Paatsch, J. Barry, C. Bow, R. Wales, M. Wright, C. Psarros, K. Rattigan & R. Tooher. 2001. Relationships among speech perception, production, language, hearing loss, and age in children with impaired hearing. *Journal of Speech, Language, and Hearing Research* 44. 264–285.

Boons, T., J. Brokx, I. Dhooge, J. Frijns, L. Peeraer, A. Vermeulen & A. van Wieringen. 2012a. Predictors of spoken language development following pediatric cochlear implantation. *Ear & Hearing* 33 (5). 627–639.

Boons, T., J. Brokx, I. Dhooge, J. Frijns, L. Peeraer, A. Vermeulen & A. van Wieringen. 2012b. Effect of pediatric bilateral cochlear implantation on language development. *Archives of Pediatric and Adolescence Medicine* 166 (1). 28–34.

Botting, N. 2005. Non-verbal cognitive development and language impairment. *Journal of Child Psychology and Psychiatry* 46 (3). 317–326.

Bourgeois-République, C., J.-J. Chabrier & P. Collet. 2004. Automatic fitting of cochlear implants with evolutionary algorithms. *Proceedings of the 2004 ACM symposium on applied computing*, 296–300.

Campbell, A., M. Dillon, C. Buchman & O. Adunka. 2013. Hearing preservation cochlear implantation. *Current Otorhinolaryngology Reports* 1. 69–79.

Caselli, M., P. Rinaldi, C. Varuzza, A. Giuliani & S. Burdo. 2012. Cochlear implant in the second year of life: Lexical and grammatical outcomes. *Journal of Speech, Language, and Hearing Research* 55. 382–394.

Clark, G. 1989. The bionic ear and beyond. *Journal of the Otolaryngological Society of Australia* 6 (4). 244–249.

Clark, G., Y. Tong & R. Dowell. 1983. Clinical results with a multichannel pseudobipolar system. *Annals of the New York Academy of Science* 404. 370–377.

Colletti, L., M. Mandalà, L. Zoccante, R. Shannon & V. Colletti. 2011. Infants versus older children fitted with cochlear implants: Performance over 10 years. *International Journal of Pediatric Otorhinolaryngology* 75. 504–509.

Colletti, V., M. Carner, V. Miorelli, M. Guida, L. Colletti & F. Fiorino. 2005. Cochlear implantation at under 12 months: Report on 10 patients. *The Laryngoscope* 115. 445–449.

Connor, C., H. Craig, S. Raudenbush, K. Heavner & T. Zwolan. 2006. The age at which young deaf children receive cochlear implants and their vocabulary and speech-production growth: Is there an added value for early implantation? *Ear & Hearing* 27. 628–644.

Cosetti, M. & S. Waltzman. 2012. Outcomes in cochlear implantation: Variables affecting performance in adults and children. *Otolaryngology Clinics North America* 45 (1). 155–171.

De Raeve, L. 2006. Making the case for early hearing detection and intervention in Flanders, Belgium. *Volta Voices*. 14–17.

De Raeve, L. 2014. *Paediatric cochlear implantation: Outcomes and current trends in education and rehabilitation.* Radboud Universiteit Nijmegen Ph.D. thesis.

De Raeve, L. & G. Lichtert. 2012. Changing trends within the population of children who are deaf or hard of hearing in Flanders (Belgium): Effects of 12 years of universal newborn hearing screening, early intervention, and early cochlear implantation. *The Volta Review* 112 (2). 131–148.

De Raeve, L. & A. Wouter. 2013. Accessibility to cochlear implants in Belgium: State of the art on selection, reimbursement, habilitation, and outcomes in children and adults. *Cochlear Implants International* 14 (S1). 18–25.

Desloovere, C., N. Verhaert, E. Van Kerschaver & F. Debruyne. 2013. Fifteen years of early hearing screening in Flanders: Impact on language and education. *B-ENT* 9. 81–90.

Dettman, S., D. Pinder, R. Bruggs, R. Dowell & J. Leigh. 2007. Communication development in children who receive the cochlear implant younger than 12 months: Risks versus benefits. *Ear & Hearing* 28. 11S–18S.

Dowell, R., A. Brown, P. Seligman & G. Clark. 1985. Patient results for a multiple-channel cochlear prosthesis. In R. Schindler & M. Merzenich (eds.), *Cochlear implants (10th Anniversary Conference on Cochlear Implants)*, 421–431. New York: Raven Press.

Duchesne, L., A. Sutto & F. Bergeron. 2009. Language achievement in children who received cochlear implants between 1 and 2 years of age: Group trends and individual patterns. *Journal of Deaf Studies and Deaf Education* 14 (4). 465–485.

Eisenberg, L. & W. House. 1982. Initial experience with the cochlear implant in children. *Annals of Otology, Rhinology & Laryngology* 91 (2). S67–S73.

Ely, R. 2005. Language and literacy in the school years. In J. Berko Gleason (ed.), *The development of language*, 395–443. Boston: Allyn & Bacon.

Eriks-Brophy, A., S. Gibson & S. Tucker. 2013. Articulatory error patterns and phonological process use of preschool children with and without hearing loss. *The Volta Review* 113 (2). 87–125.

Ertmer, D., & Goffman, L. 2011. Speech production accuracy and variability in young cochlear implant recipients: Comparisons with typically developing age-peers. *Journal of Speech, Language and Hearing Research* 54 (1). 177–189.

Ertmer, D., D. Kloibe, J. Jung, K. Connell Kirleis & D. Bradford. 2012. Consonant production accuracy in young cochlear implant recipients: Developmental sound classes and word position effects. *American Journal of Speech-Language Pathology* 21. 342–353.

Ertmer, D. J. & Mellon. 2001. Beginning to talk at 20 months: Early vocal development in a young cochlear implant recipient. *Journal of Speech, Language, and Hearing Research* 44. 192–206.

Faes, J., J. Gillis & S. Gillis. 2015. Syntagmatic and paradigmatic development of cochlear implanted children in comparison with normally hearing peers up to age 7. *International Journal of Pediatric Otorhinolaryngology* 79. 1533–1540.

Faes, J., J. Gillis & S. Gillis. 2016. Phonemic accuracy development in children with cochlear implants up to five years of age by using Levenshtein Distance. *Journal of Communication Disorders* 59. 40–58.

Fink, N., N.-Y. Wang, J. Visaya, J. Niparko, A. Quittner, L. Eisenberg E. & Tobey. 2007. Childhood development after cochlear implantation (CDaCI) study: Design and baseline characteristics. *Cochlear Implants International* 8 (2). 92–116.

Fletcher, K. & E. Reese. 2005. Picture book reading with young children: A conceptual framework. *Developmental Review* 25. 64–103.

Frush Holt, R., J. Beer, W. Kronenberger, D. Pisoni & K. Lalonde. 2012. Contribution of family environment to pediatric cochlear implant users' speech and language outcomes: Some preliminary findings. *Journal of Speech, Language, and Hearing Research* 55. 848–864.

Geers, A. 2002. Factors affecting the development of speech, language, and literacy in children with early cochlear implantation. *Language, Speech, and Hearing Services in Schools* 33. 172–183.

Geers, A. 2006. Spoken language in children with cochlear implants. In P. Spencer & M. Marschark (eds.), *Advances in spoken language development of deaf and hard-of-hearing children*, 244–270. Oxford: Oxford University Press.

Geers, A., C. Brenner & L. Davidson. 2003. Factors associated with development of speech perception skills in children implanted by age five. *Ear & Hearing* 24 (1S). 24S–35S.

Geers, A., J. Moog, C. Biedenstein, C. Brenner & H. Hayes. 2009. Spoken language scores of children using cochlear implants compared to hearing age-mates at school entry. *Journal of Deaf Studies and Deaf Education* 14 (3). 371–385.

Geers, A. & J. Nicholas. 2013. Enduring advantages of early cochlear implantation for spoken language development. *Journal of Speech, Language, and Hearing Research* 56. 643–653.

Geers, A., J. Nicholas & A. Sede. 2003. Language skills of children with early cochlear implantation. *Ear & Hearing* 24 (1S). 46S–58S.

Geers, A., E. Tobe, J. Moog & C. Brenner. 2008. Long-term outcomes of cochlear implantation in the preschool years: From elementary grades to high school. *International Journal of Audiology* 47 (Suppl. 2). 21–30.

Gérard, J.-M., N. Deggouj, C. Hupin, A.-L. Buisson, V. Monteyne, C. Lavis & M. Gersdorff. 2010. Evolution of communication abilities after cochlear implantation in prelingually deaf children. *International Journal of Pediatric Otorhinolaryngology* 74. 642–648.

Gilley, P., A. Sharma & M. Dorman. 2008. Cortical reorganization in children with cochlear implants. *Brain Research* 1239. 56–65.

Guo, L., L. Spencer & B. Tomblin. 2013. Acquisition of tense marking in English-speaking children with cochlear implants: A longitudinal study. *Journal of Deaf Studies and Deaf Education* 18 (2). 187–205.

Hammer, A. 2010. *The acquisition of verbal morphology in cochlear-implanted and specific language impaired children*. Universiteit Leiden Ph.D. thesis.

Hammes, D., M. Novak, L. Rotz, M. Willis, D. Edmondson & J. Thomas. 2002. Early identification and cochlear implantation: Critical factors for spoken language development. *Annals of Otology, Rhinology & Laryngology* 111. 74–78.

Hart, B. & T. Risley. 1995. *Meaningful differences in the everyday experience of young American children*. Baltimore: Brookes.

Hoff, E. 2003. The specificity of environmental influence: Socioeconomic status affects early vocabulary development via maternal speech. *Child Development* 74. 1368–1378.

Hoffman, M., A. Quittner & I. Cejas. 2014. Comparisons of social competence in young children with and without hearing loss: A dynamic systems framework. *Journal of Deaf Studies and Deaf Education*.

Holt, R. & M. Svirsky. 2008. An exploratory look at pediatric cochlear implantation: Is earliest always best? *Ear & Hearing* 29 (4). 492–511.

Houston, D., J. Beer, T. Bergeson, S. Chin, D. Pisoni & R. Miyamoto. 2012. The ear is connected to the brain: Some new directions in the study of children with cochlear implants at Indiana University. *Journal of the American Academy of Audiology* 23. 446–463.

James, C., B. Fraysse, O. Deguine, T. Lenarz, D. Mawman, A. Ramos & O. Sterkers. 2006. Combined electroacoustic stimulation in conventional candidates for cochlear implantation. *Audiology & Neurotology* 11 (S1). 57–62.

Johnson, C. & U. Goswami. 2010. Phonological awareness, vocabulary, and reading in deaf children with cochlear implants. *Journal of Speech, Language, and Hearing Research* 53. 237–261.
Jusczyk, P. 1997. *The discovery of spoken language*. Cambridge: MIT Press.
Kirk, K., R. Miyamoto, C. Lento, E. Ying, T. O'Neill & B. Fears. 2002. Effects of age at implantation in young children. *Annals of Otology, Rhinology & Laryngology* 111. 69–73.
Kochkin, S. 2010. The efficacy of hearing aids in achieving compensation equity in the workplace. *The Hearing Journal* 63 (10). 19–28.
Koopmans-van Beinum, F., C. Clement & I. van den Dikkenberg-Pot. 2001. Babbling and the lack of auditory speech perception: A matter of coordination? *Developmental Science* 4:1. 61–70.
Kral, A. & G. O'Donoghue. 2010. Profound deafness in childhood. *The New England Journal of Medicine* 363 (15). 1438–1450.
Kral, A. & A. Sharma. 2011. Developmental neuroplasticity after cochlear implantation. *Trends in Neurosciences* 35. 111–122.
Laaha, S., M. Blineder & S. Gillis. 2015. Noun plural production in preschoolers with early cochlear implantation: An experimental study of Dutch and German. *International Journal of Pediatric Otorhinolaryngology* 79. 561–569.
Leigh, J., S. Dettman, R. Dowell & R. Briggs. 2013. Communication development in children who receive a cochlear implant by 12 months of age. *Otology & Neurotology* 34. 443–450.
Lesinski, S., A. Illg, R. Heermann, B. Bertram & M. Lenarz. 2004. Pediatric cochlear implantation in the first and the second year of life: A comparative study. *Cochlear Implant International* 5 (4). 146–159.
Liker, M., V. Mildner & B. Sindij. 2007. Acoustic analysis of the speech of children with cochlear implants: A longitudinal study. *Clinical Linguistics & Phonetics* 21 (1). 1–11.
Mahdieh, N., B. Rabbani & I. Inoue. 2012. Genetics of hearing loss. In S. Naz (ed.), *Hearing loss*, 211–246. Rijeka: InTech Europe.
McDonald Connor, C., S. Hiebr, H.A. Arts & T. Zwola. 2000. Speech, vocabulary, and the education of children using cochlear implants: Oral or total communication? *Journal of Speech, Language, and Hearing Research* 43. 1185–1204.
Mitchell, R. & M. Karchmer. 2004. Chasing the mythical ten percent: Parental hearing status of deaf and hard of hearing students in the United States. *Sign Language Studies* 4. 138–163.
Moeller, M., B. Hoover, C. Putman, K. Arbataitis, G. Bohnenkamp, B. Peterson & P. Stelmachowicz. 2007. Vocalizations of infants with hearing loss compared with infants with normal hearing: Part I – Phonetic development. *Ear & Hearing* 28. 605–627.
Molemans, I. 2011. *Sounds like babbling. A longitudinal investigation of aspects of the prelexical speech repertoire in young children acquiring Dutch: Normally hearing and hearing-impaired children with a cochlear implant*. University of Antwerp Ph.D. thesis.
Molemans, I., R. van den Berg, L. Van Severen & S. Gillis. 2012. How to measure the onset of babbling reliably? *Journal of Child Language* 39. 523–552.
Möller, A. 2006. History of cochlear implants and auditory brainstem implants. *Advances in Otorhinolaryngology* 64. 1–10.
Montag, J., A, AuBuchon, D. Pisoni & W. Kronenberger. 2014. Speech intelligibility in deaf children after long-term cochlear implant use. *Journal of Speech, Language, and Hearing Research* 57. 2332–2343.
Moore, J. & S. Bass-Ringdahl. 2002. Role of infant vocal development in candidacy for and efficacy of cochlear implantation. *Annals of Otology, Rhinology & Laryngology* 111. 52–55.
Moreno-Torres, I. & S. Torres. 2008. From 1-word to 2-words with cochlear implant and cued speech: A case study. *Clinical Linguistics & Phonetics* 22. 491–508.
Nathani, S., D. Oller & A. Neal. 2007. On the robustness of vocal development: An examination of infants with moderate-to-severe hearing loss and additional risk factors. *Journal of Speech, Language, and Hearing Research* 50. 1425–1444.

Neumeyer, V., J. Harrington & C. Draxler. 2010. An acoustic analysis of the vowel space in young and old cochlear-implant speakers. *Clinical Linguistics & Phonetics* 24 (9). 734–741.

Nicholas, J. & A. Geers. 2006. Effects of early auditory experience on the spoken language of deaf children at 3 years of age. *Ear & Hearing* 27. 286–298.

Nicholas, J. & A. Geers. 2007. Will they catch up? The role of age at cochlear implantation in the spoken language development of children with severe to profound hearing loss. *Journal of Speech, Language, and Hearing Research* 50. 1048–1062.

Nicholas, J. & A. Geers. 2008. Expected test scores for preschoolers with a cochlear implant who use spoken language. *American Journal of Speech-Language Pathology* 17. 121–138.

Nicolaidis, K. & A. Sfakiannaki. 2007. An acoustic analysis of vowels produced by Greek speakers with hearing impairment. *Proceedings of 16th International Congress of Phonetic Sciences*, 1969–1972. Saarbrücken.

Nikolopoulos, T. 2015. Neonatal hearing screening: What we have achieved and what needs to be improved. *International Journal of Pediatric Otorhinolaryngology* 79 (5). 635–637.

Nikolopoulos, T., S. Archbold, C. Wever & H. Lloyd. 2008. Speech production in deaf implanted children with additional disabilities and comparison with age-equivalent implanted children without such disorders. *International Journal of Pediatric Otorhinolaryngology* 72. 1823–1828.

Niparko, J., E. Tobey, D. Thal, L. Eisenberg, N.-Y. Wang, A. Quittner & N. Fink. 2010. Spoken language development in children following cochlear implantation. *JAMA – Journal of the American Medical Association* 303 (15). 1498–1506.

Nittrouer, S. & C. Chapman. 2009. The effects of bilateral electric and bimodal electric–acoustic stimulation on language development. *Trends in Amplification* 13 (3). 190–205.

O'Donoghue, G. 2013. Cochlear implants – science, serendipity, and success. *New England Journal of Medicine* 369 (13). 1190–1193.

Oller, D. & R. Eilers. 1988. The role of audition in infant babbling. *Child Development* 59 (22). 441–449.

Oller, K. 2000. *The emergence of the speech capacity*. Mahwah, NJ: Lawrence Erlbaum.

Peng, S., L. Spencer & J. Tomblin. 2004. Speech intelligibility of pediatric cochlear implant recipients with 7 years of device experience. *Journal of Speech, Language, and Hearing Research* 47. 1227–1236.

Philips, B., P. Corthals, L. De Raeve, W. D'haenens, L. Maes, A. Bockstael & I. Dhooge. 2009. Impact of newborn hearing screening: Comparing outcomes in pediatric cochlear implant users. *The Laryngoscope* 119. 974–979.

Philips, B., L. Maes, H. Kepple & I. Dhooge. 2014. Cochlear implants in children deafened by congenital cytomegalovirus and matched Connexin 26 peers. *International Journal of Pediatric Otorhinolaryngology* 78 (3). 410–415.

Quittner, A., P. Leibac & K. Marciel. 2004. The impact of cochlear implants on young deaf children. *Archives of Otolaryngology – Head & Neck Surgery* 130. 547–554.

Ramirez Inscoe, J., & Nikolopoulos, T. 2004. Cochlear implantation in children deafened by cytomegalovirus: Speech perception and speech intelligibility outcomes. *Otology & Neurotology*, 25 (4), 479–482.

Redford, M. 2015. The acquisition of temporal patterns. In M. Redford (ed.), *The handboook of speech production*, 379–403. Hoboken, NJ: John Wiley & Sons.

Rowe, M. 2008. Child-directed speech: Relation to socioeconomic status, knowledge of child development and child vocabulary skill. *Journal of Child Language* 35. 185–205.

Ruffin, C., W. Kronenberger, B. Colson, S. Henning & D. Pisoni. 2013. Long-term speech and language outcomes in prelingually deaf children, adolescents and young adults who received cochlear implants in childhood. *Audiology and Neurotology* 18. 289–296.

Sarant, J. 2012. Cochlear implants in children: A review. In S. Naz (ed.), *Hearing loss*, 331–382. Rijeka: InTech.

Sarant, J., D. Harris, L. Bennet & S. Bant. 2014. Bilateral versus unilateral cochlear implants in children: A study of spoken language outcomes. *Ear & Hearing* 35 (4). 396–409.

Schauwers, K., S. Gillis, K. Daemers, C. De Beukelaer & P. Govaerts. 2004. The onset of babbling and the audiological outcome in cochlear implantation between 5 and 20 months of age. *Otology & Neurotology* 25. 263–270.

Schauwers, K., S. Gillis & P. Govaert. 2008. The characteristics of prelexical babbling after cochlear implantation between 5 and 20 months of age. *Ear and Hearing* 29. 627–637.

Schorr, E., F. Roth & N. Fox. 2008. A comparison of the speech and language skills of children with cochlear implants and children with normal hearing. *Communications Disorders Quarterly* 29. 195–210.

Schramm, B., A. Bohnert & A. Keilmann. 2009. The prelexical development in children implanted by 16 months compared with normal hearing children. *International Journal of Pediatric Otorhinolaryngology* 73. 1673–1681.

Sharma, A., M. Dorman & A. Kral. 2005. The influence of a sensitive period on central auditory development in children with unilateral and bilateral cochlear implants. *Hearing Research* 203. 134–143.

Sharma, A., E. Tobey, M. Dorman, S. Bharadwaj, K. Martin, P. Gilley & F. Kunkel. 2004. Central auditory maturation and babbling development in infants with cochlear implants. *Archives of Otolaryngology – Head and Neck Surgery* 130. 511–516.

Sparreboom, M., M. Langerei, A. Snik & E. Mylanus. 2015. Long-term outcomes on spatial hearing, speech recognition and receptive vocabulary after sequential bilateral cochlear implantation in children. *Research in Developmental Disabilities* 36. 328–337.

Spencer, P., M. Marschark & L. Spencer. 2011. Cochlear implants: Advances, issues, and implications. In M. Marschark & P. Spencer (eds.), *The Oxford handbook of deaf studies, language, and education*, 452–470. New York: Oxford University Press.

Svirsky, M., A. Robbins, K. Kirk, D. Pisoni & R. Miyamoto. 2000. Language development in profoundly deaf children with cochlear implants. *Psychological Science* 11. 153–158.

Svirsky, M., S. Teoh & H. Neuburger. 2004. Development of language and speech perception in congenitally, profoundly deaf children as a function of age at cochlear implantation. *Audiology and Neuro-otology* 9. 224–233.

Szagun, G. 2001. Language acquisition in young German-speaking children with cochlear implants: Individual differences and implications for conceptions of a 'sensitive phase'. *Audiology and Neuro-otology* 6. 288–297.

Szagun, G. & B. Stumper. 2012. Age or experience? The influence of age at implantation and social and linguistic environment on language development in children with cochlear implants. *Journal of Speech, Language, and Hearing Research* 55. 1640–1654.

Tobey, E., A. Geers, C. Brenner, D. Altuna & G. Gabbert. 2003. Factors associated with development of speech production skills in children implanted by age five. *Ear & Hearing* 24. 36S–45S.

Tomblin, B., B. Barker, L. Spencer, X. Zhang & B. Gantz. 2005. The effect of age at cochlear implant initial stimulation on expressive language growth in infants and toddlers. *Journal of Speech, Language, and Hearing Research* 48. 853–867.

Tomblin, B., S.-C. Peng, L. Spencer & N. Lu. 2008. Long-term trajectories of the development of speech sound production in pediatric cochlear implant recipients. *Ear & Hearing* 51. 1353–1368.

Tribushinina, E., S. Gillis & S. De Maeyer. 2013. Infrequent word classes in the speech of two- to seven-year-old children with cochlear implants and their normally hearing peers: A longitudinal study of adjective use. *International Journal of Pediatric Otorhinolaryngology* 77. 356–361.

Van Kerschaver, E., A. Boudewijns, L. Stappaerts, F. Wuyts & P. Van den Heyning. 2007. Organisation of a universal newborn hearing screening programme in Flanders. *B-ENT* 3. 185–190.

Vanormelingen, L., S. De Maeyer & S. Gillis. 2015. Interaction patterns of mothers of children with different degrees of hearing: Normally hearing children and congenitally hearing-impaired children with a cochlear implant. *International Journal of Pediatric Otorhinolaryngology* 79. 520–526.

Vanormelingen, L., S. De Maeyer & S. Gillis. 2016. A comparison of maternal and child language in normally hearing and children with cochlear implants. *Language, Interaction and Acquisition* 7 (2). 145–179.

Vanormelingen, L. & S. Gillis. in preparation. Babbling onset and consonant characteristics in babbles of children with different SES.

Verhoeven, J., O. Hide, S. De Maeyer & S. Gillis. 2016. Hearing impairment and vowel production. A comparison between typically developing, hearing-aided and cochlear implanted Dutch children. *Journal of Communication Disorders* 59. 24–39.

Vernon-Feagans, L., N. Pancsofar, M. Willoughby, M. Odom, E. Quade & M. Cox. 2008. Predictors of maternal language to infants during a picture book task in the home: Family SES, child characteristics and the parenting environment. *Journal of Applied Developmental Psychology* 29. 213–226.

Vincent, C., J. Bebear, E. Radafy, F. Vaneecloo, I. Ruzza, S. Lautissier & P. Bordure. 2012. Bilateral cochlear implantation in children: Localization and hearing in noise benefits. *International Journal of Pediatric Otorhinolaryngology* 76. 858–864.

Vlastarakos, P., K. Proika, G. Papacharalampous, I. Exadaktylou, G. Mochloulis & T. Nikolopoulos. 2010. Cochlear implantation under the first year of age – The outcomes. A critical systematic review and meta-analysis. *International Journal of Pediatric Otorhinolaryngology* 74. 119–126.

Vos, B., R. Lagasse & A. Leveque. 2014. Main outcomes of a newborn hearing screening program in Belgium over six years. *International Journal of Pediatric Otorhinolaryngology* 78 (9). 1496–1502.

Wright, M., A. Purcell & V. Reed. 2002. Cochlear implants and infants: Expectations and outcomes. *Annals of Otology, Rhinology & Laryngology* 111. 131–137.

Yoshinaga-Itano, C. 2004. Levels of evidence: Universal newborn hearing screening (UNHS) and early hearing detection and intervention systems (EHDI). *Journal of Communication Disorders* 37. 451–465.

Yoshinaga-Itano, C. 2006. Early identification, communication modality, and the development of speech and spoken language skills: Patterns and considerations. In P. Spencer & M. Marschark (eds.), *Advances in spoken language development of deaf and hard-of-hearing children*, 298–327. Oxford: Oxford University Press.

Yoshinaga-Itano, C., A. Sedey, D. Coulter & A. Mehl. 1998. Language of early- and later-identified children with hearing loss. *Pediatrics* 102. 1161–1171.

Young, G. & D. Killen. 2002. Receptive and expressive language skills of children with five years of experience using a cochlear implant. *Annals of Otology, Rhinology & Laryngology* 111. 802–811.

Sara Ingber and Tova Most
38 Parental involvement in early intervention for children with hearing loss

1 Introduction

Most children with permanent hearing loss (92%) are born to typically hearing parents (Mitchell & Karchmer, 2004) who are not familiar with the effects of hearing loss (HL) on a child's pathways to communication. Typically, hearing children learn to communicate through spontaneous interaction within their natural environment. This is not the case with children with HL. The presence of the HL may affect the child's language acquisition and development which normally occur in natural environments and through significant parent-child interactions (Bodner-Johnson & Sass-Lehrer, 2003). Early detection and intervention are believed to be critical steps toward proactive management of these children because of the critical window available for auditory neural development and speech and language acquisition (Cole & Flexer, 2011). As a result, for children with HL, early family involvement in intervention is crucial and should be implemented in their natural environment – such as at home – while maximizing the active participation and involvement of parents and other family members in the habilitation process (Yoshinaga-Itano, 2014).

Consequently, professionals encourage parents to take an active role in the intervention process and they often develop programs for the whole family in order to help the child realize the maximum benefit possible, by providing a consistent emphasis upon developing the different aspects of spoken language skills (Dromi & Ingber, 1999; Ingber & Dromi, 2009; Kaiser & Hancock, 2003; Moeller, 2000; Bodner-Johnson & Sass-Lehrer, 2003; Moog & Geers, 2003).

2 Definition of parental involvement

Parent involvement has been endorsed as a fundamental component of successful early intervention (Smith & Zaslow, 1995). Studies on early intervention for children with special needs present different definitions of the term **parental involvement** (Baily, 2001; Korfmacher et al, 2008; Raikes, Summers & Roggman, 2005). In explaining **parental involvement**, Baily (2001) emphasizes parental behaviors as being those that define the activities in which parents participate in order to be involved in their child's intervention program. He includes behaviors that range from bringing the

Sara Ingber and Tova Most, Tel Aviv University

child to the intervention center, at the second level: attending the therapy sessions, then following up on the professionals' recommendations, and on the highest level is the parental involvement in decision making, parental involvement in initiating and giving ideas to the child's therapist as well as supporting other parents. Along the same lines, the range from Head Start Program defined the activities that describe and typify parental involvement as being: volunteering in the child's classroom, observing the child in the classroom, helping with field trips, preparing materials for use in the classroom, attending parent/teacher conferences, workshops and social events, participating in the program's policy council and raising funds for the program (Raikes, Summers, & Roggman, 2005). Korfmacher et al (2008) defined parental involvement as including two broad dimensions: (a) the family's participation and manner of involvement in the child's intervention program, which includes the actions and behavior of the parents; and (b) the family's emotional engagement and commitment to the program and the professionals who operate it. Thus, Korfmacher et al (2008) not only highlighted practical behaviors and activities that typify parental involvement but also emphasized the degree of engagement and emotional interaction of family members in the intervention.

In addition to the above, parental involvement in the case of children with HL focuses particularly upon behavior and activities which involve language development and interaction with the children. Moeller (2000) defined parental involvement in early intervention for children with HL as the quality of family participation in early intervention, emphasizing their contribution to the child's communication and language development. The focus is placed upon what the parent can do to enhance and help his/her child's language acquisition. DesJardin, Eisenberg & Hodapp (2006) emphasize parental collaboration with professionals. Parental involvement is accomplished by following guidelines prescribed by the early interventionists. Ingber, Alyagon and Dromi (2011), described five kinds of parental involvement on a range from a passive involvement like bringing the child to the intervention center through participating in child's therapeutic sessions, communicating with professionals on a basic daily level, participating in decision making, taking responsibility on their child's development and being involved in parents' groups.

Brown, Bakar, Rickards & Griffin (2006) added a unique aspect to parental involvement in early intervention for children with HL that relates to the need for parental collaboration with professionals and their involvement when crucial decision-making is required. With regards to the optimal mode of communication for the child for example, parental involvement is essential when a decision has to be made as to whether the child will be educated through the use of spoken language, total communication (spoken language accompanied by signs) or sign language. Such a cardinal decision should take into account the parents' views, beliefs and hopes for their child's future. Parents can be involved also in decisions about the kind of vocabulary their child will be exposed to or what activities should be taught at home or in the intervention center. A second major decision that warrants close parental participation pertains to the optimal choice of personal amplification devices (i.e. hearing aids, cochlear implants, etc.) which may have different medical, social and habilitation implications for children of different ages. Yet another decision that requires close parental involvement relates to the choice of educational placement: oral inclusion (individual or group) or segregation (a class with only children with HL) (Ingber & Dromi, 2010).

3 Types of parental involvement

Parental involvement may express itself in many forms. It may be conveyed through a variety of activities such as: attending the child in an early intervention program, communicating with teachers and other school staff about the child's special needs, volunteering in schools and classrooms of children with disabilities, and attending parent-teacher conferences (Turnbull et al, 2009). Epstein (1996) related to more types of parental involvement. He listed five major types of parental involvement in early intervention programs for children with special needs:

- **Parenting**: Carrying out child-rearing duties (including health care), understanding the child's development and establishing home conditions that support safe daily life. In the case of children with HL parenting includes taking care of the child's hearing device, taking responsibility on the listening conditions at home etc.
- **Communicating**: Being in constant contact with professionals (general and specific information on the child's progress). In the case of children with HL parents should follow up the professional's guidelines and implement them at home.
- **Volunteering** to take part in activities in educational settings. Parents of children with HL should participate in the child's therapeutic sessions and take an active part in implementing the program strategies in everyday activities
- **Learning at home**: Active involvement in learning activities at home that are related to the child's disability. Parents of children with HL should be active in mediating everyday activities to the child enhancing his vocabulary and communication with others.
- **Decision-making**: Active involvement in governance and advocacy as decision makers. In the case of children with HL parents should be involved in the decision about the communication options of the child, the preference of the hearing device as well as the decision on the educational setting's.

As mentioned above, the ways in which parents are involved in their child's intervention differ. The degree and nature of parental involvement is linked to the parents' beliefs and expectations, as well as personality issues that are related to the parent's communication skills and the rapport they can establish with professionals (Beckman, 2002; Ingber & Dromi, 2009). Understanding how parental involvement is expressed in each family may help professionals encourage and enhance various types of involvement.

Ingber (Ingber & Dromi, 2010) identified five types of parental involvement in early intervention for children with HL. Some of them are similar to those cited by Epstein (1996) and others typify mothers' involvement in the early intervention for young children with HL. These activities focus upon the unique styles of involvement in early intervention that parents' of children with HL need to address:

- **Communication** with professionals illustrates standard general communication of mothers with professionals that is aimed at an exchange of information about the child's language and amplification. This feature is a basic activity that typifies all parent-professional co-operation.
- **Attendance** describes those activities that mothers perform to promote basic interaction with professionals. This factor indicates the mother's commitment to bring the child to therapeutic sessions and to obtain up-to-date information about the child's progress. It should be noted that the mother's attendance at therapeutic meetings does not necessarily demonstrate her active involvement or her readiness to act in accordance with the ongoing guidance from professionals.
- **Active collaboration** with professionals defines those activities that parents carry out to be involved and committed, and fully engaged in their child's therapy and habilitation process. This factor emphasizes mutual cooperation between parents and professionals that is expressed by the exchange of ideas about the child's communication performance.
- **Initiative and responsibility** expresses parental involvement in decision-making with regard to their child's rehabilitation process (e.g. type of hearing device and mode of communication) and in taking a greater part in the child's development by expanding therapy to the home environment.
- **Social involvement** demonstrates the highest level of involvement. Mothers are not only involved in their own child's intervention but also support other parents and take part in volunteer activities.

All of these types of parental involvement in early intervention for children with HL represent the wide range of styles in which parents can be involved. Different studies show that families choose to participate in diverse activities and may elect to adopt different styles of collaboration with professionals. Parents have a range of activities that are possible for them to choose and that best correspond to their own distinctive style (Ingber & Dromi 2010; Ingber et al., 2014).

In a study by Zaidman-Zait, Most, Tarrasch, Haddad & Brand, et al (2016) on the involvement of fathers and mothers of children with HL in the Arab sector, it was found that mothers and fathers both reported that their involvement was, for the most, passive. The parents maintained regular contact with the professionals and received information from them, however, they were not dominant in their initiations, activities or criticism. According to the reports, they were less involved in the decision-making process, in the assessments and evaluations, or less prone to provide ideas to improve the services than to participate in other involvement activities. In addition, they were not socially involved with other parents of children with HL.

The results reported in a previous study on mothers of children with HL in the Jewish sector were, in part, similar to those regarding mothers in the Arab sector but not completely so. Ingber & Dromi (2010) reported that for the most part, mothers in the Jewish sector insisted on constant contact with the child's professional team and ensured that the professionals were updated with regard to any new information about their child's health. In addition, the parents expected the professionals to provide them with any and all available information related to their child's development and they then applied the guidelines and advice they received. However, just as parents in the Arab sector, they were not very involved in active domains and were taking less initiative, not being very active in the decision-making process or in the assessments and evaluations, or when it came to initiating ideas to improve the services. They were also much less socially involved with other parents of children with HL than was expected. All those studies highlight the importance of parental involvement and the contribution to the child's development and outcomes.

4 What is the contribution of parental involvement?

Studies on the effects of parental involvement on the development of the child with HL have resulted in two major findings. First, information provided by the parents about various experiences have accounted for a significant portion of the inconsistency in the developmental outcomes of the children. In other words, despite the fact that biological or genetic conditions compromise the ability of children to learn and develop, the manner in which parents interact with their children still plays an important role in contributing to the developmental achievements that the children attain. Second, the parents' level of responsiveness is one of the main factors that contribute to children's development, at least during the first five years of their lives. Children whose parents are able to respond to their needs attain higher levels of communication, better cognitive and academic functions, as well as social relationships (Mahoney, 2009; Moeller et al, 2013).

Most of the studies on the effectiveness of parental involvement in early interventions for children with HL have highlighted the association between the types and levels of parental involvement and the child's achievements. Different kinds of parental activities such as constant involvement in therapy sessions, encouraging active communication with the child, close collaboration with professionals, participating in their children's social events in the early intervention programs have a significant influence on the children's language development (DesJardin, 2005; Henderson & Mapp, 2002; Jordan, Orozco & Averret, 2001), behavioral and social competence (Dunst & Trivette, 2009; King, Teplicky & Rosenbaum, 2004), cognitive development

(Ingber & Eden 2011) and early literacy development (Aram, Ingber & Konkol, 2010). Research has documented the fact that the active involvement of parents in early detection of the HL and early amplification are significant positive predictors of young children's language development, reading skills, social competence and everyday life management (Bruder & Dunst, 2008; DesJardin et al., 2006; Roush, Wilson & Alberg, 2008; Zaidman-Zait & Young, 2008). When parents are actively and constructively involved, and extend and utilize communication activities in the home environment, they contribute to facilitating their children's rehabilitation and language development during the early years, especially where communication, motivation to learn and self-esteem are concerned (Kahan et al., 2009; Patrikakou, Weissberg, Redding & Walberg, 2005a). To be more specific, parental level of responsiveness to their children's needs is one of the main factors that contribute to the cognitive and communication functions, as well as to the social emotional well-being of the child with HL, at least during the first five years of their lives (Mahoney 2009). In other words, progress in children's overall development has been associated not only with the level of parental responsiveness but with the extent and type of the mothers' involvement during early intervention. Mothers who participated in training groups that focused upon responsive behaviors such as reciprocity-interactions, contingency-interactions, shared control-match-interactions, and who followed professionals' guidance and directions, were able to adjust to their children's level of development and improved their children's functioning with regard to communication, as well as social and cognitive areas (Mahoney 2009).

5 Parental involvement and child's language and communication development

One major area that was reported to be influenced by parental involvement in early intervention for the child with HL is language and communication (Quittner et al, 2012; Moeller, 2000; Yoshinaga-Itano & Sedey, 2000; 2014). Holzinger, Fellinger & Beitel's (2011) research found that when a child's family intervened close to the time of diagnosis, there was a great impact on the childs' language achievements despite the age of the child at the time of diagnosis. In other words, the short time span between diagnosis and intervention was a very significant factor and it had a greater impact than the child's age and time of diagnosis. These authors reported that the age at which child's exposure to early intervention took place explained only about 4% of the variance in language outcomes. Their findings emphasized the fact that early intervention helps parents to gain a positive perspective, to use the prescribed hearing aids properly and to apply adapted communication strategies along with their child. Parents who were involved in their children's early intervention program had better communication with their children and contributed more to their children's progress in language development. Furthermore, parental involvement in the early stages of development was found to be critical for future language acquisition and educational development (Yoshinaga-Itano & Sedey, 2000), while limited family involvement was associated with significant child language delays at 5 years of age, especially when enrollment in intervention was delayed (Moeller, 2000). In other words, when parents were involved and expended the strategies of intervention into everyday situations, the child could learn how to generalize and communicate in different schemes. This activities had a critical influence on the child progress. Quittner et al. (2010) confirmed that parenting behavior and involvement in a child's early intervention, including a mother's sensitivity to her child's needs, affected the development of oral language. This conclusion was made after accounting for a child's early hearing experience and for the child and family demographics. Calderon (2000) pointed out that parental involvement, when added to maternal communication skills, were the strongest predictors for child's language development.

6 Parental involvement and child's academic success

Parental involvement was also positively related to the child's **academic successes** and **pre-reading** skills (Calderon, 2000). Cognitive readiness at kindergarten entry and parental involvement in school were incorporated as primary mediators of preschool effectiveness, and predictive of pre-reading skills in children with HL. The children of mothers who were involved in early intervention of their children, read them books, encouraged them to "write" notes and demonstrated better communication skills with their children, had higher language and reading scores and less behavior problems, after taking HL into account, in comparison to children of uninvolved mothers (Calderon, 2000; Calderon & Naidu, 2000; Reynolds et al., 1996).

Aram et al. (2010) conducted an intervention program for young children with HL. 79 children aged 5–6 and their parents participated in the program that included parental involvement in storybook reading, games and activities that encouraged letter knowledge, phonological awareness and functional writing. The study compared the performance of the children who attended two educational inclusion tracks: individual inclusion (a single student with HL fully integrated into a regular classroom) and co-enrollment (a group of students with HL partially integrated into a regular classroom and co-taught by a regular teacher and a special education teacher). Another group of children with HL studying in a co-enrollment track served as a control group. The program lasted one year, during which parents participated in four workshops that focused upon reading strategies. Results showed that children who had participated in the program and whose parents had encouraged storybook-telling at home had progressed more rapidly in the intervention with regard to phonological awareness and word writing than the control group, regardless their educational setting.

Griffith (1996) examined the influence of parental involvement as perceived by parents of children with HL in elementary schools. Data were collected from 41 elementary schools in a large suburban school district. Over 83% of parents who received surveys returned a completed survey, with a large sample of over 11,000 parents responding. Using the state's criterion-reference test as a measure of student achievement, the results indicated that schools with higher levels of perceived involvement of parents had higher student test scores than those with lower levels. This correlational relationship was positive and significant when other school and student characteristics were accounted for. Results also indicated that parents who had children in the same school showed agreement regarding feelings of involvement and empowerment. In other words, results indicate that parental involvement and empowerment accounted for substantial variance in the students' performance on standardized tests at school.

7 Parental involvement and child's socio-emotional functioning

A few research studies pointed out the impact of parental involvement on **socio-emotional functioning** of children with HL. For example, Calderon (2000) examined the impact of school-based, teacher-rated parental involvement on four achievements by children: language development, early reading skills, and positive and negative measures of social-emotional development. 28 children, aged 45 to 88 months, participated in the study. The author reported that teachers rated children of involved parents as being better adjusted and more competent with regards to social relations. Furthermore, examination of the relationship between parental involvement and child achievements demonstrated that maternal communication with the child and maternal use of additional services were positively related to the child's emotional understanding and social problem-solving skills (Calderon, 2000).

In summary, researchers concluded that: (1) parents are the major influence on their children's development – more than professionals – even when their children participate in an intervention program, and that (2) the effectiveness of the intervention is closely associated with the fact that parents have become more involved with their children during the course of the intervention.

8 What motivates parents of children with HL to be involved?

As mentioned above, early family involvement in early intervention for children with HL is crucial. This involvement contributes to the child's development in many domains: language and communication, social competence, cognition, etc. (Moores, 2001; Quittner et al. 2010). Mahoney (2009) demonstrated that the effectiveness of early intervention programs was related to the degree of parental responsiveness to their children's needs. In his study Mohoney encouraged parents to engage in highly responsive interactions during daily routines with their children. The results showed that the effectiveness of intervention was related to the degree to which parents were involved in and become more responsive with their children. As such, Mohoney recommended to encourage parent involvement and responsive interaction as they are key elements of successful early intervention practice. Caldron (2000) also demonstrated the impact of parental involvement on child's achievements. The study's findings indicate that not only parental involvement in their child with HL education program can positively contribute to academic performance. A more important and significant predictor to child's language and academic performance was parental communication skill with the child.

Although parental involvement was found, and is recognized, to be a major component in influencing a child's development, not all parents can or are able to be equally involved in their child's' early intervention and rehabilitation process. In addition, because of the many different definitions attributed to "parental involvement", this concept cannot be perceived as a single entity and should be thoroughly examined.

Encouraging parents to take a more meaningful role in their children's early intervention and education has proven to be a significant challenge (Yoshinaga-Itano, 2014). It is even more challenging with parents who have limited education or limited financial resources, or when parents come from cultural backgrounds that do not appreciate professional involvement and interference in their child's rearing (Epstein, 2001; Kahan, Stempler & Berchin-Weiss, 2009; Patrikakou et al., 2005). Researchers claim that professionals should inform parents about the positive aspects of their contribution to their children's current and future development and thereby enhance the families' motivation to be involved (Dempsey, Keen, Pennell, O'Reilly & Neilands, 2009; DesJardin et al, 2006). Moeller et al. (2013) stated that early intervention programs must take into consideration family differences, choices and manners of involvement. Professionals should tailor the intervention program according to family preferences and choices. Laosa (1999) emphasized the importance of recognizing how the interplay between culture, cognition, and social and emotional processes determines the ultimate success of parental involvement in early intervention. In Ingber and Dromi's study (2009), mothers considered their involvement to be a satisfactory component in the intervention and they suggested that parents should be offered a wider range of services such as various kinds of imformation, guidance and support, in order to be better able to respond to the diverse needs of their children. The mothers believed that this approach would help parents to become increasingly involved.

While searching for the variables that affect the motivation of parents to be more involved in the intervention process than others, several variables were reported to be crucial. Some of these variables are **personal parental attributes** (e.g. parental competence, self-efficacy, emotional state, parental level of education, parental hearing status and parental gender), **family characteristics** (e.g. family support)) and the **child's attributes** (e.g. child's age, type of sensory aid required, etc.) (Calderon, 2000; DesJardin et al., 2009; Ingber, Al-Yagon & Dromi, 2011; Ingber & Most 2012; Siebes et al., 2007; Zhang et al., 2011).

9 Parental and family characteristics

Parental **self-efficacy** was found to affect parental involvement in early intervention for children with HL (DesJardin, 2005). Parental **self-efficacy** refers to the feeling that a parent possesses about his/her knowledge, motivation and effectiveness as a parent in promoting his/her child rearing behaviors (Bandura, 1989 in DesJardin, 2005). For example, parental self-efficacy and competence were found to affect parental involvement in the children's language interventions (Dempsey, et al., 2009; DesJardin, 2005; Ingber, Most & Goldenberg, 2014). In other words, the mothers' sense of competence was associated with their use of strategies that enhanced their children's performance in language and communication. Strategies such as the mother's competence in the daily care of her child's sensory device, the mother's active involvement in her child's speech and language development, the quality of communicative interactions with the child, and the mother's ability to facilitate language strategies and linguistic mapping, imitations and directives. (For more details, see DesJardin, 2005).

A study carried out by Ingber, Most & Goldenberg (2014), evaluated the mothers' involvement with intervention for preschool children with HL. It was assumed that the child's language level was related to the degree of the mother's involvement in early intervention practices such as attending in the therapeutic session, implementing the intervention strategies at home etc. The results demonstrated that all the mothers were very highly involved and thus, there was no significant link between their involvement and the child's language level. However, the variable that was related to the language level was that of the mother's self-efficacy. Children of mothers who felt more competent exhibited higher language levels.

Different studies focused upon the role of the maternal **emotional state** as a risk factor in parental functioning. These studies highlighted the correlation found between mothers' depression and their general lack of motivation, energy and confidence, which, in turn, influenced a mother's ability to be involved in her child's early intervention (Ingber & Dromi, 2009; Epps & Jackson, 2000; Kohl, Lengua, McMahon & Conduct Problems Prevention Group, 2000). Moreover, Ingber et al. (2011) reported that high levels of anger and frustration were found to contribute significantly to reduced parental involvement in early intervention. Mothers who felt more frustrated and angry about having a child with HL exhibited difficulties in bringing their child to the early intervention center.

In contrast, mothers who exhibited an emotional state characterized by high levels of curiosity and motivation tended to make intensive efforts to be involved (Layzer, Goodson, Bernstein & Price, 2001; Ingber et al., 2010). Mothers of children with HL, who rated themselves as having a high level of curiosity, tended to perceive situations as interesting and challenging. These mothers had higher levels of involvement than mothers with a lower level of curiosity (Ingber et al., 2011). Furthermore, when critical decision-making was required, such as a decision regarding cochlear implant surgery, parents with high motivation were found to be more cooperative with professionals with regard to attempts to promote their child's rehabilitation (Zaidman-Zait, 2007).

Parental levels of involvement were found to be influenced by several **social support** systems. The social support systems could be formal ones, such as professionals and community services, or informal ones such as friends, neighbors and the extended family (Turnbull & Turnbull, 2001). Recently, Poon and Zaidman-Zait (2014) suggested that when designing early interventions for parents of children with HL, it is recommended that focus be centered upon enhancing mothers' sources of formal and informal support. These sources of support can provide emotional guidance and counseling, thereby enhancing the mother's ability to be involved in the intervention and to adjust to the needs of a child with HL.

Ingber et al., (2010) reported on the effect of informal social support upon maternal involvement. Mothers were asked to describe the kind and the amount of support they have in different areas (child rearing, household, emotional support etc.') with a greater level of social support from family and friends to whom they can turn for assistance or advice, were found to be more involved in the intervention programs for their children with HL. Moreover, mothers whose load of their many pressing daily tasks was lightened had more free time to deal with and be more involved in the upbringing of their child.

Another factor that was found to be linked to parental involvement was the **parents' level of education**. This variable was directly related to or was mediated by parental motivation for their involvement. Ingber (2004) reported on a negative correlation between maternal level of education and the mother's involvement in early intervention program of her child with HL. Mothers with higher levels of education reported less involvement, while mothers with lower levels of education mediated with high motivation reported a greater level of active involvement in the program. In other words, mothers with higher level of education were occupied with career progression and could not find the time to participate in their childs' early intervention. On the other hand, mothers with lower levels of education that had high levels of motivation found the involvement and participation in their child's early intervention as challenging yet satisfactory. These findings reinforced the argument that facing the child's HL may be more difficult for parents with higher levels of education based upon their higher expectations from the child. But when parents are motivated to be involved in the child's development, their motivation can enhance their willingness to take part in their child's early intervention program (Ingber et al., 2010; Marshrack, 2003).

Another variable that was reported to affect maternal involvement is the **maternal hearing status**. Hearing mothers were more involved in the intervention program than deaf or hard-of-hearing mothers. Other researchers reported limited involvement of deaf parents in early interventions. They attributed this behavior to these parents' difficulties in communicating and understanding the guidelines proposed by the professionals (Meadow-Orlans et al., 2003; Moores et al., 2001). These researchers claimed that when deaf parents were involved, it was possible to enhance their motivation and willingness to be involved in their child's rehabilitation process through accessible support and guidance. This claim was supported by Ingber (2004) who discovered that having formal and informal social support encouraged deaf/hard-of-hearing mothers to be more involved in the intervention.

Another factor that was found to be associated with parental involvement in intervention is **parental gender**. In fact, in most studies, the reports on parental involvement relate to the mother's involvement where she is usually the child's principal caregiver (Ingber et al., 2010; Ingber & Dromi, 2009; Mahoney, 2009; DesJardin, 2005). These findings are supported by research in different Western countries that reported that mothers are the principal caregivers of young children (Bianchi & Milkie, 2010) or people with various disabilities (Allen, 1999; Brett, 2002; Read, 2003) and therefore mothers are those who participate in early interventions, have a constant relationships with professionals and implement recommended intervention strategies at home. A recent study by Zaidman-Zait et al. (2016) compared the involvement of fathers from the Arab sector in Israel with young children with HL with that of mothers of young children with HL in the same sector. Their findings revealed that the mothers were significantly more involved than the fathers in taking care of the child in general, and in particular, with respect to children with HL. This finding supports previous findings in Arab society, showing that mothers are in charge of their young children while fathers take no active part in their care (Bouhdiba, 1997; Young, 1997). However, several studies have shown an interesting shift in fathers' involvement during the last decade. For example, a study by Ingber & Most (2012) evaluated the fathers' involvement. The authors examined fathers of preschool children with and without HL. Fathers completed the Inventory of Father Involvement developed by Hawkins et al., (2002) and adapted to Hebrew by Al-Yagon, (2009).

The results demonstrated that both groups of fathers were highly involved in their children's early development. Thus, when examining parental involvement, it is important to refer to both the mother and the father.

10 Child attributes

An additional group of factors that was reported to influence parental involvement in early intervention relates to the child's characteristics. These factors include characteristics such as the child's age or his/her hearing device (DesJardin, 2005; Ingber & Dromi, 2009; Ingber et al., 2010). DesJardin (2005), for example, reported on the influence of a **child's hearing device** upon maternal involvement in early intervention. Mothers of children with cochlear implants were found to be more involved than mothers of children with hearing aids. The author assumed that mothers who had decided to have an implant placed in their child through elective surgery were more motivated to be involved and to take part in their child's rehabilitation. DesJardin (2005), emphasized that the mothers perceived their role as advocates by being involved in the type, quantity and quality of child's therapy, and by being responsible for the management of their child's implant. These mothers were involved in a parent support group that was guided by professionals. In this group, the parents acquired knowledge and ideas of how to encourage the child's activities of listening, as well as language learning at home and in natural situations. By contrast, mothers of children with hearing aids rather than implants did not have to be as involved in managing the hearing device and did not have sense of commitment and responsibility of being involved and managing the child's progress (DesJardin, 2005).

Another factor that was reported to have an influence on parental involvment was the **child's age**. Reseachers reported that parents of younger children were very motivated to be involved and to take part in the rehabilitation process (DesJardin, 2005; Ingber & Dromi, 2009; Ingber et al., 2011). Furthermore, these studies emphasized that parental involvement in the child's early stages contributed not only to the child's emotional state but to that of the parents as well. Being involved in the early intervention of a very young child helped to significantly reduce parents' feelings of pressure. It enhanced the parents' knowledge about their child's needs, enabling them to apply the guidance and information they received from professionals as soon as their child had been diagnosed. These parents felt increasingly competent and possessed the motivation to be involved in their child's development (Ingber & Dromi, 2009).

Assessment of the parents' and the child's characteristics can assist professionals when tailoring the intervention in accordance to the family's and child's needs. This can lead to finding the optimal way to enable the parents to express their individual style for their involvement in the early intervention program for their child with HL (Dempsey et al., 2009). Programs must be based upon outlooks that are sensitive to a family's willingness to be part of the intervention, in conjunction with exhibiting sensitivity to parental competence and confidence with regard to parenting in order to promote the child's development.

11 Summary and Conclusions

Studies report high levels of parental involvement among parents of children with HL. This is a very important factor since it was found to be very significant in the effects upon various aspects in the child's development (DesJardin, 2005; Henderson & Mapp, 2002; Jordan, Orozco & Averret, 2001). In fact, the results suggest that success is achieved when early identification is paired with early intervention that actively involve the families (Moeller, 2000).

Parental involvement is a broad concept. It is related to various factors within the family, to the parent and the child, and it may be expressed in many different ways. Professionals should be aware of the various factors related to parental involvement and tailor the intervention according to the needs of each family, supporting and encouraging the family's way of dealing with the situation. This makes it possible for the parents to maximize their own involvement and enables them to have a positive effect on the child's development. Furthermore, parents still need to be encouraged to take an active role in the decision-making process and initiating improvements in services, and they should be socially involved in early intervention activities.

Future studies and research should continue to explore the crucial factors that affect parental involvement. Since more fathers have recently become more involved in their child's upbringing, additional research should focus upon examining the father's involvement in addition to that of the mother. Finally, future research should continue to examine this domain in the various cultures and societies in order to be able to meet the family's needs accordingly.

References

Al-Yagon, Michal. 2009. Comorbid LD and ADHD in childhood: Socioemotional and behavioral adjustment and parents' positive and negative affect. *European Journal of Special-Needs Education* 24. 371–391.

Aram, D., Sara Ingber & Smadar Konkol. 2010. Promoting alphabetic skills of young children with hearing loss in co-enrollment versus individual inclusion. L1- *Education studies in Language and Literature* 10(1). 139–165.

Bailey, Donald B. 2001. Evaluating parent involvement and family support in early intervention and preschool programs. *Journal of Early Intervention* 24(1). 1–14

Beckman, Paula J. 2002. Providing family-centered care. In M. L. Batshaw (ed.), *Children with disabilities*, 5th edition, 683–691. Baltimore: Brooks.

Brown, Margaret P. Zaharah Abu Bakar, Field W. Rickards & P. Griffin. 2006. Family functioning, early intervention support and spoken language and placement outcomes for children with profound hearing loss. *Deafness and Education International* 8(4). 207–226.

Bodner-Johnson, Barbara & Marilyn Sass-Lehrer. 2003. *The young deaf or hard of hearing child: A family-centered approach to early education*. Baltimore, MD: Paul H. Brooks.

Bruder, Mary Beth & Carl J. Dunst. 2008. Factors related to the scope of early intervention service coordinator practices. *Infants & Young Children* 21(3). 176–185.

Calderon, Rosemary. 2000. Parental involvement in deaf children's education programs as a predictor of child's language, early reading and social-emotional development. *Journal of Deaf Studies and Deaf Education* 4(2). 140–156.

Calderon, Rosemary & Susan Naidu. 2000. Further support for the benefits of early identification and intervention for children with hearing loss. *Volta review* 100(5). 53–84.

Cole, Elizabeth B. & Carol Flexer. 2011. Children with hearing loss: Developing listening and talking, birth to six, 2nd edition. San Diego: Plural Publishing, Inc.

Dempsey, Ian, Deb Keen, Donna Pennell, Jess O'Reilly & Judy Neilands. 2009. Parent stress, parenting competence and family-centered support to young children with an intellectual or developmental disability. *Research in Developmental Disabilities* 30(3). 558–566.

Desjardin, Jean L. 2005. Maternal perceptions of self-efficacy and involvement in the auditory development of young children with pre-lingual deafness. *Journal of Early Intervention* 27. 193–209.

DesJardin, Jean L., Laurie S. Eisenberg & Robert M. Hodapp. 2006. Sound beginnings: Supporting families of young deaf children with cochlear implants. *Infants & Young Children* 19. 179–189

Dromi, Esther & Sara Ingber. 1999. Israeli mothers' expectations from early intervention with their pre-school deaf children. *Journal of Deaf Studies and Deaf Education* 4. 50–68.

Dunst, Carl J. & Carol M. Trivette. 2009. Meta-analytic structural equation modeling of the influences of family-centered care on parent and child psychological health. *International Journal of Pediatrics (2009)*. 1–9.

Epps, Susan Ed. & Barbara J. Jackson. 2000. *Empowered families, successful children: Early intervention programs that work*. Washington, DC: American Psychological Association.

Epstein, Joyce L. 1996. Advances in family, community and school partnerships. *New schools, new communities* 12, 5–13.

Epstein, Joyce L. 2001. *School, family and community partnerships: Preparing educators and improving schools*. Boulder, CO: Westview Press.

Griffith, James. 1996. Relation to parental involvement, empowerment and school traits to student academic performance. *The Journal of Educational Research* 90(1). 33–41.

Hawkins, Alan J. Kay P. Bradford, Rob Palkovitz, Shawn L. Christiansen, Randal D. Day & Vaughn RA Call. 2002. The inventory of father involvement: A pilot study of a new measure of father involvement. *Journal of Men's Studies* 10(2). 183–196.

Henderson, Anne T. & Karen L. Mapp. 2002. *A new wave of evidence: The impact of school, family and community connections on student achievement*. Austin, TX: Southwest Educational Development Laboratory.

Holzinger, Daniel, Johannes Fellinger & Christoph Beitel. 2011. Early onset of family-centered intervention predicts language outcomes in children with hearing loss. *International journal of pediatric otorhinolaryngology* 75(2). 256–260.

Ingber, Sara. 2004. *The philosophy and practice of parental involvement in early intervention for children with hearing impairment in Israel*. Tel Aviv: Tel Aviv University Dissertation. (Hebrew)

Ingber, Sara, Michal Al-Yagon & Esther Dromi. 2011. Mothers' involvement in early intervention for children with hearing loss the role of maternal characteristics and context-based perceptions. *Journal of Early Intervention* 32(5). 351–369.

Ingber, Sara & Esther Dromi. 2009. Demographics affecting parental expectations from early deaf intervention. *Deafness Education International* 11(2). 83–111.

Ingber, Sara & Esther Dromi. 2010. Actual versus desired family-centered practice in early intervention for children with hearing loss. *The Journal of Deaf Studies and Deaf Education* 15(1). 59–71.

Ingber, Sara & Sigal Eden. 2011. Enhancing sequential time perception and storytelling ability among deaf and hard-of-hearing children. *American Annals of the Deaf* 156(4). 391–401.

Ingber, Sara & Tova Most. 2012. Fathers' involvement in preschool programs for children with and without hearing loss. *American Annals of the Deaf* 157(3). 273–285.

Ingber, Sara, Tova Most & N. Goldenberg. 2014. Mothers' perception of their involvement in their child's intervention program and its relations to the child's language performance. *DASH* 33. 37–60 (Hebrew)

Jordan, Catherine, Evangelina Orozco & Amy Averett. 2001. *Emerging issues in school, family & community connections*. Austin, TX: Southwest Educational Development Laboratory.

Kahn, Ruth, Steven Stemler & Janice Berchin-Weiss. 2009. Enhancing parent participation in early intervention through tools that support mediated learning. *Journal of Cognitive Education and Psychology* 8(3). 269–287.

Kaiser, Ann P. & Terry B. Hancock. 2003. Teaching parents new skills to support their young children's development. *Infants & Young Children* 16(1). 9–21.

King, Susanne, Rachel Teplicky, Gillian King & Peter Rosenbaum. 2004. Family-centered services for children with cerebral palsy and their families: A review of the literature. *Seminars in Pediatric Neurology* 11(1). 78–86.

Kohl, Gwynne O. Liliana J. Lengua, Robert J. McMahon & Conduct Problems Prevention Group. 2000. Parent involvement in school: Conceptualizing multiple dimensions and their relations with family and demographic risk factors. *Journal of School Psychology* 38. 501–523.

Korfmacher, Jon, Beth Green, Fredi Staerkel, Carla Peterson, Gina Cook, Lori Roggman, Richard A. Faldowski & Rachel Schiffman. 2008. Parent involvement in early childhood home visiting. *Child and Youth Care Forum* 37(4). 171–196.

Laosa, Luis M. 1999. Intercultural transitions in human development and education. *Journal of Applied Developmental Psychology* 20. 355–406.

Layzer, Jean I. Barbara D. Goodson, Lawrence Bernstein & Cristofer Price. 2001. *National evaluation of family support programs. Volume A: The meta-analysis. Final report*. Cambridge, MA: Abt Associates Inc. http://www.abtassociates.com/reports/NEFSP-VolA.pdf. (accessed 22 December 2009)

Mahoney, Gerald. 2009. Relationship Focused Intervention (RFI): Enhancing the role of parents in children's developmental intervention. *International Journal of Early Childhood Special Education* 1(1). 79–94.

Marschark, Marc & Patricia Elizabeth Spencer. 2003. *Oxford handbook of deaf studies, language and education*. New York: Oxford University Press.

Meadow-Orlans, Kathryn P. Marilyn Sass-Lehrer & Donna M. Mertens. 2003. *Parents and their deaf children: The early years*. Washington DC: Gallaudet University Press.

Mitchell, Ross E. & Michael A. Karchmer. 2004. Chasing the mythical ten percent: Parental hearing status of deaf and hard-of-hearing students in the United States. *Sign Language Studies* 4(2). 138–163.

Moeller, Mary Pat. 2000. Early intervention and language development in children who are deaf and hard-of-hearing. *Pediatrics* 106(3). 1–9.

Moeller, Mary Pat, Gwen Carr, Leeanne Seaver, Arlene Stredler-Brown & Daniel Holzinger. 2013. Best practices in family-centered early intervention for children who are deaf or hard of hearing: An international consensus statement. *Journal of Deaf Studies and Deaf Education* 18(4). 429–445.

Moog, Jean Sachar & Ann E. Geers. 2003. Epilogue: Major findings, conclusions and implications for deaf education. *Ear and Hearing Monograph* 24(1). 121S–125S.

Moores, Donald F. 2001. *Educating the deaf: Psychology, principles and practices*. Boston: Houghton Mifflin.

Moores, Donald F. Jerry Jatho & Cynthia Dunn. 2001. Families with deaf members: American Annals of the Deaf, 1996 to 2000. *American Annals of the Deaf* 146(3). 245–250.

Most Tova, Ricardo Tarrasch, Eliana Haddad & Devora Brand. 2016. The impact of childhood hearing loss on the family: Mothers and fathers stress and coping resources. *Journal of Deaf Studies and Dead Education* 21. 23–33.

Patrikakou, Evanthia N. & Amy R. Anderson (eds.). 2005. *School-family partnerships for children's success*. New York, NY: Teachers College Press.

Poon, Brenda T. & Anat Zaidman-Zait. 2014. Social support for parents of deaf children: Moving toward contextualized understanding. *Journal of Deaf Studies and Deaf Education* 19(2). 176–188.

Quittner, Alexandra L. David H. Barker, Ivette Cruz, Carolyn Snell, Mary E. Grimley, Melissa Botteri & CDaCI Investigative Team. 2010. Parenting stress among parents of deaf and hearing children: Associations with language delays and behavior problems. *Parenting: Science & Practice* 10. 136–155

Raikes, Helen H. Jean Ann Summers & Lori A. Roggman. 2005. Father involvement in Early Head Start research programs. *Fathering* 3(1). 29–52.

Reynolds, David. 1996. *Making good schools: Linking school effectiveness and school improvement*. London: Routledge.

Roush, Jackson, Kathryn Wilson & Joni Alberg. 2008. Audiologists and speech-language pathologists collaborate in successful program. *ASHA Leader* 13(2). 14–17.

Sass-Lehrer, Marilyn & Barbara Bodner-Johnson. 2003. Early intervention: Current approaches to family-centered programming. In Marc Marschark & Patricia Elizabeth Spencer (Eds.), *Deaf studies, language and education*, 65–81. New-York: Oxford University Press.

Siebes, Renate C. Lex Wijnroks, Marjolijn Ketelaar, Petra E.M. Van Schie, Jan Willem Gorter & Adri Vermeer. 2007. Parent participation in paediatric rehabilitation centres in the Netherlands: A parent's viewpoint. *Child: Care, Health and Development* 33(2). 196–205.

Smith Shila & Martha Zaslow. 1995. Rationale and policy context for two-generation interventions. In Shila Smith (Ed.), *Two-generation programs for families in poverty: A new intervention strategy*, 1–36. Norwood, NJ: Ablex.

Turnbull, Ann P. Jean Ann Summers, George Gotto, Matt Stowe, Donna Beauchamp, Samara Klein, Kathleen Kyzar, Rud Turnbull & Nina Zuna. 2009. Fostering wisdom-based action through web 2.0 communities of practice: An example of the early childhood family support community of practice. *Infants & Young Children* 22(1). 54–62.

Turnbull, Ann P. & Rutherford H. Turnbull. 2001. *Families, professionals and exceptionality: Collaboration for empowerment*. Des Moines, IA: Merrill Prentice Hall.

Yoshinaga-Itano, Christine & Allison Sedey. 2000. Early speech development in children who are deaf or hard-of-hearing: Interrelationships with language and hearing. *The Volta Review* 100(5). 181–211.

Yoshinaga-Itano, Christine. 2014. Principles and guidelines for early intervention after confirmation that a child is deaf or hard-of-hearing. *Journal of Deaf Studies and Deaf Education* 19(2). 143–175.

Zaidman-Zait, Anat. 2007. Parenting a child with a cochlear implant: A critical incident study. *Journal of Deaf Studies and Deaf Education* 12(2). 221–41.

Zaidman-Zait, Anat & Richard A. Young. 2008. Parental involvement in the habilitation process following children's cochlear implantation: An action theory perspective. *Journal of Deaf Studies and Deaf Education* 13(2). 193–214.

Esther Dromi, Yonat Rum and Jessica Goldberg Florian
39 Communication, language, and speech in young children with autism spectrum disorder (ASD)

1 Introduction

In recent years there has been a growing increase in the awareness about the merit of early intensive intervention for young children with autism spectrum disorder (ASD). Research has indicated that early diagnosis of ASD using standardized assessment tools, such as the Autism Diagnostic Observation Schedule (ADOS) and the Autism Diagnostic Interview-Revised (ADI-R), is valid and consistent (Zuddas, 2013). Studies on the efficacy of intervention point to the noteworthy gains in language and in cognition when appropriate targets are selected and the intervention is intensive (Dawson et al., 2010; Warren et al., 2011).

This chapter reviews findings on the development and impairments of communication, language comprehension, and expressive speech that are associated with ASD. In the opening section of this chapter we address the heterogeneity that exists with respect to language abilities in young children with ASD. In the following sections we summarize findings on emotional bonding, social communication, language comprehension, and speech production. The objective of this review is to assist language clinicians in identifying goals for intervention for young children with ASD.

2 Variability in language learning and use by young children with ASD

According to the *Diagnostic and Statistical Manual of Mental Disorders, Fifth Edition* (DSM-5) published by the American Psychiatry Association (2013), ASD is a neurobiological developmental disability that is characterized by two essential areas of impairments: persistent deficits in communication and in social interaction across multiple contexts; and restricted repetitive patterns of behaviors, interests, or activities. The symptoms must be present early in life, even if not all of them are fully manifested, and the impairments must cause obvious adjustment problems. The disorder may appear with or without intellectual or linguistic impairments, domains in which children vary greatly from one another (Norbury, 2013).

Esther Dromi, Yonat Rum and Jessica Goldberg Florian, Tel Aviv University, Accord, Communication, Language and Speech Clinic

Language abilities in ASD may range from no or minimal speech to a full range of linguistic competency in comprehension, production, and even in literacy (Kim et al., 2014). According to current estimates, 15–20% of individuals with ASD fail to learn even single words for communication purposes, while approximately 50% obtain complex expressive skills by adolescence, and the remainder attain fluent and functional speech (Luyster and Lord, 2009). While phonology and syntax are generally viewed as less affected in ASD, semantics and pragmatics are areas of salient difficulty. The use of language in context, which includes both conversational skills as well as narrative abilities, is the core deficit in ASD. It is one which is noted even in individuals who acquire functional speech (Losh and Gordon, 2014), and which persists in a subtle way even in individuals with "optimal outcome" (Suh et al., 2014). The prognosis of children with ASD with respect to educational, adaptive, and emotional outcomes is closely linked to their linguistic abilities during the preschool years (Kuhl et al., 2013; Norbury, 2013).

Language impairments in children with ASD were traditionally attributed to reduced social interest and limited interaction during infancy, as well as to a lack of social learning from adults throughout childhood (Tomblin, 2011). Deficits in Theory of Mind (Astington and Jenkins 1999; Peterson, Wellman, and Liu 2005) and Weak Central Coherence (Happé and Frith, 2006) were invoked to explain the difficulty these children experience in learning language. Some researchers have argued that executive dysfunctions (e.g., limitations in working memory, inhibition, goal oriented behaviors, planning, and self-monitoring) impede the process of language learning in this population (Norbury, 2013).

Over the last decade, it has often been argued that ASD and specific language impairment (SLI) are comorbid conditions. Kjelgaard and Tager-Flusberg (2001) were the first to argue for the need to differentiate between autistic children with language impairment (ALI) and autistic children with normal language (ALN) whose scores are within the typical range on formal language tests (Loucas et al., 2008; Tomblin, 2011). Norbury (2013) argued that ASD should be seen as a multifactorial disorder. She cited an article by Bishop (2010) and posited that co-morbidity occurs much more frequently in neurodevelopmental disorders than was estimated in the past.

3 Engagement: Bonding with the adult caretaker

Ample research shows that typical cognitive and social development is largely dependent on the baby's emotional relationship with the primary caretakers. An emotional attachment between the parents and the baby is formed immediately following birth and grows over the first year of life. The intimate dyadic encounters between the mother and her baby involve co-regulation, in which each participant contributes their respective part (Feldman, 2003). During the first months of life, the baby's activities (e.g., alertness, cooing sounds, crying, and opening eyes) invite adult responses and interpretations (Bates et al., 1979; Meltzoff, 2013). The interpretations that adults give to the baby's activities lead to recurring experiences and to consistency in adult-child socio-emotional transactions.

The development of mutual engagement during the first year of life is highly cultivated by the baby's visual behaviors. Babies whose development is intact are able to respond, initiate, and maintain eye contact and face-to-face gaze from the age of several weeks old (Aslin, 1987). Stern (1974) claimed that both adult and baby are active in exchanging glances. The baby's gaze towards the mother provides a positive response to parental attempts to create eye contact and increases the chances that she will continue to play with her baby. Papousek and Borenstein (1992) found that parents tend to position their faces at the center of the child's visual field and use different methods of stimulation to direct the baby's visual attention to their face. Adults frequently use facial expressions, various gestures, and vocal productions in response to the baby's visual attention. The appearance of a social smile around the age of 6 weeks also leads to the consolidation of the bonding between the adult and the baby (Reddy, 1999).

Around the age of 6 months, babies begin to show visual interest in the objects and events in their surroundings (Trevarthen, 1979). This behavior encourages the adult to describe the object that the child is observing. Towards the end of the first year of life, the ability to initiate and participate in intentional mutual communication emerges (Harding, 1983). The baby begins to separate both physically and emotionally from his primary caregiver. This separation is particularly apparent in the independent explorations that the baby displays, and has a seminal role in the establishment of interpersonal communication between the child and the adults (Adamson, 1995). Adamson, Bakeman, and Deckner (2004) describe the interaction patterns between adults and babies and how symbol-infused joint engagement (i.e., a triad) leads to language learning.

3.1 Early signs for ASD: Red flags

Very little is known about the early emotional experiences of children with ASD. Initial findings that are not yet conclusive, and which are based on various models of data collection (e.g., retrospective research, prospective sibling studies and neuroimaging), suggest that during the first year of life not all infants who later were diagnosed with ASD showed signs of being less engaged with their parents, or exhibited different developmental trajectories than TD infants (Landa et al., 2013).

Several studies utilized retrospective analyses of home video recordings of diagnosed children during their first year of life. The findings suggested that some children demonstrated avoidance of visual orientation to faces of other people, reduced eye contact, limited attempts to initiate body contact (e.g., to be held in parents' arms), less social responses to appearance of parents, and reduced head-turn to human voice or parents calling their names (Baranek, 1999; Clifford and Dissanayake, 2008; Paul, 2008).

The prevalence of ASD among siblings of diagnosed children is five times higher than in the general population (Ozonoff et al., 2011). Therefore, longitudinal prospective studies of sibling cohorts provide invaluable information concerning those infants who are at risk for developing ASD (Zwaigenbaum et al., 2007; Landa et al., 2013; Zwaigenbaum et al., 2015a). Sibling studies suggest that early signs of ASD do not emerge before age 18 months (Zwaigenbaum et al., 2015a; Macari et al., 2012), however, it has been suggested that some children who were later diagnosed with ASD showed impairments at around 12 months of age in terms of eye contact and social smiles, as well as reduced rates of canonical babbling and a lack of overt enjoyment while interacting with their parents (Dromi, in press). Paul and associates (2011) found that infants at risk for ASD show differences in some paralinguistic vocal behaviors when compared to their peers at low risk for ASD. The former produce fewer speech-like vocalizations, more non-speech vocalizations, fewer consonant types, and fewer canonical syllable shapes. The presence of these differences in the first year of life was associated with autistic symptomatology in the second year, leading the researchers to conclude that early vocal behavior is a sensitive indicator of heightened risk for ASD in infants with a family history of this disorder (Paul et al., 2011).

Many researchers share the view that it is not yet possible to identify a distinctive group of infants who are at risk for ASD as early as 12–18 months. Pierce et al., (2011) reported that the general screening procedure at age 12 months efficiently distinguished TD children from those who exhibited a wide range of developmental disorders, but did not necessarily identify children with ASD (Pierce et al., 2011; Landa et al., 2013)

An international multidisciplinary panel of researchers and practitioners has recently published a statement regarding the best practice standards for early identification, screening, and intervention with children below 24 months of age (Zwaigenbaum et al., 2015b). They claimed that the long-term stability of an ASD diagnosis is viable for children older than two years. ASD screening of the general population before the second birthday may result in false-positive results, and therefore should not take place too early. Siblings of children with ASD who are at substantial risk for the disorder, as well as other developmental challenges, should receive repeated examinations by pediatricians and clinicians between the ages of 18–36 months. Landa et al. (2013) also proposed beginning therapy around age two, to refer to relevant professionals if developmental delays are noticed, and to refer families for more specific assessments around age 36 months in order to verify an ASD diagnosis.

Dromi and Shteiman (2011) proposed that the following non-verbal social-emotional behaviors should be examined in children who are at risk for ASD: initiation, response and sustaining of eye contact; interest in facial expressions and mouth movement of the adult; social smile and level of emotional engagement; pleasure derived from participation in dyadic games; attention to human voice and especially head turn in response to hearing their name. These behaviors are prerequisites for the acquisition of more advanced communicative attainments that are described in section 4.

3.2 Visual behaviors and face processing in individuals with ASD

The difficulty in establishing eye contact and in processing facial expressions is found among individuals with ASD across all levels of functioning (Dawson, Webb, and McPartland, 2005). The deficits in the ability to process faces seem to be primarily centered on the area around the eyes, which is an emotionally charged region of the face (Tanaka and Sang, 2016). High-functioning adults with ASD report that eye contact, processing faces, and reading facial cues constitute extremely difficult tasks for them (Nadig et al., 2010; Pascal, 2012). The difficulty of integrating visual and auditory information for processing linguistic input, especially in terms of shifting from one modality to the other, has been proposed as an explanation for the visual withdrawal of individuals with ASD (Nadig et al., 2010; Pascal, 2012, Norbury, 2013).

Avoiding the eyes may be an adaptive strategy which protects individuals with ASD from the discomfort and threat perceived to be posed by the eyes. However, this approach exacerbates the social challenges for persons with ASD, as it affects the ability to encode and to discriminate information about facial identity, expression, and intention, further interfering with social processing (Tanaka and Sang, 2016).

An interesting theory on why eye gaze is such an area of difficulty for babies at risk for ASD was recently proposed by Jones and Klin (2013): They report a steady decline in eye fixation throughout the first two years of life in siblings of children with ASD. Klin and associates (2015) suggest that looking behaviors during the first three months of life are guided by automatic low-level brain procedures. From age 3 months and onward the underlying mechanisms that control gaze are cortical and reinforced by social interactions. The hypothesis is that in the transition from automatic to cortical eye gaze control mechanisms, babies with an atypical course of brain development fail to appropriately develop visual fixation and therefore exhibit a decline pattern. This hypothesis requires further testing.

4 Intentional communication: Pre-verbal behaviors

Towards the beginning of the second year of life, toddlers become active participants in pre-linguistic communication, as they successfully direct the attention of partners towards the object of their interest (i.e., proto-declaratives), and begin to influence the actions of other people (i.e., proto-imperatives) (Dromi and Zaidman-Zait, 2011). The appearance of intentional communication indicates fusion between "object schemes" and "social schemes" that during infancy developed in parallel (Sugarman,

1983). Researchers emphasize the important achievement of being able to differentiate between the "self" and the "other", as well as the ability to conceptualize the notion of an agent as related to the emergence of intentional communication (Harding 1983; Meltzoff, 2013; Tomasello, 1995).

During this developmental phase, the toddler and the adult take reciprocal roles of initiating and responding, and also increasing the length of episodes of joint attention (Dromi and Zaidman-Zait, 2011). This is manifested by the alternation of gaze between the object and the communication partner (i.e., the adult or toddler). Social referencing also appears around 13–15 months, shortly before the emergence of symbolic representation and first words (Repacholi 1998). During the second year of life, sensory-motor dyadic activities occur alongside triadic episodes involving the adult, the toddler, and a book or a toy, to which both partners simultaneously direct their attention (Adamson, Bakeman, and Deckner, 2004; Ringwald-Frimerman, 2003). It is through these triadic interactions that the toddler acquires the notion that there are multiple points of view with regard to objects or events, and that mental states such as thoughts, emotions, and beliefs direct and influence observable behaviors (Hobson, 1993; Tomasello, 1995).

Even before the first words appear, toddlers express a wide range of communicative intentions: They use intonation patterns and gestures for conveying agreement or disagreement, requests, and descriptions; they also provide answers in response to questions and carry out simple instructions. Even before language appears, it is possible to observe imitations of actions or vocal productions that are modeled by an adult (Dromi and Ringwald-Frimerman, 1996).

As indicated earlier, social communication presents a genuine challenge for the ASD population. Paul (2008) lists a number of problem areas for children with ASD that are noted prior to the emergence of their first words: following an adults' gaze, pointing, gesturing, and vocalizing. She and other researchers described the limited abilities of pre-linguistic children with ASD to use gestural and visual means of communication. The communicative intentions that young children with ASD express are often limited to a single function, such as proto-imperatives (i.e., early forms of requests for an activity or food). These are often expressed through crying or pulling a parent's hand toward a desired object or place, and often go unnoticed by the parents (Shteiman and Dromi, 2007). Deictic gestures such as showing, giving, or pointing occur very rarely in children with ASD, and they hardly use proto-declaratives (i.e., early forms of commenting or describing, such as pointing out a dog on the street) (Shteiman and Dromi, 2007).

In a series of pioneering studies, Mundy and colleagues (1986, 1990) looked at emerging social abilities in young children with ASD, and compared them to TD children and children with Down syndrome (DS) at the same language levels. These researchers concluded that the core deficit in ASD is the inability to initiate, respond, or sustain joint attention, leading to a failure to learn from others (Mundy, Sigman, and Kasari, 1986, 1990; Mundy et al., 1986). This claim was supported in subsequent studies that reported low rates of joint attention episodes among children with ASD, and much shorter triadic episodes when they did occur (Clifford and Dissanayake, 2008; Kasari, Freeman, and Paparella, 2006). The deficit in joint attention, which is so notable in ASD, is often attributed to the inability of the child to internalize the idea that another person may hold different desires, beliefs, expectations, and perspectives than his. Moreover, as was argued by Adamson et al. (2004, 2009), this deficit has severe consequences for future learning of conventional language.

In their developmental model, Dromi and Shteiman (2011) proposed that the following communicative behaviors should be evaluated in all children suspected for ASD: initiation and response to pointing; episodes of joint attention; triadic play episodes; turn taking; switching attention from a person to an object and vice versa; social referencing; and producing declarative and imperative communicative intentions.

5 Language comprehension

Internalized rules of grammar (i.e., phonology, morphology, semantics, syntax and pragmatics) enable the child to understand words, syntactic constructions, and connected discourse. The ability to fully comprehend language is based on a process of identifying units, memorizing, organizing, analyzing, and processing them (Peters, 1983). Controlled experiments show that several months before they begin to talk, TD children identify the phonotactic attributes of the language they hear, identify syllabic units in the input, differentiate between possible words in their mother tongue and show a preference for listening to the language to which they are exposed (Jusczyk, 1997). Toddlers begin to respond to simple instructions such as "where is the light?", "wave bye-bye", "what does a fish do?", "where is daddy?", "give me a kiss", and so on, towards the end of the first year of life (Kuhl et al., 2008).

The ability to comprehend language is closely related to the ability to connect phonological representations with cues perceived through the visual and other sensory channels. The child must associate between the linguistic symbols he hears and the designated object, event, relation, or complete experience in the real world. The scientific term for this designation is "reference" or "extension" (Dromi, 1987). Relationships between linguistic terms and real world entities are random and therefore require processing, organization, and memorization.

Abstract syntactical rules are derived by the child from the repeated experience listening to the language and deciphering its structure (Bowerman, 1988). A strong link exists between syntactic knowledge and lexical learning (McGregor et al., 2012; Tovar, Fein, and Naigles, in press). Recent research indicates the importance of learning language through interactive activities during which the toddler utilizes bi-directional social mechanisms for learning (Meltzoff, 2013; Kuhl et al., 2013). For this reason, the question of how children with ASD go about learning grammar is intriguing.

Due to their limited response to instructions and lack of interest in joint attention episodes, testing language comprehension in young children with ASD is a highly complicated task. Indirect evidence indicates that syntax and morphology are areas of relative strength in children with ASD. Some studies reported on children with ASD, particularly those classified as "high-functioning", who were developing along similar trajectories of grammatical learning as TD children (McGregor et al., 2012). Interestingly, syntactic complexity is not associated with symptom severity in ASD. Thus it is possible to observe children with severe ASD symptoms exhibiting better grammatical skills than children with mild ASD symptoms (Loucas et al., 2008). As previously mentioned, in recent years groups of children with ASD have been divided into those who demonstrate better grammatical skills (i.e., ALN) and those with grammatical deficits (i.e., ALI) that resemble those of children with SLI (Norbury, 2013; McGregor et al., 2012).

In a series of innovative experimental studies, Naigles and colleagues utilized the Intermodal Preferential Looking Paradigm for testing language comprehension in preschool children with ASD. By measuring percentages of looking at each scene, as well as latency of first look on the matching scene, these researchers were able to demonstrate that participants demonstrated understanding of both simple (e.g., SVO word order) and more complex (e.g., subject and object WH-questions) in English. In another experiment, they found that four-year-olds with ASD could correctly distinguish between simple past tense and progressive forms by differentially looking at contrasting scenes (Tovar, Fein and Naigles, in press). These results indicate that the utilization of an objective methodology opens new ways to measure comprehension skills in both very young TD children and children with ASD, for whom collaboration with examiners and direct testing situations are highly challenging (Naigles and Tovar, 2012).

It has been suggested that children in the ALI group compensate for their difficulty in acquiring grammar by depending on rote learning. They often produce memorized sets of words and sentences (e.g., citations from television shows or books), that they do not fully analyze or comprehend. For example, a girl who wanted her mother to open a box approached the mother and asked, "Do you want me to open it for you?", while a boy who was afraid of the noise made by a popping balloon quoted a sentence from the Israeli book *A Tale of Five Balloons*: "Boom, bang, what happened? The balloon exploded, the balloon was torn" (Shteiman and Dromi, 2007). Parents also frequently report that their children can remember books verbatim after only having heard them once or only a few times. Such children are able to recount entire stories by heart, but cannot identify the referents of simple words, such as "ball", "car", or "take". The use of memorized sequences, including, numbers, letters, and geometric forms, indicates an impairment in linguistic processing and a difficulty in internalizing grammatical rules.

Some individuals with ASD exhibit echolalia which is an exact, immediate or delayed imitation of sentences that they hear, often including the intonation of the original speaker. Echolalia was previously regarded as one of the most salient irregular speech behavior of individuals with ASD, and a red flag for referral to diagnosis. McEvoy, Loveland, and Landry (1988) found that immediate echolalia was recorded in children with ASD who had minimal spontaneous expressive language. They argued that this behavior was not reflective of participants' chronological age or nonverbal IQ. Tager-Flusberg and Calkins (1990) compared echolalic and non-echolalic productions of participants with ASD. They reported that echoed utterances were significantly shorter and less grammatically advanced than the spontaneous utterances of the same speakers. Prizant and Duchan (1981) identified six communicative functions of echolalic expressions: turn taking, assertions, affirmatives, answers, requests, rehearsal in order to aid processing, and self-regulation. They argued that delayed echoes are used communicatively to request activities or objects, as well as a means for self-regulation. Echolalia is not unique to ASD and is thought of as a sign of lack of linguistic processing as well as a pragmatic means of keeping conversation going when productive speech is limited. Research has indicated that this behavior is desirable as it may serve as a route for eliciting productive speech (Shteiman and Dromi, 2007).

Pronoun reversal, in which the child fails to shift reference between the first and second person, is highly common in the speech of individuals with ASD. Pronoun reversal sometimes occurs in blind children, in children with SLI, and it may be briefly recorded even in the speech of young TD children (Chiat, 1982). Kim, Tager-Flusberg, Paul, and Lord (2014) argued that most young children with ASD go through a stage of reversing pronouns and that the more linguistically advanced children stop making these errors.

Rice and colleagues (1994) argued that the information processing demands of having to shift and mark reference between the speaker and the listener makes pronoun acquisition a highly demanding task for young children in general and for children with language impairments in particular (Rice, Oetting, and Marquis, 1994). Other researchers attributed pronoun errors to the difficulty that children with ASD have in conceptualizing the notions of "self" and "other" as these are embedded in shifting discourse (Lee, Hobson, and Chiat, 1994).

An area which is of great difficulty for individuals with ASD is integrating information in order to fully comprehend connected discourse, be it spoken or written. Deficits in understanding ambiguities, jokes, figurative expressions, idioms, and metaphors are regularly reported in this population. Making inferences also causes difficulty for individuals with ASD (Norbury, 2013). In a series of studies, Norbury (2005a, 2005b) showed that ALN and ALI children significantly varied in their ability to process and comprehend jokes, metaphors, and idioms. She argued that this difference is associated with the overall deficit in structural language abilities in the two groups. In her opinion, difficulties integrating information within a linguistic context are not specific to ASD, and do appear in other pathologies. When she matched clinical groups according to their linguistic scores, ALI children and non-ASD groups with language disorders did not differ with respect to their narrative scores (Norbury, 2013). Her hypothesis was that difficulties observed in narrative comprehension result from shifting between literal and figurative meanings, as well as inhibition of interpretations that are irrelevant to the communication context at hand.

6 Speech production: Canonical babbling, words, phrases, and sentences

In most cases, children with ASD are brought for an assessment due to a delay in the emergence of their first words (Shteiman and Dromi, 2007; Freund, 2012). In TD children, one-word utterances emerge around 18 months and accumulate over several months to a year (Dromi, 1987). Initially, children learn their new words slowly. After a few months, most children experience a significant acceleration in the rate at which they acquire new words. This acceleration reflects a qualitative change in symbolic abilities and is termed a "lexical spurt" (Dromi, 1987, 2009).

It has been shown that the timing in which canonical babbling first appears is a crucial milestone in word learning (Kuhl et al., 2008). Oller and Eiler (1988), and Oller, Eiler, Neal, and Schwartz (1999) claimed that the production of canonical babbling implies that the baby attends to the input language directed to him and is able to segment it into basic units. A strong link has been identified between late emergence of canonical babbling, or lack of canonical babbling, and subsequent impairments in cognition and language (Oller and Eiler, 1988; Oller et al., 1999).

Few studies directly examined canonical babbling in children with ASD, however, many parents report that their children did not go through this phase at all during the pre-linguistic period (Freund, 2012). There is empirical evidence for toddlers with ASD having difficulty attending to motherese (Kuhl et al., 2008), as well as poor performance in nonsense word repetition (McGregor et al., 2012).

Howlin (2003) compared ADI-R questionnaire data of 38 adults diagnosed with High Functioning Autism (HFA) and 42 adults with Asperger syndrome (AS). He found that the average timing of first words in individuals with HFA was 38 months in comparison to 15 months in the AS group. He also reported that the rate of learning words in the first group was significantly prolonged and in some cases lasted until 9 years of age. Similar reports on significant delays in the appearance of first words as well as extended period of constructing lexicons appear in other publications (Naigles and Chin, in press; Tek et al., 2013). At the same time, there are reports on lexical learning by children with ASD occurring on time, and in some children even accelerated rates of learning new words or nonsense words (Loucas et al., 2008; Kjelgaard and Tager-Flusberg, 2001). Rescorla and Safyer (2013) analyzed in detail the first words that toddlers were reported by their parents to say. Vocabulary composition of the first 100 words was remarkably similar for both TD and ASD groups, consisting mostly of labels for food, body parts, and people; however, vocabulary composition of lexicons greater than 100 words began to differ by group, with children with ASD producing fewer words for actions and household items.

The establishment of a rich productive vocabulary of meaningful words requires the discovery of the arbitrary connections between the word (i.e., the signifier) and its reference (i.e., the signified), and an internalization of the symbolic relations between language and real world experiences. The extension of new words beyond a single context or time requires representational abilities that enables thinking about objects, events, and relationships among them even at a distant time or place, as well as an understanding that a single word labels categories and not single exemplars (Dromi, 2009).

There is a dearth of in-depth studies on referential knowledge, categorization abilities, semantic organization, definitions, recall of semantic information, as well as priming effects in ASD. In a few recent publications, the semantic abilities of children with ASD were found to be inferior to those in TD control groups who were matched by language skills rather than by age. Norbury, Griffiths, and Nation (2010) report that even when children with ASD were matched with controls on the basis of comparable receptive scores in the British Picture Vocabulary Scale-II (1997), their scores on a definition test were lower than controls by more than one standard deviation. Moreover, the children with ASD, unlike the TD children, faced serious difficulties in the consolidation of meaning over time (Norbury, Griffiths, and Nation, 2010).

McGregor et al. (2012) found that picture naming, definitions, and word associations were much more sensitive indicators of lexical learning in school-age children with ALI than tests of lexical comprehension. They argued that there is a similarity between the ALI and SLI groups with regards to the acquisition of syntax and lexical semantics. These results provide unique evidence of qualitative differences in word learning and consolidation of meaning among young children with ASD (Norbury, Griffiths and Nation, 2010).

Shteiman and Dromi (2007) described a child with ASD who at age 4 began to utter his first words. This child named a set of photos of everyday objects (e.g., a ball, a book, a doll, a box), but could not extend these words to the same real objects that were presented to him by the clinician (Shteiman and Dromi, 2007). Difficulties in word extension are common in ASD and it is therefore important to carefully examine the different contexts in which these children's words are uttered. Tek et al. (2008) presented novel objects paired with a novel noun to toddlers with ASD and examined whether the children would extend this label to new objects of the same shape or new objects of the same color. Whereas TD toddlers as young as 24 months of age showed the expected tendency to extend the labels to same-shape objects, language-matched children with ASD did not, even after multiple presentations over the course of two years (Tek et al., 2008). As was suggested by McGregor et al. (2012), simple quantitative measures, such as the number of words a child uses, do not reveal much about the depth or the richness with which a given word is represented in the child's mental lexicon. Future research should explore the underlying processes of word learning and use by individuals with ASD in much more detail (Norbury, Griffiths, and Nation, 2010; Naigles and Chin, in press).

Paul (2008) points to the unique supra-segmental patterns and voicing or pitch variability in children with ASD that often calls unwanted attention to the speaker and contributes to low speech intelligibility. More often than not, children with ASD use flat intonation, while others use intonation characterized by their caregivers as "strange", excessive, or "robotic" (Green and Tobin, 2009; Naigles and Chin, in press).

As stated above, several studies revealed that the patterns of syntactic and morphological learning of English speaking children with ALI resembled those of children with SLI at a similar linguistic stage (McGregor et al., 2012). Findings on syntax and morphology are not universal and are highly linked to the features of the target language. For example, it was argued that difficulties in marking tense is a clinical marker for English speaking children with SLI, however, this is not the case for Hebrew children with SLI (Dromi et al., 1999). In Hebrew, the marking of gender (which is not required in English) is a challenge for children with ASD and with SLI. One reason for the vulnerability of this distinction might be associated with its opaque representation in the real world, another explanation might be its arbitrary nature, and finally, feminine forms in Hebrew are derivative and much more structurally complex than masculine forms (Dromi et al., 1999). Moreover, errors of gender in ASD might occur either as a result of rote learning, or due to the requirement to coordinate between several sources of information.

In addition to testing the grammaticality of a child's productions, it is important to examine whether the productions of a child with ASD are directed towards another person during the interaction, or whether they serve for self-monitoring or self-stimulation purposes. In cases where the productions cannot undergo syllabic analysis and are classified as "gibberish", it may be the case that a child with ASD is producing sounds, words, and even sentences for himself in a state of detachment or for self-stimulation (Shteiman and Dromi, 2007). Often children with ASD can respond appropriately to questions, but violate communicative conventions such as looking at the addressee or being able to talk while playing and shifting gaze appropriately. For the above reasons, language assessment should be multidimensional in cases of children who are at risk for ASD or who have already received a diagnosis. It should include a number of parameters and cover phonology, semantics, syntax, and pragmatics.

7 Conclusions

The most important generalization from the rich review of research on communication, language, and speech in children with ASD is the great variability that exists in this population. Within-group heterogeneity is the rule rather than the exception in this population. Furthermore, each child with ASD presents a unique clinical profile. Thus, in a talk at the American Speech-Language-Hearing Association annual convention, Patricia Prelock (2011) said: "When you've seen one child with autism, you've seen one child".

Language impairment is not a criterion necessary for a diagnosis of ASD; at the same time, it often occurs in this population and should be seen as co-morbid with this diagnosis. While segmental phonology, morphology, and syntax are generally less affected in ASD, prosody, semantics, and pragmatics are areas of salient difficulty. Language comprehension and language processing are also highly challenging areas that need to be cultivated in therapy. A careful examination of the similarities and specificities of ALI versus SLI is also warranted, since very little research has been conducted to date in languages other than English.

The diversity in this population, as well as the great number of cognitive and linguistic factors that appear to be involved in the communication and language of patients with ASD, call for detailed and in-depth evaluations in order to carefully identify developmentally justified targets for intervention. The scope of the assessment should be broad in order to cover a wide range of behaviors. Clinicians should pay particular attention to the salient characteristics that have been highlighted in this chapter.

References

Adamson, Lauren B. 1995. *Communication development during infancy*. Madison, WI: Brown & Benchmark.

Adamson, Lauren B., Roger Bakeman & Deborah F. Deckner. 2004. The development of symbol-infused joint engagement. *Child Development* 75 (4). 1171–1187.

Adamson, Lauren B., Roger Bakeman, Deborah F. Deckner & MaryAnn Romski. 2009. Joint engagement and the emergence of language in children with autism and Down syndrome. *Journal of Autism and Developmental Disorders* 39 (1). 84–96.

American Psychiatric Association. 2013. *Diagnostic and statistical manual of mental disorders fifth edition: DSM 5*. Arlington, VA: American Psychiatric Association.

Aslin, Richard N. 1987. Visual and auditory development in infancy. In Joy D. Osofsky (ed.), *Handbook of infant development*, 5–97. New York: Wiley.

Astington, Janet W. & Jennifer M. Jenkins. 1999. A longitudinal study of the relation between language and theory-of-mind development. *Developmental Psychology* 35 (5). 1311.

Baranek, Grace T. 1999. Autism during infancy: A retrospective video analysis of sensory-motor and social behaviors at 9–12 months of age. *Journal of Autism and Developmental Disorders* 29 (3). 213–224.

Bates, Elizabeth, Laura Benigni, Inge Bretherton, Luigia Camaioni & Virginia Volterra. 1979. *The emergence of symbols: Communication and cognition in infancy*. New York: Academic Press.

Bishop, Dorothy V.M. 2010. Overlaps between autism and language impairment: Phenomimicry or shared etiology? *Behavior Genetics* 40 (5). 618–629.

Bowerman, Melissa. 1988. Inducing the latent structure of language. In Frank Kessel (ed.), *The development of language and language researchers: Essays in honor of Roger Brown*. New York: Lawrence Erlbaum.

Chiat, Shulamith. 1982. If I were you and you were me: The analysis of pronouns in a pronoun-reversing child. *Journal of Child Language* 9 (2). 359–379.

Clifford, Sally M. & Cheryl Dissanayake. 2008. The early development of joint attention in infants with autistic disorder using home video observations and parental interview. *Journal of Autism and Developmental Disorders* 38 (5). 791–805.

Dawson, Geraldine, Sarah J. Webb & James McPartland. 2005. Understanding the nature of face processing impairment in autism: Insights from behavioral and electrophysiological studies. *Developmental Neuropsychology* 27 (3). 403–424.

Dawson, Geraldine, Sally Rogers, Jeffrey Munson, Milani Smith, Jamie Winter, Jessica Greenson, Amy Donaldson & Jennifer Varley. 2010. Randomized, controlled trial of an intervention for toddlers with autism: The Early Start Denver Model. *Pediatrics* 125 (1). e17–e23.

Dromi, Esther. 1987. *Early lexical development*. New York: Cambridge University Press.

Dromi, Esther. In press. *Autism: A scientific journey into the spectrum and early intervention*. (Hebrew).

Dromi, Esther 2009. Old data – New eyes: Theories of word meaning acquisition. In Virginia C. Mueller Gathercole (ed.), *Routes to language: Studies in honor of Melissa Bowerman*, 39–59. London: Psychology Press.

Dromi, Esther, Laurence B. Leonard, Galit Adam & Sara Zadoneisky-Erlich. 1999. Verb agreement morphology in Hebrew-speaking children with specific language impairment. *Journal of Speech, Language and Hearing Research* 42 (6). 1414–1431.

Dromi, Esther & Michal Shteiman. 2011. A developmental model for the assessment of communication and language. In Ofra Korat and Dorit Aram (eds.), *Literacy and language: Interrelations, bilingualism and disorders*. Jerusalem: Magnes Publishing House. (in Hebrew).

Dromi, Esther & Dalia Ringwald-Frimerman. 1996. *Communication and language intervention with hearing impaired children: The prelinguistic stage*. Tel Aviv: Tel Aviv University, Ramot. (in Hebrew).

Dromi, Esther & Anat Zaidman-Zait. 2011. Interrelations between communicative behaviors at the outset of speech: Parents as observers. *Journal of Child Language* 38 (01). 101–120.

Dunn, Lloyd M., Leota M. Dunn, Chris Whetton & Juliet Burley. 1997. British Picture Vocabulary Scale, 2nd edn. [Measurement instrument]. NFER-Nelson, Windsor, Berks.

Feldman, Ruth. 2003. Infant-mother and infant-father synchrony: The coregulation of positive arousal. *Infant Mental Health Journal* 24 (1). 1–23.

Freund, Keren. 2012. Pre-verbal communicative skills of toddlers with autism spectrum disorders as compared to toddlers with typical development. Bar Ilan University MA dissertation. (in Hebrew).

Green, Hila & Yishai Tobin. 2009. Prosodic analysis is difficult – but worth it: A study in high functioning autism. *International Journal of Speech-Language Pathology* 11 (4). 308–315.

Happé, Francesca & Uta Frith. 2006. The weak coherence account: Detail-focused cognitive style in autism spectrum disorders. *Journal of Autism and Developmental Disorders* 36 (1). 5–25.

Harding, Carol G. 1983. Setting the stage for language acquisition: Communication development in the first year. In Roberta M. Golinkoff (ed.), *The transition from prelinguistic to linguistic communication*. Hillsdale, NJ: Earlbaum.

Hobson, R. Peter. 1993. *Autism and the development of mind*. New York: Psychology Press.

Howlin, Patricia. 2003. Outcome in high-functioning adults with autism with and without early language delays: Implications for the differentiation between autism and Asperger syndrome. *Journal of Autism and Developmental Disorders* 33 (1). 3–13.

Jones, Warren & Ami Klin. 2013. Attention to eyes is present but in decline in 2–6-month old infants later diagnosed with autism. *Nature* 504. 427–430.

Jusczyk, Peter W. 1997. *The discovery of spoken language*. Cambridge, MA: MIT Press.

Kasari, Connie, Stephanny Freeman & Tanya Paparella. 2006. Joint attention and symbolic play in young children with autism: A randomized controlled intervention study. *Journal of Child Psychology and Psychiatry* 47 (6). 611–620.

Kim, So Hyun, Rhea Paul, Helen Tager-Flusberg & Catherine Lord. 2014. Language and communication in autism. In Fred R. Volkmar, Rhea Paul, Sally J. Rogers, Kevin A. Pelphrey (eds.), *Handbook of autism and pervasive developmental disorders, volume 2, Assessment, interventions, and policy*, 4th edn., 230–262. Hoboken, NJ: Wiley.

Kjelgaard, Margaret M. & Helen Tager-Flusberg. 2001. An investigation of language impairment in autism: Implications for genetic subgroups. *Language and Cognitive Processes* 16 (2–3). 287–308.

Klin, Ami, Sarah Shultz & Warren Jones. 2015. Social visual engagement in infants and toddlers with autism: Early developmental transitions and a model of pathogenesis. *Neuroscience and Behavioral Reviews* 50. 189–203.

Kuhl, Patricia K., Sharon Coffey-Corina, Denise Padden & Geraldine Dawson. 2005. Links between social and linguistic processing of speech in preschool children with autism: Behavioral and electrophysiological measures. *Developmental Science* 8 (1). F1–F12.

Kuhl, Patricia K., Sharon Coffey-Corina, Denise Padden, Jeffrey Munson, Annette Estes & Geraldine Dawson. 2013. Brain responses to words in 2-year-olds with autism predict developmental outcomes at age 6. *PLoS One* 8 (5). e64967.

Kuhl, Patricia K., Barbara T. Conboy, Sharon Coffey-Corina, Denise Padden, Maritza Rivera-Gaxiola & Tobey Nelson. 2008. Phonetic learning as a pathway to language: New data and native language magnet theory expanded (NLM-e). *Philosophical Transactions of the Royal Society of London. Series B, Biological sciences* 363 (1493). 979–1000.

Landa, Rebecca J., Aiden L. Gross, Elizabeth A. Stuart & Ashley Faherty. 2013. Developmental trajectories in children with and without autism spectrum disorders: The first 3 years. *Child Development* 84 (2). 429–442.

Le Couteur, Ann, Catherine Lord & Michael Rutter. 2003. Autism Diagnostic Interview – Revised. [Measurement instrument.] Western Psychological Services.

Lee, Anthony, Peter Hobson & Shulamith Chiat. 1994. I, you, me and autism: An experimental study. *Journal of Autism and Developmental Disorders* 24. 155–176.

Lord, Catherine, Michael Rutter, Pamela C. DiLavore & Susan Risi. 1989. Autism Diagnostic Observation Schedule. [Measurement instrument]. Western Psychological Services.

Losh, Molly & Peter C. Gordon. 2014. Quantifying narrative ability in autism spectrum disorder: A computational linguistic analysis of narrative coherence. *Journal of Autism and Developmental Disorders*. 1–10.

Loucas, Tom, Tony Charman, Andrew Pickles, Emily Simonoff, Susie Chandler, David Meldrum & Gillian Baird. 2008. Autistic symptomatology and language ability in autism spectrum disorder and specific language impairment. *Journal of Child Psychology and Psychiatry* 49 (11). 1184–1192.

Luyster, Rhiannon & Catherine Lord. 2009. The language of children with autism. In Edith L. Bavin (ed.), *The Cambridge handbook of child language*. Cambridge: Cambridge University Press.

Macari, Suzanne L., Daniel Campbell, Grace W. Gengoux, Celine A. Saulnier, Ami J. Klin & Katarzyna Chawarska. 2012. Predicting developmental status from 12 to 24 months in infants at risk for autism spectrum disorder: A preliminary report. *Journal of Autism and Developmental Disorders* 42 (12). 2636–2647.

McEvoy, Robin E., Katherine A. Loveland & Susan H. Landry. 1988. The functions of immediate echolalia in autistic children: A developmental perspective. *Journal of Autism and Developmental Disorders* 18 (4). 657–668.

McGregor, Karla K., Amanda J. Berns, Amanda J. Owen, Sarah A. Michels, Dawna Duff, Alison J. Bahnsen & Melissa Lloyd. 2012. Associations between syntax and the lexicon among children with or without ASD and language impairment. *Journal of Autism and Developmental Disorders* 42 (1). 35–47.

Meltzoff, Andrew N. 2013. Origins of social cognition: Bidirectional self-other mapping and the "Like-Me" hypothesis. In Mahzarin R. Banaji & Susan Gelman (eds.), *Navigating the social world: What infants, children, and other species can teach us*, 139–144. New York: Oxford University Press.

Mundy, Peter, Marian Sigman & Connie Kasari. 1990. A longitudinal study of joint attention and language development in autistic children. *Journal of Autism and Developmental Disorders* 20 (1). 115–128.

Mundy, Peter, Marian Sigman, Judy Ungerer & Tracy Sherman. 1986. Defining the social deficits of autism: The contribution of non-verbal communication measures. *Journal of Child Psychology and Psychiatry* 27 (5). 657–669.

Nadig, Aparna, Iris Lee, Leher Singh, Kyle Bosshart & Sally Ozonoff. 2010. How does the topic of conversation affect verbal exchange and eye gaze? A comparison between typical development and high-functioning autism. *Neuropsychologia* 48 (9). 2730–2739.

Naigles, Letitia R. & Andrea T. Tovar. 2012. Portable intermodal preferential looking (IPL): Investigating language comprehension in typically developing toddlers and young children with autism. *Journal of Visualized Experiments* 70.

Naigles, Letitia R. & Iris Chin. 2015. Language development in children with autism. In Edith L. Bavin & Letitia R. Naigles (eds.), *The Cambridge handbook of child language, 2nd edition*. New York: Cambridge University Press.

Norbury, Courtenay F. 2005a. The relationship between theory of mind and metaphor: Evidence from children with language impairment and autistic spectrum disorder. *British Journal of Developmental Psychology* 23 (3). 383–399.

Norbury, Courtenay F. 2005b. Barking up the wrong tree? Lexical ambiguity resolution in children with language impairments and autism spectrum disorders. *Journal of Experimental Child Psychology* 90. 142–171.

Norbury, Courtenay F. 2013. Autism spectrum disorders and communication. In L. Cummings (ed.), *The Cambridge handbook of communication disorders*. New York: Cambridge University Press.

Norbury, Courtenay F., Helen Griffiths & Kate Nation. 2010. Sound before meaning: Word learning in autistic disorders. *Neuropsychologia* 48 (14). 4012–4019.

Oller, D. Kimbrough & Rebecca E. Eilers. 1988. The role of audition in infant babbling. *Journal of Child Language* 59. 441–449.

Oller, D. Kimbrough, Rebecca E. Eilers, A. Rebecca Neal & Heidi K. Schwartz. 1999. Precursors to speech in infancy: The prediction of speech and language disorders. *Journal of Communication Disorders* 32. 223–245.

Ozonoff, Sally, Gregory S. Young, Alice Carter, Daniel Messinger, Nurit Yirmiya, Lonnie Zwaigenbaum, Leslie J. Carber, John N. Constantino, Karen Dobkins, Ted Hutman, Jana M. Iverson, Rebecca Landa, Sally J. Rogers, Marian Sigman & Wendy L. Stone. 2011. Recurrence risk for autism spectrum disorders: A baby siblings research consortium study. *Pediatrics* 128 (3). e488–95.

Papousek, Hanous & Marc H. Bornstein. 1992. Didactic interactions: Intuitive parental support of vocal and verbal development in human infants. In Hanous Papousek, Uwe Jurgens & Mechthild Papousek (eds.), *Nonverbal vocal communication: Comparative and developmental approaches*. New York: Cambridge University Press.

Pascal, Meital. 2012. Autistic individuals' perceptions of autistic communication as they emerge from the discussions in online forums. Tel Aviv University MA thesis. (in Hebrew).

Paul, Rhea. 2008. Communication development and assessment. In Katarzyna Chawarska, Ami Klin & Fred R. Volkmar (eds.), *Autism spectrum disorders in infants and toddlers: Diagnosis, assessment, and treatment*, 76–103. New York: Guilford Press.

Paul, Rhea, Yael Fuerst, Gordon Ramsay, Katarzyna Chawarska & Ami Klin. 2011. Out of the mouths of babes: Vocal production in infant siblings of children with ASD. *Journal of Child Psychology and Psychiatry* 52 (5). 588–598.

Peters, Ann M. 1983. *The units of language acquisition*. Cambridge: Cambridge University Press.

Peterson, Candida C., Henry M. Wellman & David Liu. 2005. Steps in Theory-of-Mind development for children with deafness or autism. *Child Development* 76 (2). 502–517.

Pierce, Karen, Cindy Carter, Melanie Weinfeld, Jamie Desmond, Roxana Hazin, Robert Bjork & Nicole Gallagher. 2011. Detecting, studying, and treating autism early: The one-year well-baby check-up approach. *The Journal of Pediatrics* 159 (3). 458–465.

Prelock, Patricia. 2011. *Innovations in Theory of Mind assessment & intervention for children with ASD*. Presentation at the annual convention of the American Speech-Language-Hearing Association, San Diego, CA.

Prizant, Barry M. & Judith F. Duchan. 1981. The functions of immediate echolalia in autistic children. *Journal of Speech and Hearing Disorders* 46 (3). 241–249.

Reddy, Vasudevi. 1999. Prelinguistic communication. In Martyn Barrett (ed.), *Early lexical development*. London: UCL Press.

Repacholi, Betty M. 1998. Infants' use of attentional cues to identify the referent of another person's emotional expression. *Developmental Psychology* 34 (5). 1017–1025.

Rescorla, Leslie A. & Paige Safyer. 2013. Lexical composition in children with autism spectrum disorder (ASD). *Journal of Child Language* 40. 47–68.

Rice, Mabel L., Janna B. Oetting, Janet Marquis, John Bode & Soyeong Pae. 1994. Frequency of input effects on word comprehension of children with specific language impairment. *Journal of Speech and Hearing Research* 37 (1). 106–121.

Ringwald-Frimerman, Dalia. 2003. *Mother-child dyad as a dynamic system: The emergence of linguistic symbols in multi-modalities environments*. Tel Aviv University Ph.D. dissertation. (in Hebrew).

Shteiman, Michal & Esther Dromi. 2007. Communication, language and speech in young children with autism: Assessment and intervention principles. In S. Lowinger (ed.), *Interactive approaches to the treatment of children with communication disorders*. Haifa: Ach Publishing House. (in Hebrew)

Stern, Daniel N. 1974. Mother and infant at play: The dyadic interaction involving facial, vocal, and gaze behaviors. In Michael Lewis & Leonard A. Rosenblum (eds.), *The effect of the infant on its caregiver*, 187–213, New York: Wiley & Sons.

Sugarman, Susan. 1983. Empirical versus logical issues in the transition from prelinguistic to linguistic communication. In: Roberta Michnick Golinkoff (ed.), *The transition from prelinguistic to linguistic communication*. Hillsdale, NJ: Lawrence Erlbaum.

Suh, Joyce, Inge-Marie Eigsti, Letitia Naigles, Marianne Barton, Elizabeth Kelley & Deborah Fein. 2014. Narrative performance of optimal outcome children and adolescents with a history of an autism spectrum disorder (ASD). *Journal of Autism and Developmental Disorder*. 1–14.

Tager-Flusberg, Helen & Susan Calkins. 1990. Does imitation facilitate the acquisition of grammar? Evidence from a study of autistic, Down syndrome and normal children. *Journal of Child Language* 17 (3). 591–606.

Tanaka, James & Andrew Sang. 2016. The "Eye Avoidance" hypothesis of Autism face processing. *Journal of Autism and Developmental Disorders* 46. 1538–1552.

Tek, Saime, Gul Jaffery, Deborah Fein & Letitia Naigles. 2008. Do children with autism spectrum disorders show a shape bias in word learning? *Autism Research* 1 (4). 208–222.

Tek, Saime, Laura Mesite, Deborah Fein & Letitia Naigles. 2013. Longitudinal analyses of expressive language development reveal two distinct language profiles among young children with autism spectrum disorders. *Journal of Autism and Developmental Disorders* 44 (1). 75–89.

Tomasello, Michael. 1995. Joint attention as social cognition. In Chris Moore, Philip J. Dunham (eds.), *Joint attention: Its origins and role in development*. 103–130. New York: Psychology Press.

Tomblin, Bruce. 2011. Co-morbidity of autism and SLI: Kinds, kin and complexity. *International Journal of Language & Communication Disorders* 46 (2). 127–137.

Tovar, Andrea, Deborah Fein & Letitia Naigles. 2015. Grammatical aspect is a strength in the language comprehension of young children with autism spectrum disorder. *Journal of Speech, Language and Hearing Research* 58. 301–310.

Trevarthen, Colwyn. 1979. Communication and cooperation in early infancy: A description of primary intersubjectivity. In Margaret Bullowa (ed.), *Before speech: The beginning of interpersonal communication*, 321–347. New York: Cambridge University Press.

Warren, Zachary, Melissa L. McPheeters, Nila Sathe, Jennifer H. Foss-Feig, Allison Glasser & Jeremy Veenstra-Vanderweele. 2011. A systematic review of early intensive intervention for autism spectrum disorders. *Pediatrics* 127 (5). e1303–e1311.

Zuddas, Alessandro. 2013. Autism assessment tools in the transition from DSM-IV to DSM-5. *European Child & Adolescent Psychiatry* 22 (6). 325–327.

Zwaigenbaum, Lonnie, Susan Bryson & Nancy Garon, N. 2013. Early identification of autism spectrum disorders. *Behavioural Brain Research* 251. 133–146.

Zwaigenbaum, Lonnie, Audrey Thurm, Wendy Stone, Grace Baranek, Susan Bryson, Jana Iverson, Alice Kau, Ami Klin, Cathy Lord, Rebecca Landa, Sally Rogers & Mirian Sigman. 2007. Studying the emergence of autism spectrum disorders in high-risk infants: Methodological and practical issues. *Journal of Autism and Developmental Disorders* 37. 466–480.

Zwaigenbaum, Lonnie, Susan E. Bryson, Jessica Brian, Isabel, M. Smith, Wendy Roberts, Peter Szatmari, Caroline Roncadin, Nancy Garon and Tracy Vaillancourt. 2015a. Stability of diagnostic assessment for Autism Spectrum Disorder between 18 and 36 months in high risk cohorts. *Autism Research*.

Zwaigenbaum, Lonnie, Margaret L. Bauman, Deborah Fein, Karen Pierce, Timothy Buie, Patricia A. Davis, Craig Newschaffer, Diana L. Robins, Amy Wetherby, Roula Choueiri, Connie Kasari, Wendy L. Stone, Nurit Yirmiya, Annette Estes, Robin L. Hansen, James C. McPartland, Marvin R. Natowicz, Alice Carter, Doreen Granpeesheh, Zoe Mailloux,Susanne Smith Roley & Sheldon Wagner. 2015b. Early screening of autism spectrum disorder: Recommendations for practice and research. *Pediatrics* 136. 41–59.

Yonata Levy
40 Language in people with Williams syndrome

1 Introduction

William syndrome (WS) is a rare genetic disorder with a prevalence of 1 in 20,000 live births (Morris, et al., 1988), although more recent studies suggest it is more common, with a frequency of 1:7,500 (Stromme, Bjornstad and Ramstad, 2002). WS is caused by a hemizygous deletion on chromosome 7q11.23 that can be confirmed by fluorescent in situ hybridization (FISH test). The typical WS deletion contains ~26 genes, including one copy of the elastin gene (Peoples et al, 2000), although there exist genetic variabilities that are a function of the exact size of the deletion.

People with WS have connecting tissue abnormalities, cardiovascular disorders (most frequently, supravalvular aortic stenosis), facial dysmorphology, decreased muscle tone and unusual sensitivity to noise (Hyperacusis; Gothelf, et al. 2006). Neurophysiological studies showed atypicalities of brain morphology. Decreased overall brain and cerebellar volumes, disproportionate volume reduction of the brainstem, relative preservation of temporo-limbic structures and relative preservation of gray matter along with disproportionate reduction in white matter have been reported (Reiss et al. 2000; Jones, et al. 2002). Interestingly, there have been reports of cases of duplication or inversion within the relevant WS region which caused disorders of language that were quite unlike WS (Tassabehji 2003; Tassabehji and Donnai 2006). A recent case study described a patient with de novo 7q11.23 duplication and autistic symptoms with opposite effects on brain morphology compared to WS. In this patient, the limbic structure appeared hypo-functional and total brain volume was increased. These results highlight the effects on brain development of gene-dosage in this area (Prontera et al. 2014; see also Malenfant et al. 2012).

Relative preservation of frontal structures with reductions in parietal and occipital structures, increased number of gyri, and abnormal forms of the hippocampus were observed in people with WS (Meyer-Lindenberg et al. 2005; Thompson et al. 2005). Although cerebrum volume was significantly smaller, cerebellar volumes relative to intracranial volumes were relatively enlarged (Osorio et al. 2014). Sampaio et al. (2013) found morphological differences in the corpus callosum (CC) relative to typical controls. Importantly, atypicalities were seen regarding the association between CC measures, age, white matter volume and cognitive performance (Haas et al. 2014). A recent study of laterality in WS found that similar to other neurodevelopmental disorders, in a significant proportion of individuals laterality was poorly defined, with an adverse effect on general and verbal IQ (Perez-Garcia et al. 2015).

Yonata Levy, Psychology Department and Hadassah-Hebrew University Medical School

1.1 Cognitive and behavioral profile of people with WS

The majority of individuals with WS have mild to moderate cognitive deficits within an IQ range of 50–70. Verbal IQ typically exceeds performance IQ and language is considered a relative strength. This advantage is driven mainly by an exceptionally poor performance on the spatial motor sub-tests. Deficits seem highly specific and universal (Mervis et al. 1999). Numerical skills are likewise poorer than predicted by general cognition (Paterson, et al., 2006). Face recognition is relatively preserved although, similar to other populations with cognitive impairments, recognition of facial expressions is impaired (Levy, Pluber, and Bentin, 2011). A dominant feature of WS personality profile is their hypersociability. People with WS are characterized by overfriendliness, anxiety and empathy and an indiscriminant positive approach to people (Klein-Tasman and Mervis 2003). Several studies however, reported co-existence of WS gene deletion along with a range of autistic-like features including lack of language (Tordjman et al. 2012).

In their seminal paper, later followed by several other publications, Bellugi, Sabo and Vaid (1988) argued that although mentally atypical, children and adolescents with WS had intact language abilities. While their understanding of numerosity, perceptual-motor abilities and performance on Piagetian conservation tasks were severely deficient, they could comprehend and produce complex linguistic structures such as reversible passives, conditionals and tag questions. Furthermore, according to these authors, people with WS had excellent vocabularies, exceeding age matched typical individuals, and an atypical lexico-semantic organization (Bellugi et al.). Based on these claims, interest in WS soared. The syndrome was considered as providing evidence for the independence of language, supporting a modular view of cognition (Fodor 1985). The linguistic profile of WS was of significance clinically as well, as it addressed questions concerning the uniqueness of WS relative to other syndromes with mental disabilities, the effects of general cognitive level on language and syndrome-specific vs. general interventions.

Whereas in earlier studies language and related skills in people with WS were frequently compared to mental age (MA) matched people with Down syndrome (DS; e.g. Reilly, Klima, and Bellugi 1990; Wang, et al. 1992), in more recent studies comparison to DS has been carried out with greater caution. Researchers realized that the pronounced difficulties in language and in auditory short-term memory that characterized DS set relatively low standards for people with WS.

Nevertheless, comparative studies among clinical populations are important in order to address the theoretical and translational issues that concern language disorders (Rice, Warren, and Betz 2005). Three comparison groups are of interest in the study of language in people with WS. If language in WS is indeed exceptional and independent of general cognition, then the expectation is that it will match that of same-age typically developing (TD) individuals. However, if language is correlated with general cognition, it will approximate that of MA TD controls. In this case the issue of the significant age differences among the groups must be taken into consideration (Levy, in press). Finally, a comparison with people with other neurodevelopmental conditions is critical in order to address the question of the uniqueness of language in WS.

1.2 Neuroconstructivism vs. the 'normalcy' approach

An up-to-date version of the dispute concerning the modularity of language can be seen in the debate between neuroconstructivism and the 'normalcy' approach, which has engaged the field in the past 15 years. Proponents of the 'normalcy' approach have typically adopted a nativist view of language, espousing a generative model of mature grammatical knowledge and a modular view of cognition (e.g. Musolino, Chunyo, and Landau 2010; Zukowski 2009). It has been argued that the developmental trajectories are characterized by types of rules and categories that do not differ from the building blocks of typical grammars. The typicality of the developmental trajectory, however, remained a topic of empirical investigations.

Neuroconstructivism (Karmiloff-Smith 1998; Thomas and Karmiloff-Smith 2003; 2005) rejected the tenets of the 'normalcy' approach. It has been argued that in view of brain alterations characteristically brought about by neurodevelopmental disorders, neither the developmental trajectories nor the end state of mature grammars were likely to be typical. Consider the following quote from a paper by Karmiloff-Smith et al. (2012: 393) "Brain volume, brain anatomy, brain chemistry, hemispheric asymmetry and the temporal patterns of brain activity are all atypical in people with WS. How could the resulting system be described as a normal brain with parts intact and parts impaired, as the popular view holds?". In other words, according to this view, a global re-organization of developmental trajectories is a necessary, almost a logical, outcome of the anatomical and physiological state of the WS brain.

Language in people with WS has often served as a model case for both positions. Arguing for a 'normalcy' approach to language in people with WS, Musolino et al. (2010) highlighted the fact that, while neuroconstructivism objected to generative accounts of language in mature individuals with WS, it did not provide a competing account of the linguistic knowledge base in these individuals. This followed on Zukowski (2009) who argued that the evidence that was put forth by the 'normalcy' approach and by neuroconstructivism in fact aimed at different explanatory levels.

To the best of my knowledge, Thomas and Karmiloff-Smith (2003) was the only proposed account of atypical knowledge base in WS. It was hypothesized that an atypical phonology-semantics imbalance underlies linguistic competence in WS and this accounted for an alternative route to acquisition. Reliance on and sensitivity to phonology, lexical-semantic impairment, semantic lag and impairment in integrating semantics and phonology were offered as potential characteristics of an altered acquisitional course. Reviewing the evidence, Brock (2007) rejected this proposal, arguing that there was relatively little direct support for an unusual relationship between vocabulary and phonological short term memory in WS. Furthermore, Brock found little evidence to support the claim that the knowledge base of language in WS was atypical.

Within this context, it is important to point to the differences between the set of behaviors or functions that are subsumed under the term "language" in research conducted within linguistics, psychology and clinical neuropsychology. It is often the case that psycholinguists of generative persuasion focus on morphosyntax and formal semantics, whereas clinicians and neuropsychologists as well as linguists of other persuasions and communicative-pragmatic theorists tend to consider language as an umbrella term, covering multiple aspects of verbal behavior. Clarifying the focus of the research is important when one evaluates the theoretical status of the debate between neuroconstructivism and the normalcy approach along with its clinical implications.

For the most part, the debate between neuroconstructivism and the normalcy approach focused on the structural typicality of the developmental trajectories and the nature of the underlying knowledge base. Nevertheless, delay in the onset of combinatorial language and a protracted acquisitional course have received some attention in this debate (e.g. Thomas, Karaminis, and Knowland 2010). In light of recent neurobiological research highlighting the role of chronology in gene expression, maturational schedules and epigenetic processes (Courchesne, Campbell, and Solso 2011; Lenroot et al. 2009), and the critical role of timing in setting up a synchronized structural and functional brain networks (Alexander-Bloch, Giedd, and Bullmore 2013), developmental timing, i.e. age, deserves in depth consideration in behavioral theorizing.

The current review considers language in WS with a special emphasis on aspects of the WS linguistic profile that are relevant to the theoretical and clinical issues raised by the debate between neuroconstructivism and the normalcy approach. When information concerning age of acquisition and the way it compares with typical development is given in the study, it will be reported as well.

2 Language in WS

2.1 Phonology and speech

Most children with WS have intelligible and fluent speech, which far exceeds that of learning impaired (LI) children matched on age and verbal IQ (Udwin and Yule 1990). Speech quality is significantly better than in matched individuals with developmental disabilities or people with DS (Gosch, Stading, and Pankau 1994; Laws and Bishop 2004). However, a recent study suggests oromotor praxis in fluent individuals with WS, perhaps contributing to the delay in language development that characterizes people with WS (Krishnan et al. 2015). Older children and adults with WS performed as well as age-matched controls when required to repeat syllables of various structures (Bohning, Campbell, and Karmiloff-Smith 2002). However, toddlers with WS remained dependent on prosodic cues for 1–3 years longer than TD children (Nazzi, Paterson, and Karmiloff-Smith 2003). Importantly, the severity of hyperacusis predicted individual variability in speech perception (Elsabbagh et al. 2011).

Mervis and Bertrand (1997) observed the expected co-occurrence of hand banging and canonical babbling in babies with WS. Masataka (2001) reported similar results, although overall delay was found in terms of the onset of canonical babbling, first words, as well as various motor milestones. The degree to which acquisition of each of the milestones was delayed was individually variable. Once canonical babbling was produced, the onset of first words was recorded during the following 2–3 months period. Unlike TD children, toddlers with WS produced words before they used pointing and word production preceded serial ordering (Mervis and Bertrand 1997; Laing et al. 2002).

Phonological short term memory (STM), typically tested on digit and word span tasks, was an area of preserved competence in people with WS, when compared to people with DS in whom phonological memory was a pronounced weakness (Reilly et al. 1990; Mervis et al. 1999; 2003). However, performance of people with WS was no better than that of TD children or LI children matched on non-verbal abilities or vocabulary (e.g. Brock 2007; Jarrold et al. 2004; Laing et al. 2001; Robinson et al. 2003 and more). Importantly, studies that have controlled for potential confounding variables such as level of overall performance, have consistently failed to find evidence for atypical phonological effects such as word or non-word length, phonological similarities, semantic priming and performance on semantic fluency tasks (Brock 2005; Lee and Binder 2014; Levy and Bechar 2003). Contrary to expectations based on their STM and language abilities, people with WS did not show evidence of phonological recoding (Danielsson, Henry, Messer, Carney and Ronnberg, 2016).

2.2 Lexicon and semantics

First words appear around 28 months in children with WS. This delay can be predicted on the basis of their overall MA whereas a longer delay characterizes children with DS of similar MA (Harris et al. 1997; Levy and Eilam 2013; Paterson et al. 1999). Harris et al. (1997) and Mervis and Robinson (2000) reported advantages on expressive vocabulary of children with WS when compared to children with DS but no differences on receptive vocabulary (Klein and Mervis 1999). Six year old Greek children with WS, however, had an advantage over children with DS in receptive as well as expressive vocabularies (Ypsilanti, Grouios, Alveriadou, and Tsapkini (2005). Contrary to the above, Laing et al. (2002) reported comparable early vocabularies in children with WS, children with DS and TD children matched on MA.

Children with WS do not engage in joint attention when new words are introduced. Instead, they focus on the speaker's face (Klein-Tasman et al. 2004). Similarly, children with WS did not show "fast mapping" which is the tendency to attribute a novel name to an unfamiliar object, nor did they organize objects by categories, or formed name-based categories prior to acquiring a significant vocabulary (Nazzi, Gopnik, and Karmiloff-Smith 2005). These results reinforce the view that there are multiple ways to acquire words (Bloom 2000). It suggests that while pointing and activities related to joint attention characteristically precede word learning, and "fast mapping" along with object categorization precede lexical growth, these are not necessary preconditions for vocabulary acquisition.

Receptive vocabulary is a noticeable strength in adolescents and young adults with WS (Brock et al. 2006). However, unlike TD children, the advantage seen in receptive vocabulary in WS was not accompanied by the expected advantage in phonological short term memory (e.g. Brock 2005; Jarrold et al. 2004). Productive vocabulary and word definition did not show an advantage either, and performance of people with WS matched their MA (Bello et al. 2004; Stojanvik and van Ewijk 2008).

Several measures of semantic knowledge have been applied in an effort to better understand the claim that lexical-semantic organization and representation in WS was atypical (Bellugi et al. 1988). Semantic fluency was comparable to LI groups and to MA controls (Jarrold et al. 2000; Johnson and Carey 1998; Levy and Bechar 2003; Volterra et al. 1996). Semantic priming effects and word frequency were normal (Lee and Binder 2014). Concrete vocabulary emerged as a relative strength in children with WS, while relational language was remarkably weak (Mervis and John 2008). Purser et al. (2011) investigated semantic knowledge in people with WS through definition and categorization tasks. Performance of the WS group (age 12–45 years; verbal MA 4–17 years) on the Definitions task began at a level commensurate with an MA matched TD group (age 5–10 years; verbal MA- 5–13 years), but soon diverged from it. Performance on the Categorization task was markedly poorer than predicted by verbal MA. This pattern of results indicated that individuals with WS have less lexico-semantic knowledge than expected given their level of receptive vocabulary. It further suggests that we need to rethink the meaning of MA in interaction with chronological age. Is a 9 year old child with MA of 10 the right control for a 30 year old person with WS with a similar MA? Recent neurobiological research and its emphasis of the role of synchronicity in gene expression and brain development suggests that chronological age has significant effects (Levy, In press).

In sum, group studies have not confirmed the claims concerning exceptional lexical knowledge in people with WS. Whereas receptive vocabulary showed an unexpected strength, productive vocabulary and semantic knowledge were at the expected MA level. The fact remains, however, that in natural conversations, people with WS impress their interlocutors, among them experienced clinicians, with their rich lexicon. This inconsistency awaits further research.

2.3 Grammar

Grammar is the focus of the debate surrounding modularity of language in WS and studies of grammar in WS are of central importance to the debate between neuroconstructivism and the normalcy approach. Significant delays in the onset of combinatorial language in toddlers with WS, with two-word combinations occurring at 40–46 months on average, have been observed (Harris et al. 1997; Levy and Eilam 2013). Interestingly, 8–20 months old infants with WS were able to discriminate statistically defined "words" and "part-words" in an artificial language. These findings suggest that inability to track statistical regularities in the speech stream is unlikely to be the prime reason for the delay in the onset of language in children with WS (Cashon, Ha, Estes, Saffran and Mervis, 2016). Grammatical development in toddlers with WS is characterized by a normal relationship between syntax, vocabulary and MA. Typical relationship between number of words and complexity of grammar in English speaking children with WS and an overall typical acquisitional course were reported by Harris et al. as well as by Mervis et al. (2003). In a longitudinal follow-up of Hebrew speaking children with WS, children with DS and language-matched TD children, Levy and Eilam reported typical growth trajectories of grammatical features and size of the lexicon. However, statistically significant differences were seen in age of onset of combinatorial language and in rate of achieving developmental milestone.

Few studies did find atypicalities in the early phases of grammatical development in WS. Capirci, Sabbadini, and Volterra (1996) pointed to abnormal error patterns in a young Italian speaking girl with WS. Karmiloff-Smith et al. (1997) observed atypical morphological development with respect to French gender compared to TD children. Note that the results by Karmiloff-Smith et al. could not be replicated with Hebrew speaking children with WS (Levy and Hermon, 2003).

Adolescents with WS performed similarly to MA matched TD children on test of comprehension of complex syntax (Ring and Clahsen 2005). Reception of grammar was poorer than receptive vocabulary and did not exceed the expected MA level (Robinson et al. 2003; Vicari et al. 2004). Regular and irregular morphology (e.g. past tense forms or gender inflections) provided opportunities to study rule governed vs. rote memorized forms in WS. Some studies found that people with WS performed better on regular past tense verbs than on irregulars (Clahsen et al. 2003; Pleh et al. 2003), suggesting intact rule use and impaired lexical memory. Others have not found evidence of an advantage of regulars over irregulars (Thomas et al. 2001; Zukowski 2005; Karmiloff-Smith et al. 1997). A mixed picture emerged from Jacobson and Cairns (2010) who reported a profile of regular and irregular past tense use in an adolescent with WS that both approximated and diverged from normal expectations.

Working within a generative type framework, Perovic and Wexler (2007) reported intact binding principles in 6–16 year old children with WS, along with delays in the acquisition of constraints regulating coreferential interpretation of pronouns. More recently, these authors found deficits relating to the structure of verbal passives that were not directly predicted by the children's level of nonverbal abilities, receptive vocabulary, or general comprehension of grammar (Perovic and Wexler 2010). Perovic, Modyanova, and Wexler (2013) pointed to the structural typicality of the developmental trajectory of binding in children with WS, whereas atypicalities were seen in the developmental trajectory of language impaired children with autism. In a similar vein, Musolino et al. (2010) results suggested knowledge of core syntactic and semantic relations (scope and c-command, entailment and the effects of negation on conjunction and disjunction) in people with WS, reinforcing the perspective on language offered by the normalcy approach.

An interesting perspective on cognition-language interdependence in WS is offered through the study of spatial language. If language is modular and hence dissociated from cognition, can spatial language be preserved, given the noticeable difficulties of people with WS with visuospatial construction tasks? Results do not support this hypothesis. Most studies of spatial language in people with WS show specific difficulties with spatial terms in comparisons with MA controls (Landau and Zukowski 2003) or controls matched on other language measures (Philips et al. 2004). However, when controls were matched on relational language, for which children with WS show a noticeable weakness, spatial language did not differ among the groups (Mervis and John 2008). A recent study by Farran, Atkinson and Broadbent (2016) suggests that non-verbal mental age significantly contributes to spatial category representation, whereas the influence of spatial language ability is only marginally significant.

2.4 Pragmatics

People with WS talk a lot, often incessantly. They ask persistent questions, use an excess of emotional and evaluative terms, switch topics and fail to provide relevant information (Stojanovik, Perkins, and Howard 2001; Semel and Rosner 2003; Udwin et al. 1987). Importantly, in natural speech, there is a significant increase in the frequency of hesitations, repetitions and pauses resulting in disfluencies (Rossi et al. 2011). Nevertheless, language is a significant feature of WS hypersociable personality. This has been recently reinforced in the finding of a significant association between a brain index of language processing and judgment of approachability of faces as an index of sociability (Fishman et al. 2011). Such an association was not found in TD controls. Children and young adults with WS were significantly poorer on coherence, stereotyped conversation, inappropriate initiation, conversational context and conversational rapport as well as on global coherence and informativeness (Marini et al. 2010; Reilly et al. 2004). They made fewer inferences of motivation and mental states, abundant use of social engagement devices and emotional inferences (Reilly et al.) and gave fewer verbal clarifications, although overall they spoke as much as TD controls (Asada et al. 2010). While both children with autism and children with WS were impaired on the Children's Communication Check List (CCC-2; Nurbury and Bishop 2003), children with WS were less impaired on several subscales than children with autism spectrum disorder (Philofsky, Fidler, and Hepburn 2007). Children with WS did not outperform children with Prader-Willie or with learning disabilities in understanding jokes or lies, and were poorer on second order knowledge questions (e.g. Does Mum know that John knows that Sally did not go to school today?; Sullivan, Winner, and Tager-Flusberg 2003). Children and adults with WS selected less abstract terms in a comparison task of figurative language (Thomas et al. 2010), while non-literal language such as sarcasm and metaphor was similar to MA controls (Godbee and Porter 2013). In a critical review of the literature, Mervis and Becerra (2007) concluded that language and communicative skills provided evidence for the interdependence of language and general cognition in WS. In a similar vein, a recent study of Spanish adults with WS suggested that while narrative skills were structurall equivalent to overall linguistic knowledge, they were primarily affected by general cognition (Diez-Itza, Marinez and Anton, 2016).

3 Summary and conclusion

The majority of the work that has been carried out in recent years suggests that language in WS develops normally and is commensurate with MA level. The significant brain abnormalities have but minimal effect on the robust course of language acquisition, certainly in what concerns comprehension and production of basic language in natural conversations.

Vocabulary growth in children with WS is normal, running in parallel to syntactic development. There is no evidence of an unusual semantic organization although word acquisition does not correlate with joint attention, pointing, serial ordering or categorical organization the way it does in typical development. Lexico-conceptual knowledge is poor although receptive vocabulary exceeds that of MA controls. Trajectories of basic syntax are normal. Whereas there is some controversy about the level of syntactic knowledge beyond basic production and comprehension, there is scant evidence of atypical grammatical structures or idiosyncratic developmental trajectories.

Pragmatic skills such as staying on topic, providing relevant information, inferring the interlocutor's mental state, telling jokes, uncovering lies and maintaining the right register do not match those of TD controls. Nevertheless, people with WS are good conversationalists, often impressing their listeners with their rich vocabularies and good syntax. It seems that linguistic skills play a crucial role in WS hypersociability.

Importantly, while the developmental course is mostly similar to the normal, first words and word combinations are delayed relative to TD children and language develops at a significantly slower pace. In other words, contrary to the structural properties of the developmental trajectories, **developmental timing** is definitely aberrant. WS thus mirrors other neurodevelopmental syndromes in which one often sees late language onset and an abnormal developmental time course alongside near-typical structural trajectory. The extent and nature of the time setback in children with neurodevelopmental disorders, however, is syndrome specific, suggesting that the developmental clock is differentially reflected in distinct neurobiological conditions, or perhaps differentially affecting them. Since the data is mostly correlational, the establishment of causal relations awaits further research.

What is the impact of the emerging language profile of children with WS on the debate between neuroconstructivism and the normalcy approach? Is the developmental trajectory typical in children with WS? The answer depends on the definition of 'normalcy'. If one considers structural properties of the developmental course of language in children with WS then the answer is probably YES. However, if typical age of onset and acquisitional pace are necessary components of normality, and if disorders of timing can impact the developmental course in a non-transitory ways, as argued by recent neurobiological research, than trajectories of language development in people with WS cannot be considered typical.

The structural similarities between developmental trajectories vis a vis the syndrome-specific time course of language development that characterize neurodevelopmental disorders have clinical implications as well. It reinforces the clinical wisdom behind intervention programs that are general rather than specific. It suggests that, in what concerns the development of basic language skills, intervention programs need not be different in terms of the linguistic details they target, because the developmental trajectories do not differ in systematic ways among syndromes. However, intervention programs need to pay attention to age differences and to the time course that is required for children with different disorders to reach the expected outcome, and work out the consequences of those age gaps for the classroom situation.

References

Alexander-Bloch, Aaron, Jay N. Giedd & Ed Bullmore. 2013. Imaging structural co-variance between human brain regions. *Nature Reviews Neuroscience* 14. 322–336.
Asada, Kosuke, Kiyotaka Tomiwa, Masako Okada & Shoji Itakura. 2010. Fluent language with impaired pragmatics in children with Williams syndrome. *Journal of Neurolinguistics* 23(6). 540–552.
Bellugi, Ursula, Helene Sabo & Jyotsna Vaid. 1988. Spatial deficits in children with Williams Syndrome. In Stiles-Davis, Joan, Mark Kritchevsky & Ursula Bellugi (Eds.), *Spatial cognition: Brain bases and development*, 273–298. Hillsdale, NJ: Lawrence Erlbaum Associates.
Bello, Arianna, Olga Capirci & Virginia Volterra. 2004. Lexical production in children with Williams syndrome: Spontaneous use of gesture in a naming task. *Neuropsychologia* 42(2). 201–213.
Bloom, Paul. 2000. *How children learn the meanings of words: Learning, development, and conceptual change.* Cambridge, MA: MIT Press.

Böhning, Marita, Ruth Campbell & Annette Karmiloff-Smith. 2002. Audiovisual speech perception in Williams syndrome. *Neuropsychologia* 40(8). 1396–1406.

Brock, Jon. 2007. Language abilities in Williams syndrome: A critical review. *Development and Psychopathology* 19(1). 97–127.

Brock, Jon, Gordon DA. Brown & Jill Boucher. 2006. Free recall in Williams syndrome: Is there a dissociation between short- and long-term memory? *Cortex* 42(3). 366–375.

Brock, Jon, Teresa McCormack & Jill Boucher. 2005. Probed serial recall in Williams syndrome: Lexical influences on phonological short-term memory. *Journal of Speech, Language, and Hearing Research* 48(2). 360–371.

Brock, Jon, Christopher Jarrold, Emily K. Farran, Glynis Laws & Deborah M. Riby. 2007. Do children with Williams syndrome really have good vocabulary knowledge? Methods for comparing cognitive and linguistic abilities in developmental disorders. *Clinical Linguistics & Phonetics* 21(9). 673–688.

Cashon, Cara, H., Oh-Ryeong Ha, Katharine G. Estes, Jenny R. Saffran & Carolyn Mervis. 2016. Infants with Williams syndrome detect statistical regularities in continuous speech. *Cognition* 154. 165–168.

Capirci, Olga, Leticia Sabbadini & Virginia Volterra. 1996. Language development in Williams syndrome: A case study. *Cognitive Neuropsychology* 13. 1017–1039.

Clahsen Herald & Christin C. Temple. 2003. Words and rules in children with Williams syndrome. In Yonata Levy & Jeanette Schaeffer (Eds.), *Language competence across populations: Toward a definition of specific language impairment*, 323–352. Mahwah, NJ: Lawrence Erlbaum.

Courchesne, Eric, Kathleen Campbell & Stephanie Solso. 2011. Brain growth across the life span in autism: Age-specific changes in anatomical pathology. *Brain Research* 1380. 138–145.

Danielsson, Henrik, Lucy Henry, David Messer, Daniel P. J. Carney & Jerker Ronnberg. 2016. Developmental delays in phonological recoding among children and adolescents with Down syndrome and Williams syndrome. *Research in Developmental Disabilities* 55. 64–76.

Diez-Itza, Eliseo, Veronica Martinez & Aranzazu, Anton. 2016. Narrative competence in Spanish speaking adults with Williams syndrome. *Psicothema* 28. 291–297.

Elsabbagh, Mayada, H. Cohen, M. Cohen, S. Rosen & Annette Karmiloff Smith. 2011. Severity of hyperacusis predicts individual differences in speech perception in Williams syndrome. *Journal of Intellectual Disability Research* 55(6). 563–571.

Farran, Emily, K., Lauren Atkinson & Hannah Broadbent. 2016. Impaired spatial category representation in Williams syndrome: an investigation of the mechanistic contribution of non-verbal cognition and spatial language performance. *Frontiers in Psychology* 7, article 1868.

Fishman, Inna, Anna Yam, Ursula Bellugi & Deborah Mills. 2011. Language and sociability: Insights from Williams syndrome. *Journal of Neurodevelopmental Disorders* 3(3). 185–192.

Fodor, Jerry A. 2005. Précis of the modularity of mind. *Behavioral and Brain Sciences* 8(1). 1–42.

Godbee, Kali & Melanie Porter. 2013. Comprehension of sarcasm, metaphor and simile in Williams syndrome. *International Journal of Language & Communication Disorders* 48(6). 651–665.

Gosch, Angela, Gabriele Städing & Rainer Pankau. 1994. Linguistic abilities in children with Williams-Beuren syndrome. *American Journal of Medical Genetics* 52. 291–296.

Gothelf, Doron, N. Farber, E. Raveh, Alan Apter & J. Attias. 2006. Hyperacusis in Williams syndrome: Characteristics and associated neuroaudiologic abnormalities. *Neurology* 66(3). 390–395.

Haas, Brian W. Naama Barnea-Goraly, Kristen E. Sheau, Bun Yamagata, Shruti Ullas & Alan L. Reiss. 2014. Altered microstructure within social-cognitive brain networks during childhood in Williams syndrome. *Cerebral Cortex* 24(10). 2796–806.

Singer Harris, Naomi G. Ursula Bellugi, Elizabeth Bates, Wendy Jones & Michael Rossen. 1997. Contrasting profiles of language development in children with Williams and Down syndromes. *Developmental Neuropsychology* 13(3). 345–370.

Jacobson, Peggy F. & Helen Smith Cairns. 2010. Exceptional rule learning in a longitudinal case study of Williams syndrome: Acquisition of past tense. *Communication Disorders Quarterly* 31(4). 231–242.

Jarrold, Christopher, Nelson Cowan, Alexa K. Hewes & Deborah M. Riby. 2004. Speech timing and verbal short-term memory: Evidence for contrasting deficits in Down syndrome and Williams syndrome. *Journal of Memory and Language* 51(3). 365–380.

Jarrold, Christopher, Samantha J. Hartley, Caroline Phillips & Alan D. Baddeley. 2000. Word fluency in Williams syndrome: Evidence for unusual semantic organization? *Cognitive Neuropsychiatry* 5(4). 293–319.

Johnson, Susan C. & Susan Carey. 1998. Knowledge enrichment and conceptual change in folk biology: Evidence from Williams syndrome. *Cognitive Psychology* 37(2). 156–200.

Jones, Wendy, John Hesselink, Tim Duncan, Kevin Matsuda & Ursula Bellugi. 2002. Cerebellar abnormalities in infants and toddlers with Williams syndrome. *Developmental Medicine & Child Neurology* 44(10). 688–694.

Karmiloff-Smith, Annette. 1998. Development itself is the key to understanding developmental disorders. *Trends in Cognitive Sciences* 2(10). 389–398.

Karmiloff-Smith, Annette, Dean D'Souza, Tessa M. Dekker, Jo Van Herwegen, Fei Xu, Maja Rodic & Daniel Ansari. 2012. Genetic and environmental vulnerabilities in children with neurodevelopmental disorders. *PNAS 109* (Supplement 2). 17261–17265.

Karmiloff-Smith, Anentte, Julia Grant, Ioanna Berthoud, Mark Davies, Patricia Howlin & Orlee Udwin. 1997. Language and Williams syndrome: How intact is "intact"? *Child Development* 68(2). 246–262.

Klein, Bonita P. & Carolyn B. Mervis. 1999. Contrasting patterns of cognitive abilities of 9- and 10-year-olds with Williams Syndrome or Down Syndrome. *Developmental Neuropsychology* 16(2). 177–196.

Klein-Tasman, Bonita P. & Carolyn Mervis. 2003. Distinctive personality characteristics of 8-, 9-, and 10-year-olds with Williams syndrome. *Developmental Neuropsychology* 23(1–2). 269–290.

Klein-Tasman, Bonita P. Carolyn B. Mervis, Catherine Lord & Kristin D. Phillips. 2007. Socio-communicative deficits in young children with Williams syndrome: Performance on the Autism Diagnostic Observation Schedule. *Child Neuropsychology* 13(5). 444–467.

Krishnan, Saloni, Lina Bergström, Katherine J. Alcock, Frederic Dick & Annette Karmiloff-Smith. 2015. Williams syndrome: A surprising deficit in oromotor praxis in a population with proficient language production. *Neuropsychologia* 67. 82–90.

Laing, Emma, George Butterworth, Daniel Ansari, Marisa Gsödl, Elena Longhi, Georgia Panagiotaki, Sarah Paterson & Annette Karmiloff-Smith. 2002. Atypical development of language and social communication in toddlers with Williams syndrome. *Developmental Science* 5(2). 233–246.

Laing, Emma, Julia Grant, Michael Thomas, Charlotte Parmigiani, Sandra Ewing & Annette Karmiloff-Smith. 2005. Love is… an abstract word: The influence of lexical semantics on verbal short-term memory in Williams syndrome. *Cortex* 41(2). 169–179.

Landau, Barbara & Andrea Zukowski. 2003. Objects, motions, and paths: Spatial language in children with Williams syndrome. *Developmental Neuropsychology* 23(1–2). 105–137.

Laws, Glynis & Dorothy V.M. Bishop. 2004. Pragmatic language impairment and social deficits in Williams syndrome: A comparison with Down's syndrome and specific language impairment. *International Journal of Language and Communication Disorders* 39. 45–64.

Lee, Cheryl S. & Katherine S. Binder. 2014. An investigation into semantic and phonological processing in individuals with Williams syndrome. *Journal of Speech, Language, and Hearing Research* 57(1). 227–235.

Lenroot, Rhoshel K. James E. Schmitt, Sarah J. Ordaz, Gregory L. Wallace, Michael C. Neale, Jason P. Lerch, Kenneth S. Kendler, Alan C. Evans & Jay N. Giedd. 2009. Differences in genetic and environmental influences on the human cerebral cortex associated with development during childhood and adolescence. *Human Brain Mapping* 30(1). 163–74.

Levy, Yonata. (In press). Developmental delay reconsidered: The impact of disrupted developmental timing.

Levy, Yonata & Talma Bechar. 2003. Cognitive, lexical, and morpho-syntactic profiles of Israeli children with Williams syndrome. *Cortex* 39. 255–271.

Levy, Yonata & Shulamit Hermon. 2003. Morphological abilities of Hebrew speaking adolescents with Williams syndrome. *Developmental Neuropsychology* 23. 59–83.

Levy, Yonata & Ariela Eilam. 2013. Pathways to language: A naturalistic study of children with Williams syndrome and children with Down syndrome. [Special Issue on language acquisition in a-typical populations]. *Journal of Child Language* 40(1). 106–138.

Levy, Yonata, Hadas Pluber & Shlomo Bentin. 2009. Covert processing of facial expressions by people with Williams syndrome. *Cortex* 47(1). 23–34.

Malenfant, P., X. Liu, M. L. Hudson, Y. Qiao, M. Hrynchak, N. Riendeau, M. J. Hildebrand, I. L. Cohen, A. E. Chudley, C. Forster-Gibson, E. C. R. Mickelson, E. Rajcan-Separovic, M. E. S. Lewis & J. J. A. Holden. 2012. Association of GTF2i in the Williams-Beuren syndrome critical region with autism spectrum disorders. *Journal of Autism and Developmental Disorders* 42(7). 1459–1469.

Marini, Andrea, Sara Martelli, Chiara Gagliardi, Franco Fabbro & Renato Borgatti. 2010. Narrative language in Williams syndrome and its neuropsychological correlates. *Journal of Neurolinguistics* 23(2). 97–111.

Masataka, Nobuo. 2001. Why early linguistic milestones are delayed in children with Williams syndrome: Late onset of hand banging as a possible rate-limiting constraint on the emergence of canonical babbling. *Developmental Science* 4(2). 158–164.

Mervis, Carolyn B. & Angela M. Becerra. 2007. Language and communicative development in Williams syndrome. *Mental Retardation and Developmental Disabilities Research Reviews* 13(1). 3–15.

Mervis, Carolyn B. & Angela E. John. 2008. Vocabulary abilities of children with Williams syndrome: Strengths, weaknesses, and relation to visuospatial construction ability. *Journal of Speech, Language, and Hearing Research* 51(4). 967–982.

Mervis, Carolyn B. Colleen A. Morris, Jacquelyn Bertrand & Byron F. Robinson. 1999. Williams syndrome: Findings from an integrated program of research. In: Helen Tager-Flusberg (Ed.), *Neurodevelopmental disorders*, 65–110. Cambridge, MA: MIT Press.

Mervis, Carolyn B. & Byron F. Robinson. 2000. Expressive vocabulary ability of toddlers with Williams syndrome or Down syndrome: A comparison. *Developmental Neuropsychology* 17(1). 111–126.

Mervis, Carolyn B. Byron F. Robinson, Melissa L. Rowe, Angela M. Becerra & Bonita P. Klein-Tasman. 2003. Language abilities of individuals with Williams syndrome. In Leonard Abbeduto (Ed.), *International review of research in mental retardation: Language and communication in mental retardation*, Vol 27, 35–81. San Diego: Academic Press.

Meyer-Lindenberg, Andreas, Carolyn B. Mervis, Deepak Sarpal, Paul Koch, Sonya Steele, Philip Kohn, Stefano Marenco, Colleen A. Morris, Saumitra Das, Shane Kippenhan, Venkata S. Mattay, Daniel R. Weinberger & Karen F. Berman. 2005. Functional, structural, and metabolic abnormalities of the hippocampal formation in Williams syndrome. *Journal of Clinical Investigation* 115. 1888–1895.

Morris, Colleen A. Susan A. Demsey, Claire O. Leonard, Constance Dilts & Brent L. Blackburn. 1988. Natural history of Williams syndrome: Physical characteristics. *Journal of Pediatrics* 11. 318–326.

Musolino, Julien, Gitana Chunyo & Barbara Landau. 2010. Uncovering knowledge of core syntactic and semantic principles in individuals with Williams syndrome. *Language Learning and Development* 6(2). 126–161.

Nazzi, Thierry, Alison Gopnik & Annette Karmiloff-Smith. 2005. Asynchrony in the cognitive and lexical development of young children with Williams syndrome. *Journal of Child Language* 32(2). 427–438.

Nazzi, Thierry, Sarah Paterson & Annette Karmiloff-Smith. 2003. Early word segmentation by infants and toddlers with Williams syndrome. *Infancy* 4. 251–271.

Norbury, Cortney F. & Dorothy V. M. Bishop. 2003. Narrative skills of children with communication impairments. *International Journal of Language & Communication Disorders* 38(3). 287–313.

Osório, Ana, José Miguel Soares, Montse Fernández Prieto, Cristiana Vasconcelos, Catarina Fernandes, Sónia Sousa, Ángel Carracedo, Óscar F. Gonçalves & Adriana Sampaio. 2014. Cerebral and cerebellar MRI volumes in Williams syndrome. *Research in Developmental Disabilities* 35(4). 922–928.

Paterson, Sarah J., J. H. Brown, M. K. Gsödl, Mark H. Johnson & Annette Karmiloff-Smith. 1999. Cognitive modularity and genetic disorders. *Science* 286(5448). 2355–2358.

Paterson, Sarah J. Luisa Girelli, Brian Butterworth & Annette Karmiloff-Smith. 2006. Are numerical impairments syndrome specific? Evidence from Williams syndrome and Down's syndrome. *Journal of Child Psychology and Psychiatry* 47(2). 190–204.

Peoples, Risa, Yvonne Franke, Yu-Ker Wang, Luis Pérez-Jurado, Tamar Paperna, Michael Cisco & Uta Francke. 2000. A physical map, including a BAC/PAC clone contig, of the Williams-Beuren syndrome-deletion region at 7q11.23. *American Journal of Human Genetics* 66(1). 47–68.

Pérez-García, D., R. Flores, C. Brun-Gasca & L. A. Pérez-Jurado. 2015. Lateral preference in Williams–Beuren syndrome is associated with cognition and language. *European Child & Adolescent Psychiatry* 24(9). 1025–1033.

Perovic, Anna, Nadya Modyanova & Ken Wexler. 2013. Comparison of grammar in neurodevelopmental disorders: The case of binding in Williams syndrome and autism with and without language impairment. *Language Acquisition: A Journal of Developmental Linguistics* 20(2). 133–154.

Perovic, Anna & Ken Wexler. 2007. Complex grammar in Williams syndrome. *Clinical Linguistics & Phonetics* 21(9). 729–745.

Perovic, Anna & Ken Wexler. 2010. Development of verbal passive in Williams syndrome. *Journal of Speech, Language, and Hearing Research* 53(5). 1294–1306.

Phillips, Caroline E. Christopher Jarrold, Alan D. Baddeley, Julia Grant & Annette Karmiloff-Smith. 2004. Comprehension of spatial language terms in Williams syndrome: Evidence for an interaction between domains of strength and weakness. *Cortex* 40(1). 85–101.

Philofsky, Amy, Deborah J. Fidler & Susan Hepburn. 2007. Pragmatic language profiles of school-age children with autism spectrum disorders and Williams syndrome. *American Journal of Speech-Language Pathology* 16(4). 368–380.

Pléh, Csaba, Agnes Lukács & Mihály Racsmány. 2003. Morphological patterns in Hungarian children with Williams syndrome and the rule debates. *Brain and Language* 86(3). 377–383.

Prontera, Paolo, Domenico Serino, Bernardo Caldini, Laura Scarponi, Giuseppe Merla, Giuseppe Testa, Marco Muti, Valerio Napolioni, Giovanni Mazzotta, Massimo Piccirilli & Emilio Donti. 2014. Brief report: Functional MRI of a patient with 7q11.23 duplication syndrome and autism spectrum disorder. *Journal of Autism and Developmental Disorders* 44(10). 2608–2613.

Purser, Harry RM, Michael SC Thomas, Sarah Snoxall, Denis Mareschal & Annette Karmiloff-Smith. 2011. Definitions versus categorization: Assessing the development of lexico-semantic knowledge in Williams syndrome. *International Journal of Language & Communication Disorders* 46(3). 361–373.

Reilly, Judith, Edoward S. Klima & Ursula Bellugi. 1990. Once more with feeling: Affect and language in atypical populations. *Development and Psychopathology* 2(4). 367–391.

Reilly, Judy, Molly Losh, Ursula Bellugi & Beverly Wulfeck. 2004. "Frog, where are you?" Narratives in children with specific language impairment, early focal brain injury, and Williams syndrome. *Brain and Language* 88(2). 229–247.

Reiss, Allan L. Stephan Eliez, Eric J. Schmitt, Anil Patwardhan & Michael Haberecht. 2000. Brain imaging in neurogenetic conditions: Realizing the potential of behavioral neurogenetics research. *Mental Retardation and Developmental Disabilities Research Reviews* 6(3). 186–197.

Rice, Mabel L. Steven F. Warren & Stacy K. Betz. 2005. Language symptoms of developmental language disorders: An overview of autism, Down syndrome, fragile X, specific language impairment, and Williams syndrome. *Applied Psycholinguistics* 26(1). 7–27.

Ring, Melanie & Harald Clahsen. 2005. Distinct patterns of language impairment in Down's syndrome and Williams syndrome: The case of syntactic chains. *Journal of Neurolinguistics* 18(6). 479–501.

Robinson, Byron F. Carolyn B. Mervis & Bronwyn W. Robinson. 2003. The roles of verbal short-term memory and working memory in the acquisition of grammar by children with Williams syndrome. *Developmental Neuropsychology* 23(1–2). 13–31.

Rossi, Natalia Freitas, Adriana Sampaio, Óscar F. Gonçalves & Célia Maria Giacheti. 2011. Analysis of speech fluency in Williams syndrome. *Research in Developmental Disabilities* 32(6). 2957–2962.

Sampaio, Adriana, Sylvain Bouix, Nuno Sousa, Cristiana Vasconcelos, Montse Férnandez, Martha E. Shenton & Oscar F. Gonçalves. 2013. Morphometry of corpus callosum in Williams syndrome: Shape as an index of neural development. *Brain Structure & Function* 218(3). 711–720.

Semel, Eleanor Messing & Sue R. Rosner. 2003. *Understanding Williams syndrome: Behavioral patterns and interventions*. Mahwah, NJ: Lawrence Erlbaum Associates.

Stojanovik, Vesna, Mick Perkins & Sara Howard. 2001. Language and conversational abilities in Williams syndrome: How good is good? *International Journal of Language & Communication Disorders*, 36(Supplement). 234–239.

Stojanovik, Vesna & Lizet van Ewijk. 2008. Do children with Williams syndrome have unusual vocabularies? *Journal of Neurolinguistics* 21(1). 18–34.

Strømme, Petter, Per G. Bjømstad, & Kjersti Ramstad. 2002. Prevalence estimation of Williams syndrome. *Journal of Child Neurology* 17. 269–271.

Sullivan, Kate, Ellen Winner & Helen Tager-Flusberg. 2003. Can adolescents with Williams syndrome tell the difference between lies and jokes? *Developmental Neuropsychology* 23(1–2). 85–103.

Tassabehji May. 2003. Williams-Beuren syndrome: A challenge for genotype-phenotype correlations. *Human Molecular Genetics*. 12 supplement 2. 229–37.

Tassabehji May & Diane Donnai. 2006. Williams-Beuren Syndrome: More or less? Segmental duplications and deletions in the Williams-Beuren syndrome region provide new insights into language development. *European Journal of Human Genetics* 14(5). 507–8.

Thomas, Michael S.C. Julia Grant, Zita Barham, Marisa Gsödl, Emma Laing, Laura Lakusta, Lorraine K. Tyler, Sarah Grice, Sarah Paterson & Annette Karmiloff-Smith. 2001. Past tense formation in Williams syndrome. *Language and Cognitive Processes* 16(2–3). 143–176.

Thomas, Michael S.C. Themis N. Karaminis & Victoria C.P. Knowland. 2010. What is typical language development? *Language Learning and Development* 6(2). 162–169.

Thomas, Michael S. C. & Annette Karmiloff-Smith. 2003. Modeling language acquisition in atypical phenotypes. *Psychological Review* 110(4). 647–682.

Thomas, Michael S. C. & Annette Karmiloff-Smith. 2005. Can developmental disorders reveal the component parts of the language faculty? *Language Learning and Development* 1. 65–92.

Thomas, Michael S. C. Mike Van Duuren, Harry R. M. Purser, Dennis Mareschal, Daniel Ansari & Annette Karmiloff-Smith. 2010. The development of metaphorical language comprehension in typical development and in Williams syndrome. *Journal of Experimental Child Psychology* 106(2–3). 99–114.

Thompson, Paul M. Agatha D. Lee, Rebecca A. Dutton, Jennifer A. Geaga, Kiralee M. Hayashi, Mark A. Eckert, Ursula Bellugi, Albert M. Galaburda, Julie R. Korenberg, Debra L. Mills, Arthur W. Toga & Alan L. Reiss. 2005. Abnormal cortical complexity and thickness profiles mapped in Williams syndrome. *Journal of Neuroscience* 25. 4146–4158.

Tordjman, Sylvie, George M. Anderson, Michel Botbol, Annick Toutain, Pierre Sarda, Michèle Carlier, Pascale Saugier-Veber , Clarisse Baumann, David Cohen, Celine Lagneaux, Anne-Claude Tabet & Alain Verloes. 2012. Autistic disorder in patients with Williams-Beuren Syndrome: A reconsideration of the Williams-Beuren Syndrome phenotype. *PLOS ONE* 7(3). e30778.

Udwin, Orlee, William Yule & Neil Martin. 1987. Cognitive abilities and behavioural characteristics of children with idiopathic infantile hypercalcaemia. *Child Psychology & Psychiatry & Allied Disciplines* 28(2). 297–309.

Vicari, Stefano, Elisabeth Bates, Maria Cristina Caselli, Patrizio Pasqualetti, Chiara Gagliardi, Francesca Tonucci & Virginia Volterra. 2004. Neuropsychological profile of Italians with Williams syndrome: An example of a dissociation between language and cognition? *Journal of the International Neuropsychological Society* 10(6). 862–876.

Volterra, Virginia, Olga Capirci, Grazia Pezzini & Leticia Sabbadini. 1996. Linguistic abilities in Italian children with Williams syndrome. *Cortex* 32(4). 663–677.

Wang, Paul P. Sally Doherty, John R. Hesselink & Ursula Bellugi. 1992. Callosal morphology concurs with neurobehavioral and neuropathological findings in two neurodevelopmental disorders. *Archives of Neurology* 49(4). 407–411.

Ypsilanti, A. & G. Grouios. 2008. Linguistic profile of individuals with Down syndrome: Comparing the linguistic performance of three developmental disorders. *Child Neuropsychology* 14(2). 148–170.

Zukowski, Andrea. 2005. Knowledge of constraints on compounding in children and adolescents with Williams syndrome. *Journal of Speech, Language, and Hearing Research* 48(1). 79–92.

Zukowski, Andrea. 2009. Elicited production of relative clauses in children with Williams syndrome. *Language and Cognitive Processes* 24(1). 1–43.

Sigal Uziel-Karl and Michal Tenne-Rinde

41 Making language accessible for people with cognitive disabilities: Intellectual disability as a test case

1 Introduction

Information and communication play a central role in our modern daily lives. An abundance of language-based information is available to us through the internet, the media (newspapers, radio, or television), books, signage and face-to-face interactions. However, this information may not be equally accessible to everyone. For individuals with cognitive disabilities, coping with written or spoken information may pose a considerable challenge, as they often experience difficulties understanding and responding to language presented in these modalities. Thus, people with cognitive disabilities often need to get information in an accessible manner in order to understand it. The lack of accessible information forms a major barrier for their full participation in the community and for their independent functioning in everyday life (Yalon-Chamovitz, 2009, Collier, Blackstone and Taylor, 2012).

To get a sense of what is involved in coping with inaccessible information, try to recall the helplessness you must have felt when trying to find your way around in a foreign country without speaking the local language, when struggling to navigate through a complicated interactive voice menu, or to understand the terms and conditions of a standard rental agreement. Frustration often increases at the face of legal, financial or medical information written in a highly professional language, using jargon, abstract expressions, complicated logical reasoning and complex sentences. These examples, like many others, illustrate the distress one may feel in the absence of proper communication or in the lack of clear and accessible information.

The present paper provides a state-of-the-art overview of the current situation regarding information and language accessibility for individuals with cognitive disabilities in Israel, zooming in on a major sub-group within this range – persons with intellectual disabilities. We outline the major language accessibility guidelines for this sub-group, and demonstrate their implementation, pointing out dilemmas along the way. The guidelines are set to reduce structural complexity, while maintaining semantic content, yielding information that is clear, comprehensible and adapted to the needs, world-knowledge and linguistic proficiency of persons with intellectual disabilities (Uziel-Karl, Tenne-Rinde and Yalon-Chamovitz, 2011).

Sigal Uziel-Karl, Achva Academic College
Michal Tenne-Rinde, Ono Academic College

The past three decades have been characterized by dramatic social and constitutional changes in the realm of accessibility, mainly as a result of social demand for equal rights for people with disabilities. Consequently, most equal rights laws include sections that emphasize accessibility as a significant enabler of participation (Yalon-Chamovitz, 2009). Moreover, policy-makers world-wide have recognized the need for making information accessible for people with disabilities and acted to ensure this right via legislation, regulations and international treaties. In 1990, the United States enacted the *Americans with Disabilities Act [ADA]*. This human rights law protects people with disabilities from discrimination and ensures them accessibility and equal opportunities. The law requires that all states in the United States and all local authorities take measures to ensure that their communication with people with disabilities is as effective as with the general public. That is, everything said or written must be clear and understandable to all. Similarly, many Western countries (e.g., Canada, United-kingdom, Ireland, Sweden, Australia and New-Zealand) have developed accessibility guidelines for people with disabilities (e.g., SAIF, 2011). In 2008, the *United Nations Convention on the Rights of Persons with Disabilities* entered into force. The Convention aims to promote, protect and ensure that all persons with disabilities enjoy the full and equal rights and fundamental freedoms, and that their inherent dignity in all realms of life is respected (work, education, health, and more).

The term a*ccessibility* refers to a person's ability to reach a place, to move and orient oneself in that place, to use a service and enjoy it, to receive information and take part in programs and activities in that place, all in an equal, respectable, independent, and safe manner (*Americans With Disabilities Act [ADA]*, 1990; *Israeli Equal Rights for Persons With Disabilities Law – Accessibility Amendment*, 2005).

In Israel, accessibility was first brought to public attention in 1996, when the Supreme Court recognized the right to accessibility for persons with disabilities as part of their right for social integration (Supreme Court Appeal, 1996). The court noted in its ruling that accessibility should not be based on the concept of grace and charity, but on the concept of human rights and equal opportunities. In 1998, Israel enacted the *Equal Rights for People with Disabilities Act*. The purpose of this law is to protect the dignity, freedom and rights of people with disabilities to run their lives independently. The term **negishut** 'accessibility' was defined in the Amendment to the *Equal Rights for People with Disabilities Act* (2005, Amendment No. 2), where reference to accessibility of service and information was first made. The definition aims to ensure that a person with disability will not be excluded because of his disability. "It is not individual limitations, of whatever kind, which are the cause of the problem but society's failure to provide appropriate services and adequately ensure [that] the needs of disabled people are fully taken into account in its social organization" (Oliver 1996:32). Thus, the responsibility for the implementation of the law is bestowed on society as a whole, and in particular, on public service providers (Feldman, Danieli-Lahav and Haimovitz, 2007). On March 31, 2007 Israel signed the

UN Convention on the Rights of Persons with Disabilities, and ratified it on September 28th, 2012. The convention lists the measures that should be taken in order to enable people with disabilities to live independently and to fully participate in all aspects of life. These measures include: identification of obstacles and barriers to accessibility and disabling them, developing and formulating standards and guidelines for accessibility and monitoring their implementation, initiating and promoting research, developing new technologies and promoting design for all (Universal Design – UD). In April 2013, the *Regulations for the Equal Rights for People with Disabilities* were enacted (to include service accessibility). These regulations place great emphasis on the accessibility of information and communication in the public service. They require the adaptation of practices and procedures of the service, and the provision of means and auxiliary services to enable a person to obtain information given or produced in a place, or to participate in programs and activities that take place in it (*Regulations for Accessibility of Service*, 2013, section 29). Accessibility to information is also currently discussed in a revision of the Israeli standard dealing with access to the media (*Israeli Standard* 1918, Part 4, The Standards Institution of Israel, 2015). Consequently, all public and private service providers will be required to meet the standard (Israeli Standard 1918, Part 4, 2015), the regulations and the law, as applicable.

2 Cognitive disabilities, intellectual disability

In the International Classification of Functioning, Disability and Health [ICF] (2001) **disability** is defined as a multi-dimensional concept relating to functions and structures of the human body, people's activities and the life areas in which they participate, and factors in their environment that affect these experiences. Within this framework, a person's disability is conceived as the dynamic interaction between health conditions, environmental and personal factors. Disabilities may be physical or motor, sensory (e.g., visual or hearing impairments), cognitive or developmental, mental or psycho-social. A person may have one or multiple disabilities.

The term **cognitive disabilities** refers to a broad range of clinical diagnoses (which may be inherited, congenital, developmental or acquired) that may impair one's ability to perform certain cognitive functions (Carmien et al., 2005). Among these are autism, intellectual disabilities, mental health disabilities, traumatic brain injury, dementia, as well as Attention Deficit Disorder [ADD], Complex Learning Difficulties and Disabilities (CLDD) and others. Persons with cognitive disabilities may experience memory and attention deficits, language comprehension difficulties, difficulties with solving problems, concentrating on a task, understanding inference, understanding abstract or metaphorical content, distinguishing important from peripheral information, and reading; additional difficulties may include way-finding, math comprehension and visual comprehension. Consequently, these difficulties affect their ability to receive, to process and to produce information successfully.

Intellectual disability is a developmental cognitive disability. In the Welfare Law (1969), a person with intellectual disability is defined as "a person who, due to lack of development or poor development of his mental capacity, has limited ability for adaptive behavior and is in need of care". But the actual assessment and assignment of intellectual disability in Israel today, adopted by the Division for Intellectual and Developmental Disabilities of the Ministry of Social Affairs and Social Services, is largely based on the definition of the American Association on Intellectual and Developmental Disabilities [AAIDD] (Schalock et al., 2010):

*"**Intellectual disability** is a disability characterized by significant limitations both in **intellectual functioning** (reasoning, learning, problem solving) and in **adaptive behavior** (a range of everyday social and practical skills). This disability originates before the age of 18".*

2.1 Language skills of people with intellectual disabilities

Research has shown that persons with intellectual disabilities may experience diverse cognitive difficulties, among which are difficulties in long and short term memory which can affect their ability to acquire complex linguistic structures and to expand their vocabulary; difficulties with cognitive processes such as reasoning, symbolization, generalization and abstraction, understanding concepts like time and quantity and understanding idiomatic or multiple-meaning expressions (Harris, 2006; Rhea, 2004). The vocabulary of persons with intellectual disability consists mostly of concrete nouns and verbs, and includes only a small set of descriptive words such as adjectives and adverbs (Yoder and Warren, 2004). They tend to generate short, simple sentences. They may find it difficult to produce and understand passive sentences (e.g., *the book was written by Danny*), sentences with non-canonical word-order (e.g., *out jumped the rabbit = The rabbit jumped out*), conditional sentences (e.g., *if it rains, I will not go for a walk*), and complex sentences with relative clauses (e.g., *the man [that [Danny met]] is a famous actor*), or embedded clauses (e.g., *Danny thought [that [tomorrow I will buy him another book]]*) (Zukowski, 2004).

Additional challenges that might impair the linguistic and communicative abilities of persons with intellectual disability include **pace, complexity, literacy,** and **stigma** (Yalon-Chamovitz, 2009):

- **Pace:** People with intellectual disabilities show relatively slow processing and reaction time in many different tasks (for a review, see Kail, 2000). Therefore, pace accommodations should be applied both to environmental design and procedures of service provision, e.g. provide instructions at a slower pace, allow more time to complete activities, etc. (Yalon-Chamovitz, 2007, 2009:396).

- **Complexity**: people with intellectual disabilities often experience difficulties in verbal communication, in way-finding in the physical and virtual environment, in understanding and following product-operating instructions and in coping with procedures. Thus, it is recommended that the procedures and language be simplified to accommodate their needs, e.g., maps, clear design that facilitates orientation, simple operating instructions, etc.
- **Literacy**: Literacy is an important means for independent functioning, and for improving the quality of life of people with intellectual disability (Downing, 2005; Shengross, 2011). People with intellectual disabilities often exemplify low literacy level, and many of them experience difficulties reading simple texts (Yong et al. 2004). A survey conducted by the U.S. Department of Education in the 90's found that 87% of the Americans with intellectual disability are at the lowest literacy level (Irwin et. al., 1993, Cohen et al., 2001). People with intellectual disability may also experience difficulties receiving and integrating information, organizing knowledge and planning agenda, which might increase the need to receive external support on a daily basis in order to perform tasks that require literacy skills, thus damaging a person's self-esteem and his or her sense of competence. This may lead people with intellectual disabilities to avoid challenging experiences which could improve their skills for full participation in the community. The recommended accommodations in this case are easy-to-read language and the use of graphic representation of information (Salmi, Ginthner, and Guerin, 2004).
- **Stigma**: is perhaps the predominant barrier to accessibility. Despite rights granted by legislation, in practice, people with intellectual disabilities cannot actively claim or implement their rights. They are often still treated as patients or people in need of protection, and are expected to be escorted or supervised when accessing community programs and services. Although this might be appropriate for some, the range of functional abilities and support needs of people with intellectual disabilities is very wide (Luckasson et al., 2002), and many could function independently given appropriate accommodations. To remove stigma, it is necessary to increase awareness to accessibility needs of people with intellectual disabilities and provide practical guidelines for the provision of accessible, equal, and respectful service to all (Yalon-Chamovitz, 2009:398).

2.2 Linguistic accessibility for persons with intellectual disability

Access to information is one of the most important accommodations for people with intellectual disabilities. As part of the general effort to develop the body of knowledge and means to help implement regulations concerning information accessibility, the Division for Intellectual and Developmental Disabilities of the Ministry of Social Affairs and Social Services recently published a set of guidelines (Uziel-Karl, Tenne-Rinde and Yalon-Chamovitz, 2011). These guidelines form the basis for the definition of **linguistic simplification** in the Regulations for Accessibility of Service (2013), and are a product of comprehensive applied research on language accessibility for individuals with intellectual disability sponsored by the Ministry. The guidelines are intended to direct service providers and professionals in the preparation and production of accessible materials for persons with intellectual disabilities.

Linguistic accessibility refers to the process of adapting written or spoken information to the needs of people with disabilities in order to make it clear, understandable and inviting for them, using diverse linguistic and sensory means (i.e., visual, audio or tactile). Visual means rely on sight for communication and transmission of information (e.g., accessible print and symbols). **Audio means** rely on hearing for communication and transmission of information (e.g., screen readers, public address systems). **Tactile means** rely on touch to communicate and transfer information (e.g., embossed signs, maps). The outcome of this process is accessible information adapted to the needs of the target audience.

The process of making information linguistically accessible to persons with intellectual disabilities consists of three main phases: (1) **Planning** – a preparatory phase which includes formulating ideas, selecting the mode of information transfer (spoken or written) and the appropriate means of delivering the message to the target audience; (2) **implementation** – adapting various linguistic aspects of the message to the needs of the target audience (e.g., vocabulary, sentence structure). This process is also known as *easy-to-read* or *language simplification*; Printed easy-to-read materials are marked as such with a designated symbol and caption to allow easy identification (see Figure 1)[1]; (3) **Quality assurance** – ensures that the simplified information suits the needs of the target population.

מסמך בפישוט לשוני

Figure 1: Easy-to-Read (simple language) Symbol

Language simplification can be performed at different levels. *Easy-to-read language* should be distinguished from **Plain language**. The latter constitutes an intermediate level between non-simplified, expert language and *easy-to-read (simple) language*. It is defined as everyday language, a language that the lay person can understand, with no jargon or professional terms. Yet, it is not sufficiently adapted to the needs of persons with intellectual disabilities as described above.

---

[1] This symbol is based on the EU easy-to-read symbol. It is currently considered for inclusion in the revision of the *Israeli standard* 1918, part 4.

Table 1: Key simplification guidelines

Category	Guidelines
Content Plan what you want to say	Present only necessary and important information
	Present the information in a logical sequence, one step at a time
	Express only one main idea per sentence
	Use respectful language
	Use adult language when addressing adults
	Do not assume previous knowledge about your subject
Structure Adapt the language to the needs of the target audience (vocabulary and sentence structure)	Use only words that are common in the everyday language of persons with intellectual disability
	Avoid jargon, foreign words or abbreviations
	Avoid abstract words
	Explain difficult words and give examples
	Refrain from using metaphors and uncommon figures of speech
	Be consistent in the way you use words to refer to particular objects or concepts
	Use active rather than passive verbs
	Make direct reference to your audience using pronouns such as "you" and "we"
	Otherwise, prefer lexical noun phrases over pronouns or null subjects
	Keep sentences short
	Avoid complex sentences
	Use positive language
Design Adapt the text layout and design to the needs of the target audience	Divide the text into separate paragraphs
	Make sure the layout and text-flow support the content of the text
	Use bullet points when forming a list
	Use simple punctuation (, . ?)
	Use digits rather than words to refer to numbers (e.g., '3' instead of 'three')
	Use symbols to support your text
	Use matt paper of good quality
	Use a clear typeface such as Arial
	Use a large type-size, 16–22 point
	Make sure there is good contrast between type and paper
Quality Assurance (QA) Check the simplified product	Consult persons with intellectual disability on whether the simplified product is clear and understandable to them

Language simplification requires adjustment of the content, structure and design (for written information only) of the original message. Table 1 lists the major guidelines for language simplification in each one of these domains.

To illustrate language simplification in action, compare the compound "aquatic insects" with its simplified counterpart "water bugs". In this example the Latinate denominal adjective (aquatic) and noun (insects), were replaced by the everyday English words of Germanic origin – "water" and "bugs" to yield "water bugs", in accordance with the requirement (in Table 1) to use common, familiar vocabulary.

- **Content**: The number of ideas expressed in a text determine its level of complexity. Paragraphs which contain sentences with multiple abstract ideas are hard to remember and to understand (Haramati, 1991). To make information accessible to individuals with intellectual disabilities, it is essential to reduce information density (express one idea per sentence, delete information that does not contribute directly to understanding the main ideas), to focus on a small number of main ideas and to fill in pragmatic and logical gaps (e.g. *unlock the door* vs. *to unlock the door, do the following: 1. Insert the key in the keyhole, 2. Turn the key to the left*). It is also necessary to reduce stylistic density (e.g. refrain from using high register words) and to use examples and explanations to facilitate understanding. Additional guidelines relating to content are listed in Table 1.
- **Structure**: to adapt the vocabulary of a message to individuals with intellectual disabilities, it is necessary to reduce vocabulary density, to use common familiar words and to ensure consistency in word usage throughout the message. It is necessary to keep to a minimum the use of constructions like conditionals (*if the weather is good, we'll go swimming*), modals (*I must read this book*), double negation (*not allowed not to testify*), and clefts (*it is Dan who won the game*). As for sentence structure, the longer the sentence, the more likely it is to be syntactically complex, and the harder it is to follow, to remember and to understand. Thus, complex and compound sentences should be broken down into simple sentences (one subject and one predicate per sentence), and should follow canonical word order (subject-verb-object). Additional guidelines are listed in Table 1.
- **Design** (written information): Visual means are often necessary and extremely helpful in supporting written information e.g., accessible print, clear headers, spaces between paragraphs and symbols (Nir, 1989). The use of accessible page layout, print and symbols to support a written message is illustrated in Figure 2.

As shown in Figure 2, various visual and graphic elements can be used to enhance the accessibility of a message: (1) The header, distinctly marked (bold, underline), gives a clear idea of the topic; (2) Line spacing and numbering allow the reader to follow the sequence of actions and their relative ordering more easily, provided the order is significant; (3) Large and readable font (Arial 16) and black print over white

How to write a letter?

1. Prepare a pen, a sheet of paper and an envelope.	
2. Write the letter on the sheet of paper.	
3. Carefully fold the letter in two.	
4. Put the letter in an envelope.	
5. Seal (close) the envelope.	

Figure 2: Writing a letter

background allow the reader to focus on the written message with no distractions. Font size may also facilitate reading for individuals who are visually impaired (Regulations for the Equal Rights for People with Disabilities, Accessibility of Service, chapter 1: 968 – Accessible Print, 2013); (4) Symbols, defined as clear and simple graphic representations of information delivered to the public (the *Regulations for Equal Rights for People with Disabilities, Access to Service, 2013*), enable individuals whose reading ability is not sufficient or functional, or who cannot read or write, to figure out the content of the message without having to fully read it. Why symbols? Individuals with intellectual disabilities tend to think very concretely, so that using a photograph of an object or a person might be interpreted as referring only to that specific object or person. To avoid association with specific objects or people, symbols are schematic; they are black and white to avoid dependence on colors for their interpretation (which might be problematic in photocopying or for individuals who are color blind, for example). Conventional symbols are universally acceptable, and are created according to an obligatory set of requirements set in the international ISO standards of graphic symbols [ISO 7001]. Symbols are placed to the right of the message in languages like English (read from left to right), or to the left of the message in Semitic languages like Hebrew (read from right to left), to enable reading with the aid of electronic reading devices.

- **Quality assurance (QA):** is an important step in the simplification process. This step is designed to make sure the simplified information meets the needs of the target population. QA is not necessarily limited to the end product, but can be performed throughout the simplification process. Since the simplified information is intended for individuals with intellectual disabilities, it is important that members of this target group check whether they comprehend the simplified content.

Note that while some easy-to-read guidelines are universal and may be shared cross-linguistically (e.g. use simple sentences), others are not, and should be adapted to a particular language, culture or locale. Since the present paper reviews the situation of language accessibility for persons with intellectual disability in Israel, the following examples of language simplification are from Hebrew (Tables 2–3 below).

A Semitic language like Hebrew with a dense morphology makes use of morphological structure in most lexical classes, with diverse systems to express different classes of inflection and derivation (Berman, 1978; Bolozky, 2007; Schwarzwald, 2001, 2002). Nouns, adjectives, verbs, and even prepositions are heavily inflected and demonstrate rich and complex allomorphy. The opacity of the system and its complexity pose special challenges for Hebrew-speaking individuals with intellectual disability. To make the necessary adaptations, language specific simplification guidelines were formulated. Consider the following specific examples:

- **Possession:** Hebrew marks possession in one of two ways – analytically, by using the possessive particle *shel* 'of' [*ha-sefer shel ha-yeled* 'the book of the boy'] and synthetically, by attaching an inflectional suffix to a noun [*sifr-o* 'the-boy's-book']. The former option is more transparent than the latter, and structurally invariant and so should be preferred: To express possession, prefer analytic to bound forms (Dekel, 2014).
- **Null subjects:** Null subjects are morphologically licensed by Hebrew verbs in past and future tense, 1st and 2nd person (e.g., *halaxnu la-avoda* 'went-1-PL to work'), as the missing subject can be reconstructed from the inflectional affixes on the verb (*-nu* '1-PL-PAST). Yet, individuals with intellectual disabilities find sentences with null subjects harder to process. Thus, overt subjects should be preferred: Use overt subjects (e.g., *anaxnu halaxnu* 'we went-1-PL').
- **Gender:** Hebrew overtly marks grammatical gender on nouns, verbs, adjectives, prepositions and pronouns. Thus, a message addressed to males and females requires using both feminine and masculine forms. This creates an overload for persons with intellectual disabilities. Moreover, in formal documents, both forms are often listed using a "/" separator (e.g., *kax/kxi* 'take-MS/take-FM' or *kax/i* 'take-MS/FM'). This creates additional cognitive burden. To overcome this: Use the imperative in the plural form (e.g., *kxu* 'take-PL'), or the infinitive form (e.g., *lakaxat* 'to take'). Alternatively, create two separate gender-oriented versions of the message.

- **Homography**: Hebrew has two orthographic versions, pointed and non-pointed, differing in the amount of phonological information they supply to readers. In the deep non-pointed orthography, consonants are fully represented, but vowels are only partially and ambiguously represented, resulting in pervasive homography that challenges readers. For example, the written string חומה "ḤWMH" which does not represent vowels overtly, may be read as /xoma/ 'wall' or /xuma/ 'brown' (Bar-On and Ravid, 2011; Ravid, 2012). To facilitate the understanding of homographic words, it is recommended that these words be used with *nikud* "pointing" diacritics, which supply full information about vocalization. Contextual clues in the form of examples or explanations may also be provided.

To illustrate the implementation of the easy-to-read guidelines in Hebrew, consider the following example. Tables 2 and 3 present two versions of an excerpt from the *UN Convention for the Rights of People with Disabilities (2006)* – the original text (Table 2) and an easy-to-read version of the same excerpt (Table 3), both accompanied by a Hebrew translation.

Table 2: Original non-simplified text

Article 9	סעיף 9
Accessibility	נגישות
To enable persons with disabilities to live independently and participate fully in all aspects of life, States Parties shall take appropriate measures to ensure to persons with disabilities access, on an equal basis with others, to the physical environment, to transportation, to information and communications, including information and communications technologies and systems, to other facilities and services open or provided to the public, both in urban and in rural areas.	על מנת לאפשר לאנשים עם מוגבלויות לחיות בצורה עצמאית ולהשתתף באופן מלא בכל היבטי החיים, תנקוטנה מדינות שהן צדדים אמצעים הולמים כדי להבטיח לאנשים עם מוגבלויות גישה לסביבה הפיזית, לתחבורה, למידע ולתקשורת, לרבות לטכנולוגיות ומערכות מידע ותקשורת, ולמתקנים ושירותים אחרים הפתוחים או ניתנים לציבור, באזורים עירוניים וכפריים כאחד, בשוויון עם אחרים.

Table 3: An Easy-to-Read version

Accessibility	נגישות
The states that take part (in the agreement) will do everything to give people with disabilities access (possibility to get and use): • a place • transportation (bus, train, car) • information and to tools for getting information • facilities and other services for the public This will enable people with disabilities • to live independently • to participate in all the activities in their community like any other person	המדינות השותפות (להסכם) יעשו כל מה שצריך כדי לתת לאנשים עם מוגבלויות **נגישות** (אפשרות להגיע להשתמש): • במקום • בתחבורה (אוטובוס, רכבת, מכונית) • במידע ולכלים לקבלת מידע • במתקנים ושירותים אחרים לציבור (לכולם) זה יעזור לאנשים עם מוגבלויות: • לנהל את החיים שלהם בעצמם • להשתתף בפעילויות בקהילה כמו כל אדם אחר

The original text (Table 2) consists of a single, complex, multi-clausal sentence. In the simplified version, this sentence is divided into smaller units (phrases). The order of presentation of the purpose and action clauses in the original text is reversed to match the default order [main clause – adjunct] and the logical order of cause and effect. Explanations of unfamiliar words and examples are given in parentheses, e.g. *taxbura (otobus, rakevet, mexonit)* 'transportation (bus, train, car)', *tsibur* (everbody) 'public', *atsma'it* 'independently', etc. High register words like *holmim* 'appropriate', *sviva fizit* 'physical environment', *texnologya* 'technology' and others are replaced or eliminated. Similarly, construct state *hebetey ha-xayim* 'aspects of life', passive verbs *nitanim* 'given', richly inflected verbs *tinkotna* 'will-take-3-PL-FM measures' and adjectives *kafriyim* 'rural-PL-MS', *ironiyim* 'urban-PL-MS' are substituted or deleted in the simplified version. Source or possession is marked analytically (*bli ezra* **shel** *anashim axerim* 'without the help **of** other people', *nihul ha-xayim* **shelahem** 'managing their own lives') rather than synthetically (*ezratam* 'help-theirs = their help', *xayehem* 'lives-theirs = their lives') (see discussion above). Finally, the layout of the text is modified to facilitate understanding. For example, each sentence or phrase is presented on a separate line; list items that appear in the original text as concatenated phrases separated by commas, are listed on separate lines and marked by bullet points for easy detection.

The examples discussed so far, related to the simplification of written information; but a lot of information is delivered to the public orally, in face-to-face interactions or through the media. This type of information should also be accessible to persons with intellectual disabilities. For example, a person requesting medical care may receive an explanation from the doctor about his medical condition, the treatment and the medications that he needs to take. In order for that person to understand the doctor's instructions, these instructions should be conveyed at a slow pace, and be clearly articulated. The speaker should use short sentences and familiar vocabulary. To refer to discourse entities, lexical NPs should be used, as well as repetitions and clarification questions to ensure understanding. When giving information to a person with intellectual disability, the speaker should address the person with the disability himself and not his companion.

In addition to language simplification, it is important to simplify the procedures of service provision. For example, when navigating through an interactive voice menu, the navigation procedure should be limited to a small number of chronologically ordered steps, an option to receive help at any point in the process, an option to talk to a human responder, sufficient time to select an option and to press the right button, a possibility to go back to a previous option in the menu, etc. Such accommodations will increase the feeling of control that a person with disability has over his actions and will reduce anxiety, consequently, affecting the level of his or her cooperation with the service provider.

3 Conclusion

The advent of the *Regulations for Accessibility of Service (2013)*, increased the need for linguistic accessibility, i.e., adapting the information delivered to people with disabilities when providing service. This need is reinforced when the information is abstract, complex or highly professional.

Language Accessibility is a tool for mediating different content worlds – professional terminology and everyday language. Given accessible or simplified information, the person who receives the service is able to fully understand what is required of him and to make thoughtful decisions. The ability to understand what is said or written, and to be a true partner in a conversation or a process, gives people a sense of security and control over their lives, let alone people with disabilities.

Yet, language simplification poses numerous dilemmas for language editors or authors engaged in this process, some of which are listed here: (1) an oversimplified message might seem childish and inappropriate for adults with intellectual disability whereas an under-simplified message would miss its goal. What is the appropriate balance between language simplification and language "lowering"? (2) Simplified information might keep the language of individuals with intellectual disability stagnant, rather than enrich and develop it, as it should. How can we simplify information in a way that would encourage the development of linguistic abilities and knowledge in individuals with intellectual disability? (3) Persons with intellectual disability exhibit heterogeneous functional and linguistic abilities. How can a simplified message be made to suit the needs of as many people in the target audience as possible? (4) A different kind of dilemma is how to remain faithful to the original message throughout the simplification process; (5) Still other dilemmas have to do with the legal aspects of language simplification, e.g., what is the legal validity of simplified documents (e.g., medical informed consent forms or legal contracts), and who owns the copy rights for simplified materials? (Uziel-Karl, Tenne-Rinde and Yalon-Chamovitz, 2016).

The process of language accessibility is complex, and requires professional expertise, as well as familiarity with the relevant content areas and the relevant target groups. Nonetheless, it is a well structured process backed by the Service Accessibility Regulations (2013). It combines linguistic simplification and auxiliary or alternative means for providing accessible information to the service recipient as well as monitoring the simplification process and the coherence of the outcome for people with disabilities. It is, thus, recommended that simplification be done by "an expert in language simplification who has knowledge of the subject matter and is familiar with the needs of the target audience". Likewise, symbols should be designed by professionals with specific expertise in accessible graphic design. It is also recommended that the outcome be reviewed by an expert as well as by a person with intellectual disability, to ensure its appropriateness for the target audience.

Accessibility could make the difference between a person who cannot deal with the authorities and services and a person who is an independent, active participant in the community. Thus, despite its complexity and the many issues involved, it is important to remember that the products of language accessibility may considerably improve the quality of life of persons with intellectual disability, but not just theirs – we may all benefit from clear and accessible information.

References

Bar On, Amalia & Dorit Ravid. 2011. Morphological analysis in learning to read pseudowords in Hebrew. *Applied Psycholinguistics* 32. 553–581.

Berman, Ruth A. 1978. *Modern Hebrew structure*. Tel Aviv: University Publishing Projects.

Bolozky, Shmuel. 2007. Israeli Hebrew morphology. In Alan S. Kaye (ed.), *Morphologies of Asia and Africa (including the Caucasus)*, 283–308. Winona Lake: Eisenbrauns.

Carmien, Stefan, Melisa Dawe, Gerhard Fischer, Andrew Gorman, Anja Kintsch & James F. Sullivan Jr. 2005. Socio-technical environments supporting people with cognitive disabilities using public transportation. *ACM Transactions on Computer-Human Interaction* 2(12). 233–262.

Cohen, David, Jean Philippe Riviere, Monique Plaza, Caroline Thompson, Dominique Chauvin, Nicole Hambourg, Odile Lanthier, Philippe Mazet & Martine Flament. 2001. Word identification in adults with mental retardation: Does IQ influence reading achievement? *Brain and Cognition* 46(1–2). 69–73.

Collier, Barbara, Sara W. Blackstone & Andrew Tyalor. 2012. Communication access to businesses and organizations for people with complex communication needs. *Augmentative and Alternative Communication* 28(4). 205–218.

Dekel, Nurit. 2014. *Colloquial Israeli Hebrew: A corpus-based survey*. Berlin: De Gruyter Mouton.

Downing, June E. 2005. Teaching literacy to students with significant disabilities. *Literacy and Public Education*. 12–25.

Feldman, D., Y. Danieli-Lahav & S. Haimovitz. 2007. *The accessibility of the Israeli society for persons with disabilities on the threshold of the 21st century*. Jerusalem: Ministry of Justice. [in Hebrew]

SAIF Guide to Easy Read. 2011. Retrieved [September 16th, 2014] from https://www.st-andrews.ac.uk/media/human-resources/equality-and-diversity/SAIF%20Guide%20to%20Easy%20Read.pdf

Haramati, S. 1991. *Didactic re-writing: Goals, principles, implementation with basic text list, graded for educating Hebrew readers in the diaspora*. Jerusalem: Magnes. [in Hebrew]

Harris, James C. 2006. *Intellectual disability: Understanding its development, causes, classification and treatment*. Oxford: Oxford University Press.

International Classification of Functioning, Disability and Health [ICF]. 2001. Fifty Fourth World Health Assembly. [Retrived September 17th, 2014] http://apps.who.int/gb/archive/pdf_files/WHA54/ea54r21.pdf?ua=1

Kirsch, Irwin S., Ann Jungeblut, Lynn Jenkins & Andrew Kolstad. 1993. *Adult literacy in America: A first look at the findings of the National Adult Literacy Survey*. Washington, DC: U.S. Department of Education, National Center for Education Statistics.

Luckasson, Ruth, Sharon Borthwick-Duffy, Wil HE Buntinx, David L. Coulter, Ellis M. Pat Craig, Alya Reeve, Robert L. Schalock et al. 2002. *Mental retardation: Definition, classification, and systems of support* (10th Edition).Washington, DC: American Association on Mental Retardation.

Kail, Robert. 2000. Speed of information processing: Developmental change and links to intelligence. *Journal of School Psychology* 38. 51–61.

Nir, Refael. 1989. *Language, medium and message*. Jerusalem: Posner and Sons. [in Hebrew]

Oliver, Michael. 1996. *Understanding disability: From theory to practice*. Basingstoke, UK: Macmillan.
Ravid, Dorit. 2012. *Spelling morphology: The psycholinguistics of Hebrew spelling*. New York: Springer.
Rhea, Paul. 2004. *Language disorders from infancy through adolescence: Assessment and intervention*. New York: John Wiley & Sons.
Salmi, P., D. Ginthner & D. Guerin. 2004. Critical factors for accessibility and way-finding for adults with intellectual disabilities. *Designing for the 21st century III: An international conference on universal design, adaptive environments*, Rio de Janeiro.
Schalock, Robert L., Sharon A. Borthwick-Duffy, Valerie J. Bradley, Wil H. E. Buntinx, David L. Coulter, Ellis M. Craig, Sharon C. Gomez, Yves Lachapelle, Ruth Luckasson, Alya Reeve, Karrie A. Shogren, Martha E. Snell, Scott Spreat, Marc J. Tasse, James R. Thompson, Miguel A. Verdugo-Alonso, Michael L. Wehmeyer & Mark H. Yeager. 2010. *Intellectual disability: Definition, classification, and systems of supports* (11th edn.). Washington: AAIDD.
Shengross, Avivit. 2011. "Reading the world" – *A second chance for learning to read: The effects of a literacy intervention program on reading skills and well being*. Haifa University MA thesis. [in Hebrew]
Schwarzwald, Ora R. 2001. *Modern Hebrew*. Muenchen: Lincom Europa.
Schwarzwald, Ora R. 2002. *Hebrew morphology*. Tel Aviv: Open University. [In Hebrew]
Uziel-Karl, Sigal, Michal Tenne-Rinde & Shira Yalon-Chamovitz. 2011. *Linguistic accessibility for individuals with intellectual disabilities: Guidelines booklet*. Ono Academic College and the Division for Intellectual and Developmental Disabilities of the Ministry of Social Affairs and Social Services.
Uziel-Karl, Sigal, Michal Tenne-Rinde & Shira Yalon-Chamovitz. 2016. Accessibility to law and justice in Israel: Linguistic accessibility for individuals with intellectual disability as a test-case. *Hukim* 8. 287–307. [in Hebrew]
Yalon-Chamovitz, Shira. 2007. Explicit disability–implicit accessibility: The story of people with intellectual disabilities. In Dina Feldman, Y. Danieli-Lahav & S. Haimovitz (eds.), *The accessibility of the Israeli society for persons with disabilities on the threshold of the 21st century*. 573–596. Jerusalem: Ministry of Justice.
Yalon-Chamovitz, Shira. 2009. Invisible access needs of people with intellectual disabilities: A conceptual model of practice. *Intellectual and Developmental Disabilities* 47. 395–400.
Yoder, Paul J. & Steven F. Warren. 2004. Early predictors of language in children with and without Down Syndrome. *American Journal on Mental Retardation* 109(4). 285–300.
Young, Louise, Karen B. Moni, Anne Jobling & Christinavan E. Kraayenoord. 2004. Literacy skills of adults with intellectual disabilities in two community-based day programs. *International Journal of Disability, Development and Education* 51(1). 83–97.
Zukowski, Andrea. 2004. Investigating knowledge of complex syntax: Insights from experimental studies of Williams Syndrome. In Mabel L. Rice & Steven F. Warren (eds.), *Developmental language disorders: From phenotypes to etiologies*, 99–120. London: Lawrence Erlbaum Associates.

Bills, Laws, Regulations and Standards

Americans with Disabilities Act [ADA] of 1990, Pub. L. No. 101–336, §2, 104 Stat. 328 (1991). Retrieved [September 16th, 2014] from http://www.ada.gov/pubs/ada.htm
Equal Rights for Persons with Disabilities Law, 5758–1998. Retrieved [September 17th, 2014] http://www.moital.gov.il/NR/exeres/007B3BF6-3091-42F4-BAF1-D394DC0A334E.htm
International ISO standards: Graphical symbols – Public information symbols [ISO 7001], 2007.
Israeli Equal Rights of Persons with Disabilities Law, 5765–2005, (Amendment No. 2 Accessibility). Retrieved [November 24th, 2015] http://index.justice.gov.il/Units/NetzivutShivyon/documents/1000_hokshivionzchuyotleanashimimmugbalut13.pdf

Israeli standard – IS 1918: Part 4: Environmental Accessibility in Construction: Communications. The Standards Institution of Israel, 2015. Retrieved [July 11th, 2017] http://www.iame.org.il/uploadimages/negishot/negisotteken19186.pdf

Regulations for the Equal Rights for People with Disabilities, Accessibility of Service (section 29), 2013. Retrieved [September 17th, 2014] http://www.isoc.org.il/docs/1160_TakHanegishutLeSherut.pdf

Regulations for the Equal Rights for People with Disabilities, Accessibility of Service (chapter 1:968 – Accessible Print), 2013. Retrieved [September 18th, 2014] http://www.isoc.org.il/docs/1160_TakHanegishutLeSherut.pdf

United Nations Convention on the Rights of Persons with Disabilities (2006) Retrieved [September 17th, 2014] http://www.un.org/disabilities/convention/conventionfull.shtml

Welfare Law, 5729–1969. Retrieved [September 17th, 2014] http://www.dinimveod.co.il/hashavimcmsfiles/Pdf/sh558.pdf

Supreme Court appeal 7801/03 Botser vs. Maccabim-Reut municipality, ruling 19(1), 1996.

Websites

Division for Intellectual and Developmental Disabilities of the Ministry of Social Affairs and Social Services (definition of intellectual disability). Retrieved [September 17th, 2014]
http://www.molsa.gov.il/Populations/Disabilities/MentalRetardation/Diagnosis/Pages/Pigur_Ivhun.aspx

IV Language and communication disorders

Section 9: Disorders in aging

IV Language and communication disorders

Section 1 Disorders in aging

Eve Higby, Dalia Cahana-Amitay and Loraine K. Obler
42 Brain and language in healthy aging

1 Introduction

As adults age, they often complain about difficulties recalling names and/or understanding incoming speech in challenging conditions, such as noisy contexts or when the material is grammatically complex. However, not all aspects of language processing decline with aging. A prime example is older adults' vocabulary knowledge, which remains quite stable, or even grows, over time. From a brain perspective, this observation raises the question of what it is about the aging brain that produces these particular patterns of age-related changes in language production and perception.

With the emergence of brain imaging technologies and their widespread use in research, a picture incorporating links among neural structure, brain function, and language behaviors among healthy older adults is starting to emerge. This picture reveals that age-related neural and cognitive factors play a role in the performance of older adults on certain linguistic tasks. The general consensus is that a reshaping of the division of labor between the right and left hemispheres in the service of language functions occurs over time, resulting in these behavioral patterns (for a recent review see Shafto and Tyler 2014). Indeed, the degree to which language processing is lateralized to one hemisphere changes over the lifetime, increasing in childhood until age 20, plateauing from 20–25 years of age, and then slowly decreasing from 25–90 years of age (Szaflarski et al. 2006; Zhang et al. 2013). What we are concerned with here, of course, are the neural underpinnings of late-life language changes, in other words, of older adults.

Language processing in the aging brain is often characterized by differences in neural activation patterns compared to younger brains. Decreased activity is frequently interpreted in terms of deficits, such as the inability to up-regulate key regions to aid effortful processing, while increased activity is typically considered compensatory (Grady 2012). There are a variety of possible causes for these patterns, such as a lack of efficient use of neural resources, alterations in cerebral vasculature, microstructural changes, reductions in the selectivity of neural networks, and undetected neuropathological changes, among others (Grady 2012).

The question of how these age-related neurological changes affect behavioral outcomes in older adults has been much more widely explored in the context of

---

Eve Higby, University of California, Riverside
Dalia Cahana-Amitay, Boston University School of Medicine, VA Boston Healthcare System
Loraine K. Obler, VA Boston Healthcare System, Boston University School of Medicine, The Graduate Center of the City University of New York

age-related cognitive declines than in the context of language declines. Declines in certain cognitive processes, such as inhibition, mental set-shifting, and working memory, have consequences for language processes as well. Thus, we consider theories of neurocognitive change in aging in order to explore their application to the empirical findings of brain and language in aging. These models focus primarily on either the allocation of cognitive resources or the reorganization of the aging brain into less localized functions.

2 Brain reorganization in aging and its effects on task performance

Age-related neural changes are typically characterized in terms of (1) brain atrophy, measured by observing the density or volume of gray matter comprising the neural tissue on the surface of the cerebral cortex and areas of the subcortex, and (2) white matter damage to fiber tracts connecting various gray matter regions. Older adults show gradual, widespread gray matter volume reduction starting in middle age and continuing linearly over time (Giorgio et al. 2010; Good et al. 2001; Jernigan et al. 2001; Shafto et al. 2007).

The earliest observed reductions in gray matter are usually detected in the frontal cortex (Giorgio et al. 2010; Jernigan et al. 2001; Kalpouzos et al. 2009; Meunier, Stamatakis, and Tyler 2014). Similarly, deterioration of white matter microstructure is related to age and is detected starting as early as young adulthood (Giorgio et al. 2010; Stamatakis et al. 2011). Age-related changes to white matter are also more pronounced in prefrontal regions (Grieve et al. 2007). Decreased white matter integrity has been linked to poorer performance on cognitive tasks, particularly for speed of processing and executive functions (Grieve et al. 2007; Gunning-Dixon and Raz 2000; Madden, Bennett, and Song 2009).

These observations of age-related changes in frontal areas led to the formulation of the *frontal lobe hypothesis*, which posits that the frontal cortex is more vulnerable to change in aging than other cortical regions (Raz and Rodrigue 2006; West 1996). Given the role of the prefrontal cortex in a variety of executive control tasks, thinning in this region is expected to have consequences for cognitive functioning, and in fact is consistent with a large number of studies demonstrating declines on tasks measuring executive control in aging (see reviews in Braver and West 2008; Rabbitt and Anderson 2006).

The *Posterior-Anterior Shift in Aging (PASA)* complements this hypothesis, as it describes a pattern in which older adults show weaker activity than younger adults in posterior brain regions, such as occipital and posterior temporal cortex, accompanied by enhanced activity in anterior brain regions, such as the frontal cortex (Dennis and Cabeza 2008; Davis et al. 2008). These patterns have also been placed in an ontogenetic context, such as the *developmental theory of aging*, which posits that pathways that develop later in maturation (e.g., the frontal cortex) are those that show early age-related loss of functionality (Gunning-Dixon et al. 2009).

Two hypotheses have attempted to account specifically for the more diffuse activation patterns seen for older adults. The first, the *dedifferentiation hypothesis*, focuses on the loss of efficiency of neural networks with aging (Li and Lindenberger 1999). Young adults tend to exhibit more focal patterns of activation in networks that are specialized for and optimized for specific types of task demands. Older adults show reduced activity in some of these same regions (e.g., left inferior frontal cortex and middle temporal lobe for many language tasks) accompanied by activity in other regions not observed in the patterns of young adults. Additional evidence for dedifferentiation comes from behavioral studies showing increased correlations in performance on different cognitive tasks with age (e.g., Baltes and Lindenberger 1997) as well as less distinguishable patterns of neural activity for different tasks in older adults (e.g., Cabeza 2002; Ghisletta and Lindenberger 2003; Park et al. 2004).

Functional dedifferentiation appears to be more closely linked to changes in gray matter density than to chronological age, however (Meunier, Stamatakis, and Tyler 2014). The *Scaffolding Theory of Aging and Cognition (STAC)* follows a similar idea by proposing that neural declines prompt the functional reorganization of networks that provide a scaffold for processing that may be less efficient but still maintain a high level of cognitive functioning (Park and Reuter-Lorenz 2009).

It would appear, then, that the same cortical regions that show the greatest amount of atrophy in aging (prefrontal and parietal cortices) are those that tend to show increased functional activation in older adults during task performance (Greenwood, 2007). In some instances, however, greater activation is associated with greater gray matter density (Shafto et al. 2010). Moreover, there is evidence of a link between gray matter density and the degree of functional connectivity in the brain. Meunier, Stamatakis, and Tyler (2014) found that decreased gray matter integrity in older adults led to poorer connectivity within key language regions, but increased functional connectivity overall. Nevertheless, this altered network organization was less efficient than specialized networks. Thus, the relationship between structure and function, particularly in older adults, is far from clear-cut.

A common explanation of this relationship in reference to language performance in aging is the *Hemispheric Asymmetry Reduction in Older Adults (HAROLD) model* (Cabeza 2002). This model proposes that aging is accompanied by a reduction in hemispheric lateralization for verbal and non-verbal cognitive tasks from a predominantly within-hemisphere pattern to a more bilateral (i.e., cross-hemisphere) pattern of processing. The HAROLD model is supported by a sizable number of studies showing a more bilateral pattern of activation for older adults compared to young adults on a variety of tasks (e.g., Davis et al. 2011; Manenti et al. 2013; Obler et al. 2010; Reuter-Lorenz 2002; Wierenga et al. 2008).

It is unclear, however, whether the recruitment of right-hemisphere networks is beneficial, playing a compensatory function in the context of reduction in neural density, or whether it reflects decreased functional connectivity among language regions in the left hemisphere. While some studies have found that increased right-hemisphere activation was associated with better performance (e.g., Cabeza 2002; Obler et al. 2010; Reuter-Lorenz et al. 2000), others report the opposite pattern, namely, greater right-hemisphere activation associated with poorer performance (e.g., Meunier, Stamatakis, and Tyler 2014). Thus, the relation between hemispheric activation and language performance is still unclear.

The *Production Affects Reception in Left Only (PARLO) model* (Federmeier 2007) presents a more specific description of age-related hemispheric shifts by proposing that the left hemisphere is more specialized for predictive, top-down processes, while the right hemisphere operates on bottom-up processes. Thus, a shift to increased right-hemisphere involvement in aging would result in a shift from greater top-down recruitment to more reliance on bottom-up processes.

3 The aging brain, cognitive changes, and language performance

Some researchers have noted that age-related impairments in language performance are associated with declines in certain aspects of cognition that adversely affect the availability of cognitive resources for task performance. A well-known example is the effect of impaired inhibition on older adults' word recognition abilities (Peelle et al. 2011; Sommers and Danielson 1999; Wingfield, Tun, and McCoy 2005). This theory is known in the cognitive aging literature as the *inhibitory deficit theory* (Hasher and Zacks 1998; Healey, Campbell, and Hasher 2008). Neuroimaging evidence supporting this theory demonstrates that older adults exhibit an inability to suppress neural activity from distracting information (Gazzaley and D'Esposito 2007).

Relatedly, some have argued that older adults are less able to deactivate the "default mode network," which is a neural network that is active during resting states when no task demands are imposed, but which is deactivated when one performs a task. Older adults deactivate this network like young adults for tasks that impose low demands on cognitive control, but show lesser degrees of deactivation than young adults for more demanding task requirements (Persson et al. 2007). The magnitude of the deactivation correlates with task performance, suggesting that the ability to flexibly switch off the default mode network in response to task demands has behavioral consequences and may reflect the available resources for performance of, say, a language task.

Similarly, older adults show more diffuse neural activation than younger adults during relatively low-demand tasks, whereas younger adults tend to show this kind of pattern only for more challenging task conditions. In terms of language performance, older adults are presumed to up-regulate support networks, such as working memory, more frequently than younger adults during language comprehension tasks (Wingfield and Grossman 2006). This idea is also encompassed in the *Compensation-Related Utilization of Neural Circuits Hypothesis (CRUNCH)*, which proposes that older adults recruit more neural resources at lower levels of cognitive load than young adults (Reuter-Lorenz and Cappell 2008). In a recent study, Kennedy and colleagues (2015) reported that neural modulation in response to increased task demands during performance of a language task assessing semantic knowledge revealed a gradient progression, from early changes to frontoparietal networks, through altered subcortical nuclei in middle age, to effects in the midbrain and brain stem among the very old.

By contrast, others have proposed that older adults adopt a less proactive strategy for language processing, instead relying on reactive cognitive control mechanisms, which adjust the level of control in reaction to task demands rather than in anticipation of them and which are less resource-intensive (Federmeier 2007; Jimura and Braver 2010). Thus, cognitive control may be engaged at later stages of processing for older adults compared to younger adults, termed the *Early to Late Shift in Aging (ELSA)* (Dew et al. 2012). These proposals are in line with a general cognitive pattern found in aging, which is that deliberative or controlled processing skills decline while automatic language skills are more preserved (Harley, Jessiman, and MacAndrew 2011).

At present, it is hard to determine which of these theoretical accounts are more or less reconcilable with evidence from studies of the neural basis of lexical retrieval and sentence processing in aging. The methods exploring these age-related declines are diverse, sample sizes vary, and findings are mixed, leading to a somewhat murky picture of how language-cognition-brain might be linked in aging. Nonetheless, some patterns are emerging, as we show in what follows.

4 Lexical retrieval and sentence processing in the aging brain

Research on language and aging has focused primarily on two areas of language processing for which age-related impairments are frequently observed: word retrieval and certain aspects of sentence comprehension. Recent brain studies of these patterns have been moving away from a strict localizationist approach, which attempts to identify which brain regions subserve specific language or cognitive functions, towards a dynamic network approach, which investigates how the connectivity patterns between regions relate to brain function and behavioral performance.

4.1 Lexical retrieval

The process of word retrieval involves at least two basic stages: access to the word's representation in semantic memory and retrieval of the word's phonological form. Semantic memory, particularly for lexical information, is relatively well preserved in older adults (Gold et al. 2009; Grieder et al. 2012), and activity in brain areas associated with semantic memory is similar for younger and older adults (Wierenga et al. 2008). By contrast, retrieval of a word's phonological form presents particular difficulty for older adults. This is evident from studies examining the occurrence of tip-of-the-tongue states (TOTs) among different age groups. A TOT is described as an instance of word retrieval difficulty for which the semantic and grammatical content of a word can be retrieved but for which the phonological form is elusive, resulting in retrieval of only partial phonological information, if any (e.g., the initial phoneme or number of syllables).

Older adults exhibit higher rates of TOTs than younger adults (e.g., Burke et al. 1991; Gollan and Brown 2006; Juncos-Rabadán et al. 2010). In an investigation of brain activity associated with TOT states during naming, Shafto et al. (2010) reported that brain activation for trials on which the word was successfully retrieved was similar for younger and older adults, but for trials on which participants experienced a TOT, younger adults exhibited a boost of activity in left insular cortex while older adults did not. Furthermore, among the older adults, those with greater brain activity during TOTs showed fewer TOTs overall, suggesting that the ability of some of the older adults to generate additional activity during a TOT state might have led to successful word retrieval on a subset of the trials. This is supported by Shafto et al.'s (2010) observation that those older adults with better overall performance on the word retrieval task showed more brain activity during successful trials than those with poorer overall performance, in line with the CRUNCH theory.

When overall brain activation patterns of older and younger adults on lexical retrieval tasks are compared, older adults often show greater and more widespread activation, consistent with the dedifferentiation theory. Activation in classical left-hemisphere language areas, such as Broca's area in the frontal lobe and Wernicke's area in the temporal lobe, increases with age (Fridriksson et al. 2006). Frequently, older adults also exhibit greater right-hemisphere activation than young adults, such as the right-hemisphere homologue to Broca's area (right inferior frontal lobe) (Fridriksson et al. 2006). This right-hemisphere recruitment appears to be compensatory, as the HAROLD theory would predict. For example, while higher activation in right inferior frontal lobe was associated with poorer performance among young adults, higher activation was associated with better performance among older adults. Specifically, greater right inferior frontal lobe activation was seen among older adults who performed better on the task while older adults who performed more poorly behaviorally showed a pattern similar to the young adults (Wierenga et al. 2008). These findings suggest that similar activation patterns in right inferior frontal lobe between younger and older adults do not necessarily imply similar behavioral outcomes. Rather, the recruitment of this right hemisphere region was associated with better performance among the older adults.

Shafto and Tyler (2014) have proposed that the difference between younger and older adults' neural activation during lexical retrieval lies in their ability to engage cognitive control networks (as the notion of older adults' difficulty up-regulating support networks predicts). They posit that although both younger and older adults appear to recruit neural networks involved in cognitive control to support word retrieval processes, older adults' weakened phonological system impacts the conditions for cognitive recruitment. When retrieval is successful, activation of occipital, temporal, and frontal networks is observed, alongside the anterior cingulate and the inferior frontal and insular cortices bilaterally. However, in an overly weakened phonological activation, engagement of this cognitive support is compromised and fails to trigger the neural correlates to support language performance.

Further evidence that points to age-related brain changes underlying word retrieval comes from studies using repetitive transcranial magnetic stimulation (rTMS). These studies support the Scaffolding model and the HAROLD model, and are consistent with the frontal-lobe vulnerability hypothesis. Young adults' lexical retrieval is more enhanced by rTMS applied over left dorsolateral prefrontal cortex than the same region in the right hemisphere, while stimulation of both left and right regions improves word retrieval in older adults (Cotelli et al. 2010, 2012; Manenti et al. 2013). As in the Wierenga et al. (2008) study, older adults with better word retrieval performance were those who relied on both left and right hemisphere regions (in this case, the prefrontal cortex) while older adults with greater left-hemisphere dominance for word retrieval – despite this dominance being similar to that seen in younger adults – exhibited poorer performance (Manenti et al. 2013).

Interestingly, while functional activation during language tasks becomes more prominent in the right hemisphere with increasing age, this does not mean that structural atrophy is asymmetrical, differentially impacting the left hemisphere and therefore requiring the "stronger" hemisphere to take over some of the functions. In fact, white matter atrophy appears to be similar in the two hemispheres (Stamatakis et al. 2011). Nevertheless, findings from structural brain studies are largely consistent with functional activation studies. Consistent with the HAROLD model, the integrity of right-hemisphere regions (most notably, in the frontal and temporal lobes) has been found to be associated with successful word retrieval performance in older adults (Obler et al. 2010). Not inconsistent with the PARLO and PASA models, the number of TOTs among older adults has been associated with the degree of gray matter atrophy in left insula, with greater atrophy associated with more TOTs (Shafto et al. 2007). Greater TOT frequency was also associated with lower integrity of a specific white matter tract important for language processing, the left superior longitudinal fasciculus, which connects frontal, posterior temporal, and inferior parietal regions (Stamatakis et al. 2011). In line with the PASA model, the negative correlation between TOTs and fascicle integrity was found only for posterior portions of this anterior-posterior white matter fiber tract.

In summary, the studies we reviewed here are consistent with HAROLD, Scaffolding, and CRUNCH models in that they indicate that the integrity of white and gray matter regions in both left and right hemispheres underlies successful word retrieval abilities in older adults. Successful performance hinges on activation of core language networks alongside networks associated with cognitive control, which are suggestive of a neural system in the aging brain which is essentially neurally multifunctional (Cahana-Amitay and Albert 2014); that is, both linguistic and non-linguistic functions are engaged to create a correct linguistic representation.

4.2 Sentence comprehension

Overall, older adults' sentence comprehension skills are quite well preserved when their hearing and visual acuity are unimpaired or corrected. Relative to word retrieval, the impairments seen in sentence comprehension are subtler (Shafto and Tyler 2014). Comprehension of complex syntactic structures, such as object-relative embedded clauses, exhibits age-related declines (Caplan et al. 2011; Goral et al. 2011; Obler et al. 1991; Yoon et al. 2015) as does resolution of syntactic ambiguity (Payne et al. 2014). Nevertheless, spared sentence comprehension abilities have been observed for older adults, particularly when on-line measures are used such as self-paced reading or eye-tracking measures (DeDe et al. 2004; Kemper, Crow, and Kemtes 2004; Stine-Morrow et al. 2001). The relative maintenance of this language function in the face of age-related brain atrophy has prompted researchers to investigate whether patterns of neural functioning that support sentence processing are also maintained in aging or, as the Scaffolding theory would predict, whether older brains adapt to the changes in neural density and volume by recruiting new or additional areas of the brain and networks.

Studies by Grossman and colleagues indicate that older adults activate the same core sentence processing network in the left hemisphere as young adults, including inferior frontal cortex, middle temporal gyrus, and parietal cortex (Grossman et al. 2002a; Peelle et al. 2010). However, consistent with the Scaffolding theory, the activation pattern for older adults but not younger ones appears to also involve areas outside the core language processing network including additional left-hemisphere regions as well as right-hemisphere regions (Grossman et al. 2002a; Peelle et al. 2010).

It is unclear, however, whether the recruitment of right-hemisphere brain areas improves performance on sentence processing tasks. Tyler et al. (2010), for example, reported that increased activity in right-hemisphere frontotemporal regions (cross-hemispheric homologues of the core left-hemisphere sentence processing network) was associated with preserved task performance in older adults. This pattern was associated with atrophy in left-hemisphere language regions, suggesting that the right-hemisphere contribution to task performance was compensatory, as would be predicted by the dedifferentiation, HAROLD and Scaffolding models. However, Grossman et al. (2002b) found that among older adults, those with increased right-hemisphere activity in inferior frontal cortex showed worse sentence comprehension, while those with high comprehension showed increased left-hemisphere activity, as CRUNCH would predict. Moreover, increased functional connectivity within the right hemisphere was associated with decreased syntactic sensitivity in Meunier, Stamatakis, and Tyler (2014), indicating, consistent with the dedifferentiation approach but contradictory to the HAROLD model, that right-hemisphere involvement in sentence processing is not fully compensatory.

Impairments in processing syntactically complex sentences are well documented for older adults (e.g., Caplan and Waters 1999; DeDe et al. 2004). The idea that the brain networks underlying syntactic processes change with age is supported by structural and functional imaging studies, as well as studies using electrophysiological methods. Meunier, Stamatakis, and Tyler (2014), for example, found that lower sensitivity to syntactic structures among older adults was associated with decreased connectivity in the left-hemisphere network underpinning syntactic processing coupled with increased connectivity within the entire language network of the brain, indicating a less specialized – dedifferentiated – system.

Furthermore, less engagement of the core left-hemisphere language system (inferior frontal and posterior-superior temporal cortices) was found among older adults with poor comprehension of complex syntax (object relative clauses) as compared to older adults with better syntactic comprehension (Wingfield and Grossman 2006). In other words, the preservation of this core network leads to preservation of behavioral performance on comprehension tasks involving complex syntax. This finding does not support a Scaffolding approach, as the utilization of classic pathways within the left hemisphere for dealing with complex syntax was associated with better performance.

However, there is evidence that clearly supports the idea proposed in the Scaffolding model of novel pathways being used among older adults for practiced tasks. Antonenko et al. (2013), for example, reported that for young adults, performance on sentences with embedded clauses was associated with integrity of the superior longitudinal fasciculus, a dorsal fiber tract that connects the posterior portion of Broca's area to the posterior temporal lobe. Performance by older adults, by contrast, was associated with a more ventral pathway, the uncinate fasciculus, which connects the frontal operculum to the anterior temporal lobe. This implies not only a PASA shift in the networks utilized for processing syntactically complex sentences, but also perhaps a PARLO shift in strategy from more global to more local phrase-structure building as the ventral pathway is typically associated with local phrase-structure building in young adults (Antonenko et al. 2013).

Patterns of activation seen for more complex sentence processing among young adults are sometimes observed even for less complex sentences among older adults. For example, activation in the left inferior frontal cortex or the striatum has been found only for more complex sentences among young adults, but is seen even for less complex sentences among older adults (Grossman et al. 2002a; Wingfield and Grossman 2006). Grossman et al. (2002a) suggest that older adults up-regulate the working memory support network at lower levels of demand in order to compensate for less efficient functioning. Their older adults who showed poor comprehension of syntactically complex sentences showed less activity in left inferior frontal cortex compared to older adults with good comprehension, a region that has been implicated for tasks with high working memory demands (Wingfield and Grossman 2006). This finding lends support to the idea that reduced working memory resources contribute to older adults' errors on syntactically complex sentences.

Structural and functional connectivity differences between the brains of young and older adults also affect sentence comprehension. Older adults showed reduced correlations between activated regions compared to younger adults during sentence comprehension (Peelle et al. 2010). Moreover, certain types of inter-hemispheric connections appear to be beneficial for older adults. The forceps minor connects the anterior frontal lobes. Older adults with better sentence comprehension show greater structural integrity of the forceps minor but lower connectivity between left and right inferior frontal gyrus (Antonenko et al. 2013). Thus, it appears that the weakening of intra-hemispheric connections (not inconsistent with PASA) and increased inter-hemispheric connections (potentially reconcilable with HAROLD) characterize some of the age-related patterns found for sentence processing.

Electrophysiological studies employing Event-Related Potentials (ERPs) have been used to show that older adults' sentence processing problems are perhaps more pervasive than we think. These problems appear to also involve difficulties with online integration of semantic and syntactic information. Typically, lexical-semantic processes are indexed in the electrophysiological response as a negative-going peak at around 400 msec after the onset of a word, termed the N400 component. The N400 thus indexes both the automatic spread of activation within the semantic network and the semantic expectancy of a word within the semantic context. Older and younger adults tend to show a similar N400 pattern for semantic priming tasks, a task considered to tap into automatic spread of activation (Grieder et al. 2012; Gunter, Jackson, and Mulder 1998). This conclusion is supported by fMRI data, demonstrating that priming leads to similar degrees of activation decreases in both younger and older adults (Gold et al. 2009; Lustig and Buckner 2004).

Unlike the priming effect, the effect of semantic expectancy does exhibit age-related differences. Older adults typically demonstrate an N400 that is smaller in amplitude than that seen for young adults (Federmeier et al. 2002, 2003; Federmeier and Kutas 2005; Gunter, Jackson, and Mulder 1995; Gunter, Vos, and Friederici 1999; Wlotko and Federmeier 2012) and sometimes also delayed in terms of latency

(Federmeier and Kutas 2005; Gunter, Jackson, and Mulder 1995; Gunter, Vos, and Friederici 1999; Wlotko and Federmeier 2012). Kutas and Iragui (1998) reported that the N400 effect for semantic congruency shows a linear decrease in amplitude and increase in latency with advancing age.

Young adults tend to engage in predictive processes during sentence comprehension, building contextual meaning incrementally over time and predicting the appearance of specific words or a set of words with a particular set of semantic features. Federmeier and colleagues have demonstrated that older adults do not engage in predictive processing during sentence comprehension to the same extent as younger adults (Federmeier et al. 2002; Federmeier and Kutas 2005; Federmeier, Kutas, and Schul 2010; Wlotko, Lee, and Federmeier 2010), consistent with the Early to Late Shift in Aging hypothesis.

The ERP literature on sentence processing thus provides good evidence for a selective pattern of decline, whereby the N400 to automatic spread of activation in the semantic network is not affected in aging, while the N400 to semantic expectancy is (Federmeier et al. 2003; Wlotko, Lee, and Federmeier 2010). Although the ability to use message-level contextual information to facilitate word processing may be compromised with aging (see also Cahana-Amitay et al., 2016) a subset of older adults does show evidence of predictive processing, namely those who exhibit higher vocabulary and higher verbal fluency scores (Federmeier et al. 2002; Federmeier, Kutas, and Schul 2010). Linking these findings to brain changes in aging, Federmeier (2007) has suggested that left-hemisphere processing is more expectancy driven while the right hemisphere is driven by more bottom-up processes; a HAROLD-model shift in the default network for sentence comprehension from left-lateralized to a more bilateral pattern in aging may thus account for the age-related changes in predictive processing observed among older adults.

In addition to the age-group differences for semantic components of sentence processing, older adults also exhibit differences in syntactic structure building during sentence comprehension. This process involves a more automatic component, termed Early Left Anterior Negativity (ELAN), and a more controlled integration process, measured as a positive wave between 500–700 msec after word onset (P600). While the ELAN appears to be similar for both older and younger adults, the P600 appears delayed and smaller in amplitude for older adults compared to younger adults (Gunter, Vos, and Friederici 1999). Moreover, the scalp distribution of the P600 is different for younger and older adults, suggesting that the neural generators for the response are somewhat modified with advancing age, as the dedifferentiation and CRUNCH models would predict (Kemmer et al. 2004).

In summary, it appears that age-related changes in sentence processing abilities implicate compromised neural activation of the left temporo-parietal syntactic networks and increased interhemispheric activation involving right hemisphere frontal networks. The role of HAROLD-model increased right hemisphere activation remains elusive, however, as it does not necessarily reflect compensatory neural reorganization (Shafto and Tyler 2014). Such neural involvement may be beneficial for offline sentence comprehension, which occurs after hearing the sentence, but it may also indicate reduced efficiency resulting in diffuse neural activity (dedifferentiation) and intrahemispheric disinhibition due to altered connectivity within the left hemisphere, potentially consistent with both the frontal lobe hypothesis and PASA. In certain cases, it may simply reflect task demands that load particular burden upon executive functions including domain-general attention.

5 Conclusion

Neural changes implicating reduced gray matter volume and compromised white matter integrity that frequently occur with advancing age play a critical role in the behavioral changes that are observed over the adult lifespan, including those specifically associated with lexical retrieval and sentence processing. In fact, these age-related brain changes may affect how language is processed even when behavioral performance on a task is unimpaired relative to young adults. From a theoretical perspective, it seems that the neural underpinnings of older adults' linguistic performance are intertwined with neural networks supporting nonlinguistic cognitive processes, representing a dynamic neurally multifunctional brain which continues to be reshaped throughout the lifespan (Cahana-Amitay and Albert 2014). This reshaping involves observable changes in between- and within-hemisphere structural integrity and functional connectivity, consistent with all the theoretical accounts of neurocognitive aging we reviewed above, and not ruling out any, as they are not mutually exclusive. The jury is still out regarding whether the neural changes older adults demonstrate reflect a reduction in availability of cognitive resources that adversely affects language performance and/or whether the reorganization of the aging brain becomes less focalized over time, leading to successful compensation in some instances, but perhaps to less efficient cognitive and linguistic processing as well. What is clear, however, is that to fully understand how the aging brain engages in linguistic processes, we must consider three different components as well as the interactions among them: neural structure, functional organization, and behavioral language and cognitive performance.

References

Antonenko, Daria, Jens Brauer, Marcus Meinzer, Anja Fengler, Lucia Kerti, Angela D. Friederici & Agnes Flöel. 2013. Functional and structural syntax networks in aging. *Neuroimage* 83. 513–523.

Baltes, Paul B. & Ulman Lindenberger. 1997. Emergence of a powerful connection between sensory and cognitive functions across the adult life span: A new window to the study of cognitive aging? *Psychology and Aging* 12 (1). 12–21.

Braver, Todd S. & Robert West. 2008. Working memory, executive control, and aging. In Fergus I. M. Craik & Timothy A. Salthouse (eds.), *The handbook of aging and cognition*, 311–372. New York, NY: Psychology Press.

Burke, Deborah M., Donald G. MacKay, Joanna S. Worthley & Elizabeth Wade. 1991. On the tip of the tongue: What causes word finding failures in young and older adults? *Journal of Memory and Language* 30 (5). 542–579.

Cabeza, Roberto. 2002. Hemispheric asymmetry reduction in older adults: The HAROLD model. *Psychology and Aging* 17 (1). 85–100.

Cahana-Amitay, Dalia & Martin L. Albert. 2014. Brain and language: Evidence for neural multifunctionality. *Behavioural Neurology* 2014 (260381). 1–16.

Cahana-Amitay, Dalia, Avron Spiro III, Jesse T. Sayers, Abigail C. Oveis, Eve Higby, Emmanuel A. Ojo, Susan Duncan, Mira Goral, JungMoon Hyun, Martin L. Albert & Loraine K. Obler. 2016. How older adults use cognition in sentence-final word recognition. *Aging, Neuropsychology, and Cognition* 23 (4). 418–444.

Caplan, David N. & Gloria S. Waters. 1999. Verbal working memory and sentence comprehension. *Behavioral and Brain Sciences* 22 (1). 77–94.

Caplan, David N., Gayle DeDe, Gloria Waters, Jennifer Michaud & Yorghos Tripodis. 2011. Effects of age, speed of processing, and working memory on comprehension of sentences with relative clauses. *Psychology and Aging* 26 (2). 439–450.

Cotelli, Maria, Rosa Manenti, Michela Brambilla, Orazio Zanetti & Carlo Miniussi. 2012. Naming ability changes in physiological and pathological aging. *Frontiers in Neuroscience* 6 (120). 1–13.

Cotelli, Maria, Rosa Manenti, Sandra Rosini, Marco Calabria, Michela Brambilla, Partizia S. Bisiacchi, Orazio Zanetti & Carlo Miniussi. 2010. Action and object naming in physiological aging: An rTMS study. *Frontiers in Aging Neuroscience* 2 (151). 1–7.

Davis, Simon W., Nancy A. Dennis, Sander M. Daselaar, Mathias S. Fleck & Roberto Cabeza. 2008. Que PASA? The posterior-anterior shift in aging. *Cerebral Cortex* 18. 1201–1209.

Davis, Simon W., James E. Kragel, David J. Madden & Roberto Cabeza. 2011. The architecture of cross-hemispheric communication in the aging brain: Linking behavior to functional and structural connectivity. *Cerebral Cortex* 22 (1). 232–242.

DeDe, Gayle, David Caplan, Karen Kemtes & Gloria Waters. 2004. The relationship between age, verbal working memory, and language comprehension. *Psychology and Aging* 19 (4). 601–616.

Dennis, Nancy A. & Roberto Cabeza. 2008. Neuroimaging of healthy cognitive aging. In Fergus I. M. Craik, & Timothy A. Salthouse (eds.), *The handbook of aging and cognition*, 3rd edn., 1–54. New York, NY: Psychology Press.

Dew, Ilana T. Z., Norbou Buchler, Ian G. Dobbins & Roberto Cabeza. 2012. Where is ELSA? The early to late shift in aging. *Cerebral Cortex* 22 (11). 2542–2553.

Federmeier, Kara D. 2007. Thinking ahead: The role and roots of prediction in language comprehension. *Psychophysiology* 44 (4). 491–505.

Federmeier, Kara D. & Marta Kutas. 2005. Aging in context: Age-related changes in context use during language comprehension. *Psychophysiology* 42 (2). 133–141.

Federmeier, Kara D., Marta Kutas & Rina Schul. 2010. Age-related and individual differences in the use of prediction during language comprehension. *Brain and Language* 115 (3). 149–161.

Federmeier, Kara D., Devon B. McLennan, Esmeralda De Ochoa & Marta Kutas. 2002. The impact of semantic memory organization and sentence context information on spoken language processing by younger and older adults: An ERP study. *Psychophysiology* 39 (2). 133–146.

Federmeier, Kara D., Cyma Van Petten, Tanya J. Schwartz & Marta Kutas. 2003. Sounds, words, sentences: Age-related changes across levels of language processing. *Psychology & Aging* 18 (4). 858–872.

Fridriksson, Julius, K. Leigh Morrow, Dana Moser & Gordon C. Baylis. 2006. Age-related variability in cortical activity during language processing. *Journal of Speech, Language and Hearing Research* 49. 690–697.

Gazzaley, Adam & Mark D'Esposito. 2007. Top-down modulation and normal aging. *Annals of the New York Academy of Sciences* 1097 (1). 67–83.

Ghisletta, Paolo & Ulman Lindenberger. 2003. Age-based structural dynamics between perceptual speed and knowledge in the Berlin Aging Study: Direct evidence for ability dedifferentiation in old age. *Psychology and Aging* 18. 696–713.

Giorgio, Antonio, Luca Santelli, Valentina Tomassini, Rose Bosnell, Steve Smith, Nicola De Stefano & Heidi Johansen-Berg. 2010. Age-related changes in grey and white matter structure throughout adulthood. *Neuroimage* 51 (3). 943–951.

Good, Catriona D., Ingrid S. Johnsrude, John Ashburner, Richard N. A. Henson, Karl J. Friston & Richard S. J. Frackowiak. 2001. A voxel-based morphometric study of ageing in 465 normal adult human brains. *Neuroimage* 14 (1). 21–36.

Gold, Brian T., Anders H. Andersen, Greg A. Jicha & Charles D. Smith. 2009. Aging influences the neural correlates of lexical decision but not automatic semantic priming. *Cerebral Cortex* 19. 2671–2679.

Gollan, Tamar H. & Alan S. Brown. 2006. From tip-of-the-tongue (TOT) data to theoretical implications in two steps: When more TOTs means better retrieval. *Journal of Experimental Psychology: General* 135 (3). 462–483.

Goral, Mira, Manuella Clark-Cotton, Avron Spiro III, Loraine K. Obler, Jay Verkuilen, and Martin L. Albert. 2011. The contribution of set switching and working memory to sentence processing in older adults. *Experimental Aging Research* 37 (5). 516–538.

Grady, Cheryl. 2012. The cognitive neuroscience of ageing. *Nature Reviews Neuroscience* 13. 491–505.

Greenwood, Pamela M. 2007. Functional plasticity in cognitive aging: Review and hypothesis. *Neuropsychology* 21 (6). 657–673.

Grieder, Matthias, Raffaella M. Crinelli, Thomas Koenig, Lars-Olof Wahlund, Thomas Dierks & Miranka Wirth. 2012. Electrophysiological and behavioral correlates of stable automatic semantic retrieval in aging. *Neuropsychologia* 50 (1). 160–171.

Grieve, Stuart M., Leanne M. Williams, Robert H. Paul, C. Richard Clark & Evian Gordon. 2007. Cognitive aging, executive function, and fractional anisotropy: A diffusion tensor MR imaging study. *American Journal of Neuroradiology* 28 (2). 226–235.

Grossman, Murray, Ayanna Cooke, Christian DeVita, David Alsop, John Detre, Willis Chen & James Gee. 2002a. Age-related changes in working memory during sentence comprehension: An fMRI study. *Neuroimage* 15 (2). 302–317.

Grossman, Murray, Ayanna Cooke, Christian DeVita, Willis Chen, Peachie Moore, John Detre, David Alsop & James Gee. 2002b. Sentence processing strategies in healthy seniors with poor comprehension: An fMRI study. *Brain and Language* 80 (3). 296–313.

Gunning-Dixon, Faith M., Adam M. Brickman, Janice C. Cheng & George S. Alexopoulos. 2009. Aging of cerebral white matter: A review of MRI findings. *International Journal of Geriatric Psychiatry* 24 (2). 109–117.

Gunning-Dixon, Faith M. & Naftali Raz. 2000. The cognitive correlates of white matter abnormalities in normal aging: A quantitative review. *Neuropsychology* 14 (2). 224–232.

Gunter, Thomas C., Janet L. Jackson & Gijsbertus Mulder. 1995. Language, memory and aging: An electrophysiological exploration of the N400 during reading of memory-demanding sentences. *Psychophysiology* 32. 215–229.

Gunter, Thomas C., Janet L. Jackson & Gijsbertus Mulder. 1998. Priming and aging: An electrophysiological investigation of N400 and recall. *Brain and Language* 65. 333–355.

Gunter, Thomas C., Sandra H. Vos & Angela D. Friederici. 1999. Memory or aging? That's the question: An electrophysiological perspective on language. In Susan Kemper & Reinhold Kliegl (eds.), *Constraints on language: Memory, aging, and grammar*, 249–282. Norwell, MA: Kluwer Academic Publishers.

Harley, Trevor A., Lesley J. Jessiman & Siobhan B. G. MacAndrew. 2011. Decline and fall: A biological, developmental, and psycholinguistic account of deliberative language processes and ageing. *Aphasiology* 25 (2). 123–153.

Hasher, Lynn & Rose T. Zacks. 1988. Working memory, comprehension, and aging: A review and a new view. In Gordon H. Bower (ed.), *The psychology of learning and motivation*, Vol. 22, 193–225. San Diego, CA: Academic Press.

Healey, M. Karl, Karen L. Campbell & Lynne Hasher. 2008. Cognitive aging and increased distractibility: Costs and potential benefits. In Wayne S. Sassin, Jean-Claude Lacaille, Vincent F. Castellucci & Sylvie Belleville, *Essence of memory* (Progress in Brain Research Vol. 169), 353–363. Amsterdam & Oxford: Elsevier.

Jernigan, Terry L., Sarah L. Archibald, Christine Fennema-Notestine, Anthony C. Gamst, Julie C. Stout, Julie Bonner & John R. Hesselink. 2001. Effects of age on tissues and regions of the cerebrum and cerebellum. *Neurobiology of Aging* 22 (4). 581–594.

Jimura, Koji & Todd S. Braver. 2010. Age-related shifts in brain activity dynamics during task switching. *Cerebral Cortex* 20 (6). 1420–1431.

Juncos-Rabadán, Onésimo, David Facal, Maria Soledad Rodríguez & Arturo Pereiro. 2010. Lexical knowledge and lexical retrieval in ageing: Insights from a tip-of-the-tongue (TOT) study. *Language and Cognitive Processes* 25 (10). 1301–1334.

Kalpouzos, Grégoria, Gaël Chételat, Jean-Claude Baron, Brigitte Landeau, Katell Mevel, Christine Godeau, Louisa Barré, Jean-Marc Constans, Fausto Viader, Francis Eustache & Béatrice Desgranges. 2009. Voxel-based mapping of brain gray matter volume and glucose metabolism profiles in normal aging. *Neurobiology of Aging* 30 (1). 112–124.

Kemmer, Laura, Seana Coulson, Esmeralda De Ochoa, & Marta Kutas. 2004. Syntactic processing with aging: An event-related potential study. *Psychophysiology* 41. 372–384.

Kemper, Susan, Angela Crow & Karen Kemtes. 2004. Eye-fixation patterns of high- and low-span young and older adults: Down the garden path and back again. *Psychology and Aging* 19 (1). 157–170.

Kennedy, Kristen M., Karen M. Rodrigue, Gérard N. Bischof, Andrew C. Hebrank, Patricia A. Reuter-Lorenz & Denise C. Park. 2015. Age trajectories of functional activation under conditions of low and high processing demands: An adult lifespan fMRI study of the aging brain. *NeuroImage* 104. 21–34.

Kutas, Marta & Vicente Iragui. 1998. The N400 in a semantic categorization task across 6 decades. *Electroencephalography and Clinical Neurophysiology* 108 (5). 456–471.

Li, Shu-Chen & Ulman Lindenberger. 1999. Cross-level unification: A computational exploration of the link between deterioration of neurotransmitter systems and dedifferentiation of cognitive abilities in old age. In Lars-Goran Nilsson & Hans J. Markowitsch (eds.), *Cognitive neuroscience of memory*, 103–146. Ashland, OH: Hogrefe & Huber Publishers.

Lustig, Cindy & Randy L. Buckner. 2004. Preserved neural correlates of priming in old age and dementia. *Neuron* 42 (5). 865–875.

Madden, David J., Ilana J. Bennett & Allen W. Song. 2009. Cerebral white matter integrity and cognitive aging: Contributions from diffusion tensor imaging. *Neuropsychology Review* 19 (4). 415–435.

Manenti, Rosa, Michela Brambilla, Michela Petesi, Carlo Miniussi & Maria Cotelli. 2013. Compensatory networks to counteract the effects of ageing on language. *Behavioural Brain Research* 249. 22–27.

Meunier, David, Emmanuel A. Stamatakis & Loraine K. Tyler. 2014. Age-related functional reorganization, structural changes, and preserved cognition. *Neurobiology of Aging* 35 (1). 42–54.

Obler, Loraine K., Deborah Fein, Marjorie Nicholas & Martin L. Albert. 1991. Auditory comprehension and aging: Decline in syntactic processing. *Applied Psycholinguistics* 12. 433–452.

Obler, Loraine K., Elena Rykhlevskaia, David Schnyer, Manuella R. Clark-Cotton, Avron Spiro III, JungMoon Hyun, Dae-Shik Kim, Mira Goral & Martin L. Albert. 2010. Bilateral brain regions associated with naming in older adults. *Brain and Language* 113 (3). 113–123.

Park, Denise C., Thad A. Polk, Rob Park, Meredith Minear, Anna Savage & Mason R. Smith. 2004. Aging reduces neural specialization in ventral visual cortex. *Proceedings of the National Academy of Sciences* 101. 13091–13095.

Park, Denise C. & Patricia Reuter-Lorenz. 2009. The adaptive brain: Aging and neurocognitive scaffolding. *Annual Review of Psychology* 60. 173–196.

Payne, Brennan R., Sarah Grison, Xuefei Gao, Kiel Christianson, Daniel G. Morrow & Elizabeth A. L. Stine-Morrow. 2014. Aging and individual differences in binding during sentence understanding: Evidence from temporary and global syntactic attachment ambiguities. *Cognition* 130 (2). 157–173.

Peelle, Jonathan E., Vanessa Troiani, Murray Grossman & Arthur Wingfield. 2011. Hearing loss in older adults affects neural systems supporting speech comprehension. *Journal of Neuroscience* 31 (35). 12638–12643.

Peelle, Jonathan E., Vanessa Troiani, Arthur Wingfield & Murray Grossman. 2010. Neural processing during older adults' comprehension of spoken sentences: Age differences in resource allocation and connectivity. *Cerebral Cortex* 20. 773–782.

Persson, Jonas, Cindy Lustig, James K. Nelson & Patricia A. Reuter-Lorenz. 2007. Age differences in deactivation: A link to cognitive control? *Journal of Cognitive Neuroscience* 19 (6). 1021–1032.

Rabbitt, Patrick & Mike Anderson. 2006. The lacunae of loss? Aging and the differentiation of cognitive abilities. In Ellen Bialystok & Fergus I. M. Craik (eds.), *Lifespan cognition: Mechanisms of change*, 331–343. New York: Oxford University Press.

Raz, Naftali & Karen M. Rodrigue. 2006. Differential aging of the brain: Patterns, cognitive correlates and modifiers. *Neuroscience and Biobehavioral Reviews* 30 (6). 730–748.

Reuter-Lorenz, Patricia A. 2002. New visions of the aging mind and brain. *Trends in Cognitive Sciences* 6 (9). 394–400.

Reuter-Lorenz, Patricia A. & Katherine A. Cappell. 2008. Neurocognitive aging and the compensation hypothesis. *Current Directions in Psychological Science* 17 (3). 177–182.

Reuter-Lorenz, Patricia A., John Jonides, Edward E. Smith, Alan Hartley, Andrea Miller, Christina Marshuetz & Robert A. Koeppe. 2000. Age differences in the frontal lateralization of verbal and spatial working memory revealed by PET. *Journal of Cognitive Neuroscience* 12 (1). 174–187.

Shafto, Meredith A., Deborah M. Burke, Emmanuel A. Stamatakis, Phyllis P. Tam & Loraine K. Tyler. 2007. On the tip-of-the-tongue: Neural correlates of increased word-finding failures in normal aging. *Journal of Cognitive Neuroscience* 19 (12). 2060–2070.

Shafto, Meredith A., Emmanuel A. Stamatakis, Phyllis P. Tam & Loraine K. Tyler. 2010. Word retrieval failures in old age: The relationship between structure and function. *Journal of Cognitive Neuroscience* 22 (7). 1530–1540.

Shafto, Meredith A. & Loraine K. Tyler. 2014. Language in the aging brain: The network dynamics of cognitive decline and preservation. *Science* 346 (6209). 583–587.

Sommers, Mitchell S. & Stephanie M. Danielson. 1999. Inhibitory processes and spoken word recognition in young and older adults: The interaction of lexical competition and semantic context. *Psychology and Aging* 14 (3). 458–472.

Stamatakis, Emmanuel A., Meredith A. Shafto, Guy Williams, Phyllis P. Tam & Loraine K. Tyler. 2011. White matter changes and word finding failures with increasing age. *PLoS One* 6. e14496.

Stine-Morrow, Elizabeth A. L., Le-Ann Milinder, Olivia Pullara & Barbara Herman. 2001. Patterns of resource allocation are reliable among younger and older readers. *Psychology and Aging* 16 (1). 69–84.

Szaflarski, Jerzy P., Scott K. Holland, Vincent J. Schmithorst & Anna W. Byars. 2006. fMRI study of language lateralization in children and adults. *Human Brain Mapping* 27. 202–212.

Tyler, Lorraine K., Meredith A. Shafto, Billi Randall, Paul Wright, William D. Marslen-Wilson & Emmanuel A. Stamatakis. 2010. Preserving syntactic processing across the adult life span: The modulation of the frontotemporal language system in the context of age-related atrophy. *Cerebral Cortex* 20 (2). 352–364.

West, Robert L. 1996. An application of prefrontal cortex function theory to cognitive aging. *Psychological Bulletin* 120 (2). 272–292.

Wierenga, Christina E., Michelle Benjamin, Kaundinya Gopinath, William M. Perlstein, Christiana M. Leonard, Leslie J. Gonzalez Rothi, Tim Conway, M. Allison Cato, Richard Briggs & Bruce Crosson. 2008. Age-related changes in word retrieval: Role of bilateral frontal and subcortical networks. *Neurobiology of Aging* 29 (3). 436–451.

Wingfield, Arthur & Murray Grossman. 2006. Language and the aging brain: Patterns of neural compensation revealed by functional brain imaging. *Journal of Neurophysiology* 96 (6). 2830–2839.

Wingfield, Arthur, Patricia A. Tun & Sandra L. McCoy. 2005. Hearing loss in older adulthood: What it is and how it interacts with cognitive performance. *Current Directions in Psychological Science* 14 (3). 144–148.

Wlotko, Edward W. & Kara D. Federmeier. 2012. Age-related changes in the impact of contextual strength on multiple aspects of sentence comprehension. *Psychophysiology* 49 (6). 770–785.

Wlotko, Edward W., Chia-Lin Lee & Kara D. Federmeier. 2010. Language of the aging brain: Event-related potential studies of comprehension in older adults. *Language and Linguistics Compass* 4 (8). 623–638.

Yoon, Jungmee, Luca Campanelli, Mira Goral, Klara Marton, Naomi Eichorn & Loraine K. Obler. 2015. The effect of plausibility on sentence comprehension among older adults and its relation to cognitive functions. *Experimental Aging Research* 41 (3). 272–302.

Zhang, Haobo, Perminder S. Sachdev, Wei Wen, Nicole A. Kochan, John D. Crawford, Henry Brodaty, Melissa J. Slavin, Simone Reppermund, Kristan Kang & Julian N. Trollor. 2013. Grey matter correlates of three language tests in non-demented older adults. *PloS One* 8 (11). e80215.

Rosemary Varley and Vitor Zimmerer
43 Language impairments in acquired aphasia: Features and frameworks

1 Introduction

A typical case report of aphasia would be that of an individual who previously had normal language function, but then experienced a sudden loss of these capacities following a brain lesion. Aphasia can vary in severity. In mild forms a person might complain of word retrieval difficulties, problems in understanding speech under challenging listening conditions (for example, noisy environments and where there are many speakers), and loss of pleasure in reading due to the attentional demands of decoding large amounts of text. In its severest form (global aphasia), an individual is likely to display minimal understanding of either spoken or written language, while language production is restricted to small numbers of single words or frozen formulas.

Definitions of aphasia include a number of elements, which together assist in clinical diagnosis and allow differentiation of aphasia from other types of language impairment and other conditions that can follow brain injury. Key components are that aphasia is an *acquired* impairment of language, thus differentiating it from developmental language disabilities. Aphasia typically occurs in adults and most often as a consequence of damage to the language-dominant cerebral hemisphere (usually the left in right handers, and also the majority of left handers; Pujol et al. 1999). Aphasia is often defined as a disorder *specific* to language. Difficulties in understanding or producing language cannot be attributed to peripheral sensory-perceptual impairments (such as hearing loss), or paralysis of muscles necessary for realising linguistic messages in various modalities such as speech (dysarthria), writing or signing. Similarly, higher-order cognitive systems such as reasoning and inference-making may be relatively unimpaired (Varley 2014). Aphasia is viewed as a consequence of disruption to the central stores of linguistic knowledge and/or the processing systems that implement this knowledge in comprehension or production. The extent of language impairment is both disproportionate to deficits in non-linguistic cognitive systems and cannot be explained by such extra-linguistic disruptions.

The notion of specific language impairment has some ambiguities at the interfaces of language with peripheral sensory-motor systems or with other central cognitive systems. For example, phonological perceptual impairment might also be associated with deficits in processing music and environmental sounds. But the criterion has clinical utility in differentiating aphasia from communicative impairments that follow diffuse brain injury such as occur in Alzheimer's disease or traumatic brain injury

Rosemary Varley and Vitor Zimmerer, University College London

(e.g., resulting from a traffic accident, fall or blast). In the latter conditions, there is typically bilateral brain damage/degeneration and, although language areas of the brain might be damaged, injury extends to other regions of grey and white matter outside of the core linguistic system. For example, in Alzheimer's disease there is degeneration of neurons in the medial temporal lobe, with profound consequences for the encoding and retrieval of various types of declarative memory. As a result, the individual displays linguistic impairments such as difficulty in retrieving words from lexical memory or in recalling earlier contributions to a conversation, but there are also non-language deficits such as confusion and disorientation. A person with aphasia will also have word retrieval difficulties, but this linguistic impairment is disproportionate to impairments in other cognitive domains. The aphasic person knows when it is, who and where they are, and to whom they are talking.

2 Biology of aphasia

Aphasia is typically caused by damage to cortical zones bordering the large horizontal fissure (Sylvian or lateral fissure) that separates the temporal lobe from the parietal and frontal lobes. This perisylvian region includes Broca's area in the inferior frontal lobe, the supramarginal and angular gyri that lie at the intersection of temporal and parietal lobes, and the superior and middle temporal gyri, including Wernicke's area. These neural zones are critical processing hubs for understanding and formulating language expressions. However, functional neuroimaging reveals that activations associated with language processing extend beyond the perisylvian region to other left hemisphere sites, as well as subcortical structures such as the thalamus and putamen and homologous areas of the right hemisphere (Price 2012). Given this widely distributed neural network, not only the cortical outer mantle of grey matter is involved in language, but also white matter pathways that connect these distributed sites. While a lesion of significant size within the left hemisphere perisylvian region is likely to cause marked and long-lasting aphasic impairment, damage outside this area may also result in transient or subtle disruptions of language.

There are various ways in which perisylvian cortex and its interconnecting white matter pathways can be damaged. The lesions that cause aphasia are usually vascular in origin, with disruption of blood supply to areas of brain as a result of blockage (thrombosis or embolism) or rupture (haemorrhage) of an artery. Vascular lesions (or strokes) usually result in focal damage, i.e., there is a clear boundary to the area of structural brain injury. Although strokes are more prevalent in older adults, they can occur at any point in the lifespan. Younger adults or children can experience stroke-linked aphasia and, in the case of aphasia in early life, there can be a complex interplay between loss of established language function and impact on subsequent language learning. Although strokes are a common cause of focal injury, other forms of pathology can result in focal damage, such as a tumour affecting the perisylvian area. More recently, the impact of focal degeneration or cell loss in perisylvian cortex has been described with the identification of primary progressive aphasias (PPA). Three forms of PPA have been reported to date (*semantic, non-fluent, logopenic*; Gorno-Tempini et al. 2011). These variants differ in language profiles, loci of initial brain atrophy, and possibly also the neurobiological triggers of degeneration. Whereas focal stroke aphasia is typically of sudden onset and then displays either a stable pattern of impairment or a gradual improvement in function, in PPA there is slow and insidious loss of language capacities. The initial profile of disability is in language (hence, the *primary* component of the label), but over a period of years the degeneration extends into other brain areas (the *progressive* element), ultimately leading to a broader profile of cognitive impairment typical of other forms of degenerative dementias such as Alzheimer's disease.

3 Frameworks in aphasia

3.1 Early anatomical approaches and the fluent/non-fluent aphasia dichotomy

Although there are reports of likely cases of aphasia in Classical antiquity (Tesak and Code 2008), the beginnings of modern study of aphasia are traced to the mid-late nineteenth century. In 1861, Broca described a man who had a severe impairment of speech production (he only used the syllable *tan* and a few expletives), but seemed to retain good understanding of language. At autopsy, although the patient was found to have a large left hemisphere lesion, Broca inferred that the damage responsible for his aphasia was centred in the third convolution of the inferior frontal gyrus (subsequently named Broca's area). Broca suggested that this region was the location of the 'motor images' of words. He went on to report a series of patients in 1865 and, although other neurologists had noted the association between language impairment and the left hemisphere, Broca is generally recognised at the first clinician-scientist to widely disseminate this observation. In 1874, Wernicke described a series of patients with a different form of aphasia that followed damage to the posterior portion of the left superior temporal gyrus (subsequently Wernicke's area). By contrast to Broca's non-fluent case, these patients spoke fluently in the sense that speech was well-articulated and with normal prosodic contours, although the content was often difficult to follow. In further contrast to Broca's patient, these patients displayed impaired understanding of language. Wernicke suggested that the posterior temporal lobe was the site of 'auditory images' of words and played an important role in language comprehension.

The behavioural and neuroanatomical distinctions established by Broca and Wernicke between fluent and non-fluent variants remain at the core of many contemporary clinical classifications of aphasia. An initial decision in clinical diagnosis is whether the speaker displays fluent or non-fluent output. At a behavioural level, this distinction is based upon an amalgam of linguistic and phonetic characteristics. Patients with anterior (frontal) lesions are more likely to have involvement of motor cortex and therefore the possibility of phonetic-phonological impairment in speech production. As a result, prosodic groupings in non-fluent speech tend to be short and often there are articulatory errors, altered voice quality, and general increase in speech effort. Anterior lesions, particularly in the region of the inferior frontal gyrus and Broca's area, can also give rise to grammatical impairments (*agrammatism*) and speech is characterised by reduced and simplified clause structures, including an underuse of verbs, missing verb arguments and bare noun phrases.

(1) It's alright. Yes. Mate... Jack comes and all... but... oh dear... Jack... er... old ... er seventy. No. Sixty eight Jack... but swim. Me like this [gesture].... swimming... er... I can't say it.... but Jack... er.... swimming on front... er... back

The output is often described as telegrammatic as speech is stripped down to content items. Function words such as articles and verb auxiliaries are often omitted (but note that they are sometimes present in higher frequency phrases such as *I can't say it*). By contrast, fluent aphasic speech is prosodically normal, with few articulatory errors and, relative to reduced telegrammatic production, it appears syntactically near normal. There might be errors on function words, but these are often viewed as a consequence of lexical retrieval errors occurring within the closed sets of grammatical words. Notice the inconsistent use of pronouns in the fluent aphasic sample below. This is likely to derail the listener's understanding of the intended meaning. These grammatical abnormalities that might be a consequence of lexical selection problems are termed *paragrammatism*.

(2) I saw a niece of one. Comes from London. And she came with her mother first and he said that if I were her, he would go into hospital.

Despite the fluent/non-fluent contrast representing a basic diagnostic distinction, there is often some confusion surrounding its use: most aphasic speakers display non-fluencies in connected speech. For example, a patient with word-finding difficulty (*anomia*) will produce speech with pauses that reflect word retrieval failure. There may be fragments of sentences which have been abandoned due to formulation difficulties (Extract 3). Typically anomic aphasia would be classified as a fluent form of aphasia because, amidst these non-fluencies, there is ample evidence of large prosodic groupings that are produced without error or struggle and include syntactically well-formed complex structures. But the evidence of *some* non-fluencies, and certainly more non-fluencies than typical/healthy speech, might lead to the novice aphasiologist to an incorrect judgement.

(3) Had a pub. We had a pub in ... in ... where we're out. Where we're now. Not far away. We had it for twenty ... one ... two ... thirty ... thirty two at the pub

The initial dichotomy of the aphasias into Broca's/non-fluent and Wernicke's/fluent types was subsequently elaborated. In addition to auditory and motor language areas, Wernicke identified a fibre tract that appeared necessary for repetition. This tract (*arcuate fasciculus*) connected the posterior auditory area and the anterior motor area. He suggested that damage to the tract disconnects the two systems, resulting in *conduction aphasia* and a specific impairment of speech repetition. Further syndromes were added to this anatomically-based model, including *anomia, transcortical motor* and *transcortical sensory aphasia*. These various syndromes were identified on the basis of performance on four behavioural measures: speech fluency, auditory comprehension, repetition and naming. For example, anomic aphasia represents an impairment specific to naming with behaviour on other dimensions relatively unaffected. In instances where all behaviours are seriously impaired the syndrome of *global aphasia* was described.

This 'classical' model of aphasia – based in nineteenth century neurology – was 'rediscovered' in the 1960's by clinician-scientists such as Norman Geschwind working from Boston and is now referred to as the Boston or neoclassical model of aphasia classification (Goodglass and Kaplan 1983; Catani and ffytche 2005). It remains influential, particularly in clinical aphasiology in North America. With 20th century advances in neuroimaging and linguistic analysis, both the anatomical and behavioural features of the various syndromes have been elaborated. Key characteristics of the approach include close coupling of brain structure and language function and emphasis on syndromes or categories of aphasia.

Despite the impact and longevity of the neoclassical approach, it faced considerable opposition from its inception. The opponents (such as John Hughlings Jackson, Pierre Marie, Henry Head and Hildred Schuell) are often grouped under the label of 'holists' as they objected to both the behavioural and anatomical fractionation of the language system. A key observation was that only a small proportion of people with aphasia displayed impairments that fit easily into neoclassical syndromes, and there was marked variability between individuals who were grouped within a syndrome. Prins, Snow and Wagenaar (1978) reported that only 20% of their sample of 74 aphasic participants could be allocated to a syndrome. Instead many were classed as 'mixed' in their profiles. However, they also note that the fluent/non-fluent dichotomy was more robust and allowed classification of 75% of patients. Furthermore, there were concerns regarding the behavioural dimensions upon which the syndromes were based. As we have already described, speech fluency is a product of many linguistic components. Similarly, a term such as auditory comprehension encompasses multiple psycholinguistic processes, each of which might have distinct neurobiological substrates.

3.2 Linguistic investigations of aphasia

The application of linguistic theory and analytic tools to aphasia began in the 1960s and 1970s. An early and striking demonstration of the potential value of linguistic concepts was in investigation of the comprehension ability of speakers with agrammatic, Broca's aphasia. Under the neoclassical approach, these individuals were believed to display non-fluent speech but intact comprehension. However, two significant studies revealed that agrammatic speakers displayed difficulties in making decisions about sentence structure and comprehension failures that paralleled their syntactic deficits in production (Caramazza and Zurif 1976; von Stockert and Bader 1976). Caramazza and Zurif employed a sentence-picture matching task. Participants with agrammatic speech matched sentences with a centre-embedded relative clause to an appropriate picture in the presence of distracter pictures that depicted either changed referents (lexical) or reversed agency (grammatical). Where sentences were semantically-constrained (e.g., *the balloon that the clown is holding is round*), performance was relatively normal. However, when sentences were either implausible or semantically unconstrained (e.g., *the lion that the baby is scaring is yellow*; *the fish that the frog is biting is green*), performance on picture selection dropped to chance level. Von Stockert and Bader revealed that while agrammatic patients used semantic plausibility information in a sentence assembly task, fluent Wernicke's-type patients used syntactic information in making judgements. These remarkable experiments suggested that in agrammatic aphasia there is impairment of a central syntactic competence that mediates behaviour across both comprehension and production and, when impaired, parallel deficits across modalities occur. Not only would syntactic difficulties be evident in spoken and written production, but also in comprehension where successful decoding rests upon interpretation of syntactic features. Furthermore, Wernicke's aphasia began to be characterised as primarily a lexical-semantic deficit, accounting for prominent word-finding and comprehension difficulties.

These investigations inspired by linguistic theory established important shifts in the study of aphasia. First, subsequent research was more closely informed by psycholinguistics. Second, the tradition of 'words' versus 'rules' was established within aphasiology: some patients may have difficulties with words and lexical-semantic processing (linked to posterior perisylvian injury), while others may have impaired rule-based mechanisms that allow combination (and decomposition) of morphemes into complex words, and words into phrases and clauses (following frontal injury). This distinction between words and rules had a powerful effect on management of aphasia. The notion of a central competence that governed processing in both comprehension and production held a particular allure for clinicians. Directing therapy at a modality-free competence might result in generalised improvements in performance across modalities. For example, an intervention based around making semantic judgements might facilitate both word comprehension and retrieval in speech and orthography (e.g., Drew and Thompson 1999). This phase of clinical aphasiology saw the development of metalinguistic therapies that involved judgements about language content and form. These interventions were abstract in the sense they involved judgements about language rather than actual language use. Unfortunately, subsequent research revealed that these interventions often result only in item- and task-specific training effects (Best, Greenwood, Grassly, Herbert, Hicken and Howard 2013).

3.3 Psycholinguistic and cognitive neuropsychological investigations of aphasia

Syndromes such as Broca's/syntactic or Wernicke's/semantic aphasia are often used as high-order abstractions to divide up the problem-space of aphasia. Within these categories there is considerable heterogeneity in the behavioural profiles of individuals who share the same diagnostic label (Caramazza 1988; Berndt, Mitchum, & Haendiges 1996). Although differences in severity might account for some within-syndrome variability, there are also qualitative differences among individuals. For example, there were reports of agrammatic speakers who did not have syntactic comprehension difficulties, or cases in which there were dissociations between elements of syntactic processing (Badecker and Caramazza 1985; Howard 1985). Miceli, Silveri, Romani and Caramazza (1989) described differences between 'agrammatic' patients in use of morphology. Some patients showed relatively preserved use of prepositions or articles, but high levels of substitution or omission of verb auxiliaries. Other 'agrammatic' patients, however, displayed the reverse profile and preservation of verb auxiliaries in face of abnormalities in article use. These patterns of *dissociation* are critical in creating and testing psycholinguistic models of language processing. In the case of dissociations within morphology, this might indicate that the processing mechanisms for each type of information are both functionally and neuroanatomically distinct.

In response to within-syndrome heterogeneity, approaches shifted to exploring the behaviour of individuals against the predictions generated by psycholinguistic models which decomposed complex behaviours such as sentence or word production into a series of semi-autonomous processing steps. The objective was to identify intact and impaired sub-processes in order both to understand the behaviour of individual patients and to test the architecture of the underpinning model. A number of psycholinguistic models have been influential in investigations of aphasia. For example, lexical impairments have been analysed from the perspective of Morton's logogen model (e.g., Morton and Patterson 1980) and Levelt's (1992) word production model. Garrett (1982) described a multi-stage sentence production model that influenced investigations of sentence processing. The description we provide of the features of aphasic language in Section 4 is informed by these approaches. Furthermore, psycholinguistic approaches had powerful impacts on the treatment of aphasia. Once a processing deficit is identified, specific therapies are designed that attempt to target the impairment, with the aspiration that these focused interventions will be more effective than generalised language training. For example, in the case of a naming impairment, a psycholinguistic approach probes the possible source of the processing failure through error analysis, the impact of different variables on naming success (e.g., a semantic variable such as abstractness/imageability), and the effect of upgrading information at various processing phases through the provision of cues as to meaning or word form. If disruption at a specific level is identified, a therapy can then be administered which is narrowly targeted on, for example, semantic organisation or facilitating phonological access (Whitworth, Webster and Howard 2014).

4 Features of aphasia

In most cases of aphasia, there is cross-modality impairment of language with disruption in understanding and formulating linguistic messages across spoken/written/ signed modalities. There are rare reports of individuals with impairments restricted to a single modality (e.g., Varley et al. 2005), but in these cases the breakdown lies at the interface between central linguistic and perceptual or motor systems. The expressive deficits of aphasia are most evident with errors or failure of word retrieval, abnormalities of sentence structure and frequent expressions of frustration and embarrassment at communicative difficulties. However, most aphasic individuals have some degree of comprehension deficit. In particular, less frequent and abstract (or low imageability) words, and sentence structures requiring maintenance and tracking of multiple dependencies across phrases, are challenging to aphasic comprehension. Fortunately, as natural language interactions do not always involve such forms and structures, the person with aphasia can sometimes use alternative sources to achieve a degree of understanding (e.g., partial linguistic information, redundancies in a message, supporting contextual information, interpretation of speaker intonation and non-verbal behaviours).

4.1 Lexical impairments

4.1.1 Lexical comprehension

Decoding of spoken and/or written words involves a series of phases in processing. These different phases are conceptualised as autonomous sub-modules in serial information processing models (Levelt 1992). For example, where an individual shows retained ability to understand written words but fails to decode those same words when spoken, this pattern of deficit suggests some autonomy between decoding of phonological versus orthographic form, and the likely separation of semantic processing from form decoding systems.

The recognition and understanding of words is often conceived as involving three phases of processing. First, at the interface of the language system with sensory-perceptual mechanisms, acoustic (speech) or visual (writing) feature detectors determine the nature of the input (/pa/ or /ta/?). The second phase involves activation of an entry in lexical memory that matches the perceived input (word recognition). In the healthy system, once a form is recognised there is automatic activation of associated meaning (word comprehension). This may not be the case in aphasic processing. A patient might successfully classify words and pseudo-words (e.g., *fence vs. lence*) as real and non-words respectively, indicating adequate word recognition, but fail to make accurate judgements with regard to the meaning of the real word (e.g., matching *fence* to a picture of wall rather than the appropriate referent). In the aphasic case, words which are perceptually unique (e.g., *hippopotamus vs. hip*), used frequently, and refer to entities with rich sensory-perceptual and motor characteristics (having high imageability, e.g., *dog vs. dogma*) are more likely to be decoded successfully. Psycholinguistic testing often manipulates these variables in a series of perceptual, recognition and comprehension tasks in order to discover the stage at which word processing fails. For example, a perceptual failure might be reflected in errors of processing minimally different (e.g., *hip – ship*) but not maximally-different (e.g., *hip – dog*) word pairs.

4.1.2 Lexical production

Lexical retrieval or word-finding difficulties are pervasive in aphasia. They are also a common report of healthy older adults (Shafto et al. 2007). However, aphasic word-finding difficulty occurs more frequently and on vocabulary that typically does not present a challenge to healthy speakers. Just as word understanding is conceived of as a multiphase process, so too is word retrieval. Standard models of lexical retrieval (e.g., Levelt 1992) suggest that the first phase of processing involves activation within semantic memory of a relevant meaning representation and then mapping to its associated phonological or orthographic form. Failure of word-finding in healthy speakers typically represents a breakdown of this mapping: the speaker has a clear idea of content but is unable to retrieve the appropriate word form. The speaker may experience a tip-of-the tongue state where there is partial access to the word form. Subsequent to word form retrieval, and at a linguistic-motor system interface, forms must engage learned movement coordinates (motor memory) that govern realisation in speech, writing or sign.

Aphasic lexical retrieval impairments may reflect failure at one or more of these processing steps. In clinical investigations the source of a problem is examined by determining sensitivity to a range of variables (e.g., imageability, word frequency, word length) and undertaking an analysis of errors in naming tasks. Imageability (the extent of sensory, perceptual and motor representation associated with a word) is viewed as a semantic variable and a patient who displays differential performance across high and low imageability words, when other key variables such as word frequency are kept constant, is hypothesised to suffer from an impairment at the semantic level. The semantic system is conceived as a central system which is involved both in comprehension and production across spoken and written modalities. Therefore, the performance of a patient suspected of having a semantic deficit will be examined across modalities. Naming errors will be evaluated for signs of semantic under-specification (e.g., *hospital – place*) or semantically-related error (*semantic paraphasias* e.g., *cushion – sponge*). Both nouns and verbs may be replaced with semantically-light or deictic forms as retrieval of lower frequency words with more specific reference is aborted in favour of forms such as pronouns (*he, it, they*), proverbs (*do*) and generic nouns such as *thing* or *man*.

In the case of post-semantic failure, sometimes described as breakdown at the phonological/orthographic output lexicon, a patient might show a different pattern of errors, with greater sensitivity to lexical variables such as word frequency rather than imageability. Typical errors might include circumlocution in which the intended meaning is described in a multiword utterance (e.g., *signpost – these posts stuck up in the air with these here doings [+ gesture for writing] on them*), formal (phonological or orthographic) paraphasias (e.g., *parasol – paracetamol*), or *conduite d'approach* behaviour, where the speaker might be able to access only partial form information (often the word onset) and makes repeated approximations to the target form. There is also the possibility of dissociation in performance between phonological and orthographic retrieval. Individuals might be able to write a word that they cannot retrieve in spoken naming, or vice versa. Other aphasic lexical retrieval errors such as neologisms, where a nonword is produced (e.g., *toast – gatchind*), are more difficult to localise to a single level of processing failure. Some aphasic speakers display frequent neologisms in their spoken and written output and are described as having *jargon aphasia*. There are a number of different forms: in *neologistic* jargon aphasia, output consists of strings of fluently produced non-word syllables, with both content and grammatical words produced as neologisms. In *semantic* and *phonemic* forms errors predominate on content words. In the semantic variant errors consist of real but inappropriate words, while in the phonemic variant errors may result in nonwords, but also formal or phonemic paraphasias where there is a form relationship to the intended target.

Although tracking sensitivity to lexical variables and error analysis can provide insights into the sources of a processing failure, it is often the case that individual aphasic speakers display signs that suggest multiple processing deficits. For example, a person has difficulty in retrieving both low-imageability and low-frequency words, producing a range of errors such as semantic and phonemic paraphasias, as well as neologisms.

4.2 Grammatical impairments

4.2.1 Sentence comprehension

Hildred Schuell, a pioneer of aphasia treatment in the mid-20th century, indicated that just as word-finding difficulty is a pervasive symptom of aphasia, so too is failure of sentence comprehension (Schuell, Jenkins and Jiminez-Pabon 1967). However, whereas failure of word retrieval is overt, sentence comprehension difficulty is less evident and careful testing is often necessary to determine the extent and nature of impairment. There are multiple streams of information supporting language decoding (e.g., prosodic, contextual, gestural) and a patient with significant grammatical processing difficulties may still gain some understanding of an interlocutor's intentions, particularly in the case where that individual retains considerable lexical comprehension ability. The sentence *the man eats the apple* can be understood with little awareness of the grammatical role of each of the referents (as can *the apple is eaten by the man*). Events involving interactions of people and apples do not require interpretation of the word order of the active sentence or the morphological information of the passive (e.g., NP be+TNS V+en) in order to determine that *man* is agent and *apple* is patient. However, when sentences are manipulated so as to remove lexical cues as to agency, aphasic comprehension failures are more likely to be revealed. In *reversible* sentences, the head of either the subject or object noun phrase is a potential agent (e.g., *the diver splashed the dolphin/the dolphin splashed the diver*) and aphasic listeners/readers are in general prone to error in their interpretation through impairments in use of word order and/or morphological information to assign agency (Schwartz, Saffran and Marin 1980).

The sources of aphasic sentence processing deficits are complex. There are multiple mechanisms involved in processing sentences which are closely coupled. There have been a number of attempts to develop single deficit accounts of asyntactic comprehension (Martin 2006). For example, a number of influential studies motivated by generative approaches to syntax propose that sentences that undergo transformation from canonical order (e.g., the movement of an object NP to the subject position in passive formation) are problematic (Grodzinsky 2000). However, it is unlikely that a single processing deficit is at the source of sentence comprehension failures and analyses of large numbers of patients reveal heterogeneity of deficits (Caramazza et al. 2005). Key processes involved in sentence decoding include lexical processing, particularly of the verbs in the sentence but also other content words such as nouns (see the discussion of plausible agents above), sensitivity to functional morphology, and the capacity to maintain sequentially-presented information in order to determine the configurational relationship between the various sentence sub-components, as well as access to stored templates for possible configurational patterns in a language.

The processing of verbs provides crucial cues to sentence structure. Verbs are inherently relational in that they link the various noun, adverbial and prepositional phrases into a coherent representation of an event. Strongly associated with the verb is argument structure or subcategorisation information which provides a framework for the sentence (Thompson, Bonakdarpour and Fix 2010). For example, the verb 'arrive' works well in an intransitive frame (*John arrived* is perfectly acceptable, while **John arrived London* is less so). By contrast, the transitive verb 'reach' is odd if an object is not specified (**John reached*), but acceptable when the object slot is filled. A number of studies suggest greater impairment in verb relative to noun processing in aphasia (Bastiaanse and Jonkers 1998). If this is the case, then access is reduced to both the structural and semantic templates for the sentence.

Grammatical morphemes are drawn from closed sets of forms including articles, verb auxiliaries, prepositions, conjunctions and affixes (e.g., *a/the; will/shall; in/from; and/but/or; -ed/-ing*). These forms are very frequent in a language, but at the same time do not refer to specific entities, i.e., they are of very low imageability. Furthermore, they are generally short, unstressed and not prosodically prominent. However, grammatical morphemes provide indications as to the structural role of a sentence component (e.g., articles cue identification of a noun phrase). They also mark boundaries between sentence units and guide parsing decisions regarding the structure of a sentence. One possibility is that the low perceptual and semantic salience of these words makes them vulnerable to aphasic impairment and contributes to sentence processing difficulties (Goodglass, Fodor and Schulhoff 1967).

While processing of function words and verbs reflect essentially lexical contributions to sentence processing, sensitivity to sequence information is also important. Serially-presented information must be briefly maintained in order to enable activation of matching structural templates for phrases and whole sentence patterns in long-term memory. Some sentences are particularly demanding on short-term maintenance/buffering resources. In particular, sentences with complex subordinate structures require maintenance of sub-units until the hierarchical relationships within the sentence can be recognised (Haarmann, Just and Carpenter 1997). Aphasia comprehension tests often probe understanding of sentences such as *The dog chasing the cat is brown* or *The dog chased by the cat is brown* and sentences of this type are invariably challenging to aphasic comprehension.

Finally, the input has to be mapped to a semantic/thematic representation (who did what to who?) as the listener aims to reconstruct the speaker's communicative intentions. One influential account of aphasic sentence comprehension failure suggests that the capacity to structurally parse a sentence is retained in aphasia. Linebarger, Schwartz, and Saffran (1983) explored the ability of four agrammatic participants to make grammaticality judgements on a range of sentence types (i.e., deciding if a string was grammatically well- or ill-formed). They reported retained ability on most sentence types, although participants displayed some difficulty on sentences involving longer-range dependencies (e.g., **the little boy fell down, didn't it?*). In subsequent elaborations of this research, sentence comprehension failure was seen as a failure to map the syntactically-parsed input to its thematic roles, with processing of verbs as a key component of this process (Schwartz, Saffran and Marin 1980). However, in addition to a general caution regarding single-processing failure accounts of aphasic sentence comprehension, the original finding of retained grammaticality judgement in aphasia has not always been replicated (Wilson and Saygin 2004).

The area of aphasic grammatical comprehension has been the subject of considerable (and often polarised) debate. In the account we have developed above, we have described multiple information streams that contribute to sentence processing and any one (or combination) of these processes may be impaired in an aphasic disorder, resulting in heterogeneity within aphasic sentence comprehension impairments.

4.2.2 Sentence production

As well as impairments in sentence comprehension, aphasic disorders result in abnormalities of sentence production. These are usually discussed with reference to the grammatical impairments of non-fluent, Broca's-type aphasia. However, most speakers with aphasia display abnormalities in sentence production. There may be abnormal numbers of incomplete sentences, i.e., structures that have been abandoned due to formulation problems, or which are incomplete due to failures of word retrieval. Lexical retrieval errors are not restricted to naming tasks and sentences may display any of the errors in lexical retrieval described in Section 4.1.2.

With regard to grammatical impairment, extract (1) represents prototypical agrammatic production, with simplification of word and phrase combinations. Heads of phrases are often unmodified, with omission of grammatical words and inflections. However, the extract also displays the syntactically well-formed structure *I can't say it*. The elaboration of the verb phrase is noteworthy and atypical of the remainder of this speaker's spoken and written output. This variability is typical of aphasic speech and theories both of grammatical processing and agrammatism have to account for such phenomena. The presence of islands of syntactically-normal output might be regarded as evidence that grammatical knowledge is intact in agrammatism, but that its implementation is disrupted by intermittent failure of processing mechanisms such as requirement for integration with other levels of representation (e.g., lexical-semantic). An alternative account partitions these atypical forms into *formulas* or *stereotypes* and separates them from the generation of novel sentences (van Lancker Sidtis and Postman 2006). Sometimes they are described as *automatic* or *non-propositional* speech. However, the validity of the latter terms is questionable given these formulas are used intentionally by aphasic speakers with a useful communicative function such as signalling formulation difficulty to listeners.

The characteristics of agrammatic output extend beyond omission of function words from sentences. Some speakers display word order problems and difficulties in retrieval of verbs. In Section 4.2.1 we described the importance of sub-categorisation information packaged within the verb in providing a template for the sentence. For example, an intransitive verb (e.g. *smile*) provides a different structural plan from that of a transitive verb (e.g., *build*). Agrammatic speakers are reported to use verbs in gerundive form (e.g., *swimming*) as if naming actions (or 'nounifying verbs'; Saffran, Schwartz, and Marin 1980), but also to 'verbify nouns'. For example, in a conversation regarding his sleeping pattern the fluent aphasic speaker reported in extract (2) said:

(4) I won't know until it alarmclocks.

Difficulties with verbs may therefore not be restricted to agrammatic speakers. As with all aspects of aphasic language, within-syndrome variability and cross-syndrome overlap are pervasive. Bastiaanse and Jonkers (1998) confirm that verb retrieval difficulties are apparent in both non-fluent/agrammatic and fluent anomic speakers, with both groups displaying more difficulties on verbs than nouns. Furthermore, verbs with more complex argument structures (e.g., three argument verbs such as *put*) were more problematic than those with simple structures. Argument structure also affects production of adjectives, as Meltzer-Asscher and Thompson (2014) demonstrated. Adjectives with complex argument structure (e.g., *fond of* NP) are under-represented in aphasic speech.

5 Summary: Current and future directions

The distinction between words and rules, or lexicon and grammar, has had a powerful impact upon the classification and treatment of aphasia. Aphasia is a complex neurobiological disorder and abstract distinctions drawn in theoretical linguistics may not always be simply reflected in aphasic language impairments. Approaches to language which are based upon foundational principles of neurobiology and cognitive psychology may offer more in enhancing understanding of aphasia. One key idea is that mainstream linguistics has under-estimated the role of memory in language and the potential to store not only words but large chunks of information such as verbs and their associated constructional frame, or even whole utterances when these are used frequently and where language forms have a strong relationship with a particular communicative function (Goldberg 2006). The preserved construction *I can't say it*, observed in the extract of agrammatic speech, is one such example. In regard to formulas, frequency and other usage variables play an important role. While these variables are commonly considered in the lexical domain, they have often been ignored in the context of multiword utterances. A ground-breaking study by Gahl et al. (2003) examined the impact of the frequency with which a verb appeared in active or passive constructions. In the case of passive-dominant verbs (e.g., *injure*) Gahl et al. showed that comprehension of passives was significantly better when the sentence contained a passive-biased verb than one with an active bias. The results of this study indicate that breaking down strict distinctions between grammar/rules and lexical-semantics/words is likely to be productive in future understanding of the mosaic of intact and disrupted features in aphasic language. Furthermore, usage-based approaches which consider factors such as frequency and function of words and larger constructions, offer considerable therapeutic potential. In particular, they inter-link linguistic units with issues of function and use; and it is the latter that is central to the concerns of aphasic people and their communicative partners.

References

Badecker, William & Alfonso Caramazza. 1985. On considerations of method and theory governing the use of clinical categories in neurolinguistics and cognitive neuropsychology: The case against agrammatism. *Cognition* 20. 97–125.

Bastiaanse, Roellen & Roel Jonkers. 1998. Verb retrieval in action naming and spontaneous speech in agrammatic and anomic aphasia. *Aphasiology* 12. 951–969.

Berndt, Rita S., Charlotte C. Mitchum & Anne N. Haendiges. 1996. Comprehension of reversible sentences in "agrammatism": a meta-analysis. *Cognition* 58(3). 289–308.

Best, Wendy, Alison Greenwood, Jenny Grassly, Ruth Herbert, Julie Hicken & David Howard. 2013. Aphasia rehabilitation: does generalisation from anomia therapy occur and is it predictable? A case series study. *Cortex* 49. 2345–2357.

Caramazza, Alfonso. 1988. When is enough, enough? A comment on Grodzinsky and Marek's "Algorithmic and heuristic processes revisited". *Brain and Language* 33. 390–399.

Caramazza, Alfonso, Rita Capasso, Erminio Capitani & Gabriele Miceli. 2005. Patterns of comprehension performance in agrammatic Broca's aphasia: A test of the Trace Deletion Hypothesis. *Brain and Language* 94(1). 43–53.

Caramazza, Alfonso & Edgar Zurif. 1976. Dissociation of algorithmic and heuristic processes in language comprehension: evidence from aphasia. *Brain and Language* 3. 572–582.

Catani, Marco & Dominic H. Ffytche. 2005. The rises and falls of disconnection syndromes. *Brain* 128(10). 2224–2239.

Drew, Ruby L. & Cynthia K. Thompson. 1999. Model-based semantic treatment for naming deficits in aphasia. *Journal of Speech, Language, and Hearing Research* 42. 972–989.

Gahl, Susanne, Lise Menn, Gail Ramsberger, Daniel S. Jurafsky, Elizabeth Elder, Molly Rewega & Audrey Holland. 2003. Syntactic frame and verb bias in aphasia: plausibility judgments of undergoer-subject sentences. *Brain and Cognition* 53. 223–228.

Garrett, Merrill F. 1982. Production of speech: Observations from normal and pathological language use. In Andrew W. Ellis (ed.), *Normality and pathology in cognitive functions*. London: Academic Press.

Goldberg, Adele. 2006. *Constructions at work: The nature of generalization in language*. Oxford: Oxford University Press.

Goodglass, Harold & Edith Kaplan. 1983. *The assessment of aphasia and related disorders*. Philadelphia: Lea & Febiger.

Goodglass, Harold, Iris G. Fodor & Celia Schulhoff. 1967. Prosodic factors in grammar: evidence from aphasia. *Journal of Speech, Language and Hearing Research* 10. 5–20.

Gorno-Tempini, Maria Luisa, Argye E. Hillis, Sandra Weintraub, Andrew Kertesz, Mario Mendez, Stefano F. Cappa & Murray Grossman. 2011. Classification of primary progressive aphasia and its variants. *Neurology* 76. 1006–1014.

Grodzinsky, Yosef. 2000. The neurology of syntax: Language use without Broca's Area. *Behavioral and Brain Sciences* 23. 1–71.

Haarmann, Henk J., Marcel Adam Just & Patricia A. Carpenter. 1997. Aphasic sentence comprehension as a resource deficit: a computational approach. *Brain and Language* 59(1). 76–120.

Howard, David. 1985. Agrammatism. In Newman, S. & Epstein, R. (eds.) *Current perspectives in dysphasia*. Edinburgh: Churchill Livingstone.

Levelt, Willem J. M. 1992. Accessing words in speech production: Stages, processes and representations. *Cognition* 42. 1–22.

Linebarger, Marcia C., Myrna F. Schwartz & Eleanor M. Saffran. 1983. Sensitivity to grammatical structure in so-called agrammatic aphasics. *Cognition* 13(3). 361–392.

Marshall, Jane, Tim Pring & Shula Chiat. 1998. Verb retrieval and sentence production in aphasia. *Brain and Language* 63. 159–183.

Martin, Randi C. 2006. The neuropsychology of sentence processing: Where do we stand? *Cognitive Neuropsychology* 23(1). 74–95.

Meltzer-Asscher, Aya & Cynthia K. Thompson. 2014. The forgotten grammatical category: Adjective use in agrammatic aphasia. *Journal of Neurolinguistics* 30. 48–68.

Miceli, Gabriele, Catarina M. Silveri, Cristina Romani & Alfonso Caramazza. 1989. Variation in the pattern of omissions and substitutions of grammatical morphemes in the spontaneous speech of so-called agrammatic patients. *Brain and Language* 36. 447–492.

Morton, John & Karalyn E. Patterson. 1980. A new attempt at an interpretation, or, an attempt at a new interpretation. In Max Coltheart, Karalyn E. Patterson and John C. Marshall (eds.), *Deep dyslexia*. London: Routledge and Kegan Paul.

Prins, Ronald S., Catherine E. Snow & Erin Wagenaar. 1978. Recovery from aphasia: Spontaneous speech versus language comprehension. *Brain and Language* 6(20). 192–211.

Pujol, Jesús, Juan Deus, Josep M. Losilla & Antoni Capdevila. 1999. Cerebral lateralization of language in normal left-handed people studied by functional MRI. *Neurology* 53(5). 1038–1043.

Saffran, Eleanor M., Myrna F. Schwartz & Oscar S. M. Marin. 1980. The word order problem in agrammatism: 2. Production. *Brain and Language* 10. 263–280.

Schuell, Hildred, James Jenkins & Edward Jimenez-Pabon. *Aphasia in adults: Diagnosis, prognosis and treatment*. New York: Hoeber Medical.

Schwartz, Myrna F., Eleanor M. Saffran & Oscar S. M. Marin. 1980. The word order problem in agrammatism: 1. Comprehension. *Brain and Language* 10. 249–262.

Shafto, Meredith A., Deborah M. Burke, Emmanuel A. Stamatakis, Phyllis P. Tam & Lorraine K. Tyler. 2007. On the tip-of-the-tongue: neural correlates of increased word-finding failures in normal aging. *Journal of Cognitive Neuroscience* 19. 2060–2070.

Tesak, Juergen & Chris Code. 2008. *Milestones in the history of aphasia: Theories and Protagonists*. Hove: Psychology Press.

Thompson, Cynthia K., Borna Bonakdarpour & Stephen C. Fix. 2010. Neural mechanisms of verb argument structure processing in agrammatic aphasia and healthy age-matched listeners. *Journal of Cognitive Neuroscience* 22(9). 1993–2011.

Tomasello, Michael. 2003. *Constructing a language: A usage-based theory of language acquisition*. Cambridge, MA: Harvard University Press.

Van Lancker Sidtis, Diane & Whitney A. Postman. 2006. Formulaic expressions in spontaneous speech of left- and right-hemisphere-damaged subjects. *Aphasiology* 20(5). 411–426.

Varley, Rosemary. 2014. Reason without much language. *Language Sciences*. 46, 232–244.

Varley, Rosemary, Patricia E. Cowell, Andrew Gibson & Charles A. J. Romanowski. 2005. Disconnection agraphia in a case of multiple sclerosis: The isolation of letter movement plans from language. *Neuropsychologia* 43(10). 1503–1513.

Von Stockert, Theodor Ritter & Luisa Bader. 1976. Some relations of grammar and lexicon in aphasia. *Cortex* 12. 49–60.

Whitworth, Anne, Janet Webster & David Howard. 2014. *A cognitive neuropsychological approach to assessment and intervention in aphasia: a clinician's guide*. Hove: Psychology Press.

Wilson, Stephen M. & Ayse Pinar Saygin. 2004. Grammaticality judgment in aphasia: deficits are not specific to syntactic structures, aphasic syndromes, or lesion sites. *Journal of Cognitive Neuroscience* 16(2). 238–252.

Frédéric Assal and Ariane Laurent
44 Language in neurodegenerative diseases

1 Introduction

In the last decade, language in neurodegenerative diseases has been increasingly recognized as a specific marker not only for distinguishing different language isolated syndromes, or primary progressive aphasia (PPA) and its variants, but also for diagnosing various neurodegenerative disorders manifesting with language impairment amongst other cognitive deficits, and emotional and neurological signs and symptoms. Starting from the PPA syndrome that will be presented in details, we briefly extend the discussion to overlapping clinical phenotypes of heterogeneous neurodegenerative diseases such as corticobasal degeneration (CBD), supranuclear palsy (SP), Alzheimer's Disease (AD), the Parkinson's Disease (PD)-Dementia with Lewy Bodies (DLB) and fronto-temporal dementia (FTD)-Amyotrophic Lateral Sclerosis (ALS) spectra. Apart from diagnosis, a better understanding of linguistic profiles in such conditions is very important. Patients with communication difficulties and neurodegenerative diseases are going to increase drastically because of the growing elderly population, and disease modifying treatments still have a long way to go before showing clinical efficacy. There is therefore a real need to improve our knowledge in linguistic profiles of patients with neurodegenerative disease in order to better help patient's and caregiver's quality of life.

2 Primary progressive aphasia

Primary progressive aphasia (PPA) is a heterogeneous neurodegenerative clinical syndrome characterized by a progressive isolated language impairment in the early stages of the disease process. The changes are therefore at first restricted to communication in everyday life. The understanding of PPA is very important since it served as a model of language impairment in neurodegenerative diseases, initially frontotemporal dementias. In the last decade, a new consensus of criteria for primary progressive aphasia (PPA) has emerged (Gorno-Tempini et al., 2004; Gorno-Tempini et al., 2011; Hillis and Caramazza, 1989), based on Mesulam's classification (Mesulam, 2001), offering us a potential model to asses and classify these disorders. These developments represent significant progress, even if controversies exist concerning the period of two years during which the language difficulties have to be isolated, and if a classification in three variants fails to take into account unclassifiable disorders (Harris et al., 2013; Sajjadi et al., 2012).

Frédéric Assal and Ariane Laurent, Geneva University Hospitals

2.1 Basic criteria

The International Consensus Criteria were published in 2011 in order to define and classify PPA (Gorno-Tempini et al., 2011).

Table 1: Inclusion and exclusion criteria for the diagnosis of PPA (based on criteria by Mesulam (Gorno-Tempini et al., 2011)

Inclusion criteria 1–3 must be answered positively:
1. The most prominent clinical feature is the language disorder
2. The language deficit is the principal cause of impairment at the level of activities of daily living (ADL).
3. Language disorder should be the most prominent deficit at symptom onset and for the initial phases of the disease

Exclusion criteria 1–4 must be answered negatively for a PPA diagnosis
1. Pattern of deficits is better accounted for by other nondegenerative nervous system disorders or by medical criteria
2. Cognitive disturbances are better accounted for by a psychiatric diagnosis
3. Initial prominent of episodic memory, visual memory, and visuoperceptual impairments
4. Initial prominence of behavioral disturbance [Table 2]

Table 2: Diagnosis of PPA variants

A. Clinical diagnosis of nonfluent/agrammatic variant (PPA-A):
At least one of the following core features must be present:
1 Agrammatism in language production
2 Effortful, halting speech with inconsistent speech sound errors and distortions (apraxia of speech)

At least 2 of 3 of the following other features must be present:
1 Impaired comprehension of syntactically complex sentences
2 Spared single-word comprehension
3 Spared object knowledge

Imaging-supported PPA-A diagnostic criteria include clinical diagnosis and neuroimaging showing predominant left posterior fronto-insular atrophy on MRI or hypoperfusion/hypometabolism on SPECT/PET

B. Clinical diagnosis of semantic variant PPA (PPA-S):
Both of the following core features must be present:
1 Impaired confrontation naming
2 Impaired single word comprehension

At least 3 of the following other diagnostic features must be present:
1 Impaired object knowledge, particularly for low-frequency or low-familiarity items
2 Surface dyslexia or dysgraphia
3 Spared repetition
4 Spared speech production (grammar and motor speech)

Imaging supported PPA-S diagnostic criteria include clinical diagnosis and neuroimaging showing anterior temporal lobe atrophy on MRI or hypoperfusion/hypometabolism on SPECT/PET

C. Clinical diagnosis of logopenic variant PPA (PPA-L):
Both of the following core features must be present:
1 Impaired single-word retrieval in spontaneous speech and naming
2 Impaired repetition of sentences and phrases

At least 3 of the following other feature must be present:
1 Speech (phonologic) errors in spontaneous speech and naming
2 Spared single-word comprehension and object knowledge
3 Spared motor speech
4 Absence of frank agrammatism

Imaging supported PPA-L diagnostic criteria include clinical diagnosis and neuroimaging showing predominant left posterior perisylvian or parietal atrophy on MRI or hypoperfusion/hypometabolism on SPECT/PET.

As we know, language impairments in progressive disease are heterogeneous and tend to develop in an insidious fashion. However, in all variants of PPA, we expect specific linguistic domains to be affected: loss of verbal fluency, anomia, or deficits in word/sentence repetition, in comprehension, and in reading (Leyton et al., 2011). Then, we expect other specific linguistic features to be present: phonetic and syntactic in the non-fluent/agrammatic variant (PPA-A), phonological and verbal working memory deficits in the logopenic variant (PPA-L) and semantic impairment in the semantic variant (PPA-S).

2.2 The non-fluent/agrammatic variant of primary progressive aphasia

The hallmark of the non-fluent/agrammatic variant of primary progressive aphasia (PPA-A) is dysfluent speech. Patients often complain of effortful speech. Their speech rate is low (Ash and Grossman, 2015). They may produce a greater number of false starts, filled pauses and repaired sequences (Wilson et al., 2010). The production of phonetic distortions and articulatory impairments can lead to apraxia of speech. Discriminant function analyses reveal that a measure of relative vowel duration differentiated non-fluent variant PPA cases from logopenic variant cases with 88% agreement, with expert judgment of the presence of apraxia of speech in non-fluent variant PPA cases (Ballard et al., 2014). This apraxia can become so severe that the patient becomes mute.

Concerning phonology, some patients also produce non-distorted phonological paraphasias. This presentation can be attributed to phonological impairment. Errors are characterized by substitutions, insertions, deletions, or transpositions (Bonner, Ash, and Grossman, 2010). Repetition of phrases and sentences will be impaired with similar speech sound errors.

Regarding to the lexical level and semantics, some patients, but not all, tend to produce fewer closed class words and/or fewer verbs than controls. However, according to Wilson et al. (Wilson et al., 2010), these lexical features cannot be considered diagnostic for the non-fluent variant. Single-word comprehension and object knowledge is on the whole relatively spared.

At the level of syntax, many patients produce utterances that are not complete sentences, omitting determiners or failing to produce appropriate subject-verb agreement (Bonner, Ash, and Grossman, 2010). Some produce syntactic errors. The ability to generate complex syntactic structures is reduced. So is the mean length of utterances and the number of embeddings. According to Wilson et al. (Wilson et al., 2010) the fact that some patients produce no syntactic errors and others only a few, shows that most patients with the non-fluent/agrammatic variant are not agrammatic in the same way of patients with Broca's aphasia are. These authors found that the patients they studied were less impaired than the typical non-fluent vascular patient, in terms of speech errors and syntactic structure. Patients also had difficulties in comprehending grammatical phrases, particularly complex ones (Gorno-Tempini et al., 2011).

Regarding pragmatics, patients' communication with PPA-A can be quite similar to those with Broca's aphasia, but with executive difficulties that patients with Broca's aphasia do not necessarily display.

When it comes to written language, an assessment of writing may reveal early grammatical errors (Gorno-Tempini et al., 2011). Phonological dysgraphia and/or dyslexia can be present. Patients demonstrate difficulties in writing, spelling and reading unfamiliar words aloud, due to deficits in the phonology-orthography conversion system (Brambati et al., 2009).

2.3 The logopenic variant of primary progressive aphasia

The hallmark of the logopenic variant of primary progressive aphasia (PPA-L) – logopenic meaning "lack of words" – is slowed speech and frequent word finding.

Speech rate is generally described as intermediate between the non-fluent and the semantic variant (Ash and Grossman, 2015). There are few or no distortions or misarticulations. Production is marked by a great number of false starts, filled pauses and repaired sequences. For this reason, these patients fall into the "fluent" category.

At the segmental level, phonological paraphasias may occur. The errors are typically full-blown phonemic errors (e.g., substitutions of different phonemes) probably reflecting a phonological impairment.

At the lexical and semantic levels, the production of more pronouns and somewhat more verbs than controls is observed (Wilson et al., 2010). Repetition of single words and digits is possible but that of sentences, word and letter span, as well as digit span all prove to be difficult due to a phonological loop or auditory short-term memory impairment (Gorno-Tempini et al., 2008). Single-word comprehension, preserved at the beginning of the disease, is increasingly impaired as the disease progresses.

Syntax is not characterized by agrammatism as such: most of the syntactic errors observed are paragrammatic rather than agrammatic. In addition to the verbal working memory deficits described by Gorno-Tempini (Gorno-Tempini et al., 2008), Wilson (Wilson et al., 2010) attributed the repaired sequences and constant rephrasing to a difficulty in resolving syntactic dependencies. Comprehension is not enhanced by syntactic simplification.

Concerning written language, phonological dysgraphia and/or dyslexia can be present, as in the non-fluent variant PPA (Macoir et al., 2014).

2.4 The semantic variant of primary progressive aphasia (PPA-S)

The semantic variant of primary progressive aphasia (PPA-S) is considered as a fluent variant of PPA and characterized by a progressive deterioration in the production and comprehension of language due to semantic impairment. Overall speech rate is nevertheless reduced; patients pause significantly more frequently than controls, and they pause more often in the environment of noun phrases than of verb phrases (Ash and Grossman, 2015). Reduction in the speech rate is not due to motor speech or syntactic factors, but to difficulties in higher-level discourse processes (Ash et al., 2006). Speech sound errors are rare; false starts, filled pauses or repaired sequences generally do not differ from controls.

At the phonological level, speech is relatively fluent and phonologically correct.

At the semantic and lexical levels, spontaneous speech is often empty or repetitive with the use of generic filler terms (e.g., a thing) or superordinate categories (e.g., animal for lion) (Ash and Grossman, 2015; Bayles, Tomoeda, and Trosset, 1990). Semantic difficulties appear in naming. Moreover, produced nouns tend to be of a higher frequency than in other PPA subgroups, a finding shared by several studies (Bird et al., 2000; Patterson and MacDonald, 2006). Difficulties also manifest in task such as verbal semantic category fluency. Relative to open class items, there is a greater proportion of closed class items. There is also a greater proportion of pronouns relative to nouns, and more verbs in comparison of nouns. Comprehension of single word is impaired due to loss of knowledge of objects (Ash and Grossman, 2015). Patients often question the meaning of common words. A word can be better recognized insofar as it is presented in a familiar or personally relevant context (Bozeat et al., 2002; Giovannetti et al., 2006). As the disease progresses patient's skills in topic maintenance and elaboration decline (Wong et al., 2009). Another point is the relative preservation of numerical and musical knowledge.

These observations can contribute to the debate regarding a semantic system based on modality-specific feature representations, over an amodal system supporting conceptual representations in all modalities (e.g., verbal, visual) (Bonner, Ash, and Grossman, 2010).

At the level of syntax, errors are not abundant. When they occur, they tend to be paragrammatic rather than agrammatic. The mean length of utterance tends to be reduced, but more embeddings are produced than by controls (Wilson et al., 2010). These authors attributed this finding to patients' anomia. Connected speech production is preserved if lexical content is set aside.

Concerning written language, surface dysgraphia or/and surface dyslexia can be present. Patients demonstrate difficulties in writing, spelling and reading aloud familiar words. Writing samples can display phonologically plausible errors due to deficits in the orthographic lexicon.

Most authors do not distinguish between PPA-S (Gorno-Tempini et al., 2004; Grossman, 2010) and semantic dementia, a term proposed by Snowden et al., whereas the semantic deficits are respectively restricted to the language modality (unimodal) or associated with other modalities, mainly visual agnosias/prosopagnosia (multimodal or amodal) (Snowden, Goulding, and Neary, 1989); (Moreaud et al., 2008). In this variant, visuospatial skills and day-to-day memory are relatively spared (Hodges and Patterson, 2007), and behavior and social symptoms such as loss of empathy and impaired emotion recognition commonly occur (Duval et al., 2012).

2.5 Limitations concerning PPA criteria

Starting from PPA consensus recommendation, some authors found a variable proportion of patients could not be classified into the three main variants (Harris et al., 2013). More recently, Mesulam and Weintraub (Mesulam and Weintraub, 2014) have suggested some modifications to the classification of Gorno-Tempini et al. (Gorno-Tempini et al., 2011). First, a core criterion for the logopenic variant should be the absence of a specific grammatical/syntactic impairment (affecting both production and comprehension). Secondly, patients who fit the clinical description of the logopenic variant, but do not present abnormal sentence and phrase repetition, may still be classifiable within this variant if the repetition impairment is a secondary, rather than a core criterion. The logopenic variant can therefore be subdivided according to the status of repetition of sentences and phrases. Finally, broader recognition of a fourth "mixed" variant would allow a decrease in the number of unclassifiable cases, for patients with a combination of agrammatism and semantic impairments (Mesulam and Weintraub, 2014).

2.6 Approach to the assessment of language in PPA

Until recently, the assessment of language in neurodegenerative diseases has been carried out using essentially the same approach as for focal vascular lesions. Certain linguistic domains tended to be under-investigated and assessment tools or normed data were lacking (Leyton et al., 2011). This hampered researchers in establishing differential hypotheses between syndromes, based on the presence of specific disorders, such as apraxia of speech, agrammatism, disorders of lexical comprehension, and disorders of sentence repetition, as described by Leyton (Leyton et al., 2011) and Gorno-Tempini (Gorno-Tempini et al., 2011).

A fine analysis of the hallmark features of PPA and more specific disorders, such as those affecting phonetic and syntactic processes, phonological and verbal working memory and semantics, is sometimes missing in patients' description of speech and language deficits. This analysis is essential, not only for classificatory purposes amongst progressive disorders, but also, to propose specific and appropriate therapy. The classification of PPA subtypes revolves around the core language domains of grammatical ability, word comprehension, object naming, repetition and motor aspect of speech. Ancillary features include syntactic comprehension, object knowledge, phonologic integrity of speech and phonological or surface dyslexia.

In practice, taking a case history allows also the clinician to screen patients' communication before entering a more formal assessment. Generally, the assessment of language begins with the evaluation of spontaneous speech, based on several minutes of informal conversation in order to assess language and communicative incentive, fluency, pausing, circumlocutions, phonological transformations, motor speech disorders, agrammatism, and the general semantic appropriateness of discourse.

Leyton et al., (2011) found that the distinction between the different variants of PPA could be made by considering four discriminant language variables: single-word comprehension, motor speech disorder, agrammatism, and impaired sentence repetition. They proposed a language scale, based on an algorithm which allowed them to correctly classified 96% of their patients. This raises questions regarding the need to include features such as anomia, word repetition, sentence comprehension, and reading in assessment, because these features are present in all variants of progressive aphasia and will not be discriminant to classify PPA into the different variants. Although the International Consensus Criteria include features revealed by non-verbal-based semantic tasks, such as object knowledge and spelling/reading tasks, all patients with the PPA-S were correctly classified applying the *Progressive Aphasia Language Scale*.

In order to differentiate PPA-A from PPA-L, sentences repetition is impaired in both variants but in the former, patients present with motor speech disorders, in the form of distortions and omissions, and frequent expressive agrammatism.

Patients with the logopenic variant commonly omit words and can only repeat the first two or three words. Both variants demonstrate preservation of single-word comprehension.

Patients with PPA-S show an homogeneous pattern compared to other variants. Speech articulation, sentence repetition, and grammatical language production are preserved whereas word comprehension is impaired.

Because the course of the disease varies, and the distinction between the three variants can lead to various treatment options, some authors (Savage et al., 2013) introduced another language battery to classify the PPA variants. This battery is part of a standard assessment of cognition and targets key distinctive features in four subtests, which are confrontational naming, repetition, word comprehension, and semantic association. It is hypothesized that each PPA variant demonstrates a distinct profile across these subtests.

In the non-fluent variant, patients had difficulties in speech related tasks, such as word repetition, but only half of them were impaired on the word comprehension task. Only a small proportion (10%) of patients was impaired in the semantic association subtest.

In the logopenic variant, patients displayed obvious difficulties in confrontation naming. As in non-fluent variant, patients were poor at word repetition. Performance on the word comprehension task was significantly lower than for controls. A quarter of the patients were impaired on the semantic association task.

In the semantic variant, severe impairments in confrontation naming was noted (through a word-picture matching task with imageable, living, and non-living nouns of three or more syllables, with decreasing frequencies). Repetition errors were not frequent. Patients were impaired on word comprehension and semantic association subtests.

Second line assessments help specify both the diagnosis and the therapeutic project (Croot et al., 2009). For instance, patient's word-finding abilities can be further assessed using a more detailed test of action naming or verb fluency. In a quantitative classification of PPA at early and mild stages, Mesulam (Mesulam et al., 2012) supplemented the WAB by more specialized tests and a systematic analysis of recorded narrative speech. A sample of narrative speech and a picture description is obtained in order to capture the fluency of connected speech. Verbal fluency is a complex construct consisting of features such as speech rate, phrase length, articulatory agility and syntactic structure. These features do not always decline in parallel (Wilson et al., 2010). A sentence construction task from given words, including verbs, will inform about the potential for syntactic elaboration. For instance, the Northwestern Anagram Test (NAT[1]); (Weintraub et al., 2009) is designed to test the grammaticality of sentence production, as is the Sentence Production Priming Test (SPPT) of the Northwestern Assessment of Verbs and Sentences (NAVS) (Cho-Reyes and Thompson, 2012). These tools have been developed and are used and validated as reliable measures for patients with PPA (Dickerson, 2011). As for written language, production is assessed using dictation of letters, words, sentences, and numbers, first spontaneously, then to dictation.

---

1 NAT: the patient is asked to order single words to be syntactically consistent with an action depicted in a target picture.

For a review of the most common assessment tools used in English, see Volkmer (Volkmer, 2013).

To complement formal testing, qualitative assessment of discourse, conversational and functional communication will also be valuable. Evaluation at the level of pragmatic abilities and communication effectiveness concerns the ability to transpose ideas into verbal or non-verbal communication. This extends from generation of novel ideas to automatic over-learned responses (Chapman and Ulatovska, 1997), and usage of the functions of communication, for instance, the instrumental function (e.g., I want...), or the personal function (e.g., I feel...) (Halliday, 1977).

Moreover, informal discourse assessment can reveal a specific activity that the patient reports as difficult and for which therapy will be particularly meaningful.

3 Therapeutic approaches, their adaptation to the different variants of PPA

Speech-language therapists are accustomed to re-adjusting treatments and their goals according to the patient's progression. Published evidence-based practices are not numerous in progressive diseases. However, in a special issue of Aphasiology "Progressive Language Impairments: Intervention and management, Croot (Croot et al., 2009) distinguished between two types of interventions, namely those which were primarily directed at remediating the patient's language impairments, as opposed to those that focus on improving capacity in a given real-life situation, such as in the home. These participation-directed interventions are, as emphasized by the authors, compatible with the World Health Organization revised dynamic classification system. Routhier et al. (Routhier, Gravel-Laflamme, and Macoir, 2013), presented the behavioral interventions and the augmentative/alternative communication tools reported in the literature to improve language performances or to compensate for language difficulties. The authors reviewed fourteen articles reporting the efficiency of at least one intervention. Beside the efficiency of these interventions, inconsistent results were found regarding maintenance of improvement and generalization to untreated language abilities.

4 Goals and anticipated outcomes

Impairment-directed therapies developed for non-progressive aphasias can be readily utilized in progressive language impairments. However, goal setting and treatment planning with patients presenting progressive communication and language impairments is a challenge since an absence of change does not necessarily indicate an absence of benefit.

Goals of therapy are guided by the social and functional usefulness of communicative activities that are affected by the impairment. It is important to work with a vocabulary which makes sense and is useful for the patient and in his (her) environment (Reilly, 2015). In the same way, to work with personal objects (or photographs of these) of a familiar environment will allow the concepts to be better maintained.

Language rehabilitation techniques share common principles with those of memory rehabilitation, based as they are on memory function facilitations, on the exploitation of preserved capacities and on the use of prosthetic tools. The facilitation of memory functioning uses the creation of a mental image. Repetition, graded cueing, spaced retrieval, and errorless learning contribute, among other factors, to mobilizing preserved/remaining capacities. The use of external reminders involves the adaptation of the environment, such as promoting the use of a communication chart or of a diary.

Principles relating to repetition and intensity of practice have been highlighted in a recent research report (Savage et al., 2013). In patients suffering from severe deficits, these authors found strong effect of treatment.

Graded cueing requires providing graded sequences of cues or vanishing cues to the patient in order to access information. For example, increasing or decreasing amounts of semantic and/or phonological information is given with phonemes, written letters, and words. A good example of a method with semantic self-cueing, and orthographic and phonemic self-cues, is the *Lexical Retrieval Cascade Treatment* developed at the University of Arizona (Henry et al., 2013).

Spaced retrieval involves systematic recall of information with increasing time intervals. The gaps are first close enough to ensure memorizing: 15 seconds, then 30 seconds, then one minute. Then intervals are proposed as a function of patient's performances. For an example of this method, see Bier et al. (Bier et al., 2009).

Errorless learning techniques are considered important for accurate learning in people with neurodegenerative diseases, as their ability to self-monitor and correct is often impaired. According to Bourgeois and Hickley (Davis, 2013), patients will probably show deficits in declarative memory. So, in order to prevent inaccurate learning, errors in new learning should be inhibited. For an example of this approach, see Jokel et al. (Jokel and Anderson, 2012; Jokel, Rochon, and Anderson, 2010).

Even if at the conclusion of the assessment, there is no proposal for therapy centered on the patient, a meeting with the caregivers gives the opportunity to discuss the best way of communicating with her/him.

Reports drawn from the evidence-based therapy literature will allow one to choose among the possible therapeutic approaches. Before beginning the therapy, establishing a base line is essential and after the various sessions, post-therapy measures should be taken.

It is also important to re-asses the progression of comprehension impairments and associated cognitive disorders to end a treatment if it is no longer benefitting the patient. The results of a longitudinal study in three cases of PPA-L, over a period of 18 months, showed how patients' resilience decreased with the progressing severity of their disease (Etcheverry et al., 2012).

Communication needs may change as the disease progresses. In her exhaustive work on the question of assessment and therapy in progressive diseases, Volkmer (Volkmer, 2013) tackled the complex question of discharge from therapy. She emphasized the emotional dimensions in patients' reactions to treatment, both positive and negative.

In the context of degenerative impairments, Volkmer's views converged with those of Duffy and McNeil (Duffy and McNeil, 2008) in considering that therapy and treatment options may no longer be reasonable; that is, communication goals may no longer be a priority and non-compliance may become an issue, with the deterioration of awareness.

5 Complexity of PPA and overlaps within and amongst neurodegenerative diseases

Since neurological signs and behavioral symptoms frequently appear during the course of PPA, such cases must be followed up over time from a multidisciplinary point of view and should have a frequent neurological and neuropsychiatric assessments. Corticobasal syndrome (ideomotor apraxia, parkinsonism, dystonia, alien hand and parietal sensory deficits) or supranuclear palsy syndrome (vertical gaze palsy, axial parkinsonism and gait difficulties with falls) or behavioral symptoms reaching diagnostic criteria for the behavioral variant of frontotemporal dementia may appear either sequentially, in any order of apparition (Kertesz et al., 2005) – and in that case, aphasia is not a primary progressive syndrome and one may prefer the term *progressive aphasia* – or in parallel. PPA, mainly PPA-A and or isolated apraxia of speech even represent isolated subtypes of autopsy-proved Corticobasal Degeneration, Supranuclear Palsy, or Frontotemporal Degeneration (Armstrong et al., 2013; Assal et al., 2012; Dickson et al., 2010; Josephs et al., 2006; Laganaro et al., 2012; Uyama et al., 2013). The comprehension of these overlaps is very important from a pathophysiological point of view of neurodegenerative diseases and disease prognosis but does not change the treatment approach of one single patient. In this section, we discuss other neurodegenerative diseases that present with language difficulties amongst other neuropsychological, neurological and neuropsychiatric symptoms including the classic form of AD and the FTD-ALS and PD-DLB spectra. We will just mention at this stage that the most common form of prion disease, Creutzfeldt-Jakob disease (CJD) may present with atypical isolated language presentation of long duration mimicking PPA-A and/or PPA-L (Kobylecki et al., 2012; Krasnianski et al., 2006; Martory et al., 2012). This is important to know for diagnostic purposes – since MRI including DWI sequences have to be performed – and for prognosis as well as appropriate information to both patient and caregivers.

5.1 Alzheimer's disease

AD neuropathology probably represents the most common pathology underlying PPA-L (Gorno-Tempini et al., 2011) but patients with the classic sporadic form of AD do obviously not fulfill PPA criteria and present with prominent episodic memory deficits. In a sample of 18 post mortem confirmed AD cases compared to 18 healthy controls, analysis of spoken language revealed that only one patient had a typical PPA-L profile, and most patients had reduction in syntactic complexity measures (Ahmed et al., 2012). In AD, language impairments are heterogeneous, both qualitatively and dynamically, occurring at disease onset or later during its course (Cummings et al., 1985; Goldblum et al., 1994). At an early stage, language difficulties are mild, associated to semantic impairment, and therefore AD is often difficult to distinguish from PPA-S (Libon et al., 2013; Rogers and Friedman, 2008). Semantic processing measured by semantic units of discourse samples is abnormal particularly for nouns and verbs in early stage of AD Ahmed (et al., 2013a). Word-retrieval anomia, literal and neologistic errors, reduction in phrase length, difficulties in sentence repetition, and impaired comprehension, mainly for written sentences are frequent (Mendez et al., 2003). Patient then typically show deficits at the level of oral production, semantic dissociations and both quantitative and qualitative discourse impoverishment (Ripich and Terrell, 1988). A decline in written production and in comprehension is usually observed later in the disease and the severity of language deficits globally parallels global cognitive impairment (Bschor, Kuhl, and Reischies, 2001). Even at the prodromal stage of AD, in a longitudinal cohort of 15 patients with autopsy confirmed patients, two thirds of them showed significant connected speech decrease using quantitative production analysis technique of the Cookie Theft Picture (Ahmed et al., 2013b). Word finding difficulties, decrease in pictorial themes and informative contents, increase in error-monitoring difficulties, more frequent pauses and hesitations or use of ohs and hums, longer formulaic phrases, self-referential tags augmentation and more regular checking on the certainty of the question commonly occur (Asp and Rockwood, 2006; Davis and Maclagan, 2009; Gayraud and Barkat-Defradas, 2011). Difficulties both at the microlinguistic level (lexico-semantic) and at macrolinguistic one (supra-sentential, thematic coherence) are found together with preserved speech outflow, speech articulation, and syntax and non-verbal communication (Glosser and Deser, 1991; Rousseaux, Vérigneaux, and Kozlowski, 2010; Venneri, Forbes-Mckay, and Shanks, 2005). Pragmatics, using a referential communication task (trial repetition in order to achieve common references), was altered in AD whereas patients benefited from the task repetition but were significantly worse integrating previous shared information and referential expressions, when compared to healthy controls, that did not parallel executive deficits (Feyereisen, Berrewaerts, and Hupet, 2007). Contemporary conversational gesture reduction suggested parallelism between speech and gesture degradation (Carlomagno et al., 2005).

5.2 Parkinson's disease and Dementia with Lewy Bodies spectrum

In Parkinson disease (PD), language impairment has been studied only recently although language complaints are not rare at an early stage (Bastiaanse and Leenders, 2009). The processing of long complex sentences is altered because of multiple breakdowns at the level of working memory, executive resources, sequencing, semantic priming and set switching abilities, verb generation, and metaphoric comprehension difficulties PD patients without dementia showed deficits of verbs and also of proper names generation (Fine et al., 2011; Péran et al., 2003). Corticostrial circuits might be involved since subthalamic nucleus stimulation significantly increased object and action naming (Silveri et al., 2012). In a very innovating study from the perspective of listeners of PD patients, who were naïve of the diagnosis, parkinsonian discourse was linguistically appropriate but patients less interested, less involved, less happy and less friendly than controls, probably explaining negative social impressions of parkinsonian patients (Jaywant and Pell, 2010).

In Dementia with Lewy Bodies (DLB) whereas patients share parkinsonian signs but have prominent cognitive and neuropsychiatric symptoms, aphasia or language impairment is not a core cognitive diagnostic criteria (McKeith, 2006). Nevertheless, when compared to AD matched for age and dementia severity, DLB patients have similar language profile consisting on diminished confrontation naming, letter and category fluencies, repetition, and oral and written comprehension (Noe et al., 2004). When compared to PD, DLB patients present with script comprehension difficulties (loss of accuracy in ordering judgment and significantly slower) and sentence processing difficulties correlating respectively to executive and working memory deficits (Ash, McMillan, et al., 2012; Gross et al., 2012). Narrative discourse is also disturbed in non-aphasic DLB patients (Ash, Xie, et al., 2012). Interestingly, cases of PPA followed by hallucinations, delusions and parkinsonism and partly meeting DLB diagnostic criteria have been described suggesting mixed AD-DLB pathology (Caselli et al., 2002; Teichmann et al., 2013).

5.3 Frontotemporal dementia and Amyotrophic Lateral Sclerosis Spectrum

The behavioral variant of fronto-temporal degeneration or bv-FTD, along with PPA-A and PPA-S differs neuropathologically from AD. Moreover, language impairment is usually faster than in AD and overlaps with PPA (mainly PPA-A, or PPA-S) suggesting a continuum (Blair et al., 2007). Speech output and conversational initiation is decreased as well as frequent occurrence of echolalia, word finding difficulties and semantic paraphasias, verbal stereotypia (such as ah, ah, ah), sentence comprehension deficits in relation with syntactic complexity and discourse difficulties (fewer accurate and more incomplete events, diminished global and local connectedness, difficulties in maintaining the theme of the story) and pragmatics (greeting, attention) (Ash et al., 2006; Pasquier et al., 1999; Rousseaux et al., 2010).

Motoneuron Disease, or Amyotrophic Lateral Sclerosis (ALS) can be isolated (amyotrophic lateral sclerosis, ALS) or accompanied by dementia and more specifically bv-FTD (FTD-ALS) consecutively to common neuropathological and genetic bases. At a very early stage of the disease, when standardized language tests are normal, subtle but quantitative differences in discourse content significantly occur in ALS patients compared to controls (Roberts-South et al., 2012), and, contrary to common knowledge, language deficits might be more frequent than executive ones in ALS patients, occurring respectively in 35–43% and 23–31% (Abrahams et al., 2014; Taylor et al., 2013). In the latter study, language deficits did parallel bulbar difficulties and both category fluency and semantic associations were not significantly different from normal controls.

6 Conclusion

Neurodegenerative diseases are heterogeneous conditions that disrupt neuroanatomical language networks at different levels and therefore overpassing classic aphasia syndrome also explaining why PPA variants differ from the classic Lichtheim Wernicke model of language. Although most language phenotypes are not specific and many clinical overlaps exist between different neuropathologic entities, recent advances in our understanding in language mechanisms at the cognitive/linguistic level greatly improved our detection of language deficits. Benefiting from the PPA model presented in this review and extended to other common neurodegenerative diseases, language is now increasingly recognized as a clinical marker of neurodegenerative diseases (see Table 3). Because of better understanding at the linguistic level and recent development of standardized batteries, rehabilitation techniques are now available mostly in patients with PPA. Structural and molecular neuroimaging as well as CSF markers pinpointing to neuromolecular pathology correlated with more quantified language analysis will probably allow to better understand language deficits in vivo in the future and improve rehabilitation techniques and communication with caregivers.

Table 3: Language as a clinical marker of disease. Main linguistic features in common neurodegenerative diseases (see text for abbreviations)

Disease/PPA variant	Linguistic features
PPA-A	Phonetic and syntactic difficulties
	Agrammatism
(Pure or predominant AOS)	Effortful speech
PPA-L	Phonological and verbal working memory deficits
PPA-S	Semantic deficits
Early AD	Lexico-semantic impairment
	Decreased connected-speech
FTD	Reduced speech – echolalia
	Changes in pragmatics
MND	Changes in discourse content
PD	Complex sentences processing difficulties, verb generation deficits, metaphoric comprehension difficulties
DLB	Same as in AD, sentence processing difficulties, slow output

Acknowledgments

Special thanks to Mary Overton, speech and language therapist, and Charlotte Edelsten, Ph.D., for help with translation and a careful reviewing of this chapter. Dr Assal is supported by the Swiss National Science Foundation (grant n°320030_138163).

References

Abrahams, Sharon, Judith Newton, Elaine Niven, Jennifer Foley & Thomas Bak. 2014. Screening for cognition and behaviour changes in ALS. *Amyotrophic Lateral Sclerosis and Frontotemporal Degeneration* 15(1–2). 9–14.

Ahmed, Samrah, Celeste A. de Jager, Anne-Marie F. Haigh & Peter Garrard. 2012. Logopenic aphasia in Alzheimer's disease: clinical variant or clinical feature? *Journal of Neuroogy,l Neurosurgery and Psychiatry* 83(11). 1056–1062.

Ahmed, Samrah, Celeste A. de Jager, Anne-Marie Haigh & Peter Garrard. 2013a. Semantic processing in connected speech at a uniformly early stage of autopsy-confirmed Alzheimer's disease. *Neuropsychology* 27(1). 79–85.

Ahmed, Samrah, Anne-Marie F. Haigh, Celeste A. de Jager & Peter Garrard. 2013b. Connected speech as a marker of disease progression in autopsy-proven Alzheimer's disease. *Brain* 136 (Pt 12). 3727–3737.

Armstrong, Melissa J., Irene Litvan, Anthony E. Lang, Thomas H. Bak, Kailash P. Bhatia, Barbara Borroni & William J. Weiner. 2013. Criteria for the diagnosis of corticobasal degeneration. *Neurology* 80(5). 496–503.

Ash, Sharon & Murray Grossman. 2015. Why study connected speech production? In Roel M. Willems (ed.), *Cognitive neuroscience of natural language use*, 29–58. Cambridge: Cambridge University Press.

Ash, Sharon, Corey McMillan, Rachel G. Gross, Philip Cook, Delani Gunawardena, Brianna Morgan & Murray Grossman. 2012. Impairments of speech fluency in Lewy body spectrum disorder. *Brain and Language* 120(3). 290–302.

Ash, Sharon, P. Moore, S. Antani, G. McCawley, M. Work & Murray Grossman. 2006. Trying to tell a tale: discourse impairments in progressive aphasia and frontotemporal dementia. *Neurology* 66(9). 1405–1413.

Ash, Sharon, Sharon X. Xie, Rachel Goldmann Gross, Michael Dreyfuss, Ashley Boller, Emily Camp & Murray Grossman. 2012. The organization and anatomy of narrative comprehension and expression in Lewy body spectrum disorders. *Neuropsychology* 26(3). 368–384.

Asp, Elissa, Xiaowei Song & Kenneth Rockwood. 2006. Self-referential tags in the discourse of people with Alzheimer's disease. *Brain and Language* 97(1). 41–52.

Assal, Frédéric, Marina Laganaro, Corinne D. Remund, & Claire Ragno Paquier. 2012. Progressive crossed-apraxia of speech as a first manifestation of a probable corticobasal degeneration. *Behavioral Neurology* 25(4). 285–289.

Ballard, Kirrie J., Sharon Savage, Cristian E. Leyton, Adam P. Vogel, Michael Hornberger & John R Hodges. 2014. Logopenic and nonfluent variants of primary progressive aphasia are differentiated by acoustic measures of speech production. *PLoS One* 9(2). e89864.

Bastiaanse, Roelien & Klaus L. Leenders. 2009. Language and Parkinson's disease. *Cortex* 45(8). 912–914.

Bayles, Kathryn A., Cheryl K. Tomoeda & Michael W. Trosset. 1990. Naming and categorical knowledge in Alzheimer's disease: the process of semantic memory deterioration. *Brain and Language* 39(4). 498–510.

Bier, Nathalie, Joël Macoir, Lise Gagnon, Martial Van der Linden, Stéphanie Louveaux & Johanne Desrosiers. 2009. Known, lost, and recovered: Efficacy of formal-semantic therapy and spaced retrieval method in a case of semantic dementia. *Aphasiology* 23(2). 210–235.

Bird, Helen, Ralph M.A. Lambon, Karalyn Patterson & John R. Hodges. 2000. The rise and fall of frequency and imageability: noun and verb production in semantic dementia. *Brain and Language* 73(1). 17–49.

Blair, Mervin, Cecile A. Marczinski, Nicole Davis-Faroque & Andrew Kertesz. 2007. A longitudinal study of language decline in Alzheimer's disease and frontotemporal dementia. *Journal of International Neuropsychology Society* 13(2). 237–245.

Bonner, Michael F, Sharon Ash & Murray Grossman. 2010. The new classification of primary progressive aphasia into semantic, logopenic, or nonfluent/agrammatic variants. *Current Neurology and Neuroscience Reports* 10(6). 484–490.

Bozeat, Sasha, Ralph M.A. Lambon, Karalyn Patterson & John R. Hodges. 2002. When objects lose their meaning: what happens to their use? *Cognitive, Affective & Behavioral Neuroscience* 2(3). 236–251.

Brambati, Simona M., Jennifer Ogar, John Neuhaus, Bruce L. Miller & Maria Luisa Gorno-Tempini. 2009. Reading disorders in primary progressive aphasia: a behavioral and neuroimaging study. *Neuropsychologia* 47(8–9). 1893–1900.

Bschor, T, K. P. Kuhl & F. M. Reischies. 2001. Spontaneous speech of patients with dementia of the Alzheimer type and mild cognitive impairment. *International Psychogeriatrics* 13(3). 289–298.

Carlomagno, Sergio, Anna Santoro, Antonella Menditti, Maria Pandolfi & Andrea Marini. 2005. Referential communication in Alzheimer's type dementia. *Cortex* 41(4). 520–534.

Caselli, Richard J., Thomas G. Beach, Lucia I. Sue, Donald J. Connor & Marwan N. Sabbagh. 2002. Progressive aphasia with Lewy bodies. *Dementia and Geriatric Cognitive Disorders* 14(2). 55–58.

Chapman, Sandra B. & Hanna Ulatovska. 1997. Discourse in dementia: Consideration of consciousness. In M. Stamenov (ed.), *Language structure, discourse and the access to consciousness*, 155–188. Philadelphia: John Benjamins.

Cho-Reyes, Soojin & Cynthia K. Thompson. 2012. Verb and sentence production and comprehension in aphasia: Northwestern Assessment of Verbs and Sentences (NAVS). *Aphasiology* 26(10). 1250–1277.

Croot, Karen, Lyndsey Nickels, Felicity Laurence & Margaret Manning. 2009. Impairment- and activity/participation-directed interventions in progressive language impairment: Clinical and theoretical issues. *Aphasiology* 23(2). 125–160.

Cummings, Jeffrey L., F. Benson, M. A. Hill & S. Read. 1985. Aphasia in dementia of the Alzheimer type. *Neurology* 35(3). 394–397.

Davis, Boyd. 2013. Dementia: from diagnosis to management – a functional approach, by Michelle S. Bourgeois and Ellen M. Hickey. *Activities, Adaptation & Aging* 37(3). 265–266.

Davis, Boyd, H. & Margaret Maclagan. 2009. Examining pauses in Alzheimer's discourse. *American Journal of Alzheimer's Disease & Other Dementias* 24(2). 141–154.

Dickerson, Bradford C. 2011. Quantitating severity and progression in primary progressive aphasia. *Journal of Molecular Neuroscience* 45(3). 618–628.

Dickson, Dennis W, Ahmed Zeshan, Avi A. Algom, Yoshio Tsuboi & Keith A. Josephs. 2010. Neuropathology of variants of progressive supranuclear palsy. *Current Opinions in Neurology* 23(4). 394–400.

Duffy, Joseph R. & Malcolm R. McNeil. 2008. Primary progressive aphasia. *Language intervention Strategies for Aphasia* (5th edn.). Baltimore: Williams & Wilkins.

Duval, Celine, Alexandre Bejanin, Pascale Piolino, Mickael Laisney, Vincent de La Sayette, Serge Belliard & Beatrice Desgranges. 2012. Theory of mind impairments in patients with semantic dementia. *Brain* 135(Pt 1). 228–241.

Etcheverry, Louise, Barbara Seidel, Marion Grande, Stephanie Schulte, Peter Pieperhoff, Martin Sudmeyer & Stefan Heim. 2012. The time course of neurolinguistic and neuropsychological symptoms in three cases of logopenic primary progressive aphasia. *Neuropsychologia* 50(7). 1708–1718.

Feyereisen, Pierre, Joelle Berrewaerts & Michel Hupet. 2007. Pragmatic skills in the early stages of Alzheimer's disease: an analysis by means of a referential communication task. *International Journal of Language Communication Disorders* 42(1). 1–17.

Fine, Eric M, Dean C. Delis, Brianna M. Paul & J. Vincent Filoteo. 2011. Reduced verbal fluency for proper names in nondemented patients with Parkinson's disease: a quantitative and qualitative analysis. *Journal of Clinical and Experimental Neuropsychology* 33(2). 226–233.

Gayraud, Frederique, Hye-Ran Lee & Melissa Barkat-Defradas. 2011. Syntactic and lexical context of pauses and hesitations in the discourse of Alzheimer patients and healthy elderly subjects. *Clinical Linguistics and Phonerics* 25(3). 198–209.

Giovannetti, Tania, Nicole Sestito, David J. Libon, Kara S. Schmidt, Jennifer L. Gallo, Matthew Gambino & Evangelia G. Chrysikou. 2006. The influence of personal familiarity on object naming, knowledge, and use in dementia. *Archives of Clinical Neuropsychology* 21(7). 607–614.

Glosser, G & T Deser. 1991. Patterns of discourse production among neurological patients with fluent language disorders. *Brain and Language* 40(1). 67–88.

Goldblum, Marie-Claire, Catherine Tzortzis, Jean-Luc Michot, Michel Panisset & François Boller. 1994. Language impairment and rate of cognitive decline in Alzheimer's disease. *Dementia* 5(6). 334–338.

Gorno-Tempini, Maria Luisa, Simona M. Brambati, Valeria Ginex, Jennifer Ogar, Nina F. Dronkers, Alessandra Marcone & Bruce L. Miller. 2008. The logopenic/phonological variant of primary progressive aphasia. *Neurology* 71(16). 1227–1234.

Gorno-Tempini, Maria Luisa, Nina F. Dronkers, Katherine P. Rankin, Jennifer M. Ogar, L. Phengrasamy, Howard J. Rosen & Bruce L Miller. 2004. Cognition and anatomy in three variants of primary progressive aphasia. *Annals of Neurology* 55(3). 335–346.

Gorno-Tempini, Maria Luisa, Argye E. Hillis, Sandra Weintraub, Andrew Kertesz, Mario Mendez, Stefano F Cappa & Murray Grossman. 2011. Classification of primary progressive aphasia and its variants. *Neurology* 76(11). 1006–1014.

Gross, Rachel G., Corey T. McMillan, Keerthi Chandrasekaran, Michael Dreyfuss, Sharon Ash, Brian Avants & Murray Grossman. 2012. Sentence processing in Lewy body spectrum disorder: the role of working memory. *Brain and Cognition* 78(2). 85–93.

Grossman, Murray. 2010. Primary progressive aphasia: clinicopathological correlations. *National Review of Neurology* 6(2). 88–97.

Halliday, Michael, A K. 1977. *Learning how to mean: Explorations in the development of language.* New York: Elsevier.

Harris, Jennifer M., Claire Gall, Jennifer C. Thompson, Anna M. Richardson, David Neary, Daniel du Plessis & Matthew Jones. 2013. Classification and pathology of primary progressive aphasia. *Neurology* 81(21). 1832–1839.

Henry, Maya L., Kindle Rising, Andrew T. DeMarco, Bruce L. Miller, Maria Luisa Gorno-Tempini & Pélagie M. Beeson. 2013. Examining the value of lexical retrieval treatment in primary progressive aphasia: two positive cases. *Brain and Language* 127(2). 145–156.

Hillis, Argye E., & Alfonso Caramazza. 1989. The graphemic buffer and attentional mechanisms. *Brain and Language* 36. 208–235.

Hodges, John R & Karalyn Patterson. 2007. Semantic dementia: a unique clinicopathological syndrome. *Lancet Neurology* 6(11). 1004–1014.

Jaywant, Abhishek & Marc D. Pell. 2010. Listener impressions of speakers with Parkinson's disease. *Journal of the International Neuropsychology Society* 16(1). 49–57.

Jokel, Regina & Nicole D. Anderson. 2012. Quest for the best: effects of errorless and active encoding on word re-learning in semantic dementia. *Neuropsychological Rehabilitation* 22(2). 187–214.

Jokel, Regina, Elizabeth Rochon & Nicole D. Anderson. 2010. Errorless learning of computer-generated words in a patient with semantic dementia. *Neuropsychological Rehabilitation* 20(1). 16–41.

Josephs, Keith A., Joseph R. Duffy, Edyth A. Strand, Jennifer L. Whitwell, Kenneth F. Layton, Joseph E. Parisi & Ronald C. Petersen. 2006. Clinicopathological and imaging correlates of progressive aphasia and apraxia of speech. *Brain* 129 (Pt 6). 1385–1398.

Kertesz, Andrew, Paul McMonagle, Mervin Blair, Wilda Davidson & David G. Munoz. 2005. The evolution and pathology of frontotemporal dementia. *Brain* 128 (Pt 9). 1996–2005.

Kobylecki, Christopher, Jennifer C. Thompson, Matthew Jones, Samantha J. Mills, Sandip Shaunak, James W. Ironside & Anna M Richardson. 2012. Sporadic Creutzfeldt-Jakob disease presenting as progressive nonfluent aphasia with speech apraxia. *Alzheimer Disease and Associated Disorders.*

Krasnianski, Anna, Bettina Meissner, Walter Schulz-Schaeffer, Kai Kallenberg, Mario Bartl, Uta Heinemann & Inga Zerr. 2006. Clinical features and diagnosis of the MM2 cortical subtype of sporadic Creutzfeldt-Jakob disease. *Archives of Neurology* 63(6). 876–880.

Laganaro, Marina, Michèle Croisier, Odile Bagou & Frederic Assal. 2012. Progressive apraxia of speech as a window into the study of speech planning processes. *Cortex* 48(8). 963–971.

Leyton, Cristian E., Victor L. Villemagne, Sharon Savage, Kerryn E. Pike, Kirrie J. Ballard, Olivier Piguet & John R. Hodges. 2011. Subtypes of progressive aphasia: application of the International Consensus Criteria and validation using beta-amyloid imaging. *Brain* 134 (Pt 10). 3030–3043.

Libon, David J, Katya Rascovsky, John Powers, David J. Irwin, Ashley Boller, Danielle Weinberg & Murray Grossman. 2013. Comparative semantic profiles in semantic dementia and Alzheimer's disease. *Brain* 136 (Pt 8). 2497–2509.

Macoir, Joel, Robert Laforce, Laura Monetta & Maximiliano Wilson. 2014. [Language deficits in major forms of dementia and primary progressive aphasias: an update according to new diagnostic criteria]. *Geriatrie et Psychologie Neuropsychiatrie du Vieillissement* 12(2). 199–208.

Martory, Marie-Dominique, Serge Roth, Karl-Olof Lövblad, Manuela Neumann, Johannes Alexander Lobrinus & Frédéric Assal. 2012. Creutzfeldt-Jakob disease revealed by a logopenic variant of primary progressive aphasia. *European Neurology* 67(6). 360–362.

McKeith, Ian G. 2006. Consensus guidelines for the clinical and pathologic diagnosis of dementia with Lewy bodies (DLB): report of the Consortium on DLB International Workshop. *Journal of Alzheimer's Disease* 9 (3 Suppl). 417–423.

Mendez, Mario F., David G. Clark, Jill S. Shapira & Jeffrey L. Cummings. 2003. Speech and language in progressive nonfluent aphasia compared with early Alzheimer's disease. *Neurology* 61(8). 1108–1113.

Mesulam, M.-Marsel. 2001. Primary progressive aphasia. *Annals of Neurology* 49(4). 425–432.

Mesulam, M.-Marsel & Sandra Weintraub. 2014. Is it time to revisit the classification guidelines for primary progressive aphasia? *Neurology* 82(13). 1108–1109.

Mesulam, M.-Marsel, Christina Wieneke, Cynthia Thompson, Emily Rogalski & Sandra Weintraub. 2012. Quantitative classification of primary progressive aphasia at early and mild impairment stages. *Brain* 135 (Pt 5). 1537–1553.

Moreaud, O., S. Belliard, J. Snowden, S. Auriacombe, S. Basaglia-Pappas, F. Bernard & M. E. Virat-Brassaud. 2008. Semantic dementia: reflexions of a French working group for diagnostic criteria and constitution of a patient cohort. *Revue Neurologique (Paris)*. 164(4). 343–353.

Noe, Enrique, Karen Marder, Karen L. Bell, Diane M. Jacobs, Jennifer J. Manly & Yaakov Stern. 2004. Comparison of dementia with Lewy bodies to Alzheimer's disease and Parkinson's disease with dementia. *Movement Disorders* 19(1). 60–67.

Pasquier, F., F. Lebert, I. Lavenu & B. Guillaume. 1999. The clinical picture of frontotemporal dementia: diagnosis and follow-up. *Demententia and Geriatric Cognitive Disorders*, 10 Suppl 1. 10–14.

Patterson, Karalyn & Maryellen C. MacDonald. 2006. Sweet nothings: narrative speech in semantic dementia. In S. Andrews (ed.), *From inkmarks to ideas: current issues in lexical processing*, 229–317. Hove: Psychology Press.

Péran, Patrice, Olivier Rascol, Jean-Francois Demonet, Pierre Celsis, Jean-Luc Nespoulous, Bruno Dubois & Dominique Cardebat. 2003. Deficit of verb generation in nondemented patients with Parkinson's disease. *Movement Disorders* 18(2). 150–156.

Reilly, Jamie. 2015. How to constrain and maintain a lexicon for the treatment of progressive semantic naming deficits: Principles of item selection for formal semantic therapy. *Neuropsychological Rehabilitation*. 1–31.

Ripich, D. N. & B. Y. Terrell. 1988. Patterns of discourse cohesion and coherence in Alzheimer's disease. *Journal of Speech and Hearing Disorders* 53(1). 8–15.

Roberts-South, Angela, Kate Findlater, Michael J Strong & J. B. Orange. 2012. Longitudinal changes in discourse production in amyotrophic lateral sclerosis. *Seminars in Speech and Language* 33(1). 79–94.

Rogers, Sean L. & Rhonda B. Friedman. 2008. The underlying mechanisms of semantic memory loss in Alzheimer's disease and semantic dementia. *Neuropsychologia* 46(1). 12–21.

Rousseaux, Marc, Amandine Seve, Marion Vallet, Florence Pasquier & Marie Anne Mackowiak-Cordoliani. 2010. An analysis of communication in conversation in patients with dementia. *Neuropsychologia* 48(13). 3884–3890.

Rousseaux, Marc, Clarisse Vérigneaux & Odile Kozlowski. 2010. An analysis of communication in conversation after severe traumatic brain injury. *European Journal of Neurology* 17(7). 922–929.

Routhier, Sonia, Karine Gravel-Laflamme & Joel Macoir. 2013. [Non-pharmacological therapies for language deficits in the agrammatic and logopenic variants of primary progressive aphasia: a literature review]. *Geriatrie et Psychologie Neuropsychiatrie du Vieillissement* 11(1). 87–97.

Sajjadi, Seyed Ahmad, Karalyn E. Patterson, Robert J. Arnold, P. C. Watson & Peter J Nestor. 2012. Primary progressive aphasia: a tale of two syndromes and the rest. *Neurology* 78 (21). 1670–1677.

Savage, Sharon A., Kirrie J. Ballard, Olivier Piguet, & John R. Hodges. 2013. Bringing words back to mind – Improving word production in semantic dementia. *Cortex* 49(7). 1823–1832.

Savage, Sharon, Sharpley Hsieh, Felicity Leslie, David Foxe, Olivier Piguet & John R. Hodges. 2013. Distinguishing subtypes in primary progressive aphasia: application of the Sydney language battery. *Demententia and Geriatric Cognitive Disorders* 35(3–4). 208–218.

Silveri, Maria Caterina, Nicoletta Ciccarelli, Eleonora Baldonero, Carla Piano, Massimiliano Zinno, Francesco Soleti & Antonio Daniele. 2012. Effects of stimulation of the subthalamic nucleus on naming and reading nouns and verbs in Parkinson's disease. *Neuropsychologia* 50(8). 1980–1989.

Snowden, Julie S., P. J. Goulding & David Neary. 1989. Semantic dementia: a form of circumscribed cerebral atrophy. *Behavioural Neurology* 2. 167–182.

Taylor, Lorna J., Richard G. Brown, Stella Tsermentseli, Ammar Al-Chalabi, Christopher E. Shaw, Catherine M. Ellis & Laura H. Goldstein. 2013. Is language impairment more common than executive dysfunction in amyotrophic lateral sclerosis? *Journal of Neurology, Neurosurgery and Psychiatry* 84(5). 494–498.

Teichmann, Marc, Raffaella Migliaccio, Aurelie Kas & Bruno Dubois. 2013. Logopenic progressive aphasia beyond Alzheimer's–an evolution towards dementia with Lewy bodies. *Journal of Neurology, Neurosurgery and Psychiatry* 84(1). 113–114.

Uyama, Naoto, Fusako Yokochi, Mitsuaki Bandoh & Toshio Mizutani. 2013. Primary progressive apraxia of speech (AOS) in a patient with Pick's disease with Pick bodies: a neuropsychological and anatomical study and review of literatures. *Neurocase* 19(1). 14–21.

Venneri, Annalena, Katrina E. Forbes-Mckay & Michael F. Shanks. 2005. Impoverishment of spontaneous language and the prediction of Alzheimer's disease. *Brain* 128 (Pt 4). E27.

Volkmer, Anna. 2013. *Assessment and therapy for language and cognitive communication difficulties in dementia and other progressive diseases*. Croydon: J&R Press.

Weintraub, Sandra, M.-Marsel Mesulam, Christina Wieneke, Alfred Rademaker, Emily J Rogalski & Cynthia K. Thompson. 2009. The northwestern anagram test: measuring sentence production in primary progressive aphasia. *American Journal of Alzheimer's Disease and Other Dementias* 24(5). 408–416.

Wilson, Stephen M., Maya L. Henry, Max Besbris, Jennifer M Ogar, Nina F. Dronkers, William Jarrold & Maria Luisa Gorno-Tempini. 2010. Connected speech production in three variants of primary progressive aphasia. *Brain* 133. 2069–2088.

Wong, Stéphanie, Raksha Anand, Sandra B Chapman, Audette Rackley & Jennifer Zientz. 2009. When nouns and verbs degrade: Facillitating communication in semantic dementia. *Aphasiology* 23(2). 286–301.

Index

Introductory Note

References such as '128–9' indicate (not necessarily continuous) discussion of a topic across a range of pages. Wherever possible in the case of topics with many references, these have either been divided into sub-topics or only the most significant discussions of the topic are listed. Because the entire work is about 'communication disorders', the use of this term (and certain others which occur constantly throughout the book) as an entry point has been restricted. Information will be found under the corresponding detailed topics.

AABR (automated auditory brainstem responses) 766
ability 34–6, 91–3, 124–6, 139–40, 405–8, 555–6, 569–72, 624–5, 675–6, 815–17
- academic 383, 429
- communicative 270, 848
- early 260–1
- emerging 124, 555
- limited 816, 848
- linguistic 11, 123, 204, 312–13, 548, 617, 622–3, 625, 771, 857
- mind 260, 266, 271, 273
- narrative 357–9, 368, 371, 373, 381, 383, 711, 812
- pragmatic 237, 710, 907
- reading 205, 408, 412, 505, 516, 853
- syntactic 622, 632, 744
- verbal 517
abjads 444, 447
abnormalities 27, 289, 705, 714, 829, 837, 887–8, 893
ABR (auditory brainstem responses) 26–7, 575, 766
Abrahamsson, N. 678–9
abstract concepts 140, 142
abstract identities 723, 731–2
abstract letters 723, 732–3
abstract words 108, 742, 851
abstraction 139, 848, 887
academic achievement 7, 9, 137–9, 141–2, 146, 358, 415, 547, 573, 576
academic performance 247, 567, 801
academic success 119, 415, 431, 628, 799
ACC, *see* anterior cingulate cortex
access to semantics 167, 743–4

accessibility 480, 483, 485, 510, 513, 846–7, 849, 852, 855, 857–8
- language 14, 845, 850, 854, 857–8
- linguistic 850, 857
accessible information 845, 850, 857–8
accessible print 850, 852–3
accuracy 32–3, 127, 161–2, 164, 225–6, 571–2, 631, 634, 737, 774–5
- phonemic 774–5
- reading 224, 659, 742
accusative 206–7, 622, 698
achievement, academic 7, 9, 137–9, 141–2, 146, 358, 415, 547, 573, 576
acoustic hearing aids 765–6, 768, 770, 780, 785
acoustic information 23, 26, 47
acoustic properties 50, 52
acoustic signals 19, 34, 45, 49, 55, 477, 765
acoustic stimulation 766, 769, 781
acoustic stimuli 19, 22, 29
acoustic-phonetic information 53, 55–6
acquired aphasia, language impairments in 881–95
acquired deep dyslexia 721, 743
acquired dyslexia 722, 733, 741
acquired neglect dyslexia 733
acquired neglexia 734
acquisition
- agglutinative language 203–14, 531
- derivational morphology 8, 221, 225, 227
- figurative language, *see* figurative language, acquisition/development
- lexical 93, 107, 110, 272
- literacy 5, 330, 416, 439
- morpho-lexical 219–29

- reading 10, 441, 452, 461, 463, 466, 509, 512, 734, 743
- second language 667–81
- spelling 461–72
- vocabulary 93, 594, 627–9, 675, 834
action naming 894, 906, 911
action sequences 369, 852
action structure 329, 336, 340, 343, 346
actional-eventive perspective 335–6
activation 25–6, 155–7, 160–1, 164, 493–4, 740, 865, 868–70, 872–3, 889
- cascading 160–1
- neuronal 571–2, 574, 576
active involvement 396, 795–6, 798, 802–3
active participation 392, 399, 401, 793
activity context 283, 285
Adam, G. 66–8, 146, 438, 477, 556, 630
Adamson, L.B. 280, 282, 286, 813, 816–17
adaptation 102, 572, 623, 628, 691, 847, 854, 907–8
adjectives 219, 221–2, 240–1, 270, 670, 674, 852, 854, 856, 894
adolescence 117, 119, 137, 139–42, 145–6, 148, 245, 706, 710, 713–15
- late 197, 226, 706, 716
adolescents 117, 119–22, 137, 139–43, 145–9, 235, 237, 248–51, 712, 834–5
adoptees, international 104, 108, 111, 603, 609
adult input 301–2
adult languages 75, 92, 155, 207, 238, 851
adult model 376, 705, 713
adult readers 451, 512, 515
adult speakers 121, 155, 164, 189
adult thresholds 44–5, 47
adult-child conversations 251, 330, 332
adult-child interaction 8, 297, 592
adulthood 52, 117, 119, 130, 141, 219, 250, 578
- early 104, 119, 571, 574, 864
adults 43–8, 118–23, 125–8, 196–8, 296–8, 318–20, 388–93, 399–400, 423–5, 705–8
- older 863–74, 882
- young 119, 467, 834, 836, 865–74
- younger 864, 866–9, 872–3, 882
adverbial clauses 236, 241–2, 244–5, 251, 372
adverbs 222, 228, 340–1, 365, 378–9, 382, 670, 674, 848
- temporal 143, 340
adverse neonatal conditions 8, 203–14

affixes 220, 222, 227–8, 492, 495, 497–9, 725, 727, 734, 742
- morphological 725, 735–6, 742
- neutral 220, 222
- non-neutral 220, 222, 228
affordances 187–8
affricates 72, 774
African Americans 334, 345, 370, 551, 589, 697
Afrikaans 699
age 103–9, 118–22, 238–45, 337–40, 590–4, 651–4, 677–81, 705–13, 766–80, 813–15
- chronological, see chronological age
- differences 51, 128, 338, 678, 831, 838
- effects 54, 104, 125–6, 428, 779
- gestational 50, 98, 205, 207–10, 213
- mental 106, 294, 504, 830
- of onset (AoO) 620, 623, 627, 633
- ranges 13, 110, 205, 223, 371, 705, 713
- school 2, 5, 10, 222, 245, 248, 251–2, 705, 709, 714
- young 50, 250, 424, 570, 620, 766
age-matched peers 626, 775
agentive suffixes 221–2, 226, 229
agents 222, 431, 622, 628, 816, 891
- mental 345–6
age-of-acquisition 163
age-related changes 45, 863–4, 869, 873–4
age-related differences 244, 872
age-related impairments 866–7
age-related patterns 51, 872
agglutinative languages 203–14, 531
aging, healthy 863–74
AGL, see Artificial Grammar Learning
agrammatic aphasia 886
agrammatic speech 886, 894
agrammatism 884, 886–7, 892–4, 900, 903–5
agreement, markers 206
air flow 75–6
air pressure 21, 24
Akhtar, N. 260, 263–4, 282, 295, 297, 317, 554–5
aksharas 444, 448, 453
Albanian 649–50, 652
Albert, L. 346, 870, 874
Alberta Language and Development Questionnaire 623
Alberta Language Environment Questionnaire 623
Alexander, R. 126, 382, 388–9

algorithms 769, 905
alliterations 419–20
Allusional Pretense Theory of verbal irony 130–1
alphabetic knowledge 416, 418, 420, 423
alphabetic skills 10, 415, 417, 422, 424, 428–9
alphabetical scripts 449, 461, 463, 512
alphabets 195, 407, 409, 411, 438, 440–1, 444, 446–8, 452
alternations 74, 206–7, 313–14, 536, 692, 694
Alzheimer's disease 145, 881–3, 899, 910
ambient language 4, 11, 27–9, 49–52, 68, 78, 82, 252, 778
ambiguity 140, 287–8, 342, 405, 446–7, 450, 881
− linguistic 139–40
− referential 269–70
− syntactic 870
ambiguous words 516–17
American children 120, 298
American mothers 298, 334
American Sign Language 681, 706
amplitude 21–2, 92, 872–3
Amyotrophic Lateral Sclerosis 899, 911–12
anchor tense 336, 340
Andringa, S. 678, 680
Angeleri, R. 119, 126
Anglin, J.M. 103–4, 219–22, 225, 227
animal models 183, 574
anomia 167, 170, 884–5, 901, 904–5, 910
anomic aphasia 884–5
anterior cingulate cortex (ACC) 571, 574, 578
Antonenko, D. 871–2
anxiety 400, 574, 668, 830, 856
AoO, see age of onset
Apel, K. 224, 226–7
aphasia 160, 162, 164–5, 168, 170–1, 689, 881–9, 891–4, 909, 911
− acquired, see acquired aphasia
− agrammatic 886
− anomic 884–5
− biology of 882
− Broca's 707, 713, 715, 886, 893, 902
− global 881, 885
− primary progressive, see PPA
− progressive 14, 905, 909
− stroke-linked 882–3
− treatment 887, 891, 894
− Wernicke's 886–7
aphasic comprehension 888, 891–3

aphasic language 14, 887, 894–5
aphasiology 886, 907
− clinical 885–6
Appelbaum, M. 713
appropriateness 330, 530, 857, 905
apraxia 901, 909
− ideomotor 909
− of speech 167, 900–1, 905
Arab sector 796–7, 804
argument structure 690, 698–9, 892, 894
Arial 851–2
Arnbak, E. 446, 471
Arnold, J.E. 330, 344
articles
− definite 270, 316–17, 626
− indefinite 313, 626
articulation 22, 30, 36, 51, 74, 76, 91–3, 156, 159, 192
− place of 36, 51, 54, 74, 76
Artificial Grammar Learning (AGL) 753–5, 758–61
artificial languages 676, 755, 835
ASD, see autism spectrum disorder
Asperger syndrome 820
assertions 130–1, 345, 819
assessment 143, 145–9, 362, 606–11, 622–4, 628–9, 646, 797, 904–5, 908–9
− tools 156, 595, 619, 628, 632, 696–7, 904
Astington, J.W. 125–6, 268, 330, 345–6, 812
attention 32–4, 197–8, 262–3, 282–3, 285–6, 290, 299–300, 314–16, 571–3, 674–7
− deficits 729, 731, 847
− selective 34, 570–2
− visual 813
attentional dyslexia 723, 730–2, 735, 744–6
attitude 125, 130, 267–8, 667, 669
attrition 606, 608–10
atypical development 75, 77–8, 81–2, 101, 103, 105, 205, 279, 288–9, 301–2
atypical populations 80, 104–5, 288, 302
atypically developing children 66, 71, 78, 705
auditory brainstem responses, see ABR
auditory cortex 19, 25, 197, 778
auditory information 3, 573, 753, 785, 815
auditory neuropathy spectrum disorder (ANSD) 27
auditory perception 19, 22, 27–30, 34, 47, 97
auditory processing 19, 33, 97
auditory stimuli 26, 29, 44, 760–1

auditory system 36, 46, 48, 51
Australia 102, 590, 652, 846
autism 27, 96, 117, 285, 289–90, 292–3, 299–301, 812, 836–7, 847
autism spectrum disorder (ASD) 107, 126, 131, 272, 288, 602, 811–23, 837
– high-functioning 126
automated auditory brainstem responses (AABR) 766
automatic processes 486, 493–4, 498, 755
automaticity 444, 509, 757–8
automaticity deficit hypothesis 754, 758
automatization 130, 440, 449, 754, 757
– incomplete 754
autopsies 883, 909–10
auxiliaries 106, 318–19, 481, 619, 674, 692–3, 857
– verb 884, 887, 892
awareness 221–2, 395, 401, 406, 427, 431, 471, 479, 672, 675
– morphological 8, 221, 223–7, 466–7, 471–2, 477–9, 528, 531, 657
– orthographic 415, 419, 424–5
– phonemic 466, 477
– phonological 415–16, 418–20, 422, 424–6, 428–30, 462–3, 471–2, 567, 657, 799
– print 415, 418–20, 422–6, 428–31
– of spelling 411

Babayiğit, S. 528, 531, 534
babbling 27–30, 71, 97, 569, 708, 773–4, 784
– canonical, *see* canonical babbling
– onsets 29, 773, 784
background noises 27, 34, 47
backgrounds
– cultural 147, 593, 601, 801
– linguistic 146, 586
– social 586, 589, 595
backward readers 504
– general 504–5, 518
Baddeley, A.D. 104, 107, 439, 630, 675–6
Baird, J.A. 108, 330, 345–6, 630
Bakeman, R. 280, 282, 286, 813, 816
Baker, A.E. 147, 300, 320, 342, 517, 554, 643
balance 32–3, 374, 531
Baldwin, D. 260, 262–3, 272, 286, 293, 554
Bamberg, M. 330, 332, 335, 337, 339, 341, 343, 345, 347
Baron-Cohen, S. 272, 280, 282, 285, 289, 294

barriers 280–3, 286, 537, 845, 847, 849
Barsky, V. 205
base forms, percentage of 209, 211–14
baselines 77, 291, 347, 360, 362, 365–6, 369, 371–2, 379
basic learning mechanisms 36, 183
Basque, M. 478
Bastiaanse, R. 892, 894, 911
Bates, E. 94–6, 102, 283–4, 708, 710, 736, 813
Bedore, L.M. 110–11, 618, 630
Beers, S.F. 532–4, 536, 736–7, 783
beginning readers 451, 507, 510, 514, 517
beginning signers 681
behavioral measures 570, 576
behavioral performance 572, 574, 757, 867, 871, 874
behavioral symptoms 143, 909
Behney, J. 674–5
Belgium 766–8
belief questions 124, 128
belief states 344, 346
beliefs 122, 124–7, 129, 265, 267–8, 273, 409, 551, 794–5, 816–17
– false 123, 260–1, 273, 346
– first-order 128, 131
Belletti, A. 619
Bellugi, U. 321, 618, 830, 834
Bengali 650, 656
Bennett, I.J. 755–6, 864
Berber 650, 656
Berger, A. 571, 573–4
Berko, J. 221–3, 229, 528
Bernstein, B. 586, 589
Beron, K. 546–7
Bertram, R. 54, 495–6
between-word errors 732
between-word migrations 730, 732, 735
BFLA (bilingual first language acquisition) 602, 604–11
bias 10, 103, 122, 297, 529, 570, 697, 895
– initial left hemisphere 713, 716
– noun 101, 103, 108
– trochaic 65, 67–8
bidirectional influence 620, 622
bi-directional social mechanisms 817
bidirectional transfer 618
bigram frequencies 464
bilateral implantation 767, 779–80
bilaterality 715–16

bilingual children 12, 109–11, 601, 606–8, 617, 619–35, 643–6, 648, 651, 653
– English 625, 628, 630–1, 633
– with SLI 617, 620, 631, 635
– Spanish-English 651, 653–5, 657, 661
– vocabulary 110, 627
– young 601, 606, 611
bilingual development 617, 619–21, 623, 625, 627, 629, 631, 633, 635
bilingual first language acquisition, *see* BFLA
bilingual learners 12, 643–4, 648, 651–4, 658–61
bilingual lexicon 626, 629
bilingual norms 621
Bilingual Parents' Questionnaire, *see* BIPAQ
bilingual populations 628, 646–7, 660–1
bilingual preschool children 607–8
bilingual situation/settings 606, 619, 621, 623, 626
bilingual typical language development, *see* biTLD
bilingualism 3, 12, 111, 605, 617, 619, 630, 632, 634–5, 667
– early child 601–11
– and SLI 617, 619, 630, 634
bimodal implantation 781
bi-morphemic words 220, 497
biology 441, 453
– of aphasia 882
BIPAQ (Bilingual Parents' Questionnaire) 623–4
BIPAQ scores 624
birth 50, 56, 92, 97, 197, 602–3, 605, 607, 609, 765–6
birth weights 98, 203, 207–11, 213
biSLI, *see* bilingual children, with SLI
biTLD (bilingual typical language development) 617–19, 626, 628–9, 631, 633–5
Blamey, P. 774
blind children 106, 819
blind decomposition 487–8
blindness 106, 111
– feature 694–5
Bliss, L.S. 346, 618, 711
blogs 209, 670
Boada, R. 508
Boder, E. 721–2
Boers, F. 147, 675
Bollt, E.M. 760
bonding 445, 811–13

bookreading 375, 380, 550
bookreading interventions 418, 422
books, children's 375–6, 379–80, 382, 430
bootstrapping
– logical 95
– syntactic 96, 698
Bornstein, M. 103, 554, 603, 606, 628
Bottleneck Hypothesis 671–2
bound stems 220, 222, 228, 482–3, 487, 494
Bowerman, M. 235, 238, 817
Bowers, E.P. 111, 221, 226–7, 746
boys 67, 241–2, 244–5, 247–9, 312, 314, 689–90, 692, 694, 783
Bradley, R.H. 483, 509, 548–50, 565–6, 578, 760
brain 25–6, 197, 437, 442, 571–5, 706–7, 714–15, 864–5, 870–2, 882
– activity 571, 831, 868
– damage 268, 689, 721–2
– development 139, 197, 203, 706, 815, 829, 834
– function 14, 574, 576, 863, 867
– imaging techniques 144, 863
– networks 757, 832, 871
– plasticity 566, 712
– regions 145, 573, 575–6, 864, 867
– structures 566, 575, 705, 714, 885
brainstem 766–7, 829
breakdown 36, 164, 171–2, 250, 334, 888–90, 911
Brinton, B. 138, 145–6
Bristol 554, 586
Broca, P. 705–6, 883, 885, 887
Broca's aphasia 707, 713, 715, 886, 893, 902
Broca's area 568, 754, 868, 871, 882–4
Brock, J. 831–4
Brooks, R. 280–1, 555
Bruck, M. 468
Bruner, J.S. 284, 329–30
Brunsdon, R. 732
Bryant, P. 224, 407, 449, 465, 471, 478, 509, 517, 760
Brysbaert, M. 467, 489
buffer 35, 166, 724–5, 734
– episodic 34
– phonological input 737
building blocks 28, 79, 91, 415, 440, 444, 453, 493, 725, 831
Burgoyne, K. 656, 659

bursts 374, 527, 773–4
bus story 361, 370
Bush, G. 571, 574

CA (conversation analysis) 388, 390, 392, 399, 782
Cacciari, C. 123, 147
Cain, K. 123, 138, 440, 513, 517–18
Calderon, R. 799–802
Calkins, S. 819
Callanan, M.A. 263, 297, 317
Camarata, S.M. 96–7, 318, 320
Canada 128, 284, 652–3, 655, 658, 846
– French-speaking 109
canonical babbling 569–70, 708, 774, 814, 820, 833
– onset 773, 778, 833
Cantonese 102, 649–50, 655–6, 700
capacity
– emerging 92, 285, 301
– general 13, 754, 761
– infant hearing 6, 43
– sensory 32, 37
– social-emotional 548
Capirci, O. 284, 835
Caramazza, A. 160–3, 165, 170, 172, 220, 483, 886–7, 891, 899
caregiver-child dyads 296, 298, 301
caregivers 102–3, 205, 285, 296–8, 313, 318–23, 552, 557–8, 804, 908
– primary 206, 812–13
– speech 551, 553–5
caretakers, see caregivers
Carlisle, J. 221–5, 227, 465–6, 656
Carpenter, M. 143, 260, 264–5, 282–4, 297–9, 531, 892
cascading of activation 160–1
case markers 206–7, 670
Castles, A. 223, 446, 509–11, 736, 743, 746, 754
CAT (comprehensive aphasia test) 156
categorization 51–3, 187–8, 609, 778, 821
– tasks 760, 834
category fluencies 903, 911–12
causal conjunctions 340, 371, 383
causal links 107, 272, 345
causal relationships 361, 508–9, 838
causality 346, 357, 365, 379
CBE (consolidation-based enhancement) 756–7

CBM (curriculum-based measures) 529
CBS (consolidation-based stabilization) 756
CC, see clause-combining
CD, see communication disorders
CDI (Communicative Developmental Inventory) 102, 108, 110, 590, 622, 625, 628, 708
ceiling 80, 120, 138, 634
– accuracy 774
– effect 221
CELF-3, see Clinical Evaluation of Language Fundamentals III
center-embedded relative clauses 241, 514
cerebellum 754, 758
cerebral cortex 25, 575, 864
cerebral palsy 29, 379
chaining 244
– causal 245
– linear 243
– para-tactic 249
channels 34, 55, 295, 769
– nonverbal 296
– sensory 817
Chapman, R.S. 106, 251, 907
character intentionality 336–7
characters 267, 269, 335–7, 341–3, 346, 371–2, 374–5, 381–2, 420–1, 447–9
– Chinese 439–40, 448–51, 453
Chiat, S. 168, 631–4, 819
child language 66, 74, 624
child-directed speech 102, 108, 323, 550, 552–3, 557–8, 623
– exposure to 552, 557–8
– quantity and quality 553
child-external factors 104, 111
childhood 30, 101, 111, 117, 137, 139, 146, 568, 574–5, 714–15
– late 261, 338
child-internal factors 104
child-parent interactions 286, 302
children, young 102–3, 417–18, 422–5, 428–31, 601–3, 605–7, 804, 811, 815–19, 821
children's books 375–6, 379–80, 382, 430
China 447, 449, 451, 453, 568
Chinese 65, 440, 443–5, 447, 449, 621, 623, 650, 656–7, 678–9
– characters 439–40, 448–51, 453
Chomsky, N. 3, 68, 428, 437, 450, 691, 707
Chondrogianni, V. 620, 627

chronological age 55, 105–6, 470–2, 504, 692–3, 771–3, 776, 819, 834, 865
chronological age-matched children 469, 471–2
chunking 245, 340–1, 440, 444, 448, 531, 894
cingulate cortex 577
– anterior 571, 574, 578
– inferior 577
cingulo-frontal-parietal (CFP) cognitive network 571
circumlocutions 621, 629, 890, 905
CIs, *see* cochlear implants
CJD (Creutzfeldt-Jakob disease) 909
Clahsen, H. 618, 673, 692, 695, 835
classification 13, 569, 733, 745, 885, 894, 899, 904–5
classmates 34, 246, 425
classroom activities 141, 375–6, 380
classroom contexts 677–8
classroom discourse 10, 389, 399
classroom interactions 390, 392
classroom teachers 141, 375, 420
classrooms 142, 361, 367, 369–72, 375, 378, 380, 672, 678, 794–5
– experimental 378
– inclusive 387–401
clause boundaries 240, 242
clause length 525, 532, 534
clause types 235, 237, 250, 338
clause-combining (CC) 235, 237–42, 244, 247–51, 253, 537, 829
– complex syntax 248, 250–3
clause-linkage 235
clauses 235–52, 329–30, 338, 340, 365, 367, 526–7, 532–4, 537, 626
– action 856
– complement 236–7, 241–3, 249, 340–1, 345
– coordinate 236–7, 243, 246, 249, 251, 632
– dependent 238, 243, 251, 532
– embedded 848, 870–1
– independent 251, 338
– isolated 240, 245, 252
– main 235–7
– matrix 241
– non-finite 236–7, 243, 246, 249
– simple 526, 632
– single 239, 532
– subordinate 246, 250–2, 338–9, 345, 379, 533, 690, 711

CLDD (Complex Learning Difficulties and Disabilities) 847
Cleave, P. 320, 470, 602, 694
CLI (contextualized language interventions) 364, 374–9
clinical aphasiology 885–6
clinical diagnoses 847, 881, 883, 900–1
Clinical Evaluation of Language Fundamentals III (CELF-3) 633–4
clinical markers 13–14, 618, 690, 694, 696–7, 700, 822, 912–13
clinical populations 117, 143, 149, 272, 830
clinical practice 137, 139, 141, 143, 145, 147, 149, 601–11, 690, 695
clinical syndromes 274, 899
clinical tools 26, 161, 624
clinical trials 359, 624
clinician-child interactions 374–5
clinicians 19, 21, 143–4, 367, 370, 374, 377, 379, 587, 821
clinician-scientists 883, 885
clitic pronouns 313, 618, 634
closed class words 94–5, 108, 902–3
closed eyes 280–2
clouds 106, 406–7, 727
clues 259, 262, 396–7, 445, 465, 855
clusters 407, 410, 468, 494, 496, 631, 695
– consonant 50, 167, 462–3, 468, 477
– of letters 407, 410
CMV (cytomegalovirus) 782
coaching 422, 427–31
Cobo-Lewis, A.B. 109, 627
cochlea 24–6, 35, 47, 53, 575, 765–6, 768
cochlear implants (CIs) 13, 26–7, 30, 35–6, 43, 53–5, 106, 765–85, 795, 805
– hybrid 766, 781
co-constructions 8, 238, 240
codaless productions 79–80
codas 63–5, 69–72, 81, 334, 337, 371
– complex 64, 69–71
– final 80–1
– medial 80–1
– position 63, 77
code interference 621, 625
co-enrollment 799
cognates 110–11, 358, 627, 629, 654–5, 661
cognition 1–2, 5, 20, 23, 33, 37, 573–5, 801, 830–1, 836
– general 14, 830, 837

- irony 126, 132
- and language 565–79, 820, 836
- social 20, 23, 124, 147, 341
- spatial 578
cognitive abilities 26, 32, 55, 94, 104, 126, 147, 504, 507, 565–7
- advanced 108
- general 33, 36, 517
- nonverbal 782
cognitive control 578, 866–7, 869–70
cognitive deficits 11, 503–4, 519, 830, 899
cognitive development 12, 24, 26, 91, 97, 142, 145, 567, 576, 578
cognitive difficulties 370, 783, 848
cognitive disabilities 14, 503, 845–58
cognitive functions 139, 570, 574, 847, 867
cognitive impairments 111, 167, 830, 883, 910
cognitive models 164, 382, 722, 746
cognitive neuropsychological approach 164, 173, 887
cognitive performance 566, 829, 874
cognitive processes 2, 11, 121, 144, 503–4, 506, 513, 519, 864, 874
cognitive psychology 117, 894
cognitive representations 329, 534
cognitive resources 507, 515, 864, 866, 874
cognitive science 117, 182, 186, 439–40, 452
cognitive skills 11, 37, 93, 109, 111, 119, 123, 125, 260, 272
cognitive stimulation 549–51, 566
cognitive system 156, 575, 881
cognitive tasks 571–3, 675–6, 864–5
cognitive theories 170, 723
cognitive-psychological approach 506
coherence 142, 330, 344, 535, 836, 857
- global 11, 527, 836
- relations 506, 515
coherent mental representation 506, 514, 516
cohesion 249, 330, 339, 365, 531, 711
cohesive devices 339–40
coincidence detection 755
Colé, P. 223–4, 471, 483
college students 104, 534
college-educated mothers 550
Collins, E.E. 601, 650–2, 654
collocational knowledge 679
color 193, 199, 266, 368, 445, 571, 821, 853
colored cue cards 361, 368–9, 373
combinatorial language 832, 835

combinatorial structure 440, 449
combinatoriality 445–6, 452–3
communication deficits 19–20, 27
communication difficulties 387, 392, 395, 400, 585, 899
communication disorders (CD) 1–7, 9, 11–14, 20–1, 37
communication skills 284, 566, 795, 799
communicative adequacy 9, 329–30, 332, 341, 344
communicative competence 7, 137, 548
communicative contexts 1, 4, 8, 253, 279, 286, 296, 301, 440, 535
communicative cues 280, 282, 286, 290, 292–4, 299, 302
communicative development 9, 24, 259, 261, 272, 274, 279, 285, 548, 551
Communicative Developmental Inventory, see CDI
communicative functions 142, 819, 893–4
communicative intentions 125, 259, 265–8, 272–4, 294, 311, 313, 405, 407, 816–17
communicative interactions 374, 545, 548–9, 551, 802
communicative partners 94, 271, 281–2, 286, 289–91, 295–7, 299, 301–2, 551, 895
communicative situations 259, 288, 290, 295
communicative units, see C-units
communities 140, 295, 298, 437–8, 586, 593, 845, 849, 855, 858
- Caucasian 551
- cultural 295, 298, 302
- Mayan 285
- working-class 551
comparability 587, 629
comparison
- direct 132, 376–7, 713, 783
- groups 140, 143, 649, 655–6, 680
Compensation-Related Utilization of Neural Circuits Hypothesis (CRUNCH), see CRUNCH (Compensation-Related Utilization of Neural Circuits Hypothesis)
competence 33, 341, 347, 406, 409, 411, 525, 670, 673, 802
- communicative 7, 137, 548
- grammatical 11, 525–6, 528, 530–1, 537
- linguistic 9, 556, 831
- native-like 678, 680
- social 405, 797–8, 801

competencies 132, 286, 405, 408, 411, 423, 812
complement clauses 236-7, 241-3, 249, 340-1, 345
complex codas 64, 69-71
complex constructions 8, 242, 531
complex language 400, 589, 708, 784-5
Complex Learning Difficulties and Disabilities (CLDD) 847
complex linguistic structures 830, 848
complex onsets 64, 69-72, 80-2
complex sentences 251-2, 357-8, 514-15, 547, 845, 848, 851, 871-2, 911, 913
complex structures 632, 634, 679, 884, 892
complex syntactic structures 249, 329, 340, 553, 589, 744, 870, 902
complex syntax 8, 143, 346, 552, 568, 620, 710-11, 713, 835, 871
– development 235-53
– use 251, 712
complex words 465, 467, 477, 492, 494, 496, 498, 724-5, 740, 742-4
complexity 332-3, 339, 526, 528, 532-4, 536, 644, 646, 759-60, 848-9
– cumulative 70, 74
– grammatical 95, 251, 531-5, 537, 550
– levels 210, 533, 760, 852
compliments 125, 127, 129-30, 267-8, 273
– ironic 126-31, 268
– literal 124-5, 129, 268
component processes 505-6, 518-19
component skills 347, 505-6, 514, 517-18
compositionality 225, 529
compounds 449, 451, 472, 483, 494-5
comprehension 23, 121-5, 131-2, 142-5, 166-7, 645-7, 660-1, 737, 744, 903-4
– abilities 318, 383, 870, 886
– aphasic 888, 891-3
– deficits 609, 888
– good 706, 872
– idiom 121-3, 141-2
– impaired 744, 900, 910
– impairments 706, 893, 908
– irony 124-7, 130-1
– language 147, 203, 546-7, 590, 608, 780, 785, 811, 817, 823
– lexical 106, 821, 888, 905
– listening 138, 416, 422, 507, 657-9
– narrative 377, 383
– predicting 648, 661
– process 144, 517
– and production 252, 629, 771, 837, 886, 890
– reading, see reading, comprehension
– sentence 14, 422, 515, 744, 867, 870, 872-3, 891, 893, 905
– single-word 902-3, 905
– skills 97, 120, 507, 513-14, 606
– spoken language 556, 771
– text 421, 511, 516-17, 643
– verbal irony 124, 127, 130
– vocabulary and reading 643-4, 646-7, 660
comprehensive aphasia test (CAT) 156
computer screens 291, 293
concatenation 479, 487, 492, 856
conceptual representations 156, 726, 904
conceptualization 144, 188, 410, 528, 646, 726, 816
conceptual-semantic system 725-6, 737, 742-3
conditionals 240, 244, 634, 830, 852
conductive impairments 25
conflict 111, 197, 247, 671
congenital hearing loss 26, 56, 765, 782
congenitally deaf children 765-85
conjunctions 5, 236, 240, 339-40, 375-6, 382, 490, 690, 805, 836
– causal 340, 371, 383
– connective 236
connected speech 783, 884, 904, 906, 910
connectionist models 511, 755
connective conjunctions 236
connectives 341
– non-temporal 248
– overt 236, 240
– required 238, 240
connectivity 235, 244, 249, 340, 527, 533, 865, 867, 871, 874
– functional 865-6, 871-2, 874
Conscious Compensation Hypothesis 754
consecutive consonants 477, 490
consistency 461, 463, 480, 489, 813, 852
consolidation 756-8, 813, 821
consolidation-based enhancement (CBE) 756-7
consolidation-based stabilization (CBS) 756
consonant clusters 50, 167, 462-3, 468, 477
consonant harmony 76-9
consonantal stems 489-90, 495-7
consonants 54, 63-4, 70, 72-4, 76-80, 468, 471, 489-91, 630, 725-7

- consecutive 477, 490
- random 490–1
consonant-vowel, see CV
constituent morphemes 479, 482, 487, 496
constraints 6, 64–5, 70, 82, 188, 323, 330, 347, 671–2, 681
- ONSET 65, 69
constructions 4, 123–4, 239, 241, 244, 248–9, 252, 337, 365, 448
- complex 8, 242, 531
- conditional 536
- grammatical 7, 359, 528, 532–3, 535–7
- narrative 240, 343
- particle 122
- passive sentence 697
- subordinating 252, 340
containers 269, 283
content words 95–6, 552, 890–1
contexts 31–3, 77–8, 122–3, 170, 187–92, 329–32, 342–3, 645–6, 710–11, 863–4
- activity 283, 285
- communicative 1, 4, 8, 253, 279, 286, 296, 301, 440, 535
- conversational 286, 716, 836
- educational 389, 529
- familiar 586, 603
- interactive 240, 374, 554
- linguistic 11, 35, 206, 553, 819
- obligatory 207, 693
- semantic 514–15, 872
- sentence 466, 516, 726, 743
- supportive 131, 238
- syntactic 338, 446, 498
contextual cues 140, 147, 266
contextual evidence 19, 32–3, 37
contextual information 35, 123, 126, 144, 468, 516, 873, 888
contextual knowledge 125, 265
contextual support 121, 123, 447
contextualized approaches 366, 373–4, 379–80
contextualized intervention 366, 375, 380
contextualized language interventions, see CLI
contextualized narrative interventions 373, 378, 380, 383
contingent responses 318–19, 321–3
continuity 7, 375–6, 415
Conti-Ramsden, G. 107, 139, 141, 143, 145–6, 319–20, 622, 632, 707–8

contrast enhancement 75–6
control, cognitive 578, 866–7, 869–70
control classroom 377–9
control condition 283, 377
control groups 97, 171, 367–8, 370–1, 373, 419–22, 424–8, 470, 472, 799
- no-treatment 367, 378, 381
- visuo-motor skills 428
control words 465, 470, 488
conventionality 121–2, 198
conventions 197–8, 319, 408, 415, 535, 601, 822, 846–7, 855
conversation, learning from 311–23
conversation analysis, see CA
conversational contexts 286, 716, 836
conversational exchanges 9, 311–12, 314, 318, 321, 323
conversational partners 271, 295, 312–13
conversational skills 9, 271, 273–4, 311–13, 317, 322, 812
- basic 315
- learning 311–23
conversations 145–7, 238, 246, 311–23, 331, 416, 418–19, 548, 554, 625
- adult-child 251, 330, 332
- face-to-face 313, 608
- informal 390, 905
- natural 834, 837
conversion
- grapheme-to-phoneme 509, 511, 726, 736–41, 744, 746
- letter-to-phoneme 740
- phoneme-to-grapheme 468
- sound-to-spelling 461
Conway, M.C. 33, 36, 205, 676
co-occurrence 50, 183, 185, 196, 250, 489, 753, 833
cooperation 237, 856
coordinate clauses 236–7, 246, 251, 632
coordination 237, 240, 242–3, 245, 249, 252, 346, 357, 533
- complex 10, 357
- and subordination 237, 249
Coppieters, R. 678
copulas 206, 319–20, 674
core deficits 758, 812, 816
core skills 294, 301
Corkum, V 281, 291–2
coronals 74–7

corpora 4–5, 118, 189, 195, 206, 449
correction, grammatical 318, 392–3
corrections 318, 392–4, 401, 669
corrective reformulations 320
corrective responses 319–20
corrective turn 393–4
correlational relationships 509, 643, 800
correspondence 28
– grapheme-phoneme 446
– many-to-one 78
– orthography-meaning 449
– strong 125
– target-child output 72
Corson, D. 219–21, 226
cortex
– auditory 19, 25, 197, 778
– frontal, see frontal cortex
– parietal 574, 578, 754, 870
– prefrontal 145, 197, 566, 571, 573–4, 576–8, 754, 864, 869
– visual 753
cortical areas 25, 29, 197, 571
cortical regions 571, 864–5
cortical thickness 573
corticobasal syndrome 909
Corwyn, R.F. 548–50, 565–6, 578
count nouns 168–70
countability 168, 170
covariation 131, 190, 263
CP (clause packages) 235, 237, 244–7, 250–1, 532–3, 694
Crago, M. 2, 607, 618–19, 651, 696, 700
creative activities 418, 420
Creusere, M. 130
Creutzfeldt-Jakob disease (CJD) 909
criterion-referenced tests 696, 700
criticisms
– ironic 124–31, 267–8, 273
– literal 129, 267–8
Croatian 775
Croft, W. 4–5, 72
crosscultural work 9, 102, 279, 298
cross-linguistic differences 118, 729
cross-linguistic relationships 649, 655, 657
cross-linguistic studies 7, 11, 102, 117, 206, 213, 335, 342, 658, 661
cross-modal priming 484, 491–3, 496
cross-sectional studies 512, 594, 646–7
Crowhurst, M. 534–5

CRUNCH (Compensation-Related Utilization of Neural Circuits Hypothesis) 867–8, 870–1, 873
Crutchley, A. 122
cue cards, colored 361, 368–9, 373
cued-attention tasks 291–2
cues 183–6, 191, 193, 197–8, 262–3, 265, 287, 290–4, 888, 891
– appropriate 189, 192
– communicative 280, 282, 286, 290, 292–4, 299, 302
– contextual 140, 147, 266
– generic 190
– informative 184, 190–1, 295
– morphological 96, 207, 477
– rhythmic 50, 92
– socio-pragmatic 285–6, 295, 301
cultural backgrounds 147, 593, 601, 801
cultural communities 295, 298, 302
cultural differences 102, 124, 128, 130, 333, 593
cultures 102, 295, 297–8, 302, 437, 441, 586, 592, 801, 806
– European 295, 438
– independent 298
– interdependent 298
cumulative complexity 70, 74
C-units 338, 370
curriculum-based measures (CBM) 529
CV (consonant-vowel) 28, 63–4, 69–70, 631, 741
Cypriot Greek 629
cytomegalovirus (CMV) 782

Dale, P.S. 94, 96, 99, 298, 552, 556, 590, 628
Daneman, M. 36, 515
Danish 447, 463, 624
Dasinger, L. 242, 248, 252
dative 206, 699
Davidi, O. 167, 252, 533
Davies, P. & K. 188, 288, 342, 359, 361, 368–9, 373, 445
Davis, C. 104, 288, 437, 485–6, 488, 493, 499, 864–5, 908, 910
Davison, M. 606, 650–1, 656
Dawson, G. 35, 289–91, 321, 811, 815
DD, see developmental dyslexia
de Saussure, F. 437, 443
de Villiers, J. 2, 260, 345, 553, 691, 697

deaf children 13, 20, 33
- congenitally 765–85
deaf parents 804
Deák, G.O. 198
deceleration 108, 653–4, 658
decipherability 446, 450–2
deciphering 446–7, 449, 817
Deckner, D.F. 813, 816
declarative gestures 282, 289, 300
declarative memory 882, 908
- long-term 753
declarative pointing 284–5, 294
decoding 182, 227, 408, 416, 426, 507, 514, 645–6, 881, 888
- orthographical 510–11, 513
- successful 471, 886
decomposability 121
decomposable idioms 122–3
decomposition 187, 222, 225, 489, 886
- blind 487–8
- process 219–20, 489–91
- morphological 482, 484, 491, 498
decontextualized language interventions, see DLI
decontextualized narrative interventions 366, 374
decontextualized skills 376, 380
dedifferentiation 865, 868, 871, 873–4
deep dyslexia 721–2, 742–3, 745–6
deficient processes 505, 508, 514
deficits 504–11, 707–8, 727–8, 732–3, 735–6, 738–41, 743–4, 746–7, 755, 759–61
- attention 729, 731, 847
- cognitive 11, 503–4, 519, 830, 899
- communication 19–20, 27
- core 758, 812, 816
- general 34, 708, 758
- implicit learning 759, 761
- language 14, 24, 618, 715, 900, 905, 910, 912
- patterns 11, 272, 518, 713, 715, 888, 900
- phonological 470, 508–11, 736, 738, 753–4
- in phonological recoding 507–8, 513
- selective 723, 727, 735, 741, 746
- semantic 513, 743, 890, 904, 913
- syntactic 671, 743, 886
- visual 732, 746
definite articles 270, 316–17, 626
degeneration 882–3, 911

degenerative dementias 883
degenerative impairments 909
deictic gestures 292, 294, 299, 301, 816
deictic pronouns 618
DeKeyser, R. 672, 678–80
delayed onsets 104, 111, 765
delays, language 30, 97, 110, 148, 203, 369, 556, 558, 587, 590–1
deletion 65–6, 71, 73–4, 204, 238, 568, 829, 901
dementia 847, 899, 911–12
- degenerative 883
- fronto-temporal 899, 909, 911–13
- with Lewy bodies 899, 911, 913
- semantic 904
- severity 911
Demir, O.E. 711
demonstrations 126, 264, 266, 484, 491–2, 496, 733, 886
dense orthographic neighbourhoods 734, 741
density 247, 301, 864
- clausal 338
- differences 573
- measures 533
- neural 866, 870
- phonological neighbourhood 168
- structural 247
- stylistic 852
- syntagmatic 533
dependencies 8, 229, 246, 252–3, 696, 888, 892
dependent clauses 238, 243, 251, 532
depression 551, 574, 802
deprivation, social 585–6, 589–91, 593, 595
derivational morphology 8, 219–23, 226–7, 229, 339
- acquisition 8, 221, 225, 227
derivational processes 195, 228, 494
derivational suffixes 222, 478
derivations 464, 477–8, 483–4, 486, 488–9, 492–5, 497–9, 854
- masked 487, 489
- opaque 488, 491–3, 499
- prefixed 483, 494
- transparent 487, 491–3, 495, 499
derived forms 226, 465–7, 470–1
derived verbs 219, 478, 494
derived words 103–4, 219, 223, 225, 464, 467, 471–2, 482–6, 497–9

Dérouesné, J. 722
descriptive sequences 336, 340, 369
DesJardin, J.L. 794, 797–8, 801–2, 804–6
detection 22–3, 26, 43–6, 330, 745, 755, 768, 856, 912
– early 766–7, 777, 793, 798
determiners 157, 169–70, 342–3, 618, 690, 694–5, 902
developing phonology 63–82
developmental delays 37, 284, 291–3, 300–1, 814
developmental disabilities 832, 848–9, 881
developmental disorders 2, 566, 689, 698, 707, 722, 814
developmental dyslexia (DD) 13, 467–8, 503–4, 721–47, 753–61
developmental milestones 336, 624, 835
developmental neglexia 733–4
developmental neuroscience 12, 567
developmental paths 8, 69, 237, 245, 250, 252, 681
developmental phonological dyslexia 721, 739–40
developmental psychology 143, 148, 186
developmental studies 222, 466, 534, 565, 567, 660
developmental trajectories 224, 245, 249, 343, 347, 708–9, 712, 771, 831–2, 836–8
developmental trends 227, 332, 345, 712
devices 53, 279, 315, 531, 536, 766, 768–9, 771–3, 779–81, 785
– cohesive 339–40
– depersonalization 536
– experience 54, 769–70, 779
– length of use 772, 774–6, 779
– nonverbal 9, 279–80
– use 54, 772, 779, 785
diacritics 451–2
– lexical-syntactic 160
diagnosis 1–3, 11, 13, 20–1, 412–13, 695, 697, 798, 822–3, 899–900
– of dyslexia 508, 518
– of language impairment 138, 709
Diagnostic and Statistical Manual of Mental Disorders 504, 811
diagnostic criteria 2, 138, 167, 504, 900–1, 909, 911
diagnostic tools 506, 617, 621, 628, 632–3
dialect 28, 52, 148, 441, 446, 586, 697

dialogic discourse 387, 400
dialogic teaching 10, 388–9
dialogues 35, 228, 296, 371–2, 399–400
dictation 426–7, 429, 439, 480, 906
Diessel, H. 235–6, 238–9, 241–2, 252
digits 441, 675, 833, 902
direct comparisons 132, 376–7, 713, 783
disabilities 412–13, 767, 776, 783, 795, 804, 846–8, 850, 853, 855–7
– cognitive 14, 503, 845–58
– developmental 832, 848–9, 881
– equal rights for people with 846–7, 853
– intellectual 845–58
– learning 2, 146, 167, 412, 630, 837
– literate 405–13
– reading 359, 468, 503, 507
disadvantaged neighborhoods 566, 572
discourse 9–10, 250–2, 312–13, 316–17, 342, 344, 388–9, 417, 535–6, 705
– content 912–13
– development 567, 569, 709
– extended 8, 314, 317, 323
– function 332, 339–42, 535
– genres 237, 248, 251–2, 534–7, 710
– structures 4, 340, 534
– units of 245, 533
discrimination 22, 26, 36, 43, 47, 51, 186, 282, 289, 555
– learning 182, 184, 186, 193–6
– skills 53, 92
discriminative learning 185–6, 188, 198–9
discriminative models 185, 195, 199
disempowerment 437, 442
disorders 2–3, 5–6, 8, 19–20, 117, 590–1, 690–1, 814, 838, 905
– in aging 14
– language 2, 5, 357–83, 585, 587, 589, 591, 593, 595, 900
– mental 504, 811
– neurodevelopmental 812, 829, 831, 838
– neurological 12–13, 379
– primary 19–20, 27, 37
dispersion principle 71
dissociations 196, 268, 470, 483, 496, 535, 694, 698, 887, 890
– double 510, 730
distortions 30, 900, 902, 905
distractions 587, 676, 853
distractors 123, 284, 293–4, 297

distributed representations 155, 511
disyllabic words 65-7, 80
diversity 5, 381, 383, 417, 438, 442, 452, 553, 628, 632
- lexical 338-9, 367, 376, 382, 550, 592, 710-11
DLB, see dementia, with Lewy bodies
DLI (decontextualized language interventions) 72, 364, 374-6, 378, 528
DLPFC (dorsolateral prefrontal cortex) 571, 573-4
domain-general attention 50, 676, 874
Donlan, C. 251, 330, 338-9, 345-6
dorsolateral prefrontal cortex, see DLPFC
double dissociation 510, 730
doubled letters 728, 731
Down syndrome (DS) 104, 106-7, 111, 145, 288, 290, 816, 830, 832-3, 835
Droop, M. 645, 650, 656, 659-60
DS, see Down syndrome
du Gard, R.M. 689
dual patterning 440, 452
dual-route models of visual word recognition 461-2, 506, 511-12, 723-4, 742
Dubé, R.V. 331, 344
Duchan, J.F. 819
Duchesne, L. 772
Duffy, J.R. 909
Dunham, P.J. 128, 131, 315, 555
Dutch, verb forms 479-81
dyadic interactions 13, 280, 291-2, 295-7, 557, 815
dyads, caregiver-child 296, 298, 301
dyseidetic dyslexia 721-2
dyslexia 97-9, 467-9, 471-2, 503-5, 721-3, 727, 729-30, 732, 734-6, 739-47
- attentional 723, 730-2, 735, 744-6
- deep 721-2, 742-3, 745-6
- developmental 13, 467-8, 503-4, 721-47, 753-61
- dyseidetic 721-2
- dysphonetic 721-2
- graphemic buffer 735-6
- letter identity 732-3, 735
- letter position 723, 727-32, 735, 741, 744-6
- phonological, see phonological dyslexia
- phonological buffer 740-1, 744-5
- surface 510, 722, 736-9, 741, 744-6, 900, 905

- visual 721-2, 735-6, 745
- vowel letter 741, 745
dyslexic readers 11, 504-5, 508-11, 516, 760
dyslexics 468-9, 504, 506, 731
- English-speaking 469
dysphasia, see aphasia

ear infections 24, 575
early adulthood 104, 119, 571, 574, 864
early bilingual development 12, 601-2, 607
early child bilingualism 601-11
early childhood 102, 204, 285, 416, 429, 569, 576, 604, 706
early detection 766-7, 777, 793, 798
early educational settings 423, 430
early expressive lexicon 94-6, 98-9
early grammar 63, 98, 694
early intervention 30, 53, 585, 766, 793-806
- programs 795, 797-8, 801, 803-5
early language 209, 555, 576, 590, 709
- development 12, 98, 228, 545, 709
- socioeconomic differences 545-58
Early Language in Victoria Study (ELVS) 590
Early Left Anterior Negativity (ELAN) 873
early lexical development 6-7, 91, 93-4, 96, 98, 101-2, 108
- predictive value 96-8
early lexicon 7, 91-9, 318
early literacy 415-31, 569, 798
- skills 415, 418, 421, 424, 427, 430
early second language acquisition, see ESLA
early speech perception 43, 92, 555
early speech processing 555
Early to Late Shift in Aging (ELSA) 867, 873
early vocabulary 96, 101, 103, 645, 833
- development 93, 98, 546
ears 19, 21, 24, 766, 779-80
easy-to-read 849-50, 854-5
echolalia 818-19, 912-13
ecological validity 5, 132, 697
economic investment 429-30
educated mothers 214, 550
education
- maternal 103, 285, 546, 575, 588-90, 594, 623
- parental 566, 569, 573, 575, 577, 588, 784, 803-4
- secondary 466, 644
educational settings 423, 585-6, 593, 795

educators 425, 439, 444, 503, 518, 526, 594, 604
effect sizes 377–8, 577
effective communication 9, 279, 294, 531
effectiveness 47, 140, 320, 358, 367, 394, 426, 430, 797, 799–802
efficacy 366–7, 374–5, 380, 416, 811, 899
effortlessness 10, 437, 440, 444, 705
Eilers, R.E. 29, 47, 52, 109, 773, 820
Eklund, K.M. 97
elaboration 8, 319, 334, 534–5, 711, 892–3, 903, 906
elaborative mothers 333
ELAN (Early Left Anterior Negativity) 873
Elbro, C. 138, 440, 446–7, 472
electrical stimulation 765, 769
electrodes 765, 769, 781
electrophysiological measures 44, 766
electrophysiological responses 44–5, 872
elementary school 138, 527, 547, 655, 709, 713, 715–16, 800
elicitation 4, 245, 250, 331, 344, 347, 377, 625–6
ellipsis 249, 340, 342, 690
ELSA (Early to Late Shift in Aging) 867, 873
ELVS (Early Language in Victoria Study) 590
embedded clauses 848, 870–1
embodiment 117, 132
emergent literacy 333, 417, 569
emerging capacities 92, 285, 301
Emmen, R.A.G. 654
Emmerzael, K. 623
Emmorey, K. 680–1
emotional engagement 794, 814
emotional states 32, 316, 802–3, 805
emotional understanding 271, 800
emotions 32, 129, 137, 141, 148, 271, 283, 566, 573, 578
empathy 126, 830, 904
encoding 102, 118, 181–2, 330, 426, 440, 723, 727–9, 815, 882
– letter position 723–4, 728–9, 746
– process 425–7, 431
– skills 425
encouragement 393–4, 422, 426
endurance 124
engagement 3, 296, 299–300, 417, 794, 812, 869, 871
– emotional 794, 814

– mutual 289, 291, 813
– social 9, 279
Engle, R.W. 548–9, 676
English bilingual children 625, 628, 630–1, 633
English children 463, 627, 631, 633
English orthography 438, 450, 452, 462, 464, 469
English receptive vocabulary 651–4, 657
English speakers 119, 192, 621, 652, 667, 677, 713, 822, 835
English vocabulary 657–8
– development 654
– growth rates 653
– knowledge 651, 657
English-speaking children 94–5, 120, 222, 238, 251, 694, 774
English-speaking dyslexics 469
environment 20, 93–4, 183–4, 186, 188–9, 198, 566–8, 574–5, 667, 908
– communicative 20, 286, 295
– home 205, 567, 623, 667, 796, 798
– learning 188, 190, 192, 558, 754
– linguistic 7, 185, 192, 198–9, 553, 623
– physical 548, 855–6
– social 108, 572
– structured 13, 754, 761
environmental effects 6, 11, 587, 593
environmental factors 4, 13, 35, 503, 548, 555–6, 558, 570, 576, 776
environmental input 7, 30, 104
environmental settings 565–79
epenthesis 65–6, 72
episodic memory 485–6, 900
– deficits 910
episodic structures 336, 339, 379
epistemic states 313, 316, 346
Epstein, J.L. 795–6, 801
equal rights for people with disabilities 846–7, 853
ERIC database 358, 648
ERPs (event-related potentials) 92, 571–3, 872–3
errors 163–7, 190–3, 392, 480–1, 618–19, 727–9, 731–2, 734–6, 739–41, 888–91
– analysis 470, 626, 888–90
– grammatical 393, 469, 531
– letter position 723, 727, 735, 741, 744
– migration 727, 729

- morphological 634, 709, 711–13
- neglect 734
- patterns 617, 634, 735, 773, 835, 890
- phonological 166, 168, 469, 629
- semantic 164–6, 168, 393, 401, 629, 721, 743
- speech 164–5, 172, 902
- spelling 469, 477, 498
- syntactic 619, 902–3
- types 13, 168, 727, 742, 745–6
- visual 469, 742

ESLA (early second language acquisition) 602–11
etiologies 289, 705, 753
Euro-Americans 333–4
European cultures 295, 438
European Portuguese 72, 81
evaluative functions 329, 341, 344–5
evaluative language 9, 331
Evans, J.L. 4–5, 95, 423, 438, 548–9, 572, 574–5, 578
event-related potentials, *see* ERPs
everyday activities 34, 634, 795
everyday communications 141, 312, 430
everyday interactions 273, 371
everyday language 141, 144, 850–1, 857
everyday life 329, 798, 845, 899
everyday situations 311, 799
evidence-based practices 358, 907–8
exchange 167, 311, 314, 316, 323, 390, 392, 397, 796
- social 126, 389
exclusion criteria 689, 707, 900
executive functions 139, 145–6, 185, 566–7, 570, 573–6, 635, 864, 874
experience 2, 4, 28, 53, 190–1, 196, 329–30, 408–9, 593–4, 769–70
- early 556, 630
- personal 236, 331–2, 371
- social 268, 572
experimental conditions 226, 293
experimental procedures 287, 293, 485, 556
experimental studies 105, 286, 294–5, 552, 554, 818
experimenters 262–6, 269, 271–2, 286–8, 290–2, 294, 300
- head turns 282, 291–2
experts 417, 449–50, 452, 857
explicitness 221–3, 226

exploration 389, 548, 566, 647, 813
expository genres 226, 237, 248, 251, 534–6
exposure
- to child-directed speech 552, 557–8
- quantity and quality of 552–3, 603, 620–1, 627, 633
- variables 620–1, 627, 629, 631, 633
expressions
- facial 290, 298, 345, 813–15, 830
- figurative 138, 144–5, 147, 819
expressive language 54–5, 379, 391, 556, 585, 592, 772, 819
- development 778, 780
expressive lexicon 91–2, 94–6; *see also* expressive vocabulary
- early 94–6, 98–9
- growth 98
expressive skills 9, 248, 331, 339, 395, 812
expressive vocabulary 102, 107–9, 111, 617, 622, 626, 628, 651–3, 657–9, 833; *see also* expressive lexicon
- size 95, 108
- tasks 110–11
Expressive vocabulary ability of toddlers 653
extended discourse 8, 314, 317, 323
extension 29, 106, 157, 261–2, 817, 821
- problem 262–3, 265
external entities 282–3, 285–6, 289, 291, 296, 298–9
extremely low birth weight (ELBW) 207–8
eyes 244, 269, 280–1, 290, 296, 440, 442, 445, 813, 815
- closed 280–2
- contact 289, 291–2, 296, 813–15
- movements 439, 673, 675, 680
- role 280, 282
eye-trackers 673, 680–1
eye-tracking 127, 516, 673–6, 870

faces 280, 289, 421, 813, 836
- cartoon 289
- scrambled 280
face-to-face interactions 32, 263, 280, 286, 295–6, 298, 313, 608, 813, 845
facial expressions 290, 298, 345, 813–15, 830
facilitation 485–6, 488, 490, 908
false beliefs 123, 260–1, 273, 346
false starts 901–3

familiar words 49, 92, 437, 443–5, 448, 547, 556, 558, 722, 852
familiarity 121–2, 332–3, 415, 443, 528, 630, 857
families 420–1, 427, 545–8, 550–1, 568–9, 578–9, 586, 588–95, 783–4, 805–6
– extended 551, 803
family environments 12, 555
family history 97, 570, 591, 623, 814
family income 565, 572–3, 575, 577, 588
family involvement 105, 799
– early 793, 800
family size 495–7, 784
– effect 495–6
– morphological 494–7, 499
family stress 545, 549–50
Farah, M.J. 565–6, 573, 576
Farran, L.K. 225, 836
Farsi 451, 650
fathers 126, 223, 689, 796, 804, 806
Faust, M.E. 167, 516
Fawcett, A.J. 753–4
Fayol, M. 464, 470, 481, 532
feasibility 55, 375, 383
feature blindness 694–5
Federmeier, K.D. 866–7, 872–3
feedback 29–30, 104, 161, 301, 323, 370, 398, 425–7, 429, 488
– explicit 194, 394
feminine 157, 464, 466, 621, 822, 854
Fernald, A. 3, 110, 546–7, 554–7, 618
fictional narratives 9, 316, 331–7, 344–5, 347, 710
– spontaneous 335, 337
Fighel, A. 223, 489, 491
figurative expressions 138, 144–5, 147, 819
figurative forms 117, 124, 132, 140, 147
figurative language 7, 138–41, 143–4, 146–7, 149, 837
– acquisition/development 7, 117–32, 139, 141, 143, 145, 147, 149
– implications for assessment and clinical practice 137–49
– comprehension 7, 117, 143, 147
– impairment 7, 141–3, 148
– processing 145–6
figurative meanings 121, 123, 137, 144–5, 147, 820
Filippova, E. 125–6, 128, 132, 268

filled pauses 901–3
filtering 55, 145, 198, 481, 572
final codas 80–1
final letters 464–5, 487–8, 498, 723–4, 727, 730
– silent 465, 467
final sibilants 187, 190, 192
final sounds 398, 479–80
finiteness 696, 698
Finnish 73, 95, 203, 339, 416, 495
first graders 511, 576, 629, 649, 655, 657
first language 108, 147, 593, 602, 617, 619, 623, 628, 654, 668–9
first words 28, 94, 101–2, 106–7, 284, 708–9, 816, 820–1, 833, 837
first year of life 27, 31, 45, 50, 92, 280, 283, 778–9, 812–14, 817
first-order beliefs 128, 131
five year olds 98, 270, 336, 338, 709, 711
Flahive, L. 359, 366–7
Flanders 766–7
Fleming, S. 359–60, 366–7
Flemish 416, 766
Fletcher, P. 29, 102, 450–1, 693, 695, 698, 700, 753, 756
Fluctuation Hypothesis 671–2
fluency 371, 605, 661, 676, 754, 905–6
– verbal 575, 901, 906
fluent speech 49–50, 95, 556
fluorescent in situ hybridization 829
Foley, W.A. 235
font 723, 852–3
foreign languages 30, 54, 643, 667, 674
– learning 667, 674
formal schooling 415, 437, 602
form-function relations 330, 338–9, 341, 343
form-meaning relations 8, 101, 110–11, 195, 219, 225, 229, 672
Forster, K.I. 219, 437, 443–4, 482–3, 485–90, 492–4, 499
France 634, 667
free stems 220, 222, 228
French
– orthography 462, 464
– spellers 478, 481
French-speaking Canada 109
French-speaking children 126, 478, 515
frequency
– of occurrence 102, 691, 709

- specificity 46–7
fricatives 52, 72, 75–6, 774
Frith, U. 445, 470, 507, 510, 812
frog stories 236, 335, 345
frontal cortex 864–5
- inferior 568, 575, 865, 870–2
frontal lobes 139, 145, 571, 864, 868–9, 872, 874, 882
fronto-temporal degeneration 909, 911
fronto-temporal dementia (FTD) 899, 909, 911–13
Frost, R. 5, 438, 441–2, 451, 463, 489–90, 497, 512
Frota, S. 674
FTD (fronto-temporal dementia) 899, 909, 911–13
Fujiki, M. 138, 145–6
function words 65, 725, 742–3, 884, 892–3
functional categories 670, 672, 694
functional connectivity 865–6, 871–2, 874
functional neuroanatomy 714–15
functional neuroimaging 706, 714, 882
functions
- cognitive 139, 570, 574, 847, 867
- discourse 332, 339–42, 535
- evaluative 329, 341, 344–5
- executive 139, 145–6, 185, 566–7, 570, 573–6, 635, 864, 874
- language 568, 576, 706–7, 716, 863, 870, 882, 885
- referential 280, 329
- social 126, 128–30, 273

Gafni, C. 76–9
Gagarina, N. 209, 331, 619, 621, 633
Gahl, S. 195–6, 894–5
games 296, 300, 359, 362, 364, 373, 377, 423, 427–8, 430
gaps 48, 109–10, 300, 302, 412, 416, 628–9, 631–2, 652, 771–3
- detection 48
Garnett, M. 273
Garrett, M.F. 320, 887
Gathercole, V. 104, 107, 601, 607, 628, 630–2, 676, 707
Gatt, D. 628
gaze 198–9, 262, 281–2, 285, 294, 673, 816
- alternations 280, 295, 300, 816
- direction 262–3, 265, 282, 292–4

- mutual 280
- spontaneous 280, 289, 294, 301
gaze-following trials 291–2
Geers, D. 54, 105, 767–70, 772, 776, 778–80, 782–3
Geiger, V. 227
Gelman, R. 270–1
gender 32, 52, 515, 590, 674, 775, 783, 822, 854
- grammatical 157–8, 160, 166, 670
gene expression 566, 832, 834
general backward readers 504–5, 518
general capacity 13, 754, 761
general cognition 14, 830, 837
general cognitive abilities 33, 36, 517
general neurocognitive systems 567, 575
general purpose words 618–19, 626
generalizability 368–9, 373, 510
generalization 106, 227, 332, 360–5, 379, 419, 604–5, 677, 755, 822
generative approaches 6, 68, 235, 891
Genesee, F. 109, 607, 679, 700
genetic factors 556, 591, 782, 829, 912
genres 253, 331, 333, 335–6, 347, 530, 535–7
- discourse 237, 248, 251–2, 534–7, 710
German 494, 509
- bilinguals 621–2
- children 471, 511, 629, 633, 652
Germanic languages 494–5
Germanic origin 220, 852
Germany 387, 652
Gernsbacher, M.A. 117, 144, 282, 285, 295, 516
gestational age 50, 98, 205, 207–10, 213
gestures 279, 283–5, 288, 290, 296, 301–2, 546, 552–4, 813, 816
- declarative 282, 289, 300
- intended 28
- pointing 285–6, 294
Geva, E. 225, 650–1, 653, 656, 658, 660–1
Gibbon, F. 589
Gibson, T.A. 110
Gillam, S. & R. 330, 338–9, 343, 357–8, 362, 364–6, 373–4, 376–9, 625, 630
Gillenwater, J.M. 44–5, 47–8
Ginsborg, J. 585, 587, 589
girls 118, 122, 236, 241–2, 244, 391, 586, 619, 621, 783
Glenwright, M. 124–6, 129
global coherence relations 506, 515

goal-directed activity 260, 359, 381
Godfroid, A. 672–3, 675
Golberg, H. 650–4
Gold, E.M. 317, 868, 872
Goldfield, B.A. 101
Goldin-Meadow, S. 284–5, 546, 552–4, 711
Goldrick, M. 155
Gonnerman, L. 220, 224, 493
Goodman, E. 94–6, 263, 438, 552, 574
Goodwin, A.P. 220, 224–5, 227, 229, 301
Gopnik, M. 103, 260, 273, 694, 834
Goralnik Screening Test 633
Gorno-Tempini, M.L. 883, 899–900, 902–5, 910
Grainger, K. 491, 586–7, 723
grammar 96–7, 361–2, 415–16, 525–38, 671–2, 675–6, 690–2, 694–6, 699, 835–6
– early 63, 98, 694
– emergence 94–5, 98
– reception 515, 835
– story, *see* story grammar
– systems 760
– text-embedded 531, 533
grammatical categories 619, 670, 693
grammatical choices 331, 536
grammatical competence 11, 525–6, 528, 530–1, 537
grammatical complexity 95, 251, 531–5, 537, 550
grammatical constructions 7, 359, 528, 532–3, 535–7
grammatical correction 318, 392–3
grammatical development 94, 203, 330, 546, 552, 556, 776, 835
grammatical errors 393, 469, 531
grammatical features 320, 525–6, 533–5, 537–8, 693–4, 835
grammatical gender 157–8, 160, 166, 670
grammatical impairments 884, 891, 893
grammatical knowledge 196, 311, 330, 831, 893
grammatical markers 528, 694
grammatical morphemes 319, 329, 693, 699, 892
grammatical morphology 693, 696, 699
grammatical problems 690–1, 697
grammatical processing 713, 891, 893
grammatical roles 207, 553, 891
grammatical rules 186, 528, 759, 818

grammatical skills 529, 569, 818
grammatical structures 5, 137, 330, 514, 554, 677
grammatical symptoms 690–1, 700
grammaticality 317, 378, 525, 537, 822, 892, 906
graphemes 407, 410, 461, 463, 465–6, 726, 739
grapheme-to-phoneme conversion 509, 511, 726, 736–41, 744, 746
graphemic buffer dyslexia 735–6
graphic signs 406–7, 410, 412
graphotactic regularities 461, 466
Grassmann, S. 286–7
gray matter 829, 864–5, 869–70, 874
Greek 65–6, 69, 72, 76, 343, 452, 469, 624, 649, 652
– Cypriot 629
Grice, P. 144, 312, 315, 405
Griffin, Z.N. 330, 344, 358, 383, 416, 421, 547, 794
Griffith, P.L. 143, 331, 508, 529, 800
Grossman, M. 867, 870–2, 901–4
growth rates 103, 110, 651–4
Grunwell, P. 78, 80–1
Guarini, A. 203–4
guidance 372, 425, 427, 429, 566, 611, 796, 798, 801, 804–5
guidelines 14, 31, 347, 438, 767, 797, 804, 845, 847, 849–52
– easy-to-read 854–5
Gujerati 649–50, 655–6
Gutierrez-Clellen, V.F. 625, 630–1, 633
Guttorm, T.K. 92
Gvion, A. 723, 727, 741, 745
gyri 577, 829, 882

Hackman, D.A. 565–6
Haddad-Hanna, M. 727, 730, 733, 742–3
hair cells 24–7, 765
Håkansson, G. 620
Halliday, M.A.K. 235, 250, 329, 339, 526–7, 531, 535, 907
Haman, E. 628–9
Hammer, B. 546–7, 603, 606, 650–1, 775–6
Hancock, J.T. 128, 131, 267, 793
HAROLD model 865, 868–73
Hart, L. 3, 330, 507, 512, 546–7, 550, 552–4, 587, 589, 591–2

Hasan, R. 329, 339, 531, 535
Hawkins, A.J. 28, 52, 67, 671, 804
Hayward, D. 336, 359, 368–9, 371, 373, 625
head turns 280–1, 291, 294, 815
– experimenters 282, 291–2
health 32, 335, 429, 622, 624, 846–7
– mental 143, 549–50, 574
healthy aging 863–74
hearing 6, 19–25, 29–31, 33, 35, 37, 267, 680–1, 768, 770–1
– aids 25–6, 35, 43, 53–4, 765–8, 770, 777, 780, 785, 805
– devices 55, 795–6, 805
– impairment 19–20, 105, 111, 601, 610, 767, 777, 782, 847
– loss (HL) 6, 13, 19–22, 25–6, 29–30, 43–56, 765–8, 770, 777, 782
– early intervention 795–806
– role 6, 20, 23, 30–1
– role in speech and language acquisition and processing 19–37
hearing peers 105, 770–1, 779, 785
hearing-impaired children 36, 776–7, 782, 785
Heath, B.S. 74, 334, 551
Hebrew 65–6, 70, 72–3, 76–80, 249–51, 489–90, 494–9, 620–2, 633, 853–5
Hebrew-speaking children 244, 430
heterogeneity 11, 505, 611, 621, 887, 891, 893, 899, 901, 910
heuristic scaffolding 389, 395, 397–8, 401
Hickmann, M. 317, 330–1, 336, 338–9, 342–4
hierarchy 65, 69–70, 398–9, 691
higher order/figurative language 7, 137–41, 143–4, 147–9
high-functioning Autism Spectrum Disorder 126
high-point analysis 334
HL, see hearing, loss 13, 19–22, 25–6, 29–30, 43, 53–6, 765–8, 770, 777, 793–806
Hobson, P. 289, 291, 816, 819
home environment 205, 567, 623, 667, 796, 798
home language 601, 604, 617, 621–5, 628, 644, 649, 652, 655
homophone intrusions 480–1, 498
homophones 170–2, 195, 445, 450, 479–81, 498–9, 512, 516, 737–8
Hood, B. 262, 293, 321, 423
hospitals 204, 244, 884, 890

Hudson, J.A. 330, 333, 336, 339–40, 344–5
Hulme, C. 146, 447, 509, 513, 515, 528
humor 126, 129, 268, 423, 706
Hurtado, N. 110, 555–6, 618
Hutchinson, J.M. 651, 653, 659
Huttenlocher, J. 239, 547, 552–3, 589
hyperbole 7, 117, 120, 126, 267

Icelandic 95, 463
identification 1, 148–9, 226–7, 518–19, 692, 696, 722–4, 777, 847, 850
– early 53, 503, 777, 806, 814
idioms 7, 117, 121–3, 139–41, 145, 147, 819
– comprehension 121–3, 141–2
– decomposable 122–3
IFG, see inferior frontal gyrus
imageability 162–3, 742, 889–90
images, mental 119–21, 908
imitations 298, 300, 321, 802, 816
impaired children 35, 323, 369, 374, 379, 587, 770–1, 775–6, 778, 783
impaired performance 160, 168, 290, 754
impairments 25–6, 164–8, 360–3, 594–5, 619–20, 735–6, 746–7, 882–3, 885–6, 890–3
– cognitive 111, 167, 830, 883, 910
– grammatical 884, 891, 893
– language, see language impairments
– reading 13, 31, 467, 727, 735, 746, 754, 761
– semantic 167, 901, 903–4, 910
– sensory 25, 707, 753
– visual 204, 735, 746, 783
implant use 772, 774–5, 780
implantation 105, 768, 770–1, 773–4, 778–83, 785
– bilateral 767, 779–80
– bimodal 781
implanted children 770–2, 779–80, 785
implants, cochlear, see cochlear implants
implicit learning 13, 753–9, 761
inclusive classrooms 387–401
income, family 565, 572–3, 575, 577, 588
inconsistency 462–3, 517, 537, 797, 834
indefinite articles 313, 626
independence 397, 399–401, 428, 830
independent clauses 251, 338
independent cultures 298
index finger pointing 283–5, 294
indirect evidence 299, 317, 375, 818

infancy 20, 47–8, 51–2, 55, 261, 537, 546, 556, 812, 815
infants 27–30, 43–56, 259–60, 262–3, 280–6, 295–6, 298, 313–14, 551–8, 813–14
– older 43–4, 50–3
– young 45, 47–9, 51
inferences 123, 139, 142, 145, 147, 262, 274, 311, 332, 516–17
– making 140–1, 333, 377, 819
inferior frontal gyrus (IFG) 568, 575, 577, 883–4
inflected words 103, 195, 210, 470, 479, 498
inflectional morphology 96, 472, 494, 621, 671–2, 690, 775, 785
inflectional paradigm 480–1, 489, 491, 498, 776
inflections 206, 620–1, 626, 694, 775, 854, 893
information 24–6, 35–6, 93–4, 269–70, 516–18, 571–3, 724–5, 795–7, 845–53, 855–7
– accessible 845, 850, 857–8
– acoustic 23, 26, 47
– acoustic-phonetic 53, 55–6
– auditory 3, 573, 753, 785, 815
– contextual 35, 123, 126, 144, 468, 516, 873, 888
– morphological 11, 464–6, 469, 471, 891
– phonological 52, 160, 462–3, 508, 725, 760, 855, 908
– processing 145, 440
– semantic 35, 145, 449, 515, 821
– simplified 850, 854, 857
– syntactic 160, 872, 886
informative cues 184, 190–1, 295
Ingram, D. 75, 80, 470, 692
inhibition 35, 110, 145, 163, 586, 812, 820, 864
initiating events 334, 366, 368, 372, 378, 381, 618
initiation 299–300, 314, 554, 571, 796, 814, 817, 836
input 11–12, 70, 301–2, 554–5, 591–3, 595, 601–3, 607–11, 667–71, 676–8
– linguistic 4, 104, 199, 319, 545, 555, 620, 815
integration 8, 125, 139, 330, 345, 428, 516, 893
integrity 26, 105, 447, 869–71
intellectual disabilities 845–58
intelligence 141, 504, 753

intelligibility, speech 23, 769, 777, 783
intensity 43–6, 48, 56, 908
intent 19, 23, 31, 33, 127–8, 587
– questions 124–5, 127–9
intentionality 260, 262, 284, 313, 316, 329, 344, 346, 813, 815–16
– character 336–7
intentions 125–6, 259, 262–3, 267, 280, 282, 340, 342, 405–7, 409
– communicative 125, 259, 265–8, 272–4, 294, 311, 313, 405, 407, 816–17
– referential 262–4, 266
interactions 125–6, 295–7, 301–2, 387–8, 399–400, 490–1, 548–9, 552–3, 592, 743
– communicative 374, 545, 548–9, 551, 802
– face-to-face 263, 298, 845, 856
– parent-child 199, 298, 333–4, 389, 427, 548–51, 558, 595
– social 34, 137–40, 146, 148, 204, 209, 332, 342, 811, 815
– triadic 285, 291–2, 296, 816
– verbal 545, 551, 558
interactive activation model 159, 161, 170, 172
interference 145, 193, 621, 754, 756–7, 801
interlocutors 126, 238, 240, 259, 270, 272, 311–18, 322, 834, 837
internal responses 334, 366, 372, 378
internal states 280, 296, 316, 336, 346
internal structures 159, 219, 222, 477, 495–6, 499, 526
international adoptees 104, 108, 111, 603, 609
intervention 300–1, 358–62, 367–74, 376–81, 383, 418–30, 793–4, 798–806, 886–8, 907
– groups 371, 419–22, 424–6, 428
– materials 368–9, 372–3
– morphological 227, 471
– narrative 357–83
– programs 300, 366–7, 369, 381, 427, 429, 511, 799–801, 803–4, 838
– reading 417–19, 424, 503, 519
– story grammar 359, 368–9, 373
– studies 11, 168, 226–7, 300–1, 359, 418, 427
intonation 270, 407–8, 781, 818
IQ scores 505, 590
Ireson, J. 390–4
ironic compliments 126–31, 268
ironic criticisms 124–31, 267–8, 273
irony 117, 125–6, 130–1, 259, 273, 706
– comprehension 124–7, 130–1

– gestural 132
– verbal, see verbal irony
irregular words 186, 188, 190–1, 193, 721–2, 736, 743, 745, 835
isolated clauses 240, 245, 252
isolation 36, 49, 93, 197, 465–6, 478, 553, 566, 592, 732
Israel 417, 424, 430, 623–4, 679, 804, 845–8, 854

Jackson, C.W. 138, 505, 651–2, 654, 746, 872–3
James, T. 129, 186, 270, 339, 766
Japanese 66, 82, 298, 333, 345, 407, 444, 448, 450, 453
– Kanji 444, 448, 450, 453
Jean, M. 651, 653
Johnson, J. 50, 140, 144, 198, 260, 280, 294, 606, 678, 709
joint attention 279, 282, 288, 295–6, 300–1, 551, 554–5, 816–18, 834, 837
– episodes 282, 298–9, 302, 555, 816–18
– skills 93, 106, 282, 291–3, 300–1
Jusczyk, P.W. 48–52, 196, 380, 678, 766, 778, 817, 874
justice 332–4, 338–9, 343, 345–6, 416, 420

Kail, M. 167, 317, 336, 342–4, 708, 848
Kanji 444, 448, 450, 453
Karmiloff-Smith, A. 119, 221, 242, 280, 331, 338, 342–3, 528, 831, 833–5
Karni, N. 72–3, 757
Katzenberger, A. 248, 250, 343
Keller, H. 298, 604
Kelly, A 145, 273, 755, 759
Kemps, R. 191, 195
Kerbel, N. 730–2
Kieffer, M.J. 224–5, 227, 646–7, 651–3, 655–9
kindergarten 10, 138, 141, 246, 508–9, 515, 649, 652, 654–5, 657–8
– children 138, 344, 346, 359, 368, 373, 575, 707
– entry 546–7, 799
Kintsch, W. 440, 506, 516
Kirby, J.R. 220–1, 223–4, 226–7, 513
Kjelgaard, M.M. 812, 820
Klecan-Aker, J. 359–60, 366–7
Kneile, L.A. 225
Knopman, D.S. 757

knowledge 19–20, 53, 122–4, 130, 269–72, 329–31, 412, 526–7, 630, 694–6
– grammatical 196, 311, 330, 831, 893
– lexical 6–8, 451, 483, 490, 627, 629
– linguistic 1, 10, 34, 186, 198, 238, 341, 525, 618, 627
– morphological 8, 221–2, 226–7, 467, 469
– mutual 342–4
– object 901–3, 905
– orthographic 419, 464, 471
– prior 19, 23, 32–3, 37, 357, 516–17
– semantic 123, 491, 834
– syntactic 222, 514, 629, 658, 817, 837
– vocabulary, see vocabulary, knowledge
Kohnert, K. 601, 607, 610, 631
Korfmacher, J. 793–4
Kuhl, P.K. 47, 51–2, 92, 554–6, 812, 817, 820, 910

L1 610, 620, 622, 625–6, 631, 634, 652, 654, 658, 669–71
L2 110, 610, 620, 622–4, 626, 634, 652, 654–6, 658, 669–71
labels 106, 227, 235, 262–6, 286, 295, 298, 821, 883, 885
– novel 262, 265–6, 272, 286–7, 293, 295
labials 74–7
Lam, K. 110, 225, 655, 657
Landa, R.J. 813–14
Landerl, K. 438, 463, 469, 471
language abilities 2, 27, 91, 147, 271, 370, 380, 711, 783, 811
– receptive 92, 97–8, 770
language accessibility 14, 845, 850, 854, 857–8
language acquisition 1, 3, 6–7, 66–7, 319, 321–3, 585–6, 590–1, 593–4, 776–8
– and development 1, 13, 776, 778
– figurative 7, 117
– and processing 19, 21, 23, 25, 27, 29, 31, 33, 35, 37
language assessment 12, 607, 620, 624, 696, 822
language comprehension 147, 203, 546–7, 590, 608, 780, 785, 811, 817, 823
– figurative 7, 117, 143, 147
– spoken 556, 771
language deficits 14, 24, 618, 715, 900, 905, 910, 912

language delays 30, 97, 110, 148, 203, 369, 556, 558, 587, 590–1
language development 91–2, 96–9, 203–5, 545–6, 585–90, 705–6, 708–9, 714–15, 767–9, 797–800
– atypical 71, 205, 620, 705
– early 12, 98, 228, 545, 709
– figurative 137, 139, 141, 143, 145, 147, 149
– spoken 770, 776, 778
– typical 97, 226, 617, 620, 624, 626, 631, 711–12
Language Development Survey (LDS) 102, 108, 627
language difference 148, 585–95, 680
language difficulties 146, 373, 378, 388, 390, 392–3, 399, 708, 907, 909–10
language disorders 2, 5, 173, 199, 203, 357–83, 467, 820, 830, 900
– and language difference 585–95
language functions 568, 576, 706–7, 716, 863, 870, 882, 885
language growth 545, 547, 554, 556, 654
language impairment, late emerging 139, 146
language impairments 2–3, 145–8, 318–20, 358–9, 587–8, 621–3, 689, 705–9, 711–16, 910–11
– in acquired aphasia 881–95
– figurative 7, 141–3, 148
language inputs 111, 156, 552, 554, 587, 591, 602
language learning 5, 197, 374, 387–92, 554–6, 558, 601–2, 668–70, 677–8, 811–13
– foreign 667, 674
language outcomes 26, 54–5, 105, 109, 548, 551, 555–6, 590, 770, 781–3
language processing 14, 26, 31, 148, 164, 863, 867, 869, 882, 887
language production 63, 155, 167, 237, 323, 609, 691, 863, 881, 900
language profiles 148, 606, 709, 712, 883, 911
language scores 97, 652, 772, 784
language skills 98, 372, 374–5, 377, 380, 546, 548, 569, 576, 770–1
– oral 26, 415, 417–18, 422, 425, 428, 430, 547, 766, 793
language tasks 371, 566, 568, 705, 714, 865–7, 869
language tests 203, 593, 696
language typologies 4–5, 248, 343, 347, 528

language use 50, 65, 195, 204, 224, 238, 250–1, 547, 779, 887
late language emergence, see LLE
latency 124, 127, 162, 818, 872–3
lateralization 714–15
late-talkers (LT) 96–9, 590, 709
Lawrence, J. 594, 603, 606, 650–2
LBW, see low birth weight
LDS, see Language Development Survey
Le Sourn-Bissaoui, S. 121, 123
learning
– conversational skills/from conversation 311–23
– disabilities 2, 146, 167, 412, 630, 837
– environment 188, 190, 192, 558, 754
– lexical 101–2, 105, 108–9, 111, 603, 670, 817, 820–1
– literacy 11, 411, 413, 437–8
– mechanisms 8, 181, 190, 759
– orthographic 447–8
– procedural 757–8
– processes 56, 101, 198–9, 412, 448–9, 477, 669, 754, 758
– to read 437–53
– second language 3, 12, 593, 667, 672
– sequences 757–9
– statistical 13, 50, 754, 761
– theory of 197, 439, 441
– universal model of learning to read 437–53
– vocabulary 7, 102, 105, 111, 553, 647
Leekam, S. 289–94
left hemisphere 568, 577, 705, 708, 713–15, 863, 866, 869–71, 874, 883
left hemisphere lesion (LHL) 709, 713–16, 883
left inferior frontal gyrus 568, 575
left perisylvian 574–6, 578
length of exposure, see LoE
Leow, R. 675
Lesaux, N.K. 224–5, 227, 509, 645, 647, 650–3, 655, 657
Leseman, P. 593, 603, 631
lesions 14, 571, 706–7, 709, 711, 713–15, 882, 884
letter identity dyslexia 732–3, 735
letter knowledge 410, 419–20, 424–5, 427, 430, 462
letter migrations 722, 727, 730–1, 735
letter names 423, 426, 429, 758
letter position 723–4, 728, 735

- dyslexia (LPD) 723, 727–32, 735, 741, 744–6
- encoding 723–4, 728–9, 746
- errors 723, 727, 735, 741, 744
letter strings 444, 470, 483, 487–8, 492, 733, 759
letter substitutions 735–6
letters 409–12, 423–9, 440, 461–4, 477–9, 721–4, 726–34, 736–7, 739, 853
- abstract 723, 732–3
- middle 727–9, 735
- naming 415, 420, 422, 426
- silent 478–9, 481, 736, 739
- single 407, 437, 736, 739–40
- vowel 451, 727, 741
- written 415, 732–3, 908
Levelt, C.C. 64–5, 69–70, 74–5, 78, 155, 157–8, 160–1, 170, 172, 887–9
Levin, I. 417, 419, 421, 423, 426–7, 431
Levine, S.C. 142, 284, 547, 554, 711
Levorato, C. 123, 147
Lewy bodies, see dementia, with Lewy bodies
lexica, bilingual 626, 629
lexical access 167, 483–4, 486, 488, 492, 618
- process 482–3, 485–6
lexical acquisition 93, 107, 110, 272
lexical comprehension 106, 821, 888, 905
lexical development 7, 67, 91, 98, 101, 104, 108, 111, 274, 554
- atypical 101–11
- early 6–7, 91, 93–4, 96, 98, 101–2, 108
- factors influencing 104
- typical 101–4
lexical diversity 338–9, 367, 376, 382, 550, 592, 710–11
lexical knowledge 6–8, 451, 483, 490, 627, 629
lexical learning 101–2, 105, 108–9, 111, 603, 670, 817, 820–1
lexical processing 462, 480, 484–5, 491, 493, 557, 891
lexical quality hypothesis 445, 507
lexical representations 53, 482–3, 485–7, 490–1, 496, 498–9, 512–13, 558
lexical retrieval 14, 706, 746, 867–9, 874, 884, 889, 893
lexical route 461, 506, 725–6, 736–9, 741, 743
lexical semantics 157–8, 821
lexical syntax 157–8, 160–1, 168, 170
lexical-semantics 156, 158, 168, 893

lexicon 91, 93–4, 195–6, 219–20, 618, 629–30, 724–6, 728, 741–3, 833–5
- early 7, 91–9, 318
- mental 140, 171, 173, 219–20, 225, 227, 229, 479–85, 491–9, 506
- orthographic 444, 725, 742, 904
- orthographic input 724–5, 728, 731, 736–9, 742–4, 747
- phonological output 156, 163, 165–6, 725, 737–40, 742–3, 746
- semantic 725–6, 737–8, 743–4
- size 94–5, 98
lexomes 188–9, 191
Leyton, C.E. 901, 905
LHL, see left hemisphere lesion
LI, see language impairments
Liberman, A.M. 28, 51, 437, 450
Liebal, K. 282–3, 297–8, 317
Liles, B.Z. 331, 338–9, 344, 711
Limber, J. 235, 241
Limbird, C.K. 651–2, 659–60
linear scripts 446–7
linguistic abilities 11, 123, 204, 312–13, 548, 617, 622–3, 625, 771, 857
linguistic context 11, 35, 206, 553, 819
linguistic environments 7, 185, 192, 198–9, 553, 623
linguistic input 4, 104, 199, 319, 545, 555, 620, 815
linguistic knowledge 1, 10, 34, 186, 198, 238, 341, 525, 618, 627
linguistic literacy 10, 248
linguistic processing 143, 194, 461, 595, 818–19, 874
linguistic profiles 620, 693, 830, 832, 899
linguistic skills 37, 99, 221, 227, 338, 366, 586, 755, 837
linguistic structures 226, 279, 293, 339, 343, 377, 380–1, 677
linguistic theories 3–4, 181–2, 690, 695, 886
linguistic units 525–6, 533, 895
linguistics 2–3, 5, 439–40, 452, 832
- theoretical 690, 894
lips 93, 407, 769
listeners 19, 26, 28, 32–4, 36, 52, 317, 341–2, 344, 357
listening
- comprehension 138, 416, 422, 507, 657–9
- conditions 23, 105, 795, 881

literacy 8, 10, 26, 224, 358, 405–13, 416, 437–8, 441–3, 848–9
- achievements 224, 226, 415–16, 423, 547
- acquisition 5, 330, 416, 439
- development 20, 253, 425, 498, 576, 585–6
- early, see early literacy
- learning 11, 411, 413, 437–8
- linguistic 10, 248
- skills 227, 425, 430, 569, 645, 849
literal compliments 124–5, 129, 268
literal criticisms 129, 267–8
literal meanings 125, 140, 142, 144–5, 268, 273
literate disabilities 405–13
Liu, H-M. 52, 92, 260, 416, 451, 555, 812
LLE (late language emergence) 570
localisation 43, 47, 164, 167, 280, 689
Locke, A. 585, 587, 589, 707
LoE (length of exposure) 620–1, 627, 633–4
logic 186, 195, 440, 442, 448–9, 511
Logogen model 156–7, 161, 164, 170, 172
logopenic PPA 883, 901, 904–6
longitudinal studies 96, 101, 139–40, 321, 515, 517, 534, 594, 709, 772
long-lag priming paradigm 485–6, 494
long-term memory 34–5, 443, 527, 892
Longtin, C-M. 486–9
Lonigan, C.J. 415, 429
Lopez, L. 289, 291, 298, 606
Lord, C. 107, 289, 293, 812, 819
low birth weight (LBW) 203–5, 207–14, 566
low-frequency words 485–6, 890
LPD, see letter position dyslexia
LT, see late-talkers
Lu, Y. 650, 653, 755
Lust, B. 235, 602
Luyster, R. 293, 812
Lyytinen, P.&H. 97–8

McCabe, A. 331, 333–4, 338–40, 345–6, 618, 711
McClelland, J.L. 186–8, 483, 511, 731, 755
McCormick, S. 203, 489
McFadden, S. 330, 338–9, 366, 374, 711
McGregor, K. 105, 107, 168, 359, 362, 368, 370–1, 373, 817–18, 820–2
Mackey, T.A. 138, 667, 674, 680
McLeod, S. 138, 592, 602, 605, 607
McNamara, D.S. 4, 506, 526, 534

macronarrative 360–5
macrostructure 330, 334, 338, 357–8, 364, 370, 377–82, 619, 626
magnetic resonance imaging, see MRI
Mahon, M. 390–4
Mahoney, G. 223, 797–8, 801, 804
main clauses 235–7
mainland China 447, 449, 451, 453
Mäkinen, L. 336–9
Mandarin 103, 343, 650, 653, 661
Manis, F.R. 510–11, 570, 645, 657–8, 755
Marin, O.S.M. 891, 893–4
Marinellie, S.A. 122, 225, 251
Marinis, T. 446, 620, 836
markedness 63–4, 72, 680
- constraints 63–4, 70, 74, 81–2
markers 49, 206–7, 289, 480, 530, 535, 618, 690, 696, 899
- agreement 206
- clinical 13–14, 618, 690, 694, 696–7, 700, 822, 912–13
- grammatical 528, 694
Marshall, J. 164, 172, 721–2, 731, 735, 739–40, 742
Marslen-Wilson, W. 74, 489, 492–4
masked priming technique 486, 488, 492–3, 498
maskers 45–6
mass nouns 168, 170
maternal education 103, 285, 546, 575, 588–90, 594, 623
mathematics lessons 388, 390, 395–7
matrix clauses 241
Matthews, D. 219, 225, 269, 279, 288, 316
maturation 25, 370, 373, 568, 571, 715, 865
Mayan infants 285
mean length
- of utterance 205, 207, 209–11, 319, 362, 692, 776, 784, 902, 904
- of word (MLW) 209, 211–13
meaning
- literal 125, 140, 142, 144–5, 268, 273
- representations 156, 407, 512–13, 889
- units of 182, 187, 194, 407
media 142, 411, 437, 845, 847, 856
medial codas 80–1
mediation 329, 423, 430, 493, 628
- maternal 428

Meltzoff, A.N. 260, 281, 289–90, 555, 813, 816–17
memory 23, 32–3, 331–2, 439, 566, 573–4, 577–8, 675–6, 904, 908
– episodic, see episodic memory
– long-term 34–5, 443, 527, 892
– phonological 620, 630, 632, 833
– semantic 204, 868, 889
– short-term 623, 632, 724, 830, 832–3, 848
– verbal 97, 104–5, 107, 140, 905
– working, see working memory
mental age 106, 294, 504, 830
mental disorders 504, 811
mental health 143, 549–50, 574
mental images 119–21, 908
mental lexicon 140, 171, 173, 219–20, 225, 227, 229, 479–85, 491–9, 506
mental model 342, 440, 516
mental states 9, 259–61, 268, 281–2, 289–90, 301–2, 313, 315, 345–6, 836–7
Menyuk, P. 205, 691–2
Mervis, C. 289, 830, 833–7
Messer, M.H. 167, 631, 833
Mesulam, M-M. 899–900, 904, 906
meta-analysis 320, 333, 416, 418, 505, 509
metaphors 7, 117–19, 132, 139–40, 144, 267, 273, 406, 411, 819
methodologies 55, 124, 205, 331, 366, 673, 676, 768
metonymy 7, 117, 132
Meunier, F. 488, 864–6, 871
micronarrative 360–5
microstructure 338, 357–8, 364, 370, 377–8, 382, 618–19
middle childhood 137–8, 245, 251, 253
middle letters 727–9, 735
migratable words 728–30, 744
migration errors 727, 729
migrations 11, 617, 723, 729–32, 735
– between-word 730, 732, 735
– letter 722, 727, 730–1, 735
milestones 101, 336, 624, 773, 777, 820, 833, 835
Miller, J.F. 34, 51, 185, 251, 331, 337, 342, 345, 527, 533
mind 117, 119, 259–61, 263, 265–73, 341, 345–6, 484, 768, 770
– abilities 260, 266, 271, 273
– skills, theory of 262, 265, 268, 270–2, 347

– understandings 260, 262, 267, 272, 274
minimal words 36, 64–6
MISL (Monitoring Indicators of Scholarly Language) 364, 377–8
MLU, see mean length, of utterance 205, 207, 209–12, 319, 362, 692, 776, 784, 902, 904
MLW, see mean length, of word
modalities 149, 165, 170, 297, 301–2, 484, 881, 886, 890, 904
– visual 104, 106, 297, 733, 760
modifiers 101, 251, 553
Moeller, M.P. 30, 105, 773, 793–4, 797–9, 801, 806
Moll, H. 260, 265, 280–4, 463, 469
Monitoring Indicators of Scholarly Language, see MISL
monolingual children 109–11, 593, 603–5, 607–10, 618–19, 627–9, 631–3, 643–7, 651–4, 659–61
monolingual norms 109–10, 607, 621, 632–3, 652, 654
Montag, J. 769–70
Montrul, S. 678–9
Moore, C. 24–5, 32–3, 47, 52, 280–2, 289, 291, 801, 804
moraic scripts 450
morphemes 181–2, 209–10, 212–14, 407, 444–6, 449–50, 482, 489–90, 492–4, 496–7
– constituent 479, 482, 487, 496
– grammatical 319, 329, 693, 699, 892
morphemic scripts 450
morpho-lexical acquisition 219–29
morphological affixes 725, 735–6, 742
morphological awareness 8, 221, 223–7, 466–7, 471–2, 477–9, 528, 531, 657
morphological complexity 209, 213–14, 222
morphological decomposition 225, 482, 484, 487–8, 490–2, 494, 498, 724, 734
morphological development 8, 181–99, 211, 835
morphological effects 224, 465, 494, 734
morphological errors 634, 709, 711–13
morphological family size 494–7, 499
morphological information 11, 464–6, 469, 471, 891
morphological knowledge 8, 221–2, 226–7, 467, 469
morphological priming 223, 494

morphological processing 8, 11, 182, 188, 221, 229, 461, 470
morphological relationships 478–9, 489, 498
morphological rules 692–3, 738
morphological skills 227, 472
morphological status 483, 487, 492, 498
morphological structure 226, 470, 479, 482, 487, 492–3, 496–7, 499, 732, 854
morphology 186–8, 223–5, 464–6, 472, 477, 481–3, 489, 493–5, 497–9, 632
– grammatical 693, 696, 699
– inflectional 96, 472, 494, 621, 671–2, 690, 775, 785
– role in reading and writing 477–99
– use 481, 494, 497, 887
– verb 694–5, 698, 776
– verbal 320, 623, 775–6
morphosyntax 107, 618, 675, 679–80, 711, 832
Morrongiello, B.A. 46–8
Morton, J. 155–7, 280, 483, 485, 887
mothers
– college-educated 550
– elaborative 333
MRI (magnetic resonance imaging) 573, 900–1, 909
multiletter phonological dyslexia 739–40
multilingualism 12, 621–2; *see also* bilingualism
Murrell, G. 485
Musolino, J. 831, 836
mutism, selective 27, 610
mutual engagement 289, 291, 813
mutual gaze 280
Myklebust, H.R. 721–2

Nachman-Katz, I. 733–4
Nagy, W.E. 219–23, 225, 229, 466, 532–4, 536, 603, 645–6
Naigles, L.R. 108, 207, 301, 552–3, 817–18, 820, 822
Nakamoto, J. 645, 655, 657–8
Nakamura, M. 279, 345, 669
naming 165, 170, 203, 426, 628–9, 738, 743, 885, 901, 903
– letter 415, 420, 422, 426
– object 905
– picture 161–2, 164, 168, 646, 821
narrations 10, 357–8, 366, 372, 376, 379, 382

narrative abilities 357–9, 368, 371, 373, 381, 383, 711, 812
narrative analysis 347, 617, 622
narrative coherence 334, 347, 382
narrative competence 9, 330, 337–8, 347
narrative comprehension 377, 383
narrative development 331–2, 334–5, 338, 710, 712
narrative discourse 251, 329–47, 535, 911
narrative interventions 357–83
– contextualized 373, 378, 380, 383
– decontextualized 366, 374
narrative production 330, 373, 383
narrative skills 332–4, 336, 346, 366, 373, 378–9, 837
narrative structure 338–9, 341, 369, 713–14
narrative styles 333–4
narratives 329–32, 334–7, 339–40, 357–65, 369, 378–80, 534–6, 618–19, 624–6, 710–13
– children's 333, 339–41, 373, 619, 711
– fictional, *see* fictional narratives
– oral 226, 236, 249–50, 368, 532
– personal 331, 334, 336–7, 344, 347, 372, 711
– written 251, 375, 534
narrators 251, 329, 331, 334, 340–1, 344, 357
Nation, K. 104, 289, 291, 447, 513, 515–17, 821–2
National Early Literacy Panel (NELP) 416, 418
national norms 649, 652–5
native language (NL) 27–8, 30, 50, 54, 91–2, 555, 558, 667, 670, 672
native speakers (NSs) 147, 225, 441, 625, 670–1, 673, 678–80
native-like competence 678, 680
NAVS, *see* Northwestern Assessment of Verbs and Sentences
NBW, *see* normal birth weight
near-native speakers 673, 678
negation 206, 376, 699, 836
neglect dyslexia, *see* neglexia
neglect errors 734
neglexia 733–5, 745
– developmental 733–4
neighbourhoods 196, 419, 565–6, 578, 585, 588, 591, 594
NELP (National Early Literacy Panel) 416, 418
Nelson, K. 4, 101, 319–20, 329–30, 332, 337, 345–6, 554, 556, 706

neonatal conditions, adverse 8, 203–14
neonates 24, 27, 765–6
Nettelbladt, U. 620, 699
networks 160, 240, 405, 499, 512, 706, 865–6, 870–1
– neural 863, 865–6, 869, 874
neural development 716, 778, 793
neural networks 863, 865–6, 869, 874
neural structure 14, 183, 863, 874
neuroanatomy, functional 714–15
neurobiology 452, 894
neurocognitive systems 567, 574, 576–8
neuroconstructivism 831–2, 835, 838
neurodegenerative diseases 14, 899–913
neurodevelopmental disorders 812, 829, 831, 838
neuroimaging 813, 885, 900–1
– functional 706, 714, 882
neurological disorders 12–13, 379
neuronal activation 571–2, 574, 576
neuroplasticity 572, 705–16
neuroscience, developmental 12, 567
neutral affixes 220, 222
newborns 50, 280, 766
Newcombe, F. 721–2, 735, 740, 742
Newport, E. 50, 67–8, 198, 678
NH, see normal hearing
Niparko, J.K. 771–2, 778, 780–1, 784
Nir, B. 221, 226, 235, 237, 245, 249–51, 525, 527, 529–35, 537
Nissen, M.J. 756–7
NL, see native language
Noble, K.G. 565–6, 568–9, 575–6
noise 23, 32, 34–5, 48, 105, 130, 192, 299, 442, 780
non-alphabetic scripts 512
nonce words 222, 229, 316
non-finite clauses 236–7, 243, 246, 249
non-fluent PPA 883, 885, 893, 902, 906
non-literal language 267–8, 273–4, 706, 837
nonsuccesses 667, 669, 671, 673, 675, 677, 679, 681
non-verbal communication 97, 570, 907, 910
non-verbal devices 9, 279–80
non-words 165–6, 419, 482, 486, 508–10, 629–30, 725–8, 736–7, 740–5, 889–90
Norbury, C.F. 2, 138, 279, 288, 330, 345–6, 358, 811–12, 815, 818–22
normal birth weight (NBW) 207–8, 210–14

normal hearing (NH) 21, 26, 29, 31, 43, 53, 55, 768, 771–6, 784
normally hearing children 770–1, 773–4
norms 20, 149, 207, 621, 628
– monolingual 109–10, 607, 621, 632–3, 652, 654
– national 649, 652–5
Northwestern Assessment of Verbs and Sentences (NAVS) 906
noun bias 101, 103, 108
noun phrases 168, 248, 318, 340, 342, 379, 515, 535, 619, 626
nouns 103, 107–8, 157–8, 189, 206, 489–91, 629, 694–5, 854, 890–1
– count 168–70
– mass 168, 170
novel labels 262, 265–6, 272, 286–7, 293, 295
novel objects 55, 263–6, 287, 821
novel verbs 186, 264
novel words 53, 55, 96, 259, 261, 264, 266, 287, 297, 552
novices 440, 444, 448–50, 452
Novogrodsky, R. 237, 242, 252, 744
NSs, see native speakers
Nunes, T. 224, 407, 471
nurseries 585–6, 589, 594–5

Oakhill, J.V. 138, 142, 440, 517–18
object knowledge 901–3, 905
object naming 905
O'Grady, W. 668–9
OIORs, see other-initiated other-repairs
OISRs (other-initiated self-repairs), see other-initiated self-repairs (OISRs)
older adults 863–74, 882
older children 119–20, 125, 127, 129, 335, 339, 405, 465, 593–4, 712–13
Olinghouse, N.G. 526, 528, 530
Oller, K.D. 92–3, 110, 557, 569, 627, 766, 773, 820
Olsson, J. 471
omissions 207, 618–19, 621, 626, 692, 695–6, 728, 731–6, 740, 893
onsets
– of babbling 29, 773, 784
– of canonical babbling 773, 778, 833
– complex 64, 69–72, 80–2
– delayed 104, 111, 765
opaque derivations 488, 491–3, 499

open questions 377, 397, 634, 735
optimality theory 73
oral language 10, 415, 418–20, 422, 428, 430–1, 783, 799
– skills 415, 417–18, 422, 425, 428, 430, 547
oral narratives 226, 236, 249–50, 368, 532
orthographic awareness 415, 419, 424–5
orthographic input buffer 724, 734, 742
orthographic input lexicon 724–5, 728, 731, 736–9, 742–4, 747
orthographic knowledge 419, 464, 471
orthographic lexicon 444, 725, 742, 904
orthographic patterns 471, 478, 483, 485, 487–8, 498
orthographic representations 448–9, 512–13
orthographic retrieval 890
orthographical decoding 510–11, 513
orthographic-visual analyser 722–3, 727, 731, 733, 735, 737–8, 741
orthographies 5, 439, 441–2, 444–7, 462, 464, 729–30, 732, 734, 741
– deep 463
– English 438, 450, 452, 462, 464, 469
– shallow 463, 471
– transparent 447, 461, 471, 509, 511
other-initiated other-repairs (OIORs) 392–3
other-initiated self-repairs (OISRs) 392, 394, 401
Ouellette, M. 424, 429
overhearing 263, 297, 780
over-regularization 192–4

Pacton, S. 224, 464–7, 478
Papagno, C. 145, 676
Papousek, H. 314, 813
Paradis, J. 2, 76, 601, 605, 607, 618–21, 623, 651, 696, 700
parental education 566, 569, 573, 575, 577, 588, 784, 803–4
parental involvement 13, 793–806
parent-child interactions 199, 298, 333–4, 389, 427, 548–51, 558, 595
parenting 298, 430, 549–51, 558, 566, 795, 805
parietal cortex 574, 578, 754, 870
Parkinson's Disease (PD) 899, 911, 913
partners 259, 265, 270–1, 279, 286, 293–4, 299, 313–18, 321–2, 815–16
– communicative 94, 271, 281–2, 286, 289–91, 295–7, 299, 301–2, 551, 895
– conversational 271, 295, 312–13
– social 9, 93–4, 286, 301–2
PASA, see posterior-anterior shift in aging
past tense 186–9, 393–4, 498, 536, 692–3, 776, 835
Paul, R. 97, 319, 709, 711, 814, 816, 819, 822
pauses 398, 836, 884, 903
– filled 901–3
PBF (percentage of base forms) 209, 211–14
PD, see Parkinson's Disease
Peabody Picture Vocabulary Test (PPVT) 546, 770, 779–80
Pearson, B.Z. 109–10, 627–8, 643–4, 646, 697
Pendergast, M. 653–4
Pennington, B.F. 508, 753
Penny, S. 289, 291
penultimate stress 67–8
percentage of base forms (PBF) 209, 211–14
perception 4, 19, 23, 33, 46–7, 55, 69, 525–6, 778, 781
– auditory 19, 22, 27–30, 34, 47, 97
– speech, see speech, perception
perceptual processing 33, 37
Perfetti, C.A. 5, 225, 437–9, 441, 444–5, 447–8, 450, 453, 506–7, 512
performance 290–2, 294, 589–90, 630–2, 710–12, 756, 758–61, 833–4, 863–71, 885–6
– academic 247, 567, 801
– behavioral 572, 574, 757, 867, 871, 874
– cognitive 566, 829, 874
– linguistic 617, 874
– narrative 13, 705, 712
– spelling 463, 465, 467–8, 477–99
perinatal stroke (PS) 705–16
perisylvian, left 574–6, 578
Perovic, A. 835–6
personal experience 236, 331–2, 371
personal narratives 331, 334, 336–7, 344, 347, 372, 711
Petersen, D. 359, 365–6, 379, 382
Peterson, C. 273, 330–1, 333–5, 338–40, 342, 345–6, 812
Pexman, P.M. 124, 126–7, 129, 132, 268, 273
PGC (phoneme-to-grapheme correspondences) 10, 461–3, 467–8
Philips, B. 767, 782, 836

phoneme level 159–60, 163, 166–7
phonemes 32, 156–7, 159–60, 163–4, 407, 409–12, 462–3, 725–6, 736, 739–40
phoneme-to-grapheme correspondences, see PGC
phonemic accuracy 774–5
phonemic awareness 466, 477
phonemic scripts 444, 450
phonological awareness 415–16, 418–20, 422, 424–6, 428–30, 462–3, 471–2, 567, 657, 799
phonological buffer dyslexia 740–1, 744–5
phonological changes 206, 219–20, 228, 465–7
phonological complexity 80, 630–1
phonological deficits 470, 508–11, 736, 738, 753–4
phonological dyslexia 722, 739–41, 745–6
– developmental 721, 739–40
– multiletter 739–40
phonological errors 166, 168, 469, 629
phonological form 160, 162, 169–70, 186, 407, 725, 738, 868
phonological information 52, 160, 462–3, 508, 725, 760, 855, 908
phonological memory 620, 630, 632, 833
phonological output buffer 156, 725–6, 728, 737, 740, 742
phonological output lexicon (POL) 156, 163, 165–6, 725, 737–40, 742–3, 746
phonological processing 138, 461, 629, 708
phonological recoding 505–7, 509–11, 833
phonological representations 82, 167, 170–1, 508, 512
phonological skills 140, 462, 464, 469–71, 509, 754
phonological structures 6, 65, 69, 490
phonological transparency 219–20, 226, 228–9, 446, 452
phonological word form level 158–9, 163, 166, 171
phonology 2–3, 6, 28, 30, 170, 447–8, 465–6, 679, 746, 831–2
– developing 63–82
photographs 67, 289, 362, 390, 399, 407, 759, 821, 853, 908
phrase structure 691–3, 699
phrases 101–2, 137, 168–9, 437, 439–40, 525, 527, 856, 892–3, 901

physical environment 548, 855–6
picture books 118, 248, 312, 368, 382, 393, 625, 712
picture naming 161–2, 164, 168, 646, 821
pictures 268, 297–8, 344, 359–60, 363–7, 372, 378–9, 392–3, 399–400, 625
pinyin 449–51
place of articulation 36, 51, 54, 74, 76
plasticity, brain 566, 712
plot 330–1, 336–7, 391, 418–21, 423, 431, 711
plurals 189–92, 318, 481, 670, 854
pointing 14, 224, 283, 285–7, 294, 300, 816–17, 833–4, 837, 845
– declarative 284–5, 294
– gestures 285–6, 294
POL (phonological output lexicon) 156, 163, 165–6, 725, 737–40, 742–3, 746
Portuguese 649–50, 655–6
– European 72, 81
Posner, M.I. 291–2, 565–7, 576
posterior-anterior shift in aging (PASA) 864, 872, 874
posttests 360–8, 375, 378, 419, 472
poverty 3, 548, 550, 552, 565–7, 570, 572, 574, 593, 595
power 67, 75, 120, 337, 368, 484
PPA (primary progressive aphasias) 14, 883, 899–907, 909, 911–12
– variants 900–1, 905–7, 912
PPVT, see Peabody Picture Vocabulary Test
pragmatic ability 237, 710, 907
pragmatic skills 9, 138, 295, 311, 342, 837
pragmatics 2, 23, 91, 138, 812, 817, 822–3, 902, 910, 912–13
precursors 238, 240, 415, 569
predicates 238, 241, 852
predictors 97–8, 590–1, 623, 628, 657–9, 776–8, 782, 785, 799, 801
prefixes 118, 219–20, 483, 494
prefrontal cortex 145, 197, 566, 571, 573–4, 576–8, 754, 864, 869
prelexical level 482, 487, 489–90, 492–4, 497–9
prepositions 94, 619, 634, 690, 692, 699, 854, 887, 892
preschool children 9–10, 103–5, 137–8, 287–8, 368–70, 372–3, 415–31, 570, 609–10, 628–9
– bilingual 607–8

preschool teachers 111, 417, 419, 422, 424, 428, 431
present tense 182, 186, 393, 479–80
preterm children 8, 97–9, 203–5, 208, 214
Prevoo, M.J.L. 593, 654
primary progressive aphasias, see PPA
primary schools 509, 512, 585, 589, 759
primes 223, 485–6, 488–90, 492–3, 499
priming 35, 223, 484–6, 490, 872
– effects 485, 487–8, 490–1, 493–4, 821, 872
– paradigms, long-lag 485–6, 494
– semantic 494, 833, 911
– techniques, masked 486, 488, 492–3, 498
print
– accessible 850, 852–3
– awareness 415, 418–20, 422–6, 428–31
printed words 424, 437, 443, 446, 485
prior knowledge 19, 23, 32–3, 37, 357, 516–17
problem solving 140, 142, 573, 586, 847–8
problem spaces 645–6, 661
Processability Theory 674, 681
processes 155–7, 181–4, 194, 479–80, 487–94, 506–7, 527–8, 756–8, 850, 856–7
– automatic 486, 493–4, 498, 755
– encoding 425–7, 431
– lexical access 482–3, 485–6
– reading 645, 722, 746–7
– spoken word production 7, 155–73
– word-level 507, 513, 515
processing 5–6, 8–9, 21–3, 27–9, 31–7, 672–3, 815, 864–5, 888–9, 891–2
– auditory 19, 33, 97
– grammatical 713, 891, 893
– information 145, 440
– language 14, 26, 31, 148, 164, 863, 867, 869, 882, 887
– levels of 161, 163, 167, 499
– lexical 462, 480, 484–5, 491, 493, 557, 891
– linguistic 143, 194, 461, 595, 818–19, 874
– mechanisms 161, 673, 887, 893
– morphological 8, 11, 182, 188, 221, 229, 461, 470
– perceptual 33, 37
– phonological 138, 461, 629, 708
– semantic 165, 888, 910
– sentence 867, 871–4, 887, 891–3
– skills 12, 545, 555, 558
– syntactic 871, 887
– top-down 32–3, 35, 95, 338

productions, children's 63, 65, 69–70, 72–3, 78–9, 82, 318, 331, 822
productive vocabulary 101, 110, 553–4, 709, 821, 834
productivity 220, 228, 338–9, 419, 428, 497, 529, 625–6
profiles 595, 620–1, 690–2, 695, 707–9, 773, 835, 883, 885, 910
– language 148, 606, 709, 712, 883, 911
– linguistic 620, 693, 830, 832, 899
progressive aphasia 14, 905, 909; see also PPA
progressive diseases 901, 907, 909
prompts 364, 379, 395, 398–9, 401, 527, 554, 865
pronouns 316–17, 340, 342, 619, 626, 851, 854, 884, 890, 902–3
– clitic 313, 618, 634
pronunciation 443, 446–7, 478–80, 679–80, 739
prosodic word 64–7, 73, 78–80
protagonists 331, 344, 359, 381, 421, 535, 634
proverbs 7, 117, 119–20, 123, 140, 145, 890
pseudo-derivations 488, 491–2, 498
pseudowords 466, 468, 488, 490, 630, 889
psycholinguistics 1, 4, 228, 444, 525–6, 832, 886, 889
psychology 1, 3, 185, 832
– cognitive 117, 894
– developmental 143, 148, 186
psychophysical tuning curves 45–7
Punjabi 649–50, 656
puppets 124–5, 127, 129, 268, 280, 361, 369
Purser, H.R.M. 119, 834

QA, see quality assurance
qualitative changes 9, 104, 331, 820
qualitative differences 513, 692, 821, 887
quality assurance (QA) 850–1, 854
Quine, W.V.O. 187, 189, 197, 261
Quittner, A.L. 767, 798–9, 801

Rahamim, E. 723, 727, 729–30
Ramsden, C.A.H. 292, 294
Ramus, F. 463, 469, 508, 753–4
Rapp, B. 145, 155, 442
Rastle, K. 488–9, 493
rats 183–4, 187, 192, 194–5
Raveh, M. 223, 489, 491

Ravid, D. 3–5, 223, 227, 330–1, 451, 481–2, 525, 532–3, 536, 855
RCs, *see* relative clauses
RDLS (Reynell Developmental Language Scales) 770–2
reaction time (RT) 110, 756–7, 848
readers 5–6, 12–14, 406–8, 442–4, 503–6, 513–17, 725, 732–4, 736–8, 740–4
– adult 451, 512, 515
– beginning 451, 507, 510, 514, 517
– good 470, 508, 513–14, 516, 518
– normal 448, 471, 729, 758
– poor 413, 503–6, 508–19
– skilled 225, 407, 443–4, 449–51, 508, 512, 515–17, 722, 726, 731
readiness, school 137, 592
reading
– ability 205, 408, 412, 505, 516, 853
– accuracy 224, 659, 742
– acquisition 10, 441, 452, 461, 463, 466, 509, 512, 734, 743
– comprehension 11–12, 97, 138, 140–2, 224–5, 227, 415–16, 422, 503–19, 744
– skills 506, 509–10, 512–13
– and vocabulary knowledge 643–61
– difficulties 31, 409, 412, 472, 503–4, 506–7, 514–15, 518–19, 727, 732
– disabilities 359, 468, 503, 507
– impairments 13, 31, 467, 727, 735, 746, 754, 761
– intervention 417–19, 424, 503, 519
– models 225, 722–3, 727
– performance 468, 482, 509–10, 643
– process 645, 722, 746–7
– shared book 333, 417–22, 427, 430–1
– skills 98, 103–4, 437, 443–4, 461, 467–8, 504, 507, 509–10, 513
– tasks 504–5, 508–10, 518, 568, 728
receptive language ability 92, 97–8, 770
receptive vocabulary 102, 589, 592, 626, 628, 652–3, 657, 772, 779–80, 833–7
– English 651–4, 657
receptive-expressive gap 110
recoding, phonological 505–7, 509–11, 833
recordings 208–9, 409, 546, 557
referential ambiguity 269–70
referential communication 279, 288, 301, 342
referential intentions 262–4, 266
referentiality 329, 340–1, 344

referents 263–4, 266, 269–70, 283, 286, 299, 313, 316–17, 527, 536
reformulations 104, 318–19, 321, 393
regular words 165–6, 191, 193, 195–6, 736, 745
regularities 96, 194–5, 462, 738, 754–5
rehabilitation 412, 766–7, 777
Reichle, E.D. 225, 673
relative clauses 207, 236–7, 240–2, 245, 248–9, 251–2, 514, 632, 634, 848
– center-embedded 241, 514
remediation 21, 37, 412, 505, 511, 696
– programs 503–4, 519
repaired sequences 901–3
repeated sequences 93, 756, 758
repetition 23, 166, 219, 485–6, 490, 536, 885, 905–6, 908, 911
– sentence 505, 629, 632, 905, 910
representations
– cognitive 329, 534
– conceptual 156, 726, 904
– distributed 155, 511
– lexical 53, 482–3, 485–7, 490–1, 496, 498–9, 512–13, 558
– meaning 156, 407, 512–13, 889
– orthographic 448–9, 512–13
– phonological 82, 167, 170–1, 508, 512
– syntactic 673
– whole-word 220, 484, 490, 492
Rescorla, L.A. 96–7, 99, 102–3, 183–4, 194, 196, 627, 709, 820
resources 323, 368, 551, 565–6, 568, 594–5, 698, 866
– cognitive 507, 515, 864, 866, 874
– working memory 330, 343–4, 481
responses 126–8, 164, 166, 183–4, 291–2, 300–1, 319–21, 393–4, 483–5, 813–17
– contingent 318–19, 321–3
– corrective 319–20
– internal 334, 366, 372, 378
responsibility 297–8, 389, 394, 396–7, 595, 796, 805, 846
– transfer of 389, 395–6, 398, 400
retelling 331–2, 344, 346, 357–8, 363, 370, 377–8, 625
retrieval 163, 468, 508, 512, 868–9, 882, 886, 890, 893
– lexical 14, 706, 746, 867–9, 874, 884, 889, 893
– orthographic 890

- whole-word form 10, 463, 479
- word 97, 167, 575, 867–70, 881–2, 884, 888–9, 891, 893, 910
Reynell Developmental Language Scales (RDLS) 770–2
Reznick, J.S. 101, 205, 555, 734
rhetorical questions 126, 267, 296
rhymes 296, 373, 419–20, 567
Rice, K. 63, 75, 553, 618, 694, 696, 698–700, 708, 819, 830
right hemisphere 577, 709, 713–16, 866, 869–71, 873, 882
risk factors 205, 212, 576, 587–8, 590–1, 802
Risley, T.R. 3, 330, 546–7, 550, 552–4, 587, 589, 591–2, 603
Robinson, B.F. 29, 289, 550, 578, 674, 833, 835
Roeper, T. 239, 619, 697
Rowe, M.L. 3, 284–5, 546–7, 551–3, 568, 592, 784
rules 412–13, 471, 479, 527, 535, 618, 738–9, 755, 759, 886
- grammatical 186, 528, 759, 818
- grapheme-to-phoneme conversion 726, 736, 738, 740
- learning 184–5, 188
- morphological 692–3, 738
Rumelhart, D.E. 186–8, 483
Russian 67, 621–2, 624–5, 627, 631, 633–4, 649–50, 677, 679
Rutter, M. 205, 504

Saffran, E.M. 4, 43, 50, 54, 92, 155, 159, 185, 835, 891–4
Saiegh-Haddad, E. 225, 438, 447, 451
samples 102–3, 105, 195, 198, 377, 379–80, 586, 589, 625–6, 652–3
- spontaneous 624–6
- standardisation 585, 587, 589, 594
sampling 192, 195, 198–9
Samuelson, L.K. 264–5
sarcasm 139–40, 259, 267, 645, 706, 837
Saxton, M. 318–21
scaffolding 8, 10, 238, 240, 389, 395, 397, 400, 865, 870
- heuristic 389, 395, 397–8, 401
- theory 392, 400, 870
Schieffelin, B.B. 296
schizophrenia 145, 272, 274

Schmidt, R. 674, 676
Schneider, P. 44, 46–7, 331, 336, 338, 359, 361, 368–9, 371, 373
school age 2, 5, 10, 222, 245, 248, 251–2, 705, 709, 714
school entry 103, 138, 554
school readiness 137, 592
schools 243–4, 367, 369, 390, 604, 606, 625, 644–5, 651–3, 799–800
- high 246–7, 633
- primary 509, 585, 589
Schreuder, R. 488, 495–7
Scollon, R. 239, 322
scores 105, 107, 203, 209–10, 212, 587, 589, 622, 624, 651–2
- BIPAQ 624
- grammaticality judgment 528, 530, 759
- IQ 505, 590
- language 97, 652, 772, 784
screening 148, 591, 601, 608–9, 697, 766, 814
scripts 329–30, 336, 408, 441, 446–7, 450, 677–8
- alphabetical 449, 461, 463, 512
- linear 446–7
- moraic 450
- morphemic 450
- non-alphabetic 512
- phonemic 444, 450
second grade 236, 358, 415–16, 649, 652, 654–5, 657–60
second language 12, 225, 593, 617, 619, 630, 632
- acquisition 667–81
- learners 108–9, 148, 674
- learning 3, 12, 593, 667, 672
second year of life 93, 98, 285, 294, 301, 316, 415, 766–7, 815–16
secondary disorders 19–21, 37
Segal, O. 54, 68–9
segmentation 49, 222, 423, 428, 489, 553, 778
selective attention 34, 570–2
- tasks 571–2, 576
selective deficits 723, 727, 735, 741, 746
selective mutism 27, 610
self-regulation 137, 427, 574, 819
self-repair 317, 389, 392, 394, 398–9, 401
semantic context 514–15, 872
semantic deficits 513, 743, 890, 904, 913
semantic dementia 904

semantic errors 164–6, 168, 393, 401, 629, 721, 743
semantic impairments 167, 901, 903–4, 910
semantic information 35, 145, 449, 515, 821
semantic knowledge 123, 491, 834
semantic lexicon 725–6, 737–8, 743–4
semantic memory 204, 868, 889
semantic priming 494, 833, 911
semantic processing 165, 888, 910
semantic system 162, 165–6, 890, 903
semantic transparency 220, 223, 225, 229, 489, 493–4, 496, 498–9
semantics 162, 167–8, 191–3, 219–20, 228, 449, 490–1, 822–3, 890, 902–3
– access to 167, 743–4
– lexical 157–8, 821
Semitic languages 248, 492, 494, 853–4
SEN, *see* special educational needs
Sénéchal, M. 333, 336, 417, 424, 429–30, 465, 467, 478
sensitivity 24–5, 27, 45, 49–50, 228–9, 280–1, 466, 469–70, 673, 889–92
sensory impairments 25, 707, 753
sentence comprehension 14, 422, 515, 744, 867, 870, 872–3, 891, 893, 905
sentence context 466, 516, 726, 743
sentence level 342, 506, 516, 706, 772, 781
sentence processing 867, 871–4, 887, 891–3
sentence production 377, 893, 906
sentence repetition 505, 629, 632, 905, 910
– tasks 617, 622, 633
sentence structure 36, 588, 850–2, 886, 888, 891
sentences 32, 409–12, 506–7, 514–16, 528, 632–4, 673–4, 744, 851–2, 891–5
– complex 251–2, 357–8, 514–15, 547, 845, 848, 851, 871–2, 911, 913
– plausible 514–15
– simple 569, 589, 592, 848, 852, 854
sequences 93, 238–40, 321, 334–5, 340–1, 388–90, 395–7, 674–5, 756–7, 759–60
– learning 757–9
– repaired 901–3
– repeated 93, 756, 758
– symbol 729, 746, 759
sequential bilinguals 110–11, 617–20, 628–9, 632–3
Serial Reaction Time (SRT) 753–8
settings

– educational 423, 585–6, 593, 795
– environmental and socioeconomic 565–79
Seymour, P. 227, 438, 441, 469, 472, 619, 697
Shafto, M.A. 108, 863–5, 868–70, 874, 889
Shallice, T. 722, 731–2
shallow orthographies 463, 471
Shapiro, L.R. 330, 336, 339–40, 344–5
shared book reading 333, 417–22, 427, 430–1
Shatz, M. 270–1, 316
Shiro, M. 331, 336, 344–5, 347
Shneidman, L.A. 554, 591
shocks 183–4, 187
short-term memory 623, 632, 724, 830, 832–3, 848
Shteiman, M. 5, 698, 814, 816–22
Shvimer, L. 730–2
sibilants, final 187, 190, 192
Siegel, L.S. 185, 203, 205, 461–2, 504–5, 508, 742
signals 36, 47, 55, 182, 294, 299, 765
– acoustic 19, 34, 45, 49, 55, 477, 765
– speech 26–8, 34–6, 92, 769
signers, beginning 681
signs 20, 259, 407, 423, 451, 606, 610, 697, 794, 889–90
– visual 405, 408, 410–11
silent letters 478–9, 481, 736, 739
Silva, M.L. 250, 298, 340–1, 424, 429
Silverman, R.D. 655, 658
simple clauses 526, 632
simple sentences 569, 589, 592, 848, 852, 854
simplification 71, 191, 854, 856–7, 893
simplified information 850, 854, 857
simultaneity 243, 250, 340–1
single letters 407, 437, 736, 739–40
single words 23, 495, 605, 609, 722–4, 729, 744–5, 812, 902–3, 906
single-word comprehension 902–3, 905
singular forms 189–91, 193, 481
skilled readers 225, 407, 443–4, 449–51, 508, 512, 515–17, 722, 726, 731
skills
– alphabetic 10, 415, 417, 422, 424, 428–9
– cognitive 11, 37, 93, 109, 111, 119, 123, 125, 260, 272
– communication 284, 566, 795, 799
– component 347, 505–6, 514, 517–18
– conversational, *see* conversational skills
– decoding 375, 507, 510–11, 645, 661

- decontextualized 376, 380
- discrimination 53, 92
- encoding 425
- expressive 9, 248, 331, 339, 395, 812
- grammatical 529, 569, 818
- language 98, 372, 374–5, 377, 380, 546, 548, 569, 576, 770–1
- linguistic 37, 99, 221, 227, 338, 366, 586, 755, 837
- literacy 227, 425, 430, 569, 645, 849
- mind 262, 265, 268, 270–2, 347
- morphological 227, 472
- narrative 332–4, 336, 346, 366, 373, 378–9, 837
- phonological 140, 462, 464, 469–71, 509, 754
- pragmatic 9, 138, 295, 311, 342, 837
- processing 12, 545, 555, 558
- reading 98, 103–4, 437, 443–4, 461, 467–8, 504, 507, 509–10, 513
- reading comprehension 506, 509–10, 512–13
- socio-pragmatic 279–302
- speech perception 28, 48, 54, 92
- spelling 467–8, 470–1, 504, 515
- spoken language 26, 766, 793
- theory of mind (ToM) 262, 265, 268, 270–2, 347
- vocabulary 593, 646

Slabakova, R. 671, 677, 679
sleep 24, 241, 245, 757, 766
SLI (Specific Language Impairment) 2, 13, 107, 357–60, 469–70, 617–21, 623–6, 628–32, 634, 822–3
- bilingual children with 617, 620, 631, 635
- in bilingual development 617–35
- changing profile 689–700
- symptoms 690–1, 697, 699

Slobin, D.I. 207, 235–6, 239, 244–5, 248, 330–1, 334–42, 345, 530–2, 625
Slocum, T. 359, 362, 368, 371, 373
SLPs (speech-language pathologists) 1–2, 4, 358, 367, 369, 374–5, 377–8, 382, 607, 609
small group work 369, 372, 377, 387–9, 391, 394–5, 399–400, 419–20, 424
Smolensky, P. 63–4, 69, 73
Smolka, E. 493–4, 496
Snowden, J. 904

Snowling, M.J. 140–1, 146, 438, 504, 508, 513, 515–16, 753, 756, 760
social backgrounds 586, 589, 595
social class 551, 586
social cognition 20, 23, 124, 147, 341
social communication 138, 140, 288, 811, 816
social competence 405, 797–8, 801
social deprivation 585–6, 589–91, 593, 595
social disadvantage 146, 576, 593
social functions 126, 128–30, 273
social interactions 34, 137–40, 146, 148, 204, 209, 332, 342, 811, 815
social partners 9, 93–4, 286, 301–2
social relationships 7, 137, 140, 797
social stimuli 290–1
social world 37, 357, 417
social-emotional development 330, 548, 800
societal language 617, 621–2, 624–5
socioeconomic backgrounds 97, 109, 572, 575, 776
- and early language 545–58
- low 415–31
socioeconomic status 11–12, 104, 214, 545, 549, 556, 565, 567, 575, 585–95
socio-pragmatic cues 285–6, 295, 301
socio-pragmatic skills 279–302
Song, S. 5, 103–4, 141, 591, 864
sonorants 72, 75–6
sound detection 19, 25, 44
sound patterns 19, 21, 25, 32, 52
sound sensations 19, 22, 25, 27, 32–3
sound stimuli 19, 21–2, 32, 37, 766
sounds 19, 21–2, 24–5, 27–30, 43–4, 426–9, 444–6, 464, 477–80, 768
- speech 3, 21–3, 27–8, 31, 714, 768, 778
Spanish 248–9, 335, 532, 623–5, 631, 633, 649–59, 673, 677, 679
Spanish-English bilinguals 651, 653–5, 657, 661
special educational needs (SEN) 10, 387–9, 395, 416
Specific Language Impairment, *see* SLI
speech 19–21, 25–37, 47–9, 409–10, 552–4, 769–71, 773, 777–85, 883–4, 905–6
- apraxia of 167, 900–1, 905
- caregiver 551, 553–5
- children 70, 73, 78, 209, 592, 768, 773, 781, 802
- connected 783, 884, 904, 906, 910

- development 6, 20, 30, 554, 780–1
- errors 164–5, 172, 902
- intelligibility 23, 769, 777, 783
- perception 28–9, 31–3, 35, 43–56, 767, 769, 777, 780, 782, 785
- assessment 35–6
- skills 28, 48, 54, 92
- private 569–70
- production 29, 155, 741, 743, 769, 778–9, 781–2, 811, 820, 883–4
- rates 28, 901–3, 906
- sounds 3, 21–3, 27–8, 31, 714, 768, 778
- spontaneous 546–7, 553, 617, 622, 624, 773, 776, 901, 903, 905
- stream 49, 410, 413, 558, 778, 835
speech-language pathologists, *see* SLPs
spellers 461, 471, 479–82, 498
- French 478, 481
spelling 11, 224, 410–11, 426–9, 446, 461–73, 477–83, 487–9, 497–9, 754–5
- achievement 461–3, 468, 470
- acquisition 461–72
- development 448, 461–2, 472
- difficulties 461, 465, 467, 470, 472
- errors 469, 477, 498
- patterns 469, 487, 492
- performance 463, 465, 467–8, 477–99
- skills 467–8, 470–1, 504, 515
Spencer, T. 147, 219, 359, 368, 371, 373
Spinner, P. 670, 674–5
spoken language 19–20, 23, 33, 415, 437, 440–1, 450–2, 776, 779, 794
- comprehension 556, 771
- development 770, 776, 778
- skills 26, 766, 793
spoken word 156, 410–11, 423, 445–6, 477, 508, 725–6
- production 7, 155–73
spontaneous gaze 280, 289, 294, 301
spontaneous speech 546–7, 553, 617, 622, 624, 773, 776, 901, 903, 905
SRT, *see* Serial Reaction Time
SSWUs, *see* Successive Single-Word Utterances
Stainthorp, R. 528, 531, 534
Stamatakis, E.A. 864–6, 869, 871
standardisation samples 585, 587, 589, 594
standardized tests 546, 556, 587, 589–90, 595, 690, 695, 770–2, 776, 780
Stanovich, K.E. 444, 447, 504–5, 508, 515–16

statistical learning 13, 50, 754, 761
status
- morphological 483, 487, 492, 498
- socioeconomic 11–12, 104, 214, 545, 549, 556, 565, 567, 575, 585–95
stems 191, 206–7, 220–1, 223, 227–9, 477–9, 482–96, 498–9, 724–5, 742–3
- bound 220, 222, 228, 482–3, 487, 494
- consonantal 489–90, 495–7
- existing 488, 490–1
- free 220, 222, 228
- frequency 483–4
Stevens, K.N. 51, 571, 573
stigma 566, 848–9
stimulation 25, 571, 813, 869
- acoustic 766, 769, 781
- bimodal 780–1
- cognitive 549–51, 566
stimuli 22, 48, 52, 55, 183–4, 290–3, 733–4, 755–6, 758, 760
- auditory 26, 29, 44, 760–1
- central 293
- social 290–1
- sound 19, 21–2, 32, 37, 766
Stone, A.C. 224–5, 320, 462
stops 72, 75–6, 81, 193, 239, 601, 604, 738, 774
storage 23, 34, 157, 167, 480, 675–6, 726
story grammar 332, 334, 337, 357, 360–2, 364–5, 417, 421, 618–19
- approach 334, 359, 381–3
- components 366, 368, 379
- elements 336, 359, 366–70, 372–3, 376, 378–82
- interventions 359, 368–9, 373
story schemas 329–30, 332, 337–8, 346
story structure 372, 381, 710
storytelling 330, 344, 346, 358, 371
Strapp, C.M. 319–20
stress 67–8, 95, 118, 184, 345, 446, 550, 566, 570, 574
- family 545, 549–50
- patterns 65–8, 78, 167, 739
strings 29, 239, 242, 244, 410, 495, 629–30, 759–60, 890, 892
- letter 444, 470, 483, 487–8, 492, 733, 759
stroke 156, 164, 440, 447, 706, 708, 882
- perinatal 705–16
stroke-linked aphasia 882–3

structures
- grammatical 5, 137, 330, 514, 554, 677
- internal 159, 219, 222, 477, 495–6, 499, 526
- linguistic 226, 279, 293, 339, 343, 377, 380–1, 677
- morphological 226, 470, 479, 482, 487, 492–3, 496–7, 499, 732, 854
- narrative 338–9, 341, 369, 713–14
- neural 14, 183, 863, 874
- phonological 6, 65, 69, 490
- phrase 691–3, 699
- sentence 36, 588, 850–2, 886, 888, 891
- story 372, 381, 710
- syllable 63, 65, 69–71
- syntactic 121, 330, 345, 514, 547, 634, 673, 871, 902, 906
- verb argument 207, 694, 698
sublexical route 462, 725–8, 736–9, 741, 743–4
subordinate clauses 246, 250–2, 338–9, 345, 379, 533, 690, 711
subordination 237, 249, 341, 533, 535
substitutions 30, 76–7, 207, 690, 692, 732–5, 740, 887, 901–2
success, academic 119, 415, 431, 628, 799
Successive Single-Word Utterances (SSWUs) 321–2
suffixes 206–7, 219–24, 228–9, 464, 466–7, 472, 478–9, 486–9, 494–5, 498
- agentive 221–2, 226, 229
- derivational 222, 478
surface dyslexia 510, 722, 736–9, 741, 744–6, 900, 905
Swanson, L. 363, 366, 375, 509, 514, 529–30
Swedish 117, 679, 681, 699
syllable structure 63, 65, 69–71
syllables 50–1, 63–70, 73, 78–81, 159, 185, 412, 446, 721, 725
symbols 93, 198, 359, 368, 445, 729, 734, 850, 852–3, 857
- sequences 729, 746, 759
symptoms, grammatical 690–1, 700
synchronization 81–2
syntactic complexity 240–1, 250, 338–9, 341, 515, 632, 634, 710, 818, 912
syntactic context 338, 446, 498
syntactic deficits 671, 743, 886
syntactic development 260, 553, 589, 775, 837
syntactic errors 619, 902–3

syntactic knowledge 222, 514, 629, 658, 817, 837
syntactic packaging 8, 235, 252, 532
syntactic processing 871, 887
syntactic properties 122, 222, 480
syntactic representations 673
syntactic structures 121, 330, 345, 514, 547, 634, 673, 871, 902, 906
syntax 2, 7–8, 526, 569, 671–2, 675–6, 679, 710–11, 821–3, 902–4
- complex, see complex syntax
- lexical 157–8, 160–1, 168, 170
systematicity 196, 442, 493
Szagun, G. 775, 777

Taft, M. 219, 482, 484, 487–8, 492, 494, 724
Tager-Flusberg, H. 273, 345, 812, 819–20, 837
Tamil 649–50, 655–6
target objects 281–2, 284, 286–7, 291–3, 295
target words 63, 67–8, 70–1, 485, 513, 724, 727–8, 730–1, 734–5, 741–2
TAs, see teaching assistants
task demands 332, 344, 712, 865–7, 874
task performance 576, 760, 864–6, 871
tasks 123–5, 193–4, 227, 289–92, 505–6, 527–8, 571–3, 632–4, 756, 864–6
- categorization 760, 834
- cognitive 571–3, 675–6, 864–5
- complex 197, 675, 679
- cued-attention 291–2
- language 371, 566, 568, 705, 714, 865–7, 869
- reading 504–5, 508–10, 518, 568, 728
- selective attention 571–2, 576
- sentence repetition 617, 622, 633
TD, see typically developing children
teachers 236, 368–9, 378, 388–91, 395, 399–400, 412, 418–20, 429–31, 586–7
- preschool 111, 417, 419, 422, 424, 428, 431
teaching assistants (TAs) 387, 394–5
teasing 129–30, 141
technology 437, 441–2, 444, 856
Tees, R.C. 28, 43, 51
TEGI 696–7
television 67, 423, 550, 575, 818, 845
temporal lobes 865, 868–9, 882
tense 186, 378, 531, 618, 621, 690, 694, 696, 775, 854
- anchor 336

- past 186–9, 393–4, 498, 536, 692–3, 776, 835
- present 182, 186, 393, 479–80

Tesar, B. 63
Test of early grammatical impairment (TEGI) 696
Test of Narrative Language (TNL) 364, 377–8
tests
- criterion-referenced 696, 700
- standardized 546, 556, 587, 589–90, 595, 690, 695, 770–2, 776, 780

text comprehension 421, 511, 516–17, 643
text quality 11, 526, 529–32, 534, 537
Thal, D. 94, 606, 709, 712
theory of mind (ToM) 9, 108, 117, 121, 123, 125, 131, 259–74, 313, 315
- skills 262, 265, 268, 270–2, 347
- understanding 260, 272, 274

third grade 652, 655, 657–8, 739
third person entities 292
Thompson, R. 237, 320, 531, 604, 680–1, 829, 886, 892, 894, 906
Thordardottir, E.T. 95, 621–2, 631
thresholds 3, 21–2, 26, 44–5, 156, 767–8
- adult 44–5, 47

TLD, see typical language development
TNL, see Test of Narrative Language
toddlers 53–6, 137, 237–8, 288, 301, 708–9, 815–17, 820–1, 833, 835
tokens 68, 189, 450, 487, 626, 709
ToM, see theory of mind
Tomasello, M. 196–7, 260, 263–6, 280–7, 295, 297, 314–17, 320, 554–5, 816
Tomblin, J.B 54, 251, 547, 707, 773–4, 779, 812
tones 21, 44, 183–4, 187, 446–7, 534, 572
tongue 22, 36, 51, 67, 92–3
tools 12, 14, 102, 142–3, 170, 617, 621–5, 632, 855, 857
- assessment 156, 595, 619, 628, 632, 696–7, 904
- clinical 26, 161, 624
- diagnostic 506, 617, 621, 628, 632–3

top-down processing 32–3, 35, 95, 338
topic elicitors 390–1
topic invitations 391–2, 400
toys 209, 262–4, 269–72, 280, 283, 285–7, 290, 337, 375, 592
training 171, 367–8, 370, 395, 471–2, 503, 506, 509, 511, 855–6

- studies 320, 424, 508–9

transfer of responsibility 389, 395–6, 398, 400
transparency 8, 121, 511
- phonological 219–20, 226, 228–9, 446, 452
- semantic 220, 223, 225, 229, 489, 493–4, 496, 498–9

transparent derivations 487, 491–3, 495, 499
transparent orthographies 447, 461, 471, 509, 511
transpositions 727–8, 736, 740–1, 901
traumatic brain injury 847, 881
Trehub, S.E. 44, 46–8, 51
Treiman, R. 444, 462, 464, 468–9, 477–8
triadic interactions 285, 291–2, 296, 816
trochaic bias 65, 67–8
truncation 66–8
Tsao, F.M. 52, 92, 555–6
Tsesmeli, S. 227, 472
Tuller, L. 623, 634
tuning curve 45–7
T-units 250, 252, 338, 360, 367, 375, 532–3
Tunmer, W.E. 438, 446, 507, 514–15, 528
Turkish 8, 118, 206–7, 339–40, 343, 624, 633, 650, 654–6, 727
turn alternation 313–14
Two-Step model 157–61, 170, 172
Tyler, L.K. 220, 222, 225, 229, 359, 863–6, 869–71, 874
typical language development (TLD) 71, 77, 97, 289–90, 299, 617–18, 620, 626, 631–5, 711–12
typically developing children 71, 78–81, 251–2, 293–4, 298–302, 319–20, 691–3, 705–16, 759–61, 833–7
typologies, language 4–5, 248, 343, 347, 528
Tzakosta, M. 68–9, 76, 78–9

Ucelli, P. 332, 336–7, 529
UG (Universal Grammar) 667–72, 677, 681
UK, see United Kingdom
United Kingdom 102, 387–8, 585–6
United States 102, 546–7, 781, 846
units, of meaning 182, 187, 194, 407
units of sound 181, 407, 445, 448, 477
Universal Grammar, see UG
universal model of learning to read 437–53
universal principles 6, 68–9, 73, 512
Urdu 624, 650, 656

utterances 120–1, 207–8, 210, 212–14, 240–3, 267–71, 317–23, 339–40, 406–7, 409–10
- mean length of 205, 207, 209–11, 319, 362, 692, 776, 784, 902, 904

validity 132, 250, 295, 754, 893
- ecological 5, 132, 697
Vallar, G. 145, 676, 733
Van der Lely, H.K.J. 2, 630, 696–7, 699, 708
Van Dijk, T.A. 506, 516, 527
van Kleeck, A. 366, 374, 417, 421
Vanormelingen, L. 784
variability 53, 336, 381, 555, 557, 601, 604–6, 618, 621, 709
Vasilyeva, M. 111, 239, 547, 552, 569, 589
verb argument structures 207, 694, 698
verb auxiliaries 884, 887, 892
verb forms 479–81, 490–1, 498
- Dutch 479–81
verb inflection 13, 634, 694–8
verb morphology 694–5, 698, 776
verb phrases (VPs) 319, 532, 893, 903
verbal fluency 575, 901, 906
verbal irony 7, 117, 124, 128–30, 132, 267–8
- Allusional Pretense Theory 130–1
- comprehension 124, 127, 130
- social functions 128–9
verbal memory 97, 104–5, 107, 140, 905
verbal morphology 320, 623, 775–6
verbs 94–5, 107–8, 186, 206–7, 241–2, 629, 680, 698–9, 854, 890–4
- derived 219, 478, 494
- novel 186, 264
Verhoeven, L. 103–4, 236, 250, 469–70, 532, 633, 645, 656, 659–60, 775
very low birth weight (VLBW) 207–9, 211–13
videos 267, 269, 301, 676–8
visual attention 813
visual cortex 753
visual deficit 732, 746
visual dyslexia 721–2, 735–6, 745
visual impairments 204, 735, 746, 783
visual modality 104, 106, 297, 733, 760
Visual Response Audiometry SPAC (VRASPAC) 35
visual signs 405, 408, 410–11
visual targets 484, 492–3
visual word recognition 482, 497–9, 506–7, 511–12

- dual-route models 461–2, 506, 511–12, 723–4, 742
VLBW, see very low birth weight
vocabulary 102–7, 378–80, 546–7, 556–8, 588–91, 626–8, 632–4, 643–9, 651–5, 657–61
- acquisition 93, 594, 627–9, 675, 834
- bilingual children 110, 627
- children's 101, 103, 110, 417, 546, 553, 557, 568, 591–2
- composition 102, 106, 820–1
- conceptual 109–10, 627
- development 93–4, 98, 546, 552, 554, 587, 589, 593–4, 644, 647–8
- Dutch 593, 654
- English, see English vocabulary
- expressive, see expressive vocabulary
- growth 104, 547, 553, 558, 627, 648, 651, 653–4, 659
- rates 106, 547, 553, 651–4
- higher 103, 547, 658, 873
- knowledge 101, 226, 546, 558, 643–61, 863
- development 643, 645, 647, 649, 651, 653, 655, 657, 659, 661
- learning 7, 102, 105, 111, 553, 647
- productive 101, 110, 553–4, 709, 821, 834
- receptive, see receptive vocabulary
- size 103–4, 107–9, 224, 546, 554–5, 568, 623, 628, 709
- skills 593, 646
vocalizations 27, 29–30, 92, 97, 284, 296, 298, 552, 554, 557
voice onset time, see VOT
voicing 36, 51, 206, 822
Volkmer, A. 907, 909
Volterra, V. 283–4, 699, 834–5
VOT (voice onset time) 48, 51–2
vowel letters 451, 727, 741
vowel patterns 489–91, 495, 497
vowels 29–30, 74–5, 92, 451, 462–3, 725–6, 739–41, 746, 774–5, 855
VPs (verb phrases) 319, 532, 893, 903
VRASPAC (Visual Response Audiometry SPAC) 35
Vukovic, R.K. 652–3, 659
Vygotsky, L.S. 389, 424

Wagner, A.R. 184, 194, 424, 528–9, 534
Walters, J. 618–20, 623, 625–6, 629, 633

Warrington, E.K. 722, 732
Waterfall, H. 239, 547, 552, 589
Weiner, P.S. 692
Weintraub, S. 337, 904, 906
Weismer, S.E. 95, 97, 589, 714
welfare 587, 589, 591–2
Welsh 628, 631
Werker, F. 30, 43, 51–3, 263, 755
Werner, L.A. 43–5, 47–8
Wernicke, C. 706, 883, 885
Wernicke's aphasia 886–7
Wexler, K. 618, 671, 694, 696, 708, 835–6
white matter 567, 829, 864, 882
Whitehurst, G.J. 319, 333, 415, 425, 429, 569, 575
whole-word form retrieval 10, 463, 479
whole-word representations 220, 484, 490, 492
Wierenga, C.E. 865, 868–9
Williams syndrome (WS) 829–38
Wilson, S.M. 52, 132, 167, 509, 755, 893, 901–4, 906
Wimmer, H. 260, 438, 463, 470–1, 509–11
Windsor, J. 251–2, 533, 631
Winke, P. 676
WMC, see working memory, capacity
word finding difficulties 167–8, 399, 401, 910, 912
word retrieval 97, 167, 575, 867–70, 881–2, 884, 888–9, 891, 893, 910
word-finding difficulties 167, 399, 884, 889, 891
working class 546, 587, 589
working memory 34–5, 138–40, 145–6, 330, 342–3, 480–1, 573–6, 674–6, 872, 911
– capacity 330, 505, 517, 676
– resources 330, 343–4, 481
– verbal 97, 905
workshops 421, 794, 799
writers 182, 405–7, 480, 482, 525–8, 530–1, 536–8, 643, 696
written composition 525, 527
written discourse 3, 147, 228, 526, 531–2
written forms 464, 508, 725–6, 738
written language 1, 3, 141, 145, 408, 437, 440–1, 443, 902–4, 906
written letters 415, 732–3, 908
written narratives 251, 375, 534
written texts 142, 145, 406, 411, 437, 441, 525–6, 530, 533–4, 537
written words 409–10, 441, 445, 506–8, 510, 723, 725–6, 729, 743–4, 888
– comprehension 725–6, 733, 744
WS, see Williams syndrome
Wu, X. 280, 444, 447, 449, 451

young adults 119, 467, 834, 836, 865–74
young children 102–3, 417–18, 422–5, 428–31, 601–3, 605–7, 804, 811, 815–19, 821
younger adults 864, 866–9, 872–3, 882
younger children 123, 125, 127, 129–30, 335–6, 368, 424–5, 651, 653, 710
Yule, W. 504, 832

Zaidman-Zait, A. 108, 796, 803–4, 815–16
Ziegler, J. 438, 441, 446, 448, 453, 461–3, 506, 509, 511
Zoccolotti, P. 511, 737, 739, 746
Zukowski, A. 477, 831, 835–6, 848

www.ingramcontent.com/pod-product-compliance
Lightning Source LLC
Chambersburg PA
CBHW060406300426
44111CB00018B/2839